STRATEGIC MANAGEMENT AND BUSINESS POLICY

Second Edition

STRATEGIC MANAGEMENT AND BUSINESS POLICY

THOMAS L. WHEELEN
University of South Florida

J. DAVID HUNGER
Iowa State University

ADDISON-WESLEY PUBLISHING COMPANY

READING, MASSACHUSETTS · MENLO PARK, CALIFORNIA · DON MILLS, ONTARIO
WOKINGHAM, ENGLAND · AMSTERDAM · SYDNEY · SINGAPORE · TOKYO
MADRID · BOGOTÁ · SANTIAGO · SAN JUAN

Sponsoring Editors: Connie Spatz, James Heitker
Project Manager: Cindy M. Johnson
Production Supervisor: Mary Clare McEwing
Text Designer and Illustrator: Kenneth J. Wilson
Art Editor: Loretta Bailey
Cover Designer: Richard Hannus
Permissions Editor: Mary Dyer
Manufacturing Supervisor: Hugh Crawford

Library of Congress Cataloging-in-Publication Data

Wheelen, Thomas L.
Strategic management and business policy.

Includes bibliographical references and index.
1. Corporate planning. 2. Management. I. Hunger, J. David, 1941- . II. Title.
HD30.28.W43 1986 658.4′012 85-9091
ISBN 0-201-09042-2

Reprinted with corrections June, 1986

BCDEFGHIJ-HA-89876

To

Tom, Kathy, Richard

Betty
Kari, Suzi, Lori, Merry

PREFACE

This book was written in order to provide the reader with a more comprehensive understanding of the business corporation. By taking a *strategic view,* it unites the various compartments, majors, and subdisciplines usually taught within a school of business. Unlike many other areas of study, strategic management directly raises the issue of corporate existence and dares to ask *why.* Other areas deal in depth with procedures and activities designed to answer *how.* Business policy, partly because of its more holistic orientation and partly because strategic management is an emerging area of study, is often a difficult course to teach as well as to take. Consequently, this book is organized around the strategic management model that prefaces each chapter, providing a structure for both chapter content areas and complex case analyses by students.

Both the text and the cases have been course-tested in policy classes. We have included in the text those concepts that are most useful in case analysis. Our goal was to make the text as comprehensive and useful as possible while keeping the length within manageable size. All of the cases are about actual corporations. The firms range in size and maturity from large established multinationals to small entrepreneurial ventures.

Objectives

This book focuses on the following objectives, which are typically found in most business policy and strategic management courses:

- To develop *conceptual skills* so that a student is able to integrate previously learned aspects of corporations.
- To develop a *framework of analysis* to enable a student to identify central issues and problems in complex, comprehensive cases, to suggest alternative courses of action, and to present well-supported recommendations for future action.
- To develop an understanding of strategic management *concepts, research,* and *theories.*
- To develop an understanding of the *roles* and *responsibilities* of the

Board of Directors, Chief Executive Officer, and other key managers in strategic management positions.

- To develop the ability to analyze and evaluate the *performance* of the people responsible for strategic management.
- To bridge the gap between theory and practice by developing an understanding of when and how to apply *concepts* and *techniques* learned earlier in courses focusing on marketing, accounting, finance, management, and production.
- To improve the *research capabilities* necessary to gather and interpret key environmental data.
- To develop a better understanding of the *present and future environments* within which corporations must function.
- To develop and refine *analytical and decision-making skills* to deal with complex conceptual problems.

This book achieves these objectives by presenting and explaining concepts and theories useful in understanding the strategic management process. It provides studies in the field of strategy and policy in order to acquaint the student with the literature of this area and to help develop the student's research capabilities. It also describes the people who manage strategically and suggests a model of strategic management. It recommends a strategic audit as one approach to the systematic analysis of complex organization-wide issues. Through a series of comprehensive cases, it provides the student with an opportunity to apply concepts, skills, and techniques to actual, real-world corporate problems. The book focuses on the business corporation because of its crucial position in the economic system of the free world.

Structure

Part I is an overview of the subject, surveying the basic skills and competencies needed to deal with strategic issues in modern corporations. Chapter 1 presents a descriptive model as well as key terms and concepts that will be used throughout the book. Chapter 2 focuses on the development of the skills necessary to understanding and applying strategic concepts to actual situations.

Part II discusses important concepts that arise from both the external and internal environments of a corporation. It also describes key people in the corporation who are responsible for strategic management. Chapter 3 discusses the role and importance of a corporation's board of directors and top management in the strategic management process. Chapter 4 discusses both the task and societal environments of a corporation and suggests environmental scanning and forecasting as key corporate tasks. Chapter 5 examines the importance of a corporation's structure, culture, and resources to its strategic management.

Part III deals with strategy formulation. It emphasizes long-range planning and the development of alternative courses of action at both the corporate and business levels. Chapter 6 discusses situational analysis. Chapter 7 examines the many possible corporate, business, and functional strategies.

Part IV considers the implementation of strategies and policies, as well as the process of evaluation and control, with continued emphasis on corporate and division-level strategic management. Chapter 8 explains strategy implementation in terms of programs, budgets, and procedures. It tells who are in charge of implementation, what they need to do, and how they should do it. Chapter 9 focuses on evaluation and control. It considers the monitoring of corporate processes and the accomplishment of goals, as well as various methods and criteria used in evaluating performance.

Part V summarizes strategic concerns in areas of increasing importance. Chapter 10 deals with the strategic implications of operating within an international environment, and Chapter 11 describes the strategic management of not-for-profit organizations.

Part VI is composed of 38 studies of strategic issues in actual corporations. There are also three additional follow-up cases in the Instructor's Manual. These 41 cases, *38 of which are newly published,* were written by experienced case writers from a number of countries whose contributions greatly enhance the quality of the book. The cases cover a wide range of situations and illustrate the material in Parts I through V. There are four cases on strategic managers, three cases dealing with environmental issues, twenty-three comprehensive strategy cases, five cases on multinational corporations, and three cases dealing with not-for-profit organizations. In addition, a number of the cases can be grouped by business type, such as the following:

- *Brewing.* Note on U.S. Brewing Industry, Joseph Schlitz Brewing Company, Adolph Coors Brewing Company.
- *Cosmetics.* Mary Kay Cosmetics, Johnson Products.
- *Information Technology.* Xerox Corporation, Apple Computer, VLSI Technology, Hewlett-Packard, Tandy, Comshare.
- *Automobile.* Notes on the European Economic Community and the United Kingdom, Ford of Europe, plus (in the Instructor's Manual) Nissan Corporation, General Motors, Peugeot, S.A.

- *Entrepreneurial/Small Business.* Christian's, Craft Cottage, Southeastern Video, Muse Air, Vermont Tubbs, Southern Cabinet.

New, updated versions of favorite cases — Walt Disney Productions, Johnson Products, and Standard Oil of Ohio — are included. Each case is about the real problems of a real organization and helps the student bridge the gap between the theories of the ivory tower and the practices of the real world. The high quality of these cases is attested to by the fact that the majority of them have been critiqued at workshops conducted by the Case Research Association and the Midwest Case Writers Association and/or accepted for publication in leading case journals, such as the *Case Research Journal* and the *Journal of Management Case Studies.* Eighteen of the cases in this book appear in these two journals.

Instructor's Manual

A comprehensive Instructor's Manual has been carefully constructed to accompany this book. It is composed of the following four parts.

Part I: *Introduction.* Suggested course outlines, case sequences, and teaching aids.

Part II: *Text Chapters.* A strandardized format is provided for each chapter: (1) chapter abstract, (2) list of key concepts/terms, (3) suggested answers to discussion questions, and (4) multiple choice questions.

Part III: *Case Notes.* A standardized format is provided for each case: (1) case abstract, (2) case issues and subjects, (3) steps covered in the strategic decision-making process (see Fig. 6.1, p. 141), (4) case objectives, (5) suggested classroom approaches, (6) discussion questions, (7) student paper, (8) case author's teaching note, (9) student strategic audit, and (10) *a complete list of 30 calculated financial ratios* (new to this edition).

Part IV: *Transparency Masters.* Selected figures and tables from the text chapters plus other masters highlighting key strategic management concepts and techniques. *The actual transparencies are also available to those instructors who adopt the book for classroom use* (new to this edition).

Other Supplements New to This Edition

Specially prepared *decision support floppy diskettes* for use with IBM-compatible personal computers are available to instructors who adopt the book for classroom use.

- *Financial Analysis Spreadsheet Template for Lotus 1-2-3* (*FASST*), a decision support software supplement prepared by Professor A. J. Waltz of the University of South Florida, can be used by students to calculate financial ratios and generate proforma financial statements for each of the comprehensive strategic management cases in the book. By making the generation of proforma statements and ratios relatively easy, FASST allows more in-depth analysis of complicated cases and the development of more complex alternatives containing detailed implementation plans.
- A *case data diskette,* including all the key financial statements in each case where financial analysis can be performed, can be used by students in conjunction with FASST (*Financial Analysis Spreadsheet Template for Lotus 1-2-3*) or used separately with any spreadsheet software, such as Lotus 1-2-3 or Supercalc.

Acknowledgments

We are grateful to the many people who reviewed drafts of the first and second editions of this book for their constructive comments and suggestions. Their thought and effort has resulted in a book far superior to our original manuscript.

Sumer Aggarwal, University of Massachusetts, Boston
William Boulton, University of Georgia
Richard Castaldi, San Diego State University
William Crittenden, Northeastern University
Keith Davis, Arizona State University
Richard Deane, Georgia State University
Donald Del Mar, University of Idaho
Roger Evered, Naval Postgraduate School
Jerry Geisler, Eastern Illinois University
Fred Haas, Virginia Commonwealth University
Kathryn Harrigan, Columbia University
William Litzinger, University of Texas at San Antonio
John Logan, University of South Carolina
John Mahon, Boston University
Martin Marsh, California State University at Bakersfield
James Miller, Georgia State University
Thomas Navin, University of Arizona
Henry Odell, University of Virginia
Neil Snyder, University of Virginia

Jeffrey Susbauer, Cleveland State University
James Thurman, George Washington University
Robert Vichas, Old Dominion University
William Warren, College of William and Mary
Carl Zeithaml, Texas A&M University

Our special thanks go to Janis Jackson Hill, Connie Spatz, and Cindy Johnson of Addison-Wesley Publishing Company for their encouragement and concern as the book moved from being a series of interrelated ideas to a completed textbook. We are also grateful to Mary Clare McEwing, Shirley Rieger, and Jerry Moore for their comments and helpful suggestions. Their hard work is reflected in the quality of production work and in the fact that the book was published on time!

We thank Betty Hunger for her cheerful typing of the text revisions and Wayne Spies for his work in indexing. We are also grateful to Kathy, Richard, and Tom Wheelen plus Sharon James, Steven Rackleff, Irwin Heichen, Patricia Roberts, and Lori Kleiman for their help in proofreading the cases. They did a great job of spotting errors and in correcting our sometimes illegible scribbling!

In addition, we express our appreciation to Dr. Robert G. Cox, Dean of the University of South Florida's College of Business, and to Dr. Charles B. Handy, Dean of Iowa State's College of Business for their provision of the resources so necessary to write a textbook. We also thank Dr. Jerry W. Koehler and Dr. Thomas Chacko, chairs of the management departments of U.S.F. and I.S.U., respectively, for their help and encouragement. Both of us also acknowledge our debt to the University of Virginia and specifically to Dr. William Shenkir, Dean of the McIntire School of Commerce, for the provision of a work climate most supportive to the original development of this textbook.

Lastly, to the many policy instructors and students who have moaned to us about their problems with the policy course: We have tried to respond to your problems as best we could by providing a comprehensive yet usable text coupled with recent and complex cases. To you, the people who work hard in the policy trenches, we acknowledge our debt. This book is yours.

Tampa, Florida T. L. W.
Ames, Iowa J. D. H.

CONTENTS

About the Contributors

Moustafa H. Abdelsamad, D.B.A. (George Washington University) is Professor of Finance and Associate Dean for Graduate Studies in Business at Virginia Commonwealth University. He is the author of *A Guide to Capital Expenditure Analysis,* published by American Management Associations. In addition, he is author and coauthor of numerous articles. He is President of the Society for Advancement of Management and Editor-in-Chief of *SAM Advanced Management Journal.*

Sexton Adams, Ph.D., is Professor of Management at North Texas State University. He is actively engaged as consultant to various organizations in strategic planning and management development. He is the author of the textbook *Personnel Management* and coauthor of the following books: *Administrative Policy & Strategy,* 2nd ed., *The Corporate Promotables,* and *Modern Personnel Management.*

Larry Alexander, Ph.D. (U.C.L.A.) is Assistant Professor of Strategic Management in the College of Business of Virginia Polytechnic Institute & State University (V.P.I.). He previously taught at Oregon State University. He is active in the Academy of Management and his published articles have emphasized strategy implementation and how firms respond to social issues. His published cases have appeared in various textbooks. He is also coauthor of an upcoming casebook.

Roger M. Atherton, Ph.D. (University of Michigan) is Associate Dean of Faculty at Northeastern University. Previously, he was the Baldwin Professor of Business Management at the University of Oklahoma (1972–1985). He has written numerous articles in such journals as *Business Horizons,* the *Journal of Management,* and *Personnel Journal.* Prior to his academic career, he worked thirteen years in industry.

Kenneth J. Burger, D.B.A. (University of Kentucky) is an Assistant Professor at the McIntire School of Commerce at the University of Virginia. His research and teaching interests focus on business strategy development and information management. Dr. Burger is also Director of the University of Virginia's Small Business Institute and has served as consultant to several new business startup initiatives.

James W. Carland is Assistant Professor of Accounting and Computer Information Systems at Western Carolina University. He is a Certified Management Accountant and a Certified Public Accountant. He is active in a consulting company that he cofounded with his wife, Dr. Jo Ann Carland. The author of several articles, he currently focuses his research on computer information systems, entrepreneurship, and small business management.

Jo Ann C. Carland is Assistant Professor of Computer Information Systems at Western Carolina University. She is Chief Executive Officer of a microcomputer consulting company which she cofounded with her husband, Dr. James Carland. A former research assistant at the University of Georgia, the author of a book and several articles, she currently focuses her research on statistical and computer applications to businesses, entrepreneurship, and small business management.

Thomas Conquest, M.S. (Iowa State University) is an electrical engineer with Lear

Siegler, Inc., Grand Rapids, Michigan. Previously, he was with the Collins Group of Rockwell International.

William H. Davidson, M.B.A., D.B.A. (Harvard Business School) was on the faculty of the Amos Tuck School, Dartmouth College, and a Visiting Professor at INSEAD (France) and the Fletcher School, Tufts University, before joining the faculty of Colgate Darden School, University of Virginia. His most recent book is *The Amazing Race: Winning the Technorivalry with Japan.*

Steven M. Dawson, Ph.D. (University of Michigan) is Professor of Finance at the University of Hawaii. He served as a Visiting Professor at the University of Michigan, National University of Singapore, and The Chinese University of Hong Kong and on the faculties of the Advanced Management Program, the Asian Pacific Management Program, and the Executive Institute for Tourism.

Wayne H. Decker, Ph.D. (University of Pittsburgh) is Associate Professor of Management at the Fogelman College of Business and Economics of Memphis State University. His recent publications and papers have been in the areas of humor in management, job satisfaction, and occupational stereotypes.

Robert R. Dince, Ph.D. (Cornell University) is Professor of Finance at the College of Business, University of Georgia. He was formerly Deputy Comptroller of the Currency, U.S. Treasury. He has acted as consultant to such organizations as Citibank, the Mellon Bank, the Citizens & Southern National Bank. He presently is the Academic Director of the Bank Management and Strategic Planning School of the Bank Marketing Association of the American Banking Association. He is a former President of the Southern Finance Association.

Willard H. Ellis, B.A. (Queen's University), M.B.A. (University of Western Ontario), is a Visiting Professor of Management and Director of the Centre for Small Business and Entrepreneurial Studies, Concordia University, Montreal, Quebec. He served as a Professor in the Faculty of Management, McGill University, until retirement, during which time he wrote numerous cases and articles which have appeared in a number of texts and publications. He is an executive member of the International Council for Small Business-Canada and holds memberships in travel and tourism organizations.

H. Landis Gabel, Ph.D. (University of Pennsylvania) is Associate Professor at INSEAD (European Institute of Business Administration) in Fontainebleau, France. He teaches courses in economics and public policy. Previously, he was Associate Professor at the University of Virginia and a lecturer at the University of Witwatersrand, Johannesburg. He has also taught at the University of Pennsylvania and Haverford College. Professor Gabel's research interests are in industrial organization, antitrust policy, and environmental policy. He is the author of numerous articles and cases.

Adelaide Griffin, Ph.D., is Assistant Professor of Management at Texas Woman's University, and has served as Visiting Professor to the University of Texas at Arlington. She has published articles in the field of strategic planning with special emphasis on the health-care industry, as well as numerous cases and papers. She is coauthor of the textbook, *Modern Personnel Management.*

Anthony E. Hall, M.B.A. (INSEAD, France) is the Northern United Kingdom Sales Manager of General Electric Information Services (GEISCO) in Manchester, England and a Research Associate at INSEAD. Prior to taking the M.B.A. with distinction, he worked as Production Controller and General Manager for Hanson Trust. He has also taught economics and market research at City University, London, England.

J. David Hunger, Ph.D. (Ohio State University) is Associate Professor of Management at Iowa State University. Previously, he was with the University of Virginia. His research interests lie in strategic management, conflict management, and leadership. He has worked in management positions for Procter & Gamble, Lazarus Department Store, and the U.S. Army. He has been active as consultant and trainer to business corporations, as well as to state and federal government agencies. He has written and published numerous articles and cases and is a member of the Academy of Management, Midwest Case Writers Association, Case Research Association, and Strategic Management Society. He presently serves on the board of directors of the Midwest Case Writers Association and on the editorial review boards of the *Advanced Management Journal* and the *Journal of Management Case Studies.*

Per V. Jenster, Ph.D. (University of Pittsburgh) is an Assistant Professor at the McIntire School of Commerce at the University of Virginia, where he teaches and conducts research in the area of strategic management.

Paul N. Keaton, Ph.D. (University of Minnesota) is Associate Professor of Management at the University of Wisconsin-La Crosse. He previously taught at the University of Maryland at College Park and the University of Tennessee-Chattanooga. He is a member of the Midwest Case Writers Association, American Society for Personnel Administration, and the Midwest Business Administration Association. He serves as a manuscript reviewer for *Personnel Administrator* and is a contributor to *Non-Profit World Report.*

Danny G. Kinker is a Ph.D. candidate, University of Kansas, and an Instructor in the School of Business, Washburn University, Topeka, Kansas.

Robert McGlashan, Ph.D. (University of Texas at Austin) is Professor of Management at the University of Houston-Clear Lake. He is the author of numerous articles, cases, and papers. He is past President of the Academy of Management, Southwest Division and is currently Vice President and General Program Chairman of the Southwestern Federation of Administrative Disciplines.

Thomas R. Miller, Ph.D. (Ohio State University) is Associate Dean and Director of Graduate Studies of the Fogelman College of Business and Economics at Memphis State University. Dr. Miller, a Professor of Management and former Department Chairman, has published and presented many cases, articles, and papers in the fields of general management, organizational theory, and personnel administration.

William Miller, M.S. (Iowa State University) is an Industrial Engineer Specialist in the Process Development Department of the Collins Transmission Systems Division of Rockwell International, Dallas, Texas.

Robert L. Nixon, Ph.D. (Cornell University) is Assistant Professor of Management and Organizational Behavior Theory at the University of South Florida at Tampa, Florida. His publications focus on the effects of information systems in the organization. He is the author of numerous papers and articles.

Henry R. Odell, D.B.A. (Indiana University) is Associate Professor at the McIntire School of Commerce at the University of Virginia. He was one of the founders and formerly Executive Vice-President of Regal-Beloit Corporation, a manufacturing firm, of which he is currently a director.

Allan V. Palmer, Ph.D. (University of North Carolina at Chapel Hill) is Professor of Business Administration at the University of North Carolina at Charlotte. He was Dean of the College of Business at UNCC for ten years and formerly taught at Old Dominion University. Dr. Palmer serves on a number of boards and panels and teaches Business and Society in the M.B.A. program.

Bernard C. Reimann, D.B.A. (Kent State University) is Professor of Management in the James J. Nance College of Business Administration at Cleveland State University. He has been on the faculties of the Wharton School of the University of Pennsylvania, Drexel University, and Kent State University. Prior to that, he had several years of managerial experience in product development and production planning. He has had many articles published in professional journals in the areas of management and information systems. In 1983–1984 he served as a faculty intern to the Corporate Planning Department of TRW, Inc. in Cleveland, Ohio.

Foster C. Rinefort, Ph.D. (Texas A & M University) is Coordinator of Graduate Business Studies and Associate Professor at the College of Business, Eastern Illinois University. He previously served as an instructor at Texas A & M University. He has fifteen years of business experience with Procter & Gamble and a large chemical firm. As a consultant, he has provided services to a variety of clients on a worldwide basis, as well as to state and federal agencies. He is the author of numerous articles, papers, and cases. Memberships include the Academy of Management, Midwest Business Administration Association, and Midwest Case Writers Association.

Stephen J. Schewe, M.B.A. (University of Virginia) is an associate with Norwest Growth Fund, a venture capital management firm in Minneapolis, Minnesota. Previously, he was a financial analyst in the Mergers and Acquisitions Department of Morgan Stanley & Co., New York City.

Michael R. Schipper, B.B.A. (Iowa State University) is an accounting specialist with Green Holdings, Inc., Dallas, Texas. Previously, he was with International Beef Processors, Inc., as a scalehouse supervisor and with the Joseph Schlitz Brewing Company and the Stroh Brewery Company as a college representative.

Donald W. Scotton, Ph.D., is chairman and Professor of Marketing and Quantitative Business Analysis at Cleveland State University. He has served on the faculties of the University of Illinois and the University of Detroit. His business experience includes retail and sales management, marketing planning and research, operation of sales incentive plans, and commercial banking. He has published numerous articles and monographs. His business cases are included in twenty textbooks.

Arthur Sharplin, Ph.D., is Associate Professor of Strategic Management at Northeast Louisiana University. He has also taught at Mississippi State University and at Hong Kong Shue-Yan College. He is author or coauthor of four textbooks and more than 70 articles, papers, and cases. He is a member of the editorial board of the *Journal of Business Strategies,* as well as a consultant and member of various professional and civic associations.

Charles B. Shrader, Ph.D. (Indiana University) is Assistant Professor of Management, Iowa State University. He is the author or coauthor of several articles and professional papers on strategic planning, organization structure, and organization performance. He is currently serving as a reviewer for the *Journal of Management.*

Timothy M. Singleton, Ph.D. (Georgia State University) is Associate Professor of Management at the University of Houston-Clear Lake. He is coauthor of *The Practice of Management: Text, Reading, and Cases.* He is the author of many cases, articles, and papers and is an active member of the Case Research Association.

Sandra Smith, B.Sc. (University of Montreal) served as a Research Assistant while working towards advanced degrees.

Neil H. Snyder, Ph.D. (University of Georgia) is Associate Professor at the McIntire School of Commerce, University of Virginia. He is coauthor of *Readings in Policy and Strategy from Business Week* and author of numerous cases and articles in such journals as *Long Range Planning, Academy of Management Journal, Journal of Contemporary Business,* and *Strategic Management Journal.*

Matthew C. Sonfield, Ph.D. (New York University) is Professor of Management at Hofstra University. He has published two books and many journal articles in the field of management and has served on the boards of directors of several major corporations.

Melvin J. Stanford, Ph.D. (University of Illinois) is Dean of the College of Business at Mankato State University, Mankato, Minnesota. He was a faculty member at Brigham Young University for fourteen years. He is the author of *Management Policy,* 2nd ed, *New Enterprise Management,* and more than 100 cases and journal articles. His cases have been included in more than 20 major textbooks.

Laurence J. Stybel, ED.D. (Harvard University) is General Partner of Stybel, Peabody & Associates, a Boston-based management consulting firm. He was previously a management consultant for Hay Associates and Assistant Professor of Management at Babson College in Wellesley, Massachusetts. He is coauthor (with Robert Ronstadt) of *Introduction to Business: A Case Approach* (Dover, Massachusetts: Lord Press, 1983).

Allan D. Waren, Ph.D. (Case Western Reserve University) is a Professor of Computer and Information Science at the James J. Nance College of Business Administration of Cleveland State University. He has held several industrial positions in engineering and technical management. In addition, he founded and was President of Comshare, Ltd. (Canada). He is the author of more than fifty articles.

Patricia A. Watson-Kuentz, M.B.A. (University of Wisconsin-La Crosse) has taught management courses at the College of St. Teresa and is working for a health maintenance organization in Minneapolis.

Thomas L. Wheelen, D.B.A. (George Washington University) is Professor of Strategic Management, University of South Florida, and was formally the Ralph A. Beeton Professor of Free Enterprise at the McIntire School of Commerce, University of Virginia. He was Visiting Professor at both the University of Arizona and Northeastern University. He served on the Editorial Board of the *Journal of Management* and *Case Research Journal.* He is Associate Editor of *SAM Advanced Management Journal* and serves on the Editorial Board of the *Journal of Management Case Studies.* He is coeditor of *Developments in Management Information Systems* and *Collective Bargaining in the Public Sector,* and the author of numerous articles, cases, and papers. His cases appear in fifteen management textbooks. He has served on the Board of Directors of the Southern Management Association and as President of the Case Research Association.

Robert N. White, M.B.A. (Harvard University) is a Lecturer in Management at the Babcock Graduate School of Management, Wake Forest University, where he has been teaching corporate and marketing planning since 1972. Previously, he was a planning executive and consultant in industry. He is Editor of *Managing Today's Church* and author of many articles and papers.

Other Contributing Authors

Tony Arroyo
Bob Bailey
David Bellegante
Edward E. Colby, Jr.
Jeff Cury
Mike Harris
Marian Hessler
Jan Hunter
Deborah Jones
Kevin McCarey
William McCollum
Keith Morris
David Porter
Dean Salpini
Art Scibelli
Gordon Shanks
Ken Smith
Rebecca Wood

STRATEGIC MANAGEMENT AND BUSINESS POLICY

PART ONE

INTRODUCTION TO STRATEGIC MANAGEMENT AND BUSINESS POLICY

Chapter 1

INTRODUCTION

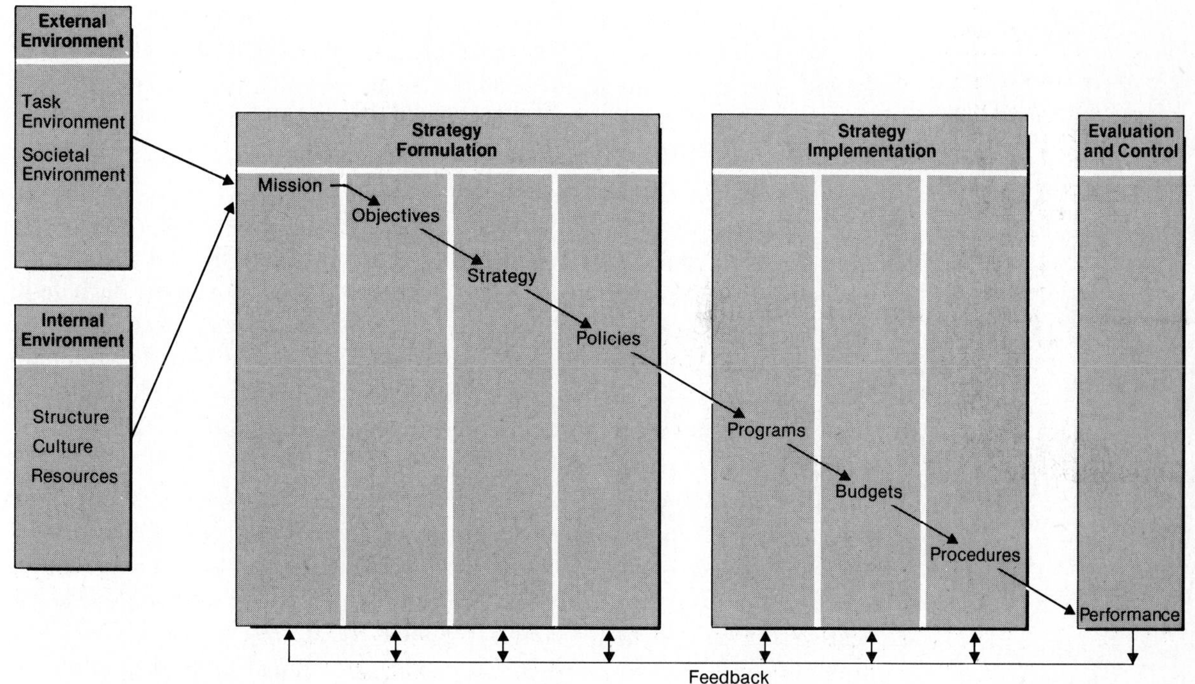

Strategic management and business policy is a fast-developing field of study. It looks at the corporation as a whole and attempts to explain why some firms develop and thrive while others stagnate and go bankrupt. Strategic management typically focuses on analyzing the problems and opportunities faced by people in top management. Unlike many decisions made at lower levels in a corporation, strategic decisions usually deal with the long-run future of the entire organization. The stakes can be very high. For instance, the strategic decision made after World War II by Sears, Roebuck and Company to expand from catalog sales into retail stores and insurance has given Sears many years of successful profits. A similar decision made independently during the 1960s by the top managements of General Motors, Ford, and Chrysler to emphasize the production of large, powerful automobiles over small, fuel-efficient ones resulted in their low profits and even the threat of bankruptcy in the early 1980s.

Other examples of strategic decisions were those made during the early 1980s by the top management of Standard Oil of Ohio (Sohio). Realizing that the $6 billion in annual revenues coming from Sohio's share in the Prudhoe Bay, Alaska, oil field was likely to begin declining by the end of the decade, the firm decided to increase significantly its oil exploration efforts and to diversify into other industries. In 1981, Sohio paid $1.77 billion for Kennecott Corporation, the largest copper producer in the United States. Market demand for copper, however, soon collapsed. In the four years since the acquisition, Kennecott lost more than $350 million. In the meantime, Sohio's top management invested $310 million in a prospective oil field called *Mukluk* in the Beaufort Sea of Alaska. The exploratory well was found in December 1983 to contain water, not oil, and was soon referred to as the most expensive "dry well" in history.

Although a number of Sohio's other acquisitions and exploratory wells have been moderately successful, none appear to have the potential to replace the Prudhoe Bay revenues. Curious about the risky nature of such high-stakes decisions, a reporter from the *Wall Street Journal* asked Alton W. Whitehouse, Jr., the chief executive officer of Sohio, if he would continue to take such strategic gambles. Mr. Whitehouse calmly stated, "If those guys come in with another [enticing prospect like Mukluk] tomorrow, I'll have my neck right back out there."[1]

Alton Whitehouse's comment suggests why top management of large business corporations must manage firms strategically. They cannot make decisions based on long-standing rules, policies, or standard operating procedures. Instead, they must look to the future to plan organization-wide objectives, initiate strategy, and set policies. They must rise above their training and experience in such functional/operational areas as accounting, marketing, production, or finance to grasp the overall picture. They must be willing to ask these key strategic questions:

1. Where is the corporation now?
2. If no changes are made, where will the corporation be in one year, two years, five years, ten years? Are the answers acceptable?
3. If the answers are not acceptable, what specific actions should the corporation undertake? What are the risks and payoffs involved?

1.1 STUDY OF STRATEGIC MANAGEMENT AND BUSINESS POLICY

Most business schools offer a strategic management or business policy course. Although this course typically serves as a capstone or final integrative class in a business administration program, it—also typically—takes on some of the characteristics of a separate discipline.

In the 1950s the Ford Foundation and the Carnegie Corporation sponsored investigations into the business school curriculum.[2] The resulting Gordon and Howell report, sponsored by the Ford Foundation, recommended a broad business education and a course in business policy to "give students an opportunity to pull together what they have learned in the separate business fields and utilize this knowledge in the analysis of complex business problems."[3] The report also suggested the content which should be part of such a course:

> The business policy course can offer the student something he [or she] will find nowhere else in the curriculum: consideration of business problems which are not prejudged as being marketing problems, finance problems, etc.; emphasis on the development of skills in identifying, analyzing, and solving problems in a situation which is as close as the classroom can ever be to the real business world; opportunity to consider problems which draw on a wide range of substantive areas in business; opportunity to consider the external, nonmarket implications of problems at the same time that internal decisions must be made; situations which enable the student to exercise qualities of judgment and of mind which were not explicitly called for in any prior course. Questions of social responsibility and of personal attitudes can be brought in as a regular aspect of this kind of problem-solving practice. Without the responsibility of having to transmit some specific body of knowledge, the business policy course can concentrate on integrating what already has been acquired and on developing further the student's skill in using that knowledge.[4]

By the late 1960s most business schools included such a business policy course in their curriculum. But since that time the typical policy course has evolved to one that emphasizes the total organization and strategic management, with an increased interest in business social responsibilities and ethics as well as nonprofit organizations. This is in line with a recent survey of business school deans that reported a primary objective of undergraduate business education is to develop an understanding of the political, social, and economic environment of business.[5] This increasing concern with the effect of environmental issues on the management of the total organization has led leaders in the field to replace the term *business policy* with the more comprehensive *strategic management.*[6] *Strategic management* is that set of managerial decisions and actions that determine the long-run performance of a corporation. It includes strategy formulation, strategy implementation, and evaluation and control. The study of strategic management therefore emphasizes the monitoring and evaluating of environmental opportunities and constraints in light of a corporation's strengths and weaknesses. In contrast, the study of *business policy,* with its integrative orientation, tends to look inward by focusing on the efficient utilization of a corporation's assets and thus emphasizes the formulation of general guidelines that will better accomplish a firm's mission and objectives. We see, then, that strategic management incorporates the concerns of business policy with a heavier environmental and strategic emphasis.

1.2 RESEARCH ON THE EFFECTIVENESS OF STRATEGIC MANAGEMENT

Many of the concepts and techniques dealing with long-range planning and strategic management have been developed and used successfully by business corporations such as General Electric and the Boston Consulting Group, among others. Nevertheless, not all organizations use these tools or even attempt to manage strategically. Many are able to succeed for a while with unstated objectives and intuitive strategies. American Hospital Supply Corporation was one such example until Karl Bays became chief executive in 1971 and introduced strategic planning to a sales-dominated management. Previously, the company's idea of long-range planning was "Maybe in December we should look at next year's budget," recalled a former AHS executive.[7]

From his extensive work in the area, Bruce Henderson of the Boston Consulting Group concludes that intuitive strategies cannot be continued successfully if (1) the corporation becomes large, (2) the layers of management increase, or (3) the environment changes substantially.[8] Research suggests that the increasing risks of error, costly mistakes, and even economic ruin are causing today's professional managers to take strategic management seriously in order to keep their company competitive in an increasingly volatile environment.[9] Research by Gluck, Kaufman, and Walleck proposes that strategic planning evolves through *four sequential phases* in corporations as top managers attempt to better deal with their changing world:

Phase 1. *Basic financial planning:* seeking better operational control through meeting budgets.

Phase 2. *Forecast-based planning:* seeking more effective planning for growth by trying to predict the future beyond the next year.

Phase 3. *Externally oriented planning:* seeking increased responsiveness to markets and competition by trying to think strategically.

Phase 4. *Strategic management:* seeking to manage all resources to develop competitive advantage and to help create the future.[10]

Concern about external as well as internal factors seems to be increasing in today's large corporations. Recent research studies conducted by Henry indicate that the planning systems of fifty large companies are becoming increasingly sophisticated. For example, there is more effort to formulate, implement, and evaluate strategic plans. There is also a greater emphasis on strategic factors in the evaluation of a manager's performance.[11] Gordon Brunton, president of Britain's International Thomson Organisation, Ltd. emphasized this point when he made the following statement:

> All International Thomson senior managers now understand that unless they demonstrate their ability to think strategically, their future career potential will be limited accordingly.[12]

William Rothschild, staff executive for business development and strategy at General Electric (GE), notes the current trend to push strategic management duties down the organizational hierarchy to operating line managers. He observes that at GE, "over half of our managers are strategic thinkers. Another 20 percent to 25 percent lean that way. The rest don't understand it, and if they're fortunate enough to be in the right business where there is a stable environment, it doesn't matter too much."[13]

Many researchers have conducted studies of corporations to learn if organizations that engage in strategic planning outperform those that do not. One analysis of five companies with sales ranging from $1 billion to $17 billion reports the impact of strategic planning has been to

- help the companies sort their businesses into "winners and losers,"
- focus attention on critical issues and choices, and
- develop a strategic frame of mind among top and upper-level managers.

The study concludes that the results management should expect from strategic planning are improved competitive position and long-term improved profits plus growth in earnings per share.[14]

Research studies attempting to measure objectively this anticipated connection between formal strategic planning and corporate performance have found mixed results.[15] For example, studies by Ansoff, Thune and House, Herold, Burt, Eastlack and McDonald, Wood and La Forge, Karger and Malik, Miller and Friesen, Welch, and Rhyne found that corporations that engaged in strategic planning outperformed those that did not.[16] On the other hand, studies by Rue and Fulmer, Leontiades and Tezel, Kudla, Frederickson and Mitchell, as well as by Lindsay, Boulton, Franklin, and Rue found no such payoff from strategic planning.[17] Rhyne, however, explains these contradictory findings as resulting from the use of different measures for planning and performance plus a typical failure to consider industry effects. When he controlled for industry variation, focused only on the total return to stockholders, and considered strategic planning as different from less-evolved stages of planning (such as budgeting or annual planning), Rhyne found a positive relationship between strategic planning and performance. He concluded that "these results provide assurance that the prescriptions of strategic management theory are indeed valid."[18]

From this evidence we may conclude that a knowledge of strategic management is very important for effective business performance in a changing environment. The use of strategic planning and the selection of alternative courses of action based upon an assessment of important external and internal factors are becoming key parts of a general manager's job.

1.3 HIERARCHY OF STRATEGY

The typical large multidivisional business firm has three levels of strategy: (1) corporate, (2) business, and (3) functional.

Corporate strategy explores the ways a firm can develop a favorable "portfolio strategy" for its many activities.[19] It includes such factors as decisions about the type of businesses a firm should be in, the flow of financial and other resources to and from its divisions, and the way a corporation can increase its return on investment (ROI).

Business strategy, in contrast, usually occurs at the divisional level, with emphasis on improving the competitive position of a corporation's products or services in a specific industry or market segment the division serves. A division may be organized as a *strategic business unit* (SBU) around a group of similar products, such as housewares or electric turbines. Top management usually treats an SBU as an autonomous unit with, generally, the authority to develop its own strategy within corporate objectives and strategy. A division's business strategy probably would stress increasing its profit margin in the production and sales of its products and services. Business strategies also should integrate various functional activities to achieve divisional objectives.

The principal focus of *functional strategy* is on maximizing resource pro-

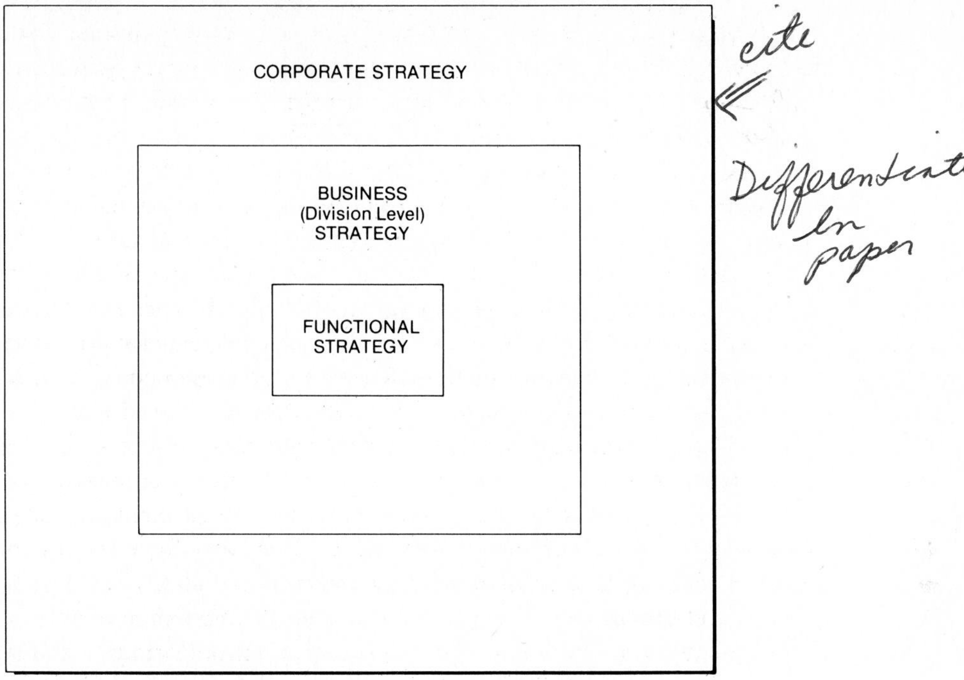

Figure 1.1 **Hierarchy of strategy.**

ductivity.[20] Given the constraints of corporate and business strategies around them, functional departments develop strategies to pull together their various activities and competencies to improve performance. For example, a typical strategy of a marketing department might center on developing the means to increase the current year's sales over those of the previous year.

The three levels of strategy—corporate, business, and functional—form a *hierarchy of strategy* within a large corporation. They interact closely with each other and must be well integrated if the total corporation is to be successful. As depicted in Fig. 1.1, each level of strategy forms the strategic environment of the next level in the corporation. (The interaction among the three levels is depicted later in the chapter in Fig. 1.5.)

1.4 DESCRIPTIVE MODEL OF STRATEGIC MANAGEMENT

The process of strategic management involves three basic elements: (1) *strategy formulation,* (2) *strategy implementation,* and (3) *evaluation and control.* Figure 1.2 shows how these three elements interact. We will discuss these interactions later in this section.

At the corporate level, the strategic management process includes activities that range from the initial statement of corporate mission to the evalua-

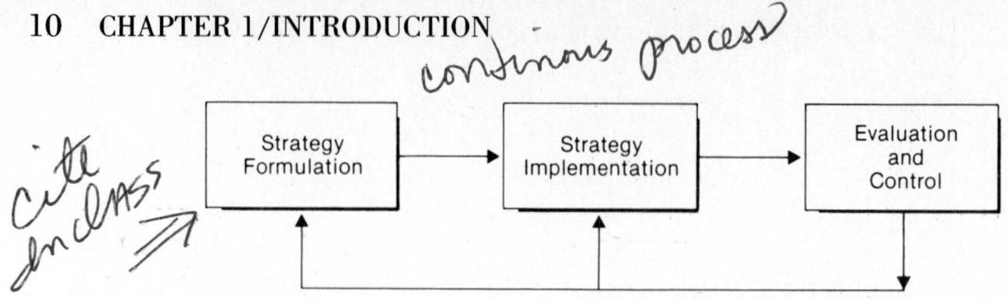

Figure 1.2 **Basic elements of the strategic management process.**

tion of performance. Top management scans both the external environment for opportunities and threats, and the internal environment for strengths and weaknesses. The most important of these to the corporation's future are referred to as strategic factors and are summarized with the acronym S.W.O.T., standing for Strengths, Weaknesses, Opportunities, and Threats. Top management then evaluates the strategic factors to determine corporate mission, which is the first step in the formulation of strategy. A statement of mission leads to a determination of corporate objectives, strategies, and policies. These strategies and policies are implemented through programs, budgets, and procedures. Finally performance is evaluated, and information is fed back into the system to ensure adequate control of organizational activities. Figure 1.3 depicts this process as a continuous one. It is an expansion of the basic model presented in Fig. 1.2.

The model in Fig. 1.3, with minor changes, also reflects the strategic management process at both divisional and functional levels of the corporation. A division's external environment, for example, includes not only task and societal variables, but also the mission, objectives, strategy, and policies of corporate headquarters. Similarly, both corporate and divisional constraints form the external environment of a functional department. The model depicted in Fig. 1.3 therefore is appropriate for any strategic level of a corporation.

External Environment

The *external environment* consists of variables (Opportunities and Threats) that exist outside the organization and are not typically within the short-run control of top management. These variables form the context within which the corporation exists. The external environment has two parts: task environment and social environment. The *task environment* includes those elements or groups that directly affect and are affected by an organization's major operations. Some of these are stockholders, governments, suppliers, local communities, competitors, customers, creditors, labor unions, special interest groups, and trade associations. The *societal environment* includes more general forces—ones that do not directly touch upon the short-run activities of the organization but that can, and often do, influence its long-run

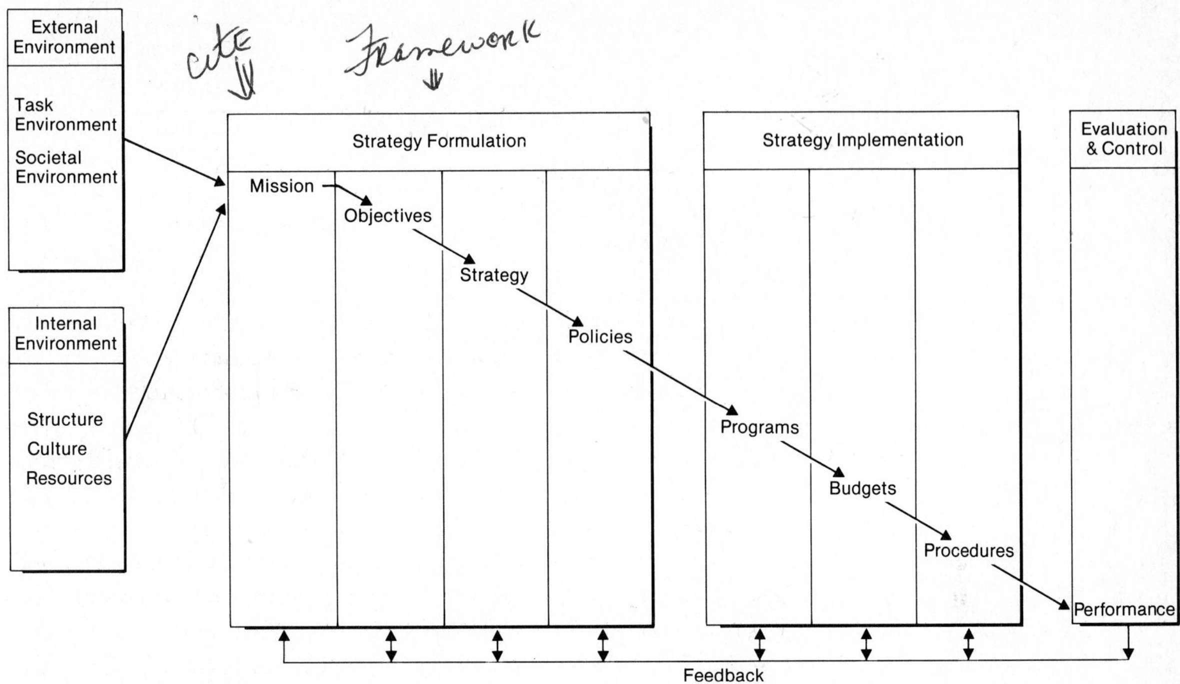

Figure 1.3 **Strategic management model.**

decisions. Such economic, sociocultural, technological, and political-legal forces are depicted in Fig. 1.4 in relation to a firm's total environment. (These external variables are discussed in more detail in Chapter 4.)

Internal Environment

The *internal environment* of a corporation consists of variables (Strengths and Weaknesses) within the organization itself that are also not usually within the short-run control of top management. These variables form the context in which work is done. They include the corporation's structure, culture, and resources. The *corporate structure* is the way a corporation is organized in terms of communication, authority, and workflow. It is often referred to as the "chain of command" and is graphically described in an organization chart. The *corporation's culture* is that pattern of beliefs, expectations, and values shared by the corporation's members. In a typical firm norms emerge that define the acceptable behavior of people from top management down to the operative employees. *Corporate resources* are those assets that form the raw material for the production of an organization's products or services. These include people and managerial talent as well as financial assets, plant facilities, and functional area skills and abilities.

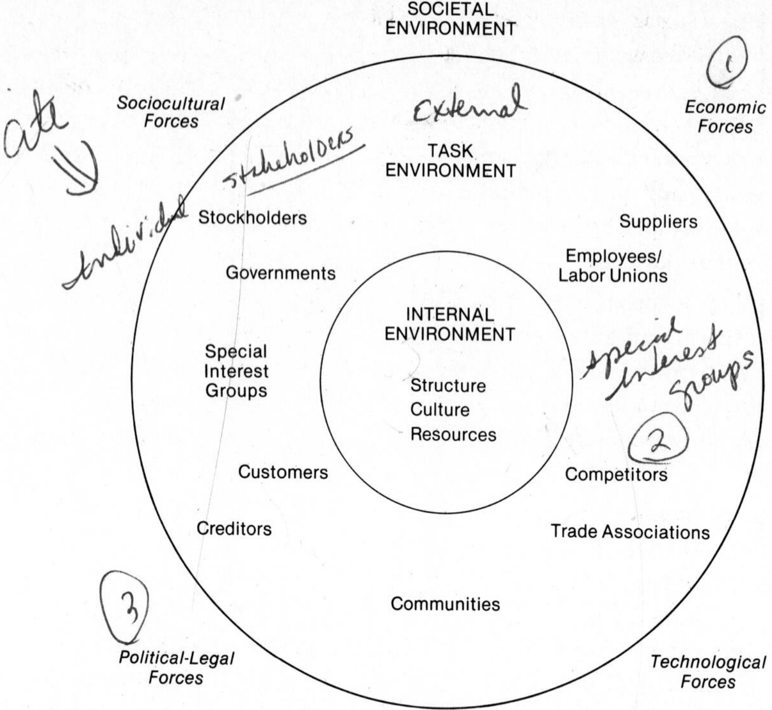

Figure 1.4 **Environmental variables.**

(These internal variables in a firm's environment are discussed in more detail in Chapter 5.)

Strategy Formulation

Strategy formulation is the process of developing long-range plans to deal effectively with environmental opportunities and threats in light of corporate strengths and weaknesses. It includes defining the corporate mission, specifying achievable objectives, developing strategies, and setting policy guidelines.

Mission

The corporate mission is the purpose or reason for the corporation's existence. For example, the mission of a savings and loan association might be to provide mortgage money to people of the community. By fulfilling this mission, the S&L would hope to provide a reasonable rate of return to its depositors. A mission may be *narrow,* like that of the S&L, or it may be *broad.* A broad statement of mission for another S&L might be to offer financial services to anyone who can pay the interest.

Objectives

The corporate mission, as depicted in Fig. 1.3, determines the parameters of the specific objectives top management chooses to achieve. These objectives are listed as an end result of planned activity. They state *what* is to be accomplished by *when* and should be quantified if possible. (The terms *goals* and *objectives* are used interchangeably.) The achievement of corporate objectives should result in a corporation's fulfilling its mission. An S&L, for example, might set an objective for the year of earning a 15% rate of return on its investment portfolio.

Strategy

The strategy of a corporation forms a comprehensive master plan stating *how* a corporation will achieve its mission and objectives. A strategy of an S&L might be to increase both demand for mortgage loans and the amount of money deposited in its savings accounts. Another strategy might be to expand its financial services so that it is not so dependent on mortgages for income.

Policies

As broad guidelines for making decisions, policies flow from the strategy. They provide guidance for decision making throughout the organization. In attempting to increase the amount of mortgage loans as well as the amount of deposits available for mortgages, an S&L might set policies of always offering the highest legal interest rate on savings deposits or to offer mortgage borrowers the best deal possible in the area. (Strategy formulation is discussed in more detail in Chapters 6 and 7.)

Strategy Implementation

Strategy implementation is the process of putting strategies and policies into action through the development of programs, budgets, and procedures. It is typically conducted by middle- and lower-level managers but reviewed by top management. Sometimes referred to as operational planning, it is concerned with day-to-day resource allocation problems.

Division and/or functional managers work to fully develop the programs, budgets, and procedures that will be used to achieve the objectives of the corporate strategy. At the same time, these managers are involved in strategy formulation at the divisional or functional level. If, for example, a corporate program for a steel company is to close down all inefficient plants within two years, a divisional objective might be to close down two specific production facilities. A divisional (business) strategy would then be developed to detail the specifics of the closing.

Programs

A program is a statement of activities or steps needed to accomplish a single-use plan. It makes the strategy action-oriented. For instance, to implement its strategy and policies, a savings and loan association might initiate an advertising program in the local area, develop close ties with the local realtors' association, and offer free silverware with every $1,000 savings deposit.

Budgets A budget is a statement of a corporation's programs in dollar terms. It lists the detailed cost of each program for planning and control purposes. The S&L might thus draw up separate budgets for each of its three programs: the advertising budget, the public relations budget, and the premium budget.

Procedures Sometimes referred to as standard operating procedures (SOP), procedures are a system of sequential steps or techniques that describe in detail how to perform a particular task or job. They typically detail the various activities that must be carried out to complete a corporation's program. The S&L, for example, might develop procedures for placing ads in newspapers and on radio. They might list persons to contact, techniques for writing acceptable copy (with samples), and details about payment. They might establish detailed procedures concerning eligibility requirements for silverware premiums. (Strategy implementation is discussed in more detail in Chapter 8.)

Evaluation and Control

Evaluation and control is the process of monitoring corporate activities and performance results so that actual performance can be compared with desired performance. Managers at all levels use the resulting information to take corrective action and resolve problems. Although evaluation and control is the final major element of strategic management, it also may serve to stimulate the beginning of the entire process by pinpointing weaknesses in previously implemented strategic plans.

For effective evaluation and control, managers must obtain clear, prompt, and unbiased feedback from the people below them in the corporation's hierarchy. The model in Fig. 1.3 indicates how feedback in the form of performance data and activity reports runs through the entire management process. Managers use this information to compare what is actually happening with what was originally planned in the formulation stage.

For example, the savings and loan would probably ask its internal information systems people to keep track of the number of mortgages being made as well as the level of deposits at the end of each week for each S&L branch office. It may also wish to develop special incentives to reward loan officers who increase their mortgage lending.

Top management of large corporations typically monitors and evaluates results by using periodic reports dealing with key performance indicators, such as return on investment, net profits, earnings per share, and net sales. Corporations are sometimes structured in ways to pinpoint performance problem areas with profit centers, investment centers, expense centers, and revenue centers. (These are discussed in detail in Chapter 9.)

Activities are much harder to monitor and evaluate than are performance results. Because of the many difficulties in deciding which activities to monitor and because of the bias inherent in evaluating job performance, some firms now manage by objectives. Management By Objectives (MBO) has been criticized, however, for ignoring many of the intermediate activities that can lead to the desired results. To counter this criticism, consulting firms have developed management "audits," which assess key organizational activities and provide in-depth feedback to consultants and managers. Management audits complement standard measures of performance and provide a more complete picture of the corporation's activities. (We discuss an example of a comprehensive audit in Chapter 2.)

1.5 ILLUSTRATION OF THE MODEL

We illustrate the strategic management model for a large, multidivisional corporation. A fictitious automobile manufacturer called Murphy Motors begins the process by scanning its external environment for any relevant information. It also scans its internal environment to assess the strengths and weaknesses in its divisions and functional areas. Officers of divisions and functional areas are normally requested to provide input in the form of proposals for top management's review. This information provides the data necessary for the formulation and implementation stages of strategic management. As depicted in Illustrative Example 1.1, the firm begins with redefining its mission and ends with developing a feedback system to aid in evaluation and control.

Illustrative Example 1.1

STRATEGIC MANAGEMENT AT MURPHY MOTORS
(Corporate Level)

STRATEGY FORMULATION

Mission

Broad. Provide transportation vehicles to people throughout the world.
Narrow. Build and sell cars and trucks in noncommunist countries.

Objectives

1. Achieve an ROI of 10% for the period 1988–1993.
2. Become number one in *global* automotive market share by 1990.
3. Increase domestic car and truck market share by 5% by 1991.
4. Reduce unit costs by 6% by 1990.

Strategies

1. Grow by concentrating all resources in the car and truck industry. Focus on developing fuel-efficient cars and trucks to meet EPA requirements and to challenge competition.

(*Continued*)

Illustrative Example 1.1
(*Continued*)

2. Vertically integrate and continually modernize manufacturing facilities with state-of-the-art technology to reduce costs and to control raw materials.
3. Engage in joint ventures with foreign auto manufacturers to build and sell cars and trucks in developing countries.

Policies

1. Emphasize research and development to reduce costs and to improve auto efficiency and safety.
2. Emphasize efficiency at all levels. Reward high performers and retire or fire unproductive workers and managers. Increase plant efficiency at all locations.
3. Emphasize the building of safe, fuel-efficient cars and trucks at a quality level equal to the number-one competitor.
4. Emphasize the international marketplace to respond to global competition.

STRATEGY IMPLEMENTATION

Programs

1. Add a new division to build and sell a new low-cost, high-quality "world car" domestically.
2. Engage in negotiations with foreign automakers to set up joint ventures to build and sell the "world car" throughout the world.
3. Purchase a steel company with the capacity to provide sufficient high-quality steel for all divisions' requirements.
4. Reduce manufacturing costs by installing robots at 50% of each division's work stations by 1990.
5. Increase fleet miles per gallon by converting 80% of all autos produced to front-wheel drive by 1990.

Budgets

Prepare budgets showing cost-benefit analysis of each planned program.

Procedures

1. Develop procedures needed to sell enough bonds and common stock to finance the construction of the "world car" division.
2. Develop procedures for negotiation teams to follow when looking for joint venture partners.
3. Develop a series of procedures to follow in order to purchase a steel company.
4. Develop procedures to convert manned to robot work stations.
5. Develop procedures to convert to front-wheel drive.

(*Continued*)

Illustrative Example 1.1
(*Continued*)

EVALUATION AND CONTROL

Require monthly status reports on the following:

1. Number of new "world car" dealerships established.
2. Actual versus planned construction time and costs for new "world car" plant.
3. Progress of negotiations with possible joint venture partners.
4. Progress of negotiations with top management of targeted steel company acquisitions.
5. Actual versus standard costs for each division.
6. Actual versus planned sales for each division.
7. Progress toward installing robots.
8. Progress toward front-wheel drive conversion.

Require annual reports on the following:

1. ROI for each division.
2. Domestic and global market shares by product and by division compared to competition in each area.
3. Raw material and manufacturing costs by product line and by division.
4. EPA rating on fleet in terms of miles per gallon.
5. Strategic audit of entire corporation and each division.

A corporation the size of a modern automobile company would tend to be structured on a divisional and a functional basis. Each car line, for example, might form its own division. Each division would have its own production facilities as well as marketing, finance, and human resource departments. As depicted in Fig. 1.5, the corporate level goes through all three stages of the strategic management process. Top management *with input from the divisions* formulates strategies and makes plans for implementation. These implementation plans stimulate the strategy formulation process at the divisional level. Each division formulates objectives, strategies, and policies in order to accomplish the corporate programs. The evaluation and control information from each division feeds upward to the corporate level for its use in evaluation and control.

Just as the implementation stage of corporate strategic planning stimulates the formulation stage of the same process at the divisional level, implementation planning at the divisional level causes each functional department to begin formulating its own strategic plans. For example, a corporate-level program of Murphy Motors might have as its goal the conversion of 80% of the auto fleet to front-wheel drive by 1990. To implement this program, each division must formulate an objective specifying which cars will be con-

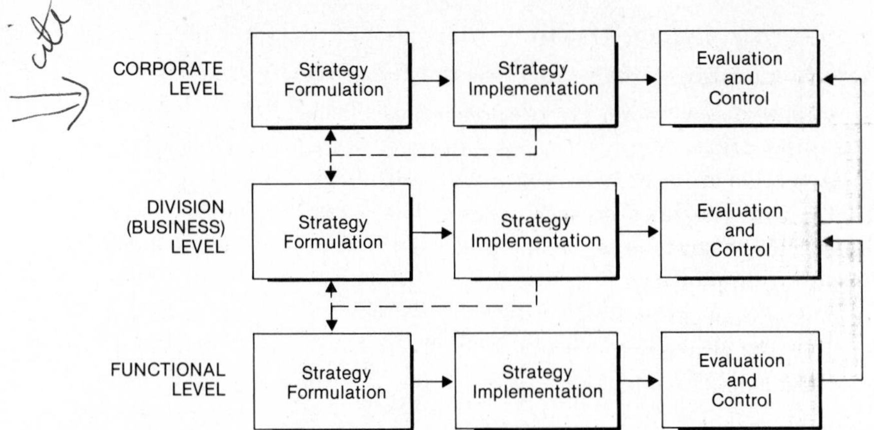

Figure 1.5 **Strategic management process at three corporate levels.**

verted by what time and at what cost and develop a strategy of how it is to be accomplished.

As each division develops its own programs for implementation, separate functional departments within each division begin to formulate their own objectives and strategies. For example, Division A's manufacturing department sets an objective of retooling its assembly line for front-wheel drive cars by 1989. The purchasing department of Division A sets objectives and plans strategies to begin ordering new parts from suppliers. Division A's marketing department initiates plans to change its advertising and promotional activities in order to ready the consumer for front-wheel drive vehicles. Each level develops its own objectives, strategies, and policies to complement the level above.

The specific operation of the hierarchy of strategy may vary from one corporation to another. The one described here of the fictitious Murphy Motors is an example of *top-down* strategic planning in which corporate-level top management initiates the strategy formulation process and calls upon divisions and functional units to formulate their own strategies as a way of implementing corporate-level strategies. Another approach may be *bottom-up* strategic planning in which the strategy formulation process is initiated by strategic proposals from divisional or functional units. This is shown in Fig. 1.5 with dotted arrows leading from functional to divisional level and from divisional to corporate level in the strategy formulation stages. Regardless of whether the initiation for strategy formulation comes from above or below, it is clear that the process involves a lot of negotiation between levels in the hierarchy to ensure that the various strategies fit together and reinforce each other.[21]

1.6 SUMMARY AND CONCLUSION

This chapter sets the stage for the study of strategic management and business policy. It explains the rationale for including the subject in a business school curriculum. In addition to serving as a capstone to integrate the various functional areas, the course provides a framework for analyzing top management's decision process and the effects of environmental issues on the corporation. Research generally supports the conclusion that corporations that manage strategically perform at higher levels than do those firms that do not. Strategic management is thus an important area of study for anyone interested in organizational productivity.

Our model of strategic management includes formulation and implementation, plus evaluation and control. The mission of a corporation derives from the interaction of internal and external environmental factors, modified by the needs and values of top management. A precise statement of mission guides the setting of objectives and the formulation of strategy and policies. Strategy is implemented through specific programs, budgets, and procedures. Management continually monitors and evaluates performance and activities on the basis of measurable results and audits of key areas. These data feed back into the corporation at all phases of the strategic management process. If results and activities fail to measure up to the plans, managers may then take the appropriate actions.

Although top management and the board of directors have primary responsibility for the strategic management process, many levels of the corporation conduct strategy formulation, implementation, evaluation, and control. Large multidivisional corporations utilize divisional and functional levels that integrate the entire corporation by focusing activities on the accomplishment of the mission.

DISCUSSION QUESTIONS

1. What is the difference between business policy and strategic management?
2. How does strategic management typically evolve in a corporation? Why?
3. What is meant by the hierarchy of strategy?
4. Does every business firm have business strategies? Explain.
5. What information is needed to properly formulate strategy? Why?

NOTES

1. G. Brooks, "After Mukluk Fiasco, Sohio Strives To Find, or Perhaps To Buy, Oil," *Wall Street Journal* (April 19, 1984), p. 22.
2. R. A. Gordon and J. E. Howell, *Higher Education for Business* (New York: Columbia University Press, 1959).
   F. C. Pierson et al., *The Education of American Businessmen* (New York: McGraw-Hill, 1959).

3. Gordon and Howell, p. 206.
4. Gordon and Howell, pp. 206–207.
5. J. D. Hunger and T. L. Wheelen, *An Assessment of Undergraduate Business Education in the United States* (Charlottesville, Va.: McIntire School of Commerce Foundation, 1980). Also summarized in "A Performance Appraisal of Undergraduate Business Education," *Human Resource Management* (Spring 1980), pp. 24–31.
6. M. Leontiades, "The Confusing Words of Business Policy," *Academy of Management Review* (January 1982), p. 46.
7. B. Lancaster, "American Hospital's Marketing Program Places Company Atop a Troubled Industry," *Wall Street Journal* (August 24, 1984), p. 19.
8. B. D. Henderson, *Henderson on Corporate Strategy* (Cambridge, Mass.: Abt Books, 1979), p. 33.
9. R. Lamb, *Advances in Strategic Management,* Vol. 2 (Greenwich, Conn.: Jai Press, Inc., 1983), p. x.
10. F. W. Gluck, S. P. Kaufman, and A. S. Walleck, "The Four Phases of Strategic Management," *The Journal of Business Strategy* (Winter 1982), pp. 9–21.
11. H. W. Henry, "Evolution of Strategic Planning in Major Corporations," *Proceedings, American Institute of Decision Sciences* (November 1980), pp. 454–456.
    H. W. Henry, "Then and Now: A Look at Strategic Planning Systems," *Journal of Business Strategy* (Winter 1981), pp. 64–69.
12. G. C. Brunton, "Implementing Corporate Strategy: The Story of International Thomson," *Journal of Business Strategy* (Fall 1984), p. 14.
13. P. Pascarella, "Strategy Comes Down to Earth," *Industry Week* (January 9, 1984), p. 51.
14. W. B. Schaffir and T. J. Lobe, "Strategic Planning: The Impact at Five Companies," *Planning Review* (March 1984), pp. 40–41.
15. R. B. Higgins, "Human Resource Management Problems in Strategic Planning: The Challenge of the 1980's," in R. Lamb (ed.) *Advances in Strategic Management,* Vol. 1 (Greenwich, Conn.: Jai Press, Inc., 1983), p. 86.
    C. B. Shrader, L. Taylor, and D. R. Dalton, "Strategic Planning and Organizational Performance: A Critical Appraisal," *Journal of Management* (Summer 1984), pp. 149–179.
16. H. I. Ansoff et al., "Does Planning Pay?" *Long Range Planning* (December 1970), pp. 2–7.
    S. Thune and R. J. House, "Where Long-Range Planning Pays Off," *Business Horizons* (August 1970), pp. 81–87.
    D. M. Herold, "Long-Range Planning and Organizational Performance: A Cross-Validation Study," *Academy of Management Journal* (March 1972), pp. 91–104.
    D. Burt, "Planning and Performance in Australian Retailing," *Long Range Planning* (June 1978), pp. 62–66.

J. O. Eastlack and P. R. McDonald, "CEO's Role in Corporate Growth," *Harvard Business Review* (May–June 1970), pp. 150–163.
D. R. Wood and R. L. LaForge, "The Impact of Comprehensive Planning on Financial Performance," *Academy of Management Journal* (September 1979), pp. 516–526.
D. W. Karger and Z. A. Malik, "Long Range Planning and Organizational Performance," *Long Range Planning* (December 1975), pp. 60–64; and Z. A. Malik and D. W. Karger, "Does Long-Range Planning Improve Company Performance?" *Management Review* (September 1975), pp. 27–31.
D. Miller and P. H. Friesen, "Strategy-Making and Environment: The Third Link," *Strategic Management Journal* (July–September 1983), pp. 221–235.
J. B. Welch, "Strategic Planning Could Improve Your Share Price," *Long Range Planning* (April 1984), pp. 144–147.
L. C. Rhyne, "The Impact of Strategic Planning on Financial Performance" (Paper presented at the Forty-Third Annual Meeting of the Academy of Management, Dallas, Texas, August 1983).

17. M. Leontiades and A. Tezel, "Planning Perceptions and Planning Results," *Strategic Management Journal* (January–March 1980), pp. 65–75.
W. Rue and R. M. Fulmer, "Is Long-Range Planning Profitable?" *Proceedings, Academy of Management* (August 1973), pp. 66–73.
R. J. Kudla, "The Effects of Strategic Planning on Common Stock Returns," *Academy of Management Journal* (March 1980), pp. 5–20.
J. W. Fredrickson and T. R. Mitchell, "Strategic Decision Processes: Comprehensiveness and Performance" (Paper presented at the Forty-Second Annual Meeting of the Academy of Management, New York, August 1982).
W. M. Lindsay, W. R. Boulton, S. Franklin, and L. W. Rue, "Strategic Management Effectiveness: A Longitudinal Study" (Paper presented at the Forty-First Annual Meeting of the Academy of Management, San Diego, California, 1981).

18. L. C. Rhyne, p. 9.

19. P. Lorange, *Corporate Planning: An Executive Viewpoint* (Englewood Cliffs, N.J.: Prentice-Hall, 1980), p. 18.

20. C. W. Hofer and D. Schendel, *Strategy Formulation: Analytical Concepts* (St. Paul, Minn.: West Publishing Co., 1978), p. 29.

21. M. E. Naylor, "Regaining Your Competitive Edge," *Long Range Planning* (February 1985), pp. 33–34.

Chapter 2

DEVELOPING CONCEPTUAL SKILLS: THE CASE METHOD AND THE STRATEGIC AUDIT

STRATEGIC MANAGEMENT MODEL

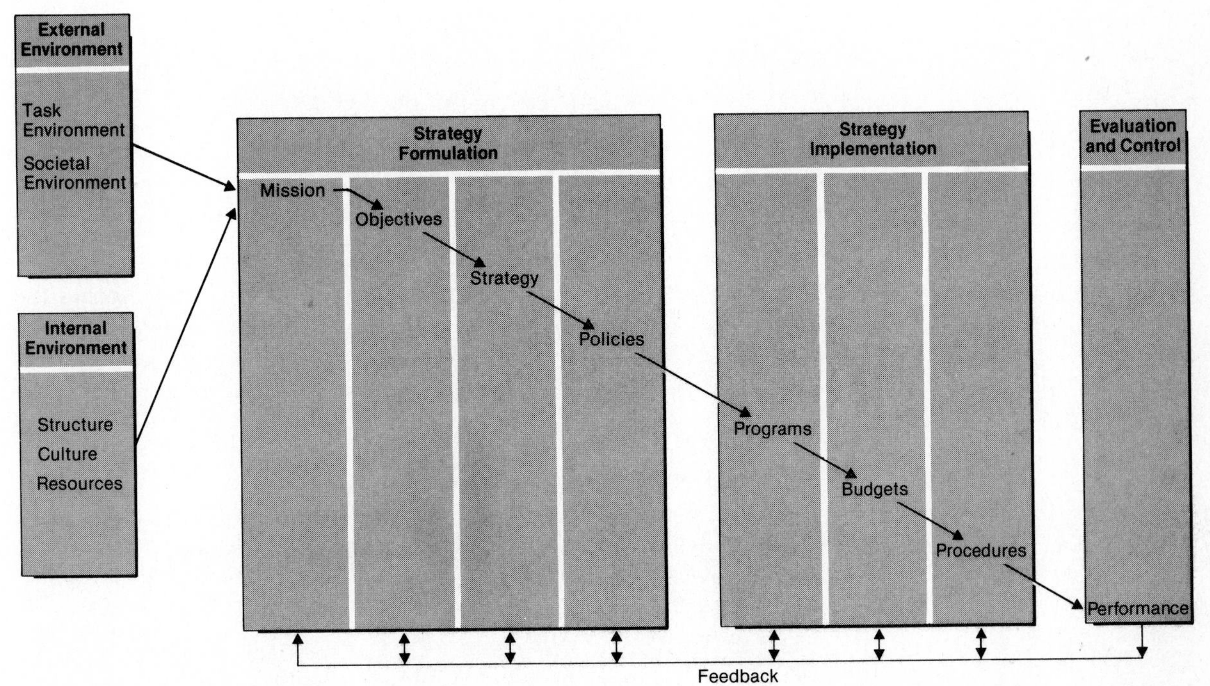

An analysis of a corporation's strategic management calls for a top-down view of the organization. In our analysis we view the corporation as an entity composed of interrelated units and systems, such as accounting, marketing, and finance. We examine the interrelationships of these areas in light of the opportunities and threats in the corporation's environment. We carry out our analysis through the use of complex cases or management simulations. These techniques will give you the opportunity to move from a narrow, specialized view to a broader, less precise analysis of the overall corporate picture. Consequently, the emphasis in case analysis is on developing and refining conceptual skills, which are different from the skills you developed in your technical and function-oriented courses. As you will see, conceptual skills are vital to performing successfully in the business world.

2.1 IMPORTANCE OF CONCEPTUAL SKILLS IN BUSINESS

Many have attempted to specify the characteristics necessary for a person to successfully advance from an entry-level position to one in top management. Few of these studies have been successful.[1] But Robert L. Katz has suggested one interesting approach. He focused on the skills successful managers exhibit in performing their jobs, an approach that negates the need to identify specific personality traits.[2] These skills imply abilities that can be developed and are manifested in performance.

Katz suggests that effective administration rests on three basic skills: technical, human, and conceptual. He defines them as follows:[3]

- *Technical skills* pertain to *what* is done and to working with *things.* They comprise one's ability to use technology to perform an organizational task.
- *Human skills* pertain to *how* something is done and to working with *people.* They comprise one's ability to work with people to achieve goals.
- *Conceptual skills* pertain to *why* something is done and to seeing the corporation as a *whole.* They comprise one's ability to understand the complexities of the corporation as it affects and is affected by its environment.

Katz further suggests that the optimal mix of these three skills varies at the different corporate levels:

> At lower levels, the major need is for technical and human skills. At higher levels, the administrator's effectiveness depends largely on human and conceptual skills. At the top, conceptual skill becomes the most important of all for successful administration.[4]

Results of a survey of 300 presidents of *Fortune's* list of the top fifty banking, industrial, insurance, public utility, retailing, and transportation firms support Katz's conclusion regarding the different skill mixes needed at

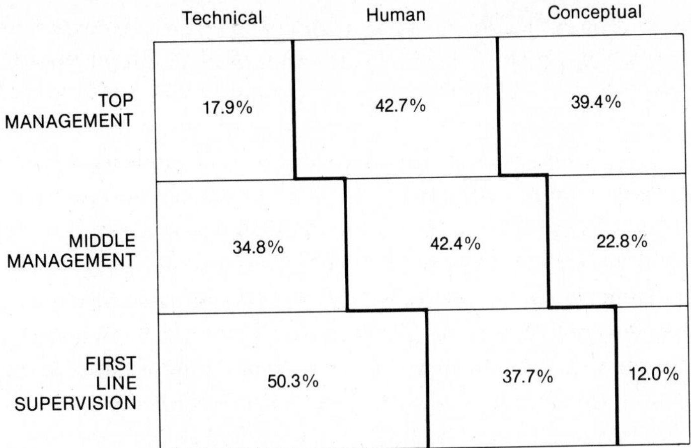

Figure 2.1 **Optimal skill mix of a manager by hierarchical level.**
SOURCE: T. L. Wheelen, G. K. Rakes, and J. D. Hunger, "Skills of an Executive," a paper presented to the Academy of Management, Kansas City, Mo., August 1976.

the different organizational levels.[5] As shown in Fig. 2.1, the need for technical skills decreases and the need for conceptual skills increases as a person moves from first line supervision to top management.

In addition, when executives were asked, "Are there certain skills necessary to move from one organizational level to another?" fifty-five percent reported conceptual skills to be the most crucial in moving from middle to top management.[6] Similar results have been reported concerning accountants in CPA firms.[7] Most theorists therefore agree that conceptual work carried out by organization leaders is the heart of strategy-making.[8]

The strategic management and business policy course attempts to develop conceptual skills through the use of comprehensive cases or complex simulations. Of course, you also need technical skills in order to analyze various aspects of each case. And you will use human skills in team presentations, study groups, or team projects. But in this course you will primarily develop and refine your conceptual skills by focusing on strategic issues. Concentrating on strategic management processes forces you to develop a better understanding of the political, social, and economic environment of business and to appreciate the interactions of the functional specialties required for corporate success.

2.2 AUDITS

Consulting firms, management scholars, boards of directors, and practicing managers are increasingly suggesting the use of audits of corporate activities.[9] An audit provides a checklist of questions by area or issue to enable a systematic analysis of various corporate activities. It is extremely useful as a diagnostic tool to pinpoint problem areas and to highlight strengths and weaknesses.

Management Audit

The National Association of Regulatory Utility Commissioners analyzed thirty-one management audits that had been completed or were in progress. The report concluded that the regulatory agencies using management audits were pleased with the results and intended to continue using them. In general, these audits recommended changes in the operating practices of management and suggested areas where substantial reductions in operating costs could be made. The audits gave the boards of directors and management the opportunity to establish new priorities in their objectives and planning, and provided specific recommendations that had impact on the "bottom line."[10]

Typically, the term *management audit* is used to describe a checklist of questions for an in-depth analysis of a particular area of importance to the corporation. Recent examples are the inflation audit, sales force management audit, the social audit, the stakeholder audit, and the forecasting audit, among others.[11] Rarely, however, does it include a consideration of more than one issue or functional area. The *strategic audit* is, in comparison, a *type of management audit* which takes a corporate-wide perspective to provide a comprehensive assessment of a corporation's strategic situation. Most business analysts predict the use of management audits of all kinds to increase. As corporate boards of directors become more aware of their expanding duties and responsibilities, they should call for more corporate-wide management audits to be conducted.

Strategic Audit

As contrasted with the typically more specialized management audit, the strategic audit considers external as well as internal factors and includes alternative selection, implementation, and evaluation and control. It therefore covers the key aspects of the strategic management process and places them within a decision-making framework. This framework is composed of the following eight interrelated steps:

1. Evaluation of a corporation's current performance results in terms of (a) return on investment, profitability, etc., and (b) the current mission, objectives, strategies, and policies.
2. Examination and evaluation of a corporation's strategic managers—its board of directors and top management.
3. A scanning of the external environment to locate strategic factors that pose opportunities and threats.

4. A scanning of the internal corporate environment to determine strategic strengths and weaknesses.
5. Analysis of the strategic factors (a) to pinpoint problem areas and (b) to review and revise the corporate mission and objectives as necessary.
6. Generation, evaluation, and selection of the best alternative strategy in light of the analysis conducted in step 5.
7. Implementation of selected strategies via programs, budgets, and procedures.
8. Evaluation of the implemented strategies via feedback systems, and the control of activities to ensure minimum deviation from plans.

This strategic decision-making process is depicted in Fig. 2.2 and basically reflects the approach to strategic management being used successfully by corporations such as Warner-Lambert and Dayton Hudson.[12] Although some research suggests that this type of "normative" approach may not work so well for firms in very unstable environments,[13] a recent survey of 956 corporate long-range planners reveals actual business practice to agree

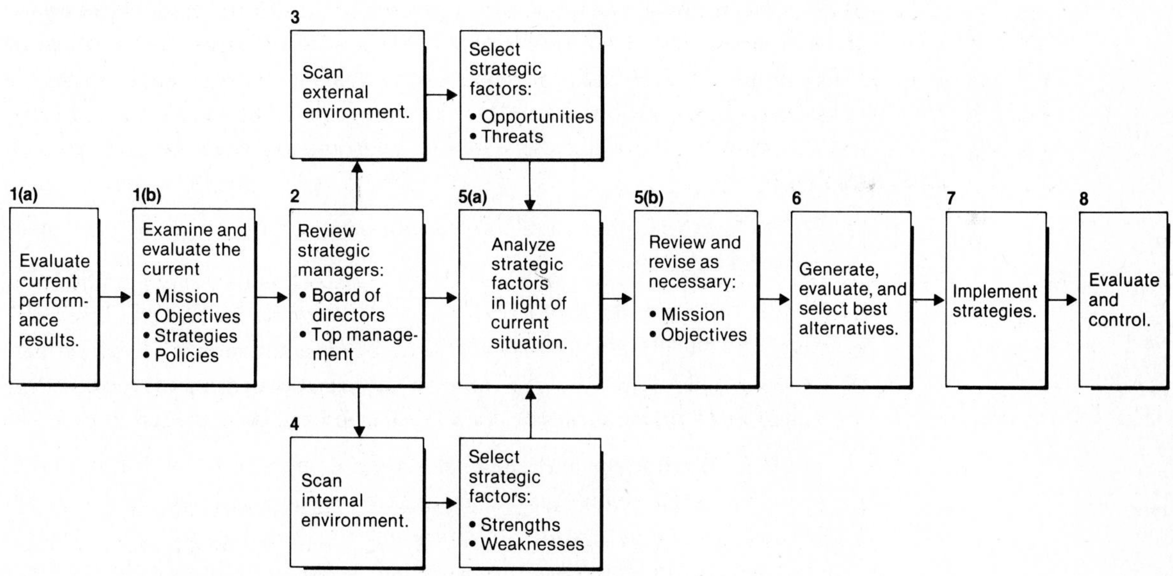

Figure 2.2 **Stategic decision-making process.**

generally with the model presented in Fig. 2.2.[14] This strategic decision-making process is made operational through the strategic audit.

The audit presents an integrated view of strategic management in action. It not only describes how objectives, strategies, and policies are formulated as long-range decisions, but also how they are implemented, evaluated, and controlled by programs, budgets, and procedures. The strategic audit, therefore, enables a person to better understand the *ways* in which various functional areas are interrelated and interdependent, as well as the *manner* in which they contribute to the achievement of the corporate mission. Consequently, the strategic audit is very useful to those people, such as boards of directors, whose job is to evaluate the overall performance of a corporation and its management.

Appendix 2.A at the end of this chapter is an example of a strategic audit proposed for use in analyzing complex business policy cases and for strategic decision making. The questions in the audit parallel the steps depicted in Fig. 2.2, the strategic decision-making process. It is *not* an all-inclusive list, but it presents many of the critical questions needed to strategically analyze any business corporation. You should consider the audit as a guide for analysis. Some questions or even some areas may be inappropriate for a particular case; in other areas, the questions may be insufficient for a complete analysis. However, each question in a particular area of the strategic audit can be broken down into an additional series of subquestions. It is up to you to develop these subquestions when they are needed.

A strategic audit fulfills three major *functions* in a case-oriented strategy and policy course:

1. It serves to highlight and review important concepts from previously studied subject areas.
2. It provides a systematic framework for the analysis of complex cases. (It is especially useful if you are unfamiliar with the case method.)
3. It generally improves the quality of case analysis and reduces the amount of time you might spend in learning how to analyze a case.

Students also find the audit helpful in organizing a case for written or oral presentation and in seeing that all areas have been considered. The strategic audit thus enables both students and teachers to maximize the amount of time spent both in analyzing why a certain area is creating problems for a corporation and in considering solutions to the problems.

2.3 CASE METHOD

The analysis/discussion of case problems has been the most popular method of teaching strategy and policy for many years.[15] Cases present actual business situations and enable you to examine both successful and unsuccessful corporations. For example, you may be asked to critically analyze a situation where a manager had to make a decision of long-run corporate importance. This approach gives you a feel for what it is like to work in a large corporation and to be faced with making a business decision.

Case Analysis and Presentation

There is no one best way to analyze or present a case report. Each instructor has personal preferences in terms of format and approach. Nevertheless, we present one suggested approach for both written and oral reports in Appendix 2.B at the end of the chapter. This approach provides a systematic method for successfully attacking a case.

The presentation of case analysis can be organized on the basis of a number of frameworks. One obvious framework to follow is the strategic audit as detailed in Appendix 2.A. Another is the McKinsey 7-S Framework composed of the seven organization variables of *structure, strategy, staff, management style, systems and procedures, skills,* and *shared values.*[16] Regardless of the framework chosen, be especially careful to include a complete analysis of key environmental variables—especially of trends in the industry and of the competition.

The focus in case discussion is on critical analysis and logical development of thought. A solution is satisfactory if it resolves important problems and is likely to be implemented successfully. What the corporation may actually have done to deal with the case problems has no real bearing on the analysis because its management may have analyzed its problems incorrectly and implemented a series of flawed solutions.

Researching the Case

You should undertake outside research to provide the environmental setting of the case. Check each case to find out when the case situation occurred and then screen the business periodicals for that time period. This background will give you an appreciation for the situation as it was experienced by the people in the case. A company's annual report from that year can be very helpful. An understanding of the economy during that period will help you avoid making a serious error in your analysis—for example, suggesting a sale of stock when the stock market is at an all-time low or taking on more debt when the prime interest rate is over 15%. Information on the industry will provide insights on its competitive activities. Some resources available for research into the economy and a corporation's industry are suggested in Appendix 2.C at the end of the chapter.

If you are unfamiliar with these business resources we urge you to read *How to Use the Business Library: With Sources of Business Information,* 5th ed., by H. W. Johnson, A. J. Faria, and E. L. Maier (Cincinnati: South-Western Publishing Co., 1984).

Table 2.1 Financial Ratios

Ratio	Formula	How Expressed
1. *Liquidity Ratios*		
Current ratio	$\frac{\text{Current assets}}{\text{Current liabilities}}$	Decimal
Quick (acid test) ratio	$\frac{\text{Current assets} - \text{Inventory}}{\text{Current liabilities}}$	Decimal
Inventory to net working capital	$\frac{\text{Inventory}}{\text{Current assets} - \text{Current liabilities}}$	Decimal
Cash ratio	$\frac{\text{Cash} + \text{cash equivalents}}{\text{Current liabilities}}$	Decimal
2. *Profitability Ratios*		
Net profit margin	$\frac{\text{Net profit after taxes}}{\text{Net sales}}$	Percentage
Gross profit margin	$\frac{\text{Sales} - \text{Cost of goods sold}}{\text{Net sales}}$	Percentage
Return on investment (ROI)	$\frac{\text{Net profit after taxes}}{\text{Total assets}}$	Percentage
Return on equity (ROE)	$\frac{\text{Net profit after taxes}}{\text{Stockholders equity}}$	Percentage
Earnings Per Share (EPS)	$\frac{\text{Net profit after taxes} - \text{Preferred stock dividends}}{\text{Average number of common shares}}$	Dollar per share
Productivity of Assets	$\frac{\text{Gross income} - \text{Taxes}}{\text{Stockholders equity}}$	Percentage
3. *Activity Ratios*		
Inventory turnover	$\frac{\text{Net sales}}{\text{Inventory}}$	Decimal
Days of inventory	$\frac{\text{Inventory}}{\text{Cost of goods sold} \div 365}$	Days
Net working capital turnover	$\frac{\text{Net sales}}{\text{Net working capital}}$	Decimal
Asset turnover	$\frac{\text{Sales}}{\text{Total assets}}$	Decimal
Fixed asset turnover	$\frac{\text{Sales}}{\text{Fixed assets}}$	Decimal
Average collection period	$\frac{\text{Accounts receivable}}{\text{Sales for year} \div 365}$	Days
Accounts receivable turnover	$\frac{\text{Annual credit sales}}{\text{Accounts receivable}}$	Decimal
Accounts payable period	$\frac{\text{Accounts Payable}}{\text{Purchases for year} \div 365}$	Days

Table 2.1 **Financial Ratios (Cont.)**

Ratio	*Formula*	*How Expressed*
Cash turnover	$\frac{\text{Cash}}{\text{Net sales for year} \div 365}$	Days
4. *Leverage Ratios*		
Debt to asset ratio	$\frac{\text{Total debt}}{\text{Total assets}}$	Percentage
Debt to equity ratio	$\frac{\text{Total debt}}{\text{Stockholders equity}}$	Percentage
Long-term debt to equity ratio	$\frac{\text{Long-term debt}}{\text{Stockholders equity}}$	Percentage
Times interest earned	$\frac{\text{Profit before taxes} + \text{Interest charges}}{\text{Interest charges}}$	Decimal
Coverage of fixed charges	$\frac{\text{Profit before taxes} + \text{Interest charges} + \text{Lease charges}}{\text{Interest charges} + \text{Lease obligations}}$	Decimal
Current liabilities to equity	$\frac{\text{Current liabilities}}{\text{Stockholders equity}}$	Percentage
5. *Other ratios*		
Price earning ratio	$\frac{\text{Market price per share}}{\text{Earnings per share}}$	Decimal
Dividend payout ratio	$\frac{\text{Annual dividends per share}}{\text{Annual earnings per share}}$	Percentage
Dividend yield on common stock	$\frac{\text{Annual dividends per share}}{\text{Current market price per share}}$	Percentage
Cash flow per share	$\frac{\text{After-tax profits} + \text{Depreciation}}{\text{Number of common shares outstanding}}$	Decimal

NOTE: In using ratios for analysis, calculate ratios for the corporation and compare them to the average ratios for the particular industry. Refer to Standard and Poor's and Robert Morris Associates for average industry data. For an in-depth discussion of ratios and their use, refer to J. F. Weston and E. F. Brigham, *Essentials of Managerial Finance,* 7th ed. (Hinsdale, Ill.: Dryden Press, 1985), pp. 59–93.

Financial Analysis: A Place To Begin

A review of key financial ratios may help you assess the company's overall situation and pinpoint some problem areas. Table 2.1 lists some of the most important financial ratios. Included are (1) *liquidity ratios,* which measure the corporation's ability to meet its financial obligations, (2) *profitability ratios,* which measure the degree of corporate success in achieving desired profit levels, (3) *activity ratios,* which measure the effectiveness of the corporation's use of resources, and (4) *leverage ratios,* which measure the contributions of owners' financing compared with creditors' financing.

In your analysis do *not* simply make an exhibit including all the ratios, but select and discuss only those ratios that have an impact on the company's problems. For instance, external resources, accounts receivable, and inventory may provide a source of funds. If receivables and inventories are double the industry average, reducing them may provide needed cash. In this situation, the case report should include not only sources of funds, but also the number of dollars freed for use.

A typical financial analysis of a firm would include a study of the operating statements for five or ten years, including a trend analysis of sales, profits, earnings per share, debt/equity ratio, return on investment, etc., plus a ratio study comparing the firm under study with industry standards. To begin, scrutinize historical income statements and balance sheets. These two basic statements provide most of the data needed for analysis. Compare the statements over time if a series of statements is available. Calculate changes that occur in individual categories from year to year, as well as the total change over the years. Determine the percentage change along with the absolute amount and the amount *adjusted for inflation.* Examination of this information may reveal developing trends. Compare trends in one category with trends in related categories. For example, an increase in sales of 15% over three years may appear to be satisfactory until you note an increase of 20% in the cost of goods sold during the same period. The outcome of this comparison may suggest that further investigation into the manufacturing process is necessary.

Another approach to analyzing financial statements is to convert them into *common-size* statements. Convert every category from dollar terms to percentages. In the case of the balance sheet, give the total assets or liabilities a value of 100%, and calculate all other categories as percentages of the total assets or liabilities. For the income statement, net sales represent 100%: calculate the percentage of each category so that the categories sum to the net sales percentage (100%). When you convert statements to this form, it is relatively easy to note the percentage each category represents of the total. Comparisons over the years may point out areas for additional analysis. To get a proper picture, however, make comparisons with industry data, if available, to see if fluctuations are merely reflecting industry-wide trends. If a firm's trends are generally in line with those of the rest of the industry, there is less likelihood of problems than if the firm's trends are worse than industry averages.

If the corporation being studied appears to be in poor financial condition, calculate its "Z-value." Developed by Edward Altman, the formula combines five ratios by weighting them according to their importance to a corporation's financial strength (see Illustrative Example 2.1). The formula predicts the likelihood of the company going bankrupt. Firms in serious trouble have Z values below 1.81.

THE ALTMAN BANKRUPTCY FORMULA

Illustrative Example 2.1

Edward I. Altman developed a formula to predict a company's likelihood of going bankrupt. His system of multiple discriminate analysis is used by stockholders to determine if the corporation is a good investment. The formula was developed from a study of 33 manufacturing companies with assets averaging $6.4 million that had filed Chapter X bankruptcies. These were paired with 33 similar but profitable firms with assets between $1 million and $25 million. The formula is:

$$Z = 1.2x_1 + 1.4x_2 + 3.3x_3 + 0.6x_4 + 1.0x_5$$

where

x_1 = Working capital divided by total assets.
x_2 = Retained earnings divided by total assets.
x_3 = Earnings before interest and taxes divided by total assets.
x_4 = Market value of equity divided by book value of total debt.
x_5 = Sales divided by total assets.
Z = Overall index of corporate fiscal health.

The range of the Z-value for most corporations is -4 to $+8$. According to Altman, financially strong corporations have Z values above 2.99. Corporations in serious trouble have Z values below 1.81. Those in the middle are question marks that could go either way. The closer a firm gets to bankruptcy, the more accurate the Z-value is as a predictor.

SOURCE: M. Ball, "Z Factor: Rescue by the Numbers," *INC.* (December 1980), p. 48. Reprinted with the permission of *INC.* Magazine, December 1980.

Adjusting for Inflation

Many of the cases in business policy/strategy textbooks take place during a period of rapid inflation. When analyzing these cases, you should calculate sales and profits in constant dollars in order to perceive the "true" performance of the corporation in comparison with that of the industry, or of the economy in general. Remember that chief executive officers wish to keep their jobs and that some will tend to bias the figures in their favor. Sales stated in current dollars may look like substantial growth, but when they're converted to constant dollars, they may show a steady decline. In 1980, Peter Drucker, a renowned author and consultant, stated, ". . . corporate profits of the last ten years would be all wiped out if they were adjusted for inflation."[17]

As of 1980, the Financial Accounting Standards Board (FASB) required the largest U.S. corporations to report the last five years' sales, dividends and market price in constant dollar terms. It also required corporations to

Table 2.2 **Scott Paper Company's Annual Report Adjusted for Inflation: An Excerpt**

(Constant dollar and current cost expressed in average 1983 dollars)	**1983**	**1982**	**1981**	**1980**	**1979**
Average consumer price index	**298.4**	289.1	272.4	246.8	217.4
(In millions, except on a per share basis)					
Sales					
As reported	**$2,465.1**	$2,293.4	$2,309.4	$2,083.2	$1,908.1
In constant dollars	**2,465.1**	2,367.2	2,529.8	2,518.8	2,619.0
Net income (loss)					
As reported	**$123.7**	$74.5	$133.3	$133.0	$136.5
In constant dollars	**(4.5)**	(40.5)	31.7	55.6	103.5
At current cost	**8.6**	(29.7)	37.4	54.7	103.7
Earnings (loss) per common share					
As reported	**$2.58**	$1.61	$3.22	$3.41	$3.50
In constant dollars	**(.24)**	(1.09)	.75	1.42	2.65
At current cost	**.05**	(.84)	.90	1.40	2.66
Dividends per common share					
As reported	**$1.00**	$1.00	$1.00	$1.00	$ .90
In constant dollars	**1.00**	1.03	1.09	1.21	1.24
Net assets at year end					
As reported	**$1,481.2**	$1,335.7	$1,287.6	$1,114.0	$1,019.8
In constant dollars	**2,515.8**	2,497.7	2,528.3	2,406.4	2,334.8
At current cost	**2,753.9**	2,741.7	2,792.3	2,681.8	2,659.0
Current cost decrease in inventory and property, plant and equipment relative to general price level	**$15.4**	$30.8	$23.7	$30.8	$42.7
Unrealized gain from decline in purchasing power of net amounts owed	**$30.7**	$31.5	$67.6	$90.0	$100.3
Market price per common share at year end					
As reported	**$31.63**	$20.50	$16.38	$21.38	$18.75
In constant dollars	**31.09**	20.92	17.36	24.69	24.34

SOURCE: Scott Paper Company, *1983 Annual Report*, p. 45.

report what they have paid for goods and services at current cost in addition to the usual historical cost.[18] In 1984, the FASB decided to continue only the current cost requirement. Table 2.2 shows a page from the 1983 annual report of the Scott Paper Company, which provided constant dollar figures so that investors could make comparisons quickly. Note that, as originally stated, Scott Paper sales increased 129 percent from 1979 to 1983. When recalculated in constant dollars, however, sales actually declined. Note also

Table 2.3 Consumer Price Index for All Items (1967 = 100.0)

Year	*CPI*	*Year*	*CPI*
1971	121.3	1978	195.4
1972	125.3	1979	217.4
1973	133.1	1980	246.8
1974	147.7	1981	272.4
1975	161.2	1982	289.1
1976	170.5	1983	298.4
1977	181.5	1984	311.1

SOURCE: U.S. Department of Commerce, *1984 Statistical Abstract of the United States*, Chart no. 809, p. 493.

Table 2.4 Changes in Prime Interest Rates*

Year	*Low*	*High*	*Year*	*Low*	*High*
1971	5¼	6¾	1978	6	11¾
1972	5	6	1979	11½	15¾
1973	6	10	1980	11	21½
1974	8¾	12	1981	15¾	20½
1975	7	10½	1982	11½	17
1976	6¼	7¼	1983	10½	11
1977	6½	7¾	1984	11	13

SOURCE: D. S. Benton, "Banking and Financial Information," Table 1.1, p. 2 in *Thorndike Encyclopedia of Banking and Financial Tables*, Revised Edition, *1984 Yearbook* (Boston, Mass.: Warren, Gorham & Lamont, 1984).

* The rate of interest that banks charge on the lowest-risk loans they make.

that when 1983 net income is calculated using constant dollars, a profit of $123.7 million becomes a $4.5 million net loss!

As an additional method of dealing with the distortions caused by inflation, firms such as DuPont and General Electric use inflation-adjusted figures throughout their operations. To adjust for inflation, most firms use the Consumer Price Index (CPI). Table 2.3 presents the index for all items. Table 2.4 provides information on prime interest rates.

2.4 SUMMARY AND CONCLUSION

The strategic management/business policy course is concerned with developing the conceptual skills that successful top management needs. The emphasis is therefore on improving your analytical and problem-solving abilities. The case method develops those skills and gives you an appreciation of environmental issues and the interdependencies among the functional units of a large corporation. The strategic audit is one recommended technique for systematizing the analysis of fairly long and complex policy cases. It also provides a basic checklist for investigating any large corporation. Nevertheless, the strategic audit is only one of many techniques with which you can analyze and diagnose case problems. We expect consultants, managers, and boards of directors to increasingly employ the audit as an analytical technique.

DISCUSSION QUESTIONS

1. Should people be selected for top management positions primarily on the basis of their having a particular combination of skills? Explain.
2. What are the strengths and weaknesses of the strategic audit as a technique for assessing corporate performance?
3. What value does the case method hold for the study of strategic management/business policy?
4. Why should one begin a case analysis with a financial analysis? When are other approaches appropriate?
5. Reconcile the strategic decision-making process depicted in Fig. 2.2 with the strategic management model depicted in Fig. 1.3.

NOTES

1. B. M. Bass, *Stogdill's Handbook of Leadership* (New York: Free Press, 1981), p. 73.
2. R. L. Katz, "Skills of an Effective Administrator," *Harvard Business Review* (January–February 1955), p. 33.
3. Katz, pp. 33–42. These definitions were adapted from the material in this article.
4. Katz, p. 42.
5. T. L. Wheelen, G. K. Rakes, and J. D. Hunger, "Skills of an Executive" (Paper presented at the Thirty-Sixth Annual Meeting of the Academy of Management, Kansas City, Mo., August 1976).
6. Wheelen, Rakes, and Hunger, p. 7.
7. W. G. Shenkir, T. L. Wheelen, and R. H. Strawser, "The Making of an Accountant," *CPA Journal* (March 1973), p. 219.
8. E. E. Chaffee, "Three Models of Strategy," *Academy of Management Review* (January 1985), pp. 89–90.
9. R. B. Buchele, "How to Evaluate a Firm," *California Management Review* (Fall 1962), pp. 5–16.
   W. T. Greenwood, *Business Policy: A Management Audit Approach* (New York: Macmillan, 1967).
   A. Elkins, *Management: Structures, Functions, and Practices* (Reading, Mass.: Addison-Wesley, 1980), pp. 441–454.
   B. H. Marcus and E. M. Tauber, *Marketing Analysis and Decision Making* (Boston: Little, Brown & Co., 1979), p. 25.
   J. A. F. Stoner, *Management,* 2nd ed. (Englewood Cliffs, N.J.: Prentice-Hall, 1982), p. 526.

J. Martindell, *The Appraisal of Management* (New York: Harper & Row, 1962).
R. Bauer, L. T. Cauthorn, and R. P. Warner, "Management Audit Process Guide," (Boston: Intercollegiate Case Clearing House, no. 9-375-336, 1975).
J. D. Hunger and T. L. Wheelen, "The Strategic Audit: An Integrative Approach To Teaching Business Policy" (Paper presented at the Forty-Third Annual Meeting of the Academy of Management, Dallas, Texas, August 1983).
M. Lauenstein, "The Strategy Audit," *Journal of Business Strategy* (Winter 1984), pp. 87–91.

10. T. Barry, "What a Management Audit Can Do for You," *Management Review* (June 1977), p. 43.
11. A. Michel, "The Inflation Audit," *California Management Review* (Winter 1981), pp. 68–74.
A. J. Dubinsky and R. W. Hansen, "The Sales Force Management Audit," *California Management Review* (Winter 1981), pp. 86–95.
A. B. Carroll and G. W. Beiler, "Landmarks in the Evolution of the Social Audit," *Academy of Management Journal* (September 1975), pp. 589–599.
R. E. Freeman, *Strategic Management: A Stakeholder Approach* (Boston: Pitman Publishing, 1984), p. 111.
J. S. Armstrong, "The Forecasting Audit," in S. Makridakis and S. C. Wheelwright (eds.), *The Handbook of Forecasting* (New York: Wiley and Sons, 1982), pp. 535–552.
A. L. Wilkins, "The Culture Audit," *Organization Dynamics* (Autumn 1983), pp. 24–38.
12. E. E. Tallett, "Repositioning Warner-Lambert as a High-Tech Health Care Company," *Planning Review* (May 1984), pp. 12–16, 41.
K. A. Macke, "Managing Change: How Dayton Hudson Meets the Challenge," *Journal of Business Strategy* (Summer 1983), pp. 78–81.
13. J. W. Fredrickson, "The Comprehensiveness of Strategic Decision Processes: Extension, Observation, Future Directions," *Academy of Management Journal* (September 1984), pp. 445–466.
14. P. M. Ginter and A. C. Rucks, "Relative Emphasis Placed on the Steps of the Normative Model of Strategic Planning by Practitioners," *Proceedings, Southern Management Association* (November 1983), pp. 19–21.
15. C. Boyd, D. Kopp, and L. Shufelt, "Evaluative Criteria in Business Policy Case Analysis: An Exploratory Study," *Proceedings, Midwest Academy of Management* (April 1984), pp. 287–292.
16. T. J. Peters and R. W. Waterman, Jr., *In Search of Excellence* (New York: Harper & Row, 1982), pp. 9–12.
17. D. Pauly, "Tomorrow's Rules for World Business," *Newsweek,* April 28, 1980, p. 71.
18. "Financial Statements Restated for General Price-Level Changes," *Financial Accounting Standards,* APB Statement no. 3 (Stamford, Conn.: Financial Accounting Standards Board, July 1, 1979).

STRATEGIC AUDIT OF A CORPORATION

Appendix 2.A

I. Current Situation

A. How is the corporation performing in terms of return on investment, overall market share, profitability trends, earnings per share, etc.?

B. What are the corporation's current mission, objectives, strategies, and policies?

1. Are they clearly stated or are they merely implied from performance?
2. *Mission:* What business(es) is the corporation in? Why?
3. *Objectives:* What are the corporate, business, and functional objectives? Are they consistent with each other, with the mission, and with the internal and external environments?
4. *Strategies:* What strategy or mix of strategies is the corporation following? Are they consistent with each other, with the mission and objectives, and with the internal and external environments?
5. *Policies:* What are they? Are they consistent with each other, with the mission, objectives, and strategies, and with the internal and external environments?

II. Strategic Managers

A. Board of Directors

1. Who are they? Are they internal or external?
2. Do they own significant shares of stock?
3. Is the stock privately held or publicly traded?
4. What do they contribute to the corporation in terms of knowledge, skills, background, and connections?
5. How long have they served on the board?
6. What is their level of involvement in strategic management? Do they merely rubber stamp top management's proposals or do they actively participate and suggest future directions?

B. Top Management

1. What person or group constitutes top management?
2. What are top management's chief characteristics in terms of knowledge, skills, background, and style?

SOURCE: T. L. Wheelen and J. D. Hunger, "Strategic Audit of a Corporation." Revised 1985.

3. Has top management been responsible for the corporation's performance over the past few years?
4. Has it established a systematic approach to the formulation, implementation, and evaluation and control of strategic management?
5. What is its level of involvement in the strategic management process?
6. How well does top management interact with lower-level management?
7. How well does top management interact with the board of directors?
8. Is top management sufficiently skilled to cope with likely future challenges?

III. External Environment: Opportunities and Threats (S.W.O.T.)

A. Societal Environment

1. What general environmental factors (that is, sociocultural, economic, political-legal, and technological factors) are affecting the corporation?
2. Which of these are the most important at the present time? In the next few years?

B. Task Environment

1. What key factors in the immediate environment (that is, customers, competitors, suppliers, creditors, labor unions, governments, trade associations, interest groups, local community, and stockholders) are affecting the corporation?
2. Which of these are most important at the present time? In the next few years?

IV. Internal Environment: Strengths and Weaknesses (S.W.O.T.)

A. Corporate Structure

1. How is the corporation presently structured?
   a) Is decision-making authority centralized around one group or decentralized to many groups or units?
   b) Is it organized on the basis of functions, projects, geography, or some combination of these?
2. Is the structure clearly understood by everyone in the corporation?
3. Is the present structure consistent with current corporate objectives, strategies, policies, and programs?
4. In what ways does this structure compare with those of similar corporations?

(*Continued*)

B. Corporate Culture

1. Is there a well-defined or emerging culture composed of shared beliefs, expectations, and values?

2. Is the culture consistent with the current objectives, strategies, policies, and programs?

3. What is the culture's position on important issues facing the corporation (that is, on productivity, quality of performance, adaptability to changing conditions)?

C. Corporate Resources

1. Marketing

a) What are the corporation's current marketing objectives, strategies, policies, and programs?

i) Are they clearly stated or merely implied from performance and/or budgets?

ii) Are they consistent with the corporation's mission, objectives, strategies, policies, and with internal and external environments?

b) How well is the corporation performing in terms of analysis of market position and marketing mix (that is, of product, price, place, and promotion)?

i) What trends emerge from this analysis?

ii) What impact have these trends had on past performance and how will they probably affect future performance?

iii) Does this analysis support the corporation's past and pending strategic decisions?

c) How well does this corporation's marketing performance compare with those of similar corporations?

d) Are marketing managers using accepted marketing concepts and techniques to evaluate and improve product performance? (Consider product life cycle, market segmentation, market research, and product portfolios.)

e) What is the role of the marketing manager in the strategic management process?

2. Finance

a) What are the corporation's current financial objectives, strategies, policies, and programs?

i) Are they clearly stated or merely implied from performance and/or budgets?

ii) Are they consistent with the corporation's mission, objectives, strategies, policies, and with internal and external environments?

b) How well is the corporation performing in terms of financial analysis? (Consider liquidity ratios, profitability ratios, activity ratios, leverage ratios, capitalization structure, and constant dollars.)

i) What trends emerge from this analysis?

ii) What impact have these trends had on past performance and how will they probably affect future performance?

iii) Does this analysis support the corporation's past and pending strategic decisions?

c) How well does this corporation's financial performance compare with that of similar corporations?

d) Are financial managers using accepted financial concepts and techniques to evaluate and improve current corporate and divisional performance? (Consider financial leverage, capital budgeting, and ratio analysis.)

e) What is the role of the financial manager in the strategic management process?

3. Research and Development (R&D)

a) What are the corporation's current R&D objectives, strategies, policies, and programs?

i) Are they clearly stated or implied from performance and/or budgets?

ii) Are they consistent with the corporation's mission, objectives, strategies, policies, and with internal and external environments?

iii) What is the role of technology in corporate performance?

iv) Is the mix of basic, applied, and engineering research appropriate given the corporate mission and strategies?

b) What return is the corporation receiving from its investment in R&D?

c) Is the corporation technologically competent?

d) How well does the corporation's investment in R&D compare with the investments of similar corporations?

e) What is the role of the R&D manager in the strategic management process?

4. Manufacturing/Service

a) What are the corporation's current manufacturing/service objectives, strategies, policies, and programs?

(*Continued*)

i) Are they clearly stated or merely implied from performance and/or budgets?

ii) Are they consistent with the corporation's mission, objectives, strategies, policies, and with internal and external environments?

b) What is the type and extent of production capabilities of the corporation?

i) If product-oriented, consider plant facilities, type of manufacturing system (continuous mass production or intermittent job shop), age and type of equipment, degree and role of automation and/or robots, plant capacities and utilization, productivity ratings, availability and type of transportation.

ii) If service-oriented, consider service facilities (e.g., hospital, theater, or school buildings), type of operations systems (continuous service over time to same clientele or intermittent service over time to varied clientele), age and type of supporting equipment, degree and role of automation and/or use of mass communication devices (e.g., diagnostic machinery, videotape machines), facility capacities and utilization rates, efficiency ratings of professional/service personnel, availability and type of transportation to bring service staff and clientele together.

c) Are manufacturing or service facilities vulnerable to natural disasters, local or national strikes, reduction or limitation of resources from suppliers, substantial cost increases of materials, or nationalization by governments?

d) Is operating leverage being used successfully with an appropriate mix of people and machines in manufacturing firms or of support staff to professionals in service firms?

e) How well is the corporation performing compared to the competition? Consider costs per unit of labor, material, and overhead; downtime; inventory control management and/or scheduling of service staff; production ratings; facility utilization percentages; and number of clients successfully treated by category (if service firm), or percentage of orders shipped on time (if product firm).

i) What trends emerge from this analysis?

ii) What impact have these trends had on past performance and how will they probably affect future performance?

iii) Does this analysis support the corporation's past and pending strategic decisions?

f) Are manufacturing/service managers using appropriate concepts and techniques to evaluate and improve current performance? Consider cost systems, quality control and reliability systems, inventory control management, personnel scheduling, learning curves, safety programs, engineering programs to improve efficiency of manufacturing or of service.

g) What is the role of the manager of manufacturing or services in the strategic management process?

5. Human Resources Management (HRM)

a) What are the corporation's current HRM objectives, strategies, policies, and programs?

i) Are they clearly stated or merely implied from performance and/or budgets?

ii) Are they consistent with the corporation's mission, objectives, strategies, policies, and with internal and external environments?

b) How well is the corporation's HRM performing in terms of improving the fit between the individual employee and the job? Consider turnover, grievances, strikes, layoffs, quality of work life.

i) What trends emerge from this analysis?

ii) What impact have these trends had on past performance and how will they probably affect future performance?

iii) Does this analysis support the corporation's past and pending strategic decisions?

c) How does this corporation's HRM performance compare with that of similar corporations?

d) Are HRM managers using appropriate concepts and techniques to evaluate and improve corporate performance? Consider job analysis program, performance appraisal system, up-to-date job descriptions, training and development programs, attitude surveys, job design programs, quality of relationship with unions.

e) What is the role of the HRM manager in the strategic management process?

6. Information Systems (MIS)

a) What are the corporation's current MIS objectives, strategies, policies, and programs?

(Continued)

i) Are they clearly stated or merely implied from performance and/or budgets?

ii) Are they consistent with the corporation's mission, objectives, strategies, policies, and with internal and external environments?

b) How well is the corporation's MIS performing in terms of providing a useful database, automating routine clerical operations, assisting managers in making routine decisions, and providing information necessary for strategic decisions?

i) What trends emerge from this analysis?

ii) What impact have these trends had on past performance and how will they probably affect future performance?

iii) Does this analysis support the corporation's past and pending strategic decisions?

c) How does this corporation's MIS performance and stage of development compare with that of similar corporations?

d) Are MIS managers using appropriate concepts and techniques to evaluate and improve corporate performance? Do they know how to build and manage a complex database, conduct system analyses, and implement interactive decision support systems?

e) What is the role of the MIS manager in the strategic management process?

V. Analysis of Strategic Factors

A. What are the key internal and external factors (S.W.O.T.) that strongly affect the corporation's present and future performance?

1. What are the short-term problems facing this corporation?

2. What are the long-term problems facing this corporation?

B. Are the current mission and objectives appropriate in light of the key strategic factors and problems?

1. Should the mission and objectives be changed? If so, how?

2. If changed, what will the effect be on the firm?

VI. Strategic Alternatives

A. Can the current or revised objectives be met by simply implementing more carefully those strategies presently in use (for example, fine tuning the strategies)?

B. What are the feasible alternative strategies available to this corporation?

1. Do you recommend stability, growth, retrenchment, or a combination of these strategies?
2. What are the pros and cons of each?

C. What is the *best* alternative (that is, *your* recommended strategy)?
1. Does it adequately resolve the long- and short-term problems?
2. Does it take into consideration the key strategic factors?
3. What policies should be developed or revised to guide effective implementation?

VII. Implementation

A. What kinds of programs (for example, restructuring the corporation) should be developed to implement the recommended strategy?
1. Who should develop these programs?
2. Who should be in charge of these programs?

B. Are the programs financially feasible? Can *pro forma* budgets be developed and agreed upon? Are priorities and timetables appropriate to individual programs?

C. Will new standard operating procedures need to be developed?

VIII. Evaluation and Control

A. Is the current information system capable of providing sufficient feedback on implementation activities and performance?
1. Can performance results be pinpointed by area, unit, project, or function?
2. Is the information timely?

B. Are adequate control measures in place to ensure conformance with the recommended strategic plan?
1. Are appropriate standards and measures being used?
2. Are reward systems capable of recognizing and rewarding good performance?

SUGGESTED TECHNIQUES FOR CASE ANALYSIS AND PRESENTATION

Appendix 2.B

A. Case Analysis

1. Read the case rapidly to get an overview of the nature of the corporation and its environment. Note the date the case was written so that you can put it into proper context.

(Continued)

2. Read the case a second time, giving it a detailed analysis according to the strategic audit (see Appendix 2.A) when appropriate. The audit will provide a conceptual framework to examine the corporation's objectives, mission, policies, strategies, problems, symptoms or problems, and issues. You should end up with a list of the salient issues and problems in the case. Perform a financial analysis.
3. Undertake outside research, when appropriate, to uncover economic and industrial information. Appendix 2.C suggests possible sources for outside research. These data should provide the environmental setting for the corporation. Conduct an in-depth analysis of the industry. Analyze the important competitors. Consider the bargaining power of suppliers as well as buyers which may affect the firm's situation. Consider also the possible threats of future competitors in the industry as well as the likelihood of new or different products or services which may substitute for the company's present ones.
4. Marshal facts and evidence to support selected issues and problems. Develop a framework or outline to organize the analysis. Your method of organization could be one of the following:
   a) The case as organized around the strategic audit.
   b) The case as organized around the key individual(s) in the case.
   c) The case as organized around the corporation's functional areas: production, management, finance, marketing, and R&D.
   d) The case as organized around the decision-making process.
   e) The case as organized around the seven variables (McKinsey 7-S Framework) of structure, strategy, staff, management style, systems and procedures, skills, and shared values.
5. Clearly identify and state the central problem(s) as supported by the information in the case. Use the S.W.O.T. format to sum up the key strategic factors facing the corporation: Strengths and Weaknesses of the company; Opportunities and Threats in the environment.
6. Develop a logical series of alternatives that evolve from the analysis to resolve the problem(s) or issue(s) in the case.
7. Evaluate each of the alternatives in light of the company's environment (both external and internal), mission, objectives, strategies, and policies. For each alternative, consider both the possible obstacles to its implementation and its financial implications.
8. Make recommendations on the basis of the fact that action must be taken. (Don't say, "I don't have enough information." The individuals in the case may have had the same or even less information than is in the case.)

a) Base your recommendations on a total analysis of the case.
b) Provide the evidence gathered in step A4 to justify suggested changes.
c) List the recommendations in order of priority—those to be done immediately and those to be done in the future.
d) Show how your recommendation(s) will solve each of the problems mentioned in step A5.
e) Explain how each recommendation will be implemented. How will the plan(s) deal with anticipated resistance?
f) Suggest feedback and control systems to ensure that the recommendations are carried out as planned and to give advance warning of needed adjustments

B. Written Presentation

1. Use the outline from step A4 to write the first draft of the case analysis.
   a) Don't rehash the case material; rather supply the salient evidence and data to support your recommendations.
   b) Develop exhibits on financial ratios and other data for inclusion in your report. The exhibits should provide meaningful information. Mention key elements of an exhibit in the text of the written analysis. If you include a ratio analysis as an exhibit, explain the meaning of the ratios in the text and cite only the critical ones in your analysis.
2. Review your case analysis after it is written for content and grammar. Remember to compare the outline (step A4) with the final product. Make sure you've presented sufficient data or evidence to support your problem analysis and recommendations. If the final product requires rewriting, do so. Keep in mind that the written report is going to be judged not only on *what* is said but also on the *manner* in which it is said.
3. If your written or oral presentation requires *pro forma* statements, you may wish to develop a scenario for each quarter and/or year in your forecast. A well-constructed scenario will help improve the accuracy of your forecast. Chapters 4 and 8 suggest methods to develop scenarios.

C. Oral Presentation by Teams

1. Each team member should develop his or her own outline from step A4.
2. The team should consolidate member outlines into one comprehensive team outline.
3. Divide the work of the case analysis among the team members for further modification and for presentation.

(*Continued*)

4. Modify the team outline, if necessary, and have one or two rehearsals of the presentation. If there is a time constraint, apply it to the practice presentation. If exhibits are used, make sure to allow sufficient time to explain them. Critique one another's presentations and make the necessary modifications to the analysis.
5. During the class presentation, if a presenter misses a key fact, either slip a note to him or her, or deal with it in the summary speech.
6. Answer the specific questions raised by the instructor or classmates. If one person acts as a moderator for the questions and refers the questions to the appropriate team member, the presentation runs more smoothly than it will if everyone (or no one!) tries to deal with each question.

RESOURCES FOR CASE RESEARCH

Appendix 2.C

A. Company Information
   1. Annual Reports
   2. *Moody's Manuals on Investment* (a listing of companies within certain industries that contains a brief history of each company and a five-year financial statement)
   3. Securities and Exchange Commission Annual Report Form 10-K
   4. *Standard and Poor's Register of Corporations, Directors, and Executives*
   5. *Value Line Investment Survey*

B. Economic Information
   1. Regional statistics and local forecasts from large banks
   2. *Business Cycle Development* (Department of Commerce)
   3. Chase Econometric Associates' publications
   4. Census Bureau publications on population, transportation, and housing
   5. *Current Business Reports* (Department of Commerce)
   6. *Economic Indicators* (Joint Economic Committee)
   7. *Economic Report of the President to Congress*
   8. *Long-Term Economic Growth* (Department of Commerce)
   9. *Monthly Labor Review* (Department of Labor)
   10. *Monthly Bulletin of Statistics* (United Nations)

11. "Survey of Buying Power," *Sales Management*
12. Standard and Poor's Statistical Service
13. *Statistical Abstract of the United States* (Department of Commerce)
14. *Statistical Yearbook* (United Nations)
15. *Survey of Current Business* (Department of Commerce)
16. *U.S. Industrial Outlook* (Department of Defense)
17. *World Trade Annual* (United Nations)
18. *Overseas Business Reports* (published by country by U.S. Department of Commerce)

C. Industry Information
   1. Analysis of companies and industries by investment brokerage firms
   2. *Annual Report of American Industry* (a compilation of statistics by industry and company published by *Fortune*)
   3. *Business Week* (provides weekly economic and business information and quarterly profit and sales rankings of corporations)
   4. *Fortune Magazine* (publishes listings of financial information on corporations within certain industries)
   5. *Industry Survey* (published quarterly by Standard and Poor Corporation)

D. Directory and Index Information
   1. *Business Information: How to Find and Use It*
   2. *Business Periodical Index*
   3. *Directory of National Trade Associations*
   4. *Encyclopedia of Associations*
   5. *Funk and Scott Index of Corporations and Industries*
   6. *Thomas's Register of American Manufacturers*
   7. *Wall Street Journal Index*

E. Ratio Analysis Information
   1. *Almanac of Business and Industrial Ratios* (Prentice-Hall)
   2. *Annual Statement Studies* (Robert Morris Associates)
   3. *Dun's Review* (Dun and Bradstreet: published annually in September–December issues)

F. General Sources
   1. *Commodity Yearbook*
   2. *U.S. Census of Business*

(*Continued*)

   3. *U.S. Census of Manufacturers*
   4. *World Almanac and Book of Facts*

G. Business Periodicals
   1. *Business Week*
   2. *Forbes*
   3. *Wall Street Journal*
   4. *Fortune*
   5. Industry-specific periodicals (e.g., *Oil and Gas Journal*)

H. Academic/Practitioner Journals
   1. *Harvard Business Review*
   2. *Journal of Business Strategy*
   3. *Long-Range Planning*
   4. *Strategic Management Journal*
   5. *Planning Review*
   6. *Academy of Management Review*

PART TWO

SCANNING THE ENVIRONMENT

Chapter 3

STRATEGIC MANAGERS

STRATEGIC MANAGEMENT MODEL

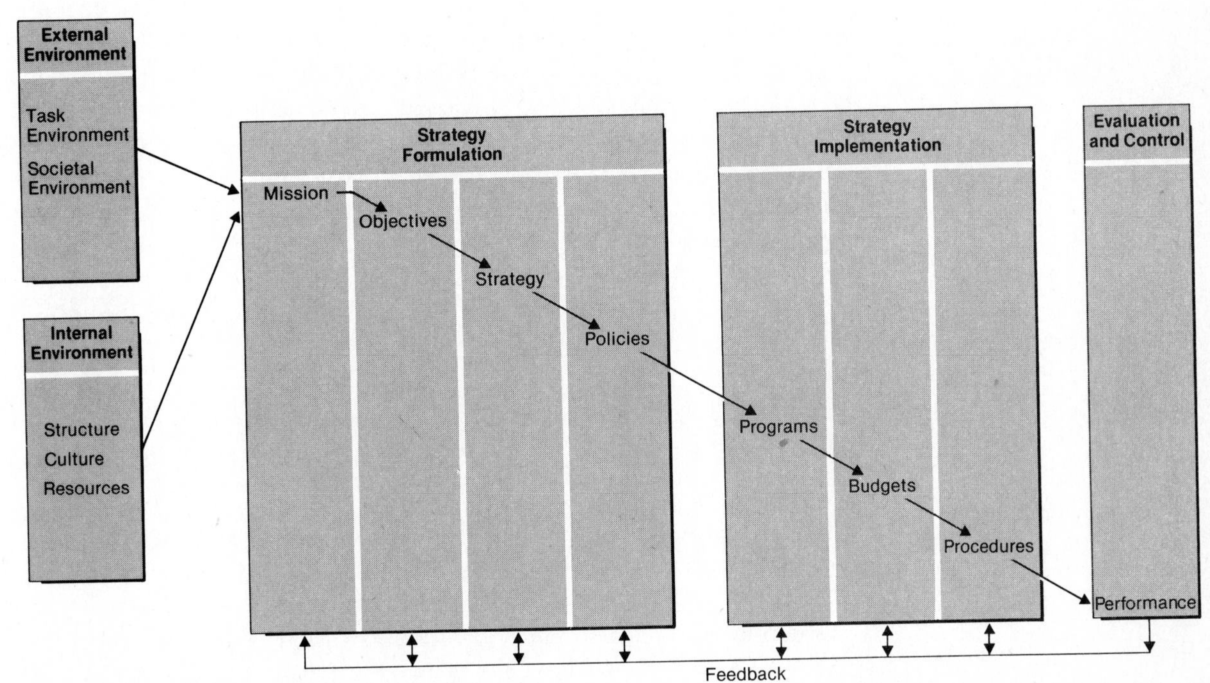

Strategic managers are the people in a corporation who are involved in the strategic management process. They are the people who scan the internal and external environments, formulate and implement objectives, strategies and policies, and evaluate and control the results. The people with direct responsibility for this process are the board of directors and top management. The chief executive officer (CEO), the chief operations officer (COO) or president, the executive vice-president, and the vice-presidents in charge of operating divisions and functional areas typically form the top management group. Traditionally, boards of directors have engaged in strategic management only to the extent that they passively approved proposals from top management and hired and fired their CEOs. Their role, however, is changing dramatically. The strategic management process, therefore, is also changing.

3.1 CORPORATE BOARD OF DIRECTORS

> Directors conduct a far different meeting from those in the past. Pressures—from regulatory agencies, shareholders, lenders, and the public—have practically forced greater awareness of directors' responsibilities. The board as a rubber stamp or a bastion of the "old-boy" selection system has largely been replaced by more active, more professional boards.[1]

Even in the recent past, boards of directors have functioned rather passively. Members were selected because of their prestige in the community, regardless of their knowledge of the specific functioning of the corporation they were to oversee. Traditionally, members of the board were requested to simply approve proposals by top management or the firm's legal counsel, and the more important board activities generally were conducted by an executive committee composed of insiders.[2] Even now, the boards in some family-owned corporations are more figureheads than overseers; they exist on paper because the laws of incorporation require their presence, but rarely, if ever, do they question management's plans.

Lee Iacocca describes how such a situation existed at the Ford Motor Company.

> The Ford Motor Company had gone public in 1956, but Henry never really accepted the change. As he saw it, he was like his grandfather, the rightful owner—Henry Ford, Prop. (Proprietor)—and the company was his to do [with] as he pleased. When it came to the board, he, more than most CEO's, believed in the mushroom treatment—throw manure on them and keep them in the dark. That attitude, of course, was fostered by the fact that Henry and his family, with only 12% of the stock, held on to 40% of the voting rights.[3]

Over the past decade, stockholders and various interest groups have seriously questioned the role of the board of directors. As a result, the general public has become more aware and more critical of many boards' apparent lack of responsibility for corporate activities. Who is responsible for radioactive leaks in nuclear power plants? For the manufacture and sale of unsafe toys? For not properly safeguarding employees from hazards in the workplace? For bribery attempts by corporate officers? Can boards, especially those of multinational corporations, realistically monitor the decisions and actions of corporate employees in countries halfway around the world? What are the legal liabilities of a board for the actions taken by the corporation?

Responsibilities of the Board

At this time, there are no national standards defining the accountability or responsibility of a board of directors. The law offers little guidance on this question. Specific requirements of directors vary, depending on the state in which the corporate charter is issued. According to Conference Board reports authored by Bacon and Brown, "State corporation laws give boards of directors rather sweeping powers couched in general language that does not specify to whom they are accountable nor clarify what it is they are accountable for.[4] There is, nevertheless, a developing consensus concerning the major responsibilities of a board.

The board of directors of a corporation is appointed or elected by the stockholders for the following purposes:

- To oversee the management of the corporation's assets;
- To establish or approve the corporation's mission, objectives, strategy, and policies;
- To review management's actions in light of the financial performance of the corporation; and
- To hire and fire the principal operating officers of the corporation.

In a legal sense, the board is required to direct the affairs of the corporation but not to manage them. It is charged by law to act with "due care." As Bacon and Brown put it, "Directors must act with that degree of diligence, care and skill which ordinarily prudent men would exercise under similar circumstances in like positions."[5] If a director or the board as a whole fails to act with due care and, as a result, the corporation is in some way harmed, the careless director or directors may be held personally liable for the harm done.

For example, after the Federal Deposit Insurance Corporation (FDIC) put together a $4.5 billion package to rescue the failing Continental Illinois Bank of Chicago in 1984, it dismissed nine of the bank's sixteen directors.

Two other directors resigned. Even though each director had sworn the Joint Oath of the National Bank Directors to "diligently and honestly administer the affairs" of the bank, the FDIC contended that the directors should have monitored more carefully what was happening at Continental Illinois.[6]

The increasing popularity of personal liability insurance for board members suggests that a number of people on boards of directors are becoming very concerned that they might be held personally responsible not only for their own actions but also for the actions of the corporation as a whole. This is reinforced by the requirement of the Securities and Exchange Commission (SEC) that a majority of directors must sign the Annual Report Form 10-K. A recent survey found that of 606 major U.S. corporations, 51% go beyond the SEC requirement by requiring that *all* directors sign the 10-K.[7]

In addition to these duties, directors must make certain that the corporation is managed in accordance with the laws of the state in which it is incorporated. They must also ensure management's adherence to laws and regulations, such as those dealing with the issuance of securities, insider trading, and other conflict-of-interest situations. They must also be aware of the needs and demands of constituent groups so that they can achieve a judicious balance among the interests of these diverse groups while ensuring the continued functioning of the corporation.

Role of the Board in Strategic Management

In terms of strategic management, a board of directors has three basic tasks.[8]

- *To initiate and determine.* A board can delineate a corporation's mission and specify strategic options to its management.
- *To evaluate and influence.* A board can examine management proposals, decisions, and actions; agree or disagree with them; give advice and offer suggestions; outline alternatives.
- *To monitor.* By acting through its committees, a board can keep abreast of developments both inside and outside the corporation. It can thus bring to management's attention developments it may have overlooked.

Even though any board will be composed of people with varying degrees of commitment to the corporation, we can make some generalizations about a board of directors as a whole in its attempt to fulfill these three basic tasks. We can characterize a board as being at a specific point on a continuum on the basis of its degree of involvement in corporate strategic affairs. As types, boards may range from phantom boards with no real involvement to catalyst boards with a very high degree of involvement. Highly involved boards tend

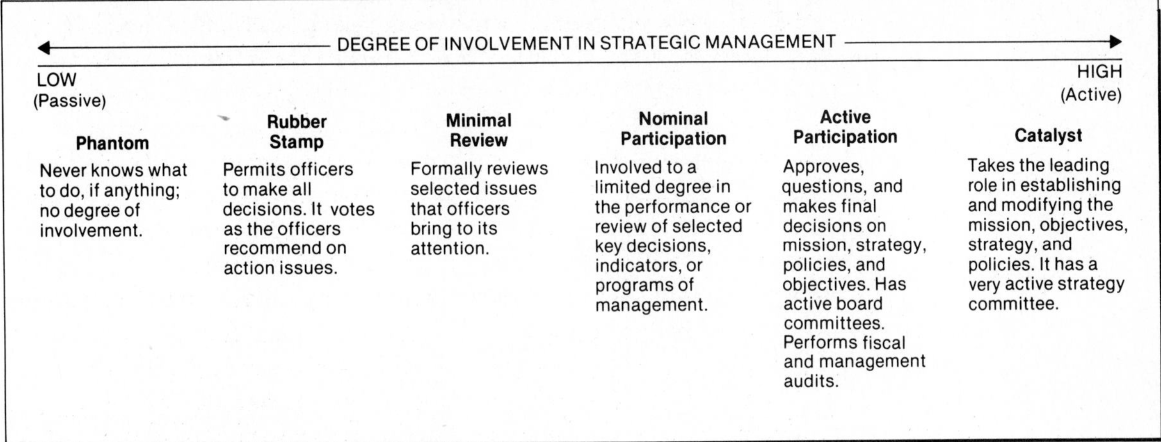

Figure 3.1 **Board of directors continuum.**

to be very active. They take their tasks of initiating, evaluating and influencing, and monitoring very seriously by providing advice when necessary and keeping management alert. As depicted in Fig. 3.1, they may be deeply involved in the strategic management process. At Texas Instruments, for example, the board attends a four-day strategic planning conference each year to discuss business opportunities of the next decade. Several members of the board also attend, during the following two days, management meetings attended by 500 managers from throughout the company. Kenneth Andrews, an authority on the role of the board of directors in strategic management, indicates the result:

> By the time the board comes to approve the company's plans, via ten days' annual work of the corporate objectives committee, it is presumably informed enough to play an important role in the company's planning processes.[9]

As a board becomes less involved in the affairs of the corporation, it is found further to the left on the continuum. These are passive boards that typically *never* initiate or determine strategy unless a crisis occurs. Most large, publicly owned corporations probably have boards that operate at some point between nominal and active participation. Few have catalyst boards, except for those with major problems (that is, pending bankruptcies, mergers, or acquisitions).

A recent survey of the nation's 2,235 largest commercial banks by Egon Zehnder International, a management consulting firm, supports this characterization of boards of directors.[10] The chief executive officers were asked:

"What phrase best characterizes the role of your Board of Directors in the *strategic* success of your bank?" They responded as follows:

• Critical contributor to our strategic success (catalyst)	5%
• Very active contributor (active participation)	22%
• Somewhat active contributor (nominal participation)	45%
• Passive (minimal review)	21%
• Largely ceremonial (phantom/rubber stamp)	8%

Surprisingly, only *one* CEO from the very biggest banks viewed his board as a critical contributor to his bank's strategic success.

Many CEOs and board members do not want the board to be involved in strategy matters at more than a superficial level. Andrews suggests why:

> Many chief executive officers, rejecting the practicality of conscious strategy, preside over unstated, incremental, or intuitive strategies that have never been articulated or analyzed—and therefore could not be deliberated by the board. Others do not believe their outside directors know enough or have time enough to do more than assent to strategic recommendations. Still others may keep discussions of strategy within management to prevent board transgression onto management turf and consequent reduction of executives' power to shape by themselves the future of their companies.[11]

Nevertheless, a recent survey of more than 1,000 outside directors reveals that one of the most pressing concerns of these directors is strategic management. "In the past," said one director, "strategic planning has been exclusively a management function. But now it has been intertwined with the role and functions of the board."[12] As a result, board members are now coming to think of themselves as being participants in the corporation's strategic management.[13]

Board Membership: Inside versus Outside Directors

The boards of most publicly owned corporations are comprised of both inside and outside directors. Inside directors are typically officers or executives employed by the corporation. The outside director may be an executive of another firm but is not an employee of the board's corporation. A survey sponsored by the Financial Executives Institute found that an average of 72% of the board members of nearly 800 responding *publicly* held corporations were nonmanagement (outside) directors. In comparison, only 55% of the board members of approximately 200 *privately* held corporations were outside directors.[14]

Although the 1984 Hay Survey of Directors reported outside directors to be compensated for their work at an average rate of $21,661 in industrial companies and $17,210 in financial companies,[15] the median pay in the largest companies is probably closer to the $20,000 to $30,000 range.[16] Few inside directors are paid for assuming this extra duty.

The American Law Institute, an association of 1,800 leading lawyers, judges, and law professors proposes in its "Principles of Corporate Governance and Structure: Restatement and Recommendations" that all corporations be required to have outside directors form a majority of the membership of their boards of directors.[17] The Securities and Exchange Commission (SEC) now requires corporations whose stock is listed on the New York Exchange to have at least two outside directors. The ALI and the SEC apparently take the view that outside directors are less biased and more likely to evaluate objectively management's performance than are inside directors. Vance, an authority on boards of directors, contends, however, that outside directors are less effective than are insiders because of their "questionable interest, availability, or competency."[18] Recent research by Pearce found that a director's orientation toward the external environment was more associated with corporate performance than was the ratio of outsiders to insiders.[19] Nevertheless, the general trend seems to be one of an increasing percentage of outsiders on the boards of U.S. corporations.

Surveys of manufacturing companies disclose that a majority (51%) of the outside directors are presidents, managing partners, or chairmen of the boards of other corporations. Outside directors come from a variety of organizations, some even from the ministry, but a majority of them come from the manufacturing, banking, law, and investment industries. With the current concern for productivity, there appears to be a movement toward having more executives on boards with strong operating experience and away from investment bankers and attorneys. A majority (58%) of the inside directors include the president, chairman of the board, and vice-presidents; the rest are key officers or former employees. Lower-level operating employees, including managers, form only 1% of the total employee board membership of the companies surveyed.[20]

Codetermination

The dearth of nonmanagement employee directors on the boards of U.S. corporations may be changing. Codetermination, the inclusion of a corporation's workers on its board, began only recently in the United States. The addition of Douglas Fraser, President of the United Auto Workers, to the board of Chrysler Corporation in 1980 was a controversial move designed to placate the union while Chrysler was attempting to avoid bankruptcy. Critics of this plan raise the issue of conflict of interest. Can a member of the board who is privy to confidential managerial information function as a union leader whose primary duty is to fight for the best benefits for his members?

With the replacement of Douglas Fraser in 1984 by Owen Bieber, the newly elected president of the UAW, a seat for labor in the Chrysler boardroom appeared to become permanent. Eastern Airlines and Western Air Lines have also added representatives from employee associations to their boards. As in the case of Chrysler, both corporations had appointed employee directors as part of an agreement with their union to accept major pay concessions. Research in fourteen other U.S. firms with workers on the board found that "worker board representation is no guarantee that workers will have an effective role in the governance of the organization."[21] The need to work for the corporation as a whole as well as to represent the workers creates role conflict and stress among the worker directors—thus cutting into their effectiveness.

While the movement to place employees on the boards of directors of American companies is only just beginning, the European experience reveals an increasing acceptance of worker participation on corporate boards. The Federal Republic of Germany pioneered the practice with its Co-Determination Acts of 1951 and 1976 and Works Constitution Act of 1952. Worker representatives in the coal, iron, and steel industries were given equal status with management on policy-making boards. Management in other industries, however, retained, a two-thirds majority on policy-making boards.

Other countries, such as Sweden, Denmark, Norway, and Austria have passed similar codetermination legislation. Belgium, Luxembourg, France, Italy, Ireland, and the Netherlands use worker councils to work closely with management, but are seriously considering moving closer toward the German model. The British government in the 1960s established the codetermination concept in nationalized industries but found it to be a failure. It did not cause better labor–management relations.[22] Recent research on German codetermination found that legislation requiring firms to put employee representatives on their boards "lowered dividend payments, led to a more conservative investment policy, and reduced firm values."[23]

Interlocking Directorates

Boards that are primarily composed of outside directors will not necessarily be more objective than those primarily composed of insiders. CEOs may nominate for board membership chief executives from other firms for the purpose of exchanging important information and guaranteeing the stability of key marketplace relationships. One or more individuals serving on the boards of directors of two or more corporations create an *interlocking directorate.* Although the Clayton Act and the Banking Act of 1933 prohibit interlocking directorates by companies competing in the same industry,[24] interlocking continues to occur in almost all corporations, especially large ones.[25] Research has shown that the larger the firm, the greater the number of different corporations represented on its board of directors. Corporations also have members of their management teams on the boards of other corporations. General Motors, for example, has 284 connections (11 through ownership, 67 through direct interlocking, and 206 through indirect interlocking).[26] Interlocking occurs because large firms have a large impact on other corporations; and these other corporations, in turn, have some control over the firm's inputs and marketplace. Interlocking directorates are also a useful method to gain both inside information about an uncertain environment and objective expertise about a firm's strategy. As a result, capital-intensive firms tend to be involved in extensive interlocking.[27] Family-owned corporations, however, are less likely to have interlocking directorates than are corporations with highly dispersed stock ownership, probably because family-owned corporations do not like to dilute their corporate control by adding outsiders to boardroom discussions.[28]

Nomination and Election of Board Members

Traditionally, the CEO of the corporation decided whom to invite to board membership and merely asked the stockholders for approval. This practice continues to occur in approximately 40% of all corporations. The chief criteria used by most CEOs in nominating board members are that the persons be compatible with the CEO and that they bring some prestige to the board.[29]

There are some dangers, however, in allowing the CEO free reign in nominating directors. The CEO may select board members who, in the CEO's opinion, will not disturb the company's policies and functioning. More importantly, directors selected by the CEO often feel that they should go along with any proposals made by the CEO. Thus, board members find themselves accountable to the very management they are charged to oversee. Because of the likelihood of these occurrences, there is an increasing tendency for a special board committee to nominate new outside board members.

A survey by Korn and Ferry reveals that the percentage of corporations using nominating committees to select new directors rose from less than 20% in the 1970s to approximately 60% in the 1980s.[30]

Term of Office

A recent survey by The Hay Group reports that 65% of industrial corporations and 69% of banks elect all directors annually for a one-year term of office. In contrast, 60% of insurance companies elect directors for a three-year term.[31] Virtually every corporation whose directors serve terms of more than one year divide the board into classes and stagger elections so that only a portion of the board stands for election each year. Arguments in favor of this practice are that it provides continuity by reducing the chance of an abrupt turnover in its membership and that it reduces the likelihood of people unfriendly to management being elected through cumulative voting.

Among the many companies recently attempting to switch from one-year terms to longer-term staggered elections to reduce the likelihood of a takeover are Beatrice Foods, Union Oil, Sterling Drug, and Quaker Oats.

Cumulative Voting

The practice of cumulative voting allows a stockholder to concentrate his or her votes in an election of directors. Cumulative voting is required by law in 18 states and is mandatory on request or permitted as a corporate option in 32 other states or territories. Under cumulative voting, the number of votes allowed is determined from multiplying the number of voting shares held by the number of directors to be elected. Thus, a person owning 1,000 shares in an election of 12 directors would have 12,000 votes. These votes may then be distributed in any manner—for instance, divided evenly (or unevenly) between two directors or concentrated on one. This is contrasted with straight voting in which the stockholder votes simply yes or no for each director to be elected.[32]

Only a minority of companies surveyed provide for cumulative voting in their bylaws or certificate of incorporation.[33] Although few stockholders use this privilege, it is a powerful way for them to influence a board of directors. For example, a minority of stockholders could concentrate their voting power and elect one or more directors of their choice. In contrast, straight voting allows the holders of the majority of outstanding shares to prevent the election of any director not to their liking.

Those in favor of cumulative voting argue that it is the only system under which a candidate not on the management slate can hope to be elected to the board. Otherwise, under straight voting, an entrenched management could insulate itself from criticism and use the board as a rubber stamp. Critics of cumulative voting argue that it allows the board to deteriorate into interest groups more concerned with protecting their own special concerns than in working for the good of the corporation. This could become a serious problem if the corporation is in danger of being bought or controlled by another firm. For instance, by purchasing some shares, another firm (such as a potential acquirer) could, through cumulative voting, elect enough board members to directly influence or even incapacitate the board. Nevertheless, the practice of cumulative voting has been recommended as a way to achieve minority representation on the boards of directors of major corporations.

Organization of the Board

The size of the board is determined by the corporation's charter and its bylaws in compliance with state laws. Although some states require a minimum number of board members, most corporations have quite a bit of discretion in determining board size. Surveys of U.S. business corporations reveal that the average *privately* held company has eight board members who meet four times a year as compared to the average *publicly* held corporation with thirteen directors who meet seven times a year. In addition, there appears to be a direct relationship between company size as measured by sales volume and the number of people on the board.[34]

Chairman

A fairly common practice in U.S. corporations is to have the chairman of the board also serve as the chief executive officer. The CEO concentrates on strategy, planning, external relations, and responsibility to the board. The chairman's responsibility is to ensure that the board and its committees perform their functions as stated in their charter. Further, the chairman schedules board meetings and presides over the annual stockholders' meeting. In over 75% of the Fortune 500 corporations, the CEO also serves as chairman of the board.[35]

Committees

The most effective boards of large corporations accomplish much of their work through committees.[36] Although the committees do not have legal duties, unless detailed in the bylaws, most committees are granted full power to act with the authority of the board between board meetings. Typical standing committees are the executive committee, audit committee, compensation committee, finance committee, and nominating committee. The executive committee is formed from local directors who can meet between board meetings to attend to matters that must be settled quickly. This committee acts as an extension of the board and, consequently, may have almost unrestricted authority in certain areas. A recent survey reports that in 68% of industrial and 72% of financial corporations, the executive committee includes at least a majority of outside directors.[37] Other less common committees are the strategy, corporate responsibility, investments (pension funds), and conflict-of-interest committees.[38]

Trends for the Future

A study by Northwestern University and McKinsey & Company, Inc. sees several following trends for future responsibilities and organizations of boards.[39] Although the study concludes that it is not likely there will be significant changes in the typical board structure, it does predict a reduction in board size and a greater use of committees. The board of the future will tend to direct its own affairs with less reliance on the CEO. It will have fewer inside members and will be under less CEO influence in the selection of its members. There will be greater emphasis on systematically monitoring and appraising top management's performance, with more involvement by the board in the management succession process. Boards will also have more influence in determining executive compensation, and there will probably be more open communication between the board and management as the boards become more active. Boards will most likely form audit committees for the purpose of ensuring a formalized evaluation of overall corporate performance. Their membership will become more representative of minorities and women. In addition, there will be a continuing pressure on board members in terms of their liabilities, plus greater expectations by the public for higher standards of public responsibility.

3.2 TOP MANAGEMENT

The top management function is usually conducted by the CEO of the corporation in coordination with the COO or president, executive vice-president, and vice-presidents of divisions and functional areas. As we mentioned earlier in this chapter, some corporations combine the office of CEO with that of chairman of the board of directors. Although this plan has the advantage of freeing the president or COO of the firm from many strategic responsibilities so that he or she may focus primarily on operational matters, it has been criticized because it gives the combined CEO/chairman too much power and serves to undercut the independence of the board.[40]

Responsibilities of Top Management

Top management, and especially the CEO, is responsible to the board of directors for the overall management of the corporation. It is tasked with getting things accomplished through and with others in order to meet corporate objectives. Top management's job is thus multidimensional and oriented toward the welfare of the total organization. Specific top management tasks vary from firm to firm and are developed from an analysis of the mission, objectives, strategies, and key activities of the corporation. But all top managers are people who see the business as a whole, who can balance the present needs of the business against the needs of the future, and who can make final and effective decisions.[41] The chief executive officer, in particular, must successfully handle three responsibilities crucial to the effective strategic management of the corporation: (1) fulfill key roles; (2) provide corporate leadership; and (3) manage the strategic planning process.

Fulfill Key Roles

From five weeks of in-depth observation of five chief executives, Henry Mintzberg concluded that the job of a top manager contains ten interrelated *roles*. The importance of each role and the amount of time demanded by each probably varies from one job to another. These roles are as follows:

Figurehead	Acts as legal and symbolic head; performs obligatory social, ceremonial, or legal duties (hosts retirement dinners, luncheons for employees, and plant dedications; attends civic affairs; signs contracts on behalf of firm).
Leader	Motivates, develops, and guides subordinates; oversees staffing, training, and associated activities (intro-

	duces Management By Objectives [MBO], develops a challenging work climate, provides a sense of direction, acts as a role model).
Liaison	Maintains a network of contacts and information sources outside top management in order to obtain information and assistance (meets with key people from the task environment, meets formally and informally with corporate division managers and with CEOs of other firms).
Monitor	Seeks and obtains information in order to understand the corporation and its environments; acts as nerve center for the corporation (reviews status reports from vice-presidents, reviews key indicators of corporate performance, scans *Wall Street Journal* and key trade journals, joins select clubs and societies).
Disseminator	Transmits information to the rest of the top management team and other key people in the corporation (chairs staff meetings, transmits policy letters, communicates five-year plans).
Spokesman	Transmits information to key groups and people in the task environment (prepares annual report to stockholders, talks to the Chamber of Commerce, states corporate policy to the media, participates in advertising campaigns, speaks before congressional committees).
Entrepreneur	Searches the corporation and its environment for projects to improve products, processes, procedures, and structures; then supervises the design and implementation of these projects (introduces cost reduction programs, makes plant trips to divisions, changes forecasting system, brings in subcontract work to level the work load, reorganizes the corporation).
Disturbance Handler	Takes corrective action in times of disturbance or crisis (personally talks with key creditors, interest groups, congressional committees, union leaders; establishes investigative committees; revises objectives, strategies, and policies).
Resource Allocator	Allocates corporate resources by making and/or approving decisions (reviews budgets, revises program

scheduling, initiates strategic planning, plans personnel load, sets objectives).

Negotiator — Represents the corporation in negotiating important agreements; may speak directly with key representatives of groups in the task environment or work through a negotiator; negotiates disagreements within the corporation by working with conflicting division heads (works with labor negotiator; resolves jurisdictional disputes between divisions; negotiates with key creditors, suppliers, and customers).[42]

Provide Corporate Leadership

People who work in corporations look to top management for leadership. Their doing so, says Drucker, reflects a need for standard setting and example setting.[43] According to Mintzberg, this is a key role of any manager.

Corporate leadership is important because it sets the tone for the entire corporation. Since most middle managers look to their boss for guidance and direction, they will tend to emulate the characteristics and style of successful top managers. People in an organization want to have a vision of what they are working toward—a sense of mission. Only top management is in the position to specify and communicate this sense of mission to the general work force. Top management's enthusiasm (or lack of it) about the corporation tends to be contagious.

For instance, a positive attitude characterizing many well-known industrial leaders—such as Alfred Sloan at General Motors, Ed Watson at IBM, Robert Wood at Sears, Ray Kroc at McDonald's, and Lee Iacocca at Chrysler—have energized their respective corporations. In their book *In Search of Excellence,* Peters and Waterman report that "associated with almost every excellent company was a strong leader (or two) who seemed to have a lot to do with making his company excellent in the first place."[44] A two-year study by McKinsey & Co. found the CEOs of midsized high-growth companies to be "almost inevitably consummate salesmen who radiate enormous contagious self-confidence" . . . and "take pains to communicate their strong sense of mission to all who come in contact with them."[45]

Chief executive officers with a clear sense of mission are often perceived as dynamic and charismatic leaders. They are able to command respect and to influence strategy formulation and implementation because they tend to have three key characteristics.

1. The CEO *presents a role* for others to identify with and to follow. The leader sets an example in terms of behavior and dress. The CEO's attitudes and values concerning the corporation's purpose and activities are clear-cut and constantly communicated in words and deeds.

2. The CEO *articulates a transcendent goal* for the corporation. The CEO's vision of the corporation goes beyond the petty complaints and grievances of the average work day. This vision puts activities and conflicts in a new perspective, giving renewed meaning to everyone's work activities and enabling them to see beyond the details of their own jobs to the functioning of the total corporation.
3. The CEO *communicates high performance standards* but also *shows confidence* in the followers' abilities to meet these standards. No leader ever improved performance by setting easily attainable goals that provide no challenge. The CEO must be willing to follow through by coaching people.[46]

Manage Strategic Planning

Top management must initiate and manage the strategic planning process. It must take a very long-range view in order to specify the corporate mission, delineate corporate objectives, and formulate appropriate strategies and policies. As depicted in Fig. 3.2, the ideal time horizon varies according to one's level in the corporate hierarchy. The president of a corporation, for example, should allocate the largest proportion of planning time to looking two to

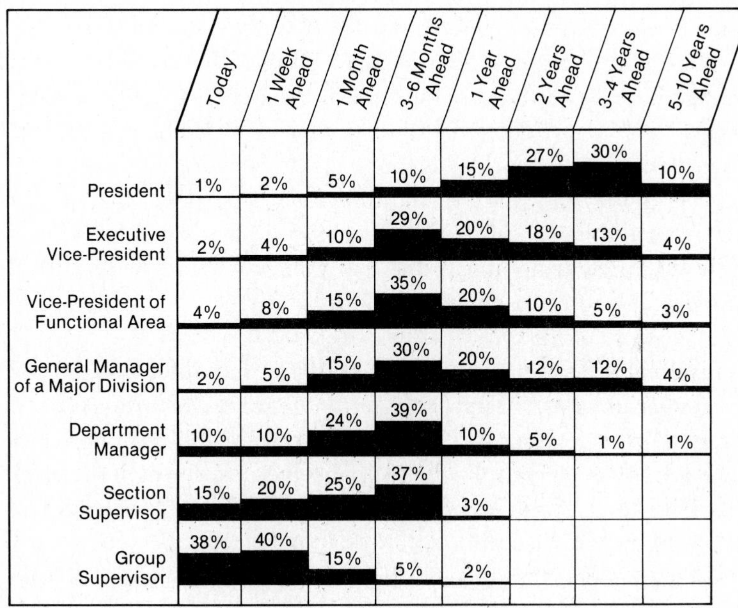

Figure 3.2 **"Ideal" allocations of time for planning in the "average" company.**
SOURCE: Reprinted with permission of The Free Press, a division of Macmillan, Inc. from *Top Management Planning* by G. A. Steiner. Copyright © 1969 by the Trustees of Columbia University in the City of New York.

four *years* ahead. A department manager, however, should put the heaviest proportion of planning time on looking only three to six *months* ahead.

To accomplish its tasks, top management must use information provided by three key corporate groups: a long-range planning staff, division or SBU managers, and managers of functional departments.

A *long-range planning staff* typically consists of six people, headed by a senior vice-president or director of corporate planning.[47] It continuously monitors both internal and external environments in order to generate data for strategic decisions by top management. It also suggests to top management possible changes in the corporate mission, objectives, strategies, and policies. Although only one in five companies with sales under $100 million have a separate, formal planning department, nearly all corporations with sales of at least $2 billion have such departments.[48]

Divisional or SBU managers, with the assistance of the long-range planning staff and with input from their product managers, perform the strategic planning function for each division. These SBU managers typically initiate proposals for top management's consideration and/or respond to requests for such proposals by corporate headquarters. They may also be tasked to carry out strategies and policies decided upon at the corporate level for organization-wide implementation. These division managers typically work with the heads of various functional units within the division to develop the appropriate functional strategies to implement planned business-level strategies.

Managers of functional departments (marketing, engineering, R&D managers, etc.) report directly either to divisional managers in a multidivision corporation or to top management if the corporation has no divisions. Although they may develop specific functional strategies, they generally do so within the framework of divisional or corporate strategies. They also respond to initiatives from above that ask them for input or require them to develop strategies to implement divisional plans.

Characteristics of Top Management Tasks

Top management tasks have two characteristics that differentiate them from other managerial tasks.[49] First, *very few of them are continuous.* Rarely does a manager work on these tasks all day. The responsibilities, however, are always present, even though the tasks themselves are sporadic. And when the tasks do arise, they are of crucial significance, such as the selection of a person to head a new division.

Mintzberg reports that the activities of most executives are characterized by brevity, variety, and fragmentation: "Half of the observed activities were completed in less than nine minutes and only one-tenth took more than an hour. In effect, the managers were seldom able or willing to spend much time on any one issue in any one session."[50]

It is likely that serious objective-setting and strategy formulation will not occur in corporations if most top managers are as activity-oriented as those in the Mintzberg study. John De Lorean suggests as much in his comments about "The Fourteenth Floor" (the executive offices) of General Motors.

> I was trying to bring a set of new eyes to the job of group executive, as one only can do in the first few months in a new position. But I had no time to perform the real function of my position. Instead, I was being tied down and totally consumed by this constant parade of paperwork and meetings.[51]

The second characteristic of top management tasks is that *they require a wide range of capabilities and temperaments*. Some tasks require the capacity to analyze and carefully weigh alternative courses of action. Some require an awareness of and an interest in people; whereas others call for the ability to pursue abstract ideas, concepts, and calculations.

One result of these two task characteristics is that top managers are often drawn back into the functional work of the corporation. Since the activities of top management are not continuous, people in top management often have unplanned free time. They tend therefore to get caught up in the day-to-day work in manufacturing, marketing, accounting, engineering, or in other operations of the corporation. They may find themselves constantly solving crises that could probably have been better handled by lower-level managers. These managers are also usually fond of protesting, "How can I be expected to drain the swamp when I'm up to my eyeballs in alligators!?"

A second result of the task characteristics is that top managers tend to perceive only those aspects and responsibilities of the top management function that are compatible with their abilities, experience, and temperaments. And, if the board of directors fails to state explicitly what it considers to be the key responsibilities and activities of top management, the top managers are free to define the job themselves. As a result, important tasks may be overlooked until a crisis occurs.

Top Management Team

Many executives believe that top management work is a job for a team rather than for one person. The large amount and variety of the work may be too great for one person to handle capably. Furthermore, when one person is in charge, he or she becomes extremely involved in the organization and tends to take personally any criticism of corporate activities. Consequently, that person is less willing to change personal management practices as situations change. According to Drucker, ". . . one-man top management is a major reason why businesses fail to grow."[52]

Analysts argue, therefore, that a large complex corporation needs a clearly structured top management team. This team may be organized as an office of the president in which a number of people serve as equals, each with an assigned area of primary responsibility. Corporations such as DuPont, Standard Oil of New Jersey, Royal Dutch Shell, and Unilever have taken this approach.[53] Or the team may include one person who carries the title of CEO and several colleagues, each of whom has clearly assigned authority and responsibility for a segment of the top management task. Another common structure is a three- or four-person team, each person having clearly assigned top management responsibilities even though one person is officially in charge. General Motors and Xerox Corporation use this structure. GM's team includes a chairman, a vice-chairman, a chairman of the executive committee, and a president. General Electric has taken a similar approach, although it refers to its four-man top management group as the Corporate Executive Office.

The use of top management teams has increased dramatically from only 37 in 1970 to 113 in 1980.[54] An advantage of the team approach to top management is the sharing of roles, responsibilities, and tasks, a sharing that depends on the strengths and weaknesses of the people involved. It makes more sense for large corporations to put together a top management team to achieve synergy, rather than try to find the perfect person to be CEO. Certainly succession problems are minimized by the team approach; decisions can be made even though the CEO has resigned, is incapacitated or otherwise absent.

3.3 STRATEGIC MANAGEMENT STYLES

Just as boards of directors vary widely on a continuum of involvement in the strategic management process, so do top management teams. For example, a top management team with low involvement in strategic management will tend to be functionally oriented and will focus its energies on day-to-day operational problems; this type of team is likely either to be disorganized or to have a dominant CEO who continues to identify with his or her old division. In contrast, a top management team with high involvement will be active in long-range planning. It will try to get division managers involved in planning so that it will have more time to scan the environment for challenges and opportunities.

Both the board of directors and top management can be placed on a matrix to reflect four basic styles of corporate strategic management. These styles are depicted in Fig. 3.3.

Chaos Management

When both the board of directors and top management have little involvement in the strategic management process, their style is referred to as chaos management. The board waits for top management to bring it proposals. Top management is operationally oriented and continues to carry out strate-

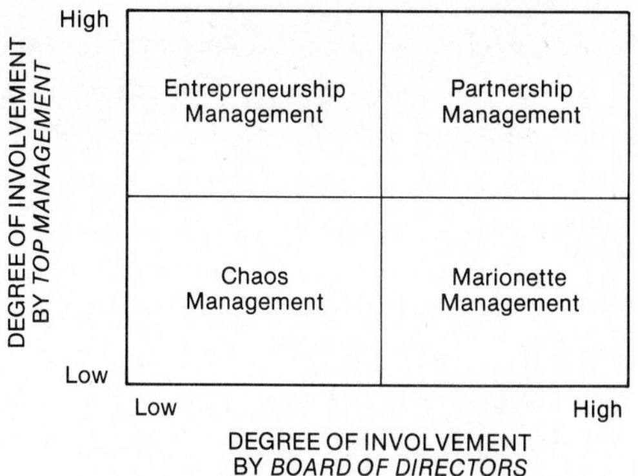

Figure 3.3 **Strategic management styles.**

gies, policies, and programs specified by the founding entrepreneur who died years ago. The basic strategic philosophy seems to be, "If it was good enough for old J. B., it's good enough for us." There is no strategic management being done here.

Entrepreneurship Management

A corporation with an uninvolved board of directors but with a highly involved top management has entrepreneurship management. The board is willing to be used as a rubber stamp for top management. The CEO, operating alone or with a team, dominates the corporation and its strategic decisions. An example is the Calhoun First National Bank of Calhoun, Georgia, whose CEO is Bert Lance. Returning to the bank after serving in the cabinet of President Jimmy Carter, Lance tried to regain control of the corporation as its president. He wanted, among other things, the bank to initiate new loan policies and to hire his 26-year-old son as an officer. After the board turned him down, Lance began a proxy fight for control of the bank. The resulting new board not only approved all the changes desired by Lance, it fired both the previous chairman of the board and the president without severance pay. Lance, of course, returned to his job as president of the bank and gained total control of all strategic management.[55]

Marionette Management

Probably the rarest form of strategic management styles, marionette management occurs when the board of directors is deeply involved in strategic decision making, whereas top management is primarily concerned with operations. Such a style evolves when a board is composed of key stockholders who refuse to delegate strategic decision making to the president. The president is forced into a COO role and can do only what the board allows him to do. This style also occurs when a board fires a CEO but is slow to find a replacement. The COO or executive vice-president stays on as "acting" president or CEO until the selection process is complete. In the meantime, strategic management is firmly in the hands of the board of directors. In one specific bank (which will remain unnamed), the board of directors is so involved in managing that it requires the president to ask its permission before offices are painted. The board actually votes on the color!

Partnership Management

Probably the most effective style of strategic management, partnership management is epitomized by a highly involved board and top management. The board and the top management team work closely to establish mission, objectives, strategies, and policies. Board members are active in committee work and utilize strategic audits to provide feedback to top management on its actions in implementing agreed-upon strategies and policies. This appears to be the style emerging in a number of successful corporations such as Texas Instruments, Dayton Hudson Corporation, and General Electric Company.[56]

3.4 SUMMARY AND CONCLUSION

The strategy makers of a modern corporation are the board of directors and top management. Both must be actively involved in the strategic management process if the corporation is to have long-term success in accomplishing its mission.

An effective board is the keystone of the modern corporation. Without it, management would tend to focus on short-run problems and solutions or go off on tangents at odds with the basic mission. The personal needs and goals of executives would tend to overrule the interests of the corporation. Even the strongest critics of boards of directors are more interested in improving and upgrading boards than in eliminating them.[57] An active board is critical in determining an organization's mission, objectives, strategy, and policies.

Top management, in contrast, is responsible for the overall functioning of the corporation. People in top management must view the corporation as a whole rather than as a series of functional departments or decentralized divisions. They must constantly visualize and plan for the future, setting objectives, strategies, and policies that will allow the corporation to successfully meet that future. They must set standards and provide a vision not only of what the corporation is but also of what it is trying to become. They must develop working relationships with the board of directors, key staff personnel, and managers from divisions and functional areas.

The interaction between the board of directors and the top management of a corporation usually results in an overall strategic management style. The long-run success of a corporation is best ensured through a partnership style in which both the board and top management are genuinely involved in strategic issues.

DISCUSSION QUESTIONS

1. Does a corporation really need a board of directors? Why or why not?
2. What aspects of a corporation's environment should be represented on a board of directors?
3. Should cumulative voting for the election of board members be *required* by law in all political jurisdictions?
4. Do you agree that a chief executive officer (CEO) should fulfill Mintzberg's ten roles in order to be effective?
5. Is partnership management always the best style of strategic management?

NOTES

1. W. L. Shanklin and J. K. Ryans, Jr., "Should the Board Consider This Agenda Item?" *MSU Business Topics* (Winter 1981), p. 35.
2. W. R. Boulton, "The Evolving Board: A Look at the Board's Changing Roles and Information Needs," *Academy of Management Review* (October 1978), p. 828.
3. L. Iacocca, *Iacocca: An Autobiography* (Toronto: Bantam Books, 1984), p. 104.
4. J. Bacon and J. K. Brown, *Corporate Directorship Practices: Role, Selection and Legal Status of the Board* (New York: The Conference Board, Report no. 646, 1975), p. 7.
5. Bacon and Brown, p. 75.
6. G. Smith, "Who Was Watching the Store?" *Forbes* (July 30, 1984), pp. 37–38.
   "Rolling Heads," *Time* (December 17, 1984), p. 69.
7. L. B. Korn and R. M. Ferry, *Board of Directors Ninth Annual Study* (New York: Korn/Ferry International, February 1982), p. 8.
8. Bacon and Brown, p. 15.
9. K. R. Andrews, "Corporate Strategy as a Vital Function of the Board," *Harvard Business Review* (November–December 1981), p. 175.
10. *Third Annual Banking Survey of Chief Executive Officers* (Atlanta, Chicago, New York: Egon Zehnder International, Inc., 1984), p. 9.
11. K. R. Andrews, "Directors' Responsibility for Corporate Strategy," *Harvard Business Review* (November–December 1980), p. 30.
12. T. R. Horton, "The Case for Planning Committees," *Directors & Boards* (Summer 1984), p. 26.
13. A. Tashakori and W. Boulton, "A Look to the Board's Role in Planning," *Journal of Business Strategy* (Winter 1983), pp. 64–70.
14. E. Mruk and J. Giardina, *Organization and Compensation of Boards of Directors* (New York: Financial Executives Institute, Arthur Young & Co., 1981), pp. 11 and 39.

15. L. Barker, "Director Compensation 1984," *Directors & Boards* (Spring 1984), p. 35.

16. S. C. Vance, *Corporate Leadership: Boards, Directors, and Strategy* (New York: McGraw-Hill Book Company, 1983), p. 64.

17. K. R. Andrews, "The American Law Institute's Proposals for Regulating Corporate Governance," *Harvard Business Review* (November–December 1982), p. 34.

18. S. C. Vance, p. 274.

19. J. A. Pearce, "The Relationship of Internal versus External Orientations to Financial Measures of Strategic Performance," *Strategic Management Journal* (December 1983), pp. 297–306.

20. E. S. Buffa, "Making American Manufacturing Competitive," *California Management Review* (Spring 1984), p. 39.
J. Bacon, *Corporate Directorship Practices: Membership and Committees of the Board* (New York: The Conference Board, Report no. 588, 1973), pp. 28–29.

21. T. H. Hammer and R. N. Stern, "Worker Representation on Company Boards of Directors," *Proceedings, Academy of Management,* 1983, p. 368.

22. R. J. Kuhne, *Co-Determination in Business* (New York: Praeger Publishers, 1980), pp. 41–71.

23. L. H. Clark, Jr., "What Economists Say about Business—and Baboons," *Wall Street Journal* (June 7, 1983), p. 33. Article summarizes a research paper by G. Benelli, C. Loderer, and T. Lys presented to the Interlaken Seminar on Analysis and Ideology, Interlaken, Switzerland, 1983.

24. E. F. Donaldson and J. K. Pfahl, *Corporate Finance,* 3rd ed. (New York: Ronald Press, 1969), p. 742.
F. D. Schoorman, M. H. Bazerman, and R. S. Atkin, "Interlocking Directorates: A Strategy for Reducing Environmental Uncertainty," *Academy of Management Review* (April 1981), p. 244.

25. M. H. Bazerman and F. D. Schoorman, "A Limited Rationality Model of Interlocking Directorates," *Academy of Management Review* (April 1983), pp. 206–217.
M. Ornstein, "Interlocking Directorates in Canada: Intercorporate or Class Alliance?" *Administrative Science Quarterly* (June 1984), pp. 210–231.

26. R. S. Burt, "Cooptive Corporate Actor Networks: A Reconsideration of Interlocking Directorates Involving American Manufacturing," *Administrative Science Quarterly* (December 1980), p. 566.

27. Burt, p. 559.

28. For a more in-depth discussion of this topic, refer to J. M. Pennings, *Interlocking Directorates* (San Francisco: Jossey-Bass, 1980), and M. S. Mizruchi, *The American Corporate Network 1904–1974* (Beverly Hills, Calif.: Sage Publications, 1982).

29. R. F. Lewis, "Choosing and Using Outside Directors," *Harvard Business Review* (July–August 1974), p. 71.

30. Korn and Ferry, p. 5.
31. Barker, p. 40.
32. Bacon, pp. 7–8.
33. Bacon, p. 6.
34. Korn and Ferry, p. 3; and Mruk and Giardina, p. 39.
35. H. S. Geneen, "Why Directors Can't Protect the Stockholders," *Fortune* (September 17, 1984), p. 29.
36. W. Wommack, "The Board's Most Important Function," *Harvard Business Review* (September–October 1979), p. 48.
37. Barker, p. 39.
38. For further information on board committees, refer to Bacon and Brown, pp. 99–140. For detailed information on the audit committee, see L. Braiotta, *The Audit Director's Guide* (New York: John Wiley & Sons, 1981).
39. R. P. Neuschel, Conference Summary (p. 60), "The Changing Role of the Corporate Board," proceedings of a conference held in Chicago on April 13, 1977, and sponsored jointly by Northwestern University's Graduate School of Management and McKinsey & Company, Inc. Privately published by the sponsors.
40. Bacon and Brown, p. 25.
    Andrews, 1980, p. 36.
    W. R. Boulton, "Effective Board Development: Five Areas of Concern," *Journal of Business Strategy* (Spring 1983), pp. 94–100.
    H. S. Geneen, "Why Directors Can't Protect the Stockholders," *Fortune* (September 17, 1984), p. 29.
41. P. F. Drucker, *Management: Tasks, Responsibilities, Practices* (New York: Harper & Row, 1974), p. 613.
42. Adapted from H. Mintzberg, *The Nature of Managerial Work* (New York: Harper & Row, 1973), pp. 54–94.
43. Drucker, pp. 611–612.
44. T. J. Peters and R. H. Waterman, *In Search of Excellence* (New York: Harper & Row, 1982), p. 26.
45. A. Levitt, Jr., and J. Albertine, "The Successful Entrepreneur: A Personality Profile," *Wall Street Journal* (August 29, 1983), p. 12.
46. Adapted from R. J. House, "A 1976 Theory of Charismatic Leadership," *Leadership: The Cutting Edge*, eds. J. G. Hunt and L. L. Larson (Carbondale, Ill.: SIU Press, 1977), pp. 189–207. Bernard M. Bass refers to this model as *transformational leadership* in his article "Leadership: Good, Better, Best" in *Organizational Dynamics* (Winter 1985), pp. 26–40.
47. S. Matlins and G. Knisely, "Update: Profile of the Corporate Planners," *Journal of Business Strategy* (Spring 1981), pp. 75 and 77.
48. C. D. Burnett, D. P. Yeskey, and D. Richardson, "New Roles for Corporate

Planners in the 1980's," *Journal of Business Strategy* (Spring 1984), p. 67.

49. Drucker, pp. 615–617.
50. Mintzberg, p. 33.
51. J. P. Wright, *On a Clear Day You Can See General Motors* (Grosse Pointe, Mich.: Wright Enterprises, 1979), p. 28.
52. Drucker, p. 618.
53. Drucker, p. 619.
54. S. C. Vance, p. 203.
55. D. Russakoff, "Bert Lance on the Rebound," *Washington Post* (May 17, 1981), pp. A6–A7.
56. K. Andrews, "Corporate Strategy as a Vital Function of the Board," *Harvard Business Review* (November–December 1981), p. 175.
    K. N. Dayton, "Corporate Governance: The Other Side of the Coin," *Harvard Business Review* (January–February 1984), p. 35.
57. R. P. Neuschel, Introductory Remarks (p. 11), "The Changing Role of the Corporate Board," proceedings of a conference held in Chicago on April 13, 1977 and sponsored jointly by Northwestern University's Graduate School of Management and McKinsey & Company, Inc. Privately published by the sponsors.

Chapter 4

THE EXTERNAL ENVIRONMENT

STRATEGIC MANAGEMENT MODEL

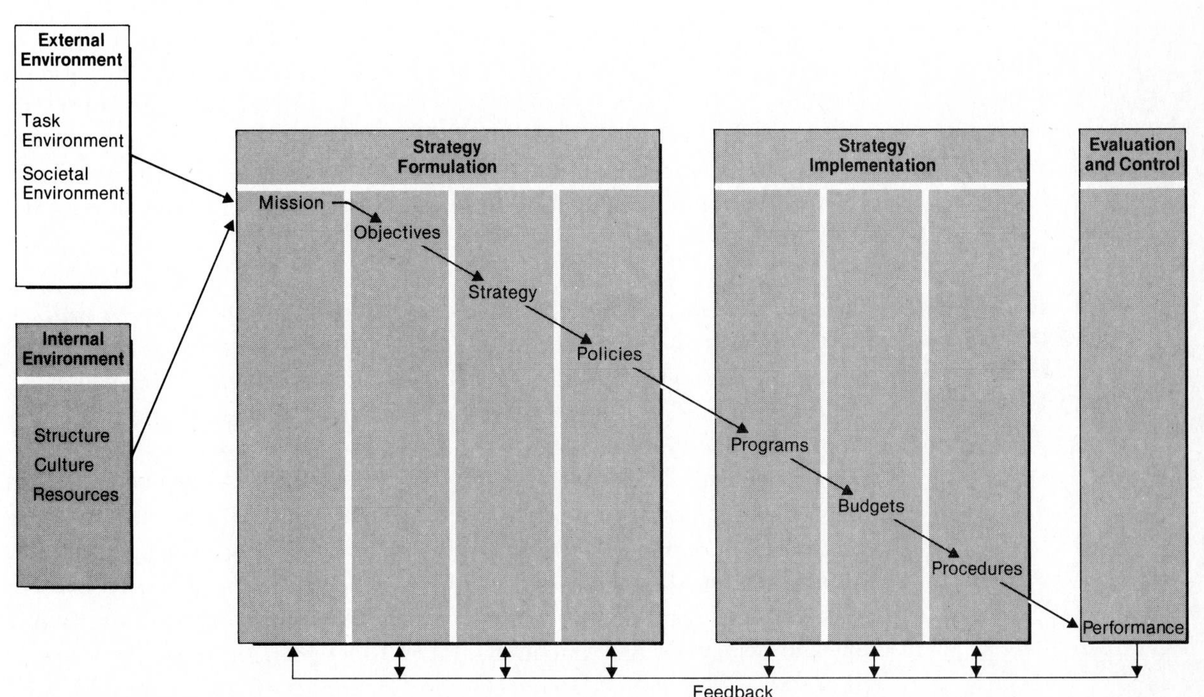

Business corporations do not exist in a vacuum. They arise out of society's need for a particular product or service and can continue to exist in freedom only so long as they acknowledge their role in the larger society. As a result, corporations must constantly be aware of the key variables in their environment. These variables may be within a firm's task environment or in its larger societal environment (see Fig. 4.1). The *task environment* includes those elements or groups that directly affect the corporation and, in turn, are affected by it. These are governments, local communities, suppliers, competitors, customers, creditors, employees/labor unions, special interest groups, and trade associations. The *societal environment* includes the more general forces that do not directly touch on the short-run activities of the organization but that can, and often do, influence its long-run decisions. These, also shown in Fig. 4.1, are as follows:

- *Economic forces* that regulate exchange of materials, money, energy, and information.
- *Sociocultural forces* that regulate values, mores, and customs.
- *Technological forces* that generate problem solving inventions.
- *Political-legal forces* that allocate power and provide constraining and protecting laws and regulations.

All of these variables and forces constantly interact with each other. In the short run, societal forces affect the decisions and actions of a corporation through the groups in its task environment. In the long run, however, the corporation also affects these groups through its activities. For example, the possible collapse of Chrysler Corporation in 1980 had wide-ranging and serious effects upon almost every group and force in its task and societal environment.

4.1 BUSINESS AND SOCIETY: A DELICATE RELATIONSHIP

For centuries, business corporations have lived in an uneasy truce with society. Exchange and commercial activities, along with laws governing them, are as old as recorded history. The Code of Hammurabi, established about 2000 B.C., provided guidelines for merchants and peddlers.[1] The Old Testament is filled with examples of commercial activity and the laws and regulations governing them. Greek philosophers, in general, regarded commercial activities as necessary but distasteful. The Romans, like the Greeks, were necessarily tolerant of commercial activity, but gave those so engaged a low status.[2] During the early years of the Middle Ages, the Roman Christian Church held business and commercial activity in disdain and governed it through strict rules and limitations. Usury, the lending of money at interest, for instance, was decreed a mortal sin for Christians, who were forbidden the

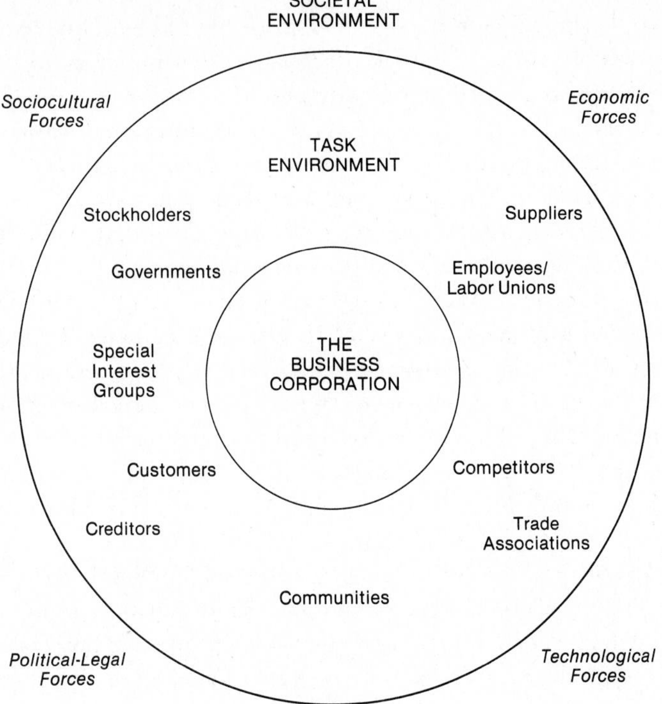

Figure 4.1 Key environmental variables.

practice, although Jews were permitted to engage in it. Trade itself was of dubious purity, and the gathering of wealth was considered an action directly opposed to the charitable teachings of Jesus Christ. This view of trade and commerce and the associated accumulation of capital as necessary evils was commonly accepted in the Western world until the Protestant Reformation. The Eastern world, in contrast, was much more tolerant and accepting of business activities.

Development of the Capitalistic Ethic

With the end of the Middle Ages, values began to change in the West, and business activities were viewed more positively. Max Weber, noted economist and sociologist, postulated that changes in the religious ethic resulting from the Reformation and the Protestant movement provided an economic climate highly favorable for the development of capitalism.[3] A new spirit of individualism developed out of the Renaissance and was encouraged by humanism and Protestantism. Society placed a high value on frugality, thrift, and hard work—key elements of what is commonly referred to as the *Protestant ethic.*

Free trade was not, however, commonly accepted until much later. After the Reformation, kings and queens replaced the Church as earthly rulers. They established their right to regulate business activity through the concept of *mercantilism.* According to this concept, the individual was subordinate to the state, and all economic and business activity was dedicated to support the power of the state. Under mercantilism, Europeans set up organizations, such as the East India Company, to trade with the natives of distant lands and to return with goods valuable to crown and country.

In 1776, however, economist Adam Smith advanced a theory justifying and underlying capitalism in his book *An Inquiry into the Nature and Causes of the Wealth of Nations.* Smith argued that economic freedom would enable individuals through self-interest to fulfill themselves and thereby benefit the total society. He used the term *laissez-faire* to suggest that government should leave business alone. The "invisible hand" of the marketplace would, through pure competition, ensure maximum benefit to society.

The doctrine of *laissez-faire,* as postulated by Smith and refined by others, called for society to give business corporations increasing autonomy so that they could accomplish their work—the production and sale of goods and services. In the rapidly changing world of the eighteenth and nineteenth centuries such work was considered worthwhile and valuable to society. For example, James Watt's development of a usable steam engine permitted muscle power to be replaced by an external power source and resulted in enormous increases in the production and distribution of scarce goods. Because of these benefits, governments relaxed many of their restrictions on commerce and trade, and allowed capital to accumulate and business to flourish.

Society Supports Free Enterprise

With changes in sociocultural values fed by the benefits of new technology and *laissez-faire* economics, governments in the West began to support independent businesses. During much of the early part of the nineteenth century in the United States, government favored the development of commerce and industry. The Supreme Court, for example, ruled that the private corporation was a legal entity, and Congress passed tariff laws protecting business interests. In addition, the government provided vast sums of money and land for the rapidly expanding railroads.[4] As pointed out by McGuire,

> . . . the Federal government attempted to encourage business activities with a minimum of regulation and intervention. . . . Government's task in these years, it was thought by many politicians and businessmen, was to aid business enterprise in accord with the best principles of mercantilism and still leave business free to grow and develop without restraint, as set

> forth in the doctrine of *laissez-faire*. The tradition thus grew that businessmen in the United States could do what so few people were able to do—have their cake and eat it too.[5]

Beginnings of Regulation

In the late 1800s and early 1900s, the public began to find some business practices antisocial. This dissatisfaction was expressed increasingly. Karl Marx, who wrote *The Communist Manifesto* with Friedrich Engels in 1848 and *Das Kapital* in 1867, put into words much of this dissatisfaction. He, as well as many others, rejected the capitalistic ethic because of its many unsavory side-effects, such as child labor, unsafe working conditions, and subsistence wages. The development of monopolistic corporations and cartels caused various groups within the United States to demand some form of regulation. Although most U.S. citizens rejected the Marxist view, they challenged the *laissez-faire* concept by suggesting that Adam Smith's economic system was based on a pure, competitive model that was ineffective in a system of entrenched monopolies and oligopolies. As a result, the federal government reclaimed some of the freedom and autonomy it had granted business by enacting such legislation as the Interstate Commerce Act (1887), the Sherman Antitrust Act (1890), the Pure Food and Drug Act (1906), the Clayton Act (1914), and the Federal Trade Commission Act (1914). More restrictive laws were to follow.

A Question of Autonomy

The Great Depression of the 1930s, Keynesian economics, and the increasing popularity of socialism as a political force resulted in business losing even more of its autonomy to government. Governments all over the world assumed responsibility for their economies. In 1946, the U.S. Congress passed the Fair Employment Act, which states that the federal government has prime responsibility for the maintenance of full employment and full utilization of economic resources.[6] Through the decades of the 50s, 60s, and 70s, *laissez-faire*, if not dead, was certainly forgotten as people put their faith in a democratically elected central government rather than the self-interest of capitalists.

Consecutive years of profits earned by American big business during these prosperous decades suggested to a number of people that business was not truly paying its way in society. Increasingly, problems with product safety and environmental pollution were seen as the negative consequences of a selfish concern only with profits by business people. Some of these feelings were expressed in 1962 by President Kennedy after the U.S. steel industry ignored his request to refrain from raising prices during a time of inflation.

> Some time ago I asked each American to consider what he would do for his country, and I asked steel companies. In the last 24 hours we had their an-

> swer. . . . My father always told me that all businessmen were sons of bitches, but I never believed it until now.[7]

Business people were increasingly constrained in their decision making by laws regarding air and water pollution, product safety, and employment practices, among others. In the United States, the number of federal agencies involved in regulating business activity increased from 49 in 1960 to 83 in 1970. Firms in the steel industry alone faced 5,600 regulations from 27 federal agencies.[8] All around the world businesses were threatened by governments with more regulation or even outright nationalization. Business autonomy was seriously threatened.

National Policy—Modern Mercantilism?

With the coming of the 1980s, the relationship between business and government changed. The labor productivity growth rate which had steadily increased in the United States for nearly two hundred years slowed and became negative during the period from 1978 to 1980.[9] Focusing upon high-volume standardized production, major Western firms found to their chagrin that companies in the developing nations had copied their technology. With lower production costs due to lower wages, among other factors, these companies in the third world were able to seriously erode the market share and profits of the business corporations in the industrialized countries of the West. Faced with serious problems of unemployment and balance of trade problems, governments of the United States, Great Britain, and other Western nations acted to reduce some of the constraints they had previously placed on business activity.

A number of people argued that not only should business be given more autonomy, but also that the national government in the United States be an active supporter of business development. Stating that other nations with supportive industrial policies—such as Japan, Korea, and Singapore—had more competitive business corporations than did many Western nations, proposals for a sort of modern mercantilism were developed. Reich, in his influential book *The Next American Frontier,* contended that the federal government should develop a better system to help move U.S. industry more quickly out of high-volume standardized production into more flexible, quality-oriented systems of production using skilled labor.[10] National governments throughout the world were coming to think of business activity as the key to economic well-being. Questions of social responsibility were temporarily forgotten as people worried more about unemployment than pollution. Nevertheless, by the mid-1980s, problems of toxic waste, hazardous chemical plants, and unsafe products again became important topics for discussion as people once more became concerned about the distasteful side-effects of economic activity.

4.2 SOCIAL RESPONSIBILITY

The concept that business must be socially responsible sounds appealing until one asks, "Responsible to whom?" As was shown in Fig. 4.1, the task environment includes a large number of groups with interest in a corporation's activities. These groups are referred to as *stakeholders* because they affect or are affected by the achievement of the firm's objectives.[11] Should a corporation be responsible only to some of these groups, or does business have a responsibility to society at large?

The corporation must pay close attention to its task environment because its stakeholders are very responsive to the general trends in the societal environment and will typically translate these trends into direct pressure to affect corporate activities. Even if top management assumes the traditional *laissez-faire* stance that the major concern of its corporation is to make profits, it will find (often to its chagrin) that it must also be concerned with the effect of its profit making on stakeholders within its task environment. Each stakeholder uses its own criteria to determine how well a corporation is performing, and each is constantly judging top management's actions by their effect on itself. Therefore top management must be aware not only of the key stakeholders in the corporation's task environment but also of the criteria each group uses to judge the corporation's performance. The following is a list of some of these stakeholders and their probable criteria.

Stockholders	Price appreciation of securities. Dividends (How much and how often?).
Unions	Comparable wages. Stability of employment. Opportunity for advancement.
Governments	Support of government programs. Adherence to laws and regulations.
Suppliers	Rapidity of payment. Consistency of purchases.
Creditors	Adherence to contract terms. Dependability.
Customers/Distributors	Value given for the price paid. Availability of product or service.
Trade associations	Participation in association programs (*time*). Participation in association programs (*money*).

Competitors	Rate of growth (encroachment on their markets). Product or service innovation (source of new ideas to use).
Communities	Contribution to community development through taxes, participation in charitable activities, etc. Employment of local people. Minimum of negative side-effects (e.g., pollution).
Special interest groups	Employment of minority groups. Contributions to urban improvement programs. Provision of free services to the disadvantaged.

Priority of Concerns

In any one decision regarding corporate strategy, the interests of one stakeholder can conflict with another. For example, a business firm's decision to build a plant in an inner-city location may have a positive effect on community relations but a negative effect on stockholder dividends. Which group's interests have priority?

In a survey sponsored by the American Management Association, 6,000 managers and executives were asked to rate on a seven-point scale the importance of a number of corporate stakeholders.[12] As shown in Table 4.1, executives felt customers to be the most important concern. Employees were also rated highly. Interestingly, the general public was felt to be of similar

Table 4.1 **Importance to Executives of Various Stakeholders**

Stakeholder	*Rank*
Customers	6.40
Employees	6.01
Owners	5.30
General public	4.52
Stockholders	4.51
Elected public officials	3.79
Government bureaucrats	2.90

SOURCE: Adapted from B. Z. Posner and W. H. Schmidt, "Values and the American Manager: An Update." Copyright © 1984 by the Regents of the University of California. Adapted by permission of the Regents from *California Management Review*, vol. xxvi, no. 3, p. 206.

NOTE: The ranking is calculated on a scale of 7 (most important) to 1 (least important).

importance to stockholders. Owners (presumably those who own large blocks of stock), however, were rated as more important than either the public or more typical stockholders. Government representatives were rated as least important of all the groups considered.

Pressures on the Business Corporation

Given the wide range of interests and concerns present in any corporation's task environment, one or more groups, at any one time, probably will be dissatisfied with a corporation's activities. For example, consider General Motors' decision to build a new plant in a run-down area of Detroit (sometimes referred to as "Poletown"). In 1980, when corporate profits were turning to losses, General Motors advised the city of Detroit that in 1983 it would close its Cadillac and Fisher Body plants, both of which were located within city boundaries. Realizing its responsibility to Detroit, GM suggested that if the city could find a rectangular area of 450 to 500 acres with access to highways and long-haul railroad lines, it would build a new plant within the city. The city government in cooperation with the town of Hamtramck decided on the vacant Dodge "main plant" (abandoned previously by Chrysler Corporation), along with the adjacent area. As Detroit and Hamtramck began to appropriate the homes, factories, and churches in the area, protests developed. Lawsuits were filed. General Motors was in a situation of being damned if it left Detroit and damned if it stayed.[13]

Another controversial issue is the presence of over 300 United States business corporations in South Africa. Given the apartheid policy of strict racial segregation and discrimination against non-whites of the South African government, many critics of apartheid have been urging U.S. firms to withdraw their business. With American corporations controlling nearly 70% of South Africa's computer industry and half of its petroleum business, anti-apartheid spokespeople argue that the presence of such important firms as IBM, Exxon, G.E., GM, Kodak, Johnson and Johnson, Hewlett-Packard, Ford, among others, gave tacit approval and financial support to a "racist" government. Calls for the *disinvestment* of American business in South Africa were criticized, however, by other black South Africans with a different point of view. Mangosutu Gatsha Buthelezi, hereditary prime minister of the Zulu nation, commented: "No one has proved to us that the suffering which will ensue within the black community as a result of disinvestment will actually force the regime to effect the fundamental changes all of us are clamoring for."[14] Torn between two conflicting demands, around 150 U.S. business corporations have chosen a compromise position. They remained in South Africa, but signed and followed the *Sullivan Code,* a set of equal opportunity and fair treatment principles drawn up by Leon H. Sullivan, minister of Philadelphia's Zion Baptist Church and a director of General Motors. Nevertheless, by mid-1985 approximately forty U.S. universities had removed more than $300 million in investments from firms dealing with South Africa as had more than eighteen cities and five states.[15]

The previous examples indicate how easily a business corporation can run into problems—even when top management is trying to achieve the best outcome for all involved. There are other examples, however, of business firms engaging in very questionable, unethical, or even illegal actions. These examples reveal the dark side of corporate decision making and support those who favor more governmental regulation and less business autonomy. There is no doubt that top management of some business firms has sometimes made decisions emphasizing short-term profitability or personal gain over long-term relations with governments, local communities, suppliers, and even customers and employees. For example, here are some of the questionable practices that have been exposed in recent years:

- Possible negligent construction and management practices at nuclear power and chemical plants (for example, nuclear plants at Three Mile Island and Diablo Canyon and Union Carbide's chemical plant in Bhopal, India).[16]
- Improper disposal of toxic wastes (for instance, at Love Canal).[17]
- Production and sale of defective products (for example, A. H. Robbins' Dalkon Shield birth control device).[18]
- Declaring bankruptcy to cancel a labor contract and cut wages (for instance, Wilson Foods).[19]
- Insufficient safeguarding of employees from exposure to dangerous chemicals and materials in the workplace (for instance, the asbestos problem at Johns-Manville).[20]
- Continuous instances of fraud, bribery, and price fixing at corporations of all sizes and locations (for example, National Semiconductor's defrauding the Defense Department by failing to test electronic components properly and General Electric's illegal claims for more than $800,000 in cost overruns on Minuteman missile contracts).[21]

Ethics: A Question of Values

Such questionable practices by business corporations run counter to the values of society as a whole and are justly criticized and prosecuted. Why are actions taken that so obviously harm important stakeholders in the corporation's task environment? Are business corporations and the people who run them amoral, or are they simply ignorant of the many consequences of their actions?

Cultural Differences

One reason for such behavior is that there is no worldwide standard of conduct for businesspeople. Cultural norms and values vary between countries and even between different geographic regions and ethnic groups within a country. One example is the use of payoffs and bribes to influence a potential customer to buy from a particular supplier. Although this practice is considered illegal in the United States, it is deeply entrenched in many countries. In Mexico, for instance, the payoff, referred to as *la mordida* (the bite), is considered a fringe benefit or *propina* (a tip).[22]

Personal Differences

Another possible reason for a corporation's questionable practices lies in differences in values between top management and key stakeholders in the task environment. Some businesspeople may believe profit maximization is the key goal of their firm, whereas concerned interest groups may have other goals, such as the hiring of minorities and women or the safety of their neighborhoods.

Economist Milton Friedman, in urging a return to a *laissez-faire* style worldwide economy, argues against the concept of social responsibility. If a businessperson acts "responsibly" by cutting the price of the firm's product to prevent inflation, or by making expenditures to reduce pollution, or by hiring the hard-core unemployed, that person, according to Friedman, is spending the stockholder's money for a general social interest. Even if the businessperson has stockholder permission or encouragement to do so, he or she is still acting from motives other than economic and may, in the long run, cause harm to the very society the firm is trying to help. By taking on the burden of these social costs, the business becomes less efficient; and either prices go up to pay for the increased costs, or investment in new activities and research is postponed. These results negatively affect—perhaps fatally—the long-term efficiency of a business. Friedman thus referred to the social responsibility of business as a "fundamentally subversive doctrine" and stated that "there is one and only one social responsibility of business—to use its resources and engage in activities designed to increase its profits so long as it stays within the rules of the game, which is to say, engages in open and free competition without deception or fraud."[23]

Friedman's stand on free enterprise has been both criticized and praised. Businesspeople tend to agree with Friedman because his views are compatible not only with their own self-interests but also with their hierarchy of values. Research by Guth and Tagiuri points out that high-level U.S. executives hold most highly a combination of economic, theoretical, and political values. Religious, asthetic, and social values have less importance in their lives. The following comparison of the value systems of business executives and ministers shows large differences (the values are arranged in order from most important to least important).[24]

Executives	*Ministers*
Economic	Religious
Theoretical	Social
Political	Aesthetic
Religious	Political
Aesthetic	Theoretical
Social	Economic

Imagine the controversy that would result if a group composed of ministers and executives had to decide the following strategy issues: Should business firms close on Sunday? Should the corporation hire handicapped workers and accept the increased training costs associated with their employment? In discussing these issues, the executive would probably be very concerned with the effects on the "bottom line" (profits), whereas the minister would probably be concerned with the effects on society and salvation (a very different bottom line).

This conclusion is supported by a study of 6,000 executives and managers who were asked to rate a representative sample of typical organizational goals as depicted in Table 4.2. The results clearly show community service and public service ranked at the bottom of the list under organizational effectiveness and profit maximization.[25] This study generally agrees with previous studies which revealed a desire by businesspeople to limit their social responsibilities to those areas where they can clearly see benefits to the corporation in terms of reduced costs and less governmental regulation.[26]

This very narrow view of businesses' responsibilities to society typically will cause conflicts between the business corporation and certain members of

Table 4.2 **Importance to Executives of Various Organizational Goals**

Organizational Goal	*Degree of Importance*
Organizational effectiveness	6.26
High productivity	6.16
High morale	6.01
Organizational efficiency	5.93
Profit maximization	5.44
Organizational growth	5.20
Organizational value to community	4.82
Service to the public	4.68

SOURCE: Adapted from B. Z. Posner and W. H. Schmidt, "Values and the American Manager: An Update." Copyright © 1984 by the Regents of the Univesity of California. Adapted by permission of the Regents from *California Management Review,* vol. xxvi, no. 3, p. 205.

NOTE: The ranking is calculated on a scale of 7 ("very important to me") to 1 (" of little or no importance to me").

its task environment. Carroll, in his research on social responsibility, suggests that in addition to the obvious economic and legal responsibilities, businesses have ethical and discretionary ones.[27] The *economic* responsibilities of a business corporation are to produce goods and services of value to society. Its *legal* responsibilities are defined by governments in the laws that corporations are expected to obey. Its *ethical* responsibilities are to follow the generally held beliefs about how one should act in a society. *Discretionary* responsibilities, in contrast, are the purely voluntary obligations a corporation assumes. Examples are philanthropic contributions, training the hard-core unemployed, and providing day-care centers. Carroll suggests that to the extent that business corporations fail to acknowledge discretionary or ethical responsibilities, society, through government, will act, making them legal responsibilities. This may be done by governments, moreover, without regard to a corporation's economic responsibilities. As a result, the corporation may have greater difficulty in earning a profit than it would have had in assuming voluntarily some ethical and discretionary responsibilities. For example, it has been suggested by some people in the American automobile industry that the large number of safety and pollution regulations passed in the 1960s and 1970s were partially responsible for the poor health of the industry in the early 1980s.[28]

Nevertheless, studies in the area have *failed* to find any significant relationship between a business corporation's social responsibility and its financial performance. Examples can be cited of both highly profitable and marginally profitable companies with both poor and excellent social records.[29] One interesting example is Control Data Corporation. Under the leadership of socially concerned William C. Norris as founder, chairman, and CEO, Control Data has organized assembly plants in ghettos and prisons and spent millions of dollars on computer systems for education and training in schools and industry. Unfortunately, corporate earnings have fallen and Norris has been criticized for allowing his "pet businesses" to drain investment away from the company's profitable ventures.[30]

Even with the finding that social responsibility has no relationship to profits, one conclusion seems clear. The *iron law of responsibility* applies: If business corporations are unable or unwilling to police themselves by considering their responsibilities to all stakeholders in their task environment, then society—usually in the form of government—will police their doing so, and once again governments will reduce business's autonomy via increased rules and regulations.

4.3 ENVIRONMENTAL SCANNING

Because they are a part of a larger society that constantly affects them in many ways, corporations must be aware of changes and potential changes within the key variables in their task and societal environments. In 1973, for example, the Arab oil embargo caught many firms completely by surprise, with the result that goods dependent on oil as a raw material or energy source could not be produced. The resulting shortages and price adjustments caused chaos throughout the world's economy. The top management of many business corporations then realized just how dependent they were on seemingly unpredictable external events. It was at this time, in the early 1970s, that many corporations established for the first time formal strategic planning systems. By 1984, between 92 and 95% of the world's largest corporations were using planning departments to monitor the environment and to prepare forecasts.[31]

Before strategy makers can begin formulating specific strategies, they must scan the external environment to identify possible *opportunities* and *threats.* Environmental scanning is the monitoring, evaluating, and disseminating of information from the external environment to key people within the corporation.[32] It is a tool used by a corporation to avoid strategic surprise and to ensure its long-run health.[33] Both the societal and task environments must be monitored to detect strategic factors that are likely to have a strong impact on corporate success or failure.

Monitoring Strategic Factors

Usually environmental scanning begins with the identification of strategic factors in the societal and task environments. *Strategic factors* are those variables that top management believes have great potential for affecting its corporation's activities. They are the patterns of events that will influence the corporation in the future. These factors are typically ones that have strongly affected a corporation in the past or are presently doing so. But, unfortunately, few firms attempt to anticipate them.[34] Furthermore, the values of the top managers are likely to bias both their perceptions of what is or is not important to monitor in the external environment and their interpretations of what they perceive.

For example, a recent research study of presidents of savings and loan associations revealed that a president's perception of the environment strongly affected strategic planning. Those presidents who believed the present uncertain environment to be only temporary used no long-term planning staff or planning committees. They simply chose to wait for the "good old days" to return. In contrast, those presidents who believed the days of the stable, regulated environment to be long gone spent 30 to 50% of their time considering long-range strategic issues and using planning staffs extensively.[35]

Societal Environment

The number of possible strategic factors in the societal environment is enormous. As noted in Table 4.3, large corporations categorize the societal en-

Table 4.3 Some Important Factors in the Societal Environment

Sociocultural	*Economic*	*Technological*	*Political-Legal*
Life-style changes	GNP trends	Total federal spending for R&D	Antitrust regulations
Career expectations	Interest rates	Total industry spending for R&D	Environmental protection laws
Consumer activism	Money supply	Focus of technological efforts	Tax laws
Rate of family formation	Inflation rates	Patent protection	Special incentives
Growth rate of population	Unemployment levels	New products	Foreign trade regulations
Age distribution of population	Wage/Price controls	New developments in technology transfer from lab to marketplace	Attitudes toward foreign companies
Regional shifts in population	Devaluation/revaluation	Productivity improvements through automation	Laws on hiring and promotion
Life expectancies	Energy availability and cost		Stability of government
Birth rates	Disposable and discretionary income		

vironment into four areas and focus their scanning in each area on trends with corporate-wide relevance. The economic area is usually the most significant, followed by the technological, political–legal, and sociocultural in decreasing order of importance.[36] Obviously, trends in any one area may be very important to the firms in one industry but of lesser importance to firms in other industries. For example, the demographic bulge in the U.S. population caused by the "baby boom" in the 1950s strongly affects the brewing industry, among others. As this demographic group becomes older during the decade of the 80s, the percentage of the population in the 18–25 years of age category—prime beer drinking age—decreases. Thus sales and profits of breweries decrease and corporations like Anheuser-Busch find that they must diversify if they are to stay profitable. In contrast, as the number of people in the 25–34 years of age category becomes larger, demand increases considerably for day-care facilities like Kinder-Care Learning Centers. As this group of "Yuppies" (young urban professionals) have children, businesses are forced to alter their product and service offerings. For example, Jerry Jones, senior vice-president of Colorado's Keystone Resort, says that the baby boomers who once flocked to the ski slopes are now young parents who ski less often and spend fewer dollars when they do. To survive, even fashionable resorts are now using discount rates and promotions to lure families.[37]

John Naisbitt, in his influential book, *Megatrends,* states that America's present societal environment is turbulent because we are moving from one era to another. From a content analysis of newspapers, he proposes that

American society is being restructured by *ten broad influences* or "megatrends" that are defining the new society.

1. We are moving from an industrial to an information society.
2. We are moving from forced technology to matching each new technology with a compensatory human response ("Hi tech–hi touch").
3. We are moving from a national to a world economy.
4. We are moving from short-term to long-term considerations with an emphasis on strategic planning.
5. We are moving from a period of centralization to decentralization of power.
6. We are shifting from reliance on institutional help to more self-reliance.
7. We are moving from representative democracy to more participative democracy in politics as well as in the workplace.
8. We are giving up our dependence on traditional hierarchical structures in favor of informal networks of contacts.
9. We are moving geographically from the North to the South and West.
10. We are moving from a society with a limited number of personal choices to a multiple-option society.[38]

If Naisbitt is correct, these changes will have enormous impact on business corporations. Strategic planners will need to closely monitor the environment for any trends or issues which will have serious impact on the future of

PROBABILITY OF OCCURRENCE \ PROBABLE IMPACT ON CORPORATION	High	Medium	Low
High	High Priority	High Priority	Medium Priority
Medium	High Priority	Medium Priority	Low Priority
Low	Medium Priority	Low Priority	Low Priority

Figure 4.2 **Issues priority matrix.**

SOURCE: Adapted from L. L. Lederman, "Foresight Activities in the U.S.A.: Time for a Re-Assessment?" *Long-Range Planning* (June 1984), p. 46. Copyright © 1984 by Pergamon Press, Ltd. Reprinted by permission.

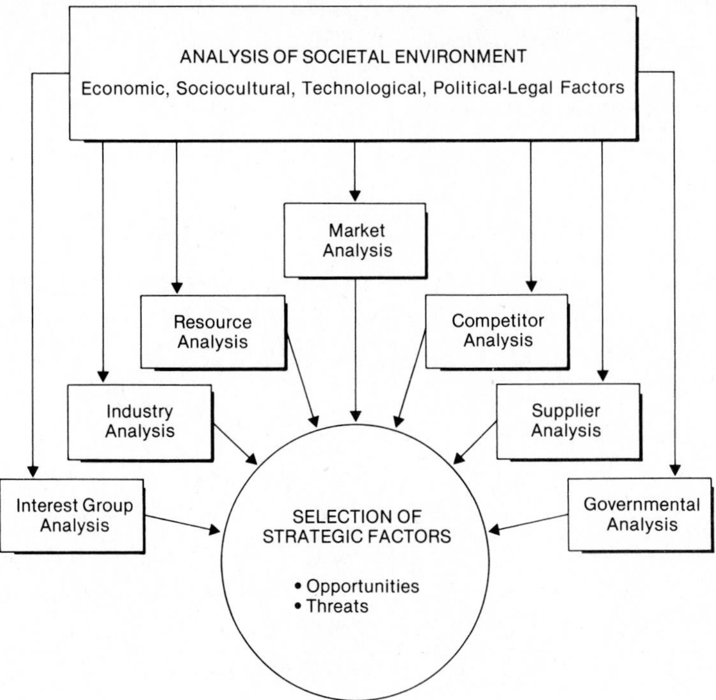

Figure 4.3 **Scanning the external environment.**

their corporation. To avoid information overload, planners should use an *issues priority matrix,* as shown in Fig. 4.2, to help them decide which issues to monitor closely (high priority) and which issues to merely scan (low priority).

Task Environment

As was noted earlier, changes in the societal environment tend to be reflected in pressures on the corporation from task environment groups. As shown in Fig. 4.3, a corporation's scanning of the environment will include analyses of all the relevant elements in the task environment—interest groups, its industry, resources, the marketplace, competitors, suppliers, and governments.

Porter, an authority on competitive strategy, contends that a corporation is most concerned with the intensity of competition within its industry. The level of this intensity is determined by basic competitive forces, which are depicted in Fig. 4.4. "The collective strength of these forces," he contends, "determines the ultimate profit potential in the industry, where profit potential is measured in terms of long-run return on invested capital."[39] Although Porter only mentions five forces, a sixth—other stakeholders—is added to

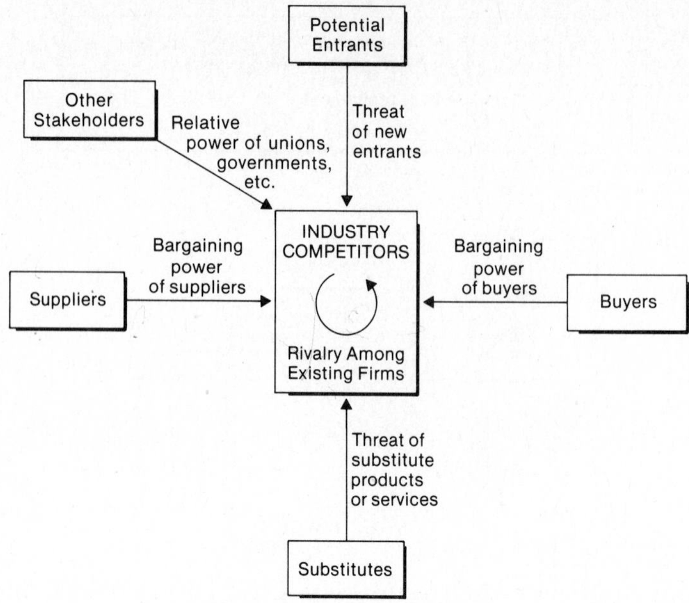

Figure 4.4 **Forces driving industry competition.**
SOURCE: Adapted with permission of The Free Press, a division of Macmillan, Inc. from *Competitive Strategy* by M. E. Porter. Copyright © 1980 by The Free Press.

reflect the power of unions, governments, and other groups from the task environment on industry activities.

A corporation must carefully scan the task environment to assess the importance to its success of each of the following six forces.[40]

1. *Threat of New Entrants:* New entrants to an industry typically bring to it new capacity, a desire to gain market share, and substantial resources and are, therefore, threats to an established corporation. The threat of entry depends on the presence of entry barriers and the reaction that can be expected from existing competitors. For example, there have been very few new automobile companies successfully established since the 1930s because of the high capital requirements to build production facilities and to develop a dealer distribution network.
2. *Rivalry among Existing Firms:* In most industries, corporations are mutually dependent. A competitive move by one firm can be expected to have a noticeable effect on its competitors and thus may cause retaliation or efforts to counter the move. For example, the entry of Philip Morris into the beer industry through the acquisition of Miller Brewing

increased the level of competitive activity to such an extent that a new product or promotion is now quickly followed by similar moves from other brewers.

3. *Threat of Substitute Products or Services:* In effect, all corporations in an industry are competing with industries that produce substitute products. According to Porter, "Substitutes limit the potential returns of an industry by placing a ceiling on the prices firms in the industry can profitably charge."[41] In the 1970s, for example, the high price of cane sugar caused soft drink manufacturers to turn to high fructose corn syrup as a sugar substitute. Sometimes a difficult task, the identification of possible substitute products or services means searching for products or services that can perform the same *function,* even though they may not appear to be easily substitutable. Videotape recorders, for example, are becoming substitutes for home motion picture projectors. The television screen thus substitutes for the portable projection screen.

4. *Bargaining Power of Buyers:* Buyers affect an industry through their ability to force down prices, bargain for higher quality or more services, and play competitors against each other. A buyer or a group of buyers is powerful if some of the following hold true:

   - It purchases a large proportion of the seller's product or service.
   - It has the potential to integrate backward by producing the product itself.
   - Alternative suppliers are plentiful.
   - Changing suppliers costs very little.

   For example, to the extent that General Motors purchases a large percentage of Firestone's total tire production, GM's purchasing department can easily make all sorts of demands on Firestone's marketing people. This would be the case especially if GM could easily get its tires from Goodyear or General Tire at no extra trouble or cost. Increasing demands by large manufacturing companies for "just-in-time delivery" means that in order to get the orders, a small supplier dependent on the large firm's business must take over the warehousing functions previously handled by the large firm.

5. *Bargaining Power of Suppliers:* Suppliers can affect an industry through their ability to raise prices or reduce the quality of purchased goods and services. A supplier group is powerful if some of the following apply:

- The supplier industry is dominated by a few companies, but sells to many.
- Substitutes are not readily available.
- Suppliers are able to integrate forward and compete directly with their present customers. An example is the construction of oil refineries by Saudi Arabia.
- A purchasing industry buys only a small portion of the supplier group's goods and services.

For example, major oil companies in the 1970s were able to raise prices and reduce services because so many companies that purchased oil products had heavy energy needs and, in the short run, were unable to switch to substitute fuels, such as coal or nuclear power. Wishing to be less dependent on suppliers for the raw material so necessary to produce synthetic materials, Dupont chose to buy Conoco, a major oil company.

6. *Relative Power of Other Stakeholders:* Freeman recommends adding this sixth force to Porter's list to include a variety of stakeholder groups from the task environment.[42] Some of them are governments, unions, local communities, creditors (if not included with suppliers), trade associations, special interest groups, and stockholders. The importance of these stakeholders will vary by industry. For example, environmental groups successfully fought to pass bills in Maine, Michigan, Oregon, and Iowa outlawing disposable bottles and cans, thus requiring deposits for most drink containers. Although Porter contends that government influences the level of competitive activity through the previously mentioned five forces, it is suggested here that governments deserve a special mention because of their strong relative power in all industries.

Strategic Groups

In analyzing the level of competitive intensity within an industry, it is useful to categorize the various competitors for predictive purposes. According to Miles and Snow, competing firms within a single industry can be grouped on the basis of similar patterns of behavior into one of four basic types: the Defender, the Prospector, the Analyzer, and the Reactor. Each of these types has its own favorite strategy for responding to the environment. Each has its own combination of structure, culture, and processes consistent with that strategy. These general types have the following characteristics:

- *Defenders* are corporations with a limited product line that focus on improving the efficiency of their existing operations. Their focus makes them less likely to innovate in new areas. An example would be the Schlitz Brewing Company.

- *Prospectors* are corporations with fairly broad product lines that focus on product innovation and market opportunities. They tend to emphasize creativity over efficiency. An example would be the Miller Brewing Company.
- *Analyzers* are corporations that operate in two different product-market areas, one stable and one changing. In the stable area, efficiency is emphasized. In the changing area, innovation is emphasized. An example would be Anheuser-Busch (beer and snack food).
- *Reactors* are corporations that lack a consistent strategy-structure-culture relationship. They tend to respond (often ineffectively) to environmental pressures with piecemeal strategic changes. An example would be the Pabst Brewing Company.[43]

Lumping the competition into one of these four groups enables the strategic manager to not only monitor the effectiveness of certain strategic orientations, it also aids in the development of future industry scenarios (to be discussed later in this chapter).

Sources of Information

Studies have shown that much environmental scanning is done on an informal and individual basis. Information is obtained from a variety of sources such as customers, suppliers, bankers, consultants, publications, personal observations, subordinates, superiors, and peers. For example, scientists and engineers working in a firm's R&D lab may learn about new products and competitors' ideas at professional meetings; or speaking with supplier representatives' personnel in the purchasing department may uncover valuable bits of information about a competitor. A study of product innovation in the scientific instruments and machine tool industries found that 80% of all product innovations were initiated by the *customer* in the form of inquiries and complaints.[44] In these industries, the sales force and service departments must be especially vigilant.

Some of the main sources of information about an industry's environment are shown in Fig. 4.5. Because people throughout a corporation may obtain an extraordinary amount of data in any given month, top management must develop a system to get these data from those who obtained it to the people who can integrate it with other information to form a comprehensive environmental assessment.

As one would suspect, research suggests that corporations develop and implement more scanning procedures for following, anticipating, and responding to changes in the activities of *competitors* than for any other stakeholder in the environment.

There is danger in focusing one's scanning efforts too closely on one's

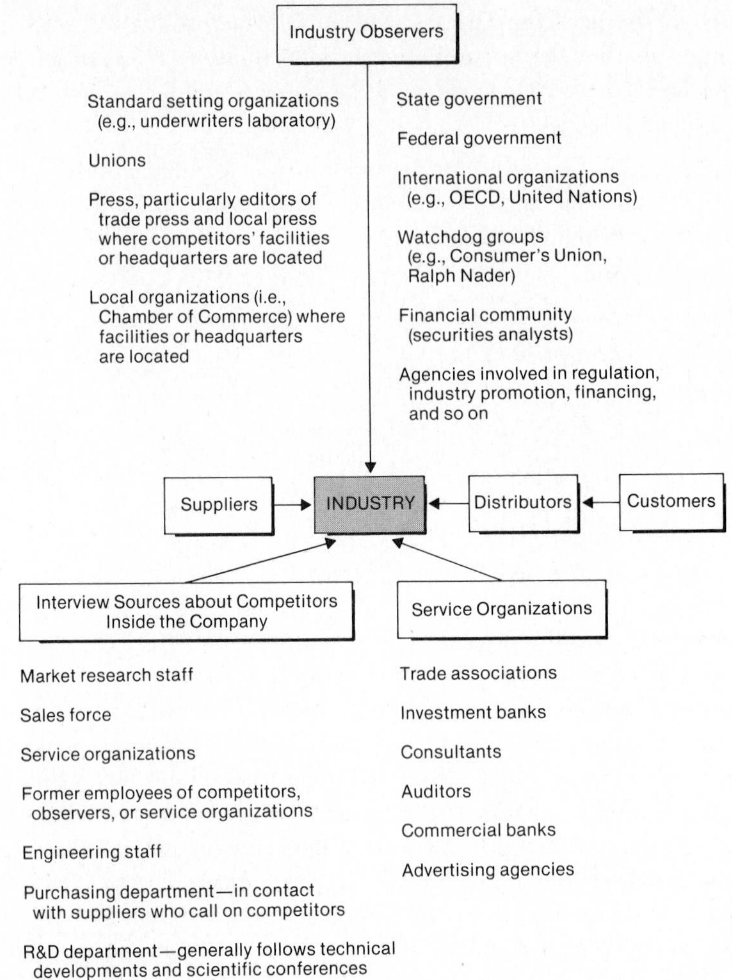

Figure 4.5 **Sources of data for industry analysis.**
SOURCE: Reprinted with permission of The Free Press, a division of Macmillan, Inc. from *Competitive Strategy* by M. E. Porter. Copyright © 1980 by The Free Press.

own industry, though. According to research by Snyder, "History teaches that most new developments which threaten existing business practices and technologies do not come from traditional industries."[45] For instance, *technology transfer*, the process of taking new technology from the laboratory to the marketplace, has become an important issue in recent decades. Consider just one example. With the development of the integrated circuit, electronics firms, such as Texas Instruments, were able to introduce high-volume, low-cost electronic digital watches. These firms' entry into the watch-making industry took well-established mechanical watchmakers by surprise. Timex,

Seiko, and especially the Swiss firms found that their market had changed overnight. Their production facilities, however, had not; and they spent a lot of money buying the new technology.

Most corporations rely on outside organizations to provide them with environmental data. Firms such as A. C. Nielsen Co. provide subscribers with bimonthly data on brand share, retail prices, percentages of stores stocking an item, and percentages of stock-out stores. These data can be used to spot regional and national trends as well as to assess market share. Information on market conditions, government regulations, competitors, and new products can be bought from "information brokers." Such firms as FIND/SVP, a New York company, get their data from periodicals, reference books, computer data banks, directors, and experts in the area. Other firms, like Chase Econometrics, offer various data bases plus a software package to enable corporate planners to gain computer access to a large number of key indicators. Typically, the largest corporations spend from $20,000 to $25,000 a year for database services. Close to 6,000 firms in the United States and Canada have established their own in-house libraries to deal with the growing mass of available information.[46]

Some companies, however, chose to get their information straight from their competitors through industrial espionage or other intelligence gathering techniques. For example, Hitachi Ltd, the large Japanese electronics firm, pleaded guilty in 1983 to conspiring to transport stolen IBM material to Japan.[47] In 1984, Procter & Gamble filed a patent-infringement suit against Nabisco Inc, Keebler Co., and Frito-Lay Inc., accusing them of *cookie espionage.* Procter & Gamble (P&G) claimed to have invented the process to make the "dual texture" cookies—crispy outside and soft inside. P&G charged that one competitor took aerial photographs of its cookie manufacturing plant during construction and that another learned the recipe by penetrating a restricted area where the secret technology was being used. The competitors denied all allegations.[48] Other legal, but still questionable, approaches to intelligence gathering are hiring people away from competitors, getting customers to put out phony bid requests, and analyzing a competitor's garbage, to name a few![49]

4.4 FORECASTING

Once a business corporation has collected data about its current environmental situation, it must analyze present trends to learn if they will continue into the future. The strategic planning horizon for many large corporations is from five to ten years in the future. A long-term planning horizon is especially necessary for large, capital-intensive corporations, such as automobile or heavy-machinery manufacturers. These corporations require many years to move from an accepted proposal to a finished product. As a result, most

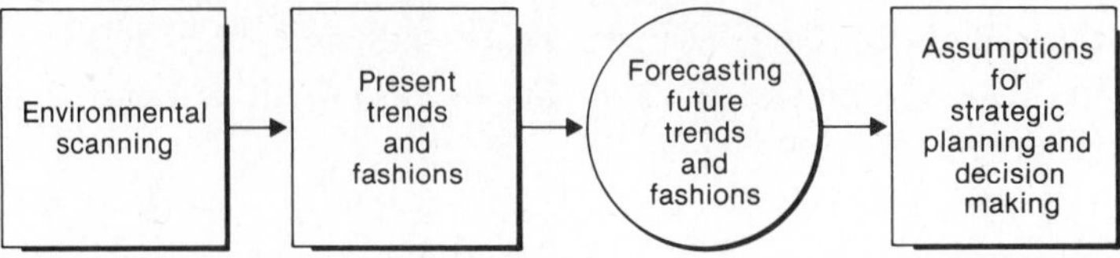

Figure 4.6 **The role of forecasting.**

corporations must make future plans on the basis of a forecast, a set of assumptions about what that future will look like. These assumptions may be derived from an entrepreneur's vision, from a head-in-the-sand hope that the future will be similar to the present, or from the opinions of experts. Figure 4.6 depicts the role of forecasting in the strategy formulation process.

The Danger of Assumptions

A forecast is nothing more than a leap of faith into the future. Environmental scanning provides reasonably hard data on the present situation, but intuition and luck are needed to predict the future. Nevertheless, many firms formulate and implement strategic plans with little or no realization that their success is based on a series of assumptions. Many long-range plans are simply based on projections of the current situation. One example of what can happen when corporate strategy rests on the very questionable assumption that the future will simply be an extension of the present is that of the Pacific Coal Corporation.

In 1981, the Pacific Coal Corporation decided to build a coal-export terminal near Portland, Oregon. One of a score of coal-export terminals proposed for the West Coast, the terminal was planned after the world's second oil crisis when Asian nations sought new supplies of steam coal for electric generating plants. West Coast ports, coal developers, and railroads expected a coal-export boom. Unfortunately, a global recession coupled with an unforeseen drop in oil prices reduced Asian energy demands. Construction of the $60 million Portland facility was suspended in March 1983 with only 80% completion. The facility, with a planned annual capacity of 12 million tons of coal, had no long-term contracts. "The situation is pretty bleak," stated another developer. "Our assessment of the future is it may be unlikely to turn around until the early 1990's—we may be talking about ten years."[50]

Techniques

As depicted in Table 4.4, various techniques are used to forecast future situations. Each has its proponents and critics. A recent study of nearly 500 of the world's largest corporations revealed *trend extrapolation* to be the most widely practiced form of forecasting—over 70% use this technique either occasionally or frequently.[51] Simply stated, extrapolation is the extension of present trends into the future. Like the Pacific Coal Corporation example, it

Table 4.4 **Degree of Usage of Forecasting Techniques***

Technique	*Top 1,000 U.S. Industrials* (n=*215*)	*Top 100 U.S. Industrials* (n=*40*)	*Top 300 U.S. Non-Industrials* (n=*85*)	*Top 500 Foreign Industrials* (n=*105*)
Trend extrapolation	73%	70%	74%	72%
Statistical modeling (i.e., regression analysis)	48	61	51	45
Scenarios	57	67	67	61
Relevance trees	5	3	7	4
Simulation	34	45	38	27
Brainstorming	65	61	69	52
Trend impact analysis	34	33	31	29
Expert opinion/Delphi	33	42	24	35
Morphological analysis	2	0	0	5
Signal monitoring	15	19	14	18
Cross-impact analysis	12	22	11	5

SOURCE: H. E. Klein and R. E. Linneman, "Environmental Assessment: An International Study of Corporate Practices," *Journal of Business Strategy* (Summer 1984), p. 72.

* Figures reflect the percentage of respondents indicating either "frequent" or "occasional" use. Respondents had been asked to classify their frequency of technique use as "not used," "rarely used," "used occasionally," or "used frequently."

rests on the assumption that the world is reasonably consistent and changes slowly in the short run. Time series methods are approaches of this type which attempt to carry a series of historical events forward into the future. The basic problem with extrapolation is that a historical trend is based upon a series of patterns or relationships among so many different variables that a change in any one can drastically alter the future direction of the trend. As a rule of thumb, the further back into the past one can find relevant data supporting the trend, the more confidence one can have in the prediction. Nevertheless, even experts in forecasting admit: "Forecasts that cover a period of two years or more are typically very inaccurate."[52]

As shown in Table 4.4 brainstorming and statistical modeling are also very popular forecasting techniques. *Brainstorming* is a nonquantitative approach requiring simply the presence of people with some knowledge of the situation to be predicted. The basic ground rule is to propose ideas without first mentally screening them. No criticism is allowed. Ideas tend to build upon previous ideas until a consensus is reached. This is a good technique to use with operating managers who have more faith in "gut feel" than in more quantitative "number crunching" techniques.

Statistical modeling is a quantitative technique that attempts to discover causal or at least explanatory factors that link two or more time series together. Examples of statistical modeling are regression analysis and other econometric methods. Although very useful to grasp historic trends, statistical modeling, like trend extrapolation, is based on historical data. As the patterns of relationships change, the accuracy of the forecast deteriorates.[53]

Other forecasting techniques, such as *cross-impact analysis, trend impact analysis,* and *relevance trees* have not established themselves successfully as regularly employed tools. Research by Klein and Linneman reports that corporate planners found these techniques to be complicated, time-consuming, expensive, and academic. Usage was therefore concentrated among the very largest companies.[54]

Research further reports that *scenario-writing* appears to be the most widely used forecasting technique after trend extrapolation. Among corporations in the top Fortune 1,000 Industrials, the usage of scenarios increased from 22% in 1977 to 57% in 1981. Klein and Linneman predict increasing usage of this popular forecasting technique, but point out that "most companies follow a very informal scenario-writing approach with little reliance on rigorous methodologies."[55] The scenario may thus be merely a written description of some future state in terms of key variables and issues or it may be generated from other forecasting techniques in combination. A more complex version used by General Electric is depicted in Fig. 4.7 and is based upon a Delphi panel of experts, a trend impact analysis, and a cross-impact analysis. The *Delphi* technique involves an anonymous panel of experts who are asked individually to estimate the probability of certain events occurring in the future. Each member of the panel is given several opportunities to revise his/her estimate after seeing the anonymous responses from the other experts on the panel.

In his recent book *Competitive Advantage,* Michael Porter strongly recommends the use of scenarios because they: (1) allow a firm to move away from dangerous, single-point forecasts of the future in instances when the future cannot be predicted, and (2) encourage managers to make their assumptions explicit.[56] He recommends the use of *industry scenarios* which utilize variables from the societal environment as they affect the key stakeholders in a corporation's task environment. The process may operate as follows.[57]

1. *Examine possible shifts in the societal variables* (e.g., economic, sociocultural, technological, and political-legal). Begin with the obvious factors in Table 4.3 and plot them on the issues priority matrix depicted in Fig. 4.2.
2. *Identify uncertainties in each of the six forces from the task environment* (e.g., competitors, buyers, suppliers, likely substitutes, potential

entrants, and other key stakeholders) as depicted in Fig. 4.4. Make sure that all the high-priority societal issues identified in the first step are specified as they affect the appropriate forces in the task environment.

3. *Identify the causal factors behind the uncertainties.* These sources of uncertainty may be inside the industry (e.g., competitor behavior) or outside the industry (e.g., new regulations). It is likely that many of these causal factors were identified earlier when analyzing the societal environment. It is also likely that new ones surfaced when analyzing the task environment.
4. *Make a range of plausible assumptions about each important causal factor.* For example, if the price of oil is a causal factor, make reason-

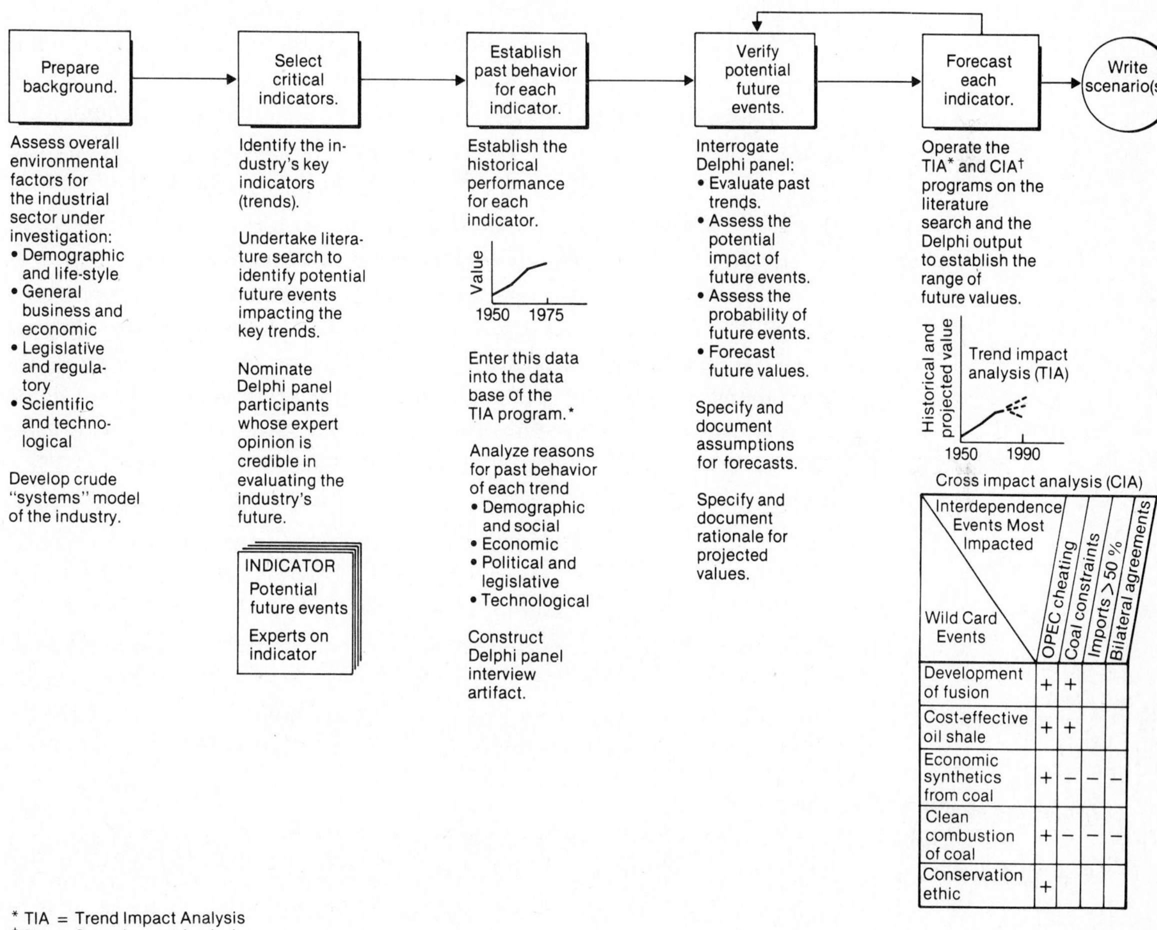

Interdependence Events Most Impacted / Wild Card Events	OPEC cheating	Coal constraints	Imports > 50 %	Bilateral agreements
Development of fusion	+	+		
Cost-effective oil shale	+	+		
Economic synthetics from coal	+	–	–	–
Clean combustion of coal	+	–	–	–
Conservation ethic	+			

Figure 4.7 **Scenario construction at General Electric.**
SOURCE: General Electric Company. Used by permission.

able assumptions about its future level in terms of high, low, and most probable price.

5. *Combine assumptions about individual causal factors into internally consistent scenarios.* Put various combinations of the assumptions together into sets of scenarios. Since one assumption may affect another, ensure that the scenarios are internally consistent. For example, if a scenario includes the assumptions of high oil prices and a low level of inflation in the economy, that scenario is not internally consistent and should be rejected. It is an unlikely event because high oil prices tend to drive inflation upward.
6. *Analyze the industry situation that would prevail under each scenario.* For example, if one scenario assumes that generic (no-name) drugs will be more in demand than brand-name drugs, the situation in the drug industry will be very different than if one assumed that the demand for generic drugs will be negligible. For example, an industry dominated by generic drugs would mean low profit margins for all firms and a very heavy degree of competition. It is likely that a few firms would leave the drug industry.
7. *Determine the sources of competitive advantage under each scenario.* For example, in an industry dominated by generic drugs, the combination of low price backed up by low operating costs would provide competitive advantage to a firm. If brand-name drugs dominated, the combination of strong advertising, high-quality production, and heavy promotion would provide competitive advantage to the firm using them.
8. *Predict competitor behavior under each scenario.* As the industry moves toward a particular scenario each competitor will make some adjustment. Some may leave the industry. New competitors may enter. Estimate what each competitor is likely to do given its history and what is known about its management. Once this is done, management should be able to specify the *strategic factors* necessary for success in a variety of future scenarios. One may also attach probabilities to each of the developed scenarios in order to choose the ones most likely to occur.

4.5 SUMMARY AND CONCLUSION

Anyone concerned with how strategic decisions are made in large corporations should be aware of the impact of the external environment on top management and the board of directors. Long-run developments in the economic, technological, political-legal, and sociocultural aspects of the societal environment strongly affect the corporation's activities through the more immediate pressures in its task environment.

Business and commerce have lived an uneasy truce with society for centuries. Vacillating between heavy regulation and *laissez-faire* economics, business corporations are learning that they must be socially responsible if they are to operate with some autonomy. Top management and the board of directors must constantly balance the needs of one stakeholder in the corporation's task environment against the needs of another. They must work to ensure that their priorities do not get too far away from those valued by society.

Before strategy can be formulated, strategy makers must scan the external environment for possible opportunities and threats. They must identify which strategic factors to monitor, as well as assess which are likely to affect the corporation in the future. Then they must analyze the resulting information and disseminate it to the people involved in strategic planning and decision making.

Just as environmental scanning provides an understanding of present trends in the environment, forecasting provides assumptions about the future that are crucial for strategic management. Modern corporations primarily use the techniques of trend extrapolation, scenario-writing, brainstorming, and statistical modeling to predict their likely future environment. Even if the predictions prove to be wrong, the very act of scanning and forecasting the environment helps managers take a broader perspective. These techniques also help prevent the development of reactive managers who dare not take the time to plan for the future because they are caught up in the crises and problems of the present.

DISCUSSION QUESTIONS

1. Should U.S. corporations be allowed to operate in South Africa under an "apartheid"-oriented government?
2. How appropriate is the theory of *laissez-faire* in today's world?
3. Why should a business corporation be socially responsible?
4. What can a corporation do to ensure that information about strategic environmental factors gets to the attention of strategy makers?
5. To what extent do you agree with the conclusion that the ultimate profit potential of an industry depends on the collective strength of six key forces: the threat of new entrants, the rivalry among existing firms, the threat of substitutable products or services, the bargaining power of buyers, the bargaining power of suppliers, and the relative power of other stakeholders? Defend your view.
6. If most long-term forecasts are usually incorrect, why bother doing them?
7. Compare and contrast trend extrapolation with scenarios as forecasting techniques.

NOTES

1. E. C. Bursk, D. T. Clark, and R. W. Hidy, "The Oldest Business Code: Nearly 4000 Years Ago," *The World of Business,* vol. 1 (New York: Simon and Schuster, 1962), pp. 9–10.
2. F. E. Kast and J. E. Rosenzweig, *Organization and Management,* 2nd ed. (New York: McGraw-Hill, 1974), p. 28.
3. M. Weber, *The Protestant Ethic and the Spirit of Capitalism,* trans. Talcott Parsons (New York: Charles Scribner's Sons, 1958).
4. Kast and Rosenzweig, p. 35.
5. J. W. McGuire, *Business and Society* (New York: McGraw-Hill, 1963), p. 78.
6. Kast and Rosenzweig, pp. 37–39.
7. *New York Times* (April 23, 1962) as quoted by H. L. Gabel, G. A. Becker, and B. S. Seng, "Armco—The 1978 Wage and Price Guidelines," in T. L. Wheelen and J. D. Hunger, *Strategic Management and Business Policy,* 1st ed. (Reading, Mass.: Addison-Wesley, 1983), p. 397.
8. G. A. Steiner, *The New CEO* (New York: Macmillan Publishing, 1983), p. 6.
9. K. Hughes, *Corporate Response to Declining Rates of Growth* (Lexington, Mass.: Lexington Books, 1982), p. 14.
10. R. B. Reich, *The Next American Frontier* (New York: Times Books, 1983).
11. R. E. Freeman, *Strategic Management: A Stakeholder Approach* (Boston: Pitman Publishing Co., 1984), p. 25.
12. B. Z. Posner and W. H. Schmidt, "Values and the American Manager: An Update," *California Management Review* (Spring 1984), pp. 202–216.
13. "Pushing the Boundaries of Eminent Domain," *Business Week* (May 4, 1981), p. 174.
14. "Kennedy, Zulu Leader Discuss Investments," *Ames Tribune* (United Press International), Ames, Iowa, January 10, 1985, p. 20.
15. S. P. Sherman, "Scoring Corporate Conduct in South Africa," *Fortune* (July 9, 1984), pp. 168–172.
    M. Maremont, "Fire on Campus, Tremors in the Boardroom," *Business Week* (April 29, 1985), pp. 98–99.
16. "Three Mile Island's Lingering Ills," *Business Week* (October 22, 1979), p. 75.
    T. Redburn, "Stalled Nuclear Power Plant: PG&E Feels Powerless," *Los Angeles Times* (February 24, 1980), part 4, p. 1.
    J. H. Dobrzynski, W. B. Glaberson, R. W. King, W. J. Powell, Jr., and L. Helm, "Union Carbide Fights for Its Life," *Business Week* (December 24, 1984), pp. 52–56.
17. "Who Will Be Liable for Toxic Dumping?" *Business Week* (August 28, 1978), p. 32.
18. M. W. Walsh, "A. H. Robbins Seeks a Consolidated Trial for All Dalkon Punitive-Damage Claims," *Wall Street Journal* (October 23, 1984), p. 4.
19. L. Sorenson, "Chapter 11 Filing by Wilson Foods Roils Workers' Lives, Tests Law," *Wall Street Journal* (May 23, 1983), p. 25.

20. S. Soloman, "The Asbestos Fallout at Johns-Manville," *Fortune* (May 7, 1979), pp. 197–206.

21. "Test Case: A Defense Contractor Is Fined," *Time* (March 19, 1984), p. 47.
F. Schwadel, "General Electric Pleads Guilty in Fraud Case," *Wall Street Journal* (May 14, 1985), p. 119.
I. Ross, "How Lawless Are Big Companies?" *Fortune* (December 1, 1980), pp. 58–61.

22. W. M. Pride and O. C. Ferrell, *Marketing,* 2nd ed. (Boston: Houghton Mifflin, 1980), p. 720.

23. M. Friedman, "The Social Responsibility of Business Is to Increase Its Profits," *New York Times Magazine* (September 13, 1970), pp. 30, 126–127; and *Capitalism and Freedom* (Chicago: University of Chicago Press, 1963), p. 133.

24. W. D. Guth and R. Tagiuri, "Personal Values and Corporate Strategy," *Harvard Business Review* (September–October 1965), pp. 126–127.

25. Posner and Schmidt, pp. 203–205.

26. S. N. Brenner and E. A. Molander, "Is the Ethics of Business Changing?" *Harvard Business Review* (January–February 1977), p. 70.

27. A. B. Carroll, "A Three-Dimensional Conceptual Model of Corporate Performance," *Academy of Management Review* (October 1979), pp. 497–505.

28. L. Iacocca, *Iacocca: An Autobiography* (Toronto: Bantam Books, 1984), pp. 196–197.

29. K. E. Aupperle, A. B. Carroll, and J. D. Hatfield, "An Empirical Examination of the Relationship between Corporate Social Responsibility and Profitability," *Academy of Management Journal* (June 1985), p. 459.
L. E. Preston, *Research in Corporate and Social Performance and Policy,* Vol. 3 (Greenwich, Conn.: Jai Publishing, 1981), p. 9.

30. "Control Data Starts a Painful Retrenchment," *Business Week* (October 22, 1984), pp. 94–96.

31. H. E. Klein and R. E. Linneman, "Environmental Assessment: An International Study of Corporate Practices," *Journal of Business Strategy* (Summer 1984), p. 67.

32. N. H. Snyder, "Environmental Volatility, Scanning Intensity and Organization Performance," *Journal of Contemporary Business* (September 1981), p. 7.

33. H. I. Ansoff, "Managing Strategic Surprise by Response to Weak Signals," *California Management Review* (Winter 1975), pp. 21–33.

34. F. J. Agvilar, *Scanning the Business Environment* (New York: Macmillan, 1967).

35. M. Javidan, "The Impact of Environmental Uncertainty on Long-Range

Planning and Practices of the U.S. Savings and Loan Industry," *Strategic Management Journal* (October–December 1984), pp. 381–392.

36. S. C. Jain, "Environmental Scanning in U.S. Corporations," *Long Range Planning* (April 1984), p. 119.
37. S. D. Atchison, "What's Giving Some Ski Resorts a Lift," *Business Week* (January 14, 1983), p. 32.
38. J. Naisbitt, *Megatrends* (New York: Warner Books, 1982).
39. M. E. Porter, *Competitive Strategy* (New York: Free Press, 1980), p. 3.
40. This summary of the forces driving competitive strategy is taken from M. E. Porter, *Competitive Strategy* (New York: Free Press, 1980), pp. 7–29.
41. Porter, p. 23.
42. R. E. Freeman, *Strategic Management: A Stakeholder Approach* (Boston: Pitman Publishing, 1984), p. 140–142.
43. R. E. Miles and C. C. Snow, *Organizational Strategy, Structure, and Process* (New York: McGraw-Hill Book Co., 1978).
44. R. T. Pascale, "Perspective on Strategy: The Real Story Behind Honda's Success," *California Management Review* (Spring 1981), p. 70.
45. Snyder, p. 16.
46. J. L. Roberts, "As Information Swells, Firms Open Libraries," *Wall Street Journal* (September 25, 1983), p. 25.
47. J. Drinkhall, "Hitachi Ltd. Pleads Guilty in IBM Case," *Wall Street Journal* (February 9, 1983), p. 4.
48. L. Renner, "Smart Cookies Stay Soft and Chewy on Store Shelves," *Des Moines Register* (September 16, 1984), p. 9E.
49. S. Flax, "How to Snoop on Your Competition," *Fortune* (May 14, 1984), pp. 28–33.
R. Eells and P. Nehemkis, *Corporate Intelligence and Espionage* (New York: Macmillan, 1984).
50. N. Thorpe, "Grand Plans for Coal Ports Fade in West," *Wall Street Journal* (July 20, 1983), p. 27.
51. H. E. Klein and R. E. Linneman, "Environmental Assessment: An International Study of Corporate Practices," *Journal of Business Strategy* (Summer 1984), p. 72.
52. S. Makridakis and S. C. Wheelwright, "Introduction to Management Forecasting," *The Handbook of Forecasting* (New York: Wiley and Sons, 1982), p. 8.
53. Makridakis and Wheelwright, p. 6.
54. Klein and Linneman, p. 72.
55. Klein and Linneman, p. 73.
56. M. E. Porter, *Competitive Advantage* (New York: The Free Press, 1985), p. 447.
57. This process of scenario development is adapted from M. E. Porter, *Competitive Advantage* (New York: The Free Press, 1985), pp. 448–470.

Chapter 5

THE INTERNAL ENVIRONMENT

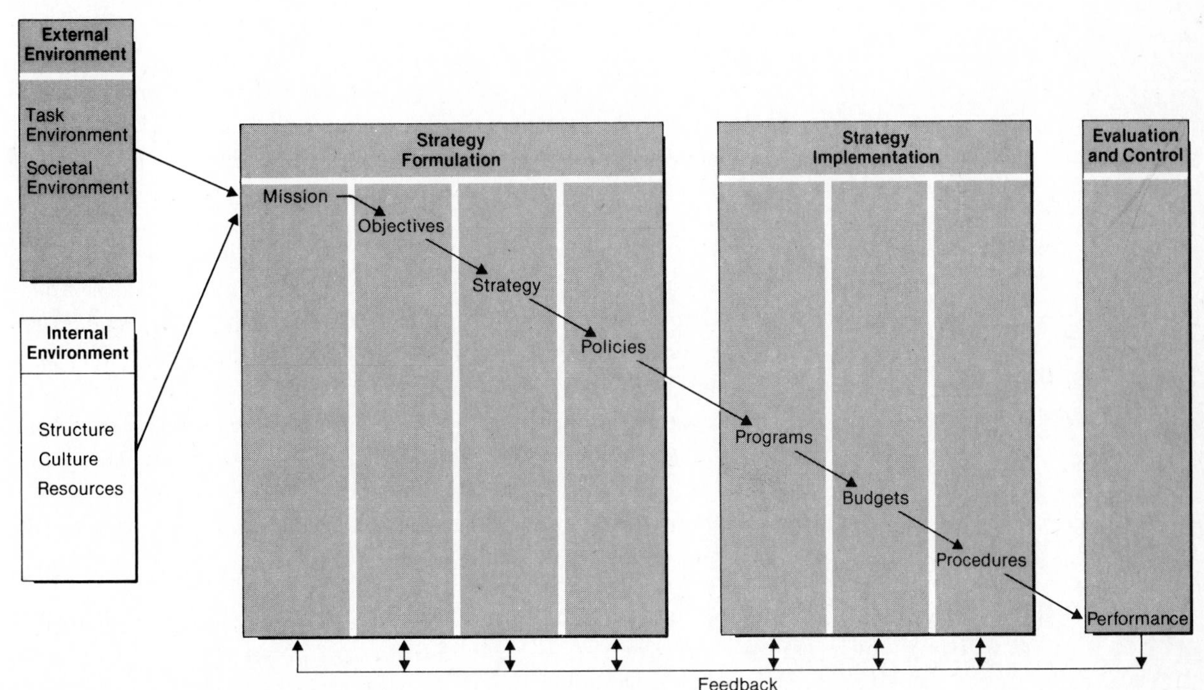

Strategic planning and decision making cannot be successful at the corporate level without an in-depth understanding of the strategic factors within the corporation. These factors are the internal *strengths* and *weaknesses* that act to either constrain or support a strategy. Part of a firm's internal environment, these factors are not within the short-run control of strategic managers. Instead they form the context within which work is accomplished. Strategic factors in a corporation's internal environment are *structure, culture,* and *resources.*

5.1 STRUCTURE

The structure of a corporation is often defined in terms of communication, authority, and work flow. It is the corporation's pattern of relationships, its "anatomy." It is a formal arrangement of roles and relationships of people so that the work is directed toward meeting the goals and accomplishing the mission of the corporation.[1] Sometimes it is referred to as the chain of command and is often graphically described in an organization chart.

Although there is an almost infinite variety of structural forms, certain types are predominant in modern complex organizations. These are simple, functional, divisional, matrix, and conglomerate structures.[2] Figure 5.1 illustrates some of these structures.

Simple Structure

Firms having a simple structure are usually small in size and undifferentiated laterally—that is, there are no functional or product categories. A firm with a simple structure is likely to be managed by an owner-manager who either does all the work or oversees a group of unspecialized people who do whatever needs to be done to provide a single product or service. A simple structure is appropriate if the owner-manager can grasp all the intricacies of the business and if the demand for the product or service is reasonably stable.

Functional Structure

In a functional structure, work is divided into subunits on the basis of such functions as manufacturing, finance, and sales. Functional structure enables a firm to take advantage of specialists and to deal with complex production or service-delivery problems more efficiently than it could if everyone performed an undifferentiated task. The functional structure is appropriate as long as top management is willing to invest a lot of energy in coordinating the many activities. The typical long vertical channels of communication and authority tend to make the firm rather inflexible to the requirements of a changing environment, but very successful when adaptability is not required and predictability is important.

Divisional Structure

When a corporation is organized on the basis of divisions, an extra management layer—division chiefs—is added between top management and functional managers. The standard functions are then designed around products,

I. SIMPLE STRUCTURE

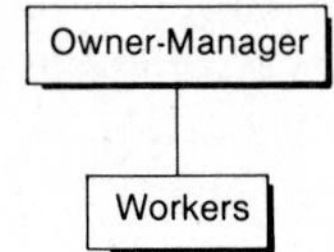

II. FUNCTIONAL STRUCTURE

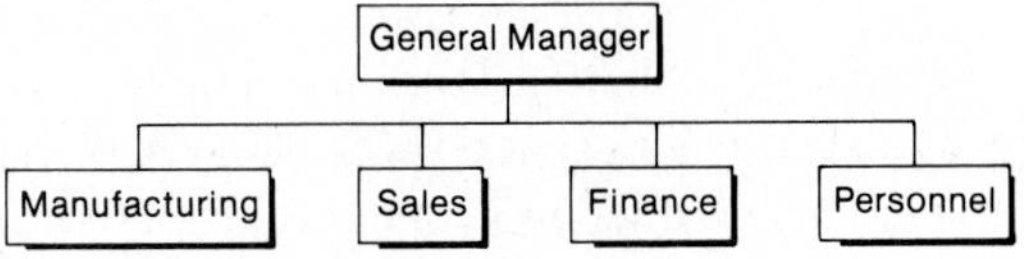

III. DIVISIONAL STRUCTURE*

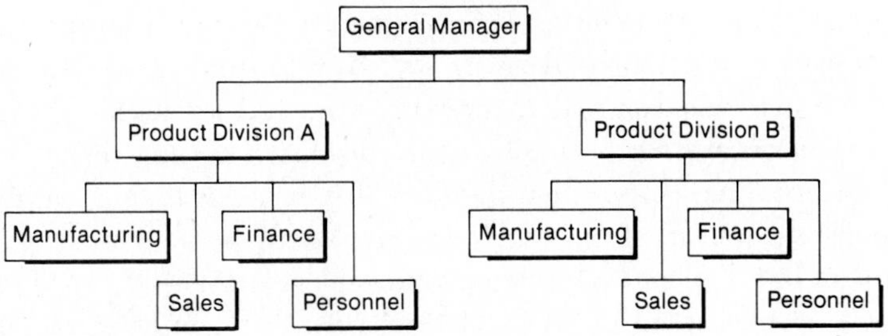

*Conglomerate structure is a variant of the division structure.

IV. MATRIX STRUCTURE

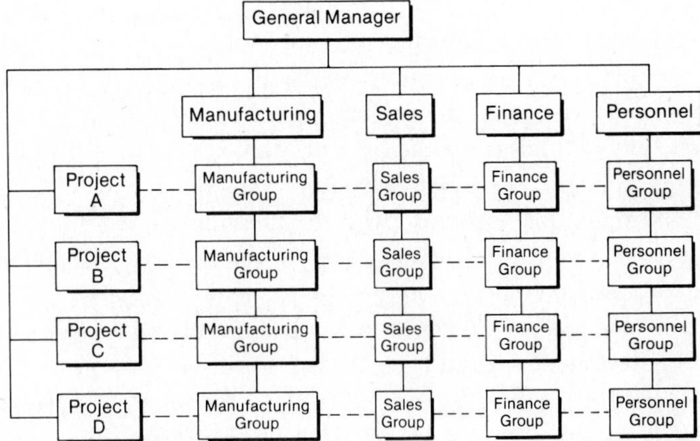

Figure 5.1 **Basic structures.**

clients, or territories.[3] A recent innovation in this area is the use of *strategic business units* (SBUs). Organizational groups composed of discrete, independent *product-market* segments are identified and given primary responsibility and authority to manage their functional areas. For example, instead of food preparation appliances being housed in three different divisions—such as large appliances, small appliances, and cookware—they can be merged into a single SBU serving the housewares market.

An SBU may be of any size or level, but it must have (1) a unique mission, (2) identifiable competitors, (3) an external market focus, and (4) control of its business functions.[4] Once a large corporation is organized on a divisional basis around strategic business units, there still may be too many SBUs for top management to effectively manage. In this case, an additional management layer—*group executives*—is added between top management and the division or SBU chiefs. The group executive is thus responsible for the management of a number of similar SBUs, such as housewares, building materials, and auto accessories. Approximately 70% of the Fortune 500 corporations are combining divisions or SBUs around group executives.[5] (For more information on SBUs, refer to Chapter 8.) The divisional structure is appropriate for a firm with many products serving many different markets. It gives the corporation the flexibility it needs to deal with a complex and changeable environment. It can be potentially inefficient, however, if there is much duplication of equipment and support staff. Furthermore, one division can be operating at overcapacity while in another division much of its facilities and staff are idle.

Matrix Structure

In matrix structures, functional and divisional areas are combined *simultaneously* at the same level of the corporation. Employees have two superiors, a project manager and a functional manager. The "home" department—that is, engineering, manufacturing, or sales—is usually functional and is reasonably permanent. People from these functional units are assigned on a temporary basis to one or more project units. The project units act like divisions in that they are differentiated on a product-market basis. Pioneered in the aerospace industry, the matrix structure was developed to combine the stability of the functional structure with the flexibility of a project organization. The matrix structure is very useful when the external environment (especially the technological and market aspects) is very complex and changeable. It does, however, result in conflicts revolving around duties, authority, and resource allocation.

Conglomerate Structure

A variant of a divisional structure organized by product, the conglomerate structure is typically an assemblage of separate firms having different products in different markets but operating together under one corporate umbrella. The divisions are independent of each other but share a dependence on central headquarters for financial resources and corporate planning. Its chief advantages to the corporation lie in the limitation of liability, a possible reduction in taxes, and, for the various divisions, the appearance of autonomy.[6] In addition, risks are spread over many different segments of the marketplace. The disadvantages of conglomerate structure derive from its heavy legalistic and financial orientation. In order to keep the legal advantages, the corporation cannot easily combine divisions to generate operating or marketing synergy. The investment orientation at the corporate level can easily prevent top management from understanding divisional problems in any sense other than financial. Furthermore, the ability to sell off a troubled division can lead to a short-run strategic orientation concerned only with the year-end bottom line.

An understanding of how a particular corporation is structured is very useful when formulating strategy. If the structure is compatible with a proposed change in strategy, it is a corporate strength. If, however, the structure is not compatible with either the present or proposed strategy, it is a definite weakness, and will act to keep the strategy from being implemented properly. Data General, for example, has had some serious problems because its growth strategy was incompatible with its centralized decision-making structure. Opportunities were not grasped quickly enough because all decisions had to be approved by the president.[7] In another example, a study by Fouraker and Stopford revealed that diversified corporations using a divisional structure were more likely to move into foreign operations than were centralized companies using a functional structure.[8]

5.2 CULTURE

A corporation's culture is the collection of beliefs, expectations, and values shared by the corporation's members and transmitted from one generation of employees to another. These create norms (rules of conduct) that define acceptable behavior of people from top management to the operative employee. Myths and rituals, often unrecorded, emerge over time to emphasize certain norms or values and to explain why a certain aspect of the culture is important. Like the retelling of the vision and perseverance of the founder(s) of the corporation, the myth is often tied closely to the corporate mission.

Corporate culture shapes the behavior of people in the corporation. Analysts Schwartz and Davis point this out: "Apparently, the well-run corporations of the world have distinctive cultures that are somehow responsible for their ability to create, implement, and maintain their world leadership positions."[9] Since these cultures have a powerful influence on the behavior of managers, they may strongly affect a corporation's ability to shift its strategic direction. For example, in 1975, the CEOs of two major oil companies changed the strategy of their respective firms from concentration in oil to diversification. They did so because they believed that their current business could neither support long-term growth nor deal with serious political threats. The strategy was announced, and elaborate implementation plans were developed and put into action. By 1980, however, both companies were again firmly concentrating in oil after five years of floundering in attempts to acquire and build new businesses. Both CEOs had been replaced. As *Business Week* reported, "Each of the CEOs had been unable to implement his strategy, not because it was theoretically wrong or bad but because neither had understood that his company's culture was so entrenched in the traditions and values of doing business as oilmen that employees resisted—and sabotaged—the radical changes that the CEOs tried to impose."[10]

Peters and Waterman, in their best-selling book *In Search of Excellence,* argue persuasively that the dominance and coherence of culture is an essential ingredient of the excellent companies they studied.

> The top performers create a broad, shared culture, a coherent framework within which charged-up people search for appropriate adaptations. Their ability to extract extraordinary contributions from very large numbers of people turns on the ability to create a sense of highly valued purpose. Such purpose invariably emanates from love of product, providing top-quality services, and honoring innovation and contribution from all.[11]

Peters and Waterman also state that poorer performing companies tend to have cultures that focus on internal politics instead of the customer and on "the numbers" instead of the product or the people who make it.

A recent study of thirty-four corporations by Denison supports the conclusions of Peters and Waterman. Denison found that companies with participative cultures (i.e., strong employee involvement in corporate decision making) not only have better performance records than those without such a culture, but that the performance difference widens over time. The evidence thus suggests a possible cause and effect relationship between culture and performance.[12]

Corporate culture fulfills several important functions in an organization:

- First, culture conveys a sense of identity for employees;
- Second, culture helps generate commitment by employees to something greater than themselves;
- Third, culture adds to the stability of the organization as a social system; and,
- Fourth, culture serves as a frame of reference for employees to use to make sense out of organization activities and to use as a guide for appropriate behavior.[13]

Corporate culture generally reflects the mission of firms. It gives a corporation a sense of *identity:* "This is who we are. This is what we do. This is what we stand for." The culture includes the dominant orientation of the company.[14] Some companies are *market-oriented.* Like IBM and John Deere they define themselves in terms of their customers and their customers' needs. For example, one of the secrets given for the success of Deere and Company during a period of agricultural recession is its rural roots. Unlike International Harvester, which has its headquarters in downtown Chicago, Deere has its headquarters in East Moline, Illinois, in the heart of an agricultural region responsible for two of the nation's major crops, corn and soybeans. Deere has "geographical awareness, because most of its executives live on a farm or near one . . ."[15] Other companies may be *materials-* or *product-oriented.* They define themselves in terms of the material they work on, the product they make, or the service they provide. As in the example given earlier of the two oil companies, they are first and foremost oil companies, steel companies, railroads, banks, or hospitals. This means that the people working for the company tend to identify themselves in the same way. They don't just work for a company; they *are* truckers, railroaders, bankers. For example, when he left Ford Motor Company, Lee Iacocca stated that he had no interest in pursuing possible offers from International Paper, Lockheed, or Tandy Corporation. Said Iacocca, ". . . cars were in my blood."[16] Other companies are *technology-oriented.* These companies define themselves in terms of the technology they are organized to exploit. Eastman Kodak, for example, ignored the development of xerography because of its strong commitment to the chemical film technology pioneered by George Eastman.[17] Similarly, high-tech firms in Silicon Valley think of themselves primarily as technological entrepreneurs.

An understanding of a corporation's (or division's) culture is thus imperative if the firm is to be managed strategically. A change in mission, objectives, strategies, or policies is not likely to be successful if it is in opposition to the accepted culture of the corporation. As was true for structure, if the culture is compatible with the change, it is an internal strength. But if the corporate culture is not compatible with the change, it is, under circumstances of a changing environment, a serious weakness. This does not mean that a manager should *never* consider a strategy that runs counter to the established culture. However, if such a strategy is to be seriously considered, top management must be prepared to attempt to change the culture as well, a task that will take much time, effort, and persistence.

5.3 RESOURCES

William Newman, an authority in strategic management, points out that a practical way to develop a master strategy of the corporation is to "pick particular roles or niches that are appropriate in view of competition and the company's resources."[18] Company resources are typically considered in terms of financial, physical, and human resources, as well as organizational systems and technological capabilities. Because these resources have functional significance, we can discuss them under the commonly accepted functional headings of marketing, finance, research and development, manufacturing/operations, human resources, and information systems. These resources, among others, should be audited to ascertain internal strengths and weaknesses.

Corporate-level strategy formulators must be aware of the many contributions each functional area can make to divisional and corporate performance. Functional resources include not only the people in each area but also that area's ability to formulate and implement under corporate guidance functional objectives, strategies, and policies. Thus they include the knowledge of analytical concepts and procedural techniques common to each area and the ability of the people in the area to utilize them effectively. These are some of the most valuable and well-known concepts and techniques: market segmentation, product life cycle, capital budgeting, financial leverage, technological competence, operating leverage, experience curve analysis, job analysis, job design, and decision support systems. There are many others, of course, but these are the basic ones. If used properly, these resources can improve overall strategic management.

Marketing

The primary task of the marketing manager from a corporation's point of view is to regulate the level, timing, and character of demand in a way that will help the corporation achieve its objectives.[19] The marketing manager is the corporation's primary link to the customer and the competition. The manager must therefore be especially concerned with the market position and marketing mix of the firm.

Market position deals with the question, "Who are our customers?" It refers to the selection of specific areas for marketing concentration, and can be expressed in terms of market, product, and geographical locations. Through market research, corporations are able to practice market segmentation with various products or services so that a family of products does not directly compete with each other. For example, Procter & Gamble Company positions Crest as a toothpaste for young children, whereas it positions Gleem as an adult toothpaste.

The *marketing mix* refers to the particular combination of key variables under the corporation's control that can be used to affect demand and to gain competitive advantage. These variables are *product, place, promotion,* and *price.* Within each of these four variables are several subvariables, listed in

Table 5.1 Marketing Mix Variables

Product	*Place*	*Promotion*	*Price*
Quality	Channels	Advertising	List price
Features	Coverage	Personal selling	Discounts
Options	Locations	Sales promotion	Allowances
Style	Inventory	Publicity	Payment periods
Brand name	Transport		Credit terms
Packaging			
Sizes			
Services			
Warranties			
Returns			

SOURCE: Philip Kotler, *Marketing Management: Analysis, Planning, and Control,* 4th ed. (Englewood Cliffs, N.J.: Prentice-Hall, 1980), p. 89. Copyright © 1980. Reprinted by permission of Prentice-Hall, Inc.

Table 5.1, which should be analyzed in terms of their effect upon divisional and corporate performance.

One of the most useful concepts in marketing insofar as strategic management is concerned is that of the *product life cycle.* As depicted in Table 5.2, the product life cycle is a graph showing time plotted against the dollar sales of a product as it moves from introduction through growth and maturity to decline. Table 5.2 lists the functional strategic objective at each developmental stage, as well as appropriate approaches for each stage in terms of design, pricing, promotion, and distribution. This concept enables a marketing manager to examine the marketing mix of a particular product or group of products given its position in its life cycle. Although marketing people agree that different products will have differently shaped life cycles, research concludes that a consideration of the product life cycle is an important factor in strategy formulation.[20]

Finance

The job of the financial manager is the management of funds. The manager must ascertain the best *sources* of funds, *uses* of funds, and *control* of funds. Cash must be raised from internal or external financial sources and allocated for different uses. The flow of funds in the operations of the corporation must be monitored. Benefits must be given to the sources of outside financing in the form of returns, repayments, or products and services. All these tasks must be handled in a way that complements and supports overall corporate strategy.

From a strategic point of view, the financial area should be analyzed to see how well it deals with funds. The mix of externally generated short-term and long-term funds in relation to the amount and timing of internally generated funds should be appropriate to corporate objectives, strategies, and

Table 5.2 Dynamic Competitive Strategy and the Market Life Cycle

	MARKET DEVELOPMENT (Introductory period for high learning products only)	RAPID GROWTH (Normal introductory pattern for a very low learning product)	COMPETITIVE TURBULENCE	SATURATION (MATURITY)	DECLINE
	Low Learning Products — TIME				
STRATEGY OBJECTIVE	Minimize learning requirements; locate and remedy offering defects quickly; develop widespread awareness of benefits; and gain trial by early adopters.	To establish a strong brand market and distribution niche as quickly as possible.	To maintain and strengthen the market niche achieved through dealer and consumer loyalty.	To defend brand position against competing brands and product category against other potential products, through constant attention to product-improvement opportunities and fresh promotional and distribution approaches.	To milk the offering dry of all possible profit.
OUTLOOK FOR COMPETITION	None is likely to be attracted in the early, unprofitable stages.	Early entrance of numerous aggressive emulators.	Price and distribution squeezes on the industry, shaking out the weaker entrants.	Competition stabilized, with few or no new entrants and market shares not subject to substantial change in the absence of a substantial perceived improvement in some brand.	Similar competition declining and dropping out because of decrease in consumer interest.
PRODUCT DESIGN OBJECTIVE	Limited number of models with physical product and offering designs both focused on minimizing learning requirements. Designs cost-and-use engineered to appeal to most receptive segment. Utmost attention to quality control and quick elimination of market-revealed defects in design.	Modular design to facilitate flexible addition of variants to appeal to every new segment and new use-system as fast as discovered.	Intensified attention to product improvement, tightening up of line to eliminate unnecessary specialties with little market appeal.	A constant alert for market pyramiding opportunities through either bold cost- and price-penetration of new markets or major product changes. Introduction of flanker products. Constant attention to possibilities for product improvement and cost cutting. Reexamination of necessity of design compromises.	Constant pruning of line to eliminate any items not returning a direct profit.

PRICING OBJECTIVE	To impose the minimum of value perception learning and to match the value reference perception of the most receptive segments. High trade discounts and sampling advisable.	A price line for every taste, from low-end to premium models. Customary trade discounts. Aggressive promotional pricing, with prices cut as fast as costs decline due to accumulated production experience. Intensification of sampling.	Increased attention to market-broadening and promotional pricing opportunities.	Defensive pricing to preserve product category franchise. Search for incremental pricing opportunities, including private label contracts, to boost volume and gain an experience advantage.	Maintenance of profit-level pricing with complete disregard of any effect on market share.
PROMOTIONAL GUIDELINES *Communications Objectives*	a) Create widespread awareness and understanding of offering benefits. b) Gain trial by early adopters.	Create and strengthen brand preference among trade and final users. Stimulate general trial.	Maintain consumer franchise, and strengthen dealer ties.	Maintain consumer and trade loyalty, with strong emphasis on dealers and distributors. Promotion of greater use frequency.	Phase out, keeping just enough to maintain profitable distribution.
Most valuable media mix	In order of value: Publicity. Personal Sales. Mass communications.	Mass media. Personal sales. Sales promotions, including sampling. Publicity.	Mass media. Dealer promotions. Personal selling to dealers. Sales promotions. Publicity.	Mass media. Dealer-oriented promotions.	Cut down all media to the bone—use no sales promotions of any kind.
DISTRIBUTION POLICY	Exclusive or selective, with distributor margins high enough to justify heavy promotional spending.	Intensive and extensive, with dealer margins just high enough to keep them interested. Close attention to rapid resupply of distributor stocks and heavy inventories at all levels.	Intensive and extensive, and a strong emphasis on keeping dealer well supplied, but with minimum inventory cost to him/her.	Intensive and extensive, with strong emphasis on keeping dealer well supplied, but at minimum inventory cost to him/her.	Phase out outlets as they become marginal.
INTELLIGENCE FOCUS	To identify actual developing use-systems and to uncover any product weaknesses.	Detailed attention to brand position, to gaps in model and market coverage, and to opportunities for market segmentation.	Close attention to product improvement needs, to market-broadening chances, and to possible fresh promotion themes.	Intensified attention to possible product improvements. Sharp alert for potential new inter-product competition and for signs of beginning product decline.	Information helping to identify the point at which the product should be phased out.

SOURCE: C. R. Wasson, *Dynamic Competitive Strategy and Product Life Cycles,* 3rd ed., (Austin, Tex.: Austin Press, 1978), pp. 256–257. Copyright © 1978 by Chester R. Wasson. Reprinted by permission.

NOTE: Strictly speaking, this is the cycle of the category market, and only a high-learning introduction passes through all the phases indicated above. The term *product life cycle* is sometimes applied indiscriminately to both brand cycles and category cycles. Most new brands are only emulative of other products already on the market, have a much shorter life cycle than the product category, and must follow a strategy similar to any low-learning product.

policies. The concept of *financial leverage* (the ratio of total debt to total assets) is very useful in describing the use of debt to increase the earnings available to common stockholders.[21] Financial leverage can be used to boost earnings per share. Although interest paid on debt reduces taxable income, the higher debt means there are fewer stockholders to share the profits. There are fewer stockholders because the corporation finances its activities by selling bonds or notes instead of stock. The debt, however, gives the firm a higher break-even point than it would have if the firm financed from internally generated funds only. High leverage may therefore be perceived as a corporate strength in times of prosperity and ever-increasing sales, or as a weakness in times of a recession and dropping sales. This is because leverage

Table 5.3 **Costs and Benefits of Increasing Financial Leverage**

Costs	*Benefits*

Increased financial risk:
• Greater volatility of earnings and stock price
• Increased probability of financial disruption of existing operations
Increased potential for restrictive loan covenants:
• Reduced flexibility to respond financially to opportunity or competitive threats
• Reduced autonomy for management
Possibility of lower credit rating:
• Higher interest rates
• If rating falls below "A":
  • Reduced institutional demand for common stock
  • Possibly forced to private placement market during credit crises (to the extent not "insured" by bank lines)
Cost of larger bank lines to ensure against capital unavailability during credit crises
Possible stimulation of excessive investment (i.e., investment in projects with returns less than the cost of capital)
	Increased return on investment from an expanded investment program:
	• Ability to undertake projects with returns greater than the cost of capital
	• Strengthened competitive position (lower costs, increased product differentiation, higher market share, etc.)
	• Increased number of future investment options
	For a given ROI, increased return on equity because of financial leverage
	Increased sustainable rate of growth
	Reduced risk because of stronger competitive position
	Lower cost of capital:
	• Tax deductibility of interest
	• Repayment of debt with inflated currency

SOURCE: Reprinted by permission of the *Harvard Business Review*. An exhibit from "Subordinate Financial Policy to Corporate Strategy" by Richard E. Ellsworth (November/December 1983).

acts to magnify the effect on earnings *per share* of an increase or decrease in dollar sales. The costs and benefits of increasing financial leverage (that is, increasing the amount of debt used to fund new programs) is shown in Table 5.3.

The knowledge and use of *capital budgeting* techniques is an important financial resource. A good finance department will be able to analyze and rank possible investments in such fixed assets as land, buildings, and equipment in terms of additional outlays a corporation must make as well as the additional receipts that will result. Then it can rank investment proposals on the basis of some accepted criteria or "hurdle rate" (for example, years to pay back investment, rate of return, time to break-even point, etc.) and make a decision.

Break-even analysis is an analytical technique for studying the relations among fixed costs, variable costs, and profits. It is a device for determining the point at which sales will just cover total costs. Figure 5.2 shows a basic break-even chart for a hypothetical company. The chart is drawn on a unit basis, with volume produced shown on the horizontal axis and with costs and revenues measured on the vertical axis. Fixed costs are $80,000, as represented by the horizontal line; variable costs are $2.40 per unit. Total costs rise by $2.40, the amount of the variable costs, for each additional unit produced past $80,000, and the product is sold at $4.00 per unit. The total revenue line is a straight line increasing directly with production. As is usual, the slope of the total revenue line is steeper than that of the total cost line because, for every unit sold, the firm receives $4.00 of revenue for every

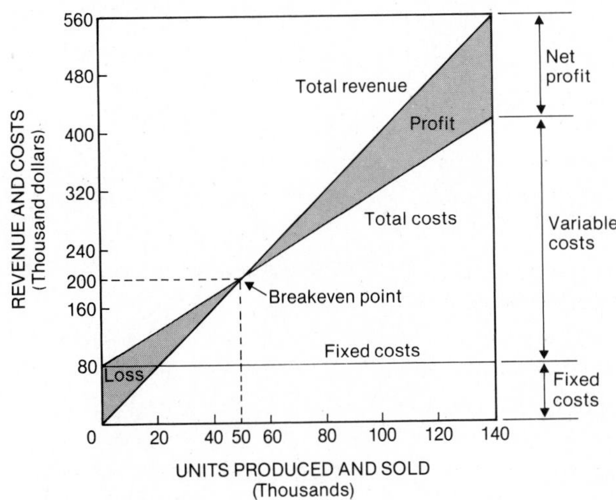

Figure 5.2 Break-even chart.

$2.40 paid out for labor and material. Up to the break-even point (the intersection of the total revenue and total cost lines), the firm suffers losses. After that point, the firm earns profits at an increasing amount as volume increases. In this instance, the break-even point for the firm is at a sales and cost level of $200,000 and a production level of 50,000 units.

The financial manager must be very knowledgeable of these and other more sophisticated analytical techniques if management is to implement functional strategies successfully, such as internal financing or leveraged buyouts (discussed in Chapter 7).

Research and Development

The R&D manager is responsible for suggesting and implementing a corporation's technological strategy in light of corporate objectives and policies. The manager's job therefore involves (1) choosing among alternative new technologies to use within the corporation, (2) developing methods of embodying the new technology in new products and processes, and (3) deploying resources so that the new technology can be successfully implemented.[22]

The term *research and development* is used to describe a wide range of activities. In some corporations R&D is conducted by scientists in well-equipped expensive laboratories where the focus is on theoretical problem areas. In other firms, R&D is heavily oriented toward marketing and is concerned with product or product-packaging improvements. In still other firms, R&D takes on an engineering orientation concentrating on quality control, the manufacturing of design specifications, and the development of improved production equipment. Most corporations will have a mix of basic, applied, and engineering R&D. The balance of these types of research is known as the *R&D mix* and should be appropriate to corporate strategy.

A corporation's R&D unit should be evaluated for *technological competence* in both the development and use of innovative technology. Not only should the corporation make a consistent research effort (as measured by reasonably constant corporate expenditures that result in usable innovations), it should also be proficient in managing research personnel and integrating their innovations into its day-to-day operation.

Corporations operating in technology-based industries must be willing to make substantial investments in R&D. For example, the computer and pharmaceutical industries spend an average of 7.2% and 6.7% respectively of their sales dollars for R&D. As shown in Table 5.4 other industries, such as steel and tobacco, spend less than 1%. General Electric, for example, spends a large amount of money on R&D. Michael Carpenter, vice-president of corporate business development and planning at GE, points out that much of the company's growth has developed internally out of its R&D efforts. He

Table 5.4 **R&D Industry Expenditures**

Industry		Sales (Million Dollars)	Profits (Million Dollars)	R&D Expenses (Million Dollars)	Percent of Sales	Percent of Pretax Profits	Dollars per Employee
Aerospace	[17]	56,023	2,007	2,575	4.6	79.2	4,176
Appliances	[11]	10,304	345	192	1.9	30.7	1,362
Automotive:							
Cars, Trucks	[6]	140,366	5,081	4,906	3.5	61.8	3,968
Parts, Equipment	[15]	10,312	203	186	1.8	49.5	1,400
Building Materials	[16]	12,297	396	172	1.4	25.6	1,474
Chemicals	[44]	112,486	4,039	3,355	3.0	40.0	3,870
Conglomerates	[13]	56,827	2,039	1,480	2.6	43.5	1,840
Containers	[6]	12,900	418	103	0.8	18.9	794
Drugs	[29]	51,411	5,477	3,422	6.7	39.6	5,641
Electrical	[32]	53,648	3,473	1,690	3.2	31.7	2,317
Electronics	[74]	39,114	1,463	1,592	4.1	66.7	2,567
Food & Beverage	[31]	81,376	3,566	657	0.8	10.4	858
Fuel	[19]	387,557	18,578	2,367	0.6	6.1	2,910
Informational Processing:							
Computers	[33]	81,725	7,680	5,853	7.2	43.7	5,958
Office Equipment	[16]	13,686	711	730	5.3	66.4	4,169
Peripherals	[47]	6,461	392	445	6.9	68.3	4,524
Software, Services	[18]	1,962	182	145	7.4	44.9	5,105
Instruments	[66]	16,663	642	894	5.4	87.9	3,372
Leisure Time	[18]	22,343	425	1,133	5.1	110.9	3,978
Machinery:							
Farm, Construction	[19]	20,527	−353	702	3.4	NEG	3,047
Machine Tools, Industrial, Mining	[39]	13,171	51	396	3.0	422.0	2,101
Metals & Mining	[14]	19,968	−380	211	1.1	NEG	1,480
Miscellaneous Manufacturing	[95]	51,935	2,457	1,311	2.5	32.2	1,796
Oil Service & Supply	[23]	31,165	1,124	790	2.5	51.5	2,146
Paper	[15]	30,499	1,175	301	1.0	17.0	1,083
Personal & Home Care Products	[23]	32,031	1,951	789	2.5	22.8	2,869
Semiconductors	[15]	8,830	60	735	8.3	NEG	4,140
Steel	[7]	27,363	−1,974	174	0.6	NEG	803
Telecommunications	[17]	88,050	7,073	1,296	1.5	11.0	2,081
Textiles, Apparel	[14]	9,748	296	75	0.8	14.7	492
Tires, Rubber	[9]	22,786	617	517	2.3	46.0	1,751
Tobacco	[2]	4,816	461	19	0.4	2.2	242
All-Industry Composite	[803]	1,528,300	69,500	39,200	2.6	31.0	2,983

SOURCE: Adapted from "R&D Scoreboard," *Business Week* (July 9, 1984), pp. 65–78.

NOTE: Numbers in brackets represent the number of corporations in that industry grouping.

states: "We spend half as much money each year on R&D as all the money going into the venture capital industry . . . As a result GE has always been at the leading edge of technology."[23] Simply spending money on R&D or new projects does not mean, however, that the money will produce useful results. Between 1950 and 1979, the United States steel industry spent 20% more on plant maintenance and upgrading for each ton of production capacity added or replaced than did the Japanese steel industry. Nevertheless, U.S. steelmakers failed to recognize and adopt two "breakthroughs" in steelmaking—the basic oxygen furnace and continuous casting. Their hesitancy to adopt new technology caused them to lose the world steel market.[24]

In addition to money, another important consideration in the effective management of research and development is the time factor. It is generally accepted that the time needed to obtain meaningful profits from the inception of a specific R&D program is typically seven to eleven years.[25] If a corporation is unwilling to invest the large amounts of money and time for its own program of research and development, it may be able to purchase or lease the equipment, techniques, or patents necessary to stay abreast of the competition. Ford Motor Company, for instance, invested $20 million during 1985 in American Robot Corporation in order to gain some manufacturing advantage over General Motors. Ford and American Robot planned to fully automate Ford's new electronic components plant near Toronto by 1987—well before GM would be able to complete a comparable facility. Ford's Chairman Donald E. Petersen reported that similar investments may follow: "If the best way to get technology is through acquisitions, we have an open-door policy."[26]

Those corporations that do purchase an innovative technology must, nevertheless, have the technological competence to make good use of it. Unfortunately, some corporations introduce the latest technology into their processes without adequately assessing the competence of their organization to handle it. For example, the U.S. Navy contracted with Tano Corporation to replace the existing manually operated propulsion controls of five amphibious assault vessels (at a cost of $6 million per ship) with new automatic, computer-controlled, electro-pneumatic systems. When in place the systems failed to operate as planned. A few months after installation, the Navy was forced to spend $30 million to have Tano take out the new automatic systems on all five ships and to replace them with the previously used manual systems. According to an executive from Tano, the removal was "a very unfortunate situation for us. We assumed that a certain level of technicians would be on the ships to operate this equipment. They weren't."[27]

The R&D manager must determine when to abandon present technology and when to develop or adopt new technology. After several years of studying progress and patterns in various technologies, Richard Foster of McKinsey and Company states that the displacement of one technology by another (*Technological Discontinuity*) is a frequent and strategically important phenomenon. For each technology within a given field or industry, the plotting of product performance against research effort/expenditures on a graph results in an S-shaped curve. Foster describes the process depicted in Fig. 5.3.

> Early in the development of the technology a knowledge base is being built and progress requires a relatively large amount of effort. Later, progress comes more easily. And then, as the limits of that technology are approached, progress becomes slow and expensive. *That* is when R&D dollars should be allocated to technology with more potential. That is also—not so incidentally—when a competitor who has bet on a new technology can sweep away your business or topple an entire industry.[28]

The presence of such a *technological discontinuity* in the world's steel industry during the 1960s may explain why the large capital expenditures by U.S. steel companies failed to keep them competitive with the Japanese firms adopting the new technologies. As Foster points out: "History has shown that as one technology nears the end of its S-curve, competitive leadership in a market generally changes hands."[29] The conclusion is that the

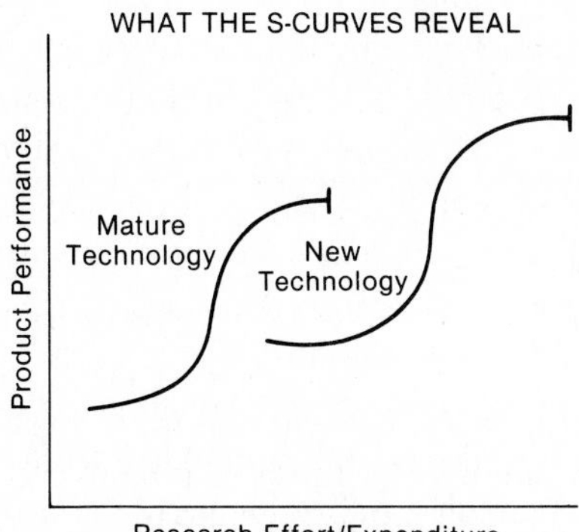

In the corporate planning process, it is generally assumed that incremental progress in technology will occur. But past developments in a given technology cannot be extrapolated into the future, because every technology has its limits. The key to competitiveness is to determine when to shift resources to a technology with more potential.

Figure 5.3 **Technological discontinuity.**

SOURCE: P. Pascarella, "Are You Investing in the Wrong Technology?" *Industry Week* (July 25, 1983), p. 38.

essence of managing technology well is the ability and willingness of all concerned to make timely transitions to new technologies.

Manufacturing/ Service

If the corporation is in business to transform tangible raw materials, like iron ore or petroleum, into usable products, like automobiles, machine parts, or plastic raincoats, the transformation process can be called *manufacturing*. If, however, the corporation is in the business of using people's skills and knowledge, such as those of doctors, lawyers, or loan officers, to provide services via hospitals, legal clinics, or banks, the work involved may be called *service*. These functions can be found in any corporation producing and providing either a tangible product or an intangible service. Many of the key concepts and techniques popularly used in manufacturing can therefore be applied to service businesses.

The primary task of the manufacturing or service manager is to develop and operate a system that will produce the required number of products or services, with a certain quality, at a given cost, within an allotted time. However, manufacturing plants vary significantly depending on the type of product made. In very general terms, manufacturing may be intermittent or continuous. In *intermittent systems* (job shops), the item normally goes through a sequential process, but the work and sequence of the process vary. At each center, the tasks determine the details of processing and the time required for them: "Work flows through the system in batches or special orders and commonly waits for a time before being processed at service facilities required by the products."[30] In contrast, *continuous systems* are those laid out as lines on which products can be assembled or processed. An example is an automobile assembly line.

The type of manufacturing system used by a corporation determines divisional or corporate strategy. It makes no sense, for example, to plan to increase sales by saturating the market with low-priced products if the corporation's manufacturing process was designed as an intermittent "job shop" system that now produces one-time-only products to a customer's specifications. Conversely, a plan to produce a number of specialty products may not be economically feasible if the manufacturing process was designed to be a mass-producing, continuous system using low-skilled labor or special purpose robots.

Continuous systems are popular because they allow a corporation to take advantage of manufacturing *operating leverage*. According to Weston and Brigham, "The degree of operating leverage is the percentage change in operating income that results from a percentage change in units sold."[31] For example, a highly labor-intensive firm has little automated machinery and thus a small amount of fixed costs. It has a fairly low break-even point, but its variable cost line has a relatively steep slope. Since most of the costs associated with the product are variable (many employees earning piece rate wages), its variable costs are higher than those of automated firms. Its advantage over other firms is that it can operate at low levels and still be profitable. Once it reaches break-even, however, the huge variable costs as a percentage of total costs keep the profit per unit at a relatively low level. Its low operating leverage prevents it from gathering the huge profits possible from a high volume of sales. In terms of strategy, this firm should look for a niche in the marketplace where it can produce and sell a reasonably small quantity of goods.

In contrast, a capital-intensive firm has a lot of money in fixed investments, such as automated processes and highly sophisticated machinery. Its labor force is relatively small but highly skilled, earning salaries rather than piece-rate wages. Consequently, it has a high amount of fixed costs. It also has a relatively high break-even point, but its variable cost line rises slowly. Its advantage over other firms is that once it reaches break-even, its profits rise faster than do those of less automated firms. In terms of strategy, this firm needs to find a high-demand niche in the marketplace where it can produce and sell a large quantity of goods. Its high operating leverage makes it an extremely profitable and competitive firm once it reaches its high break-even point. Changes in the level of sales have a magnified (leveraged) impact on profits. In times of recession, however, it is likely to suffer huge losses. During an economic downturn, the firm with less automation and thus less leverage is more likely to survive comfortably, since a drop in sales primarily affects variable costs. It is often easier to lay off labor than to sell off specialized plants and machines.

In terms of a service business, operations may also be continuous or intermittent. Continuous operations describe fairly similar services provided to the *same* clientele over a period of time (such as patients in a long-term care hospital), whereas intermittent operations describe somewhat different services provided to *different* clientele over a period of time (such as once-a-year auditing or income tax counseling by a CPA firm). Service firms that use continuous operations may be able to use operating leverage by substituting diagnostic machinery or videotape machines for highly paid professional personnel. Those using batch or intermittent operations may be able to substitute lower-paid support personnel for some of the more routine services performed by highly paid professionals.

A conceptual framework that many large corporations have used successfully is the *experience curve.*[32] The concept applied to manufacturing is that unit production costs decline by some fixed percentage (commonly 20%–30%) each time the total accumulated volume of production in units doubles. The actual percentage varies by industry and is based upon the time it takes a person to learn a new task, scale economies, product and process improvements, lower raw materials costs, and other variables. For example, in an industry where an 85% experience curve can be expected, a corporation might expect a 15% reduction in costs for every doubling of volume. The total costs per unit (adjusted for inflation) can be expected to drop from $100 when the total production is 10 units, to $85 ($100 × 85%) when production increases to 20 units, and to $72.25 ($85 × 85%) when it reaches 40 units.[33] To achieve these results often means making investments in R&D and fixed assets, thus resulting in higher operating leverage and less flexibility. Nevertheless, the manufacturing strategy is one of building capacity ahead of demand in order to achieve the lower unit costs of the experience curve. Price the product or service very low on the basis of some future point on the experience curve so as to preempt competition and increase market demand. The resulting high number of units sold and high market share should result in high profits given the low unit costs.[34] This idea of using the anticipated experience curve to price low in order to gain high market share and thus high profits underlies the Boston Consulting Group's portfolio matrix (discussed in Chapter 6).

The experience curve concept is commonly used in estimating the production costs of (1) a product never before made with the present techniques and processes or (2) current products produced by newly introduced techniques or processes. The concept was first applied in the airframe industry and may be applied in the service industry as well. While many firms have used experience curves extensively, an unquestioning acceptance of the industry norm (such as 80% for the airframe industry or 70% for integrated circuits) is very risky. The experience curve for an industry may not hold for a particular corporation for a variety of reasons.[35]

Recently, the use of large mass-production facilities to take advantage of experience curve economies has been criticized. The introduction of CAD/CAM (computer-assisted design and computer-assisted manufacturing) with robot technology means shorter learning times and the ability to economically manufacture products in small customized batches. Emphasizing *economies of scope* over *economies of scale*, a number of firms have introduced "flexible manufacturing."[36] The new flexible factories permit low-volume output of custom-tailored products at a profit. It is thus possible to have the cost advantages of continuous systems with the customer-oriented advantages of intermittent systems. For example, Deere's new tractor assembly plant in Waterloo, Iowa, can produce more than 5,000 variations of its tractors to suit its customers' needs.[37]

Human Resources

The primary task of the manager of human resources is to improve the match between individuals and jobs. The quality of this match influences job performance, employee satisfaction, and employee turnover.[38] Consequently, human resource management (HRM) is concerned with the selection and training of new employees, appraisal of employee performance, the assessment of employees' promotion potential, and recruitment and personnel planning for the future. HRM is also highly involved in wage and salary administration, labor negotiations, job design, and employee morale.

A good HRM department should be competent in the use of attitude surveys and other feedback devices to assess employee satisfaction with their jobs and with the corporation as a whole. HRM managers should also be knowledgeable in *job analysis* and competent in its use. Job analysis is a means of obtaining information for job descriptions about what needs to be accomplished by each job in terms of quality and quantity. Up-to-date job descriptions are essential not only for proper employee selection, appraisal, training, and development; wage and salary administration; and labor negotiations—but also for summarizing the human resources of a corporation in terms of employee-skill categories. Just as a corporation must know the number, type, and quality of its manufacturing facilities, it also must know the kinds of people it employs and the skills they possess. This knowledge is essential for the formulation and implementation of corporate strategy. The best strategies are meaningless if employees do not have the skills to carry them out or if jobs cannot be designed to accommodate the available workers. Honeywell, Inc., for example, uses *talent surveys* to ensure that it has the right mix of talents to implement its planned strategies.[39]

A good human resource manager should be able to work closely with the unions if the corporation is unionized. A recent development is the increasing desire by union leaders to work jointly with management in formulating and implementing strategic changes. For example, when General Electric announced its intention to close its Charleston, South Carolina, steam turbine generator plant in 1985, the United Electrical Workers proposed to management eleven alternative products the plant could produce. To save jobs, other unions are making the same argument. Jerome M. Rosow, president of the Work in America Institute, states that the involvement of union leaders in business decision making is a "major breakthrough which has great potential for improving the competitive edge of those companies."[40]

Human resource departments have found that to reduce employee dissatisfaction and unionization efforts (or conversely, to improve employee satisfaction and existing union relations), they must consider the *quality of work life* (QWL) in the design of jobs. Partially a reaction to the traditionally heavy emphasis upon technical and economic factors in job design, QWL emphasizes the human dimension of work. Corporations such as General Motors, General Foods, Procter & Gamble, Cummins Engine, and Shell Canada, Ltd., have been involved actively in improving QWL through extensive job and plant redesigning.[41] In general, quality of work life is "the degree to which members of a work organization are able to satisfy important personal needs through their experiences in the organization."[42] The knowledgeable human resource manager should therefore be able to improve the corporation's quality of work life by (1) introducing participative problem solving, (2) restructuring work, (3) introducing innovative reward systems, and (4) improving the work environment.[43] This will lead to hopefully a more participative corporate culture and thus higher performance.

The quality of work life becomes especially important in today's world of global communication and transportation systems. Advances in technology are copied almost immediately by competitors around the world. People, however, are not as willing to move to other companies in other countries. It is therefore argued that the only long-term resource advantage remaining to a corporation lies in the area of human resources. Paul Hagusa, president of the American subsidiary of Sharp Corporation of Japan, makes this point very clearly.

> Once there was a time when the Americans had very efficient machines and equipment, and Japan did not. At that time—regardless of the workers—those with the most modern machines had the competitive advantage. But now, one country soon has the same machinery as another. So, what makes the difference today is the quality of the people.[44]

Information Systems

The primary task of the management of information systems (MIS) department is to design and manage the information flow of the corporation in order to improve productivity and decision making. Information must be collected, stored, and synthesized in such a manner that it will answer important operating and strategic questions. This function is growing in importance for three reasons: (1) Corporations are growing in size and complexity. Managers must increasingly rely on second-hand, written information. (2) As corporations become more dispersed and decentralized, more sophisticated control techniques are needed to ensure that managers are operating according to agreed plans. (3) The widespread application and increasing low cost of the computer make it an ideal aid to information processing.[45]

Information systems can fulfill four major purposes.[46]

- *Provide a basis for analyzing early warning signals that can originate both externally and internally.* Any information system has a database. Like a library, the system collects, categorizes, and files the data so that the system can be used by other departments in the corporation.
- *Automate routine clerical operations.* Payroll, inventory reports, and other records can be generated automatically from the database and thus reduce the need for fileclerks.

- *Assist managers in making routine (programmed) decisions.* Scheduling orders, assigning orders to machines, and reordering supplies are routine tasks which can be automated through a detailed analysis of the company's work flow.
- *Provide the information necessary to make strategic (nonprogrammed) decisions.* Increasingly, personal computers coupled with sophisticated software are being used to analyze large amounts of information and to calculate likely payoffs from alternate strategies. In order to fulfill this purpose, decision suport systems are needed which allow more interaction by the user with the computer.

In assessing the corporation's strengths and weaknesses, it is important to note the level of development of the firm's information system. There are at least four distinct stages of development.[47] These are depicted in Table 5.5. Stage one, *initiation,* generally involves accounting applications. The information systems personnel are computer technicians who work to reduce clerical costs. Stage two, *growth,* emerges as applications spread beyond accounting into production and marketing. People now use the system to process information like budgets and sales forecasts. Stage three, *moratorium,* is a consolidation phase and calls for a stop to new applications. The spread of information systems is matched by increasing frustration in attempting to use it and by concern over the large costs of operating the system. Stage four, *integration,* stresses the acceptance of information systems as a major activity that must be integrated into the total corporation. Decision support systems are now developed to aid managers at all levels of the corporation. A stage-four system is a significant internal strength for a corporation.

The requirements of a well-designed information system include the following:[48]

1. The system must focus managers' attention on the critical success factors in their jobs.
2. The system must present information that is accurate and of high quality.
3. The system must provide the necessary information when it is needed to those who most need it.
4. The system must process raw data so that it can be presented in a manner useful to the manager.

A corporation's information system can be a strength in all three elements of strategic management: formulation, implementation, and evaluation and control. For example, it can not only aid in environmental scanning

Table 5.5 Stages of Development of Information Systems

	Stage One *Initiation*	*Stage Two* *Growth*	*Stage Three* *Moratorium*	*Stage Four* *Integration*
Application Focus	Accounting and cost reduction	Expansion of applications in many functional areas	Halt on new applications; emphasis on control	Integrating existing systems into the organization; decision support systems
Example Applications	Accounts payable, accounts receivable, payroll, billing	*Stage one plus:* cash flow, budgeting, forecasting, personnel inventory, sales, inventory control	*Stage two plus:* purchasing control, production scheduling	*Stage three plus:* simulation models, financial planning models, on-line personnel query system
MIS Staffing	Primarily computer experts and other skilled professionals	User-oriented system analysts and programmers	Entry of functional managers into MIS unit	Balance of technical and management specialists
Location of MIS in Structure	Embedded in accounting department	Growth in size of staff, still in accounting area	Separate MIS unit reporting to head financial officer	Same as stage three, or decentralization into divisions
What Top Management Wants from MIS	Speed computations with a reduction in clerical staff	Broader applications into operational areas	Concern over MIS costs and usefulness	Acceptance as a major organizational function, involved in planning and control
User Attitudes	Uncertainty; hands-off approach; anxiety over applications	Somewhat enthusiastic; minimum involvement in system design	Frustration and dissatisfaction over developed systems; concern over costs of developing and operating systems	Acceptance of MIS in their work; involvement in system design, implementation, and operation

SOURCE: Reprinted by permission of the *Harvard Business Review.* An exhibit from "Controlling the Costs of Data Services" by Richard L. Nolan (July/August 1977).

and in controlling a corporation's many activities, it can also be used as a strategic weapon to gain competitive advantage. For example, American Hospital Supply (AHS), a leading manufacturer and distributor of a broad line of products for doctors, laboratories, and hospitals, has developed an order entry-distribution system that directly links the majority of its customers to AHS computers. The system has been successful because it simplifies ordering processes for customers, reduces costs for both AHS and the customer, and allows AHS to provide pricing incentives to the customer. As a result, customer loyalty is high and AHS's share of the market has become large.[49] Other examples are the automated reservations systems American Airlines and United Airlines make available to travel agents. Since the reservations systems feature either American or United most prominently in the listings, other airlines complain that American and United have an unfair advantage in attracting customers. The advantage appears to be real given that American and United have successfully obtained 65% of the market in automated reservations systems.[50]

5.4 SUMMARY AND CONCLUSION

Before strategies can be developed, top management needs to assess its internal corporate environment for strengths and weaknesses. It must have an in-depth understanding of the internal strategic factors, such as the corporation's structure, culture, and resources.

A corporation's *structure* is its anatomy. It is often described graphically with an organization chart. Corporate structures range from the simple structure of an owner-manager operated business to the complex series of structures of a large conglomerate. If compatible with present and potential strategies, a corporation's structure is a great internal strength. Otherwise, it may be a serious weakness that will either prevent a good strategy from being implemented properly or reduce the number of strategic alternatives available to a firm.

A corporation's *culture* is the collection of beliefs, expectations, and values shared by its members. A culture produces norms that shape the behavior of employees. Top management must be aware of this culture and include it in its assessment of strategic factors. Those strategies that run counter to an established corporate culture are likely to be doomed by the poor motivation of the workforce. If a culture is antagonistic to a strategy change, the implementation plan will also have to include plans to change the culture.

A corporation's *resources* include not only such generally recognized assets as people, money, and facilities, but also those analytical concepts and procedural techniques known and in use within the functional areas. Since most top managers view their corporations in terms of functional activities, it is simplest to assess resource strengths and weaknesses by functional area. Each area should be audited in tems of financial, physical, and human resources, as well as its organization and technological competencies and capabilities. Just as the knowledge of key functional concepts and techniques is a corporate strength, its absence is a weakness.

DISCUSSION QUESTIONS

1. In what ways can a corporation's structure act as an internal strength or weakness to those formulating corporate strategies?

2. Why should top management be aware of a corporation's culture?
3. What kind of internal factors help determine whether a firm should emphasize the production and sales of a large number of low-priced products or a small number of high-priced products?
4. What is the difference between operating and financial leverage? What are their implications to strategic planning?
5. Why is technological competence important in strategy formulation?
6. How can a knowledge of technological discontinuity help to improve a corporation's efficiency?
7. What are the pros and cons of using the experience curve to determine strategy?
8. Why should MIS be considered when analyzing a corporation's strengths and weaknesses?

NOTES

1. R. N. Osborn, J. G. Hunt, and L. R. Jauch, *Organization Theory: An Integrated Approach* (New York: John Wiley & Sons, 1980), p. 274.
2. R. H. Miles, *Macro Organizational Behavior* (Santa Monica, Calif.: Goodyear Publishing, 1980), pp. 28–34.
3. Osborn, Hunt, and Jauch, pp. 288–289.
4. M. Leontiades, "A Diagnostic Framework for Planning," *Strategic Management Journal* (January–March 1983), p. 14.
5. J. M. Stengrevics, "Managing the Group Executive's Job," *Organization Dynamics* (Winter 1984), p. 21.
6. Osborn, Hunt and Jauch, p. 293.
7. "Data General's Management Trouble," *Business Week* (February 9, 1981), pp. 59–61.
8. L. E. Fouraker and J. M. Stopford, "Organization Structure and the Multinational Strategy," *Administrative Science Quarterly* (June 1968), pp. 47–64.
9. H. Schwartz and S. M. Davis, "Matching Corporate Culture and Business Strategy," *Organizational Dynamics* (Summer 1981), p. 30.
10. "Corporate Culture," *Business Week* (October 27, 1980), p. 148.
11. T. J. Peters and R. H. Waterman, Jr., *In Search of Excellence* (New York: Harper & Row, 1982), pp. 293–294.
12. D. R. Denison, "Bringing Corporate Culture to the Bottom Line," *Organizational Dynamics* (Autumn 1984), pp. 5–22.
13. L. Smircich, "Concepts of Culture and Organizational Analysis," *Administrative Science Quarterly* (September 1983), pp. 345–346.
14. S. C. Wheelwright, "Manufacturing Strategy: Defining the Missing Link," *Strategic Management Journal* (January–March 1984), p. 79.

15. D. Muhm, "John Deere's Company: 145 Years of Farming History," *Des Moines Register* (November 11, 1984), p. 2F.
16. L. Iacocca, *Iacocca: An Autobiography* (Toronto: Bantam Books, 1984), p. 141.
17. T. Moore, "Embattled Kodak Enters the Electronic Era," *Fortune* (August 22, 1983), pp. 120–130.
18. W. H. Newman, "Shaping the Master Strategy of Your Firm," *California Management Review,* vol. 9, no. 3 (1967), p. 77.
19. P. Kotler, *Marketing Management,* 4th ed. (Englewood Cliffs, N.J.: Prentice-Hall, 1980), p. 22.
20. C. A. Anderson and C. P. Zeithaml, "Stage of the Product Life Cycle, Business Strategy, and Business Performance," *Academy of Management Journal* (March 1984), p. 22.
21. J. F. Weston and E. F. Brigham, *Managerial Finance,* 7th ed. (Hinsdale, Ill.: Dryden Press, 1981), pp. 555–569.
22. M. A. Maidique and P. Patch, "Corporate Strategy and Technological Policy" (Boston: Intercollegiate Case Clearing House, no. 9-769-033, 1978, rev. March 1980), p. 3.
23. R. J. Allio, "G.E. = Giant Entrepreneur?" *Planning Review* (January 1985), p. 21.
24. T. F. O'Boyle, "Steel's Management Has Itself to Blame," *Wall Street Journal* (May 17, 1983), p. 32.
25. E. F. Finkin, "Developing and Managing New Products," *Journal of Business Strategy* (Spring 1983), p. 45.
26. R. Brandt, M. Rothman, and A. Gabor, "Will Ford Beat GM in the Robot Race?" *Business Week* (May 27, 1985), p. 44.
27. "Navy Scraps $6 Million Computer Systems Sailors Couldn't Operate" (Charlottesville, Va.) *Daily Progress* (April 22, 1981), p. B11.
28. P. Pascarella, "Are You Investing in the Wrong Technology?" *Industry Week* (July 25, 1983), p. 37.
29. Pascarella, p. 38.
30. E. S. Buffa, *Modern Production/Operations Management,* 6th ed. (New York: John Wiley & Sons, 1980), p. 487.
31. Weston and Brigham, p. 231.
32. Buffa, p. 48.
33. A. C. Hax and N. S. Majuf, "Competitive Cost Dynamics: The Experience Curve," in A. C. Hax (ed.), *Readings on Strategic Management* (Cambridge, Mass.: Ballinger Publishing Co., 1984), pp. 49–60.
34. B. D. Henderson, *Henderson on Corporate Strategy* (Cambridge, Mass.: Abt Books, 1979), p. 11.
35. R. B. Chase and N. J. Aquilano, *Production and Operations Management,* rev. ed. (Homewood, Ill.: Richard D. Irwin, Inc., 1977), pp. 526–531.
36. J. D. Goldhar and M. Jelinek, "Plan for Economies of Scope," *Harvard*

Business Review (November–December 1983), pp. 141–148.
G. G. Anderson, "Planning for Restructured Competition," *Long Range Planning* (February 1985), p. 27.

37. J. Holusa, "Deere & Co. Leads the Way in 'Flexible' Manufacturing," *Des Moines Register* (January 29, 1984), p. 10F.
38. H. G. Heneman, D. P. Schwab, J. A. Fossum, and L. D. Dyer, *Personnel/Human Resource Management* (Homewood, Ill.: Richard D. Irwin, Inc., 1980), p. 7.
39. N. Tichy, "Conversation with Edson W. Spencer and Foster A. Boyle," *Organization Dynamics* (Spring 1983), p. 30.
40. J. Hoerr, "Now Unions Are Helping to Run the Business," *Business Week* (December 24, 1984), p. 69.
"A Bold Tactic to Hold On to Jobs," *Business Week* (October 29, 1984), pp. 70–72.
41. E. F. Huse, *Organization Development and Change,* 2nd ed. (St. Paul, Minn.: West Publishing Co., 1980), pp. 236–244.
42. J. L. Suttle, "Improving Life at Work—Problems and Perspectives," *Improving Life at Work: Behavioral Science Approaches to Organizational Change,* eds. J. R. Hackman and J. L. Suttle (Santa Monica, Calif.: Goodyear Publishing, 1976), p. 4.
43. D. A. Nadler and E. E. Lawler III, "Quality of Work Life: Perspectives and Directions," *Organization Dynamics* (Winter 1983), p. 27.
44. L. E. Calonius, "In a Plant in Memphis, Japanese Firm Shows How to Attain Quality," *Wall Street Journal* (April 29, 1983), p. 14.
45. R. F. Neuschel, *Management Systems for Profit and Growth* (New York: McGraw-Hill, 1976), p. 270.
46. R. G. Murdick, *MIS: Concepts and Designs* (Englewood Cliffs, N.J.: Prentice-Hall, 1980), p. 253.
47. R. L. Nolan, "Controlling the Costs of Data Services," *Harvard Business Review* (July–August 1977), p. 117.
48. R. H. Gregory and R. L. Van Horn, "Value and Cost of Information," in J. D. Cougar and R. W. Knapp (eds.), *Systems Analysis Techniques* (New York: Wiley, 1974), pp. 473–489.
49. R. I. Benjamin, J. F. Rockart, M. S. S. Morton, and J. Wyman, "Information Technology: A Strategic Opportunity," *Sloan Management Review* (Spring 1984), p. 5.
50. "Business Is Turning Data into a Potent Strategic Weapon," *Business Week* (August 22, 1983), p. 92.

PART THREE

STRATEGY FORMULATION

Chapter 6

STRATEGY FORMULATION: SITUATION ANALYSIS

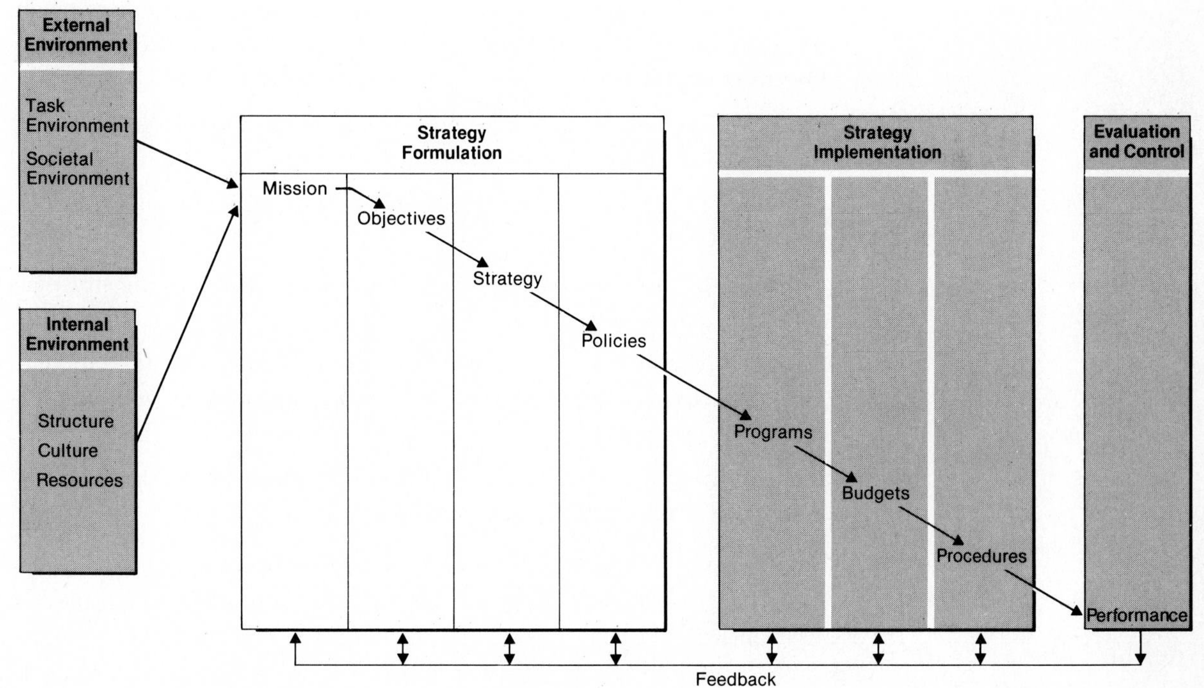

Strategy formulation is often referred to as strategic planning or long-range planning. Regardless of the term used, the process is primarily analytical, not action-oriented. The basic Strategic Management Model, shown first in Chapter 1, reflects the distinction between strategy formulation and strategy implementation. As shown in the model, the formulation process is concerned with developing a corporation's *mission, objectives, strategy,* and *policies.* In order to do this, corporate strategy makers must scan both the *external* and *internal environments* for needed information on strategic factors.

The Strategic Management Model does not show how the formulation process occurs. It merely describes the key *input variables* (internal and external environments) and the key *output factors* (mission, objectives, strategy, and policies). Chapters 6 and 7 therefore provide a more detailed discussion of the key activities in the process in order to supplement the Strategic Management Model.

In Chapter 2, a strategic decision-making process was introduced as a graphic representation of the strategic audit. It is also included in this chapter as Fig. 6.1.

The first six steps commonly found in strategy formulation are a series of interrelated activities:

1. *Evaluation* of (a) the corporation's current performance results in terms of return on investment, profitability, etc., and (b) the corporation's current mission, objectives, strategies, and policies.
2. *Examination* and *evaluation* of the corporation's strategic managers—board of directors and top management.
3. *Scanning* of the *external* environment to locate strategic opportunities and threats.
4. *Scanning* of the *internal* corporate environment to determine strategic strengths and weaknesses.
5. *Analysis* of the strategic factors from steps 3 and 4 to (a) pinpoint problem areas and (b) review and revise the corporate mission and objectives as necessary.
6. *Generation, evaluation,* and *selection* of the best alternative strategy appropriate to the analysis conducted in step 5.

Situation analysis is the first part of the strategy formulation process. Beginning with an evaluation of current performance and ending with the review and possible revision of mission and objectives, the process includes steps one through five. These steps are discussed in this chapter. Step six,

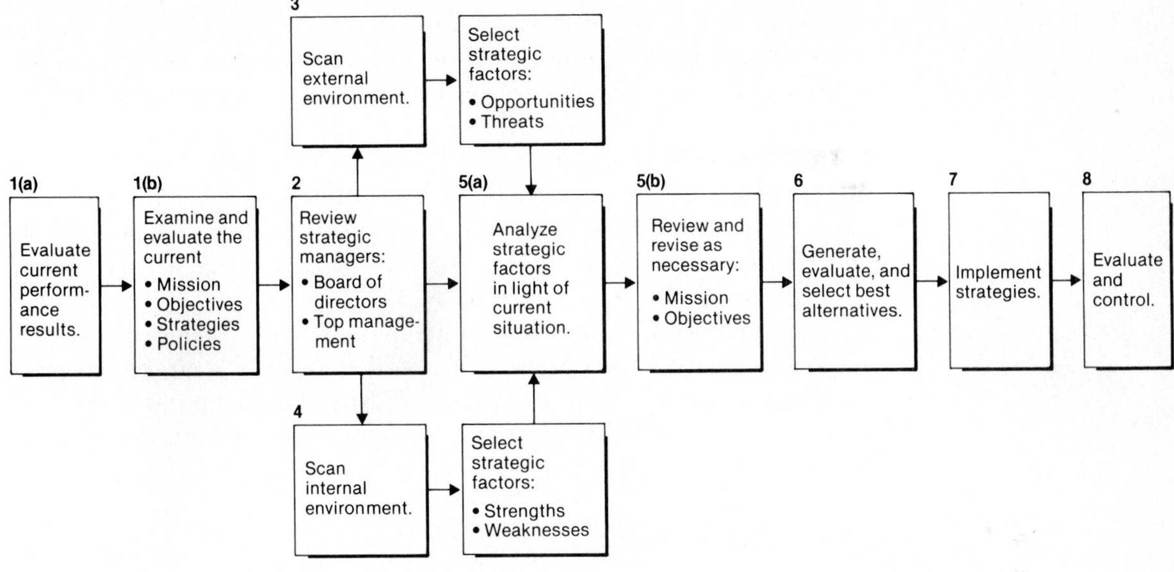

NOTE: Steps 1 through 6 are *strategy formulation.*
Step 7 is *strategy implementation.*
Step 8 is *evaluation and control.*

Figure 6.1 **Strategic decision-making process.**

the generation, evaluation, and selection of the best alternative strategy, is discussed in Chapter 7.

6.1 EVALUATION OF CURRENT RESULTS

After much research, Henry Mintzberg found that strategy formulation is typically not a regular, continuous process: "It is most often an irregular, discontinuous process, proceeding in fits and starts. There are periods of stability in strategy development, but also there are periods of flux, of groping, of piecemeal change, and of global change."[1] This view of strategy formulation as an irregular process may be explained by the tendency of most people to continue on a particular course of action until something goes wrong. In a business corporation, the stimulus for a strategy review lies, in most instances, in current performance results.

Performance results are generally periodic measurements of developments that occur during a given time period. At the corporate level, for example, the board and top management would be most concerned with overall measurements such as return on investment (ROI), profits after taxes, and earnings per share. The measurements for the current year would be compared to similar measurements from previous years to see whether a trend exists. At the business or divisional level, the manager might be concerned with the return on division assets or the net contribution to corporate profits. At the functional level, various managers would be concerned with total sales and market share, plant efficiency, or number of new patents.

Current performance results are compared with current objectives (desired results). If the results are equal to or greater than current objectives, most strategic managers are likely to assume that current strategies and policies are appropriate, as is. In this instance, only incremental changes to present objectives and strategy are likely to be recommended. The strategy formulation process may thus end rather abruptly with a summary statement suggesting that the corporation continue doing what it's already doing—only do it a little better next year. This is basically what occurred at Coca Cola Company a number of years ago. Hugh Schwarz, director of corporate planning at that time for Coca Cola, stated:

> If a person is happy with the present situation, he will not want to change. The very success of The Coca Cola Company works against its planning for change.[2]

If, however, the results of performance are less than what is desired, the formulation process begins in earnest. People at all levels are urged by the board and top management to question present objectives, strategies, and policies. Even the mission may be questioned. Are we aiming too high? Do our strategies make sense? Environmental scanning of both internal and external variables begins. What went wrong? Why? Questions such as these prompt top management to review the corporation's mission, objectives, strategies, and policies. Certainly Coca Cola's top management spent many hours during 1985 agonizing over their decision to change the traditional flavor of "Coke" to improve the brand's deteriorating market position. As discussed in Illustrative Example 6.1, General Foods Corporation and H&R Block both used a deteriorating situation to stimulate a strategy review.

EVALUATING CURRENT PERFORMANCE RESULTS: GENERAL FOODS AND H&R BLOCK

Illustrative Example 6.1

GENERAL FOODS CORPORATION

James Ferguson, CEO of General Foods, noticed in 1981 increasing stagnation in several of General Foods' businesses, such as cereals and pet foods. Even though General Foods' earnings had been increasing at an average annual rate over the last five years of 17%, the increase had come at the expense of product innovation and diversification. The corporation generated only enough new products between 1974 and 1980 to add $375 million to revenues in the 1980–81 fiscal year. Executive vice-president

(*Continued*)

Philip Smith commented, "Against a mass of $7 billion [estimated sales for the fiscal year ending March 31, 1981], $375 million is an inadequate addition." General Foods' top management reported that it wanted to make its businesses grow at a rate of 2 to 3% over time rather than the industry average of 1% per year. As a result, it began to develop a series of strategies focusing on diversification and growth.

H&R BLOCK

Founded by Henry and Richard Bloch in 1955, the Kansas City, Missouri-based H&R Block (spelled with a "k" to avoid mispronunciation) has built a very successful business out of helping people to complete their income tax forms. The company prepared 10% of all returns filed in the United States, so top management was concerned to see its growth in tax preparing level off and begin to decline in 1981. The number of forms processed by Block fell 3% from 1982 to 1983—the year the much simplified Form 1040EZ was introduced. The company was able to stay profitable chiefly by increasing prices. Nevertheless, its 1.6% (in 1982) and 6.5% (in 1983) increases in profits were far below the 15% annual growth goal set by Henry Bloch.

Believing that the company had reached a saturation point in its basic business, management decided that it had to do other things if the firm was to recapture its earlier profit growth rate. To become more than just a tax preparer, H&R Block decided to diversify into computer information services, employment services for temporary health and clerical workers, and legal advisory services. "You can't stand still," commented Jerome Grossman, executive vice president and chief operating officer. "You are either moving forward or going backward. This is an attempt to move forward."

SOURCES: "Changing the Culture at General Foods," *Business Week* (March 30, 1981), pp. 136–140. "Simpler Tax Forms Force H&R Block to Become Much More Than a Tax Preparer," *Des Moines Register* (April 22, 1984), p. 8F.

Evaluation of Mission

The breadth or narrowness of the corporate mission has an important effect upon performance.[3] The definition of the corporate mission determines the broad limits of a company's growth.[4] For example, amusement parks traditionally defined themselves as in-place carnivals. After floundering in the 1950s, many such businesses went bankrupt. The success of Disneyland in the 1960s caused many parks such as Cedar Point, Inc. in Sandusky, Ohio to redefine themselves as "theme" parks with entertainment "packages" of shows, rides, and nationally known performers. With the aging of the American population, that mission is being further broadened to include a wider spectrum of entertainment, including golf courses.

The concept of a corporate mission implies that throughout a corporation's many activities there should be a *common thread* or unifying theme and that those corporations with such a common thread are better able to direct and administer their many activities.[5] In acquiring new firms or in developing new products, such a corporation looks for "strategic fit," that is, the likelihood that new activities will mesh with present ones in such a way that the corporation's overall effectiveness and efficiency will be increased. There may be common distribution channels or similar customers, warehousing economies or the mutual use of R&D, better use of managerial talent or any of a number of possible synergistic effects.[6]

Evaluation of Objectives

As pointed out in Chapter 4, each stakeholder in a corporation's task environment will have its own way of measuring the corporation's performance. Stockholders may want dividends and price appreciation, whereas unions want good wages, stability of employment, and opportunities for advancement. Customers, distributors, creditors, suppliers, local communities, and other governments, to name only a few, have their own criteria to judge the corporation. The objectives and the priorities attached to them by the corporation are one way to recognize these outside forces and to deal with them in a logical fashion. Some of the possible objectives a corporation might pursue are the following:

- Profitability (net profits)
- Efficiency (low costs, etc.)
- Growth (increase in total assets, sales, etc.)
- Shareholder wealth (dividends plus stock price appreciation)
- Utilization of resources (ROE or ROI)
- Contributions to customers (quality/price)
- Contributions to employees (employment security, wages)
- Contributions to society (taxes paid, participation in charities)
- Market leadership (market share, reputation)
- Technological leadership (innovations, creativity)
- Survival (avoiding bankruptcy)
- Personal needs of top management (using the firm for personal purposes, such as providing jobs for relatives)

It is likely, however, that many small corporations have no formal objectives; rather, they have vague, verbal ones. It is even more likely that even though a corporation has specified, written objectives, they will not be ranked on the basis of priority.

Evaluation of Strategies and Policies

Just as a number of firms have no formal objectives, many CEOs have "unstated, incremental, or intuitive strategies that have never been articulated or analyzed. . . ."[7] If pressured, these executives may state that they are following a certain strategy. This stated or "explicit" strategy is one with which few could quarrel, such as the development and acquisition of new product lines. Further investigation, however, may reveal the existence of a very different "implicit" strategy. For example, the prestige of a banker in one community is strictly a function of bank size. Top management, therefore, tends to choose strategies that will increase total bank assets rather than profits. An extremely profitable "small" bank is still just a "small" bank.

Often the only way to spot the implicit strategies of a corporation is to look not at what top management says, but at what it does. Implicit strategies can be derived from examining corporation policies, programs approved (and disapproved), and authorized budgets. Programs and divisions favored by budget increases and staffed by managers who are considered to be on the fast promotion track reveal where the corporation is putting its money and its energy.

It is, nevertheless, not always necessary for strategic planning to be a formal process for it to be effective. Small corporations, for example, may plan informally and irregularly.[8] The president and a handful of top managers may get together casually to resolve strategic issues and plan their next steps. They need no formal, elaborate planning system, for "The number of key executives involved in such decisions is usually small, and they are located close enough for frequent, casual get-togethers."[9]

In large, multidivisional corporations, however, the planning of strategy can become quite complex. A formalized system is needed to ensure that a hierarchy of objectives and strategy exists. Otherwise, top management becomes isolated from developments in the divisions and lower-level managers lose sight of the corporate mission.

6.2 EVALUATION OF STRATEGIC MANAGERS

As discussed in Chapter 3, the interaction of a corporation's board with its top management is likely to reflect one of four basic styles of strategic management: chaos, entrepreneurial, marionette, and partnership. Firms like Adolph Coors Company, Cannon Mills Company, and Tandy Corporation have for years been so dominated by their founders that their boards probably operated passively as an instrument of the founder. Once the founder dies and an outsider is brought in to head the firm, however, the board may take a more active role in representing the interests of the family. In such instances, the new CEO may be quite constrained by the board in terms of strategic options.

The strategic management style of such a corporation may thus change abruptly from entrepreneurial (where the founder dominates the board) to marionette management (where the board, made up of the founder's family and friends, dominates top management and makes the significant decisions).

In many instances where the board is only moderately involved in strategic management, the CEO has a free hand to set the direction of the corporation. Then the success or failure of a corporation's strategy must be evaluated in light of the CEO's managerial style.

For example, William Ylvisaker, chairman and CEO of Gould Inc., has a reputation of being "mercurial" and "cavalier" with his people. Credited with reshaping the stodgy battery maker into a high-tech electronics concern, "the unpredictable Mr. Ylvisaker bought and sold properties like someone playing Monopoly."[10] In contrast, Stephen Pistner, who took over the job of president of Montgomery Ward in 1981 and subsequently left in 1985 to join Rapid-American Corporation, has a reputation of being a strategic planner who "drives right for the meat of the situation" and builds strong management teams.[11] The personal style of J. Peter Grace heavily determines the strategic directions taken by W. R. Grace and Company. When Mr. Grace was on a business trip in California a few years ago, he stopped at a coffee shop called Coco's for breakfast. He liked the meal so much that, after some research, he bought the company that owned the restaurant chain![12]

Henry Mintzberg has pointed out that a corporation's objectives and strategies are strongly affected by top management's view of the world.[13] This view determines the approach or "mode" to be used in strategy formulation. He names three basic modes: entrepreneurial, adaptive, and planning. Characteristics of each mode are listed in Table 6.1.

- *Entrepreneurial mode.* Strategy is made by one powerful individual. The focus is on opportunities. Problems are secondary. Strategy is guided by the founder's own vision of direction and is exemplified by large, bold decisions. The dominant goal is growth of the corporation.

  As mentioned earlier, Gould Inc. under William Ylvisaker and W. R. Grace and Company under Peter Grace are examples of corporations being run in the entrepreneurial mode. Surprisingly, both are old, established firms with extremely dynamic and creative CEOs who have striven to change the character of their respective firms to match their vision of the future.

- *Adaptive mode.* Sometimes referred to as "muddling through," this strategy-formulation mode is characterized by reactive solutions to existing problems, rather than a proactive search for new opportunities. Much bargaining goes on concerning priorities of objectives. Strategy is

Table 6.1 Characteristics and Conditions of the Three Modes

Characteristic	*Entrepreneurial Mode*	*Adaptive Mode*	*Planning Mode*
Motive for decisions	Proactive	Reactive	Proactive and reactive
Goals of organization	Growth	Indeterminate	Efficiency and growth
Evaluation of proposals	Judgmental	Judgmental	Analytical
Choices made by	Entrepreneur	Bargaining	Management
Decision horizon	Long-term	Short-term	Long-term
Preferred environment	Uncertainty	Certainty	Risk
Decision linkages	Loosely coupled	Disjointed	Integrated
Flexibility of mode	Flexible	Adaptive	Constrained
Size of moves	Bold decisions	Incremental steps	Global strategies
Vision of direction	General	None	Specific
Condition for Use			
Source of power	Entrepreneur	Divided	Management
Objectives of organization	Operational	Nonoperational	Operational
Organizational environment	Yielding	Complex, dynamic	Predictable, stable
Status of organization	Young, small, or strong leadership	Established	Large

SOURCE: H. Mintzberg, "Strategy Making in Three Modes." Copyright © 1973 by the Regents of the University of California. Reprinted by permission of the Regents from *California Management Review*, vol. xvi, no. 2, p. 49.

fragmented and is developed to move the corporation forward in incremental steps.

This mode is typical of most universities, many large hospitals, a large number of government agencies, and a surprising number of large corporations. Western Union, for example, has for years successfully plodded along earning a small but predictable annual profit from businesses that largely were outgrowths of the telegraph. Only recently, when it tried to change modes and become more aggressive, did it fall on hard times.

- *Planning mode.* Analysts assume major responsibilities for strategy formulation. Strategic planning includes both the proactive search for new opportunities and the reactive solution of existing problems. Systematic comprehensive analysis is used to develop strategies that integrate the corporation's decision-making processes.

  Sears, Roebuck and Company, in its strategic move into financial services, exemplifies this mode. Rather than simply working to improve their then-stagnant merchandising group, top management chose to capitalize on the firm's successes in insurance and real estate to take advantage of unique opportunities emerging in the financial services industry.

In the *entrepreneurial* mode, top management believes that the environment is a force to be used and controlled. In the *adaptive* mode, it assumes the environment is too complex to be completely comprehended. In the *planning* mode, it works on the assumption that systematic scanning and analysis of the environment can provide the knowledge necessary to influence the environment to the corporation's advantage. The specific planning mode used reflects top management's perception of the corporation's environment. If we categorize a corporation's top management according to one of these three planning modes, we can better understand how and why key decisions are made. Then if we look at these decisions in light of the corporation's mission, objectives, strategies, and policies, we can then determine whether the dominant planning mode is appropriate.

In addition, strategy-making modes may change as a corporation increases in size and complexity, or changes top management personnel. Tandy Corporation, for example, has changed from the entrepreneurial mode characteristic of the reign of its founder Charles Tandy to the more adaptive mode under his successor, Phil North. If Tandy Corporation continues to be successful, North's successor may move toward a more planning-oriented mode.[14]

6.3 SCANNING THE EXTERNAL ENVIRONMENT

At the point in the strategy formulation process where the external environment is scanned, strategic managers must examine both the societal and task environments for those strategic factors that are likely to strongly influence their corporation's success—factors that are, in other words, opportunities and threats. Long-run developments in the economic, technological, political-legal, and sociocultural aspects of the societal environment tend to affect strongly a corporation's activities by asserting more immediate pressures on the corporation's task environment. Such societal issues as consumerism, governmental regulations, environmental pollution, energy cost and availability, inflation-fed wage demands, and heavy foreign competition tend to emerge from stakeholders in the firm's task environment.

As discussed in Chapter 4, strategic managers should evaluate environmental issues in terms of the probability of their occurring and their probable impact on the corporation. In this manner, the possible societal issues listed in Table 4.3 can be placed on an issues priority matrix as shown in Fig. 4.2. Special emphasis may then be placed on monitoring these high-priority issues. Each of the six forces from the task environment depicted in Fig. 4.4, such as the threat of substitute products and services, also can be evaluated in this same manner and marked for special attention. Top management should then request its divisions and functional areas to report to it any significant developments in any of the high- or even medium-priority issues.

6.4 SCANNING THE INTERNAL ENVIRONMENT

Before top management can properly address what possible future strategies are appropriate for the corporation, it must assess its own internal situation—the environment within the firm itself. Strategic decisions should not be made until top management understands the strengths and weaknesses in the division and functional areas.

Management audits can be very useful in this instance as a diagnostic aid. As mentioned in Chapter 5, the key internal variables to consider are the corporation's structure, culture, and resources. An example of a corporation (IBM) in which a basic weakness in a functional area seriously hurt the implementation of a reasonable strategy is given in Illustrative Example 6.2.

INTERNAL WEAKNESS NEGATIVELY AFFECTS IMPLEMENTATION OF STRATEGIC DECISION AT IBM

Illustrative Example 6.2

In 1980, IBM began opening grandly decorated computer retail stores called IBM Product Centers in selected locations throughout the United States. Although the 81 stores achieved more than $100 million in sales during 1983, IBM decided to cancel its plans to add 100 additional stores during 1984. Burdened with start-up costs and high overhead, the stores were making far less than the 20% return IBM was accustomed to earning. It had become apparent that IBM's immense internal strengths in marketing to business customers did not transfer to standard retailing. Serious merchandising weaknesses translated into significant errors at the store level. Anxious not to appear cold and remote, IBM decorated its stores in bright red. To give its stores an image of class, IBM chose to avoid flashy, in-store displays, brochures, and racks of impulse items near the cash registers. It also staffed the stores entirely with the company's own career salespeople, few of whom had retailing experience. Using the approach that worked extremely well with its business customers, IBM stressed service over price-cutting and special offers. The retailing customers, however, were not impressed. The color of the stores caused mood problems. Commented Warren Winger, chairman of CompuShop, a Dallas-based retail chain, "Red doesn't just irritate bulls, it makes salesmen hostile and alarms customers." IBM's career salespeople intimidated first-time customers. The lack of store displays and competitive pricing caused customers to leave the stores disappointed and disillusioned. Jim Turner, the IBM vice president in charge of the stores, hinted that the Product Centers might change offerings to concentrate on selling office automation systems. In reviewing the retail stores' failure to generate the anticipated profits, Turner confessed: "The in-store merchandising—we never realized how important it was."

SOURCE: P. Petre, "IBM's Misadventures in the Retail Jungle," *Fortune* (July 23, 1984), p.80.

A current research effort to help pinpoint relevant strategic factors for business corporations is being made by the Strategic Planning Institute. Its *PIMS Program* (Profit Impact of Market Strategy) is composed of a data bank containing about 100 items of information on the strategic experiences of over 2,000 companies covering a four- to eight-year period. The research conducted with the data has been aimed at discovering the empirical "laws" that determine which strategy, under which conditions, produces what results in terms of return on investment and cash flows regardless of the specific product or services. To date, PIMS research has identified nine major strategic factors which account for around 80% of the variation in profitability across the businesses in the database.[15] In working with these factors, the Strategic Planning Institute has prepared profiles of high ROI companies as contrasted with low ROI companies. They found that the high rate of return companies had the following characteristics:

- Low investment intensity (the amount of fixed capital and working capital required to produce a dollar of sales)
- High market share
- High relative product quality
- High capacity utilization
- High operating effectiveness (the ratio of actual to expected employee productivity)
- Low direct costs per unit relative to competition[16]

These and other PIMS research findings are quite controversial. For example, PIMS research has reported consistently that a large market share should lead to greater profitability.[17] The reason appears to be that high market share results in low unit costs because of economies of scale. A company could therefore take advantage of the experience curve (discussed in Chapter 5) to gain share through low price. Unfortunately, a number of studies have found that high market share does not always lead to profitability. Firms selling products of high quality relative to the competition have been found to be very profitable even though they do not have large market share.[18] From a practitioner's point of view, the most important criticism of PIMS research is that the "significant predictors of performance (investment intensity, market share, relative product quality, capacity utilization, etc.) generally have tended to be variables outside of management's control, at least in the short run."[19] As a result of these and other limitations, one can conclude that we are still quite a distance away from discovering "univeral strategic laws." Nevertheless, the PIMS program is useful to help strategic managers identify some key internal strategic factors, such as investment intensity, market share, product quality, capacity utilization, operating effectiveness, and direct costs per unit. These factors can be measured and compared to other firms in the same industry to assess a corporation's relative strengths and weaknesses.

6.5 ANALYSIS OF STRATEGIC FACTORS

The analysis of the strategic factors in the strategic decision-making process calls for an integration and evaluation of data collected earlier from the scanning of the internal and external environments. External strategic factors are those opportunities and threats found in the present and future task and societal environments. Internal strategic factors are those important strengths and weaknesses within the corporation's divisional and functional areas. Step 5(a) in Fig. 6.1 requires that top management attempt to find a "strategic fit" between external opportunities and intentional strengths.

S.W.O.T. Analysis

S.W.O.T. is a term used to stand for a summary listing of a corporation's key internal *Strengths* and *Weaknesses* and its external *Opportunities* and *Threats*. These are the strategic factors to be analyzed in step 5(a) of Fig. 6.1. They should include not only those external factors that are most likely to occur and to have a serious impact on the company, but also those internal factors that are most likely to affect the implementation of present and future strategic decisions. In the case of Illustrative Example 6.2 discussing IBM, a S.W.O.T. analysis should reflect the great *opportunities* for profits emerging in the early 1980s for retail computer stores. It would also show the increasing *threat* from consumer-oriented Apple to dominate the developing personal computer market. S.W.O.T. analysis should also list IBM's impressive marketing, research, and personnel *strengths*. Nevertheless, an objective assessment of *weaknesses* should have highlighted IBM's lack of experience at the retail level and raised a "red flag" for management to seriously consider before choosing this particular strategy. Since IBM failed to note the seriousness of its retailing weaknesses, it was forced to (1) train its salespeople in retail selling, (2) install a point-of-sale computer system (which it had failed to do initially), and (3) change to a new store design with cozier colors and point-of-sale promotions.

Finding a Niche

William Newman suggests that a corporation should seek to obtain a "propitious niche" in its strategy formulation process.[20] This niche is a corporation's specific competitive role. It should be so well-suited to the firm's internal and external environment that other corporations are not likely to challenge or dislodge it.

The finding of such a niche is not always easy. A firm's management must always be looking for *strategic windows,* that is, market opportunities.[21] As in the case of Electronic Technology Corporation, presented in Illustrative Example 6.3, the first one through the strategic window (if the firm has the required internal strengths) can occupy a propitious niche and discourage competition. Zayre's decision to improve and emphasize its inner-city discount stores at a time when competitors were leaving inner-city locations in droves enabled it to build a niche successfully where none previously existed. Other examples are the many commuter airlines which sprouted throughout the country in the early 1980s after deregulation allowed major airlines to desert the smaller cities. Because these regional airlines fly smaller planes than the majors, their operating costs are lower and thus allow profits to well-managed firms.

A recent study of high-performing mid-sized growth companies found these successful corporations to have four characteristics is common:

- They innovate as a way of life.
- They compete on value, not price.
- They achieve leadership in *niche markets.*
- They build on their strengths by competing in *related niches.*[22]

The finding of a specific niche where a corporation's strengths fit well with environmental opportunities is therefore a desired outcome of situation analysis.

HIGH-TECH ELECTRONIC TECHNOLOGY CORPORATION AND *LOW-TECH* ZAYRE'S DISCOUNT STORES FIND PROPITIOUS NICHES

Illustrative Example 6.3

SILICON VALLEY IN CEDAR RAPIDS?

Just one year after its founding, Electronic Technology Corporation (ETC), is succeeding beyond its founder's fondest dreams. The firm manufactures semi-custom integrated circuits and sells to customers throughout the Midwest. Founder Scott Clark brought the idea to Iowa from the famed "Silicon Valley" of northern California where such companies are more common than hamburger stands. "When we began, our plan was to have a typical production order of $35,000," says Clark. "Within six months, we revised it to $90,000. And by September, orders were averaging $240,000. In fiscal year 1985, orders will average $400,000. . . . We can't grow fast enough to keep up." A significant reason for its success is its location in Cedar Rapids. Since an estimated 90% of the industry is located in Silicon Valley, about 5% on the East Coast, and the remainder

(*Continued*)

scattered throughout the United States, ETC leads the way in the upper Midwest. "We're between Chicago, Minneapolis, Milwaukee, St. Louis, and Kansas City. We're accessible and we're interested in our customers," states Clark. ETC offers its customers *service* and *security*. Clark says that it's not unusual for Silicon Valley engineers to stay with a company only a matter of months. When a company receives a big contract, it can hire the necessary design engineers from one of its competitors. "These guys jump from one job to another and think nothing of it. But what they do when they jump is take the secrets of the last company they did a contract for. They can offer it to a contractor's competitor. And that doesn't happen here. Our engineers come here planning to stay. They like the security of the job and they like being out of the rat race in California. We can guarantee our customers the security they must have," comments Clark. ETC's plans to expand over the next five years conjure up dreams of a Silicon Valley of the Midwest—located in Iowa. "I really believe it will happen," predicts Clark. "The business is here and our only real competitors are in California."

ZAYRE'S FINDS SUCCESS IN INNER-CITIES

In the late 1970s, Zayre Corporation was suffering from low earnings because of the "rummage sale" nature of its discount stores. Zayre responded by renovating its stores and improving its merchandise presentation and inventory. Unlike other discounters, who were leaving the inner-city in droves, Zayre decided to stay. The chain made a "significant commitment to become very good at something that [other retailers] were running away from," says President Malcolm L. Sherman. Inner-city Chicago stores were the first to be upgraded. By 1984, approximately 20% of Zayre's 276 stores were in or near black and Hispanic neighborhoods in Chicago, Pittsburgh, Atlanta, Indianapolis, and other cities. They are generally the chain's profit leaders. Zayre has few competitors in the inner-city. The inventory of the inner-city stores is tailored to the specific needs and tastes of area residents. The emphasis is on apparel. The inner-city stores stock more apparel than do suburban stores because inner-city residents "have fewer places to shop" and tend to have larger families, states Mr. Sherman. Its hiring and advertising practices also reflect the ethnic mix. Apparently, Zayre's concern for its inner-city customers is reciprocated by the people in the Zayre locations. When riots shook Miami's Liberty City in March, 1984, some residents of the area intervened to protect the store from troublemakers. "We had no damage," said Charles Howze, the inner-city store's manager.

SOURCES: J. Carlson, "Silicon Valley Comes to Iowa—and Sprouts," *Des Moines Register* (January 27, 1985), p. 6X. J. L. Roberts, "Zayre's Strategy of Ethnic Merchandising Proves To Be Successful in Inner-City Stores," *Wall Street Journal* (September 25, 1984), p. 37.

Portfolio Analysis

The business portfolio is the most recommended approach to aid the integration and evaluation of environmental data. Research suggests that "at least 200 of the Fortune 500 companies [and probably substantially more] are using the portfolio planning concept in some manner and informal discussions suggest a similar rate of adoption in Western Europe."[23]

All corporations, except the simplest and smallest, are involved in more than one business. Even though a corporation sells only one product, it may benefit from handling separately a number of distinct product-market segments. Procter & Gamble, for example, managed Prell Liquid and Prell Concentrate as two separate brands for a number of years because of their appeal to two separate and distinct market segments.

Portfolio analysis recommends that each product, strategic business unit (SBU), or division be considered separately for purposes of strategy formulation.[24]

There are a number of matrixes available to reflect the variables under consideration in a portfolio. SBUs or products can be compared for growth rate in sales, relative competitive position, stage of product/market evolution, market share, and industry attractiveness.

Four Cell BCG Growth-Share Matrix

The simplest matrix is the *growth-share matrix* developed by the Boston Consulting Group as depicted in Fig. 6.2. Each of the corporation's SBUs or products is plotted on the matrix according to both the growth rate of the industry in which it competes and its relative market share. A product's or SBU's relative competitive position is defined as its market share in the industry divided by that of the largest other competitor. The business growth rate is the percentage of market growth—that is, the percentage of increased sales of a particular product or SBU classification of products.

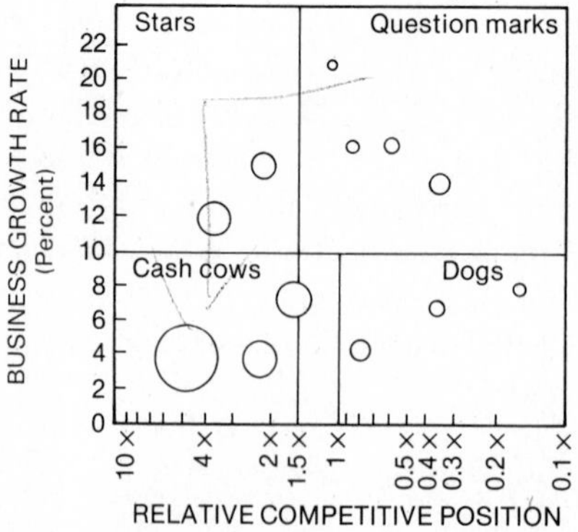

Figure 6.2 **The BCG portfolio matrix.**

SOURCE: B. Hedley, "Strategy and the Business Portfolio," *Long Range Planning* (February 1977), p. 12. Reprinted by permission.

The line separating areas of high and low relative competitive position is set at 1.5 times. Relative strengths of this magnitude are needed to ensure the dominant position needed to be a star or cash cow. On the other hand, a product or SBU should be 1 times or less to ensure its dog status.[25] Each product or SBU is represented in Fig. 6.2 by a circle. The area of the circle represents the relative significance of each SBU or product to the corporation in terms of assets used or sales generated.

The growth-share matrix has a lot in common with the product life cycle. New products are typically introduced in a fast-growing industry. These initially are termed *question mark* products. To gain enough market share to become a market leader and thus a *star*, money must be taken from more mature *cash cow* products to spend on the *question marks. Stars* are typically at the peak of their product life cycle and are usually able to generate enough cash to invest in keeping a high share of the market. Once the market growth rate slows, *stars* become *cash cows.* These products typically bring in far more money than is needed to sustain their market share. As these products move along the decline stage of their life cycle, they are "milked" for cash to invest in new *question mark* products. Those products unable to obtain a dominant market share by the time the industry growth rate inevitably slows become *dogs* which are either sold off or managed carefully for the small amount of cash they may generate.

Once a corporation's current position has been plotted on a matrix, a projection can be made of its future position, assuming no changes in strategy. Present and projected matrixes can thus be used to assist in the identification of major strategic issues facing the corporation.

Research on the growth-share matrix generally supports its assumptions and recommendations except for the advice that dogs should be promptly harvested or liquidated.[26] Products with a low share in declining industries may be very profitable if the products have niches where market demand remains stable and predictable.[27] If enough of the competition leaves the industry, a product's market share may increase by default until the dog becomes the market leader and thus a cash cow. All in all, the BCG growth-share matrix is a very popular technique. It is quantifiable and easy to use. The barnyard analogies of cash cows and dogs have become trendy buzzwords in management circles.

The growth-share matrix has been criticized for a number of reasons nevertheless:

- The use of highs and lows to make just four categories is too simplistic.
- The link between market share and profitability is not necessarily strong. Low share businesses can be profitable, too (and vice versa).

- The highest-growth rate markets may not always be the best.
- It only considers the product or SBU in relation to one competitor—the market leader. It misses small competitors with fast-growing market shares.
- Growth rate is only one aspect of industry attractiveness.
- Market share is only one aspect of overall competitive position.[28]

Nine Cell GE Business Screen

A more complicated matrix is that developed by General Electric with the assistance of the McKinsey and Company consulting firm. As depicted in Fig. 6.3, it includes nine cells based on long-term industry attractiveness and business strength/competitive position. Interestingly, this nine-cell matrix is almost identical to the *Directional Policy Matrix* developed by Shell Oil and used extensively by European firms. Both use the same factors and both use nine cells. The GE Business Screen, in contrast to the BCG growth-share matrix, includes much more data in its two key factors than just business growth rate and comparable market share. For example, at GE, industry attractiveness is defined as a composite projection of—among other character-

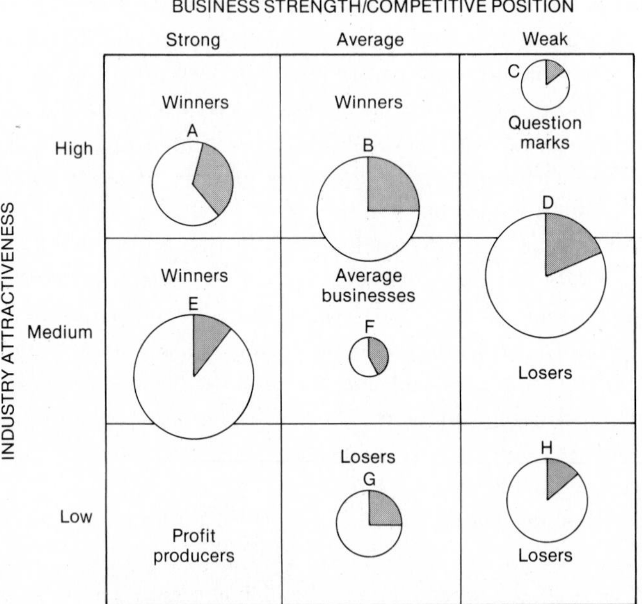

Figure 6.3 **General Electric's business screen.**
SOURCE: Adapted from *Strategic Management in GE,* Corporate Planning and Development, General Electric Corporation. Used by permission of General Electric Company.

istics—*market size, market growth rate, competitive diversity, competitive structure,* and *profitability.*[29] Business strength or competitive position can be a combination of, among others, *market share, facilities, technological position, image in marketplace,* and *caliber of management.* The individual products or SBUs are identified by a letter and plotted on the GE Screen. The area of the circles is in proportion to the size of the industry in terms of sales. The pie slices within the circles depict the market share of each product or SBU.[30]

The following four steps are recommended for plotting products or SBUs on the GE Business Screen.[31]

1. *Assess industry attractiveness.*
   a) Select general criteria to rate the industry. These criteria should be key aspects of the industry, such as its potential for sales growth and likely profitability. Table 6.2 lists fifteen criteria for one specific industry.

Table 6.2 **An Example of an Industry Attractiveness Assessment Matrix**

Attractiveness Criteria	*Weight**	*Rating***	*Weighted Score*
Size	0.15	4	0.60
Growth	0.12	3	0.36
Pricing	0.05	3	0.15
Market diversity	0.05	2	0.10
Competitive structure	0.05	3	0.15
Industry profitability	0.20	3	0.60
Technical role	0.05	4	0.20
Inflation vulnerability	0.05	2	0.10
Cyclicality	0.05	2	0.10
Customer financials	0.10	5	0.50
Energy impact	0.08	4	0.32
Social	GO	4	—
Environmental	GO	4	—
Legal	GO	4	—
Human	0.05	4	.20
	1.00		3.38

SOURCE: C. W. Hofer and D. Schendel, *Strategy Formulation: Analytical Concepts* (St. Paul, Minn.: West Publishing Co., 1978), p. 73.

* Some criteria may be of a GO/NO GO type. For example, many *Fortune 500* firms probably would decide not to invest in industries that are viewed negatively by our society, such as gambling, even if it were both legal and very profitable to do so.

** 1 (*very unattractive*) through 5 (*highly attractive*).

b) Weight each criterion according to management's perception of the criterion's importance to achieving corporate objectives. For example, because the key criterion of the corporation in Table 6.2 is profitability, it receives the highest weight, 0.20.

c) Rate the industry on each of these criteria from 1 (very unattractive) to 5 (very attractive). For example, if an industry is facing a long-term decline in profitability, this criterion should be rated 2 or less.

d) Multiply the weight for each criterion by its rating to get a weighted score. These scores are then added to get the weighted attractiveness score for the industry as a whole for a particular SBU.

2. *Assess business strength/competitive position.*

a) Identify the SBU's key factors for success in the industry. Table 6.3 lists seventeen such factors for a specific industry.

b) Weight each success factor (market share, for instance) in terms of its relative importance to profitability or some other measure of success within the industry. For example, since market share was believed to have a relatively small impact on most firms in the industry of Table 6.3, this success factor was given a weight of only 0.10.

c) Rate the SBU on each of the factors from 1 (very weak competitive position) to 5 (very strong competitive position). For example, as the products of the SBU of Table 6.3 have a very high market share, it received a rating of 5.

d) Multiply the weight of each factor by its rating to get a weighted score. These scores are then added to provide a weighted business strength/competitive position score for the SBU as a whole.

3. *Plot each SBU's current position.* Once industry attractiveness and business strength/competitive position are calculated for each SBU, the actual position of all the corporation's SBUs should be plotted on a matrix like the one illustrated in Fig. 6.3. The areas of the circles should be proportional to the size of the various industries involved (in terms of sales), the company's current market share in each industry should be depicted as a pie-shaped wedge, and the circles should be centered on the coordinates of the SBU's industry attractiveness and business strength/competitive position scores.

To develop a range of scores for the *industry attractiveness* axis of the matrix, look back at Table 6.2. A highly attractive industry

Table 6.3 An Example of a Business Strength/Competitive Position Assessment Matrix for an SBU

Key Success Factors	*Weight*	*Rating***	*Weighted Score*
Market share	0.10	5	.50
SBU growth rate	X*	3	—
Breadth of product line	.05	4	.20
Sales distribution effectiveness	.20	4	.80
Proprietary and key account advantages	X	3	—
Price competitiveness	X	4	—
Advertising and promotion effectiveness	.05	4	.20
Facilities location and newness	.05	5	.25
Capacity and productivity	X	3	—
Experience curve effects	.15	4	.60
Raw materials cost	.05	4	.20
Value added	X	4	—
Relative product quality	.15	4	.60
R&D advantages/position	.05	4	.20
Cash throw-off	.10	5	.50
Caliber of personnel	X	4	—
General image	.05	5	.25
	1.00		4.30

SOURCE: C. W. Hofer and D. Schendel, *Strategy Formulation: Analytical Concepts* (St. Paul, Minn.: West Publishing Co., 1978), p. 76.

* For any particular industry, there will be some factors that, while important in general, will have little or no effect on the relative competitive position of firms within that industry. It is usually better to drop such factors from the analysis than to assign them very low weights.

** 1 (*very weak competitive position*) through 5 (*very strong competitive position*).

should have mostly 5s in the rating column. An industry of medium attractiveness should have mostly 3s in the rating colum. An industry of low attractiveness should have mostly 1s in the rating column. Since the weights of the criteria used for each industry must sum to 1.00 regardless of the number of criteria used, the attractiveness axis of the GE Business Screen matrix should range from 1.00 (low attractiveness) to 5.00 (high attractiveness) with 3.00 as the midpoint.

Similarly, the range of scores for the *business strength/competitive position* axis of the GE Business Screen matrix should also range from 1.00 (weak) to 5.00 (strong) with 3.00 as the midpoint (average). This can be more clearly understood by again looking at Table 6.3.

Given that the criteria weights must sum to 1.00 regardless of the number of criteria used for each SBU, an SBU with a very strong competitive position might have all 5s in the rating column and thus a total weighted score of 5.00.

The resulting matrix shows the corporation's current portfolio situation. This situation is then contrasted with an ideal portfolio. Figure 6.4 depicts what Hofer and Schendel consider to be such a portfolio. It is considered ideal because it includes primarily winners, with enough winners and profit producers to finance the growth of developing (or potential) winners. In reality, however, even a successful firm would probably have a few question marks and perhaps a small loser.

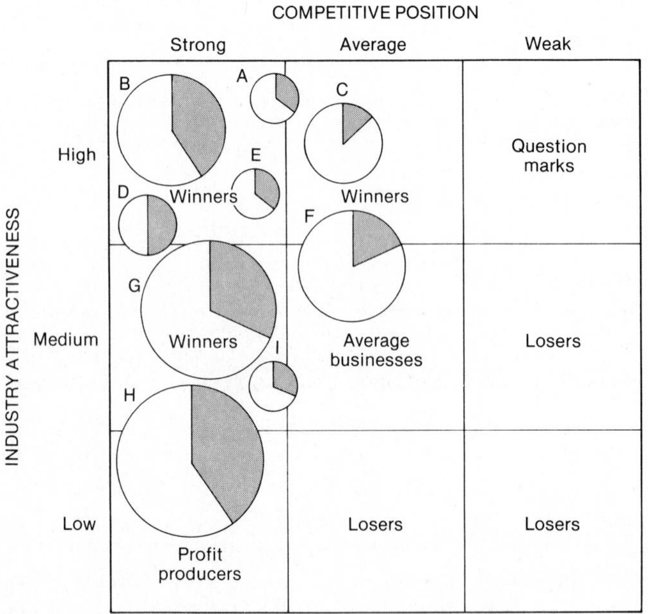

Figure 6.4 **An ideal multi-industry corporate portfolio.**

SOURCE: C. W. Hofer and D. Schendel, *Strategy Formulation: Analytical Concepts* (St. Paul, Minn.: West Publishing Co., 1978), p. 83. Copyright © 1978 by West Publishing Company. All rights reserved. Reprinted by permission.

NOTE: It is impossible to identify the orientation (i.e. growth, profit, or balance) of an ideal portfolio based solely on the information contained in the GE Business Screen, because the screen does not reflect all the information needed to do so. For instance, SBUs B, C, F, G, and H could be developing winners in very large markets or established winners in smaller markets. Likewise, SBUs A, D, E, and I could represent either developing potential winners in large markets or established winners in small markets. In the majority of instances, however, the pattern of SBU sizes and positions depicted in this figure would correspond to a balanced ideal portfolio.

4. *Plot the firm's future portfolio.* An assessment of the current situation is complete only when the present portfolio is projected into the future. Assuming the present corporate and SBU strategies continue unchanged, top management should assess the probable impact likely changes to the corporation's task and societal environments will have on both future industry attractiveness and SBU competitive position. They should ask themselves whether future matrixes show an improving or deteriorating portfolio position. Is there a performance gap between projected and desired portfolios? If the answer is yes, there is a *strategic gap* that should be the stimulus to review the corporation's current mission, objectives, strategies, and policies.

Overall, the nine cell GE Business Screen is an improvement over the Boston Consulting Group growth-share matrix. It considers many more variables and does not lead to such simplistic conclusions. Nevertheless, it can get quite complicated and cumbersome. The calculations used in Tables 6.2 and 6.3 give the appearance of objectivity but are in reality subjective judgments that may vary from one person to another. Another shortcoming of this portfolio matrix is that it cannot effectively depict the positions of new products or SBUs in developing industries.

Fifteen Cell Product/Market Evolution Matrix

This matrix, based on the product life cycle, was developed by Hofer to depict the developing types of products or SBUs that cannot be easily shown on the GE Business Screen. Products or SBUs are plotted in terms of their competitive positions and their stages of product/market evolution.[32] As with the GE Business Screen, the circles represent the sizes of the industries involved with the pie wedges representing the market shares of the firm's SBUs or products. Present and future matrixes can be developed to identify strategic issues. In Fig. 6.5, for example, one could ask why product or SBU B does not have a greater share of the market, given its strong competitive position.[33]

6.6 REVIEW OF MISSION AND OBJECTIVES

A reexamination of a corporation's current mission and objectives must be done before alternative strategies can be generated and evaluated. The seriousness of this step is emphasized by Tregoe and Zimmerman.

> When making a decision, there is an almost universal tendency to concentrate on the alternatives—the action possibilities—rather than on the objectives we want to achieve. This tendency is widespread because it is much easier to deal with alternative courses of action that exist right here

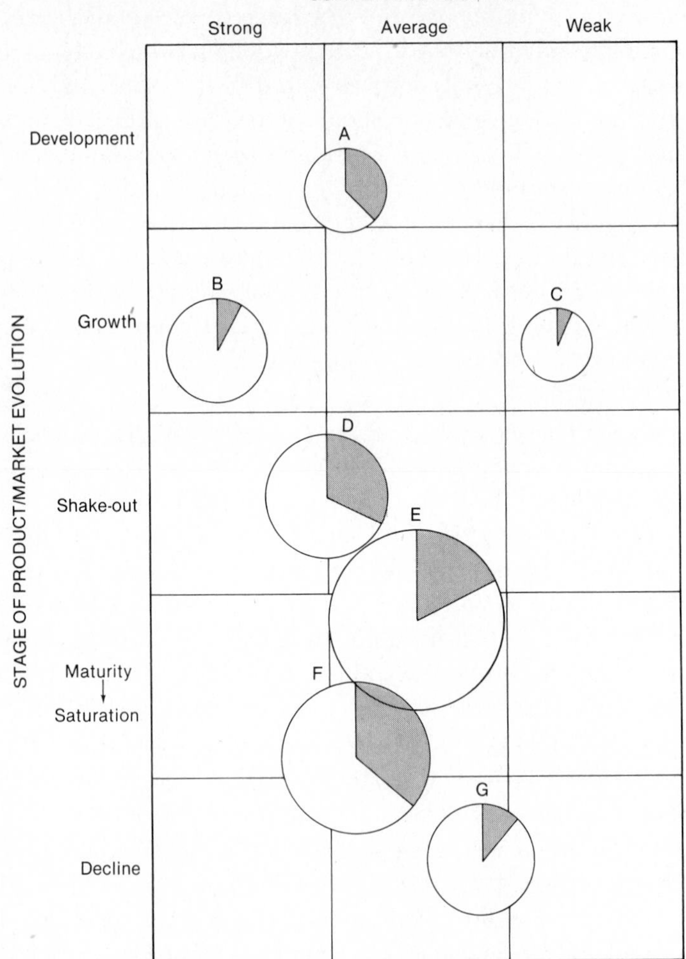

Figure 6.5 **Product/market evolution portfolio matrix.**

SOURCE: C. W. Hofer and D. Schendel, *Strategy Formulation: Analytical Concepts* (St. Paul, Minn: West Publishing Co., 1978), p. 34. From C. W. Hofer, "Conceptual Constructs for Formulating Corporate and Business Strategies" (Dover, Mass: Case Publishing), no. BP-0041, p. 3. Copyright © 1977 by Charles W. Hofer. Reprinted by permission.

> and now than to really think about what we want to accomplish in the future. Projecting a set of values forward is hard work. The end result is that we make choices that set our objectives for us, rather than having our choices incorporate clear objectives.[34]

Problems in corporate performance may derive from an inappropriate statement of mission, which may be too narrow or too broad. If the mission does not provide a common thread for a corporation's businesses, managers may be unclear about where the corporation is heading. Objectives and strategies may be in conflict with each other. Divisions may be competing against one another, rather than against outside competition—to the detriment of the corporation as a whole. According to Lorange, "Rapid changes in the environment suggest that the definition of businesses should be reviewed frequently, so that the relevance of the business definitions can be maintained."[35]

An example of a revision of a corporation's mission statement is that by American Telephone and Telegraph (AT&T). The revised mission was published in AT&T's 1980 annual report to the stockholders and had important implications for future corporate strategy:

> No longer do we perceive that our business will be limited to telephony or, for that matter, telecommunications. Ours is the business of information handling, the knowledge business. And the market that we seek is global.

A corporation's objectives may also be inappropriately stated. They may either focus too much on short-term operational goals or be so general that they provide little real guidance. Consequently, objectives should be constantly reviewed to ensure their usefulness.

6.7 SUMMARY AND CONCLUSION

This chapter describes the key activities involved in the process of formulating strategy. Following the strategic decision-making process introduced in Chapter 2, formulation is described as being composed of six distinct steps. Situation analysis incorporates five steps beginning with the evaluation of current performance results and ending with the review and revision of mission and objectives. Step six—the generation, evaluation, and selection of the best alternative strategy—is discussed in the next chapter.

Step 1—the evaluation of current performance results and the review of the corporation's mission, objectives, strategies, and policies—deals with the initial stimulus to start the formulation process. *Step 2*, the review of strategic managers, includes an evaluation of the competencies, level of involvement, and performance of the corporation's top management and board of directors. *Step 3*, scanning the external environment, focuses on collecting information, selecting strategic factors, and forecasting future events likely to affect the corporation's strategic decisions. *Step 4*, scanning the internal environment, deals with the assessment of internal strengths and weaknesses in terms of structure, culture, and resources. *Step 5(a)*, analysis of strategic factors in light of the current situation, proposes S.W.O.T. analysis and portfolio analysis as techniques to locate a business' propitious niche. Matrixes developed by the Boston Consulting Group, General Electric, and Hofer are described as three ways to compare business strengths with industry attractiveness. *Step 5(b)*, review and revision of the mission and objectives, completes the situation analysis by forcing a strategic manager to reexamine corporate purpose and objectives before initiating alternative strategies.

DISCUSSION QUESTIONS

1. Does strategy formulation need to be a regular continuous process? Explain.
2. Is it necessary that a corporation have a "common thread" running through its many activities in order to be successful? Why or why not?
3. What set of objectives might a typical university have?
4. What is likely to happen to an SBU that loses its propitious niche?
5. What value has portfolio analysis in the consideration of strategic factors?
6. Compare and contrast S.W.O.T. analysis with portfolio analysis.
7. Is the GE Business Screen just a more complicated version of the Boston Consulting Group growth/share matrix? Why or why not?
8. Is portfolio analysis used to formulate strategy at the corporate, divisional, or functional level of the corporation?

NOTES

1. H. Mintzberg, "Planning on the Left Side and Managing on the Right," *Harvard Business Review* (July–August 1976), p. 56.
2. P. Lorange, *Implementation of Strategic Planning* (Englewood Cliffs, N.J.: Prentice-Hall, 1982), p. 130.
3. J. A. Pearce, III, "The Company Mission as a Strategic Tool," *Sloan Management Review* (Spring 1982), pp. 15–24.
   W. R. Stone and D. F. Heany, "Dealing with a Corporate Identity Crisis," *Long Range Planning* (February 1984), pp. 10–18.
4. B. E. Gup, *Guide to Strategic Planning* (New York: McGraw-Hill, 1980), p. 12.
5. H. I. Ansoff, *Corporate Strategy* (New York: McGraw-Hill, 1965), pp. 104–108.
6. A. A. Thompson, Jr., and A. J. Stricklin, III, *Strategic Management: Concepts and Cases,* 3rd ed. (Plano, Tex.: Business Publications, Inc., 1984), pp. 48–49.
7. K. R. Andrews, "Directors' Responsibility for Corporate Strategy," *Harvard Business Review* (November–December 1980), p. 30.
8. R. B. Robinson, Jr., and J. A. Pearce, III, "Research Thrusts in Small Firm Strategic Planning," *Academy of Management Review* (January 1984), pp. 128–137.
9. F. R. Vancil and P. Lorange, "Strategic Planning in Diversified Companies," *Harvard Business Review* (January–February 1975), p. 81.

10. J. Bussey, "Gould Reshapes Itself into High-Tech Outfit amid Much Turmoil," *Wall Street Journal* (October 3, 1985), p. 1.

11. S. Weiner, "Much of Old Montgomery Ward May Go as Pistner Seeks Profitability, New Image," *Wall Street Journal* (June 15, 1981), p. 23.

12. T. Hall, "For a Company Chief, When There's a Whim There's Often a Way," *Wall Street Journal* (October 1, 1984), p. 1.

13. H. Mintzberg, "Strategy-Making in Three Modes," *California Management Review* (Winter 1973), pp. 44–53.

14. J. Kirkpatrick, "Tandy Corp. Survives Loss of Legendary Entrepreneur," (Charlottesville, Va.) *Daily Progress* (July 8, 1981), p. B14.

15. S. Schoeffler, "The PIMS Program," in K. J. Albert (ed.), *The Strategic Management Handbook* (New York: McGraw-Hill, 1983), pp. 23.1–23.10.

16. G. Badler, "Strategizing for a Spectrum of Possibilities," *Planning Review* (July 1984), pp. 28–31.

17. Badler, p. 28.
R. G. Wakerly, "PIMS: A Tool for Developing Competitive Strategy," *Long Range Planning* (June 1984), p. 95.

18. C. Y. Woo, "Market-Share Leadership—Not Always So Good," *Harvard Business Review* (January–February 1984), pp. 50–54.
J. K. Newton, "Market Share—Key to Higher Profitability?" *Long Range Planning* (February 1983), pp. 37–41.

19. V. Ramanujan and N. Venkatraman, "An Inventory and Critique of Strategy Research Using the PIMS Database," *Academy of Management Review* (January 1984), p. 147.

20. W. H. Newman, "Shaping the Master Strategy of Your Firm," *California Management Review*, vol. 9, no. 3 (1967), pp. 77–88.

21. D. F. Abell, "Strategic Windows," *Journal of Marketing* (July 1978), pp. 21–26, as reported by K. R. Harrigan, "Entry Barriers in Mature Manufacturing Industries" in R. Lamb (ed.), *Advances in Strategic Management*, Vol. 2 (Greenwich, Conn.: Jai Press, 1983), pp. 67–97.

22. D. K. Clifford and R. E. Cavanagh, "The Winning Performance of Midsized Growth Companies," *Planning Review* (November 1984), pp. 18–23, 35.

23. R. A. Bettis and W. K. Hall, "Strategic Portfolio Management in the Multibusiness Firm," *California Management Review* (Fall 1981), p. 23.

24. B. Hedley, "Strategy and the Business Portfolio," *Long Range Planning* (February 1977), p. 9.

25. Hedley, pp. 12–13.

26. D. C. Hambrick, I. C. MacMillan, and D. L. Day, "Strategic Attributes and Performance in the BCG Matrix—A PIMS-Based Analysis of Industrial Product Businesses," *Academy of Management Journal* (September 1982), pp. 510–531.
D. C. Hambrick and I. C. MacMillan, "The Product Portfolio and Man's Best Friend," *California Management Review* (Fall 1982), pp. 84–95.

27. C. Y. Woo and A. C. Cooper, "The Surprising Case for Low Market Share," *Harvard Business Review* (November–December 1982), pp. 106–113.

28. C. W. Hofer and D. Schendel, *Strategy Formulation: Analytical Concepts* (St. Paul: West Publishing Co., 1978), pp. 31–32.
P. McNamee, "Competitive Analysis Using Matrix Displays," *Long Range Planning* (June 1984), pp. 98–114.
R. E. Walker, "Portfolio Analysis in Practice," *Long Range Planning* (June 1984), pp. 63–71.
J. A. Seeger, "Reversing the Image of BCG's Growth/Share Matrix," *Strategic Management Journal* (January–March 1984) pp. 93–97.

29. W. K. Hall, "SBUs: Hot, New Topic in the Management of Diversification," *Business Horizons* (February 1978), p. 20.

30. Hofer and Schendel, pp. 32–33.

31. Hofer and Schendel, pp. 72–87.

32. Similar to the Hofer model, but using twenty instead of fifteen cells is the Arthur D. Little (ADL) strategic planning matrix. For details see M. B. Coate, "Pitfalls in Portfolio Planning," *Long Range Planning* (June 1983), pp. 47–56.

33. Hofer and Schendel, pp. 33–34.

34. B. B. Tregoe and J. W. Zimmerman, "The New Strategic Manager," *Business* (May–June 1981), p. 19.

35. Lorange, p. 211.

Chapter 7

STRATEGY FORMULATION: STRATEGIC ALTERNATIVES

STRATEGIC MANAGEMENT MODEL

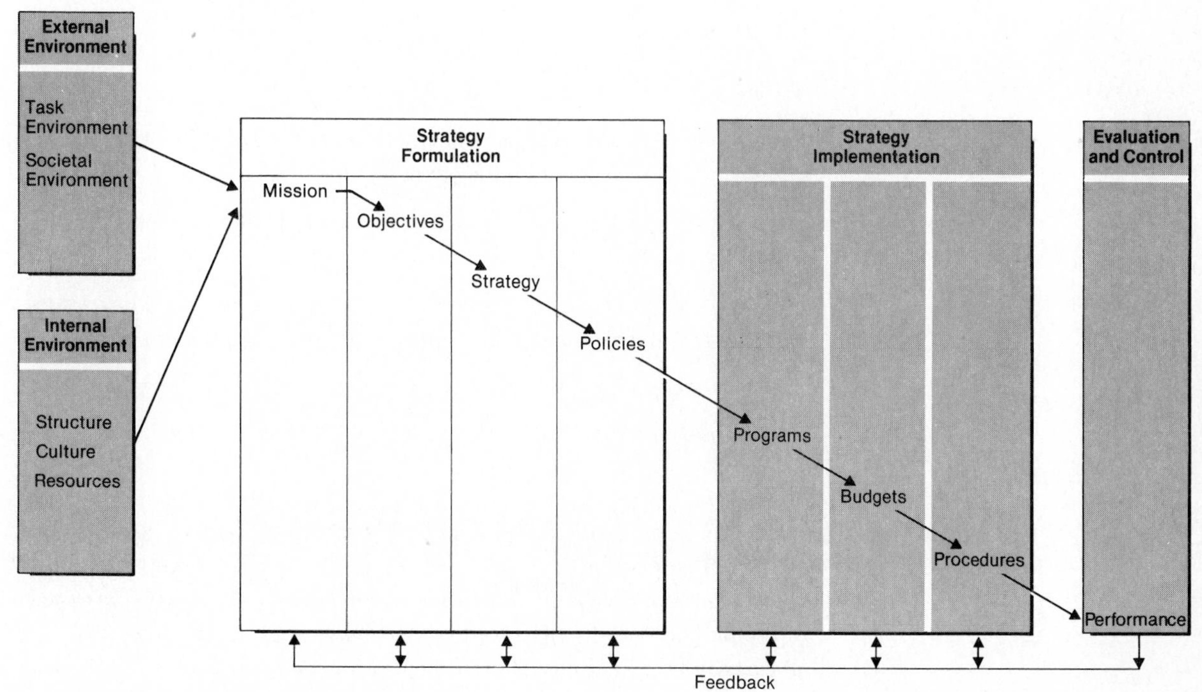

A key part of strategy formulation is the development of alternative courses of action that specify means by which the corporate mission and objectives are to be accomplished. As explained in Chapter 6 and depicted in Fig. 6.1, the generation, evaluation, and selection of the best strategic alternative is the sixth step of the strategic decision-making process. Once the best strategy is selected, appropriate policies must be established to define the ground rules for implementation. This chapter, therefore, will (a) explain the many alternative strategies available at the corporate, divisional, and functional levels of the corporation; (b) suggest criteria to use in the evaluation of these strategies; (c) explain how an optimal strategy is selected; and (d) suggest how strategy is translated into policies.

7.1 ALTERNATIVE STRATEGIES

There is no one set of strategies that can be used at all levels of a corporation. Most likely, a company will need both corporate and functional-level strategies. If it is in many different industries, the corporation will also have to develop divisional or SBU strategies for its families of related products or businesses.

Corporate Strategies

Prefaced by the broad question, "What should our corporation be like in the future?" top management should ask the following questions in order to develop strategic alternatives:[1]

1. Should we stay in the same business(es)?
2. Should we leave this business entirely or just some parts of it by merging, liquidating, and/or selling part of our corporation?
3. Should we become more efficient or effective in the business(es) we are presently in?
4. Should we try to grow in this business by (a) increasing our present size and market or (b) acquiring corporations in similar businesses?
5. Should we try to grow primarily by expanding into other businesses?
6. Should we use different strategies in different parts of the corporation?

If question 1 is answered yes, top management will probably choose a *stability* strategy. If question 2 or 3 is yes, *retrenchment* is a likely strategy. If either question 4 or 5 is yes, a *growth* strategy is appropriate. If question 6 is yes, top management should adopt a *combination* of strategies.

An analysis by Glueck of the strategic choices of 358 executives over a period of 45 years found the following frequency of usage of the four overall strategies:[2]

Stability:	9.2%
Growth:	54.4%
Retrenchment:	7.5%
Combination:	28.7%

Stability Strategies

The *stability* family of strategies is appropriate for a successful corporation operating in a reasonably predictable environment. Epitomized by a steady-as-she-goes philosophy, these strategies involve no major changes. A corporation concentrates its resources on its present businesses in order to build upon and improve its competitive advantage. It retains the same mission and similar objectives; it simply increases its level of achievement by approximately the same percentage each year. Its main strategic decisions concern improving the performance of functional areas. Some stability strategies are as follows:

No-change strategy In this strategy, a corporation continues on its course only with an adjustment for inflation in its objectives. Rarely articulated as a definite strategy, the success of a no-change strategy depends on a lack of change in a corporation's internal or external environments. This strategy may evolve from a lack of interest in or need to engage in hard strategic analysis. After all, if everything is going along fine, why change anything?

Profit strategy The profit strategy involves the sacrifice of future growth for present profits. The result is often short-term success coupled to long-term stagnation. By reducing expenditures for R&D, maintenance, or advertising, short-term profits increase and are reflected in the stockholders' dividends. If a corporation has a number of "cash cow" divisions, they can be "milked" of more cash than they spend. For example, when times were tough for railroads in the 1960s, a number of firms chose to meet expenses and prop up their annual dividends by cutting back on track maintenance. Unfortunately, difficulties continued into the 1970s, and the railroad track continued to deteriorate. On some sections, the trains were restricted to less than 20 miles per hour because of the poor track conditions! Obviously, the profit strategy is only useful to help a company get through a temporary difficulty. Unfortunately, the profit strategy is seductive and if continued long enough will lead to bankruptcy.

Pause strategy After a period of prolonged fast growth, a corporation may become inefficient or unmanageable. The addition of new divisions through acquisition or internal development can stretch management and resources thin. A pause strategy involves reducing the levels of a corporation's objectives so that it is able to consolidate its resources. The strategy is generally considered temporary—a way to get a corporate house in order. For example, after acquiring more than 150 companies and selling off about 75 of them since 1952, W. R. Grace and Company turned to consolidating organizationally its myriad holdings in chemicals, natural resources, and consumer goods.[3]

Proceed-with-caution strategy This strategy results from a specific decision to proceed slowly because of important factors developing in the external environment. Top management may feel that a growth strategy is no longer feasible given, for instance, a sudden scarcity of needed raw materials, new governmental regulations, or a poor economic climate.

Growth Strategies

Growth strategies are extremely popular because most executives tend to equate growth with success. Those corporations that are in dynamic environments *must* grow in order to survive. Growth means greater sales and a chance to take advantage of the experience curve to reduce the per unit cost of products sold, thereby increasing profits. This becomes extremely important if a corporation's industry is growing quickly and competitors are engaging in price wars in order to gain larger shares of the market. Those firms that have not reached "critical mass" (that is, gained the necessary economy of large-scale production) will face large losses unless they can find and fill a small, but profitable, niche.

Growth is a very seductive strategy for two key reasons:

- A growing firm can cover up mistakes and inefficiences more easily than can a stable one. A growing flow of revenue into a highly leveraged corporation can create a large amount of "organization slack"[4] (unused resources) that can be used to quickly resolve problems and conflicts between departments and divisions.
- There are more opportunities for advancement, promotion, and interesting jobs in a growing firm. Growth, per se, is exciting and ego-enhancing for CEOs. A growing corporation tends to be seen as a "winner" or "on the move" by the marketplace and by potential investors.

Vertical integration strategy The vertical integration strategy is the strategy of a corporation that enters one or more businesses that are necessary to the manufacture and distribution of its own products but that were previously purchased from other companies. These can range from the obtaining of raw materials to the merchandising of the product. *Backward integration* is the corporation's entry into the business of supplying some of its present raw materials. Henry Ford I achieved this when he built his own steel mill to supply Ford's assembly lines. *Forward integration* is the entry of the corporation into the business of distributing its product by entering marketing channels closer to the ultimate consumer. This is common in the tire industry where manufacturers, such as Firestone and Goodyear, own and manage their own retail outlets. More recently, IBM has opened retail stores in order to market its personal computers directly to the consumer. Backward and forward integration as well as other popular growth strategies are depicted in Fig. 7.1.

Vertical integration is quite common in the oil, rubber, basic metal, automobile, and forest products industries. As pointed out in Table 7.1, some of the advantages are lower costs and improved coordination and control. Although backward integration is usually more profitable than forward integration,[5] it can reduce a corporation's strategic flexibility by an

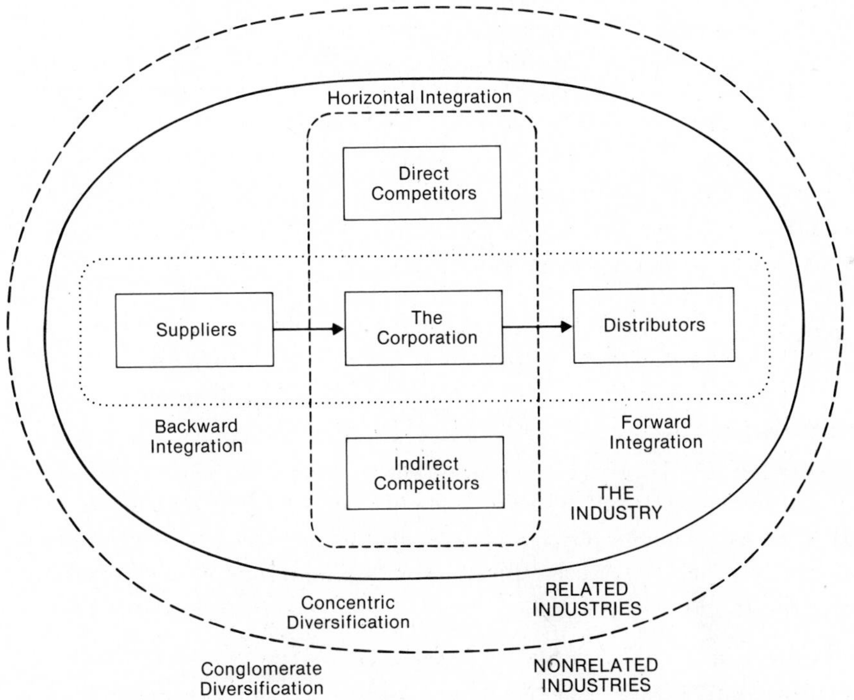

Figure 7.1 **Basic growth strategies.**
SOURCE: Suggested by C. W. Hofer as part of his presentation with J. J. Chrisman of "First Diversification and the Strategic Management Process: A New Perspective," a paper presented to the Academy of Management, Boston, Massachusetts, August 1984.

Table 7.1 Some Advantages and Disadvantages of Vertical Integration

Advantages	Disadvantages
Internal benefits	*Internal costs*
Integration economies reduce costs by eliminating steps, reducing duplicate overhead, and cutting costs (technology dependent)	Need for overhead to coordinate vertical integration increased costs
Improved coordination of activities reduces inventorying and other costs	Burden of excess capacity from unevenly balanced minimum efficient scale plants (technology dependent)
Avoid time-consuming tasks, such as price shopping, communicating design details, or negotiating contracts	Poorly organized vertically integrated firms do not enjoy synergies that compensate for higher costs
Competitive benefits	*Competitive dangers*
Avoid foreclosure to inputs, services, or markets	Obsolete processes may be perpetuated
Improved marketing or technological intelligence	Creates mobility (or exit) barriers
Opportunity to create product differentiation (increased value added)	Links firm to sick adjacent businesses
Superior control of firm's economic environment (market power)	Lose access to information from suppliers or distributors
Create credibility for new products	Synergies created through vertical integration may be overrated
Synergies could be created by coordinating vertical activities skillfully	Managers integrated before thinking through the most appropriate way to do so

SOURCE: K. R. Harrigan, "Formulating Vertical Integration Strategies," *Academy of Management Review* (October 1984), p. 639.

encumbrance of expensive assets that may be hard to sell and thus create an exit barrier to leaving that particular industry.[6]

A study by Harrigan reveals at least four types of vertical integration ranging from *full integration* to *long-term contracts.*[7] For example, if a corporation does not want to have the disadvantages of full vertical integration, it may choose either *taper* or *quasi-integration* strategies. With taper integration, a firm partially produces its own requirements and buys the rest from outside suppliers. In the case of quasi-integration, a company gets most of its requirements from an outside supplier which is under its partial control. IBM, for example, purchased 20% of the common stock of Intel Corporation in order to guarantee IBM's access to 16-bit microprocessors for its personal computers.[8]

Horizontal integration strategy The acquisition by a corporation of another corporation in the same industry is called horizontal integration. The term is applied primarily to those corporations that predominantly operate in one industry, such as Ford Motor Company or Heileman Brewing Company. Since the acquiring firm is thus buying a competitor, such a transaction is liable to antitrust suits. The corporation's objective may be to become more efficient through larger economies of scale, to enter another geographic market, or simply to reduce competition for supplies and customers. Renault's acquisition of American Motors is one example of horizontal integration. United Airlines' acquisition in 1985 of Pan American World Airways' Pacific division was another example.

Diversification strategy This is the strategy of adding *different* products or divisions to the corporation. There are two types of diversification—concentric and conglomerate.

Concentric diversification is the addition to a corporation of *related* products or divisions. The corporation's lines of business still possess some "common thread" that serves to relate them in some manner. The point of commonality may be similar technology, customer usage, distribution, managerial skills, or product similarity. An example of concentric diversification was the addition of "Eagle Snacks" to Anheuser-Busch's successful line of beers.

Conglomerate diversification, in contrast to concentric diversification, is the addition to the firm of *unrelated* products or divisions. Rather than keeping a common thread throughout their corporation, top managers who adopt this strategy are primarily concerned with a return on investment criterion: Will it increase the corporation's level of profitability? The addition may, however, be justified in terms of strategic fit. A cash-rich corporation with few opportunities for growth in its industry may, for example, move into another industry where opportunities are great, but cash hard to find. An example of this strategy was the purchase of Vydec Corporation, a maker of word processors, by Exxon Corporation, the oil company. Another instance of conglomerate diversification might be the purchase by a corporation with a seasonal and, therefore, uneven cash flow of a firm in an unrelated industry with complementing seasonal sales that will level out the cash flow.

Beginning with a classic study of Rumelt, researchers in the area have concluded consistently that diversification into other industries (unrelated or conglomerate) does *not* increase the profitability of a business corporation.[9] Peters and Waterman support the developing chorus in favor of concentric over conglomerate diversification.

> Our principal finding is clear and simple. Organizations that do branch out (whether by acquisition or internal diversification) but stick very close to their knitting outperform the others. The most successful of all are those diversified around a single skill—the coating and bonding technology at 3M, for example.

> The second group, in descending order, comprises those companies that branch out into related fields—the leap from electric power generation turbines to jet engines (another turbine) from GE, for example.
>
> Least successful, as a general rule, are those companies that diversify into a wide variety of fields. Acquisitions especially, among this group, tend to wither on the vine.[10]

Supporting this argument is the recent increase in spinoffs by conglomerate corporations of formerly acquired units. In the past few years ITT, RCA, Gulf & Western, Beatrice Foods, Quaker Oats, General Electric, Exxon, and R. J. Reynolds have sold off major nonrelated holdings.

Nevertheless, a study by *Fortune* magazine provides contrary results. The study compared the performance of the 39 largest conglomerates with the performance of the 226 largest nondiversified industrial companies on the Fortune 500 list. It found that although nondiversified companies did produce a higher median return on shareholder equity in 1978 and 1979 than did conglomerates, results were about equal in 1980. During the next three years (1981–1983), however, the conglomerates outperformed the nondiversified companies. In examining the results, Roy Little, founder of the huge conglomerate Textron, International, concluded:

> My basic concept of unrelated diversification is as sound as ever. The bad reputation the conglomerates acquired in the late 1960s and early 1970s just doesn't square with the facts today. . . . A well-run diversified company shouldn't ever lose money.[11]

The argument appears to be far from settled.

Mergers, acquisitions, and joint ventures Corporations may engage in strategic mergers, acquisitions, and joint ventures in order to attain *synergy* (the 2 + 2 = 5 effect). Two corporations so involved are able to achieve more by working together than they could by acting separately. Different types of synergy are possible:

1. *Sales synergy* exists when many products use the same distribution channels.
2. *Operating synergy* exists when many products use the same manufacturing facilities and personnel, thereby distributing the overhead among more products.
3. *Management synergy* exists when managerial skills and abilities can be transferred from one corporation or industry to solving problems in another.
4. *Technological synergy* exists when R&D personnel and techniques can be combined for greater effectiveness.

A *merger* is a transaction involving two or more corporations in which stock is exchanged, but from which only one corporation survives. Mergers are usually between firms of somewhat similar size and are usually "friendly." The resulting firm is likely to have a name derived from its composite firms. One example is the merging of Allied Corporation and Signal Companies to form Allied Signal.

An *acquisition* is the purchase of a corporation that is completely absorbed as an operating subsidiary or division of the acquiring corporation. An example is the acquisition by U.S. Steel of Marathon Oil. Acquisitions are usually between firms of different sizes and can be either "friendly" or "unfriendly." A friendly acquisition usually begins with the acquiring corporation discussing its desires with the other firm's top management. In return for fair consideration after acquisition, the top management of the firm to be acquired agrees to work for the acquisition. Friendly acquisitions are thus very similar to mergers. Unfriendly acquisitions, in contrast, are often called "takeovers." The acquiring firm ignores the other firm's top management or board of directors and simply begins buying up the other firm's stock until it owns a controlling interest. The takeover target, in response, begins defensive maneuvers, such as buying up its own stock, calling in the Justice Department to initiate an anti-trust suit in order to stop the acquisition, or looking for a friendly merger partner (as Gulf Oil did with Standard Oil of California when Texas oilman T. Boone Pickens mounted a takeover effort to buy Gulf's stock).

Slang terms are very popular in mergers and acquisitions. For example, a "pigeon" (highly vulnerable target) or "sleeping beauty" (more desirable than a pigeon) may take a "cyanide pill" (taking on a huge long-term debt on the condition that the debt falls due immediately upon the firm's acquisition) in order to avoid being "raped" (forcible hostile takeover sometimes accompanied by looting the target's profitability) by a "shark" (extremely predatory takeover artist) using "hired guns" (lawyers, merger and acquisition specialists, and certain investment bankers).[12] To avoid takeover threats, a number of corporations have chosen to stagger the elections of board members (discussed in Chapter 3), prohibit two-tier tender offers (the offering of a higher price to stockholders who sell their shares first), prohibit "greenmail" (the buying back of a company's stock from a "shark" at a premium price), and require an 80% shareholder vote to approve a takeover. The ultimate countermeasure appears to be the *poison pill*, a procedure granting present shareholders the right to acquire at a substantial discount a large equity stake in an acquiring company whose offer does not have the support of the acquired company's board of directors. For an interesting application of a "takeover" strategy, see Illustrative Example 7.1.

Illustrative Example 7.1

USE OF TAKEOVER STRATEGY AT TYCO LABORATORIES, INC.

Tyco Laboratories, Inc., a miniconglomerate based in New Hampshire, has adopted an interesting growth strategy. The stated aim of Tyco's president, Joseph S. Gaziano, is to make Tyco grow through acquisitions. Gaziano, according to Lynch, ". . . likes to muse that Tyco one day might be as well known as International Telephone and Telegraph Co.—with Mr. Gaziano ranked right up there with his idol, former ITT chairman Harold Geneen."

Tyco usually begins by buying the stock of another corporation on the open market. If the other firm objects, Mr. Gaziano becomes very aggressive. He once appeared at a takeover target's stockholders meeting and loudly demanded a meeting with the CEO. As in the case of his attempt to acquire Leeds and Northrup, he sometimes promises to fire the top executives, so his demand was tantamount to a threat. In 1979, Tyco acquired some shares of Trane Company, an air-conditioner manufacturer, for $43 each. So fearful was Trane of Gaziano's takeover tactics, it paid Tyco $50 per share to get its shares back. At the time, Trane's common stock was trading at less than $40 a share.

Tyco's attempt to acquire Ludlow Corporation took two and a half years to complete. Ludlow, a packaging and furniture concern, fought Tyco's advances at every step. At the beginning of his takeover attempt, Mr. Gaziano cited Ludlow's $22 million in cash as a reason for the bid. In order to avoid Tyco's grasp, Ludlow used the cash to acquire a packaging concern—a decision that has resulted in lower profits for Ludlow.

So far, Mr. Gaziano's use of the takeover strategy has been extremely profitable. Even in those attempts when a second bidder wins a takeover battle by paying a higher price, Tyco is able to sell the acquired stock at a much higher price than it paid for it. On three takeover attempts that failed, Tyco earned approximately $15 million.

SOURCE: M. C. Lynch, "Tyco's Successful Acquisition Still Leaves Questions about Gaziano's Grand Design," *Wall Street Journal* (August 27, 1981), p. 21.

A *joint venture* is the strategy of forming a temporary partnership or consortium for the purpose of gaining synergy. Joint ventures occur because the corporations involved do not wish to or cannot legally merge permanently. Joint ventures provide a way to temporarily fit the different strengths of partners together in order to achieve an outcome of value to both. For example, IBM, CBS, and Sears have formed a joint venture to develop and market *videotex*—the sending and receiving of words and pictures to at-home video screens by which people can order merchandise, do banking, and carry out other functions. A major innovation in the joint venture plan is to send the data to computers instead of to special-purpose video-screen terminals. CBS has experience with advertisers, news reporting, and publishing. Sears can use the venture to market its merchandise catalogue and financial services products electronically.[13] Joint ventures are extremely popular in international undertakings because of financial and political–legal constraints. They are also a convenient way for a privately owned and publicly owned (state-owned) corporation to work together. Joint ventures are discussed further in Chapter 10.

Mergers, acquisitions, and joint ventures are often combined with vertical and horizontal integration, and with diversification. As mentioned earlier, Henry Ford I vertically integrated backward by using his own and Ford Motor's cash to build a steel mill for his River Rouge Plant. Cincinnati Milacron diversified concentrically with its own resources into making industrial robots on the basis of its traditional excellence in manufacturing high-quality machine tools. In contrast, many corporations, such as DuPont and Philip Morris, grew externally; DuPont vertically integrated by acquiring Conoco to assure oil supplies for the manufacture of its petroleum-based synthetics; Philip Morris diversified concentrically in the acquisitions of Miller Brewing Company and Seven-Up Corporation so that it could apply its consumer marketing expertise to other industries.

Concentration strategy A corporation may choose to grow by concentrating all of its resources in the development of a single product or product line, single market, or single technology. Corporations such as McDonald's (fast food), Caterpillar (construction equipment), and Gerber (baby products) that concentrate their efforts on a single product line are able to stay ahead of competitors who dilute their effort in many industries. Gerber, for example, failed miserably when it tried to diversify into adult foods, mail-order insurance, and day-care centers. With a 71% share of the baby food market, Gerber decided that concentrating on selling a little more each year to a few more mothers was its best strategy.[14]

These firms can organize on a functional or geographical basis with no need for divisions. The very real advantages inherent in a concentration strategy may have been one reason why many large multi-industry, multi-product corporations have begun to reorganize themselves around strategic business units. Such concentration allows the corporation to put more time, energy, and resources into developing innovative product strategies through market penetration, market development, and product development. For an example of an effective use of the concentration strategy, see Illustrative Example 7.2.

Illustrative Example 7.2

CONCENTRATION STRATEGY AT CUMMINS ENGINE COMPANY

Cummins Engine Company has always been well known as a diesel-engine producer. Its real growth began after World War II, when truckers began clamoring for engines that cost less to run, lasted longer, and needed less maintenance than gasoline engines. In the late 1960s, however, top management at Cummins feared that the demand for diesel engines would slow. Noting the success of other corporations that tried diversification, Cummins acquired companies making products as unrelated as skis and computer software.

In the mid-1970s, top management reassessed the corporation. It had underestimated the demand for diesels. "We hadn't anticipated inflation or the beginning of the energy crisis," said Henry B. Schacht, Cummin's CEO and chairman. "The other businesses weren't bad, but we needed all of our capital to expand our diesel production." So in 1975 and 1976, Cummins divested itself of everything but its truck-engine line.

The crisis came in 1979. Cummins faced slumping demand for its engines. The economy was fading and the heavy truck industry was in recession. Top management made another strategic decision. They chose to stay in the diesel business and to devote the company's resources to its new engine line. This meant spending $900 million—nearly twice its net worth—to retool the engine line and develop new low-horsepower models to broaden its markets and to fend off Japanese and European competitors. Cummins cut the work force by 22% while pushing production to record levels. Break-even was reduced 31%; inventories were trimmed 40%. The union backed the strategy by signing a new contract three months ahead of schedule to keep up customer confidence in the firm.

The next four years were difficult ones for Cummins Engine. Truck-engine shipments dropped 36% in 1982. Earnings in 1983 were only $5.2 million. By 1984, sales and net income appeared to be improving at last. Mr. Schacht is optimistic about Cummin's single-product strategy. "We never felt we put the company in danger," he insists. Someday Cummins might try diversification again, he says, "but for quite a while, we think we can stick to our knitting."

SOURCE: H. S. Byrne, "Cummins Decides to Go with Its Strength as It Pins Hopes on Diesel Truck Engines," *Wall Street Journal* (July 3, 1984), p. 23.

Investment strategy Investment strategy is sometimes referred to as "grow to sell out." It is a way to maximize stockholder investment when the corporation is sold at an attractive price. An entrepreneur may build successfully a corporation for the purpose of selling it just at the point when competition becomes heavy and when further growth would require giving up control. The corporation is therefore viewed as an investment not only by the stockholders, but also by top management and the board of directors.

One example is that of Walter Cornett, an entrepreneur who started a nursing home chain, several medical supply companies, and a venture to raise Brahman bulls. Once each company became successful, Cornett sold it for a profit, paid the investors, and began a new company. The venture capitalists were interested in a quick return on their investment and Cornett was interested in starting (but not managing) a series of new businesses.[15]

Retrenchment Strategies

Retrenchment strategies are relatively unpopular because retrenchment seems to imply failure—that something has gone wrong with previous strategies. With these strategies there *is* a great deal of pressure to improve performance. As with the coaches of losing football teams, the CEO is typically under pressure to do something quickly or be fired.

Turnaround strategy The turnaround strategy emphasizes improving operational efficiency. It is appropriate when a corporation's problems are pervasive, but not yet critical. Analogous to going on a diet, a turnaround strategy includes two initial phases. The first phase is *contraction,* the initial effort to reduce size and costs. It typically involves a general cutback in personnel and all noncritical expenditures. Hiring stops, and across-the-board reductions in R&D, advertising, training, supplies, and services are usual. The second phase is *consolidation,* the development of a program to stabilize the leaner corporation. An in-depth audit is conducted in order to identify areas where long-run improvements can be made in corporate efficiency. Plans are developed to streamline the corporation by reducing unnecessary overhead and to make functional activities "cost-effective." Financial expenditures in all areas must be justified on the basis of their contribution to profits. This is a crucial time for the corporation. If the consolidation phase is not conducted in a positive manner, many of the best people will leave the organization. If, however, all employees are encouraged to get involved in productivity improvements, the corporation likely may emerge from this strategic retrenchment period a much stronger and better organized company.

If the corporation successfully emerges from these two phases of contraction and consolidation, it is then able to enter a third phase, *rebuilding.* At this point, an attempt is made to once again expand the business.[16] For an example of an effective use of the turnaround strategy, see Illustrative Example 7.3.

TURNAROUND STRATEGY AT TORO COMPANY

Illustrative Example 7.3

Top management at Toro Company was astonished when a 1974 marketing survey showed the brand name of the little lawn-mower manufacturer ranked second only to Hershey chocolate in consumer recognition. They

(*Continued*)

Illustrative Example 7.3 (Continued)

rushed to transform Toro by broadening both its product lines and distribution system. By 1979 the company had 33,000 new chain-store outlets to sell a stream of new products, such as lightweight snow-throwers and chain saws. Sales of $358 million with earnings of $17.4 million both tripled 1974 levels. "The idea is to make the Toro name an umbrella under which we can market just about anything," said Chairman David T. McLaughlin.

Seeds for disaster had been planted. The pressure to increase sales led to a slide in product quality. New products were rushed to market in the late 1970s and early 1980s without the usual time-consuming development and testing phases. The distribution of mowers and snow-throwers through mass merchandisers like K-Mart and J. C. Penney infuriated Toro's traditional dealer network. Not only were the dealers forced to compete with their own products being sold at lower prices by discounters; they were being stuck with servicing the products the discounters sold! Some dealers refused to service machines they did not sell and actually told prospective customers not to buy a Toro.

The crisis arrived when the two snowless winters of 1979–80 and 1980–81 plunged the company into ten straight quarters of losses. In early 1981, as sales fell from $400 million to $247 million annually, McLaughlin resigned as chairman. Before leaving, he fired 125 managers including Toro's president, John Cantu. The dismissals were probably long overdue. One manager admitted that the firm's staff was that of a billion-dollar company—far too large for a small company like Toro.

Executive Vice-President Kendrick Melrose was named president. The fight for survival began. Dividends were suspended. Melrose acted to cut the work force in half, to 1,800 people; cut sales and administrative costs by 23%; consolidated production to five plants from eight; and suspended production of snow-throwers until sales caught up with inventories two years later. More importantly, Melrose worked to salvage the dealer network by stopping sales to discounters of equipment that required servicing. He also improved Toro's inventory-support program, giving independent dealers and distributors more protection from losses when their inventories exceeded a "normal year's" level.

"The toughest decision was to terminate half the employment force," admitted President Melrose. "The second toughest was to go to the half that remained and tell them that not only do we have fewer resources, but we still need greater productivity, and that they're going to have to make some financial sacrifices." That meant no incentive compensation for executives for at least four years, salary freezes and mandatory furlough days for office employees, and wage freezes or reductions for hourly workers. Stringent controls were set in place to keep management aware of inventory levels. "Now we can go through a year with little snow and still be fairly solid," says Mr. Melrose. Embarrassed by Toro's poor-quality image,

(Continued)

the new president re-dedicated the company to quality and appointed a vice-president for product excellence.

By 1985, the Minneapolis firm was a much slimmer, more carefully managed, and apparently healthier company. Fiscal 1984 earnings were $8.3 million on sales of $280 million compared with a modest profit in 1983. Sales have not returned to pre-disaster levels and probably will not for some time. Nevertheless, the dividend has been restored and top management is cautiously optimistic. To keep costs down, some manufacturing is done outside the U.S. Parts are being produced in South Korea, Taiwan, Japan, and Singapore. An assembly plant has opened near Winnepeg, Manitoba. Fabrication joint ventures are under way in New Zealand and Venezuela.

As a result of its successes, Toro management has switched from what it called "a defensive, survival mode" to "a more opportunistic direction." Mr. Melrose put two executive vice-presidents in charge of day-to-day operations so that he could focus on new ventures. According to Melrose, the company is "emphasizing businesses that deliver high margins and don't have a lot of vulnerability on the downside," such as turf irrigation and commercial lawn care equipment. "Long-range planning is something new at Toro," he says. "In the past we didn't spend much time thinking about the future. We thought only about how we're going to get out of the mess."

SOURCES: R. Gibson, "Toro Breaks Out of Its Slump after Taking Drastic Measures," *Wall Street Journal* (January 23, 1985), p. 7. "Toro: Coming to Life after Warm Weather Wilted Its Big Plans," *Business Week* (October 10, 1983), p. 118.

Divestment strategy Divestment is appropriate when corporate problems can be traced to the poor performance of an SBU or product line or when a division or SBU is a "misfit," unable to synchronize itself with the rest of the corporation. This was the situation Exxon faced with its office systems division. The big oil company was unable to properly manage the acquired entrepreneurial units of Qwip, which made facsimile machines; Vydec, an early leader in word processors; and Qyx, which produced the first electronic typewriter. "Every move had to be reviewed and approved by oil men who just didn't understand the industry," said a former Exxon manager.[17]

Still another situation appropriate for divestment is that of a division's needing more resources to be competitive than a corporation is willing to provide. Some corporations, however, select divestment instead of the more painful turnaround strategy. With divestment, top management is able to do one of two things: (1) select a scapegoat to blame for all of the corporation's problems, or (2) generate a lot of cash in the sale, which can be used to reduce debt and buy time. The second rationale may explain why Pan American chose to sell the most profitable parts of its corporation, the Pan Am Building in New York and Intercontinental Hotels, while keeping its money-losing airline.[18]

Captive company strategy Rarely discussed as a separate strategy, the captive strategy is similar to divestment; but instead of selling off divisions or product lines, the corporation reduces the scope of some of its functional activities and becomes "captive" to another firm. In this manner, it reduces expenses and achieves some security through its relationship with the stronger firm. An agreement is reached with a key customer that in return for a large number of long-run purchases, the captive company will guarantee delivery at a favorable price. Since 75% or more of its product is sold to a single purchaser, the captive company can reduce its marketing expenditures and develop long-run production schedules that reduce costs. If supplies ever become a problem for the captive company, it can call on its key customer to help put pressure on a reluctant supplier.

One interesting version of this strategy has developed out of the recent popularity of "just-in-time" deliveries. Emulating successful Japanese firms, General Motors is building a plant for its new Saturn company. It plans to require its key suppliers to build *satellite plants* around the Saturn facility for the sole purpose of manufacturing parts to Saturn specifications and delivering them to the Saturn assembly lines as they are needed. These satellite plants will thus be *captive* to General Motors.

Liquidation strategy A strategy of last resort when other retrenchment strategies have failed, an early liquidation may serve stockholder interests better than an inevitable bankruptcy. To the extent that top management identifies with the corporation, liquidation is perceived as an admission of failure. Pride and reputation are liquidated as well as jobs and financial assets.

From their research of companies in difficulty, Nystrom and Starbuck conclude that top management very often does not perceive that crises are developing. When top managers do eventually notice trouble, they are prone to attribute the problems to temporary environmental disturbances and tend to follow profit strategies of postponing investments, reducing maintenance, halting training, liquidating assets, denying credit to customers, and raising prices. They adopt a weathering-the-storm attitude. "A major activity becomes changing the accounting procedures in order to conceal the symptoms."[19] Even when things are going terribly, there is a strong temptation for top management to avoid liquidation in the hope of a miracle. It is for this reason that a corporation needs a strong board of directors who can safeguard stockholder interests by telling top management when to quit.

Combination Strategies

Combination strategies can be composed of any number of variations of the preceding strategies. The main focus is on the conscious use of several overall strategies (stability, growth, retrenchment) in several SBUs at the same time or at different times in the future.[20]

Evaluation of Corporate Strategies

Before the selection of a particular corporate strategy, top management must critically analyze the pros and cons of each feasible alternative in light of the corporation's situation. The tendency to select the most obvious strategy can sometimes lead to serious trouble in the long run. The orientation of most top management toward growth strategies has resulted in a high value being placed on acquisitions and mergers as preferred alternatives. In fact, a survey of 236 chief executive officers of the largest 1,000 U.S. industrial firms found that CEOs prefer diversification and acquisition over new product planning and development as a growth strategy.[21] A similar survey of chief financial officers found that the major motive for acquiring another firm was to generate fast growth.[22] Not surprisingly, W. T. Grimm and Company, a merger broker which keeps records on mergers, acquisitions, and divestitures, reported these transactions for the first nine months of 1984 to total $103.2 billion—more than $20 billion higher than the prior period for a full year![23]

Nevertheless, it is estimated that because of poor planning, high prices, mismanaged consolidation, or bad luck, one-half to two-thirds of all acquisitions are ultimately failures.[24] The explanation may lie in top management's overestimating the benefits to be derived or from valuing too highly their own skills in managing a new business.

A number of techniques are available to aid strategic planners in estimating the likely effects of strategic changes. One of these was derived from the research project on the profit impact of market strategies (PIMS), which was discussed in Chapter 6. From the analysis of data from a large number of business corporations, key factors were identified in regression equations to explain large variations in ROI, profitability, and cash flow. As part of PIMS, reports are prepared for a participating corporation's business units showing how its expected level of ROI is influenced by each factor. A second report shows how ROI can be expected to change, both in the short and long runs, if particular changes are made in its strategy.[25]

Business (SBU) Strategies

Sometimes referred to as division strategy, business strategy focuses on improving the competitive position of a corporation's products or services within the specific industry or market segment that the division serves. It is a strategy developed by a division to complement the overall corporate strategy. Although many business strategies appear to be similar to corporate strategies, they differ in terms of their orientation to a specific market and to a specific line of business or product.

Portfolio Strategies

The nine cell matrix discussed in Chapter 6 as the GE Business Screen or the Directional Policy Matrix may be used to identify suggested business level strategies. The combination of industry attractiveness and competitive strengths provides a matrix of strategies, as depicted in Fig. 7.2.

Depending on the cell in which a division or product is placed, the matrix recommends one of the following eight strategies:[26]

1. *Disinvest.* Products falling in this area will probably be losing money—not necessarily every year; but losses in bad years will outweigh the gains in good years. It is unlikely that any activity will surprise management by falling within this area because its poor performance should already be known.

2. *Phased withdrawal.* A product with an average-to-weak position with low, unattractive market prospects, or a weak position with average market prospects is unlikely to be earning any significant amounts of cash. The indicated strategy is used to realize the value of the assets on a controlled basis in order to make resources available for employment elsewhere.

3. *Cash generator.* A typical situation in this matrix area is that of a product moving toward the end of its life cycle, which is being replaced in the market by other products. No finance should be allowed for expansion; and the product, so long as it is profitable, should be used as a source of cash for other areas. Every effort should be made to maximize

INDUSTRY ATTRACTIVENESS	BUSINESS STRENGTH/COMPETITIVE POSITION: Strong	Average	Weak
High	Leader	Try Harder	Double or Quit
Medium	Leader Growth	Growth Proceed with Care	Phased Withdrawal
Low	Cash Generator	Phased Withdrawal	Disinvest

Figure 7.2 Portfolio strategies.

profits, because activity concerning the product has no long-term future.

4. *Proceed with care.* In this position, some investment may be justified, but major investments should be made with extreme caution.
5. *Growth.* Investment should be made to allow the product to grow with the market. In general, the product will generate sufficient cash to be self-financing and will not be making demands on other corporate cash resources.
6. *Double or quit.* Tomorrow's breadwinners among today's R&D projects may come from this area. Putting the strategy simply, those with the best prospects should be selected for full backing and development. The rest should be abandoned.
7. *Try harder.* The implication is that the product can be moved toward the leader box by judicious application of resources. In these circumstances the division may wish to make available resources in excess of what the product can generate for itself.
8. *Leader.* The strategy should be to maintain a leading position. At certain stages this may imply that resources to expand capacity may be required, but that the cash required need not be met entirely from funds generated by the product, although its earnings should be above average.

The nine cell portfolio matrix can help a division or SBU develop appropriate alternative strategies. It is *not,* however, a push-button technique. It should be used sensibly and in conjunction with other methods. Portfolio analysis by its very nature tends to be somewhat simplistic. It may, for example, rule out what might be the very profitable strategy of being a minority producer in certain niche markets when industry attractiveness is very low.[27] When the eight portfolio strategies are considered in their most simplified form, they form the three popular strategies of *build, hold, or harvest.* Unfortunately, these are short-run cash-oriented terms that provide little, if any, guidance in developing a product line's business strength or competitive position.

Porter's Competitive Strategies

Porter, an authority on business level strategies, proposes three generic strategies for outperforming other corporations in a particular industry: overall cost leadership, differentiation, and focus.[28]

1. *Overall cost leadership.* This strategy requires "aggressive construction of efficient-scale facilities, vigorous pursuit of cost reductions from

experience, tight cost and overhead control, avoidance of marginal customer accounts, and cost minimization in areas like R&D, service, sales force, advertising, and so on."[29] Having a low-cost position gives an SBU a defense against rivals. Its lower costs allow it to continue to earn profits during times of heavy competition.

Backward vertical integration (a corporate-level strategy that can also be used at the divisional level) is one route to an overall low-cost position. For example, Humana, Inc., the hospital operator, has moved into the health insurance field as the low-cost competitor. It is able to underprice Blue Cross, Blue Shield because it controls the source of 60% of all medical bills, the hospital. "The one feature of our product that is clearly understood by employers is that because we own and operate hospitals, we can control costs," states William Werroven, chief operating officer of Humana's group health division.[30]

2. *Differentiation.* This strategy involves the creating of a product or service that is perceived throughout its industry as being unique. It may be accomplished through design or brand image, technology, features, dealer network, or customer service. Differentiation is a viable strategy for earning above-average returns in a specific business because the resulting brand loyalty lowers customer sensitivity to price.

   Examples of the successful use of a differentiation strategy are Walt Disney Productions, Maytag appliances, Mercedes-Benz automobiles, and Beech-Nut Nutrition Corporation. Owned by Nestlé, Beech-Nut has chosen to attack Gerber's 70% share of the baby food market by launching *Stages,* a line of 123 baby foods. The Stages line of products is color-coded to correspond to different stages of an infant's development. "Baby food was just a commodity sold entirely on price," says Niels Hoyvald, Beech-Nut's president and CEO. "I wanted to set us apart." Even though Stages costs 10 to 30% more than comparable products offered by the competition, it has managed to earn 50% of the business in a few of the markets in which it competes. Profits are up nicely.[31]

3. *Focus.* Similar to the corporate strategy of concentration, this business strategy focuses on a particular buyer group, product line segment, or geographic market. The value of the strategy derives from the belief that an SBU that focuses its efforts is better able to serve its narrow strategic target more effectively or efficiently than can its competition. Focus does, however, necessitate a trade-off between profitability and overall market share.

   The focus strategy has two variants: *cost focus* and *differentiation focus*. In cost focus, the company seeks a cost advantage in its target segment, while in differentiation focus, a company seeks differentiation in its target segment. "The target segments must either have buyers with unusual needs or else the production and delivery system that best serves the target must differ from that of the other industry segments."[32] A good example of cost focus is Hammermill Paper's move into low-volume, high-quality specialty papers. By focusing on the quality niche of the market, Hammermill is able to compete against larger companies which need high-volume production runs to reach break-even. Johnson Products, in contrast, has successfully used a differentiation focus by manufacturing and selling hair care and cosmetic products to black consumers. This strategy was most successful when the large cosmetics companies ignored the product preferences of the black community.

Porter argues that a business unit must achieve one of these three "generic" business strategies to be successful. Otherwise, the business unit is *stuck in the middle* of the competitive marketplace with no competitive advantage and is doomed to below-average performance.[33] Research generally supports Porter's contention.[34] Before selecting one of these strategies for a particular corporate business or SBU, it is important to assess its feasibility in terms of divisional strengths and weaknesses. Porter lists some of the commonly required skills and resources, as well as organizational requirements, in Table 7.2.

It is interesting to note that the strategic groups of Miles and Snow discussed in Chapter 4 can be characterized by their usage of Porter's competitive strategies. *Defenders* tend to use overall cost leadership, whereas *prospectors* tend to follow a differentiation or focus strategy. *Reactors* are those companies with no real competitive strategy who are "stuck in the middle." *Analyzers* use whichever competitive strategy is most appropriate for each of their various product lines or businesses.

Functional-Area Strategies

The principal focus of functional-area strategy is to maximize corporate and divisional resource productivity. Given the constraints of corporate and divisional strategies, functional-area strategies are developed to pull together the various activities and competencies of each function to improve performance. For example, a manufacturing department would be very concerned with developing a strategy to reduce costs and to improve the quality of its output. Marketing, in comparison, typically would be concerned with developing strategies to increase sales.

Some of the many possible functional strategies are listed in the decision

Table 7.2 Requirements for Generic Competitive Strategies

Generic Strategy	*Commonly Required Skills and Resources*	*Common Organizational Requirements*
Overall cost leadership	Sustained capital investment and access to capital Process engineering skills Intense supervision of labor Products designed for ease in manufacture Low-cost distribution system	Tight cost control Frequent, detailed control reports Structured organization and responsibilities Incentives based on meeting strict quantitative targets
Differentiation	Strong marketing abilities Product engineering Creative flair Strong capability in basic research Corporate reputation for quality or technological leadership Long tradition in the industry or unique combination of skills drawn from other businesses Strong cooperation from channels	Strong coordination among functions in R&D, product development, and marketing Subjective measurement and incentives instead of quantitative measures Amenities to attract highly skilled labor, scientists, or creative people
Focus	Combination of the above policies directed at the particular strategic target	Combination of the above policies directed at the particular strategic target

SOURCE: Reprinted with permission of The Free Press, a division of Macmillan, Inc. from *Competitive Strategy* by M. E. Porter, pp. 40–41. Copyright © 1980 by The Free Press.

tree depicted in Fig. 7.3. These are some of the many functional-area strategy decisions that need to be made if corporate and divisional strategies are to be implemented properly by functional managers. For example, once top management decides to acquire another publicly held corporation, it must decide how it will obtain the funds necessary for the purchase. A very popular financial strategy is the *leveraged buyout.* In a leveraged buyout, a company is acquired in a transaction financed largely by borrowing. Ultimately, the debt is paid with money generated by the acquired company's operations or by sales of its assets. This is what happened when Westray Transportation, Inc., an affiliate of Westray Corporation, purchased Atlas Van Lines in 1984. Under the leveraged buyout plan Atlas stockholders received $18.35 for each share of stock outstanding and the company was taken private by Westray. The money was funded by Merrill Lynch Interfunding, Inc. and Acquisition Funding Corp. Westray then paid the debt from the operations of its new subsidiary, Atlas Van Lines.[35]

A functional area that has received a great deal of attention recently in

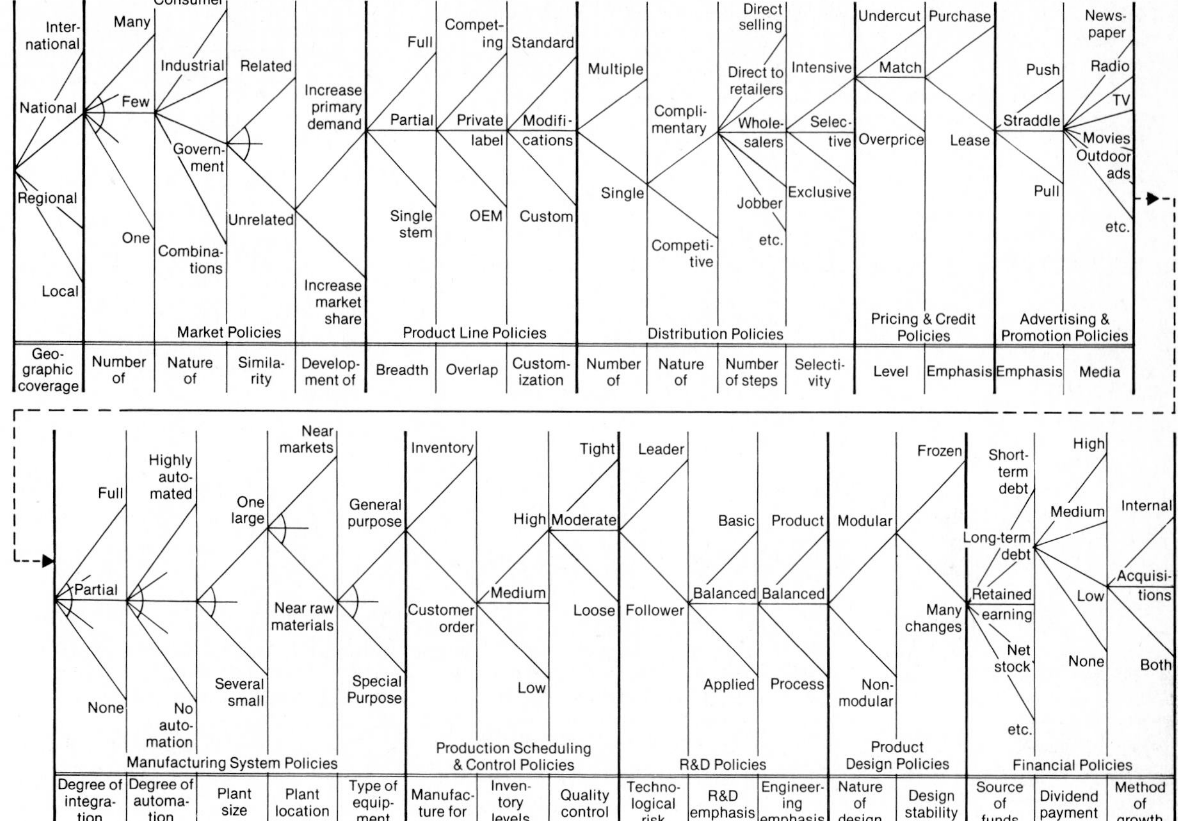

Figure 7.3 **Functional strategy decision tree.**
SOURCE: C. W. Hofer, "The Uses and Limitations of Statistical Division Theory" (Boston: Intercollegiate Case Clearing House), no. 9-171-653, 1971, p. 34. Copyright © 1971 by C. W. Hofer. Reprinted by permission.

terms of strategy is technology (R&D). Those corporations that are dependent on technology for their success are becoming concerned increasingly with developing R&D strategies that complement business level strategies.[36] As shown in Fig. 7.3, one of the R&D choices is to either be a *leader* or a *follower.* Porter suggests that the decision to become a technological leader or follower can be a way of achieving either overall low cost or differentiation.[37] This choice is described in more detail in Table 7.3.

Other functional strategies, such as the location and scale of manufacturing facilities, distribution channels, and the choice of push (promotion) versus pull (advertising) marketing emphasis can only be mentioned briefly in this book. For a detailed discussion of functional strategies, refer to ad-

Table 7.3 Technological Leadership and Competitive Advantage

	Technological Leadership	*Technological Followership*
Cost Advantage	Pioneer the lowest-cost product design Be the first firm down the learning curve Create low-cost ways of performing value activities	Lower the cost of the product or value activities by learning from the leader's experience Avoid R&D costs through imitation
Differentiation	Pioneer a unique product that increases buyer value Innovate in other activities to increase buyer value	Adapt the product or delivery system more closely to buyer needs by learning from the leader's experience

SOURCE: Reprinted with permission of The Free Press, a division of Macmillan, Inc. from *Competitive Advantage* by M. E. Porter, p. 181. Copyright © 1985 by Michael E. Porter.

vanced texts in each of the functional areas (e.g., *Marketing Planning and Strategy* by S. C. Jain, among others) or *Strategy, Policy, and Central Management* by Newman, Logan, and Hegarty.[38]

Strategies to Avoid

There are a number of strategies used at various levels that are very dangerous. They may be considered by managers because of a poor analysis or lack of creativity.[39]

1. *Follow the leader.* Imitating the strategy of a leading competitor may seem good, but it ignores a firm's particular strengths and weaknesses. Atari learned this when it attempted to move into the personal computer business against Apple and Commodore.
2. *Hit another home run.* If a corporation is successful because it pioneered an extremely successful product, it has a tendency to search for another superproduct that will ensure growth and prosperity. Like betting on "long shots" at the horse races, the probability of finding a second winner is slight. Polaroid spent a lot of money developing an "instant" movie camera, but the public ignored it.
3. *Arms race.* Entering into a spirited battle with another firm for increased market share may increase sales revenue, but will probably be more than offset by increases in advertising, promotion, R&D, and manufacturing costs. Since the deregulation of airlines, price wars and rate "specials" have contributed to low profit margins or bankruptcy for many major airlines.
4. *Do everything.* When faced with a number of interesting opportunities, there may be a tendency to take all of them. At first, a corporation may have enough resources to develop each into a project, but it soon runs short as the many projects demand large infusions of time, money, and

energy. Convinced that its brand name would serve as an effective umbrella for a whole series of new products, Toro Company quickly ran out of money and time (see Illustrative Example 7.3 on page 179).

5. *Losing hand.* A corporation may have invested so much in a particular strategy that top management is unwilling to accept the fact that the strategy is not successful. Believing that it has "too much invested to quit," the corporation continues to throw good money after bad. Pan American chose to sell its Pan Am Building and Intercontinental Hotels, the most profitable parts of the corporation, to keep its money-losing airline flying. It then agreed to pay $1.1 billion to Airbus Industries for 28 new jet planes.

7.2 SELECTION OF THE BEST STRATEGY

Once potential strategic alternatives have been identified and evaluated in terms of their pros and cons, top management must select one to implement. By this point, it is likely that a number of alternatives will have emerged as feasible. How is the decision made to determine the "best" strategy?

Choosing among a set of acceptable alternative strategies is often not easy. Each alternative is likely to have its proponents as well as critics. Steiner and Miner suggest using the twenty questions listed below before selecting one strategy over another. Perhaps the most important criterion to use is the ability of each alternative to satisfy agreed-upon objectives with the least use of resources and with the fewest number of negative side effects. It is therefore important to develop a tentative implementation plan in order to address the probable difficulties management is likely to face. Is the alternative worth the probable short-term as well as long-term costs?

TWENTY QUESTIONS TO USE IN EVALUATING STRATEGY

1. Does the strategy conform with the basic mission and purpose of the corporation? If not, a new competitive arena may be entered with which management is not familiar.
2. Is the strategy consistent with the corporation's external environment?
3. Is the strategy consistent with the internal strengths, objectives, policies, resources, and personal values of managers and employees? A strategy may not be completely in tune with all of these, but major dissonance should be avoided.
4. Does the strategy reflect the acceptance of minimum potential risk, balancing it against the maximum potential profit consistent with the corporation's resources and prospects?

(*Continued*)

5. Does the strategy fit a niche in the corporation's market not now filled by others? Is this niche likely to remain open long enough for the corporation to return capital investment plus the required level of profit? (Niches have a habit of filling up fast.)
6. Does the strategy conflict with other corporate strategies?
7. Is the strategy divided into substrategies that interrelate properly?
8. Has the strategy been tested with appropriate criteria (such as consistency with past, present, and prospective trends) and by the appropriate analytical tools (such as risk analysis, discounted cash flows, and so on)?
9. Has the strategy been tested by developing feasible implementation plans?
10. Does the strategy really fit the life cycles of the corporation's products?
11. Is the timing of the strategy correct?
12. Does the strategy pit the product against a powerful competitor? If so, reevaluate carefully.
13. Does the strategy leave the corporation vulnerable to the power of one major customer? If so, reconsider carefully.
14. Does the strategy involve the production of a new product for a new market? If so, reconsider carefully.
15. Is the corporation rushing a revolutionary product to market? If so, reconsider carefully.
16. Does the strategy imitate that of a competitor? If so, reconsider carefully.
17. Is it likely that the corporation can get to the market first with the new product or service? (If so, this is a great advantage. The second firm to market has much less chance of high returns on investment than the first.)
18. Has a really honest and accurate appraisal been made of the competition? Is the competition under- or overestimated?
19. Is the corporation trying to sell abroad something it cannot sell in the United States? (This is not usually a successful strategy.)
20. Is the market share likely to be sufficient to assure a required return on investment? (Market share and return on investment generally are closely related but differ from product to product and market to market.) Has this relationship of market and product been calculated?

SOURCE: Adapted with permission of Macmillan Publishing Company from *Management Policy and Strategy* by G. A. Steiner and J. B. Miner, pp. 219–221. Copyright © 1977 by Macmillan Publishing Company.

Scenario Construction

Detailed *scenarios* are often constructed using pro forma balance sheets and income statements to forecast the likely effect of each alternative strategy and its various programs on division and corporate return on investment. These scenarios are simply extensions of the industry scenarios discussed in Chapter 4. If, for example, industry scenarios suggest the probable emergence of a strong market demand for certain products, a series of alternative strategy scenarios can be developed. The alternative of acquiring another company having these products can be compared with the alternative of developing the products internally. Using three sets of estimated sales figures (optimistic, pessimistic, and most likely) for the new products over the next five years, the two alternatives can be evaluated in terms of their effect on future (pro forma or spread sheet) company financial statements. These scenarios can quickly become very complicated, especially if three sets of acquisition prices as well as development costs are also calculated. Nevertheless, this sort of detailed "what if" analysis is needed in order to realistically compare the projected outcome of each reasonable alternative strategy and its attendant programs, budgets, and procedures.

Regardless of the quantifiable pros and cons of each alternative, the actual decision will probably be influenced by a number of subjective factors that are difficult to quantify. Some of these factors are management's attitude toward risk, pressures from the external environment, influences from the corporate culture, and the personal needs and desires of key managers.

Management's Attitude toward Risk

The attractiveness of a particular strategic alternative is partially a function of the amount of risk it entails. The risk is composed not only of the *probability* that the strategy will be effective, but also of the amount of *assets* the corporation must allocate to that strategy, and the length of *time* the assets will be unavailable for other uses. To quantify this risk, a number of people suggest the use of the *Capital Asset Pricing Model* (CAPM). CAPM is a financial method for linking the risk involved in a particular alternative with expected returns on a company's equity.[40]

The greater the amount of assets involved and the longer they are tied up, the more likely top management will demand a higher probability of success. This may be one reason why innovations seem to occur more often in small firms than in large, established corporations.[41] The small firm managed by an entrepreneur is willing to accept greater risk than would a large firm of diversified ownership. It is one thing to take a chance if you are the primary stockholder. It is something else if throngs of widows and orphans depend on your corporation's monthly dividend checks for living expenses.

Decision Style

The decision style of top management and the board of directors will heavily affect the way a decision is made. Thompson points out that there are two basic variables to each decision: (1) preferences about possible outcomes (the amount of agreement about the key objectives to be met), and (2) beliefs about cause/effect relationships (the amount of certainty that a specific means will cause a specific end).[42] These are depicted graphically in Fig. 7.4.

If there is total agreement among top management and the board about the corporation's mission and key objectives, one of two decision styles is likely to be used—computational or judgmental. A *computational* style is appropriate in those situations when there is a high degree of certainty about cause/effect relationships. The "best" alternative in this situation is either "obvious" or can be programmed on a computer using quantitative techniques. A *judgmental* style is typically used when there is no clear-cut connection between cause and effect. The ability of a specific strategy to achieve specific objectives is considered in terms of probabilities. This calls for executive judgment. This decision-making style is most likely to epitomize strategy makers who operate in what Mintzberg calls a "planning mode."

If, however, there is little agreement about the mission and key objectives of the corporation, one of two decision styles is likely to be used—compromising or inspirational. A *compromising* style is appropriate in those situations where there is a high degree of certainty about cause/effect relationships. The selection of the "best" strategy boils down to a compromise regarding which objectives top management and the board are willing to pursue. This style is characteristic of what Mintzberg calls the "adaptive

BELIEFS ABOUT CAUSE/EFFECT RELATIONS	PREFERENCES REGARDING POSSIBLE OUTCOMES: Certainty	Uncertainty
Certain	Computational	Compromise (Adaptive Mode)
Uncertain	Judgmental (Planning Mode)	Inspirational (Entrepreneurial Mode)

Figure 7.4 **Four basic decision styles.**
SOURCE: Adapted from J. D. Thompson, *Organizations in Action* (New York: McGraw-Hill, 1967), p. 134. Copyright © 1967 by McGraw-Hill, Inc. Used by permission.

mode." An *inspirational* style is likely to be used not only when there is no clear-cut connection between strategy and the accomplishment of objectives, but also when there is no agreement about which objective has priority. This style is characteristic of Mintzberg's "entrepreneurial mode." In this mode the founder of a corporation makes strategic decisions based on the personal need to achieve a vague goal such as success. To outsiders, such decisions may appear to be arbitrary and capricious.

Pressures from the External Environment

The attractiveness of a strategic alternative will be affected by its perceived compatibility with the key stakeholders in a corporation's task environment. These stakeholders are typically concerned with certain aspects of a corporation's activities. Creditors want to be paid on time. Unions exert pressure for comparable wages and employment security. Governments and interest groups demand social responsibility. Stockholders want dividends. All of these pressures must be considered in the selection of the best alternative.

As previously stated in Chapter 4, most strategy makers will probably lean toward satisfying pressures from stakeholders in their corporation's task environment in the following order:

1. Customers
2. Employees
3. Owners
4. General public
5. Stockholders
6. Elected public officials
7. Government bureaucrats[43]

Questions to raise in attempting to assess the importance to the corporation of these pressures are the following:

1. Which stakeholders are most crucial for corporate success?
2. How much of what they want are they likely to get under this alternative?
3. What are they *likely* to do if they don't get what they want?
4. What is the probability that they will do it?

By ranking the key stakeholders in a corporation's task environment and asking these questions, strategy makers should be better able to choose strategic alternatives that minimize external pressures.

Pressures from the Corporate Culture

As pointed out in Chapter 5, the norms and values shared by the members of a corporation do affect the attractiveness of certain alternatives. If a strategy is incompatible with the corporate culture, the likelihood of its success will be very low. Footdragging and even sabotage will result as employees fight to resist a radical change in corporate philosophy.

Precedents from the past tend to restrict the kinds of objectives and strategies that can be seriously considered. The "aura" of the founding father of a corporation lingers long past his lifetime because his values have been imprinted on the corporation's members. According to Cyert and March,

> Organizations have memories in the form of precedents, and individuals in the coalition are strongly motivated to accept the precedents as binding. Whether precedents are formalized in the shape of an official standard operating procedure or are less formally stored, they remove from conscious consideration many agreements, decisions, and commitments that might well be subject to renegotiation in an organization without a memory.[44]

In considering a strategic alternative, the strategy makers must assess its compatibility with the corporate culture. To the extent that there is little fit, management must decide if it should (1) take a chance on ignoring the culture, (2) manage around the culture by changing the implementation plan, (3) try to change the culture to fit the strategy, or (4) change the strategy to fit the culture.[45] If the culture will be strongly opposed to a possible strategy, it is foolhardy to ignore the culture. Further, a decision to proceed with a particular strategy without being committed to changing the culture or managing around the culture (both very tricky and time consuming) is dangerous. Nevertheless, restricting a corporation to only those strategies that are completely compatible with its culture may eliminate from consideration the most profitable alternatives. For an example of an attempt to change a corporate culture in order to implement a change in strategy, see Illustrative Example 7.4.

CHANGING THE CULTURE AT PROCTER & GAMBLE

Illustrative Example 7.4

In choosing to emphasize overall low cost as the key competitive strategy for each of its product lines, Procter & Gamble under President Smale is attempting a turnaround strategy of large proportions. By firing people to boost overall management performance, Smale risks undermining the employee loyalty that has been one of the company's greatest strengths. Apparently some board members are unsettled by what they see as a conflict

(Continued)

between P&G's time-honored dedication to quality, high-performance products and its new emphasis on controlling costs. Similarly, the drive to move quickly and to take more risks with new products goes counter to the firm's traditional cautious style. Nevertheless, P&G must do something. Because its detergent and consumer paper goods markets are maturing, the company has been unable to attain its cherished goal of doubling its unit volume every ten years. The reason given is that consumers are increasingly responsive to price. The question remains, nonetheless: Will Smale be successful in changing P&G's corporate culture to implement a change from its traditional quality differentiation strategy to one of overall low cost?

SOURCE: "Why Procter & Gamble Is Playing It Even Tougher," *Business Week* (July 18, 1984), pp. 176–186.

Needs and Desires of Key Managers

Even the most attractive alternative may not be selected if it is contrary to the needs and desires of important top managers. A person's ego may be tied to a particular proposal to the extent that all other alternatives are strongly lobbied against. Key executives in operating divisions, for example, may be able to influence other people in top management in favor of a particular alternative so that objections to it are ignored.

An example of such a situation was described by John DeLorean when he was at Pontiac Division of General Motors in 1959. At that time, General Motors was developing a new rear-engined auto called Corvair. Ed Cole, the General Manager of Chevrolet Division, was very attracted to the idea of building the first modern, rear-engine American automobile. A number of engineers, however, were worried about the safety of the car and made vigorous attempts to either change the "unsafe" suspension system or keep the Corvair out of production. "One top corporate engineer told me that he showed his test results to Cole but by then he said, 'Cole's mind was made up.' "[46] By this time, there had developed quite a bit of documented evidence that the car should not be built as designed. However, according to DeLorean,

> . . . Cole was a strong product voice and a top salesman in company affairs. In addition, the car, as he proposed it, would cost less to build than the same car with a conventional rear suspension. Management not only went along with Cole, it also told the dissenters in effect to "stop these objections. Get on the team, or you can find someplace else to work." The ill-fated Corvair was launched in the fall of 1959.
>
> The results were disastrous. I don't think any one car before or since produced as gruesome a record on the highway as the Corvair. It was designed and promoted to appeal to the spirit and flair of young people. It was sold in part as a sports car. Young Corvair owners, therefore, were

> trying to bend their cars around curves at high speeds and were killing themselves in alarming numbers.[47]

In only a few years, General Motors was inundated by lawsuits over the Corvair. Ralph Nader soon published a book primarily about the Corvair called *Unsafe at Any Speed,* launching his career as a consumer advocate.

Strategic Choice Model

A technique found to be useful in methodically comparing various strategic alternatives is that of the Strategic Choice Model developed by Snyder.[48] As shown in Table 7.4, the model incorporates both the alternatives under consideration and the decision criteria considered most relevant by the strategic managers using the model.

The specific alternatives, criteria, and numbers given in Table 7.4 are those for a specific computer corporation and, of course, will vary depending upon the corporation and situation under consideration. The choice model is developed by going through the following seven steps:

1. List the feasible alternatives on the vertical axis. (Six are given in Table 7.4—for example, personal home computers and software development.)

Table 7.4 **Strategic Choice Model**

	Weighted Decision Criteria						
Alternatives	*Internal Consistency* (5×)	*External Consistency* (4×)	*Short Run Return* (3×)	*Long Run Return* (5×)	*Marketability* (4×)	*Investment Feasibility* (5×)	***Total of Multiplied Weights***
Personal home computers	4 = **20**	5 = **20**	3 = **9**	5 = **25**	3 = **12**	4 = **20**	**106**
Software development	5 = **25**	5 = **20**	4 = **12**	5 = **25**	5 = **20**	4 = **20**	**122**
Expansion/ retail stores	4 = **20**	3 = **12**	3 = **9**	5 = **25**	3 = **12**	3 = **15**	**93**
Management consulting	3 = **15**	5 = **20**	2 = **6**	5 = **25**	3 = **12**	2 = **10**	**88**
Computer networking	5 = **25**	4 = **16**	4 = **12**	5 = **25**	5 = **20**	5 = **25**	**123**
Communications satellite	2 = **10**	4 = **16**	1 = **3**	5 = **25**	2 = **8**	3 = **15**	**77**

SOURCE: N. H. Snyder, "A Strategic Choice Model," A Working Paper (Charlottesville, Va.: McIntire School of Commerce, University of Virginia), 1982. Used by permission.

2. List important internal and external considerations (decision criteria) along the horizontal axis. Although it is not done in Table 7.4, internal consistency can be subdivided into separate columns showing internal consistency with each functional area. Likewise, external consistency can be subdivided into external consistency with each element in the task environment. Obviously, other criteria in addition to those given in Table 7.4 can be listed for any particular situation.
3. Weight each decision criterion listed on the horizontal axis from 1 to 5 according to its importance to the firm. For example, the strategists who prepared Table 7.4 believed that long-run return on investment was more important than was short-run return. Thus, short-run return was weighted 3 and long-run return was weighted 5.
4. Evaluate each feasible alternative in terms of its effect on each criterion listed on the horizontal axis. The effect may be positive, neutral, or negative. Use a scale ranging from −5 (negative effect) to +5 (positive effect). The numerical weight of each criterion for each alternative is the left side of each "equation" at the intersection of each row and column. For example, in Table 7.4 software development is thought to have a positive effect (+4) on the corporation's short-run return and an extremely positive effect (+5) on its long-run return.
5. Multiply the numerical weight for each criterion in the horizontal axis (calculated in step 3) by the numerical weight on the left side of each equation (calculated in step 4). The resulting product of each multiplication is recorded on the right side of each "equation." For example, the value of software development on short-run return is $3 \times 4 = 12$.
6. Sum the products for each row. Record that total in the column on the far right. For example, we find the sum of the products for the "personal home computers" alternative by adding thus: $20 + 20 + 9 + 25 + 12 + 20 = 106$.
7. Find the "best" alternative; it has the highest numerical total. Given the decision criteria and weights stated in Table 7.4, "computer networking" is the best alternative. If the corporation has the resources to develop more than one alternative at a time, the model is of use in establishing the priority of each selected alternative.

7.3 DEVELOPMENT OF POLICIES

The selection of the best strategic alternative is not the end of strategy formulation. Policies must now be established to define the ground rules for implementation. As defined earlier, policies are broad guidelines for making decisions. They flow from the selected strategy to provide guidance for decision making throughout the organization. Corporate policies are broad guidelines for divisions to follow in order to comply with corporate strategy. These policies are interpreted and implemented through each division's own objectives and strategies. Divisions may then develop their own policies that will be guidelines for their functional areas to follow.

One example of a corporate-level policy is that developed by Ford Motor Company. Concerned with the historic lack of cooperation between Ford U.S. and Ford of Europe, Ford's top management developed a company-wide policy requiring any new car design to be easily adaptable to any market in the world. Previous to this policy, Ford of Europe developed cars strictly for its own market, while engineers in the United States separately designed their own products. The policy was a natural result of Ford's emphasis on manufacturing efficiency and becoming more globally integrated as a corporation. One result of this new policy was the program to produce the European Sierra and its U.S. counterpart the Merkur. The cost to convert the European Sierra to meet all U.S. safety and emission standards was about one-fourth of what it would have cost to convert previous European models. The Taurus and Sable models have also been engineered for easy conversion to overseas markets, as well.[49]

Some policies will be expressions of a corporation's *critical success factors* (CSF). Critical success factors are those elements of a company that determine its strategic success or failure. They vary from company to company. IBM, for example, sees customer service as its critical success factor. McDonald's CSF is quality, cleanliness, and value. Hewlett-Packard is concerned with new product development.[50] Policies may therefore be guidelines for decision making based on a corporation's critical success factors. At Lazarus Department Store in Columbus, Ohio, for example, customer service is a critical success factor. Store policies state that the customer is *always* right. Even if a department manager believes that a customer bought a particular shirt from a competitor, the manager is bound by policy to accept the shirt and to give back money to the customer. Lazarus' top management believes that even though the store may be taken advantage of in the short run by a few people, the store will make up for it in the long run with good will and increased market share.

Policies tend to be rather long lived and may even outlast the particular strategy that caused their creation. Interestingly, these general policies, such as "The customer is always right" or "Research and development should get first priority on all budget requests," can become, in time, part of a corporation's culture. Such policies may make the implementation of specific strategies easier. They may also restrict top management's strategic options in the future. It is for this reason that a change in strategy should be followed quickly by a change in policies. It is one way to manage the corporate culture.

7.4 SUMMARY AND CONCLUSION

This chapter has focused on the last stage of the strategy formulation process: generating, evaluating, and selecting the best strategic alternative. It also has discussed the development of policies for implementing strategies.

There are three main kinds of strategies: corporate, business (divisional), and functional. Corporate strategies fall into four main families: stability, growth, retrenchment, and a combination of these. Epitomized by a steady-as-she-goes philosophy, *stability* strategies are (1) no change, (2) profit, (3) pause, and (4) proceed with caution. The very popular *growth* strategies are (1) vertical integration, (2) horizontal integration, (3) diversification, (4) merger, acquisition, and joint ventures, (5) concentration, and (6) investment. *Retrenchment* strategies are generally unpopular because they imply failure. They include (1) turnaround, (2) divestment, (3) captive company, and (4) liquidation. *Combination* strategies are composed of a number of these strategies.

Business or divisional strategies are described as the logical result of portfolio analysis. The nine cell portfolio matrix suggests eight recommended strategies based upon a division's or product line's situation in terms of industry attractiveness and business strengths. Porter's three generic competitive strategies—*overall cost leadership, differentiation,* and *focus*—are also suggested. Functional-area strategies are described briefly in terms of their effect upon maximizing corporate and divisional resource productivity.

The selection of the best strategic alternative from projected scenarios will probably be affected by a number of factors. Among them are management's attitude toward risk, pressures from the external environment, influences from the corporate culture, and the personal needs and desires of key managers. A Strategic Choice Model is recommended as a means of comparing feasible alternatives.

Corporate policies operate as broad guidelines for divisions to follow in order to assure their compliance with corporate strategy. Divisions may then generate their own internal policies for their functional areas to follow. These policies define the ground rules for strategy implementation and serve to align corporate activities in the new strategic direction.

DISCUSSION QUESTIONS

1. Is the profit strategy really a stability strategy? Why or why not?
2. Why is growth the most frequently used corporate-level strategy?
3. How does horizontal integration differ from concentric diversification?

4. In what situations at the corporate level might Porter's generic competitive strategies be useful?
5. Can corporate-level strategies also be used at the divisional or functional levels?
6. How can scenarios be used in conjunction with the Strategic Choice Model?

NOTES

1. W. F. Glueck, *Business Policy and Strategic Management*, 3rd ed. (New York: McGraw-Hill, 1980), p. 199.
2. Glueck, p. 290. Glueck uses the term *stable growth* instead of *stability*.
3. J. F. Berry, "Amazing Grace and Unbelievers," *Washington Post* (December 6, 1981), pp. F1 and F3.
4. R. M. Cyert and J. G. March, *A Behavioral Theory of the Firm* (Englewood Cliffs, N.J.: Prentice-Hall, 1963).
5. J. Vesey, "Vertical Integration: Its Effects on Business Performance," *Managerial Planning* (May–June 1978), pp. 11–15.
6. R. H. Hayes and W. J. Abernathy, "Managing Our Way to Economic Decline," *Harvard Business Review* (July–August 1980), pp. 72–73.
   A. R. Burgess, "Vertical Integration in Petrochemicals—1. The Concept and Its Measurement," *Long Range Planning* (August 1983), p. 55.
   K. R. Harrigan, "Exit Barriers and Vertical Integration," *Academy of Management Proceedings* (August 1983), p. 34.
7. K. R. Harrigan, *Strategies for Vertical Integration* (Lexington, Mass.: D. C. Heath–Lexington Books, 1983), pp. 16–21.
8. P. Richter, "Intel Corp. Rations Products, Scrambles to Meet Demand," *Des Moines Register* (April 22, 1984), p. 9F.
9. R. P. Rumelt, *Strategy, Structure, and Economic Performance* (Cambridge, Mass: Harvard University Press, 1974).
   R. W. Hearn, "Fighting Industrial Senility: A System for Growth in Mature Industries," *Journal of Business Strategy* (Fall 1982), pp. 3–20.
   M. Lubatkin, "Mergers and the Performance of the Acquiring Firm," *Academy of Management Review* (April 1983), p. 218.
   C. A. Montgomery and H. Singh, "Diversification Strategy and Systematic Risk," *Strategic Management Journal* (April–June 1984), pp. 181–191.
10. T. J. Peters and R. H. Waterman, Jr., *In Search of Excellence* (New York: Harper & Row, 1982), pp. 293–294.
11. R. Little, "Conglomerates Are Doing Better Than You Think," *Fortune* (May 28, 1984), p. 60.
12. P. M. Hirsch, "Ambushes, Shootouts, and Knights of the Roundtable: The Language of Corporate Takeovers" (Paper presented to the 40th Meeting of the Academy of Management, Detroit, Mich., August 1980).
13. D. Kneale and L. Landro, "IBM, CBS and Sears Plan a Joint Venture in

At-Home Marketing through Videotex," *Wall Street Journal* (February 15, 1984), p. 3.

14. "Gerber: Concentrating on Babies Again for Slow, Steady Growth," *Business Week* (August 22, 1983), p. 80.
15. B. Morris, "Making a Killing," from Special Report on Small Business, *Wall Street Journal* (May 20, 1985), pp. 32c, 36c–37c.
16. D. C. Hambrick, "Turnaround Strategies," in W. D. Guth (ed.), *Handbook of Business Strategy* (Boston: Warren, Gorham & Lamont, 1985), pp. 10.1–10.32.
17. "Exxon Wants Out of the Automated Office," *Business Week* (December 17, 1984), p. 39.
18. D. Brand, "Pan Am to Sell Its Hotel Chain to Grand Met," *Wall Street Journal* (August 24, 1981), p. 6.
19. P. C. Nystrom and W. H. Starbuck, "To Avoid Organizational Crises, Unlearn," *Organizational Dynamics* (Spring 1984), p. 55.
20. Glueck, pp. 229–331.
21. R. Hise and S. McDonald, "CEOs' Views On Strategy: A Survey," *Journal of Business Strategy* (Winter 1984), pp. 81 and 86.
22. H. K. Baker, T. O. Miller, and B. J. Ramsperger, "An Inside Look at Corporate Mergers and Acquisitions," *MSU Business Topics* (Winter 1981), p. 51.
23. T. Metz, "Debate over Mergers Intensifies amid Record Surge of Transactions," *Wall Street Journal* (January 2, 1985), p. 6B.
24. S. Prokesch and W. J. Powell, "Do Mergers Really Work?" *Business Week* (June 3, 1985), p. 88.
25. S. Schoeffler, R. D. Buzzell, and D. F. Heany, "Impact of Strategic Planning on Profit Performance," *Harvard Business Review* (March–April 1974), pp. 144–145.
26. D. E. Hussey, "Portfolio Analysis: Practical Experience with the Directional Policy Matrix," *Long Range Planning* (August 1978), pp. 3–4.
27. K. R. Harrigan, *Strategies for Declining Businesses* (Lexington, Mass.: D. C. Heath–Lexington Books, 1980).
    K. R. Harrigan, "End-Game Strategies for Declining Industries," *Harvard Business Review* (July–August 1983), pp. 111–120.
28. M. E. Porter, *Competitive Strategy* (New York: Free Press, 1980), pp. 36–46.
29. Porter, 1980, p. 35.
30. J. B. Hull, "Hospital Chains Battle Health Insurers, But Will Quality Care Lose in the War?" *Wall Street Journal* (February 5, 1985), p. 35.
31. J. Fierman, "Beech-Nut Bounces Up in the Baby Market," *Fortune* (December 24, 1984), p. 56.
32. M. E. Porter, *Competitive Advantage* (New York: Free Press, 1985), p. 15.
33. Porter, 1985, p. 16.

34. G. G. Dess and P. S. Davis, "Porter's Generic Strategies as Determinants of Strategic Group Membership and Organizational Performance," *Academy of Management Journal* (September 1984), p. 484.

35. J. Zaslow, "Atlas Van Lines Agrees to Buyout for $71.6 Million," *Wall Street Journal* (June 25, 1984), p. 10.

36. A. L. Frohman and D. Bitondo, "Coordinating Business Strategy and Technical Planning," *Long Range Planning* (December 1981), pp. 58–67.

37. Porter, 1985, p. 181.

38. S. C. Jain, *Marketing Planning* and *Strategy* (Cincinnati: South-Western Publishing Co., 1981).
W. H. Newman, J. P. Logan, and W. H. Hegarty, *Strategy, Policy, and Central Management,* 9th ed. (Cincinnati: South-Western Publishing Co., 1985).

39. A. A. Thompson, Jr., and A. J. Strickland, III, *Strategy and Policy* (Plano, Tex.: Business Publications, 1981), pp. 106–107.

40. D. R. Harrington, "Stock Prices, Beta, and Strategic Planning," *Harvard Business Review* (May–June 1983), pp. 157–164.
M. B. Coate, "Pitfalls in Portfolio Planning," *Long Range Planning* (June 1983), pp. 53–54.

41. Peters and Waterman, pp. 115–116.

42. J. D. Thompson, *Organizations in Action* (New York: McGraw-Hill, 1967), p. 134.

43. B. Z. Posner, and W. H. Schmidt, "Values and the American Manager: An Update," *California Management Review* (Spring 1984), p. 206.

44. R. M. Cyert and J. G. March, "A Behavioral Theory of Organizational Objectives," *Management Classics,* eds. M. T. Matteson and J. M. Ivancevich (Santa Monica, Calif.: Goodyear Publishing, 1977), p. 114.

45. H. Schwartz and S. M. Davis, "Matching Corporate Culture and Business Strategy," *Organizational Dynamics* (Summer 1981), p. 43.

46. J. P. Wright, *On a Clear Day You Can See General Motors* (Grosse Point, Mich.: Wright Enterprises, 1979), p. 54.

47. Wright, p. 55.

48. N. H. Snyder, "A Strategic Choice Model," a Working Paper (Charlottesville, Va.: McIntire School of Commerce, University of Virginia, 1982).

49. M. Edid and W. J. Hampton, "Now That It's Cruising, Can Ford Keep Its Foot on the Gas?" *Business Week* (February 11, 1985), pp. 48–52.

50. A. L. Mendlow, "Setting Corporate Goals and Measuring Organizational Effectiveness—A Practical Approach," *Long Range Planning* (February 1983), p. 72.

PART FOUR

STRATEGY IMPLEMENTATION AND CONTROL

Chapter 8

STRATEGY IMPLEMENTATION

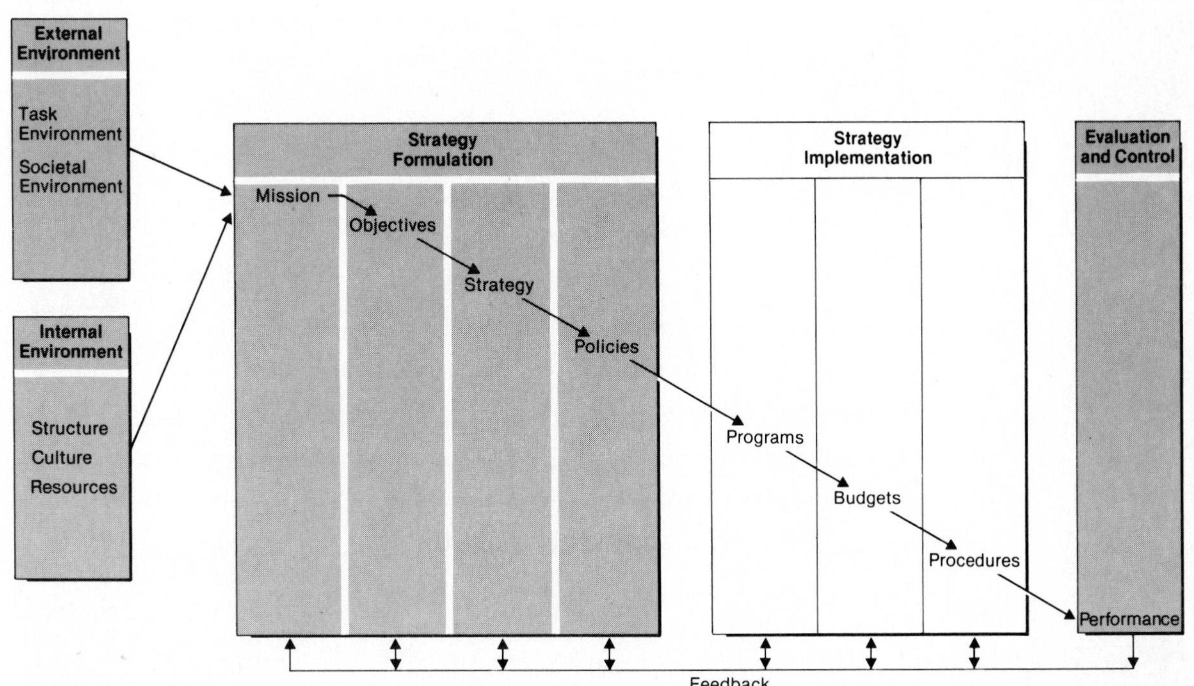

Once a strategy and a set of policies have been formulated, the focus of strategic management shifts to implementation. Corporate strategy makers must consider these three questions:

Who are the people who will carry out the strategic plan?

What must be done?

How are they going to do what is needed?

These questions and similar ones should have been addressed initially when the pros and cons of strategic alternatives were anlayzed. They must also be addressed now before appropriate implementation plans can be made. Unless top management can answer these basic questions in a satisfactory manner, even the best planned strategy will be unlikely to have the desired results.

For example, Fisher-Price's plan to expand from durable toys into children's playwear was a well-conceived strategy but failed in its introduction because of a strike and production problems at its partner's plant in Jamaica. Clothing arrived in stores six weeks late or not at all. Some retailers received shirts and no pants. Both Fisher-Price and the purchasing stores took a loss on the new line of clothes.[1]

Alexander's survey of ninety-three company presidents and divisional managers revealed the following ten problems experienced by over half of the group when attempting to implement a strategic change. These problems are listed in order of frequency of occurrence.

1. More time needed for implementation than originally planned.
2. Unanticipated major problems.
3. Ineffective coordination of activities.
4. Crises that distracted attention away from implementation.
5. Insufficient capabilities of the involved employees.
6. Uncontrollable external environmental factors.
7. Inadequate leadership and direction by departmental managers.
8. Inadequate training and instruction of lower-level employees.
9. Poor definition of key implementation tasks and activities.
10. Inadequate monitoring of activities by the information system.[2]

As shown in Fig. 8.1, poor implementation of an appropriate strategy may result in failure of the strategy. An excellent implementation plan, however, will not only cause the success of an appropriate strategy; it may also

STRATEGY FORMULATED

STRATEGY IMPLEMENTED	Appropriate	Inappropriate
Excellent	*Success* Targets for growth, share, profits are met.	*Rescue or Ruin* Good execution may save a poor strategy or may hasten failure.
Poor	*Trouble* Poor execution hampers good strategy. Management may conclude strategy is inappropriate.	*Failure* Cause of failure hard to diagnose. Poor strategy marked by inability to execute.

Figure 8.1 **Interaction of strategy formulation and implementation.**
SOURCE: Reprinted by permission of the *Harvard Business Review*. An exhibit from "Making Your Marketing Strategy Work" by Thomas V. Bonoma (March/April 1984). Copyright © 1984 by the President and Fellows of Harvard College; all rights reserved.

rescue an inappropriate strategy. This is why an increasing number of chief executives are turning their attention to the problem of implementation. Now more than ever before, they realize that the successful implementation of a strategy depends on having the right organization structure, resource allocation, compensation program, information system, and corporate culture.[3]

8.1 *WHO* IMPLEMENTS STRATEGY?

Depending on how the corporation is organized, those who implement corporate strategy may be a different set of people from those who formulate it. In most large, multi-industry corporations, the implementers will be everyone in the organization except top management and the board of directors. Vice-presidents of functional areas and directors of divisions or SBUs will work with their subordinates to put together large-scale implementation plans. From these plans, plant managers, project managers, and unit heads will put together plans for their specific plants, departments, and units. As a result, every operational manager down to the first-line supervisor will be involved in some way in implementing corporate, divisional, and functional strategies.

It is important to note that most of the people in the corporation who are crucial to successful strategy implementation probably had little, if anything, to do with the development of the corporate strategy. As a result, they may be entirely ignorant of the vast amount of data and work that went into the formulation process. Unless changes in mission, objectives, strategies, and policies and their importance to the corporation are communicated clearly to all operational managers, there may be a lot of resistance and footdragging. In those instances when top management formulates strategy that challenges the corporation's culture, lower-level managers may even sabotage the implementation. These managers may hope to influence top management to abandon its new plans and return to the old ways.

8.2 *WHAT* MUST BE DONE?

The managers of divisions and functional areas work with their fellow managers to develop *programs, budgets,* and *procedures* for the implementation of strategy. A *program* is a statement of activities or steps needed to accomplish a single-use plan, the purpose of which is to make the strategy action-oriented. For example, top management may have chosen forward vertical integration as its best strategy for growth. The corresponding divisional strategy might be to purchase existing retail outlets from another firm rather than to build and develop its own outlets. Various programs—such as the following—would have to be developed to integrate the new stores into the corporation:

1. An advertising program ("Jones Surplus is now a part of Ajax Continental. Prices are lower. Selection is better.")
2. A training program for newly hired store managers as well as for those Jones Surplus managers the corporation has chosen to keep.
3. A program to develop reporting procedures that will integrate the stores into the corporation's accounting system.
4. A program to modernize the stores and to prepare them for a "grand opening."

Once these and other programs are developed, the budget process begins. A *budget* is a statement of a corporation's programs in terms of dollars. The detailed cost of each program is listed for planning and control purposes. Planning a budget is the last real check a corporation has on the feasibility of its selected strategy. An ideal strategy may be found to be completely impractical only after specific implementation programs are costed in detail. A good example was President Reagan's 1981 attempt to implement his strategy of reducing taxes, increasing defense spending, and balancing the federal budget without hurting the poor or the old. In theory, everyone agreed. In practice, conflict reigned. No member of Congress was willing to cut Social Security, the school lunch program, or any of a number of other social programs.

Once program, divisional, and corporate budgets are approved, procedures must be developed to guide the employees in their day-to-day actions. Sometimes referred to as Standard Operating Procedures, *procedures* are a system of sequential steps or techniques specified to perform a particular task or job. They typically detail the various activities that must be carried out to complete a corporation's programs. In the case of the corporation that decided to acquire another firm's retail outlets, new operating procedures must be established for, among others, in-store promotions, inventory ordering, stock selection, customer relations, credits and collections, warehouse distribution, pricing, paycheck timing, grievance handling, and raises and promotions. These procedures ensure that the day-to-day store operations will be consistent over time (that is, next week's work activities will be the same as this week's) and consistent among stores (that is, each store will operate in the same manner as the others). McDonald's, for example, has done an excellent job of developing very detailed procedures (and policing them!) to ensure that its policies are carried out to the letter in every one of its fast food retail outlets.

8.3 *HOW* IS STRATEGY TO BE IMPLEMENTED?

Up to this point, both strategy formulation and implementation have been discussed in terms of planning. Programs, budgets, and procedures are simply more detailed plans for the eventual implementation of strategy. The total management process includes, however, several additional activities crucial to implementation, such as organizing, staffing, directing, and controlling. Before *plans* can lead to actual performance, top management must ensure that the corporation is appropriately *organized,* programs are adequately *staffed,* and activities are being *directed* toward achieving desired objectives. These activities are reviewed briefly in this chapter. Top management must also ensure that there is progress toward objectives according to plan; this is a *control* function that will be discussed in Chapter 9.

Organizing

It is very likely that a change in corporate strategy will require some sort of change in the way a corporation is structured and in the kind of skills needed in particular positions. In a classic study of large American corporations, such as DuPont, General Motors, Sears Roebuck, and Standard Oil, Chandler concluded that changes in corporate strategy lead to changes in organization structure. He also concluded that American corporations follow a pattern of development from one kind of structural arrangement to another as they expand. According to him, these structural changes occur because inefficiences caused by the old structure have, by being pushed too far, become too obviously detrimental to live with: "The thesis deduced from these several propositions is then that structure follows strategy and that the most complex type of structure is the result of the concatenation [linking together] of several basic strategies."[4] Chandler therefore proposed the following as the sequence of what occurs:

1. New strategy is created.
2. New administrative problems emerge.
3. Economic performance declines.
4. New appropriate structure is invented.
5. Profit returns to its previous level.

Structure Follows Strategy

Chandler found that in their early years, corporations such as DuPont tend to have a centralized organizational structure that is well suited to their producing and selling a limited range of products. As they add new product lines, purchase their own sources of supply, and create their own distribution networks, they become too complex for highly centralized structures. In order to remain successful, this type of successful organization needs to shift to a decentralized structure with several semi-autonomous divisions.

In his book, *My Years with General Motors,* Alfred P. Sloan detailed how General Motors conducted such structural changes in the 1920s.[5] He saw decentralization of structure as centralized policy determination coupled with decentralized operating management. Once a strategy was developed for the total corporation by top management, the individual divisions, such as Chevrolet, Buick, etc., were free to choose how they would implement that strategy. Patterned after DuPont, GM found the decentralized multidivisional structure to be extremely effective in allowing the maximum amount of freedom for product development. Return on investment was used as a financial control.

Research generally supports Chandler's proposition that structure follows strategy (as well as the reverse proposition from Chapter 5 that structure influences strategy).[6] The recent decision by General Motors to restructure its automobile divisions into the three large-car divisions of Buick, Cadillac, and Oldsmobile and the two small-car divisions of Chevrolet and Pontiac is another example of how implementing strategic decisions may often require structural changes.

There is some evidence, however, that a change in strategy may not necessarily result in a corresponding change in structure if the corporation has very little competition. If a firm occupies a monopolistic position, with tariffs in its favor or close ties to a government, it can raise prices to cover internal administrative inefficiencies. This is an easier path for these firms to take than going through the pain of corporate reorganization.[7]

Although it is agreed that organizational structure must vary with different environmental conditions, which, in turn, affect an organization's strategy, there is no agreement about an optimal organizational design.[8] What was appropriate for DuPont and General Motors in the 1920s may not be appropriate today. Firms in particular industries do, however, tend to organize themselves in a similar fashion. For example, automobile manufacturers tend to emulate General Motors' decentralized division concept, whereas consumer-goods producers tend to emulate the brand-management concept pioneered by Procter & Gamble Company. The general conclusion seems to be that firms following similar strategies tend to adopt similar structures.[9]

Organic and Mechanistic Structure

Research by Burns and Stalker concluded that a "mechanistic" structure with its emphasis on the centralization of decision making and bureaucratic rules and procedures appears to be well suited to organizations operating in a reasonably stable environment. In contrast, however, they found that successful firms operating in a constantly changing environment, such as those in the electronics and aerospace industries, find that a more "organic" structure, with the decentralization of decision making and flexible procedures, is more appropriate.[10] Studies by Lawrence and Lorsch support this conclusion. They found that successful firms in a reasonably stable environment, such as the container industry, coordinate activities primarily through fairly centralized corporate hierarchies, which place some reliance on direct contact by managers as well as on paperwork directives. Successful firms in more dynamic environments, such as the plastics industry, coordinate activities through integrative departments and permanent cross-functional teams as well as through the hierarchical contact and paperwork.[11] These differences in the use of structural integrating devices are detailed in Table 8.1.

Table 8.1 **Integrating Mechanisms in Three Different Industries**

	Plastics	*Food*	*Container*
Percent new products in last 20 years	35%	15%	0%
Integrating devices	Rules. Hierarchy. Goal setting. Direct contact. Teams at 3 levels. Integrating departments.	Rules. Hierarchy. Goal setting. Direct contact. Task forces. Integrators.	Rules. Hierarchy. Goal setting. Direct contact.
Percent integrators/ managers	22%	17%	0%

SOURCE: J. Galbraith, *Designing Complex Organizations* (Reading, Mass.: Addison-Wesley, 1973), p. 111. Copyright © 1973 by Addison-Wesley Publishing Co. Reprinted by permission.

The container industry is most stable; foods, intermediate; plastics, the least stable.

Strategic Business Units

A successful method of structuring a large and complex business corporation was developed in 1971 by GE. Referred to as *strategic business units* or SBUs, organizational groups composed of discrete, independent product-market segments served by the firm were identified and given primary responsibility and authority to manage their own functional areas. Recognizing that its structure of decentralized operating divisions was not working efficiently (massive sales growth was not being matched by profit growth), GE's top management decided to reorganize. They restructured nine groups and forty-eight divisions into forty-three strategic business units, many of which crossed traditional group, divisional, and profit center lines. For example, food preparation appliances in three separate divisions were merged into a single SBU serving the "housewares" market.[12] The concept thus is to decentralize on the basis of strategic elements rather than on the basis of size or span of control.

General Electric was so pleased with the results of its experiment in organizational design that it reported ". . . the system helped GE improve its profitability, and return on investment has been rebuilt to a healthier level. In the last recession, General Electric's earnings dropped much less than the overall decline for the industry generally."[13] As a result, other firms such as General Foods, Mead Corporation, Eastman Kodak, Campbell Soup, Union Carbide, and Armco Steel, have implemented the strategic business unit concept. General Foods introduced the concept by organizing certain products on the basis of menu segments like breakfast food, beverage, main meal, dessert, and pet foods.

Typically, once a corporation organizes itself around SBUs, it combines similar SBUs together under a group or sector (mentioned earlier in Chapter 5). In 1985, Eastman Kodak, for example, reorganized into seventeen business units under three operating groups. This type of reorganization on the basis of markets is a way to develop a *horizontal strategy* based upon competitive considerations which cut across divisional boundaries. The group or sector executive therefore is responsible for developing and implementing a horizontal strategy to coordinate the various goals and strategies of related business units.[14] This can help a firm compete with *multipoint competitors*—that is, firms that compete with each other not only in one business unit but in a number of related business units.[15] For example, Procter & Gamble, Kimberly-Clark, Scott Paper, and Johnson and Johnson compete with each other in varying combinations of consumer paper products from disposable diapers to facial tissue. If (purely hypothetically), Johnson and Johnson had just developed a toilet tissue with which they chose to challenge

Procter & Gamble's high-share Charmin brand in a particular district, they might charge a low price for their new brand to build sales quickly. Procter & Gamble might not choose to respond to this attack on its share by cutting prices on Charmin. Because of Charmin's high-market share, Procter & Gamble would lose significantly more sale dollars in a price war than would Johnson and Johnson with Johnson and Johnson's initially low-share brand. Procter & Gamble might thus wish to retaliate by challenging Johnson and Johnson's high-share baby shampoo with Procter & Gamble's own low-share brand of baby shampoo in a different district. Once Johnson and Johnson had perceived the response by Procter & Gamble, it might choose to stop challenging Procter & Gamble's Charmin brand of toilet tissue in one district so that Procter & Gamble would stop challenging Johnson and Johnson's baby shampoo in a different district.

Matrix Structure

As pointed out in Chapter 5, the matrix structure simultaneously combines the stability of the functional structure with the flexibility of the project organization. It is likely to be used within an SBU when the following three conditions exist:

- There is a need for cross-fertilization of ideas across projects or products.
- Resources are scarce.
- There is a need to improve the ability to process information and to make decisions.[16]

The matrix structure is appealing but must be carefully managed. To the extent that the goals to be achieved are vague and the technology used is poorly understood, there is likely to be a continuous battle for power between project and functional managers.[17]

Organizing for Innovation

Those corporations that emphasize the latest technology as part of their missions, objectives, and strategies are finding that their structure tends to lag behind their technology. Keen suggests there is a lag time before a technology can be fully exploited because more change is expected than a system can handle. An infrastructure needs to be built within a corporation to deal with the implications and impact of rapid technological change.[18] Frohman makes a similar argument: "Many aspects of an organization—from technical talent to reward systems, from climate to equipment—affect the payoff a company will receive from its investments in technology."[19]

Large corporations that wish to encourage innovation and creativity within their firms must choose a type of structure that will give the new business unit an appropriate amount of freedom with headquarters still having

OPERATION RELATEDNESS	Very Important	Uncertain	Not Important
Unrelated	3. Special Business Units	6. Independent Business Units	9. Complete Spin-Off
Partly Related	2. New Product Business Department	5. New Venture Division	8. Contracting
Strongly Related	1. Direct Integration	4. Micro New Ventures Department	7. Nurturing and Contracting

STRATEGIC IMPORTANCE

Figure 8.2 **Organization designs for corporate entrepreneurship.**
SOURCE: Reprinted from R. A. Burgelman, "Designs for Corporate Entrepreneurship in Established Firms." Copyright © 1984 by the Regents of the University of California. Reprinted by permission of the Regents from *California Management Review,* vol. xxvi, no. 3, p. 161.

some degree of control. In Fig. 8.2, Burgelman proposes that the particular organization design should be determined by the *strategic importance* of the new business to the corporation and the *relatedness* of the unit's operations to those of the corporation.[20] The combination of these two factors results in nine organizational designs for corporate entrepreneurship (or *intrapreneurship,* as it is called by Pinchot).[21]

1. *Direct integration.* High strategic importance and operational relatedness mean that the new business must be a part of the corporation's mainstream. Product "champions"—people who are respected by others in the corporation and who know how to work the system—are needed to manage these projects. When he was with Ford Motor Company, Lee Iacocca, for example, championed the Mustang.
2. *New product business department.* High strategic importance and partial operational relatedness require a separate department organized around an entrepreneurial project in the division where skills and capabilities can be shared.
3. *Special business units.* High strategic importance and low operational relatedness require the creation of a special new business unit with specific objectives and time horizons. General Motor's new Saturn unit is one example of this approach.
4. *Micro new ventures department.* Uncertain strategic importance and high operational relatedness seem typical for "peripheral" projects which are likely to emerge in the operating divisions on a continuous basis. Each division thus has its own new ventures department.

5. *New venture division.* When the new business has uncertain strategic importance and is only partly related to present corporate operations, it belongs in a new venture division. It brings together projects which may exist in various parts of the corporation or can be acquired externally to build sizable new businesses. Allied Corporation, for example, established a new ventures unit to try to commercialize technologies the company had neglected. It invests $20 million a year in the unit's new businesses in the hope that one will be successful.[22]

6. *Independent business units.* Uncertain strategic importance coupled with no relationship to present corporate activities may make external arrangements attractive. As in the case of Monsanto, the corporation owns Fisher Controls but controls it through membership on a separate Fisher Controls' board of directors. Monsanto's executive vice-president, Earle Harbison, serves as chairman of the separate board and presses Fisher to grow overseas and to achieve what he calls "an Arabian Nights of product development."[23]

7. *Nurturing and contracting.* When an entrepreneurial proposal may not be important strategically to the corporation but is strongly related to present operations, top management may help the entrepreneurial unit "spin off" from the corporation. This allows a friendly competitor to capture a small niche instead of one of the corporation's major competitors. For example, Tektronix, a maker of oscilloscopes, formed a unit to act as an in-house venture capitalist to its own employees by swapping the parent company's operational knowledge for equity in the new company. The arrangement is intended to provide Tektronix with a better return on its R&D expenditures and to help it maintain ties with innovative employees who want to run their own companies.[24]

8. *Contracting.* As the required capabilities and skills of the new business are less related to those of the corporation, the parent corporation may spin off the unit yet keep some relationship through a contractual arrangement with the new firm. The connection is useful in case the new firm develops something of value to the corporation.

9. *Complete spin off.* If both strategic importance and operational relatedness are negligible, the corporation is likely to completely sell off the unit to another firm or to the present employees in some form of ESOP (Employee Stock Ownership Plan). Or the corporation may sell off the unit through a leveraged buyout (executives of the unit buy the unit from the parent company with money from a third source to be repaid out of the unit's anticipated earnings).[25]

Organizing for innovation has become especially important for those corporations in "high tech" industries that wish to recapture the entrepreneurial spirit but are really too large to do so. Apple Computer, for example, turned to a small group to help develop its portable computer Lisa. IBM has formed "independent business units," each with its own mini-board of directors. One such IBU produced the company's successful personal computer. Even Levi Strauss and Company, the clothing manufacturer, is encouraging "in-house entrepreneurs" by financing new fashion-apparel businesses.

Rather than attempting such in-house innovation, a number of corporations are investing venture capital in existing small firms. Wang, for example, purchased a minority interest in InteCom, Inc., a maker of telephone switching equipment. General Motors did the same with Teknowledge, Inc. GM hopes Teknowledge will develop a diagnostic software program to prescribe repairs for troubled cars. This form of minority equity ownership is really quasi-vertical integration and raises a question of organizational identity. In such corporations, it becomes difficult to tell when one firm begins and the other leaves off.

Stages of Corporate Development

A key proposition of Chandler's was that successful corporations tend to follow a pattern of structural development as they grow and expand. Further work by Thain, Scott, and Tuason specifically delineates three distinct structural stages.[26]

Stage I is typified by the entrepreneur, who founds the corporation to promote an idea (product or service). The entrepreneur tends to make all the important decisions personally, and is involved in every detail and phase of the organization. The Stage I corporation has a structure allowing the entrepreneur to directly supervise the activities of every employee (see Fig. 8.3). The corporation in Stage I is thus characterized by little formal structure. Planning is usually short range or "fire-fighting" in nature. The typical managerial functions of planning, organizing, directing, staffing, and controlling are usually performed to a very limited degree, if at all. The greatest strengths of a Stage I corporation are its flexibility and dynamism. The drive of the entrepreneur energizes the corporation in its struggle for growth. Its greatest weakness is its extreme reliance on the entrepreneur to decide general strategies as well as detailed procedures. If the entrepreneur falters, the corporation usually flounders.

Stage I described Polaroid Corporation, whose founder Dr. Edwin Land championed *Polarvision*, a financially disastrous instant movie system, while ignoring industrial and commercial uses. Growing concern by stockholders over declines in sales and net income resulted in Dr. Land's resignation from his top management position in 1980 and from the board of directors in

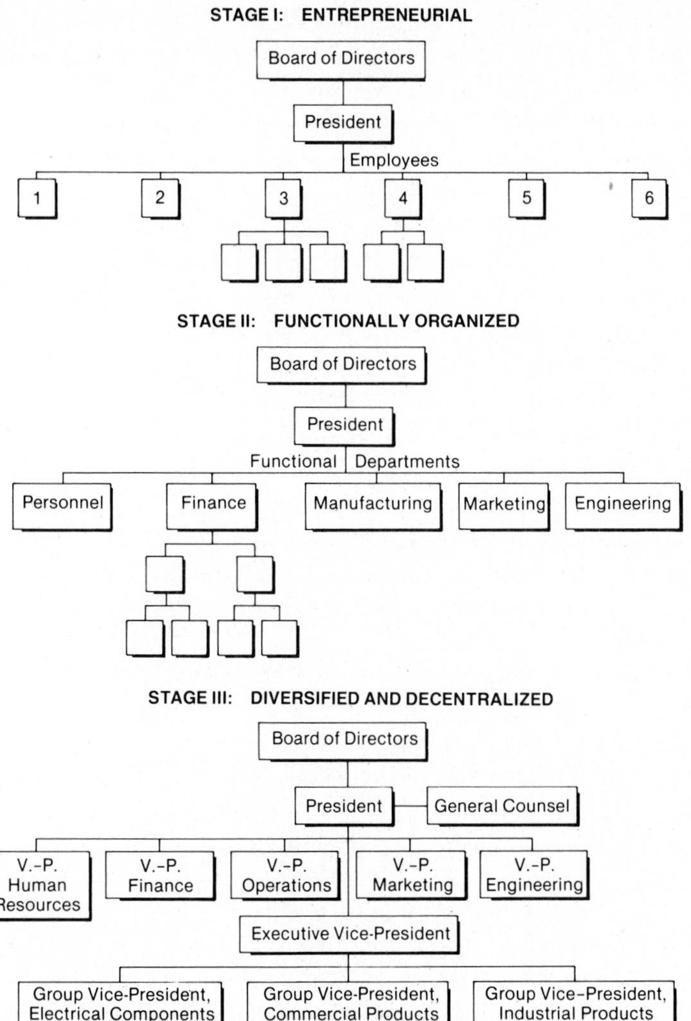

Figure 8.3 **Stages of corporate development.**

1982. In 1983, analysts reported that Polaroid was in the throes of a "mid-life crisis," worrying about its mortality and the loss of Dr. Land's inspiring vision.[27] Polaroid Corporation was, in effect, a Stage II corporation being managed by Dr. Land as if it still were a Stage I corporation.

At *Stage II,* the entrepreneur is replaced by a team of managers with functional specializations (see Fig. 8.3). The transition to this state requires a substantial managerial style change for the chief officer of the corporation, especially if the chief officer was the Stage I entrepreneur. Otherwise, having additional staff members yields no benefits to the corporation. At this juncture, the corporate strategy favors protectivism by trying to dominate the industry, often through vertical or horizontal integration. The great strength of a Stage II corporation lies in its concentration and specialization in one industry. Its great weakness is that all of its eggs are in one basket.

McDonald's, the world's largest food service company, is a Stage II corporation that is concentrating on fast food. Fred Turner, chairman of the board, commented in 1984 on the company's specialization in one industry:

> My view is that we can maintain a growth rate in the teens through this decade. And if you believe that, it makes the question of diversification beside the point.[28]

The *Stage III* corporation focuses on internal operating efficiencies. These corporations grow by diversifying their product lines and expanding to cover wider geographical areas. These corporations move to a divisional structure with a central headquarters (see Fig. 8.3). Headquarters attempts to coordinate the activities of its operating divisions through performance and results-oriented control and reporting systems, and by stressing corporate planning techniques. The divisions are not tightly controlled, but are held responsible for their own performance results. Therefore, to be effective, there has to be a decentralized decision process. The greatest strength of a Stage III corporation is its almost unlimited resources. Its most significant weakness is that it is usually so large and complex that it tends to become relatively inflexible.[29] General Electric, DuPont, and General Motors are Stage III corporations.

These descriptions of the three stages of corporate development are supported by research.[30] The differences among the stages are specified in more detail by Thain in Table 8.2.

In his study, Chandler noted that the empire builder was rarely the person who created the new structure to fit the new strategy, and that, as a result, the transition from one stage to another is often a painful one. This was true of General Motors Corporation under the management of William Durant, Ford Motor Company under its founder Henry Ford, and Polaroid Corporation under Edwin Land. Thain, in Table 8.3, summarizes the internal and external blocks to movement from one stage to another.

Table 8.2 **Key Factors in Top Management Process in Stage I, II, and III Companies**

Function	*Stage I*	*Stage II*	*Stage III*
1. Size-up: Major problems	Survival and growth dealing with short-term operating problems.	Growth, rationalization, and expansion of resources, providing for adequate attention to product problems.	Trusteeship in management and investment and control of large, increasing, and diversified resource. Also, important to diagnose and take action on problems at division level.
2. Objectives	Personal and subjective.	Profits and meeting functionally oriented budgets and performance targets.	ROI, profits, earnings per share.
3. Strategy	Implicit and personal; exploitation of immediate opportunities seen by owner-manager.	Functionally oriented moves restricted to "one product" scope; exploitation of one basic product or service field.	Growth and product diversification; exploitation of general business opportunities.
4. Organization: Major characteristic of structure	One unit, "one-man show."	One-unit, functionally specialized group.	Multiunit general staff office and decentralized operating divisions.
5. (a) Measurement and control	Personal, subjective control based on simple accounting system and daily communication and observation.	Control grows beyond one man; assessment of functional operations necessary; structured control systems evolve.	Complex formal system geared to comparative assessment of performance measures, indicating problems and opportunities and assessing management ability of division managers.
5. (b) Key performance indicators	Personal criteria, relationships with owner, operating efficiency, ability to solve operating problems.	Functional and internal criteria such as sales, performance compared to budget, size of empire, status in group, personal relationships, etc.	More impersonal application of comparisons such as profits, ROI, P/E ratio, sales, market share, productivity, product leadership, personnel development, employee attitudes, public responsibility.
6. Reward-punishment system	Informal, personal, subjective; used to maintain control and divide small pool of resources to provide personal incentives for key performers.	More structured; usually based to a greater extent on agreed policies as opposed to personal opinion and relationships.	Allotment by "due process" of a wide variety of different rewards and punishments on a formal and systematic basis. Company-wide policies usually apply to many different classes of managers and workers with few major exceptions for individual cases.

SOURCE: D. H. Thain, "Stages of Corporate Development," *The Business Quarterly* (Winter 1969), p. 37. Copyright © 1969 by *The Business Quarterly*. Reprinted by permission.

Table 8.3 **Blocks to Development**

a) Internal Blocks Stage I to II	Stage II to III
Lack of ambition and drive.	Unwillingness to take the risks involved.
Personal reasons of owner-manager for avoiding change in status quo.	Management resistance to change for a variety of reasons including old age, aversion to risk taking, desire to protect personal empires, etc.
Lack of operating efficiency.	Personal reasons among managers for defending the status quo.
Lack of quantity and quality of operating personnel.	Lack of control system related to appraisal of investment of decentralized operations.
Lack of resources such as borrowing power, plant and equipment, salesmen, etc.	Lack of budgetary control ability.
Product problems and weaknesses.	Organizational inflexibility.
Lack of planning and organizational ability.	Lack of management vision to see opportunities for expansion.
	Lack of management development, i.e., not enough managers to handle expansion.
	Management turnover and loss of promising young managers.
	Lack of ability to formulate and implement strategy that makes company relevant to changing conditions.
	Refusal to delegate power and authority for diversification.

b) External Blocks Stage I to II	Stage II to III
Unfavorable economic conditions.	Unfavorable economic, political, technological, and social conditions and/or trends.
Lack of market growth.	Lack of access to financial or management resources.
Tight money or lack of an underwriter who will assist the company "to go public."	Overly conservative accountants, lawyers, investment bankers, etc.
Labor shortages in quality and quantity.	Lack of domestic markets necessary to support large diversified corporation.
Technological obsolescence of product.	"The conservative mentality," e.g., cultural contentment with the status quo and lack of desire to grow and develop.

SOURCE: D. H. Thain, "Stages of Corporate Development," *The Business Quarterly* (Winter 1969), pp. 43–44.

Although it has been suggested that an additional phase in a corporation's development is the multinational or "global" stage,[31] this could be viewed as just a variation of the Stage III, multidivisional corporation. A truly multinational or global corporation usually has decentralized investment centers based on geography rather than on product line or strategic business unit. (Refer to Chapter 10 for additional information on multinational corporations.)

Organizational Life Cycle

A more recent approach to better understanding the development of corporations is that of the organizational "life cycle."[32] Instead of considering stages in terms of structure, this approach places the primary emphasis on the dominant issue facing the corporation. The specific organizational structure, therefore, becomes a secondary concern. These stages are *Birth* (Stage I), *Growth* (Stage II), *Maturity* (Stage III), *Decline* (Stage IV), and *Death* (Stage V). The impact of these stages on corporate strategy and structure is summarized in Table 8.4. Note that the first three stages of the organizational life cycle are basically the same as the three stages of corporate development mentioned previously. The only significant difference is the addition of the decline and death stages to complete the cycle.

The Stage IV firm became widespread in the Western world during the 1970s as many corporations in basic industries such as steel and automobiles seemed to lose their vitality and competitiveness. Most of the product lines of a Stage IV firm are at the mature or declining phase of their product life cycle. Sales are stagnant and actually declining if adjusted for inflation. An emphasis on company-wide cost-cutting further erodes future competitiveness. The major objective changes from stability to survival. Retrenchment coupled with pleas for government assistance is the only feasible

Table 8.4 **Organizational Life Cycle**

	Stage I	*Stage II*	*Stage III*	*Stage IV*	*Stage V*
Dominant Issue	Birth	Growth	Maturity	Decline	Death
Popular Strategies	Concentration in a niche	Horizontal and vertical integration	Concentric and conglomerate diversification	Profit strategy followed by retrenchment	Liquidation or bankruptcy
Likely Structure	Entrepreneur-dominated	Functional management emphasized	Decentralization into profit or investment centers	Structural surgery	Dismemberment of structure

strategy. Chrysler Corporation was a good example of a Stage IV corporation in the early 1980s.

Unless a corporation is able to resolve the critical issues facing it in Stage IV (as Chrysler was able to do), it is likely to move into Stage V, corporate death. This is what happened in the mid-1980s to AM International (previously known as the Addressograph-Multigraph Corporation), Baldwin-United, and Osborne Computers, as well as many other firms. The corporation is forced into bankruptcy. As in the cases of Rolls Royce and Penn Central, both of which went bankrupt in the 1970s, a corporation may nevertheless rise like a phoenix from its own ashes and live again. The company may be reorganized or liquidated, depending upon the individual circumstances. In some liquidations, the corporation's name is purchased, and the purchasing corporation places that name on some or all of its products. For example, Wordtronix, a maker of stand-alone word processors, acquired in 1983 the Remington Rand trademark, even though Remington Rand no longer made typewriters. Top management planned to change the Wordtronix name to Remington Rand to give its machines some name recognition in the marketplace.[33]

It is important to realize that not all corporations will move through these five stages in order. Some corporations, for example, may never move past Stage II. Others, like General Motors, may go directly from Stage I to Stage III. A large number will go from Stage I into Stages IV and V. Ford, for example, was unable to move from Stage I into Stage II as long as Henry Ford, I was in command. Its inability to realign itself no doubt contributed to its movement into Stage IV just before World War II. After the war, Henry Ford, II's turnaround strategy successfully restructured the corporation as a Stage II firm.

Staffing

The implementation of new strategy and policies often calls for a different utilization of personnel. If growth strategies are to be implemented, new people need to be hired and trained. Experienced people with the necessary skills need to be found for promotion into newly created managerial positions. For example, if a firm has decided to integrate forward by opening its own retail outlets, one key concern is the ability of the corporation to find, hire, and train store managers. If a corporation adopts a retrenchment strategy, however, a large number of people may need to be laid off or fired; and top management, as well as the divisional managers, need to specify criteria used to make these personnel decisions. Should employees be fired on the basis of low seniority or on the basis of poor performance? Sometimes corporations find it easier to close an entire division rather than choosing which individuals to fire. The University of Michigan followed this approach in

1981 when it cut back expenses by dropping its entire Geography Department.

Some authorities have suggested that the type of general manager needed to effectively implement a new divisional, corporate, or SBU strategy varies depending upon the desired strategic direction of that business unit.[34] Illustrative Example 8.1 tells how this approach was followed by the board of AM International in selecting the corporation's chief executive officer.

AM INTERNATIONAL MATCHES THE MANAGER WITH THE STRATEGY

Illustrative Example 8.1

The board of directors of AM International followed the theory that the general manager should match the firm's desired strategy when it both hired and fired Joe B. Freeman as the corporation's chief executive officer. Hired originally when the company filed for Chapter 11 bankruptcy in April 1982, Freeman worked hard to turn the firm around. He concentrated on cutting costs, boosting sales, and soothing both creditors and employees. By January 1984, the corporation was beginning to show a profit—and Joe B. Freeman was fired by the board. Looking back on the experience, Freeman admitted that some of the problem had been with his analytically oriented accounting background.

> The company had reached a new phase. My skills had been successful in bringing it to this phase but the board wanted a person with a different set of skills to lead it. . . . [The board wanted] an orientation toward business strategy and people skills. . . . I chose to devote most of my time to managing the company, to working with the creditors, and didn't spend much time on the image side with shareholders and directors.

SOURCE: R. Johnson, "AM International's Ex-Chief Freeman Tells How His Success Got Him Fired," *Wall Street Journal* (August 27, 1984), p. 21.

Depending on the situation of a specific division as determined by the GE Business Screen Matrix (Fig. 6.3), the "best" or most appropriate division manager may need to have a specific mix of skills and experiences. Some of these suggested "types" are depicted in Fig. 8.4.

One research study of business executives found that strategic business units with a "build" strategy as compared to SBUs with a "harvest" strategy tend to be headed by managers with a greater willingness to take risks and a higher tolerance for ambiguity.[35] Another study also found that managers with a certain mix of behaviors, skills, and personality factors tend to be linked with a different strategy than those with a different mix. For example,

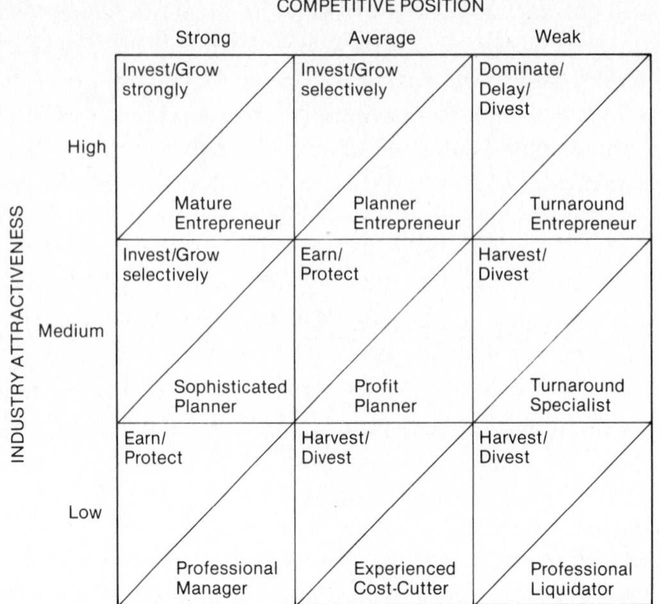

Figure 8.4 **The types of general managers needed to strategically manage different types of businesses.**
SOURCE: Adapted from C. W. Hofer and M. J. Davoust, *Successful Strategic Management* (Chicago: A. T. Kearney, Inc., 1977), pp. 45 and 82. Used by permission.

SBUs with a stability strategy tend to be run by a manager with a conservative style, a production or engineering background, and experience with controlling budgets, capital expenditures, inventories, and standardization procedures.[36] In summary, there is growing support for matching executive "types" with the dominant strategic direction of a business unit. Unfortunately, there is little help available to select the most appropriate manager when a corporation or SBU does not have a specific strategy formulated for that manager to implement.

There are a number of ways to ensure a continuous development of people for important managerial positions. One approach is to establish a sound *performance appraisal system* to identify good performers with managerial potential. A number of large organizations have started to use *assessment centers* to evaluate a person's suitability for a management position. Popularized by AT&T in the mid-1950s, corporations such as Standard Oil of Ohio and GE now use them.[37] Since each is specifically tailored to its corporation, these assessment centers are unique. They use special interviews, management games, in-basket exercises, leaderless group discussions, case analyses, decision-making exercises, and oral presentations to assess the potential of employees for higher-level positions. People are promoted into specific positions based on their performance in the assessment center. Many assessment centers have proved to be highly predictive of subsequent managerial performance.[38]

The implementation of strategy should not only be concerned with the selection of strategic managers, but also with the selection of the appropriate mix of professional, skilled, and unskilled labor. At IBM, for example, top management decided in 1984 to emphasize software development in order to reach its corporate growth objectives. Key divisions were then directed to expand their programming staffs by 20% per year for the next ten years.[39]

Directing

To effectively implement a new strategy, appropriate authority and responsibility must be delegated to the operational managers. People should be motivated to act in desired ways. Further, the actions must be coordinated to result in effective performance. Managers should be stimulated to find creative solutions to implementation problems without getting bogged down in conflict. When the proper people have been placed in the proper positions, a corporation needs a system to direct them toward the proper implementation of corporate, business, and functional strategies. Sometimes this is informally accomplished through a strong corporate culture with well-accepted norms and values regarding teamwork and commitment to the company's objectives and strategies. New employees are "socialized" into the culture through a series of planned training experiences.[40] Even if such a culture is not in place, activities can be directed toward accomplishing strategic goals through programs such as Management By Objectives (MBO) and incentive management.

Management By Objectives

Management By Objectives (MBO) is one organization-wide approach to help assure purposeful action toward desired objectives. MBO links organizational objectives and the behavior of individuals. Since it is a system that links plans with performance, it is a powerful implementation technique.

Although there is some disagreement about the purpose of MBO, most authorities agree that this approach involves (1) establishing and communicating organizational objectives, (2) setting individual objectives that help implement organizational ones, and (3) periodically reviewing performance as it relates to the objectives.[41] MBO provides an opportunity to connect the objectives of people at each level to those at the next higher level: "If carried out logically and ideally, the goals at each level would be contributing most directly toward overall organizational objectives. . . . MBO provides a potential method of integrating the physical, financial, and human resource plans of the organization to the goals that an individual is expected to achieve."[42] MBO, therefore, acts to tie together corporate, business, and functional objectives as well as the strategies developed to achieve them.

This forms a hierarchy of objectives similar to the hierarchy of strategy discussed earlier in Chapter 1. The MBO process is depicted in Fig. 8.5.

Research on corporate MBO programs is mixed but tends to support the belief that MBO should result in higher levels of performance than other approaches that do not include performance goals, relevant feedback, and joint supervisor/subordinate goal setting.[43] Galbraith and Nathanson point out that the existence of an MBO program at Dow-Corning permits its matrix structure (as discussed in Chapter 5) to function effectively: "Because people work against goals and problems, rather than against each other, they have less need for hierarchy and tie-breaking."[44] At Dow-Corning, the agreed-upon objectives are used to help reach consensus and thus reduce the potential for the conflict inherent in a matrix-style organization.

Incentive Management To ensure that there is a congruence between the needs of the corporation as a whole and the needs of the employees as individuals, managers should develop an incentive system that rewards desired performance. Research confirms the conventional wisdom that when pay is tied to performance, it motivates higher productivity, strongly affecting both absenteeism and work quality.[45] Corporations have, therefore, developed various types of incen-

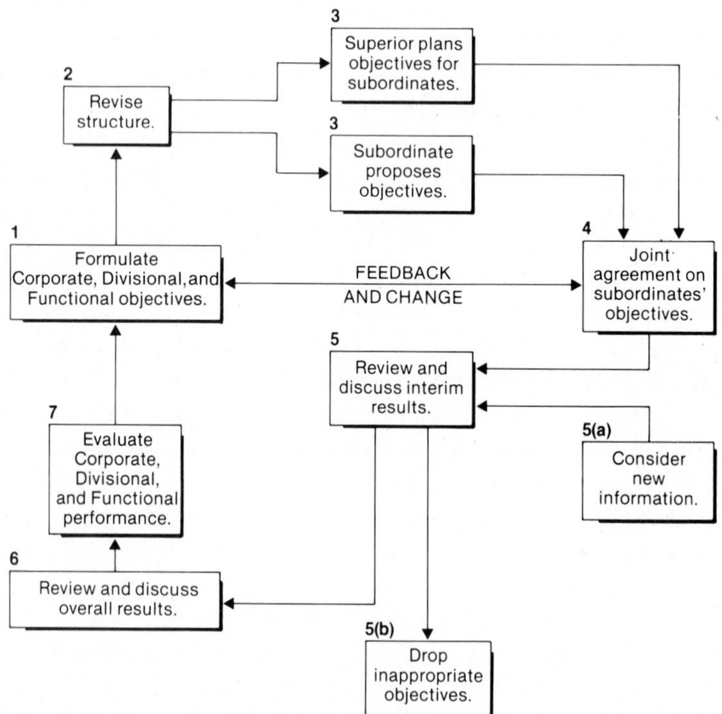

Figure 8.5 **The process of Management By Objectives.**

tives for executives that range from stock options to cash bonuses. All these incentive plans should be linked in some way to corporate and divisional strategy. Performance appraisal and incentive systems are discussed in more detail under Evaluation and Control in Chapter 9.

8.4 SUMMARY AND CONCLUSION

This chapter explains the implementation of strategy in terms of (1) *who* the operational managers are who must carry out strategic plans, (2) *what* they must do in order to implement strategy, and (3) *how* they should go about their activities. Vice-presidents of functional areas and directors of divisions or SBUs work with their subordinates to put together large-scale implementation plans. These plans include *programs, budgets,* and *procedures* and become more detailed as they move down the corporate "chain of command."

Strategy is implemented by management through planning, organizing, staffing, and directing activities.

Planning results in fairly detailed programs, budgets, and procedures.

Organizing deals with the design of an appropriate structure for the corporation. Research generally supports Chandler's proposal that changes in corporate strategy tend to lead to changes in organizational structure. The growing use of strategic business units, matrix structures, and entrepreneurial units reflects a need for more flexible structures to manage increasingly diversified corporations. Not only should a firm work to make its structure congruent with its strategy, it should also be aware that there is an organizational life cycle composed of stages of corporate development through which a corporation is likely to move.

Staffing focuses on finding and developing appropriate people for key positions. Without capable and committed managers and staff, strategy can never be implemented satisfactorily. To this end, performance appraisal systems and assessment centers are used by a number of large corporations.

Directing deals with organization-wide approaches that direct operational managers and employees to effect the implementation of corporate, business, and functional strategies. One such approach is Management By Objectives (MBO), which links organizational objectives and the behavior of operational managers. Its ability to tie planning with performance makes it a powerful implementation technique. The proper use of incentives, when integrated with a goal-centered approach such as MBO, is another method of directing effort toward achieving desired results.

DISCUSSION QUESTIONS

1. Japanese corporations typically involve many more organizational levels and people in the development of implementation plans than do U.S. corporations. Is this appropriate? Why or why not?
2. To what extent should top management be involved in strategy implementation?

3. Does structure follow strategy or does strategy follow structure? Why?
4. What can be done to encourage innovation in large corporations?
5. Should corporations select a certain type of person to be a general manager of a division depending on the strategic situation of that particular division? Why or why not?

NOTES

1. *Wall Street Journal* (December 27, 1984), p. 15.
2. L. D. Alexander, "Towards an Understanding of Strategy Implementation Problems," *Proceedings, Southern Management Association* (November 1982), p. 147.
3. P. Miesing, "Integrating Planning with Management, " *Long Range Planning* (October 1984), pp. 118–124.
   "The Future Catches Up with a Strategic Planner," *Business Week* (June 27, 1983), p. 62.
4. A. D. Chandler, *Strategy and Structure* (Cambridge, Mass.: MIT Press, 1962), p. 14.
5. A. P. Sloan, Jr., *My Years with General Motors* (Garden City, N.Y.: Doubleday, Anchor Books, 1972).
6. J. R. Galbraith and D. A. Nathanson, *Strategy Implementation: The Role of Structure and Process* (St. Paul, Minn.: West Publishing Co., 1978), p. 47.
   P. H. Grinyer and M. Yasai-Ardekani, "Strategy, Structure, Size, and Bureaucracy," *Academy of Management Journal* (September 1981), pp. 471–486.
   P. Lorange, *Implementation of Strategic Planning* (Englewood Cliffs, N.J.: Prentice-Hall, 1982), p. 109.
   L. G. Hrebiniak and W. F. Joyce, *Implementing Strategy* (New York: Macmillan, 1984), pp. 65–92.
7. Galbraith and Nathanson, p. 139.
8. D. R. Dalton, W. D. Todor, M. J. Spendolini, G. J. Fielding, and L. W. Porter, "Organization Structure and Performance: A Critical Review," *Academy of Management Review* (January 1980), pp. 49–64.
9. Hrebiniak and Joyce, p. 70.
10. T. Burns and G. M. Stalker, *The Management of Innovation* (London: Tavistock Publications, 1961).
11. P. R. Lawrence and J. W. Lorsch, *Organization and Environment* (Homewood, Ill.: Richard D. Irwin, Inc., 1967), p. 138.
12. William K. Hall, "SBUs: Hot New Topic in the Management of Diversification," *Business Horizons* (February 1978), p. 19.
13. "Evolving the GE Management System," *General Electric Monogram* (November–December 1977), p. 4.
14. M. E. Porter, *Competitive Advantage* (New York: The Free Press, 1985), pp. 395–398.
15. Porter, p. 322.
16. Hrebiniak and Joyce, pp. 85–86.

17. J. L. Brown and N. M. Agnew, "The Balance of Power in a Matrix Structure," *Business Horizons* (November–December 1982), pp. 51–54.

18. P. G. W. Keen, "Communications in the 21st Century: Telecommunications and Business Policy," *Organizational Dynamics* (Autumn 1981), pp. 54–67.

19. A. L. Frohman, "Technology as a Competitive Weapon," *Harvard Business Review* (January–February 1982), p. 97.

20. R. A. Burgelman, "Designs for Corporate Entrepreneurship," *California Management Review* (Spring 1984), pp. 154–166.

21. G. Pinchot, *Intrapreneuring, or Why You Don't Have to Leave the Corporation to Become an Entrepreneur* (New York: Harper & Row, 1985) as reported by J. S. DeMott, "Here Come the Intrapreneurs," *Time* (February 4, 1985), pp. 36–37.

22. E. C. Gottschalk, "Allied Unit, Free of Red Tape, Seeks To Develop Orphan Technologies," *Wall Street Journal* (September 13, 1984), p. 29.

23. M. Magnet, "Acquiring without Smothering," *Fortune* (November 12, 1984), p. 26.

24. C. Dolan, "Tektronix New-Venture Subsidiary Brings Benefits to Parent, Spinoffs," *Wall Street Journal* (September 18, 1984), p. 31.

25. Burgelman, pp. 162–164.

26. D. H. Thain, "Stages of Corporate Development," *The Business Quarterly* (Winter 1969), pp. 32–45.
B. R. Scott, "Stages of Corporate Development" (Boston: Intercollegiate Case Clearing House, no. 9-371-294, 1971); and "The Industrial State: Old Myths and New Realities," *Harvard Business Review* (March–April 1973).
R. V. Tuason, "Corporate Life Cycle and the Evaluation of Corporate Strategy," *Proceedings, The Academy of Management* (August 1973), pp. 35–40.

27. W. M. Bulkeley, "As Polaroid Matures, Some Lament a Decline in Creative Excitement," *Wall Street Journal* (May 10, 1983), p. 1.

28. M. J. Williams, "McDonald's Refuses to Plateau," *Fortune* (November 12, 1984), p. 40.

29. Thain, p. 39.

30. N. R. Smith and J. B. Miner, "Type of Entrepreneur, Type of Firm, and Managerial Motivation: Implications for Organizational Life Cycle Theory," *Strategic Management Journal* (October–December 1983), pp. 325–340.
F. Hoy, B. C. Vaught, and W. W. Buchanan, "Managing Managers of Firms in Transition from Stage I to Stage II," *Proceedings, Southern Management Association* (November 1982), pp. 152–153.
K. Smith and T. Mitchell, "An Investigation into the Effect of Changes in Stages of Organizational Maturation on a Decision Maker's Decision Priorities," *Proceedings, Southern Management Association* (November 1983), pp. 7–9.

31. Galbraith and Nathanson, p. 118.

32. D. A. Tansik, R. B. Chase, and N. J. Aquilano, *Management: A Life Cycle Approach* (Homewood, Ill.: Richard D. Irwin, Inc., 1980).
J. R. Kimberly, R. H. Miles, and Associates, *The Organizational Life Cycle* (San Francisco: Jossey-Bass, 1980).

33. C. Waterloo, "Big Shakeout in Electronics Tests Concern," *Wall Street Journal* (November 9, 1983), p. 31.

34. C. W. Hofer, E. A. Murray, Jr., R. Charam, and R. A. Pitts, *Strategic Management: A Casebook in Business Policy and Planning* (St. Paul, Minn.: West Publishing Co., 1980), p. 19.
M. Leontiades, "Choosing the Right Manager to Fit the Strategy," *Journal of Business Strategy* (Fall 1982), pp. 58–69.
J. G. Wissema, H. W. Van Der Pol, and H. M. Messer, "Strategic Management Archetypes," *Strategic Management Journal* (January–March 1980), pp. 37–47.
L. J. Stybel, "Linking Strategic Planning and Management Manpower Planning," *California Management Review* (Fall 1982), pp. 48–56.
R. A. Bettis and W. K. Hall, "The Business Portfolio Approach—Where It Falls Down in Practice," *Long Range Planning* (April 1983), pp. 95–104.
A. D. Szilagyi, Jr. and D. M. Schweiger, "Matching Managers to Strategies: A Review and Suggested Framework," *Academy of Management Review* (October 1984), pp. 626–637.

35. A. K. Gupta and V. Govindarajan, "Business Unit Strategy, Managerial Characteristics, and Business Unit Effectiveness at Strategy Implementation," *Academy of Management Journal* (March 1984), p. 36.

36. H. Deresky and T. T. Herbert, "The Strategic Contingency in the General Manager's Role," a paper presented to the Academy of Management, San Diego, California, August 1985, p. 11.

37. J. B. Miner and M. G. Miner, *Personnel and Industrial Relations,* 3rd ed. (New York: Macmillan, 1977), pp. 194–196.

38. Miner and Miner, p. 196.

39. M. A. Harris, "IBM: More Worlds to Conquer," *Business Week* (February 18, 1985), p. 85.

40. R. Pascale, "Fitting New Employees into the Company Culture," *Fortune* (May 28, 1984), pp. 28–42.

41. S. J. Carroll, Jr. and H. L. Tosi, Jr., *Management by Objectives* (New York: Macmillan, 1973), p. 3.

42. M. D. Richards, *Organizational Goal Structures* (St. Paul, Minn.: West Publishing Co., 1978), p. 128.

43. Carroll and Tosi, p. 16.

44. Galbraith and Nathanson, p. 99.

45. E. E. Lawler III, *Pay and Organizational Effectiveness* (New York: McGraw-Hill, 1971).
E. A. Locke, "How to Motivate Employees" (Paper presented at the NATO conference on changes in the nature and quality of working life, Thessaloniki, Greece, August 19–24, 1979.) Cited in E. E. Lawler III, *Pay and Organizational Development* (Reading, Mass.: Addison-Wesley, 1981), p. 3.

Chapter 9

EVALUATION AND CONTROL

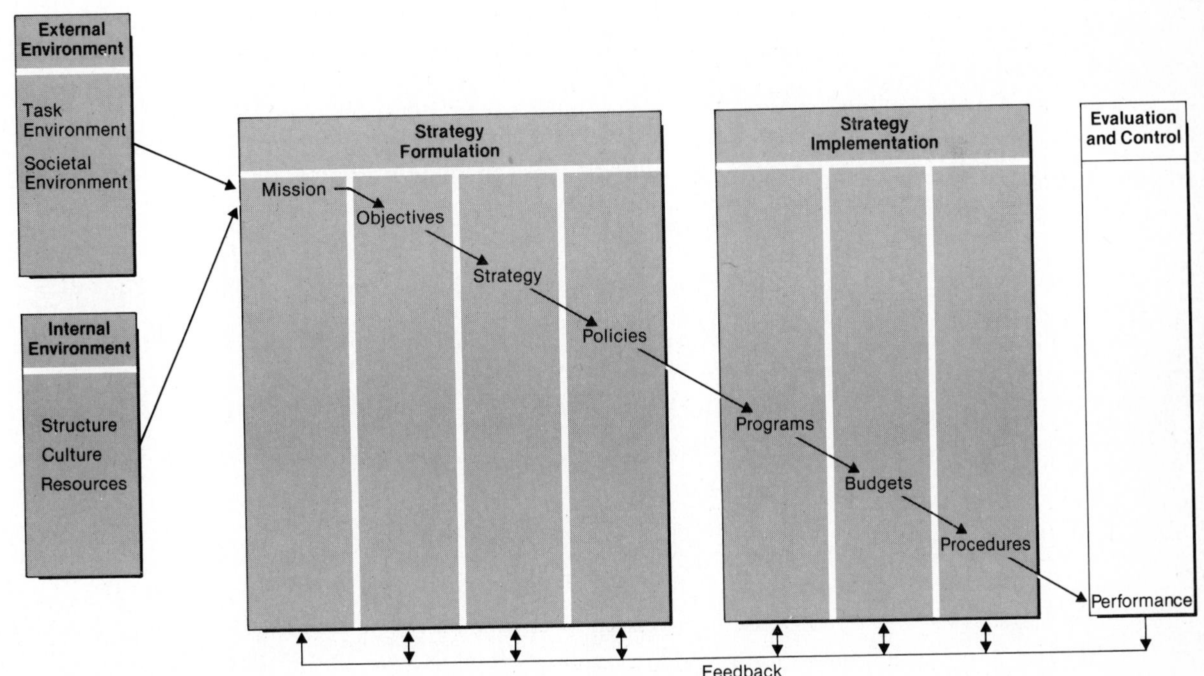

The last part of the strategic management model is the evaluation of performance and the control of work activities. Control follows planning. It ensures that the corporation is achieving what it set out to accomplish. Just as planning involves the setting of objectives along with the strategies and programs necessary to accomplish them, the control process compares performance with desired results and provides the feedback necessary to evaluate results and take corrective action, as needed.[1] This process may be viewed as a five-step feedback model as depicted in Fig. 9.1.

1. *Determine what to measure.* Top managers as well as operational managers need to specify what implementation processes and results will be monitored and evaluated. The processes and results must be capable of being measured in a reasonably objective and consistent manner. The focus should be on the most significant elements in a process—the ones that account for the highest proportion of expense or the greatest number of problems.
2. *Establish standards of performance.* Standards used to measure performance are detailed expressions of strategic objectives. They are *measures* of what are acceptable performance results. Each standard usually includes a *tolerance range* within which certain deviations will be accepted as satisfactory. Standards can be set not only for final output, but for intermediate stages of production output.
3. *Measure actual performance.* Measurements must be made at predetermined times.
4. *Compare actual performance with the standard.* If actual performance results are within the desired tolerance range, the measurement process stops here.
5. *Take corrective action.* If actual results fall outside the desired tolerance range, action must be taken to correct the deviation. The following must be determined:

   a) Is the deviation only a chance fluctuation?

   b) Are the processes being carried out incorrectly?

   c) Are the processes appropriate to the achievement of the desired standard?

   Action must be taken that will not only correct the deviation, but also prevent its happening again.

The strategic management model shows that evaluation and control information is fed back and assimilated into the entire management process.

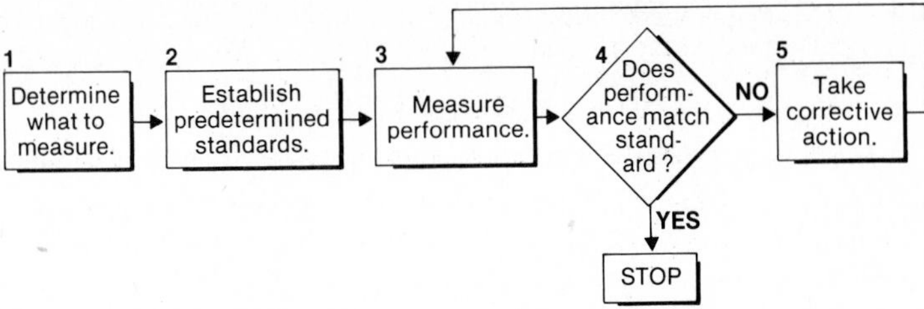

Figure 9.1 **Evaluation and control process.**

This information consists of performance data and activity reports (gathered in step 3 of Fig. 9.1). If undesired performance is the result of an inappropriate *use* of the strategic management processes, operational managers must know about it in order to correct employee activity. Top management need not be involved. If, however, undesired performance results from the processes themselves, top managers, as well as operational managers, must know about it in order to develop new implementation programs or procedures.

9.1 MEASURING PERFORMANCE

The measures used will depend on the organizational unit to be measured, as well as on the objectives to be achieved. Certain measures, such as return on investment, are very appropriate for evaluating the ability of a corporation or division to achieve a profitability objective. These measures, however, are inadequate for evaluating other objectives a corporation may want to achieve: social responsibility or employee development, for instance. Different measures are required for different objectives. Even though profitability is the major objective for a corporation, using return on investment alone may be insufficient as a control device. ROI, for example, can be computed only *after* profits are totaled for a period. It tells what happened—not what *is* happening or what *will* happen. A firm, therefore, needs to develop measures that predict likely profitability. These are referred to as "steering" or "feed-forward" controls because they measure variables that influence profitability.

Measures of Corporate Performance

The most commonly used measure of corporate performance (in terms of profits) is return on investment. As discussed in Chapter 2, it is simply the result of dividing net income before taxes by total assets. Although there are a number of advantages to using ROI, there are also a number of distinct limitations. Some of these are detailed in Table 9.1.

Other popular measures are earnings per share (EPS) and return on equity (ROE). Earnings per share also has several deficiencies when used to

Table 9.1 Advantages and Limitations of ROI as a Measure of Corporate Performance

Advantages
1. ROI is a single comprehensive figure influenced by everything that happens.
2. It measures how well the division manager uses the property of the company to generate profits. It is also a good way to check on the accuracy of capital investment proposals.
3. It is a common denominator that can be compared with many entities.
4. It provides an incentive to use existing assets efficiently.
5. It provides an incentive to acquire new assets only when doing so would increase the return.
Limitations
1. ROI is very sensitive to depreciation policy. Depreciation write-off variances between divisions affect ROI performance. Accelerated depreciation techniques reduce ROI, conflicting with capital budgeting discounted cash-flow analysis.
2. ROI is sensitive to book value. Older plants with more depreciated assets have relatively lower investment bases than newer plants (note also the effect of inflation), thus increasing ROI. Note that asset investment may be held down or assets disposed of in order to increase ROI performance.
3. In many firms that use ROI, one division sells to another. As a result, transfer pricing must occur. Expenses incurred affect profit. Since, in theory, the transfer price should be based on the total impact on firm profit, some investment center managers are bound to suffer. Equitable transfer prices are difficult to determine.
4. If one division operates in an industry that has favorable conditions and another division operates in an industry that has unfavorable conditions, the former division will automatically "look" better than the other.
5. The time span of concern here is short range. The performance of division managers should be measured in the long run. This is top management's time-span capacity.
6. The business cycle strongly affects ROI performance, often despite managerial performance.

SOURCE: James M. Higgins, *Organizational Policy and Strategic Management*, 2nd ed. Copyright © 1983 by CBS College Publishing. Reprinted by permission of The Dryden Press, CBS College Publishing.

evaluate past and future performance. For one thing, because alternative accounting principles are available, EPS may have several different but equally acceptable values, depending on the principle selected. Second, because EPS is based on accrual income, the conversion of income to cash can be near term or delayed. As a result, EPS does not consider the time value of money. Because of these and other limitations, earnings per share *by itself* is not an adequate measure of corporate performance.[2]

Stakeholder Measures

As mentioned in Chapter 4, stakeholders in the corporation's task environment are often very concerned about corporate activities and performance. Each has its own set of criteria to determine how well the corporation is performing. These criteria typically deal with the direct and indirect impact of corporate activities on stakeholder interests. Freeman proposes that top management needs to "keep score" with these stakeholders by establishing one or more simple measures for each stakeholder category.[3] A few of these measures are listed in Table 9.2.

Value Added Measures

Assuming that any one measure is bound to have some shortcomings, Hofer recommends the use of three new measures to evaluate a corporation's performance results (see Table 9.3). These measures are based on *value added* and are attempts to measure directly the contribution a corporation makes to

Table 9.2 A Sample Score Card for "Keeping Score with Stakeholders"

Stakeholder Category	*Possible Near-Term Measures*	*Possible Long-Term Measures*
Customers	Sales ($ and volume) New customers Number of new customer needs met ("tries")	Growth in sales Turnover of customer base Ability to control price
Suppliers	Cost of raw material Delivery time Inventory Availability of raw material	Growth rates of Raw material costs Delivery time Inventory New ideas from suppliers
Financial Community	EPS Stock price Number of "buy" lists ROE	Ability to convince Wall Street of strategy Growth in ROE
Employees	Number of suggestions Productivity Number of grievances	Number of internal promotions Turnover
Congress	Number of new pieces of legislation that affect the firm Access to key members and staff	Number of new regulations that affect industry Ratio of "cooperative" vs. "competitive" encounters
Consumer Advocate	Number of meetings Number of "hostile" encounters Number of times coalitions formed Number of legal actions	Number of changes in policy due to C.A. Number of C.A. initiated "calls for help"
Environmentalists	Number of meetings Number of hostile encounters Number of times coalitions formed Number of EPA complaints Number of legal actions	Number of changes in policy due to environmentalists Number of environmentalist "calls for help"

SOURCE: R. E. Freeman, *Strategic Management* (Boston: Pitman Publishing, Inc., 1984), p. 179. Copyright © 1984 by R. E. Freeman. Reprinted by permission.

Table 9.3 Three New Measures of Corporate Performance

Performance Characteristic	*Some Traditional Measures*	*Proposed New Measures*
Growth	Dollar sales, unit sales, dollar assets.	Value added*
Efficiency	Gross margin, net profits, net profits/dollar sales.	ROVA†
Asset utilization	ROI, return on equity, earnings per share.	ROVA/ROI

SOURCE: C. W. Hofer, "ROVA: A New Measure for Assessing Organizational Performance," in R. Lamb, ed., *Advances in Strategic Management*, vol. 2 (Greenwich, Conn.: JAI Press, 1983), p. 50. Copyright © 1983 by C. W. Hofer. Reprinted by permission.

* Value added = Dollar sales − Cost of raw materials and purchased parts.

† ROVA: Return on Value Added = $\frac{\text{Net profits before tax}}{\text{Value Added}} \times 100\%$.

society. Value added is the difference between dollar sales and the cost of raw materials and purchased parts. Return on value added (ROVA) is a second measure, one that divides net profits before tax by value added and converts the quotient to a percentage. Preliminary studies by Hofer suggest that ROVA tends to stabilize in the range of 12% to 18% for most industries in the maturity or saturation phases of market evolution. Hofer argues that ROVA may be a better measure of corporate performance across various industries than other measures currently in use.[4]

Shareholder Value

Because of the belief that accounting-based numbers such as return on investment and earnings per share are not reliable indicators of a corporation's economic value, many corporations are using shareholder value as a better measure of corporate performance and strategic management effectiveness.[5] *Shareholder value* (or shareholder wealth) is defined as the sum of dividends plus stock appreciation. It determines if a corporation is earning a rate of return greater than that demanded by investors in the security market. Rappaport, one of the principal advocates of this measure, explains its use.

> What I have termed the "shareholder value approach" estimates the economic value of any strategy as the expected cash flows discounted by the market discount rate. These cash flows in turn serve as the basis for expected shareholder returns from dividends and stock-price appreciation.[6]

A recent survey of the senior managers of Fortune 500 companies revealed that 30% select investment proposals on the basis of their expected contributions to shareholder wealth. The survey also noted that a number of corporations not now using this approach are starting to experiment with value-based techniques.[7]

Evaluation of Top Management

Through its strategy, audit, and compensation committees, a board of directors closely evaluates the job performance of the CEO and the top management team. Of course, it is concerned primarily with overall profitability as measured by return on investment, return on equity, earnings per share, and shareholder wealth. The absence of short-run profitability is certainly a factor contributing to the firing of any CEO.[8] The board will also, however, be concerned with other factors. For example, McSweeney recommends the incorporation of a number of areas of concern on a scorecard for use by the board. Figure 9.2 is one example of such a scorecard.

As shown in Fig. 9.2, the board should evaluate top management not only on return, but also on factors relating to its strategic management practices. Has the top management team set reasonable long-run as well as short-run objectives? Has it formulated innovative strategies? Has it worked closely with operational managers to develop realistic implementation plans, schedules, and budgets? Has it developed and used appropriate measures

General scoreboard	Good	Fair	Poor
Return on stockholders' equity			
Return on sales			
Management of stockholders' assets			
Development of sound organizational structure			
Development of successors			
Development of proprietary products			
Development of organization morale			
Development of corporate image			
Development of growth potential			
Percentage of industry by segments			
Divestments			
Acquisitions			
Application of research & development			
Application of engineering & technology			
International			

Figure 9.2 **Scorecard to rate top management.**

SOURCE: E. McSweeney, "A Scorecard for Rating Management," *Business Week* (June 18, 1974), p. 15. Reprinted from the June 18, 1974 issue of *Business Week* by special permission. Copyright © 1974 by McGraw-Hill, Inc.

of corporate and divisional performance for feedback and control? Has it provided the board with appropriate feedback on corporate performance in advance of key decision points? These and other questions should be raised by a board of directors as they evaluate the performance of top management.

The specific items that are used by a board to evaluate its top management should be derived from the objectives agreed to earlier by both the board and top management. If better relations with the local community and improved safety practices in work areas were selected as objectives for the year (or for five years), these items should be included in the evaluation. In addition, other factors should be included that tend to lead to profitability, such as market share, product quality, and investment intensity (from the PIMS research discussed in Chapter 6).[9]

Key Performance Areas

In order for top management to establish effective control systems for the entire corporation, it must identify "key performance areas." These areas must reflect important corporate objectives. According to Stoner, "Key performance or key result areas are those aspects of the unit or organization that *have* to function effectively in order for the entire unit or organization to succeed."[10] The broad controls that top management establishes for these key areas help to define the more detailed control systems and performance standards for lower-level managers. GE developed eight key performance areas and established standards for them. These areas are as follows:

1. *Profitability.* GE chose to use total dollar profits minus a charge for capital investment.
2. *Market position.* Market share, that is, the percent of available business for each product or service.
3. *Productivity.* Two measures were used—payroll dollar cost and the depreciation dollar costs of goods produced. These enabled GE to assess the efficiency with which labor and equipment were being used.
4. *Product leadership.* In each of GE's businesses, members of the engineering, manufacturing, marketing, and finance departments annually evaluated the costs, quality, and market position of each existing and each planned product.
5. *Personnel development.* Various reports were compiled to evaluate the manner in which GE was providing for present and future personnel needs.
6. *Employee attitudes.* Attitudes of employees toward the company were measured directly by regular attitude surveys, as well as indirectly by absenteeism and turnover.

7. *Public responsibility.* Indicators were developed to assess how well GE was carrying out its responsibilities to its employees, suppliers, and local communities.
8. *Balance between short-range and long-range goals.* An in-depth study of the interrelationships between key performance areas was carried out to ensure that immediate goals were not being attained at the expense of future profits and stability.[11]

Strategic Audits

Audits of corporate activities are used by various consulting firms as a way to measure performance and are increasingly suggested for use by boards of directors as well as by others in managerial positions. Management audits have been developed to evaluate activities such as corporate social responsibility, functional areas such as the marketing department, divisions such as the international division, as well as to evaluate the corporation itself in a strategic audit (see Chapter 2). The strategic audit approach is likely to be increasingly used by corporations that become concerned with closely monitoring those activities that affect overall corporate effectiveness and efficiency. To be effective, the strategic audit should be developed to parallel the corporation's strategic management process and/or model.

Measures of Divisional and Functional Unit Performance

Corporations use a variety of techniques to evaluate and control performance in divisions, SBUs, and functional units. If a corporation is composed of SBUs or divisions, it will use many of the same performance measures (ROI, for instance) that it uses to assess overall corporation performance. To the extent that it can isolate specific functional units, such as R&D, the corporation may develop responsibility centers.

Budgets are certainly an important control device. During strategy formulation and implementation, top management approves a series of programs and supporting operating budgets from its business units.[12] During evaluation and control, actual expenses are contrasted with planned expenditures to assess the degree of variance. This is typically done on a monthly basis. In addition, top management will probably require *periodic statistical reports* summarizing data on key factors, such as the number of new customer contracts, volume of received orders, and productivity figures, among others.[13]

Evaluating a Division or SBU

At Norton Company, each SBU is evaluated in depth every two years. This evaluation is conducted by the Strategy Guidance Committee, composed of the CEO, the financial vice-president, eight vice-presidents in charge of operations, the controller, assistant controller, vice-president for corporate development, and an assistant vice-president. At the same time that the line manager in charge of an SBU comes before the committee with a detailed strategy for each major segment of the unit's operations, the committee is evaluating the unit's performance according to past objectives, and arriving at its strategic position within the corporation and, therefore, its potential.

> The Strategy Guidance Committee looks at a strategic business unit from many viewpoints—return on net assets, return on sales, asset turnover, market share strategy. The committee might test sales growth rate against market growth rate against market share strategy. The committee also looks at competition, relative strengths and weaknesses, and cash generation plotted against market share strategy. It also places the unit on a balloon chart or growth/market share matrix for the entire company, to see how this unit fits in with all the others.[14]

The Strategy Guidance Committee looks at the SBU from all angles and asks a number of penetrating questions. Some of these questions are listed below.

Evaluation of a Strategic Business Unit at Norton Company

- How does this unit contribute to the overall scheme of things?
- Does it help to balance the total?
- Does it increase or decrease the cyclical nature of the company?
- How does it relate to other Norton technologies, processes, or distribution systems?
- How successfully does it compete?
- How is it regarded by its customers and by its competitors?
- Does it hurt or improve the company's image with the investment community?
- What are its mission and mode of operation in terms of build, maintain, or harvest?
- Is its current strategy appropriate?
- Can we win and, if so, how?
- If it has changed its strategy or performance since the last review, why has it changed?
- What does our analysis suggest about the unit's profitability in comparison with similar businesses?

SOURCE: D. R. Melville, "Top Management's Role in Strategic Planning," *The Journal of Business Strategy,* vol. 1, no. 4, (Spring 1981), p. 63. Reprinted by permission from the *Journal of Business Strategy.*

Responsibility Centers

Control systems can be established to monitor specific functions, projects, or divisions. Budgets typically are used to control the financial indicators of performance. Responsibility centers are used to isolate a unit so that it can be evaluated separately from the rest of the corporation. A responsibility center is headed by a manager responsible for the center's performance. It uses resources (measured in terms of costs) to produce a service or a product (measured in terms of volume or revenues). There are five major types of responsibility centers. They are determined by the way these resources and services or products are measured by the corporation's control system:[15]

1. *Standard cost centers.* Primarily used in manufacturing facilities, standard (or expected) costs are computed for each operation on the basis

of historical data. To evaluate the center's performance, its total standard costs are multiplied by the units produced to give the expected cost of production, which is then compared to the actual cost of production.

2. *Revenue centers.* Production, usually in terms of unit or dollar sales, is measured without consideration of resource costs (e.g., salaries). The center is thus judged in terms of effectiveness rather than efficiency. The effectiveness of a sales region, for example, is determined by its actual sales compared to its projected or previous year's sales. Profits are not considered because sales departments have very limited influence over the cost of the products they sell.

3. *Expense centers.* Resources are measured in dollars without consideration of service or product costs. Thus budgets will have been prepared for "engineered" expenses (those costs that can be calculated) and for "discretionary" expenses. Typical expense centers are administrative, service, and research departments. They cost an organization money, but they only indirectly contribute to revenues.

4. *Profit centers.* Performance is measured in terms of the difference between revenues (which measure production) and expenditures (which measure resources). A profit center is typically established whenever an organizational unit has control over both its resources and its products or services. By having such centers, a corporation can be organized into divisions of separate product lines. The manager of each division is given autonomy to the extent that she or he is able to keep profits at a satisfactory (or better) level. Some organizational units that are not usually thought of as potentially autonomous can, for the purpose of profit-center evaluations, be made so. A manufacturing department, for example, may be converted from a standard cost center (or expense center) into a profit center by allowing it to charge a *transfer price* for each product it "sells" to the sales department. The difference between the manufacturing cost per unit and the agreed-upon transfer price is the unit's "profit."

5. *Investment centers.* As with profit centers, investment center performance is measured in terms of the difference between its resources and its services or products. Since most divisions in large manufacturing corporations use huge assets, such as plants and equipment, to make their products, evaluating their performance on the basis of profits alone ignores the size of their assets. For example, two divisions in a corporation make identical profits, but one division owns a \$3 million plant, whereas the other owns a \$1 million plant. Both make the same profits,

but one is obviously more efficient: The smaller plant provides the stockholders with a better return on their investment.

The most widely used measure of investment center performance is ROI. Another measure, called residual income, is found by subtracting an interest charge from the net income. This interest charge could be based on the interest the corporation is actually paying to lenders for the assets being used. It could also be based on the amount of income that could have been earned if the assets had been invested somewhere else.

Sloan reports that the concept of rate of return on investments was crucial to General Motors' exercise of its permanent control of the whole corporation in a way consistent with its decentralized organization.[16] Donaldson Brown, who came to GM from DuPont in 1921, defined return on investment as a function of the profit margin and the rate of turnover of invested capital. Multiplying the profit margin by the investment turnover equals the percent of return on investment. Management can, therefore, increase the return on investment by increasing the rate of capital turnover in relation to sales (that is, increase volume) as well as by increasing profit margins (increase revenue and/or cut costs and expenses).[17]

Investment center performance can also be measured in terms of its contribution to *shareholder value.* One example is given by the CEO of a large corporation.

> We value our businesses by computing the net present value of each unit's equity cash flow, using the appropriate cost of capital. Then we subtract out the market value of assigned debt and arrive at an estimate of the warranted market value of the unit. These techniques allow us to evaluate and rank our units based on their relative contribution to the creation of overall corporate equity value, which is our overall objective.[18]

9.2 STRATEGIC INFORMATION SYSTEMS

Before performance measures can have any impact on strategic management, they must be communicated to those people responsible for formulating and implementing strategic plans. Strategic information systems can perform this function. They may be computer-based or manual, formal or informal. They serve the information needs of top management.[19] As discussed in Chapter 5, an information system is meant to provide a basis for early warning signals that can originate both externally or internally. These warning signals grow out of the corporation's need to ensure that programs and procedures are being implemented to achieve corporate and divisional objectives.

As mentioned in Chapter 5, the information system should focus managers' attention on the critical success factors in their jobs. *Critical success factors* are those few things that must go well to ensure success in a corporation. They therefore represent those areas that must be given special and continuous attention to bring about high performance.[20] These critical success factors provide a focal point for directing the development of a computer-based information system. Taking this approach should result in an information system useful to strategic managers as it pinpoints key areas that require a manager's attention.

At the divisional or SBU level of a corporation, the information system should be used to support, reinforce, or enlarge its business-level strategy.[21] An SBU pursuing a strategy of overall cost leadership could use its information system to reduce costs either by improving labor productivity or the utilization of other resources such as inventory or machinery. Another SBU, in contrast, might wish to pursue a differentiation strategy. It could use its information system to add uniqueness to the product or service and contribute to quality, service, or image through the functional areas.[22] American Hospital Supply and both United and American Airlines took this approach to increase their market shares by offering unique information systems services to their customers. The choice of the business-level strategy will thus dictate the type of information system needed in the SBU to both implement and control strategic activities. Table 9.4 lists the differences between an information system needed to evaluate and control a low-cost strategy and an information system needed for product differentiation. The information systems will be constructed differently to monitor different activities because the two types of business-level strategies have different critical success factors.

9.3 PROBLEMS IN MEASURING PERFORMANCE

The measurement of performance is a crucial part of evaluation and control. The lack of quantifiable objectives or performance standards and the inability of the information system to provide timely, valid information are two obvious control problems.[23] Without objective and timely measurements, it would be extremely difficult to make operational, let alone strategic, decisions. Nevertheless, the use of timely, quantifiable standards does not guarantee good performance. The very act of monitoring and measuring performance can cause side-effects which interfere with overall corporate performance. Among the most frequent negative side-effects are a *short-term orientation* and *goal displacement.*

Short-Term Orientation

Hodgetts and Wortman state that in many situations top executives do not analyze *either* the long-term implications of present operations on the strategy they have adopted *or* the operational impact of a strategy on the corporate mission. They report that long-run evaluations are *not* conducted because executives (1) may not realize their importance, (2) may feel that

Table 9.4 Use of Information Systems to Monitor Implementation of Business Strategies

	Generic Strategies	
	Low Cost	*Product Differentiation*
Product Design & Development	Product engineering systems Project control systems	R&D data bases Professional work stations Electronic mail CAD Custom engineering systems Integrated systems for manufacturing
Operations	Process engineering systems Process control systems Labor control systems Inventory management systems Procurement systems Quality monitoring systems	CAM Quality assurance systems Systems for suppliers Quality monitoring systems
Marketing	Streamlined distribution systems Centralized control systems Econometric modeling systems	Sophisticated marketing systems Market data bases Graphic display systems Telemarketing systems Competition analysis systems Modeling systems Service-oriented distribution systems
Sales	Sales control systems Advertising monitoring systems Systems to consolidate sales function Strict incentive/monitoring systems	Differential pricing systems Office/field communications Customer/sales support systems Dealer support systems Customer order entry systems
Administration	Cost control systems Quantitative planning & budgeting systems Office automation for staff reduction	Office automation to integrate functions Environment scanning & nonquantitative planning systems Teleconferencing systems

SOURCE: G. L. Parsons, "Information Technology: A New Competitive Weapon," *Sloan Management Review* (Fall 1983), p. 12. Reprinted by permission of the publisher.

short-run considerations are more important than long-run considerations, (3) may not be personally evaluated on a long-term basis, or (4) may not have the time to make a long-run analysis.[24] There is no real justification for the first and last "reasons." If executives realize the importance of long-run evaluations, they make the time needed to conduct them. The short-term nature of most incentive and promotion plans, however, provides a rationale for the second and third reasons.

A study of 112 large U.S. corporations revealed that only 44.4% had an explicit policy for rewarding the contribution of key line managers to strategic planning.[25] A similar study found that whereas 79% of the corporations sampled rewarded executives for short-term performance (typically an annual bonus linked to pretax profit), only 42% of the same firms offered longer-term incentive plans.[26]

Table 9.1 indicates that one of the limitations of ROI as a performance measure is its short-term nature. In theory, ROI is not limited to the short run, but in practice it is often difficult to use this measure to realize long-term benefits for the corporation. If the performance of corporate and division managers is evaluated primarily on the basis of an annual ROI, the managers tend to focus their effort on those factors that have positive short-term effects. As a result, division managers often undertake capital investments with early paybacks to establish a favorable division track record. Results are often inconsistent with corporate long-run objectives. Since managers can often manipulate both the numerator (earnings) as well as the denominator (investment), the resulting ROI figure becomes meaningless. Advertising, maintenance, and research efforts might be reduced. Mergers may be undertaken that will do more for this year's earnings than for the division's or corporation's future profits. Expensive retooling and plant modernization can be delayed as long as a manager can manipulate figures on production defects and absenteeism. Efforts to compensate for these distortions tend to create a burdensome accounting control system which stifles creativity and flexibility, leading to even more questionable "creative accounting" practices.[27] For example, the manager of Doughtie's Foods' wholesaling operation in Richmond, Virginia, admitted to SEC investigators that he routinely gave false inventory figures to his superiors in order to overstate his division's profits. He admitted that he did it "just to look good." His division had not been doing well and his bosses would regularly single him out for criticism at corporate planning meetings.[28]

A more insidious danger resulting from heavy emphasis on short-term performance measures is their effect on top-level strategic decisions. Hayes and Abernathy contend that such control measures have helped cause a decline in technological innovations: "Conditioned by a market-driven strategy and held closely to account by a 'results now' ROI-oriented control system, American managers have increasingly refused to take the chance on innovative product/market development."[29] Even the highly touted PIMS research (discussed in Chapter 6) has contributed to this short-run tendency by focusing on only those variables that affect ROI as a measure of corporate performance. For example, PIMS research has concluded that "increased investment almost invariably reduced ROI and cash flow in the short run. . . ."[30]

Goal Displacement

The very monitoring and measuring of performance (if not carefully done) can actually result in a decline in overall corporate performance. A dysfunctional side-effect known as *goal displacement* can occur. This is the confusion of means with ends. Goal displacement occurs when activities originally intended to help attain corporate objectives become ends in themselves—or are adapted to meet ends other than those for which they were intended.[31] Two types of goal displacement are *behavior substitution* and *suboptimization*.

Behavior Substitution

Not all activities or aspects of performance can be easily quantified and measured. It may be very difficult to set standards for such desired activities as cooperation or initiative. As a result, managers of divisions or functional units tend to focus more of their attention on those behaviors that are measurable than on those that are not.[32] They thus reward those people who do well on these types of measures. Since the managers tend to ignore behaviors that are either unmeasurable or difficult to measure, people receive little to no reward for engaging in these activities. The problem with this phenomenon is that the easy-to-measure activities may have little to no relationship to the desired good performance. Rational people, nevertheless, will tend to work for the rewards the system has to offer. As a result, employees will tend to substitute behaviors that are recognized and rewarded for those behaviors that are ignored without regard to their contribution to goal accomplishment. A U.S. Navy quip sums up this situation: "What you inspect is what you get." If the evaluation and control system of an auto plant rewards the meeting of quantitative goals while paying only lip-service to qualitative goals, consumers can expect to get a very large number of very poorly built cars!

The most frequently mentioned problem with Management By Objectives (MBO) is that the measurement process partially distorts the realities of the job. Objectives are made for areas where the measurement of accomplishments is relatively easy, such as with ROI, increased sales, or reduced cost. But these may not always be the most important areas. This problem becomes crucial in professional, service, or staff activities where quantitative measurements are difficult. If, for example, a manager is achieving all of the quantifiable objectives, but in so doing, alienates the work force, the result may be a long-term drop in performance. If promotions are strictly based on measurable short-term performance results, this manager may very likely be promoted or transferred before the negative employee attitudes result in complaints to the personnel office, strikes, or sabotage. The law governing the effect of measurement on behavior seems to be: *Quantifiable measures drive out nonquantifiable measures.*

Suboptimization

The emphasis in large corporations to develop separate responsibility centers can create some problems for the corporation as a whole. To the extent that a division or functional unit views itself as a separate entity, it may refuse to cooperate with other units or divisions in the same corporation if cooperation may in some way negatively affect its performance evaluation. The competition between divisions to achieve a high ROI can result in a refusal to share new technology or work process improvements. One division's attempt to optimize the accomplishment of its goals can cause other divisions to fall behind and thus negatively affect overall corporate performance. One common example of this type of suboptimization occurs when a marketing department approves an early shipment date to a customer as a means of getting an order and forces the manufacturing department into overtime production for this one order. Production costs are raised, which reduces the manufacturing department's overall efficiency. The end result may be that, although marketing achieves its sales goal, the corporation fails to achieve its expected profitability.

9.4 GUIDELINES FOR PROPER CONTROL

In designing a control system, top management should remember that controls should follow strategy. Unless controls are a means to ensure the use of the proper strategy to achieve objectives, there is a strong likelihood that dysfunctional side-effects will completely undermine the implementation of the objectives. The following guidelines are recommended:

1. Control should involve only the minimum amount of information needed to give a reliable picture of events. Too many controls create confusion.
2. Controls should monitor only meaningful activities and results, regardless of measurement difficulty. If cooperation between divisions is important to corporate performance, some form of qualitative or quantitative measure should be established in order to monitor cooperation.
3. Controls should be timely so that corrective action can be taken before it is too late. *Steering controls,* controls that monitor or measure the factors influencing performance, should be stressed in order to give advance notice of problems.
4. Long-term as well as short-term controls should be used. If only short-term measures are emphasized, a short-term managerial orientation is likely.
5. Controls should aim at pinpointing exceptions. Only those activities or results that fall outside a predetermined tolerance range should call for action.
6. Emphasize the reward of meeting or exceeding standards rather than punishment for failing to meet standards. Heavy punishment of failure

will typically result in goal displacement. Managers will "fudge" reports and lobby for lower standards.

Surprisingly, the best-managed companies may have only a few formal objective controls. They focus on measuring the critical success factors—hose few things that must go well to ensure success. Other factors are controlled by the social system in the form of the corporate culture. To the extent that the culture complements and reinforces the strategic orientation of the firm, there is less need for an extensive formal control system. In their book, *In Search of Excellence,* Peters and Waterman state that "the stronger the culture and the more it was directed toward the marketplace, the less need was there for policy manuals, organization charts, or detailed procedures and rules. In these companies, people way down the line know what they are supposed to do in most situations because the handful of guiding values is crystal clear."[33]

9.5 STRATEGIC INCENTIVE MANAGEMENT

In an assessment of the strategic planning performance of large U.S. corporations, Steiner reports a significant weakness in rewarding managers for strategic thinking.[34] His view agrees with the data reported earlier that fewer than half of the large U.S. corporations have long-term incentive plans. Traditionally, the emphasis of executive compensation has been on equity and competitiveness.[35] This means that the level of compensation for chief executive officers has been a function of how much CEOs are paid at comparable firms. As a result, CEO compensation is related more to the size of the corporation than to the size of its profits.[36] This association between firm size and executive compensation, according to Rappaport, can only fuel top management's natural inclination to grow businesses as fast as possible.[37]

Boards of directors need to take the initiative in developing long-term controls and corresponding incentive plans. According to Andrews, "The best criterion for appraising the quality of management performance, in the absence of personal failures or unexpected breakdowns, is management's success over time in executing a demanding and approved strategy that is continually tested against opportunity and need."[38]

Executive compensation must be linked more clearly to strategic performance—to the management of the corporate portfolio, to the business unit's mission, to short-term financial as well as long-term strategic performance, and to the degree of risk involved in managing a portfolio effectively and efficiently.[39] The following three approaches are tailored to help match measurements and rewards with explicit strategic objectives and timeframes: (1) the *weighted-factor method,* (2) the *long-term evaluation method,* and

(3) the *strategic-funds method.* These approaches can also be combined to best suit a corporation's circumstances.[40]

1. *Weighted-factor method.* The *weighted-factor method* is particularly appropriate for measuring and rewarding the performance of top SBU managers and group-level executives when performance factors and their importance vary from one SBU to another. One corporation might contain the following variations: the performance of high-growth SBUs measured in terms of market share, sales growth, designated future payoff, and progress on several future-oriented strategic projects; the performance of low-growth SBUs, in contrast, measured in terms of ROI and cash generation; and the performance of medium-growth SBUs measured for a combination of these factors. Refer to Table 9.5 for an example of how the weighted-factor method could be applied to three different SBUs.

2. *Long-term evaluation method.* The *long-term evaluation method* compensates managers for achieving objectives set over a multiyear period. An executive is promised some company stock or "performance units" (convertible into dollars) on the basis of long-term performance. An executive committee, for example, might set a particular objective in

Table 9.5 **A Weighted-Factor Approach to Strategic Incentive Management**

Strategic Business Unit Category	*Factor*	*Weight*
High growth	Return on assets	10%
	Cash flow	0%
	Strategic-funds programs	45%
	Market-share increase	45%
		100%
Medium growth	Return on assets	25%
	Cash flow	25%
	Strategic-funds programs	25%
	Market-share increase	25%
		100%
Low growth	Return on assets	50%
	Cash flow	50%
	Strategic-funds programs	0%
	Market-share increase	0%
		100%

SOURCE: Paul J. Stonich, "The Performance Measurement and Reward System: Critical to Strategic Management," *Organizational Dynamics* (Winter 1984), p. 51.

terms of growth in earnings per share during a five-year period. The giving of awards would be contingent on the corporation's meeting that objective within the designated time limit. Any executive leaving the corporation before the objective is met receives nothing.

As of 1984, approximately 15% of corporations with sales over $550 million had long-term income programs that compensated managers with some sort of deferred stock to achieve set goals over a multiyear period. The typical emphasis on stock price, however, makes this approach more applicable to top management than to business unit managers.[41]

3. *Strategic-funds method.* The *strategic-funds method* encourages executives to look at developmental expenses as different from expenses required to sustain current operations. The accounting statement for a corporate unit enters strategic funds as a separate entry below the current ROI. It is therefore possible to distinguish between those expense dollars consumed in the generation of current revenues and those invested in the future of the business. As a result, the manager can be evaluated on *both* a short- and a long-term basis and has an incentive to invest strategic funds in the future. Refer to Table 9.6 for an example of the strategic-funds method applied to a business unit.

According to Stonich, "An effective way to achieve the desired strategic results through a reward system is to combine the weighted-factor, long-term evaluation, and strategic funds approaches."[42] To do this, first segregate strategic funds from short-term funds, as in the strategic-funds method. Second, develop a weighted-factor chart for each SBU. Third, measure performance on three bases: the pre-tax profit in the strategic-funds approach; the

Table 9.6 **A Strategic-Funds Approach Applied to an SBU Profit and Loss Statement**

Sales	$ 12,300,000
Cost of sales	6,900,000
Gross margin	$ 5,400,000
Operating (general and administrative expense)	−3,700,000
Operating (return on sales)	$ 1,700,000 or 33%
Strategic funds	−1,000,000
Pre-tax profit	$ 700,000 or 13.6%

SOURCE: Paul J. Stonich, "The Performance Measurement and Reward System: Critical to Strategic Management," *Organizational Dynamics* (Winter 1984), p. 52.

weighted factors; and the long-term evaluation of the SBU's and the corporation's performance. These incentive plans will probably gain increasing acceptance with business corporations in the near future. General Electric and Westinghouse are two firms using a version of these measures.

9.6 SUMMARY AND CONCLUSION

The evaluation and control of performance is a five-step process: (1) determine what to measure, (2) establish standards for performance, (3) measure actual performance, (4) compare actual performance with the standard, and (5) take corrective action. Information coming from this process is fed back into the strategic management system so that both strategic and operational managers can correct performance deviations.

Although the most commonly used measures of corporate performance are the various return ratios, measures based on a value-added or shareholder value approach may be of some use. A number of corporations also monitor key factors related to ROI that may have predictive value. If a corporation has objectives other than profitability, it may wish to follow GE's example by establishing "key performance areas" for special attention. A stakeholder "scorecard" may also be of some value in assessing the corporation's impact on its environment. The strategic audit is recommended as a method to evaluate activities throughout the corporation.

Divisions, SBUs, and functional units are often broken down into responsibility centers to aid control. Such areas are often categorized as standard cost centers, revenue centers, expense centers, profit centers, and investment centers. Budgets and periodic statistical reports are important control devices to monitor the implementation of major programs in business units.

A strategic information system is an important part of the evaluation and control process. By focusing on critical success factors, it can provide early warning signals to strategic managers. The system can be tailored to the business-level strategy being implemented in the SBU in order to ensure the success of the strategy.

The monitoring and measurement of performance can result in dysfunctional side effects that negatively affect overall corporate performance. Among the likely side effects are a short-term orientation and goal displacement. These problems can be reduced if top management remembers that controls must focus on strategic goals. There should be as few controls as possible, and only meaningful activities and results should be monitored. Controls should be timely to both long-term as well as short-term orientations. They should pinpoint exceptions but should be used more to reward than to punish individuals.

Incentive plans should be based upon long-term as well as short-term considerations. Three suggested approaches are the weighted-factor method, the long-term evaluation method, and the strategic-funds method.

A proper evaluation and control system should act to complete the loop shown in the strategic management model. It should feed back information important not only to the implementation of strategy, but also to the initial formulation of strategy. In terms of the strategic decision-making process depicted in Fig. 6.1, the data coming from evaluation and control are the basis for step 1—evaluating current performance results. Because of this feedback effect, evaluation and control is the beginning as well as the end of the strategic management process.

DISCUSSION QUESTIONS

1. Is Fig. 9.1 a realistic model of the control process? Why or why not?
2. Why bother with value-added, shareholder value, or a stakeholder's scorecard? Isn't it simpler to evaluate a corporation and its SBUs just using standard measures like ROI or earnings per share?
3. What are the values to a corporation of establishing "key performance areas"?
4. How much faith can a division or SBU manager place in a *transfer price* as a surrogate for a market price in measuring a profit center's performance?
5. Why are goal displacement and short-run orientation likely side effects of the monitoring of performance? What can a corporation do to avoid them?
6. Why do less than half of the large U.S. corporations use long-term incentive plans?
7. Is the evaluation and control process appropriate for a corporation that emphasizes creativity? Are control and creativity compatible? Explain.

NOTES

1. L. G. Hrebiniak and W. F. Joyce, *Implementing Strategy* (New York: Macmillan, 1984), p. 195.
2. V. E. Millar, "The Evolution Toward Value-Based Financial Planning," *Information Strategy: The Executive's Journal* (Winter 1985), p. 28.
3. R. E. Freeman, *Strategic Management: A Stakeholder Approach* (Boston: Pitman Publishing Co., 1984), pp. 177–181.
4. C. W. Hofer, "ROVA: A New Measure for Assessing Organizational Performance," in R. Lamb (ed.), *Advances in Strategic Management,* Vol. 2 (Greenwich, Conn.: Jai Press, 1983), pp. 43–55.
   C. W. Hofer and D. Schendel, *Strategy Formulation: Analytical Concepts* (St. Paul, Minn.: West Publishing Co., 1978), p. 130.
5. A. Rappaport, "Corporate Performance Standards and Shareholder Wealth," *Journal of Business Strategy* (Spring 1983), pp. 28–38.

6. A. Rappaport, "Have We Been Measuring Success with the Wrong Ruler?" *Wall Street Journal* (June 25, 1984), p. 22.
7. Millar, pp. 29–30.
8. L. R. Jauch, T. N. Martin and R. N. Osborn, "Top Management Under Fire," *Journal of Business Strategy* (Spring 1981), p. 39.
9. G. Badler, "Strategizing for a Spectrum of Possibilities," *Planning Review* (July 1984), pp. 28–31.
10. J. A. F. Stoner, *Management,* 2nd ed. (Englewood Cliffs, N.J.: Prentice-Hall, 1982), pp. 603–604.
11. J. A. F. Stoner, *Management,* 1st ed. (Englewood Cliffs, N.J.: Prentice-Hall, 1978), pp. 583–586.
12. C. H. Roush, Jr., "Strategic Resource Allocation and Control," in W. D. Guth (ed.), *Handbook of Business Strategy* (Boston: Warren, Gorham, and Lamont, 1985), pp. 20.1–20.25.
13. R. L. Daft and N. B. Macintosh, "The Nature and Use of Formal Control Systems for Management Control and Strategy Implementation," *Journal of Management* (Spring 1984), pp. 43–66.
14. D. R. Melville, "Top Management's Role in Strategic Planning," *Journal of Business Strategy* (Spring 1981), p. 63.
15. This discussion is based on R. N. Anthony, J. Dearden, and R. F. Vancil, *Management Control Systems* (Homewood, Ill.: Richard D. Irwin, Inc., 1972), pp. 200–203.
16. A. P. Sloan, Jr., *My Years with General Motors* (Garden City, N.Y.: Doubleday, Anchor Books, 1972), p. 159.
17. Sloan, p. 161.
18. Millar, p. 30.
19. J. A. Turner and H. C. Lucas, Jr., "Developing Strategic Information Systems," in W. D. Guth (ed.), *Handbook of Business Strategy* (Boston: Warren, Gorham and Lamont, 1985), p. 21.2.
20. A. C. Boynton and R. W. Zmud, "An Assessment of Critical Success Factors," *Sloan Management Review* (Summer 1984), p. 17.
21. G. L. Parsons, "Information Technology: A New Competitive Weapon," *Sloan Management Review* (Fall 1983), p. 11.
22. Parsons, p. 11.
23. Hrebiniak and Joyce, pp. 198–199.
24. R. M. Hodgetts and M. S. Wortman, *Administrative Policy,* 2nd ed. (New York: John Wiley & Sons, 1980), p. 128.
25. R. B. Higgins, "Human Resource Management Problems in Strategic Planning," in R. Lamb (ed.), *Advances in Strategic Management,* Vol. I (Greenwich, Conn.: Jai Press, 1983), p. 90.
26. J. B. Quinn, "Why Executives Think Short," *Newsweek* (July 13, 1981), p. 11c.

27. J. Dutton and A. Thomas, "Managing Organizational Productivity," *Journal of Business Strategy* (Summer 1982), p. 41.

28. R. L. Hudson, "SEC Charges Fudging of Corporate Figures Is a Growing Practice," *Wall Street Journal* (June 2, 1983), p. 1.

29. R. H. Hayes and W. J. Abernathy, "Managing Our Way to Economic Decline," *Harvard Business Review* (July–August 1980), p. 72.

30. C. P. Zeithaml, C. R. Anderson, and F. T. Paine, "An Empirical Re-examination of Selected PIMS Findings," *Proceedings, Academy of Management* (August 1981), p. 14.

31. H. R. Bobbitt, Jr., R. H. Breinholt, R. H. Doktor, and J. P. McNaul, *Organizational Behavior,* 2nd ed. (Englewood Cliffs, N.J.: Prentice-Hall, 1978), p. 99.

32. K. Cameron, "A Study of Organizational Effectiveness and Its Predictions," Working Paper, Center for Higher Education Management Systems, Boulder, Colorado, September 1983, p. 2.

33. T. J. Peters and R. H. Waterman, *In Search of Excellence* (New York: Harper & Row, 1982), pp. 75–76.

34. G. A. Steiner, "Formal Strategic Planning in the United States Today," *Long Range Planning* (June 1983), pp. 12–17.

35. M. R. Hurwich and R. A. Furniss, "Measuring and Rewarding Strategic Performance," in W. D. Guth (ed.), *Handbook of Business Strategy* (Boston: Warren, Gorham, and Lamont, 1985), p. 24.5.

36. G. R. Ungson and R. M. Steers, "Motivation and Politics in Executive Compensation," *Academy of Management Review* (April 1984), pp. 313–323.

37. A. Rappaport, "How To Design Value-Contributing Executive Incentives," *Journal of Business Strategy* (Fall 1983), p. 50.

38. K. R. Andrews, "Directors' Responsibility for Corporate Strategy," *Harvard Business Review* (November–December 1980), p. 32.

39. L. J. Brindisi, Jr., "Paying for Strategic Performance: A New Executive Compensation Imperative," in R. B. Lamb (ed.), *Competitive Strategic Management* (Englewood Cliffs, N.J.: Prentice-Hall, 1984), p. 334.

40. P. J. Stonich, "The Performance Measurement and Reward System: Critical to Strategic Management," *Organizational Dynamics* (Winter 1984), pp. 45–57.

41. Stonich, p. 52.

42. Stonich, p. 53.

PART FIVE

OTHER STRATEGIC CONCERNS

Chapter 10

STRATEGIC MANAGEMENT OF MULTINATIONAL CORPORATIONS

STRATEGIC MANAGEMENT MODEL

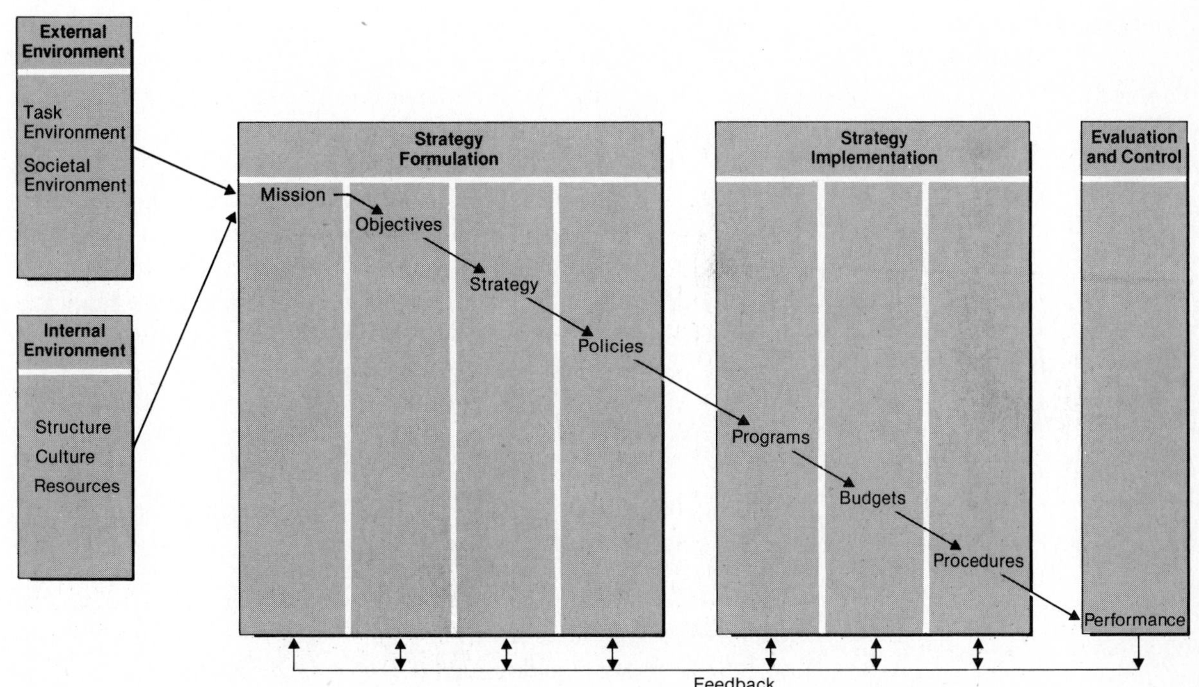

Throughout much of its history, the United States has been virtually self-sufficient. During the 1700s and 1800s, the distance between North America and Europe encouraged the United States to develop its own industries. As late as the 1960s, combined exports and imports of merchandise represented only 7% to 8% of the U.S. gross national product—the lowest of any major industrialized nation.[1] A large domestic market, plus a bountiful supply of natural resources and labor, enabled major corporations to grow and become successful with only a casual interest in "foreign" markets. High tariff laws served to keep the business interests of other countries out of the United States while the infant domestic companies matured.

Since World War II, however, international trade has increased dramatically. In the past quarter century, the volume of goods traded between nations has climbed from less than $100 billion to more than $1 trillion.[2] The United States became much more concerned about international trade. From 1973 to 1983, U.S. exports expanded 281% from $71.4 billion to $200.5 billion. At the same time, U.S. imports increased 368% from $70.1 billion to $258.1 billion.[3] Manufactured exports now equal approximately 20% of U.S. manufacturing output.[4] International considerations have become crucial to the strategic decisions of any large business corporation.

10.1 THE COMING GLOBAL VILLAGE

In 1965, Marshall McLuhan suggested that advances in communications and transportation technologies were drawing the people of the world closer together. As intercontinental travel times decreased, the world went toward becoming a "global village" of interdependent people.[5] People in all countries were finding themselves affected by huge multinational corporations (MNCs).

In 1984, for example, the Chicago Mercantile Exchange linked with a futures exchange in Singapore in a major step toward global 24-hour financial trading. The world's automobile manufacturers, as shown in Fig. 10.1, were heavily involved by 1984 in a series of joint ventures and complicated equity arrangements. Not only did General Motors and Chrysler have minority ownership in the Japanese firms of Suzuki, Isuzu, and Mitsubishi, French government-owned Renault had 15% equity in Swedish Volvo and almost majority ownership of American Motors.[6]

Going International

Three basic reasons can be listed for business corporations expanding their operations internationally:

1. Corporations can earn increased sales and profits by expanding market outlets and by exploiting growth opportunities. Foreign sales can thus absorb extra capacity and reduce unit costs. They can also spread economic risks over a wider number of markets. For example, while Ford's

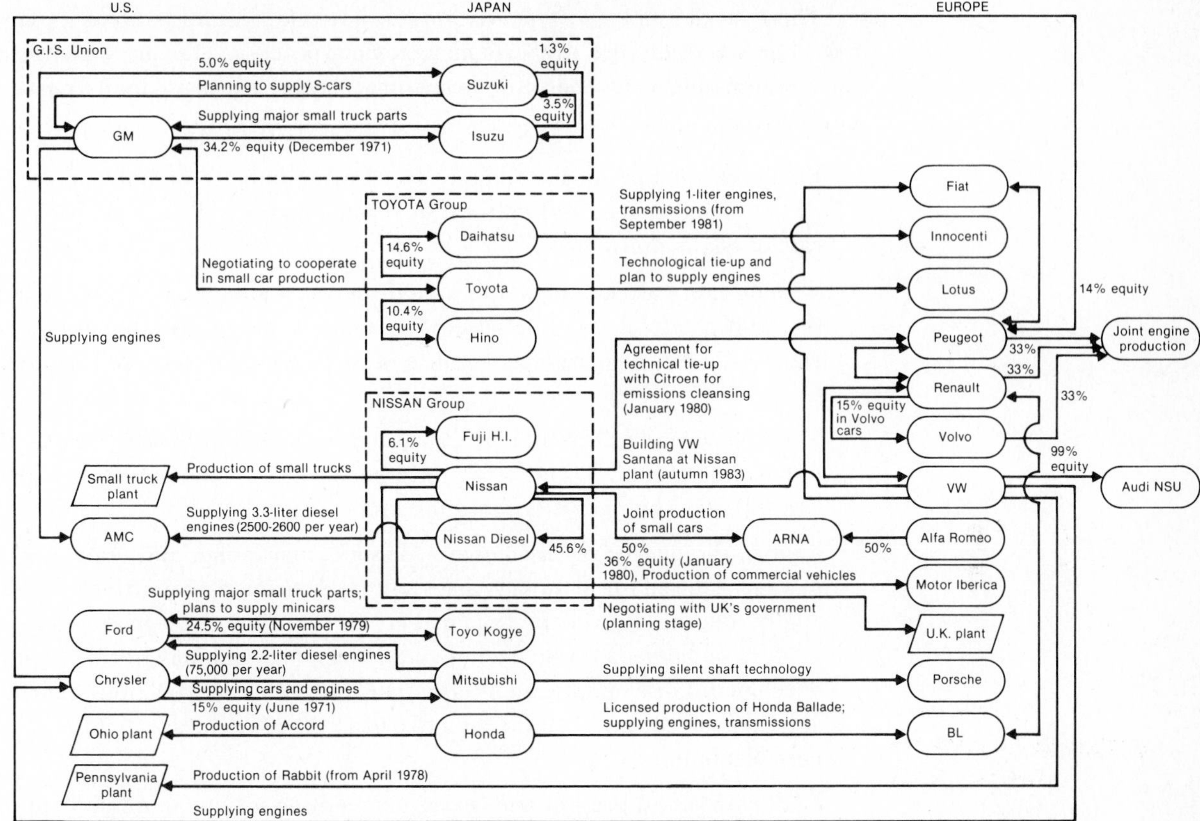

Figure 10.1 **International cooperation among auto manufacturers.**
SOURCE: J. McElroy, "Cheaper by the Dozen," *Road and Track* (June 1984), p. 122. Courtesy Dodwell Associates. Reprinted with permission.

U.S. market share dropped below 25% in 1980, Ford of Britain's had risen to 32%, up six percentage points in four years.[7]

2. Corporations can gain competitive advantages by seeking low-cost production facilities in locations close to raw materials and/or cheap labor. They can achieve wider channels of distribution and access to new technology through joint ventures. Both General Electric and Société Nationale d' Étude et de Construction de Moteurs d'Aviation (SNECMA), the French engine maker, benefited from their joint venture in forming CFM International to produce and sell jet engines to airlines.[8]

3. In addition, companies can secure raw material resources by engaging in the worldwide exploration for, and the processing, transportation, and marketing of raw materials. For years, the major rubber companies have owned rubber plantations in Southeast Asia. Oil companies have, of course, gone international for the same reason.

There are a number of *disadvantages,* however, in international expansion. For one thing, the strategic management process is far more complex for a multinational than for a domestic firm. Dymsza lists six limitations to international expansion.[9]

> First, the multinational company faces a multiplicity of political, economic, legal, social, and cultural environments as well as a differential rate of change in them.
>
> Second, there are complex interactions between a multinational firm and the multiplicity of its national environments because of national sovereignties, widely disparate economic and social conditions, as well as other factors.
>
> Third, geographical distance, cultural and national differences, variations in business practices, and other differences make communications difficult between the parent corporation and its subsidiaries.
>
> Fourth, the degree of significant economic, marketing, and other information required for planning varies a great deal among countries in availability, depth, and reliability. Furthermore, in any given host country, modern techniques for analyzing and developing data may not be highly developed. For example, an international corporation may find it difficult and expensive to conduct the effective market research essential for business planning.
>
> Fifth, analysis of present and future competition may be more difficult to undertake in a number of countries because of differences in industrial structure and business practices.
>
> Sixth, the multinational company is confronted not only with different national environments but also with regional organizations such as the European Economic Community, the European Trade Area, and the Latin American Free Trade Area, all of which are achieving various degrees of economic integration. The United Nations and specialized international organizations such as the International Bank for Reconstruction and Development, the International Finance Corporation, and the General Agreement of Tariffs and Trade (GATT) may also affect its future opportunities.

Becoming International

Perhaps the best reason for U.S. corporations taking an international viewpoint in strategic management is the increasing rate of international investment and the marketing of imports in the United States. Investments by foreign interests in U.S. corporations and properties have increased from $416 billion in 1979 to $833 billion in 1984.[10] By year-end 1983, 13.5

million acres (1% of all privately owned U.S. agricultural land) was in non-U.S. hands.[11] During 1984, Nestlé S. A. of Switzerland paid $2.9 billion for Carnation Company. Saatchi and Saatchi PLC, Britain's largest advertising agency, bought the U.S. market research firm of Yankelovich, Skelly, and White. Over a one-year period, five of Japan's six largest steelmakers spent more than $500 million to buy U.S. assets and forge partnerships in metals-related industries. One example of this type of acquisition is Nippon Kokan K.K.'s purchase of 50% interest in Pittsburgh's National Steel Corporation.[12] A survey of 193 chief executives in 15 European countries in 1984 revealed that 45% preferred to invest in the United States than in any other country.[13]

The average U.S. consumer is becoming more involved and increasingly affected by international trade. Peoria-based Caterpillar Tractor Company laid off 22,000 U.S. workers in 1983 because of a worldwide sales slump aggravated by a debt crisis in Latin American countries.[14] Out of every dollar spent by Americans, 20 cents is now spent on imported items. During 1983, for example, K-Mart, J. C. Penney, and Sears Roebuck purchased a total of $5.2 billion worth of imported goods for resale to U.S. consumers.[15] The old slogan, "Buy American," no longer makes sense at a time when a large proportion of many U.S. products includes foreign-made parts. Chrysler Corporation, for example, is importing Plymouth Reliants and Dodge Aries from its Toluca, Mexico plant for sale in the United States. In an almost "Alice in Wonderland" manner, the reverse is also true. So-called foreign products are being made in the United States. Volkswagen produces (German-American?) cars in its New Stanton, Pennsylvania plant. Japan's Matsushita Electric Industrial Company purchases air conditioners from the U.S.'s General Electric Company for sale in the United States under the Panasonic brand name![16]

The Multinational Corporation

The multinational corporation is a very special type of international firm. Any U.S. company can call itself "international" if it has a small branch office in, say, Juarez or Toronto. An *international company* is one that engages in any combination of activities from exporting/importing to full-scale manufacturing in foreign countries. The *multinational corporation,* in contrast, is a highly developed international company with a deep worldwide involvement, plus a global perspective in its management and decision making.[17] A more specific definition of an MNC is suggested by Dymsza:[18]

1. Although a multinational corporation may not do business in every region of the world, its decision makers consider opportunities throughout the world.

2. A considerable portion of its assets are invested internationally. One authority suggests that a firm becomes global when 20% of its assets are in other countries. Another suggests that the point is reached when operations in other nations account for at least 35% of the corporation's total sales and profits.
3. The corporation engages in international production and operates plants in a number of countries. These plants may range from assembly to fully integrated facilities.
4. Managerial decision making is based on a worldwide perspective. The international business is no longer a sideline or segregated activity. International operations are integrated into the corporation's overall business.

Refer to Table 10.1 for a list of the world's largest multinational corporations in terms of total revenue. Note the strong presence of the Japanese trading companies and various oil firms.

Table 10.1 **World's Largest Multinational Corporations**

Rank	*Company*	*Total Revenue (millions)*	*Corporate Headquarters*	*Industry*
1.	Exxon	$88,651	U.S.A.	Energy
2.	Royal Dutch/Shell Group	80,610	Neth/U.K.	Energy
3.	General Motors	74,582	U.S.A.	Automobiles
4.	Mitsui & Co., Ltd.	63,149	Japan	Wholesaler
5.	Mitsubishi Corp.	62,831	Japan	Wholesaler
6.	Mobil	55,609	U.S.A.	Energy
7.	British Petroleum Co. Plc.	49,231	U.K.	Energy
8.	C. Itoh & Co. Ltd.	48,436	Japan	Wholesaler
9.	Marubeni Corp.	46,816	Japan	Wholesaler
10.	Sumitomo Corp.	45,806	Japan	Wholesaler
11.	Ford Motor	44,455	U.S.A.	Automobiles
12.	IBM	40,180	U.S.A.	Computers
13.	Texaco	40,068	U.S.A.	Energy
14.	Sears, Roebuck	35,883	U.S.A.	Wholesale/retail
15.	E.I. du Pont de Nemours	35,173	U.S.A.	Chemicals
16.	Nissho Iwai Corp.	34,039	Japan	Wholesaler
17.	Phibro–Salomon	29,757	U.S.A.	Minerals/metals
18.	Standard Oil, Indiana	27,937	U.S.A.	Energy
19.	General Electric	27,681	U.S.A.	Electrical equipment
20.	Standard Oil, California	27,342	U.S.A.	Energy

SOURCE: *Forbes* (July 2, 1984), pp. 129–132 and 134.

10.2 STRATEGY FORMULATION

As described in Chapter 1, the strategic management process includes strategy formulation, implementation, and evaluation and control. In order to formulate strategy, the top management of a multinational corporation must scan both the external environment for opportunities and threats, and the internal environment for strengths and weaknesses.

Scanning the External Environment

The dominant issue in the strategic management process of a multinational corporation is the external environment. The type of relationship an MNC can have with each factor in its task environment varies from one country to another and from one region to another. International societal environments vary so widely that a corporation's internal environment and strategic management process must be very flexible. Cultural trends in West Germany, for example, have resulted in the inclusion of worker representatives in corporate strategic planning. Differences in the sociocultural, economic, political-legal, and technological aspects of societal environments among countries strongly affect how an MNC conducts its marketing, financial, manufacturing, and other functional activities.

Sociocultural Forces

Different sociocultural norms and values among nations will affect MNC activities importantly. For example, some cultures accept bribery and payoffs as a fact of life, whereas others punish them heavily. In Nigeria the accepted "dash" (money under the table) ranges from 15% of a multibillion dollar contract to a few naira to get a hotel operator to place a phone call.

Most countries differentiate between "lubrication" or "grease" payments made to minor officials to expedite the execution of their duties and large-scale "whitemail" bribes intended to allow either a violation of the law or an illegal contribution designed to influence government policy. In some countries grease payments may be viewed by their citizens as an entitlement—necessary income to supplement low public salaries.[19] Since the dividing line between these two forms of extra payment is indistinct, an MNC must carefully monitor each country's norms to ensure its actions are in line with local practice. Ethics tend to become pragmatically bound to situations, and the top managers of MNCs may find themselves open to charges of being amoral.

In less developed countries (LDCs), most of the working population may be illiterate. As a result, there will likely be a shortage of skilled labor and supervisors. Manufacturing facilities that mesh with the technical sophistication of the work force must be designed. If U.S. managers are used in LDCs, they must be aware of the wide variance in working practices around the world and totally familiar with those in the country where they are stationed. For example, it is common in Europe for employees to get added compensation according to the number of their family members or because of unpleasant working conditions. Finish paper mill workers get a "sauna premium" for missing baths when they are asked to work on Sunday. Fiji Island miners receive a daily half-hour "sex break" to fulfill marital obligations.[20] Other examples abound.

Differences in language and social norms will affect heavily the marketing mix for a particular country. Product presentation, packaging, distribution channels, pricing, and advertising must be attuned to each culture. For example, Western cosmetic firms such as Max Factor, Revlon, and Avon have had little success in selling their usual products in Japan. Certain cultural factors affect their sales: in Japan perfume is hardly used; suntans are considered ugly; and bath oil is impractical in communal baths.[21] In contrast, Mr. Donut franchise shops are very successful in Japan, even though there is no coffee and doughnut custom there. Doughnuts are presented as a snack rather than as a breakfast food and located near railroad stations and supermarkets. All the signs are in English in order to appeal to the Western interests of the Japanese.

Even if a product is desired by the public, literal translation of product names and slogans can ruin sales. For example, Pepsi Cola's "Come alive" jingle was translated into German as "Come alive out of the grave."[22] When General Motors introduced its Nova model into Latin America, it believed the name would translate well. Nova means constellation in Spanish. Nevertheless, people began to pronounce it "no vá," which in Spanish means "it does not go."[23] An advertisement for ink by the Parker Pen Company when translated into Spanish gave the false impression that the product helped prevent pregnancy.[24]

Religious beliefs may also make a significant impact on a country's business practices. For example, banks in Pakistan stopped paying interest to depositors in 1985 to conform with Islamic law. The alternative is a profit-sharing and loss-sharing system. Sudan and Iran are also moving toward a totally Islamic banking system.[25] In Japan, each time Mazda manufactures a new car model, a Shinto priest clad in traditional white robe, sandals, and black lacquered hat conducts "honorable purification" rites on the new product with top management in attendance.[26]

Economic Forces

The type of economic system in a country can affect strongly the kind of relationship an MNC can establish with a host country. The managers of an MNC based in a free-market capitalistic country may have difficulty understanding the regulations affecting trade with a centrally planned socialistic country. Licensing, acquisition, and joint ventures may be restricted severely by such a host country. In addition, in most countries inflation and currency exchange rates create further difficulties for an MNC. In Argentina, for example, the inflation rate during 1985 was around 1000%! An

MNC's financial policy in an economy subject to rapid inflation must be altered to protect the firm against inflationary losses. Cash balances must be minimized. Credit terms must be restricted. Prices must be constantly watched. In addition, balance of payments problems in a host country may lead to currency devaluation, as occurred in Mexico from 1980 through 1985 and in Italy during 1985. Such devaluation leads to an MNC's taking large losses in terms of the assets and profits of its subsidiary in the devaluating country. In addition, a socialistic country may control the prices of the products sold by the MNC in that country but may increase the price of the raw materials it sells to the MNC. This results in a severe profit squeeze as the host government attempts to pass the burden of inflation to "rich" multinational corporations.

As a result of these and other economic problems throughout the world, an MNC must be prepared to engage in countertrade and in hedging its foreign currency. *Countertrade* is a modern form of bartering which ranges from relatively simple barter transactions to intricate arrangements that can involve many nations and goods as well as complex financing and credits. Because less developed countries are often unable to pay cash for needed goods, exchanging goods and services is becoming increasingly attractive for them. From 1976 to 1984, countertrade grew from an estimated 2% to 33% of world commerce. For example, Sorimex, a Renault subsidiary, accepts coffee, phosphates, and other commodities in exchange for autos in agreements with such countries as Colombia, Tunisia, Turkey, Egypt, Rumania, and the People's Republic of China. Almost one-fifth of General Electric's $4 billion in exports in 1983 were under countertrade contracts. Banks now have countertrade divisions to turn commodities into cash for the bank's commercial customers.[27] Multinational corporations must also deal with fluctuating exchange rates by *hedging* their foreign-currency exposures in the forward foreign-exchange market where currencies are bought and sold for delivery at specific dates.[28] For example, if a U.S.-based multinational is scheduled to receive 100 million German marks in exchange for machine tools one year from today, it may lose money if the dollar rises in value in relation to that of the mark. One-hundred million marks may be worth 30 million U.S. dollars today, but only 25 million U.S. dollars next year. To avoid this risk, an MNC may choose to sell marks for dollars in the forward market for delivery in one year. This hedge "locks in" the MNC's dollar revenue at 30 million U.S. dollars regardless of currency fluctuations.

Political-Legal Forces

The system of laws and public policies governing business formation, acquisitions, and competitive activities constrains the strategic options open to a multinational company. It is likely that a particular country will specify guidelines for hiring, firing, and promoting people, as well as giving employment ratios of "foreigners" to its citizens and restricting management prerogatives regarding unions. In addition, there are likely to be government policies dealing with ownership, licensing, repatriation of profits (profits leaving the host country for the MNC's home country), royalties, importing, and purchasing. Beyond these, there are likely to be both some sentiment for keeping out foreign goods by erecting tariff barriers and some strong negative feeling about foreign control by an MNC of the host country's assets.

There are many examples of countries expropriating and nationalizing foreign as well as domestic holdings. In 1981, for example, France, under socialist leader François Mitterand, ordered a number of foreign-owned firms (among them, Honeywell-Bull Computers, ITT-France, and Rouseel-Uclaf Drugs) to sell a large percentage of their stock to the French government. Other countries have passed laws forbidding foreign nationals (including MNCs) from having majority control of firms in key industries. Mexico and India restricted foreign ownership during the 1970s. Canada passed legislation in 1981 requiring U.S. energy companies operating in Canada to sell a majority of their stock to Canadian owners by 1990. Responding to Malaysia's requirement that Malaysians have majority control of rubber plantations, Uniroyal sold its profitable rubber plants to a Malaysian company in 1984 and left the country.[29]

By the mid-1980s two international trends were evident. One was the desire by a number of countries to sell to private interests previously state-owned firms and to welcome the presence of foreign-owned MNCs. Similar to President Reagan's deregulation of government agencies, this *denationalization* or *privatization* of state-owned corporations was taking place in Canada, Japan, and most Western European nations. Great Britain, for example, sold the assets of Jaguar automobiles and 51% of British Telecom, the telecommunications monopoly. The second international trend was an increasing amount of trade barriers, local content regulations, and other *protectionist measures* designed to help domestic industry compete with foreign competition. Murray Weidenbaum, former Chairman of the U.S. Council of Economic Advisers, stated in 1984 that "Protectionist sentiment around the world is stronger now than it has been in decades."[30] As an example of local content laws, Mexico requires its six foreign-car manufacturers to use locally produced parts and material equal to half of each vehicle's value. Similar protectionist sentiment exists in the United States in the form of "voluntary" quotas on Japanese cars and foreign steelmakers and quotas on sugar and other imported goods.[31] There are examples like these for most nations in the world. Such protectionist and nationalistic tendencies serve to short-circuit the basic logic underlying the economic concept of *comparative advantage* (see Illustrative Example 10.1), resulting in higher prices for consumers and inefficient domestic industries.[32]

In order to introduce some stability into international trade, a number of countries have formed alliances and negotiated mutual cooperation agreements. One such agreement is the General Agreement on Tariffs and Trade (GATT) established in 1948 by twenty-three countries. This agreement was formed to create a relatively free system of trading, primarily through the reduction of tariffs. It provides a forum for negotiating mutual reduction of trade restrictions. Since 1948, most nations in the "free" world have become parties to GATT. According to Daniels, Ogram, and Radebaugh, "Through the most-favored-nation provision of GATT, countries have agreed to apply the same trade regulations to nearly all countries in the world. This greatly simplifies the negotiation process and allows exporters from almost any nation to have the same access, in terms of restrictions, to the market in any participating country."[33] An example of a political/trade alliance is the European Economic Community (Common Market), which agreed not only to reduce duties and other trade restrictions among member countries, but also to have a common tariff against nonmember countries. This provision was a major factor in encouraging firms from nonmember countries, such as the United States, to locate some manufacturing and marketing facilities inside the EEC to avoid tariffs.[34]

THE BASICS OF ABSOLUTE AND COMPARATIVE ADVANTAGE IN INTERNATIONAL TRADE

Illustrative Example 10.1

Suppose a country presently produces 1 million bushels of corn and 5 million bushels of beans each year. Its people desire more corn. Should it simply plant more corn and less beans? This seems like a reasonable solution until one notes that the soil and water are much better for growing beans than for corn. Each acre planted can produce twice as much bean crop as corn. It takes the same amount of work, and the seeds, fertilizer, and other costs are the same for the farmers regardless of the crop planted. Suppose that the neighboring country has different soil and on every acre planted is able to produce twice as much corn as beans.

The concept of *absolute advantage* in international trade suggests that when both countries are considered, the first country has advantage over the second country in producing beans, but the second has advantage over the first in producing corn. The logical conclusion is that the first country should specialize in producing beans (where it has absolute advantage) and the second should plant only corn (where it also has absolute advantage). The result would be that the first country would produce 7 million bushels of beans each year and *no* corn (with the 2 to 1 advantage of beans to corn,

(*Continued*)

Illustrative Example 10.1 (Continued)

the 1 million bushels of corn would be replaced by 2 million bushels of beans). The reverse would be true in the second country. If the countries are able to trade freely with each other, both countries would be able to have more corn and beans if they specialize in the crop with which there is advantage than if both countries tried to produce both crops.

Therefore, in answer to the question posed earlier, if a country wants more corn but has an absolute advantage in the production of beans, it should plant more beans. The excess beans can be exported to another country in exchange for more corn than the first country could ever produce with the same resources.

What happens, however, when the first country can produce more corn *and* beans per acre planted than can its neighboring country? Is there any benefit to trade? According to the concept of *comparative advantage,* it still makes sense to specialize as long as the first country is able to grow more of one crop than another crop per acre planted. As an analogy, suppose the best architect in town also happens to be the best carpenter. Would it make sense for him to build his own house? Certainly not, because he can earn more money per hour by devoting all his time to his job as an architect even though he has to employ a carpenter less skillful than himself to build the house. In the same manner, the first country will gain if it concentrates its resources on the production of that commodity it can produce most efficiently. It will earn enough money from the export of that commodity to still import what it needs from its less efficient neighbor country.

SOURCE: J. D. Daniels, E. W. Ogram, Jr., and L. H. Radebaugh, *International Business: Environments and Operations,* 3rd ed. (Reading, Mass.: Addison-Wesley, 1982), pp. 107–113.

There are also trade associations, such as the Organization of Petroleum Exporting Countries (OPEC), the International Tin Council, and the International Cocoa Organization, which attempt to stabilize commodity supplies and prices to the benefit of their member nations.

Technological Forces

As mentioned in Chapter 4, the question of technology "transfer" has become an important issue in international dealings. Most less developed countries welcome multinational corporations into their nation as conduits of advanced technology and management expertise. They realize that not only will local labor be hired to work for the firm, but that the MNC will have to educate the work force to deal with advanced methods and techniques. Reich, in his book *The Next American Frontier,* argues that production technologies are rapidly moving from the developed to the developing nations of the world.[35] Countries such as Korea, Hong Kong, Taiwan, Singapore, Brazil, and Spain, which specialized in the 1960s in simple products like clothing and toys, are now mass producing technologically complex products like automobiles, televisions, and ships. At the same time, the less developed countries of Malaysia, Thailand, the Philippines, Sri Lanka, and India have taken over the production of clothing, toys, and the like. With Korea and Taiwan on its heels technologically, Japan reduced its steelmaking capacity and began orienting itself in the 1980s beyond consumer electronics toward telecommunications.[36]

Political-legal considerations become important when aerospace firms, with their heavy dependence on government contracts, want to transfer technology developed for military purposes into profitable commercial products sold internationally. General Electric, for example, had a great deal of difficulty forming a joint venture with the French national engine firm SNECMA in the early 1970s. The venture involved the sharing of jet engines developed specifically for the prototype of the B-1 bomber. Although the U.S. federal government refused, for political reasons, to put the B-1 bomber into production, it did not like the idea of GE's selling such advanced technology to another country.[37] In the 1980s, the U.S. government has similar fears of semiconductor technology being sold to countries behind the "iron curtain." The Coordinating Committee for Multilateral Export Controls (Cocom), composed of the fifteen members of the North Atlantic Treaty Organization (NATO) minus Spain and Iceland plus Japan, compiles lists of items that cannot be sold to Communist countries without its approval. This has created a number of problems for MNCs wishing to sell high-technology products to China.[38]

Another technological issue raised in international trade is the determination of the appropriate technology to use in production plants located in host countries. For example, labor-saving devices (robots, for instance) that are economically justifable in highly developed countries where wage rates are high, may be more costly than labor-intensive types of production in less developed countries with high unemployment and low wage rates. The knowledge of technology may be so low in a country that the MNC may be tempted to employ very few local people and automate the plant as much as possible to gain operating leverage. The host country's government, however, faced with massive unemployment, may strongly desire a labor intensive plant.[39] The basic question an MNC may face is whether the benefits to be gained by modifying technologies for the unique conditions of each country are worth the costs that must be incurred.

Assessing International Opportunities and Risks

In searching for an advantageous market or manufacturing location, a multinational corporation must gather and evaluate data on strategic factors in a large number of countries and regions. Given the global perspective of MNCs, one company may use comparative advantage to its benefit by making machine parts in Brazil, assembling them as engines in Germany, installing the engines in auto bodies in Italy, and shipping completed cars to the United States for sale. This strategy serves to reduce the risk to the MNC of operating in only one country, but exposes it to a series of smaller risks in a greater number of countries. As a result, multinational corporations must be able to deal with political and economic risk in many diverse countries and regions.[40]

Some firms, such as American Can Company, develop an elaborate computerized system to rank investment risks. Smaller companies may hire outside consultants like Chicago's Associated Consultants International or Boston's Arthur D. Little, Inc. to provide political risk assessments. Among the many systems that exist to assess political and economic risks are the Political System Stability Index, the Business Environment Risk Index, Business International's Country Assessment Service, and Frost and Sullivan's World Political Risk Forecasts.[41] (For a summary of Frost and Sullivan's risk index, see the May 1985 issue of *Planning Review.*)[42] Regardless of the source of data, a firm must develop its own method of assessing risk. It must decide upon the most important factors from its point of view and assign weights to each. An example of such a rating method is depicted in Table 10.2.

Scanning the Internal Environment

Any corporation desiring to move into the international arena will need to assess its own strengths and weaknesses. Chang and Campo-Flores suggest that a corporation's chances for success are enhanced if it has or can develop the following capabilities:

1. *Technological lead.* An innovative approach or a new product or a new process gives one a short-term monopoly position.
2. *A strong trade name.* Snob appeal of a well-known product can permit a higher profit margin to cover initial entry costs.
3. *Advantage of scale.* A large corporation has the advantage of low unit costs and a financial base strong enough to weather setbacks.
4. *A scanning capability.* An ability to search successfully and efficiently for opportunities will take on greater importance in international dealings.
5. *An outstanding product or service.* A solid product or service is more likely to have staying power in international competition.
6. *An outstanding international executive.* The presence of an executive who understands international situations and is able to develop a core of local executives who can work well with the home office is likely to result in the building of a strong and long-lasting international organization.[43]

Table 10.2 Example of Weighted Rating of Investment Climate

	Country A			Country B		
Factors Listed in Order of Importance	(1) *Assigned Weights Considering Importance of Adverse Developments*	(2) *Rating of Factor from 0 (Completely Unfavorable) to 100 (Completely Favorable)*	(3) *Weighted Rating (Column 1 × Column 2)*	(1) *Assigned Weights Considering Importance of Adverse Developments*	(2) *Rating of Factor from 0 (Completely Unfavorable) to 100 (Completely Favorable)*	(3) *Weighted Rating (Column 1 × Column 2)*
1. Possibility of expropriation.	10	90	900	10	55	550
2. Possibility of damage to property from rebellion or war.	9	80	720	9	50	450
3. Remission of earnings.	8	70	560	8	50	400
4. Governmental restrictions of foreign business compared to domestic-owned enterprise.	8	70	560	8	60	480
5. Availability of local capital at reasonable cost.	7	50	350	7	90	630
6. Political stability.	7	80	560	7	50	350
7. Repatriation of capital.	7	80	560	7	60	420
8. Currency stability.	6	70	420	6	30	180
9. Price stability.	5	40	200	5	30	150
10. Taxes on business (including any discriminatory provisions).	4	80	320	4	90	360
11. Problems of dealing with labor unions.	3	70	210	3	80	240
12. Government investment incentives.	2	0	0	2	90	180
TOTAL WEIGHTED RATING OF INVESTMENT CLIMATE			5,360			4,390

SOURCE: W. A. Dymsza, *Multinational Business Strategy* (New York: McGraw-Hill Book Co., 1972), p. 90.

Evaluating the Mission

Once a corporation has decided to become multinational in orientation, the first step is to restate the corporate mission. An example of such a mission statement is from General Electric Company:

> To carry on a diversified, growing, and profitable world-wide manufacturing business in electrical apparatus, appliances, and supplies, and in related materials, products, systems, and services for industry, commerce, agriculture, government, the community, and the home.[44]

Setting Objectives

Upon completing an assessment of its external and internal environments, a multinational corporation can determine specific objectives for foreign affiliates, corporate divisions, and the entire firm. Dymsza states that a multinational corporation usually starts with profitability goals in terms of amounts: return on investment, assets, or sales; rate of growth per year; or growth in earnings per share by major unit. It then sets specific marketing, production, logistics, technology, personnel, acquisition, and other goals for a given period. These goals provide the basis for determining strategies.[45]

Developing International Strategies

A multinational corporation can pick from a number of strategic options the ways to enter a foreign market or to establish manufacturing facilities in another country. An experienced firm with a global orientation will usually select a strategy based on specific product strengths and on host country attractiveness.

Exporting

Exporting is a good way to minimize risk and to experiment with a specific product; it can be conducted in a number of ways. An MNC could choose to handle all critical functions itself, or it could contract these functions to an export management company. To operate in a country such as Japan, which has a series of complex regulations, an MNC could use the services of an agent or distributor.

Licensing

Under a *licensing* agreement, the licensing firm grants rights to a firm in the host country to produce and/or sell a product. The licensee pays compensation to the licensing firm in return for technical expertise. This is an especially useful strategy if the trademark or brand name is well known, but the MNC does not have sufficient funds to enter the country directly. La Chemise Lacoste, the French sportswear concern, for example, sold the U.S. and Canadian licenses for the Lacoste trademark and its alligator emblem to General Mills to use in its Izod, Ltd. fashion unit. Anheuser-Busch is also using this strategy to produce and market Budweiser beer in Great Britain, Japan, Israel, Australia, Korea, and the Philippines. It also becomes an important strategy if the country makes entry via investment either difficult or impossible. Examples are Japan and Eastern European countries. There is always the danger, however, that the licensee may develop its competence to the point that it becomes a competitor to the licensing firm.

Joint Ventures

Joint ventures are very popular with MNCs. The corporation engages in international ownership at a much lower risk. A joint venture will typically be an association between an MNC and a firm in the host country or a government agency in that country. A quick method of obtaining local management, it also reduces the risks of expropriation and harassment by host country officials. Some of the joint ventures engaged in recently by U.S. firms with foreign partners are listed in Table 10.3.

When more than two organizations participate in a joint venture, it is sometimes referred to as a *consortium*. For example, Airbus Industrie, the European producer of jet airplanes is a consortium owned by four partners from four countries: Aerospatiale of France (37.9%), Messerschmitt-Bokkow-Blohm of West Germany (37.9%), British Aerospace Corp. (20%), and Construcciones Aeronauticas S. A. of Spain (4.2%). Disadvantages of joint ventures include loss of control, lower profits, probability of conflicts with partners, and the likely transfer of technological advantage to the local partner. Joint ventures typically are meant to be temporary, especially by the Japanese who view them as a way to rectify a competitive weakness until they can achieve long-term dominance in the partnership.[46]

Acquisitions

If an MNC wishes total control of its operations, it may want to start a business from scratch or acquire a firm already established in the host country.

Table 10.3 **Some Recent Joint Ventures**

Joint Venture	*U.S. Parent*	*Foreign Partner*	*Products*
New United Motor Mfg.	General Motors	Toyota (Japan)	Subcompact cars
National Steel	National Intergroup	Nippon Kokan (Japan)	Steel
Siecor	Corning Glass Works	Siemens (Germany)	Optical cable
Honeywell/Ericsson Development	Honeywell	L. M. Ericsson (Sweden)	PBX systems
Himont	Hercules	Montedison (Italy)	Polypropylene resin
GMFanuc Robotics	General Motors	Fanuc (Japan)	Robots
International Aero Engines	United Technologies	Rolls-Royce (Britain)	Aircraft engines

SOURCE: "Are Foreign Partners Good for U.S. Companies?" *Business Week* (May 28, 1984), p. 59. Reprinted from the May 28, 1984 issue of *Business Week* by special permission. Copyright © 1984 by McGraw-Hill, Inc.

An *acquisition* has merits because assets can be bought in their entirety rather than on a piecemeal basis. Synergistic benefits may result if the MNC acquires a firm with strong complementary product lines and a good distribution network. Nestlé S. A. of Switzerland, for example, purchased Beech-Nut (baby foods), Libby, McNeill and Libby (fruit juices), Stouffer (hotels and frozen dinners), Ward-Johnson (candy), Hills Brothers (coffee), and Carnation (evaporated milk) to complement its successful Nescafé, Quik, Nestea, and L'Oreal consumer products. In some countries, however, acquisitions may be difficult to arrange due to a lack of available information about potential candidates. Government restrictions on ownership, such as Canada's requirement that all energy corporations in Canada be controlled by Canadians, also may discourage acquisitions. It may be possible, however, to have control of a foreign enterprise even though the MNC cannot attain more than 49% of the ownership. One way is to maintain control over some asset required by the foreign firm. Another device is to separate equity into voting and nonvoting stock so that the minority MNC investor has a majority of the voting stock.[47]

Green-Field Development

If a corporation does not wish to buy another firm's existing facilities via acquisition, it may choose a *green-field development,* or the building of a manufacturing facility from scratch. This is usually far more complicated and expensive than acquisition, but it allows the MNC more freedom in designing the plant, choosing suppliers, and hiring a work force. An Italian semiconductor manufacturer, SGS-Ates Componenti Elettronici S. p. A., selected this strategy. According to its vice-president of marketing, Richard Pieranunzi: "To find a company that exactly matched our needs would be difficult. And we didn't want to buy other people's problems."[48]

Production Sharing

Coined by Peter Drucker, the term *production sharing* combines the higher labor skills and technology available in the developed countries with lower-cost labor available in developing countries. Since 1970, U.S. imports under production-sharing arrangements have been increasing at a rate of more than 20% per year.[49] Among the multinational corporations using this strategy are Texas Instruments, RCA, Honeywell, General Electric, and GTE. By locating assembly plants in Ciudad Juarez, Mexico and packaging plants across the border in Texas, these firms are able to take advantage of Mexico's low labor costs. This was a result of the Mexican government's relaxation of its laws against foreign ownership of factories and its reduction of import taxes on raw materials.[50]

Management Contracts

A large multinational corporation is likely to have a large amount of management talent at its disposal. *Management contracts* offer a means through which an MNC may use part of its personnel to assist a firm in a host country for a specified fee and period of time. Such arrangements are common when a host government expropriates part or all of an MNC's holdings in its country. This allows the MNC to continue to earn some income from its investment and keep the operations going until local management is trained. Management contracts are also used by a number of less developed countries that have the capital but neither the labor nor the managerial skills required to utilize available technology.

Turnkey Operations

Turnkey operations are typically contracts for the construction of operating facilities in exchange for a fee. The facilities are transferred to the host country or firm when they are complete. The customer is usually a government agency of, say, an Eastern European or Middle Eastern country that has decreed a given product must be produced locally and under its control. MNCs that perform turnkey operations are frequently industrial equipment manufacturers that supply some of their own equipment for the project and that commonly sell to the host country replacement parts and maintenance services. They thereby create customers as well as future competitors.

Subcontract Arrangements

MNCs may find that in times of national fervor in the less developed countries, facilities that mine and process raw materials are prime targets for expropriation. As a result, an MNC may *contract* with a foreign government or local firm to trade raw materials for certain resources belonging to the MNC. For example, several oil-producing countries have made arrangements with oil firms to let the firms take all exploration and development risks in exchange for a share of the sales of the oil produced.[51]

International Product Portfolio

Broadly viewed, strategic planning seeks to match markets with products and other corporate resources in order to strengthen a firm's competitive position. Since most multinational corporations manufacture and sell a wide range of products, it is necessary, when formulating strategy, to keep track of country attractiveness as well as product strength. Nevertheless, there is a strong tendency for top management in MNCs to plan around either products or markets, but not both.[52]

To aid international strategic planning, Harrell and Kiefer have shown how portfolio analysis can be applied to international markets. As depicted in Fig. 10.2, each axis summarizes a host of data concerning the attractiveness of a particular country and the competitive strength of a particular product.

Country attractiveness is composed of market size, market rate of

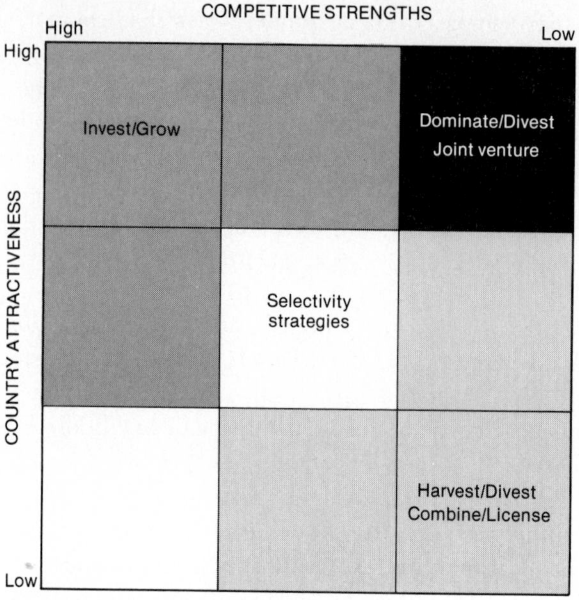

COMPETITIVE STRENGTHS
High
Low
High
Invest/Grow
Dominate/Divest
Joint venture
COUNTRY ATTRACTIVENESS
Selectivity
strategies
Harvest/Divest
Combine/License
Low

Figure 10.2 **Matrix for plotting products.**
SOURCE: G. D. Harrell and R. O. Kiefer, "Multinational Strategic Market Portfolios," *MSU Business Topics* (Winter 1981), p. 7. Reprinted by permission.

growth, government regulation, and economic and political factors. *Competitive strength* is composed of market share, product fit, contribution margin, and market support. The two scales form the axes of the matrix in Fig. 10.2. Those countries falling in the upper left generally should receive funding for growth, whereas countries in the lower right are prime for "harvesting," or divesting. Those countries falling on the lower left to upper right diagonal require selective funding strategies. Those falling in the upper right block require additional funding if the product is to contribute in the future to the firm's profits. Joint ventures or divestitures would be most appropriate if cash is limited. Those falling in the center and lower left blocks are probably good candidates for "milking." They can produce strong cash flows in the short run.[53]

10.3 STRATEGY IMPLEMENTATION

To be effective, international strategies must be implemented with national and cultural differences in mind. Among the many considerations an MNC must deal with, three of the most important are (1) selecting the local partner for a joint venture or licensing arrangement, (2) organizing the firm around the most appropriate structure, and (3) encouraging global rather than national management practices.

Partner Selection

Joint ventures and licensing agreements between a multinational company and a local partner in a host country are increasingly popular as a means of entry into other countries, especially less developed countries.[54] National policies as well as the complexity of the host country market often make these the preferred strategies for balancing country attractiveness against financial risk. The key to the successful implementation of these strategies is the selection of the local partner. In Fig. 10.3, Lasserre proposes a model describing the many variables to be considered by both sides when assessing a partnership. Each party needs to assess not only the strategic fit of each company's project strategy, but also the fit of each company's respective re-

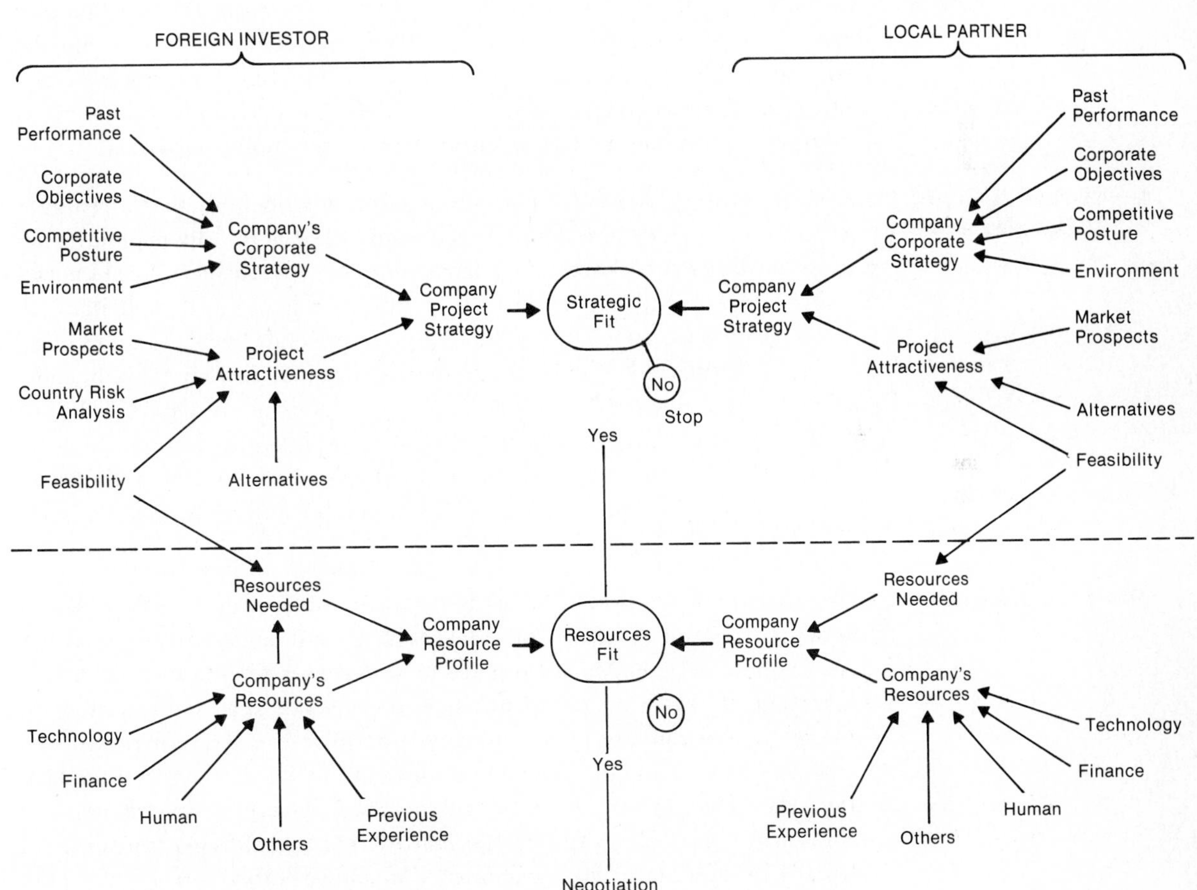

Figure 10.3 **Assessing partners to implement joint venture and licensing strategies.**
SOURCE: P. Lasserre, "Selecting a Foreign Partner for Technology Transfer," *Long Range Planning* (December 1984), p. 45. Copyright © 1984 Pergamon Press, Ltd. Reprinted by permission.

sources. Lasserre contends that this process requires a minimum of one to two years of prior contacts between both parties.[55] The fact that joint ventures tend to have a high rate of costly failures suggests that few multinationals use such a careful selection process.[56]

Organization Structure

Rarely, if ever, do multinational corporations suddenly appear as full-blown worldwide organizations. They tend to go through three common evolutionary stages both in their relationships with widely dispersed geographic markets and in the manner in which they structure their operations and programs.

Stage 1: Initial Entry

The "parent" corporation is attracted to a particular market in another country and seeks to test the potential of its products in this market with minimal risk. The firm thus introduces a number of product lines into the market through home-based export programs, licensing agreements, joint ventures, and/or through local commercial offices. The product divisions at headquarters continue to be responsible for all functional activities.

Stage 2: Early Development

Success in Stage 1 leads the parent corporation to believe that a stronger presence and broader product lines are needed if it is to fully exploit its advantage in the host country. The parent company establishes a local operating division or company in the host country, such as Ford of Britain, to better serve the market. The product line is expanded. Local manufacturing capacity is established. Managerial functions (product development, finance, marketing, etc.) are organized locally. As time goes by, other related businesses are acquired by the parent company to broaden the base of the local operating division. As the subsidiary in the host country successfully develops a strong regional presence, it achieves greater autonomy and self-sufficiency.

Stage 3: Maturity

As the parent corporation becomes aware of the success of its subsidiaries in other countries and the skills of its local managers, it consolidates operations under a regional management organization. Greater attention is given to a wider range of investment opportunities, such as mergers and acquisitions. Although the regional or local company continues to maintain ties with the parent corporation and the product divisions in the home country, it tends to enjoy relative autonomy in terms of local policy-setting and managerial practices. As was the case with the North American Philips Corporation, originally an affiliate of N. V. Philips' Gloeilampenfabrieken, a subsidiary may become a totally separate company with local shareholders and publicly traded stock.[57] Table 10.4 summarizes some of the structural arrangements possible in each stage of MNC development.

Table 10.4 **International Activity and Structure**

Stage	*Activities of Company*	*Organization Responsible for International Activities*	*Executive In Charge*
1	Exports directly and indirectly, but trade is minor.	Export department.	Export manager, reporting to domestic marketing executive.
	Exports become more important.	Export division.	Division manager.
2	Company undertakes licensing and invests in production overseas.	International division.	Director of international operations, usually vice-president.
	International investments increase.	Sometimes international headquarters company as wholly owned subsidiary [of domestic parent company].	President, who is vice-president in parent company.
3	International investments substantial and widespread; diversified international business activities.	Global organizational structure by geographic areas, product lines, functions, or some combination. Also worldwide staff support.	No single executive in charge of international business.

SOURCE: Adapted from W. A. Dymsza, *Multinational Business Strategy* (New York: McGraw-Hill Book Company, 1972), p. 22. Copyright © 1972 by McGraw-Hill, Inc. Reprinted by permission.

Even though most international and multinational corporations move through these stages in their involvement with host countries, any one corporation may be at different stages with different products in different markets. An example of diversity in international operations is Hewlett-Packard. The company began international activity by exporting its products. It used its own staff for exports to Canada and export management companies (export intermediaries operating on a buy-and-sell basis and providing financing for export shipments) for exports to other countries. These exports were then sold in both cases to middlemen abroad. As sales expanded, Hewlett-Packard took over the exporting functions, opened its own sales office in Mexico, purchased a warehousing facility in Switzerland, organized a wholly owned manufacturing subsidiary in West Germany, and entered into a partly owned venture in Japan.[58]

A basic dilemma facing the globally oriented multinational corporation is how to organize authority centrally in order to operate as a vast interlocking system to achieve synergy and at the same time decentralize authority to allow local managers to make the decisions necessary to meet the demands of the local market or host government.[59] To deal with this problem, many mature MNCs structure themselves along the lines of a matrix organization combining *product* and *geography.*

Typically, multinational corporations do not organize themselves around business functions, such as marketing or manufacturing, unless they are in an extractive raw-materials industry. Basic functions are thus subsumed under either product or geographic units.[60] Two extremes of the usual matrix are Nestlé and American Cyanamid. Nestlé's structure is one in which significant power and authority have been decentralized to geographic entities. This structure is similar to that depicted in Fig. 10.4, with each geographic set of operating companies having a similar set of products. In contrast, American Cyanamid has a series of product groups with worldwide responsibilities. To depict this structure, the geographical entities in Fig. 10.4 would have to be replaced by product or strategic business unit names. There does appear to be a trend, however, toward the Nestlé version of the matrix structure in which the geographic unit dominates the product unit.[61] Each regional unit in this case is fairly self-sufficient and independent but will be loosely coordinated by headquarters to avoid duplication of effort, achieve economies of scale, or ensure uniformity of procedures.[62]

Management Practices

As is true of people from any highly developed society, U.S.-trained managers tend to believe that what works well in their society will work well anywhere. Thus, someone well-schooled in the virtues of MBO, participative decision making, theory Y practices, job enrichment, and management science will have a tendency to transplant these practices without alteration to foreign nations. Unfortunately, just as products often need to be altered to appeal to a new market, so too do most management practices.

In a study of forty different cultures, Hofstede found that he could ex-

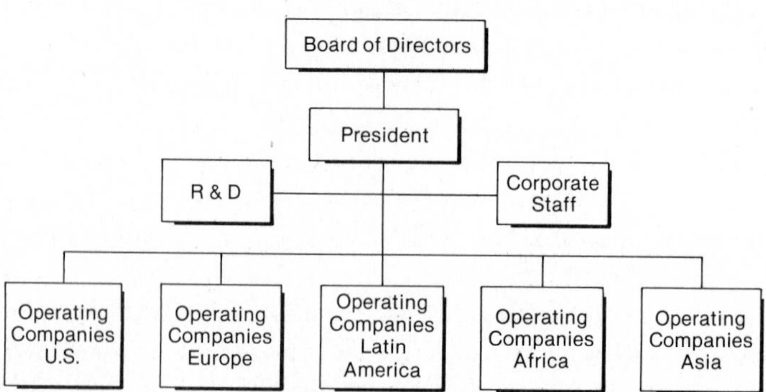

Figure 10.4 **Structure of a mature MNC.**

plain the success or failure of certain management practices on the basis of four cultural dimensions: power distance, uncertainty avoidance, individualism–collectivism, and masculinity–feminity.[63] He points out that management by objectives (MBO) has been the single most popular management technique "made in U.S.A." It has succeeded in Germany because the idea of replacing the arbitrary authority of the boss with the impersonal authority of mutually agreed-upon objectives fits the small power distance and strong uncertainty avoidance that are dimensions in the German culture. It has failed in France, however, because the French are used to large power distances—to accepting orders from a highly personalized authority. This cultural dimension goes counter to key aspects of MBO: small power distance between superior and subordinate and impersonal, objective goal setting. This same cultural dimension explains why the French, for whom vertical authority lines are very important, are significantly more reluctant than Americans to accept the multiple authority structures of project management or matrix organization.[64]

Because of these cultural differences managerial style and practices must be tailored to fit the situations in other countries. Most multinational corporations based in the United States, therefore, attempt to fill executive positions in their subsidiaries with well-qualified citizens of the host countries. IBM, for example, fills executive positions with the citizens of the many countries in which it operates.[65] This serves to placate nationalistic governments and to better attune IBM management practices to the host country's culture. Another approach to staffing the managerial positions of multinational corporations is to use people with an "international" orientation regardless of their country of origin or host country assignment. This approach allows for more promotion opportunities than does IBM's policy but it may result in a greater number of misunderstandings and conflicts with the local employees and with the host country government. In addition, it is estimated that anywhere from 25 to 40% of *expatriate* managers (people from a different country than the host country) fail to adjust to the host country's social and business environment. This is costly in terms of management performance, operations efficiency, and customer relations.[66]

10.4 EVALUATION AND CONTROL

In evaluating the activities of its international operations, the MNC should consider not only return on investment and other financial measures, but also the effect of its activities on the host country.

Financial Measures

The three most widely used techniques for international performance evaluation are return on investment, budget analysis, and historical comparisons. In one study, 95% of the corporate officers interviewed stated that they use the same evaluation techniques for foreign and domestic operations. Rate of return was mentioned as the single most important measure.[67] The use of ROI, however, can cause problems when applied to international operations: "Because of foreign currencies, different rates of inflation, different tax laws, and the use of transfer pricing, both the net income figure and the investment base may be seriously distorted."[68] Consequently, Daniels, Ogram, and Radebaugh recommend that MNC top management emphasize budgets as a means of differentiating between the worth of the subsidiary and the performance of its management.

Since differences among countries magnify the usual problems of comparability, multiple performance indicators should be used. Dymsza suggests that MNCs use management audits for their operations in foreign countries.[69]

MNC/Host Country Relationships

As multinational corporations grow and spread across the world, nations find themselves in a dilemma. Most countries, especially the less-developed ones, want to have the many benefits an MNC can bring: technology transfer, employment opportunities, tax revenues, and the opportunity to build domestic business corporations in partnership with powerful and well-connected foreign-based companies. These countries also fear the problems an MNC can bring. After having welcomed an MNC with tax benefits and subsidies of various types, the host country may find itself in a double bind regarding the repatriation of profits. It can either allow the MNC to export its profits to corporate headquarters—thereby draining the nation of potential investment capital—or it can allow the MNC to send home only a small portion of its profits—thereby making the host country unattractive to other MNCs as a place to invest. For example, research reveals that between 1960 and 1968, profits sent to the United States from Latin America by MNCs exceeded new investment by $6.7 billion.[70] Host countries also note that less-developed countries seldom receive much benefit from MNC technology transfer in the form of increasing their exports. MNCs also have a tradition of placing business values above the cultural values of the host country.[71]

Given the pros and cons of the multinational corporation's presence in the world, Fayerweather proposes four basic relationships an MNC can assume vis-à-vis a host country. They range from positively *contributing* to the country's development to negatively *undermining* the basic culture of the country.[72]

Contributory Relationships

An MNC acts to directly augment or contribute to the goals or achievement of a host nation without any negative effect. In this relationship both the MNC and the local partner (if any) positively help each other as well as their respective countries. Renault's investment in American Motors Corporation has resulted in keeping AMC from going bankrupt, thus saving American jobs. Recent AMC profits have helped compensate for Renault's poorer performance in Europe, thus helping Renault's owner, the French government.

Reinforcing Relationships

The actions of an MNC reinforce the goals or achievement of a host nation but tend to have some negative side-effects. This is a somewhat less than ideal relationship. The MNC invests heavily in the country's development and may build the transportation and communication systems so necessary for economic development. Nevertheless, the MNC sends all its profits to its headquarters and its emphasis on its own cultural values sometimes conflicts with host country values. This is probably the type of relationship existing between the U.S.-based MNCs that are production sharing in Mexico.

Frustrating Relationships

Actions of an MNC challenge the goals of the nation or impede its immediate functioning in ways to which the nation cannot respond effectively so that its government is frustrated. Nestlé's aggressive marketing of baby formula to mothers in less-developed countries is an example of this type of relationship. In countries where breast-feeding is more nutritious and healthier for babies than bottle-feeding (due to the poor quality of water and sanitary conditions) the use of Nestlé's baby formula contributed to malnutrition and other sickness in the babies. Because many LDC governments were unable to deal with the situation, church groups from the developed countries plus the United Nations put enough pressure on Nestlé to cause it to stop its aggressive marketing practices in the LDCs.[73]

Undermining Relationships

The effect of an MNC is to reduce the basic logic (in terms of norms, values, and philosophy) of a nation so that its functioning is weakened or undermined. MNCs' development of oil resources in the Middle Eastern countries caused a clash between traditional Moslem values and Western values; this probably contributed to the Iranian revolution and disruptions in other Moslem countries. The resulting antagonism from such a relationship is reflected in the following comment by a Third World representative:

> Poor countries have often been swindled out of a decent return for their produce in the name of market mechanism, deprived of their economic independence, seduced by imported life styles, foreign value systems, irrelevant research designs—all in the name of freedom of choice.[74]

To the extent that an MNC fails to contribute to or reinforce the functioning of a host country, it may find its assets expropriated and its home-country management team asked to leave. For those corporations that go to less-developed countries to locate and extract needed raw materials but see the host countries only as something to manipulate and use, a certain cycle results:

> *First,* they are welcomed by the host country as a source of foreign currency, a major employer, a means of upgrading the country's skills, a stimulant to the economy, and a catalyst to attract other investors. *Second,* after a few years, pressure increases on the firm to process in addition to only extracting the material. This often leads to a second phase of investment by the company and more benefits to the country. *Third,* the company is now sufficiently dependent to be vulnerable to a request to have local participation in ownership, either through private parties or directly by the host government. *Fourth,* nationalization advances to a takeout stage after more years of evolving relationships, usually involving compensation for assets and some arrangement of management. *Fifth,* recalling that the primary reason for the original investment was a source of materials, and recognizing that government owned operations are almost always inefficient, the company is forced to pay increasing prices and turns to alternative sources if they exist.[75]

10.5 SUMMARY AND CONCLUSION

A knowledge of international considerations is becoming extremely important for the proper understanding of the strategic management process in large corporations. Just as U.S. firms are becoming more involved every year with operations and markets in other countries, imports and subsidiaries from other countries are becoming more a part of the American landscape. International corporations have been transforming themselves slowly into multinational corporations (MNCs) with a global orientation and flexible management styles.

The dominant issue in the strategic management process of a multinational corporation is the effect of widely different external environments on internal activities. A firm's top management must therefore be well schooled in the differences among nations in terms of their sociocultural, economic, political-legal, and technological environment variables. Data search procedures and analytical techniques must be used to assess the many possible investment opportunities and their risks in world business. Assuming that top management feels that the corporation has the requisite internal qualifications to become multinational, it must determine the appropriate set of strategies for entering and investing in potential host countries. These may vary from simple exportation to the formation with other companies of very complex consortiums. The corporation's product portfolio must be constantly monitored for strengths and weaknesses.

Attention must also be paid to selecting the most appropriate local partner, organization structure and management system for a worldwide enterprise. An overall system of control and coordination must be balanced against a host country's need for local flexibility and autonomy. An MNC should use a series of performance indicators so that return on investment, budget analysis, and historical comparisons can be viewed in the context of a strategic audit of operations in the host country. Above all, the top management of a multinational corporation has the responsibility to ensure that the MNC contributes to and reinforces the functioning of the host nation rather than frustrating or undermining its government and culture.

DISCUSSION QUESTIONS

1. What differentiates a multinational corporation from an international corporation?
2. If the basic concepts of absolute and comparative advantage suggest free trade as the best route to prosperity for all nations, why do so many countries use protectionist measures to keep out imports?
3. Should MNCs be allowed to own more than half the stock of a subsidiary based in a host country? Why or why not?
4. Should the United States allow unrestricted trade between corporations in the United States and communist countries? Why or why not?
5. In developing an international product portfolio matrix, what specific factors should be included to assess a country's attractiveness?
6. Given the many disadvantages of joint ventures (loss of control, lower profits, probability of conflicts with partners, and the likely transfer of technological advantage to a partner), plus its typical temporary nature, why is it such a popular strategy?
7. What is the overall impact of multinational corporations on world peace? How do they help? How do they hinder?

NOTES

1. B. D. Henderson, *New Strategies for the New Global Competition* (Boston: Boston Consulting Group, 1981), p. 1.
2. A. L. Malabre, Jr., "World Trade Suffers as Economies Slow," *Wall Street Journal* (August 3, 1981), p. 1.
3. *International Financial Statistics Yearbook*, Volume XXXVII (Washington, D.C.: International Monetary Fund, 1984), p. 595.
4. B. R. Scott, "National Strategy for Stronger U.S. Competitiveness," *Harvard Business Review* (March–April 1984), p. 77.
5. M. McLuhan, *Understanding Media: The Extensions of Man* (New York: McGraw-Hill Paperbacks, 1965).
6. J. McElroy, "Cheaper by the Dozen," *Road and Track* (June 1984), pp. 122–128.
7. L. Birger, "Once Threatened by Henry Ford II, European Fords Carrying Detroit," *The Tribune*, Albuquerque, N. Mex. (June 2, 1980), p. C-10.
8. "USAir Orders Engines for Its Boeing Jets," *Wall Street Journal* (August 3, 1981), p. 22.

9. Adapted from W. A. Dymsza, *Multinational Business Strategy* (New York: McGraw-Hill, 1972), pp. 50–51.
10. United States Commerce Department, Washington, D.C. Reported by B. Boyd in "Moneylist," *Ames Tribune*, Ames, Iowa (February 11, 1985), p. 1.
11. *Wall Street Journal* (May 24, 1983), p. 35.
12. G. Anders, "European Executives Consider U.S. Prime Area for Expansion Abroad, Journal Poll Shows," *Wall Street Journal* (December 5, 1984), p. 34.
"Saatchi and Saatchi PLC To Buy Yankelovich; Price Is $13.5 Million," *Wall Street Journal* (October 31, 1984), p. 37.
T. F. O'Boyle, "Some Japanese Steelmakers Are Weighing Making Investments in U.S. Steel Industry," *Wall Street Journal* (October 12, 1984), p. 2.
13. Anders.
14. O. Ullmann, "Third World Debt Plays Poorly for Caterpillar, Peoria," *Des Moines Register* (September 25, 1983), p. 5F.
15. "Drastic New Strategies To Keep U.S. Multinationals Competitive," *Business Week* (October 8, 1984), p. 172.
16. A. Nag, "Chrysler Tests Consumer Reaction to Mexican-Made Cars Sold in U.S.," *Wall Street Journal* (July 23, 1984), p. 13.
"Matsushita Selling G. E. Products in U.S.," *Des Moines Register* (July 8, 1984), p. 3F.
17. Dymsza, p. 5.
18. Dymsza, pp. 5–6.
19. S. J. Kobrin, "Morality, Political Power and Illegal Payments by Multinational Corporations," *Columbia Journal of World Business* (Winter 1976), p. 106.
20. J. D. Daniels, E. W. Ogram, Jr., and L. H. Radebaugh, *International Business: Environments and Operations,* 3rd ed. (Reading, Mass.: Addison-Wesley, 1982), p. 640.
21. Daniels, Ogram, and Radebaugh, 3rd ed. (1982), p. 513.
22. D. Ricks, M. Y. C. Fu, and J. S. Arpan, *International Business Blunders* (Columbus, Ohio: Grid, Inc., 1974).
23. Daniels, Ogram, and Radebaugh, 3rd ed. (1982), pp. 522–523.
24. D. A. Ricks and V. Mahajan, "Blunders in International Marketing: Fact or Fiction," *Long Range Planning* (February 1984), pp. 78–82.
25. "Banks in Pakistan To Stop Paying Interest in 1985," *Wall Street Journal* (June 18, 1984), p. 23.
26. S. Chang, "The Gods and the U.A.W. Are Smiling: Mazda's New Boss Plans To Make Cars, and Jobs, for Yanks," *People* (February 18, 1985), pp. 90–91.
27. R. T. Grieves, "Modern Barter," *Time* (June 11, 1984) p. 48.
D. B. Yoffie, "Profiting from Countertrade," *Harvard Business Review* (May–June 1984), pp. 8–12, 16.

28. P. F. Drucker, "Insulating the Firm from Currency Exposure," *Wall Street Journal* (April 30, 1985), p. 28.
29. "Uniroyal Sells a Unit for Over $71 Million to Malaysian Concern," *Wall Street Journal* (December 24, 1984), p. 12.
30. M. L. Weidenbaum, "Facing the Problems of the World Economy," *Journal of Business Strategy* (Winter 1984), p. 68.
31. H. DeNero and A. Mahini, "Local-Content Laws Abroad Needn't Cut Profitability," *Wall Street Journal* (July 23, 1984), p. 10.
    W. R. Cline, "Protectionism: An Ill Trade Wind Rises," *Wall Street Journal* (November 6, 1984), p. 30.
32. A. Pine, "Study Says Curb on Japan's Cars Lifts U.S. Prices," *Wall Street Journal* (February 14, 1985), p. 3.
33. Daniels, Ogram, and Radebaugh, 3rd ed. (1982), p. 28.
34. Y. N. Chang and F. Campo-Flores, *Business Policy and Strategy* (Santa Monica, Calif.: Goodyear Publishing, 1980), p. 601.
35. R. B. Reich, *The Next American Frontier* (New York: Times Books, 1983).
36. R. A. Shaffer, "Japanese Now Target Communications Gear as a Growth Industry," *Wall Street Journal* (January 13, 1982), p. 1.
37. G. W. Weiss, Jr., "The General Electric-SNECMA Jet Engine Development Program" (Boston: *Intercollegiate Case Clearing House*, no. 9-380-739, 1980).
38. J. Mark, "High-Tech Exports to China Still Being Delayed, Despite Eased Rules, U.S. Firms Finding," *Wall Street Journal* (January 3, 1985), p. 16.
39. R. Stobaugh and R. T. Wells, Jr., *Technology Crossing Borders* (Boston: Harvard Business School Press, 1984), p. 4.
40. P. Banker, "You're the Best Judge of Foreign Risks," *Harvard Business Review* (March–April 1983), pp. 157–165.
41. T. N. Gladwin, "Assessing the Multinational Environment for Corporate Opportunity," in W. D. Guth (ed.), *Handbook of Business Strategy* (Boston: Warren, Gorham and Lamont, 1985), pp. 7.28–7.41.
42. W. D. Coplin and M. K. O'Leary, "The 1985 Political Climate for International Business: A Forecast of Risk in 82 Countries," *Planning Review* (May 1985), pp. 36–43.
43. Chang and Campo-Flores, pp. 602–604.
44. Dymsza, p. 1.
45. Dymsza, pp. 96–102.
46. V. Pucik and N. Hatvany, "Management Practices in Japan and Their Impact on Business Strategy," in R. Lamb (ed.), *Advances in Strategic Management,* Vol. I (Greenwich, Conn.: Jai Press, 1983), p. 124.
47. Daniels, Ogram, and Radebaugh, 3rd ed. (1982), p. 490.
48. S. P. Galante, "Foreign Semiconductor Firms Try New Strategy in U.S.," *Wall Street Journal* (August 23, 1984), p. 20.
49. K. P. Power, "Now We Can Move Office Work Offshore To Enhance Output," *Wall Street Journal* (June 9, 1983), p. 30.

50. S. Koepp, "Hands across the Border," *Time* (September 10, 1984), p. 36.
51. For further discussion of these strategies, refer to a text on international business such as that by Daniels, Ogram, and Radebaugh.
52. G. D. Harrell and R. O. Kiefer, "Multinational Strategic Market Portfolios," *MSU Business Topics* (Winter 1981), p. 5.
53. Harrell and Kiefer, p. 8.
54. P. Lasserre, "Selecting a Foreign Partner for Technology Transfer," *Long Range Planning* (December 1984), pp. 43–49.
55. Lasserre, pp. 48–49.
56. J. P. Killing, "How To Make a Global Joint Venture Work," *Harvard Business Review* (May–June 1982), p. 120–127.
57. R. L. Drake and L. M. Caudill, "Management of the Large Multinational: Trends and Future Challenges," *Business Horizons* (May–June 1981), pp. 84–85.
58. Daniels, Ogram, and Radebaugh, 2nd ed. (1979), p. 359.
59. Stobaugh and Wells, pp. 16–17.
60. S. M. Davis, *Managing and Organizing Multinational Corporations* (New York: Pergamon Press, 1979), p. 241.
61. Drake and Caudill, p. 87.
62. T. T. Herbert, "Strategy and Multinational Organization Structure: An Interorganizational Relationship Perspective," *Academy of Management Review* (April 1984), p. 264.
63. G. Hofstede, "Motivation, Leadership, and Organization: Do American Theories Apply Abroad?" *Organizational Dynamics* (Summer 1980), pp. 42–63.
    G. Hofstede, "National Cultures in Four Dimensions: A Research-Based Theory of Cultural Differences among Nations," *International Journal of Management and Organization* (Spring–Summer 1983), pp. 46–74.
    G. Hofstede, "The Cultural Relativity of the Quality of Life Concept," *Academy of Management Review* (July 1984), pp. 389–398.
64. G. Inzerilli and A. Laurent, "Managerial Views of Organization Structure in France and the USA," *International Studies of Management and Organization* (Spring–Summer 1983), p. 113.
65. W. H. Newman, J. P. Logan, and W. H. Hegarty, *Strategy, Policy, and Central Management,* 9th ed. (Cincinnati, Ohio: South-Western Publishing Company, 1985), p. 611.
66. M. Mendenhall and G. Oddou, "The Dimensions of Expatriate Acculturation: A Review," *Academy of Management Review* (January 1985), pp. 39–47.
67. Daniels, Ogram, and Radebaugh, 3rd ed. (1982), p. 552.
68. Daniels, Ogram, and Radebaugh, 3rd ed. (1982), p. 552.
69. Dymsza, pp. 74–78.
70. K. Paul and R. Barbato, "The Multinational Corporation in the Less Devel-

oped Country: The Economic Development Model versus the North–South Model," *Academy of Management Review* (January 1985), p. 9.

71. P. Wright, "MNC-Third World Business Unit Performance: Application of Strategic Elements," *Strategic Management Journal* (July–September 1984), pp. 231–240.

72. Adapted from J. Fayerweather, *International Business Strategy and Administration* (Cambridge, Mass.: Ballinger Publishing, 1978), p. 124.

73. J. E. Post, "Assessing the Nestlé Boycott," *California Management Review* (Winter 1985), pp. 113–131.

74. M. Ul Haq, *The Poverty Curtain: Choices for the Third World* (New York: Columbia University Press, 1976) as quoted by Wright, p. 232.

75. F. T. Haner, *Business Policy, Planning and Strategy* (Cambridge, Mass.: Winthrop Publishers, 1976), p. 441.

Chapter 11

STRATEGIC MANAGEMENT OF NOT-FOR-PROFIT ORGANIZATIONS

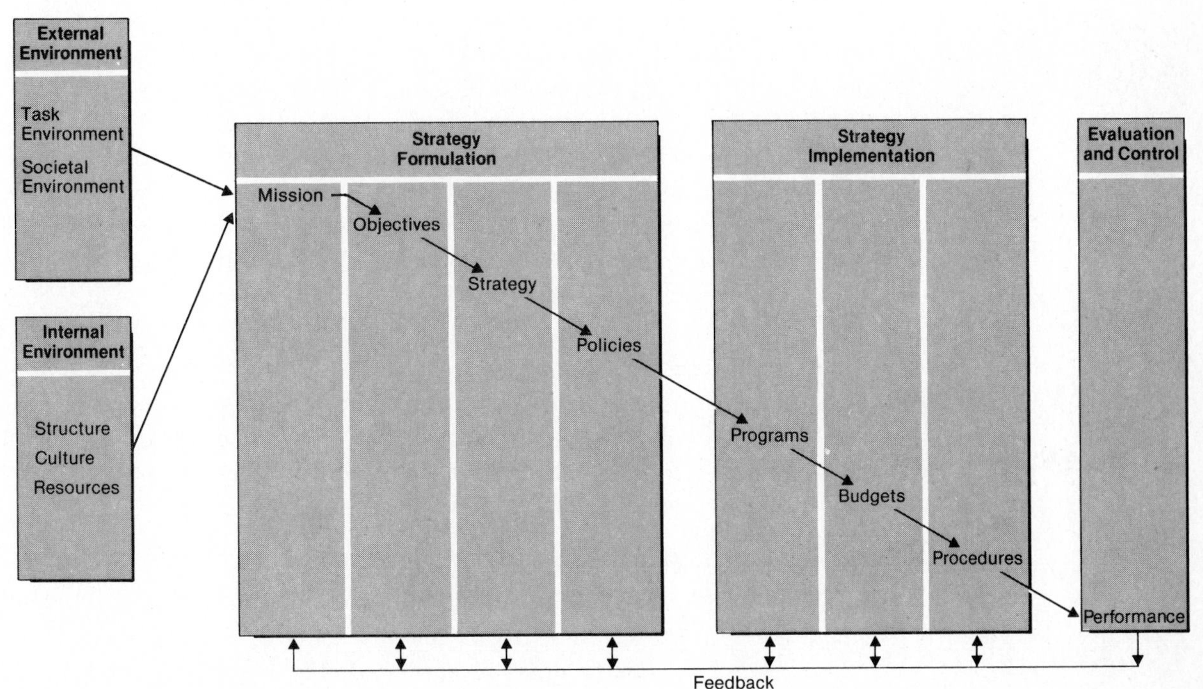

Traditionally, studies in strategic management have dealt with profit-making firms to the exclusion of nonprofit or governmental organizations. The little existing empirical research suggests that not-for-profit organizations are in the initial stage of using strategic management.[1] From their study of 103 not-for-profit organizations, Unterman and Davis conclude: "Not only have not-for-profit organizations failed to reach the strategic management stage of development, but many of them have failed to reach even the strategic planning stages that for-profit enterprises initiated 15 to 20 years ago."[2] Nevertheless, an increasing number of not-for-profits, especially hospitals, are concerned with strategic issues and strategic planning, even though it may be only an informal process.[3] A knowledge of not-for-profit organizations is important if for no other reason than the fact that they employ over 20 million people in the United States (compared to approximately 70 million in the profit-making sector).[4] Private nonprofit organizations, in particular, represent 5.2% of all corporations, partnerships, and proprietorships in the United States, receive 3.5% of all revenue, and hold about 4.3% of the total assets of business firms. During the 1970s, nonprofit firms increased both in total number and revenues *faster* than did profit-making firms.[5] It is estimated that over one-third of the world's gross product is generated by "non-market" corporations (which include state-owned corporations and regulated utilities).[6] In the United States alone, in addition to various federal, state, and local government agencies, there are about 3,500 not-for-profit hospitals; 3,000 colleges and universities; and approximately 300 national church and synagogue bodies, plus hundreds of thousands of local churches, synagogues, and charities.[7]

The first ten chapters of this book dealt primarily with the strategic management of profit-making corporations. The purpose of this chapter, however, is to highlight briefly the major differences between the profit-making and the not-for-profit organization to indicate how their differences might affect the strategic management process.

11.1 CATEGORIES OF ORGANIZATIONS

All profit-making and not-for-profit organizations can be grouped into four basic categories. In some instances, it is difficult to clearly state where one category leaves off and another begins: "The wide and growing involvement of government in all aspects of life has caused a convergence or blurring of the various sectors."[8] Four categories are as follows:

1. *Private for-profit* businesses dependent on the market economy for generating the means of survival (ranging from small businesses to major corporations).
2. *Private quasi-public* organizations created by legislative authority and

given a limited monopoly to provide particular goods or services to a population subgroup (primarily public utilities).

3. *Private nonprofit* organizations operating on public goodwill (donations, contributions, and endowments or government stipends), but constituted outside the authority of governmental agencies or legislative bodies.
4. *Public* agencies of government (federal, state, and local) constituted by law and authorized to collect taxes and provide services.[9]

Typically, the term *not-for-profit* includes private nonprofit corporations such as hospitals, institutes, private colleges, and organized charities, as well as public governmental units or agencies such as welfare departments, prisons, and state universities. Regulated public utilities are in a grey area somewhere between profit and not-for-profit. They are profit making and have stockholders, but take on many of the characteristics of the not-for-profit organization, such as a greater dependence on rate-setting government commissions than on customers.

11.2 WHY NOT-FOR-PROFIT?

The not-for-profit sector of the American economy is becoming increasingly important for a number of reasons. *First,* society desires certain goods and services that profit-making firms cannot or will not provide. These are referred to as "public" or "collective" goods because people who may not have paid for the goods also receive benefits from them. Paved roads, police protection, museums, and schools are examples of public goods. A person cannot use a private good unless she or he pays for it. Generally once a public good is provided, however, anyone can partake of it.

Second, a private nonprofit firm tends to receive benefits from society that a private profit-making firm cannot obtain. Preferred tax status to nonstock corporations is given in section 501(c)(3) of the Internal Revenue Code in the form of exemptions from corporate income taxes. Private nonprofit firms also enjoy exemptions from various other state, local, and federal taxes. Under certain conditions they also benefit from the tax deductibility of donor contributions and membership dues. In addition, they qualify for special third-class mailing privileges.[10] These benefits are allowed because private nonprofit organizations are typically service organizations which are expected to use any excess of revenue over costs and expenses to either improve service or reduce the price of their service. This service orientation is reflected in the fact that not-for-profit organizations do not use the term *customer* to refer to the consumer or recipient of the service. The recipient is typically referred to as a patient, student, client, case, or simply "the public."

11.3 IMPORTANCE OF REVENUE SOURCE

The feature that best differentiates not-for-profit organizations from each other as well as from profit-making corporations is their source of income.[11] The profit-making firm depends upon revenues obtained from the sale of its goods and services to customers. Its source of income is the customer who buys and uses the product, and who typically pays for the product when it is received. Profits result when revenues are greater than the costs of making and distributing the product, and are thus a measure of the corporation's *effectiveness* (a product is valued because customers purchase it for use) and *efficiency* (costs are kept below selling price).

The not-for-profit organization, in contrast, depends heavily on dues, assessments, or donations from its membership or on funding from a sponsoring agency such as the United Way or the federal government. Revenue, therefore, comes from a variety of sources—*not* just from sales to customers/clients. It may come from people who do not even receive the services they are subsidizing. Such charitable organizations as the American Cancer Society and CARE are examples. In another type of not-for-profit organization—such as unions and voluntary medical plans—revenue comes mostly from the people, the members, who receive the service. Nevertheless, the members typically pay dues *in advance* and must accept later whatever service is provided whether they want it or not, whether it is what they expected or not. The service is often received long after the dues are paid. As a result, some members who have paid into a fund for many years may leave the organization or die without receiving services, whereas newcomers may receive many services even though they have paid only a small amount into it.

Therefore, in profit-making corporations, there is typically a simple and direct connection between the customer or client and the organization. The organization tends to be totally dependent on sales of its products or services to the customer for revenue and is therefore extremely interested in pleasing the customer. As shown in Fig. 11.1, the profit-making organization (organization A) tries to influence the customer to continue to buy and use its services. The customer, in turn, directly influences the organization's decision-making process by either buying or not buying the item offered.

In the case of the typical not-for-profit organization, however, there is likely to be a very different sort of relationship between the organization providing and the person receiving the service. Since the recipient of the service typically does not pay the entire cost of the service, outside sponsors are required. In most instances, the sponsors receive none of the service but may provide from partial to total funding of needed revenues. As indicated earlier, these sponsors may be the U.S. Congress (using taxpayers' money) or charitable organizations, such as the United Way (using voluntary donations). As shown in Fig. 11.1, the not-for-profit (NFP) organization may be

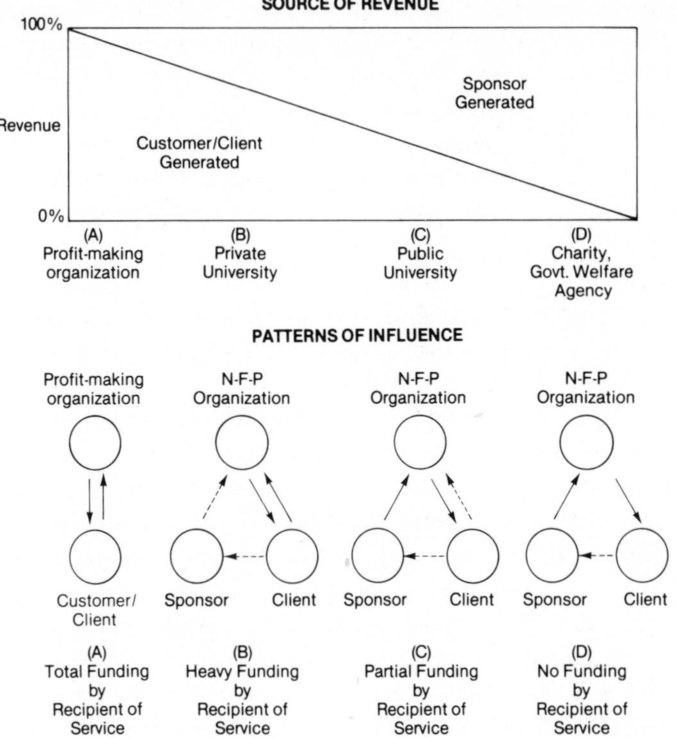

Figure 11.1 **The effect of sources of revenue on patterns of client-organization influence.**
SOURCE: Thomas L. Wheelen and J. David Hunger, "The Effect of Revenue upon Patterns of Client-Organization Influence." Copyright © 1982 by Wheelen and Hunger Associates. Reprinted by permission.

partially dependent on sponsors for funding (organizations B and C) or totally dependent on the sponsors (organization D).

The pattern of influence on the organization's strategic decision making derives from its sources of revenue. As shown in Fig. 11.1, a private university (organization B) is heavily dependent on student tuition and other client-generated funds for around 71% of its revenue.[12] As a result, student desires are likely to have more influence (as shown by an unbroken line) on the university's decision making than are the desires of the various sponsors, such as alumni and private foundations. The relatively marginal influence on the organization by the sponsors is reflected by a broken line. In contrast, a public university (depicted in Fig. 11.1 as organization C) is more heavily dependent on outside sponsors, such as a state legislature, for revenue funding. Student tuition and other client-generated funds form a smaller percentage (typically only 37%) of total revenue. As a result, decision making is heavily influenced by the sponsors (unbroken line) and only marginally influenced directly by the students (broken line). In the case of organization D in Fig. 11.1, however, the client has no direct influence on the organization because the client pays nothing for the services received. In this type of situation, the organization tends to measure its effectiveness in terms of sponsor satisfaction. It has no real measure of its efficiency other than its ability to carry out its mission and achieve its objectives within the dollar contribution it has received from its sponsors. In contrast to other organizations where the client contributes a significant proportion of the needed revenue, this type of not-for-profit organization (D) actually may be able to increase the amount of its revenue by heavily lobbying its sponsors while reducing the level of its service to its clients!

Regardless of the percentage of total funding generated by the client, the client may attempt to influence indirectly the not-for-profit organization through the sponsors. This is depicted by the broken lines connecting the client and the sponsor in organizations B, C, and D in the figure. Welfare clients or prison inmates, for example, may be able to improve indirectly the services they receive by pressuring government officials by writing letters to legislators or, even, by rioting. And students at public universities may lobby state officials for student representation on governing boards.

The key to understanding the management of a not-for-profit organization is thus to learn who pays for the delivered services. To the extent that the recipients of the service pay only a small proportion of the total cost of the service, it is likely that top management will be more concerned with satisfying the needs and desires of the funding sponsors or agency than those of the people receiving the service. As previous studies indicate, acquisition of resources may become an end in itself.[13]

11.4 CONSTRAINTS ON STRATEGIC MANAGEMENT

Because not-for-profit organizations are truly different from profit-making organizations, there are a number of characteristics peculiar to the former that constrain its behavior and affect its strategic management. Newman and Wallender list the following five constraining characteristics:

1. Service is often intangible and hard to measure. This difficulty is typically compounded by the existence of multiple service objectives developed in order to satisfy multiple sponsors.
2. Client influence may be weak. Often the organization has a local monopoly, and payments by customers may be a very small source of funds.
3. Strong employee commitment to professions or to a cause may undermine their allegiance to the organization employing them.

4. Resource contributors—notably fund contributors and government—may intrude upon the organization's internal management.
5. Restraints on the use of rewards and punishments may result from characteristics 1, 3, and 4.[14]

It is true that a number of these characteristics may be found in profit-making as well as in not-for-profit organizations. Nevertheless, as Newman and Wallendar state, the ". . . frequency of strong impact is much higher in not-for-profit enterprises. . . ."[15] As a result, the strategic management process for any given situation will be different in a not-for-profit organization than in the typical profit-making corporations discussed in earlier chapters.

Impact on Strategy Formulation

Long-range planning and decision making are affected by the listed constraining characteristics and serve to add at least four *complications* to strategy formulation.

1. *Goal conflicts interfere with rational planning.* Since the not-for-profit organization typically lacks a single clear-cut performance criterion (such as profits), divergent goals and objectives are likely.[16] This is especially true if there are multiple sponsors. Differences in the concern of various important sponsors may prevent top management from stating the organization's mission in anything but very broad terms, fearing a sponsor may disagree with a particular narrow definition of mission and cancel funding. In such organizations it is the reduced influence of the clients that *permits* this diversity of values and goals to occur without a clear market check.
2. *An integrated planning focus tends to shift from results to resources.* Since not-for-profit organizations tend to provide services that are hard to measure, there is rarely a net "bottom line." Planning, therefore, becomes more concerned with resource inputs, which can easily be measured, than with service, which cannot. Goal displacement, therefore, becomes even more likely than in business organizations.
3. *Ambiguous operating objectives create opportunities for internal politics and goal displacement.* The combination of vague objectives and a heavy concern with resources allows managers considerable leeway in their activities. Such leeway makes possible political maneuvering for personal ends. In addition, since the effectiveness of the not-for-profit organization hinges on the satisfaction of the sponsoring group, there is a tendency to ignore the needs of the client while focusing on the desires of the powerful sponsor. This problem is compounded by the fact

that boards of trustees are often selected not on the basis of their managerial experience, but on the basis of their ability to contribute money, raise funds, and work with politicians. Board members therefore tend to ignore the task of determining strategies and policies—leaving this to the paid executive director.[17]

4. *Professionalization simplifies detailed planning but adds rigidity.* In those not-for-profit organizations where professionals hold important roles (as in hospitals or colleges), professional values and traditions may prevent the organization from changing conventional behavior patterns to fit new service missions to changing social needs. This, of course, can occur in any organization that hires professionals. The strong service orientation of most not-for-profit organizations, however, tends to encourage the development of static professional norms and attitudes.

Impact on Strategy Implementation

The five constraining characteristics affect how a not-for-profit organization is organized in both its structure and job design. Three *complications,* in particular, can be highlighted.

1. *Decentralization is complicated.* The difficulty of setting objectives for an intangible, hard-to-measure service mission complicates the delegation of decision-making authority. Important matters are therefore centralized and lower-level managers are forced to wait until top management makes a decision. With the heavy dependence on sponsors for revenue support, the top management of a not-for-profit organization always must be alert to how the sponsors may view an organizational activity. This leads to "defensive centralization" in which top management retains all decision-making authority to avoid any actions to which the sponsors may object.
2. *Linking pins for external-internal integration become important.* Given the heavy dependence on outside sponsors, a special need arises for people in "buffer" roles who can relate to both inside and outside groups. This is especially necessary when the sponsors are diverse (revenue comes from donations, membership fees, and federal funds) and the service is intangible (for instance, a "good" education) with a broad mission and multiple shifting objectives. The job of a "Dean for External Affairs," for example, consists primarily of working with school alumni and fund raising.
3. *Job enlargement and executive development may be restrained by professionalism.* In organizations that employ a large number of professionals, managers must design jobs that appeal to prevailing professional norms. Professionals have rather clear ideas about which

activities are, and which are not, within their province. Enriching a nurse's job by expanding his or her decision-making authority regarding drug dosage, for example, may cause conflict with medical doctors who feel such authority is theirs alone. In addition, promoting a professional into a managerial job may be viewed as a punishment rather than as a reward.

Impact on Evaluation and Control

Special *complications* arising from the constraining characteristics also affect how behavior is motivated and performance is controlled. Two problems, in particular, are often noticed.

1. *Rewards and penalties have little or no relation to performance.* When desired results are vague and the judgment of success is subjective, predictable and impersonal feedback cannot be established. Performance is judged either intuitively ("You don't seem to be taking your job seriously") or on the basis of those small aspects of a job that can be measured ("You were late to work twice last month").
2. *Inputs rather than outputs are heavily controlled.* Since inputs can be measured much more easily than outputs, the not-for-profit organization tends to focus more on the resources going into performance than on the performance itself. The emphasis is thus on setting maximum limits for costs and expenses. Because there is little to no reward for meeting these standards, people usually respond negatively to controls.

11.5 TYPICAL RESPONSES TO CONSTRAINTS

Not-for-profit organizations tend to deal with the complications resulting from constraining characteristics in a number of ways. Although these responses may occur in profit-making organizations as well, they are more typical of not-for-profit organizations.

Select a Dynamic and Forceful Leader

One approach, which is also used in profit-making firms at times, is to appoint a strong leader to the top management position: "The leader has personal convictions about the values to be used in decision-making and either has enough power to make important choices, or is so influential that her or his values are accepted by others who make decisions."[18] This manager thus can force a change in the planning of the organizational mission and objectives without antagonizing the sponsors, as well as in the organizing and controlling of activities. The danger with this approach, however, is that change can occur only from the top down. Rather than accepting the normal risks inherent in making an important decision, lower-level managers "play it safe" and either wait for guidance from above to see which way "the wind is blowing" or pass the decision upward in the hierarchy.

Develop a Mystique

The organization can be integrated toward successful goal accomplishment by developing a "mystique" that dominates the enterprise and attracts likely sponsors. A strong conviction shared by all employees, as well as the sponsors, about the importance of a particular mission or service objective can also serve to motivate unusually high performance and client satisfaction. This sense of mission typically focuses on providing a unique service to a highly visible client group, such as mentally retarded children. Once established, the mystique sets the character and values decision makers and others are expected to follow.[19] Thus it is similar to the corporate culture discussed earlier. One danger in using mystique to focus activities and to motivate performance is that the mission can move far afield from that desired by the sponsoring groups.

Generate Rules and Regulations

Since the constraints may force people in not-for-profit organizations to be concerned more with pleasing the sponsors than with achieving a mission of satisfying the client, top management may respond by generating rules and regulations regarding activities with the client. Minimum standards may be developed regarding the number of contact hours spent with each client, the number of reports completed, and/or the "proper" method of working. The danger inherent in this approach is that it tends to emphasize form over substance and to confuse looking good and keeping busy with actual performance. More goal displacement develops and feeds upon itself. "Burnout" develops among dedicated employees who may feel they are being forced to spend too much energy fighting the system rather than helping the client.

Appoint a Strong Board

A board of directors or trustees can help ensure vigilance in setting and monitoring the objectives of the organization. To the extent that the board actively represents the sponsors and special interest groups that determine the organization's revenues, it has a great deal of power: "The potential for control by some not-for-profit boards far exceeds that of the boards of a corporation which represents only the owners."[20] The board can perform a watchdog role over the organization by demanding clear-cut, measurable objectives and a mission of client satisfaction. The danger with this approach, however, is that the board may get too involved in operational activities. In organizations with a large number of professional employees, the senior administrator may be viewed as a "hybrid" professional—part professional and part manager (for instance, a physician serving as a hospital administrator). The board thus tends to involve itself not only with strategic matters, but also with operational matters such as hiring, directing, and developing the budget.[21] Nevertheless, like the boards discussed in Chapter 3, not-for-profit boards can range in their degree of involvement in strategic management from the passive phantom or figurehead boards to the active catalyst type.

Establish Performance-Based Budgets

A fifth approach to dealing with complications in a not-for-profit organization is to institute an information system that ties measurable objectives to budgeted line items. One such system is the *planning, programming, budgeting system* (PPBS) developed by the U.S. Department of Defense. It assists not-for-profit administrators in choosing among alternative programs in terms of resource use. It includes five steps:

1. Specify objectives as clearly as possible in quantitative, measurable terms.
2. Analyze the actual output of the not-for-profit organization in terms of the stated objectives.
3. Measure the cost of the particular program.
4. Analyze alternatives and search for those that have the greatest effectiveness in achieving the objectives.
5. Establish the process in a systematic way so that it continues to occur over time.[22]

Another system is *zero base budgeting* (ZBB). It is a planning process that requires each manager to justify budget requests in detail each year a budget is constructed. This procedure serves to avoid developing annual budgets based upon the previous year's budget plus a certain percentage increase. ZBB forces a manager to justify the use of money for old established programs as well as for new ones. The system requires three steps:

1. Identify each activity with a program in order to relate input to output.
2. Evaluate each activity by systematic analysis.
3. Rank all programs in order of performance.[23]

Zero base budgeting has been used by the U.S. Department of Agriculture since 1971 and has been employed in nearly a dozen state and local governments as well as in other federal agencies and in over one hundred business firms.[24] Its main value is to tie inputs with outputs and to force managers to set priorities on service programs. It is also a very useful adjunct to MBO, which is being increasingly adopted by many not-for-profit organizations.

The danger with emphasizing performance-based budgets is that members of an organization become so concerned with justifying the existence of pet programs that they tend to forget about the effect of these programs on achieving the mission. The process may become very political. It gives the appearance of rational decision making, but it can be just another variant of trying to please the sponsors and looking good on paper.[25]

11.6 POPULAR NOT-FOR-PROFIT STRATEGIES

Because the mission of the not-for-profit organization is typically to satisfy an unmet need of a segment of the general public, its objective becomes one of satisfying that need as much as is possible. To the extent that revenues exceed costs and expenses, the not-for-profit therefore is likely to use the surplus (otherwise known as "profit") to expand or improve its services. If, however, revenues are less than costs and expenses, strong pressures from both within and without the organization often prevent it from reducing its services. To the extent that management is able to find new sponsors, all may be well. For many not-for-profits, however, there is an eventual limit to contributions with no strings attached. The organization is thus painfully forced to reject contributions from sponsors who wish to alter a portion of the organization's basic mission as a requirement of the contribution.

As a result of various pressures to provide more services than the sponsors and clients can pay for, not-for-profit organizations are developing strategies to meet their desired service objectives. Two popular strategies are *strategic piggybacking* and *interorganizational linking*.

Strategic Piggybacking

Coined by Nielsen, the term *strategic piggybacking* refers to the development of a new activity for the not-for-profit organization for the purpose of generating funds needed to make up the difference between revenues and expenses.[26] The new activity is related typically in some manner to the not-for-profit's mission, but its purpose is to help subsidize the primary service programs. In an inverted use of portfolio analysis, top management invests in new, safe *cash cows* to fund its current cash-hungry stars, question marks, and dogs.

Although this strategy is not a new one, it is becoming increasingly popular in the 1980s. As early as 1874, for example, the Metropolitan Museum of Art retained a professional to photograph its collections and to sell copies of the prints. Profits were used to defray the museum's operating costs. Surpluses generated from the sale of food, wine, liquor, and tickets to the Boston Pops performances help support the primary mission of the Boston Symphony Orchestra—the performance of classical music. More recently, various income generation ventures have appeared under various auspices, from the Girl Scouts to UNICEF, and in numerous forms, from small gift shops to vast real estate developments.[27] The Small Business Administration, however, views this activity as "unfair competition."[28] The Internal

Revenue Service advises that a not-for-profit that engages in a business "not substantially related" to the organization's exempt purposes may jeopardize its tax-exempt status, particularly if the income from the business exceeds approximately 20% of total organizational revenues.[29]

Edward Skloot, president of the New York consulting firm New Ventures, suggests that a not-for-profit organization have five resources before beginning a revenue-earning activity.[30]

1. *Something to sell.* The organization should assess its resources to see if people might be willing to pay for a good or service closely related to the organization's primary activity.
2. *Critical mass of management talent.* There must be enough people available to nurture and sustain an income venture over the long haul.
3. *Trustee support.* If the trustees have strong feelings against earned-income ventures, they may actively or passively resist commercial involvement.
4. *Entrepreneurial attitude.* Management must be able to combine an interest in innovative ideas with businesslike practicality.
5. *Venture capital.* Given that it often takes money to make money, engaging in a joint venture with a business corporation can provide necessary start-up funds as well as marketing and management support. For example, Massachusetts General Hospital receives $50 million from Hoechst, the West German chemical company for biological research, in exchange for exclusive licenses to develop commercial products from certain research discoveries. The Children's Television Workshop, in partnership with Anheuser-Busch, developed a theme park for young children in Langhorne, Pennsylvania.[31]

Inter-organizational Linking

A major strategy often used by not-for-profit organizations to enhance their capacity to serve clients or to acquire resources is developing cooperative ties with other organizations.[32] Not-for-profit hospitals increasingly are using this strategy as a way to cope with increasing costs and declining revenues. Through cooperation with other hospitals, services can be purchased and provided more efficiently than if done alone. Currently, close to one-third of all nongovernmental not-for-profit hospitals in the United States are part of a *multihospital system,* defined as "two or more acute care hospitals owned, leased, or contract-managed by a corporate office."[33] By belonging to a system, a formerly independent hospital can hope to benefit in terms of staff utilization and management efficiency.[34]

11.7 SUMMARY AND CONCLUSION

Strategic management in not-for-profit organizations is in its initial stages. Approaches and techniques, such as MBO, which work reasonably well in profit-making corporations, are being tried in a number of not-for-profit organizations. Nevertheless, private nonprofit and public organizations differ in terms of their sources of revenue and thus must be treated differently. The relationship between the organization and the client also is more complicated. Moreover, not-for-profit organizations have certain constraining characteristics that affect their strategic management process. These characteristics cause variations in the way managers in not-for-profit organizations formulate and implement strategic decisions. Not-for-profit organizations therefore are more likely than profit-making corporations to look for dynamic and forceful leaders who can pull together various constituencies, develop a mystique about their activities, generate many rules and regulations regarding the client, appoint a strong board of directors/trustees to represent sponsoring agencies and special interest groups, and develop performance-based budgets. As increasing numbers of not-for-profit organizations find it difficult to generate the necessary funds from sponsors to achieve key service objectives, they are turning to *strategic piggybacking* and *interorganizational linking* strategies.

Not-for-profit organizations form an important part of society. It is therefore important to understand their reason for existence and what makes them different from profit-making corporations. The lack of a profit motive often results in vague statements of mission and unmeasurable objectives. This, coupled with a concern for funding from sponsors, may cause a lack of consideration for the very client the organization was designed to serve. Programs may develop that have little or no connection with the organization's mission. Nevertheless, it is important to remember that not-for-profit organizations usually are established to provide goods and services judged valuable by society that profit-making firms cannot or will not provide. It is dangerous to judge their performance on the basis of simple economic considerations because they are designed to deal with conditions under which profit-making corporations could not easily survive.

DISCUSSION QUESTIONS

1. Are not-for-profit organizations less efficient than profit-making organizations? Why or why not?
2. Do you agree that the source of revenue is the best way to differentiate between not-for-profit and profit-making organizations as well as among the many kinds of not-for-profit organizations? Why or why not?
3. Is client influence always weak in the not-for-profit organization? Why or why not?

4. Why does the employment of a large number of people who consider themselves to be professionals complicate the strategic management process? How may this also occur in profit-making firms?
5. How does the lack of a clear-cut performance measure, such as profits, affect the strategic management of a not-for-profit organization?
6. What are the pros and cons of *strategic piggybacking?*
7. In the past, a number of profit-making businesses such as city bus lines and railroad passenger services have changed their status to not-for-profit as governmental agencies took them over. Recently, however, a number of not-for-profit organizations have been converting to profit-making. For example, more than 20 of the 115 nonprofit Health Maintenance Organizations (HMOs) formed with federal money have converted to for-profit status.[35] Why would a not-for-profit organization want to change its status to profit-making?

NOTES

1. M. S. Wortman, Jr., "Strategic Management: Not-for-Profit Organizations," *Strategic Management*, eds. D. E. Schendel and C. W. Hofer (Boston: Little, Brown, 1979), pp. 353–381.
M. S. Wortman, Jr., "Strategic Management in Voluntary and Nonprofit Organizations: Reality, Prescriptive Behavior and Future Research," in M. Moyer (ed.), *Managing Voluntary Organizations* (Toronto, Ontario: York University, 1983), pp. 146–167.
2. I. Unterman and R. H. Davis, "The Strategy Gap in Not-For-Profits," *Harvard Business Review* (May–June 1982), p. 30.
3. W. F. Crittenden and D. D. White, "An Examination of Strategic Planning Characteristics in Voluntary Organizations," *Proceedings, Southern Management Association* (November 1982), pp. 140–142.
S. M. Vonderhaar, J. Strauss, and H. LeVan, "Impact of Selected Environmental Variables on the Long-Range Planning Process in U.S. Hospitals," *Proceedings, Southern Management Association* (November 1982), pp. 212–214.
4. B. P. Keating and M. O. Keating, *Not-For-Profit* (Glen Ridge, N.J.: Thomas Horton & Daughters, 1980), p. 18.
5. D. R. Young, *If Not For Profit, For What?* (Lexington, Mass.: D. C. Heath, Lexington Books, 1983), p. 9.
6. J. Ruffat, "Strategic Management of Public and Non-Market Corporations," *Long Range Planning* (April 1983), p. 74.
7. W. F. Glueck, *Business Policy and Strategic Management*, 3rd ed. (New York: McGraw-Hill, 1980), pp. 22–24.
8. M. D. Fottler, "Is Management Really Generic?" *Academy of Management Review* (January 1981), p. 2.
9. Fottler, p. 2.

10. Keating and Keating, pp. 23–24.
11. Keating and Keating, p. 21.
12. "Revenues and Expenditures of Colleges and Universities, 1981–82," *The Chronicle of Higher Education* (April 4, 1984), p. 14.
13. D. Mott, *Characteristics of Effective Organizations* (San Francisco: Harper & Row, 1972) as reported by H. L. Tosi, Jr. and J. W. Slocum, Jr., "Contingency Theory: Some Suggested Directions," *Journal of Management* (Spring 1984), p. 11.
14. W. H. Newman and H. W. Wallender, III, "Managing Not-For-Profit Enterprises," *Academy of Management Review* (January 1978), p. 26.
15. Newman and Wallender, p. 27. The following discussion of the effects of these constraining characteristics is taken from Newman and Wallender, pp. 27–31.
16. P. C. Nutt, "A Strategic Planning Network for Non-Profit Organizations," *Strategic Management Journal* (January-March 1984), p. 57.
17. Unterman and Davis, pp. 30–32.
18. Newman and Wallender, p. 27.
19. Newman and Wallender, p. 28.
20. Keating and Keating, p. 130.
21. E. H. Fram, "Changing Expectations for Third Sector Executives," *Human Resource Management* (Fall 1980), p. 9.
22. Keating and Keating, pp. 140–141.
23. Keating and Keating, pp. 143–144.
24. S. M. Lee and J. P. Shim, "Zero-Base Budgeting—Dealing with Conflicting Objectives," *Long Range Planning* (October 1984), p. 103.
25. M. W. Dirsmith, S. F. Jablonsky, and A. D. Luzi, "Planning and Control in the U.S. Federal Government: A Critical Analysis of PPB, MBO, and ZBB," *Strategic Management Journal* (October–December 1980), pp. 303–329.
    E. E. Chaffee, "The Link between Planning and Budgeting," Working Paper, National Center for Higher Education Management Systems, Boulder, Colorado, October 1981, p. 12–13.
26. R. P. Nielsen, "SMR Forum: Strategic Piggybacking—A Self-Subsidizing Strategy for Nonprofit Institutions," *Sloan Management Review* (Summer 1982), pp. 65–69.
    R. P. Nielsen, "Piggybacking for Business and Nonprofits: A Strategy for Hard Times," *Long Range Planning* (April 1984), pp. 96–102.
27. E. Skloot, "Should Not-For-Profits Go into Business?" *Harvard Business Review* (January–February 1983), pp. 20–26.
28. "When Should the Profits of Nonprofits Be Taxed?" *Business Week* (December 5, 1983), p. 191.
29. Skloot, p. 21.
30. Skloot, pp. 20–24.

31. Skloot, p. 24.
32. K. G. Provan, "Interorganizational Cooperation and Decision Making Autonomy in a Consortium Multihospital System," *Academy of Management Review* (July 1984), pp. 494–504.
33. *Directory of Multihospital Systems* (Chicago: American Hospital Association, 1980).
34. Provan, p. 496.
35. D. Wellel, "As HMOs Increasingly Become Big Businesses, Many of Them Convert to Profit-Making Status," *Wall Street Journal* (March 26, 1985), p. 4.

PART SIX

CASES IN STRATEGIC MANAGEMENT

SECTION A

STRATEGIC MANAGERS

Case 1

THE WALLACE GROUP

Laurence J. Stybel

Frances Rampar, President of Rampar Associates, drummed her fingers on the desk. Scattered before her were her notes. She had to put the pieces together in order to make an effective sales presentation to Harold Wallace.

Hal Wallace was the president of The Wallace Group. He had asked Frances Rampar to conduct a series of interviews with some key Wallace Group employees in preparation for a possible consulting assignment for Rampar Associates.

During the past three days, Rampar had been talking with some of these key people and had received background material about the company. The problem was not in finding the problem. The problem was that there were too many problems!

BACKGROUND OF THE WALLACE GROUP

The Wallace Group, Inc., is a diversified company dealing in the manufacture and development of technical products and systems (see Exhibit 1.1). The company currently consists of three operational groups and a corporate staff. The three groups include Electronics, Plastics, and Chemicals, each operating under the direction of a Group Vice-President (see Exhibits 1.2, 1.3, and 1.4). The company generates $70 million in sales as a manufacturer of plastics, chemical products, and electronic components and systems. Principal sales are to large contractors in governmental and automotive markets. With respect to sales volume, Plastics and Chemicals are approximately equal in size, and both of them together equal the size of the Electronics Group.

This case was prepared by Dr. Laurence J. Stybel. It was prepared as a basis for class discussion rather than to illustrate either effective or ineffective handling of an administrative situation.

Exhibit 1.1 (FROM THE ANNUAL REPORT)

To the Shareholders:

This past year was one of definite accomplishment for The Wallace Group, although with some admitted soft spots. This is a period of consolidation, of strengthening our internal capacity for future growth and development. Presently, we are in the process of creating a strong management team able to meet the challenges we will set for the future.

Despite our failure to achieve some objectives, we turned in a profit of $3,521,000 before taxes which was a growth over previous year earnings. And we have declared a dividend for the fifth consecutive year, albeit one that is less than the year before. However, the retention of earnings is imperative if we are to lay a firm foundation for future accomplishment.

Currently, The Wallace Group has achieved a level of stability. We have a firm foothold in our current markets and we could elect to simply enact strong internal controls and maximize our profits. However, this would not be a growth strategy. Instead, we have chosen to adopt a more aggressive posture for the future, to reach out into new markets wherever possible, and to institute the controls necessary to move forward in a planned and orderly fashion.

The Electronics Group performed well this past year and is engaged in two major programs under defense department contracts. These are developmental programs that provide us with the opportunity for ongoing sales upon testing of the final product. Both involve the creation of tactical display systems for aircraft being built by Lombard Aircraft for the Navy and the Air Force. Future potential sales from these efforts could amount to approximately $56 million over the next five years. Additionally, we are developing technical refinements to older, already installed systems under Army Department contracts.

In the future, we will continue to offer our technological competence in such tactical display systems and anticipate additional breakthroughs and success in meeting the demands of this market. However, we also believe that we have unique contributions to make to other markets and to that end we are making the investments necessary to expand our opportunities.

Plastics also turned in a solid performance this past year and has continued to be a major supplier to Chrysler, Martin Tool, Foster Electric, and, of course, to our Electronics Group. The market for this group continues to expand and we believe that additional investments in this group will allow us to seize a larger share in the future.

Chemicals' performance, admittedly, has not been as satisfactory as anticipated during the past year. However, we have been able to realize a small amount of profit from this operation and to halt what was a poten-

(*Continued*)

tially dangerous decline in profits. We believe this situation is only temporary and that infusions of capital for developing new technology, plus the streamlining of operations, has stabilized the situation. The next step will be to begin more aggressive marketing to capitalize upon the group's basic strengths.

Overall, the outlook seems to be one of modest but profitable growth. The near term will be one of creating the technology and controls necessary for developing our market offerings and growing in a planned and purposeful manner. Our improvement efforts in the various company groups can be expected to take hold over the years with positive effect on results.

We wish to express our appreciation to all those who participated in our efforts this past year.

Harold Wallace
Chairman and President

Electronics offers competence in the areas of microelectronics, electromagnetic sensors, antennas, microwave, and mini-computers. Presently, these skills are devoted primarily to the engineering and manufacture of countermeasure equipment for aircraft. This includes radar detection systems that allow an aircraft crew to know they are being tracked by radar units either on the ground, on ships, or on other aircraft. Further, they manufacture displays that provide the crew with a visual "fix" on where they are relative to the radar units that are tracking them.

In addition to manufacturing tested and proven systems developed in the past, The Wallace Group is currently involved in two major and minor programs, all involving display systems. The Navy-A Program calls for the development of a display system for a tactical fighter plane; Air Force-B is another such system for an observation plane. Ongoing production orders are anticipated following flight testing. The other two programs, Army-LG and OBT-37, involve the incorporation of new technology into existing aircraft systems.

The Plastics Group manufactures plastic components utilized by the electronics, automotive, and other industries requiring plastic products. This includes switches, knobs, keys, insulation materials, and so on, used in the manufacture of electronic equipment and other small made-to-order components found on automobiles, planes, and so forth.

The Chemicals Group produces chemicals used in the development of plastics. They supply bulk chemicals to the Plastics Group and other companies. These chemicals are then injected into molds or extruded to form a variety of finished products.

Exhibit 1.2 THE WALLACE GROUP

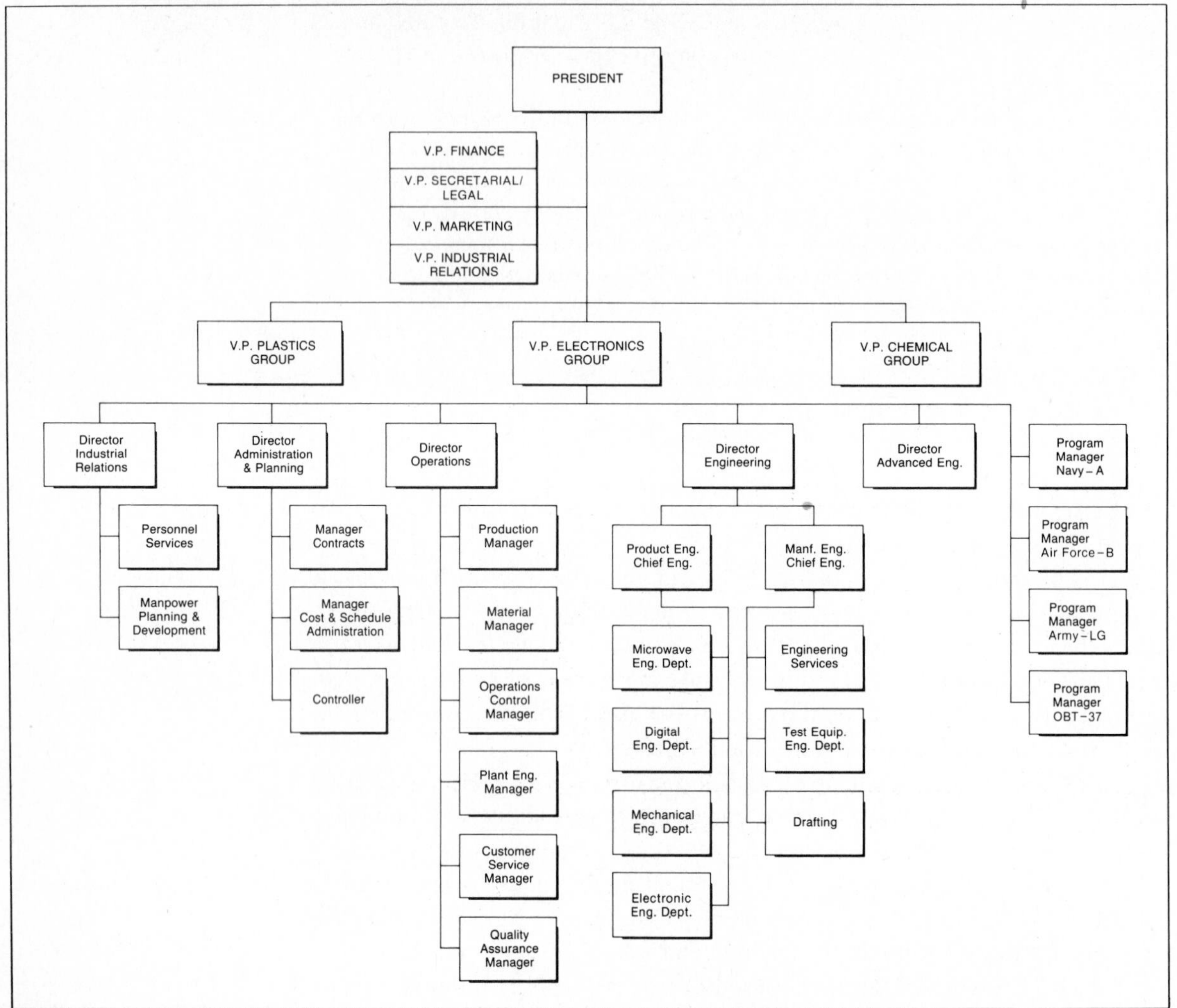

HISTORY OF THE WALLACE GROUP

Each of the three groups began its existence as a sole proprietorship under the direct operating control of an owner/manager. Several years ago, Harold Wallace, owner of the original electronics company, determined to undertake a program of diversification. Initially, he attempted to expand his market by product development and line extensions entirely within the electronics industry. However, because of initial problems, he drew back and sought other opportunities. Wallace's primary concern was his almost total dependence upon defense-related contracts. He had felt for some time that he should take some strong action to gain a foothold in the private markets.

THE WALLACE GROUP

Exhibit 1.3

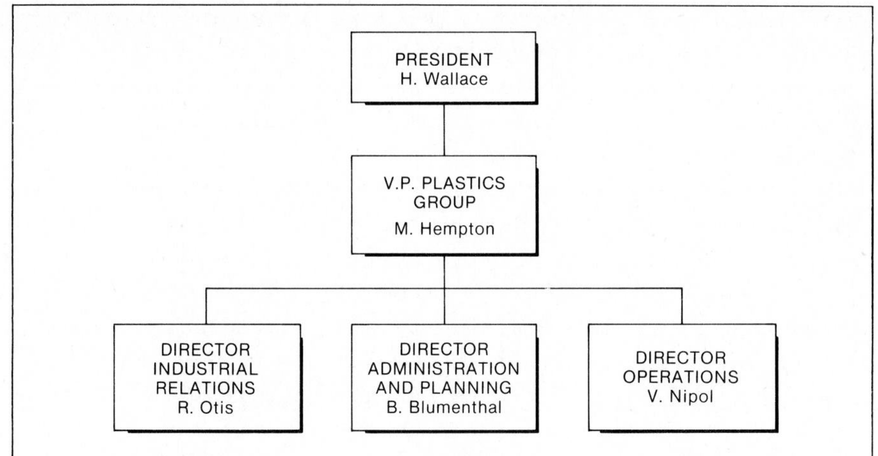

The first major opportunity which seemed to satisfy his various requirements was the acquisition of a former supplier, a plastics company whose primary market was not defense related. The company's owner desired to sell his operation and retire. At the time, Wallace's debt structure was not able to manage such an acquisition and so equity capital had to be attracted. He was able to gather together a relatively small group of investors and form a closed corporation. A Board of Directors was established with Wallace as Chairman and President of the new corporate entity.

With respect to operations, little changed. Mr. Wallace continued direct operational control over the Electronics Group. As holder of 60% of the

THE WALLACE GROUP

Exhibit 1.4

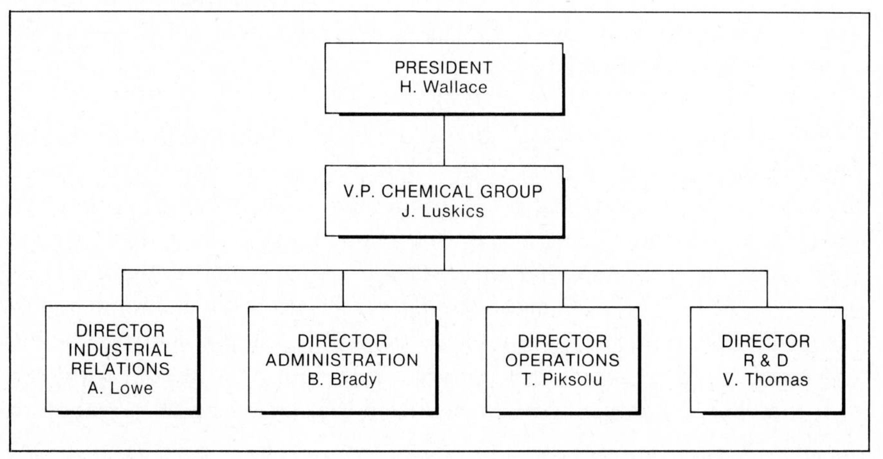

stock, he maintained his effective control over policy and operations. However, given his personal interests, the Plastics Group, now under the direction of a newly hired Vice-President, Martin Hempton, was pretty much left to its own devices except for yearly progress reviews by the President. All Wallace asked for the time being was that the Plastics Group continue its profitable operation, which it did.

Several years ago, Wallace and the Board decided upon further diversification because two-thirds of their business was still defense-dependent. It became known that one of their major suppliers of the Plastics Group, a chemical company, was on the verge of bankruptcy. The company's owner, Jerome Luskics, was approached and a sale was consummated. However, this acquisition required a public stock offering, with most of the monies going to pay off debts incurred by the three groups, especially the Chemicals Group. The net result was that Wallace now holds 45% of The Wallace Group, Jerome Luskics 5%, with the remainder distributed among the public.

ORGANIZATION AND PERSONNEL

Presently, Harold Wallace serves as Chairman and President of The Wallace Group. The Electronics Group had been run by LeRoy Tuscher, who just resigned as Vice-President. Hempton continued as Vice-President of Plastics and Luskics served as Vice-President of the Chemicals Group.

Given the requirements for a corporate perspective and approach, a corporate staff has grown up consisting of Vice-Presidents for Finance, Secretarial/Legal, Marketing, and Industrial Relations. This staff has assumed many functions formerly carried on with the group offices.

Because these positions are recent additions, many of the job accountabilities are still in the process of being defined. Problems have arisen over the responsibilities and relationships existing between corporate and group positions. Most of the disputes have been settled by President Wallace as soon as they appear because of the inability of the various parties to resolve differences among themselves.

CURRENT TRENDS

Presently, there is a mood of lethargy and drift within The Wallace Group. Most managers feel that each of the three groups functions as an independent company. And, with respect to group performance, not much change or progress has been evidenced in recent years. Electronics and Plastics are still stable and profitable, but there does not seem to be growth in either market or profit. The infusion of capital breathed new life and hope into the Chemicals operation but did not relieve most of the old problems and failings that had brought about its initial decline. It was for all of these various reasons that Wallace decided that strong action was necessary. His greatest disappointment was with the Electronics Group in which he had placed high hopes for future development. Thus, he acted by requesting and getting the Electronics Group Vice-President's resignation. Jason Matthews has been hired from a computer company, to replace LeRoy Tuscher, and joined The Wallace Group a week ago.

Last year, Wallace's net sales were $70 million. On a group basis, this was:

Electronics	$35,000,000
Plastics	$20,000,000
Chemicals	$15,000,000

On a consolidated basis, the financial highlights of the last two years are as follows:

	1983	1982
Net sales	$70,434,000	$69,950,000
Income (pre-tax)	3,521,000	3,497,500
Income (after-tax)	1,760,500	1,748,750
Working capital	16,200,000	16,088,500
Shareholder's equity	39,000,000	38,647,000
Total assets	59,869,000	59,457,000
Long-term debt	4,350,000	3,500,000
Per Share of Common Stock		
Net income	$.37	$.36
Cash dividends paid	.15	.25

Of the net income, approximately 70% came from Electronics, 25% from Plastics, and 5% from Chemicals.

SELECTED PORTIONS OF A TRANSCRIBED INTERVIEW WITH H. WALLACE

RAMPAR: What is your greatest problem right now?

WALLACE: That's why I called you in! Engineers are a high-strung, temperamental lot. Always complaining. It's hard to take them seriously.

Last month we had an annual stockholders' meeting. We have an Employee Stock Option Plan, and many of our long-time employees attended the meeting. One of my managers—and I won't mention any names—introduced a resolution calling for the resignation of the President—me! The vote was defeated. But, of course, I own 45% of the stock!

(Continued)

Now I realize that there could be no serious attempt to get rid of me. Those who voted for the resolution were making a dramatic effort to show me how upset they are with the way things are going.

I could fire those employees who voted against me. I was surprised by how many did. Some of my key people were in that group. Perhaps I ought to stop and listen to what they are saying.

Businesswise, I think we're O.K. Not great, but O.K. Last year we turned in a profit of $3.5 million before taxes, which was a growth over previous years' earnings. We declared a dividend for the fifth consecutive year.

We're currently working on the creation of a tactical display system for aircraft being built by Lombard Aircraft for the Navy and the Air Force. If Lombard gets the contract to produce the prototype, then future sales could amount to $56 million over the next five years.

Why are they complaining?

RAMPAR: You must have some thoughts on the matter.

WALLACE: I think the issue revolves around how we manage people. It's a personnel problem. You were highly recommended as someone with expertise in high-technology human-resource management.

I have some ideas on what is the problem. But I'd like you to do an independent investigation and give me your findings. Give me a plan of action.

Don't give me a laundry list of problems, Fran. Anyone can do that. I want a set of priorities I should focus on during the next year. I want a clear action plan from you. And I want to know how much this plan is going to cost me!

Other than that, I'll leave you alone and let you talk to anyone in the company you want.

SELECTED PORTIONS OF A TRANSCRIBED INTERVIEW WITH FRANK CAMPBELL, VICE-PRESIDENT OF INDUSTRIAL RELATIONS

RAMPAR: What is your greatest problem right now?

CAMPBELL: Trying to contain my enthusiasm over the fact that Wallace brought you in!

Morale is really poor here. Hal runs this place like a one-man operation, when it's grown too big for that. It took a palace revolt to finally get him to see the depths of the resentment. Whether he'll do anything about it, that's another matter.

RAMPAR: What would you like to see changed?

CAMPBELL: Other than a new President?

RAMPAR: Uh-huh.

CAMPBELL: We badly need a management development program for our group. Because of our growth, we have been forced to promote technical people to management positions who have had no prior managerial experience. Mr. Tuscher agreed on the need for a program, but Hal Wallace vetoed the idea because developing such a program would be too expensive. I think it is too expensive *not* to move ahead on this.

RAMPAR: Anything else?

CAMPBELL: The IEWU negotiations have been extremely tough this time around, due to excessive demands they have been making. Union pay scales are already pushing up against our foreman salary levels, and foremen are being paid high in their salary ranges. This problem, coupled with union insistence on a no-layoff clause, is causing us fits. How can we keep all our workers when we have got production equipment on order that will eliminate 20% of our assembly positions?

RAMPAR: Wow.

CAMPBELL: We have been sued by a rejected candidate for a secretarial position on the basis of discrimination. She claimed our entrance qualifications are excessive because we require shorthand. There is some basis for this statement since most reports are given to secretaries in hand-written form or on audio cassettes. In fact, we have always required it and our executives want their secretaries to have skill in taking dictation. Not only is this case taking time, but I need to reconsider if any of our position entrance requirements are, in fact, excessive. I am sure we do not want another case like this one.

RAMPAR: That puts The Wallace Group in a vulnerable position, considering the amount of government work you do.

CAMPBELL: We have a tremendous recruiting backlog, especially for engineering positions. Either our pay scales are too low, our job specs are too high, or we are using the wrong recruiting channels. Kane and Smith (Director of Engineering and Director of Advanced Systems) keep rejecting everyone we send down there as being unqualified.

RAMPAR: Gee.

CAMPBELL: Being head of Human Resources around here is a tough job. We don't act. We react.

SELECTED PORTIONS OF A TRANSCRIBED INTERVIEW WITH MATTHEW SMITH, DIRECTOR OF ADVANCED SYSTEMS

RAMPAR: What is your greatest problem right now?

SMITH: Corporate brass keeps making demands on me and others that don't relate to the job we are trying to get done. They say that the information they need is to satisfy corporate planning and operations review requirements, but they don't seem to recognize how much time and effort is required to provide this information. Sometimes it seems like they are generating analyses, reports, and requests for data just to keep themselves busy. Someone should be evaluating how critical these corporate staff activities really are. To me and the Electronics Group, these activities are unnecessary.

An example is the Vice-President, Marketing (L. Holt), who keeps asking us for supporting data so he can prepare a corporate marketing strategy. As you know, we prepare our own group marketing strategic plans annually, but using data and formats that are oriented to our needs, rather than Corporate's. This planning activity, which occurs at the same time as Corporate's coupled with heavy work loads on current projects, makes us appear to Holt as though we are being unresponsive.

Somehow we need to integrate our marketing planning efforts between our group and Corporate. This is especially true if our group is to successfully grow in nondefense-oriented markets and products. We do need corporate help, but not arbitrary demands for information that divert us from putting together effective marketing strategies for our group.

I am getting too old to keep fighting these battles.

RAMPAR: This is an old, long-standing problem?

SMITH: You bet! Our problems are fairly classic in the high-tech field. I've been at other companies and it's not much better. We spend so much time firefighting, we never really get organized. Everything is done on an ad hoc basis.

I'm still waiting for tomorrow.

SELECTED PORTIONS OF A TRANSCRIBED INTERVIEW WITH RALPH KANE, DIRECTOR OF ENGINEERING

RAMPAR: What is your greatest problem right now?

KANE: Knowing you were coming, I wrote them down. They fall into four areas:

a. Our salary schedules are too low to attract good, experienced EEs. We have been told by our Vice-President (Frank Campbell) that corporate policy is to hire new people below the salary grade midpoint. All qualified candidates are making more than that now and in some cases are making more than our grade maximums. I think our Project Engineer job is rated too low.

b. Chemicals Group asked for and the former Electronics Vice-President (Tuscher) agreed to "lend" six of our best EEs to help solve problems they are having developing a new battery. That is great for the Chemicals Group, but meanwhile how do we solve the engineering problems that have cropped up in our Navy-A and OBT-37 programs?

c. As you know, Matt Smith (Director of Advanced Systems) is retiring in six months. I depend heavily on his group for technical expertise and in some areas he depends heavily on some of my key engineers. I have lost some people to the Chemicals Group and Matt has been trying to lend me some of his people to fill in. But he and his staff have been heavily involved in marketing planning and trying to identify or recruit a qualified successor soon enough before his retirement to be able to train him. The result is that his people are up to their eyeballs in doing their own stuff and cannot continue to help me meet my needs.

d. IR has been preoccupied with union negotiations in the plant and has not had time to help me deal with this issue of management planning. Campbell is working on some kind of system that will help deal with this kind of problem and prevent them in the future. That is great, but I need help now—not when his "system" is ready.

SELECTED PORTIONS OF A TRANSCRIBED INTERVIEW WITH BRAD LOWELL, PROGRAM MANAGER, NAVY-A

RAMPAR: What is your . . . ?

LOWELL: . . . great problem? I'll tell you what it is.
I still cannot get the support I need from Kane in Engineering. He commits and then doesn't deliver and it has me quite concerned. The excuse now is that in "his judgment," Sid Wright needs the help for the Air Force program more than I do. Wright's program is one week ahead of schedule, so I disagree with "his judgment." Kane keeps complaining about not having enough people.

RAMPAR: Why do you think Kane says he doesn't have enough people?

LOWELL: Because Hal Wallace is a tight-fisted S.O.B. who won't let us hire the people we need!

SELECTED PORTIONS OF A TRANSCRIBED INTERVIEW WITH PHIL JONES, DIRECTOR, ADMINISTRATION AND PLANNING

JONES: Wheel spinning—that's our problem! We talk about expansion, but we don't do anything about it. Are we serious or not?

For example, a bid request came in from a prime contractor seeking help in developing a countermeasure system for a medium-range aircraft. They needed an immediate response and concept proposal in one week. Tuscher just sat on my urgent memo to him asking for a go/no go decision on bidding. I could not give the contractor an answer (because no decision came from Tuscher), so they gave up on us.

I am frustrated because: (1) we lost an opportunity we were "naturals" to win, and (2) my personal reputation was damaged because I was unable to answer the bid request. Okay, Tuscher's gone now, but we need to develop some mechanism so an answer to such a request can be made quickly.

Another thing is our MIS being developed by the Corporate Finance Group. More wheel spinning! They are telling us what information we need rather than asking us what we want! E. Kay (our Group Controller) is going crazy trying to sort out the input requirements they need for the system and understanding the complicated reports that come out. Maybe this new system is great as a technical achievement, but what good is it to us if we can't use it?

SELECTED PORTIONS OF A TRANSCRIBED INTERVIEW WITH BURT WILLIAMS, DIRECTOR OF OPERATIONS

RAMPAR: What is your biggest problem right now?

WILLIAMS: One of our biggest problems we face right now stems from corporate policy regarding transfer pricing. I realize we are "encouraged" to purchase our plastics and chemicals from our sister Wallace groups, but we are also committed to making a profit! Because manufacturing problems in those groups have forced them to raise their prices, should *we* suffer the consequences? We can get some materials cheaper from other suppliers. How can we meet our volume and profit targets when we are saddled with noncompetitive materials costs?

RAMPAR: And if that issue was settled to your satisfaction, then would things be O.K.?

WILLIAMS: Although out of my direct function, it occurs to me that we are not planning effectively our efforts to expand into non-defense areas. With minimal alteration to existing production methods, we can develop both end-use products (e.g., small motors, traffic control devices, microwave transceivers for highway emergency communications) and components (e.g., LED and LCD displays, police radar tracking devices, word processing system memory and control devices) with large potential markets.

The problems in this regard are:

a. Matt Smith (Director, Advanced Systems) is retiring and has had only defense-related experience. Therefore, he is not leading any product development efforts along these lines.
b. We have no marketing function at the group level to develop a strategy, define markets, and research and develop product opportunities.
c. Even if we had a marketing plan and products for industrial/commercial application, we have no sales force or rep network to sell the stuff.

Maybe I am way off base, but it seems to me we need a Group/Marketing/Sales function to lead us in this business expansion effort. It should be headed by an experienced technical marketing manager with a proven track record in developing such products and markets.

RAMPAR: Have you discussed your concerns with others?

WILLIAMS: I have brought these ideas up with Mr. Matthews and others at the Group Management Committee. No one else seems interested in pursuing this concept, but they won't say this outright and don't say why it should not be addressed. I guess that in raising the idea with you I am trying to relieve some of my frustrations.

THE PROBLEM CONFRONTING FRANCES RAMPAR

As Rampar finished reviewing her notes, she kept reflecting on what Hal Wallace had told her:

> Don't give me a laundry list of problems, Fran. Anyone can do that. I want a set of priorities I should focus on during the next year. I want a clear action plan from you. And I want to know how much this plan is going to cost me!

Fran Rampar again drummed her fingers on the desk.

Case 2

SANDALWOOD RANCH

Steven M. Dawson

The Board of Directors of Sandalwood Ranch has called a special stockholders' meeting to vote on a company proposal to reduce the minimum size of the Board of Directors from five to two. The objective of this amendment to the company's Articles of Association is to prevent Nicholas Schultz from being elected to the Board. Schultz had earlier advised the company and the SEC that he intended to solicit proxies to elect himself and his attorney to the Board at the regular annual meeting. Under Hawaii's cumulative voting provision he has enough shares to gain representation on a five-man board, but not if only two are elected. In its proxy statement mailed to stockholders, the Board stated it believed Schultz's election "is not in the best interest of the company and its stockholders at large."

After reducing the Board to two members, the company intends to form a classified or staggered Board. The initial two directors will serve three-year terms. Next year another two directors will be elected for three-year terms. And a year after that either one or two more directors will get three-year terms. At the end of three years the Board will again be at either five or six members and the staggered elections will continue. Initially reducing the size of the Board and then holding staggered elections will make the company a less attractive takeover target for any outsider who does not have the support of the Board of Directors and it will enhance the continuity and stability of the company's management.

The vote to reduce the Board of Directors to two may be close. In order to be adopted, the amendment needs affirmative votes from not less than two-thirds of the total outstanding shares. Members of the Anderson family and all officers and directors own or control 51.8% of the stock. They are expected to support the amendment. John J. Anderson is President of the company and Chairman of the Board of Directors. Mr. Schultz holds or con-

Prepared by Prof. Steven M. Dawson of the University of Hawaii. Reprinted by permission.

trols 18.15% of the shares. Sandalwood Ranch has hired two investment banking firms, Cooper & Co. and Hamilton & Co., to solicit proxies. Total costs of the proxy solicitation will be approximately $125,000, including $15,000 plus expenses for Cooper and Hamilton.

Kona Corporation owns 5.28% of the outstanding Sandalwood Ranch shares and these may represent the deciding votes. If the amendment is adopted, Sandalwood Ranch will apparently become the first publicly held U.S. company to adopt a two-man Board of Directors. Nicholas Schultz also holds 5.8% of the outstanding shares of Kona Corporation.

SANDALWOOD RANCH, INC.

Sandalwood Ranch produces pineapple products and operates a growing land management and resort development program on the island of Maui. It is a Hawaii corporation originally organized in 1909 for the principal purpose of farming and ranching. The company owns 29,830 acres of land. Over 6,500 acres are located on the lower slopes of Haleakala, a 10,000 foot volcano. Most of the rest is located in a large triangular parcel on West Maui spreading from a point at the top of 5,700 foot Puu Kukui to the ocean with nine miles of shoreline, including 3,300 feet of sandy beaches. The land was acquired mostly between 1911 and 1932 and is carried on the books at its original acquisition cost.

The company, through a wholly owned subsidiary, produces a full line of pineapple products. It is the world's largest supplier of private label canned pineapple products to U.S. supermarkets and food service suppliers. In the five years ending in 1978 revenues were up 85%: from $28 million in 1973 to $52 million. Operations in 1978 exceeded previous records for profits, volume, and sales revenues (see Exhibit 2.1). The year 1979 is expected to be another good year. Pineapple production in the world continues to increase but the company remains in a strong position in its markets.

Another wholly owned subsidiary developed and operates a leading qual-

Exhibit 2.1

FIVE-YEAR RECORD—SANDALWOOD RANCH, INC.

Year	*Sales Revenues*[1]	*Net Income*[1]	*E.P.S.*	*D.P.S.*	*Book Value Per Share*
1978	$62.7	$2.8	$1.76	$.42	$19.78
1977	65.4	3.1	1.95	.40	18.44
1976	44.4	3.1	1.96	.36	16.88
1975	39.7	2.7	1.71	.32	15.28
1974	36.3	2.8	1.77	.00	13.89

[1] $ million.

ity resort, The Kapalua Bay Hotel, in West Maui. Opened in October 1978, the hotel was a loss operation in 1978, but it is expected soon to become profitable. Several condominium projects are located near the hotel and sales of units are expected to generate significant cash and profits during 1979. Advertising, promotion, interest, and general and administrative expenses have been written off when incurred. Demand has been high for the units and resales have shown excellent appreciation. Sales contracts have been signed for units totalling $69 million which have not yet been reported in the income statement. Total closings were $16.4 million in 1977 and $6.3 million in 1978. The large increases in pineapple earnings have enabled the company to provide all of the equity requirements for the land development projects without including a joint partner.

In the closing paragraph of his letter to stockholders in the 1979 Annual Report, John Anderson said: "In summary, 1978 was a good year and 1979 promises to be a better one, with another fine pineapple year in the offing and a strong positive swing in Kapalua's results."

OWNERSHIP OF SANDALWOOD RANCH STOCK

In 1969 the Anderson group completed a complex transaction with Alexander and Baldwin, another Hawaii company, which involved the exchange of Sandalwood shares held by Alexander and Baldwin for Alexander and Baldwin shares held by the Anderson group. After this exchange the Anderson group held 99% of the Sandalwood shares. Later in 1969 there was a public offering for $21.50 a share of 100,000 newly issued shares and 775,000 previously issued shares held by the Anderson group (see Exhibit 2.2). This dropped their ownership to 44%. Kona Corporation was one of the buyers, purchasing 80,000 shares. The prospectus for the issue stated that the holders of the company's common stock had waived preemptive

Exhibit 2.2

COMMON STOCK PRICES—SANDALWOOD RANCH, INC.

Year/Quarter		*High*		*Low*
1979	April		$31.00 ask price 29.50 bid price	
1978	4th quarter	$39.00		$25.50
	3rd quarter	34.50		23.25
	2nd quarter	24.25		18.00
	1st quarter	19.50		13.25
1977	4th quarter	13.50		12.75
	3rd quarter	14.50		12.00
	2nd quarter	14.75		12.50
	1st quarter	13.00		11.00

SANDALWOOD RANCH, INC. STOCK OWNERSHIP
April 1979: Month of the Special Stockholders' Meeting

Exhibit 2.3

Stockholders	*Shares*	*% of Total*
The Anderson family, Officers and Directors	932,402[1]	51.80%
Nicholas Schultz	326,650	18.15
Kona Corporation	95,000	5.28
All other stockholders	445,948	24.77
	1,800,000	100.00%

[1] Includes 205,533 in the ESOP.

rights to subscribe for authorized shares of stock up to 1.8 million shares. For shares issued in excess of 1.8 million, the preemptive right again applies (see Exhibit 2.3).

In 1979, shortly before the special stockholders' meeting, the Anderson family and all officers and directors owned or controlled 932,402 shares or 51.8% of the 1.8 million shares outstanding. Nicholas Schultz owned or controlled 326,650 shares or 18.15%. The only other large investor was Kona Corporation with 95,000 shares or 5.28%. A total of almost 1,500 investors owned the remaining 24.77%.

THE SCHULTZ SHARES

In December 1976, after a lengthy series of open market purchases, Nicholas Schultz, a well-known businessman in Hawaii (see Exhibit 2.4), controlled 171,852 Sandalwood shares. This was 10.78% of the outstanding shares and in a Schedule 13D filed with the SEC, he said the shares were held "for investment." In 1977 and 1978, he increased his holdings, accounting for about 35% of the total shares traded. On November 6, 1978, he filed an amended Schedule 13D showing 296,752 shares, 18.61% of the then outstanding shares, and stated he wished to change his purpose of holding to "interested in representation on the Board and to have a voice in management." On January 8, 1979, he filed a Schedule 14B with the SEC indicating he intended to solicit proxies for the 1979 annual meeting and would propose two nominees for the Board of Directors. Schultz stated he had reviewed the company's financial statements and determined it would be appropriate to have outside directors who were not involved in the formulation of the company's business planning. Citing losses in resort development, higher administrative expenses, increased interest and debt burdens, and several corporate writeoffs as examples of "extremely poor business judgment" and wasted assets, Schultz proposed as nominees himself and his attorney, Lawrence Chun. At the time there were five directors and 1,594,467 shares outstanding. Nicholas Schultz controlled 318,350 shares. Cumulative voting could be called for by any stockholder up to 48 hours before the stockholders' meeting.

MAGAZINE EXCERPTS ABOUT NICHOLAS SCHULTZ

Exhibit 2.4

Nicholas Schultz is a shrewd, often abrasive entrepreneur who has been taking on the Establishment—any establishment—for years now and making big money at it. He's gone to the mat with politicians and entrenched management in cities as diverse as Honolulu, Scranton, Dallas, and New York. Thanks partly to his skills as a proxy fighter—and his appreciation that the threat of a fight can be as potent as the real thing—Schultz has wound up laughing all the way to the bank.

Schultz is now in his early 70s but feisty as ever. In his latest assault, he is taking on what may be the tightest establishment of them all—the *kamaainas* who control such land-rich members of Hawaii's "Big Five" or its satellites as C. Brewer & Co., Alexander & Baldwin, and Sandalwood Ranch.

The confrontation is classic. On one side, the Austrian-born Schultz, whose formal education ended around the sixth grade. On the other side, antagonists like John J. Anderson, the 52-year-old chairman of Sandalwood Ranch whose family has been on the island for five generations, and who personifies the *kamaaina* and Harvard Business School with his crisp but casual aloha shirt and his well-tended fingernails.

Schultz is the quintessential *malahini*—an outsider despite being one of the largest individual landowners and investors in Hawaii. With an investment of $35 million at stake, he is the biggest outside shareholder in Kona Corporation, Alexander & Baldwin, and Sandalwood. He also owns a sizable chunk of another Big Five agribusiness, C. Brewer & Co.

Like all of the Big Five, A&B and Brewer—and Sandalwood—are tied to the uncertainties of the commodities business—sugar and shipping in the case of A&B; sugar, molasses and macadamia nuts, among others, in the case of Brewer. But commodities are not what attracts Schultz. The one commodity all the major Hawaiian companies have going for them is land—land that was put on the books (and is still carried) at low, low 1900 to 1930 prices.

Sandalwood Ranch, for example, owns and manages almost 30,000 acres, including about nine miles of beachfront on the island of Maui, one of the most beautiful—and eminently developable—spots in Hawaii. The land is carried at an average cost of $91 an acre in an area where even outback and moose pasture sells for $1,000 an acre. Prime beachfront acreage, assuming it could be bought, might go for $4 to $5 a square foot.

Sandalwood's stated book value is $19 a share. The stock, currently selling at around 29, is one of the few *kamaaina* companies that trade above generally understated book. How much is Sandalwood truly worth? Who knows? Schultz contends at least one tender offer has been broached to him at $60 a share. John Anderson questions the authenticity of the bid but obviously thinks his company is worth a lot more than its stock sells for.

Schultz is a kind of perpetual motion Benjamin Graham. As a young man in Baltimore he and his brother William would buy houses at tax sales, fix them up with a bit of sweat equity, and resell them at a profit. He learned early to see opportunity where others saw only problems. Schultz likes to buy below book.

Honolulu Rapid Transit, for example, like most bus companies, had no sex appeal whatever back in 1957, when Schultz first took a position in the stock. Members of one of the Big Five families, the Castles, were happy to unload on Schultz, outsider or no, shares of the bus company they had owned for years. Nicholas asked for a seat on the board, was rebuffed, started a proxy fight, continued to buy stock, and in 1960 became chairman of the board. Nicholas Schultz didn't want to run buses. His eye was on land and cash—"nonutility assets"—that Schultz argued weren't needed in operating the business. He parlayed those into control of bus companies in Dallas and New York.

Schultz soon made himself so unpopular—cutting back services, fighting with the unions, demanding higher fares—that the politicians finally paid him to go away. The local governments bought out the transit companies at prices that left Schultz with cash to plow back into rich, Hawaiian earth.

For example, he took a position in Amfac, Inc., another of the Big Five, demanded a board seat, threatened a proxy fight: He finally sold his shares back to the company at a fat profit. He repeated the pattern at Kona Corporation, the big Hawaiian construction company, where he persuaded management to swap his $5.3 million worth of stock for $7 million worth of land.

SOURCE: Richard Phalon, "Nicholas Schultz versus John Anderson," *Forbes* (July 9, 1979), pp. 61–64. Used by permission.

If there's any name that sends shivers through every corporate boardroom in Hawaii, the odds are that the name is Nicholas Schultz. For more than a decade, the burly financier, who looks and talks much more like the boss of a tough labor union than a captain of industry, has pummelled and pillaged some of the state's oldest and most prestigious companies seemingly at will. With the cunning of a street fighter he has bullied their boards and bamboozled their management into making him one of the richest men in

(*Continued*)

Exhibit 2.4
(*Continued*)

town. In another, less rarefied context, Schultz's tactics would smack of extortion. But at the level and manner in which he practices them they're not only legal but fascinating, even to his victims.

Part of their fascination is that, while larger business communities have many Nicholas Schultzes, he is, perhaps fortunately, the only one of his breed in the Islands. And while watching Nicholas operate may not always be comfortable and is often expensive, the experience never fails to be educational. Schultz has, in fact, become something of a folk hero, a lone bull in the china closet of local big business who fearlessly bangs heads with the most blue-blooded names in town.

Schultz works hard at maintaining his maverick image. Even to those who know him, he's an enigma. Though he could afford much better, the capital of his sprawling commercial empire is a Spartan, tile-floored office just steps from the Honolulu waterfront and the whizzing traffic on Nimitz Highway. Maybe the noise of the traffic is why Nicholas talks so loud. "Talks" is a serious understatement. Schultz thunders. Words come spilling from his lips not in sentences but in cacophonous, rolling barrages.

But that, too, is probably part of Schultz's MO. It's helped him drive to distraction many a cool and professional executive. He's done it with sheer firepower. Rather than surrender hours of their valuable time to absorbing Schultz's salvos, they have bought his silence. Kona Corporation did it in the 1960s by trading $7 million worth of its land for the $5.3 million worth of Kona stock that Nicholas had accumulated and used to get a seat on the company's board. Thereupon, Nicholas turned his guns on Amfac, Inc. This time he sold out for cash to other investors, but Schultz has made some subsequent buys of choice Amfac real estate that indicate that he has at least kept close to the company.

Such maneuvers have made Schultz quite possibly the biggest individual commercial real estate owner in the Islands, and almost certainly the wealthiest. A financial officer at one of Nicholas's "victims" estimates that he can lay his hands on $200 million with a single phone call. Even if that's an exaggeration, it still gives Schultz an extraordinary amount of maneuverability in conducting his one-man raids.

SOURCE: "The Not-So-Enigmatic Nicholas Schultz," *Hawaii Business Magazine* (August 1979), Vol. 25, No. 2, pp. 83–88. Used by permission.

THE COMPANY'S RESPONSE

In a proxy statement mailed to stockholders, the Board of Directors of Sandalwood Ranch proposed amending the company's Articles of Association to allow the reduction of the Board from a minimum of five members to two. Hawaii corporate law allows the Board of Directors to reduce its size, but since the Board is already at the minimum level set in the Articles of Association, stockholder approval will be needed. If just two directors are elected,

Schultz will be unable to elect anyone to the Board of Directors unless he gains the support of other stockholders.

The Board stated in its proxy statement that their objection to Schultz was substantive, not personal. After a review of the public record of his investments, board memberships, and subsequent transactions in other companies over the last 20 years, they determined that Schultz's representation on the Board would not be in the best interests of the company and its stockholders. The proxy statement sent to the shareholders prior to the special meeting contained a summary of the Board's material and it is presented in Exhibit 2.5. It reported Schultz started his business activity in Hawaii in 1958 with the acquisition of a large block of Honolulu Rapid Transit Company (HRT) shares. He then requested a board seat, was rebuffed, announced a proxy fight, got on the board, and in 1960 became Board Chairman. By the end of 1959, $400,000 of HRT funds were used by a subsidiary to acquire stock in the Dallas Transit Co. The State Public Utilities Commission ordered HRT to return the funds but in 1960 HRT transferred an additional $200,000 to the same subsidiary. In 1961 the PUC and HRT worked out a compromise with regard to the transferred funds. From 1959 to 1962 Schultz and his associates acquired control of Dallas Transit Co. and used it, in turn, to obtain control of Fifth Avenue Coach Co. of New York. After lengthy disputes with these companies, both the City of Dallas and New York City ended up buying the transit systems.

In other companies (e.g., Amfac, Inc., and Kona Corporation) Schultz has followed the pattern of purchasing a substantial minority position, insisting on board membership, threatening proxy fights (or obtaining board membership without a fight), and ending by resigning and exchanging his stock for corporate landholdings or cash.

The Board said the decision to call a special meeting of stockholders was influenced by Schultz's accumulation of stock, by his proposed proxy contest to obtain representation on the Board, and by certain proposed state legislation. A year ago the State Legislature amended the Hawaii corporation law and reduced the minimum number of directors in any Hawaii corporation to one. The prior law required at least three directors. The State Department of Regulatory Agencies has proposed a bill, which is pending in the legislature, that would restore the minimum number of directors to three for all companies with three or more stockholders.

According to the proxy statement, the Board intends to amend the bylaws later so that two directors are nominated for three-year terms at the start. The following year, two more directors would be elected for three-year terms. And the year after that another one or two directors would be elected for three-year terms. The company would then have a classified or staggered

Board. This means stockholders would elect at most two directors each year and there would be continuity on the Board since directors will serve for a longer time and terms will expire at different times.

An even number of directors creates the possibility the Board will encounter an impasse. In this case, Hawaii law provides for a court-appointed director, who is neither a stockholder nor a creditor, to join the Board.

If approved, this would be the second time in recent years that the Board of Directors had been reduced in size. At the 1977 annual stockholders' meeting the Board was reduced from nine to five. At the same time, the company was restructured into a parent holding company and two principal, wholly owned, operating subsidiaries, one for land development and one for pineapple production. As a holding company it was deemed advisable to reduce the number of directors on the parent company Board while strengthening the Boards of the two operating subsidaries.

SCHULTZ SUMMARY

Summary of Nicholas Schultz's Investments and Board Memberships over 20 Years—Contained in Proxy Statement Issued by Sandalwood Ranch

Exhibit 2.5

1958: Nicholas Schultz ("Schultz") owns approximately one-third of outstanding Honolulu Rapid Transit Company, Ltd. ("HRT") common stock. Schultz represented on HRT Board by his attorney, Lawrence Chun ("Chun"). Schultz asks to be put on HRT board and to be given operational control of HRT. Schultz's request for HRT board seat denied. Schultz starts proxy fight to place himself on HRT board. HRT reduces board to six members and proposes a real estate spin-off of Honolulu, Limited in attempt to maintain control of HRT.

February 1959: HRT agrees to put Schultz on board of Honolulu, Limited, Chun to remain on HRT board, and boards of both companies are to be reduced in size; real estate spin-off cancelled. Schultz is elected president of Honolulu, Limited.

July 1959: Schultz is named to board of HRT. HRT transfers $400,000 to its subsidiary, Honolulu, Limited. With the $400,000, Honolulu, Limited buys block of stock in Dallas Transit Company (DTC).

September 1959: Public Utilities Commission of the State of Hawaii ("PUC") finds $400,000 transfer improper and orders funds returned to HRT.

January 1960: Schultz becomes Chairman of the board of DTC. Schultz's attorney becomes a director of DTC. HRT seeks to become a subsidiary of Honolulu, Limited. PUC orders investigation and seeks to prevent corporate changes.

March 1960: Schultz is named Chairman of the board of both HRT and Honolulu, Limited. His attorney also becomes a member of both boards. HRT transfers an additional $200,000 to Honolulu, Limited.

April 1960: PUC files a lawsuit in Honolulu Circuit Court alleging that HRT transferred $200,000 and other assets to Honolulu, Limited in violation of a 1959 PUC order.

June 1960: DTC transfers more than $2.0 million in assets to its subsidiary, DalTran Service Co. ("DalTran").

August 1960: The last pre-Schultz outside director resigns from HRT. In 1960, HRT cuts its second quarter dividend by 50% and omits dividends for last two quarters of 1960 and first two quarters of 1961.

January 1961: Four Schultz brothers are directors or executives of DTC. PUC holds a public hearing on HRT's requested fare increase.

February 1961: DTC requests bus fare increase. PUC disputes HRT earnings figures.

March 1961: Dallas City Council holds hearing regarding DTC bus fare increase and transfer of funds to DalTran. Evidence presented to PUC establishes that Schultz and his associates own more than 50% of HRT common stock.

April 1961: City of Dallas ("Dallas") and DTC settle; Dallas denies fare increase but approves transfer of assets from DTC to DalTran; transferred funds used to buy stock in Fifth Avenue Coach Lines, Inc. ("Fifth Avenue Coach").

April 1961: Bills in both houses of Hawaii legislature propose new HRT franchise; bills would also require the City of Honolulu to pay a higher price for HRT calculated on a broader valuation formula.

May 1961: In trial of lawsuit filed by DalTran against Fifth Avenue Coach, DalTran alleges an improper "voting trust" and seeks to enjoin Fifth Avenue Coach annual meeting. Schultz associate, attorney Roy M. Cohn ("Cohn") representing DalTran.

December 1961: HRT and PUC settle question of transferred $600,000 by permitting transfer but crediting HRT with a 6% return on the funds for rate-making purposes.

January 1962: HRT and Wahiawa Transport System enter into a purchase memorandum.

February 1962: Schultz is elected Chairman of the board of Fifth Avenue Coach and Chairman of the company's executive committee after 11 members of old board resign. Schultz requests a fare increase for Fifth Avenue Coach. Schultz owns 16.2% of Fifth Avenue Coach stock.

March 1962: New York City ("NYC") moves to seize control of Fifth Avenue Coach bus routes as the bus strike continues. NYC Mayor Wagner and City officials attack Schultz in press release.

April 1962: Schultz controls large block of Hawaiian Airlines ("HAL") stock.

May 1962: Schultz backs H. Everest Clements in HAL proxy fight. Victorious Clements names Schultz to board of HAL.

June 1962: Fifth Avenue Coach sues NYC regarding takeover of the Fifth Avenue Coach bus routes.

(*Continued*)

Exhibit 2.5
(Continued)

February 1963: Schultz resigns as President of Fifth Avenue Coach. His attorney becomes President of Fifth Avenue Coach.

March 1963: Daniel Schultz becomes President of DTC. Four other brothers remain as officers and directors.

April 1963: Schultz renamed to HAL board.

August 1963: Dallas files suit to determine whether DTC should lose its franchise for cutting bus service and for alleged mismanagement of transit company.

December 1963: Dallas to pay $5.5 million for DTC assets; City to operate bus system itself. Major HAL stockholder, J. H. Magoon, Jr., buys out Schultz's interest in HAL.

February 1964: Fifth Avenue Coach and NYC continue to disagree on the value of the bus line in condemnation proceedings: Fifth Avenue Coach asking $92.5 million plus damages. BSF Company takes over control of Fifth Avenue Coach from Schultz interests.

August 1964: Fifth Avenue Coach stock drops 14 points.

March 1966: Schultz and his corporations own approximately 5% of Amfac, Inc. ("Amfac") stock. Schultz submits his name for election to Amfac board; Schultz becomes an Amfac director.

February 1967: Schultz, seeking three more seats on Amfac board, threatens Amfac proxy fight. Amfac reduces number of board members from 14 to 7. Schultz withdraws request for additional board seats and resigns from Amfac board. Schultz's interests in Amfac are bought out for cash.

March 1967: Schultz, a director of Kona Corporation ("Kona"), owns 7% of Kona's common stock and 6% of preferred stock. Kona redeems Schultz's stock worth $5.3 million by trading land worth $7 million; Schultz resigns from Kona board.

January 1968: Schultz is large stockholder of American Pacific Group, Inc. ("APG") (10%); Schultz's 100 Corporation threatens court action if APG violations, including alleged undervaluation of stock, not corrected; APG denies violations. Schultz's 100 Corp. files suit against six of seven directors of APG; Director George D. Gannon, who sold stock to Schultz, not named in suit.

May 1968: Schultz-APG suit dismissed: Schultz is given three nominations to eight-man slate of directors.

July 1968: Schultz and his two nominees win three seats on APG board.

January 1969: NYC Grand Jury indicts Cohn for conspiracy to bribe and names Schultz's lawyer and John Schultz as co-conspirators but not as defendants.

June 1969: His lawyer testifies that Cohn and John Schultz bribed a NYC appraiser for confidential information during the condemnation case of Fifth Avenue Coach; also states that Cohn threatened him into giving up control of Fifth Avenue Coach. Schultz sells interests in APG to National Environment Corp.

December 1969: Cohn acquitted of bribery charges.

January 1970: Schultz and interests currently own 14.05% of stock of Peoples Drug Stores, Inc. of Washington D.C. ("Peoples Drug").

August 1970: PUC enters order denying Schultz's August 1969 request for a bus fare increase.

September 1970: Honolulu City Council decides to pursue HRT purchase.

1971: Schultz elected to board of Peoples Drug.

June 1972: State files criminal charges against Schultz, Wahiawa Transit System, Leeward Bus Company, and others, charging collusion in bidding for contracts for bus services.

March 1973: Hawaii State Supreme Court rules that City and County of Honolulu should pay only $2,917,715 for purchase of HRT and not the $9,621,129 asked by HRT. Court clears Schultz, Wahiawa Transit System, Leeward Bus Company, and others from collusion charges.

March 1975: Schultz sells out interests in Peoples Drug to Lane Drug Corp. for $12 per share when shares selling for $6.62 on New York Stock Exchange.

December 1976: Schultz files Schedule 13D with SEC showing ownership of 8% of Sandalwood Ranch ("SR") stock; states purpose "for investment." Schultz files amended Schedule 13D showing he now owns 10.78% of SR stock; states purpose "for investment."

August 1978: C. Brewer & Co. ("Brewer") stockholders approve merger with subsidiary of IU International Corp.

November 1978: Schultz's 200 Corp. and Honolulu, Limited sue Brewer and IU International Corp. over alleged undervaluation of Brewer stock. Schultz files amended Schedule 13D showing he now owns 18.61% of SR stock, but changes purpose to seeking "representation on the board and to have a voice in management."

January 1979: Schultz files Schedule 14B with SEC showing intent to start SR proxy fight for seats on SR board for himself and Chun at 1979 annual meeting. Schedule 14B also shows Schultz owning more than 90% of HRT stock and that since 1971 the business of HRT and of its subsidiaries has been buying and developing real estate in Hawaii and on the mainland. Consolidated Balance Sheets of HRT and its wholly owned subsidiaries, as of December 31, 1977, show total assets of $46,480,000 and total stockholders' equity of $21,399,305.

February 1979: Schultz's companies, owners of 6% common stock of Alexander & Baldwin, Inc. ("A&B"), a Hawaii corporation with large landholdings, sue A&B alleging undervaluation of A&B stock in proposed A&B merger with Pacific Resources, Inc.

RELEVANT DEVELOPMENTS

Several important changes in stockholder holdings and the total number of shares outstanding occurred between January 8, when Schultz announced he wanted to be elected to the Board, and the special stockholders' meeting called to reduce the number of directors.

On February 5, 53,625 shares were purchased by the Lahaina Publishing Company from a mainland investor with $1.9 million borrowed from a bank. John Anderson is president of Lahaina Publishing Company.

Near the end of 1978, an Employee Stock Ownership Plan (ESOP) was established for the benefit of salaried nonunion employees. Such a plan had been under consideration as early as 1970. After reviewing the existing plan, comparing it with the benefit plan for union employees, and doing a cost benefit analysis, the company determined that an ESOP had several advantages over a conventional insured benefit plan. John Anderson and three company vice-presidents became members of the ESOP's controlling committee.

An ESOP is similar to a profit sharing plan except that distributions are in the form of employer company common stock. An ESOP is allowed to borrow money from a bank, with the loan guaranteed by the company, and to use those funds to pay for new shares issued by the company. The company then makes periodic payments to the ESOP which are tax deductible as retirement plan payments. The ESOP in turn repays the bank loan. An ESOP, in effect, is a deferred compensation plan that can be used to raise capital.

The plan was implemented on February 7 by the sale of 205,533 shares, including 9,883 Treasury shares and 195,650 authorized but previously unissued shares. At $21 a share, $4,316,193 was raised at a time the company needed to pay off maturing loans and stay out of a bank line of credit for 30 days. An earlier study by a pension fund consultant recommended that the company should increase its retirement plan by 18 percent of covered payroll, which would be about $390,000 per year. A comparison with other Hawaiian companies produced a range of $260,000 to $360,000. The repayment on the loan is approximately $305,000 plus interest. Since this loan will only replace other loans, the interest would have been incurred anyhow and could thus be ignored, leaving $305,000 as the annual cost of the ESOP.

The $21 price per share for the ESOP purchase was arrived at by Gandalf & Co., a firm knowledgeable in the field of ESOP's. The methods used to value the stock are in Exhibit 2.6. Gandalf & Co. was founded in 1971 by W. Gandalf and in the course of its work as an investment banking firm has had extensive experience in determining the fair market value of securities for stock ownership plans. Mr. Gandalf, a former corporate and financial lawyer, originated ESOPs as a financing technique which would make employees capital owners of their company. Since the shares are not taken from the existing shareholders, Mr. Gandalf felt the ESOP would "make haves out of the have-nots without making have-nots out of the haves." Shares bought by the ESOP must not exceed their fair market value. The market price did not change noticeably during the time of the purchase. During the week before the announcement of the ESOP, the stock traded at $30.50 (bid) and $32 (ask). Several weeks later the stock was at $29.50 (bid) and $31 (ask). The ESOP paid for the stock with proceeds from an interim "bridge" bank loan soon to be replaced by a fifteen-year bank loan guaranteed by the company and to be repaid by annual company contributions to the ESOP. Thus the ESOP provided the company long-term financing replacing short-term, high-cost borrowings and the repayments of both principal and interest were to be made with tax-deductible payments.

As a result of the purchase of 53,625 shares by Lahaina Publishing Company and the issuance of 205,533 shares to the ESOP, the shares held or controlled by the Anderson family and the officers and Directors of Sandalwood Ranch increased from 673,244 to 932,402 and the total number of shares outstanding rose from 1,594,467 to 1,800,000.

DERIVATION OF THE $21 PRICE FOR SHARES SOLD TO THE ESOP

Exhibit 2.6

The price of $21 per share was set on the recommendation of Gandalf & Co. since it was felt that market price was not a fair price to the ESOP because of the size of the block and other market and plan considerations. Under IRS and Treasury regulations, the price of the stock issued to an ESOP must be "fair." Gandalf & Co. used the following methods in arriving at the value of Sandalwood Ranch stock.

1. Price/Earnings multiple method using 1978 earnings and a five-year average PE:

Year	*PE*
1978	15.44
1977	6.86
1976	5.29
1975	4.22
1974	8.34
Average	8.03

(8.03 PE) ($1.76 EPS) = $14.13

2. Price/Earnings method using five-year averages:

Year	*PE*	*EPS*
1978	15.44	$1.76
1977	6.86	1.95
1976	5.29	1.96
1975	4.22	1.71
1974	8.34	1.77
Average	8.03	$1.83

(8.03 PE) ($1.83 EPS) = $14.69

(Continued)

Exhibit 2.6
(Continued)

3. Market price to book value ratio method using five-year averages and book value as of September 30, 1978:

Year	*Market/Book Value*
1978	1.24
1977	0.76
1976	0.67
1975	0.59
1974	0.57
Average	0.77

$$(.77)\ (\$30{,}443{,}000 \text{ Book value}) = \$23{,}441{,}110$$

$$\frac{\$23{,}441{,}110 \text{ Adjusted book value}}{1{,}594{,}467 \text{ Shares}} = \$14.70$$

4. Book value method using current book value:

$$\frac{\$30{,}443{,}000 \text{ Current book value}}{1{,}594{,}46) \text{ Shares}} = \$19.09$$

5. Calculate effect on market price of common stock after sale of 205,-533 shares to the ESOP. (This assumes that the market price for the company's stock will decrease in value due to the sale of a large new issue of stock. The following simultaneous equation should hold):

$$\frac{\text{ESOP } \$}{\text{ESOP shares}} = \frac{\text{Total market value}}{\#\text{ of shares + ESOP shares}}$$

given that

ESOP $ equals total dollars spent by the ESOP to purchase 205,533 shares.

ESOP shares equal total shares purchased by the ESOP.

Total market value equals the current value of all shares outstanding at the market price of $30 before the ESOP shares are issued.

Number of shares equal the shares outstanding before the ESOP shares are issued.

Then

$$\frac{\text{ESOP } \$}{205{,}533} = \frac{\$30\ (1{,}594{,}467)}{1{,}594{,}467 + 205{,}533}$$

$$\text{ESOP } \$ = \$5{,}461{,}012$$

$$\text{Price per share} = \frac{5{,}461{,}012}{205{,}533} = \$26.57$$

6. Historical Valuation Method

In recent years there have been two occasions for estate tax purposes where the market price has been discounted to determine the value of a block of common stock. The valuations were accepted by the IRS. The discounts were 40% and 36.8%, respectively. Using the smaller of the discounts, the price would be:

$$\$30\ (1 - 0.368) = \$18.96$$

7. Discounts applied to Stock Valuations
   a) *Restrictive Agreements:* Stock held by the ESOP will contain restrictions. It cannot be sold to the public until the participant receives the shares after retirement and/or possibly after termination of employment. Second, the plan requires that the Company be allowed the "right of first refusal" which prevents the shareholder from selling his stock on the open market until he has first offered the shares at current fair market value to the company.
   b) *Minority Interest Discount:* A majority block is generally worth more than a minority block. Since the ESOP and its participants will not have a majority position, a discount should be applied.
   c) *Blockage Discount:* It often takes a lower price to sell a large block. Hence a discount should apply for selling such a large block of stock.
   d) *Costs of Marketing Discount:* New issues have costs, such as legal fees, registration expenses, advertising, and underwriting fees. Discounts applied for marketing costs range from 5% to 10% of total value.
   e) *Extraordinary Market Pressures:* The market for the stock is thin and an individual has purchased a large number of shares over the last three years, possibly driving up the price and reducing the shares available. Withdrawal of this large purchaser could dramatically decrease the price.

Case 3

THE DIXIEVILLE NATIONAL BANK (A)

Robert R. Dince

Mr. Edward Smith, 63, President and Chairman of the Board of Dixieville National Bank of Dixieville, Tennessee, was sitting in his private office late in the afternoon of the day before the mid-year Board meeting. As he sat deep in his chair, his eyes glided over the many certificates, diplomas, awards and photographs which covered his career of forty years in banking. As he daydreamed, his thoughts continually returned to his major achievements—he and the Dixieville bank were synonymous. The Chapman family may have founded and controlled it, but he felt that the Tennessee Bankers Association and the town saw the bank as *his* bank. The current comings and goings of the Chapman family still attracted some attention in the local newspaper's society columns, but the family was now widely scattered and, with one exception, had little impact on the town. One Chapman aunt still lived on the family estate; the oldest part of the plantation house built in 1815 was still preserved intact within the present mansion. But Smith and his family were the real social leaders of the town. As a prominent Mason and Rotarian, Smith would never identify himself as an aristocrat. But he had a strong sense of personal accomplishment. He snorted and mumbled half aloud his distaste for the Chapmans who had the effrontery to feel that, after forty years, he could be set aside to make room for a retired government bureaucrat who now wanted to be head of the bank.

THE SUCCESSION ISSUE

At the regularly scheduled June Board meeting of the Dixieville National Bank of Dixieville, Tennessee, the following matters were moved by Mr. Edward Smith, the president of the bank:

SOURCE: Robert R. Dince, "The Dixieville National Bank (A)," *Journal of Case Research 1984*, pp. 81–96. Reprinted by permission of the author and the Case Research Association.

1. That an unspecified amount of loans in the Hollowville Branch should be written off.
2. That all the (nonequipment) decorating cost of the bank's handsome new branch in a suburb of Dixieville should be written off.
3. That the regular semi-annual dividend of $.50 should be paid.

These matters were all passed without any discussion by the bank's eleven directors.

Mr. Smith then went on to a discussion of a large previously defaulted loan. He said, "I am very happy to report to the Board that we have been able to arrange a new loan on the property that we foreclosed. This means that the loan is a fresh loan and that there are no losses for the bank to absorb. We are not going to have to charge our loan loss reserves. I think we have done a very good day's work here." After these business matters were discussed, the president then took up the key problem of management succession faced by the Board.

At the December meeting of the Board, Mr. Smith had announced that he was considering retirement. He was then sixty-three years old and had spent over thirty years as President and Chairman of the Board. At the December Board meeting, the succession to the presidency had been discussed. While several alternatives were discussed, it was agreed to postpone any decision for six months (see Exhibit 3.1).

Smith started the present discussion by stating his thoughts on his son William Smith, a Vice-President in charge of the branch.

"Willy has done a marvelous job of opening our beautiful branch in the new section of Dixieville. So far as I can see, this branch is a complete success." He went on, "However, new branches take time to get established and the deposit gains we thought we were going to get have not been up to our expectations. We seem to have gained an additional $450,000 in governmental deposits and perhaps an extra $400,000 from workers living and working in the area. But the branch is very convenient for our other depositors and so far our additional operating costs are very low. Willie is the branch manager and we have two fulltime teller/bookkeepers and a couple of part-time girls. We don't make loans out there since Willie refers almost everyone downtown. But the branch is so beautiful we expect to see it featured in the next issue of *Banking.* And I would like to tell you that because of its beautiful interior and exterior decoration, the Senior Ladies Garden Club is going to use the branch for their monthly meetings. We surely will get some business out of that. We let anyone use the bank for civic meetings and we think it is great advertising. We thought the branch might develop some trust business but nothing has come our way yet."

CORPORATE OFFICERS

Exhibit 3.1

The Chapmans: Joseph Chapman, corporate executive, member of the Board of Directors, Dixieville National Bank, first cousin of Walter Chapman. Walter Chapman, Vice-President and member of the Board of Dixieville National Bank, candidate for Presidency of the bank.

The Smiths: Edward Smith, President and Chairman of the Board of Dixieville National Bank. Appointed as President by Walter Chapman's uncle 30 years ago.

William Smith, Vice-President and branch manager, Dixieville National Bank. Edward Smith's only son.

Bank Officers: Ward McGolrick, Vice-President in charge of bank lending.

Mr. Kellogg, Vice-President and Board Member in charge of investments and operations.

After Mr. Smith extolled the branch, one of the Directors pointedly asked, "Come on Ed, how can we justify the expenditure of that much money when it hasn't brought us any new business? Just what did this place really cost us?" Smith answered, "Well the total deal came to $970,000—we bought the land twenty years ago for peanuts. Frankly, it doesn't seem much to me in terms of current building costs."

Smith then went on to say a few more words about his son in the context of his review of all the officers' presidential capabilities. Mr. Smith reminded the Board that Willie had been in complete charge of the planning, construction, and decoration of the bank. He extolled the new branch in terms of its impact on future growth of the bank. "Willie has done a great job and I am proud of him." Mr. Smith then turned to a discussion of Mr. Kellogg, the bank's senior Vice-President in charge of bank investments and operations. Smith praised Kellogg, "We are lucky to have such an astute money manager in such a small bank. He really can handle our funds. He is a real market manipulator and can handle those Fed Funds like we were the Mellon Bank. In my opinion, he has added thousands of dollars of net income just by his cash letter direct clearing technique."

The President then reviewed the work of Mr. Ward McGolrick, the senior loan officer. Mr. McGolrick, who had been working for the bank for ten years, handled almost all of the business loans and personal loans (excluding consumer installment credit). Since much of this work had been handled by Mr. Edward Smith in prior years, Mr. McGolrick's work received special attention. Over $1,500,000 of new loans had been put on the books in the last year. There had been some fairly large write-offs, many of which had occurred from loans made prior to Mr. McGolrick's sole responsibility in this area. However, the bank's loan-loss reserve was large enough to handle this without impairing the capital position. Mr. McGolrick, a very personable young man of thirty-eight, was praised highly by Mr. Smith.

The next officer discussed was Mr. Walter Chapman, who had been with the bank only six months. Mr. Chapman had been elected Vice-President and Director of the bank despite the fact that he had no prior banking experience. He came to the bank after thirty years in the Diplomatic Service. Mr. Chapman was the largest single stockholder in the bank, controlling 10% of the stock. Most of this had been inherited from his mother, and the remainder he had purchased in the last few years. Mr. Chapman's family controlled almost exactly 51% of the outstanding stock of the bank, and it was Mr. Chapman's great uncle who had founded the bank and had left the stock to his heirs. Mr. Chapman's cousin Joseph was on the bank's Board, but other than going to Board meetings, he took little active interest, having left all management decisions directly to Mr. Smith. But he was not totally happy with Smith's stewardship. In 1981, before his first cousin Walter had expressed an interest in joining the bank, Joseph Chapman had written a rather hard letter to Ed Smith (see Exhibit 3.2).

Exhibit 3.2

July 28, 1981

Mr. Edward Smith
President
Dixieville National Bank
Dixieville, Tennessee

Dear Ed:

Frankly after receiving the financial statements of the first six months of this year, I was keenly disappointed with the small dividend you declared out of earnings. Paying out only 20 percent of earnings is an extremely short-sighted policy on the part of both you and the Board.

I would like to remind you that we stockholders own the bank and that we are all entitled to a fair return on our investment. Certainly, a bank should not endanger its capital by overpaying dividends, but a 50% payout of earnings would not be excessive. I have discussed this matter with other family stockholders and they share my views.

My objection to your present and past policy seems to make no impression on you. Using even a conservative capitalization rate, the stock should

(*Continued*)

Exhibit 3.2
(*Continued*)

sell for at least 50 percent more than its present price. The present market price is less than book value—and that book value ignores the written-off value of the main bank building and the reserve for losses.

Unless we secure better treatment from you and the Board, it will be my recommendation to the other family stockholders that we do not give you our proxies. I would like to remind you that we can exercise our right to cumulative voting at the next Annual Meeting.

Sincerely,

Joseph Chapman

After discussing Walter Chapman's background and Chapman's interest in becoming the chief executive officer of the Dixieville National Bank, Smith went on to say, "I want everyone to understand that I agree to step down and let Walter and the Chapman family take over the bank. But I really think that after all the years I spent in building the bank, Chapman should work his way up through the bank. In that way, he will be trained as a successor and not just an inheritor. I have set up a training program so that he can accomplish this objective. We have had him on the teller line, working in operations, seeing how we handle cash and due-forms. Right now we have him working in consumer credits. In fact, McGolrick informs me that Walter has made his first few loans this past week. Of course, he is going to have to learn our ways. You know in a town like Dixieville, you don't have to be able to read a financial statement to know who does or does not get credit. That kind of experience and judgment you don't get with a couple of weeks of lending. But all this will come in time."

The remaining directors were representatives of the local business community. None of the outside directors owned more than the minimum of shares needed to qualify as directors. When Mr. Chapman had joined the bank, one of Mr. Smith's close friends on the Board made a formal motion that Smith continue as President, and upon Mr. Smith's retirement he should be paid the sum of $35,000 a year for the rest of his life as a consultant to the bank. His particular responsibility would be to review policy with the officers and to maintain the bank's friendly relationships with its large corporate and government depositors.

After his discussion, Mr. Smith said, his voice heavy with emotion, "But you must remember, the Smiths are investors in this bank just like the Chapmans. Old man Chapman, your uncle, gave me my big chance 30 years ago, but that was after I had ten years of banking experience. I think Walter will be just fine—just fine. But he needs some experience before we can turn all this over to him. I am reaching the end of my road and I am ready to turn the reins over to someone else."

BACKGROUND

The Dixieville National Bank was founded by Mr. Chapman's family in 1880. A Chapman had always been associated with the running of the bank until 1951 when Mr. Smith was elected President. Except for the Bank Holiday, the bank had never been in difficulty and it always had been noted as a well-run, profitable, and extremely sound bank. It was the largest bank in Dixieville, with deposits three times greater than its only local competitor, a state bank. While the national firms who had offices and factories in Dixieville did the bulk of their banking in large city banks, they all maintained active balances with the Dixieville Bank and used the banks as a depository for payroll and local working balances. The bank was extremely successful in getting fairly substantial state and local government balances. While these state balances tended to be volatile, they still averaged considerably higher than other banks in the area. Dixieville was located about thirty miles from Nashville, which did create some competition. In addition to the competition from the large banks thirty miles away, the bank faced the competition of two savings and loan associations in the town whose total accounts were 50% greater than the total deposits of the two commercial banks together. At the time of the directors' meeting, the banks were paying 1½% less for Money Market Accounts than the S & L's.

Foremost of the major problems that the bank faced was deposit volatility (see Exhibit 3.3). Generally speaking, the first half of the year saw a decline in deposits, with the deposits increasing in the second half of the year. The large government deposits, coupled with the large industrial deposits, made the management of the bank's money position difficult. For many years, the bank had maintained an exceptionally heavy investment position at the expense of loans. This position in highly liquid government debt was taken in order to guard against possible illiquid periods.

The investment officer, Mr. Kellogg, was pushed by the President to maximize investment income. The President delegated his authority to the investment officer, whose only policy requirement was that funds would always be available to meet the bank's liquidity needs. Mr. Kellogg was able to balance the bank's position without maintaining large correspondent balances or an excess reserve position at the Federal Reserve. He performed this mainly by taking substantial positions in the Federal Funds Market, which Kellogg felt was the most liquid investment he could make on a very short term basis. He much preferred the Federal Funds Market to govern-

Exhibit 3.3

TOTAL ASSETS FIGURES FOR DIXIEVILLE NATIONAL BANK
(000 Eliminated)

12/75	31,036
12/76	25,739
12/77	26,670
3/78	24,415
6/78	26,009
9/78	27,554
12/78	28,707
3/79	28,406
6/79	30,302
9/79	27,884
12/79	25,466
3/80	25,158
6/80	24,816
9/80	25,965
12/80	26,646
3/81	26,791
6/81	26,475
9/81	30,090
12/81	30,589
3/82	27,663
6/82	29,043

Exhibit 3.4

MATURITY SCHEDULE OF DIXIEVILLE NATIONAL BANK
As of June 31, 1982 (Thousands of Dollars)

	U.S. and Agency Securities	*State and Local*
Due in 90 days	70	80
Due in 91–180 days	280	300
Due in 181 days to one year	1,050	400
Due in 1–5 years	2,101	1,830
Due in 5–10 years	560	2,890
Due in more than 10 years	300	3,460
	4,270	8,960

ment bills, since the bank often gained or lost a million dollars in government and large industry balances in a two-week period. In addition, the bank, because of its weak loan position, had taken a heavy position in long-term governments (see Exhibit 3.4).

At the time of the June Board meeting, the bank was in a tight liquidity position. The increasing commitment of funds to loans and investments had drawn down the bank's cash position (see Exhibits 3.5 and 3.6). At the time of the Board meeting, the bank held only a tiny position in short term government bills. It was Kellogg's custom to maintain correspondent balances with fifteen banks (though his major correspondent held 25% of the total). He did this in order to send directly to the proper correspondent any checks

CALL REPORT BY COMPTROLLER OF THE CURRENCY FOR DIXIEVILLE NATIONAL BANK
(Thousands of Dollars)

Exhibit 3.5

	December 1981	*June 1982*
ASSETS		
Cash	3,976	2,873
U.S. Government Securities	5,589	4,270
Obligations of State and Local Governments	5,889	8,960
Federal Funds Sold	1,500	1,000
Other	617	1,315
Loans and Discounts	8,164	10,098
Stock in Federal Reserve	36	36
Bank Premises	972	491
TOTAL ASSETS	$30,589	$29,043
LIABILITIES		
Deposits of Individuals and Corporations	9,206	8,849
U.S. Deposits	2,652	1,502
State and Local Deposits	3,104	5,418
Certified Checks	146	379
Time Certificates and Savings Deposits	11,594	9,105
Other Liabilities	686	783
Total Liabilities	27,388	26,036
Capital Accounts	3,201	3,007
TOTAL LIABILITIES	$30,589	$29,043

Exhibit 3.6

1981 INCOME STATEMENT FOR DIXIEVILLE NATIONAL BANK
(Thousands of Dollars)

Income		% (X)	% (XX)
Total Interest on Securities	1,123	44	23
Interest on Loans	1,067	42	68
Service Charges	215	8	5
Other Income	164	6	4
TOTAL INCOME	$2,569	100	100
Expense			
Salaries, Officers	335	13	10
Salary and Wages Other	237	9	13
Interest on Time and Savings	1,090	42	50
Occupancy and Equipment Expense	200	8	5
Other Expense	67	3	10
Net Provision for Loan Losses	210	8	2
TOTAL EXPENSE	$2,139	83	90
Net Current Operating Earnings	430	17	10
Income before Tax	430	17	10
Tax	76	3	3
Net Income	354	14	7
Dividend	70		

(X) All percentages calculated as % of Total Income.
(XX) Peer group banks.

deposited by one of the major industrial accounts. In some cases, to gain a day, he would send a bank messenger directly to a city as far as one hundred and fifty miles away to present the check for immediate clearing. In cases where the deposits of the major companies were too far to be directly delivered, he would send a bank messenger into Nashville so cash letters could be sent by air mail without delay. Kellogg avoided the use of the Federal Reserve Clearing system and normal clearing systems available to System members despite the fact that the Fed offered reserve deposit credit on a basis ranging from immediate credit up to a maximum of two days deferred credit. By such agile handling of the bank's money position he was often able to gain as much as two days over sending the items on a normal cash letter clearing basis. While he had little formal investment training, he was apparently well grounded in his knowledge of the investment market. Kellogg, however, made little effort to solicit help or advice on his investments from his major correspondents. Kellogg even avoided purchase of government securities through his correspondents and dealt directly with the large government bond dealers in order to save two or three thirty-seconds on bid/ask prices. Kellogg was the main operations officer of the bank and technically was in control of all of the internal operations, though the President actually supervised many of the internal operations. Kellogg made no loans and was in no way responsible for any of the loan policy decisions. The increase in the loans of the bank in the last year with little increase in deposits had apparently caught him unawares.

Lending had been under the direct control of Edward Smith until Mr. McGolrick's duties had been enlarged. Mr. McGolrick's original prime duty had been installment lending and working as an assistant to Mr. Smith. Prior to Mr. McGolrick's taking over as a loan officer, the Dixieville National had another officer, Mr. George Lee, who had left the bank in 1980. Mr. Lee had been the officer in charge of the Hollowville Branch, located in a community within the county. Mr. Lee had always worked independently of the main office, and since almost all the loans were agricultural it was left pretty much to his jurisdiction. The branch operated with an advisory Board separate from the bank's main Board of Directors. This advisory Board reviewed all loans made at the branch over $5,000. A routine examination of the bank had shown that a large number of small notes, all in amounts less than $5,000, had been discounted by one borrower. None of the original makers of these notes could be identified. Upon closer examination it was found that $250,000 worth of such small notes were in fact forged. In the ensuing clean-up proceedings, the Chapman family first began to be concerned about some of the operations under Smith's direction. Neither Mr. Lee nor Mr. Smith apparently had taken the proper precautions to guard against such a major, and with hindsight, such an apparent fraud. Mr. Lee resigned his position and a new young man was put in charge of the branch under Mr. McGolrick's direction.

The bank did not press for prosecution. Part of the loss was covered by insurance and the remainder was charged off. When the bank threatened legal action against the discounter of the notes, he turned over most of his real property to them. The property was purchased from the bank by a holding company controlled by Mr. Smith with funds borrowed from another bank. This company had then sold the property to a new buyer with the Dixieville Bank holding the mortgage. One effect of this complicated transaction was to save the bank from charging off any further losses and thus removing the stigma from Mr. Smith that the loss had been his responsibility. It was this property which was mentioned at the June Board meeting.

Mr. McGolrick's loan record procedures were somewhat typical of those found in many country banks. An accurate note file was kept in which the number of times the note had been renewed was kept on record. It was the usual procedure to renew a good note rather than force the borrower to repay. But in the few cases where the number of renewals became so large that they might attract the examiners' attention, the loan was switched to demand notes which did not require renewal. Mr. McGolrick switched those few notes to demand (with Mr. Smith's approval) when the underlying collateral or the borrower's net worth was strong enough to protect the bank.

Because the bank had such vigorous competition from local savings and loan associations, the level of time deposits was relatively low. The National Bank Act at that time prohibited a bank from lending on real estate, other than government insured mortgages, more than 100% of its unimpaired capital and surplus or 70% of its time deposits, whichever was larger.[1] This restriction had limited the Dixieville National's real estate loans. As a result, Mr. McGolrick had devised a technique for avoiding the intent of the law.

His technique was quite simple. He would use an ordinary term loan or combination of term loan and renewable short-term notes. These notes were shown in the note files as ordinary loans. In addition, a separate mortgage was taken out pledging the property to the bank. These mortgage arrangements were not shown on the bank's books and were in fact kept in a "secret" file, which was not known to anyone except Mr. McGolrick and Mr. Smith. In June, the total of such "under-the-counter" mortgage loans was approximately $285,000.

Mr. McGolrick did emphasize that in the last year he had done everything possible to put more loans on the books in order to increase the bank's earnings. He said this was done under Mr. Smith's direction and the bank had actually solicited loans all over that part of the state. By June, $1.5 million worth of new loans had been added to the bank's books.

Before leaving the government, Mr. Chapman had visited Dixieville and expressed to his relatives his interest in becoming the chief officer of the bank. Although they expressed some reservations about his lack of banking experience, they agreed to support his ambition. Chapman then informed Mr. Smith of the family support. Mr. Smith in the interview expressed great pleasure at the news, pointing out that he had tremendous respect for Chapman's cousin and always had a very pleasant relationship with members of the family. According to Mr. Chapman, Mr. Smith gave the clear impression that he would relinquish the presidency to Chapman as soon as possible.

In a meeting later that week, Mr. Smith, discussing the matter with Mr. Chapman and other Chapman family stockholders, pointed out that the bank was in a better earnings position than ever before. Under his direction, a more ambitious lending program had been inaugurated. He pointed out that the slow growth of the bank was due to Dixieville's laggard expansion. He emphasized that whatever growth had occurred in the bank was due solely to his efforts, and to his position in the community (not that of the Chapman family). He further vehemently pointed out that the large industrial and governmental deposits which were in the bank were due to his political and business connections. At this point, Mr. Smith, in a rather dramatic fashion talking to the assembled members of the family, pointed to the large and ornate silver loving cup, displayed in a special niche, which had been presented to him by the local Chamber of Commerce in honor of his twenty-fifth anniversary of being President of the bank. The cup detailed Mr. Smith's activities in community affairs and was signed by all the town's leading citizens. At this point he said that he would certainly welcome Mr. Chapman's joining the bank, but he felt that the man would have to gain banking experience. He would be glad, however, to train him as his successor.

It was agreed therefore that Mr. Chapman would join the bank as Vice-President and Board member. When Mr. Chapman felt he had sufficient knowledge to take over the bank, Mr. Smith said that he would happily retire and that he looked forward to Mr. Chapman's future appointment as President.

Shortly after this meeting in Dixieville, Ward McGolrick paid Mr. Chapman a surprise visit at his Washington office. McGolrick assured Chapman of his support since he felt that the President should be from a family with large stock interests in the bank. McGolrick admitted that his long-run ambition was to be President but only if the younger Mr. Smith and now Mr. Chapman would not accept the position. He voiced the hope that meanwhile the Chapman family would support his candidacy to the Board of Directors.

EDWARD SMITH

Over the years, Edward Smith had become a dominating figure not only in the Dixieville National Bank, but also in the town of Dixieville. He had founded an insurance agency which was premised in the banking building and which handled all the insurance on the bank's loans (not only credit insurance, but property, casualty, and other). He was known as an important local real estate investor and developer. Through clever investment in the surrounding town properties and farm real estate. Mr. Smith's equity in the bank was only a small part of his total holdings. Nevertheless, the bank was the center of his life, and he felt responsible for seeing the bank grow from total resources of $3 million to its present size. All during this period, there was a member of the Chapman family on the Board, but Mr. Smith was given carte blanche to run the bank exactly as he saw fit. It was only during the early seventies that some family dissatisfaction with his management became evident. It is interesting to notice that Mr. Smith had acquired almost all of his holding for himself and his son from outsiders and that the Chapman family had never sold any of their stock to him. But, when outside directors were elected to the bank's Board, he was able to persuade one of the Chapman family to release enough shares to allow the new Board members to qualify as directors. The bank's stock traded infrequently and was usually bought either by the Smiths or the Chapmans. As is often the case for small banks, the stock sold at a small discount from its book value. As of June 1982, it sold for $80–$85 per share.

It is not clear whether Mr. Smith's long term strategy was to break the control of the Chapmans, but some of his actions had the effect of reducing their majority position. The first such move occurred in the 1970s when the Bank merged with a small country bank (state charter) located in Hollowsville. In order to perform the merger without involving any cash outlay for the bank, a stock switch was arranged. The capitalization of the Dixieville National was increased by 50% and stock was issued to the former shareholders of the country bank. This move reduced the holdings by the Chapman family from approximately 75% of the total stock down to 51%.

The next such move occurred when a bank located within the same county, and closer to Nashville, was suggested by Mr. Smith as a possible merger candidate. This bank was roughly half the size of the Dixieville National. In order to have made the merger effective it would have been necessary for the Dixieville National to issue additional stock in such a proportion that the holdings of the Chapman family would have been reduced to approximately 35% of the outstanding stock after the merger. Considering the strategic location of the other bank, and its growth possibilities, many good arguments were advanced by Mr. Smith and his supporters on the Board. The merger appeared to be an excellent strategic move for the Bank despite the fact that the stock switch arrangement was clearly for the present benefit of the smaller bank's shareholders. The advantages of growth by merger, possible lower operating costs, and a better loan spread were quite obvious to a majority of the Board. There is no doubt that a merger would have gone through except for the objection by Walter Chapman. It was Chapman's hostility and his refusal to sign the merger proposal which prevented, or at least postponed, a final agreement. While the majority of the Board favored the merger, Mr. Chapman's intransigence had the implicit support of the Chapman family's controlling interest.

It was from this time that Mr. Smith's hostility toward William Chapman and the Chapman family became evident. This was in contrast to his earlier cordiality when Chapman had announced his intention of joining the bank.

However, prior disaffection by the Chapman family over Mr. Smith's dividend policy and overall management had already been expressed.

NOTE

1. Construction loans made on the security of real estate for a period not exceeding eighteen months were exempted from the mortgage loan restriction provided the total of such loans did not exceed 100% of capital and surplus (Public Law 87-717).

Case 4

THE DIXIEVILLE NATIONAL BANK (B)

Robert R. Dince

At the next regular meeting, which was scheduled to be nothing more than a routine affair, Mr. Joseph Chapman, Walter Chapman's first cousin and an executive Vice-President of a large Southern steel company, asked for the floor.

"As you all know, I have spent many years on the Board of this bank. All in all, my views representing the majority stockholders in the bank have been to support management. However, recent occurrences inside the bank make it necessary for me to bring my opinions before this Board. The Chapman family has not had a member of the family working within the bank for many years, but this is no longer true.

"Certain policies of the bank," Joseph Chapman continued, "are literally beyond belief. On checking around, I can't find anyone else in the state of Tennessee like us. Why should the bank have such a high cash position? If we are so good at operating in the Fed Funds market then why can't we do better with our cash? This idea of running old Hank the bank porter around the countryside with the bank car directly presenting checks for payment is ridiculous. What do we save by all this? What do we make?" He went on, "In my business, we don't do anything unless we can prove it is cost effective. As far as I can see, all this does is expose us to the ridicule of all the other banks in this part of the state who think we are some sort of loonies for doing it. They are all laughing at us behind our backs.

"Furthermore, the whole business at the Hollowville branch and the things that fell out of it are really disreputable. Sure you can get embezzlements and defalcations, that's why we carry insurance. Every bank faces

SOURCE: Robert R. Dince, "The Dixieville National Bank (B)," *Journal of Case Research 1984*, pp. 96–99. Reprinted by permission of the author and the Case Research Association.

that. But this is really crazy." Joseph Chapman was now really warming to the subject and continued in an even louder voice. "This is a small town. For a chief executive officer to let a lending officer make a bunch of loans to nonexistent folks in a place this small is hard to believe. All the CEO had to do, as head of the loan committee reviewing new credits, was to ask 'do I know this person?' His carelessness cost the bank money—money it will never be able to get back. And then at the last meeting, Mr. Smith gets up and proudly tells us all how he has arranged a new loan on the basis of a foreclosed property. Don't you all realize that we are lending money to Smith through this holding company that we all know he controls? He was buying a property at a bargain price through the bank's foreclosure and then having the bank refinance it. Sure, he made the loan whole on the bank's books, but wasn't it improper using his insider position for his own benefit?"

Chapman was now quite excited. "My God, look at this nonsense with the mortgage loans. Sooner or later the examiners are going to find it out and come down on us like a ton of bricks. And what for? It's no big deal. Why expose ourselves to a possible writeup and censure—maybe even add administrative order? Why should we do anything like this? We don't gain anything and we are all exposing ourselves to possible suits on the basis of negligence."

Chapman continued, "My cousin and I now feel that the Board should go on record as censuring Mr. Smith and asking him to fix his date of retirement."

At this point, Mr. Ed Smith rose to his feet almost apoplectic and asked that the meeting be adjourned. The majority of the Board, quite embarrassed by all the accusations and heat, quickly voted to adjourn. Mr. Smith, closely followed by his son, rushed out of the room without saying another word to the two Chapmans.

One week later, Ed Smith asked the members of the Chapman family to come to the bank for a discussion of the bank and its future. Mr. Smith opened the meeting by saying "As we all know, the accusations made at the last Board meeting, with the apparent support of the Chapman family, have distressed me greatly. I don't see any reason why I should have to take these accusations from you people. You turned over the management of the bank to me thirty years ago and the bank has always made money and paid a good dividend. I have done my job for thirty years and now that one of your family has nothing to do and decides to come back to Dixieville, all sorts of accusations are being made."

Smith's voice got even lower and he growled, "Well, you folks have put it to me that it is time for me to get out. Let me tell it to you another way—it's time for you to get out. I am going to make you an offer that I don't think you can refuse.

"Providing that the family tenders all the stock to me, not only in personal holdings but in all trusts and the like, I am willing to pay $2.3 million for the whole block. That is better than 40% higher than book and about 55 to 60% higher than the last trade in the stock. If you don't take this generous offer then we are going to have a war in the bank that is going to hurt everyone's investment. The fact is, Walter here is still learning and I don't think he can run the bank profitably. I don't have that problem. Further, I have the friends who control the deposits and they are not going to look kindly at my expulsion for a new untried management. You seem to think you have a monopoly on banking in this town. I think maybe it's time for me to call in some of my political chips and ask the state of Tennessee for a new charter for Dixieville. And then we'll see who will get the town's business."

Smith continued, "I think I am making more than a fair offer. The offer is made only to the Chapman family, and I must have all Chapman shares to make my offer effective. I need to know your answer by the end of the week. Thank you very much for your attention." And with that he left the room.

The Chapmans sitting around the table were stunned by this announcement. In the babble of voices following Smith's leaving the room, all sorts of resentments against Smith and his high-handed ways with the family were voiced. "Can you imagine—he is so insulting—are we the ones that want him out? The nerve of that man." But as the din quieted down, Mr. Joseph Chapman, the Chapman with the most business experience and the family's Board member for many years said, "You know, that old b———d really has made us an offer we can't refuse. There is no way we can get this much for the bank unless we can find a buyer for our shares from a Nashville bank. The laws of the state are somewhat restrictive in this case. The usual way is to give us stock in the holding company. That provides the capital gain tax but still leaves us as investors in the banking business. This guy is willing to pay us cash. For example, Walter, that means approximately $460,000 for you before taxes. After taxes you can make $45,000–$50,000 tax free invested in long-term 'munis' this summer. Besides, I don't think the old guy's threat is an idle boast. I really think he could turn to the banking commission and get a charter in Dixieville so quick you would not believe it. If he does that, then the value of our holdings are that much less. Let's face it, Walter is a great guy but he still is not ready to run this bank. If we are going to get some young hot shot to run it for us, that frustrates Walter and his plans. And we can't get anybody really decent unless we offer him a chance at an equity position."

Joseph Chapman now had everyone's attention and he continued,

"Frankly, I don't see any reason why we should not accept his offer. Looking at it from a strictly monetary point of view, our cash income will jump five times from what it is now; even after we pay the taxes. I for one have no longer any sentimental attachment to the bank as a family enterprise and except for Aunt Susan, none of us live here anymore. Walter lives here, but as you all know I think his wife would be happy to move back to Washington where all their friends live. I would just as soon have the money. Why not?"

Walter Chapman got up and said, "Joe, with all due respect, I am shocked to hear you state the position as if money was the only thing we should concern ourselves with. This is a family business. This is a commitment of the Chapmans to the past, present and future of Dixieville. I was doing more than just finding a way to fill up my hours. I was investing my time and my being to the preservation of our family's interest in this enterprise. If you accept this offer, you are letting that old goat rub our noses in it one more time. I say reject it and the hell with him."

SECTION B

ENVIRONMENTAL ISSUES

Case 5

THE McGUIRE NUCLEAR POWER PLANT

Allen Palmer/William McCollum

INTRODUCTION

On June 29, 1981, the Nuclear Regulatory Commission (NRC), the group within the federal government charged with controlling the use of atomic energy for commercial purposes, authorized the issuance of a license allowing Duke Power Company of Charlotte, N.C. to operate Unit 1 of the two-unit McGuire Nuclear Station at the full design power output level. This was the final license necessary to allow Duke Power Company to place the first unit of the McGuire plant into operation and begin producing electricity for the first time. The authorization of the full power license followed by approximately eleven and one-third years the formal announcement by Duke Power Company of the plans for building the McGuire power plant, and followed by over ten years the beginning of construction of the station.[1]

In the official news release by Duke Power Company following the announcement of the NRC decision, Carl Horn, Chairman of the Board of Duke Power was quoted as saying, "We have waited a long, long time for this day. . . . With this plant in operation a more secure supply of electricity is assured for our customers."[2] Bill Grigg, the Senior Vice-President of Legal and Finance for Duke, was quoted soon after the announcement as saying, ". . . I was always comfortable that eventually we would solve the technical problems. I had complete confidence in that . . . the major concerns that I've had have been financial." "We've had to raise over the last

Prepared by Prof. Allen Palmer of the University of North Carolina at Charlotte, and William McCollum of Duke Power Co. Presented at the Case Research Association Meeting, 1983. Distributed by the Case Research Association.

four or five years about $500 million a year. So the McGuire expenditure represents about four years of our financing requirements. That's a lot of money."[3] The total cost of the two-unit station had risen from an estimate of $372 million (made in 1969, when the projected operating dates for Units 1 and 2 were March 1976 and March 1977, respectively) to a total estimated cost in January 1981 of over $1,842 million.[4]

In December 1982, Mr. Horn, reflecting on his long involvement with nuclear power, stated:

> I predict the day will come when electric customers of utilities who fought the many battles (environmental, economic and political) to build today's nuclear plants will be thankful rather than hostile. Their electric bills will be lower and their air will be cleaner.[5]

THE COMPANY

Duke Power Company ranks among the ten largest investor-owned electric utilities in the United States. The company has been ranked consistently as one of the top companies in the industry by financial and industry analysts. Duke Power Company has had the most efficient fossil-fired (powered by coal) generating system in the United States for ten of the twelve years from 1970 through 1981, and was ranked second in the United States the other two years. In 1981, Duke operated the most efficient nuclear generating unit in the United States, compared to other nuclear units of similar design.

Duke Power Company is unusual in that the company maintains its own in-house Design Engineering staff, and designs and builds its own power plants, as opposed to contracting the design and construction work to outside firms. Partly because of this fact, Duke's cost of generating facilities has been among the lowest in the utility industry.

Duke Power Company serves the central portion of North Carolina and the northwestern portion of South Carolina, an area of 20,000 square miles with a population of about 4 million (see Exhibit 5.1). The company headquarters is located in Charlotte, North Carolina.

HISTORICAL BACKGROUND—DUKE POWER COMPANY'S NUCLEAR PROGRAM

The Atomic Energy Act of 1954 established federal responsibility for the promotion and regulation of the commercial use of atomic energy for non-military purposes. This dual responsibility was delegated to the Atomic Energy Commission (AEC), an agency of the federal government. Throughout the 1950s and early 1960s, the government promoted the development of atomic energy, both directly through research and development efforts, and indirectly through tax incentives which allowed electric utilities to write off investments for nuclear energy research. Exhibit 5.2 is a selection of quotations from leaders in government, industry, science, and the international community that illustrate the predominant view in the early and mid-1960s. Utilities had already recognized a growing problem in the energy supply

DUKE POWER COMPANY SERVICE AREA

Exhibit 5.1

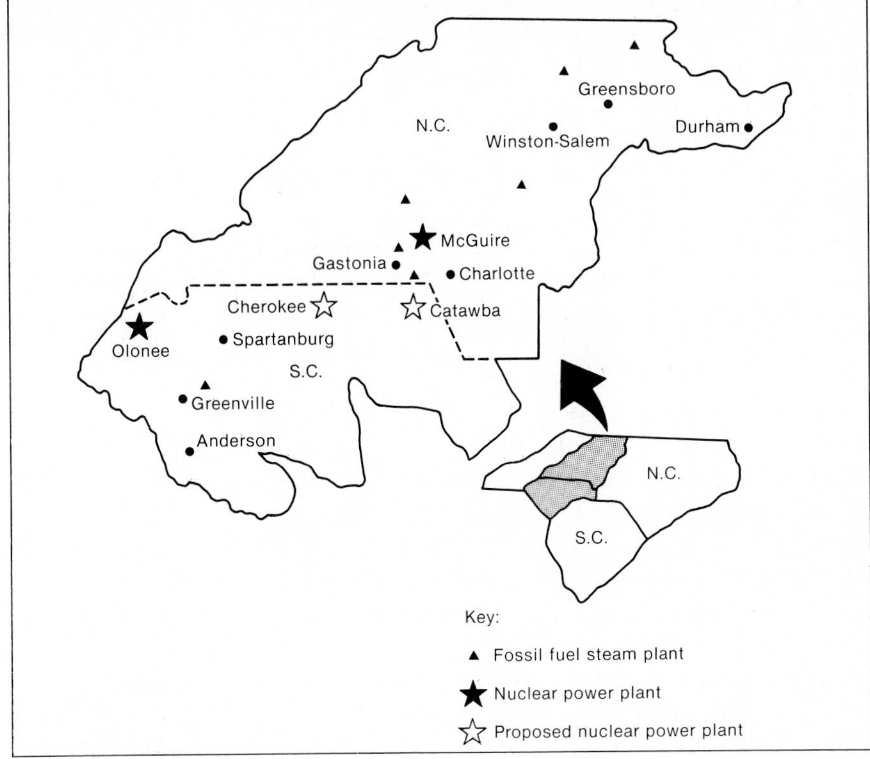

field. Fossil-fueled generating plants could not continue to supply the growing demand for electricity, because of limited resources and increasing fuel cost. Further expansion of hydroelectric production was not feasible in many areas due to lack of suitable sites. Thus the industry was looking for a new source of power, and nuclear power appeared to be the answer to industry's problem.

COMMENTS ON NUCLEAR POWER FROM THE 1960s

Exhibit 5.2

"An Institute of Business Analysts convention report on atomic energy said that by 1965 nuclear power would be produced at a cost competitive with that generated by hydroelectric and steam plants."

The *New York Times*, November 30, 1961

"Atomic fuels offer a valuable supplement to conventional fuels in the short term and an essential replacement for them in the much longer term. Numerous large power reactors have been and are being constructed from

(Continued)

Exhibit 5.2
(Continued)

which valuable technical information will be obtained. Expenditures for the development of civilian atomic power and directly related supporting technology will considerably exceed $200 million in 1963."

From President John F. Kennedy's budget
message on January 19, 1962

"The International Atomic Energy Agency, a U.N. affiliate, predicts that in many countries nuclear power will be able to compete with other forms of energy within the next ten years."

From an editorial in the *New York Times*
entitled "Glimpses of the Atomic Future"

"The director of the Atomic Energy Commission's division of reactor development said today that peaceful nuclear power can lead to savings in the cost of electricity to American consumers of 'between four and five billion a year by the year 2000. . . . Probably the most spectacular benefit to the nation from nuclear power is in the savings which the power consumer—the American public—could realize through a reduced cost of electricity.' "

Quoted from a statement made by Dr.
Frank K. Pittman, Director of Reactor
Development, A.E.C. before the American
Power Conference on March 28, 1963

"Atomic power will be on a competitive commercial basis with other forms of fuel within about four years."

Sir William Cook, Member United Kingdom
Atomic Energy Commission, December 3, 1963

"Today's atomic power plants have been developed to the point where large size units can compete neck and neck with fossil-fueled plants in most parts of the nation."

James F. Young, General Manager,
General Electric Company Atomic Products
Division, February 27, 1964

"Nuclear power plants for generating electricity in large blocks of power are today competitive with fossil fuel in a number of areas where the cost of fuel delivered is above the national average."

J. E. Rengel, General Manager,
Atomic Power Division, Westinghouse
Electric Corporation, June 1964

"It is safe to predict that nuclear power stations will be substituting for conventional ones in the early nineteen-seventies."

Olaf Berg, Chairman of the Board,
Swedish Electric Power Stations, June 1964

"President Johnson gave the industry its full stature last week when he told the graduating class of Holy Cross College in Worcester, Massachusetts, 'that the [electric power] industry had achieved an economic breakthrough in the field of atomic power.' He said 'the long promised day of economical nuclear power is close at hand.' "

June 14, 1964

"The age of nuclear power now has begun. By 1975 the atom will be the source of at least half of all the additional electric power needed by the expanding American economy."

Dr. Glenn T. Seaborg, Chairman, Atomic Energy Commission, August 29, 1964

"In the next few years, nuclear power in many parts of the world will be the main source of energy."

Professor Vasil S. Emelyanov, USSR President of the UN Conference on Peaceful Uses of Atomic Energy, Geneva, August 31, 1964

"The Director of one of the nation's chief atomic research centers [Dr. Alvin M. Weinberg, director of the Oak Ridge National Laboratory] believes that immensely cheap nuclear power is a real possibility and that a new industrial revolution will result. . . . Dr. Weinberg talks about atomic power produced at half or even a quarter of present costs. 'What would we do,' he asks, 'with unlimited power at such a price?' "

January 24, 1965

"The economic advantages of nuclear power spring from several factors. In recent years, one of the major inducements for building huge steam generating plants at the mouths of coal mines was the fact that little or no money had to be spent on equipment to control air pollution. This, however, is no longer the case and utilities are faced with many pressures for the installation of such costly equipment.

"In theory, at least, atomic power plants have the advantage of requiring absolutely no air pollution equipment. They are clean.

"Large plants under construction today promise to produce power competitive in cost with coal from mines only a few miles away. And nuclear engineers expect more favorable economics as additional innovations are applied to future plants."

The *New York Times,* November 28, 1965

Exhibit 5.3 shows the peak electricity demand in the Duke Power Company service area for each year from 1955 through 1973. As the data show,

Exhibit 5.3

PEAK LOAD GROWTH—DUKE POWER SERVICE AREA

Year	*Annual Peak Load (kw)*
1955	1,934,000
1956	2,041,000
1957	2,177,000
1958	2,306,500
1959	2,474,000
1960	2,661,000
1961	2,820,000
1962	3,192,000
1963	3,370,000
1964	3,522,700
1965	3,826,365
1966	4,439,700
1967	4,579,460
1968	5,364,165
1969	5,613,625
1970	6,283,915
1971	6,622,125
1972	7,449,500
1973	8,235,585

the peak demand doubled approximately every ten years, implying an average compound annual growth rate in excess of 7%. In the late 1960s, the annual growth was even greater. Thus, Duke Power Company management was forced to plan for a construction program which would double the company's production capacity within ten years. In planning this program, management decided that since the present production facilities were almost totally coal burning units, addition of capacity through the construction of nuclear power plants offered a way to obtain a balanced generating "mix" of nuclear and fossil generation.

Plans were made to build a nuclear station at Seneca, S.C., to be named the Oconee Nuclear Station. Construction was started on the site in March 1967 and the first unit was put into operation in July 1973. By this time, work was well underway at the site of the McGuire Nuclear Station as well as the Catawba Nuclear Station, to be built close to York, S.C. (Exhibit 5.1 shows the approximate locations of these plants in the Duke Power service area.) Nuclear reactors had been ordered for two more future stations for which sites had been selected, bringing the total nuclear generating facilities either planned, under construction, or in operation by Duke Power Company to thirteen reactors located at five separate sites. McGuire was to be the second of the five. The experience with building the Oconee plant had indicated that there would be no unusual problems in completing the plant on schedule, and on or close to budget. This was the backdrop against which Duke applied for construction work permits in September 1970.

LICENSING APPROVAL PROCESS FOR THE McGUIRE NUCLEAR STATION

As the first step in the lengthy process of obtaining the necessary licenses and permits to allow construction and operation of the McGuire Nuclear Station, Duke Power had to obtain approval from the North Carolina Utilities Commission for the facility. In February 1971, a local environmental/antinuclear group, the Carolina Environmental Study Group (CESG), formally opposed the building of the McGuire Nuclear Station before the N.C. Utilities Commission. This group, consisting of 100 to 150 Charlotte area residents, was led by Jesse Riley, a fifty-seven-year-old chemist and inventor with Charlotte-based Celanese Corporation. The organization is supported by $10 annual dues from members and by donations estimated at about $2,000 per year, Riley has been described as founder, guiding force, media contact, technical advisor, typist, and impromptu lawyer for CESG.[6]

Work on the next step of the required licensing process began with the filing of an application for a construction permit by Duke Power with the Atomic Energy Commission (AEC) in September 1970. Since state and federal regulations allow the performance of limited site preparation work prior to issuance of permission to construct the facility, and because Duke needed to begin work as soon as possible to complete the McGuire facility in time to supply the projected load growth based upon the data in Exhibit 5.3, site work began in April 1971, while the matter was still under consideration by the N. C. Public Utilities Commission. In May 1971, the Utilities Commission gave approval for the facility.

On June 25, 1971, a notice of a hearing to be held on the application was published in the Federal Register by the AEC,[7] as was required by law. The CESG filed a petition to intervene in the proceedings in July 1971. The hearings on Duke's application for a construction permit were held before the Atomic Safety and Licensing Board (the group within the AEC which conducts license hearings) between June 27–30, 1972 (4 days), September 6–15, 1972 (7 days), October 24, 1972 (1 day), and November 1–4, 1972 (4 days).

In these hearings, the CESG brought up a variety of contentions concerning the location of the site: the radiological programs which Duke Power Co. had proposed to put into practice at McGuire; the likelihood of severe earthquakes in the vicinity of the McGuire site; and the general technical and financial qualifications of Duke Power Company to operate and maintain a nuclear power plant. In addition, the CESG contended on technical grounds that the design of the reactor vessel closure head (the reactor vessel contains the uranium fuel during operation) and the design of the building surrounding the reactor vessel were deficient. As a part of the final decision of the hearing board, it was found on the basis of the evidence presented by the parties to the hearing that

> The Board is satisfied that the weight of evidence clearly supports the findings and conclusions adopted herein. CESG's proposed conclusions are rejected as contrary to fact and law.[8]

The Atomic Safety and Licensing Board issued its Initial Decision on February 22, 1973 (two years from the time of application for the permits). The construction permits were issued to Duke Power on February 28, 1973. The issuance of these permits allowed Duke to expand the scope of the construction work at the site to begin building the nuclear reactor systems and major support systems. The CESG filed an appeal to the ASLB decision, which went to the Atomic Safety and Licensing Appeal Board. The Appeal Board reviewed the decision and denied all of the contentions of the CESG, with the exception of the contention concerning Duke Power Company's quality assurance program. The case was returned to the ASLB for further review of this point. The ASLB reopened hearings on July 10, 1973. After further evidence on Duke Power's quality assurance program was entered into the record, the ASLB reviewed the evidence and decided in favor of Duke Power on the contention concerning quality assurance.

Before the final decision had been rendered on the quality assurance issue, the CESG filed a complaint in Federal District Court in June 1973 which asked the court to review the issuance of the construction permits for McGuire and, further, asked the court to declare that a federal law, 42 USC 2210, commonly known as the Price-Anderson Act, was unconstitutional. The Price-Anderson Act was passed by Congress in 1957 and basically limited the liability of nuclear power plant owners to $500 million in the event of an accident. The CESG also petitioned for review in the U.S. Court of Appeals (Washington, D.C. circuit). During this time period, Congress passed the Energy Reorganization Act of 1974, which abolished the AEC and set up the Nuclear Regulatory Commission to oversee the construction and operation of nuclear facilities. In January 1975 the Court of Appeals affirmed the AEC decision in all respects, and the District Court dismissed all of the counts of the CESG complaint, with the exception of the request concerning the Price-Anderson Act. The District Court agreed that it would hear arguments on the constitutionality of the Price-Anderson Act. Arguments were heard in December 1975 and hearings were held in September 1976, with the CESG contending that the law was unconstitutional because it denied the persons who might be affected by an accident at a nuclear facility the right of due process as guaranteed by the Constitution, the right to just compensation for injury, and that the Act violated the equal protection component of the Fifth Amendment to the U.S. Constitution "by forcing the victims of a nuclear accident to bear the burden of injury, whereas society as a whole benefits from the existence and development of nuclear power." Duke Power Company contended that the law should not be set aside because it represented a legislative attempt to achieve a reasonable balancing of economic interests, and therefore, was within the powers accorded to the legislative branch under the U.S. Constitution unless it could be shown to be irrational or arbitrary.[9] Because of the potential impact of this decision on the electric utility industry as a whole, several organizations, including the Atomic Industrial Forum, the Edison Electric Institute and the Southeastern Legal Foundation, filed friend of the court briefs supporting the constitutionality of the Price-Anderson Act.

On April 15, 1977 the District Court judgment was entered, declaring the Price-Anderson Act (42 USC 2210 (e)) unconstitutional. Duke Power Co. filed an appeal to the United States Supreme Court in May 1977. The Supreme Court agreed to hear the case, and it was argued before the court on March 20, 1978. The Supreme Court entered its decision on June 26, 1978, reversing the District Court decision. The effect of the lengthy hearing and court suit process had been to force Duke to proceed, at its own risk, to build the McGuire facility for over seven years after beginning of initial site work, with the construction permits and liability issues in doubt. In the meantime, the process of obtaining an operating license had been pursued in parallel, to avoid even greater delays. But the years between 1971 and 1978 had brought other problems which had an even greater impact upon the McGuire project.

FINANCIAL PROBLEMS AND McGUIRE CONSTRUCTION CUTBACK

During the period of the 1960s the cost of electricity, which had been decreasing steadily for years, began to climb. Exhibit 5.4 shows the cost of residential electric service, by year, for the period from 1950 through 1980. As this exhibit illustrates, the cost of electricity generation had risen enough to turn around the decline in electricity prices by 1969. Electric rates hit their lowest point in 1969 and climbed steadily thereafter. This was due primarily to the impact of inflation on the capital equipment costs and construction costs. In previous years, continuing improvements in power plant technology had allowed new power plants to be operated more efficiently, at a much

RESIDENTIAL ELECTRIC RATES

Exhibit 5.4

	Avg Rate per KWH (c) Total Utility	
Year	***Duke***[1]	***Industry***[2]
1950	2.25	2.88
1951	2.18	2.81
1952	2.18	2.77
1953	2.16	2.74
1954	2.12	2.70
1955	2.09	2.65
1956	2.05	2.61
1957	2.04	2.56
1958	2.00	2.54
1959	1.99	2.51
1960	1.97	2.47
1961	1.95	2.45
1962	1.95	2.41
1963	1.90	2.37
1964	1.86	2.31
1965	1.84	2.25
1966	1.80	2.20
1967	1.79	2.17
1968	1.75	2.12
1969	1.72	2.09
1970	1.73	2.10
1971	1.90	2.19
1972	2.00	2.29
1973	2.08	2.38
1974	2.61	2.83
1975	3.00	3.21
1976	3.29	3.45
1977	3.40	3.78
1978	3.62	4.03
1979	3.90	4.33
1980	4.11	4.93

SOURCES: (1) *Duke Power Company Annual Report*, 1980. (2) EEI *Source & Disposal of Electricity* Monthly Report

lower cost than previous plants. Thus as new plants were constructed to meet the rapidly growing electricity demand, the average cost of electricity production for a utility would decrease, allowing the utility to lower its rates. But by the late 1960s the methods for increasing the efficiency of coal and oil burning power plants had been practically exhausted, prohibiting the continuance of the efficiency increases of the past. The technology for designing, building, and operating had run up against some fundamental physical limits which could not be overcome by application of ingenuity and with each new plant addition, the increasing cost of materials and labor used in plant construction made the cost of generating electricity higher than that of previous plants. Exhibit 5.5 provides selected producer price indices which show the rates of increase of these costs from 1965 through 1981.

PRICE INDEXES 1965–1982

Exhibit 5.5

Date	*Materials and Components for Construction*[1]	*Capital Equipment*[1]	*All Commodities*[1]	*Index of Hourly Compensation in Manufacturing*[2]
1965	95.8	101.3	96.6	92.5
1966	105.9	104.9	99.8	95.6
1967	106.1	108.0	100.0	100.0
1968	105.6	110.5	102.5	106.1
1969	111.9	111.0	106.5	112.4
1970	112.6	112.0	110.4	119.4
1971	119.5	114.5	115.0	127.3
1972	126.2	119.5	119.1	135.3
1973	136.7	123.5	134.7	143.6
1974	161.6	141.0	160.1	155.9
1975	176.0	163.0	175.0	171.4
1976	188.0	173.0	183.0	184.6
1977	203.0	185.0	194.0	199.3
1978	224.0	199.0	209.0	215.9
1979	247.0	217.0	236.0	234.6
1980	268.3	239.8	268.8	262.3
1981	291.1	274.1	295.7	291.4
1982*	293.8	277.1	300.9	308.3

* 1st quarter 1982 (est.).

SOURCES: (1) Producer Price Index, Bureau of Labor Statistics, U.S. Department of Labor. (2) Handbook of Labor Statistics, U.S. Department of Labor.

Faced with the increasing operating costs and higher interest rates (see Exhibit 5.6) of the early 1970s, Duke Power was forced to attempt to raise rates to cover the costs of service and allow a fair rate of return. But the system of rate regulation was not capable of responding to the rapid rise in costs. In the past, when labor costs, material costs and interest rates changed slowly, a one- or two-year lag time between a change in costs and an increase in the price of electricity would not seriously hurt the company financially. With inflation running over 10% annually, and with construction costs of new plants rising rapidly, Duke found itself in a difficult situation. It was not possible to recover current costs, because the company would only get rate increases based upon a level of costs which was one to two years old by the time the rate increase was granted. Thus, in a time of steadily increasing costs, the company could never "catch up" to earn the rate of return on cap-

PUBLIC UTILITY BOND YIELDS

"A" Rating

Exhibit 5.6

Year	*High*	*Low*
1965	4.9%	4.5%
1966	5.7	5.0
1967	6.6	5.3
1968	6.9	6.2
1969	8.8	6.9
1970	9.1	8.0
1971	8.4	7.9
1972	8.0	7.5
1973	8.2	7.5
1974	10.7	8.2
1975	10.4	9.7
1976	10.0	8.5
1977	8.6	8.4
1978	9.8	8.8
1979	12.8	9.7
1980	15.1	12.0
1981	17.4	14.2
1982*	17.0	16.0

* 1st quarter 1982.

SOURCE: Moody's *Bond Record,* July 1982.

ital necessary to sustain a strong financial position. Consequently, the price of Duke Power Company Stock, which had been over $40 per share in the period from 1965 through 1969, fell to a low of around $10 per share in 1974. Duke Power Company's corporate earnings dropped to a level which would not support an AA bond rating, and the rating on Duke bonds slipped to A in November 1972.[10] Thus, Duke management did not feel that it could sell long-term bonds because the company's earnings would not support the additional burden, particularly at the higher interest rate necessitated by the lower bond rating. Exhibit 5.7 gives selected financial statistics for Duke Power Company for the period from 1965 through 1981.

The projected cost of completing the McGuire plant had increased sharply from $372 million in 1970 to almost $588 million in 1973. This increase, plus the similar increases in the cost of other Duke nuclear units

Exhibit 5.7

DUKE POWER CO.
Summary Financial Statistics

Year	*Gross Revenue ($ mill.)*	*Net Income ($ mill.)*	*Common Equity %*	*Dividends per Share*	*Price Range*	*Price Earnings Ratio*
1965	236.7	39.8	44.2	1.00	44–35	23.8
1966	261.1	41.7	44.5	1.10	43–35	22.8
1967	284.7	46.2	41.5	1.20	43–30	19.8
1968	312.2	49.1	38.1	1.30	43–33	20.0
1969	342.2	54.4	32.8	1.40	43–27	17.4
1970	386.1	51.2	30.9	1.40	29–20	15.8
1971	451.5	71.9	31.3	1.40	27–20	12.9
1972	510.7	80.4	31.7	1.40	25–21	13.6
1973	603.1	99.6	31.1	1.40	23–16	10.5
1974	825.3	105.1	33.5	1.40	20–10	8.5
1975	954.0	128.2	34.1	1.40	19–10	8.3
1976	1,108.4	173.7	38.3	1.53	23–16	8.3
1977	1,267.0	192.4	40.2	1.63	23–20	9.0
1978	1,396.7	230.6	42.9	1.74	22–18	7.7
1979	1,492.6	247.8	42.9	1.83	20–16	6.4
1980	1,682.8	311.1	43.4	1.95	19–14	5.4
1981	1,908.4 (est.)	326.3 (est.)		2.08	22–16	6.0

SOURCE: Moody's *Financial Handbook*. For more extensive financial data, see Moody's *Public Utility Manual*.

under construction, greatly increased the burden of financing necessary to support the construction program. Due to the company's weakened financial position, Duke could not raise the necessary capital to maintain the needed level of construction expenditures. In August 1974, Duke announced a cutback in the construction program affecting the McGuire and Catawba projects. This cutback included a slowdown in the construction effort at McGuire (resulting in a two-year delay in project completion), in order to cut expenditures on that project, plus a cessation of work at the Catawba Nuclear Plant site. The management of the company realized that this delay would save current expenditures, but would result in greatly increased final project cost, due to increased labor and material costs associated with maintenance of the site during the increased duration of the project and construction of additional plant structures required because of the delay, and due to the increased carrying charges because of the two-year delay. In October 1974, Duke revised the cost estimate for the McGuire project to reflect the two-year delay resulting in an increased projected cost of $126.3 million, or 20.5% of the most recent previous cost estimate, to push the total projected project cost to over $741 million. Of this increase, half came from increased carrying charges on investment, and the other half from all other sources. Though the cost increase exacerbated the problem of raising capital to finance construction, management felt that there was no choice but to delay completion.

OPERATING LICENSE APPLICATION

Duke proceeded with the application for an operating license for Unit 1 of the McGuire station prior to the final resolution of the construction permit issues, by filing an application with the NRC for an operating license on April 4, 1974. In July 1974, the CESG filed a third petition to intervene, opposing the issuance of an operating license. Because the announcement of the construction cutback at McGuire occurred in August 1974, causing a two-year delay in the estimated completion date of the facility, the NRC postponed hearings on the operating license application until 1977. Hearings were held March 28–April 1977; April 19–22, 1977; and August 22–31, 1978. The contentions which were given by the CESG as supporting a denial of the license centered around four basic issues, as follows:[11]

1. That the growth in electricity demand within the Duke Power service area would not be as great as Duke had forecast, and thus the McGuire facility would not be needed, at least not within the current century. The reasoning behind this contention focused in two areas: first, a challenge to the basic assumptions of the Duke Power load forecast such as price elasticity, per capita energy use, and the relationship between energy

use and industrial production; and second, the claim that Duke had failed to properly consider the impact of emerging solar technology on the overall electricity demand. In support of this latter point, the statement was made that by 1985, one-half of 1% of the total energy needs of the Duke Power service area would be supplied by solar energy, and that this percentage would increase rapidly after 1985, thus obviating the need for further nuclear generating plants.

2. That the likelihood of occurrence of earthquakes more severe than those planned for in the McGuire design was far greater than Duke Power Company had claimed previously. The CESG presented a witness who testified that faults which had been found in the vicinity of the McGuire site, which had been judged inactive by other experts, could not be said to be inactive with total certainty, and that therefore there did exist the possibility that an earthquake, centered at one of these nearby faults, and of a magnitude greater than that considered in the McGuire design process, could occur.

3. That Duke Power was not financially qualified to build or operate the McGuire facility. The CESG noted the decline in the market price of Duke common stock, and the lowering of Duke's corporate bond rating, as indicators of poor financial condition.

4. That Duke Power Company had not performed properly the cost-benefit comparison with alternative types of power plants—most notably, coal burning plants—which is required by regulations. The regulations require each applicant for a license for a nuclear power plant to demonstrate not only that the facility will be cost-effective, but also that the reasonable alternative types of generating plants which would be built in place of the nuclear power plant would not be more cost-effective than the nuclear plant. The regulations also require the applicant to include in his cost-benefit analysis such "external" costs as health effects of the "fuel cycle" of the plant in question. The fuel cycle is defined as including all activities directly associated with the extraction of the fuel material (mining, in the case of uranium for nuclear reactors); any processing necessary before use; use of the fuel in the power plant; and disposal of any waste products left after use. The CESG presented witnesses who testified that Duke Power had underestimated the health effects of the uranium fuel cycle by considering only the releases of radioactive gases from the wastes created by the processing of the uranium occurring during the first 100 years after processing. The CESG maintained that the analysis should include radioactive gases which would occur over the first 1,000 years following processing. The CESG

concluded that if the effects of the releases over the 1,000-year time period had been properly considered, the cost-benefit analysis would have shown that a coal burning plant would be more cost-effective than a nuclear power plant at the McGuire site.

In response to these contentions, Duke Power presented witnesses who stated:

1. That Duke's load forecast was sound and reasonable and that while load forecasting was not an exact science, and while it was possible to make assumptions different from those made by Duke which could result in a projected demand substantially lower than the demand forecast by Duke, the assumptions used by Duke Power in its forecast were reasonable in light of historical evidence, and that when a significant doubt existed as to the assumption which should be made, the responsibility of the power company to provide dependable, reliable service dictated that they err in the conservative (high) direction, in order to avoid the potentially severe economic impact of brownouts or blackouts.
2. That, based upon the accepted practices of seismology, there was not a reasonable risk of severe earthquakes occurring within the immediate vicinity of the McGuire site, and that even in the unlikely event that an earthquake centered at one of the faults near the McGuire site occurred, the probability that the vibrations experienced at the McGuire plant would exceed those assumed in the design would be extremely low.
3. That Duke Power had embarked upon a program of financial rebuilding based upon sound business principles, which had included the restructuring of Duke's construction program and an aggressive load management program, which would assure the continued financial health of the company, and thus ensure that Duke would be financially capable of constructing and operating the McGuire facility.
4. That Duke Power Co. had performed a reasonable cost-benefit analysis, including health effects considerations, which showed that the cost of power from the McGuire Nuclear Plant would be cheaper than power produced by alternative means. Duke maintained that the costs which CESG wished to include in the analysis, to cover health effects of the uranium fuel cycle over a 1,000-year time horizon, were excessive and unsound. Duke also pointed out that it was ridiculous to recalculate the comparative cost of alternatives without considering the sunk cost in the McGuire Project which Duke had incurred to this point, and that if the analysis were done comparing the cost of completing the McGuire

facility with the cost of building an alternative plant, the analysis would show that completing the McGuire facility was the most cost-effective alternative, regardless of the assumptions used concerning fuel cycle effects.

The final segment of these hearings concluded on August 31, 1978. Based upon the evidence presented in the hearings, Duke was confident of a favorable decision on the operating license application. But on March 28, 1979, the first major nuclear power plant accident in the history of the United States occurred at the Three Mile Island Nuclear Plant, near Harrisburg, Pa. The accident caused an instant reaction of fear that another accident (or a more serious one) could occur at one of the other nuclear plants in the country, and precipitated a call by several congressmen, numerous private citizens, and even the President of the United States for a reevaluation of the safety of nuclear power plants. The chairman of the senate committee studying the accident, Senator Gary Hart of Colorado, was quoted as saying: "The accident has revolutionized the economics of nuclear power and the real question is whether there will be any more real growth in the nuclear industry."[12] A *Wall Street Journal* staff article summarized the outlook by saying: "Talks with officials at utilities and in the nuclear power industry, and their critics, indicate that the Harrisburg accident will add billions of dollars to nuclear generating costs that are already vastly higher than imagined in the industry's pioneer days."[13]

In addition to investigations by congressional committees and a special Presidential Commission, numerous parallel studies were launched by the NRC itself, mostly with the intent of proposing new regulations aimed at increasing the safety of nuclear power plants. Following the accident, the NRC announced a moratorium on the issuance of new operating licenses, pending the completion of these safety studies. In April 1979, acting upon Duke Power Company's pending application for the McGuire plant, the Atomic Safety and Licensing Board ruled in Duke's favor with respect to each of the issues which had been argued during the hearings on the application for an operating license for McGuire, and ruled that a license would be issued to Duke, pending issuance of a supplement to the NRC safety evaluation report, addressing the significance of the resolution of generic safety issues then under study.

During the next thirteen months, Duke Power worked to complete the construction of the McGuire facility. In May 1980, the NRC staff issued a report on the investigation of the safety issues in question, and Duke immediately filed a motion asking the ASLB to lift the stay of the issuance of the license for McGuire Unit I. On June 9, 1980, the CESG filed in opposition to

Duke Power Company's request, and asked that hearings on the operating license application be reopened, for the purpose of discussing the issue of the possibility of hydrogen gas buildup and burning in the reactor containment building during an accident. This was an issue which had come up as a result of the Three Mile Island accident and had been investigated by the NRC, but the CESG contended that there were special circumstances in the case of the McGuire containment design which made it more dangerous. The ASLB agreed to reopen the hearings to hear testimony on the hydrogen issues. While the parties involved were waiting for the hearings to be scheduled, Duke asked the ASLB to grant the company a special license to allow it to load the nuclear fuel into the reactor, begin a chain reaction, and conduct some required tests, without producing significant power. Duke made the request in an attempt to minimize further delays; the company argued that the only issues remaining to be decided were concerned with phenomena which would not happen with the reactor at a very low power level. The ASLB eventually agreed, and the special low-power license was granted on November 25, 1980. The hearings on the hydrogen questions were held between February 24 and 27, 1981; March 2 through 6, 1981; March 10 through 13, 1981; and March 17 through 19, 1981.

In June 1981, the ASLB rendered a final decision that all of the issues had been satisfactorily resolved, and authorized the issuance of a full power operating license for the McGuire Unit I reactor.[14]

DESIGN CHANGES AND COST ESCALATION

In looking at the cost increases which added to the worsening financial situation facing Duke Power Company, it can be seen from Exhibit 5.8 that between 1969 and 1979, the total estimated cost of the McGuire Nuclear Station rose from $372 million to $1,529 billion, an increase of 411% over the base estimate. In terms of cost per kilowatt of production capacity, a measure generally used by the utility industry, the cost rose from $162 per kilowatt in 1969 to $648 per kilowatt in 1979. The three major cost categories shown in Exhibit 5.8 illustrate that the cost of materials increased by 80% during this time period (during the same period, the consumer price index rose 100%), the cost of labor increased by 740%, and the cost of Interest During Construction (IDC), the carrying charges incurred during the construction period, increased by 900%. While the increase in material cost is relatively straightforward and follows the general inflation experienced during the period, the increases in labor and interest charges require further explanation.

During the period between 1969 and 1979, labor rates for skilled workers increased (see Exhibit 5.5), as did interest rates (see Exhibit 5.6), but not enough to account for the tremendous increases seen at McGuire. The

McGUIRE NUCLEAR STATION COST ESTIMATES

Exhibit 5.8

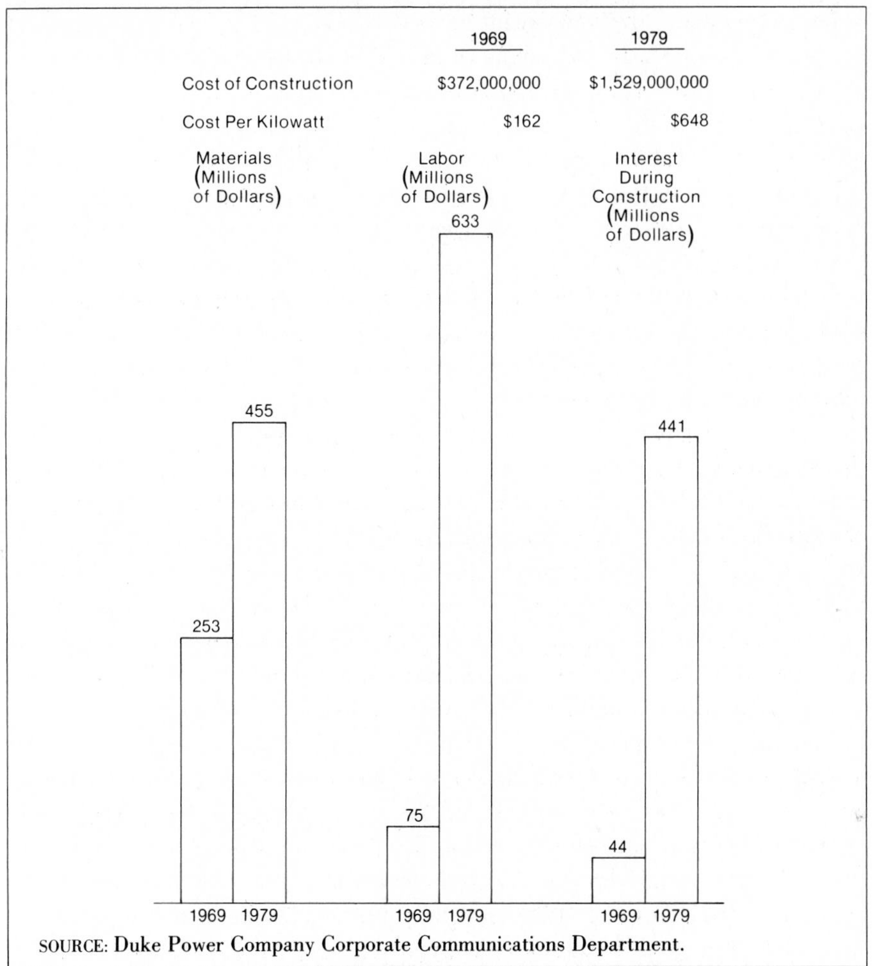

SOURCE: Duke Power Company Corporate Communications Department.

major factor behind these increases, according to Duke Power Company, is the explosion of regulatory requirements which occurred during this time period, in the total numbers of new or expanded regulations. While it is true that these regulations had widely varying amounts of impact upon the construction process, virtually all had some impact, and many caused major changes to have to be made to designs of systems and structures, or to procedures for quality assurance. The net result of these requirements was that Duke had to expand the construction work force at the McGuire site, and because many requirements were issued after work had begun at the site, the regulations which required changes in the design resulted, in many cases, in construction workers tearing down work which had been complete and rebuilding it to meet the new requirements.

As an example, a large portion of the piping in the plant (that portion associated with systems important to reactor safety) must be supported by structural restraints designed to meet very strict criteria specified by the NRC and on the ability of the supports and piping to withstand earthquake loadings. These supports, in many cases, are large structures which are difficult to build. In a large number of cases, the design criteria changed during the course of work at McGuire, requiring redesign of the structures after they had initially been erected. Thus in these cases, the company paid for triple the necessary labor (first installation, teardown, second installation) to accomplish a given amount of progress in building the plant. Since performing this rework took longer than the time originally allotted for performing the work, the changes resulted in delays in the project schedule. These delays greatly increased the amount of interest on funds used during construction, particularly since the interest rates for commercial borrowing rose sharply during this period, making the cost of carrying this construction investment over an extended period even higher.

Another major cause of the dramatic rise in labor charges was the fact that Duke Power Company, as well as other utilities involved in building nuclear power plants, did not initially realize the difference between nuclear power plant construction and the construction of conventional fossil-fueled or hydroelectric plants. As an example, the requirements for structural supports for piping in a nuclear plant require the use of more manpower to build and inspect the supports. But the manpower estimates used originally were extrapolated from the times which had been used in estimating conventional plant construction. Even when Duke Power began to revise the estimates for McGuire the true impact of the increased requirements was not apparent immediately. Thus cost estimates continued to be revised, to reflect inflation, interest increases, and experience.[15]

COMMERCIAL OPERATION OF McGUIRE UNIT I

On December 1, 1981, Unit 1 of the McGuire Nuclear Station was declared to be in commercial operation. The second unit of the McGuire Station was scheduled to be in commercial operation in 1983.

NOTES

1. Duke Power Company news release, dated June 30, 1981.
2. Ibid.
3. *Duke Power News* (Duke Power Company newspaper), Volume 7, July 1981, p. 8.
4. Letter from J. L. Zapata, Manager of Cost Engineering, to Michael Demback, dated November 23, 1981.

5. Letter to the author from Mr. Carl Horn, dated December 17, 1982. Quoted with permission.
6. *The Charlotte Observer,* December 13, 1981, p. 4C.
7. *Federal Register,* June 25, 1971 (36 Fed. Reg. 12323).
8. Atomic Energy Commission transcript TR8723, Docket Nos. 50-369 and 50-370, Initial Decision, page 16.
9. U.S. Supreme Court Reports 438US59, 57L Ed 2nd 595, 98 S Ct 2620 (Nos. 77-262 and 77-375), page 608.
10. This and other historical information was provided by Michael Dembeck and Alex Coffin of Duke Power Company's Corporate Communications Dept.
11. Transcript of NRC/ASLB hearing board; Hearings on the Issuance of an Operating License for the W.B. McGuire Nuclear Power Station, Unit I, Transcript Nos. 135-2673.
12. *The New York Times* (staff article), September 23, 1979, p. 1.
13. *Wall Street Journal* (staff article), April 24, 1979, p. 1.
14. Ibid., McGuire Operating License Hearing, Transcript Nos 135-2673.
15. Letter from Steve C. Griffith, Jr., Duke Power Company, to Mr. Paul L. Lassiter, Staff Attorney, North Carolina Utilities Commission, dated July 1, 1981.

Case 6

MANVILLE CORPORATION

Arthur Sharplin

Manville Corporation (Johns-Manville until 1981) is a concentrically diversified mining, timber, and manufacturing company. In 1982 the company employed about 30,000 people at more than 125 facilities (plants, mines, and sales offices), about two-thirds of which are located in the United States. Until 1979, the company was engaged primarily in the mining of asbestos and manufacture of asbestos-based products. As late as 1976, sales of asbestos fiber (mostly to manufacturers outside the U.S.) provided 52% of Manville's income from operations, although it constituted only about 11% of revenues. In addition, asbestos is used by Manville in making hundreds of products such as floor tile, textiles, filters, pipe, and roofing materials. Altogether, asbestos and asbestos products accounted for more than one-half of Manville's sales in 1976 and for approximately three-fourths of operating profit.

The dangers of inhaling asbestos fibers began to be publicized widely in the 1960s and 1970s. Beginning in 1978, there were hundreds of newpaper stories, magazine articles, and television documentaries related to the problem. U.S. asbestos use declined by more than 50% from about 1973 onward. The Interior Department reports a 36% drop from 1979 to 1980 alone. Exhibit 6.1 gives more information on asbestos.

Attempts to expand and diversify Manville began in 1970, when net sales totaled $578 million. Revenues had grown at only about a 1.5% real rate since 1960, less than the rate of GNP growth. Because of the expansion effort, the company surpassed $1 billion sales in 1974 and $2 billion in 1978. However, real sales declined from 1978 onward, despite the contribution of

This case was written without the cooperation of Manville Corporation and despite the active opposition of certain Manville executives to the research upon which it is based.

This case was prepared by Prof. Arthur Sharplin of Northeast Louisiana University. Reprinted by permission.

WHAT IS ASBESTOS?

Exhibit 6.1

In an article appearing in *Sunday Review of the Society* in 1973, Bruce Porter described asbestos this way:

> Perhaps no other mineral is so woven into the fabric of American life as is asbestos. Impervious to heat and fibrous—it is the only mineral that can be woven into cloth—asbestos is spun into fireproof clothing and theater curtains, as well as into such household items as noncombustible drapes, rugs, pot holders, and ironing-board covers. Mixed into slurry, asbestos is sprayed onto girders and walls to provide new buildings with fireproof insulation. It is used in floor tiles, roofing felts, and in most plasterboards and wallboards. Asbestos is also an ingredient of plaster and stucco and of many paints and putties. This "mineral of a thousand uses"—an obsolete nickname: the present count stands at around 3,000 uses—is probably present in some form or other in every home, school, office building, and factory in this country. Used in brake linings and clutch facings, in mufflers and gaskets, in sealants and caulking, and extensively used in ships, asbestos is also a component of every modern vehicle, including space ships.

This is taken from the *Encyclopedia Britannica:*

> *asbestos,* mineral fibre occurring in nature in fibrous form. It is obtained from certain types of asbestos rock, chiefly the chrysotile variety of the serpentine groups of minerals, by mining or quarrying. Valued since ancient times for its resistance to fire, asbestos fibre achieved commercial importance in the 19th century. The fibre is freed by crushing the rock and is then separated from the surrounding material, usually by a blowing process.

$500 million in annual sales by Olinkraft Corporation, a 1979 acquisition. Exhibit 6.2 illustrates Manville's sales and earnings pattern from 1977 through 1982 while Exhibits 6.3, 6.4, and 6.5 include various financial summaries.

On August 26, 1982, Manville filed for reorganization under Chapter 11 of the U.S. Bankruptcy Code. The Supreme Court had already declared the law unconstitutional but had extended the period during which it remained in effect to give Congress time to remedy the situation. On December 24, 1982, the extension of time ran out. By that time, however, Manville was well into the Chapter 11 process. In early 1983, the company publicized a skeleton outline of its desired reorganization plan.

HISTORICAL SKETCH

Henry Ward Johns, an inventor and entrepreneur, died of "dust phthisis pneumonitis" (probably asbestosis) in 1898. Johns' son Henry combined the company his father had founded with Manville Covering Company and con-

Exhibit 6.2 SALES AND EARNINGS (all figures in 1981 dollars)

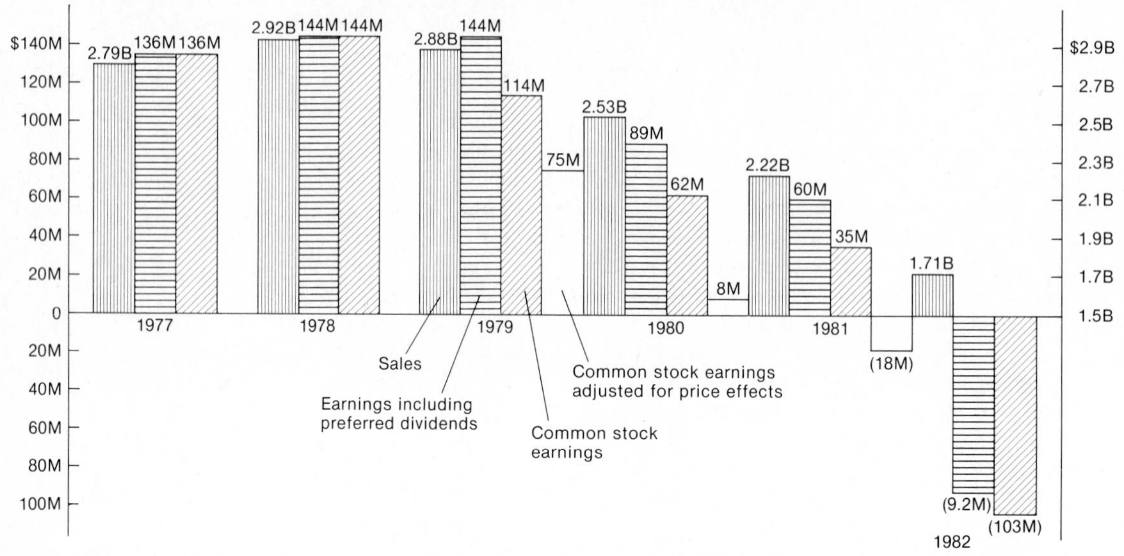

$140M
120M
100M
80M
60M
40M
20M
0
20M
40M
60M
80M
100M

2.79B 136M 136M
1977
2.92B 144M 144M
1978
2.88B 144M 114M 75M
1979
2.53B 89M 62M 8M
1980
2.22B 60M 35M (18M)
1981
1.71B (9.2M) (103M)
1982

$2.9B
2.7B
2.5B
2.3B
2.1B
1.9B
1.7B
1.5B

Sales
Earnings including preferred dividends
Common stock earnings
Common stock earnings adjusted for price effects

SOURCE: Annual reports for data through 1981; news accounts in *Wall Street Journal* for 1982 data; U.S. Bureau of Labor Statistics for CPI data.

tinued the mining of asbestos and the development and manufacture of asbestos products. Manville opened its first asbestos products plant in Hillsborough, New Jersey in 1912. The company went public and was listed on the New York Stock Exchange in 1927.

At about that time, the first of a continuing stream of asbestos health lawsuits were filed. Manville aggressively defended the early lawsuits, was able to minimize publicity about the dangers of asbestos, and continued to grow and prosper. The company consistently earned profits and paid dividends on its common stock, except for one year in the depths of the Depression and the period of financial crisis beginning in 1982. Appendix A describes Manville's acquisition and divestiture activities through 1975.

In the 1960s, several of Manville's older directors died or retired. Among them were A. R. Fisher and E. M. Voorhees, senior Manville officials since before 1930. (Both Fisher and Voorhees were involved in the early asbestos lawsuits. Also, Fisher was chief executive in the fifties and early sixties.) Compared to the 1966 Board of Directors, the 1969 Board contained a majority of new members. Departing from a tradition of promotion from within, in 1969 Manville brought in an outsider, psychologist Richard Goodwin, to a top management position. The next year, the Board of Directors

Exhibit 6.3

MANVILLE CORPORATION INCOME STATEMENTS
(Thousands of Dollars)

	1982 6 mos	1981	1980	1979	1978
Sales	$ 949,243	$2,186,005	$2,266,804	$2,276,429	$1,648,599
Cost of sales	783,860	1,730,678	1,771,448	1,747,031	1,190,318
Selling, gen. & admin. exp.	142,982	270,600	263,487	238,964	193,401
R & D and engineering exp.	16,136	33,820	34,801	31,100	32,551
Operating income	$ 6,265	$ 150,907	$ 197,068	$ 259,334	$ 232,329
Other income, net	1,283	34,674	25,547	20,933	27,990
Interest expense	35,048	72,661	65,379	62,441	22,255
Total income	$ (27,500)	$ 112,290	$ 157,236	$ 217,826	$ 238,064
Income taxes	2,400	52,600	76,600	103,220	116,462
Net income before extraord. items	$ 25,100	$ 60,320	$ 80,636	$ 114,606	$ 121,602
Div. on preferred stock	12,495	24,987	24,919	23,553	0
Extraordinary item	0	0	0	0	0
Net income avail. for common stock	$(37,595)	$ 35,333	$ 55,717	$ 91,053	$ 121,602

Exhibit 6.3 ***(Continued)***

1977	1976	1975	1974	1973	1972	1971	1970
$1,461,432	$1,308,771	$1,107,012	$1,105,508	$905,417	$796,325	$685,123	$578,157
1,066,310	983,431	852,786	838,462	674,130	584,843	500,757	433,192
173,659	166,159	176,235	170,817	152,394	134,009	116,789	93,355
28,174	25,236	0	0	0	0	0	0
$ 193,289	$ 133,945	$ 77,991	$ 96,229	$ 78,893	$ 77,473	$ 67,577	$ 46,610
18,363	(17,571)	10,737	6,731	16,230	8,439	10,037	8,958
20,105	15,153	18,990	15,798	8,852	3,749	1,551	0
$ 191,547	$ 101,221	$ 69,738	$ 87,162	$ 86,271	$ 82,163	$ 76,063	$ 55,568
88,920	47,804	31,325	36,549	30,487	32,892	30,745	22,140
$ 102,627	$ 53,417	$ 38,413	$ 50,613	$ 55,784	$ 49,271	$ 45,318	$ 33,428
0	0	0	0	0	0	0	0
0	0	0	(21,270)	0	0	(2,594)	0
$ 102,627	$ 53,417	$ 38,413	$ 71,883	$ 55,784	$ 49,271	$ 42,724	$ 33,428

SOURCE: Annual Reports and June 30, 1982 10-Q Report.

NOTE: "Asbestos health costs" of $12,756,000 for 1981 were excluded by the company from "Selling, gen. & admin. exp." but are included here.

Exhibit 6.4

MANVILLE CORPORATION BALANCE SHEETS AS OF JUNE 30
(Thousands of Dollars)

	1982	1981	1980	1979	1978
ASSETS					
Cash	$ 9,708	$ 14,081	$ 19,699	$ 18,692	$ 28,161
Marketable securities	17,059	12,013	12,186	10,023	37,868
Accounts & notes receivable	347,583	326,635	350,136	361,635	327,621
Inventories	182,215	211,129	216,749	228,988	219,249
Prepaid expenses	19,294	18,810	20,132	30,768	31,871
Total current assets	$ 575,859	$ 582,668	$ 618,902	$ 650,124	$ 644,770
Property, plant & equipment					
Land & land improvements		119,174	117,671	114,413	98,512
Buildings		363,308	357,102	352,185	320,665
Machinery & equipment		1,202,490	1,204,275	1,160,697	1,042,715
		$1,684,972	$1,679,048	$1,627,295	$1,461,892
Less: Accum. depreciation and depletion		(524,747)	(484,397)	(430,448)	(373,926)
		$1,160,225	$1,194,651	$1,196,847	$1,087,996
Timber & timberland, Less: cost of timber harvested		406,205	407,463	367,771	371,662
	$1,522,606	$1,566,430	$1,602,114	$1,564,618	$1,459,628
Invest. & adv. to assoc. cos.		0	0	0	0
Real est. sub. invest. & adv.		0	0	0	0
Other assets	148,423	148,716	117,143	109,638	112,557
Total assets	$2,246,888	$2,297,814	$2,338,159	$2,324,380	$2,216,955
LIABILITIES					
Short-term debts		$ 29,437	$ 21,749	$ 32,408	$ 23,367
Accounts payable	190,939	120,295	125,722	142,575	113,710
Comp. & employee benefits		77,477	80,191	53,537	44,678
Income taxes		30,335	21,663	50,598	84,147
Anticipated relocation costs		0	0	0	0
Other liabilities	148,642	58,031	60,946	49,727	63,390
Total current liabilities	$ 339,581	$ 315,575	$ 310,271	$ 328,845	$ 329,292
Long-term debt	498,665	507,620	519,144	532,377	543,244
Other non-current liabilities	92,564	86,411	75,430	72,644	60,497
Deferred income taxes	185,526	184,924	210,997	194,642	150,274
Total liabilities	$1,116,376	$1,094,530	$1,115,842	$1,128,508	$1,083,307

SOURCE: Annual Reports and June 30, 1982 10-Q Report.

1977	1976	1975	1974	1973	1972	1971	1970
$ 39,471	$ 25,064	$ 23,981	$ 11,829	$ 19,312	$ 18,125	$ 23,816	$ 18,274
120,553	66,132	391	5,412	1,379	6,098	35,360	37,948
262,655	239,318	205,784	187,688	171,443	147,053	112,572	99,159
148,711	144,379	145,463	160,737	117,097	94,392	89,077	65,269
29,872	26,084	20,604	20,133	14,885	19,582	25,410	13,203
$ 601,262	$ 500,977	$ 396,223	$385,799	$324,116	$285,250	$286,235	$233,853
63,674							
263,938							
642,384							
$ 969,996	$ 920,891	$ 896,873	$800,705	$728,652	$667,689	$578,917	$521,021
(336,648)	(326,887)	(316,148)	(295,962)	(285,241)	(290,728)	(276,353)	(270,069)
$ 633,348	$ 594,004	$ 580,725	$504,743	$443,411	$376,961	$302,564	$250,952
0	0	0	0	0	0	0	0
$ 633,348	$ 594,004	$ 580,725	$504,743	$443,411	$376,961	$302,564	$250,952
25,003	28,794	37,295	40,568	39,727	38,210	30,841	24,634
34,894	34,088	21,577	17,126	17,259	15,958	17,276	5,264
39,293	30,337	41,560	38,652	26,462	19,949	16,793	13,815
$1,333,800	$1,188,200	$1,077,380	$986,888	$850,975	$736,328	$653,709	$528,518
$ 18,459	$ 20,380	$ 70,327	$ 53,567	$ 69,243	$ 54,345	$ 0	$ 0
68,657	57,954	53,277	43,572	44,803	36,055	36,780	24,062
36,845	31,582	31,274	35,314	32,247	31,878	39,972	40,202
68,075	42,253	30,861	37,921	19,418	22,716	35,662	24,771
0	0	0	0	0	0	0	0
43,044	36,999	23,299	24,704	21,185	16,445	21,847	0
$ 235,080	$ 189,168	$ 209,038	$195,078	$186,896	$161,439	$134,261	$ 89,035
203,249	208,161	186,322	141,896	81,700	40,732	20,207	0
23,301	10,731	9,277	7,936	7,888	9,666	13,757	10,599
129,759	108,125	92,281	80,541	68,634	47,900	32,900	23,218
$ 591,389	$ 516,185	$ 496,918	$425,451	$345,118	$259,737	$201,125	$122,852

(Continued)

***Exhibit 6.4* (*Continued*)**

	1982	1981	1980	1979	1978
STOCKHOLDERS' EQUITY					
Preferred ($1.00 par)	$ 300,800	$ 300,800	$ 300,429	$ 299,451	$ 298,891
Common ($2.50 par)	60,071	59,102	57,526	208,370	197,413
Capital in excess of par	178,052	173,950	163,594	0	0
Retained earnings	641,666	695,362	704,725	692,420	643,317
Cum. currency translation adj.	(46,562)	(22,443)	0	0	0
Less: cost of treasury stock	(3,475)	(3,487)	(3,957)	(4,369)	(5,973)
Total stockholders' equity	$1,130,552	$1,203,284	$1,222,317	$1,195,872	$1,133,648
Total liab. & stockholder's equity	$2,246,888	$2,297,814	$2,338,159	$2,324,380	$2,216,955

voted to move long-time President C. B. Burnett to Chairman and install Goodwin as President and Chief Executive Officer. Goodwin led the company through at least twenty acquisitions and several divestitures, increasing the company's profit and sales but also increasing long-term debt, from zero in 1970 to $196 million in 1975.

Goodwin arranged to purchase the 10,000-acre Ken-Caryl Ranch near Denver in 1971, moved the company there from New York, and made plans to construct a luxurious "World Headquarters." The first phase of the project was to cost $182.2 million, 45% of Manville's net worth. The magazine *Industrial Development* called the Manville plan "a study in corporate environmental concern." *Fortune* magazine quotes Goodwin as saying, "A company's headquarters is its signature. I wanted a new signature for J-M that, frankly, would attract attention—that would tell everybody, including ourselves, that things were changing."

Things did change. With the asbestos problem growing out of control, and with the company having lost the first of many asbestos lawsuits, Manville turned back to one of its own—its chief legal officer—for leadership. In what *Fortune* magazine called "The Shoot-Out at the J-M Corral," Goodwin was deposed without explanation, and J. A. McKinney was installed as President in September 1976. In his 1977 "President's Review," McKinney charted the new course:

> We believe we can further improve the fundamental economics of a number of our operations and we will be working toward that end in the year to come. . . .
>
> Asbestos fiber, while contributing substantially to earnings, has assumed a less important position with the earnings growth of our other basic businesses. Although its profitability is expected to improve in the long term with reviving European economies, we do not expect asbestos fiber to

1977	1976	1975	1974	1973	1972	1971	1970
$ 0	$ 0	$ 0	$ 0	$ 0	$ 0	$ 0	$ 0
188,493	188,493	124,635	124,635	124,674	124,728	123,472	119,539
0	0	0	0	0	0	0	0
561,019	492,153	466,866	452,393	407,323	379,368	348,098	306,045
0	0	0	0	0	0	0	0
(7,101)	(8,631)	(11,039)	(15,591)	(26,140)	(27,505)	(18,986)	(19,918)
$ 742,411	$ 672,015	$ 580,462	$561,437	$505,857	$476,591	$452,584	$405,666
$1,333,800	$1,188,200	$1,077,380	$986,888	$850,975	$736,328	$653,709	$528,518

dominate J-M earnings to the extent that it has in the past. . . .

We have also consolidated and repositioned some businesses for more profitable growth and phased out others not important to the future direction of the company. . . .

We have begun aggressively to seek out opportunities for growth. One example is the previously announced $200 million capital expansion program which will, by 1980, double U.S. fiber glass capacity over the 1976 levels. . . . We continue seeking still other growth possibilities that would markedly change the Johns-Manville profile, possibly through substantial acquisitions. . . .

Our main thrust in 1978 will be to continue improving profitability by maintaining our expense control and pricing vigilance, by adding volume to below-capacity businesses, by better utilizing existing capacity and by adding capacity in sold-out businesses.

THE OLINKRAFT ACQUISITION

When that was written, Manville had already begun to seek a large merger candidate—a "substantial acquisition"—employing the services of the investment banking firm of Morgan Stanley to assist in the search. Using criteria provided by Manville, Morgan Stanley proposed two possibilities: Ideal Basic Industries, a producer of portland cement and potash, and Olinkraft Corporation, a forest products company.

The president of Ideal Basic Industries, John A. Love, had been a Manville director since 1976. The Ideal Basic Industries board decided in May 1978 not to authorize its officers to begin merger negotiations with Manville.

On July 13, 1978, it was announced that Texas Eastern and Olinkraft were discussing a merger. The next day, Morgan Stanley's arbitrage department began purchases of Olinkraft stock which totaled 149,200 shares. On July 17, Texas Eastern announced an offer of $51 per share for Olinkraft stock.

Exhibit 6.5

REVENUES AND INCOME FROM OPERATIONS BY BUSINESS SEGMENT
(Thousands of Dollars)

	1981	1980	1979	1978	1977	1976
Revenues						
Fiberglass products	$ 625,300	$ 610,071	$ 573,198	$ 514,287	$ 407,242	$ 357,823
Forest products	554,612	508,199	497,398	0	0	0
Non-fiberglass insulations	257,508	279,449	267,862	231,190	195,223	158,721
Roofing products	208,890	249,996	272,677	253,807	203,612	171,197
Pipe products & systems	199,322	220,084	304,856	303,334	273,512	217,526
Asbestos fiber	138,340	158,946	168,199	157,291	160,682	154,625
Industrial & spec. products	320,124	340,935	308,390	290,845	301,173	309,450
Corporate revenues, net	11,898	9,024	11,020	19,894	12,447	(22,574)
Intersegment sales	(95,315)	(84,353)	(106,238)	(94,059)	(74,096)	(55,568)
Total	$2,220,679	$2,292,351	$2,297,362	$1,676,589	$1,479,795	$1,291,200
Income from operations						
Fiberglass products	89,760	91,060	95,650	107,279	81,661	59,823
Forest products	39,434	37,001	50,320	0	0	0
Non-fiberglass insulations	19,964	26,606	27,190	35,484	28,237	18,457
Roofing products	(17,455)	9,417	14,360	23,219	13,754	8,363
Pipe products & systems	(355)	(4,773)	17,983	25,861	23,552	(2,688)
Asbestos fiber	36,821	35,048	56,477	54,592	59,815	60,237
Industrial & spec. products	50,321	54,634	43,474	35,911	25,431	18,741
Corporate expense, net	(23,335)	(37,756)	(23,436)	(22,971)	(24,290)	(48,566)
Eliminations & adj.	3,182	11,378	(1,751)	944	3,492	1,997
Total	$ 198,337	$ 222,615	$ 280,267	$ 260,319	$ 211,652	$ 116,374

	1975	1974	1973	1972
Revenues				
Thermal insulation	$ 323,134	$ 294,445	$159,654	$124,762
Pipe products & systems	192,416	231,794	164,106	147,348
General building products	166,462	172,773	383,965	347,472
Roofing products	169,928	168,122		
Industrial & other products	114,212	120,692	100,731	90,990
Mining & minerals	140,860	117,682	96,961	88,134
Non-products related earnings	0	0	0	0
Total	$1,107,012	$1,105,508	$905,417	$798,706
Income from operations				
Thermal insulation	23,098	15,273	8,437	5,568
Pipe products & systems	(3,817)	23,439	6,551	15,082
General building products	2,390	7,407	42,399	39,590
Roofing products	17,367	18,127		
Industrial & other products	10,883	7,215	10,774	3,792
Mining & minerals	20,838	22,446	18,236	19,823
Non-products related earnings	(1,021)	(6,745)	(126)	(1,137)
Total	$ 69,738	$ 87,162	$ 86,271	$ 82,718

Morgan Stanley had obtained internal—Olinkraft later said "inaccurate"—earnings projections from Olinkraft in connection with a merger analysis done a year earlier for Kennecott Copper. The earnings projections were $43.8 million in 1979, $63.6 million in 1980 and $73 million in 1981. Exhibit 6.6 provides actual earnings information for Olinkraft.

Olinkraft stock sold for a high of $34.875 in the second quarter of 1978. In September, after receiving the earnings estimates from Morgan Stanley, Manville offered $57 per share. Texas Eastern then raised its offer to $60. When Manville offered $65 per share, however, Texas Eastern bowed out.

Articles in *The Economist* and *The Wall Street Journal* suggested that Morgan Stanley may have compromised its integrity by supplying Manville the Olinkraft earnings estimates while at the same time taking a heavy arbitrage position in Olinkraft stock. Morgan Stanley maintained that it acted responsibly. A Morgan Stanley spokesman said that the company prevents compromises by maintaining a "Chinese wall" between the Merger and Acquisition and the Arbitrage departments.

OLINKRAFT, INC., AND CONSOLIDATED SUBSIDIARIES: SUMMARY OF OPERATIONS

Exhibit 6.6

	1976	1977	1978 6 mos
Net sales	$ 341,861	$ 381,226	$ 215,316
Other income	6,266	5,778	4,297
	$ 248,127	$ 387,004	$ 219,613
Cost of sales	$ 238,460	$ 276,371	$ 157,504
Depreciation & depletion	18,597	22,020	11,924
Selling, G & A	30,078	32,194	17,569
Interest	5,964	9,502	6,417
Interest capitalized	(96)	(2,777)	(3,018)
Other	3,508	5,358	2,620
Income taxes	18,047	9,740	6,611
	$ 314,558	$ 352,408	$ 199,627
Net income	$ 33,569	$ 34,596	$ 19,986
Earnings per share	$ 4.00	$ 3.91	$ 2.23
Dividends per share	$ 1.02½	$ 1.12½	$ 0.60
Common shares	8,401,071	8,859,280	8,958,148

SOURCE: December 1978 Joint Proxy Statement.
NOTE: Dollar figures in thousands except per share data.

Olinkraft and Manville completed their agreement in December 1978. The purchase price was $595 million. This was 2.24 times Olinkraft's June 1978 book value of $266 million and over twice the average total market value of Olinkraft's stock in 1978's first half.

Approximately half of the purchase price was paid in cash and the other half with preferred stock. That preferred stock was described in the 1978 Annual Report:

> On January 19, 1979, the Company issued 4,598,327 shares of cumulative preferred stock, $5.40 series, to consummate the acquisition of Olinkraft. . . .
>
> Under a mandatory sinking fund provision, the Company is required to redeem the $5.40 preferred series between 1987 and 2009 at $65 per share plus accrued dividends. The annual redemption requirements will consist of varying percentages applied to the number of outstanding shares on October 20, 1986, as follows: 5% annually from 1987 through 1996, 4% annually from 1997 through 2007, and 3% in 2008. All remaining outstanding shares are required to be redeemed in 2009.

MANVILLE CORPORATION COMMON STOCK PRICE AND TRADING VOLUME
(Thousands of Dollars)

Exhibit 6.7

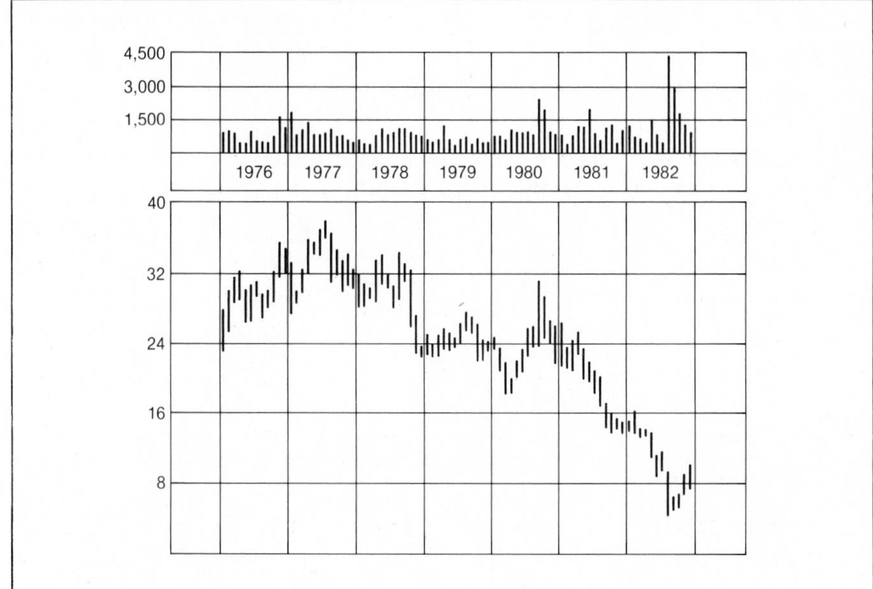

While the Olinkraft merger was being negotiated, Manville common stock declined in market value to a low of $22.125, a total decrease of over $225 million (see Exhibit 6.7). Of course, Olinkraft's stock rose to approximate the proposed acquisition price of $65 a share.

The merger was consummated on January 19, 1979. The "purchase method" of accounting was used. Essentially, the book values of Olinkraft's assets were adjusted upward by the amount by which the purchase price exceeded net worth. Exhibit 6.8 shows the adjusted and unadjusted balance sheet values.

For a time, Olinkraft's previous management stayed in power and the Olinkraft chief executive, John D. Mullins, served on the Manville Board of Directors. As financial conditions worsened in 1981 and 1982, Olinkraft top managers were replaced.

MANVILLE IN 1978

The following excerpts from the 1978 and 1979 Annual Reports describe Manville's several divisions:

> *Fiberglass products:* Residential insulations account for the largest portion of the product line, with commercial and industrial insulations and fiberglass making up the rest. . . . J-M increased production capacity by 18 percent at its eleven U.S. fiberglass insulation manufacturing facilities. . . .

PURCHASE METHOD MERGER ACCOUNTING: OLINKRAFT BALANCE SHEETS

Exhibit 6.8

	Adjusted	*Unadjusted*
Current assets	$137,557	$119,610
Investments in and advances to associated companies	6,886	6,078
Property, plant, and equipment	700,633	372,761
Deferred charges and other assets	799	3,513
	$845,857	$501,962
Current liabilities	$ 83,912	$ 67,793
Long-term debt	141,258	141,295
Other non-current liabilities	25,159	26,678
	$250,329	$235,766
Net worth	$596,546	$266,196

SOURCE: December 31, 1978 Manville-Olinkraft Joint Proxy Statement and Manville 1978 Annual Report.

through a plant modernization and expansion program started in 1977 that will double insulation production capacity by 1981. . . . New home construction represented 55 percent of the total market while [insulation for existing homes] . . . accounted for 45 percent. . . .

Non-fiberglass insulations: This business segment includes roof insulations, refractory fibers, calcium silicate insulation, and a broad range of other commercial and industrial insulating products. . . . Roof insulation production capacity will increase 30 percent. . . .

Pipe products and systems: Major products in this business segment are polyvinyl chloride (PVC) plastic pipe and asbestos cement (A-C) pipe. The company . . . will expand PVC production capacity by 17 percent during 1979 at six of its nine U.S. plants at a cost of $9 million. . . . The A-C pipe business operated at 70 percent of its six-day capacity.

Roofing products: The roofing products segment includes residential shingles and built-up roofing for commercial and industrial structures. New construction accounts for 40 percent of sales. Reroofing represents 60 percent. . . . J-M continued its gradual conversion in 1978 to fiberglass matt rather than organic materials as the base for its roofing products. . . . Several manufacturing facilities were modified in 1978 to accommodate fiberglass roofing production. . . . J-M is investing another $6.6 million to add fiberglass rolled roofing machines at three locations in 1980. . . . Fiberglass products are also expected to give J-M a competitive advantage in all roofing markets.

> *Asbestos fiber:* The asbestos fiber business area in 1978 performed better than anticipated but revenues and income from operations dropped from the 1977 level. . . . Asbestos fiber is sold in markets throughout the world. A major portion of the fiber sold is used as a raw material in products where the fiber is locked in place by cement, rubber, plastics, resins, asphalts, and similar bindings. Products include asbestos cement products, brake linings, resilient flooring, roofing, and other products that require strength and fire protection, heat resistance, dimensional stability, and resistance to rust and rot. In these applications, asbestos fiber poses no hazard to users or the public. . . . Other factors impacting performance included a decrease in the value of the Canadian dollar, shortfalls in selling certain grades of asbestos fiber and higher than planned expenses. . . . Although the asbestos fiber market in general experienced some price erosion in 1978, J-M was able to maintain its price levels in most areas. . . . A $77 million program designed to improve working operations at Jeffrey [the world's largest asbestos mine] completed its third year.
>
> *Industrial and specialty products and services:* A diverse group of businesses that have as its principal areas: Holophane lighting systems, filtration and minerals [comprised of diatomite, perlite, and fiberglass filter products] and industrial specialties. . . . The company's major diatomite mine is in Lompoc, California and J-M operates smaller facilities in France, Mexico, and Spain. . . . Perlite is mined at No Agua, New Mexico and is used by J-M in the manufacture of Fesco Board roof insulation. Other uses are in acoustical ceiling tile, horticultural applications, and in cryogenic insulations.
>
> *Forest products:* Forest products include clay-coated unbleached Kraft and other paperboards; corrugated containers; beverage carriers and folding cartons; Kraft bags; pine lumber, plywood, and particleboard; and hardwood veneer and flooring.

The dozens of asbestos injury lawsuits in the twenties and thirties, scores during the forties and fifties, and hundreds in the sixties and early seventies became thousands in the late seventies. Although the asbestos litigation was not mentioned in Manville's 1977 Annual Report, it was described, as the law required, in the company's 1977 Form 10K, submitted to the Securities and Exchange Commission in April 1978. The 10K reports 623 asbestos lawsuits against Manville, some of them multi-plaintiff cases involving many claimants. The claims for which amounts are given total $2.79 billion. The 1980 Form 10K reports that during 1978, there were 780 new suits involving 996 new asbestos disease claimants. In 1979, according to the 10K, this grew to 1,692 new suits and 2,352 claimants.

The dangers of asbestos were widely publicized in 1978. In February 1978, a federal court in Beaumont, Texas approved a $20 million settlement of lawsuits by asbestos workers against several asbestos companies. Health, Education and Welfare (HEW) Secretary Califano estimated that between

8.5 million and 11 million workers had been exposed to asbestos since World War II. In April 1978, HEW announced it was warning present and former asbestos workers and their doctors about the hazards of asbestos. The U.S. Surgeon General sent 400,000 warning letters to the nation's doctors. In May, the Raybestos-Manhattan correspondence (to be discussed later) was obtained by asbestos plaintiff lawyers and became generally available.

In June, the Environmental Protection Agency established limits for airborne asbestos caused by building demolition. In October, several asbestos manufacturers were accused of conspiracy to conceal and distort reports on the health dangers of asbestos and were sued for $1 billion in a class-action suit. Then, in December, the Environmental Defense Fund claimed that millions of school children had been exposed to cancer-causing levels of asbestos because of use of the product in school construction.

Manville's asbestos health costs were relatively insignificant (less than one-half percent of sales until 1981). But asbestos use, especially in the U.S., sharply declined after 1978. The loss of asbestos profits was compounded by a deep recession in housing and other construction, which began in mid-1978 and was to last through 1982.

MANVILLE'S KNOWLEDGE OF THE DANGERS OF ASBESTOS

Six pages of Manville's 1978 Annual Report and over half of J. A. McKinney's "Chairman's Message" were devoted to the personal injury lawsuits. Excerpts from these documents follow:

Mr. McKinney's Argument

> During the past year a great deal of publicity has appeared in the media about asbestos health hazards—most of it attacking the corporation and nearly all of it needlessly inflammatory. Your corporation has acted honorably over the years and has led the asbestos industry, medical science and the federal government in identifying and seeking to eliminate asbestos health problems. . . .
>
> Individuals exposed to asbestos-containing insulation materials are particular victims of the incomplete knowledge of earlier years. . . . It was not until 1964 that the particular risk to this category of worker [insulation workers] was clearly identified by Dr. Irving J. Selikoff of Mt. Sinai Hospital in New York City. . . .
>
> Media representatives and some elected officials have consistently ignored J-M's intensive efforts to solve asbestos health problems and, in fact, have untruthfully portrayed those efforts. . . .
>
> Litigation is based upon a finding of fault, and with respect to asbestos-related disease, there simply is no fault on the part of J-M, a fact increasingly recognized by juries throughout the nation. Litigation is, of course, favored and fostered by lawyers in search of lucrative fees and by "media personalities" in search of sensational stories. . . .

In his 1980 "Chairman's Message" Mr. McKinney says, "You can be assured that we will continue to be aggressive in asserting our defenses."

Another View

By 1929, Manville was successfully defending the first asbestos disease lawsuits. Manville's outside attorneys for the early cases were the Newark, New Jersey law firm of Hobart and Menard. On December 15, 1934, George Hobart, of that firm, wrote to Vandiver Brown, Manville's corporate Secretary and in-house attorney,

> . . . it is only within a comparatively recent time that asbestosis has been recognized by the medical and scientific professions as a disease—in fact, one of our principal defenses in actions against the company on the common law theory of negligence has been that the scientific and medical knowledge has been insufficient until a very recent period to place on the owners of plants or factories the burden or duty of taking special precautions against the possible onset of the disease in their employees.

On October 3, 1935, Mr. Brown wrote the following statement to Sumner Simpson, president of Raybestos-Manhattan Corporation: "I quite agree that our interests are best served by having asbestosis receive the minimum of publicity." He was commenting upon a letter written to Mr. Simpson by Anne Rossiter, the editor of *Asbestos,* an industry trade journal. She wrote,

> You may recall that we have written you on several occasions concerning the publishing of information [about] or discussion of, asbestosis. . . . Always you have requested that for obvious reasons, we publish nothing, and, naturally your wishes have been respected.

The letters mentioned above are part of what has been called the Raybestos-Manhattan Papers. These papers consist of hundreds of documents which were obtained by plaintiff lawyers in a South Carolina case in 1978. In ordering a new trial, the judge in that case wrote,

> The Raybestos-Manhattan correspondence reveals written evidence that Raybestos-Manhattan and Johns-Manville exercised an editorial prerogative over the publication of the first study of the asbestos industry which they sponsored in 1935. It further reflects a conscious effort by the industry in the 1930s to downplay, or arguably suppress, the dissemination of information to employees and the public for fear of the promotion of law suits. . . .
>
> On two separate occasions, September 1977, pursuant to subpoena duces tecum, and December 1977, pursuant to a Request to Produce, plaintiff sought to discover the Raybestos correspondence in question. . . . it is uncontroverted that the same documents were produced in April 1977, in a New Jersey asbestos lawsuit. . . .
>
> It is also clear that the defendant, Johns-Manville, upon whom the Decem-

> ber Request to Produce was also served, had in its possession since April 1977, the Raybestos correspondence, which also involved its corporate agents.

Also among the Raybestos-Manhattan papers was a report of an X-ray study done by Dr. Kenneth Wallace Smith. Smith was Manville's physician and Medical Director from 1945 through 1966 (except for one year). In 1949, the report shows, Dr. Smith examined 708 men who worked in a Manville asbestos plant. Of these, 704 had evidence of lung damage. The four with negative X-rays each had less than four years exposure to asbestos dust. The report continues:

> Of the 708 men, seven had X-ray evidence of early asbestosis. . . . They have not been told of this diagnosis. For it is felt as long as the man feels well, is happy at home and at work, and his physical condition remains good, nothing should be said. . . . The fibrosis of this disease is irreversible and permanent. . . .
>
> There are seven cases of asbestosis and 52 cases in a "preasbestosis group." These 59 cases are probable compensation claims. . . . There are 475 men with [fibrosis extending beyond the lung roots] all of whom will show progressive fibrosis if allowed to continue working in dusty areas.

In a 1976 deposition, Dr. Smith testified that he became "knowledgeable of the relationship between the inhalation of asbestos fibers and the lung condition known as asbestosis" during his internship in 1941–1942, before he went to work for Manville. Following are excerpts from Dr. Smith's testimony:

> Q. Did you [tell other employees of Johns-Manville] of the relationship between the inhalation of asbestos fiber and the lung condition known as asbestosis?
>
> A. Many people at Canadian Johns-Manville in supervisory positions already knew about the association of inhalation of asbestos fibers and disease. I just amplified that [and] made much more explicit the disease process.
>
> Q. Did you or did you not have discussion with Mr. A. R. Fisher with respect to the relationship between the inhalation of asbestos fiber and the pulmonary lung condition known as asbestosis, both with respect to employees of Johns-Manville and what you defined as the civilian population?
>
> A. Definitely, we discussed the whole subject many times, about dust and what it does to people, whether they are employed or not employed. . . . The good Lord gave us all the same breathing apparatus and if the asbestos fiber is present and the housewife and the asbestos worker, and the fireman, and the jeweler, and doctor, and everybody else are all in the same room, they are all going to breathe the same dust. . . . So wherever there is dust and people are breathing dust they are going to have a potential hazard.

Q. Did you at any point . . . make any recommendations to anyone at Johns-Manville in respect to the utilization of a caution label for the asbestos-containing products?

A. Hugh Jackson and I sat down with many people in other divisions suggesting that similar caution labels should be put on products which when used could create airborne dust that could be inhaled.

Q. When did you sit down with Hugh Jackson and come to that conclusion?

A. It would be late 1952 and early 1953.

Q. What was the reason . . . the asbestos-containing products were not labeled with a caution label back in 1952?

A. It was business decision as far as I could understand . . . application of a caution label identifying a product as hazardous would cut out sales. There would be serious financial implications.

Q. Did you at any time recognize the relationship between the inhalation of asbestos fibers and pulmonary malignancies, as you phrased it, or lung cancer, or pleural cancer?

A. Yes, I have recognized the alleged and sometimes factual association of malignancy with the inhalation of asbestos fibers.

Q. When would that have been, Doctor, for the first time?

A. The first time would be in the late 1940s.

Q. Had there not been studies in Britain and perhaps even in the United States prior to the beginning of the Saranac Lake Laboratories studies [1936] which had indicated [that fibrous asbestos dust caused lung disease]?

A. Very definitely. As I recall, Merriweather and his cohorts studied the effects of the asbestos textile dust many years prior to 1935 and their publications are well-documented and available worldwide.

Dr. Smith died in 1977. In 1981, a Manville lawyer (appealing a $1.9 million damage award to asbestos victim Edward Janssens) argued that the Smith deposition should not have been admitted in court. The attorney said, "J-M made a conscious policy decision not to cross-examine Dr. Smith as fully as it otherwise would have. For example, Johns-Manville decided against examining Dr. Smith regarding the fact that he was an alcoholic and under psychiatric care."

Another Manville executive, Wilbur L. Ruff, who had worked for Manville from 1929 through 1972, much of the time as plant manager at a number of Manville plants, gave an extensive deposition in 1979. Excerpts follow:

Q. Do you know whether in fact, abnormal chest findings ever were discussed with any employee of the Johns-Manville plant . . . ?

A. I know of no specific cases.

Q. Was there a policy at that time not to talk to the employees about chest findings, findings that suggested asbestosis, pneumoconiosis, or mesothelioma [asbestos cancer]?

A. That was the policy.

Q. When did the policy change?

A. In the early 1970s.

Q. Have you on other occasions, Mr. Ruff, referred to this policy that we have been discussing as a hush-hush policy?

A. Yes.

Q. Were you aware that it was company policy back in the late forties that if a man had asbestosis or industrial lung diseases that nothing would be said to him until he actually became disabled?

A. That's the way it was done.

Q. You were aware that was the company policy?

A. Whether it was policy or not, it was somebody's decision.

In 1957, the Industrial Health Foundation proposed a study on asbestos and cancer to be funded by the Asbestos Textile Institute (made up of asbestos manufacturers). The proposal was rejected by Manville and the others at the March 1957 meeting of the Institute. The minutes report, "There is a feeling among certain members that such an investigation would stir up a hornets' nest and put the whole industry under suspicion."

In 1963, Dr. I. J. Selikoff of Mt. Sinai Medical Center in New York completed an extensive study of asbestos and health. Minutes of the Asbestos Textile Institute's Air Hygiene Committee meeting of June 6, 1963 includes the following:

> The committee was advised that a Dr. Selikoff will read at the next meeting of the AMA in about 30 days a paper on a study he has made of about 1,500 workers, largely in asbestos insulation application, showing a very large incidence of lung cancer over normal expectations.

It was after the Selikoff study and the resulting symposia and publications that Manville first began to place caution labels on its asbestos products. The labels read,

> This product contains asbestos fiber.
>
> Inhalation of asbestos in excessive quantities over long periods of time may be harmful.
>
> If dust is created when the product is handled, avoid breathing the dust.
>
> If adequate ventilation control is not possible, wear respirators approved by the U.S. Bureau of Mines for pneumoconiosis producing dust.

In upholding a landmark 1972 District Court decision against Manville and other asbestos defendants, the New Orleans U.S. Court of Appeals stated,

> Asbestosis has been recognized as a disease for well over fifty years. . . . By the mid-1930s the hazard of asbestosis as a pneumoconiotic dust was universally accepted. Cases of asbestosis in insulation workers were reported in this country as early as 1934. . . . The evidence . . . tended to establish that none of the defendants ever tested its product to determine its effect on industrial insulation workers. . . . Indeed the evidence tended to establish that the defendants gave no instructions or warnings at all.

The court quoted Johns-Manville's caution label (above) and wrote,

> It should be noted that none of these so called "cautions" intimated the gravity of the risk: the danger of a fatal illness caused by asbestosis and mesothelioma or other cancers. The mild suggestion that inhalation of asbestos in excessive quantities over a long period of time may be harmful conveys no idea of the extent of the danger.

STRATEGIES OF THE EIGHTIES

The 1979 Annual Report states, "Johns-Manville has a strategy for the early 80's . . . and the commitment to succeed. . . . J-M's strategic plan embraces three major goals":

> Goal 1: To rebuild our financial reserves. . . . As expected, the Olinkraft acquisition burdened our financial resources. . . . For this reason, our most immediate short-term goal is to improve and increase the financial strength of J-M's balance sheet. We will accomplish this by increasing productivity and using the better levels of cash flow that result to provide for most of our new capital needs.
>
> Goal 2: To improve productivity and cost efficiencies. . . . We will look for ways to increase the output of our manufacturing processes, concentrating first on those projects promising the shortest payback periods. . . .
>
> Goal 3: To reaffirm J-M's position as a technological leader in terms of product performance and cost of production. . . . to increase the effort and money spent on improving manufacturing methods, enhancing the competitive strengths of present product lines and developing new products.

THE MANAGEMENT TEAM AND THEIR BENEFITS

After Richard Goodwin was expelled, top management continuity was maintained through the late seventies and eighties. The Chairman of the Board and Chief Executive Officer, J. A. McKinney; the President and Chief Operating Officer, Fred L. Pundsack; and all ten senior vice-presidents listed in the 1981 Annual Report also appear in the 1977 Annual Report. In fact, the five most highly paid executives of Manville, as shown in the March 1982 Proxy Statement, had all been with the company for twenty-nine or more years.

Only three of Manville's outside directors joined the board after the sixties. Except for brief service by John D. Mullins, former President of Olinkraft, no new director was added to Manville's board after 1976. Then, in May 1982, the existing directors were renominated.

Exhibit 6.9

EXECUTIVE BENEFITS REMUNERATION TABLE

		Cash & Cash Equivalent Forms of Remuneration		
Name of Individual or Number of Persons in Group	***Capacities in Which Served***	***Salaries, Fees, Directors' Fees, Commissions, Bonuses***	***Securities or Property, Insurance Benefits or Reimbursement Personal Benefits***	***Aggregate of Contingent Forms of Remuneration***
John A. McKinney	Chairman and Chief Executive Officer	$ 408,750	$ 11,821	$11,019
Fred L. Pundsack	President and Chief Operating Officer	$ 304,500	$ 9,515	$ 6,881
Chester E. Shepperly	Senior Vice-President	$ 248,125	$ 5,213	$ 5,099
Monroe Harris	Senior Vice-President	$ 197,150	$ 6,307	$ 1,322
Chester J. Sulewski	Senior Vice-President	$ 188,125	$ 6,298	$ 5,099
All present Directors and officers of the Corp. as a group (32 persons)		$3,882,995	$135,030	$87,071

A "Long-term Incentive Unit Plan" was adopted in 1978 to replace the executive stock option plan. At that time there were 390,950 options outstanding to purchase common stock at prices averaging about $28.00. By 1982, no officer or director of the corporation held any options under the Executive Incentive Program, having surrendered them "as a prerequisite to participation in the 'Long-term Incentive Unit Plan.' " Exhibits 6.9, 6.10, and 6.11 describe certain of the executive benefits which had been adopted by 1982 (information from the March 1982 Proxy Statement).

Special Termination Agreements

The Corporation has entered into Termination Agreements with 12 key employees including each of those individuals named in the Remuneration Table . . . upon any termination of their employment, other than termination for cause, which occurs at least sixty days prior to or within two years following a change in control of the Corporation, the terminated employee will be entitled to receive termination payments equal to one month's salary at the

EXECUTIVE BENEFITS RETIREMENT PLAN

Exhibit 6.10

Five-Year Average Final Salary + Bonuses	Annual Allowance for Representative Years of Credit Service: 20	25	30	35 or more
$200,000	$ 66,215	$ 82,769	$ 99,322	$115,876
300,000	101,643	127,054	152,465[a]	177,876[a]
400,000	137,072[a]	171,340[a]	205,608[a]	239,876[a]
500,000	172,501[a]	215,626[a]	258,751[a]	301,876[a]

[a] Retirement pay above the (current) $90,000 legal limit is to be paid by the corporation.

EXECUTIVE BENEFITS INCENTIVE UNITS

Exhibit 6.11

Cycle	J. A. McKinney	F. L. Pundsack	C. E. Shepperly	M. Harris	C. J. Sulewski	All Present Directors and Officers as a Group
1979–82	1,246	894	634	547	634	10,220
1980–83	1,358	1,118	691	642	691	11,173
1981–84	1,635	1,218	753	719	753	13,071
1982–85	1,775	1,318	828	794	813	14,687

rate in effect immediately prior to such termination for each year of credited service with the Corporation. . . .

Long-term Incentive Unit Plan

Units awarded to the individuals listed in the Remuneration Table for the four-year cycles indicated are shown in Exhibit 6.11. Each unit will have a minimum value of $25 and a maximum value of $175 if the goals set by the Compensation Committee are attained. Payments under a prior cycle to the individuals listed in the Remuneration Table amounted to: J. A. McKinney, $44,085; F. L. Pundsack, $31,664; C. E. Shepperly, $22,464; M. Harris, $19,397; C. J. Sulewski, $22,464; and all present officers and Directors as a group, including those named, $354,005.

Corporate Bonus Plan

The Corporate Bonus Plan provides that the Compensation Committee of the Board of Directors may approve cash bonuses to participants. . . . Aggregate cash awards for the five years ended December 31, 1981 under the Corporate Bonus Plan and predecessor plans were: J. A. McKinney,

$658,630; F. L. Pundsack, $520,666: C. E. Shepperly, $387,027; M. Harris, $334,856; C. J. Sulewski, $327,027; and all present officers and Directors as a group, including those named, $5,520,658. . . .

EMPLOYEE EARLY RETIREMENT PLAN

In June 1982, Manville announced an early retirement program for salaried employees with over 20 years service who were at least 55 years of age between June 1 and September 1, 1982. Employees electing retirement would get their regular retirement pay as if they had been 65 years of age as well as an extra amount to compensate for their being too young to receive Social Security payments. Fred L. Pundsack, 57 years old, then President of Manville Corporation, along with 632 other persons, retired early. Pundsack's retirement was announced in mid-August, a few days before the Chapter 11 filing.

The early retirement plan increased the actuarial deficiency in Manville's pension funds (in connection with the Olinkraft merger, Manville had reported a $6 million deficit in that fund). Manville's actuarial firm helped to design a funding plan to make up the deficit over a twenty-five-year period.

EVENTS LEADING UP TO THE BANKRUPTCY FILING

The 1981 Annual Report showed a number of non-recurring events and accounting changes which tended to elevate reported earnings. Among these were the following: (1) a $9 million increase in "Other Revenues" which resulted largely from the sale of mineral exploration rights on 586,000 acres of timberland obtained in the Olinkraft acquisition; (2) a $2.7 million increase in reported earnings due to the "reversal of a portion of the litigation reserves established at the time of the Olinkraft, Inc. acquisition"; (3) a $9.8 million increase in reported earnings because of a new way of reporting foreign currency transactions; (4) an unspecified amount due to "the sale during 1981 of eight container plants [which] occurred as part of [the] asset management program"; and (5) an $8.4 million increase in reported earnings brought about by "changes in certain actuarial assumptions in computing pension expense." Despite this, Exhibit 6.2 reveals continuously declining sales and profits after 1978, and an $18 million inflation corrected loss for 1981.

The earnings situation worsened in 1982, with the June 10-Q Report showing a $38 million loss applicable to common stock for the first half. Asbestos health costs for that period totaled $8.6 million, as compared to $12 million—0.55 percent of sales—for all of 1981. For just the second quarter of 1982, the reported loss was $26 million—an annual rate of $104 million—$5 million of which represented asbestos health costs. For the year, the loss was to total $97.6 million.

20%

Manville's mid-year 1982 10-Q Report describes the worsening situation with regard to asbestos claims:

> During the first half of 1982, J-M received an average of approximately 425 new cases per month brought by an average of approximately 495 new plaintiffs per month. . . .
>
> J-M was, for the first time in 1981, found liable by juries for punitive damages in five separate asbestos-related actions. [Punitive damages are payments above the actual damages sustained—intended to punish defendants.] All of these cases are presently subject to post-trial motions or appeals filed by J-M. The average of the punitive damages awarded against J-M in these five cases (one of which involved eleven plaintiffs) and the five cases decided during the first half of 1982 and discussed below is approximately $616,000 per case. . . .
>
> *Hansen v. Johns-Manville:* $1,060,000 in compensatory damages and $1,000,000 in punitive damages were assessed against J-M. . . .
>
> *Bunch v. Johns-Manville Corp.* A jury verdict of $420,000 in compensatory damages and $220,000 in punitive damages. . . . *Dorell v. Johns-Manville Corp.* The jury awarded the plaintiff $100,000 in compensatory damages and $1,000,000 in punitive damages. . . . *Jackson v. Johns-Manville.* A jury verdict of $195,000 in compensatory damages and $500,000 in punitive damages. . . . *Cavett v. Johns-Manville Corp.* The jury awarded the plaintiff $800,000 in compensation damages and $1,500,000 in punitive damages.

At the time of Manville's Chapter 11 filing, no punitive damages had been paid by Manville. All of the asbestos cases were stayed by the bankruptcy filing.

THE CHAPTER 11 FILING

In its August 26, 1982 petition for protection from creditors under Chapter 11 of the U.S. Bankruptcy Code, Manville explains its filing as follows:

> In early 1981, J-M commissioned outside consultants to conduct a study to try to project the future volume of asbestos cases. . . .
>
> It has been estimated that the financial burden of these litigations upon Manville could range anywhere between $2 billion to many times that amount over the next twenty years. Confronted with such potentially massive liabilities, Manville would have no recourse except to sell, liquidate or otherwise dispose of assets and dismember its businesses in order to continue to pay the costs of disposing of these suits. . . .
>
> Therefore, in order to treat all creditors of Manville evenhandedly, whether their claims at the present time be liquidated or unliquidated, contingent or non-contingent, mature or unmatured, Manville has reluctantly, but of necessity, deemed the filing of the Chapter 11 petitions to be an economic imperative.

The petition describes Manville's publicly held shares of stock and debt as follows:

> There are outstanding 9.70% senior debentures due in 1985 in the aggregate face amount of $100 million in the hands of approximately several hundred holders.

> There are outstanding 7.85% sinking fund debentures due in 2004 in the aggregate face amount of $75 million in the hands of approximately several hundred holders.

Manville listed its 59 largest unsecured creditors, with claims of $253,217,000.

In letters from J. A. McKinney dated August 27, 1982 and in a newspaper advertisement included with the letters, Manville addressed "Manville Corporation shareholders, employees, customers, suppliers, and creditors." McKinney wrote, "This is a letter I did not expect to write two weeks ago. . . . I can't tell you how agonizing it was to make this decision." In the newspaper advertisement, Mr. McKinney is quoted as saying, "Nothing is wrong with our business. . . . Our businesses will keep operating, very smoothly, we believe. . . . Thousands of asbestos health lawsuits are the problem."

Appendix A

MANVILLE CORPORATION ACQUISITIONS AND DIVESTITURES

During 1928, acquired for cash the Cellite Co. of Lompoc, Calif., miners and processors of diatomaceous earth; the Banner Rock Products Co. of Alexandria, Inc., manufacturers of rock wool and other products. During 1929, acquired for cash Weaver-Henry Manufacturing Co. of Los Angeles, Cal., manufacturers of roofings; Preformed Asphalt Products Co. of Dayton, Ohio, manufacturers of asphalt planking; E. H. Biegler Manufacturing Co. of Chicago, manufacturers of asphalt tile flooring. In January, 1929, acquired United States and Canadian rights to manufacture and sell seamless pipe of asbestos and cement under the patents of the Eternità Pietra Artificiale, Società Anonima of Genoa, Italy. In March, 1929, acquired exclusive manufacturing and sales rights to the sound-absorbing interior finish developed by the C. F. Burgess Laboratories of Madison, Wis., known as Sanacoustic Units.

In May 1930, purchased the Stevens Sound Proofing Co. of Chicago, owners of patents covering structural methods for the insulation of sound.

In March 1936, acquired sales rights for "fibretex" noise insulating building material manufactured by National Gypsum Co. of Boston.

Early in 1939, leased a plant at Billerica, Mass., for the manufacture of panels and sheathing. In 1944, a subsidiary acquired this plant.

On March 31, 1947, purchased the factories and going business of Goetze Gasket & Packing Co., Inc., New Brunswick, N.J., manufacturers of metallic gaskets.

On December 3, 1947, purchased assets of Van Cleef Bros., Inc. (sub-

SOURCE: Moody's Industrial Manuals.

sequently Johns-Manville Dutch Brand Products Corp.), Chicago, manufacturers of rubber products. Sold in 1970.

On October 6, 1952, purchased plant at Forth Worth, Tex. for manufacture of asphalt roofing.

Effective December 31, 1958, acquired assets and business of L-O-F Glass Fibers Co., in exchange for 1,094,787 common shares on 1-for-2½ basis; now operated as Johns-Manville Sales Corp. (Del.).

On September 22, 1959, acquired F. E. Schundler & Co., Inc., miners and processors of perlite in exchange for 148,000 common shares, now operated as Johns-Manville Perlite Corp. (Ill.).

On February 20, 1960, acquired for $622,898 principal assets of Franklin Plastics, Inc., makers of extruded thermoplastic pipe.

In February 1964, acquired Melamite Corp., Lawrence, Mass. (merged into Johns-Manville Products Corp. in 1972); Melamite Sales, Inc., and Melamite Distributors, Inc. for about 60,000 of company's common shares. Sold in 1974.

On December 31, 1967, acquired about 75% of gypsum capacity of Fibreboard Corp. for about $16,500,000.

In September 1968, acquired Crown Tuft Carpet, Inc., Dalton, Ga. (sold in 1972).

In August 1970, acquired Lindstrom & King Co., N.J., manufacturer of Value packing rings, for 14,934 common shares (merged into Johns-Manville Products Corp. in 1972) (sold 1975).

In 1970, Johns-Manville Products Corp. of Georgia merged into Johns-Manville Corp.

In 1971, acquired Holophane Co., Inc. for 1,584,241 Co. com. shs. (share-for-share exchange). Also acquired Silvercote Products, Inc. for 20,571 Co. com. shs. (both merged into Johns-Manville Sales Corp. in 1973).

In September 1971, acquired 75% interest in two West German Cos. for $13,038,000. (In Aug. 1972 acquired remaining 25%).

Mold, Inc. and Form Plastics, Inc. merged into Plastics Corporation of America; Holophane Export Sales Corp. and Holophane International, Inc. merged into Holophane Co., Inc.

In 1972, merged Johns-Manville Products Corp. of California into Johns-Manville Products Corp.

In December 1972, acquired Lamont & Riley, Inc., Worcester, Mass. and Hefco Inc., Lewiston, Me.

In July 1972, acquired General Sprinkler Corp. for 418,489 common shares (merged into J-M Fresno Corp. in 1973).

In September 1972, acquired Christy Metal Products, Inc. for 15,693 shares of treasury stock.

In 1973, Johns-Manville Irrigation Corp. merged into Johns-Manville Products Corp.; Johns-Manville Mining and Trading Corp. merged into Johns-Manville Corp., Mitchell.

(Continued)

In 1973 acquired Zeston, Inc. and an affiliated Co. for 180,000 shs. of treasury stock; Plastics Corp. of America for 13,974 shs. of treasury stock; Hamilton Mfg. Co. Inc. for $800,000; Club Car, Inc. for $1,531,000; and National Ceiling Systems Corp. for $752,000 (merged into Johns-Manville Corp. in 1975); also acquired Magnebras, S.A., Sao Paulo, Brazil (name changed to Johns-Manville De Brazil S.A.); Alphacoustic, Paris, France.

In 1974 acquired West Coast Silica, Overton, Nev. for 16,000 treasury shares (merged into Johns-Manville Sales Corp. in 1975); United Filigree Corp., Cranbury, N.J. for $11,038,000; Harsco Corp.'s IKG Division and controlling interest (60%) in Key Transportation, Inc., Ogden, Utah. The latter now 100% owned (merged into Johns-Manville Sales Corp. in 1976).

Also in 1974, sold all outstanding shares of Johns-Manville Timber Corp., subsidiary, to Williamette Industries, Inc. for approx. $34,000,000.

In 1975, merged the following subsidiaries into Johns-Manville Sales Corporations: Coalinga Asbestos Company, Inc.; Johns-Manville Development Corp.; Johns-Manville Fiber Glass Inc.; Johns-Manville Products Corp. of Pennsylvania; Johns-Manville Products Corp. Also in 1975, merged American Mineral Company into Desert Minerals, Inc. which was subsequently merged into L. Grantham Corporation. And sold Foresight Systems, Inc.

Case 7

A PROBLEM OF SILICOSIS

Foster C. Rinefort

BACKGROUND OF THE PROBLEM

Frank Rahman, Corporate Safety Director for International Mining and Carbon Corporation, was faced with a complex problem. Rahman was responsible for the prevention and control of work injuries and occupational diseases in the corporation. Recently, he received a copy of the first report of injury reporting a case of class I silicosis at the Emmett, North Carolina plant. The silicosis issue was brought home for Rahman every day. Walter Krutchel, who had built the Emmett plant and run it for over a decade, was now at the corporate headquarters in an office adjacent to Rahman and his silicosis-caused coughing was frequent and loud.

Frank had worked extensively with the Vice-President of the Industrial Group, Norman Dillsworth, and with the other group managers over a period of several years and had visited the Emmett plant within the year. As he tried to put the problem in perspective, Rahman thought about the corporation, its background, and its current financial position. He reviewed the operations and products of the Industrial Group, the Industrial Minerals Division, and the Emmett plant. He then took another look at the corporate safety record to date, including lost workday incidence rates and the lost workday severity rates. He reviewed the causes, symptoms, and effects of silicosis. He knew that he must take appropriate action to deal with this problem. But what should he do?

This case was prepared by Prof. Foster C. Rinefort of Eastern Illinois University. Presented at Midwest Case Writers Association Workshop, 1984. Reprinted by permission.

HISTORY OF INTERNATIONAL MINING AND CARBON CORPORATION

International Mining and Carbon Corporation was incorporated in New York in 1909 as International Mining Corporation. Its operations then consisted of an open-pit phosphate mine in central Florida and several relatively small plants in the southeast United States, where phosphates were combined with potash and some form of nitrogen and were sold in bulk and bagged form to farmers as fertilizer. The company continued to grow moderately within the agricultural fertilizer sector of the economy in the 1920s and 1930s. In the late 1930s, under the leadership of Louis Warren, a mining engineer with banking experience, the company moved its headquarters to Chicago and acquired potash mining leases near Carlsbad, New Mexico. The company opened a mine at this location in 1940. After World War II, the company obtained feldspar and bentonite mining and refining operations and built and acquired additional fertilizer plants. Then as the result of an accidental discovery in the company's research laboratories, a food flavor enhancer called "Spice" was produced from sugar beet tops in a plant in San Jose, California. The company continued through acquisitions and growth to expand at a reasonable rate and to show consistent 4 to 5% profit as a percent of sales.

In 1958 Louis Warren's son, Tom, became President and the company began a new era. A new corporate logo was prepared and a motto, "Grow," was developed to provide a statement of the objectives of the organization. A modern corporate headquarters was built in suburban Chicago and a young, capable staff was recruited. Then there followed significant growth in sales and profits, numerous acquisitions, extensive revamping of existing facilities, and the acquisition of a large potash mine which was successfully opened in Saskatchewan, Canada. This era ended in the late 1960s, when an oversupply of chemical fertilizers severely depressed prices and drastically diminished corporate profits.

In the 1970s Nelson Wilson initiated a difficult but successful turnaround period. Richard Langdon, the next Chief Executive Officer, carried on Wilson's work. From 1970 to 1980 sales increased from $588 million to $1,637 million and net earnings grew from $48 million to $146 million (see Exhibit 7.1). During this time the company expanded and further modernized existing facilities, eliminated numerous marginal operations, expanded its important Canadian and Florida mining operations, and built a large nitrogen-producing plant in Louisiana. Through acquisitions the firm expanded further into the industrial chemical and industrial minerals areas, added oil, gas and coal producing operations, and became stronger in world markets by purchasing an established New York based trading company. Since 1981 both sales and net earnings have decreased as the price of primary products has declined on a world basis.

Today the company employs 9,000 people at 121 locations throughout

Exhibit 7.1
INTERNATIONAL MINING AND CARBON CORPORATION
(Dollars in Millions except Per Share Amounts)

	1984	1983	1982	1981	1980
Revenues	1,569.9	1,464.3	1,621.8	1,824.2	1,637.6
Earnings from continuing operations before income taxes	172.7	129.9	197.0	248.7	251.8
Provision for income taxes	60.7	46.8	74.3	97.4	104.4
Earnings from continuing operations	112.0	83.1	122.7	151.3	147.4
Discontinued operations	(30.3)	(2.6)	14.7	2.5	(1.5)
Net earnings	81.7	80.5	137.4	153.8	145.9
Receivables, net	206.5	179.5	189.0	260.9	238.5
Interest expense	4.7	3.3	4.2	5.4	6.7
Inventory	246.1	253.0	323.7	348.0	297.3
Current assets	613.7	584.7	620.6	618.2	689.5
Current liabilities	326.2	306.7	316.1	358.0	345.4
Earnings from continuing operations	4.17	3.12	4.58	5.54	5.43
Discontinued operations	(1.13)	(.10)	.55	.09	(.05)
Net earnings per share	3.04	3.02	5.13	5.63	5.38
Common dividends	2.60	2.60	2.60	2.46	2.16
Average common shares (in millions)	26.7	26.5	26.7	27.3	27.1
Other Five-Year Data					
Total assets	1,965.6	1,943.9	1,941.9	1,975.2	1,848.6
Working capital	287.5	278.0	304.5	260.2	344.1
Long-term debt, less current maturities	388.1	424.6	441.8	486.3	488.4
Total debt	425.7	459.4	485.7	503.3	500.0
Deferred income taxes	112.7	124.2	125.1	106.1	93.0
Shareholders' equity	1,039.1	1,024.1	1,010.2	975.3	881.3
Invested capital	1,577.5	1,607.7	1,621.0	1,584.7	1,474.3
Number of employees	9,000	8,400	8,400	10,600	10,600

the world and continues to be a leading producer of chemical fertilizers and fertilizer materials, a major factor in the world trade of these products and an important supplier of other industrial chemicals and mineral products.

THE INDUSTRY GROUP: CARBON PRODUCTS, FOUNDRY PRODUCTS, INDUSTRIAL MINERALS

The industry group is an international supplier to heavy industry. It consists of three divisions: Carbon Products, Foundry Products, and Industrial Minerals. The *Carbon Products Division* primarily produces green petroleum coke, a by-product of petroleum refining which is sold to the steel, cement, and electrical utility industries. It also sells graphite furnace electrodes and gouging rods. The *Foundry Products Division* produces sand-bonding resins and oils for automotive and machine foundries. It is a major producer of molding sand additives, bonding clays, facing sands, and refractory mixes, and, in addition, is a manufacturer of foundry core-making machinery. The Foundry Products Division also produces Uniflo, a slag conditioner used by the steel industry which improves the efficiency of blast furnaces and the quality of the product produced. This division is a major producer of Bentonite, fireclay, facing sands, shell sand additives, resins for the paint industry, refractory mixes for lining furnace cupolas, and custom-blended moldings and additives.

The third segment, the *Industrial Minerals Division,* is a major miner and processor of feldspar and nepheline syenite materials which are primarily sold to the glass and ceramics industry. Industrial Minerals Division plants are located in Harwick, Ontario, Canada; Emmett, North Carolina; Brownwood, North Carolina; Rocky River, Virginia; and Whitman, Washington. The Industrial Minerals Division is headed by Charles Lonsbury, a Group Vice-President. He is a mining engineer with a flair for marketing and is young enough to have significant ambitions in the company. His operations manager is Phil Blasevich, a hard worker who worked his way through the Colorado School of Mines. His other principal staff assistant is Walter Krutchel, who supervised the construction of the Emmett, North Carolina plant and who was its first plant manager until an aggravated case of silicosis forced him to leave the plant or face an early death. The Division consists of a 6-person corporate staff, 325 plant-level employees, and 11 salespeople.

THE EMMETT, NORTH CAROLINA MINE AND PLANT

The Emmett open pit mine and plant is located in mountainous western North Carolina, west of the Blue Ridge Parkway. The mine was first opened and operated commercially during World War II. Workers use bulldozers to remove the earthen overburden, pneumatic drills to bore holes into the strata of feldspathic material, dynamite and ammonium nitrate-fuel oil to blast the rock free and Hough front-end loaders to load the product into heavy-duty trucks for transport to the processing plant. The refining and processing plant was constructed at the bottom of a steep valley two miles from the mine in the nearest fairly level and accessible site.

When the boulders and slabs of crystalline feldspar arrive at the plant, they are dumped into a pit, picked up by a conveyor belt, and fed into a primary or jaw crusher which breaks them into fist-sized lumps. A secondary crusher and a ball mill further reduce them in size first to the size of marbles and then, as necessary, to powder form. The product is then dried in gas-fired rotary kilns and bagged into forty-pound and eighty-pound bags, or stored in bulk form. The bagged finished product is stored in an adjacent warehouse building and is transported from the plant either by truck or by rail. The Clinchfield Railroad constructed a spur rail line to the plant so box-cars of bagged product or hopper cars of the product in bulk form can be loaded and sent to customers throughout North America.

Work in the open pit quarry is hard and can be hazardous, particularly during inclement weather. Plant work in the unheated plant is hot and dusty in the summer and bone cold in the winter. In both settings, there are hazards from moving machinery and equipment such as front-end loaders and Clark lift trucks, and from falling or flying chunks or particles of feldspar. Employees face another hazard or risk. Feldspar and napheline syenite are crystalline minerals with unique geological characteristics which make them important in the manufacture of glass and ceramics. When ground, they also produce a dust primarily consisting of crystalline silicon dioxide, or SiO_2. When this dust is inhaled, it collects in the lungs, causing irritation which results in a fibrous hardening of the lungs. This causes the occupational disease pneumoconiosis, or in this case, silicosis. Silicosis progresses from shortness of breath, to wheezing, to coughing, to pulmonary insufficiency, and, finally, to death.

The disease is diagnosed by lung x-rays and measurement of vital lung capacity by a spirometer and by medical diagnosis. The quantities of airborne dust can be measured by a Greenberg-Smith or Midget Inpinger or by a grab sample which is later analyzed in an industrial hygiene laboratory. The threshold limit value of pure crystalline SiO_2 is 2.5 million particles per cubic foot of air as calculated by the following formula:

$$\text{Concentration (mppcf)} = \frac{250}{5+\%\text{ of crystalline } SiO_2 \text{ in airborne dust}}$$

The quantity of SiO_2 in the air can be controlled and reduced in several ways. The best method—also the most expensive—is to totally enclose the dust producing process with an exhaust system which maintains a negative pressure within the enclosure. A slightly less expensive solution is a local exhaust system consisting of a hood, fan, and collector which can be installed at work stations. Significantly less adequate protection can be provided by installing fans to move and dilute dust concentrations and by mechanically supplying heated make-up air. Dust concentrations can be reduced by adding moisture at any stage of the process from drilling in the quarry to bagging the finished product in the plant. The least satisfactory—also the least expensive—solution is to provide employees with Mine Health and Safety Administration approved respirators with appropriate filters. Respirators are uncomfortable, particularly in hot weather. They can become ineffective unless they are regularly cleaned and the filters are frequently changed. Workers often will not wear them unless management consistently and vigorously requires their use.

The Emmett plant protects employees from silicosis at the quarry by wet drilling and at the plant by encouraging the use of respirators, by fans in the plant which move the air, and by wet milling when this has seemed practical. The plant superintendent is Arby Boone, who is a distant relative of Daniel Boone. He has been at the plant almost since it opened and is well respected by the men. He is completely self-educated. The seventy-two workers at the mine and at the plant are glad to have work because they are aware of their limited marketable skills and the perennial double-digit unemployment in this part of North Carolina. These workers exhibit a rugged mountaineer spirit and clannishness. Alternative local occupations include hunting, fishing and making moonshine. Many of the workers are related to one another and most have been in this part of the state for several generations. They all suspect that they are getting or will get silicosis at some point, but they are somewhat fatalistic about it, sustained by their fundamentalist religion, their close community, and their fierce pride. They know that if they report formally that they have silicosis and claim workmen's compensation benefits for their disability, they will lose their jobs and will have to live on meager amounts of money. The forty-year-old plant normally operates on very thin profit margins and has lost money at the plant level three of the past five years primarily because of a downturn in the market for glass and ceramic products.

The Plant Safety Program

There is a company safety program which this plant has adapted to a reasonable extent (see Exhibit 7.2). Central features of the program are appointment of a part-time safety supervisor; monthly safety inspections by a three-man inspection committee; and a monthly safety committee meeting of inspection committee members, three other supervisors, and the safety su-

INTERNATIONAL MINING AND CARBON CORPORATION
CORPORATE SAFETY REPORT, 1984

Exhibit 7.2

	Lost Workday Injuries	*Lost Workday Incidence Rate*[1]	*Days Time Lost*	*Lost Workday Severity Rate*[2]
Fertilizer Group				
New Mexico Mine	14	1.68	6,490	777.1
Canadian Mine	9	.62	361	24.9
Florida Mine	12	1.28	863	23.1
Florida Chemical	5	.85	152	25.8
Plant Food Division	49	4.51	7,215	661.9
	89	1.81	15,081	307.7
Industry Group	57	3.77	8,451	560.7
Chemical Group	18	1.65	6,504	585.9
Animal Products Group	8	1.24	248	36.6
Headquarters	5	1.61	122	39.1
TOTAL	176	1.85	18,406	216.3

NOTES: 1. Lost workday incidence rate is the number of disabling or lost-time work injuries or injuries in which the injured person is unable to work the next scheduled day per 100 full-time employees. 2. Lost workday severity rate is the number of days lost from disabling work injuries including actual days lost and scheduled changes for deaths, loss of a part of the body, or use of a part of the body per 100 full-time employees.

pervisor. Other parts of the program are annual safety inspections by an employee of the workmen's compensation insurance carrier, safety posters on the bulletin board, and a provisioned first aid area located near the plant superintendent's office. Excerpts from the Corporate Accident and Fire Prevention Standard Practice Manual are shown in Exhibit 7.3.

The Silicosis Claim

William "Billy" Buchanan was the youngest of a family of six children. His father and two of his brothers had worked at the Emmett mine and mill of International Mining and Carbon for most of their adult lives. Billy's father died of unknown causes when Billy was twelve years old. Billy quit school at age sixteen and was employed by the company when he was eighteen. Twelve years later he employed an attorney from a community located fifty miles east of Emmett in the valley and claimed full disability, or Class I silicosis, under the North Carolina Workmen's Compensation Act. The company, following past practices and industry custom, terminated him, and employed local counsel to fight the claim at every step.

EXCERPTS FROM THE *CORPORATE ACCIDENT AND FIRE PREVENTION STANDARD PRACTICE MANUAL*

Exhibit 7.3

Corporate Safety Policy

Safety is the first concern in all company operations. Legal and industrial safety codes, protective equipment and devices, and standard safety practices are regarded as only minimum requirements. Every possible step beyond these minimums should be taken to ensure even greater safety. Each manager or superintendent is charged with the responsibility for the safety and well-being of all employees in the plant or mine under his supervision.

Management Responsibility

The responsibility for the control of injuries and fires rests with operating management, from plant manager down to each foreman as a part of their regular management duties.

Responsibilities of the Safety Supervisor

The person designated, whether his title is Safety Supervisor or some other title, has the authority and responsibility for the effective functioning of the accident and fire prevention plan at each plant. . . . Responsibility for the functioning of the plan is carried out by the Safety Supervisor who provides staff assistance to the production supervisors in filling their responsibilities for the control of unsafe acts or conditions which cause most losses.

Instruction and Training of Employees

Because unsafe acts cause most of the accidents, fires, and other insurable losses, the development of safety rules and the thorough indoctrination, instruction, and training of each employee in the safe way of doing his work is the most important part of the plan: wherever a training program is functioning, the safety training required for each job should be incorporated into that program.

The Correction of Unsafe Practices and Conditions

It is very important to find and correct unsafe practices and conditions before they cause an accident, fire, or other type of loss. Unsafe practices are generally found by Plant Safety Inspection Committees, insurance company representatives, supervisory personnel during the daily operation of their departments, Safety Supervisors, and employees.

Safety Meetings

The Management Committee is composed of the Plant Manager or Superintendent (in his absence, his assistant), the Safety Supervisor, and other key managerial personnel. . . . The committee would meet once each month and the Safety Supervisor would act as secretary to the group.

Maintaining Interest

To maintain high interest in safety, something more than monthly safety meetings and inspections is necessary. The following are a few of the activities which are usually most effective.

1. Safety contests.
2. National Safety Council Section contests.
3. Division-wide or inter-departmental safety campaigns or contests.
4. Safety publications.
5. Safety posters.
6. Movies and sound slide films.

First Aid

Each plant should have one or more areas where first aid can be administered. Necessary first-aid supplies should be kept in the area. The area should be kept extremely clean and all employees should know where it is located.

CONCLUSION

Frank Rahman pondered what he should do. He understood the fragile and difficult economics of this plant, this Division, and the industry in general. He understood that adverse publicity could cause difficult problems at this plant and possibly trigger a visit from the Mine Health and Safety Administration, U.S. Department of Labor. As a result of his recent visit to the plant, he was painfully aware of its shortcomings regarding employee protection. What should he do?

SECTION C

CORPORATE STRATEGY

Case 8

WALT DISNEY PRODUCTIONS–1984

Charles B. Shrader/J. David Hunger

"It's kind of fun to do the impossible."
Walt Disney

As 1984 was drawing to a close, Michael Eisner sat back in his chair, looked out the office window onto the busy Burbank, California streets, and pondered the future direction of Walt Disney Productions. The last few years had been somewhat painful for the company. Except for 1984, net income had declined steadily (see Exhibit 8.1). In 1980, net income had been \$135.2 million and earnings per share (EPS) \$4.16. Net income fell to \$121.5 million in 1981, \$100.1 million in 1982, and \$93.1 million in 1983. In 1984, however, net income increased (because of an accounting change) to \$97.8 million. EPS likewise dropped from \$4.16 in 1980, to \$3.72 in 1981, \$3.01 in 1982, and \$2.70 in 1983. EPS was \$.61 in 1984 before accounting changes increased the figure to \$2.73.

Even though Walt died some twenty years ago, Eisner could almost feel his presence. Realizing that Disney Productions was an outgrowth of Walt's personal vision, Eisner was faced with making the company stand on its own, without Walt's guidance. The immediate greenmail threat was over but rumors of other takeover attempts persisted. The present relations with the Bass family, who own a large percentage of company stock, have helped stabilize the company. However, with so much ownership outside the Disney family, Eisner contemplated how the company's direction would change.

Should the new direction be toward more and better motion pictures, or toward revitalizing the theme parks? Walt Disney Productions experienced

This case was prepared by Prof. Charles B. Shrader and Prof. J. David Hunger of Iowa State University, Ames, Iowa. This case also appears in the *Case Research Journal, 1985*, pp. 79–122. Reprinted by permission of the authors and the Case Research Association. The authors thank David R. Smith, archivist, Walt Disney Productions–Burbank, and Terry McCorvie, press and publicity director, Walt Disney World, for helpful comments on earlier drafts of this case.

Exhibit 8.1 WALT DISNEY PRODUCTIONS, 1980–1984

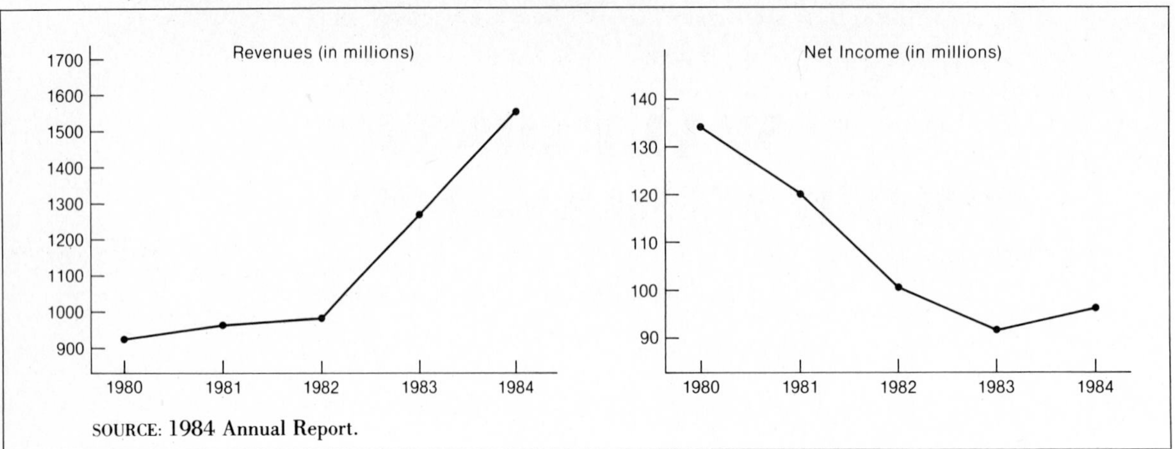

SOURCE: 1984 Annual Report.

record theme park and box office attendance in 1978–1979. With the opening of EPCOT Center in Walt Disney World during 1982, the future of the company looked bright. Even when faced with gasoline and energy shortages in the late 1970s and early 1980s, the company remained optimistic. For example, the theme of Disney's 1983 annual report was "Looking to New Horizons." Theme park revenues were down in 1984, however, and Eisner knew that the demographic trends looked bad. He also knew that one of Disney's competitors, Taft Broadcasting Company, had recently sold its theme parks in order to concentrate on expanding its communication businesses.

In 1984, Disney Productions had also suffered executive turnover, employee unrest, poor theme park attendance, and lackluster performance in the motion picture division. While top managers and board members were being shuffled, employees and shareholders had become increasingly critical of the company. The Disney image, strongly linked to family entertainment, had come under criticism for being out of date. Attempts to alter the firm's image did not sit well with much of top management. Disney encountered tough competition in its new cable TV and home video businesses. All in all, the events of 1984 caused management and the board of directors to be quite concerned about the future of Walt Disney Productions.

Michael Eisner, CEO only since September 1984, knew he would remember the past few months as a learning experience. With the year of Donald Duck's fiftieth birthday celebration coming to a close, Eisner wondered about the increasing pressure to reduce the corporation's focus on Mickey Mouse and other cartoon characters in order to emphasize more adult-oriented concepts. Did it make sense to put more money into motion pictures and to cut back investment in theme parks? What would Walt think of all the changes going on in his company, especially since it had recently been listed as "excellent" and as one of the best places in which to work?

As he rose pensively from his chair, Eisner picked up his coat and prepared to leave. He looked forward to 1985. It would certainly be an interesting year.

WALT DISNEY—COMPANY HISTORY[1,2]

"What do you do with all your money?" a friend once asked Walt. Pointing at the studio Walt said, "I fertilize the field with it."

"To the bankers I'm sure he seemed like a wild man, hell-bent for bankruptcy."

Roy O. Disney

Walter Elias Disney was born in Chicago on December 5, 1901. Walt was the fourth son of Elias Disney, a farmer, preacher, and builder, who at one time ran a hotel in Daytona Beach, Florida, only seventy miles from the present Walt Disney World. When Walt was five years old, his family moved from Chicago to a farm in Marceline, Missouri, where Walt spent most of his childhood. Walt loved the orchards and scenery of the farm. It was this memory of Marceline that provided Walt's inspiration for Disneyland's Main Street. Walt developed an interest in drawing. By the time his family moved to Kansas City during his grammar school years, his ambition was to be a cartoonist.

In World War I Walt drove an ambulance for the Red Cross. After the war, Walt returned to Kansas City to look for work as a newspaper cartoonist. Eventually his brother Roy found him a job with the Pesman-Rubin art studio where Walt made drawings for catalogues and advertisements. At Pesman-Rubin, Walt met a fellow artist, Ubbe ("Ub") Iwerks. Walt and Ub began a friendship that would last throughout Walt's life. After being laid off at the studio, Walt and Ub decided to start their own business. Using borrowed equipment and money, Walt experimented with animation in his brother Herbert's garage. He and Ub made one-minute cartoons called *Laugh-O-Grams* based on popular fairy tales and sold the cartoons for small fees. With a borrowed $15,000, Walt, Ub, and some other artists incorporated *Laugh-O-Grams* in 1922. Walt sold very few of the cartoons and the business failed one year later.

Early Hollywood Years

The company declared bankruptcy and Walt moved to Hollywood, California. In Hollywood, Walt was turned down both as a director and as an extra. He decided to give animation another try. With the help of Roy and a generous uncle, the Disney Brothers studio was started in 1923. Walt used the profits from his first series to expand the studios and to hire artists and animators, continually narrowing his profit margin. Walt hired his friend Ub to work for him in 1924. However, interest in the Disney cartoons started to fade and the Disney Studios needed a creative boost.

In 1926, Charles Mintz, Disney's distributor, suggested a new cartoon about a rabbit. Walt made the animation and Mintz gave the rabbit the name Oswald. With the creation of Oswald the Rabbit, Walt started an animation technique that would stay with him throughout most of his career. The cartoon characters first were drawn in rough form. The rough animation was then projected and checked many times over in its basic form until Walt okayed the action. After Walt's approval, the final touches and detail were added to the cartoon. This technique vastly improved the quality of the animation and made Oswald a big success.

It was with Oswald that Walt had another influential experience. Oswald was so popular that firms were using him to promote their products. Walt received no royalties from Oswald but saw the rabbit as good advertising for his studios. Therefore, he continued to spend time and money perfecting Oswald even after the cartoon was a popular success. Mintz liked the cartoon but was unhappy with the amount of money Walt was spending. Many arguments between Disney and Mintz ensued over financial matters. Finally, after a contract dispute, Mintz kept the rights to Oswald and hired all of Disney's animators (except Ub) to work for him. With Disney Studios now in dire need of a new character, Walt and Ub began work on a new cartoon featuring a mouse. From this time forward, Walt was to maintain close control over his cartoon characters.

In 1928, Walt and Ub created Mickey Mouse. Ub did the drawings and Walt did Mickey's voice. Mickey starred in the first fully synchronized sound cartoon, *Steamboat Willie,* in 1928, and was a huge success. Disney won his first Oscar in 1932, which was followed by an Oscar in 1933 for *The Three Little Pigs.* In the 1930s Disney used his cartoon characters, such as Mickey, Goofy, and Donald Duck, in the merchandising of other products. The company grew despite the Depression and Walt gave his employees a raise even though he received financial advice to the contrary.

During the company's early growth years, Walt's brother Roy acted as financial advisor while Walt was the entrepreneur, or idea man. Roy would try to find a way to finance whatever Walt wanted. Walt reinvested the money in the company as soon as it came in. Walt did no drawing after 1924, but instead, focused on developing his dreams for the company's future.

Becoming a Major Motion Picture Company

Disney made the first feature length cartoon, *Snow White and the Seven Dwarfs,* in 1937. *Snow White* was a major success. It was with this film that Walt perfected the "multiplane" animation technique. This technique further added to the quality of animation by creating the perception of depth in the cartoon. Subsequent to *Snow White,* the company experienced a spurt in growth. The staff grew from 100 to 750. Disney continued to pour the profits back into the studios, and in 1940, the studio moved to its present home in Burbank.

Also in 1940, Disney made an animated feature called *Fantasia.* Walt was especially proud of this film. *Fantasia* combined animation with classical music in a series of vignettes, such as *The Sorcerer's Apprentice.* It was artistically acclaimed, but was a failure at the box office (until the 1970s, when it became a cult film). *Fantasia* caused the studio to lose a great deal of money. As a result, the banks decided to hold off financing or advancing any more money to Walt. In an attempt to raise needed money, the Disney brothers offered stock to the public for the first time. Walt's major concerns were quality and company growth rather than stockholder returns, so he continued the practice of putting most of the profits back into the company. Walt made a profit-sharing commitment to his employees at this time, but he gave the employees stock instead of cash. The stock was not very valuable in the 1940s so the disgruntled employees went on strike for more money. The employees claimed that they were being used only for Disney's gain. Walt took the strike personally even though it lasted only a short time. As a result of the strike, the Screen Cartoonists Guild was created.

Expansion into Television and Theme Parks

The Disney studio made training films for the government during World War II. In 1950, Disney became one of the first members of the motion picture industry to become involved with television. Disney reached an agreement with ABC TV in 1954 to do weekly programs if ABC in turn would help finance Walt's newest dream, Disneyland. ABC aired a program called *Disneyland,* which was organized around the same themes as the park. For example, a *Frontierland* program might include an episode about Davy Crockett. In 1955, *The Mickey Mouse Club* was first seen on TV. In July of 1955, Disneyland opened in Anaheim, California (Disney later bought out ABC's interest in Disneyland). It was also during the early 1950s that Buena Vista Distribution Company was formed to distribute Disney films. These actions were further indications of Walt's desire to hold the rights to his work. Disney used the TV programs and Disneyland to promote his films. During the 1950s the company became financially sound.

In the 1960s Disney experimented with combining animation and live action in films. The successful film *Mary Poppins* was a good example of this process. In 1964, the company formed a subsidiary to acquire land in Florida upon which Walt Disney World would be built. Walt's dream was to build a community of the future in Florida. He died in 1966 before his dream was finished. Roy took over the company after Walt was gone and continued work on Walt Disney World. The Orlando, Florida theme park opened in October 1971. Unfortunately Roy died in December of that same year. E. Cardon Walker succeeded Roy as President of the company. Walker, who had experience in a variety of Disney operations, had been with the company for thirty-three years prior to being president. It was in 1982, during Walker's administration, that the community of the future (EPCOT), Walt's final dream, was completed.

The Dream Becomes Reality

The growth and creativity of Walt Disney Productions was largely due to Walt Disney himself. Disney was an entrepreneur and a dreamer. His full-length animated films became the state-of-the-art for the industry. His architectural genius and his landscaping designs have received international acclaim. Disney received 32 Academy awards, 5 Emmy awards, and over 900 citations for his work. All of the company's activities up through EPCOT Center were generated by Walt. Walt was fascinated with technology and much of what is seen at other theme parks was originated by Walt at Disneyland. He built a company on the philosophy of providing high-quality entertainment for all ages. Walt once said, "You can't live on things made for children or for critics. I've never made films for either of them. Disneyland is not just for children. I don't play down." When Disney died in 1966, company profits were at an all time high. Walt Disney believed his various businesses were inseparable, so he used his TV programs, Disneyland, and movies to promote one another.

The current Walt Disney Productions is a diversified international company engaged in family entertainment. It operates three major business segments:[3] *Entertainment and Recreation, Filmed Entertainment,* and *Consumer Products.* A fourth segment, *Community Development,* was added upon the purchase of Arvida during 1984. The recreation enterprise includes two major theme parks: Disneyland in California, and Walt Disney World in Florida. The company also produces full-length motion pictures, recorded music, educational media, home video products, and a variety of other consumer products. The company is also involved in real estate development and transportation. The company's financial position is presented in Exhibits 8.2, 8.3, 8.4, and 8.5.

ENTERTAINMENT AND RECREATION

Walt Disney Productions operates two major theme parks: Disneyland in California and Walt Disney World in Florida. The Walt Disney World complex includes EPCOT Center, the Magic Kingdom, three hotels, golf courses, camp grounds, shops, restaurants, a conference center, and other

Exhibit 8.2
WALT DISNEY PRODUCTIONS, INC.:
CONSOLIDATED STATEMENT OF CHANGES IN FINANCIAL POSITION
(Dollar Amounts in Thousands)

Year Ended September 30	1984	1983	1982	1981	1980
Cash Provided by Operations before Taxes on Income	$364,024	308,369	309,431	316,949	326,504
Taxes received (paid) on income—net	50,012	28,987	(34,649)	(106,144)	(121,822)
Cash provided by operations	414,036	337,356	274,782	210,805	204,682
Cash dividends	40,941	41,100	39,742	32,406	23,280
	373,095	296,256	235,040	178,399	181,402
Investing Activities					
Common stock repurchase	327,679	—	—	—	—
Attractions, property, & net payables	194,142	333,738	614,416	333,407	149,674
Film production & program costs	127,595	83,750	52,295	55,454	68,409
Rights to the Walt Disney name	—	(3,640)	40,000	—	—
EPCOT & Disney Channel start-up costs	—	18,253	19,170	1,907	—
Long-term notes receivable & other	8,542	11,406	26,881	4,023	1,619
	682,296	443,507	752,762	394,791	219,702
	(309,201)	(147,251)	(517,722)	(216,392)	(38,300)
Financing Activities					
Long-term borrowings	421,119	137,500	205,000	110,000	—
Reduction of long-term borrowings	(126,593)	(99,925)	—	—	—
Common stock offering	—	70,883	—	—	—
Common stock issued (ret.) for rights to Disney name & certain equipment	—	(3,640)	46,200	—	—
Participation fees, net of related receivables	6,892	11,169	23,867	24,745	10,361
Collection of notes & other	11,835	35,667	2,030	7,646	1,327
	313,253	151,654	277,097	142,391	11,688
Increase (Decrease) in Cash	4,052	4,403	(240,625)	(74,001)	(26,612)
Cash & short-term invest. beg. yr.	31,294*	13,652	254,277	328,278	354,890
Cash & short-term invest. end yr.	$ 35,346	$ 18,055	$ 13,652	$254,277	$328,278

SOURCE: 1984, 1983, & 1980 Annual Reports.
* Includes $13,239 for Arvida in 1984.

recreational facilities. Walt Disney Productions also receives royalties from Tokyo Disneyland, which is run by a Japanese company. The following is a summary of the recent performance of this business segment:

Entertainment and Recreation (in Thousands)

	1984	*Change*	1983	*Change*	1982
Revenues	$1,097,359	+6%	$1,031,202	+42%	$725,610
Operating Income	192,695	−2%	196,87	48%	131,645
Operating Margin	18%		19%		18%
Theme Park Attendance	30,990	48%			

SOURCE: 1984 Annual Report.

Disneyland

"... the only new towns of any significance built in America since World War II are Disneyland ... and Disney World ..."

New York Magazine

Disneyland is located in Anaheim, California, approximately 40 miles south of Los Angeles. The park covers 76.6 acres with a parking facility cov-

Exhibit 8.3

WALT DISNEY PRODUCTIONS AND SUBSIDIARIES: CONSOLIDATED FINANCIAL STATEMENTS

Consolidated Statement of Income (in thousands except per share data)

Year ended September 30	1984	1983	1982	1981	1980
Revenues					
Entertainment & recreation	$1,097,359	$1,031,202	$725,610	$691,811	$643,380
Filmed entertainment	244,552	165,458	202,102	196,806	171,965
Community development	204,384				
Consumer products	109,683	110,697	102,538	116,423	99,160
	1,655,977	1,307,357	1,030,250	1,005,040	914,505
Costs and Expenses					
Entertainment & recreation	904,664	834,324	592,965	562,337	515,848
Filmed entertainment	242,303	198,843	182,463	162,180	112,725
Community development	162,158				
Consumer products	55,819	53,815	54,706	65,869	54,632
	1,364,944	1,086,982	830,134	790,376	683,205

SOURCES: 1984, 1983, & 1981 Annual Reports.

Exhibit 8.3 **(*Continued*)**

Year ended September 30	1984	1983	1982	1981	1980
Income (Loss) Before Corporate Expenses & Unusual Charges					
Entertainment & recreation	192,965	196,878	132,645	129,474	127,532
Filmed entertainment	2,249	(33,385)	19,639	34,626	48,675
Community development	42,226				
Consumer products	53,863	56,882	47,832	50,564	55,093
	291,033	220,375	200,116	214,664	231,300
Corporate Expenses (Income)					
General & administrative	59,570	35,554	30,957	26,216	21,130
Design projects abandoned	7,032	7,295	5,147	4,598	4,294
Interest expense (income) net	41,738	14,006	(14,781)	(33,130)	(42,110)
	108,340	56,915	21,323	(2,316)	(16,686)
Income Before Unusual Charges, Taxes, & Accounting Change	182,693	163,460	178,793	216,980	247,986
Unusual charges[1]	165,960				
Income Before Taxes & Accounting Change	16,733	163,460	178,793	216,980	247,986
Taxes on income (benefit)	(5,000)	70,300	78,700	95,500	112,800
Income Before Accounting Change	21,733	93,160	100,093	121,480	135,186
Cumulative effect of change in acct. for investment tax credits[2]	76,111				
Net Income	$97,844	$93,160	$100,093	$121,480	$135,186
Earnings Per Share					
Income before accounting change	$0.61	$2.70	$3.01	$3.72	$4.16
Cumulative effect of acct. change	2.12				
	$2.73	$2.70	$3.01	$3.72	$4.16
Average number of common and uncommon equivalent shares outstanding	35,849	34,481	33,225		

NOTES: 1. The unusual charges in 1984 were due to adjustments in the carrying values and write downs for several motion picture and television properties. 2. The company changed its accounting for investment tax credits to the flow-through method in the fourth quarter of 1984.

(*Continued*)

Exhibit 8.3 **(*Continued*)**

Consolidated Balance Sheet (Dollar Amounts in Thousands)

Year ended September 30	1984	1983	1982	1981	1980
ASSETS					
Current Assets					
Cash	$35,346	18,055	13,652	5,869	9,745
Accounts receivable, net of allowances	172,762	102,847	78,968	69,302	50,711
Short term investments				248,408	318,533
Income taxes refundable	60,000	70,000	41,000		
Inventories*	312,891	77,945	66,717	59,773	54,648
Film production costs	102,462	44,412	43,850	59,079	61,127
Prepaid expenses		19,843	18,152	15,398	11,438
Total Current Assets	683,461	333,102	262,339	457,829	506,202
Film Production Costs—Non-Current		82,598	64,217	61,561	59,281
Property, Plant and Equipment					
Entertainment attractions, buildings & equipment	2,413,985	2,251,297	1,916,617	968,223	935,152
Less accumulated depreciation	(600,156)	(504,365)	(419,944)	(384,535)	(352,051)
	1,813,829	1,746,932	1,496,673	583,688	583,101
Construction & design projects in progress					
EPCOT Center		70,331	120,585	439,858	141,373
Other	94,710	37,859	39,601	29,404	21,658
Land	28,807	16,687	16,379	16,419	16,414
	1,937,346	1,871,809	1,673,238	1,069,369	762,546
Other Assets	118,636	93,686	103,022	21,250	19,378
	$2,739,443	2,381,195	2,102,816	1,610,009	1,347,407

* 1984 inventory figure includes real estate.

Exhibit 8.3 ***(Continued)***

Year ended September 30	1984	1983	1982	1981	1980
LIABILITIES AND STOCKHOLDERS EQUITY					
Current Liabilities					
Accounts payable	$239,992	187,641	210,753	158,516	109,047
Taxes on income	24,145	50,557	26,560	33,057	36,244
Total current liabilities	264,137	238,198	237,313	191,573	145,291
Long Term Borrowings	861,909	346,325	315,000		
Other Long Term Liabilities and Non-Current Advances	178,907	110,874	94,739	161,886	30,429
Deferred Taxes on Income and Investment Credits	279,005	285,270	180,980	89,432	96,889
Commitments and Contingencies					
Stockholders Equity					
Preferred & Common Shares	359,988	661,934	588,250	540,935	537,689
Retained Earnings	795,497	738,594	686,534	626,183	537,109
	1,155,485	1,400,528	1,274,784	1,167,118	1,074,798
	$2,739,443	2,381,195	2,102,816	1,610,009	1,347,407

ering 107.3 acres. There are approximately 40 acres adjacent to the park which Disney has on a long-term lease. Disneyland is the oldest "theme park" in the United States. A theme park differs from an amusement park in that a theme park offers rides, exhibits, restaurants, and shows in the context of an overall theme. For example, Sea World and Marineland are based on oceanographic themes while Disneyland and King's Island are centered around cartoon and movie characters.

When Disneyland opened in 1955, there were 17 attractions; now there are 57. Adventureland, Bear Country, Fantasyland, Frontierland, Main Street, New Orleans Square, and Tomorrowland comprise the seven major areas of the park. Disneyland leases exhibits to corporate sponsors in an attempt to continually improve and update the park. Corporate sponsors include: American Telephone and Telegraph Company, Gulf Oil Corporation, McDonnell Douglas Corporation, Oscar Meyer and Company, and Welch Foods, Inc.[4] Each sponsor pays Disney an annual participation fee for rent and the rights to use the Disney name in advertising the exhibit.

The most significant expansion project of the park in 1983–1984 was the restoration of Fantasyland. The expansion included the use of three-dimensional animation, fiber optics, black light painting, and other special effects to update attractions such as *Alice in Wonderland.*

Exhibit 8.4

WALT DISNEY PRODUCTIONS AND SUBSIDIARIES: OTHER FINANCIAL DATA
(In Thousands of Dollars)

	1984	1983	1982	1981	1980
Entertainment and Recreation					
Walt Disney World					
Admissions & rides	$ 295,921	278,320	153,504	139,326	130,144
Merchandise sales	182,804	172,324	121,410	121,465	116,187
Food sales	177,078	178,791	121,329	114,951	106,404
Lodging	104,779	98,105	81,427	70,110	61,731
Disneyland					
Admissions & rides	110,723	102,619	98,273	92,065	87,066
Merchandise sales	79,260	72,300	76,684	79,146	72,140
Food sales	46,770	45,699	44,481	44,920	41,703
Participant fees, Walt Disney Travel Co., Tokyo Disneyland royalties and other	100,024	83,044	28,502	29,828	28,005
	$1,097,359	1,031,202	725,610	691,811	643,380
Theme park total attendance					
Walt Disney World	21,121	22,712	12,560	13,221	13,783
Disneyland	9,869	9,980	10,421	11,343	11,522
	30,990	32,692	22,981	24,564	25,305
Filmed Entertainment					
Theatrical					
Domestic	$ 70,679	38,635	55,408	54,624	63,350
Foreign	38,182	43,825	64,525	76,279	78,314
Television					
Worldwide	57,479	27,992	44,420	43,672	19,736
Home video and non-theatrical					
Worldwide	78,212	55,006	37,749	22,231	10,565
	$ 244,552	165,548	202,102	196,806	171,965
Community Development					
Residential	$ 53,038	—	—	—	—
Land & commercial property	90,166	—	—	—	—
Resorts & other	61,180	—	—	—	—
	$ 204,384	—	—	—	—

SOURCE: 1984 Annual Report.

Exhibit 8.4 ***(Continued)***

	1984	1983	1982	1981	1980
Consumer Products					
Character merchandise	$ 42,750	45,429	35,912	30,555	29,631
Publications	18,184	20,006	20,821	24,658	22,284
Records & music	33,734	30,666	26,884	27,358	23,342
Educational media	11,509	10,269	15,468	21,148	21,908
Other	3,505	4,327	3,453	12,704	1,905
	$ 109,682	110,629	102,538	116,423	99,160

In each of the seven park areas there are shops and restaurants with cuisine in keeping with the area theme. For example, *Pinocchio* is the theme of the Village Inn restaurant in Fantasyland. On the average, Disneyland restaurants serve 60,000 meals a day or 4,000 people an hour. The park is covered with some 500,000 constantly groomed trees and shrubs. Disneyland is open year-round with peak season in summer. Other high attendance times are spring school vacation, Easter, Christmas, and other holidays. Financial data for Disneyland are given in Exhibits 8.4 and 8.5

In 1980, Disneyland attracted 11.5 million people, an all-time Disneyland high. Attendance has declined steadily since then. In 1984, for example, attendance was down to 9.9 million. The two Disney theme parks account for 33% of all U.S. theme park attendance. Walt Disney Productions is dependent on theme park attendance for most of its revenue. Therefore, for Disney Productions, the decline in attendance has been painful. Disney officials blame decreases in attendance on high gasoline prices, gasoline shortages, poor economic conditions, changes in U.S. demographics, and poor weather. A harsh winter was blamed for poor attendance during 1983. A low attendance summer in 1984 was blamed on the Olympics held in nearby Los Angeles.

Attendance at Knott's Berry Farm, located in Buena Park in the same county as Disneyland, however, increased by 10% in both 1983 and 1984. Attendance at Sea World in San Diego and Marineland in Los Angeles county did not drop either during that same time frame.

Knott's Berry Farm is known for restaurants and shops but also has a large section devoted to rides. Knott's reduced their admission price by 20% in 1983–1984. During 1983, Disneyland admission prices increased by 6% and per capita spending was up. Thus Disneyland is in a paradoxical situation. The park has been improved and revenues are up, but attendance and profits are down.

WALT DISNEY PRODUCTIONS, INC.

Exhibit 8.5

	Disneyland Attendance and Revenues	
	Attendance	*Revenues*
1976	10,211,000	$122,473,000
1977	10,678,000	140,555,000
1978	10,807,000	158,274,000
1979	10,760,000	177,730,000
1980	11,522,000	207,059,000
1981	11,343,000	222,391,000
1982	10,421,000	225,120,000
1983	9,980,000	220,618,000*
1984	9,869,000	$236,753,000*

	Walt Disney World and EPCOT Attendance and Revenues	
	Attendance	*Revenues*
1976	13,107,000	$275,386,000
1977	13,057,000	300,515,000
1978	14,071,000	345,638,000
1979	13,792,000	389,623,000
1980	13,783,000	433,377,000
1981	13,221,000	465,436,000
1982	12,560,000	497,445,000
1983	22,712,000	727,540,000*
1984	21,121,000	$760,582,000*

SOURCES: 1980, 1981, 1982, 1983, and 1984 Annual Reports.
* Estimates based on 1983 and 1984 aggregate data.

Walt Disney World

"You can see more respectful courteous people at Disney World in one afternoon than in New York in a year."

Wall Street Journal

"If we can bring together the technical know-how of American industry and the creative imagination of the Disney organization—I'm confident we can create right here in Disney World a showcase to the world of the American free enterprise system."

Walt Disney

Walt Disney World, the most advanced entertainment complex in the world, is located 15 miles southwest of Orlando, Florida on 28,000 acres of land. Walt Disney World is a complete "vacationland" with hotels, resorts, campgrounds, aquatic recreational facilities, sport facilities, and golf courses. There is also a shopping village and a special transportation system. Part of the park is the "Magic Kingdom" theme park located on 100 acres of the complex. EPCOT Center, Walt Disney's "living blueprint" of the future, was opened to the public in 1982. The overall area of Walt Disney World is twice that of Manhattan Island or equivalent to the area of San Francisco.[5] When Disney World originally opened in 1971 there were 35 attractions in the Magic Kingdom; now there are 45. Large corporations, such as Coca Cola Company, also sponsor exhibits at Disney World. A new pavilion at EPCOT Center, "The Living Seas," presented by United Technologies, is now under construction. It will feature the world's largest man-made tropical reef. The Living Seas is scheduled to be completed in January 1986.

The importance of Disneyland and Disney World to the company is in the cash flow they generate. The theme park properties are depreciated over ten years for tax purposes. Maintenance of the parks is a high priority and is performed meticulously.

Partially because of the opening of EPCOT Center in October 1982, Disney World attendance (including EPCOT Center) in 1983 was 22.7 million, topping the original forecast of 20 million. Attendance fell, however, during 1984 to 21.1 million guests. The profit margin at Disney World has slipped far below that of the smaller and older Disneyland.[6]

Walt Disney World has made an effort to market the recreational and resort aspects of the park by offering vacation packages and by selling three-day passes. In an attempt to appeal to a larger clientele, Disney World is now offering culinary classes, landscaping seminars, technology and transportation seminars, and instruction on other phases of Disney operations.

EPCOT

The acronym EPCOT stands for Experimental Prototype Community of Tomorrow. EPCOT Center, which is located on 600 acres of Walt Disney World land, was opened October 1, 1982. The center consists of two major theme areas: World Showcase and Future World. World Showcase presents the history and culture of countries around the world. In 1984, the "Kingdom of Morocco" was added to World Showcase. Future World explores the challenges and problems facing the world today. Future World exhibits include: "Spaceship Earth" presented by the Bell System; "Journey Into Imagination" by Kodak; "Backstage Magic," a computer show sponsored by Sperry Univac; "The World of Motion" presented by General Motors; "Horizons" sponsored by General Electric; and "The Universe of Energy" sponsored by Exxon. Another Future World attraction is "The Land," sponsored by Kraft Foods. This attraction is of particular note because it takes visitors through various earth climates and demonstrates possible agriculture of the future. Food crops can be seen growing in aluminum drums, in salt water, and out of styrofoam—all in an attempt to show the potential alternative food sources of tomorrow.

EPCOT Center was Walt's last dream. He originally planned EPCOT to be primarily funded by sponsors and other interested outside investors much in the same way Disneyland was financed. However, even though many sponsors have paid millions of dollars toward costs, Walt Disney Productions has been forced to build EPCOT at a cost of approximately $1 billion, a big part of which has had to come from internally generated funds. EPCOT Center was built primarily for adults to complement the child orientation of Fantasyland and to help attract people to the Walt Disney World complex. EPCOT Center had to close its entrances twice during the peak Christmas season of 1982 when its 6,000 space parking lot was filled. The lot has since been expanded to 9,000 spaces.

Hotels and Land[7]

Walt Disney Productions owns and operates three hotels at Walt Disney World with a capacity of 1,834 rooms. The largest Disney hotel is the Contemporary Resort with 1,046 rooms, 14 stories, and a 90-foot-high open lobby. The hotel is connected to Walt Disney World's Magic Kingdom by monorail (which runs through the fourth floor concourse of the hotel). Disney World also has the Polynesian Resort hotel and the Golf Resort. The company also operates and owns many villas, townhouses, and campgrounds which are interconnected with the golf course and other Disney World outdoor recreational facilities. The Disney World hotels run at very high capacity and help make Disney World one of the most popular vacation spots in the world. The company is currently building 541 new rooms at the Polynesian Village Resort, Golf Resort, and Club Lake Villas. See Exhibit 8.6 for hotel occupancy rates.

Disney Productions owns 40 undeveloped acres of land in Anaheim and

Exhibit 8.6

OCCUPANCY RATES:
WALT DISNEY HOTELS AND WALT DISNEY WORLD VILLAGE

	1983	1982	1981	1980	1979
Contemporary Resort	99%	96%	99%	99%	98%
Polynesian Village Resort	99%	98%	97%	98%	99%
Golf Resort	96%	89%	94%	96%	95%
Fairway and Club Lake Villas	94–97%		average 81–88%*		

SOURCES: 1983, 1982, 1981, 1980, and 1979 10K Reports.
* 1979–1982 average occupancy rate

28,000 acres in Orlando. The company on the average paid $200 an acre for the undeveloped land. Its worth is now estimated at more than $1,000 an acre.

Transportation[8]

Disneyland and Walt Disney World are known for their monorails and people movers. The monorail system at Disney World comprises some 10 trains, each with the capacity to travel an average of 45 miles an hour. These trains carry approximately 10,000,000 passengers a year, and have technologically advanced air suspensions which allow smoother rides than those offered by comparable systems. The people movers at Disney World operate at 99.8% efficiency at a cost of 9¢ a passenger mile. In August 1979, Disney accepted a joint contract to build a people mover at the Houston International Airport. The Houston people mover is now complete. Its main advantage is that it has very few belts and gears—the wheels and doors are the only moving parts in the system. Disney's transportation business is conducted in the WED Enterprises Division of the company. Walt often referred to WED as his laboratory (WED stands for Walt's initials to reflect his personal interest in technology). In 1984, Disney contracted with Bombardier Inc. of Canada to build and market people mover and monorail train systems designed by Disney Productions.[9]

Tokyo Disneyland

"From the Emperor down, Japan is presently in the grip of mouse fever!"
Harper's Magazine

The biggest Disneyland of all—Tokyo Disneyland—opened April 15, 1983 on 202 acres of landfill in Tokyo Bay, 8 miles from downtown Tokyo, Japan. Walt Disney Productions agreed to invest $2.5 million and to offer technical and strategic advice on the project. The major financing of $600 million, however, came from the Oriental Land Company of Japan. Walt Disney Productions receives 10% of the gate receipts and 5% of other sales. Disney officials are assigned as consultants to ensure the park's profitability.

Tokyo Disneyland is much like its counterpart in Southern California. The Tokyo park has Adventureland, Fantasyland, Tomorrowland, Westernland, and World Bazaar. There is little in the park that is distinctly Japanese, yet approximately 32 million Japanese people live within a 30-mile radius of the park.

The park started off well and attendance surpassed projections for the first year. In 1984, however, attendance has been reported to be off as much as 40% of capacity. The Oriental Land Company has subsequently begun an aggressive advertising campaign.

The Theme Park Industry[10,11]

Amusement parks are a traditional form of American entertainment. Theme parks in particular experienced strong growth in attendance, employment, and income during the early 1970s. For example, 1976 theme park attendance was double that of 1971. Growth, however, slowed to only 1% in 1977. Revenues for parks approached $1.2 billion, with per capita spending of $14 in 1980. In 1981, there was a 1% increase in attendance (87 million visitors), revenues climbed to $1.4 billion, and per capita spending went to $16. From 1981 to 1984 theme park revenues increased but profitability decreased. Total attendance for the industry is growing very slowly. The industry is now facing some difficulties.

Market saturation has become a serious problem. Every metropolitan area in the United States now has a theme park within or very near its boundaries. Fifty percent of those attending theme parks have to travel less than 100 miles to reach their nearest theme park. Therefore, to be successful, a park has to be centrally located and accessible, or it has to attract regional customers. In order to attract regional cutomers, a park must offer something of special appeal. Disney parks are located at either end of the United States in southern locations that can be kept open all year long. In contrast, over 50% of the country's population is within a day's drive of one of the Six Flags parks. There are five companies which operate more than one park: Walt Disney Productions, which runs Disneyland and Walt Disney World; Bally Manufacturing, which has its Six Flags parks in California, Georgia, Missouri, New Jersey, and Texas; Taft Broadcasting, which operates King's Island in Cincinnati, King's Dominion in Virginia, and Carowinds in North Carolina;* Marriott Corporation, with Great America parks in California and Illinois; and Anheuser-Busch, which owns The Dark Continent park in Tampa, Florida, and Old Country in Virginia. In addition, there are successful individual parks, such as Cedar Point which serves the Cleveland/Toledo, Ohio metropolitan areas. Exhibit 8.7 lists the 25 most popular parks.

Success in this industry is often attributed to repeat customers who return to parks for upgraded rides and attractions, spectaculars, and live shows. Many theme parks attempt to increase the number of repeat customers by cutting admission prices and by offering special values. Most companies that run theme parks feel that more revenue can be generated by expanding existing parks rather than by building new ones. For example, Six Flags, Inc. adds a new major attraction to its parks about every two years. Building a new park has almost become cost prohibitive.

In the late 1970s industry analysts blamed tapering attendance on gasoline shortages and high gasoline prices. In the 1980s, gasoline prices and quantities available have been relatively stable, yet park attendance has still dropped. Analysts feel that high gas prices may only affect those traveling

* These parks were recently sold.

AMERICA'S TOP 25 AMUSEMENT PARKS, 1984

Exhibit 8.7

Park Name and Location	*Estimated Attendance*	*% Change from 1983*
1. Walt Disney World—Orlando, Florida	22,000,000	−5.0
2. Disneyland—Anaheim, California	10,000,000	0
3. Knott's Berry Farm—Buena Park, California	3,500,000	n/a
4. Sea World—Orlando, Florida	3,050,000	8.8
5. King's Island—Cincinnati, Ohio	3,000,000	8.0
6. Sea World—San Diego, California	2,900,000	2.2
7. Busch Gardens Dark Continent—Tampa, Florida	2,900,000	n/a
8. Magic Mountain—Valencia, California	2,750,000	9.0
9. Great Adventure—Jackson, New Jersey	2,600,000	−19.0
10. Cedar Point—Sandusky, Ohio	2,600,000	n/a
11. Six Flags Over Texas—Arlington, Texas	2,300,000	−4.0
12. Six Flags Over Georgia—Atlanta, Georgia	2,100,000	−8.0
13. Opryland U.S.A.—Nashville, Tennessee	2,060,000	2.2
14. Great America—Santa Clara, California	2,000,000	n/a
15. Great America—Gurnee, Illinois	2,000,000	−19.0
16. Busch Gardens Old Country—Williamsburg, Virginia	1,960,000	0
17. King's Dominion—Doswell, Virginia	1,880,000	−2.0
18. Santa Cruz Beach Boardwalk—California	1,800,000	n/a
19. Astroworld—Houston, Texas	1,700,000	10.0

SOURCE: *Amusement Business Magazine*, December 29, 1984, p. 65.

(Continued)

Exhibit 8.7
(*Continued*)

Park Name and Location	*Estimated Attendance*	*% Change from 1983*
20. Hersheypark—Hershey, Pennsylvania	1,604,000	0
21. Darien Lake—Darien Center, New York	1,410,000	10.0
22. Worlds of Fun—Kansas City, Missouri	1,366,000	−1.0
23. Six Flags Over Mid-America—Eureka, Missouri	1,300,000	−7.0
24. Carowinds—Charlotte, North Carolina	1,138,000	2.0
25. Sea World—Aurora, Ohio	1,016,000	−8.0

long distances to parks. Admission prices may be the "real cause" of lower attendance. In order to make money, the parks have to attract large crowds. The crowds come for improved rides and new attractions. The improvements and attractions cost an increasing amount to build, so the parks are forced to raise the admission prices. This has a dampening affect on demand. As a result, large theme parks are in a difficult position. They are in a mature industry and the escalating costs of doing business are hampering growth.

Another explanation for the declining growth in amusement and theme park attendance is one of demographics. As the average age of the U.S. population increases and as average family size decreases, fewer people are likely to be interested in the child-oriented themes of the 1960s or in the teen-age–oriented thrill rides so popular in the 1970s. The Bureau of Census of the U.S. Department of Commerce projects that the annual rate of population growth will slow from .9% in 1981 to .6% in 2000 and reach zero growth by 2050. With the slowdown in growth, the median age of the U.S. population will increase from 30.3 years in 1981 to 36.3 years in 2000 and 41.6 years in 2050. A summary of U.S. population by age category in Exhibit 8.8 shows these present and projected demographic changes.

Present attendance figures indicate that about half of the people visiting theme parks today are adults. If these parks are to keep their attendance revenues up, analysts of the industry believe parks will need to change further their entertainment mix. Theme parks may be faced with having to entertain not only children and accompanying adults, but also adults without children.

Another problem facing the industry is intense competition from other

UNITED STATES RESIDENT POPULATION
AND PROJECTED POPULATION FIGURES
(In Thousands)

Exhibit 8.8

	1975	1980	1985*	1990*	2000*
Under 5 yrs.	16,121 (7.5)**	16,457 (7.2)	18,462 (7.7)	19,200 (7.7)	17,624 (6.6)
5–17 yrs.	51,044 (23.7)	47,217 (20.8)	44,352 (18.6)	45,123 (18.1)	49,762 (18.5)
18–24 yrs.	27,735 (12.8)	30,091 (13.2)	28,715 (12.0)	25,777 (10.3)	24,590 (9.2)
25–44 yrs.	54,074 (25.1)	63,238 (27.8)	73,779 (30.9)	81,351 (32.6)	80,105 (29.9)
45–64 yrs.	43,794 (20.3)	44,486 (19.6)	44,668 (18.7)	46,481 (18.6)	60,873 (22.7)
Over 65	22,696 (10.5)	25,714 (11.3)	28,673 (12.0)	31,799 (12.7)	35,036 (13.1)
TOTAL	215,464	227,203	238,649	249,731	267,990

United States Average Family Size

	1960	1970	1975	1980	1982
Average size of family	3.67	3.58	3.42	3.29	3.25

SOURCE: *Statistical Abstract of the United States,* 1984, 104th edition, pp. 32, 34, & 47.
* Years 1985–2000 contain figures projected on basis of U.S. Census Middle Series (series 14).
** Figures in parentheses are percentages of annual totals.

forms of entertainment. People now are more active and have interests such as sports and fitness activities. The prospect of going to a theme park to wait in line for a ride may not be appealing to a fast-paced, more adult-oriented society. Theme parks in the future will very likely need to involve the visitor more in the park experience. Even in the mid-1980s the trend toward water-related rides and activities with the normal side-effect of soaking the participants is beginning to replace traditional thrill rides in popularity.

FILMED ENTERTAINMENT[12]

Walt Disney Productions is involved in theatrical motion picture making and distribution, network and cable television, and home video products. In 1983, gross revenues for this segment of Walt Disney Productions totaled $165,458,000; down from $202,102,000 in 1982. In 1984, however, gross revenues for this business segment were up to $244,552,000.

Filmed Entertainment (in Thousands)

	1984	*Change*	1983	*Change*	1982
Revenues	$244,552	+48%	$165,458	−18%	$202,102
Operating income (loss)	2,249	+10%	(33,385)	−270%	19,639
Operating margin	1%		−20%		10%

SOURCE: 1984 Annual Report.

Theatrical

"It was clear we were in Never-Never Land."
Ronald Miller

Disney's film library is one of the finest anywhere and currently is worth an estimated $500 million. The library, in 1982, contained 25 full-length animated features; 8 true-life adventure films; 118 full-length live action features; and approximately 500 other films on short subjects. In 1979, films accounted for one-fifth of Disney's pretax earnings but lost $33 million in 1983. Disney Productions feels that it is the primary source of family films in the motion picture industry. Nevertheless, recent Disney films have been replaced by *Star Wars* and *E.T.* as the most popular children's movies. The Disney movies have recently been criticized for lack of imagination, creativity, and "clout" at the box office. Full-length animation efforts of other studios, such as *Watership Down* and *The Secret of NIMH,* also seemed to be less than successful in theatre receipts.

Disney makes full-length animated motion pictures, live action movies, and other types of films such as health and safety movies. Walt's personal strategy had been to make films only about stories of proven popularity. He would make a quality film and re-release it about every seven years, rarely making sequels. From 1980 to 1983, 50% of Disney's motion picture division revenues came from reissues.[13] One of the company's 1984 objectives was to reissue two or three Disney films a year. Walt also used films to promote his other businesses by generating interest in Disneyland and consumer products, like Mickey Mouse watches.

Although the Disney studios are in the geographic heart of the Hollywood movie industry, Disney has been criticized for being miles away conceptually and behind the times. E. Cardon ("Card") Walker (CEO from 1971 to 1983), once said, "We never were part of the Hollywood scene." Walker at one time wanted Disney to abandon films altogether. The company, however, decided to adapt its motion pictures to changing tastes. Ronald Miller, the chief executive in 1983, wanted to develop more innovative films with wider appeal. In June 1983, Walt Disney Pictures was created as a separate company with Richard Berger as president. Berger was hired from 20th Century Fox and began to produce films for mass audiences under the "Touchstone" label.

Disney Productions released a PG rated film—*Splash*—in 1983. The movie was a tremendous box office success and helped cause Disney's stock price to climb from 50 to 67. *Splash* was produced by Touchstone and starred John Candy, Tom Hanks, and Eugene Levy, all of whom had successful previous endeavors as comedians. The starring actress, Daryl Hannah, also had previous movie experience. Ron Howard of *Happy Days* fame directed the movie.

Some Disney executives, nevertheless, were concerned that Touchstone and *Splash* were not consistent with the Disney image. Other top Disney officials disagreed with hiring top talent from other movie companies because they felt it was giving up too much control of the company. In February of 1984, Disney ran a full-page newspaper ad that was, in effect, a disclaimer for *Splash.* Jack B. Lindquist (Exec. V.P. Marketing), and James P. Jimirro (Exec. V.P. Telecommunications) placed the ad in order to head off expected criticism by the press. People at Disney Productions were worried that Walt might not have approved of Touchstone and PG rated films. Nevertheless, Touchstone's second release, *Country,* starring Jessica Lange and Sam Shepard, received critical praise in late 1984, and the filmed entertainment segment has set objectives for making ten to twelve Touchstone films a year.

Disney has attempted other nontraditional movies in addition to *Splash. Tron,* for example, was a somewhat unsuccessful attempt to make movies primarily for teenagers. *Tron* did, however, lead to an increase of computer simulation in advertising. The movie was intended to improve Disney's creative image. Other movies, such as *Something Wicked This Way Comes,* failed at the box office and helped cause the stock price to fall. *Never Cry Wolf* was a critical success, but was not successful at the box office, either.

All of Disney's motion pictures are distributed in the United States by Disney's wholly owned subsidiary, Buena Vista Distribution Company. Buena Vista International, another wholly owned subsidiary, distributes Disney films outside the United States.

Disney Productions is not large when compared to other motion picture makers. Disney's market share was 4% in 1980, 1981, and 1982. Universal, on the other hand, had 30% box office share during that time. Major studios release fifteen movies a year on the average; whereas, Disney averages seven releases a year. Box office revenues are shown for the industry and for Disney Productions in Exhibits 8.9 and 8.10.

Television

Disney Productions first aired its TV programs in 1954. It produced forty-eight programs a year for *Walt Disney's Wonderful World* and its predecessor, *Disneyland.* Walt would use the television programs to show off his

Exhibit 8.9

MOTION PICTURE INDUSTRY SALES DATA

Box Office Sales

1983	$3,697,000,000
1982	3,452,000,000
1981	2,965,000,000
1980	2,777,000,000
1979	2,804,000,000
1978	2,665,000,000
1977	2,332,000,000

Domestic Box Office Market Shares: January 1–September 30, 1984

Company	*Percent*
Paramount	20.9
Warner Bros.	20.7
Columbia	15.5
20th Century Fox	11.5
Universal	7.5
MGM/UA	6.5
Disney	4.8
Tri-Star	4.0
Orion	3.7
Other	4.9
Total	100.0

SOURCE: Estimates for box office sales from aggregate table in *Variety,* January 11, 1984, p. 7; data for domestic box office market shares from *Standard & Poor's Industry Surveys,* 1985, p. L20.

technological achievements at Disneyland and to demonstrate the animation techniques of his latest movie. In the early 1980s Disney had contracts with CBS and had its programs seen in fifty-eight countries including: Australia, Brazil, Canada, France, Germany, Great Britain, Italy, Japan, Mexico, and Spain. The company continues to believe that its TV programs complement its marketing of motion pictures and theme parks. In 1982 TV revenues were $44.4 million, but in 1983 dropped to $27.9 million. Revenues from television, however, climbed back up to $57.5 million in 1984.

Exhibit 8.10

WALT DISNEY PRODUCTIONS:
MOTION PICTURE REVENUES
(In Thousands of Dollars)

	Theatrical/Domestic	*Theatrical/Foreign*	*Gross Revenues**
1984	$70,679	$38,182	$244,552
1983	38,635	43,825	165,458
1982	55,408	64,525	202,102
1981	54,624	76,279	196,806
1980	63,350	78,314	171,965
1979	49,594	57,288	144,058
1978	69,010	57,912	160,227

SOURCES: 1980 and 1984 Annual Reports.
* Includes television, video, and other rental revenues.

The Disney Channel[14]

"It is a curious thing that the more the world shrinks because of electronic communications, the more limitless becomes the power of the storytelling entertainer."

Walt Disney

The Disney Channel, headquartered in Burbank, was introduced to cable television in 1983. The company entered the cable market because top management believed cable channels have the potential to achieve as much as a 25% profit margin and because most cable channels experience high customer satisfaction. In 1983, approximately 532,000 people subscribed to the Disney Channel. The number jumped to 1,400,000 by September 1984. Disney expected to obtain about 15% of the cable market but was only able to get 7% of cable viewers by mid-1984. James P. Jimirro, Vice-President of telecommunications, expects the Disney Channel to break even by 1985. The Disney Channel was predicted to lose $15 million in 1983, but only lost $11 million.

Thus Disney claims the cable channel to be a success. It is the fastest growing and has the highest customer satisfaction rating of any other service in the industry. The company feels it has a major asset in instant product identification. A new television business segment has thus been formed at Disney. The Disney Channel is offered on 1,700 cable television systems covering 19 million homes in all 50 states. The company has also purchased several transponders and is optimistic about its future in cable.

Cable operators, however, claim that Disney is too rigid in its marketing strategies. The operators claim Disney does not know the cable business.

For example, they claim that Disney was asked to give the channel away free for two weeks to develop watching habits in cable viewing families. The company refused. Other operators complain the programming is no different than regular TV. Furthermore, Disney offers its own 32-page color magazine, which directly competes with cable operators' magazines. Nevertheless, Cablevision has contracted in 1984 to carry the Disney Channel on its systems for the next ten years. The agreement will pay Disney a minimum of $75 million over the period of the contract.

The format of the Disney Channel is: old TV prime time shows, family movies, and original programs. The original programming includes: Mouseterpiece Theater, Mousercise, and Good Morning Mickey. The Disney Channel competes with Home Box Office (12.5 million subscribers), Showtime (4.3 million subscribers), and Cinemax (2.5 million subscribers). Analysts report that overall demand for all cable services has been less than originally forecasted, and that demand for new subscriptions is tapering off. In addition, there have been many companies which have failed in the industry.[15] Refer to Exhibit 8.11 for cable industry subscriber data.

Home Video

Disney is also in the home video business selling video cassettes and video movie discs of such classics as *Dumbo* and *Davy Crockett.* In 1983 *Tron* and *Alice in Wonderland* were released as home videos, and total video sales were $45 million. *Splash, Never Cry Wolf, Robin Hood,* and short cartoons were released in 1984, and sales totaled $69 million. Prior to 1984, Disney had an exclusive home video distribution agreement with RCA. However, the Sony Corporation fought against the agreement in the courts and won. Disney wanted strict control over the distribution of the videos to prevent

Exhibit 8.11

PAY CABLE TV SUBSCRIBERS
(Annual Average in Millions)

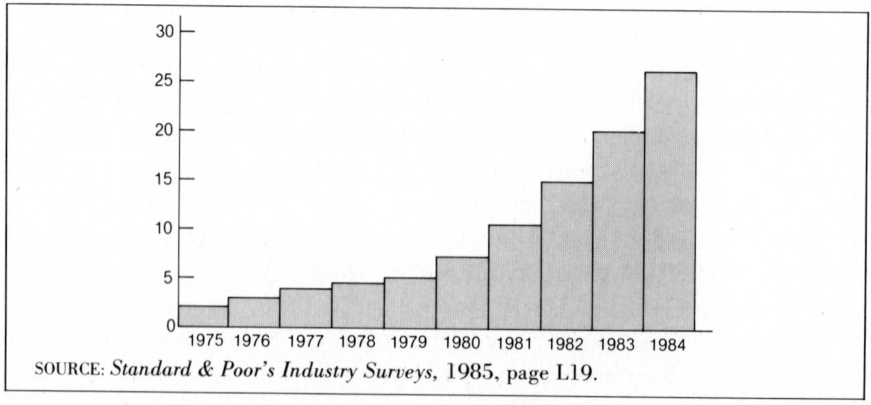

SOURCE: *Standard & Poor's Industry Surveys,* 1985, page L19.

over-exposing its movies and possibly cutting into its motion picture revenue. Disney management now claims that the expiration of the RCA agreement will work to their benefit because it will allow the company to sell movie discs to more companies. Disney home video products are now sold in eighteen countries.

CONSUMER PRODUCTS

The company markets a wide range of consumer products in this business segment. Current revenue and income figures for consumer products are listed below.

Consumer Products and Other (in thousands)

	1984	*Change*	1983	*Change*	1982
Revenues	$109,682	−1%	$110,697	+8%	$102,538
Operating income	53,863	−5%	56,882	+19%	47,832
Operating margin	49%		51%		47%

SOURCE: 1984 Annual Report.

Disney-produced records earned five certified gold records in 1984, bringing the company total to thirty-one. In character merchandising and publications, Sport Goofy became the official spokesman for the National Federation of State High School Associations. A new "Disney's Fun to Learn Library" was introduced by Bantam Books and several other new Disney books were published by companies such as World Books, Inc. and Simon & Schuster. The company has had cooperative consumer product related agreements with Atari, Coca-Cola, Hasbro Bradley, and Adidas. The educational media division expanded its educational computer software with learning games using animated graphics. Five computer manufacturers have entered into licensing agreements for the software.

Especially significant in 1984 was the announcement of a complete line of Disney designer sportswear for women, produced by J. G. Hook. Carrying the *Mickey and Co.* label, it will be on display in 2,000 stores throughout the nation. Disney Productions has also made plans to continue producing ice shows such as *Walt Disney's World on Ice* through 1989.

TOP MANAGEMENT AND BOARD OF DIRECTORS[16,17]

Upon Walt Disney's death in 1966, his financially oriented brother Roy took command of the business and continued to carry Walt's ideas forward through the completion of Walt Disney World in Florida. With Roy's death in 1971, E. Cardon ("Card") Walker, a close associate of the Disney brothers since 1938, became president and chief executive officer (CEO) of Walt

Disney Productions. A year after the completion of EPCOT, Card resigned his management position but continued as a member of the board of directors.

Ronald Miller replaced Card Walker in 1983. A former Los Angeles Rams football player, Miller had worked at Disney since 1957 and was 48 years old upon becoming the president and CEO of Disney. He had married Walt Disney's daughter Diane. Miller served as president only until September 1984. He resigned amidst a series of outside takeover attempts and disagreements with Roy E. Disney, the son of the company's co-founder, Roy O. Disney.

Miller was replaced as Chief Executive Officer by Michael Eisner, President of Paramount Pictures. Frank Wells, previously Vice Chairman of Warner Brothers, took over as President and Chief Operating Officer. Eisner's statements upon taking over the president's position at Walt Disney Productions indicated that he planned to make the company's motion picture division more creative and responsive to current trends. His most immediate problem, however, was to deal directly with the kind of acquisition threats which had given Miller so much trouble. Mr. Eisner received a one-time payment of $750,000 and options to purchase 510,000 Disney shares at $57.44 a share upon joining Walt Disney Productions. His annual base salary is $750,000. Mr. Wells received a $250,000 one-time payment and has an annual salary of $400,000.

The board of directors of Disney is, according to bylaws, to be comprised of not less than nine but not more than fifteen members. There are currently fifteen members on Disney's board. Early in 1984, Roy E. Disney quit the board after two unsuccessful outside takeover attempts. Roy was critical of Ron Miller's managing of the company and was instrumental in forcing Miller's resignation and in the hiring of Michael Eisner as CEO. Roy owns about 5% of Disney shares and runs Shamrock Holdings, Inc. Roy rejoined the company in November of 1984, assuming both board and management positions. He is now involved with the animation department. Roy is committed to new projects and to putting Disney cartoons on television on Saturday mornings.

The average board member has been serving approximately 9 years and the average age is about 59 years. The current Chairman is CEO Michael Eisner. During 1984, Sharon Disney Lund, a daughter of Walt Disney, and Joseph F. Cullman III, former CEO of Philip Morris, were added to the board. Board members Philip M. Hawley and Robert H. B. Baldwin will not stand for reelection to the board in 1986. Board members and key executives are listed in Exhibits 8.12 and 8.13.

The top management of Walt Disney Productions has been described by

WALT DISNEY PRODUCTIONS: BOARD OF DIRECTORS AND TOP MANAGEMENT, 1984

Exhibit 8.12

Board of Directors

Name	*Age*	*Year Joined Disney*	*Affiliation*
Caroline Ahmanson	65	1975	Chairman, Board of Directors, Federal Reserve Bank, San Francisco—12th District
Robert H. B. Baldwin	n/a	1983	Chairman, Morgan Stanley, Inc. (investment bankers)
Charles E. Cobb	n/a	1984	Chairman and CEO, Arvida Corp. (wholly owned subsidiary of Walt Disney Productions)
Joseph F. Cullman III	n/a	1985	Chairman Emeritus, Philip Morris
Roy E. Disney	54	1967	Vice Chairman, Walt Disney Productions
Michael D. Eisner	n/a	1984	Chairman and CEO, Walt Disney Productions
Philip M. Hawley	58	1975	President and CEO, Carter Hawley Hale Stores, Inc. (retail merchandising)
Ignacio E. Lozano, Jr.	56	1981	Publisher, LA Opinion (newspaper publishing)
Sharon Disney Lund	n/a	1984	Trustee, California Institute of the Arts
Richard A. Nunis	51	1968	Executive Vice President—Walt Disney World/Disneyland
Donn B. Tatum	70	1957	Chairman of the Finance Committee, Walt Disney Productions
E. Cardon Walker	67	1956	Former CEO, Walt Disney Productions
Raymond L. Watson	56	1974	Chairman of the Executive Committee, Walt Disney Productions
Frank G. Wells	n/a	1984	President and Chief Operating Officer, Walt Disney Productions

SOURCES: 1984 Annual Report, 1981 and 1982 10K Reports.

(*Continued*)

Exhibit 8.12 **(Continued)**

Name	Age	Year Joined Disney	Affiliation
Samuel L. Williams	n/a	1983	Partner, Hufstedler, Miller, Carlson & Beardsley (law firm)

Corporate Officers

Michael D. Eisner
Chairman of the Board and Chief Executive Officer

Frank G. Wells
President and Chief Operating Officer

Roy E. Disney
Vice Chairman of the Board

Michael L. Bagnall
Executive Vice President—Finance

Carl G. Bongirno
Executive Vice President—WED

Barton K. Boyd
Executive Vice President—Consumer Products

Ronald J. Cage
Executive Vice President—Business Affairs

James P. Jimirro
Executive Vice President—Telecommunications

Jack B. Lindquist
Executive Vice President—Marketing

Richard A. Nunis
Executive Vice President—Walt Disney World/Disneyland

Martin A. Sklar
Executive Vice President—WED Creative Development

John J. Cornwell
Vice President—Management Information Systems

Jose M. Deetjen
Vice President—Tax Administration and Counsel

Dennis M. Despie
Vice President—Entertainment

Luther R. Marr
Vice President—Corporate and Stockholder Affairs

Richard T. Morrow
Vice President—General Counsel

Peter F. Nolan
Vice President—Rights/Business Affairs—Consumer Products

Erwin D. Okun
Vice President—Corporate Communications

Howard M. Roland
Vice President—Construction Contract Administration and Purchasing

Doris A. Smith
Vice President and Secretary

Frank P. Stanek
Vice President—Corporate Planning

Donald A. Escen
Treasurer

Bruce F. Johnson
Controller

Leland L. Kirk
Assistant Secretary-Treasurer

Neal E. McClure
Assistant Secretary

Alvin L. Shelbourn
Assistant Secretary

Donald E. Tucker
Assistant Treasurer

Douglas E. Houck
Assistant Controller

Joe E. Stevens
Assistant Controller

analysts as inbred and highly tenured. A number of the managers had actually worked with Walt for as many as twenty years. In addition, Disney family interests appear to have some influence upon strategic decision making and executive succession. This is suggested by Roy E. Disney's disagreements with Ronald Miller and with 1984 news accounts of Walt's widow and one of his daughters hiring advisors so that their interests in the company could be better served.

WALT DISNEY PRODUCTIONS: CHIEF OPERATING EXECUTIVES OF SUBSIDIARIES

Exhibit 8.13

Domestic Subsidiaries

Arvida/Disney
Arvida Corporation
Disney Development Company
Charles E. Cobb, Jr., Chairman and Chief Executive Officer

Buena Vista International, Inc.
Canasa Trading Corporation
Harold P. Archinal, President

The Disney Channel
Walt Disney Telecommunications and Non-Theatrical Company
James P. Jimirro, President

Disneyland
Disneyland Inc.
Lake Buena Vista Communities, Inc.
Walt Disney World Company
WED Transportation Systems, Inc.
Richard P. Nunis, President

MAPO
WED Enterprises
Carl G. Bongirno, President

Reedy Creek Utilities Company, Inc.
Ronald J. Cayo, President

United National Operating Company
Walt Disney Educational Media Company
Barton K. Boyd, President

Vista Advertising
Walt Disney Travel Company, Inc.
Jack B. Lindquist, President

Vista Insurance Services, Inc.
Philip N. Smith, President

Vista-United Telecommunications
(a Florida Partnership)
James Tyler, General Manager

SOURCE: 1984 Annual Report.

(*Continued*)

Exhibit 8.13
(Continued)

Walt Disney Motion Pictures and Television
Walt Disney Pictures
Buena Vista Distribution Company, Inc.
Jeffrey Katzenberg, President

Walt Disney Music Company
Wonderland Music Company, Inc.
Gary Krisel, President

Foreign Subsidiaries

Belgium
Walt Disney Productions (Benelux) S.A.
Andre Vanneste

Canada
*Walt Disney M*usic of Canada Limited
James K. Rayburn

Denmark
Walt Disney Productions of A/S Denmark
Gunnar Mansson

France
Walt Disney Productions (France) S.A.
Armand Bigle, Richard Dassonville,
Dominique Bigle

Germany
Walt Disney Productions (Germany) GmbH
Horst Koblischek

Italy
Creazioni Walt Disney S.p.A.I.
Antonio Bertini

Japan
Walt Disney Enterprises of Japan Ltd.
Matsuo Yokoyama
Walt Disney Productions Japan, Ltd.
Yosaku Seki, Mamoru Morita, Mas Imai

Portugal
Walt Disney Portuguesa Criacoes Artisticas Lda.
Laszlo Hubay Cebrian

Spain
Walt Disney Iberica, S.A.
Enrique Stuyck

United Kingdom
Walt Disney Productions Limited
Dino Troni, Monty Mendelson, Terry Byrne,
Keith Bales

CORPORATE CULTURE

"We are always asking ourselves, 'What would Walt think?' "
John Mansbridge—art director

Walt Disney's force of personality and obsession with perfection were major ingredients in building Walt Disney Productions. Walt's influence on the company has been evaluated by many people as both good and bad. Some saw his obsession with perfection to be what kept the company creative and what set it apart from other film making companies. Others saw Walt's dominant personality as stifling and inhibiting to those who worked for and with him. In 1969, Walt's brother, Roy, told the following story:[18]

> Not long ago, at our Burbank, California, studio, a group of writers were holding a story conference on a new Disney cartoon feature. They were having a tough time agreeing on a story line, and the atmosphere was as stormy as the weather outside. Suddenly, lightning scribbled a jagged streak over the San Fernando Valley and there was a rolling clap of thunder. "Don't worry, Walt," one of the animators quipped, glancing heavenward. "We'll get it right."

Walt Disney's personal style, philosophies, and ideas are still very much a part of the company's way of doing things. John Mansbridge, who was a supervisory art director, says, "We are always asking ourselves, 'What would Walt think?' " Many of Walt's ideas and quotations are found in employee handbooks and training manuals. Pictures and photographs of Walt Disney are common throughout the corporate studios. New employees are educated at the "Disney University" and the informal corporate climate is referred to as the "Disney Democracy." Yet this reverence for Disney has led some to criticize the company for being too "Disney-minded." Until lately, it seemed to some that new ideas and ventures were only undertaken if Walt Disney himself had conceived of them or had approved them.

Walt Disney Productions is considered to be one of the 100 best companies to work for in America.[19] While the company only rates average on pay, benefits, and opportunities to move up in the organization, it rates extremely high on ambiance. Ambiance refers to the attractiveness of the physical work surroundings and to the company's social climate. Disneyland and Disney World are noted for their quality of landscaping, creative architecture, and the cleanliness of the buildings and grounds. Even the studios in Burbank are kept immaculately clean.

Company image is extremely important at Walt Disney Productions. It is known for creativity and is concerned that the best family entertainment is offered to its customers. Rick Fuess, a Disney training director, states that the purpose of Walt Disney Productions is to make people happy, and that in order to accomplish this purpose, employees must understand their role in creating a world of make believe. Thus, the employee orientation manual explicitly spells out proper behavior for each job position. The manual also states that the quality and integrity of Disney products must be protected at all costs. Some of the formally written company values include friendliness, public trust, integrity, uniqueness, and quality. The company has dress and moral codes with which employees must comply. An employee can be fired for moral turpitude.

Artists and animators have high status at Disney. They work in specially designed facilities. The creative work groups are kept small. There is constant striving for quality and perfected work. The Disney School of Animation was created to select and train the best and brightest potential young animators.

The organization at Disneyland and Walt Disney World is not thought of in normal terms of departments, personnel, and resources. Instead, the organization is called the "family." Employees are referred to as "cast members," and teamwork and collegiality are the norms. Each person is called by his or her first name. Cast members are encouraged to participate in the generation of ideas. Walt himself once said, "I use the whole plant for ideas. If the janitor has a good idea, I'll use it."

Disney is also very concerned that cast members feel they belong. The company sponsors cast member outings at the parks, employee group travel, regular family film festivals for cast members, and employee softball teams. All these activities are well supported by the employees.

Loyalty to the company was very important to Walt. The management of the company has primarily been kept within the family and within a group of long-time Disney associates. If a friend or family member was loyal and supportive, Walt saw to it that the person was well treated and remembered. Walt also remembered disloyalty. Walt always felt as though he was giving his employees an opportunity they could get nowhere else.

EMPLOYEE RELATIONS

"You can dream, create, design, and build the most wonderful place in the world . . . but it requires people to make the dream a reality."

Walt Disney

Walt Disney Productions employs approximately 30,000 people. The main employment centers are Anaheim and Burbank in California, and Orlando in Florida. In Anaheim, Disneyland employs 5,000 workers during the low season and 8,000 during the peak season. Walt Disney World has 13,000 low-season workers and 16,000 peak-season workers. Other employees work at the company headquarters in Burbank or for the various creative groups.

The company offers its employees pension and deferred compensation, stock option, and stock ownership plans. In 1982, about 1,025,000 options were granted at $20.77 to $64.31 per share. Stock ownership is facilitated by an investment tax credit paid to a trust fund, which is in turn used to buy stock for the employees' benefit. In 1980, approximately 11,600 shares were purchased, while 10,700 shares were purchased in 1981. Disney's aggregate retirement expense was $7,146,000 in 1980; $7,598,000 in 1981; and $9,294,000 in 1982. In general, company benefits are rated as only average.[20]

Pay, however, is rated below the average of other similar companies. The average Disneyland employee in 1984 made $7–10 an hour. Job security and opportunity for advancement are also considered to be somewhat below average at Disney. The low turnover of employees makes chances for advancement few and far between. Overall, Disney is considered to be a good company in which to work. Its heavy emphasis on training and high-quality work make its employees very attractive to other companies' personnel recruiters.

Management's concern over rising costs and falling profits at Disneyland caused them in late August 1984 to request their employees to accept a wage cut over a period of three years when the current contract expired September 15. Wages were to be reduced by 7% the first year, followed by 5% cuts each of the following two years. A Disney spokesperson said that the pay cut was necessary because of the poor 1984 summer attendance at Disneyland. Unions representing one-third of the workers at the Anaheim theme park rejected the cuts and instead demanded a two-year agreement including a pay increase.

Major strikes had occurred at Walt Disney Productions only three times in its history. In 1940, employees struck over disputes with Walt about profit sharing and pay. In 1970, two dozen talent workers at Disneyland struck for two days over pay. In 1979, 500 maintenance employees at the same theme park went on strike for 13 days over pay issues. These strikes rarely received much media exposure and did little to tarnish the company's image. In contrast, the strike beginning September 25, 1984 by 1,844 Disneyland employees represented by the Service Employees International Union, the Teamsters Local 88, the Hotel Workers Local 681, and the Bakers Local 324, became a nationwide television event, with network reporters covering every detail.

The striking employees included ride operators, wardrobe workers, food service workers, and ticket sellers. The unions voted in favor of the strike by a 69% majority. Pay was cited as the central issue for the strike. Workers said they walked out to force management into negotiations. In a television interview, a Disneyland employee stated that the employees felt Disney was different from other firms in the entertainment industry, and should be able to pay them more. Tim Stanley, a ride operator on strike, said, "It had been, basically, a big happy family out here, but now, it's like dad has taken our allowance away and given us more work to do."

On September 26, management offered a new proposal for a two-year wage freeze. The unions rejected the proposal and management said there would be no further negotiations. During this time 3,200 workers stayed on the job and the vacancies created by the strike were filled by temporary employees and by management personnel. A federal mediator sought, but was unable to bring the parties together to negotiate. On October 8, management told workers if they did not return to work in one week, they would be replaced. The previous weekend, the striking employees participated in an evening candlelight vigil, singing *When You Wish Upon a Star.* Disneyland employees eventually accepted a wage freeze and returned to work October 17.

At about the same time, Walt Disney World management also asked their employees to accept a wage freeze, but union leaders also threatened to strike. A contract calling for a 3% bonus the first year and a 4% raise the third year was finally approved to replace the one expiring October 1.[21]

On October 23, a total of 200 mid-level and top management personnel at Disney World were fired or demoted following a year-long study to cut costs. Carl Murphy, a labor leader at Disney World, commented on the changes taking place at the theme park:

> Disney's kind of facing reality. The magic's been there years and years and years. Now, they're going to have to become more productive, more efficient.
>
> The company used to be—you were hired in here for life, especially with management. They got fat on management . . . if you were a manager, you had a couple of superintendents under you. You're a superintendent, you had three supervisors under you.[22]

CRISIS IN FANTASYLAND

"Of course we were nervous!"
Ronald Miller

In March 1984, Roy E. Disney, Roy O. Disney's son, resigned from the board of directors. This took the company by surprise. At the time, Roy owned 2.3% of Disney shares, and he purchased an additional 500,000 shares immediately after leaving the company. Roy's resignation and large stock purchases started rumors of an anticipated takeover of Disney. Walt Disney Productions was considered to be a good takeover target because of its valuable film library, land holdings, low stock price, and surplus of cash. Aggressive investors could quickly liquidate company assets and make lots of money. As the takeover rumors persisted, Disney top management tried to protect the company by extending its line of credit and by hiring a consultant who was a takeover specialist.

Takeover Attempt

An investor named Saul Steinberg started acquiring Disney shares in March at a low price and at a rapid rate. By May 1984, Steinberg owned 12.2% of Disney shares and had agreed with Reliance Insurance, an investment group, to make a bid for control of Disney.

Responding to extremely heavy trading of Disney stock, top management moved to purchase in June 1984 Arvida Corporation, a real estate development company based in Boca Raton, Florida. Well known as a premier planned resort and community development company, its assets included 20,000 acres of prime landholdings in Florida, Georgia, and California. Walt Disney Productions assumed $165 million of debt to complete the acquisition. As a result, Standard and Poors lowered its rating of Disney stock. Most analysts believed the acquisition to be an attempt to make the company appear less attractive to possible takeover bids. Disney top management, however, was thinking of using Arvida to develop the unused property within Walt Disney World.

Steinberg attempted to stop the acquisition of Arvida by suing Disney. The courts, however, ruled in Disney's favor and the Arvida acquisition was allowed. Changing his tactics, Steinberg appealed directly to the Disney stockholders to vote to remove those members of the board of directors who were in favor of the acquisition. The board responded quickly by voting to change the company's by-laws to make it extremely difficult for a vote to go in Steinberg's favor. In the meantime, Roy E. Disney continued to purchase shares of Disney stock.

Problems with Gibson

Within a week of the June announcement of the Arvida acquisition, Ronald Miller announced top management's decision to also purchase the Gibson Greeting Card Company. A maker of greeting cards and gift wrappings, Gibson has exclusive rights to the cartoon characters of Garfield, Bugs Bunny, and the Road Runner plus the Sesame Street characters. Ron Miller, Disney's president and CEO, believed Gibson to be a good purchase for a number of reasons. It was seen to be a good fit with Walt Disney Productions and would provide new marketing opportunities. It would also have a desired effect of proportionally decreasing Saul Steinberg's shares of stock. The purchase called for an exchange of stock valued at $343 million.

The deal meant that Gibson stockholders would now be Disney stockholders and favorably disposed to Disney's top management. The purchase called for Disney Productions to increase its long-term debt by $30 million.

In 1983, Gibson earned $22 million on revenues of $241 million. 1984 revenues, as of mid-year, were up 30% from the previous year.

Realizing the danger to his plan, Steinberg threatened to acquire 49% of the Disney company. Rumors were flying, but never confirmed, of a possible liaison between Steinberg and Roy Disney. Before the end of June 1984 Disney top management made a deal with Steinberg. In return for a promise that he would never again attempt a takeover against Disney, Steinberg sold his 4,198,333 shares to Disney for $70.83 a share. The stock was selling at the time for around $65 a share and dropped two days later to $50.[23] Included in the agreement was $28 million in expenses which Steinberg had incurred in the takeover attempt. Since he had only paid approximately $50 a share for the stock, Saul Steinberg was more than willing to sell his stock to the company for a gain of around $59 million.[24]

With the surprise reinstatement at the end of June 1984 of Roy E. Disney to the board of directors, the crisis appeared to be over. Disney's stock price, however, continued to fall and the board of directors continued to be nervous. Their fears were realized as the summer wore on. Irwin Jacobs, an investor with a nickname in the financial community of "Irv the Liquidator" from previous takeovers, began buying Disney stock at $47 a share. Once Jacobs controlled 7.7% of the stock, he joined with the Bass family (another large stockholder) to threaten a proxy fight if Disney top management did not drop plans to acquire Gibson Greeting Cards. Over the years Jacobs had developed a reputation of moving in on a company with basic strengths, but weak top management. In August, Jacobs threatened to force a special stockholders meeting for the purpose of dismantling the company if the Gibson decision was not reversed. In response, Roy Disney vowed publicly to stop Jacobs. Nevertheless, the agreement to buy Gibson was cancelled in August by Disney's top management. Gibson's president, T. M. Conney, publicly criticized Disney stockholders for thwarting the acquisition. Many Disney stockholders, however, agreed with Jacobs that Disney top management, in their zeal to escape Steinberg's takeover, had offered more than Gibson was worth. A number were also critical of the large "greenmail" payment made to Steinberg in the form of buying back the stock at an unrealistically high price.

Management Turmoil

In September 1984, as the labor problems at Disneyland were beginning to surface, Ronald Miller resigned as Disney's president and CEO. Forced to leave by a coalition formed by Roy Disney, Miller received heavy criticism for not following Disney traditions. Michael D. Eisner, a Paramount executive, was appointed president and CEO to replace Miller. The Bass family (with the apparent blessings of Roy Disney and Walt Disney Productions top management) doubled their holdings of Disney stock. This was seen by many as a vote of confidence in the company.

Early in October, the Bass family bought Jacobs' shares of stock for $158.1 million. The Fort Worth Bass family now owned approximately 25% of the outstanding shares of common stock. The crisis appeared to be over. The strike at Disneyland had been settled and the takeover attempts by Steinberg and Jacobs had been thwarted. Some analysts, however, were more cynical and referred to Disney Production's friendly overtures to the Bass family as exchanging "one fox for another in the chicken coop."

Roy Disney rejoined the company in November. He announced a desire to revitalize the studio's animation efforts. Stock was now trading for around $57 a share. Meanwhile, the new CEO, Michael Eisner, indicated that he wished to make the motion picture division more creative and more responsive to current trends. The company announced new objectives of producing three to four new family pictures annually, ten to twelve new Touchstone films, plus acceleration of animated feature productions with new releases every eighteen months. As a whole, Disney management vowed to never again become vulnerable to a takeover. Nevertheless, as 1984 came to a close, rumors emerged that Coca-Cola might be interested in buying Walt Disney Productions.

NOTES

1. L. Gartley and E. Leebron, *Walt Disney: A Guide to References and Resources,* G. K. Hall, Boston, 1979, pp. 1–8.
2. R. O. Disney, "Unforgettable Walt Disney," *Reader's Digest,* February 1969, 94, pp. 212–218.
3. *Walt Disney Productions 1983 10K report.*
4. J. Thiel and R. C. Boals, "Walt Disney Productions—1978," in Thomas L. Wheelen and J. David Hunger, *Strategic Management and Business Policy,* Addison-Wesley, Reading, Mass., 1983, pp. 405–422.
5. D. Walker, "EPCOT 82," *Architectural Design,* 1982, Vol. 52.
6. D. Kasler, "Change Is Not a Fantasy," *Tampa Tribune,* Tampa, Fl., November 4, 1984, pp. 1E and 16E.
7. *Walt Disney Productions 1983 10K report.*
8. D. Walker, "EPCOT 82," *Architectural Design,* 1982, Vol. 52.
9. *Walt Disney Productions 1984 Annual Report.*
10. *Standard and Poor's Industry Survey,* 1983.
11. R. C. Boals, "A Note on the Theme Park Industry," University of Tennessee, 1979.
12. *Walt Disney Productions 1984 Annual Report.*
13. *Fortune Magazine,* October 4, 1982, p. 66.
14. *Walt Disney Productions 1984 Annual Report.*

15. *Business Week*, July 9, 1984, p. 40.
16. *Walt Disney Productions 1983 10K report.*
17. *Wall Street Journal*, January 16, 1985, p. 7.
18. R. O. Disney, "Unforgettable Walt Disney," *Reader's Digest*, February 1969, 94, pp. 212–218.
19. R. Levering, M. Moskowitz, and M. Katz, *The 100 Best Companies to Work For in America*, Addison-Wesley Publishing Company, Reading, Mass., 1984.
20. Levering, Moskowitz, and Katz.
21. D. Kasler, "Change Is Not a Fantasy," *Tampa Tribune*, Tampa, Fl., November 4, 1984, pp. 1E and 16E.
22. Kasler.
23. Kasler.
24. *Fortune Magazine*, October 4, 1982, p. 66.

Case 9

JOHNSON PRODUCTS COMPANY, INC. . . . THE CHALLENGES OF THE 1980S

Thomas L. Wheelen/Robert L. Nixon

Neil H. Snyder/Marian Hessler/Jan Hunter

Bob Bailey/Tony Arroyo

HISTORY

Johnson Products Company, Inc., the largest manufacturer of personal grooming products for black consumers in the world, was formed in 1954. The company was organized as an Illinois corporation in 1957, and in 1969 its state of incorporation was changed to Delaware.

George E. Johnson started the business after he became aware that blacks were unhappy with their naturally coarse, thick hair. Many blacks wanted their hair straightened so that they would have more flexibility in their hair styling. Johnson was not the first to enter the black hair-care products market, but his company became a leading firm because of his efforts to satisfy the needs of the black consumer.

George E. Johnson began his career as a door-to-door salesman in Chicago for Fuller Products, a black cosmetics company. Some time later, he had an opportunity to work as an assistant chemist with Dr. Herbert Martini

Prepared by Profs. Thomas L. Wheelen, Robert L. Nixon, Marian Hessler, Jan Hunter, Bob Bailey, and Tony Arroyo of the University of South Florida, and Prof. Neil H. Snyder of the McIntire School of Commerce at the University of Virginia.

in the lab at Fuller Products. During the 10 years Johnson worked with Martini, he learned the basics of the cosmetic industry. On these foundations, he built his own cosmetics business. The beginning of Johnson Products can be traced back to a particular day on which Johnson met a barber who had visited the managers at Fuller Products to seek help in formulating an improved hair straightener. Fuller Products was not interested, but Johnson was.

Johnson spoke with the barber, Orville Nelson, about his problem and later visited his shop to explore the matter further. At the shop Johnson found customers standing in line to have their hair straightened but the straightener being used simply did not work. Johnson and Nelson formed a short-lived partnership by putting up $250 each in capital. Johnson sought the assistance of Dr. Martini in solving the problem with existing hair straighteners, and the Johnson Products Company was underway.

In order to obtain as much information as he could about the demand for hair straighteners, Johnson visited many black beauty shop owners. He found that the problem was universal: Blacks were dissatisfied with the poor performance of the available hair straighteners. In a *New York Times* article (June 6, 1978), Johnson was quoted as saying "Black beauticians used a hot comb and grease on the hair of black women. Dr. Martini and I agreed that the smoke was bad for the health and the grease was no good for the hair, so we worked on a process to eliminate the grease and smoke, and came up with a cream press permanent, cream shampoo, and Ultra-Sheen conditioner that could be applied at home between visits to the beauty shop." With the hot-comb technique, an individual's hair had to be redone constantly, and rain or moisture would destroy the arrangement.

The emergence of black nationalism in the 1960s popularized the Afro and presented a dilemma for makers of hair straighteners. "I didn't know if it was a fad or not," said Johnson, "so I took a wait-and-see attitude until I was sure it was a trend. Then we developed Afro Sheen for the natural. But I always felt the natural wouldn't last. It's too monotonous and sure enough, women are moving from it" (*New York Times;* June 6, 1978).

Historically a vigorous, competitive hair-care products and cosmetics manufacturing enterprise, Johnson Products is also an important black institution and a growing American business. For example, Johnson Products Company, Inc. was the first black-owned firm to be listed on a major stock exchange. Through innovative product development and promotional techniques it has rapidly become one of the success stories of American business.

The Johnson story nearly ended one day in October 1964 when a devastating fire swept through the plant on Green Street in Chicago and destroyed nearly all of the production facilities. Instead of abandoning the business,

Johnson and his employees salvaged what they could and with the help of suppliers and Fuller Products Company, the company was operating from temporary headquarters within a week.

Following the fire, the company's growth was steady but unspectacular until product innovations in 1965 ushered in a period of rapid sales growth. From 1971 to 1975, gross sales increased from $13 million to $39 million. Since 1975, however, the firm has experienced a series of setbacks. Its first attempt to expand its market with an expensive men's cologne, "Black Tie," was a disaster. The failure was attributed to improper distribution channels and poor shelf space and displays at retail establishments. Coinciding with this setback was the mounting pressure exerted by major competing firms, primarily Revlon, which viewed the fast-growing black cosmetics market as an untapped well. Then in February 1975, the firm's public image was damaged seriously when management felt obligated to sign a consent order issued by the Federal Trade Commission (FTC) requiring that warning labels be placed on its best-selling hair straightener, Ultra Sheen Permanent Creme Relaxer. Johnson claims that the FTC assured him that competitors would also have to put these warning labels on their products. However, Revlon did not place this label on two of their products until nearly two years later. Compounding these problems were the generally poor state of the economy and high level of black unemployment in the late 1970s and early 1980s. The firm experienced its first operating loss in 1980 and saw a loss again in 1982. It again returned to profitability this year (1983), but the firm's future now seems uncertain.

COMPANY HIGHLIGHTS

1954	Company founded
1957	Ultra Sheen Conditioner and Hair Dress introduced
1958	Ultra Sheen line entered professional beauticians' market
1960	Ultra Sheen line introduced in retail market
1964	Fire destroys production facilities
1965	Ultra Sheen No Base Cream Relaxer introduced
1966	Completed first phase of new headquarters
1968	Afro Sheen products introduced
1968	Established The George E. Johnson Foundation
1969	Sponsored its first nationwide TV special, ". . . & Beautiful"
1969	Completed second phase of new headquarters
1969	Company made its first public stock offering
1970	Ultra Sheen cosmetics introduced

1971	Began sponsorship of "Soul Train," nationally syndicated TV show
1971	Johnson Products Company listed on American Stock Exchange
1972	Established The George E. Johnson Educational Fund
1973	Completed third phase of new headquarters
1974	Purchased eleven adjoining acres with building
1975	Entered men's fragrance market with "Black Tie" cologne and splash-on
1975	Started exporting to Nigeria
1975	Acquired Debbie's School of Beauty Culture
1978	Established its first overseas corporation in Nigeria to manufacture its products
1979	Reformulated cosmetics lines
1979	Acquired Freedom Distributors, who distributed the company's and competitors' products on the Eastern seaboard
1980	Established Johnson Products of Nigeria
1980	Introduced Ultra Sheen Precise, first of forty-two innovative product lines
1981	Undertook overseas expansion by establishing a sales and service center in Eastbourne, England
1981	Introduced new products: Gentle Treatment, Tender Treatment, and Bantu Curl
1982	Established Debbie Howell Cosmetics, direct sales line in key black market areas
1982	Introduced nineteen new products
1983	Formed Mello Touch Labs, Inc. to manufacture, market, and distribute a line of consumer products
1983	Introduced two lines of cosmetics: Ultra Sheen and Moisture Formula
1983	Sold Freedom Distributors

OFFICERS AND DIRECTORS

George E. Johnson, 56, serves as the Chairman of the Board and President. Mr. Johnson's business affiliations include board positions with Commonwealth Edison Company; Metropolitan Life Insurance Company; American Health and Beauty Aids Institute (Chairman); and the Cosmetic, Toiletry, and Fragrance Association. He is also member of a number of civic, charitable, professional, and social organizations.

Dorothy McConner, 54, serves as the Executive Vice President, Administration, and Corporate Secretary. She was elected to the Board of Directors in 1969. Mrs. McConner has been with the company for approximately twenty-five years and was selected "Blackbook's" 1975 Business Woman of the Year.

David N. Corner, 53, joined the company in December 1978 as Vice President, Finance, and Chief Financial Officer. In the preceding five years he was with Libby, McNeil & Libby, Inc., most recently as Vice President, Finance, and Treasurer.

Marilynn J. Cason, 40, has served as Corporate Counsel and was elected a Vice President in 1977. Before joining the company in 1975, she spent three years as an attorney for Kraft, Inc., and three years as an associate attorney with the Denver law firm of Dawson, Nagel, Sherman, and Horwald.

Tehsel S. Dhaliwal, 42, has been with the company since 1973. He served previously as Director of Manufacturing Operations. He was promoted to Vice President of Operations in 1983.

Michael J. Guthrie, 33, Vice President of Corporate Planning, has served as senior attorney on the company's legal staff since joining the company in 1979. He was appointed to his present position in 1983. Prior to joining the company, Mr. Guthrie was a staff attorney with Sonnenschein, Carlin, Nath, and Rosenthal.

Ezzat N. Khalil, 49, joined the company in 1975 as Director of Cosmetics. He was elected Vice President, Research and Development, in 1978. In the five years preceding 1975, Mr. Khalil held the following positions: Vice President of Research and Development with Chromex Chemical Company; Director of New Products with Kolmar Laboratories, Inc.; Laboratory Manager with Estée Lauder; Director of Research and Development with Maybelline, Inc.; and General Manager of Essencial Ohio International.

Alan N. Sym-Smith, 52, has served as Vice President, International, during the past five years and is responsible for coordinating the company's international sales and marketing activities. He joined the company in 1975. From 1971 to 1975 he served as Vice President, International, of Helene Curtis Industries, Inc.

Joan B. Johnson, 54, wife of George E. Johnson, shared in the founding of the company in 1954. She presently serves as Treasurer and Director.

Except for Tehsel S. Dhaliwal and Michael J. Guthrie, each executive officer was last elected as such on December 8, 1982 and will serve until a successor is appointed and qualified. Mr. Dhaliwal was appointed a Vice President in March 1983 and Mr. Guthrie in September 1983. Deborah A. Howell serves as President of Debbie's School of Beauty Culture, which is a wholly owned subsidiary.

The three internal directors are George E. and Joan B. Johnson, and Dorothy McConner. A brief account of the experiences of each director who is not an officer is set forth below:

John T. Schriver has served as a First Vice President of Shearson/American Express, Inc. (formally Loeb, Rhoades, Shearson, a Division of Shearson Hayden Stone, Inc.), investment bankers during the past five years.

Alvin J. Bouette has served as President of the Independence Bank of Chicago, Illinois during the past five years and was made Chairman of the Board of Independence Bank in 1980.

Melvin D. Jefferson is owner and President of Superior Beauty and Barber Supply Company (Detroit, Mich.), a full-service distributor of beauty and hair care products.

Jesse L. Howell has served as Vice President of Debbie's School of Beauty Culture, Inc. (a wholly-owned subsidiary of the company since 1975). He has served as a Director of the company since 1977.

OWNERSHIP

Because of their direct and indirect ownership of shares of the company's stock, George E. Johnson and Joan B. Johnson may be deemed to be controlling persons of the company for the purposes of the federal securities law. The Johnson family controls 62.9% of the company. (See Exhibit 9.1.)

SUBSIDIARIES AND FACILITIES

The company's corporate offices and manufacturing facilities are located at 8522 South Lafayette Avenue in Chicago. The building encompasses approximately 64,000 square feet of office space and 176,000 square feet for manufacturing and warehousing purposes.

To support its continued growth, the company acquired additional property adjacent to the South Lafayette facilities in November 1974 at a cost of $1 million. This property consists of approximately 11 acres of land (compared to the 12-acre tract of the old facility) and a 200,000 square foot building. This building currently houses the administrative offices of John-

STOCK OWNERSHIP

Exhibit 9.1

Title of Class	*Name and Address of Beneficial Owner*	*Amount Beneficially Owned*	*Percent of Class*
Common Stock	George E. Johnson, trustee of personal trust[1] 95 Brentwood Drive Glencoe, Illinois 60022	2,016,775	50.7%
Common Stock	Joan B. Johnson, trustee of personal trust[2] 95 Brentwood Drive Glencoe, Illinois 60022	180,000	4.5%
Common Stock	Joan B. Johnson, trustee for children[1, 2] 95 Brentwood Drive Glencoe, Illinois 60022	254,000	6.4%
Common Stock	Joan B. Johnson, under eleven irrevocable trusts granted by George E. Johnson[1, 2] 95 Brentwood Drive Glencoe, Illinois 60022	48,200	1.2%
Common Stock	George E. Johnson and Joan B. Johnson, as trustees of The Johnson Products Co., Inc. Employees Profit Sharing Plan and Trust[1, 2] 8522 S. Lafayette Avenue Chicago, Illinois 60620	2,700	0.07%
Common Stock	Total shares owned by George E. Johnson and Joan B. Johnson	2,501,675	62.9%
As of November 1, 1983, directors and officers of the Company (14 in group) beneficially owned the following shares:			
Common Stock		2,528,610[3]	63.5%

1. Mrs. Johnson disclaims beneficial ownership in these shares.
2. Mr. Johnson disclaims beneficial ownership in these shares.
3. Includes 5,470 shares under options exercisable within 60 days.

son's subsidiary, Debbie's School of Beauty Culture, Inc., and selected administrative offices of the company and warehousing.

The company's wholly owned subsidiary, Debbie's School of Beauty Culture, operates nine training facilities for beauticians. In 1977 Johnson Products Company purchased a Chicago building totalling 12,000 square feet. This facility now houses one of Debbie's schools. The other eight locations are leased. The locations and terms of the leases are outlined in Exhibit 9.2.

FACILITIES OF JOHNSON PRODUCTS

Exhibit 9.2

Location	*Approximate Square Footage*	*Lease Expires*
Chicago, Illinois	25,000	December 31, 1984[1]
Chicago, Illinois	12,000	December 31, 1984[1]
Chicago, Illinois	8,000	December 31, 1984[1]
Harvey, Illinois	10,000	December 31, 1984
East St. Louis, Illinois	12,000	August 31, 1984
Detroit, Michigan	7,200	July 31, 1984
Birmingham, Alabama	7,000	April 30, 1984
Indianapolis, Indiana	9,000	June 30, 1984

[1] The Chicago leases that expire in December 1984 are renewable at the option of the company and the East St. Louis lease contains a purchase option exercisable sixty days after expiration of the lease.

Since its acquisition by Johnson in 1975, Debbie's has operated profitably with the exception of fiscal 1982. Its poor performance in that year was attributed to the economic recession and curtailment in federal funding for certain types of education. The school's staff currently includes more than 100 administrators and instructors. The school's curriculum includes anatomy, hairdressing, hair weaving, personal appearance, skin and nail care, shop management, and product education. The program is 1,500 hours over nine and one-half months. In 1983, Debbie's graduated a record 1,000 students; the previous class was only 455 students. Johnson Products intends to continue expansion of Debbie's Schools, taking advantage of the scarcity of black beauty schools nationwide (there were fewer than 75 in operation in 1981). Plans call for opening a school in St. Louis, Missouri in 1984.

Debbie's operates a salon division which consists of three Ultra Precise Beauty Boutiques in Chicago, one of which is situated in a Sears department store. The other two are operating from leased space in Chicago. These leases are up for renewal in September 1986. The salons, thus far, have been only marginally profitable. All of Debbie's schools and salons use Johnson Products predominantly.

In 1982, Debbie's established Debbie Howell Cosmetics, a direct-sales organization to promote Johnson's new line of cosmetics. This division currently employs consultants in about thirty cities that the firm believes are in key black consumer markets. Losses in its first year of operation approximated $147,000, due primarily to initial start-up costs. The parent company is optimistic about the future of the endeavor because consultants have proven to be a very successful sales technique for Avon and Mary Kay Cosmetics. There are plans to expand further in existing markets and other key black consumer market areas.

INTERNATIONAL SUBSIDIARIES

Nigeria

Johnson Products owns a 40% interest in Johnson Products of Nigeria, Ltd., a manufacturing affiliate established in 1980. Johnson was the first U.S. company to manufacture hair care products in Nigeria. The Nigerian partners represent various segments of that nation's business community. The facilities include a 36,000 square foot manufacturing and warehousing building located just outside the capital, Lagos. An additional 18,000 square foot facility is available for expansion. Mr. Johnson said of the Nigerian investment:

> We have been exporting to Nigeria since 1975, but actually our products have been sold there since the 1960s. Consequently, we have excellent corporate and product name recognition. . . . By manufacturing in Nigeria we are taking what we believe is the best approach to building on our well-established reputation and maximizing the opportunities available in a developing country.

Initial investment for the Nigerian operation was $1.6 million. First-year losses totalled $380,000 and were attributed to extremely heavy living costs in accommodating a team of Johnson Products representatives from headquarters, who supervised the plant set-up and the early stages of operations. Johnson Products' managers have grown more pessimistic about the potential profitability of this venture as it has continued to operate in the red. Total losses in fiscal 1981 were $466,000. In fiscal 1982 losses were $1,802,000, including losses from operations and write-down of investment (net foreign exchange gains).

In 1983, the Nigerian operation recorded its first profitable year. Initially, problems stemmed from smuggling activities that forced Johnson Products of Nigeria, Ltd. to compete with its own product being manufactured in United States and being sold on the black market at well below retail prices. Then in 1981, in an effort to stave off illegal imports, the Nigerian government severely restricted the flow of goods, both raw materials and products, entering the country. As a result, the Nigerian plant was forced to suspend operations on several occasions due to difficulties in receiving shipments of raw materials and other goods. This operation manufactures more than 30 different products under Ultra Sheen and Afro Sheen brands.

The main problem for the past few years centers around the Nigerian government's lack of foreign exchange, which causes prolonged delays in the acquisition of raw materials. Import licenses have been granted. Therefore the company will maintain some degree of production in Nigeria despite the enduring basic raw materials problem.

In 1983, Nigeria "remains the largest market in black Africa, as well as the one most likely to provide business opportunities for American firms in the medium and long term" (*Foreign Economic Trends and Their Implications for the United States*, November 1983). Nigeria is an untapped ethnic consumer market that numbers 90 million people with an annual growth rate of 3.2%.

Great Britain Johnson Products continued its overseas expansion by establishing a sales and service center in Eastbourne, England (40 miles south of London) in October 1981. This is essentially a low-overhead central distribution center for the British and Western European markets (primarily France, Germany, Belgium, and Holland). This 3,000 square foot facility has allowed the company to offer a broader range of its professional and retail product lines to European consumers. In fiscal 1983, this distribution center "made a positive contribution" toward profit. Personal income in England increased in 1983, which prompted a 2% growth in personal consumption. These markets will be supported by an expanding advertising and promotion campaign.

Jamaica In 1981, after seven consecutive years of decline, the Jamaican economy had a growth rate of approximately 2.0%. Future growth rates were estimated in the 2.0 to 3.0% range. So in 1981 Johnson Products entered into its first licensing agreement with a Jamaican firm. The licensee currently manufactures Ultra Sheen brand products out of its facility in Kingston, Jamaica's capital city. Johnson Products supplies the raw materials as well as technical and marketing support. In return, the company receives royalties based on a percentage of sales. Although strict import regulations limit Johnson's ability to tap most of the Caribbean Islands as well as Central and South America, the Jamaican licensee is expected to be able to sell its products to the English-speaking islands, formerly the British West Indies. Puerto Rico is Johnson's biggest market in that area of the world.

Future Plans In addition to its present activities, Johnson Products is planning to establish distributorships in the Spanish-speaking islands, in order to fully develop these markets. Johnson Products is experiencing heavy competition throughout the Caribbean and Canadian markets. In the future, the company will open new markets in those Central and South American countries with the fewest import restrictions. The company's net sales and other operating revenue from international operations were $2,151,000 in 1983; $1,514,000 in 1982; and $2,690,000 in 1981.

INDUSTRY AND COMPETITION

In 1983, consumers spent $11,857,000,000 on toiletries and cosmetics. While continued gains are expected, the industry's real growth rate is expected to fall to an annual increase of 2 to 3%. (See Exhibit 9.3.) This is well below that experienced in the 1960s and 1970s. This decline is attributed to the fact that women are entering the labor force at a lower rate. This indicates that the trend of the 1960s and 1970s for the increase in multi-income families may have run its course and stabilized. Currently the country is experiencing a normal growth rate in the employment of women.

One of the fastest growing areas in the toiletries and cosmetics industry is the ethnic market. A study by Fairchild Publications estimates the ethnic toiletries and cosmetics market is growing at an annual rate of 20% through 1986. The ethnic market consists of an estimated 40 million blacks, Hispanics, and other minorities. Of Johnson's sales, 30% are accounted for by minorities other than blacks. Minority women are estimated to spend three times more on cosmetics than white women. In the 1980 U.S. Census, the black population numbered approximately 26 million with a median age of 25. (See Exhibit 9.4.) The ethnic market has potential sales of $5 billion according to estimates made by the Commerce Department.

The black consumer is experiencing an increase in disposable income greater than that of the population at large. Between 1972 and 1979, blacks' aggregate income expanded 194% from $30 billion to $88.2 billion and in 1983 was in excess of $100 billion. According to an industry analyst, blacks account for an increasing percentage (currently 13%) of the nation's population. The 25 to 34 age group—heavy toiletry and cosmetics consum-

Exhibit 9.3

U.S. TOILETRIES AND COSMETIC INDUSTRY FINANCIAL INFORMATION

Financial Indicators	1985(E)	1984(E)	1983	1982	1981	1980
Sales (millions)	13,700	12,750	11,857	11,507	10,851	10,166
Operating margins	15.5%	15.5%	14.9%	15.0%	15.9%	16.4%
Net profits (millions)	875.0	790.0	737.3	714.1	761.1	768.1
Net profit margins	6.4%	6.2%	6.2%	6.2%	7.0%	7.6%
% Earned to total capital	13.0%	13.0%	13.8%	13.5%	15.9%	16.4%
% Earned to net worth	16.0%	16.0%	16.4%	15.5%	18.2%	19.0%
% Retained to common equity	7.5%	7.0%	7.2%	6.4%	8.5%	10.0%

SOURCE: *Value Line Investment Survey,* January 25, 1985, p. 812.

NOTE: (E) means estimate.

Exhibit 9.4
BLACK DEMOGRAPHICS

	Labor Force by %						
Age	1977	1978	1979	1980	1981	1982	1983
16–19	8.5	8.8	8.4	8.0	7.5	7.3	7.0
20–24	16.0	16.0	16.1	15.8	16.0	16.3	16.1
25–34	27.9	28.0	28.6	29.5	31.0	30.8	31.5
35–44	19.5	19.4	19.5	19.7	20.0	20.3	20.6
45–54	16.2	15.8	15.7	15.6	14.5	14.2	14.0
55–64	9.3	9.2	9.1	9.0	9.0	9.0	9.0
65+	2.6	2.8	2.6	2.4	2.0	2.1	1.9

	Mean Income					
Age	1978	1979	1980	1981	1982	1983
14–24	$ 6,673	$ 7,738	$ 7,898[1]	$10,350[1]	$10,487[1]	$ 9,019[1]
25–34	11,815	12,916	14,018	15,079	16,256	15,871
35–44	14,021	15,277	16,788	18,350	19,172	20,376
45–54	14,983	16,933	18,013	19,286	19,812	21,404
55–64	11,976	14,741	16,301	17,089	18,093	19,105
65+	8,363	8,713	10,472	10,650	11,566	12,272

	Population %						
Age	1977	1978	1979	1980	1981	1982	1983
16–19	9.4[2]	9.3[2]	9.1[2]	11.3[4]	10.8[4]	10.5[4]	10.1[4]
20–24	14.3[3]	14.4[3]	13.5[3]	10.3	10.5	10.5	10.5
25–34	14.1	14.5	15.0	17.1	16.6	17.0	17.4
35–44	10.1	10.3	10.4	10.2	10.3	10.6	10.9
45–54	9.1	9.0	9.0	8.6	8.4	8.3	8.1
55–64	7.0	7.1	7.1	7.2	7.1	7.1	7.1
65+	7.7	7.8	7.9	7.9	7.9	8.0	7.9

SOURCE: *Statistical Abstract of U.S.*, 1985.

NOTES: 1. Indicates that these figures represent the age category of 15–24. 2. Indicates that these figures represent the age category of 14–17. 3. Indicates that these figures represent the age category of 18–24. 4. Indicates that these figures represent the age category of 15–19.

ers—will by the mid-1980s represent 17.4% of the total black population of the United States.

With statistics like these, the ethnic consumer is being sought after as never before. In 1983, the market penetration of the larger national companies may have peaked. The major competitors of Johnson Products Company are: (1) Revlon, with its Realistic hair straightener and Polished Amber lines; (2) Avon, with Shades of Beauty and Earth & Fire lines of makeup products for black women; and (3) Cosmair's L'Oréal of Paris, which has a product line called Radiance consisting of hair colors and formula hair relaxers. (See Exhibit 9.5.)

The competition has added a new facet in the market. The large companies such as Revlon, Avon, and Fashion Fair are still in pursuit of the ethnic dollar. Another new competition is the small regional manufacturer. These competitors offer a restricted product line offering, while competing for the same shelf space. For example, M&M Products—with their product Sta-Sof-Fro—was founded in 1973. The company's sales reached approximately $47 million in 1983, and they employed 383 people. This firm has earned a reputation as a major competitor in the black hair care industry. In 1982, Pro-Line—another competitor—had sales of approximately $23 million and had 200 employees. Pro-Line is an innovative black hair care firm that is constantly introducing new products such as Perm Repair and Cherry Fragrance Oil Shampoo.

PRODUCTS

Johnson Products currently manufactures over 100 different products. Since January 1980, the company has introduced more than forty-five new products, including nineteen in 1982. Most new products introduced by Johnson Products were matched by similar new products from their competitors. Product lines fall into two categories: those marketed to the professional industry, and those sold to the general public. (See Exhibit 9.6.) Johnson's retail sales are the company's largest segment.

Before the introduction of Ultra Sheen Precise in 1980, the company had not introduced a single innovative product in over fifteen years. As a result, the firm's public image had waned and its reputation among professional beauty operators had faltered. Each successive new product introduction in the following four years has been designed to portray the firm as an industry innovator, "personally concerned with solving the beauty problems of Black consumers" (*Black Enterprise;* June 1980).

According to Mr. Johnson, "In assessing why our business (1980) had slacked we learned several things. For one, we were no longer thought of as an innovative, sophisticated organization. We found also a low level of loyalty from professional beauticians and salon operators. In addition, there was an apparent lack of understanding among many large retail buyers that Johnson Products is a large, substantial organization."

Johnson also cited other problems including:

1. Increased competition from large and small regional competitors.
2. Competition for shelf space.

Exhibit 9.5

SELECTED FINANCIAL INFORMATION ON COMPETITORS

	Sales[1]		*Operating Margins*		*Net Profit*[1]	
Company	1983	1982	1983	1982	1983	1982
Alberto-Culver	313.7	320.4	5.2%	6.0%	3.9	6.6
Avon Products	3000.1	3000.8	13.6%	15.7%	164.4	196.6
Gillette	2183.3	2239.0	18.1%	17.7%	145.9	135.1
Helene Curtis	330.4	243.2	8.3%	5.2%	10.4	3.6
Johnson Products	45.8	42.4	9.5%	loss	1.6%	(3.6)
Mary Kay	323.8	304.3	22.2%	22.0%	36.7	35.4
Noxell Corp.	304.3	261.9	14.5%	13.7%	23.2	18.5
Redken Labs	86.3	84.6	15.7%	16.2%	6.4	6.5
Revlon, Inc.	2378.9	2351.0	13.6%	12.9%	111.2	111.1

SOURCE: *Value Line Investment Survey*, January 25, 1985, pp. 813, 814, 819, 820–825.
NOTE: 1. These figures are stated in millions of dollars.

3. Changing buying habits of the consumer due to economic conditions.
4. Bad economy which caused retailers to carry smaller inventories, causing higher stock-out conditions and loss of customer goodwill.

Hair care products and cosmetics accounted for 94% of net sales and other operating revenue in 1983. The firm also manufactures two lines of cosmetics: Ultra Sheen and Moisture Formula.

MARKETING

Sales Organization

The sales effort of Johnson Products Company is directed almost entirely toward reaching black consumers. The company's products and marketing are strategically positioned to concentrate on the ethnic markets. In 1975, Johnson Products deviated from this pattern when it introduced a men's fragrance line, Black Tie, which was marketed to the general consumer. In keeping with this marketing strategy, Johnson focuses its sales efforts in areas where there is a concentration of the black population. Therefore, most consumer purchases of Ultra Sheen, Afro Sheen, and other company products originate in the East, Midwest, West Coast, and South, with few sales being made in the Northeast, Great Plains, and Rocky Mountain regions of the United States.

Johnson Products distributes its lines mainly through retail outlets by utilizing a company/distributor/retailer channel. Johnson's professional

Net Profit Margins		*EPS*		*% Earned to Total Capital*		*% Earned to Net Worth*		*% Retained to Common Equity*	
1983	1982	1983	1982	1983	1982	1983	1982	1983	1982
1.3%	2.1%	1.01	1.17	5.6%	8.9%	5.7%	9.8%	2.7%	7.0%
5.5%	6.6%	2.21	2.75	11.9%	14.2%	13.7%	16.1%	1.3%	1.8%
6.7%	6.0%	4.78	4.45	15.3%	14.6%	19.3%	18.7%	9.9%	9.9%
3.2%	1.5%	2.84	.98	13.7%	7.1%	19.5%	8.4%	19.5%	8.4%
3.6%	loss	.41	(.91)	7.5%	loss	7.5%	loss	7.5%	loss
11.6%	10.3%	1.22	1.18	27.2%	35.6%	27.8%	37.1%	25.1%	33.8%
7.6%	7.1%	2.33	1.88	20.0%	18.7%	20.0%	18.7%	14.0%	12.9%
7.4%	7.6%	2.95	2.25	14.0%	16.0%	14.9%	17.6%	12.0%	15.0%
4.7%	4.7%	5.01	4.44	9.9%	8.7%	12.3%	9.3%	4.1%	2.8%

lines are sold to barber shops and beauty salons. Although a middleman is usually involved in product distribution, a substantial number of company sales are made directly to national and regional drug, grocery, and mass merchandising chains. In 1979, Freedom Distributors was acquired, then sold in 1983. Freedom distributed Johnson's and competitors' products on the Eastern seaboard.

With the introduction of Black Tie, Johnson's top management contracted an outside sales organization adept in the men's fragrance market to distribute the new line. Through its marketing tactics, Johnson Products hoped to create for Black Tie an image which was appealing to both the ethnic and general markets. The fragrance was perceived in the marketplace as an ethnic product and failed to achieve a profitable sales level.

Prior to 1969, all contacts with Johnson's sales organization emanated from the company's home office in Chicago. In an effort to improve the effectiveness of its sales programs, Johnson Products developed a district sales structure in 1969 to aid the control and development of its sales force and to improve its recruiting efforts. In the nine sales districts, salespeople now demonstrate the importance and profitability of ethnic products to distributors and retailers and assist them in merchandising the company's products.

Johnson Products' sales force marketing division has grown steadily over the life of the company. Each sales representative undergoes an intensive

Exhibit 9.6

MAJOR PRODUCT LINES INTRODUCED IN LAST FOUR YEARS

Major Product Lines	*Year Introduced*
Professional lines	
1. Ultra Sheen Brand	
—Precise Conditioning Relaxer	1980
—Precise Curl System	1980
—Precise No-Lye Relaxer	1983
2. Bantu Curl Brand (8 Products)	1981
3. Ultra Sheen II	1983
Retail lines	
1. Afro Sheen Brand	1980
2. Ultra Sheen Brand	
—Natural Body Formula	1980
—Ultra Sheen No-Lye Relaxer	1983
3. Classy Curl Brand	1980
4. Tender Treatment Brand	1980
5. Gentle Treatment Brand	1981
—Gentle Treatment Instant Conditioner	1983
—Super Setting Lotion	1983
—No-Lye Condition Relaxer	1983

sales training program which continues after he or she is assigned to various districts for work in the field.

Johnson's salespeople function in various capacities, all aimed at increased retail and professional sales. Some conduct store demonstrations of Johnson's facial cosmetics. Others conduct clinics in the proper use of Ultra Sheen Creme Relaxers and products designed for beauticians and barbers.

In the area of international marketing, Johnson Products Company exports to selected foreign markets. George E. Johnson's stated philosophy is that he plans to sell personal care products wherever there are blacks to buy them. It was in this spirit that Johnson Products began exporting to Nigeria in 1975. (See the section entitled International Subsidiaries.)

Consumer and Professional Markets

In an effort to improve consumer perception Johnson Products has introduced innovative products backed by elaborate promotional campaigns. In 1980, for example, the Ultra Sheen Precise line was introduced. This was the first hair relaxer to contain a substantive conditioner. This was so unique the company was issued a patent. A marketing plan, "The Precise System of Success," was developed to introduce the Precise line. Stage presentations were made in about 10 cities, with more than 10,000 beauticians attending.

This was followed by more than 100 day-long seminars in some 30 cities attended by about 20,000 beauticians. Also, the Classy Curl line was introduced for the younger market segment. For the professional market, Johnson Products introduced Natural Body Formula, Ultra Sheen Conditioning Plus Shampoo, and Curl System.

In 1981, new product introductions were Gentle Treatment, Tender Treatment, and Bantu Curl. The Tender Treatment brand includes conditioning detangling shampoo, super penetrating conditioner, and creme hair dress. Gentle Treatment has a built-in conditioning agent similar to the successful Precise brand. In addition, this product line had a significant product attribute: a calcium hydroxide base instead of the sodium hydroxide base, which had prompted the FTC in 1975 to intervene with a consent decree to place a warning on an earlier Johnson product.

Along with these product introductions, the company has experimented with several extensive promotional campaigns. The "Win a Date" contest offering a male and female winner a weekend date in Jamaica with the two Classy Curl models was used in the Classy Curl campaign. In promoting the Gentle Treatment Conditioning Creme Relaxer, the "Great Model Search" was conducted. More than 7,000 people entered this contest. The winners were used as models in promotional campaigns in 1983. Soon after these promotions, an A. C. Nielson audit survey showed an increase in market share in both product categories.

In the cosmetics lines, advertising is done mostly in magazines based on demographic and psychographic analysis. Earlier in 1979, Johnson's cosmetics line was being reformulated. The Ultra Sheen line was being designed to appeal to women under twenty-five, while Moisture Formula was directed toward the more sophisticated segment. The company accomplished the segmentation of the market by price differentials. This reformulation was done by William Pinkney, director of marketing cosmetics, in 1979. Mr. Pinkney joined the company after developing the Polished Amber lines for Revlon. Moisture Formula was advertised in such magazines as *Cosmopolitan, Ebony, Essence, Glamour,* and *Jet.* TBWA of New York was handling the advertising of the cosmetics lines.

In 1982, Johnson Products commissioned a study to research consumer opinions and/or perceptions of the company. Results from the study were: (1) a high level of name recognition (93%); (2) a feeling that its products guarantee quality (68%); and (3) a belief that the firm is reliable and trustworthy (70%).

Advertising and promotion expenses increased from 1979 through 1981. From 1982 through 1983, advertising was reduced. However, as a percentage of net sales, these expenditures have varied. (See Exhibit 9.7.)

Exhibit 9.7

ADVERTISING AND PROMOTION EXPENDITURES

Year	*Dollars*	*Percentage of Net Sales*
1983	$7,226,000	16%
1982	7,467,000	18
1981	8,076,000	17
1980	7,243,000	21
1979	6,019,000	18
1978	6,211,000	17
1977	5,731,000	18
1976	5,608,000	14
1975	4,498,000	12
1974	4,202,000	13
1973	3,733,000	15
1972	3,097,000	18
1971	2,830,000	20

In 1983, one of the company's product development goals was to increase its professional market share, which constitutes about 15% of Johnson's total hair care business. Over the past six years, sales have been increasing between 15% and 20% annually. These increases shown an expanding ethnic market. The first market introduction in 1983 was the Precise No-Lye Relaxer, which was followed by improved versions of earlier lines, Ultra Sheen II and Bantu. Special promotions and training programs are being aimed at the professional market segment.

On the retail side, the Gentle Treatment No-Lye Conditioning Creme Relaxer is being influenced by the "Great Model Search" campaign of 1982. This year's (1983) promotion plans include a fifteen market concert tour schedule featuring the "Gap Band." This tour will be sponsored by the Ultra Curl brand. Extensive couponing and sampling will be conducted concurrent with the concert tour.

RESEARCH AND DEVELOPMENT

Since January 1980, the Johnson Products Research Center has introduced, for both the retail and professional markets, more than fifty new products and line extensions. These new products contributed more than 60% of the company's sales in 1983, compared to 48% in 1982 and 36% in 1981.

The Johnson Products Research Center is considered to be the largest laboratory of its kind devoted exclusively to the research and development

R & D EXPENDITURES

Exhibit 9.8

Year	*R & D Expenditures*
1983	$ 799,000
1982	868,000
1981	870,000
1980	782,000
1979	690,000
1978	763,000
1977	739,000
1976	525,000
1975	467,000
1974	388,000

of beauty care products for black consumers. A staff of more than 30 technicians and scientists representing a variety of scientific disciplines works with the latest sophisticated equipment in a 7,000 square foot research laboratory. Approximately one-third of the research and development man-hours are spent on quality control; the rest are spent on new product development and the improvement of existing products. Research and development expenditures are shown in Exhibit 9.8. In-house capabilities are supplemented through the use of outside consultants and technical services in developing concepts and packaging design and researching the characteristics of ethnic skin and hair.

One significant aspect of the company's efforts is the capability to perform basic scientific research, which has enabled Johnson Products to develop unique technologies for producing a variety of beauty-aid products. During the past three years, the company has received four patents for products presently on the market; several other patents are pending.

FINANCE

Since 1969, Johnson Products has been a public corporation. The initial stock offering was 300,000 shares at $15 per share. Johnson was authorized to issue a total of 7,504,400 shares. They were listed on the American Stock Exchange and the stock split 2-for-1 in January 1973. The par value of the stock changed from $1 to $.50. On August 31, 1983 the market price per share of stock was $9.75. (see Exhibit 9.9.)

During the fiscal years 1980, 1981, 1982, and 1983, the company sustained losses in eight of the sixteen quarters. In 1980 and 1982, the company suffered yearly losses of $2,379,000 and $3,623,000, respectively.

Exhibit 9.9
TEN-YEAR FINANCIAL REVIEW
(Dollars in Thousands)

Years Ended August 31	**1983**	**1982**	**1981**
Summary of Operations			
Net sales	$40,937	$39,177	$43,197
Other operating revenue	4,838	3,270	3,710
Total net sales and other operating revenue	45,775	42,447	46,907
Cost of sales	16,649	18,191	19,528
Selling, general and administrative (exclusive of advertising and promotion)	18,490	19,122	17,866
Advertising and promotion	7,226	7,467	8,076
Equity in losses and write-down of investment in Nigerian affiliate	—	1,802	466
Interest, net	424	414	48
Income (loss) before income taxes	2,986	(4,549)	923
Income taxes (benefit)	1,358	(926)	538
Net income (loss)	1,628	(3,623)	385
Net income (loss) per share (EPS)	.41	(.91)	.10
Dividends per share	—	—	—
Other Financial Data[1]			
Current assets	19,894	20,082	20,112
Current liabilities	7,186	9,022	6,683
Working capital	12,708	11,060	13,429
Property, net	9,210	9,133	8,988
Total assets	29,785	29,659	30,860
Capital lease obligations	299	—	—
Shareholders' equity	21,715	20,062	23,660
Shareholders' equity per share	5.46	5.05	5.96
Capital expenditures	987	1,076	791
Ratios			
Income (loss) before income taxes to net sales and other operating revenue	6.5%	(10.7%)	2.0%
Net income (loss) to net sales and other operating revenue	3.6%	(8.5%)	.8%
Return on average shareholders' equity	7.8%	(16.6%)	1.6%
Advertising and promotion to net sales and other operating revenue	15.8%	17.6%	17.2%
Average common and common equivalent shares outstanding[2]	3,980,000	3,973,000	3,972,000
Stock price range (high)	11⅜	3½	5⅛
Stock price range (low)	3⅛	2	2⅝
Sales per share (dollars)	11.50	10.68	11.81
Number of employees	550	541	568

SOURCE: 1984 Annual Report and Value Line Investment Survey, April 19, 1985, p. 821.

NOTE: 1. In thousands of dollars except per share data, percentages and employee data. 2. Common equivalent shares consist of Class B common shares for the years 1974 through 1976.

1980	1979	1978	1977	1976	1975	1974
$32,294	$31,337	$37,246	$32,380	$39,428	$37,660	$31,585
2,842	1,801	1,416	920	703	—	—
35,136	33,138	38,662	33,300	40,131	37,660	31,585
15,250	12,291	14,854	13,071	14,327	12,993	9,877
16,773	14,657	13,776	12,812	12,232	9,431	7,917
7,243	6,019	6,211	5,731	5,608	4,498	4,202
380	—	—	—	—	—	—
(270)	(450)	(416)	(237)	(234)	(372)	(404)
(4,240)	621	4,237	2,553	8,198	11,110	9,993
(1,861)	300	2,000	1,150	3,950	5,460	4,991
(2,379)	321	2,237	1,403	4,248	5,650	5,002
(.60)	.08	.56	.35	1.05	1.40	1.24
.18	.36	.36	.36	.30	.25	.20
18,573	18,658	22,632	20,026	21,751	18,800	15,689
5,396	2,989	5,510	3,250	4,125	3,382	3,433
13,177	15,669	17,122	16,776	17,626	15,418	12,256
9,062	9,400	9,346	9,533	8,907	7,506	5,734
29,205	29,886	33,505	30,900	31,621	27,126	22,049
—	—	—	—	—	—	—
23,257	26,355	27,433	27,018	27,038	23,415	18,396
5.86	6.63	6.87	6.67	6.67	5.79	4.56
528	1,008	864	1,508	2,082	2,184	669
(12.1%)	1.9%	11.0%	7.7%	20.4%	29.5%	31.6%
(6.8%)	1.0%	5.8%	4.2%	10.6%	15.0%	15.8%
(9.6%)	1.2%	8.2%	5.2%	16.8%	27.0%	31.1%
20.6%	18.2%	16.1%	17.2%	14.0%	11.9%	13.3%
3,972,000	3,976,000	3,995,000	4,051,000	4,051,000	4,044,000	4,037,000
5⅝	6¾	11¼	8⅞	20⅝	28	25¾
2⅞	3½	8⅞	4¾	7⅝	17½	14½
8.85	8.34	9.73	8.22	9.91	9.32	7.83
563	516	553	470	490	420	410

Exhibit 9.10
JOHNSON PRODUCTS COMPANY: LAST FIVE YEARS BALANCE SHEETS
(Dollars in Thousands)

	1983	1982	1981	1980	1979
ASSETS					
Current assets					
Cash and certificates of deposit	$ 1,418	$ 1,324	$ 1,388	$ 550	$ 1,915
Receivables					
Trade less allowance for doubtful accounts of $500,000 in 1983 and $271,000 in 1982	11,120	9,962	11,423	8,061	7,149
Commercial Paper	—	—	—	—	2,654
Other	183	232	169	137	605
Refundable income taxes	—	1,170	—	2,310	749
Inventories	6,579	6,850	6,067	6,624	4,727
Prepaid expenses	594	544	1,065	891	859
Total current assets	19,894	20,082	20,112	18,573	18,685
Property, plant and equipment	17,590	16,603	15,527	14,735	14,363
Less accumulated depreciation and amortization	8,380	7,470	6,539	5,673	4,963
	9,210	9,133	8,988	9,062	9,400
Other assets					
Cash value, officers' life insurance	339	90	164	35	1,226
Investments	244	244	1,453	1,361	395
Miscellaneous receivables	57	49	63	73	86
Unamortized excess cost over net assets of business acquired	41	61	80	101	121
	681	444	1,760	1,570	1,828
Total assets	$29,785	$29,659	$30,860	$29,205	$29,886

SOURCES: Johnson Products Company, Inc., Annual Reports 1983, 1981, and 1979.

Johnson Products' return to profitability in 1983 was facilitated by the development of new products along with significant decreases in labor, material and overhead costs. Some previously contracted activities (e.g., building maintenance and silk-screening of plastic bottles) were done in-house. In 1982, total staff was cut by approximately 10% by increasing employee productivity and eliminating certain job functions.

A decrease in short-term borrowing also helped improve working capital and overall liquidity. Short-term borrowings were $963,000 in August 1983, compared to $3.5 million at the end of 1982. During 1983, the company replaced its existing line of credit with a three-year loan agreement

Exhibit 9.10 ***(Continued)***

	1983	1982	1981	1980	1979
LIABILITIES AND SHAREHOLDERS' EQUITY					
Current liabilities					
Short-term bank loans	$ 963	$ 3,500	$ —	$ 625	$ —
Accounts payable	3,376	4,556	4,971	3,829	1,917
Current capital lease obligations	133	—	—	—	—
Dividends payable	—	—	—	—	357
Income taxes					
Current	638	—	499	82	—
Deferred	440	—	—	—	—
Deferred income	303	182	321	243	402
Accrued expenses	1,333	784	892	617	313
Total current liabilities	7,186	9,022	6,683	5,396	2,989
Capital lease obligations	299	—	—	—	—
Deferred income taxes	585	575	517	552	542
Shareholders' equity					
Capital stock:					
Preferred stock, no par; authorized 300,000 shares; none issued					
Common stock, $.50 par; authorized 7,504,400 shares; issued 4,052,722 shares	2,027	2,027	2,027	2,027	2,027
Additional paid-in capital	649	670	646	628	634
Retained earnings	19,430	17,784	21,425	21,040	24,132
Treasury stock, 72,360 shares in 1983 and 77,520 shares in 1982, at cost	(391)	(419)	(438)	(438)	(438)
	21,715	20,062	23,660	23,257	26,355
Total liabilities and shareholders' equity	$29,785	$29,659	$30,860	$29,205	$29,886

which guarantees availability of funds if needed. The old agreement was set up so that credit was granted at the bank's option. The amounts of the loans are to be based on eligible trade accounts receivables as defined in the agreement. Collateral under the agreement consists of Johnson Products' trade accounts receivables and inventories. Other restrictions include provisions regarding recapitalization, mergers, consolidations, and minimum net worth requirement.

In August 1983, the unused portion of this agreement was $4,037,000. Borrowings under the agreement bear interest at 2½% above the prevailing prime interest rate. The maximum outstanding borrowings were $3.5 million at a weighted average interest rate of 15% in both fiscal 1982 and 1983.

To meet operational efficiency goals, the company spent $1 million in both 1983 and 1982 on fixed asset additions. More than $600,000 has been allocated for capital expenditures in 1984. Investment in fixed assets at year-end was $17.6 million compared to $16.6 million in 1982. Trade accounts receivable increased $1.1 million to $11.1 million in 1983 as a result of higher enrollments in the beauty school subsidiary. The allowance for doubtful accounts increased by $229,000. The company's net sales and other operating revenue for 1983 increased 8% to $45.7 million from $42.4 million in 1982, primarily reflecting an approximately 77% increase in beauty school subsidiary revenues.

Due to significant operating losses at Johnson Products of Nigeria, Ltd. and other external factors, the Johnson investment and advances to the Nigerian operation were written down in 1982. Previously, Johnson's 40% interest in this venture was carried at acquisition cost adjusted for equity in losses through July 31 of each year. Under Nigerian law, Johnson's ownership is limited to 40%. Because this affiliate is still in operation, Johnson may be required in the future to advance significant amounts of working capital to this venture.

The above financial data can be found in the schedules listed in Exhibits 9.9 through 9.11.

Exhibit 9.11

RETAINED EARNINGS OF JOHNSON PRODUCTS COMPANY, INC.

Year	*Dollars*
1983	$19,430,000
1982	17,784,000
1981	21,425,000
1980	21,040,000
1979	24,132,000
1978	25,241,000
1977	24,434,000
1976	24,491,000
1975	21,156,000
1974	16,181,000

Case 10

MARY KAY COSMETICS, INC.

Sexton Adams/Adelaide Griffin

Mary Kay Cosmetics, Inc. (MKY) was in November 1982 a relatively small manufacturer of cosmetics and skin care products, marketing its products through an international network of independent sales representatives. Located in Dallas, Texas, the company had eight distribution centers: five in the United States; one in Australia; one in Canada; and one in Argentina. Another distribution center was scheduled to open in Santo Domingo on December 1, 1982. Mary Kay Ash founded the company in 1963. Since then it has grown from 9 sales representatives to over 150,000. The company started with an initial investment of $5,500 and had grown to net sales of $235 million in 1981. With a relatively small product line that the independent sales representatives, called Beauty Consultants, carried with them, Mary Kay Cosmetics, Inc.'s target market was women aged 25 to 44 in the middle- and upper-middle income brackets.

MARY KAY—THE WOMAN

Mary Kay Ash's life story parallels, to a large extent, the story of the company that carries her name. Mary Kay was born Mary Kathlyn Wagner in Hot Wells, a small town in South Texas.[17] At age seven she was helping to support her family and her invalid father while her mother ran the family restaurant in a Houston suburb.[9]

Mary Kay did not continue her education after high school graduation even though she graduated from Reagan High School in Houston with honors and hoped to attend college. Mary Kay was married to Ben Rogers. The marriage lasted eleven years and resulted in the birth of three children:

This case was prepared by Marlene Carle, Robert Carle, Richard Edwards, and Paula Walters under the supervision of Prof. Sexton Adams, North Texas State University, and Prof. Adelaide Griffin, Texas Woman's University. Reprinted by permission.

Marylin in 1935; Ben, Jr. in 1936; and Richard in 1943. World War II meant months at a time of separation from her husband, who was drafted and unable to send home more than a few dollars each month. For a while during the time Ben was in the service, Mary Kay attended classes at the University of Houston, but her college career was cut short by the responsibility of the small children.[38]

To make ends meet, Mary Kay began to work part-time for Stanley Home Products in Houston selling household products at home parties. She had a natural aptitude for selling and quickly became one of her company's leading sales representatives. Mary Kay learned that people liked to talk to her and that her positive attitude enabled her to overcome most of the obstacles she encountered in sales.[38]

In 1953 Mary Kay left Stanley after thirteen years and went to work for World Gifts Company in Dallas where she sold decorative accessories. She moved up in this organization to become national training director. After ten years with World Gifts, Mary Kay was working 60-hour weeks and making $25,000 a year. A disagreement over proposed policy changes at World Gifts prompted Mary Kay to "retire" in 1963. She had spent almost twenty-five years in direct selling and intended to spend her time writing.[33]

Mary Kay carefully avoids discussing her age. She comments, "A woman who'd tell that would tell anything."[14] For this reason there are few times when Mary Kay's age is mentioned by writers and reporters who have interviewed her.

Retirement proved incompatible for Mary Kay. She became frustrated and, within a few days, she began writing down all the direct-selling techniques she had learned in her twenty-five years in sales. After spending two weeks on this task, she spent another two weeks compiling a list of problems she had encountered in selling, ways of solving these problems, and how she would do things differently in the future if she had the opportunity. Her initial intent was to publish a book to help women sell.[33]

In reviewing and editing her notes, Mary Kay realized that she had prepared everything needed to operate a sales organization. The only thing missing was a product.[9]

Several years earlier, while working for Stanley Home Products, Mary Kay conducted a demonstration of her company's products one evening to a group of twenty women in a Dallas suburb. After Mary Kay's demonstration, the party hostess gave the women little jars of skin treatment, which she had prepared using formulas she had been given by her grandfather, who had at one time operated a local tannery. The women attending the party were being used to test the formulas. Mary Kay had noticed the beautiful complexions of the women she had met that evening and was anxious to try the skin treatment herself. She took several of the jars, which were of various sizes and shapes and were handed to her in an old shoe box.[33] The creams smelled terrible, but they worked. Mary Kay still maintains that her own beautiful complexion is the result of using these creams which eventually became the first of the MKY product line.[33]

THE COMPANY'S BEGINNINGS

Soon after the completion of her writing, Mary Kay and her second husband, George Hallenbeck (whom she had married earlier in 1963), decided to use Mary Kay's sales and problem solving techniques to go into business. George's background included sales and administration. The idea of starting a new business appealed to both of them.[9] The formulas for the skin creams Mary Kay had been given several years earlier were purchased for $500. The woman who owned the formulas had been attempting to produce and market them by herself but had not been successful.[17]

The process of organizing the new company got underway. Mary Kay's husband was to be the administrator. He was planning the physical facilities and caring for other matters regarding the operation of the business while Mary Kay was preparing the final draft of the sales manual, designing and ordering containers, and recruiting sales people. One month before the business was to open, George died of a heart attack.[9]

Mary Kay discussed her situation with her children. Richard, who was then a 20-year old insurance salesman in Houston, moved to Dallas and helped his mother start the company in September 1963, with $5,000 capitalization.[8] Richard had attended North Texas State University for a year and a half as a marketing major; he was put in charge of administration and finance. His mother's duties included training, merchandising, and selling. Six months later Ben, Mary Kay's older son, joined to take care of warehousing and shipping.[9] Ben later became the vice-president for merchandising but left the company in 1978.[17]

The new company, called Beauty by Mary Kay, opened with two full-time employees, Mary Kay and Richard, who drew a salary of $250 a month to start, and nine women who sold the initial skin care products which were being made from the formulas purchased for $500.[30] One of MKY's strategies from the beginning was that each sales representative buy her own products at approximately 50% of retail, pay for all supplies in advance, and carry a sufficient amount of cosmetics with her to fill all orders on the spot. Thus, the company had no accounts payable and no accounts receivable.[33]

Immediate Success

The small staff of beauty consultants was successful, both in selling and in recruiting new beauty consultants. The staff grew so large that the company established a system whereby some of the beauty consultants became training directors. An incentive compensation plan was devised which enabled beauty consultants who became training directors to draw an override on the commissions earned by the beauty consultants they recruited and trained.[41] The number of beauty consultants grew from the original 9 to 318 in 1964, just one year after the company began operation. Sales for the first year amounted to $198,514. The second year sales exceeded $800,000. Growth continued at an astonishingly rapid pace both in the number of consultants and sales. MKY went public in 1967.[33]

The rapid growth in the 1960s brought MKY to the $6 million sales level—a point where expansion beyond Texas and into the four contiguous states was a logical next step. In 1969 the company found it necessary to add 102,000 square feet to the manufacturing facility in Dallas. Additional space has been added several times since. A new distribution center was added in Dallas. In the 1970s the company expanded into the California market with a branch in Los Angeles designed to serve the western states. The westward move was tremendously successful, and MKY soon had more beauty consultants in California than in Texas. An Atlanta branch was opened in 1972, and a third branch was opened in Chicago in 1975. In 1978 the first office outside the United States was opened in Toronto.[30]

The small regional company of 1970 which had sales of $6 million grew in the decade of the 1970s to an international company with sales in 1979 of $91 million. In 1980 sales were $167 million and in 1981 they reached $235 million. The sales force in 1982 included over 150,000 consultants and training directors.[30]

Annual Seminar

One factor that has contributed to the rapid growth of MKY is the ability of the company to instill the spirit of winning and the desire for success in the minds of the beauty consultants, the training directors, and the company employees. A major attraction to many of these people is the annual sales meeting (called a seminar) which is held in Dallas for three days each August. This consists of a beauty pageant, Academy Awards night, party, the sharing of ideas, classes, goal-setting, leadership training, and even bookkeeping. Each person attends the meeting at her own expense, and they come from all fifty states as well as Puerto Rico, Canada, Australia, and Argentina. The awards include mink coats, diamond rings, diamond bumblebee pins, watches, luggage, typewriters, pocket calculators, exotic vacations, and the yearlong use of pink Cadillacs and Buick Regals. Some 16,000 MKY beauty consultants and training directors have attended the seminar for each of the past two years.[6]

THE COMPANY IN 1982

Approximately 40% of the 1,400 MKY employees are housed in a modern, eight-story office building in North Dallas. This $7 million structure contains approximately 109,000 square feet of office and meeting space and was completed in 1978. The building is now completely free of encumbrance and is a showplace for employees and others; it is a rounded structure of bronzed-gold glass and beige brick, filled with plants, flowers, and trees, and a colorful display of woods, rugs, and paintings.[33]

According to management, the continued and rapid growth of MKY has necessitated the expansion of the physical plant and plans have begun to build a new facility which will be a campus. The company purchased 177 acres and in November of 1982 ground was broken for the new building. "Almost every department will have its own building, particularly production, distribution, and administrative facilities. We already have our own print shop and legal counsel. In addition, there will be a child care center and possibly in the future plans are to build a hotel."[1] Estimated cost is $100 million for this five-year project; and according to Mary Kay it will be paid for from funds generated internally.

International Operations

Attempts to broaden international operations beyond Canada have led to the opening of a subsidiary in Australia, and more recently another wholly owned subsidiary in Argentina in 1980. These two companies contributed 3% of the overall MKY sales in 1981. The Australian company appears to have reasonably good prospects for growth; however, the political and inflationary problems in Argentina and the language barrier are forcing MKY to examine this operation carefully before making a decision on whether or not to attempt to expand its efforts in this market.[27] Recruiting salespeople is difficult in Argentina, and keeping sales directors in this country is a problem for MKY. As of December 1, 1982, MKY begins operations in Santo Domingo.

> In the two where we have a different language, we have a language barrier, that we from the home office standpoint find very difficult to hurdle . . . We have tried to find someone who not only knows the cosmetics business well, but who is willing to come over here and spend a year to a year and a half learning *our* way of doing business. I don't think we will open any other market until we have someone who can speak the languages and is trained here and go there to help us.[1]

Not only is the spoken language a problem in international settings, but brochures must be rewritten in the language of the particular country.

Governmental Regulations and Legal Concerns

The rapid expansion of the business has seen the need for an increase in the number of employees. From the beginning of 1963, with the original two—Mary Kay and Richard Rogers—the company has grown to over 1,400 employees in 1982.

The beauty consultants and training directors are considered technically to be independent contractors of MKY, and not employees. However, this status of independent contractors has been under investigation by the Internal Revenue Service since 1978. The Revenue Act of 1978 contained provisions for determining an independent contractor status. With this Act, eligible taxpayers, including MKY, were relieved of all liability for ". . . federal income tax, withholding, FICA and FUTA taxes with respect to their sales persons for any period ending before January 1, 1979."[42] Congress extended the interim relief period until July 1, 1982. Any legislation enacted after the period of interim relief could present a financially adverse effect on the company's future operations. This issue has been magnified as a result of other direct sales companies whose representatives have tried to alter tax deductions.

In 1982 a bill with three provisions was introduced before Congress addressing the status of independent contractors, and was endorsed by MKY and the Direct Selling Association. In a presentation made before the New York Society of Security Analysts on July 22, 1982, Rogers said the bill ". . . would require reporting to the IRS commissions paid to sales people when those commissions exceed $600 per year. Another provision would require reporting to the IRS sales of product to individuals when their sales exceed $5,000 per person per year. The third provision which is very important to us is called a 'safe harbor provision' which includes several tests which if met would automatically classify a sales person as an independent contractor rather than an employee."[30] Mary Kay suggested that it would be difficult for her independent contractors to avoid the IRS and not report actual commissions because her company provides the needed information regarding each contractor to the IRS, with this information being maintained on a computer system.[1]

In the third quarter of 1982, the issue was resolved, at least for the time being. The IRS ruled in favor of the independent contractor status. Said Mary Kay, "We won."[1]

The company presently faces a class action suit with regard to the tender offer and purchase of MKY stock from 1979. "Nothing yet has happened," says Mary Kay. "We think, of course, that it's ridiculous. In 1978 and 1979 we as a Company had suddenly realized that our directors weren't meeting the test of a salary requirement except on a secretarial basis. They [women] will take the stable salary rather than a 'maybe' commission."[1] From this, management developed the new compensation plan which has contributed to the success of the growth of the company. "In late 1979, we found '60 Minutes' on our doorstep; and after nine days of filming, we came out smelling like a rose. Since that program, our sales have quadrupled and our numbers have tripled."[1] For most companies a loss of the suit could negatively affect financial operations and future plans. "It's just for $17 million, and we did $458 million last year in 1981. Anyway, we won't lose it."[1]

Product Line

The initial product line at MKY consisted of skin care products for women. Since its introduction in 1963, the line has remained relatively stable. Since 1976, however, there has been a gradual move toward diversification of products and additions to the Mary Kay line. In 1980, the skin care line was diversified to meet the needs of consumers. Colors have been updated to reflect the colors in fashion. The sunscreen has been reformulated and in 1981, MKY introduced the body care system. The line has also been expanded to include toiletry items, accessories, and hair care products. The skin care products for women still account for 50% of the sales revenue and will continue to be the major income producers in all likelihood.[42] Today the products at MKY are still primarily oriented toward skin care rather than the high fashion market.

In 1982, the line consisted of only forty-five products. Said Dr. Myra Barker, Vice-President for Research and Development, "our plan is to maintain the present number in our line so that our Beauty Consultants can carry the inventory with them. The best way to service our Consultants is to keep the color line basic when offering the Fashion Forecast for fall and spring." According to Dr. Barker, "this strategy allows the Consultants to sell large numbers of basic colors which sell well to our customers. This allows us to discontinue those colors which don't sell well and provide the necessary flexibility of updating our line. Mary Kay quality is instilled in all employees and products."[3]

An eleven-year veteran of the pharmaceutical industry, Dr. Bruce Rudy (former Director, Quality Assurance for the Burroughs Wellcome Company) had primary responsibility for governmental, technical, and regulatory compliance in the quality control area. Since joining the MKY organization in January 1981 as Director of Quality Assurance, Dr. Rudy was serving as Vice-President of Quality Assurance of MKY. "We have one of the strongest quality control programs in existence. Each batch of raw materials is tested in our labs. They must meet our chemical, physical, and microbiological specifications. Bulk products and finished packaged products are audited on the line, with final testing in the lab. Last week, we were inspected by the FDA which is the primary governmental agency responsible for the cosmetics industry."[51] Says Myra Barker, "We have one of the most sophisticated computer control systems in the industry. Even the FDA was impressed. Our goal is to be the best."[3]

During the past several years, MKY has experimented in the market of skin care products and toiletry items for men. These are marketed under the product name of "Mr. K.", and to date have accounted for 3% of the total company's sales in each of the past three years.[42] "Ten years ago, a man would not have gone into a beauty shop to have his hair done. As time goes on, men will find out that skin is skin. With all the emphasis on youth and keeping trim and fit in this country, skin follows right behind it. For men, skin care is a behind the door thing with cosmetics. I don't have a crystal ball," says Mary Kay, "but it's just one more step to creating the total image, even for men."[1]

"We are faced with the problem of growing too fast. We are constantly reviewing our systems and products for control measures. Typically we are understaffed and have to work a lot of overtime. Give me these problems anyday! They are nice problems to have," reflects Dr. Rudy.[51]

> With the building of our new MKY campus, we are phasing in buildings for the new facility. For example, the Glamour Products manufacturing facility is working closely with the engineering groups to ensure that we meet the criteria for a drug company and can be approved by the FDA. We are looking at meeting not only present, but future requirements for the industry and our company.[51]

Manufacturing, Research, and Development

The manufacturing and research and development facilities for MKY are located in Dallas. Products needed in other geographical areas are shipped to the various distribution centers. Raw materials, fuel, and electrical energy are available in the Dallas area at reasonable costs, and there are no plans to relocate any of the manufacturing or research and development facilities at this time, although the company does study energy-related costs. Company officials point out that a continuous research and development program is underway and is geared mainly toward the goal of improving present products; however, only a very small percentage of total income is budgeted for the research and development department.[42]

Management Philosophy

The primary reason for the success of MKY was the motivating reason for starting the company. "This company was really begun to give women an opportunity to advance, which I was denied, when I worked for others." This opportunity to become successful with rewards provided for hard work is evident in the slogan, "I can, I will, I must," which Mary Kay instills in all her employees, particularly during the training seminars. "I train the sales force by example and by relationships."[1]

Although the sales force is independent, it maintains a strong and intimate relationship with the mother company. The organization of the sales force is the brainchild of Mary Kay herself. One of the more subtle activities which takes place at the home beauty show is the recruitment of new beauty consultants. A portion of each show is reserved for explaining the MKY sales organization, compensation, and incentive plan.

Recognizing a lag in the sales force and a loss of competitive edge in 1978, MKY changed its compensation program.[38] In addition to the mark-up they receive on the products they sell, sales managers are also eligible for a series of commissions based on their monthly unit sales. To become a sales manager, the beauty consultant must recruit twenty-four women into the organizations to become consultants. The sales manager is then eligible to participate in a training program and later become a sales director. Sales directors spend time on independent sales, but they also manage, train, and recruit other sales consultants. "We expect sales directors to sell a minimum level of $3000 wholesale products per month, which is $6000 retail."[1] Mary Kay says that if a sales director falls short of that goal for two consecutive months, then the company contacts that woman to see how they can help. The Chairman of the Board doesn't just want them to be minimum. She wants to help them excel. The average sales director will earn $30,000 in 1982. New sales managers will come to Dallas for one week of training and return from time to time during the year for special training programs. The highlight of the year is the "seminar." It consists of workshops conducted by outstanding beauty consultants and directors. Training materials such as guides, manuals, tape cassettes, flip charts, films, and other materials developed by MKY staff are used during the seminar as well as at other times during the year.[20]

The incentive plan is no small contribution to the motivation strategy employed by MKY. This plan allows sales consultants and managers to set goals for themselves whereby they can earn expensive and extravagant prizes for outstanding sales. The prizes may include opera-length mink coats, diamond rings, diamond bumblebee pins, watches, luggage, typewriters, pocket calculators, exotic vacations, and yearlong use of pink Cadillacs, and Buick Regals.[27] Not only is the prize itself a motivator, but also its method of presentation serves to provide the recipient of extended measures of recognition from her peers. Promotion from sales director to national sales director is also recognized on awards night during the seminar.

Being promoted to national sales director is no small task. Each woman must have already proven what she can do. Each eligible person has at least ten offspring directors that she has brought into the company and nurtured up the ladder. These ten offspring directors must have women whom they are working with and motivating, called second-line directors. For example, Shirly Hutton earns $32,000 per month and has twenty-six offspring directors. Rena Tarbet, who is "living with cancer for seven years now" is working on her third million dollar year sales.[1]

> Richard and I are the parents of the company. We are really mother and father figures, which I am given the credit for the success, and really Richard deserves as much or at least half of everything that has been done and

> then some. When I started the company, I didn't know that Richard had an IBM head. I take care of the motivating of the sales force and the public relations work. I don't know the financial condition of the company because I don't have to. Richard knows all of that. I ask for a sales report and the number of recruits that we had for each month. That's all I need. I take it from there.[1]

Communication is considered a high priority motivational strategy at MKY. Monthly publications with circulations of 150,000; weekly bulletins; personalized letters; and 15,000 telephone calls per month keep sales directors and consultants in touch with the home office.[25] MKY also has a computerized tracking system of keeping up with its complex organization of sales consultants, sales directors, and their respective sales and recruiting data.[33]

MARY KAY COSMETICS, INC.
ORGANIZATION CHART
PRESIDENT'S STAFF

Exhibit 10.1

Board of Directors, Chairman	Mary Kay Ash
President and Chief Executive Officer	Richard Rogers
Executive Secretary	Cindy Puckett
President of Mary Kay Cosmeticos S.A. (Argentina)	Dr. Gerardo Segura
President of Mary Kay Cosmetics, Ltd. (Canada)	Richard J. Bennetts
Managing Dir. of Mary Kay Cosmetics Pty. Ltd. (Australia)	John Watt
Vice President, Administration	Gerald Allen
Vice President, Finance & Treasurer	Gene Stubbs
Vice President, Controller	Jack Dingler
Vice President, Manufacturing Group	John Beasley
Vice President, Research & Development	Dr. Myra Barker
Vice President, Manufacturing Operations	Pat Howard
Vice President, Quality Assurance	Bruce Rudy
Vice President, Marketing	Richard Barlett
Vice President, Operations	Phil Bostley
Director of Personnel	Betty Bessler
Director of Purchasing	Ron Pearce
Vice President, Secretary & General Counsel	Monty Barber
Director of Internal Audit	Wayne Furman
Director of Protective Services	Dave Leopard

It would seem that MKY would merge or be acquired by another company. Mary Kay's reply, "All the time, but no thanks. These companies believe they can bring in their male executives and take over this 2 x 4 company and show them how to run it. You can't run a direct sales company like that. We must operate in a different way. Right now we are in the top ten in the cosmetics industry. Richard's and my goal is to be the largest and best skin care company in the world. I'm sure we are the best. Now we have to concentrate on becoming the largest."[1]

MKY's future lies in the hands of the national sales directors (NSDs). These NSDs are carbon copies of Mary Kay herself. She constantly reminds them that *they* are Mary Kay. "Wherever you go, whatever you do, be careful what you do, because you are Mary Kay. You are the future of the company. When I'm not here anymore, you will be taking over. Each of you are in training to be Mary Kay."[1]

Mary Kay's goal is to touch as many of these women's lives as she can. "If I see one more woman today become greater than she ever thought she could be by my persuasion that she is great, then it's a good day."[1]

Richard Rogers, 38-year-old son of Mary Kay Ash, is positioned at the helm of Mary Kay, serving as President and CEO of the company since 1968. He is responsible for setting the tone and direction for the company. In the plans are the building of a new MKY campus. (See Exhibit 10.1.)

Sales Staff

There are over 150,000 independent beauty consultants selling MKY products. The company places a great deal of emphasis upon the rapport with others inside the organization; however, company policy is very clear on the requirements that must be fulfilled in order to be a beauty consultant. These requirements are:

- Submit a signed agreement with cashier's check or money order in advance in order to receive the beauty showcase (the basic sales kit).
- Attend three beauty shows, or sales demonstrations.
- Schedule five beauty shows for the first week's activity.
- Attend training classes conducted by a sales director in the area.

The beauty shows are the company's market place and are held in homes with no more than six customers in attendance.

THE INDUSTRY

Mary Kay Cosmetics, Inc. competes in two basic industries: (1) the cosmetics and personal care industry and (2) the direct sales industry, the latter containing approximately 2,200 direct sales companies. Among MKY's competitors in the cosmetics industry are Avon, Revlon, Estée Lauder, Gillette's Jafra, Richardson-Vick, Fabergé, Chesebrough-Ponds, Inc., and Noxell Corp. With well over $2 billion in sales in 1981 Avon, Revlon, and Gillette were the industry leaders. Chesebrough-Pond's 1981 sales were $1.5 billion. Ranked within the top ten of the cosmetics industry, sales for MKY were $235 (net) million with Fabergé and Noxell in the same sales category as MKY.[47,12] Skin care, MKY's niche, is the focus of the competition.

With their appeal to older women in middle- to high-income brackets who are entering the work force in record numbers, skin care and quality are the targets for a growing number of women according to industry analysts. They have more purchasing power but less time to spend their money. They want health, fitness, and value.[22] Appealing to these women with major marketing thrusts are: Gillette with Aapri (a facial scrub containing ground apricot pits) and Silkience (a self-adjusting moisture lotion); Richardson-Vick with Oil of Olay moisturizer; Noxell with Raintree Hand and Body Lotion and Noxema; Chesebrough-Pond's Vaseline Intensive Care; and Estée Lauder's Clinique as well as a number of products from both Revlon and Avon. Noxell and Chesebrough-Pond's sell the low-cost products. Avon and Revlon products are in the mid-price range with the Estée Lauder products in the high-price range. MKY's products are in the mid- to high-priced range. With the exception of Avon and MKY, all of these companies sell their products over the counter in department stores, drug stores, discount stores, and supermarkets.[21]

The cosmetics industry as a whole is seeing a gradual downturn for the first time in its history according to *Forbes'* Richard Stern. What has been classified as a recession-proof industry is now seeing growth that is attributed mainly to inflation. Volume sales are declining and the assumption that growth is eternal is gone. The skin care treatment portion of the industry is the only one with any expectation for growth with perhaps 2% for 1982. Even though the recession is motivating a shift to more reasonably priced products, Avon and Revlon are hurting the most. The industry has survived other recessions because of the increasing numbers of women entering the work force. But the rate of increase has been declining in recent years.[50] To further complicate the volume of sales, virtually every cosmetic company has sales promotions on the concept of a free gift with purchase. MKY is different. Says Chairman of the Board Ash, "They would love to get out of that business. We don't have to do that. We don't need to."[1]

Both Stern and Mintz of *Sales and Marketing Management* note that Avon's problems stem from a less captive home market and an inadequate compensation program for sales representatives. Retail outlets such as drug stores, mass merchandisers, and food stores are capturing some of Avon's low- to middle-income market. Avon's reward program of gifts and vacations to outstanding sales representatives has failed to improve productivity, which has been in a decline since 1979.[32]

Other industry analysts speculate that the leveling of sales in the cosmetics industry can be attributed to consumers cutting back on purchases traditionally categorized as luxury items because of inflation and recession; the number of women entering the work force leveling off; and the bulge in the teenage market which was seen in the 1960s and early 1970s beginning to decline. The portion of the cosmetics industry which has had some immunity to this decline is the skin-care portion of the industry.

Some analysts believe the biggest threat to the industry, however, is the threat of regulation by the FDA.

> If a cosmetic item is regarded as a drug, the industry could be confronted with expensive regulations. These include detailed manufacturing controls, more frequent government inspections, product registrations, labeling requirement changes, and other reviews. The Toxic Substances Strategy Committee, a special White House panel studying cancer, has asked Congress to review cosmetics legislation and bring the industry under tighter federal control.[46]

Increased regulation would mean higher production costs and higher prices to the consumer. Research and development divisions would require expansion into more scientifically oriented segments. Industry experts suggest that this would be burdensome especially to the smaller cosmetics companies and would in fact make it very hard for them to exist.

The other industry in which MKY competes is direct sales. Competition is not only for customers willing to provide their home as the marketplace but also for recruits for sales representatives upon which the industry is totally dependent. Competitors include Amway, which sells home products; Shaklee, which has organic, non-pollutant household products; Home Interiors and Gifts; and Princess House, which sells a fine line of crystal and other table accessories. All of these companies apparently understand the importance of acquiring and motivating large numbers of recruits. Contests with flashy rewards such as big cars, furs, expensive jewelry, and extravagant vacations are motivational factors used by all of these companies. Family harmony and devotion to God are emphasized not only by MKY but also by others such as Amway and Home Interiors and Gifts, the latter of which parallels many of MKY's motivational practices and was in fact founded by Mary Kay Ash's former sister-in-law, Mary Crowley.[35]

Other pressure being exerted by the Internal Revenue Service on direct sales organizations such as Amway targets individual sales representatives' use of business expenses as tax shelters. In a copyrighted article appearing in the *Fort Worth Star Telegram*, reporters Bowles, McKinsey, and Magmusson claim that Amway recruiters use the advantage of tax shelters as an enticement to become an Amway distributor. The pitch is to use the Amway distributorship as an excuse to write off new clothes, Christmas gifts, appliances, long distance calls, new cars, vacation houses, and expensive vacations. In IRS audits of the tax returns of 300 Amway distributors in Baltimore last year, all but 2 resulted in back taxes and penalties being assessed. The average payment was $1,350 not including interest and penalties. Currently 1,000 more Amway distributors in Baltimore are undergoing IRS audits. According to Roscoe Edgar, Jr., the IRS Commissioner,

> It appears that the tax benefit aspects of many of these activities may be the primary reason large numbers of people become involved. Promotional schemes, recruitment methods and other information we have on these activities frequently highlight the anticipated tax benefits above all else. This indicates to us that the individuals involved know full well what they are doing.[7]

Economic Forces There are several factors of the economy that impact on the cosmetics industry in general and MKY in particular. Among these factors are consumer demand, competition, and the general state of the national economy. For one reason or another, the once-held assumption of eternal growth for the cosmetics industry seems to have vanished. The supposedly recession-proof cosmetics industry has, for the first time in its history, experienced a downturn in business. According to Jack Salyman of Wall Street's Smith, Barney and industry consultant Allan Mottus, unit sales have been flat for years with nearly all of the growth (43%) since 1978 attributable to a 39% increase in the cost of living. The shakeout appears to be focused on the middle market. This leaves the effect on MKY uncertain.[50]

As in any other retail industry, consumer demand is the key factor that influences a company's business decisions. Competition to meet the consumer's needs has stiffened considerably in the cosmetics industry as evidenced by the fact that many companies formerly in totally unrelated businesses now have lines of cosmetics. Clothes designers are a good example. One economic factor that is affecting consumers and industry alike is the present higher cost of borrowing money, the prime lending rate. This makes it more expensive for MKY to produce and sell its products and results in higher cost to the customer.

Technological Forces If a company is not on the "leading edge" of industry technology, it will be at a competitive disadvantage. The cosmetics industry is not a high technology industry in the sense of the product produced. But a company needs the latest technology to be able to produce its product cost-effectively, which is instrumental in gaining a competitive advantage. In the cosmetics industry, technology revolves around research into how the skin relates to the rest of the body and how it relates to its environment. Of major concern is the safety and efficacy of the product.[6]

Social Forces

Two keys to the success of the cosmetics industry, which greatly influence MKY's business strategy, are population demographics and sociological changes. As noted by Richard Stern of *Forbes,* "The key is the underlying demographics. The industry rode out previous recessions by riding the skirts of ever more working women. More working women meant increased women's spending and more cosmetics to wear to the office. But the rate of increase in the number of working women has declined in recent years." Stern also sees "sociological changes afoot as well. Working women now seem to prefer convenience to ambience, prompting a shift in distribution channels toward more merchandisers, discount drugstores and even supermarkets and away from department stores."[50] These changes would appear to enhance the appeal of direct marketing because from a convenience standpoint it is much easier to have a product brought to you than it is to have to go get it. Also, the recession seems to have caused a shift in buying habits that may impact the middle market cosmetics significantly. As in other retail industries, consumers of cosmetics have gone to lower-priced goods in an effort to economize or have switched to higher-priced goods for quality.[50] Population distribution is very important to the cosmetics industry in helping determine target markets. There has been a definite change in the distribution of the population. Between 1970 and 1980 the number of people over the age of thirty increased 40% while total population grew only 11.4%. America is growing older.[21]

Political/Legal Forces

The factors that affect MKY in this area fall into two categories. First, there are laws that affect the cosmetics industry as a whole. Second, there are factors that are concerned just with regulating firms that sell through direct sales marketing techniques as does MKY. MKY, like the rest of the industry, is subject to regulation of the FDA and the Alcohol and Tax Unit of the Treasury department. The FTC regulates the company's advertising and sales practices. Plus, the company's marketing, packaging, package labeling, and product content are regulated by many other federal, state, local, and foreign laws.

Of more immediate concern to MKY and all other companies that use direct sales to market their products is a battle with the IRS over whether the sales person should be considered an employee or an independent contractor. To quote Richard Rogers, "We (MKY) are sure you can appreciate the administrative overhead and expense that we would incur if we were required to maintain employee-type records, withhold taxes, pay social security taxes, etc. for the over 150,000 persons in our sales force."[30] During the third quarter of 1982 Congress enacted The Tax Equity and Fiscal Responsibility Act of 1982. This act contains provisions which classify people in the sales force of direct sales marketing firms as "statutory non-employees." Thus ended a ten-year battle with the IRS.[30,42]

REVIEW OF INTERNAL FACTORS

Human Resources

MKY in 1982 employs approximately 1,400 persons. These employees are nonunionized. Of the 1,400, around 40% are employed in the management and administrative end of the business. The other 60% are employed in areas such as research and development, manufacturing, and so on. Even more important to the organization are the more than 150,000 beauty consultants that operate as independent contractors in selling the MKY products.

When considering human resources, the value of a company's employees must also be considered. In a direct sales organization such as MKY, motivation is the grease that keeps the wheels turning. In that respect, Mary Kay Ash is the head "cheerleader." She is ultimately responsible for motivating employees. Without the proper motivation sales would suffer. The company's motivation and communication have already been covered in detail, but the philosophy behind it all is summed up in the following quote by Mary Kay. "Somebody said, if you act enthusiastic, you will become enthusiastic. We try to generate enthusiasm by example."[19]

Physical and Production Resources

MKY is headquartered in Dallas, Texas and has facilities in Atlanta; Chicago; Los Angeles; Piscataway, New Jersey; Victoria, Australia; Toronto, Canada; and Buenos Aires, Argentina.

The executive offices are housed in an eight-story 109,000 square foot building in Dallas. The company's lone manufacturing facility is housed in a building of some 300,000 square feet, also located in Dallas. This facility is partitioned such that there are approximately 110,300 square feet for manufacturing, 51,300 square feet for office space, and 116,000 square feet for use as a warehouse. This building and the eight-story office tower are owned by the company. The company leases a third building of approximately 450,600 square feet in Dallas. This building houses operations for distribution, printing, data processing, and more warehouse space. MKY's office and warehouse facilities in Atlanta, Chicago, Los Angeles, and Australia total approximately 200,000 square feet and are owned free of encumbrance. The office and warehouse facilities in New Jersey, Argentina, and Canada total about 100,000 square feet. These facilities are leased with an option to purchase the Canadian facility. The manufacturing facilities and equipment are at least modern and in many cases state-of-the-art and well maintained.[42] Every machine that comes in contact with an MKY product is disassembled, cleaned, and sanitized at regular intervals.[38]

In the interest of future growth, MKY has purchased 177 acres in Dallas at the cost of approximately $6.5 million.[42] The project to develop this land will cost an estimated $100 million according to Mary Kay.[1] "At the present time," believes Richard Rogers, "we have in place facilities to support an annual sales volume of approximately $400 million."[25]

Market Resources

Market resources are the elements necessary to transfer possession of MKY's products to the consumer. MKY's two most important market resources are (1) channel of distribution and (2) advertising (although it has taken MKY time to understand and properly utilize this resource). MKY's channel of distribution is comprised solely of one element, a sales force of 150,000 beauty consultants who operate as independent contractors. The products are distributed via one wholesale sale and one retail sale channel. The products are transferred from the company to the consultant at wholesale, then from consultant to the consumer at retail. The beauty consultant's profit is directly derived from the sale of the product to the ultimate consumer. Her profit is the difference between the wholesale price paid MKY for the product and the price the customer paid for the product. Every consultant can sell products wherever she wishes because MKY does not set territories or sell franchises.[23]

Until recently, advertising was used infrequently in MKY's marketing plan. Historically, most advertising was done by word of mouth, relying upon direct sales personnel to spread the word. In the past, when there was an advertising budget it was set at or below 1% of sales. When national advertising was used, ads usually appeared in magazines such as *McCall's*, *Redbook*, *Better Homes and Gardens*, and *Ladies' Home Journal*.[44] Since the appearance of Mary Kay Ash on "60 Minutes" in late 1979, the company's view of advertising has been changing. Gerald Allen, MKY's Administrative Vice-President, said the company learned a lesson in the past two and one-half years thanks to "60 Minutes." He considers the show partially responsible for the tremendous growth of MKY's sales force. Mr. Allen also believes the show to have been worth the equivalent of $40 million worth of national network advertising and says, "That made believers out of us."[5] In the third quarter of 1982, MKY launched its first nationwide television advertising campaign. The advertising budget for the third and fourth quarters of 1982 will total $3 million and raise the total advertising budget for the year to $4 million (more than double the budget for any previous year).[5,28]

Research and Development Resources

According to John Beasley, Vice-President of Manufacturing for MKY, "Research and Development is the leading edge" in obtaining the corporate goal of being the finest teaching-oriented skin care company in the world with sales of $500 million by 1990. Since 1975, the company's research and development staff has grown from two to forty-seven. Mr. Beasley also said that, "We go after the top ten percent of the people in the country who have the skills that we're looking for and personal integrity."[6] MKY funds research all over the world in an effort to develop new technology. To quote Mr. Beasley again, "We (MKY) are having to stretch current technology in establishing some new standards in the industry in the area of comedogenicity, the interaction of the product, the environment, and the skin causing comedones (acne)."[6] Of great importance to the company is that research maintain a fast-response attitude because of the rate at which tastes and fashions change.[25] During a recent interview, Mary Kay Ash indicated that the research and development budget would continue to be approximately 1% of sales as has been the case in recent years.

Results of Operations

In 1981, net sales increased at a rate of 41% compared to 83% for 1980 and 70% in 1979. At the same time, the number of beauty consultants increased 42%, 64%, and 33% in 1981, 1980, and 1979, respectively. During the same period, individual productivity of the beauty consultants declined. In 1979 average annual productivity for a consultant increased 27% compared with an increase of 12% for 1980 and a decrease of 1% for 1981. At the same time, selling and general and administrative expenses held fairly constant at approximately 51% of sales. It should also be noted that MKY instituted price increases of 5% in 1980 and 15% in 1981. As a result of all the above-mentioned factors, net income increased from $4.8 million in 1978 to $24.2 million in 1981.[25] Refer to Exhibit 10.2.

Exhibit 10.2 GROWTH IN SALES AND INCOME

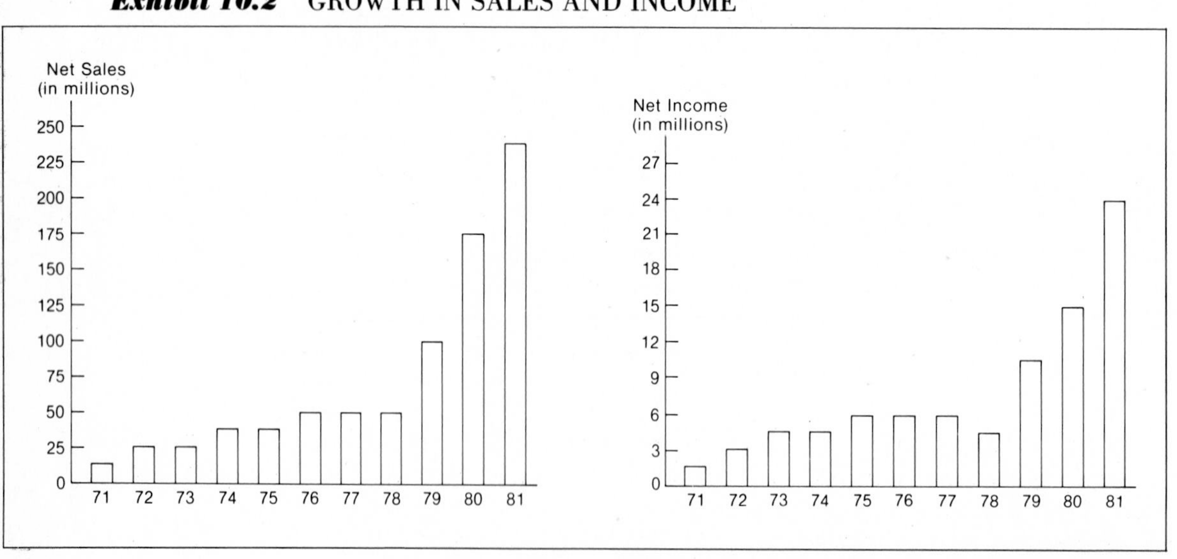

Financial Condition

In 1981 *Business Week* ranked MKY as the twelfth fastest growing company in the country.[14] When asked in a recent interview her opinion concerning the current financial condition of the company, Mary Kay Ash responded, "I think we're doing great!" However, she also admitted that she let her son Richard Rogers, the president and CEO, handle the financial matters of the company.[1]

With the phenomenal growth in the last three years, MKY's total assets have grown from $36 million in 1978 to $101 million in 1981. Working capital for the same period was $5.7 million in 1978, $2.3 million in 1979, $4.0 million in 1980, and $7.8 million in 1981. At the same time, capital expenditures were increasing faster than both working capital and total assets. In 1981 capital expenditures were $25.3 million compared to $12.5 million in 1980, $4.7 million in 1979, and $2.1 million in 1978.[14] There were approximately 14.3 million shares of common stock outstanding in 1981.[25] This represents a 25% decrease compared to the 19.6 million shares outstanding at the end of 1976.[25,39] The decrease resulted from MKY tender offers in 1977 and 1979. Other information on the company is detailed in Exhibits 10.3 through 10.5.

PRESENT STRATEGIC POSTURE OF MARY KAY COSMETICS

The most important factor in MKY's strategic posture is its niche in the skin care products area of the cosmetics market where larger competitors such as Avon are a minor factor.[39] Also, Mary Kay Ash believes that a limited product line maximizes the sales forces' efficiency.[14] Thus, the company's product line is limited to approximately 45 items.[39] The company's target market is also key. The company perceives its prime market to be women aged 25 to 44 who are in or a little above the middle-income bracket, have some college education, and live in suburbia or exurbia.[25,14]

As MKY continues to grow, it must be able to recognize and react to changes in competition, consumer demand, and economic conditions. The company believes that to do this it must be capable of supporting rapid sales volume growth with consistently high-quality products and reliable service.[25]

MARY KAY COSMETICS, INC. CONSOLIDATED BALANCE SHEETS
December 31, 1981 and 1980

Exhibit 10.3

	1981	1980
ASSETS		
Current assets:		
Cash and cash equivalents	$ 7,953,000	$11,085,000
Accounts and notes receivable	2,715,000	1,109,000
Inventories:		
Raw materials	8,888,000	6,380,000
Finished goods	18,193,000	15,218,000
	27,081,000	21,598,000
Deferred income tax benefits	2,948,000	2,036,000
Prepaid expenses	1,213,000	666,000
Total current assets	41,910,000	36,494,000
Property, plant and equipment, at cost:		
Land	12,298,000	3,793,000
Buildings and improvements	23,869,000	21,348,000
Furniture, fixtures and equipment	28,299,000	14,963,000
Construction in progress	4,829,000	3,877,000
	69,295,000	43,981,000
Less accumulated depreciation	10,519,000	7,653,000
	58,776,000	36,328,000
Notes receivable	—	1,087,000
Other assets	290,000	522,000
	$100,976,000	$74,431,000
LIABILITIES AND STOCKHOLDERS' EQUITY		
Current liabilities:		
Note payable to bank	$ 1,260,000	$ —
Accounts payable	8,061,000	8,900,000
Accrued liabilities	16,659,000	13,063,000
Income tax	5,712,000	4,214,000
Deferred sales	1,321,000	4,363,000
Current portion of long-term debt	1,058,000	1,000,000
Total current liabilities	34,071,000	31,540,000
Long-term debt	2,366,000	3,000,000
Deferred income taxes	2,587,000	1,258,000
Stockholders' equity	61,952,000	38,633,000
	$100,976,000	$74,431,000

MARY KAY COSMETICS, INC. CONSOLIDATED STATEMENTS OF INCOME

Years Ended December 31, 1981, 1980 and 1979

Exhibit 10.4

	1981	1980	1979
Net sales	$235,296,000	$166,039,000	$91,400,000
Interest and other income, net	1,485,000	712,000	493,000
	236,781,000	167,650,000	91,893,000
Cost and expenses:			
Cost of sales	71,100,000	52,484,000	27,574,000
Selling, general and administrative expenses	120,880,000	86,998,000	45,522,000
Interest expense	1,014,000	635,000	958,000
	192,994,000	140,117,000	74,054,000
Income before income taxes	43,787,000	27,533,000	17,839,000
Provision for income taxes	19,632,000	12,398,000	8,207,000
Net income	$ 24,155,000	$ 15,135,000	$ 9,632,000
Net income per common and common equivalent share	$1.65	$1.05	$.65
Average shares	14,662,000	14,442,000	14,720,000

MARY KAY COSMETICS, INC. CONSOLIDATED STATEMENTS OF CHANGES IN FINANCIAL POSITION

Years ended December 31, 1981, 1980 and 1979

Exhibit 10.5

	1981	1980	1979
Source of funds:			
Operations:			
Net income	$24,155,000	$15,135,000	$ 9,632,000
Depreciation	2,866,000	1,987,000	1,569,000
Increase in deferred income taxes	1,329,000	351,000	177,000
Gains on sales of real estate not used in business	—	—	(116,000)
Funds provided from operations	28,350,000	17,473,000	11,262,000
Proceeds from exercises of stock options	1,922,000	1,338,000	164,000
Decrease in notes receivable	1,087,000	120,000	—
Increase in long-term debt	366,000	—	5,442,000
Proceeds from sales of real estate not used in business	—	—	1,182,000
Other	325,000	—	276,000
	32,050,000	18,931,000	18,326,000
Application of funds:			
Additions to property, plant and equipment, net	25,314,000	12,457,000	4,510,000
Dividends declared	2,851,000	2,458,000	1,764,000
Reduction of long-term debt	1,000,000	1,000,000	5,000,000
Purchase of treasury shares	—	—	9,422,000
Increase in notes receivable	—	—	1,047,000
Other	—	369,000	—
	29,165,000	16,284,000	21,743,000
Increase (decrease) in working capital	$ 2,885,000	$ 2,647,000	$ (3,417,000)

NOTES

1. Ash, Mary Kay. Personal interview with Paula Walters. Dallas, Texas (November 16, 1982).
2. Barker, Monty. Telephone interview with Paula Walters (November 22, 1982).
3. Barker, Myra. Telephone interview with Paula Walters (November 22, 1982).
4. *Barron's.* "Up and Down Wall Street." (June 8, 1981): 45–46, 51.
5. Bayer, Tom. "Mary Kay Tries Net TV." *Advertising Age* (August 2, 1982).
6. Beasley, John. "Published Interview." Mary Kay Cosmetics, Inc. (May 1982).
7. Bowles, Billy, Kitty McKinsey, and Paul Magmusson. "IRS Questions the Use of Tax Shelters by Some of Amway's Distributors." *Fort Worth Star Telegram* (November 10, 1982): B1 and B3.
8. *Chemical Week.* "Mary Kay Finds Incentives That Pay Off" (May 13, 1981): 50–51.
9. *Chemical Week.* "People" (August 6, 1975): 40.
10. *Chemical Week.* "Skin-Care Elegance Hits the Suntan Scene" (February 6, 1980): 52–53.
11. *Chemical Week.* "The Chemical Week 300 Companies: 1980 Divisional Results" (April 22, 1981): 46–47.
12. *Chemical Week.* "The Chemical Week 300 Companies: 1981 Divisional Results" (February 24, 1982): 45.
13. *Chemical Week.* "Top of the News. Big Oil's Chemical Profits Slip Again" (May 5, 1982): 50–51.
14. Coburn, Marcia Froelke. "Direct's Sleeker Sell." *Advertising Age* (March 1, 1982): 14–15.
15. *Fort Worth Star Telegram.* "Off the Ticker: Mary Kay Cosmetics" (October 22, 1982): 8B.
16. Gitman, Lawrence J. *Principles of Managerial Finance,* 2nd ed. New York: Harper & Row, 1979.
17. Gordon, Mitchell. "Mary Kay's Team." *Barron's* (July 9, 1979): 32, 34.
18. Greene, Richard and Barbara Rudolph. "Toiletries and Cosmetics." *Forbes* (January 4, 1982): 218–219.
19. Gschwandtner, Gerhard. "The Make-Up of Sales Success." *Personal Selling Power* (November 1982): 1, 8.
20. *The Insiders' Chronicle.* "Analysts Caught Off Guard by Mary Kay Profit Spurt" (November 9, 1979): 1, 17–18.
21. Kesler, Lori. "Skincare Penetrates New Layers of Profits." *Advertising Age* (March 1, 1982).
22. McCable English, Mary. "Face of the 80's: What's Ahead?" *Advertising Age* (March 1, 1982): Section 2, PM-11.

23. Mary Kay Cosmetics, Inc. "A Business Perspective" (1982).
24. Mary Kay Cosmetics, Inc. "Annual Report 1980."
25. Mary Kay Cosmetics, Inc. "Annual Report 1981."
26. Mary Kay Cosmetics, Inc. "Interim Report for Three Months Ended March 31, 1982."
27. Mary Kay Cosmetics, Inc. "Interim Report for Six Months Ended June 30, 1982."
28. Mary Kay Cosmetics, Inc. "Interim Report for Nine Months Ended September 30, 1982."
29. Mary Kay Cosmetics, Inc. "News Information" (1981).
30. Mary Kay Cosmetics, Inc. "Presentation of Mary Kay Cosmetics, Inc. Before the New York Society of Security Analysts on July 22, 1982."
31. Mary Kay Cosmetics, Inc. "Notice of Annual Meeting of Shareholders To Be Held on April 21, 1982."
32. Mintz, Steven. "Avon, You're Looking Better." *Sales and Marketing Management* (April 5, 1982): 52–57.
33. *Nation's Business.* "Flying High on an Idea" (August 1978): 41–47.
34. *The Office.* "Word Processing Paces Cosmetics Firm's Growth" (November 1978): 78, 114.
35. Perkins, James. "Artful Promotions: Key to Direct Selling Success." *Direct Marketing* (April, 1980): 55–58.
36. *RMA.* "Manufacturers—Perfumes, Cosmetics & Other Toilet Preparations." Robert Morris Associates (1980): 59.
37. *RMA.* "Manufacturers—Perfumes, Cosmetics & Other Toilet Preparations." Robert Morris Associates (1981): 62.
38. Rosenfield, Paul. "The Beautiful Make-Up of Mary Kay." *The Saturday Evening Post* (October 1981): Reprint 2714B82.
39. Rudnitsky, Howard. "The Flight of the Bumblebee." *Forbes* (June 22, 1981): 104–106.
40. Rudnitsky, Howard. "You Gotta Believe." *Forbes* (June 22, 1981): 105.
41. *Sales & Marketing Management/Special Report.* "Mary Kay: Some Overriding Reasons for Success" (August 23, 1976): 54–55.
42. *Securities and Exchange Commission.* "Annual Report, Mary Kay Cosmetics, Inc." (Year Ended December 31, 1981).
43. Sloan, Pat. "Mary Kay, Jafra Show Dramatic Growth." *Advertising Age* (August 23, 1982).
44. Sloan, Pat. "Mary Kay Putting On an Ad Show." *Advertising Age* (March 24, 1980): 36, 44.
45. *Standard & Poor's Corporation Records.* "Mary Kay Cosmetics, Inc." (August 1982): 4808.
46. *Standard & Poor's Industry Surveys.* "Cosmetics and Personal Care Products" (May 20, 1982): H26–H28.

47. *Standard & Poor's Industry Surveys.* "Composite Industry Data" (1982): H31–H44.

48. *Standard & Poor's Register of Corporations/1982 Directors and Executives.* "Mary Kay Cosmetics, Inc." (1982): 1441.

49. *Standard & Poor's Stock Reports New York Stock Exchange.* "Mary Kay Cosmetics" (May 13, 1982): 1427.

50. Stern, Richard L. "The Grease Trade Skids" *Forbes* (October 25, 1982): 161–164.

51. Rogers, Richard. Telephone interview with Paula Walters (November 22, 1982).

52. Rudy, Bruce. Telephone interview with Paula Walters (November 22, 1982).

53. Tunley, Raul. "Mary Kay's Sweet Smell of Success." *Reader's Digest* (November 1978): 2–5.

54. *Wall Street Journal.* "Avon Plans To Offer $100 Million of Notes" (October 13, 1982): 42.

Case 11

THE DANNON DECISION

Danny G. Kinker

Mr. James L. Dutt, Chairman and Chief Executive Officer of Beatrice Foods Company, faced a "very difficult decision." The company had been approached by a party offering to buy their Dannon yogurt subsidiary at a very attractive price. Should he recommend to the Board of Directors that the offer be accepted or rejected?

BEATRICE FOODS COMPANY: A PROFILE

In 1894, Beatrice Foods Company had two products to sell—butter and eggs. Today, Beatrice is highly diversified, producing and distributing more than 9,000 products worldwide. The 1981 Annual Report notes that Beatrice posted records for sales, earnings, and earnings per share for the twenty-ninth consecutive year. Sales rose 6% from \$8.3 billion in fiscal 1980 to \$8.8 billion in fiscal 1981. Net earnings increased to \$304.2 million, a 5% gain from the \$290.1 million recorded in fiscal 1980. Primary earnings per share rose 5% from \$2.81 in fiscal 1980 to \$2.94 in fiscal 1981. Fully diluted earnings per share were \$2.79, up 4% from the \$2.67 posted in fiscal 1980.

Much, if not most, of the spectacular growth of Beatrice occurred during the twenty-four year reign of William G. Karnes. This was for the most part accomplished during the late 1960s and early 1970s when the market rewarded acquisitive firms with high P/E ratios. A corporate officer explained that "firms were purchased for a price representing, say, 8 times earnings with stock trading at a multiple of around 20." When asked to describe the acquisition "strategy" of this period, Mr. Dutt said, "They would buy just about anything that came along." While this may have been true, a

This case was prepared by Prof. Danny G. Kinker of Washburn University. It was presented at the Case Research Association Meeting, 1983. Distributed by the Case Research Association.

large portion of their acquisitions had similar characteristics. They were relatively small, local or regional in scope, entrepreneurially managed, and profitable. After acquisition, the firms remained quite autonomous and the entrepreneurial ex-owner remained at the helm. See Exhibit 11.1 for a depiction of the growth of Beatrice under the leadership of Mr. Karnes.

Mr. Karnes retired in 1976 and was succeeded by Wallace N. Rasmussen, who continued an acquisition strategy. Upon the retirement of Mr. Ras-

Exhibit 11.1 TWENTY-FOUR CONSECUTIVE YEARS OF GROWTH

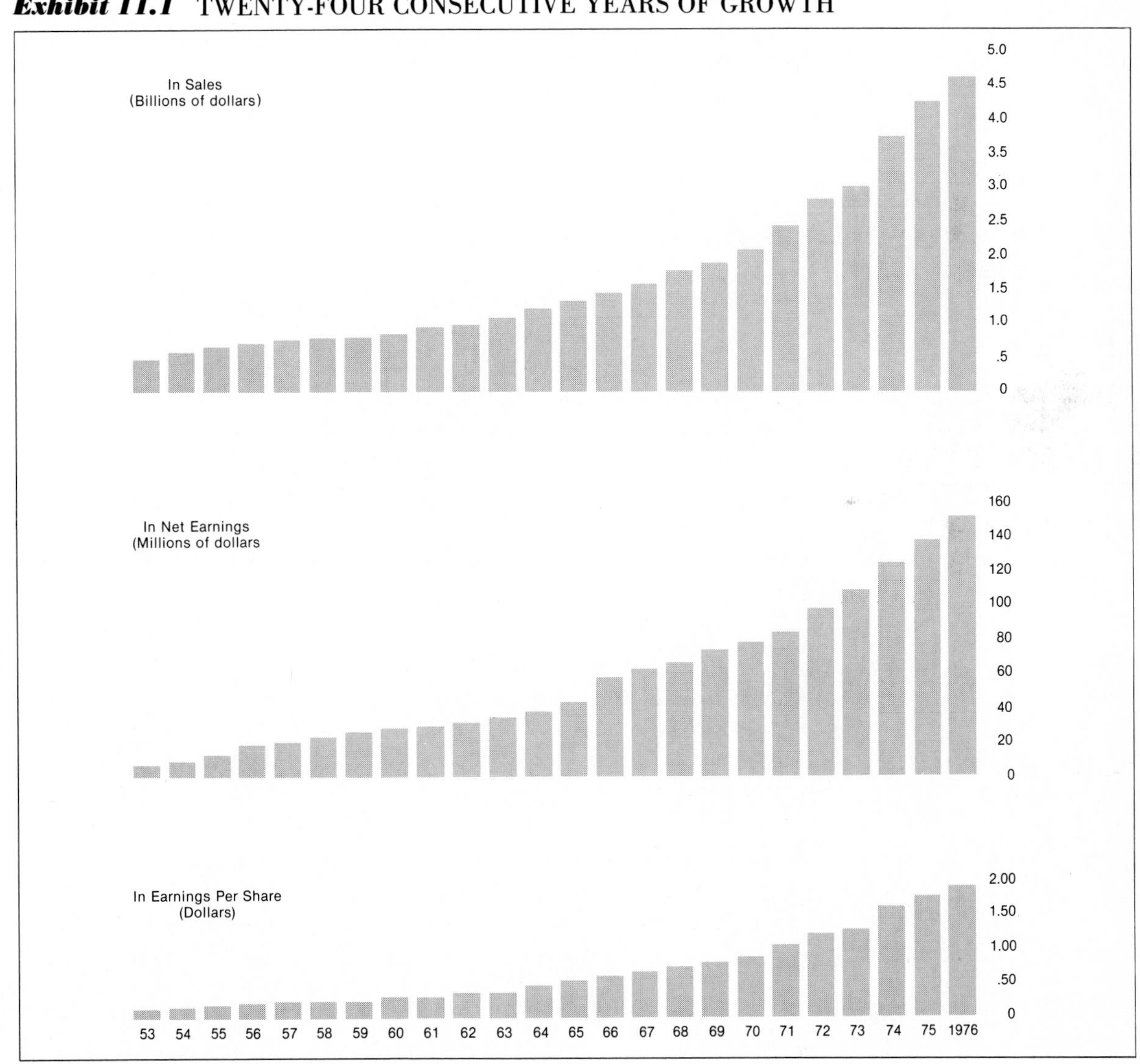

mussen in 1979, Mr. Dutt was appointed Chairman and Chief Executive Officer. It was soon noted that under the leadership of Mr. Dutt, a significant change had occurred in Beatrice's strategy. The *Wall Street Journal* called it "a quiet revolution." With all the attention placed on acquisition, a few of Beatrice's 430 autonomous businesses or "profit centers" had turned into "profit losers."

The significant change in strategy was the fact that Beatrice had begun *selling* businesses as well as acquiring them. For example, in 1979 Beatrice sold its Southwestern Investment Co. and used the proceeds to buy Fiberite Corp. While Southwestern's earnings were growing at 8% per year, Fiberite's were growing at about 30%. Mr. Dutt said, "Before, we had companies coming in, but now, we'll have companies going out as well." Walter L. Lovejoy, President of the Industrial Division, explained that (under Mr. Rasmussen), "If we weren't doing well in a business, it was because we

Exhibit 11.2

BEATRICE FOODS COMPANY: SALES AND EARNINGS
(in Thousands)

Net Sales by Major Lines of Business

	1981	1980	1979	1978
Food and Related Services				
Dairy and soft drinks	$2,297,068	$2,027,639	$1,925,631	$1,809,811
Grocery	1,313,026	1,220,735	963,184	707,623
Food distribution and warehousing	1,292,254	1,131,771	976,689	827,129
Specialty meats	677,826	688,948	657,983	548,483
Confectionery and snack	602,140	522,260	467,750	415,112
Agri-products	450,086	461,346	391,311	348,289
Manufactured and Chemical Products				
Institutional and industrial	843,886	872,561	753,325	678,382
Travel and recreational	503,325	513,017	496,751	437,507
Housing and home environment	390,216	530,293	572,765	522,440
Chemical and allied products	402,977	321,939	273,636	227,636
Net sales	$8,772,804	$8,290,509	$7,479,025	$6,522,467

Exhibit 11.2 **(*Continued*)**

Earnings by Major Lines of Business

	1981	1980	1979	1978
Food and Related Services				
Dairy and soft drinks	$ 122,499	$ 109,948	$ 106,610	$ 102,708
Grocery	125,190	113,997	82,353	50,064
Food distribution and warehousing	67,991	60,335	50,217	43,546
Specialty meats	53,224	50,009	44,964	44,520
Confectionery and snack	75,288	66,203	59,510	47,704
Agri-products	34,225	38,677	33,191	24,943
Manufactured and Chemical Products				
Institutional and industrial	106,485	126,616	111,126	106,188
Travel and recreational	54,082	47,823	45,816	38,053
Housing and home environment	22,435	22,148	42,470	53,215
Chemical and allied products	52,410	46,812	37,693	29,517
Total operating earnings	713,829	682,568	613,950	540,458
Less:[1]	409,618	392,428	351,783	313,740
Net earnings	$ 304,211	$ 290,140	$ 262,167	$ 226,718

NOTE 1. Non-operating expenses, Interest Expense, and Income Taxes.

weren't managing properly. Mr. Dutt believes there are some things maybe we just shouldn't be in." Mr. Dutt also said, "We're not going to let companies die on our vine."

By 1981, Mr. Dutt's strategy had crystallized. The 1981 Annual Report contained the following discussion of "asset redeployment."

> Beatrice has made great strides in its asset redeployment program over the past three years. During that time, the company has divested operations that generated approximately $500 million in sales in 1979. This is a managed program over time, and an ongoing review is conducted of all operations to ensure an optimum mix of companies.

> Within that diverse mix, Beatrice looks for operations to exhibit the following characteristics: they should be able to achieve a real growth rate of 5 percent; or they should be achieving a return on net assets equal to or in excess of 20 percent; or they should be generating cash to be invested in operations which are growing in real terms.
>
> When redeploying assets, Beatrice looks to profit centers or acquisition candidates that are generating returns that are higher than the corporate average.

Net sales and earnings by major lines of business, 1978–1981, are shown in Exhibit 11.2 and abbreviated income statement and balance sheet data for the company are shown in Exhibits 11.3 and 11.4.

DANNON YOGURT: A PROFILE

The history of Dannon yogurt began in 1919, when a Spaniard named Carasso created the product. He then named the product after his son, Daniel, and Danone yogurt came into existence. The Danone operation was subsequently moved from Spain to France and eventually sold to BSN. Dannon yogurt came into existence in 1942 when Daniel Carasso persuaded a friend,

STATEMENT OF CONSOLIDATED EARNINGS FOR 1981

(in Thousands)

Exhibit 11.3

Income	
Net sales	$8,772,804
Interest income	40,198
Other income	25,590
	8,838,592
Costs and Expenses	
Cost of sales, excluding depreciation	6,510,782
Selling, administrative, and general expenses, excluding depreciation	1,457,158
Depreciation expense	155,373
Interest expense	96,403
	8,219,716
Earnings before income taxes and minority interests	618,876
Provision for income taxes	301,700
Earnings before minority interests	317,176
Minority interests in net earnings of consolidated subsidiaries	12,965
Net earnings	$304,211

Juan Metzger, to come with him to the United States. They intended to produce and market yogurt. The name Dannon is an Americanization of Danone and Daniel Carasso was the same Daniel for whom the yogurt was named. The initial operation was set up in the Bronx and produced 200 bottles of plain yogurt a day. Juan Metzger recalled, "Anything would have been easier to sell than yogurt in those days." Their customers were mostly recent European immigrants.

In 1947, a daring attempt was made to enhance the product by placing strawberry preserves in the bottom of the bottle. This seemed to appeal to

CONSOLIDATED BALANCE SHEET FOR 1981

(in Thousands)

Exhibit 11.4

ASSETS	
Current assets	
Cash	$ 132,420
Short-term investments	285,108
Receivables	834,480
Inventories	
Finished goods	507,807
Work in process	138,371
Raw materials and supplies	325,854
	2,224,040
Prepaid expenses and other current assets	72,573
Total current assets	2,296,613
Investments in affiliated companies	57,021
Plant and equipment	
Land	70,171
Buildings	592,544
Machinery and equipment	1,252,049
Capitalized leases	202,745
	2,117,509
Less accumulated depreciation	803,587
	1,313,922
Intangible assets	463,363
Noncurrent receivables	80,570
Other assets	25,060
Total assets	$4,236,555

(*Continued*)

Exhibit 11.4
(Continued)

LIABILITIES AND STOCKHOLDERS' EQUITY	
Current liabilities	
Short-term debt	$ 122,410
Accounts payable	521,061
Accrued expenses	
Taxes (other than income taxes)	30,252
Other accruals	243,880
Income taxes	112,792
Current portion of long-term debt	28,813
Current obligations of capitalized leases	15,563
Total current liabilities	1,074,771
Long-term debt	564,710
Long-term lease obligations	126,728
Deferred items	
Income taxes	90,963
Investment tax credits	31,870
Other	23,368
Other noncurrent liabilities	89,293
Minority interests in subsidiaries	53,407
Stockholders' equity	
Preference stock	259,567
Common stock	180,850
Additional capital	106,930
Retained earnings	1,634,098
Total stockholders' equity	2,181,445
Total liabilities and stockholders' equity	$4,236,555

customers and, eventually, the product line was to contain sixteen flavors.

In 1952, Daniel Carasso returned to Europe to tend to his yogurt business there, but Juan Metzger remained to cultivate the yogurt business in the United States. So successful was Metzger that, realizing its potential, Beatrice sought and acquired Dannon in 1959. After the purchase by Beatrice, Metzger remained at the helm of Dannon and eventually became a member of the Board of Directors of Beatrice. With the resources of the larger company available, much faster growth was possible for Dannon. Automated equipment was installed which dramatically increased volume and the old glass bottles were replaced by waxed cups. But basic technology remained the same. The yogurt was made by keeping pasteurized low-fat milk at temperatures around 100 degrees Fahrenheit while bacteria (good ones) converted the milk's sugar into lactic acid. This caused the milk to thicken and take on the tart taste of yogurt. Beatrice also invested heavily in marketing, expanding the geographic base until it became national.

THE DECISION

The offer to buy Dannon came from a not-unfamiliar source. In fact, the offer came from BSN-Gervais-Danone. Although Dannon's recent earnings had been depressed (the previous year's sales of nearly $130 million had produced net earnings of only around $3.5 million), Beatrice had not considered selling Dannon. Income statement and balance sheet data for Dannon are presented in Exhibit 11.5.

Three reasons could be cited for Dannon's recent drop in performance. First of all, anxious to tap the West Coast market, distribution to this area was initiated prior to acquiring a production facility in California. The area was served by the Ft. Worth, Texas plant, sharply increasing distribution costs. Production in California had just recently commenced. Secondly, it was believed that the West Coast regional brands had significantly increased their promotional spending to counter the threat posed by Dannon. Thirdly,

Exhibit 11.5
DANNON INCOME STATEMENT/BALANCE SHEET INFORMATION
(in Thousands)

	1981	1980	1979	1978	1977	1976
INCOME DATA						
Total sales	$129,385	122,552	113,426	100,897	76,681	55,449
Gross margin	% 43.42	44.05	42.79	43.44	44.31	44.34
Earnings (pre-tax)	$ 6,789	6,590	5,634	10,705	9,765	6,436
Interest charges (Interco.)	(118)	(126)	98	121	130	147
	$ 6,671	6,464	5,732	10,826	9,695	6,583
Margins (pre-tax)						
After interest	% 5.28	5.40	5.01	10.79	12.86	11.62
Before interest	% 5.19	5.30	5.09	10.91	13.03	11.89
Employees	# 1,201	1,310	1,270	995	804	613
ASSET DATA						
Accounts receivable	$ 9,647	9,121	9,597	9,521	6,951	5,234
Inventory	$ 2,325	2,296	2,192	1,787	1,206	839
Accounts payable	$ (6,187)	(5,989)	(4,160)	(4,277)	(4,048)	(2,615)
Net assets	$ 19,450	21,533	23,760	22,670	17,977	12,538

Dannon encountered a new national competitor. Yoplait, a French-style yogurt, was introduced under license by General Mills.

There was one other market factor of some importance. Beatrice believed that the yogurt market was achieving maturity at about 1.3 billion containers per year. Of this 1.3 billion container market, over 30% of it belonged to Dannon. Additionally, Dannon had introduced its own French-style yogurt, Melangé. It was estimated that this product category represented roughly 15% of yogurt sales. See Exhibit 11.6 for annual production and per capita consumption of yogurt.

PRODUCTION AND PER CAPITA CONSUMPTION OF YOGURT, 1960–1981

Exhibit 11.6

Year	*Pounds (millions)*	*% Chg.*	*Sales (pounds per capita)*	*% Chg.*
1960	44	—	.26	—
1961	49	11.4	.28	7.7
1962	45	− 8.1	.25	−10.7
1963	51	13.3	.28	12.0
1964	53	3.9	.29	3.6
1965	61	15.1	.32	10.3
1966	70	14.8	.37	15.6
1967	90	28.6	.47	27.0
1968	124	37.8	.63	34.0
1969	169	36.3	.85	34.9
1970	172	1.8	.86	1.2
1971	236	37.2	1.16	34.9
1972	284	20.3	1.38	19.0
1973	318	12.0	1.52	10.1
1974	343	7.9	1.63	7.2
1975	445	29.7	2.09	28.2
1976	482	8.3	2.24	7.2
1977	534	10.8	2.45	9.3
1978	566	6.0	2.57	4.9
1979	567	0.2	2.54	− 1.2
1980	589	3.9	2.61	2.8
1981	582	− 1.2	2.55	− 2.3

SOURCE: U.S.D.A.

NOTE: 1980 figures were preliminary and 1981 figures estimated.

Production in California joined the network of plants in New York, New Jersey, Florida, Ohio, and Texas. The Texas plant had recently been enlarged as well. Dannon had considerable experience in the yogurt industry and the dominant market share. While Dannon appeared to be related to Beatrice's other dairy operations (Meadow Gold, VIVA, etc.), synergies had never been realized. Metzger was quoted as saying, "We will not depend on anyone else for storage or shipping or handling our product. Yogurt is perishable, and the minute you let it get out of your sight, someone might get careless."

Dannon's growth potential was uncertain, but Metzger's position was, "We have been a one-product company for a long time. It's time to diversify." Also, Dannon's future as a cash generator was uncertain but they had done very well in the past. The offer from BSN-Gervais-Danone was for \$384.3 million in cash. This would result in net proceeds of \$45.0 million to Beatrice. What should Mr. Dutt recommend to the Board of Directors?

Case 12

VERMONT TUBBS, INC. (B)

W. H. Ellis/Sandra Smith

During the weekend of August 7, 1982, C. Baird Morgan Jr. (45 years old), President of Vermont Tubbs, Inc., Forestdale, Vermont was thinking about the upcoming 9 A.M. meeting on Monday morning with his bankers. He was not quite sure how to prepare for it, how he might present his case, and what he should actually say to them. In other words, what strategy he should adopt and in turn what reaction he might expect from them. Sales had fluctuated over the past decade from a high of about $1.2 million in 1979 to a low of nearly $200,000 in the early years of operation. For the fiscal year ending June 30, 1982, the company had a net income of $5,000 on sales of $385,000 (Exhibits 12.1 to 12.4) compared with $30,000 and $338,000 respectively in 1971 (Exhibits 12.5 and 12.6).

HISTORY

Mr. Morgan had taken over as the president of Vermont Tubbs, Inc. in 1969. The company, founded in the 1880s, had built up a reputation as the manufacturer of high-quality snowshoes. During World War II, Tubbs' production of snowshoes reached over 100,000 pairs per year, sold entirely to the U.S. Government for use in Scandinavia, the Alps, and the Himalayas. Thereafter, the company passed through several owners until it went bankrupt in 1958. Harold Underwood, a local gasoline-station owner, was a creditor and received the business in full settlement of his claim amounting to about $250.

According to Mr. Morgan, Mr. Underwood had run the business successfully with production during the last year of Underwood's ownership reaching approximately 9,000 pairs. This rose to 15,000 in 1970–1971 and Mr. Morgan had projected an increase to 20,000 for the year 1971–1972.

This case was prepared by Mrs. Sandra Smith under the direction of Prof. W. H. Ellis of McGill University. Reprinted by permission.

Mr. Morgan, who had received his MBA from the University of Pennsylvania, Wharton School of Business Administration in 1964, had been looking for a company to buy ("I was single, independent, not afraid of hard work or long hours and did not want to work for someone else"). His search led him to Mr. Underwood, who apparently seemed to prefer fishing and hunting to owning a small business. The net result was that Mr. Morgan borrowed $10,000 from his father, borrowed $20,000 on a personal note, mortgaged the rest from Harold Underwood, and became president of Vermont Tubbs in 1969.

From 1969–1971, Mr. Morgan was able to increase sales through an improved distribution system. In New England he continued to sell directly to retail sporting-goods stores and mail-order houses.

The business continued to prosper through 1971–1975. Tubbs pur-

VERMONT TUBBS, INC.
Unaudited Balance Sheet
June 30

Exhibit 12.1

	1981	1982
ASSETS		
Current Assets		
Cash	$ 2,588	$ 15,194
Accounts receivable (less allowance for doubtful accounts)	43,707	41,865
Inventory	230,064	$124,209
Prepaid insurance	—	4,058
Total Current Assets	$276,359	$185,326
Property and Equipment		
Land	6,000	6,000
Buildings	94,098	94,098
Vehicles and equipment	164,357	166,861
Total Property and Equipment	264,455	266,959
Less accumulated depreciation	141,786	152,366
Net Property and Equipment	$122,669	$114,593
Other Assets		
Security deposits	700	700
Energy project	93,178	93,178
Total Other Assets	93,878	93,878
Total Assets	$492,906	$393,797

(*Continued*)

Exhibit 12.1
(Continued)

	1981	1982
LIABILITIES AND STOCKHOLDERS' EQUITY		
Current Liabilities		
Accounts payable	$ 27,972	3,211
Current portion of long-term debt	190,406	138,286
Taxes payable	50	1,305
Accrued expenses	11,953	—
Total Current Liabilities	$230,381	$142,802
Long-term Liabilities		
Long-term debt	228,500	215,923
Other payables	4,000	—
Total long-term debt	232,500	215,923
Total liabilities	$462,811	$358,725
Stockholders' Equity		
Common stock—20,000 shares authorized, issued and outstanding, net of discount on stock of $98,050	101,950	101,950
Retained earnings	(71,925)	(66,878)
Total Stockholder's Equity	30,025	35,072
Total Liabilities and Stockholders' Equity	$492,906	$393,797

chased a larger plant in Middletown, Vt. in 1971 and then sold it two years later when more suitable facilities were bought in Forestdale. In 1975 there were two plants in operation, one used to manufacture fiberglass canoes and a woodworking shop a quarter of a mile away.

Coincidentally, the financial problems of Vermont Tubbs began in 1975. The office procedures became so involved that Mr. Morgan hired a controller on the advice and recommendation of his banker. This employee, who appeared to have excellent references, proceeded to embezzle approximately $70,000 from the company in a short period of time. None of this money was recovered and the net result was that by the end of 1976, Vermont Tubbs was virtually bankrupt, and the plant was closed.

At this point, a benefactor appeared on the scene in the person of Mr. Howard Baker. Mr. Baker had been a former New England sales manager for Fuller Brush and currently owned a small woodworking plant outside Boston, Mass. An arrangement was made with the bank whereby he assumed the debts of Vermont Tubbs together with the controlling interest in the company. Having been a salesman all his life, Mr. Baker was accustomed to and enjoyed expense account living. The auditor, in going over the 1977

VERMONT TUBBS, INC.

Unaudited Statement of Income and Retained Earnings for the Year Ended June 30

Exhibit 12.2

	1981	1982
Revenues		
Sales	$511,348	$386,399
Less discounts and allowances	2,240	1,727
Net Revenues	$509,108	$384,672
Cost of sales		
Inventory—July 1	368,177	230,064
Purchases and freight	101,196	61,266
Labor	125,637	62,582
Total Goods Available	595,010	353,912
Less inventory—June 30	230,064	124,209
Cost of Sales	$364,946	$229,703
Gross profit from operations	$144,162	$154,969
General and administrative expenses	$207,460	$151,638
(See Exhibit 12.4.)		
Income from operations	(63,298)	3,331
Other revenues		
Proceeds from officer's life insurance	49,842	—
Gain on sale of assets	23,994	1,000
Extraordinary income (fire insurance recovery of 18,025 net of repairs of 17,259	—	766
Total Other Revenues	$ 73,836	$ 1,766
Net income before taxes	$ 10,538	$ 5,097
Income taxes		
State	50	50
Federal	0	0
Total Income Taxes	$ 50	$ 50
Net income	$ 10,488	$ 5,047
Retained earnings—July 1	$ (82,413)	$ (71,925)
Retained earnings—June 30	$ (71,925)	$ (66,878)

books, discovered that he had claimed $30,000 in personal expenses, totally unrelated to Vermont Tubbs, and had paid salaries to several of his relatives. He was highly indignant that the books should be questioned and moved the accounting records out of Vermont to an auditor in Connecticut. Mr. Morgan never saw them again until after Mr. Baker's death in May 1981.

FINANCIAL STRUCTURE

Mr. Morgan had originally owned two-thirds of the stock of Vermont Tubbs and his father had held the remaining shares. In 1975, when Mr. Baker came into the company, an additional 10,000 shares were issued, making a total of 20,000 shares outstanding of which Mr. Baker owned 10,600. The rest were divided between Mr. Morgan and his family.

Mr. Baker had set up a proprietorship called Vermont Tubbs Sales which

VERMONT TUBBS, INC.

Unaudited Statement of Changes in Financial Position for the Year Ended June 30

Exhibit 12.3

	1981	1982
Sources of Working Capital		
From operations		
Net income	$ 10,488	$ 5,047
Add back depreciation not requiring an outlay of working capital	21,841	13,561
Deduct gain on sale of property and equipment included in other sources below	(23,994)	(1,000)
	$ 8,335	$ 17,608
Other sources		
Sale of property and equipment	132,607	2,442
Increase of long-term debt	50,000	5,486
	$182,607	$ 7,928
Total Sources of Working Capital	190,942	$ 25,536
Uses of Working Capital		
Payments of long-term debt	238,064	(18,063)
Purchases of fixed assets	1,699	(6,927)
Repayment of other payables	16,037	—
Cost associated with energy project	93,178	—
Total Uses of Working Capital	$348,978	($ 24,990)
Increase in Working Capital		$ 546
Decrease in Working Capital	$158,036	

Exhibit 12.3
(*Continued*)

	1981	1982
ANALYSIS OF CHANGES IN WORKING CAPITAL		
Current Assets		
Increase in cash	—	12,606
Decrease in cash	(1,933)	—
Decrease in inventory	(138,113)	(105,855)
Increase in prepaid expenses	—	4,058
Decrease in prepaid expenses	(3,075)	—
Increase in accounts receivable	43,707	—
Decrease in accounts receivable	—	(1,842)
	($ 99,414)	($ 91,033)
Current Liabilities		
Decrease in accounts payable	(93,582)	28,761
Increase in current portion of long-term debt	162,087	
Decrease in current portion of long-term debt		52,120
Decrease in accrued expenses	(9,883)	10,698
	58,622	91,579
Increase in Working Capital		$ 546
Decrease in Working Capital	$158,036	

was a factoring agency for Vermont Tubbs and was one way of protecting the accounts receivable from the creditors of Vermont Tubbs. Vermont Tubbs Sales was to receive a 10% commission on the sales revenues of Vermont Tubbs. The intention was also that Mr. Morgan would hold a 50% interest in the sales organization.

ORGANIZATION

Prior to 1975, Mr. Morgan had handled all aspects of Vermont Tubbs' operations. He was familiar with the production techniques and would work along with the superintendents and other plant personnel.

With the entrance of Mr. Baker to the company, Mr. Morgan continued to look after production and quality control. Mr. Baker's duties and responsibilities were mainly finance, office procedures, and marketing.

PRODUCTS

Vermont Tubbs presently manufactures three products: snowshoes, snowshoe furniture, and contemporary bentwood furniture (Exhibit 12.7, 1981 catalogue, pages 528 and 529.).

Snowshoes were made from a light bentwood frame laced with rawhide or

VERMONT TUBBS, INC.

Unaudited Schedule of General and Administrative Expenses for the Year Ended June 30

Exhibit 12.4

	1981	1982
GENERAL AND ADMINISTRATIVE EXPENSES		
Auto expense	$ —	$ 1,595
Commissions	30,266	5,135
Utilities	22,738	20,433
Interest	43,321	41,575
Officers' salaries	29,004	11,685
Depreciation	21,841	13,561
Shop supplies	5,469	3,248
Office expenses	4,577	3,982
Insurance	22,366	11,053
Taxes and licenses	7,502	13,475
Travel and entertainment	2,272	1,345
Equipment repairs	1,804	4,846
Telephone	4,324	3,917
Research costs	1,366	1,365
Advertising and promotion	1,168	1,026
Professional fees	4,353	3,715
Bad debt expense	3,000	3,394
Rent	60	—
Bookkeeping expense	—	5,384
Miscellaneous	2,029	904
Total	$207,460	$151,638

neoprene strips. More recently, an additional line was added with snowshoes made by using an aluminum frame.

Snowshoe furniture, which consisted of a bentwood frame and snowshoe pattern lacings, had been manufactured by Tubbs many years ago. Some of their pieces had accompanied Admiral Byrd to the South Pole but production had ceased with the concentration on snowshoes during World War II. Tubbs began manufacturing this furniture again in 1973. A natural market was believed to exist and the company hoped to utilize the waste products from the manufacture of snowshoes in its construction.

The contemporary bentwood furniture production had begun in 1978 and consisted not only of furniture but also gourmet and gift items.

VERMONT TUBBS, INC.

Comparative Balance Sheets June 30, 1970 and June 30, 1971

Exhibit 12.5

	1970	1971
ASSETS		
Current Assets		
Cash	$ 3,945.69	$ 16,058.28
Accounts receivable (net)	5,270.34	24,576.64
Inventory	55,869.75	64,369.00
Advance to Bristol Chemical	—	50,000.00
Other	349.32	69.86
Total Current Assets	65,435.10	155,073.78
Fixed Assets (net)		
Land	3,000.00	3,000.00
Building & improvements	50,547.32	49,129.89
Machinery & equipment	39,553.62	34,303.22
Vehicle	1,833.33	2,907.61
Office equipment	—	187.03
Total Fixed Assets	94,934.27	89,527.75
Other Assets (incl. Goodwill $1,000)	1,211.52	1,159.72
Total Assets	$161,580.89	$245,761.25
LIABILITIES AND CAPITAL		
Current Liabilities		
Accounts payable	$ 6,710.50	$ 13,795.10
Accrued taxes	2,592.67	2,396.53
Accrued wages	—	1,013.85
Notes payable: Bank	10,000.00	50,000.00
Notes payable: H. Underwood (current portion)	5,572.09	6,430.50
Total Current Liabilities	24,875.26	73,635.98
Long-term Liabilities		
Due officers & stockholders	3,395.00	7,394.75
Notes payable: C. B. Morgan, Sr.	2,000.00	15,000.00
Notes payable: H. Underwood, Inc.	96,582.77	89,727.37
Total Long-Term Liabilities	101,977.77	112,122.12
Total Liabilities	126,853.03	185,758.10
Capital		
Capital stock	30,000.00	30,000.00
Retained earnings	4,727.86	30,003.15
Total Capital	34,727.86	60,003.15
Total Liabilities and Capital	$161,580.89	$245,761.25

Prepared from the books without audit.

Exhibit 12.6

VERMONT TUBBS, INC.

Comparative Income Statements F/Y 1970, 1971

	1970	1971
Sales		
Snowshoes	$180,436.22	$283,932.13
Bindings	27,669.44	52,912.75
Repairs	1,734.23	2,276.47
Sawdust & supplies	—	2,304.58
Deduct: returns & allowances	(1,378.49)	(3,481.18)
Net Sales	208,461.40	337,944.75
Cost of Sales		
Inventory July 1	37,229.62	55,869.75
Add: Lumber	31,499.40	26,293.02
Rawhide, leather, bindings, neoprene	61,531.24	107,099.72
Operating supplies	10,832.24	14,067.58
Labor	59,691.79	85,767.40
Depreciation	7,728.23	9,321.12
Taxes & licenses	5,414.83	7,162.57
Heat & lights	4,464.43	5,196.58
Freight (in)	1,930.26	2,676.03
Other (incl. repairs)	5,354.07	2,435.03
Deduct: Inventory June 30	(55,869.75)	(64,369.00)
Total Cost of Sales	169,806.36	251,519.80
Gross profit	38,655.04	86,424.95
General and administrative		
Salary: officer	3,600.00	10,000.00
Salary: office	3,666.50	5,545.22
Commission	6,293.59	9,277.03
Travel & promotion	1,741.46	1,033.25
Telephone	1,009.31	2,320.78
Interest	8,488.07	10.407.67
Advertising	2,397.76	1,821.59
Office expenses	1,465.73	2,936.00
Repairs	—	1,606.62
Legal & audit	2,551.26	1,687.51
Insurance	3,537.18	5,057.09
Bad debts	—	3,653.60
Other	447.07	2,300.84
Total G&A	35,197.93	57,647.20
Profit on operations	3,457.11	28,777.75
Other income (cash discounts)	1,270.75	1,225.40
NET PROFIT	$ 4,727.86	$ 30,003.15

Prepared from the books without audit.

From 1973–1975, Vermont Tubbs manufactured fiberglass canoes. While the design was excellent and the first-quality products got excellent acceptance, the quality control problems could not be overcome and more seconds than firsts were produced. Transportation also was a major problem; it was very expensive because of the bulky nature of the product and many canoes were damaged in transit. This business was sold in 1976 just before the hiring of the infamous controller.

DIVERSIFICATION

In 1971 Mr. Morgan had been receiving on the average of one inquiry per week to sell his business. He had rejected all offers but had considered different possibilities for diversification. He wanted to broaden his product mix so that he had year-round products. Among the possibilities he had considered to lessen dependence on a product which required snow for continued success were:

1. Bristol Manufacturing. Mr. Morgan had had the opportunity to buy out this company, which manufactured Fall Line Wax, considered to be the best wax in the world. Bristol also made Leath-R-Seal, which was a leather preservative. In addition, Bristol also manufactured paints that could be used for swimming pools and tennis courts. Tubbs advanced $50,000 on a short-term loan basis in June 1971, which held a purchase option for Tubbs. This had to be withdrawn when Tubbs itself subsequently came into financial difficulties.
2. Cross-country skis. Mr. Morgan had considered distributing a Norwegian ski under the Tubbs label. He had finally decided against it as many skiers were moving away from wooden skis to the non-wax fiberglass type. Also, the major manufacturers of downhill equipment, such as Fischer and Rossignol, were also getting into the cross-country marketplace.
3. Canoes. Reference has already been made to the attempts to diversify into this product line.

PRODUCTION

In the early 1970s Vermont Tubbs had maintained its share of the snowshoe market. During those early years, production could not keep up with demand.

However, the mid-seventies saw a number of very erratic years in terms of snowfall. If there was snow in the East, there was none in the West or vice-versa. Snowshoe production fell to a low during troubled financial times and the unstable snow conditions did not help attempts at rebuilding.

In the late seventies, efforts were made to spread out production by making snowshoes year-round, 500 to 600 pair per week or 15,000 a year. Also during this period the company produced, on the average, 40 pieces of

Exhibit 12.7 (a)

Vermont Craftsmanship

by people who put promise in their products

Vermont craftsmanship and quality are as natural and Yankee as covered bridges, fall foliage and pie for breakfast. And, in these days of mass (and sometimes careless) production, it's refreshing to find that there are still some things of value—painstakingly crafted from natural materials by people who put promise in their products. Snowshoe furniture by Vermont Tubbs—the ultimate in solid tradition and enduring, useful beauty.

Designed originally for camping, boating and canoeing, enthusiastic purchasers over the years have found other uses and enjoyment. This same furniture, taken to the South Pole by Admiral Byrd, is now serving its purpose in camps or on large estates, by the hearth or at the tennis court or in the nursery.

Each piece is carefully and individually developed from its earliest stages (select New England hardwoods and specially tanned rawhide) to its final dipped and deep-penetrating urethane finish. As a result, no two pieces are exactly alike. All finishes are weather resistant and all furniture can be used outside as well as inside. However, any wood furniture should be covered or protected from extended bad weather conditions.

Snowshoe Rocker
A clubby, comfortable addition to any porch, deck or room. A full-size chair, but still just right for a large gentleman or a small lady. The same sturdy construction used in our world-famous snowshoes. All joints are secured by countersunk screws pegged over with matching wood. 21"W x 18"D x 34"H, Seat approximately 14" from the floor.
****S101 Natural Finish $125.00**
****SA101 Antique Finish $125.00**

Exhibit 12.7 (b)

snowshoe furniture or 2,000 pieces a year. The bentwood furniture production had been very erratic, with designers changed frequently and many items manufactured to order.

MARKETING AND DISTRIBUTION

Marketing and distribution have been the major areas of concern for Vermont Tubbs over the past decade. In the early days, Mr. Morgan had hired eleven aggressive representatives who handled his snowshoes outside New England across the U.S., including Alaska. In New England he maintained Harold Underwood's network of sporting-goods stores and mail-order houses.

These dealers were a natural outlet for the snowshoe furniture and he continued with them for distribution of this product line. The sales representatives were paid 8% commission on their sales.

Mr. Baker assumed the responsibility for marketing in New England

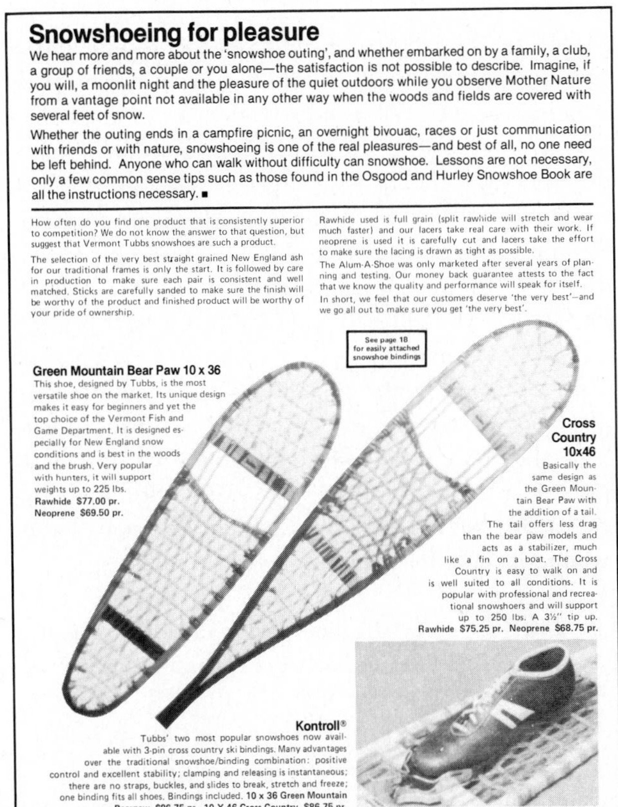

Exhibit 12.7 (c)

when he took over the company. He did not like to pay salesmen's commissions and announced that he intended to call on the dealers himself. The first year he made several trips; the second year fewer and finally since 1978 he has not made any calls. The reduced marketing effort was clearly reflected in the decline in sales.

During the three-year period of 1978–1981 with poor snowfall and limited production and sales, Mr. Morgan felt that snowshoe furniture could have been and would now have to be more strongly marketed.

The decision to manufacture upholstered bentwood furniture presented a new set of marketing and distribution problems. The market was now nationwide and not just the states of the snow-belt. This furniture could not be marketed through sporting-goods dealers.

The decision was made by both Morgan and Baker to market bentwood furniture through a distributor called Raymor-Moreddi (R-M), located in New Jersey. R-M represented about forty furniture manufacturers nationwide with showrooms in major U.S. cities. This distributor charged 22% commission on sales; Vermont Tubbs also had to pay a design fee of 3%.

Shortly after this contract was signed Mr. Morgan became disenchanted with R-M. He felt that they were not sufficiently marketing oriented and were simply order takers. At the first furniture show he attended, Vermont Tubbs was pushed off in a corner next to a lot of bric-a-brac from Taiwan.

In 1979 sales of contemporary bentwood furniture reached $200,000, the equivalent of the snowshoe furniture. However, snowshoe furniture was priced to sell with 8% commission whereas bentwood furniture had a 25% commission built into its price. In June 1981, shortly after Mr. Baker's death, Mr. Morgan cancelled the contract with R-M, who went bankrupt a year later.

He was currently dealing with a marketing consultant to whom he paid no fee. This consultant was convinced that the way to market bentwood furniture was through one or two key accounts in large cities. He was currently trying to sell it in the greater Washington area. The consultant was convinced that he could sell all the bentwood furniture that Vermont Tubbs could produce and was willing to take his fees out of future sales.

CATALOGUE SALES

Mr. Baker had decided in 1979 to enter the mail-order business. He was convinced that catalogues were where the money was to be made but Mr. Morgan was vehemently opposed to the idea. He felt that their product line was limited and that their particular market was not geared to mail-order. "Tubbs was definitely not L.L. Bean, which sells everything from soup to sleeping bags." However, Mr. Baker persisted and bought mailing lists from different companies, in the anticipation of selling $1,000 per day. In fact, they sold $8,000 worth of goods overall. Mr. Baker spent $50,000–$60,000 on the catalogue, which turned out to be a complete fiasco (Exhibit 12.7). In Mr. Morgan's opinion, the photography was poor quality and the copy very amateurish. This investment came from Vermont Tubbs Sales and had virtually wiped out all their assets. Mr. Baker had finally realized the folly of the catalogue and had promised to repay Vermont Tubbs Sales. However, he died before he could make good on this promise.

COMPETITION AND PRICING

The major competitors of Vermont Tubbs snowshoes came from Canadian manufacturers north of Quebec City. It was believed that these companies had government subsidies and used cheap Indian labour to produce a shoe that retailed for $40.00 in the U.S. Vermont Tubbs had no way of matching this price. Tubbs snowshoes were considered to be of a higher quality than the Canadian products but wholesaled for $40.00. This realization was one of the reasons Mr. Morgan had entered the furniture business.

Vermont Tubbs had very little competition in the snowshoe furniture line and it was not dependent upon snowfall. However, there were many competitors in the bentwood furniture market, and distribution and marketing seemed to be the key to success.

CURRENT PRODUCTION

In 1979 there wasn't any snow in the East until late in February. Mr. Morgan had wanted to stop production at Christmas time but Mr. Baker had insisted on manufacturing through the winter. Inventory had now been sitting there for two years incurring interest and insurance charges. Mr. Morgan had tried to reduce the inventory but had been unsuccessful. He had even offered L.L. Bean a 40% discount and still could not sell it.

All the staff except two experienced bentwood furniture makers had been let go. The payroll was now reduced to $300 per week instead of $3,000. The laid-off workers had been able to find other jobs so that when and if Vermont Tubbs resumed production, the company would have a problem finding skilled workers.

CURRENT FINANCIAL SITUATION

Mr. Morgan's meeting with his bankers will seemingly decide the fate of his company. Mr. Morgan had no plan presently to suggest to the bank beyond continuing to manufacture snowshoes and bentwood furniture in a very poor economic climate.

The total debt exceeded $350,000 with the current portion nearly $140,000. The statement of income shows $49,000 revenue from Mr. Baker's life insurance. Otherwise the loss in 1981 would have been that much greater (financial statements and sales distribution, Exhibits 12.1 to 12.6 and 12.8).

In preparing for this meeting, Mr. Morgan thought back to offers that he had entertained in the early 1970s. At that time different conglomerates had wanted to buy him out at eighteen to twenty times earnings. He had refused their offers, insisting that he would rather have his own small operation than be part of a large company.

Now he wondered if a small manufacturing company could survive the present day economic climate.

Exhibit 12.8

VERMONT TUBBS, INC.

Comparative Data on Sales Distribution

	1970		1971		1981		1982	
	$	%	$	%	$	%	$	%
Snowshoes	180,436	85.8	283,932	82.8	175,000	34.4	120,000	31.2
Bindings	27,669	13.4	52,912	15.8	50,000	9.8	30,000	7.8
Snowshoe furniture	—	—	—	—	100,000	19.6	100,000	26.0
General furniture	—	—	—	—	149,000	29.3	107,000	27.8
Repairs, sawdust, and supplies	1,734	0.8	4,581	1.4	35,108	6.9	27,672	7.2
Returns and allowances	(1,378)	—	(3,481)	—	(2,240)	—	(1,727)	—
Net Sales	208,461	100	337,944	100	509,108	100	384,672	100
Gross Sales	209,839		341,426		511,348		386,399	

SOURCE: Company statistics.

Case 13

SEARS, ROEBUCK AND COMPANY

J. David Hunger / Deborah Jones

Kevin McCarey / Keith Morris / Ken Smith

HISTORY OF THE FIRM

Sears, Roebuck and Co., the world's largest retailer of general merchandise, is an outgrowth of an enterprise established in 1886 and incorporated under the laws of New York in 1906. The Company (Sears and its consolidated subsidiaries) with general offices located at Sears Tower in Chicago, Illinois comprises the following business groups: *Merchandise Group*—which includes Merchandising (distributes goods and services in the United States), Credit (provides credit services to customers of Merchandising), and International (conducts retail merchandise and credit operations in Central and South America, Spain, Mexico and Puerto Rico, and in Canada through Simpsons-Sears Limited, approximately 40% equity-owned and 50% voting-stock-owned); *Allstate Group* (the second largest property-liability insurer in the United States—engages in various insurance and financial services businesses); and *Seraco Group* (invests in, develops, and operates real estate; performs financial services, which include savings and loan, mortgage banking, and mortage guaranty insurance activities).

For its first forty years of existence, Sears was essentially a mail-order firm. Prior to the depression of the 1930s, Sears was opening stores at an amazing rate, most in fairly large towns. The Depression began a period of consolidation, closing of marginal stores, and careful planning and research for the opening of new outlets. After World War II, Sears launched the

This case was prepared by Deborah Jones, Kevin McCarey, Keith Morris, and Ken Smith under the direction of Professor J. David Hunger, McIntire School of Commerce, University of Virginia. Developed entirely from publicly available information in periodicals and annual reports.

greatest expansion since the 1920s. It staked $300 million on the postwar economy by going through immediate expansion. In the first two years after the war, sales zoomed from one billion to almost two billion dollars.

In the period from 1945 to 1952, while other chains such as Montgomery Ward were actually closing stores, Sears was vigorously expanding from 610 stores to 684. After World War II, most population growth was taking place in major metropolitan areas, particularly the suburbs. Shopping centers were replacing downtown areas as the major business districts and Sears was taking full advantage of this situation by building almost all of its new stores in these areas.

Until the present (February 1981), Sears had continued to take advantage of the growing middle class by opening more stores and increasing sales to become the world's largest retailer (see Exhibit 13.1). However, in retailing, size alone has failed to work. Revenues in Sears's $18 billion retailing business have stagnated, and profits have tumbled since 1977, as the company has wrestled with high overhead, tough competition, and its own loss of direction in picking demographic markets in which to concentrate.

Allstate got its start fifty years ago as a mail-order insurance company doing business through the Sears catalog. Its initial growth was largely attributable to the sale of insurance in Sears stores by Allstate agents. The Seraco group's Homart Development Co.—now diversifying into several different lines of commercial construction—was launched in 1959 to build

Exhibit 13.1

TEN LARGEST RETAILERS

Rank & Chain	1978 *Volume* ($000)	1978 *Stores*	1979 *Volume* ($000)	1979 *Stores*	1979 *Sales Chng.* (%)
1. Sears Roebuck	17,946,336	3,727	17,514,212	3,680	– 2.4
2. Kmart (Kresge)	11,695,539	1,718	12,731,145	1,894	+ 8.9
3. J.C. Penney	10,845,000	2,133	11,274,000	2,145	+ 4.0
4. F.W. Woolworth	6,103,000	5,786	6,785,000	6,040	+11.2
5. Federated Dept. Stores	5,405,000	336	5,806,442	349	+ 7.4
6. Montgomery Ward	5,014,000	925	5,251,085	944	+ 4.7
7. Dayton Hudson	2,961,884	588	3,359,849	661	+13.4
8. City Products Corp.	2,666,000	1,208	3,198,162	1,228	+20.0
9. May Dept. Stores	2,567,000	166	2,747,898	169	+ 7.1
10. Carter Hawley Hale	2,116,600	679	2,408,000	760	+13.7

shopping centers where a Sears store would be one of the anchors. The financial services side of Seraco originated within Allstate. Both Allstate and Seraco are outgrowths of the merchandise business, and both have continued to expand their profit contributions to Sears.

KEY EXECUTIVES AND ORGANIZATION

Until 1980 the office of the chairman was composed of Chairman Edward R. Telling, whose background was in merchandising, and three other strictly merchandising-oriented executives. Today, Telling and Richard M. Jones, Vice-Chairman and Chief Financial Officer, are the only retailing experts at the corporate helm. They are sharing decision-making responsibilities with Donald F. Craib, Jr., Vice-Chairman, Finance, who rose from the Allstate Insurance Co. subsidiary; Phillip Purcell, Vice-President, Corporate Planning, who was recruited from McKinsey & Co. (consulting) three years ago; and Phillip M. Knox, Vice-President and general counsel. Also reporting to Mr. Telling and rounding out the strategic planning committee are the three business-group chief executives. The new team has a twofold goal: finding nonretailing expansion opportunities and making sure the Merchandise Group improves its performance. This strategic planning committee assists the chairman in setting goals, considering alternatives, monitoring performance, coordinating functions, and reporting results.

Edward R. Telling, formerly chief of retailing operations, was named chairman in 1977. At age 61, with only four years remaining in office, Telling is rapidly getting more involved in the financial area. In 1980 Telling reorganized Sears into a semi-holding company, in effect divorcing himself from the actual management of the troubled retailing operation. "We're a multiprofit-center company," said Telling, clearly displeased with the general conception of Sears as a retailer with some good sidelines.[1] The chairman went on to say that henceforth, Sears will be a parent company with three parts—real estate and financial services, retailing, and insurance—each with its own operating chief and each competing for corporate resources.

The principal role of the heads of the three business groups is the day-to-day management of their respective businesses. Edward A. Brennan, a 46-year-old territory manager, was promoted by Telling in 1980 to be the new chairman and chief executive of the Merchandising Group. When asked if Sears has problems in its retailing business, Brennan answered with comments like: "Sears is not only the biggest, it is the best."[2] Brennan, thinking positively, sees his job simply as getting the organization to do better what it has already done well, in getting buyers to generate better values for customers, for example, and in improving coordination and communication between headquarters and the field, between buyers and sellers.

While Edward Brennan struggles with Sears's accumulated retailing problems, Archie Boe, age 59, can sit comfortably in light of his accomplishments at the huge Allstate subsidiary. Although the insurance industry, particularly the property/casualty business, appears to be headed for the bottom of an economic cycle, Allstate's chairman and CEO, Mr. Boe, says that Allstate does most of its business in auto insurance which won't be hit as hard as commercial. Boe thinks the worst will come in the insurance industry during 1981, and he plans to push ahead and try to gain market share when his competitors are in disarray.

Heading Seraco is Preston Martin, the onetime head of the Federal Home Loan Bank Board, organizer of the Federal Home Loan Mortgage Corp. and finally founder of PMI, which Allstate financed. Unlike many in the industry, Martin doesn't think shopping-mall development has reached the saturation point. He says Homart will step up its investment in shopping malls from 20% to 40% in the coming years but will no longer build only where the company wants to put a Sears store. It will also put more emphasis on joint ventures. Martin is also interested in getting into commercial and industrial park development.

Thus is Sears, the world's largest retailer, consciously broadening its scope. Strategic planning means new directions for Sears and possibly more acquisitions like recent ones in mortgage insurance and executive transfer services. One key goal for the new planning committee is to ensure that capital is allocated to the projects and businesses that promise the greatest return. The new organizational structure, says Telling, makes it easy to add new groups to the existing three.

PRODUCTS OFFERED

The three main divisions of Sears (Merchandising, Allstate, and Seraco), can also be termed the company's main product lines. The Merchandising Group has been the mainstay of this firm since its inception, but has been losing ground to the financial services of Allstate and Seraco. Exhibit 13.2 shows the percentage of revenues, net profit margins, and profits for the main product lines for the past five years. As can be seen from the chart, Allstate and Seraco now constitute 26% of Sears's revenue. More importantly, though, these divisions provide 71% of Sears's profits. Following is a discussion of each major division of Sears.

Merchandising

The Merchandising Group consists of Merchandising, Credit, and International Operations. General merchandise stores carry a broad line of soft goods, including apparel and home furnishings, and most also sell such hard lines as appliances, hardware, auto supplies, and garden supplies. Staple items have been stressed in the past, but most stores are now attempting to

GROUP FINANCIAL INFORMATION

Exhibit 13.2

Group Revenue % Contribution

Group	1980	1979	1978	1977	1976
Merchandising	74	75	77	79	80
Allstate	24	23	21	20	19
Seraco	2	2	2	1	1

Group Net Income % Contribution

Group	1980	1979	1978	1977	1976
Merchandising	29	48	50	52	57
Allstate	64	47	44	41	37
Seraco	7	5	6	7	6

lure new shoppers by upgrading their fashion image, while at the same time offering competitive prices to keep their existing customers. Most stores tend to feature house brands rather than national brands, but more of the latter are being added to attract new patrons.

Sears's Merchandising Group sells a broad line of general merchandise domestically through its retail facilities as well as from catalogs. Orders for merchandise from Sears catalogs are placed by customers in person or by telephone, thus making the process very convenient for the consumer. Merchandise sales in the fourth fiscal quarter are traditionally higher than in other quarterly periods because of holiday buying patterns. Conversely, the lowest sales are typically recorded in the first fiscal quarter, normally producing a relatively high ratio of fixed costs to sales and a lower ratio of income to sales.

The Merchandising Group has announced plans to test-market five freestanding Sears business machine stores by late 1981. These specialty stores will carry a broad line of electronic equipment for small business needs. The equipment will be under Sears and other brand names. A program to develop software and related services for small businesses and individuals has been undertaken.

Suppliers

The Merchandising Group purchases goods from more than 11,300 domestic suppliers through the company's 35 buying departments in Chicago. Twenty-eight percent of Sears's purchases come from companies in which Sears owns stock. Sears has experienced an erosion of supplier relationships in the past several years. In 1978 Telling ordered a get-tough policy with the company's suppliers, informing them that Sears would no longer inventory products that were slow sellers in the stores. Instead, suppliers found new customers and expanded their lines of branded merchandise. For example, in 1972, Sears accounted for 61% of Whirlpool Corp.'s sales. In 1979, sales of refrigerators, washers, and other appliances which Sears bought from Whirlpool to sell under the Kenmore name accounted for only 47% of Whirlpool's sales. Sears had historically romanced its vendors; but since Telling's tough remarks in 1978, vendors have been scrambling for non-Sears business, Sears ending up with products that are the same as everyone else's.

Competition

The general retail merchandise industry is highly competitive. Quality, prices, styles, delivery time, repair service, and convenience of shopping facilities are the principal means of competition. Sears believes it is able to compete in every respect despite strong competitive pressures in recent years, and has increased its advertising budget from $487 million in 1979 to $545 million in 1980. K-Mart and J.C. Penney are Sears's major competitors in the merchandising field. K-Mart is a discount chain while J.C. Penney, as the second leading firm in terms of catalog sales (behind Sears), is in more direct competition with Sears. J.C. Penney, in fact, is the only real competitor in terms of volume of sales. It places most of its emphasis on soft goods, whereas Sears emphasizes hard goods, which has made J.C. Penney less vulnerable to consumer spending cutbacks. See Exhibit 13.3 for a comparison of J.C. Penney and Sears for the last five years.

Marketing Strategy

Once a retailing innovator, Sears changed to reactive marketing strategies in the 1970s, as others dramatically changed the nature of U.S. retailing. Competitors such as K-Mart Corp. created the discount market, siphoning off one segment of Sears's base, while specialty store chains such as Toys R Us, Inc. grabbed other pieces.

Exhibit 13.3

SALES
($millions)

	Sears—Merchandising	*J. C. Penney*
1980	16,865	11,353
1979	16,839	11,247
1978	17,284	10,845
1977	17,946	9,369
1976	17,224	8,354

Sears reacted first by trying to cater to upscale customers. In attempts to lure more affluent people into its solid blue-collar customer base the company began stocking expensive, high-fashion merchandise. The result—the affluent showed little interest in clothing or jewelry carrying the Sears label, and traditional customers were turned off by the new merchandise and higher prices.

Sears then attempted to attract the specialty stores' customers by stocking products in depth. Customers still saw no reason to buy sporting equipment at Sears rather than at Herman's, for example, and grew even more confused about why to buy at Sears at all. Sears wound up with expensive inventory and no increased sales.

K-Mart's customers became the next target as Sears switched to discounting. In 1977, Sears embarked on an only-too-successful price war, shooting sales up 16%. But when the final figures came in, management discovered that the price cuts had destroyed profits. Earnings for the Merchandise Group in 1977 fell more than 10%.

Sears then tried wild promotions, and later retrenched massively in promotions. The end result of all these attempts, made under the heaviest overhead burden in the industry, was a devastation of profits. And because of Sears's scattershot approach to marketing over the last decade, the company has lost customers and has clouded its long nurtured image as the provider of merchandise for America's heartland.

Allstate Group

The Allstate Group is engaged in property/liability insurance, life insurance, and financial services businesses. Allstate is authorized to sell in all fifty states, the District of Columbia, Puerto Rico, the Virgin Islands, and Canada and writes virtually all kinds of policies for individuals, businesses, and organizations. Though Allstate utilizes many systems of distribution, the nucleus of its sales force is its 10,800 employees who sell Allstate's products in booths in Sears stores or through neighborhood offices. In the past five years, Allstate has also developed an independent agent force to sell insurance in rural areas.

For 1980, passenger auto insurance accounted for approximately 65% of property/liability insurance premiums earned, and homeowners' multiple peril insurance accounted for approximately 18%. All other property/liability lines combined accounted for the remaining 17% of property/liability insurance premiums earned. Although the insurance business is generally not seasonal, claims and claims expense for the property/liability insurance operations tend to be higher for periods of inclement weather. For example, in 1979, losses incurred from hurricanes David and Frederic exceeded $1.6 billion, the largest losses on record.

The life insurance business includes most types of life insurance and certain accident insurance, as well as investment activities. Life insurance in force rose $2.4 billion in 1980 to a total of $28.9 billion. The total included $19.1 billion on individuals and $9.8 billion of group insurance. Individual insurance rose 12.9% during 1980 and group insurance rose 2.4% that year.

Financial Services consists primarily of the making of secured installment loans to consumers. Allstate Financial Corporation, a wholly owned subsidiary of Sears, obtains funds for the financial business primarily through the issuance of commercial paper and long-term debt and from borrowings under agreement with bank trust departments.

As inflation began to soar in 1978, the Allstate Group became vulnerable to lower underwriting profits. High inflation has a tendency to raise the cost of claims by customers before Allstate can adjust its rates upward. Often Allstate cannot collect the higher premiums until policies are renewed, sometimes a year or more out.

In order to maintain its position as one of the leaders in the insurance industry, Allstate is introducing a variety of new products in 1981. A broad, modernized line of life insurance products will be available during the year. The company also plans to introduce residential protection discounts and home reconstruction guarantees in the near future. In addition, Allstate will also be introducing a market-value home protection policy, a make-and-model rating program, which rates autos according to their specific property-loss potential, and new and rehabilitative home discounts.

Analysts of the property/liability insurance business predict that underwriting results will continue a downward trend in 1981. Keen competition in the insurance industry, together with regulatory and consumer pressures on prices and pricing systems, will be deterrents to obtaining adequate premium rates. However, if inflation shows signs of lessening, rate adjustments may not be as important to Allstate as they have been in the past two to three years.

Allstate's biggest competitors are State Farm Mutual Automobile Insurance Co. and Aetna Life and Casualty. Allstate is second only to State Farm in property and casualty insurance. Because State Farm is a mutually held company, no public information is available on the company. Five-year comparisons of Aetna and Allstate are shown in Exhibit 13.4.

Seraco

Seraco was formed in February of 1980 and united several ongoing and successful smaller scale financial services owned by Sears. The companies included were: Homart Development, the nation's third-largest developers of shopping malls; Allstate Savings and Loan, with $3 billion in assets and 101 branches in California; and PMI, a mortgage insurer and a mortgage banker.

Exhibit 13.4

SALES
($millions)

	Sears—Allstate	*Aetna Life & Casualty*
1980	5,723	5,548
1979	5,348	5,257
1978	4,851	4,503
1977	4,524	3,253
1976	4,342	2,832

Seraco group capabilities include real estate development, consumer savings deposits, mortgage lending, mortgage banking, mortgage insurance, and mortgage-backed security issuance. From the outset, Seraco's direction has been one of diversification, strategic positioning for the future with existing products, the introduction of new products, and the development of new market areas.

Seraco's competition is becoming more intense with each new regulatory change in the banking and thrift industry. The deregulation also opens significant areas for expansion. The banking industry was deregulated in the beginning of 1980 to better enable the banks to compete for deposits with other financial institutions. The brokerage industry was significantly deregulated in the 1970s and in 1980 scored record profits. Since the Federal Reserve changed operating procedures in October of 1979, interest rates (and the economy) have been extremely volatile. This has led to much disintermediation, which is hurting Allstate's Savings and Loan. Also, because interest rates have remained high, real estate developments have been more costly and more difficult to arrange. Additional deregulation legislation is now pending and more is certain to come with Ronald Reagan taking office. The industry that Seraco competes in is getting bigger and increasingly more competitive.

FACILITIES

On January 31, 1981, Merchandising operated 854 retail stores, including 379 full-line stores, located principally in major metropolitan areas; 361 medium-sized stores which also carry an extensive assortment of merchandise; and 114 hard-line stores serving either neighborhoods of metropolitan areas or smaller communities and stocking a limited selection of appliances, hardware, sporting goods, and automotive supplies.

In addition, there are 1,298 sales offices and other facilities, most of which are operated under short-term leases. The general offices of the company and its Merchandising Group at Sears Tower in Chicago, merchandising territorial offices in the Atlanta, Chicago, Los Angeles, and Philadelphia metropolitan areas, 14 catalog merchandise distribution centers, and 107 warehouses are owned by Sears. Additional office space in Chicago and 294 warehouses are leased for terms ranging from 2 to 99 years.

Merchandising has a continuing program of adding new retail stores and sales offices and of improving, modernizing, and replacing its retail stores and other facilities. The capital expenditures amounted to $344 million for fiscal year 1980.

The home office of the Allstate Group is located in Northbrook, Illinois.

Exhibit 13.5

SIX-YEAR SUMMARY OF CONSOLIDATED FINANCIAL DATA

Operating Results (millions)	**1980**	**1979**	**1978**	**1977**	**1976**	**1975**
Total operating revenues	$25,195	$24,549	$24,490	$22,906	$19,643	$17,711
Costs and expenses	23,480	22,615	22,437	21,106	18,216	16,536
Interest	1,134	912	737	480	365	355
Operating income	581	1,022	1,316	1,320	1,062	820
Percent of revenues	2.3	4.2	5.4	5.8	5.4	4.6
Realized capital gains and other	93	63	80	(4)	(9)	24
Net income	606	810	922	838	694	522
Percent return on average equity	8.1	11.2	13.5	13.4	12.1	9.8
Income to fixed charge ratio*	1.67	2.30	3.07	3.79	3.80	3.21
Total funds used	1,959	2,036	2,174	3,030	1,478	1,493
Funds provided from operations	1,530	1,183	1,865	660	754	1,259
Financial Position (millions)						
Customer accounts receivable	$ 7,111	$ 7,132	$ 6,723	$ 6,634	$ 5,648	$ 5,231
Merchandise inventories	2,722	2,719	2,620	2,709	2,283	1,939
Investments	11,419	10,011	9,097	8,018	5,783	4,884
Property and equipment (net)	3,156	3,053	2,944	2,850	2,760	2,692
Total assets	28,054	26,587	24,731	23,341	19,175	17,135
Short-term debt	4,304	4,185	4,132	4,237	3,293	2,988
Long-term debt	2,962	2,972	2,464	2,327	2,073	1,790
Total debt	7,266	2,972	2,464	2,327	2,073	1,790
Percent of debt to equity	94	96	93	101	91	90
Shareholders' equity	7,689	7,467	7,092	6,524	5,921	5,287

***Exhibit 13.5** (Continued)*

Shareholders' Common Stock Investment						
Book value per share (year end)	$24.38	$23.53	$21.98	$20.27	$18.56	$16.67
Shareholders (Profit Sharing Fund counted as single shareholder)	349,725	339,459	326,086	286,773	267,541	270,733
Average shares outstanding (millions)	316	319	322	320	318	316
Net income per share	1.92	2.54	2.86	2.62	2.18	1.65
Dividends per share	1.36	1.28	1.27	1.08	.80	.925
Dividend payout percent	70.8	50.4	44.4	41.2	36.7	56.1
Market price (high-low)	19⅝–14½	21⅜–17	27¼–19¾	32¾–24⅛	39⅝–30⅝	37¼–28⅝
Closing market price at fiscal year end	15¼	17⅛	21¼	25¼	31¼	34¾
Price/earnings ratio (high-low)	10–8	8–7	9–7	13–9	18–14	22–17

* Based on net income plus fixed charges and income taxes, less undistributed net income of unconsolidated subsidiaries. Fixed charges exclude interest on savings and loan deposits, but include an interest element (one-third) implicit in operating lease rentals.

The insurance company operates 35 main regional offices, 219 claim services offices, and sales facilities at approximately 2,720 locations (of which 1,210 are in Sears stores and sales offices).

FINANCIAL MATTERS

In 1980, Sears realigned its operations into three separate business groups. In connection with this organizational change, the company has changed its financial reporting. Instead of showing the affiliates as investments, it now consolidates them into a single balance sheet. Profit and loss are also consolidated now. The company believes that these changes provide financial statements that better reflect the company's organization and more clearly illustrate its results of operation and financial position (see Exhibits 13.5, 13.6, and 13.7).

One factor which indicates that Sears has dropped in the opinion of analysts and investors is the market value of Sears common stock (see Exhibit 13.8). As recently as 1975 Sears was considered one of America's great growth companies and sold for as high as 30 times earnings; at a recent price of $17.375 it actually sold at a discount of 26% from book value.

PERSONNEL

Sears has drastically cut down its work force in recent years. In 1980, Sears's employees numbered 326,000, down from 356,900 the year before (see Exhibit 13.9). In the early 1970s, while Sears was still in a period of seemingly unbridled growth, the retailing staff alone consisted of more than 400,000 employees.

All through the seventies, Sears continued to add executives, thus increasing its overhead at the same time it was superimposing an unwieldy hierarchy on the company. It gave its field people virtual autonomy on promotional pricing, store size, product selections, and the like, yet it con-

Exhibit 13.6

CONSOLIDATED STATEMENTS OF INCOME

	1981	1980	1979
(millions except per share data)	*(year ended January 31)*		
OPERATING REVENUES			
Merchandise Group			
Merchandising	$16,865.0	$16,839.6	$17,284.4
Credit	968.3	934.1	914.2
International	873.8	775.4	888.9
Total Merchandise Group	18,707.1	18,549.1	19,087.5
Allstate Group	6,197.2	5,783.8	5,238.5
Seraco Group	419.4	361.3	303.7
Corporate	71.2	14.4	—
Intergroup transactions	(200.0)	(159.2)	(139.9)
TOTAL OPERATING REVENUES	$25,194.9	$24,549.4	$24,489.8
OPERATING EXPENSES			
Costs and expenses	23,393.5	22,615.4	22,436.7
Nonrecurring expenses			
Retirement incentive	66.7	—	—
Customs settlement provision	19.8	—	—
Interest	1,133.9	912.0	737.5
TOTAL OPERATING EXPENSES	24,613.9	23,527.4	23,174.2
Operating income	581.0	1,022.0	1,315.6
Realized capital gains and other	92.8	63.2	80.0
Income before income taxes, equity in net income of consolidated companies and minority interest	673.8	1,085.2	1,395.6
Income taxes	85.2	307.1	504.9
Equity in net income of unconsolidated companies and minority interest	17.4	32.0	30.8
NET INCOME	$606.0	$810.1	$921.5

Exhibit 13.6
(Continued)

NET INCOME CONSISTS OF:			
Group income (loss)			
Merchandise Group			
Merchandising	208.6	366.8	422.4
Credit	(33.5)	14.5	36.2
International	29.7	49.9	39.1
Total Merchandise Group	204.8	431.2	497.7
Allstate Group	450.4	421.8	428.4
Seraco Group	48.8	41.2	64.1
Net corporate expense	(98.0)	(84.1)	(68.7)
NET INCOME	$606.0	$810.1	$921.5
PER SHARE	$1.92	$2.54	$2.86
Average shares outstanding	315.5	319.0	322.4

CONSOLIDATED STATEMENTS OF FINANCIAL POSITION

Exhibit 13.7

	1981	1980
(millions)	*(January 31)*	
ASSETS		
Receivables		
Retail customer	$7,110.5	$7,132.4
Financial installment notes	591.2	672.1
Insurance premium installment	589.2	528.9
Other	396.2	335.5
	8,687.1	8,668.8
Investments		
Bonds and redeemable preferred stocks (estimated market $4,542.8 and $4,899.2)	6,169.6	5,589.6
Common and preferred stocks (cost $1,166.4 and $944.2)	1,438.7	1,020.1
Mortgage loans	3,139.1	2,869.4
Real estate	578.1	468.7
Other	93.8	62.8
	11,419.3	10,010.6
Property and equipment, net	3,155.7	3,053.1
Merchandise inventories	2,721.6	2,719.2
Cash and invested cash	786.7	866.6
Investments in unconsolidated companies	533.6	517.0
Prepaid expenses and deferred charges	449.3	430.6
Other assets	300.5	321.0
TOTAL ASSETS	28,053.8	26,586.9

(Continued)

Exhibit 13.7
(Continued)

	1981	1980
LIABILITIES		
Reserve for insurance claims and policy benefits	4,508.5	4,161.2
Short-term borrowing	4,304.1	4,184.9
Long-term debt	2,961.9	2,972.2
Savings accounts and advances from Federal Home Loan Bank	2,696.1	2,411.4
Unearned revenue	2,298.6	2,126.3
Accounts payable and other liabilities	2,171.6	1,772.4
Deferred income taxes	1,424.2	1,491.3
TOTAL LIABILITIES	20,365.0	19,119.7
COMMITMENTS AND CONTINGENT LIABILITIES		
SHAREHOLDERS' EQUITY		
Common shares ($.75 par value)	244.1	243.7
Capital in excess of par value	640.4	634.3
Retained income	6,840.5	6,663.9
Treasury stock (at cost)	(188.6)	(150.7)
Unrealized net capital gains on marketable equity securities	152.4	76.0
TOTAL SHAREHOLDERS' EQUITY	$7,688.8	$7,467.2
TOTAL SHARES OUTSTANDING	315,357	317,328

Exhibit 13.8

	Market Value Shares O/S ($Millions)	*P/E Year End*
1980	4,809	8
1979	5,712	7
1978	6,372	7
1977	9,012	11
1976	11,006	16
1975	10,226	19
1974	7,615	15
1973	12,622	19
1972	18,213	30
1971	15,950	29

NUMBERS OF EMPLOYEES BY JOB CATEGORIES

Exhibit 13.9

	Employees (In thousands)	
	Jan. 80	*Jan. 81*
Officials and managers	46.0	41.0
Professionals	2.1	2.9
Technicians	2.7	2.5
Sales workers	108.7	107.5
Office and clerical	100.7	84.7
Craft workers	29.2	27.0
Operatives	10.4	10.0
Laborers	44.3	39.8
Service workers	12.7	10.8
All categories	356.9	326.2

tinually beefed up its corporate management staff in attempts to coordinate its diverse activities into a coherent whole. Sears management structures on top of management structures grew into a hindrance to timely decisions and good execution as well as a huge cost burden.

Making matters worse, while Sears was adding layers of management, its store-level work force was eroding, and its customer service was beginning to sour along with it. Throughout the 1960s and early 1970s, Sears was able to entice experienced salespeople with lucrative incentive programs based on shares of Sears stock. Once the stock started sinking, however, the incentive evaporated with it and salespeople began to leave.

Sears is starting to grapple with its personnel problems. Early last year, Telling sold his fellow directors on a massive early retirement program aimed at managers older than 55. By year end 1980, 1,600 of the 2,400 eligible employees took advantage of the plan. Sears consolidated its nine merchandising groups into seven, and dropped six of its 41 buying departments and five of its 46 field administrative units. The Southwestern territory, which employed more than 300 people, was shut down altogether. Even the national retail sales staff was appreciably reduced. By mid-1980 Sears's merchandising staff decreased to 288,000 employees.

Perhaps most significant, those managers that are left, combined with those hired to fill vacant positions, are much younger than their predecessors. "I think the group will be less set in beliefs, far more willing to take risks—all the advantages that youth brings will surface," Telling predicts.[3]

Sears is looking to the future in an attempt to infuse a more youthful orientation into what had become a stodgy management team.

NOTES

1. J. A. Briggs, "Sears Takes Stock," *Forbes* (July 21, 1980), p. 37.
2. *Ibid.*, p. 38.
3. "How Sears Became a High Cost Operator," *Business Week* (February 16, 1981), p. 54.

Case 14

CHRISTIAN'S

Thomas L. Wheelen / Moustafa H. Abdelsamad

Jeff Curry / Dean Salpini

Art Scibelli / Gordon Shanks

BACKGROUND

In the Spring Semester of 1984 four seniors at the University of Virginia were trying to decide whether they should invest in Christian's Restaurant, a small eating establishment located several miles from the University's campus in Charlottesville, Virginia.

The four students—Jeff Curry, Dean Salpini, Art Scibelli, and Gordon Shanks—were all business majors who had become involved with Christian's as the result of a management course entitled "Entrepreneurship" in which they were enrolled. The objective of this course was for the students to "set up a new company that is completely researched in all phases of the business (location, services, finance, and so on) and submit the written business plan for evaluation." The four students had decided to work together on the project at the beginning of the semester and had quickly begun investigating potential business ventures in the Charlottesville area.

The group's first idea centered on the opening of a seafood restaurant. Art believed that a restaurant offering the same product as a local chain of seafood houses near his home in Northern Virginia could prove highly successful in Charlottesville. These restaurants offered fresh seafood for relatively moderate prices in a family-type atmosphere and additionally featured several "all you can eat" items on their menu. Art had gotten in touch with one of the owner-founders of the chain, Mr. Easby-Smyth, and the group had gone to Northern Virginia to meet with him and discuss their idea.

This case was prepared by Jeff Curry, Dean Salpini, Art Scibelli, and Gordon Shanks, under the supervision of Prof. Thomas L. Wheelen, University of South Florida, and Prof. Moustafa H. Abdelsamad, Virginia Commonwealth University. This case was presented at the Case Research Association Meeting, 1984.

 Also appears in the *Journal of Management Case Studies,* 1985, Vol. 1, No. 3., pp. 220–232.

The meeting with Mr. Easby-Smyth had produced two conclusions: Charlottesville was probably too small a market to support the size restaurant the group had originally considered, and the money involved would make the project infeasible for the group. Mr. Easby-Smyth had informed them that the cost of building and outfitting a seafood house of 6,000 square feet would be approximately $300,000. The group had no desire to enter into an investment of this magnitude and were also aware of the great deal of difficulty they were sure to encounter in trying to raise the capital for such a venture.

The students still felt a smaller seafood restaurant might be successful in Charlottesville, though, and began searching for an already existing building that would be suitable for their restaurant. Ideally, they hoped to find a restaurant that was selling out and could easily be converted for their purposes. Then news of the Happy Clam reached them.

The Happy Clam was a new seafood restaurant opening up on Route 29 North, the main highway leading from Charlottesville. One visit to the new restaurant confirmed that not only was it located in the general area the group had hoped to locate in, but was also offering the same basic product mix as they had hoped to offer. In addition, the restaurant's owner had already successfully opened an identical seafood house in nearby Fredericksburg, Virginia.

Up to this point, there had been no restaurant similar to the one the students conceived in the area. Now, however, they were faced with a direct competitor who had proven he could be successful in the seafood business. It was at this point, as the students reconsidered their strategy, that Art visited a local realtor and found out about Christian's.

Christian's was a small restaurant specializing in sandwiches for lunch, and specialty dishes for dinner (see dinner menu, Exhibit 14.1). It was being sold as an ongoing business to include the name Christian's. The students met with the realtor handling the sale, William Page, who arranged a meeting with the owners of Christian's.

Peter and Mary Tarpey, a young couple from the New York area, along with a University of Virginia professor who acted as a silent partner, were the owners of Christian's. The students met with Page and the Tarpeys as arranged on a Wednesday afternoon, and the group sat down at a table in Christian's to answer each other's questions and discuss the possible purchase.

Mary Tarpey first showed the group a handwritten profit and loss statement for the period from June 13, 1983, to October 31, 1983 (see Exhibit 14.2). She explained how some of the expenses were direct payments to the banks and were being written off as business expenses, such as car payments

DINNER MENU

Exhibit 14.1

Soups
French Onion $1.50
Cream of Asparagus $1.25
Vegetable $1.00
Split Pea or Lentil $1.00

Wines
By the glass $1.25
½ Litre $3.25
Full Litre $5.75
Champagne Cocktail $1.25

Entrées
(Served with Salad & Bread)

Beef Bazaar $4.25
Marinated beef, onions & green peppers broiled & served on rice
Broccoli Casserole $3.25
Broccoli, tomatoes, onions & eggs topped with cheese
Lobster Scampi $4.25
Langostinos broiled in herb butter & served on rice
Syrian Chicken $3.85
Marinated chicken in pita bread with lettuce, tomatoes
Sausage Lasagne $4.25
An Italian dish that speaks for itself!
Omelet special $3.95
Large dinner omelet filled with pepperoni and provolone cheese
Crêpes $3.75
Chicken Divan or Sauteed Mushrooms

Desserts

Ginger Sherbet	$.75
Homemade Pecan Pie	$1.00
Cheesecake	$1.25
Carrot Cake	$1.25
Coffee or Tea	$.35
Soft Drinks	$.50
Beer	$.75

CHRISTIAN'S PROFIT AND LOSS STATEMENT

June 13, 1983–October 31, 1983

Exhibit 14.2

Sales		$100,000.00
Cost of Sales		
Beer and Wine	$2,688.30	
Food	29,189.60	
		31,877.90
Gross Profit		$ 68,122.10
Operating Expenses		
Paper	$1,079.88	
Insurance		
Store	600.00	
Car	150.00	
Health	460.00	
Workmen's Compensation	950.00	
Employment Commission	360.00	
Laundry, Linen	483.25	
Licenses	250.00	
Sales Tax (State)	4,000.00	
Repairs Maintenance	250.00	
Rent	2,500.00	
Rubbish Removal—City	448.50	
Salaries & Wages	20,000.00	
Payroll Taxes	6,000.00	
Utilities	4,000.00	
Loan Payment	1,150.00	
Equipment Payments	1,150.00	
Life Insurance	625.00	
Car Payment	1,095.00	
Maintenance	950.00	
Lease Dishwasher	448.50	
Advertising	2,750.00	
Business Association Dues & Expenses	450.00	
Administrative Salaries	5,000.00	
TOTAL		55,150.13
Income before Taxes		$ 12,971.97

NOTE: This was a handwritten statement provided by the owners.

and a life insurance policy, and need not be incurred by a new owner. She also showed the students monthly sales figures for the period of January 1983 to October 1983, as verified by a local CPA firm (see Exhibit 14.3), as well as a list of assets owned by Christian's (see Exhibit 14.4).

The Tarpeys defined their target market as "young professional." By this, they meant persons in the eighteen to thirty-five-year age group who worked in the area and came to Christian's for the menu variety and quality of food. They stated that these people eat out about twenty-two times a month for lunch and dinner, and their strategy was to try to get them at Christian's five days a month. The Tarpeys also quoted the average lunch check as being $3.76 and the average dinner check amounting to $5.92.

The Tarpeys also answered questions concerning Christian's daily operations and suppliers. One of the important issues raised was that of a transition period. The group hoped to hire an experienced, full-time manager for the restaurant, and the Tarpeys agreed they would stay on for a period of two weeks or so to help train the manager and show him the cost control and portion control procedures they had used. In addition, the Tarpeys stated that the whole employee staff had expressed their willingness to stay with the restaurant after an ownership change. The group viewed these two factors as distinct assets.

Another important issue was the future plans of the Tarpeys. As it turned out, the Tarpeys would be opening a new restaurant in a shopping center being built three-quarters of a mile from Christian's. Peter Tarpey explained that the restaurant was to be more dinner-oriented than Christian's. He described it as an "Irish cafe with French food" which would serve more expensive meals than Christian's and also serve liquor, which Christian's did not feature. Tarpey estimated that by his moving and opening a new restaurant, Christian's might lose at most 5% of its customers.

A second meeting was held with the Tarpeys at a later date, during which more of the group's questions were answered. A new lease would have to be renegotiated by any new owner in August 1984, which would be substantially higher than the current one. The students had questions about Christian's specific suppliers and asked to see the restaurant's books, but the Tarpeys wanted some sort of firm commitment on the group's part before more information about Christian's would be given out.

The price being asked for Christian's was $57,750 and the students estimated they could put up about $17,500 of their own capital. Since the rest would have to be financed by a loan of some sort, Jeff visited several banks to discuss terms. One of the banks he visited told him they only loaned money for a restaurant if it was going to be family owned and operated. At Sovran Bank, Jeff got a more positive response. The loan officer there stated that the

SALES INFORMATION

Exhibit 14.3

BROWN AND JONES COMPANY
CERTIFIED PUBLIC ACCOUNTANTS
CHARLOTTESVILLE, VIRGINIA 22906

January 9, 1984

Peter Tarpey
Christian's, Inc.
1703 Allied Lane
Charlottesville, Virginia 22901

Dear Peter:

As per your request, enclosed are sales figures for Christian's, Inc., for the ten months ending October, 1983 as filed on your monthly Virginia sales tax returns.

January 1983	$18,543.30
February 1983	19,085.43
March 1983	18,097.54
April 1983	19,984.20
May 1983	20,422.71
June 1983	21,836.37
July 1983	19,304.76
August 1983	22,231.69
September 1983	20,002.19
October 1983	20,588.86

If you need sales figures for November, 1983 and December, 1983, you will have to get these amounts from worksheets in your files. Let me know if I can be of further assistance.

Yours truly,

Thomas L. Brown
Certified Public Accountant

TLB/d

P.S.: The sales figures for November, 1983 are: $19,300.00

TLB

ADDITIONAL INFORMATION PROVIDED BY THOMAS L. BROWN

September 27, 1983

Exhibit 14.4

Attached is a schedule of fixed assets owned by Christian's, Inc., and the estimated market value of each. Since a purchaser of these would have a cost basis for depreciation and useful life different from that of Christian's, Inc., this information is not provided.

21 Tables	$ 525
43 Chairs	430
2 Banquettes	100
6 Church Pew Benches	120
Small Refrigerator	300
Walk In Box	1,500
Ice Machine	100
NCR Cash Register	150
3 Toasters	225
Jordan Box	250
Fogle Refrigerator	1,200
Hobart Slicer	1,000
Hobart Microwave	1,000
Sandwich Box	200
Stainless Prep. Table	100
Deep Fat Fryer	75
Steam Table	75
Stainless Prep. Table	125
3 Butcher Block Chef Tables	300
Small Hobart Slicer	200
3 Basin Sinks	75
Universal Freezer	100
Sears' Freezer	75
Stereo System	150
Curtains	100
Pots, Pans, Flatware, China, Glassware	600
Placemats, Salt and Pepper Mills	100
New Sign	2,000
TOTAL FIXED ASSETS	$11,175

Should you desire additional information in this matter, please contact Peter Tarpey and the data will be forthcoming.

bank would loan up to 70% of the purchase price, fully collateralized. The interest rate would be 14 or 15%.

At this point, the group decided to evaluate their objectives and "take stock" of the situation. They hoped to run the restaurant as absentee owners with the full-time manager handling daily operations. Art's immediate plans included law school in September, although he was still unsure which law school he would be attending. Dean planned on going to work in Northern Virginia after graduation, and Jeff and Gordon would be returning to the University of Virginia in the fall to complete their degrees.

The students' families, from whom they hoped to borrow some of the initial equity capital, all had reservations about the venture. Most of the doubt centered on the policy of running the restaurant as absentee owners. The families also wondered if it was wise for the students to make such an investment at this time in their careers when their futures were so undecided.

By now it was March 24, and the students knew a decision would have to be made very soon. A call to William Page had confirmed the rumor that another party had entered the scene and was seriously considering buying Christian's. A meeting was called at which the group planned to decide their next move.

At the meeting, the students decided that some sort of comprehensive analysis of the information they had gathered was necessary. Then, with the analysis in front of them, they felt they would be able to reach the best conclusion.

The group decided to break up the information into sections, with Jeff concentrating on the finance, Dean on the marketing, and Gordon and Art on the operations. When they got back together on March 31 (one week away) to put all the results together, the decision would have to be made.

MARKET ANALYSIS

Although Mr. Tarpey assured the group of the existence and loyalty of a definite market for Christian's, it was felt that a marketing survey would strengthen the group's understanding of this market. The survey was conducted among eighty-eight people who were customers at competitive restaurants, using the survey form shown (see Exhibit 14.5). The competition was determined from an assessment based on a number of factors including location, clientele, product offering, and Mr. Tarpey's estimates. Christian's, however, was not included because the group felt that their regular clientele might bias the results in favor of the restaurant.

From the results of the survey, it was discovered that most people were aware of Christian's, but were not being drawn down there to eat. In addition, only 7% of those who had eaten at Christian's did so at least five times/month, so their repeat business seemed to be lacking. Of those who

Exhibit 14.5
MARKETING SURVEY

Hello, we are students doing a research study on Christian's restaurant. Could you *please* take a little time to help us to fill out our survey and help make Christian's a better place to eat. Thank you for your cooperation. (The key results of the survey are summarized below.)

1. Have you ever eaten at Christian's? YES 50% NO 50%
   If NO, have you heard of it? YES 59% If No, no further questions. 41%
   If Yes, how often do you eat there?
   Less than 5 times a month 93%
   5 times a month 5%
   More than 5 times a month 2%
2. Which meal do you usually eat at Christian's?
   Lunch 59% Dinner 32% Both 9%
3. How would you rate Christian's on these factors:

	POOR	FAIR	AVERAGE	ABOVE AVERAGE	EXCELLENT
Location	29.5%	34%	32%	4.5%	
Food Quality			23.3%	53.5%	23.3%
Price	4.5%	11%	61.5%	16%	7%
Service		14%	48%	33%	5%
Atmosphere	9%	11.4%	41%	34%	4.6%
Menu Variety		5%	33%	45%	17%
Cleanliness	9.5%	9.5%	36%	33%	12%

4. What is the main reason(s) you eat at Christian's? Answers varied; most were complimentary.
5. How did you hear about Christian's?
   TV 2% Radio 12% Newspaper Ads 10.6% Friends 58%
   Drove By 5.8% Other (please specify) 11.6%
6. Would you like to see the following at Christian's?

	YES	NO
More Vegetarian Dishes	44%	56%
More Seafood	81%	19%
More Take-out Variety	48%	52%
Live Entertainment	19%	81%

7. An informal survey of age was conducted.

ate there regularly, most people seemed to prefer the lunch time period (60%), as opposed to the dinner period, which Mr. Tarpey had claimed would occur. Analysis of the various factors involved with Christian's showed that location was the most significant problem, with 64% of the respondents rating it below average. However, a study of traffic flow patterns in Charlottesville around the McIntyre Road area, where Christian's is located revealed that 20% of the whole day's traffic passed Christian's between 11:00 A.M. and 2:00 P.M. Price and service seemed to be average and comparable to other restaurants in most respondents' minds.

The most significant factors in a person's decision to eat at Christian's were the menu variety and food quality. Most of those who had eaten at the restaurant named specific food items as their main reason for coming. This also accounts for the major form of advertising that Christian's used, which seemed to be "word-of-mouth" advertising from satisfied customers. As far as changes in Christian's were concerned, most respondents favored the introduction of seafood into the menu (81%), whereas the same percentage felt having live entertainment would be a mistake.

One of the problems that might confront the group was the introduction of Mr. Tarpey's new restaurant down the street from Christian's. Since he had already developed a loyal clientele, the group was afraid of losing them to his new restaurant, although Mr. Tarpey assured the group that only 5% of the market would be affected. According to the survey, the figure to determine those customers that would be lost through a change in management was approximately 6.8%, a little higher than Mr. Tarpey's estimate.

Although there were no direct questions addressing demographics on the survey, respondents were asked to place themselves in one of the three age brackets: eighteen to thirty-five, thirty-five to fifty, and over fifty. Age of the customer was thought to be important in the decision to purchase Christian's so that the target market could be firmly established. Overall, it was found that 60% of those interviewed were between eighteen and thirty-five years of age, while 31% fell into the thirty-five to fifty bracket. Further analysis showed that 98% of those who presently eat at Christian's were within the eighteen to fifty age range. Those customers who were over fifty, therefore, figured to be an insignificant number of Christian's target market. Therefore, Mr. Tarpey's claim of "young professionals" as being his primary customers seems to have been supported through this age group data.

As can be seen from Exhibit 14.6, sales for eating and drinking establishments in 1982 were 10.5% above 1981, while total retail sales increased only 6.8% for the same period. Households also seem to be forming at a faster rate than the total population is growing. In addition, the Virginia State Planning Office projections show that the twenty- to thirty-four-year-old seg-

THE CHARLOTTESVILLE MARKET[1]

Exhibit 14.6

Year	*Retail Sales (in 000's)*	*Eating & Drinking[2] Sales (000's)*	*Population (in 000's)*	*Households[3] (in 000's)*
1978	153,995	N.A.[4]	38.8	13.8
1979	176,731	N.A.	38.7	14.0
1980	224,588	N.A.	39.0	14.2
1981	235,679	17,882	39.1	14.7
1982	251,766	19,753	38.9	14.7

NOTES: 1. Data provided by Virginia State Planning Service. 2. *Eating and Drinking Places:* This is a broad classification which includes any establishment selling prepared food or drink. Caterers, lunch counters, and concession stands are included as well as restaurants. 3. *Households:* All people occupying a single housing unit whether related or not. Includes single persons living alone. 4. N.A.: not available.

ment has shown disproportionate increases, which could explain the faster formation of households. These same figures also show that the twenty-five to thirty-nine-year-old age group will increase 17% between 1980 and 1985. In Albemarle County, in which Charlottesville is located, this increase will be almost 32%.

These growth figures were considered important because of the number of people who drive into Charlottesville's central business district (C.B.D.) from the county who use McIntyre Road as a major artery. The C.B.D. itself was also considered to be important, since a large part of Christian's clientele came from there. Over $2,000,000 had been privately invested in downtown since 1982; thus the C.B.D. appeared to be booming. Another important development was the county's move of their executive offices into the old Lane High School building, located down the street from Christian's. This decision would increase Christian's target market, since these people seem to fit the characteristics of their clientele.

ADVERTISING AND PROMOTION

Christian's present advertising program was very sporadic with a yearly expenditure of only $2,750. Mr. Tarpey spoke of occasional spots on television that he had used, along with local radio stations and the major newspaper in Charlottesville. However, Dean and the other members of the group felt that the effectiveness of this program was lacking.

OPERATIONS

The students were aware of their lack of experience in the restaurant business, and since the daily operations of Christian's had gone smoothly in the past, they did not plan any significant changes upon taking over.

The entire employee staff had stated they would be willing to remain at Christian's after the ownership change, and Peter and Mary Tarpey agreed they would stay on for a transition period to "show the ropes" to the new manager.

The students had realized early in their involvement with Christian's that they would need to hire a full-time manager for the restaurant were they to purchase it. It was determined that they would want someone with experience in restaurant management from the Charlottesville area. Their realtor had informed them he knew of a man who fit this description and had expressed interest in the opportunity, but the group was uanble to get in contact with him before the week ended.

The group planned on putting the manager in charge of general daily operations to include ordering, cost control, hiring, firing, scheduling, and any other operations related duty. The students planned on doing the bookkeeping themselves. They planned to pay the manager a salary of approximately $12,000, plus a commission based on the bottom line figure. This commission would be approximately 11%.

It was determined that the following employees would be needed to operate Christian's:

1 manager @ $12,000 salary plus commission
3 cooks @ $5.00/hour
1 grillman @ $4.75/hour
2 countermen @ $4.25/hour
2 prep men @ $4.25/hour
2 dishwashers @ $4.25/hour
2 cashiers @ $4.25/hour
12 waitresses @ $1.50/hour plus tips

Employees were to be allowed free drinks and one-half price meals while working.

Under the students' ownership, Christian's would continue to buy its food supplies from institutional food distributors from Richmond, Virginia, who delivered to Charlottesville. In addition, they would obtain their beer from local distributors and their soft drinks from local bottling companies.

In the past, inventory had turned over approximately once a week. Normal credit terms of suppliers had been net thirty days.

The marketing survey had indicated that Christian's menu was one of its strongest points, so the group planned few changes. The lunch menu featured over forty sandwiches along with omelets, salads, and chili. The dinner menu featured specialty dishes such as beef bazaar and Syrian chicken (see Exhibit 14.1).

In the past, Christian's had varied its dinner menu daily. The students would plan to vary it weekly, and if one combination proved particularly popular, it would be used again at a different time.

Approximately 15% of Christian's gross sales came from beer sales. The restaurant carried mainly premium and foreign beers in keeping with its target market of young professionals.

INVESTMENT

Benefiting from knowledge obtained in a business law course the previous semester, the group decided to establish Christian's as a Subchapter S corporation. This business form was chosen due to the tax advantages and flexibility it would allow the group, since the business would be taxed as a partnership, but would retain the limited liability of a corporation, to protect the shareholders. Since income tax rates for individuals in this case are substantially lower than for a corporation, the group felt that this form would offer them the best return on their investment.

LEASE

At the time of negotiations, Christian's was paying Allied Realty, the owner of the shopping plaza in which the restaurant was located, a base rent of $350 per month plus an additional percentage of gross sales (4%) not exceeding a total monthly rental of $500 per month. However, this lease would expire on August 1, 1984, and a new lease would have to be renegotiated by the new purchaser.

The new rent terms would be considerably higher than those experienced by previous owners and would consist of a minimum payment of $600 per month or 4% of sales (whichever is higher), not to exceed $750 per month. Since Christian's historical monthly sales have averaged approximately $20,000, this would mean payments of $750 per month. In addition, there would be an additional requirement that if gross sales exceeded $60,000 in any quarter, the restaurant would pay 3% of sales exceeding this amount.

Fortunately, the group was informed by its realtor, Henry Brasswell, that it might be possible to negotiate a less expensive lease, so that average monthly payments would be between $650 and $700 per month. Since the outcome of such negotiations was uncertain at the time, however, the group used a figure of $750 per month in developing pro forma statements for the business.

INCOME STATEMENTS

An examination of the 1983 sales uncovered two major factors which had to be considered in developing pro forma income statements. First, the monthly sales figures supplied by the CPA firm indicated a seasonal fluctuation in sales (see Exhibit 14.7). The effect of this on the cash flows of the restaurant and its ability to meet its debts had to be determined. Secondly, the revenue growth of this restaurant would be limited by its capacity. Jeff needed to establish how close to capacity the restaurant was operating currently. Lunch and dinner sales should be considered separately. Lunch projections would be based on 260 days a year (52 weeks × 5 days) while dinner should be based on the full 312 days which the restaurant was open. The current owners had already estimated the average check at each meal. The restaurant seated fifty-six people.

Jeff then took the handwritten income statement provided by Mrs. Tarpey and attempted to adjust it in order to get an idea of the expenses which the new management could face. Several of the perquisites the Tarpeys enjoyed had been discussed during the meeting at Christian's. Excessive long-distance calls and the car payments could be eliminated. The new management would have to add the manager's salary and bonus. A 10% annual bonus on pre-tax profits would be offered to motivate the manager to run a tight ship. These expenses had to be separated into variable and fixed expense categories to determine a break-even point. The new estimates were in line with those found in a book entitled *Restaurant Finance.*

Jeff was certain sales in the first year could be maintained at the current

SEASONALITY INDEX—1983 SALES

100 = 19,945

Exhibit 14.7

Month	*Sales*	*Actual Seasonality*
Jan	$18,543	93
Feb	19,085	96
Mar	18,097	91
Apr	19,984	100
May	20,423	102
Jun	21,836	109
Jul	19,304	97
Aug	22,231	111
Sep	20,002	100
Oct	20,589	103
Nov	19,300	97
Dec	18,948*	95*

* Assumed

level with effective advertising. Forecasted sales for the second year are based on expanding lunch sales to capacity. Years three through five assume the restaurant will operate at capacity for both lunch and dinner. Increased sales will be achieved through advertising.

THE BANK LOAN

With the income statements prepared, Jeff approached the Sovran Bank to discuss the terms of a loan (see Exhibits 14.8 and 14.9). The bank was willing to set the monthly payments at a level the cash flows of the restaurant could meet as long as the maturity of the loan did not exceed ten years. It appeared that five years would be an acceptable maturity. This would be monthly payments of approximately $1,000.

The bank would accept 50% of the book value (approximately the $11,175 listed as market value by the CPA firm) of the assets as collateral but demanded that the balance be fully collateralized also.

The loan officer was concerned that the purchase price was too high and that an excessive amount of goodwill would be involved in the new business. He was also concerned that none of the new owners had any experience with operating a restaurant. With this in mind, he wanted to know more about the manager and cook.

Exhibit 14.8

PRO FORMA INCOME STATEMENT
(In Thousands)
For the Year Ended July 31

	Year			
	Two	*Three*	*Four*	*Five*
Net Sales				
Lunch	$120.0	$120.0	$120.0	$120.0
Dinner	144.0	152.0	152.0	152.0
Total	$264.0	$272.0	$272.0	$272.0
Variable Expenses (68%)	(180.0)	(185.0)	(185.0)	(185.0)
Operating Margin (32%)	$ 84.0	$ 87.0	$ 87.0	$ 87.0
Fixed Expenses	(40.8)	(40.9)	(42.4)	(42.4)
Earnings before Interest	$ 43.2	$ 46.1	$ 44.6	$ 44.6
Interest	(3.9)	(2.9)	(1.9)	(1.0)
Earnings before Bonus (EBB)	39.3	43.2	42.7	43.6
Bonus (.10 × EBB)	3.9	4.3	4.3	4.4
Taxable Earnings	$ 35.4	$ 38.9	$ 38.4	$ 39.2

Exhibit 14.9
PRO FORMA BALANCE SHEEET
(In Thousands)
For the Year Ended July 31

	Initial	Year 1	2	3	4	5
ASSETS						
Current Assets						
Cash and Securities	.30	10.70	20.70	20.70	34.60	27.70
Inventory						
Beer and Wine (.04 month)	.80	.80	.90	.90	.90	.90
Food (.36/month)	7.20	7.20	7.90	8.20	8.20	8.20
Total Current Assets	8.30	18.70	29.50	29.80	43.70	36.80
Fixed Assets	22.30	22.30	22.30	27.30	27.30	32.30
Accumulated Depreciation	0.00	4.40	8.80	13.20	17.60	22.00
Net Fixed Assets	22.30	17.90	13.50	14.10	9.70	10.30
Intangibles						
Goodwill	35.20	35.20	35.20	35.20	35.20	35.20
Accumulated Amortization	0.00	3.52	7.04	10.56	14.08	17.60
Net Goodwill	35.20	31.68	28.16	24.64	21.12	17.60
Organization Costs	.50	.40	.30	.20	.10	0.00
Total Assets	66.30	68.68	71.46	68.74	74.62	64.70
LIABILITIES						
Current Liabilities						
Accounts Payable	7.60	7.60	7.90	8.20	8.20	8.20
Note Payable	1.00	0.00	0.00	0.00	0.00	0.00
Total Current Liabilities	8.60	7.60	7.90	8.20	8.20	8.20
Long-Term Note	40.25	32.20	24.10	16.10	8.00	0.00
Total Liabilities	48.85	39.80	32.00	24.30	16.20	8.20
EQUITY						
Stock	17.50	17.50	17.50	17.50	17.50	17.50
Retained Earnings	0.00	11.38	21.96	26.94	40.92	39.00
Total Equity	17.50	28.88	39.46	44.44	58.42	56.50
Total Liabilities and Equity	66.35	68.68	71.46	68.74	74.62	64.70

EVALUATING THE PURCHASE PRICE

Since several people had expressed concern over the price which the owners were asking, the partners wanted to decide the proper value of the restaurant. They agreed that this should be based on the present value of the income stream the restaurant could generate. In light of the fact that eight out of ten restaurants fail, the partners selected 25% as the hurdle rate which would be used to discount future earnings. The set-up costs should not exceed the present value of the income stream. The partners wanted to include the eventual sales price or liquidation value of the restaurant at the end of five years in computing the present value. Assuming various levels of sales would establish a proper price range. The set-up costs included the $57,750 asking price and $500 organizational expense for legal and accounting fees. Since this was an ongoing concern, they would not have to invest significant additional working capital.

CONCLUDING REMARKS

On March 31, at the final meeting to discuss the prospects of purchasing Christian's, the group members were fully aware of the implications such a decision would have. It was generally agreed that such an endeavor provided potential for optimum managerial skill and experience in the business world, though none of the group members was certain that this was the route he wanted to take. Faced with exams in the coming weeks, time pressure from the realtor, and the knowledge that at least one other party was interested in purchasing Christian's, the group set out to make their decision, which for better or worse would affect their immediate futures.

The students were informed by the present owners that they must reach a decision quickly since other purchasers were interested in the same business opportunity.

Case 15

AN INDUSTRY IN FLUX: THE BREWING INDUSTRY IN THE UNITED STATES

J. David Hunger

The exact origin of beer is unclear. The oldest clay document extant, dating back to the Babylonia of 6000 B.C., pictures the brewing of beer. Although Columbus found the Indians of Central America drinking a beer brewed from maize, the first brewery to be established in North America was in 1544 in Mexico. Much of the brewing in the colonial and early republican days of the United States was carried on in the household, usually by the housewife, a domestic art developed centuries earlier in Europe. The first U.S. commercial brewer was established on Manhattan Island in the early 1600s. In 1810, 132 breweries in the United States produced 185,000 barrels of beer and ale.

The type of beer consumed in America today originated in the 1840s with the introduction of lager beer. Lager beer is bottom-fermented (meaning yeast settles to the bottom during fermentation). The beer is then aged (or lagered) to mellow, resulting in a lighter, more effervescent potation. Prior to 1840, American taste closely resembled British taste (i.e., heavily oriented toward ale, porter, and stout). The influx of German immigrants in the 1840s initially increased the importance of lager beer because of the influence of German tastes and brewing skills.

SOURCE: J. David Hunger, "The United States Brewing Industry," *Journal of Case Research 1984,* pp. 101–127. Reprinted by permission. Copyright © 1984 by J. David Hunger. Special thanks are given to Neil H. Snyder, principal author of *Anheuser-Busch Companies, Inc.*, for allowing the author to use some of the information researched for his case.

By 1850, there were 431 brewers in the United States producing a total of 750,000 barrels per year. By the end of the decade, there were 1,269 brewers producing over 1,000,000 barrels per year. At that time, brewers served relatively small local areas. In the latter half of the nineteenth century, several significant technological advances were adapted to the beer industry, including artificial refrigeration, mechanized bottling equipment, and pasteurization. The latter innovation enabled brewers to ship warm beer and store it for a longer period of time without refermentation. With developments in transportation technology, the twentieth century saw the rise of the national brewer. The combined impact of these technological advances resulted in a greater emphasis on marketing and on production economies of scale as the primary instruments of competition.

The modern era of the brewing industry began with the end of World War II. Prior to that time, only a few brewers sold beer nationally, and they primarily operated out of a single plant. To offset additional transportation costs not incurred by local or even regional brewers, the national firms advertised their beers as being of premium quality and charged a premium price. This structural change in the industry from predominantly local or regional to national producers in the post-World War II time period resulted in a steady decline in the number of brewers and plants and an increase in the market concentration of the large national brewers.

As of 1980, only 88 domestic brewery plants produced 188,373,657 barrels of malt beverages compared to 465 breweries producing 87,856,902 barrels in 1947. The number of firms engaged in brewing dropped even more drastically from a total of 404 in 1947 to 41 in 1981. As shown in Exhibit 15.1, the top twelve U.S. breweries in 1981 controlled 99% of beer sales compared to only 46% in 1960. Seventy-three percent of the market in 1981 was controlled by only eleven specific brands (Exhibit 15.2). Exhibit 15.3 provides information on brewers' shipments by year from 1970 to 1981. Note that although production increased for the fourteen largest firms, shipments for the smaller (all other) firms decreased considerably. The same phenomenon of increased concentration has occurred in imported beers. As shown in Exhibit 15.4, only two brands, Heineken and Molson, accounted for 58% of imported beer sales in 1981. (The author could find no reliable figures detailing export shipments of domestic brewers. An article in the March 29, 1982 issue of *Advertising Age* reported that Miller Brewing had only modest international distribution. Anheuser-Busch, in contrast, was said to be crossing both Atlantic and Pacific Oceans. Budweiser was the largest selling import in Japan and was planning to enter Hong Kong in 1982. A locally brewed "Busch" beer was also planned to appear in France as well. Schlitz's 1981 annual report made no mention of international sales. Con-

Exhibit 15.1
LEADING U.S. BREWERS' DOMESTIC BEER MARKET SHARE

Brewer	1960	1965	1970	1975	1980	1981
Anheuser-Busch	9.7%	11.8%	18.2%	23.7%	28.9%	30.8%
Miller (Philip Morris)	2.7	3.7	4.2	8.7	21.5	22.8
Joseph Schlitz	6.5	8.6	12.4	15.7	8.6	8.1
G. Heileman	0.7	1.0	2.5	3.1	7.7	7.9
Pabst	5.4	8.2	8.6	10.5	8.7	7.6
Adolph Coors	2.2	3.6	6.0	8.0	8.0	7.5
Stroh	2.4	2.4	2.7	3.5	3.6	3.5
Olympia	1.7	2.5	2.8	3.8	3.5	3.2
Genesee	0.9	1.3	1.2	1.5	2.1	2.1
Falstaff	8.1	7.9	5.4	5.0	2.3	2.0
C. Schmidt	2.1	2.4	2.5	2.2	2.1	1.9
F.&M. Schaefer (Stroh)	3.6	4.6	4.7	4.0	2.1	1.7
Other	54.1	42.2	28.8	10.4	1.0	0.9
Total[1]	100.0%	100.0%	100.0%	100.0%	100.0%	100.0%

SOURCE: *The IMPACT American Beer Market Review and Forecast*, 1982, p. 26.
[1] Addition of the columns may not agree because of rounding.

Exhibit 15.2
SHARE OF MARKET: TREND-LEADING BEER BRANDS

Brand	1970	1975	1976	1977	1978	1979	1980	1981
Budweiser	15.4%	17.6%	13.7%	15.8%	16.1%	17.4%	19.6%	21.6%
Miller High Life	4.2	6.5	8.6	10.4	12.3	13.8	13.5	13.2
Miller Lite	—	1.8	3.1	4.2	5.6	6.1	7.0	8.3
Coors	5.9	8.0	8.9	7.9	7.2	6.6	6.6	5.8
Pabst	8.4	10.3	11.0	9.7	8.3	7.5	6.3	5.3
Michelob	0.9	3.1	3.4	4.0	4.4	4.6	4.8	4.2
Schlitz	9.4	11.7	11.3	9.7	7.7	6.4	4.2	3.1
Stroh's	2.7	3.4	3.8	3.7	3.6	3.2	3.2	3.1
Old Style	—	—	1.1	1.4	1.8	2.3	2.7	2.9
Old Milwaukee	2.0	3.0	2.9	2.5	2.1	2.0	2.2	2.8
Olympia	2.8	3.7	3.8	3.4	3.2	2.8	2.8	2.4
Total Leading Brand Share	51.7%	69.1%	71.6%	72.7%	72.3%	72.7%	72.4%	72.6%

SOURCE: *The IMPACT American Beer Market Review and Forecast*, 1982, p. 17.

Exhibit 15.3
BREWERS' SHIPMENTS 1970 THROUGH 1981
(in thousands)

	1970	1971	1972	1973	1974	1975	1976	1977	1978	1979	1980	1981
AB	22,000	24,309	26,520	29,890	34,100	35,200	29,050	36,640	41,610	46,210	50,160	54,473
Miller	5,000	5,200	5,260	6,920	9,070	12,860	18,400	24,220	31,274	35,794	37,300	40,300
Schlitz	15,129	16,708	18,910	21,343	22,661	23,179	24,162	22,130	19,580	16,804	14,954	14,305
Heileman	3,000	2,820	3,645	4,420	4,110	4,535	5,210	6,245	7,112	**11,152	13,270	13,965
Pabst	10,517	11,797	12,600	13,128	14,297	15,669	17,037	16,003	15,637	*15,115	15,091	13,465
Coors	7,250	8,525	9,788	10,947	12,330	11,860	13,545	12,824	12,566	12,912	13,779	13,261
Stroh	3,276	3,676	4,230	4,650	4,370	5,130	5,770	6,110	6,330	6,015	6,161	6,185
Olympia***	4,494	4,160	4,385	4,703	5,261	6,557	7,163	6,831	6,662	6,029	6,091	5,708
Fals-Gen-Pearl	8,433	7,934	9,327	9,099	8,840	7,406	6,918	5,183	4,589	3,489	3,821	3,500
Schmidt	3,040	3,162	3,194	3,520	3,490	3,330	3,500	3,474	3,792	3,817	3,625	3,525
Genesee	1,475	1,575	1,725	1,850	2,025	2,200	2,600	2,750	3,000	3,400	3,600	3,625
Schaefer	5,749	5,597	5,530	5,510	5,710	5,880	5,260	4,660	3,930	3,537	3,572	3,015
Pittsburgh	1,075	1,003	771	869	920	923	785	730	604	740	1,005	1,000
Carling	7,262	6,736	6,374	5,996	5,600	4,850	4,312	4,348	3,400	600	—	—
Domestic Shipments	124,393	129,583	133,440	140,317	147,345	150,341	152,291	159,136	165,331	170,816	176,580	179,402
Top 14	97,900	103,202	112,259	122,845	132,784	139,579	143,712	152,148	159,816	165,764	172,429	176,299
All Others	26,493	26,381	21,181	17,472	14,561	10,762	8,570	6,988	5,515	5,052	4,151	3,101

SOURCE: *The Beer Industry* by Beer Marketer's INSIGHTS, 1982, p. 8.

* Pabst bought Blitz 4/79. Estimate 600,000 bbls for Blitz in 78.

** Heileman bought Rainier 4/77, Falls City in 1/79, Carling 4/79.

*** Oly totals reported as in Oly 1980 annual report. Other acquisitions in the 70's: Heileman bought Associated and Grain Belt; Olympia bought Hamm's and Lone Star; Schmidt bought Rheingold, Duquesne, and Ortlieb; Schaefer bought Piels. Stroh completed acquisition of Schaefer in 1981.

Exhibit 15.4
IMPORT BRAND TRENDS
(all totals in thousands)

	Shipments				*% of Import Beer Mkt*	
Brand	**1980**	**1981**	***bbls change***	***% change***	**80**	**81**
Heineken	1,690.3	1,993.5	303.2	17.9	37.0	38.2
Molson	1,000.0	1,040.0	40.0	4.0	21.9	19.9
Beck's	232.2	332.2	100.1	43.1	5.1	6.4
Labatt	226.0	300.0	74.0	32.7	4.9	5.7
Moosehead	180.6	254.8	74.2	41.1	4.0	4.9
Dos Equis	246.8	254.2	7.4	3.0	5.4	4.9
St. Pauli Girl	83.5	105.2	21.7	26.0	1.8	2.0
Foster's Lager	72.2	72.6	.4	.6	1.6	1.4
Guinness	68.7	72.6	3.9	5.7	1.5	1.4
Tecate	67.7	72.6	4.9	7.2	under 1.5%	
Grolsch	54.8	55.8	3.3	6.0		
DAB	48.4	54.8	6.4	13.2		
O'Keefe	48.1	55.4	7.3	15.2		
Old Vienna	46.1	53.2	7.1	15.4		
Kronenbourg	25.4	47.1	21.7	85.4		
San Miguel	25.2	41.9	16.7	66.2		
Kirin	30.6	38.7	8.1	26.5		
Carta Blanca	32.2	32.6	.4	1.2		
Tsingtao	15.8	24.5	8.7	55.1		
Carlsberg	20.6	15.2	−5.4	−26.2		
Top 20 Imports	4,215.2	4,917.0	701.8	16.6		
All Others	352.6	303.9	−46.7	−13.2		
Total	4,567.4	5,220.9	635.5	14.3		
Imports as % of U.S. Total	2.6%	2.9%				

SOURCE: *The Beer Industry* by Beer Marketer's INSIGHTS, 1982, p. 57.

versations with a Schlitz sales manager revealed that international sales in 1981 totaled less than 1% of Schlitz's overall sales.)

Most U.S. brewers competed domestically with imports with super-premium products, such as Anheuser-Busch's *Michelob,* Schlitz's *Erlanger,* Pabst's *Andeker,* Heileman's *Special Export,* and Coors' *Herman Joseph's.* Miller, however, chose to obtain the right to produce and market domestically the foreign brand *Löwenbrau.* As a slightly different variation, Anheuser-Busch imported the German beer *Würzburger Hofbrau* in bulk and bottled it for sale in the United States.

In early 1982, the industry's giants, Anheuser-Busch (A-B) and Miller, were outspending and outdistancing the competition as they combined to hold 53.6% of the total U.S. beer market. This was the first time in the beer industry's history that two brewers have held more than 50% of the total U.S. beer market. A-B and Miller's market share was remarkable considering that their combined market share in 1960 and 1970 was 12.4% and 22.4%, respectively. These gains did not come without losses to other brewers, however, as seven of the next largest firms lost market share from 1970 to 1981.

Except for Miller's Philip Morris, brewers in the United States in 1982 concentrated their efforts on the production and sales of beer. Anheuser-Busch, for example, depended upon its beer division for approximately 90% of its consolidated net sales. This was typical for the industry. Nevertheless, some brewers were beginning to follow Philip Morris' lead by diversifying into other consumer products. Examples were the *Eagle* snack line of Anheuser-Busch and *Geyser Peak Winery* of Schlitz.

ECONOMIES OF SCALE

The major reasons for the growth of national firms were advertising and the economies of scale obtained in plant operations. Economies of scale in plant size enable brewers to obtain the lowest possible unit cost. According to Dr. Kenneth G. Elzinga of the University of Virginia (an authority on the brewing industry), the minimum efficient size (MES) plant capacity for the brewing industry is 1.25 million barrels per year. Cost savings accrue from water-processing equipment, sewage facilities, refrigeration equipment, management, laboratories, and custodial cost reductions. Scale economies from most of these sources continue to plant capacities of 10 million barrels per year, but beyond the size of 4.5 million barrels, cost savings are negligible. Exhibit 15.5 indicates that except for Heileman, the eight largest brewers have no plants of capacity smaller than 1.2 million barrels.

In an interview for *Advertising Age,* Mr. Peter Stroh, president of the Stroh Brewing Company, made the following analysis.

> The marketing pace being set by the two giants has resulted in the downfall of many smaller brewers. The choices for survival in the beer industry are few, but clear cut. One is to remain small, compete in narrow market segments, and brew limited volume.[1]

Beverage analyst Anton Brenner of Cyrus Lawrence & Co., New York, agreed with Mr. Stroh's assessment.

> Boutique breweries with a special product in a very limited market area can take care of that market, stroke their customers, maintain a high de-

Exhibit 15.5
CAPACITY BY BREWER (AS OF 5/82)
(all figures in millions of bbls.)

Anheuser-Busch	
St. Louis, MO	12.6
Newark, NJ	5.0
Los Angeles, CA	8.9
(11.0 by 2d qtr 82)	
Fairfield, CA	3.9
Jacksonville, FL	6.8
Tampa, FL	1.8
Houston, TX	3.5
Columbus, OH	6.7
Merrimack, NH	2.8
Williamsburg, VA	8.5
Total	60.5
Baldwinsville, NY (onstream 1983)	6.0
Schlitz	
Los Angeles, CA	3.0
Tampa, FL	1.5
Longview, TX	3.8
Winston-Salem, NC	5.0
Memphis, TN	5.5
Total	18.8
Pabst	
Milwaukee, WI	5.5
Newark, NJ	2.2
Pabst, GA	5.0
Portland, OR	2.0
Total	14.7
Stroh-Schaefer	
Detroit, MI	7.0
Allentown, PA	4.0
Total	11.0
Miller	
Milwaukee, WI	8.5
Fulton, NY	7.5
Eden, NC	8.0
Albany, GA	8.0
Fort Worth, TX	7.5
Irwindale, CA	4.5
Total	44.0
Trenton, OH (onstream late 82)	10.0
Heileman	
LaCrosse, WI	5.5
(6.0 by end of 82)	
Newport, KY	1.5
St. Paul, MN	2.2
Evansville, IN	1.2
Seattle, WA	2.0
Baltimore, MD	1.8
Frankenmuth, MI	1.1
Belleville, IL	1.2
Phoenix, AZ	.4
Auburndale, FL	.2
Total	17.1
Coors	
Golden, CO	15.3
Olympia	
Turnwater, WA	4.4
St. Paul, MN	3.25
San Antonio, TX	1.2
Total	8.85

SOURCE: *The Beer Industry* by Beer Marketer's INSIGHTS, 1982, p. 119.

> gree of brand loyalty, and may continue to do okay. On the other hand, breweries large enough to play the game (of the nationals) will survive only if they expand geographically; the in-betweens get crushed.[2]

THE EFFECTS OF MERGERS ON INDUSTRY CONCENTRATION

Leonard Weiss of the University of Wisconsin at Madison developed a means of delineating the impact of mergers on an industry's structure. Using his methodology, Dr. Elzinga found that mergers accounted for a negligible amount of the concentration occurring in the brewing industry. In fact, concentration trends in the brewing industry are rather unique in that most of the increased concentration was brought about by internal expansion rather than by merger or acquisition. Strict enforcement of the antitrust laws by the Justice Department (DOJ) is one reason why mergers have accounted for such a small share of the increase in concentration. The DOJ, nevertheless, through their rigid enforcement of the antitrust laws, may have promoted the end result they were seeking to prevent—increased national concentration. With the elimination of the merger route, the national brewers were forced to expand internally. They built large new breweries, which were more efficient than the older, smaller ones. If mergers had been permitted, the national firms might have acquired old small breweries and might have grown more slowly than they actually did.

In analyzing the effect of a proposed horizontal merger upon competition in the brewing industry, Antitrust Chief William F. Baxter was said to rely heavily upon the Herfindahl Index. Named for Orris Herfindahl, an economist, the index is a calculation based on the premise that market leaders have even greater economic power in an industry than can be assumed by simply looking at their market shares. The index is thus a measure of industry concentration obtained by the sum of the square of all participating firms' market shares. An industry in which one firm had 100% of the market would have an index of 100^2 (10,000). An industry with ten firms, each having 10% share of the market, would have an index of 10^2 (1,000). Any industry with an index over 1,000 is said to concern the Justice Department. As of April, 1982, the beer industry's Herfindahl Index was 1,600. Any merger that increases the index by around 75 points is likely to be a candidate for rejection under guidelines in effect April 1982. Other measures were used as well. The level of concentration in a local market would be a serious consideration. Given the conservative orientation of the Reagan Administration, however, industry analysts believed that the vigor of antitrust activities would soon be declining.

THE EFFECT OF ADVERTISING

Forced to expand internally in a capital intensive industry (it costs between $25 and $45 for each additional barrel of capacity), the national firms sought to ensure a steady demand for their products. The need for larger markets resulting from increased capacity coincided with the development of television which led to an increase in the firm's desired level of product identification. Advertising, particularly television spots, became the key to product differentiation in an industry where studies have shown that under test conditions most beer drinkers cannot distinguish between brands. Exhibit 15.6 lists comparative advertising expenditures for twelve major brewers by brand.

Although advertising had been important to the brewing industry since the 1950s, its importance escalated in 1970 with Philip Morris' acquisition of the Miller Brewing Company. According to Alan G. Easton, vice president for corporate affairs at Miller Brewing, Philip Morris division undertook some serious market research to "understand who was drinking beer—culturally, ethnically, socially, and economically."[3] Miller learned that its previous advertising effort to support its flagship brand had been made to the wrong market segment. Advertised as *the champagne of bottle beer,* it was very attractive to the *country club set.* These people, however, were not the high-volume beer drinkers a brand needed to generate a large number of sales. For Miller Beer to gain share, it needed to attract the everyday beer drinker who tended to drink locally made, working-man-oriented beer. Associating the product with everyday things and events, Miller invented in 1973 its famous *Miller Time* campaign. Developed by McCann-Erickson, the ad campaign presented Miller High Life beer as a reward to anyone for a job well done. The time spent in enjoying that reward was, naturally, *Miller Time.* Anheuser-Busch, noting the strong success of Miller's marketing effort, moved to a similar reward-for-work-well-done advertising campaign backed by heavy dollar expenditures. In April 1979, Anheuser-Busch began featuring "For all you do, this Bud's for you."

In 1974, Miller found a successful method for promoting a low-calorie beer, Lite, which they had purchased from Meister Brau, Inc., of Chicago in 1972. They spent heavily—around $6.00 per barrel—to introduce it nationwide. However, Lite's success was not wholly attributable to heavy advertising. Low-calorie beers had been promoted in the past with a notable lack of success. Through marketing research, Miller discovered that a significant portion of the beer market is comprised of young and middle-aged men who are sports fans with dreams of athletic prowess. In advertising Lite, Miller relied predominantly on retired athletes renowned for their speed and agility. The message was that one could drink a lot of Lite and still be fast, not that one should drink Lite to keep from getting fat.

By 1975, Schlitz and, to some extent, Anheuser-Busch had begun to increase their own advertising expenditures and made plans to enter the low-calorie beer market. This was done not only as a response to Miller's aggressiveness, but also because of a general lack of growth in demand in the face of increasing industry capacity. By 1978, nine of the ten largest brewers had light brands on the market.

The year of 1976 was a pivotal year for the beer industry. Three years into the Miller High Life campaign and two years after Lite was introduced, Anheuser-Busch was crippled by a 100-day strike. Distribution suffered as retailers ran out of Anheuser-Busch products, such as Budweiser and Michelob. Schlitz found itself in a situation of massive buyer resistance as a result of its use of cheaper ingredients. Miller's products were able to gain share rapidly without any real competition from the two top firms.

Anheuser-Busch rebounded from the strike with increased advertising budgets and new packaging. It lured people from Procter & Gamble to update its marketing efforts and rework its ad campaigns. The advertising budget was boosted from $45 million in 1977 to $112 million in 1981. Michelob Light and Natural Light were introduced. Anheuser-Busch's domestic shipments increased over the same period by 17,833,000 barrels compared to the *rest* of the entire industry which increased only 2,433,000 barrels. As Alan Easton, Vice-President at Miller's, remarked, "They (Anheuser-Busch) have been good and fast learners."[4]

A study published in 1982 suggested that the trend toward higher advertising budgets was apparently reaching a point of diminishing returns as the primary method of increasing sales and profits. Exhibit 15.7 depicts the relative advertising costs of major brewers compared with their profitability as of 1979. Miller, for example, spent $2.10 per barrel compared to only $1.33 by Heileman. Miller, which increased its brewing capacity fivefold from 1970 to 1977, and doubled it between 1977 and 1981, had in 1979 an estimated $2.94 of interest charges per barrel versus $0.19 per barrel by Heileman.

GROWTH THROUGH ACQUISITION

Heileman's growth strategy was very different from many in the industry. Instead of building new facilities and advertising heavily as did Miller Brewing, Heileman acquired small regional brewers and cut prices aggressively. In 1981, Heileman was the only major brewer outside of Anheuser-Busch and Miller to show volume, sales, and earnings increases. Russell G. Cleary, President, Chairman, and Chief Executive Officer of the G. Heileman Company, described the strategy as follows:

> We have tried to develop a collection of regional breweries by joining other regional brands with the original Heileman brands. Our objective has been to increase the penetration in the markets that are natural to us, and—secondarily—to broaden our base throughout the country . . . The goal is to get distribution on a wall-to-wall basis.[5]

Exhibit 15.6

ADVERTISING $ (000)

	1977	1978	1979	1980	1981
Anheuser-Busch					
Budweiser	22,807	24,647	29,468	32,344	42,572
Michelob	9,969	11,690	15,401	13,558	18,266
Michelob Light	—	6,476	16,293	17,109	21,605
Busch	2,995	5,468	8,187	10,476	7,748
Natural Light	9,212	14,795	16,875	18,928	18,048
Budweiser Light	—	—	—	—	2,333
Misc	238	83	1,068	1,396	978
Total	45,221	63,158	87,292	93,811	111,550
Miller					
High Life	14,623	24,410	29,685	36,747	37,568
Lite	16,218	23,332	27,700	32,516	34,122
Löwenbrau	11,284	16,284	16,966	19,000	19,493
Misc	348	264	652	256	1,743
Total	42,473	64,290	75,003	85,519	92,926
Schlitz					
Schlitz	19,032	22,815	25,535	19,666	17,618
Schlitz Light	12,546	8,027	6,623	199	20
Old Milwaukee	5,925	3,639	5,694	5,509	5,661
Old Milwaukee Light	—	—	—	1,469	2,604
Malt Liquor	3,178	5,826	7,408	4,650	4,654
Erlanger	—	—	3,016	12,138	3,305
Misc	150	410	1	443	—
Total	40,831	40,717	48,277	44,074	33,862
Heileman					
Blatz	1,333	1,246	1,861	1,263	993
Old Style	1,650	2,136	1,998	1,677	1,083
Colt 45	—	—	1,977	2,448	1,969
Carling	—	—	477	592	883
Rainier	—	558	799	777	1,072
Misc	1,650	2,781	7,722	6,851	4,130
Total	4,636	6,721	14,834	13,608	10,130

SOURCE: *The Beer Industry* by Beer Marketer's INSIGHTS, 1982, pp. 113–114.

Exhibit 15.6 **(*Continued*)**

Pabst					
Blue Ribbon	9,722	11,485	10,000	13,318	11,517
Extra Light	385	5,510	4,780	1,622	3,269
Henry Weinhard	—	—	1,173	1,359	1,340
Andeker	688	998	71	1,075	980
Misc	47	46	2,374	342	188
Total	10,842	18,039	18,398	17,716	17,294
Coors					
Coors	3,963	6,788	11,222	13,620	14,275
Coors Light	—	1,331	3,673	7,037	7,030
Herman Joseph	—	—	—	725	1,501
Misc	2	7	91	257	125
Total	3,965	8,126	14,986	21,639	22,931
Stroh					
Stroh	7,212	8,134	8,692	8,780	9,340
Stroh Light	—	663	2,414	1,926	2,051
Schaefer	—	—	—	3,634	3,889
Misc	—	194	185	1,200	703
Total	7,212	8,991	11,291	15,540	15,983
Olympia					
Oly	4,299	6,534	7,243	9,775	10,489
Hamm's	1,601	1,330	2,236	1,387	1,476
Lone Star	331	648	558	573	1,389
Oly Gold	2,239	2,204	1,835	1,788	1,929
Misc	—	—	844	1,124	43
Total	8,470	10,716	12,716	14,647	15,326
Genesee					
Total	2,784	3,007	4,440	5,951	6,292
Schmidt					
Total	3,913	3,130	3,261	2,474	2,139
Heineken					
Total	1,521	1,719	1,891	2,842	5,907
Molson					
Total	1,132	2,467	2,816	2,964	2,911

Exhibit 15.7

RETURN ON NET WORTH VS. ADVERTISING EXPENDITURES PER BARREL—1979

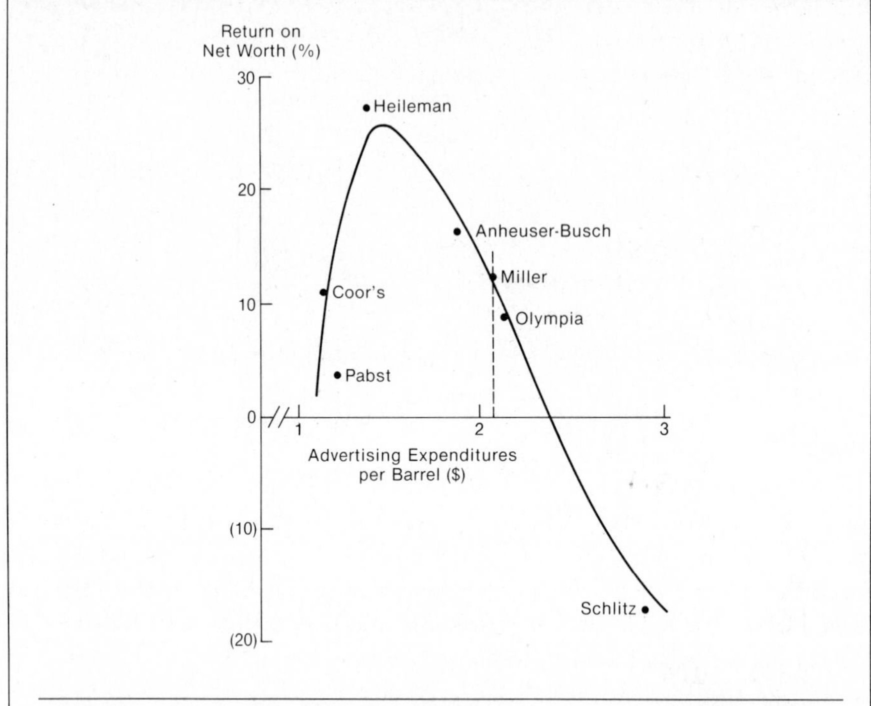

SOURCE: H. Allessro, "Market-Share-Madness," *The Journal of Business Strategy* (Fall 1982), p. 78. Reprinted by permission from *The Journal of Business Strategy*, Fall 1982, Copyright © 1982, Warren, Gorham & Lamont, Inc., 210 South Street, Boston, Mass. All Rights Reserved.

As of March 1982, Heileman produced and marketed around thirty brands with its eight major labels (Old Style, Blatz, Rainier, Colt 45, Schmidt, Black Label, Wiedemann, and Special Export) accounting for about 80% of its total output. The firm's preference has been to grow contiguously into adjacent territories. This approach allowed them to promote Heileman's chief original beer, Old Style, the largest selling beer in Wisconsin and Illinois. Analysts believe that Heileman became the industry's merger specialist out of necessity. It did not have the money to build new facilities across the country as did Anheuser-Busch, Miller, and Schlitz. It chose to grow through the acquisition of small regional breweries. In following the strategy, Heileman appeared to do everything counter to Anheuser-Busch and Miller. Aside from its LaCrosse, Wisconsin plant, it has no large modern breweries for economies of scale. It has never had to pour large sums of money into national advertising. Instead, it has chosen less expensive regional and local advertising. Nevertheless, Heileman in early 1982 was in a position to soon overtake Schlitz as the third largest selling brewer. Even though Heileman's bid to merge with Schlitz in 1981 had been opposed by the Justice Department, Russell Cleary, its CEO, was not prepared to give up Heileman's successful merger strategy.

> I think there is a legitimate concern that as the gap between the top two and the balance of the industry widens that it will be more difficult to compete. Obviously, we think that the most important aspect of preserving competition in the beer business is creating a third strong national company. The merger of Heileman and Schlitz would have done that.[6]

Cleary's thoughts were echoed by others who also felt that the country's antitrust policy was detrimental to the brewing industry as a whole. In his 1982 book, Dominick T. Armentano, an authority in the antitrust area, stated that ". . . a simple decrease in the number of competitors or an increase in the concentration ratio does not indicate anything significant with respect to the level of rivalrous competition."[7]

It was becoming accepted thinking by analysts that the brewing industry by 1982 had evolved into a three-tiered structure. The top tier was composed of Anheuser-Busch and Miller Brewing Company. The second tier was composed of firms like Schlitz, Heileman, Pabst, Coors, Stroh, and Olympia, who were conscious of their vulnerability and very concerned with survival. Genesee and Falstaff could also be put in this category. The third tier was composed of firms with less than one million barrels of capacity, such as Pittsburgh, Latrobe, Hudepohl, and Dixie, among many others. Most of these firms were likely merger targets for second-tier brewers. By 1982, Heileman had already acquired Carling, Rainier, Blatz, Wiedemann, and Schmidt, among others. Earlier, Schmidt had acquired Rheingold, Duquesne, and Ortlieb. Olympia purchased the Theodore Hamm Brewing Company and Lone Star Brewing to gain plants and markets in St. Paul and San Antonio. Stroh completed its acquisition of Schaefer in 1981. After failing to acquire Schlitz in 1981, Pabst was in the process of acquiring the Pittsburgh Brewing Company in 1982 for $7.8 million. The major question in the early 1980s revolved around the Justice Department's view of any proposed merger between two or more second-tier firms.

REGIONAL TRENDS

No brewer can be said to have uniform sales across the country. Even Anheuser-Busch, the most successful brewing firm in the United States, has done significantly better between 1977 and 1981 in the Pacific states than in the East North Central region where Miller and Heileman have been strong contenders (see Exhibit 15.8). Miller is somewhat weak in the Western states where Coors continues to have a strong but softening share of the

Exhibit 15.8
REGIONAL TRENDS OF BREWERS' SHIPMENTS 1977–1981

	BBLS (in thousands)					*Market Share by Region*				
New England	1977	1978	1979	1980	1981	1977	1978	1979	1980	1981
AB	1,967	2,289	2,549	2,652	2,882	26.8	30.1	32.8	32.9	36.0
Miller	1,785	2,370	2,592	2,853	2,758	24.3	31.2	33.3	35.4	34.4
Schlitz	1,601	1,106	848	640	586	21.8	14.6	10.9	7.9	7.2
Pabst	278	270	259	238	206	3.8	3.6	3.3	2.9	2.6
Heileman*	—	—	—	156	140	—	—	—	1.9	1.7
All Others	1,722	1,562	1,531	1,525	1,443	23.4	20.6	19.7	18.9	18.0
Total	7,353	7,596	7,779	8,063	8,015					

	BBLS (in thousands)					*Market Share by Region*				
Southeast	1977	1978	1979	1980	1981	1977	1978	1979	1980	1981
AB	6,428	6,902	7,429	8,200	8,642	35.2	35.2	36.3	38.6	39.4
Miller	4,350	5,908	6,481	6,305	6,367	23.9	30.1	31.7	29.7	29.0
Schlitz	4,086	3,638	3,188	2,885	2,794	22.7	18.5	15.6	13.6	12.8
Pabst	1,575	1,432	1,499	1,523	1,124	8.6	7.3	7.3	7.3	5.1
Heileman	—	—	—	673	829	—	—	—	3.2	3.8
Coors	—	—	—	—	337	—	—	—	—	—
Stroh	—	—	—	428	661	—	—	—	—	—
All Others	1,795	1,754	1,854	1,241	1,173	9.8	8.9	9.1	7.8	8.4
Total	18,234	19,634	20,451	21,254	21,927					

	BBLS (in thousands)					*Market Share by Region*				
East North Central	1977	1978	1979	1980	1981	1977	1978	1979	1980	1981
AB	3,578	3,780	3,798	3,859	3,783	15.6	16.1	15.9	15.8	15.5
Miller	3,342	4,369	5,430	5,855	6,312	14.6	18.6	22.7	23.9	25.9
Schlitz	1,429	1,192	988	964	967	6.2	5.1	4.1	3.9	4.0
Pabst	5,948	5,535	4,891	4,653	4,090	25.9	23.6	20.4	19.0	16.8
Heileman	1,809	2,010	2,989	3,438	3,572	7.9	8.6	12.5	14.0	14.7
Stroh	3,186	3,106	2,815	2,613	2,473	13.9	13.2	11.7	10.7	10.2
All Others	3,631	3,459	3,049	3,008	3,160	15.8	14.7	12.7	12.3	13.0
Total	22,923	23,451	23,960	24,490	24,357					

West North Central	BBLS (in thousands)					Market Share by Region				
	1977	1978	1979	1980	1981	1977	1978	1979	1980	1981
AB	2,635	2,838	2,966	3,256	3,532	21.6	22.3	22.4	4.1	25.8
Miller	1,426	2,035	2,531	2,375	2,559	11.7	16.0	19.1	7.5	18.7
Schlitz	1,696	1,374	1,189	1,090	1,177	13.9	10.8	9.0	8.1	8.6
Pabst	2,173	2,174	2,000	1,998	1,772	17.8	17.1	15.1	4.8	13.0
Heileman	—	—	—	1,883	1,912	—	—	—	3.9	14.0
Coors	916	1,335	1,631	1,608	1,459	7.5	10.5	12.3	1.9	10.7
All Others	3,361	2,988	2,936	1,325	1,259	17.5	23.4	22.2	9.7	9.2
Total	12,207	12,744	13,253	13,535	13,670					

West South Central	BBLS (in thousands)					Market Share by Region				
	1977	1978	1979	1980	1981	1977	1978	1979	1980	1981
AB	3,009	3,502	3,953	4,527	5,660	17.4	19.5	20.7	2.4	25.8
Miller	2,732	3,540	4,414	4,794	6,056	15.8	19.7	23.1	3.8	27.6
Schlitz	5,050	4,731	4,256	3,582	3,220	29.2	26.3	22.3	7.7	14.7
Pabst	251	253	280	326	302	1.5	1.4	1.5	1.6	1.4
Coors	3,680	3,695	3,929	4,588	4,473	21.3	20.6	20.6	2.7	20.4
Heileman	—	—	—	148	246	—	—	—	0.7	1.1
All Others	2,543	2,258	2,258	2,219	1,993	14.7	12.6	11.8	1.0	9.1
Total	17,265	17,979	19,090	20,184	21,950					

	BBLS (in thousands)					Market Share by Region				
Mountain	1977	1978	1979	1980	1981	1977	1978	1979	1980	1981
AB	2,155	2,686	3,112	3,161	3,469	25.5	29.2	32.2	1.4	32.3
Miller	631	1,019	1,283	1,495	1,898	7.5	11.1	13.3	4.9	17.7
Schlitz	877	879	779	697	755	10.4	9.6	8.1	6.9	7.0
Pabst	223	276	263	225	243	2.6	3.0	2.7	2.2	2.3
Heileman	—	—	—	359	420	—	—	—	3.6	3.9
Coors	3,086	2,895	2,795	3,001	2,858	36.6	31.5	28.9	9.9	26.6
All Others	1,465	1,413	1,408	1,112	1,084	17.7	15.4	14.6	1.1	10.1
Total	8,437	9,168	9,640	10,050	10,727					

(*Continued*)

Exhibit 15.8
(Continued)

	BBLS (in thousands)					*Market Share by Region*				
Pacific	1977	1978	1979	1980	1981	1977	1978	1979	1980	1981
AB	5,984	7,632	9,059	9,730	10,439	27.9	33.4	37.6	9.1	40.9
Miller	1,840	2,428	2,640	2,659	3,115	8.6	10.6	10.9	0.7	12.2
Schlitz	1,731	1,706	1,577	1,335	1,347	8.1	7.5	6.5	5.4	5.3
Pabst	518	517	1,051	1,074	1,081	2.4	2.3	4.4	4.2	4.3
Coors	5,112	4,530	4,552	4,625	4,136	23.8	19.8	18.9	8.6	16.2
Heileman	—	—	—	1,638	1,759	—	—	—	6.6	6.9
Olympia	2,864	2,583	2,326	2,165	1,974	13.4	11.3	9.6	8.7	7.7
All Others	3,385	3,442	2,901	1,628	1,648	15.8	15.1	12.0	6.5	6.5
Total	21,447	22,837	24,108	24,855	25,500					

SOURCE: *The Beer Industry* by Beer Marketer's INSIGHTS, 1982, pp. 10–16.

* In most states and regions Heileman numbers are given only for 1980 and 1981 because acquisitions from 1977–1979 prevent exact determination of Heileman barrelage during those years.

market. Only Anheuser-Busch, Miller, Schlitz, Pabst, and recently, Heileman can be said to have reasonably strong national sales. Stroh Brewing Company, for example, is strong only in the East North Central region, but along with Coors and Heileman, is trying to become important in the Southeast. Coors continues to strive for national distribution, but is frustrated by Anheuser-Busch and Miller—both targeting the key markets of California and Texas as *must have* states. Bill Keyser, corporate communication representative for Coors, states: "They're out to prove they have deeper pockets than anyone else. But we'll be competing aggressively in those two areas. We know the two majors are targeting those states, and we're up to the challenge."[8] Even though the Golden, Colorado plant was being expanded in order to reach 20 million barrel capacity by the mid-1980s, the company only used 89% of its brewing capacity in 1981 (see Exhibit 15.9). Coors top management continued to hold the land it bought in Virginia for a future 10 million barrel capacity plant to serve the East Coast.

Exhibit 15.9

U.S. BREWING INDUSTRY CAPACITY AND USAGE
(millions of barrels)

Brewer	*Number of Plants*	*Total 1981 Capacity*	*Total Shipments*[1]	*Percent of Capacity*
Anheuser-Busch	10	56.0	54.5	97.3
Miller Brewing (Philip Morris)	6	47.5	40.3	84.8
Joseph Schlitz	5	18.8	14.3	76.1
G. Heileman Brewing	10	17.1	14.0	81.9
Pabst Brewing	4	17.7	13.5	76.3
Adolph Coors	1	15.0	13.3	88.7
Stroh Brewery	1	7.3	6.2	84.9
Olympia Brewing	3	8.9	5.7	64.0
Genesee Brewing	1	4.0	3.6	90.0
Falstaff Brewing	5	6.7	3.6	53.7
C. Schmidt	2	5.0	3.3	66.0
F. & M. Schaefer (Stroh)	1	5.0	2.9	58.0
All Others	24	5.9	4.2	71.2
Total Domestic	73	214.9	179.4	83.5

SOURCE: *The IMPACT American Beer Market Review and Forecast*, 1982, p. 31.
[1]Includes 2.7 million barrels which are tax-free exports and military shipments.

Olympia was a strong contender in 1982 only in the Pacific states, but its share was dropping rapidly. Pabst Brewing Company increased its share in the Pacific area but was unable to keep its market share from dropping throughout the rest of the country.

FINANCIAL SITUATION

Exhibit 15.10 provides financial data on the eight largest brewers in the United States. This information was compiled by Beer Marketer's INSIGHTS, Inc. of West Nyack, New York. The cost and income figures have been determined in some cases from disclosed financial statements and in others from estimates.

Exhibit 15.10

ESTIMATED FINANCIAL DATA FOR EIGHT LARGEST U.S. BREWERS

(in thousands)

ANHEUSER BUSCH					
Total	1977	1978	1979	1980	1981
Barrels	36,640	41,610	46,210	50,160	54,473
Revenue	$1,683,608	$2,082,997	$2,554,027	$3,034,178	$3,544,013
Cost of goods sold	1,339,925	1,624,871	1,998,120	2,352,002	2,741,081
Marketing, general & administrative costs	174,406	253,405	328,091	394,759	474,460
Advertising	72,547	107,354	147,872	179,071	215,168
Income from operations	169,277	204,721	227,815	287,417	328,472
Interest expense	24,549	26,630	36,968	69,722	82,799
Interest income	6,962	10,819	7,856	2,006	5,447
Income tax	71,448	87,381	70,239	91,793	99,141
Extraordinary items	+4,030	+832	+52,217	+30,096	+48,481
NET INCOME	$ 84,272	$ 102,361	$ 180,681	$ 158,004	$ 200,461

MILLER					
Total	1977	1978	1979	1980	1981
Barrels	24,200	31,274	35,794	37,300	40,300
Operating revenue	$1,327,600	$1,834,500	$2,236,500	$2,542,300	$2,837,200
Operating income	106,400	150,300	181,000	144,700	115,600

Exhibit 15.10 ***(Continued)***

SCHLITZ					
Total	1977	1978	1979	1980	1981
Barrels	22,130	19,580	16,804	14,954	14,305
Revenue	$900,470	$837,828	$ 782,226	$781,795	$ 784,629
Cost of goods sold	697,980	665,328	653,171	613,866	639,720
Marketing, general & administrative costs	144,066	139,410	135,776	123,620	127,458
Advertising	53,997	56,987	70,073	64,218	56,934
Income from operations	58,423	33,090	−6,721	25,541	17,452
Interest expense	16,155	14,098	11,259	9,779	10,871
Interest income	1,770	3,133	3,865	18,536	25,892
Income tax	14,606	8,028	+43,858	16,055	+24,605
Extraordinary items	−10,401	−3,133	−74,106	4,670	−75,387
NET INCOME	$ 19,032	$ 10,965	$−44,363	$ 22,914	$−18,310

G. HEILEMAN					
Total	1977	1978	1979*	1980	1981
Barrels	6,245	7,112	11,152	13,270	13,965
Revenue	$216,358	$269,971	$478,706	$624,530	$702,319
Cost of goods sold	151,816	188,752	347,719	456,090	513,353
Marketing, general & administrative costs	39,344	49,571	80,071	104,833	119,540
Advertising	12,552	15,718	34,416	47,672	54,041
Income from operations	25,147	31,662	50,641	63,617	69,465
Interest expense	—	—	2,676	2,654	2,514
Interest income	—	—	1,227	2,389	5,307
Income tax	12,865	16,357	24,200	30,388	35,052
Extraordinary items	+62	+498	+112	−1,194	−419
NET INCOME	$ 12,365	$ 15,789	$ 25,092	$ 31,715	$ 36,728

* Heileman purchased Carling in 1979. Estimate 3400 bbls for Carling in 1978.

(Continued)

Exhibit 15.10 **(*Continued*)**

PABST

Total	1977	1978	1979*	1980	1981
Barrels	16,003	15,367	15,115	15,091	13,465
Revenue	$582,878	$598,951	$651,400	$719,902	$ 691,864
Cost of goods sold	486,126	508,544	549,447	607,526	599,324
Marketing, general & administrative costs	59,069	74,895	82,213	90,953	105,746
Advertising	26,799	39,823	43,278	45,588	47,410
Income from operations	37,683	15,512	19,740	21,423	13,206
Interest expense	1,509	1,908	2,431	2,005	1,965
Interest income	1,906	1,722	2,679	3,471	4,108
Income tax	15,775	3,150	6,500	8,528	+27,025
Extraordinary items	534	−1,090	−4,081	−1,358	−39,452
NET INCOME	$ 21,771	$ 11,086	$ 9,478	$ 12,642	$−23,536

* Pabst bought Blitz in 1979. Estimate 600,000 barrels for Blitz in 1978.

COORS

Total	1977	1978	1979	1980	1981
Barrels	12,824	12,566	12,912	13,779	13,261
Revenue	$532,251	$549,448	$638,768	$758,017	$787,739
Cost of goods sold	371,253	395,935	446,817	537,813	558,701
Marketing, general & administrative costs	40,010	66,474	84,315	121,392	150,645
Advertising	11,912	8,301	9,704	12,175	14,270
Income from operations	13,924	29,420	40,043	57,006	72,687
Operating income	108,973	78,647	97,951	86,637	64,100
Interest expense	1,550	1,588	1,419	1,388	1,423
Interest income	3,640	6,495	10,080	14,664	12,257
Income tax	48,698	35,614	42,044	36,230	24,592
Extraordinary items	+1,148	+2,422	−2,370	−6,006	−4,135
NET INCOME	$ 63,570	$ 50,337	$ 62,152	$ 57,700	$ 46,201

Exhibit 15.10 ***(Continued)***

STROH

Total	1977	1978	1979	1980	*1981	**1981
Barrels	5,791	6,392	6,112	5,924	9,791	7,184
Revenue	$223,140	$255,994	$265,104	$290,166	$516,591	$391,361
Cost of goods sold	180,079	207,204	219,387	233,204	409,893	317,916
Marketing, general & administrative costs	30,410	33,979	39,083	47,158	97,160	77,444
Advertising	11,399	13,026	16,769	na	na	na
Income from operations	12,650	14,811	6,634	9,804	9,304	−3,999
Interest expense	183	50	47	465	3,758	4,928
Interest income	848	761	864	912	3,031	1,293
Income tax	5,577	6,199	2,854	3,896	1,971	+3,788
Extraordinary items	−341	−66	−368	−257	+685	11,986
NET INCOME	$ 9,417	$ 9,258	$ 4,229	$ 6,098	$ 7,314	$ 8,140

* Cost data for 12 months estimated based on adjustment for Schaefer as if part of Stroh for full 12 months.
** 9 months through December 1981. All other years are 12 months through March of designated year.

OLYMPIA

Total	1977	1978	1979	1980	1981
Barrels	6,831	6,662	6,029	6,091	5,708
Net revenue	$273,955	$287,707	$283,616	$307,543	$303,836
Cost of goods sold	224,234	232,255	230,113	253,853	255,592
Marketing, general & administrative costs	40,713	46,741	46,754	53,811	58,210
Advertising	na	18,122	19,301	25,210	30,047
Operating income	9,008	8,711	6,749	−121	−9,966
Interest expense	928	1,759	1,636	1,464	2,280
Interest income	583	1,423	2,691	1,218	1,000
Income tax	4,376	4,629	3,988	+942	+6,393
Extraordinary items	−1,298	+2,069	+2,303	+2,205	+3,624
NET INCOME	$ 2,968	$ 5,815	$ 7,806	$ 2,780	$ −1,229

SOURCE: *The Beer Industry* by Beer Marketer's INSIGHTS, pp. 66–73.

THE FUTURE OF THE INDUSTRY

Impact, a trade newsletter published annually by M. Shanken Communications, Inc. of New York forecasts a rather difficult period ahead for the brewing industry. It believes that the eighties will be a fiercely competitive decade for the American beer market, as fewer and larger companies vie for share in a slow growth market. *Impact* forecasts a 2% annual growth rate over the years 1980–1985 with a drop to 1.9% annually from 1985–1990. This is quite a drop from the 3.7% growth rate during the 1970s. The forecast is based upon the industry's tie to the population growth of drinking age

Exhibit 15.11

DEMOGRAPHICS OF BEER DRINKERS

	Regular Domestic Beer			
	All Users		*Heavy Users*	
	000	%	000	%
Total adults	72,215	100.0	25,096	100.0
Males	46,216	64.0	20,363	18.1
Females	25,998	36.0	4,732	18.9
18–24	16,311	22.6	6,843	27.3
25–34	19,339	26.8	6,743	26.9
35–44	12,057	16.7	4,191	16.7
45–54	10,570	14.6	3,275	13.0
55–64	7,851	10.9	2,685	10.3
65 or older	6,087	8.4	1,459	5.8

	Light/Low Calorie Beer			
	All Users		*Heavy Users*	
	000	%	000	%
Total adults	31,309	100.0	11,306	100.0
Males	18,048	57.6	7,727	68.3
Females	13,261	42.4	3,579	31.7
18–24	7,361	23.5	2,525	22.3
25–34	8,953	28.6	3,453	30.5
35–44	5,194	16.6	1,987	17.6
45–54	4,527	14.5	1,598	14.1
55–64	3,072	9.8	1,081	9.6
65 or older	2,202	7.0	662	5.9

	Malt Liquor:			
	All Users		*Heavy Users*	
	000	%	000	%
Total adults	12,713	100.0	4,422	100.0
Males	8,017	63.1	2,887	65.3
Females	4,696	36.9	1,535	34.7
18–24	4,504	35.4	1,646	37.2
25–34	3,498	27.5	985	22.3
35–44	1,981	15.6	660	14.9
45–54	1,526	12.0	663	15.0
55–64	687	5.4	230	5.2
65 or older	517	4.1	238	5.4

	Imported Beer (in Cans or Bottles):			
	All Users		*Heavy Users*	
	000	%	000	%
Total adults	24,859	100.0	4,582	100.0
Males	16,439	66.1	3,683	80.4
Females	8,420	33.9	899	19.6
18–24	7,594	30.5	1,482	32.3
25–34	7,448	30.0	1,419	31.0
35–44	3,703	14.9	725	15.8
45–54	3,079	12.4	456	10.0
55–64	1,936	7.8	383	8.4
65 or older	1,099	4.4	116	2.5

SOURCE: Adapted from *The Beer Industry* by Beer Marketer's INSIGHTS, 1982, pp. 92–95.

PROJECTIONS OF UNITED STATES POPULATION
TOTAL OF AGES 20–34

Exhibit 15.12

Year	*Population in thousands*
1982	61,397
1985	63,063
1990	62,073
1995	57,618
2000	53,513

SOURCE: "Projections of the Population of the United States: 1982 to 2050 (Advance Report)," *Population Estimates and Projections, Current Population Reports,* Series P-25, No. 922 (Bureau of the Census, U.S. Department of Commerce, October 1982), Table 2.

people. Over half of all beer consumption is by the 18–34 age group (closer to 60% for malt liquor and imported beer) with a general 60–40% split between males and females, respectively (see Exhibit 15.11).

The Bureau of Census of the U.S. Department of Commerce projects that the annual rate of population growth will slow from .9% in 1981 to .6% in 2000 and reach zero growth by 2050. With the slowdown in growth, the median age of the U.S. population will increase from 30.3 years in 1981 to 36.3 years in 2000 and 41.6 years in 2050. The impact of these projections on the growth of the brewing industry is most noticeable in the all-important younger beer drinking segment of the population as shown in Exhibit 15.12.

ESTIMATED BEER CONSUMPTION BY SEGMENT
(Millions of Barrels)

Exhibit 15.13

Segment	1970	1975	1980	1981	1985	1990
Popular	71.6	65.4	26.9	26.9	22.0	17.0
Premium	46.1	71.6	107.3	107.6	114.0	120.0
Super-Premium	1.1	5.0	11.5	11.2	13.0	15.0
Light	—	2.8	22.1	25.1	32.0	41.0
Imported	0.9	1.7	4.6	5.2	8.0	12.0
Malt Liquor	3.1	3.8	5.5	5.9	8.0	11.0
Total	122.8	150.3	177.9	181.9	197.0	216.0

SOURCE: Adapted from *The IMPACT American Beer Market Review and Forecast,* 1982, pp. 8 and 51.

Simple population estimates are not the whole story, however. There is another trend which may help to counter the slow growth rate of the population. The per capita consumption has been steadily increasing from 15.4 gallons in 1960 to 18.7 gallons in 1970 to 24.6 gallons in 1981. It is possible that this trend may continue if U.S. brewers pay close attention to their changing market. A good argument can be made, however, that per capita consumption will stabilize and begin to drop around 1985–1990. By then, the largest proportion of beer drinkers (the 18–34 age group) will reduce in size. Nevertheless, based upon changing preferences in the marketplace from 1970 to 1981, *Impact* projects that popular-priced beer will tend to continue losing sales as market tastes switch more to light and imported beers. Malt liquor, with its strong popularity among black and Hispanic consumers, is projected to reach 11 million barrels in 1990 (see Exhibit 15.13).

NOTES

1. G. Sutter, "Stroh Stokes the Fires of Expansion," *Advertising Age,* March 29, 1982, p. M-42.
2. *Ibid.*
3. A. Sobczynski, "The Big 2 Strengthen Their Grip," *Advertising Age,* March 29, 1982, p. M-39.
4. *Ibid.*
5. *Ibid.*, p. M-40.
6. *Ibid.*, p. M-41.
7. D. T. Armentano, *Antitrust and Monopoly: Anatomy of a Policy Failure.* New York: Wiley, 1982, p. 232.
8. Sutter, p. M-39.

Case 16

JOSEPH SCHLITZ BREWING COMPANY: 1982

J. David Hunger / Michael Schipper

David Bellegante / David Porter / Rebecca Wood

Late Sunday night, March 28, 1982, the telephone rang at the home of Daniel McKeithan, Chairman of the Board of the Joseph Schlitz Brewing Company. "Mr. McKeithan," the voice said on the phone, "I'm with the *Wall Street Journal.* Tomorrow we plan to publish an advertisement submitted to us by the Stroh Brewing Company detailing their offer to acquire your firm. Would you like to comment on this bid?"

"I'm sorry, but I am not aware of any such offer," replied McKeithan. "What are the particulars?"

"I don't really have all the information, Sir," responded the reporter, "but it appears to be a two-step cash offer to acquire Schlitz. They're offering $16 a share for 19,740,000 shares, about 67 percent of your firm's common stock, as the first step. If successful, they plan to acquire all the remaining shares through a merger or some other combination of Schlitz into a Stroh unit. The offer is being managed by Salomon Brothers and expires April 23 unless extended. The proration date is April 7. Naturally, the *Journal* is running an article on the bid in tomorrow's edition. Do you have a comment for publication?"

McKeithan thought for a moment and replied, "Not at this time. I appre-

SOURCE: J. David Hunger, Michael Schipper, David Bellegante, David Porter, and Rebecca Wood, "Joseph Schlitz Brewing Company—1982," *Case Research Journal 1984,* pp. 129–154. Special thanks are given to Peter H. Blum, Historian of the Stroh Brewing Company, Detroit, Michigan, for his comments on an earlier draft of this case.

ciate your letting me know." He hung up the phone and immediately called Peter Stroh in Florida. The takeover had begun![1]

HISTORY OF THE COMPANY

In 1849, a German immigrant by the name of August Krug decided to go into the beer business. He already owned a restaurant on busy Chestnut Street in Milwaukee, Wisconsin. Responding to the persistent calls from his customers for beer, Krug produced 150 barrels of beer in his first year from a single 3-barrel brew kettle in his basement. In 1850, August's father, George Krug, arrived from Germany with his eight-year-old grandson, August Uihlein, and $800 in gold to invest in the business. This money was used to buy land for storage cellars and to hire four employees, among them a nineteen-year-old bookkeeper named Joseph Schiltz.

Upon the death of August Krug in 1856, Joseph Schlitz took control of the brewery and eventually gave it his name. Production continued to increase, but it was the Chicago fire of 1871 which established the brewery's reputation.

> The fire left Chicago thirsty; it was desperately short of water and its breweries were virtually destroyed. Schlitz floated a shipload of beer down Lake Michigan to his parched neighbors. They liked and remembered the Milwaukee beer long after the crisis passed, so Joseph Schlitz kept them well-supplied with it as production soared. The incident made Schlitz's product *The Beer That Made Milwaukee Famous.*[2]

Joseph Schlitz died childless in 1875 and left the brewery to August Uihlein and his three brothers—all Schlitz employees. Under the Uihleins, production rose sharply and by 1906 production reached a pre-prohibition peak of 1.5 million barrels. The company was incorporated in Wisconsin in 1920. The repeal of the Volstead Act in 1933 ended a fourteen-year prohibition of alcoholic beverages and allowed the firm to continue its expansion. Erwin Uihlein, the youngest son of August, assumed the presidency and expanded the firm geographically. Breweries were added in Brooklyn, New York in 1949, Los Angeles in 1952, and Kansas City in 1956. This increased capacity enabled consumers in 1952 to purchase more than 6 million barrels of Schlitz beer, an industry record.

The second generation of Uihleins, represented by Erwin, handed over control of the brewery to the third generation in 1961. Robert A. Uihlein, Jr., grandson of August Uihlein, became president of Schlitz and worked to modernize business methods. He closed the outdated Brooklyn and Kansas City facilities and built breweries in Tampa, Winston-Salem, Memphis, and Longview, Texas. Annual sales and production increased and hovered in the neighborhood of 20 million barrels by the mid-1970s. Only Anheuser-Busch produced and sold more beer in the United States. Anheuser-Busch, however, had greater capacity in its breweries (34 million barrels) versus Schlitz (23 million barrels) in 1974. Anheuser-Busch's sales were consequently greater: $1.1 billion (23.2% market share) in 1973 compared to Schlitz's $700 million (15.4% market share). Nevertheless, Schlitz earned 7.6% on sales and 21% on stockholders' equity in the same year. Anheuser-Busch's figures were 5.9% and 13.8%, respectively. Even though Robert Uihlein commented in 1974: "There is no way we'll pass Busch in sales in the foreseeable future," Schlitz planned to add 12 million barrels to capacity over the next three to four years.[3] Anheuser-Busch only planned to add 7 million barrels during the same time period. Given that both firms were operating their breweries at full capacity, it appeared to industry analysts in 1974 that Schlitz had a good chance to soon match the sales of Anheuser-Busch.

With catching and even surpassing Anheuser-Busch as his key objective, Robert Uihlein made some strategic decisions in the early 1970s which were starting to pay off positively in 1974. Schlitz had built, or was building in 1974, three breweries of 4 million barrel initial capacity. Anheuser-Busch had none this large. Uihlein pointed out: "In the brewhouse in our old Milwaukee brewery, we have 24 men on a shift. In our big new Winston-Salem or Memphis plants there are two."[4] The three plants were nearly equal in capacity. Schlitz's sales per employee in 1973 were approximately $110,000. Anheuser-Busch's were closer to $90,000. In addition to building larger and more modern production facilities, Uihlein worked to shorten the length of the brewing process and to reduce raw materials' costs. By changing its mix of ingredients, Schlitz paid far less for its raw materials and was able to reduce the brewing process to fifteen to twenty days (Anheuser-Busch needed thirty-two to forty days). As a result, it not only cost Schlitz less to brew a barrel of beer, Schlitz was able to increase the effective capacity of its existing breweries.

Since these changes included a reduction in the malt ratio (a certain amount of malt is required for good flavor), the taste of the Schlitz brand also changed. David Kendall, head of the Flavor Sciences unit at Arthur D. Little, said in 1974: "Today's Schlitz isn't the same product as yesterday's."[5] August A. Busch III, president of Anheuser-Busch, was reported as saying that Anheuser-Busch's was the quality beer and that Schlitz was "less drinkable."[6] Nevertheless, Schlitz's production and market share continued to increase from 22.7 million barrels (15.4% share) in 1974 to 23.3 million (15.5% share) in 1975 and 24.2 million (15.8% share) in 1976. Since taste studies seemed to indicate that only 40 to 50% of beer drinkers could reliably detect the difference between brands, Uihlein's strategic decision to shorten its production process and to switch to cheaper ingredients seemed to be a success.

During the spring of 1976, a number of critical events occurred. Under the direction of a new brewmaster, the Schlitz brand underwent a reformulation. This is a common industry practice and is used to keep up with changing consumer tastes and preferences. The new beer was brewed, packaged, and shipped to various locations. The beer tasted as it should, but when refrigerated, turned cloudy. It had an unappealing appearance when poured into a glass. This was a problem primarily in Southern markets. The change in process had been tested and approved in Milwaukee but failed when applied to the Memphis brewery whose market provided much higher temperatures for the finished product. As a consequence, sales of the Schlitz brand declined rapidly in certain locations despite the fact that Schlitz management acted quickly to replace the cloudy beer. This event, when combined with the overall poorer taste of the Schlitz beer and the heavy competition from Philip Morris' Miller Beer, resulted in falling sales throughout 1976. Lower sales meant a corresponding increase in costs per barrel as Schlitz's many large plants no longer produced at capacity. Fighting to retain share, management discounted the price of the Schlitz brand. In the midst of these events, Robert Uihlein died of leukemia at age sixty. Unfortunately, Robert had failed to groom a strong successor as he had earlier been groomed by Erwin Uihlein. The Uihlein family, who owned from 60 to 70% of the stock, were so divided that they settled on Daniel F. McKeithan, Jr. to take over as chairman of the board. McKeithan, previously married to a Uihlein, was serving at the time as a director of the company. Although his business experience had been in another industry, the family selected him because of their respect for his abilities. McKeithan began the process of searching for a product-oriented president. Meanwhile, sales continued to drop.

In 1977, Frank Sellinger was hired as Schlitz's president. Involved in the beer industry since 1936, Sellinger had run Burger, a Cincinnati-based brewery until 1964, when he took a job at Anheuser-Busch. In his thirteen years at Anheuser-Busch, he had become the company's third-ranking executive (Executive Vice-president of Management and Industry Affairs) with wide operating and financial responsibilities. He found Schlitz to be rife with problems. The entire brewing industry was in shock from the massive advertising campaigns of Miller Beer. Schlitz's former management was chastened by indictments alleging improper payments to distributors to promote Schlitz brands. In addition, constant feuding among the 200-plus descendants of the Uihlein family diverted top executives from more important things. Sellinger was especially concerned with the taste of the product. "Beer drinkers are tradition-bound," he observed. "They don't like tampering with the brew."[7] The use of cheaper ingredients plus a faster brewing process had resulted in a poorer tasting beer. Selling a premium beer at a discount also served to further cheapen Schlitz's image. Ads depicting broad-shouldered types growling at people who tried to get them to switch brands (*Don't take my gusto*) apparently backfired. Schlitz drinkers seemed to feel the company was trying to intimidate them and began switching brands in droves.

Frank Sellinger spent much of 1977 and 1978 working to achieve uniform good quality and taste from each of Schlitz's six breweries. "In the past," said Sellinger, "bad product was often allowed because the plant managers wanted to avoid showing too much variance. Our system was working against us."[8] Sellinger also served as company spokesman in television commercials. "I'm Frank Sellinger," the president would state calmly, as he stood in the midst of a beer hall. "I may be the only man running a major brewery who is a master brewer—have been for over 40 years." The camera then switched to a back lighted foam-capped seidel of beer and the Schlitz logo.

By 1980, product acceptance was confirmed by independent taste tests. With the sale to Anheuser-Busch of its new 5.4 million barrel Syracuse, New York plant, Schlitz earned around $27 million in 1980 compared to a $50.6 million loss in 1979. Frank Sellinger, 66 years old in 1980, was promoted to Vice Chairman and Chief Executive Officer. In early 1980, Jerome E. Vielehr was hired from Coca-Cola to replace Sellinger as president. Vielehr had served at Coke as vice-president of international trade. Even though the company appeared to be past its crisis, stockholders continued to be concerned. Since 1976, various members of the Uihlein family were rumored to have sold over 4 million shares behind recurring takeover rumors that momentarily raised prices.

Through 1981, Schlitz continued to face declining sales. Given Schlitz's extremely large amount of excess capacity, top management felt it had no choice but to close Schlitz's oldest and most inefficient plant—the Milwaukee brewery. With a capacity of 6.8 million barrels, approximately 25% of the company's 25.6 million barrel capacity, the brewery had a net book value of about $24 million. The closing had a heavy emotional impact upon both Schlitz and the city of Milwaukee—a name mentioned heavily in past Schlitz ads. Approximately 700 salaried and hourly workers were laid off.

In November 1981, Jerome Vielehr resigned as both president and director of Schlitz. Frank Sellinger assumed once again the responsibilities of the president's position. He acted quickly to hire Anthony J. Amendola, then 55 years old, as executive vice-president for marketing. Mr. Amendola had served as President and CEO of the Pabst Brewing Company from 1979 to 1980 after working as account executive in charge of the Anheuser-Busch

Exhibit 16.1
SCHLITZ EXECUTIVE OFFICERS AND DIRECTORS

Executive Officers

Name	*Age*	*Position*	*Past Business Experience*
Daniel F. McKeithan, Jr.	46	Chairman	Chairman since 1976, CEO 77–80 Director since 1973
Frank J. Sellinger	67	V. Chairman, Pres. & CEO	Pres. since 77, COO 77–80 Exc. VP at A-B prior two years
Anthony J. Amendola	55	Exec. VP-MKT	Pres., COO, director of Pabst 79–81 Pres. of D'Arcy, MacManus & Masius 70–78
Arthur J. Tonna	55	Exec. VP-Corp. operations	Sen. VP-operations 78–81 Exec. VP-operations for Heileman
James F. Rowe	61	Sen. VP-Subsidiaries	Sen. VP-Material Ser. 74–80
Donald A. Britt	47	VP-Finance	Finance since 77, controller 70–77
Ara A. Cherchian	43	VP-Container Div.	Since Oct. 1974
Daniel T. Coughlin	53	VP-Govt. relations	Since 77, Upjohn govt. affairs director 72–77
Robert L. Crevistion	41	VP-Personnel	Since 79, director of personnel 71–79
Hubert L. Fessler	52	VP-Labor rel.	Since 79, director of labor rel. 75–79
Paul W. Fish	48	VP-Sec. & Gen. counsel	Since Dec. 1980
William J. Hoffman	43	VP-Sales	VP-Morton Frozen Foods 78–81
Raymond D. Mendini	64	VP-Packaging	Since 1974
John A. Rourke	52	VP-Public relations	
Robert N. Wagner	53	VP-Purchasing	
J. Stephen Anderson	41	Treasurer	
Walter R. Hintz	45	Controller	

SOURCE: *10-K Report*, Joseph Schlitz Brewing Company, 1981, p. 21.

account at the St. Louis advertising firm of D'arcy-MacManus & Masius. Sellinger and Amendola knew each other well from the days when Sellinger was with Anheuser-Busch. Amendola replaced Robert A. Rechholz, who resigned as Schlitz's senior vice-president to accept a similar position at Adolph Coors Company. "With these changes . . . Schlitz has one of the best, most seasoned top management teams in the brewing industry," announced Mr. Sellinger in a formal statement to the press.[9] (Refer to Exhibit 16.1 for a listing of the Schlitz executive officers.) Nevertheless, analysts noted that Schlitz's beer shipments in the third quarter of 1981 had dropped 5.9%. This was attributed partially to the intense advertising-fueled competition by Anheuser-Busch and Philip Morris' Miller Brewing Company.

Board of Directors	
Name	*Position*
Daniel F. McKeithan, Jr.	Chairman of the Board of Schlitz
Frank J. Sellinger	Vice-chairman of the Board, CEO, and President of Schlitz
Ross F. Anderson	Retired, Foremen Group President and Director of Federated Department Stores (retailing)
Willie D. Davis	President of Willie Davis Distributing Co. (Schlitz wholesaler)
Alfred V. Elser, Jr.	Manager, IBM Corporation (business equipment)
Weston Howland, Jr.	Chairman of the Board, Warwick Mills, Inc. (textiles)
Frederick W. Patton	President and CEO, Entercom, Inc. (communications)
I. Andrew Rader	Chairman of the Board, Allen-Bradley Co. (industrial controls)
Edwin A. Seipp, Jr.	Investor, Retired, Former President of Speedmaster Engineering Co. (die castings)
Gerald J. Slade	Retired, Former Chairman of the Board and President of Western Publishing Co. (books and games)
Edgar J. Uihlein	Investor
Herman A. Uihlein	Vice-President of Thomson McKinnon Securities, Inc. (stockbrokers)
Charles S. Winston, Jr.	Retired, Former Vice-Chairman of the Board of Foote, Cone, and Belding (advertising)
R. Douglas Ziegler	President and CEO of the Ziegler Co. (chemical recycling)
Henry Uihlein, II	Investor, Honorary Lifetime Director

Board Executive Committee		
Daniel F. McKeithan, Jr.	Frank J. Sellinger	Weston Howland, Jr.
Willie D. Davis	Ross F. Anderson	Edwin A. Seipp, Jr.
I. Andrew Rader		

BEER PRODUCTION AT SCHLITZ

The ingredients in beer, which have remained basically the same over time, include: hops, which gives beer its bitter flavor and its foam clinginess; water; two varieties of barley malt, two-row or six-row; yeasts; and adjuncts, typically corn or rice. Once the ingredients are combined to form first mash and then wort, fermentation occurs. The product is then chill-lagered, carbonated, filtered, packaged, and pasteurized. All product is shipped within twenty days of its production at the brewery. The average time in inventory is two to three days. Only full truck, railcar, or container loads are shipped from the brewery. If packaged beer is not consumed within ninety to one hundred days after packaging, a noticeable degradation in quality takes place.

3 to 3½ months shelf life

Facilities

In early 1982, Schlitz had five breweries operating at around 76% of capacity as compared to only 59% capacity in 1980. The closing of the Milwaukee brewery and the sale of the new Syracuse plant to Anheuser-Busch significantly reduced overhead costs and unnecessary capacity. The Milwaukee plant, in particular, had been a problem for Schlitz management. It could not be modernized since it was spread out in different buildings over a number of city blocks. On the average, beer brewed in the Milwaukee plant cost $3 more per barrel than did beer brewed in any of the remaining five breweries. The five breweries, with a combined capacity of 18.8 million barrels in 1982, are located in Los Angeles, California; Tampa, Florida; Longview, Texas; Winston-Salem, North Carolina; and Memphis, Tennessee. The capacities of these plants interact with location in such a way so as to place the larger breweries in Schlitz's larger markets.

The Schlitz container division operated five can plants in 1982 to supply Schlitz with nearly all of its can and lid requirements. The recent reduction in brewing capacity had resulted in a significant drop in Schlitz demand for its own containers. Consequently, during 1981, the firm sold $68.7 million of cans and lids to non-affiliated third parties. These sales were expected to continue in the near future. Additional supplies Schlitz needs to produce malt beverages, such as cans, bottles, cartons, crowns, and labels, are purchased directly from suppliers under contract, and in the open market. Thus far, according to Schlitz top management, there has been no difficulty in obtaining raw materials or packaging supplies.

Research and Development

Schlitz has always been an industry innovator in packaging. In 1912, Schlitz was the first to use the brown bottle. The brown bottle filtered out the sun's ultraviolet rays, thus protecting the beer from one of its worst enemies, sunlight. Schlitz introduced the first pull-top beer can in 1964. In 1971, Schlitz became the first brewer to self-manufacture two-piece aluminum cans.

The company spent an average of $1.6 million annually in research and development during 1980 and 1981. Schlitz's 1981 *10-K Report* (published March 22, 1982) reported that company personnel are engaged in brewing operations research, concentrating on the improvement of existing products and the development of improved brewing processes and methods. Company research personnel are also employed in the development of new malt beverage products and in the improvement of packaging methods and processes. In addition to a continued concern with quality control, the company also engages in extensive market research projects dealing with consumer buying habits, advertising and merchandising effectiveness, and consumer taste preferences.

PRODUCTS OFFERED BY SCHLITZ

Schlitz's beers are sold both in package and draft form. In the domestic market, the industry's sales in 1981 averaged approximately 87% packaged beer and 13% draft beer. Schlitz's sales pattern is similar to that of the industry. Packaged beer and draft beer are sold by Schlitz in virtually all types and sizes of containers customary in the industry, with Schlitz recognizing higher profits on packaged beer than on draft beer.

The Joseph Schlitz Brewing Company brews six brands of malt beverages—Schlitz premium beer, Schlitz Light beer, Schlitz Malt Liquor, Erlanger super-premium beer, Old Milwaukee beer, and Old Milwaukee Light beer. These products are made available nationally through a network of independent beer wholesalers, who in turn sell them to retail establishments where they are purchased by consumers. Sales for Schlitz products totaled $833 million in 1981, down 4.2% from $870 million in 1980 and 6.5% from $891 million in 1979. The continuing sales decline in Schlitz's flagship brand was offset partially by increases in Old Milwaukee and Schlitz Malt Liquor sales.

Schlitz

Introduced in 1849 with the Schlitz rhomboid as its trademark, the Schlitz brand is a high-quality, two-row barley premium segment beer. It accounted for about 40% of the company's beer sales volume in 1981. This translates into 5.7 million barrels of a total of 14,305 million barrels sold during 1981.

Schlitz has never recovered from the blow dealt to its image from the use of cheaper ingredients during the four-year period from 1974 to 1978. Schlitz's sales have declined by almost 11.9 million barrels since the brand's high water mark of 17.6 million in 1975. This represented 11.9% of the total beer market in 1975. In 1981, however, the Schlitz brand could only manage 3.1% total market share or 5.3% of the premium segment market share. The Schlitz brand is expected to further deteriorate and level off at 5.0 million barrels or 4.4% of the premium segment market share by 1985.[10] This deterioration of the premium Schlitz brand does not follow the overall industry premium growth rate of 1.1%, which is expected to take Budweiser to 55 million barrels or 45.8% of the premium segment market share by 1990 from its present 36.4%. Gary Naifeh, Schlitz associate brand director, suggests that through increased trials by the consumer and a marketing program emphasizing taste and quality, the Schlitz brand should actually increase its sales.

Schlitz Light

Schlitz Light was introduced again in 1982. This is approximately the sixth time that Schlitz Light has been introduced with new formulation and new packaging to fit a particular market niche. Nevertheless, there has been some criticism of the approach being taken. Frank Spinosa, the man credited for the turnaround at Pearls Brewing said, "Schlitz . . . made a mistake by going after Miller Lite drinkers. Rather than trying to expand the market, Schlitz came in with a James Coburn macho commercial to outmacho Miller, but didn't give Miller Lite drinkers any reason to switch from their brand."[11] This explains, in part, the rather disappointing figures for Schlitz Light. Declining from its second place high in 1976 of 13.8% of the light beer market, behind Miller Lite with a 73.8% market share, it has fallen to seventh place with 1.6% of the light beer market. In total beer market terms, Schlitz Light represented a 0.6% market share in 1976 and a 0.2% market share in 1981. Another reason for its decline is its connection with the Schlitz brand.

> The success of Schlitz Light will be tied closely to the parent brand. Both products must work together in establishing consumer acceptance. Our combined investment, innovative tactics, and market concentration will result in a total comeback. When Schlitz gets rolling, Schlitz Light will be on the same track.[12]

Because of this tie, Schlitz Light experienced a 20% market share decline in 1981 and is not expected in the near future to match the projected growth rate of the light beer segment.

Old Milwaukee

"Right now, Old Milwaukee is the number one regional brand in America. That's right, Old Milwaukee is the front runner, and it's going to stay that way," proclaimed Tom Schwalm, Old Milwaukee brand director at the Schlitz 1980 Marketing Conference. Data seem to support this statement. While the national trend for popular priced beer was declining, Old Milwaukee showed an impressive 27.5% gain over 1980, thus capturing 2.8% of the total beer market. This made Old Milwaukee tenth in total consumer expenditures at $531 million. "And if Old Mil was a brewery by itself, it would be the country's ninth largest," bragged Schwalm.[13] Old Milwaukee is Schlitz's second largest selling product.

Old Milwaukee continues to be the only nationally distributed popular-priced beer. "And although Old Milwaukee competes with a host of popular brands across the country, no one competes with Old Mil on a national basis, and that gives us an important edge," added Schwalm.

Old Milwaukee Light

Introduced in August 1980, Old Milwaukee Light began national distribution during 1981. Like Schlitz and Schlitz Light, Old Milwaukee Light was closely tied to its parent brand, Old Milwaukee. It thus did fairly well in 1981, outperforming Schlitz Light by two to one in sales.

> In blind taste tests, we found Old Milwaukee Light was more preferred than either Miller Lite or Anheuser-Busch Natural Light. Since 76% of all low-calorie beer drinkers use taste as their major criteria for brand selection, Old Milwaukee Light has a significant advantage.[14]

Schlitz Malt Liquor

"No one does it like the Bull," says brand advertising. Apparently this is true, since the Bull ranks third in Schlitz's sales volume and first in the malt liquor segment, holding an amazing 40.7% of the segment. "The Bull has one of the strongest images and franchises in our industry, and it's no mistake that we outsell our nearest competitor two to one," reported Gary Truitt, the Schlitz Malt Liquor brand director. Truitt went on to say, "Rest assured that Schlitz Malt Liquor is bigger and better than ever and no other malt liquor can compete. In fact, few beer brands can."[15]

Erlanger

Erlanger, the only domestic all-barley malt beer in national distribution, was test marketed successfully in 1979. After only a few months in test markets, it was introduced into regional markets and soon thereafter was marketed nationally. Even with its relative success in regional markets, Erlanger has not been as successful as John Watson had hoped. Watson, Erlanger brand director, said, "there are a lot of obstacles in our way, a lot of competition we need to dislodge and pass by to get the major share of the market."[16] In 1981, Erlanger held a 3.6% market share in the super-premium category. This was far behind Michelob's 67.9% market share. Other beers in the category were Miller's Löwenbrau (10.7%), Tuborg (6.3%), and Special Export (4.5%).

Other Products

Geyser Peak Winery, a wholly owned subsidiary, produces and sells California premium varietals and table wines. It is the nation's fourth-largest producer of premium wines, marketed under the Geyser Peak and Summit brands. Its sales increased around 75% in 1981 over the previous year. In their February 26, 1982 letter to the Schlitz stockholders, Chairman McKeithan and President Sellinger stated that although "its sales are modest when compared to the total Schlitz sales for the year, the business is profitable. The winery has received wide recognition for its innovative packaging." Geyser Peak is experimenting with the marketing of an aluminum six-pack of Summit Chablis in test markets. Preliminary reports indicate good customer response.

In addition to Geyser Peak Winery, Schlitz owns Murphy Products Company, Inc. The company engages in the production and sale of animal feeds and feed concentrates from brewery grain by-products. These two subsidiaries (including Geyser Peak) accounted for less than 6% of the company's total consolidated net sales for 1981 and operate profitably. Schlitz also has investments in two Spanish breweries, *La Cruz del Campo* and *Henninger Espanola,* which do not contribute significantly to Schlitz's operations.

DISTRIBUTION

In 1981, approximately 99% of Schlitz's beer and malt liquor sales were made through independent wholesalers. The remaining 1% was sold, tax-free, to the U.S. Armed Forces. Throughout this distribution network, which consisted of more than 900 independently owned distributors, no wholesaler handled more than 3% of Schlitz's total sales. In order to achieve this type of distribution, Schlitz employed zone, division and district sales managers to advise and counsel wholesalers. Along with this, Schlitz provided advertising, point-of-sale materials, and promotion programs.

A major problem with Schlitz distributors in recent years has been the declining sales of the Schlitz brand. To counter this, many distributors have been going to a multi-brand house. An example of this was the Schlitz distributorship in Des Moines, Iowa. To complement its existing line of specialty beers (e.g., St. Pauli Girl), it recently bought the Coors distributor. This enabled it to carry two rather than one brand of high-volume beer. This broadening of the distributor's product line was an attempt to gain larger sales volumes than would be possible if it remained a single brand house. This move appears to be common among other beer distributors.

MARKETING

Schlitz provides advertising, point-of-sale merchandising, and promotion programs. All three are provided either free of charge or in cooperation with the wholesalers. Advertising is divided into three parts: print, television, and radio. In 1981, Schlitz spent $33,862,000 on advertising in all three media. This is down significantly from 1980's $44,074,000. Schlitz's figure represented the highest per barrel amount spent by the major brewers and has been so for the last three years. For the industry as a whole, advertising expenditures were $464.8 million in 1981, up $45.2 million from 1980. This breaks down into $426.8 million for broadcast advertising and $38 million for print and outdoor advertising.

Since Schlitz is not able to match Anheuser-Busch and Miller dollar for dollar, Schlitz strives to develop advertising that is more cost effective. A prime example of this is the Schlitz brand's *Great American Beer Taste Test,* which was carried out during the 1982 NFL playoff games. It was considered to be one of the most memorable and widely discussed advertising campaigns ever carried out in the brewing industry.

Advertising programs of Schlitz, like most other brewers, are targeted to a particular marketing group. The most highly targeted group is the young-adult market. The reason given for this by Schlitz is that once a young person picks a beer, he/she is likely to drink that beer for the rest of his/her life. Other reasons for targeting the eighteen- to twenty-four-year-old segment of the market is that these people tend to be trend leaders, accessible, and consume more beer than any other age group.

Merchandising and sales promotion activities are other important aspects of Schlitz's marketing effort. For example, Schlitz reintroduced in 1981 its neon lights for all of its brands. These lights are commonly found in the windows of most bars.

EMPLOYEE RELATIONS

According to the 1981 Schlitz *10-K Report:* "The company believes that, in general, a satisfactory relationship has been maintained with all employees." Schlitz has approximately 1,800 salaried and 3,100 hourly employees. For the most part, all hourly employees are members of labor unions, predominantly the AFL-CIO. There are fifteen labor agreements having varying terms and expiration dates. The average salary of production workers in the brewing industry increased 88.1% between 1970 and 1977, making these workers the highest paid employees in the beverage business. Non-production employee wages rose 72% during the same period. While wages have increased, the number of employees in the brewing industry has dropped 18.2% for production workers and 33.2% for non-production workers. These industry-wide trends characterized Schlitz as well.

On June 1, 1981, after extended efforts at negotiating an acceptable labor agreement, the company was struck by the Local Brewery Workers' Union at its Milwaukee Brewery. There was city-wide bargaining in Milwaukee by the union. Schlitz management did not want to settle for the same contract as Miller and Pabst because of the higher production costs and the relatively low percentage of total Schlitz production at Milwaukee. Schlitz had offered the union no wage increase and wanted the authority to hire summer help at one-half the union wage. The offer was turned down by the union. Schlitz then decided to close the Milwaukee brewery, its oldest and most inefficient plant. The Wisconsin AFL-CIO, in response, boycotted Schlitz's products in Wisconsin. Subsequent to the permanent closing of that brewery, Schlitz entered into settlement agreements with that union and most of the other affected bargaining units.

THE HEILEMAN AND PABST OFFERS

In July 1981, the G. Heileman Brewing Company, a relatively unknown company twenty years ago, made a bid of $494 million to acquire the Jos. Schlitz Brewing Co. The bid by the sixth largest brewer translated into a $17 offer per Schlitz share—40% cash and 60% stock—for the more than 29 million Schlitz shares outstanding. Heileman's current stock price was $31 per share, while Schlitz stocks were selling for only $15.75 per share. One week after the offer was made, the Schlitz board of directors announced its support of Heileman's offer. Although top management of both firms hoped the merger would be completed by October 15, the month of August found them waiting to receive approval from the Justice Department.

In early August 1981, only one week after Schlitz had accepted Heileman's offer of $494 million, the Pabst Brewing Company offered $588 million for Schlitz. This was approximately $20 per share—$200 million in cash with the remaining $388 million in debentures bearing a 15.5% interest rate. These bonds were convertible into Pabst common stock at $27 per share. Pabst executives stated that the move resulted from a fear on their part of having to compete with the company resulting from the Heileman-Schlitz merger. Such a combined company would have far surpassed Pabst as the third-largest brewer. Analysts reported that the idea for a bid for Schlitz was generated by Irwin L. Jacobs, a Minneapolis entrepreneur, after he was elected a director of Pabst one week earlier. Although industry analysts agreed that Pabst and Schlitz were ill-suited for a merger, they also felt that Heileman's offer was too low for Schlitz's plants and the $180 million in cash and marketable securities Schlitz had on its books March 31. Schlitz's top executives were very excited about the offer and commented that they had been somewhat taken by surprise by Pabst's offer.

Shortly after the Pabst offer, the Justice Department objected to the Heileman-Schlitz merger on the basis of antitrust grounds. Application of the Herfindahl Index resulted in an increase in industry concentration of around 128 points. In addition, the Heileman-Schlitz combination would have a market share of between 30 and 50% in some states—a problem of regional dominance. Heileman had no choice but to withdraw its offer. Russell Cleary, Heileman's chairman of the board and president, made the following comments in his letter to the stockholders in Heileman's 1981 Annual Report:

> We do not believe that the Department's opposition to the proposed transaction is in the best interests of the beer consumers of this nation. We believe that competition would have been enhanced by the proposed combination permitting the more effective and efficient utilization of existing industry capacity. Many, if not most, economists support the position that effective competition does not exist in a two-firm dominated industry whereas competition increases significantly through the introduction of a third major competitor.

Cleary further pointed out that the action by the Justice Department frustrated Heileman's move into the South—an area where Schlitz had excess brewing capacity. In order to continue its growth, Cleary stated that Heileman needed southern plants; the cost of building them was prohibitive.

Shortly after the objection by the Justice Department, Pabst stockholders voted against the merger. Irwin Jacobs became so enraged when Pabst withdrew its offer that he resigned his directorship and vowed to gain control of Pabst through a proxy fight to replace the present directors.

FINANCE

With the close of 1981, Schlitz's fortunes appeared to be improving. In a letter to the stockholders dated February 26, 1982, Daniel McKeithan and Frank Sellinger pointed out that the volume of beer sales had only dropped 4.3% in 1981 compared to 11% and 14.2% in 1980 and 1979, respectively.

"While management and our employees are not satisfied with sales progress to date, we are pleased to note that we are approaching the point of sales stabilization." With the sale of the Syracuse plant in 1980 and the closing of the Milwaukee brewery in 1981, the brewing capacity utilization rate improved considerably. Without the one-time charge for the Milwaukee plant closing, Schlitz would have reported net earnings of $24.5 million, or 84 cents a share. (Financial statements are included in Exhibit 16.2.) Schlitz's stock price recovered slightly in 1981 from its low of $5 a share in 1980 (refer to Exhibit 16.3). In summing up their optimism for 1982, McKeithan and Sellinger announced a dividend of 7.5 cents a share, the first since 1979.

Exhibit 16.2

FINANCIAL STATEMENTS OF THE JOSEPH SCHLITZ BREWING COMPANY

(Dollars in Thousands Except Per-Share Data)

Consolidated Balance Sheets

	***Dec. 31* 1981**	***Dec. 31* 1980**
ASSETS		
CURRENT ASSETS:		
Cash	$ 13,601	$ 8,097
Marketable securities	165,069	134,525
Accounts receivable, less reserves of $605 in 1981 and $913 in 1980	21,063	31,049
Receivable from sale of assets (Note 10)	40,000	30,000
Inventories (Note 1)	50,316	54,571
Prepaid expenses	3,488	3,756
Deferred and refundable income taxes	10,432	3,099
Total current assets	303,969	265,097
INVESTMENTS AND OTHER ASSETS:		
Notes receivable and other noncurrent assets (Note 10)	8,631	38,621
Investments	14,639	14,514
Land and equipment held for sale	12,159	6,710
	35,429	59,845
PLANT AND EQUIPMENT AT COST (NOTES 3 AND 10)	577,803	663,176
Less—Accumulated depreciation and unamortized investment tax credit	309,052	346,056
	268,751	317,120
	$608,149	$642,062

SOURCE: *1981 Annual Report,* Joseph Schlitz Brewing Company

(Continued)

Exhibit 16.2 **(*Continued*)**

LIABILITIES		
CURRENT LIABILITIES:		
Accounts payable	$ 39,425	$ 49,960
Accrued liabilities	39,084	39,790
Federal and state income taxes	898	13,383
Current portion of long-term obligations	5,020	793
Total current liabilities	84,427	103,926
LONG-TERM DEBT (NOTE 5)	111,627	119,767
ACCRUED PLANT CLOSING COSTS (NOTE 10)	45,686	—
DEFERRED INCOME TAXES	60,971	92,834
SHAREHOLDERS' INVESTMENT		
Common stock, par value $2.50 per share, authorized 30,000,000 shares, issued 29,373,654 shares	73,434	73,434
Capital in excess of par value	2,489	2,921
Retained earnings	235,204	255,808
	311,127	332,163
Less—Cost of treasury stock; 266,672 shares in 1981 and 310,672 shares in 1980	5,689	6,628
Total shareholders' investment	305,438	325,535
	$608,149	$642,062

Statements of Consolidated Earnings (Loss)

	Dec. 31 **1981**	*Dec. 31* **1980**	*Dec. 31* **1979**
SALES	$1,009,328	$1,027,743	$1,042,583
Less—Excise taxes	127,654	131,076	148,427
Net sales	881,674	896,667	894,156
COST AND EXPENSES:			
Cost of goods sold	718,751	721,278	746,415
Marketing, administrative, and general expenses	143,181	145,304	155,439
	861,932	866,582	901,854
Earnings (loss) from operations	19,742	30,085	(7,698)
OTHER INCOME (EXPENSE):			
Interest and dividend income	29,018	21,796	4,485
Interest expense	(12,223)	(11,508)	(12,784)
Gain on repurchase of debentures	2,671	4,153	1,175
Gain (loss) on disposal of assets and facilities closing (Note 10)	(87,715)	596	(86,076)
Miscellaneous, net	222	734	54
	(68,027)	15,771	(93,146)
Earnings (Loss) Before Income Taxes	(48,285)	45,856	(100,844)
Provision for Income Taxes	(27,681)	18,870	(50,199)
Net Earnings (Loss)	$ (20,604)	$ 26,986	$ (50,645)
Net Earnings (Loss) Per share	$ (.71)	$ .93	$ (1.74)

Exhibit 16.2 **(*Continued*)**

Five-Year Financial Summary

	1981	1980	1979	1978	1977
Sales including Excise Taxes	$1,009,328	$1,027,743	$1,042,583	$1,083,272	$1,134,079
NET SALES	881,674	896,667	894,156	910,841	937,424
Earnings (Loss) from Operations	19,742	30,085	(7,698)	36,048	60,855
Net Earnings (Loss)	(20,604)	26,986	4(50,645)	11,961	19,765
Depr. of Plant & Equipment	32,699	34,445	44,516	45,946	41,127
Working Capital from Operations	45,024	63,307	41,638	68,179	85,423
Capital Expenditures	10,569	9,778	11,426	14,461	35,670
Net Working Capital	219,542	161,171	87,352	40,254	47,694
Current Ratio	3.6/1	2.6/1	1.9/1	1.4/1	1.6/1
Plant & Equipment, Net	268,751	317,120	341,522	526,596	564,620
Long Term Debt	111,627	119,767	131,032	140,362	196,506
L.T. Debt to Total Capital Ratio	26.8%	26.9%	30.5%	28.3%	35.5%
Avg. #Shares Outstanding	29,081	29.063	29,063	29,063	29,063
Per Share Data:					
Net Earnings (Loss)	$ (.71)	$ .93	$ (1.74)	$ .41	$ .68
Dividends	—	—	.20	.47	.68
Shareholders' Investment	10.50	11.20	10.27	12.22	12.27
Barrels of Beer Sold (in thousands)	14,305	14,954	16,804	19,580	22,130
Brewery Capacity in Barrels (in thousands)	18,800	25,600	31,000	31,400	29,500

Notes to Consolidated Financial Statements*

1. *Inventories*

The cost of the company's inventories, calculated on a first-in, first-out basis, was in excess of the last-in, first-out basis by approximately $64,952,000 in 1981 and $63,102,000 in 1980.

Reductions of inventory quantities in 1981, 1980, and 1979 resulted in a liquidation of LIFO inventory quantities carried at costs prevailing in prior years, which were lower than current costs. The effect of these reductions was to increase net earnings by approximately $2,417,000 in 1981, $984,000 in 1980, and $764,000 in 1979.

Inventories used in the determination of cost of goods sold were as follows (in thousands):

December 31	1981	1980	1979
Raw materials and supplies	$33,526	$41,022	$41,103
Work in progress	14,001	9,855	9,315
Finished goods	2,789	3,694	5,073
	$50,316	$54,571	$55,491

The classifications are estimated because the company's LIFO method does not provide for separate determination of LIFO cost of inventory by class.

*Only notes 1, 3, 5, and 10 are included because of their relevance to the case issues.

(*Continued*)

Exhibit 16.2 **(*Continued*)**

3. *Plant and Equipment*

At December 31, 1981 and 1980, plant and equipment included the following major classifications (in thousands):

	1981	1980
Land	$ 7,161	$ 8,754
Buildings	119,656	144,782
Machinery and equipment	404,728	463,516
Cooperage and pallets	42,793	42,977
Construction in progress	3,465	3,147
	577,803	663,176
Accumulated depreciation	(300,634)	(334,431)
Unamortized investment tax credit	(8,418)	(11,625)
	$268,751	$317,120

The provision for depreciation charged to consolidated earnings was $32,699,000 in 1981, $34,445,000 in 1980, and $44,516,000 in 1979, and was calculated using the straight-line method for most of the company's depreciable assets. Lower depreciation expense in 1981 was due to the closing of the Milwaukee brewery and in 1980 was the result of the sale of the Syracuse brewery.

5. *Long-Term Debt*

At December 31, 1981 and 1980, long-term debt was as follows (in thousands):

	1981	1980
Sinking fund debentures 7.2%, due in 1966, with annual sinking fund requirements of $2,500	$ 29,710	$ 31,752
Sinking fund debentures, 9.5%, due in 1999, with annual sinking fund requirements of $3,750	58,937	64,520
Pollution control bonds, 7%, due in 1996, with annual installments of varying amounts ranging from $300 to $800	8,300	8,600
Pollution control bonds, 6.625%, due in 1997, with annual installments beginning in 1983 of varying amounts ranging from $200 to $2,700	14,600	14,600
Other notes payable	80	295
	$111,627	$119,767

The aggregate amounts of long-term debt, which will become due during the respective years, are 1982 (included in "Current Liabilities")—$380,000; 1983—$660,000; 1984—$3,307,000; 1985—$6,560,000; and 1986—$6,950,000. Prepayments of future sinking fund requirements totaled $16,353,000 at December 31, 1981.

Exhibit 16.2 **(*Continued*)**

10. *Gain (Loss) on Disposal of Assets and Facilities Closing*

For the years 1981, 1980, and 1979, the following major items were included in this classification (in thousands):

	1981	1980	1979
Loss on Milwaukee, Wisconsin brewery closing	$(85,000)	$ —	$ —
Loss on sale of Syracuse, New York, brewery	—	—	(74,945)
Loss on other capacity-related dispositions	—	(665)	(10,346)
Other	(2,715)	1,261	(785)
	$(87,715)	$ 596	$(86,076)

During the third quarter of 1981, the company announced the closing of its Milwaukee, Wisconsin brewery. A provision for losses and other expenses related to the plant closing of $85,000,000 ($43,-247,000 after income taxes) was charged to earnings in the third quarter. The earnings charge included a provision for ongoing expenses related to the closing, a write-down of the plant to estimated realizable value, and benefits for employees affected by the closing. Certain of these costs are expected to be payable over an extended period of time. The net present value of future payments is shown in the accompanying consolidated balance sheets as "Accrued Plant Closing Costs."

In addition, during the third quarter of 1981, the company sold C & D Foods, Inc., a subsidiary, and recorded a pretax loss of $2,688,000.

On February 1, 1980, the company sold its Syracuse, New York brewery to Anheuser-Busch, Incorporated, for $100,000,000 payable in three installments over a two-year period. The remaining amount due at December 31, 1981, was $40,000,000 payable January, 1982. The company recorded a loss and associated expenses of $74,945,000 on the sale of the brewery as of the fourth quarter of 1979. The loss and associated expenses were equivalent to $39,550,000 after income taxes.

During the second quarter of 1979, the company recorded a write-off of $8,799,000 relating to excess tankage and brewing facilities that had not been placed in service.

THE STROH BREWING COMPANY

On March 29, 1982, Stroh's began its takeover of Schlitz with an announcement in the *Wall Street Journal.* (Federal securities law requires that a copy of such tenders appear in a national newspaper.) The Stroh Brewing Company, a relatively small, closely held family-owned corporation, had initially proposed a merger with Schlitz in April 1981. Seeing such an acquisition as a case of *the canary swallowing the cat,* Schlitz top management had rejected Stroh's offer of $15.50 a share as not being *economically beneficial.*

The Stroh Brewing Company has brewed beer in Detroit, Michigan, for

SCHLITZ STOCK PRICES
(1972–1981)

Exhibit 16.3

1972		1973		1974		1975		1976	
High	*Low*	*High*	*Low*	*High*	*Low*	*High*	*Low*	*High*	*Low*
63¾	34½	68⅝	49	57½	13¾	30⅛	15½	24	15⅞
1977		**1978**		**1979**		**1980**		**1981**	
High	*Low*	*High*	*Low*	*High*	*Low*	*High*	*Low*	*High*	*Low*
18½	10¾	16¾	9¼	13⅜	7⅞	9⅞	5	16⅞	7⅞

SOURCE: *The Beer Industry* by Beer Marketer's INSIGHTS, 1982, p. 78.

132 years as a small, conservative corporation. Headed by Peter Stroh, the fourth generation Stroh to hold the president's position, the firm ranked seventh in 1982 in sales in the industry with a market share of 5%. Given the geographic limitation inherent in marketing from a single brewery in Detroit, Stroh Brewing acquired the F&M Schaefer Company in 1981 as part of its strategy of going national. In this acquisition, Stroh obtained Schaefer's new 5 million barrel plant in Allentown, Pennsylvania plus Schaefer's existing sales base and eastern distribution system.

Emphasizing that its fire-brewed beer was of better quality than the more typical steam-brewed beer, Stroh has been attempting to move beyond its traditional Great Lakes area market. As Stroh Bohemian beer enters a new market, it is automatically priced as a premium beer and advertised as the kind of beer people hide in their suitcases to take home. In distant markets, some consider it *the Coors of the East.* To help offset the expense of national advertising, Stroh has joined with other regionals to cooperatively purchase television time. "We found ourselves sharing with Coors certain national sporting events and from our point of view, it has worked very well," says Peter Stroh.[17] The Mississippi River divides Coors from Stroh.

Other products of Stroh Brewing are its popular-priced brands of Goebel (purchased in 1964) plus Piels and Schaefer (purchased in 1981). It also markets Stroh Light and Schaefer Light beers. Expecting that the growth segments of the 1980s and beyond will be lights, imports, and superpremiums, Stroh is introducing its superpremium beer, Signature, in May 1982 in test markets. In addition to beer, the company has an ice cream division and a recently completed can plant in Fremont, Ohio which can produce 1.2 million cans annually.

Industry analysts have mixed feelings about Stroh's future. One glowingly reports that of all the regionals Stroh has one of the best chances of going national, especially with the acquisition of Schaefer and with its ability to bring in market experts from the consumer packaging field yet retain a devotion to quality. Another points to Stroh's inability to digest its Schaefer acquisition. Stroh paid $23 million for Schaefer and has since invested another $30 million to expand the brewery and convert it to fire-brewing. Nevertheless, the Schaefer brand market share increased its usual 15% annual decline to 18% in 1981 with a corresponding loss in Schaefer's operating earnings. Another analyst points out Stroh's debt to capitalization ratio as being "an uncomfortable 47%."[18]

In order to put together its bid for Schlitz, Stroh arranged $340 million in bank loans. Stroh's top management concluded earlier that the acquisition of Schlitz by any of the second-tier brewers, such as Heileman, Pabst, and Coors, would be opposed by the Justice Department. They also assumed that the Justice Department would allow mergers of second-tier beer companies with third-tier firms, such as Olympia, Schmidt, Genesee, or Stroh, since this would yield the greatest number of competitors. The increase in the Herfindahl Index resulting from a Stroh-Schlitz merger would be a borderline case given 1980 figures. The largest overlap in regional markets would be in West Virginia, where the combined firm would control 25% of beer consumption.

THE DECISION

As Daniel McKeithan, Chairman of the Board of Schlitz, prepared to go into the office on Monday, March 29, 1982, he looked forward to the board meeting he had called quickly to discuss the Stroh offer. Is this merger the right move for Schlitz? If so, can the price be raised? Should Schlitz fight the offer and look for other more suitable merger partners? Should Schlitz continue to go it alone now that the worst seems to be over? What will the Justice Department do? To complicate things further, the latest rumors indicate that C. Schmidt and Son, the Philadelphia brewer, is bidding $167.8 million to acquire Pabst at the same time as Pabst is itself bidding $7.8 million for Pittsburgh Brewing, a small, but profitable firm. The U.S. beer industry seemed to be at a pivotal point in its history. Aside from Anheuser-Busch and Miller Brewing, the future of most brewers looked very shaky, indeed.

NOTES

1. This conversation was fabricated by the senior author from information reported in several news articles.
2. *Schlitz College Rep Network Handbook,* 1981, p. A2.
3. "Gussie Busch's Bitter Brew," *Forbes,* June 1, 1974, p. 22.
4. *Ibid.,* p. 23.
5. *Ibid.,* p. 24.

6. *Ibid.*

7. S. Ginsberg, "Is the Gusto Gone Forever?" *Forbes,* December 8, 1980, p. 35.

8. *Ibid.*

9. T. L. Lueck and D. P. Garino, "Joseph Schlitz's Vielehr Quits as President and Ex-Pabst Officer Gets Marketing Slot," *Wall Street Journal,* November 24, 1981.

10. *The Impact: American Beer Market Review and Forecast,* New York: M. Shanken Communications, Inc., 1982, p. 53.

11. T. Bayer, "Beer Exec Sees Light Growth," *Advertising Age,* July 6, 1981, p. 36.

12. J. Remitz (Schlitz Group Marketing Director), *Schlitz College Rep Network Handbook,* 1981.

13. T. Schwalm, *Schlitz College Rep Network Handbook,* 1981.

14. *Ibid.*

15. G. Truitt, *Schlitz College Rep Network Handbook,* 1981.

16. J. Watson, *Schlitz College Rep Network Handbook,* 1981.

17. G. Sutter, "Stroh Stokes the Fires of Expansion," *Advertising Age,* March 29, 1982, p. M-43.

18. "Stroh's Gamble in Swallowing Schlitz," *Business Week,* April 26, 1982, p. 31.

Case 17

THE ADOLPH COORS COMPANY

Sexton Adams / Adelaide Griffin

A cloud casts a shadow over Clear Creek Valley as Peter H. Coors, President of Administration, Sales and Marketing for the Adolph Coors Company gazes out his office window at Golden, Colorado. Mr. Coors has just returned from a meeting with the other members of the Board of Directors where they once again discussed their goal to become a national brewer. Their goal, they feel, is necessary for the firm to sustain long-term profitability.

COMPANY HISTORY

Adolph Herman Joseph Coors arrived on the coast of Baltimore, Maryland in 1868 as a stowaway at the age of 21. Coors's ultimate ambition was to open his own brewery. After serving an apprenticeship to a brewery in his native Germany and as a foreman at a U.S. brewery, Coors moved west to Colorado.

A year later, he and another businessman converted an old tannery into a brewery in the Clear Creek Valley of Golden, Colorado. In 1880, after a strong success, young Adolph bought out his partner in the Golden Brewery and renamed it the Coors Golden Brewery.

The company flourished until 1916, when Colorado voted in favor of Prohibition. Coors had to stop brewing even before the nation followed suit in 1920. Coors dumped 17,000 gallons of beer into Clear Creek, and soon after began producing a near-beer called Mannah. It was produced like their regular beer, except that the alcohol was condensed out of the product and then sold to hospitals and drug companies.

This case was prepared by Frank Reilly, Marilyn Kasko, Mark Sommer, David Kuehn, Robin Moss, Randall Green, and Tim Gottsacker under the supervision of Prof. Sexton Adams, North Texas State University and Prof. Adelaide Griffin, Texas Woman's University. Reprinted by permission.

Coors also sold malted milk, cream, butter, and buttermilk. The company also heavily relied upon the Coors Porcelain Company, which is still a major subsidiary of the firm. In 1933, when Prohibition was lifted, the Coors Brewery began producing beer. Between that time and 1965, Coors grew steadily, becoming the nation's twelfth largest brewer.

Between 1965 and 1969, Coors sales soared, and Coors became the fourth largest brewer, a position it held until 1976. Prior to 1976, Coors was the marvel of the industry, growing by leaps and bounds, gathering up a larger market share and spending little on promotion. For instance, in 1974, Coors was spending an incredibly low $807,000 in advertising, while competitors such as Anheuser-Busch (A-B) were spending as much as $18 million per year. The rapid growth with little promotion became known as the "Coors Mystique." In fact, prior to 1977, Coors could not keep up with the demand, and actually had to ration its sales.

In 1975, Philip Morris radically changed the marketing strategy of brewers after its newly acquired Miller Brewing Company introduced Miller "Lite." Lite met overwhelming consumer acceptance and was soon marketed nationally by late 1976 (see Exhibit 17.1).

Lite was promoted through clever television ads and a very expensive advertising campaign. At the same time, Miller "High Life" was also being strongly promoted. The extensive use of media vaulted Miller from being the seventh largest brewer into second place by 1979.

In 1979, Coors sidestepped tradition and introduced "Coors Light" in order to compete with Miller, Anheuser-Busch, and Schlitz, which had all introduced light beers. Even though Coors's regular beer had been considered to be a light beer and had been sold as "America's Fine Light Beer," it was losing popularity. Coors decided to introduce its light beer and change its current "Coors Banquet" to "Coors Premium." The addition to its product line and an increase in spot television and radio ads helped to increase sales for the year.

In 1980, super premium beers were beginning to gain in importance in the industry. Coors counteracted and introduced "Herman Joseph's 1868," a super premium named in tribute to the company's founder, Adolph Herman Joseph Coors.

In 1981, however, sales declined to 13.2 million barrels (see Exhibit 17.2) and Coors, in an attempt to counteract the increasing sales of imported beer, obtained a license from Pelforth Brewery of Lille, France and G. H. Lett and Company of Wexford, Ireland to brew and distribute another super premium, "George Killian's Irish Red." Red Killian's is being sold in several test market areas, such as Denver and Dallas. Killian's is the company's first non-Coors label.

COORS COMPETITORS' PRODUCT LINES

Exhibit 17.1

Anheuser-Busch	***G. Heileman***
Budweiser	Blatz
Budweiser Light	Ranier
Michelob	Colt 45
Michelob Light	Carling Black Label
A-B Natural Light	Schmidt
Classic Draft	Old Style
Busch (an export)	Special Export
Wurzburger (an import)	Mickey's Malt Liquor
	Beck's
Miller Brewing Company	***Pabst***
Miller High Life	Pabst Blue Ribbon
Miller Lite	Pabst Extra Light
Lowenbrau	Andeker Red, White and Blue
	Olde English Malt Liquor
	Henry Weinhard's Private Reserve
Stroh Brewing Company	***Olympia***
Schlitz	Olympia
Schlitz Light	Hamms
Schlitz Malt Liquor	Lone Star
Stroh	Lone Star Light
Schaeffer	Blackhorn
	Grenzquell (an import)

SOURCE: *Value Line Investment Survey.*

COMPETITION

The brewing industry has been in an upheaval with a growing number of acquisitions in the late 1970s and early 1980s. For instance, Stroh, the seventh largest brewer in 1981, merged with Joseph Schlitz, the number-three brewer. This merger put Stroh in a strong third place behind Anheuser-Busch and Miller. (31, 1558).

A-B has signed a definitive merger with Campbell-Taggart, the nation's second largest bakery goods producer (which bakes such brands as *Rainbow, Manor* and *Earth Grains*). Olympia and Pabst are in negotiations. Pabst is attempting to purchase the remaining 51% of Olympia's stock.

Exhibit 17.2

NUMBER OF BARRELS SOLD, ADOLPH COORS COMPANY

Year	*Number*	*% Change*
1981	13,201,000	− 3.76
1980	13,779,000	+ 6.52
1979	12,912,000	+ 2.38
1978	12,566,000	− 1.56
1977	12,824,000	− 5.88
1976	13,545,000	+16.24
1975	11,860,000	—
1970	7,300,000	—

Olympia and G. Heileman had, in the past, made industry history by purchasing small, regional brewers in poor shape at bargain prices and turning them around. They would reorganize the firms and greatly boost advertising expenditures to promote the products. Sales for both firms, however, have slackened.

The brewers have not been able to freely merge without encountering anti-trust allegations by the U.S. Justice Department. G. Heileman, the nation's fourth largest brewer, attempted to take over Schlitz, but the Justice Department intervened and halted the deal. Next, Heileman attempted to purchase Pabst and the government turned them down.

Heileman then arranged a deal with an investor group led by Irwin Jacobs, a major Pabst stockholder, whereby Jacobs's group would gain control of Pabst and then sell two of the company's breweries to Heileman. The Justice Department again intervened and the pact was off.

The Justice Department is also requiring Stroh to sell one of Schlitz' New England breweries in order to prevent Stroh from having too much of the market share there. Neither A-B nor Miller can purchase the brewery.

Coors has rejected at least two merger proposals in the past with unknown brewers, but with declining sales and profits, the Coors family has not ruled out an acquisition. William Coors, Chairman of the Board, surprised many long-time Coors observers by stating at the 1982 annual meeting that any merger proposal "has got to be considered." (11, 50). His nephew, Peter Coors, President of Administration, Sales and Marketing, echoed this by saying "we don't think we can brew Coors beer in anybody else's brewery, but there could be overriding reasons why it would make sense to merge." (2, 54).

Earlier, in 1973, Philip Morris, the leading cigarette producer, took over Miller Brewing Company, increasing the financial resources available for Miller by a large amount. Philip Morris indeed did use its resources to rejuvenate Miller, which soon became the number two brewer in the United States, a position which it has held since 1977.

In doing so, Philip Morris introduced the brewing industry to techniques not used there before, such as product and package segmentation, targeting audiences, and new product distribution methods.

Both Miller and A-B have greatly increased their market shares within the past five years (see Exhibit 17.3) from a combined total of 38% in 1977 to 52.7% in 1981.

COMPETITORS' GOALS

Anheuser-Busch

A-B, the largest brewer already with over 30% of the market share, has its sights upon reaching 40% of the total market by 1990. A-B has a very broad product line which includes the world's best selling beer, "Budweiser," which is 70% of the total barrels sold. A-B has also recently introduced "Budweiser Light" to compete with Miller "Lite," and it has done exceptionally well.

Industry analyst Emanuel Goldman of Sanford C. Bernstein and Company (a New York investment firm) noted that this new addition can intensify the market share erosion which plagues many other brewers. "In recent

Exhibit 17.3

THE CONCENTRATION OF THE BEER INDUSTRY, 1977–1981

Brewer	1977	*Rank & Market Share*	1981	*Rank & Market Share*
Anheuser-Busch	1	23.0%	1	30.3%
Miller	2	15.2%	2	22.4%
Joseph Schlitz	3	13.9%	3	7.9%
G. Heileman	7	3.9%	4	7.8%*
Pabst	4	10.1%	5	7.5%**
Adolph Coors	5	8.0%	6	7.4%
Stroh	8	5.0%	7	5.0%***
Olympia	6	3.2%	8	3.2%
Other	—	17.8%	—	8.5%

SOURCE: "Anheuser-Busch: The King Still Rules," *Business Week*, July 12, 1982, p. 51.

* Includes acquisition of Falls City, Carling National, and Ranier.
** Includes acquisition of Blitz-Weinhard Company.
*** Includes acquisition of F & M Schaeffer and Company.

years, the squeeze on other brewers' volume has come mainly from Budweiser and Miller Lite. Now there's a third brand to intensify the squeeze." (13, 16; 4).

A-B recently introduced "Budweiser" to Canada by special license to John LaBatt, Ltd., and within a year it became the fifth largest selling beer. Budweiser has also been introduced to France and Japan with success. "Busch," one of A-B's exports, failed in Germany, but is now sold nationally in France.

A-B began national distribution of its Eagle Snacks in June and has entered the "wine on tap" business with LaMott Winery of California, a subsidiary of John LaBatt, Ltd. Other side businesses are its Metal Container Company, which produces 40% of its needs, Busch Entertainment, owner of several theme parks, ownership of the St. Louis Cardinals Baseball Team and Busch Stadium.

With the financial strength of A-B, they will likely continue to reach their goal of 40% market share of beer as well as to continue to be very profitable. Says Peter H. Coors, Senior Vice-President of Sales and Marketing for the Adolph Coors Company, "with all the money Anheuser has, there is almost nothing it can't do." He further adds, "if they need to sell capacity, they will do it, forcing the rest of us to cut prices when margins are already low." (2, 50). This could be true for Miller, too.

A-B just recently tripled its Los Angeles brewery's capacity and is planning to increase capacity at its Houston plant by five million barrels, as well as complete a plant in New Jersey in 1983. All of these expansions (about $2 billion worth) will expand A-B's capacity to over 70 million barrels per year, a 22% increase over its current capacity of about 56 million barrels. (12, 32).

Miller Brewing Company

Miller Brewing Company, a wholly owned subsidiary of tobacco producer Philip Morris Company, the second largest brewer, has changed its pricing strategy to being a price lagger, delaying price increases by about three months after A-B, in order to increase its market share. Miller produces its premium "High Life" (about 60% of total sales), "Lite" (about 32% of total sales), and "Löwenbrau" (about 8% of all shipments).

"Lite" is the beer which gave Miller its boost from the number seven position to the number two slot within two years of production. Of the three million barrels of increased beer sales over the past year, "Lite" accounted for 2.9 million barrels. "Lite" holds a 60% market share of all of the light beers.

Philip Morris, Miller's parent company (Miller contributes about 26.1%

of the total revenues), is a very financially strong company, much larger overall than A-B and any other competitors. It is financially sound and is diversified into cigarettes (such as Marlboro, Benson & Hedges, Parliament and Merit), soft drinks, and real estate.

Both Miller and A-B are expected by industry experts to continue to hold their own nationally and begin to attack the regional brewers such as Coors, Heileman and Olympia.

Stroh Brewing Company

Stroh, which in June 1982 acquired Schlitz, thereby becoming the third largest brewer, is in the process of rebuilding Schlitz. Most of Schlitz' high level managers, including "Master Brewer" Frank Sellinger, have been replaced by Stroh officials. Peter Coors asked "How do two weak sisters make a strong match? Unless there is something on the order of miracles, I don't see this trend as a positive alternative for failing breweries." (2, 54).

G. Heileman Brewing Company

G. Heileman Brewing Company, the fourth largest brewing company in the United States, grew by 11.8% last year, jumping ahead of Coors, now the sixth largest brewer and Pabst, now the fifth largest brewer. Heileman, which grew mostly by takeover bids during the 1970s, has lost out on recent takeover bids of Schlitz and Pabst due to anti-trust problems. It seems that Heileman is too large to acquire any major brewer but must find some smaller ones in order to increase its market share; however, there are few to choose from, according to a recent *Value Line Report.* (31, 1558).

Heileman is doing quite well aside from the anti-trust problems, being one of only three major brewers to gain in volume sales in 1981. (See Exhibit 17.4.) The company is also diversified into metal parts production and bakeries.

Exhibit 17.4

1981 BREWERS' SHIPMENTS
(Millions of Barrels)

Brewer	Shipments
Anheuser-Busch	54.5
Adolph Coors	13.3
G. Heileman	14.0
Olympia	5.7
Pabst	13.5
Miller	41.0
Stroh/Schlitz	24.0

SOURCE: *Value Line Investment Survey.*

Pabst and Olympia Brewing Companies

Currently, Pabst and Olympia, which appear to be all but merged, seem to pose no serious threat of expansion as both are weak. Sales for both firms have dropped as A-B, Miller, and Heileman have gained ground, especially in the demand for their "flagship" brands. Brewing is the only business for both of these firms.

THE INDUSTRY OUTLOOK

Grain costs, at least in the short run, have been lower. Brewer's malt, sugar and hops have all decreased in cost from their highs in late 1980 and 1981, saving the industry at least $200 million in raw materials costs from 1981.

Beer sales have steadily increased over the past years at a rate of about 2.8% per year, and though steady, they are down from the 5% annual growth in the early 1970s. A reason for this decline is the aging of the prime 18–34 year old market, as well as a reversal of some state laws allowing 18 year olds to drink. The trend of slower growth in the 18–34 year old bracket will probably continue for at least ten years as estimated by *The Sales and Marketing Management's 1982 Survey of Buying Power.* (9, A-7).

The greatest growth of population is concentrated in the West, Southwest, and the South, in that order. Texas is considered to be the fastest growing beer market. Growth in the Midwest is non-existent, and in New England, only minimal. (See Exhibit 17.5.)

COORS'S DISTRIBUTION

Coors currently distributes in some twenty states, most of them being located west of the Mississippi, with the exception of Tennessee. Coors announced in October 1982 that it intends to expand distribution to several more eastern states in 1983. How many states and exactly which ones have not been announced. (1). Coors owns seven of its distributorships, and the remaining 259 are privately owned. Coors's products are, by necessity, shipped to distributors in refrigerated trucks and railcars.

Previously, people would often spend thousands of dollars on proposals for receiving distributorships. Coors would be very particular as to whom they would allow to be their distributors. People such as former Astronaut Charles Duke, the tenth man to walk on the moon, and former athletes were given distributorships. Even former Vice-President Spiro Agnew sought a distributorship.

During the mid-1970s, Coors became so popular, the firm had to ration its beer to keep up with demand. The Coors mystique had enchanted many people in the eastern portion of the United States where Coors was not distributed. Many people tried to "bootleg" the beer there by secretly transporting it across state lines. Coors was concerned about the quality of the product, as it was not being kept cold, so they ran ads asking people "not to buy Coors." (30, 14; 3).

Exhibit 17.5
1981 TOTAL SALES AND MARKET SHARES BY REGIONS

			New England				
		Change–12 months		*Past*		*Market Share*	
	Total			*6 Month*	*Change*	*12 Months*	
Brand	*Barrels*	*Barrels*	*PCT*	*Barrels*	*PCT*	*Last*	*Previous*
A-B	2,881,576	229,815	8.6	147,142	11.0	36.0	32.9
Miller	2,757,987	− 94,539	− 3.3	− 57,626	− 3.8	34.4	35.4
Schlitz	586,079	− 53,965	− 8.4	− 22,875	− 7.6	7.3	7.9
Pabst	206,163	− 31,835	−13.3	− 12,300	−10.7	2.6	3.0
All others	1,583,378	− 97,671	− 5.8	−100,446	−11.2	19.8	20.8
			Southeast and South Central				
		Change–12 months		*Past*		*Market Share*	
	Total			*6 Month*	*Change*	*12 Months*	
Brand	*Barrels*	*Barrels*	*PCT*	*Barrels*	*PCT*	*Last*	*Previous*
A-B	8,642,013	441,814	5.3	203,079	4.9	39.5	38.6
Miller	6,367,163	62,543	0.9	− 11,397	− 0.3	29.1	29.7
Schlitz	2,794,088	− 91,069	− 3.1	− 93,070	− 6.6	12.8	13.6
Pabst	1,124,495	−398,401	−26.1	−220,281	−31.4	5.1	7.2
Coors	336,964	336,964	0.0	206,782	0.0	1.5	0.0
All others	2,604,210	298,201	12.9	106,294	8.7	11.9	10.9
			Mountain				
		Change–12 months		*Past*		*Market Share*	
	Total			*6 Month*	*Change*	*12 Months*	
Brand	*Barrels*	*Barrels*	*PCT*	*Barrels*	*PCT*	*Last*	*Previous*
A-B	3,469,235	307,672	9.7	163,726	10.3	32.7	31.7
Miller	1,897,968	403,189	26.9	148,657	19.4	17.9	15.0
Schlitz	754,951	57,700	8.2	11,539	3.3	7.1	7.0
Pabst	243,389	18,349	8.1	15,417	13.8	2.3	2.3
Coors	2,858,027	−142,937	− 4.7	− 50,139	− 3.4	26.9	30.1
All others	1,401,104	13,880	1.0	− 27,681	− 4.0	13.2	13.9
			W. South Central				
		Change–12 months		*Past*		*Market Share*	
	Total			*6 Month*	*Change*	*12 Months*	
Brand	*Barrels*	*Barrels*	*PCT*	*Barrels*	*PCT*	*Last*	*Previous*
A-B	5,660,283	1,133,327	25.0	635,682	27.9	25.8	22.4
Miller	6,055,582	1,261,892	26.3	614,096	24.4	27.6	23.7
Schlitz	3,219,542	−362,600	−10.1	−167,930	−10.1	14.7	17.7
Pabst	302,227	− 24,287	− 7.4	− 27,241	−15.9	1.4	1.6
Coors	4,473,489	−114,656	− 2.4	− 33,640	− 1.5	20.4	22.7
All others	2,239,260	−128,166	− 5.4	−125,946	−10.4	10.2	11.7

(Continued)

Exhibit 17.5 **(Continued)**

E. North Central

Brand	Total Barrels	Change–12 months Barrels	Change–12 months PCT	Past 6 Month Barrels	Change PCT	Market Share 12 Months Last	Market Share 12 Months Previous
A-B	3,782,936	– 76,357	– 1.9	– 25,359	– 1.2	16.1	16.4
Miller	6,311,517	457,024	7.8	227,887	7.7	26.8	24.9
Schlitz	967,636	3,462	0.3	29,950	6.4	4.1	4.1
Pabst	4,090,460	–562,566	–12.0	–235,649	–10.5	17.4	19.8
Heileman	3,571,585	133,276	3.8	11,160	0.6	15.2	14.6
All others	4,824,314	44,634	0.9	– 22,218	– 0.8	20.5	20.3

W. North Central

Brand	Total Barrels	Change–12 months Barrels	Change–12 months PCT	Past 6 Month Barrels	Change PCT	Market Share 12 Months Last	Market Share 12 Months Previous
A-B	3,531,951	276,190	8.4	138,156	8.5	25.8	24.1
Miller	2,559,403	184,047	7.7	114,169	10.2	18.7	17.6
Schlitz	1,177,461	87,845	8.0	21,539	4.1	8.6	8.1
Pabst	1,771,727	–226,108	–11.3	–118,674	–12.2	13.0	14.8
Coors	1,458,548	–149,898	– 9.3	– 60,072	– 7.9	10.7	11.9
All others	3,170,563	– 37,180	– 1.1	–135,096	– 8.3	23.2	23.7

SOURCE: *Beer Statistics News,* "The December Report," March 1982, Copyright 1982, Beer Marketer's Insights, Inc. Reprinted with permission of the publisher.

They also took legal actions against distributors who sold the beer outside of their territorial market, claiming that the product's quality was being jeopardized. (30, 14; 3).

In 1982, with the declining sales of Coors's products, the distributorships are not in as high demand as they were previously. One-fifth of the independent franchises changed hands in the 1980s. More than half have expanded and are selling other beers or wine, whereas, in the 1970s, at least two-thirds exclusively wholesaled Coors. (10, 1; 1).

Coors requires their product to be continuously refrigerated until it reaches the retail level. This requires that distributors buy the expensive refrigerated trucks and keep the warehouses refrigerated as well. It is reported that A-B is now asking its distributors to keep their warehouses refrigerated, and other companies are expected to do so later. (10, 10; 2).

The wholesalers are also responsible for point of sale advertising which includes convincing establishments to use Coors's mementos, such as lights, ashtrays, neon signs, and other such items. They are responsible for local media advertising, merchandising, customer relations, and the placement of

Coors's products in stores and other establishments to insure best product exposure.

All of Coors's beer is brewed at its Golden, Colorado plant—the world's largest—using the natural spring water from Clear Creek. The plant has a current capacity of about 15 million barrels per year, and with expansions, can go to about 25 million barrels before reaching the limit for water, according to company information.

Coors now owns 2,100 acres near Elkton, Virginia for a potential second brewery. The site satisfies the needs of water availability and quality, fuel sources and transportation. As of late 1982, no decision has been made to begin construction.

The current brewery site can cost-effectively meet demands for the West, but industry sources say that if Coors intends to go national with its product it will have to have a brewery in the East, not only to supply the volume necessary, but also to keep transportation costs from the brewery to the retail outlet from being too prohibitive.

However, according to the *Wall Street Journal*, a "competitor" says that by moving into the East, Coors may be "walking into a hornet's nest when its own backyard isn't in order," due to price cutting techniques often used in that market. (14, 29; 4).

Coors will, if they decide to open a brewery there, have no governmental difficulties, as local officials are now welcoming them. They have also received acceptance by the Environmental Protection Agency. (15, 4; 4). If the site is used, Coors would have to drop its slogan "Brewed with Pure Rocky Mountain Spring Water."

THE PRODUCTION OF COORS

All of Coors's beer products are produced in a manner which does not require pasteurization of the product (see Exhibit 17.6). This produces a pure beer, without any preservatives or unnatural ingredients. The elimination of the pasteurization also greatly reduces the amount of energy (by 50% according to Coors) necessary to brew the product.

As mentioned earlier, the Coors Company requires that the beer be kept refrigerated from the time that it is brewed until it is sold at the retail level in order to ensure freshness and the quality of the product. According to one report, the cost of each refrigerated truck to distributors is $80,000. (10, 10). Any beer that stays in the refrigerated warehouses more than sixty days is destroyed.

Coors beer has one of the longest brewing processes in the brewing industry, taking an average of sixty-eight days to brew and package. There are six major functions in the production of Coors: malting, brewing, fermenting, aging, finishing, and packaging.

The malting process involves steeping ground barley in the famous

Exhibit 17.6

THE BREWING OF COORS BEER

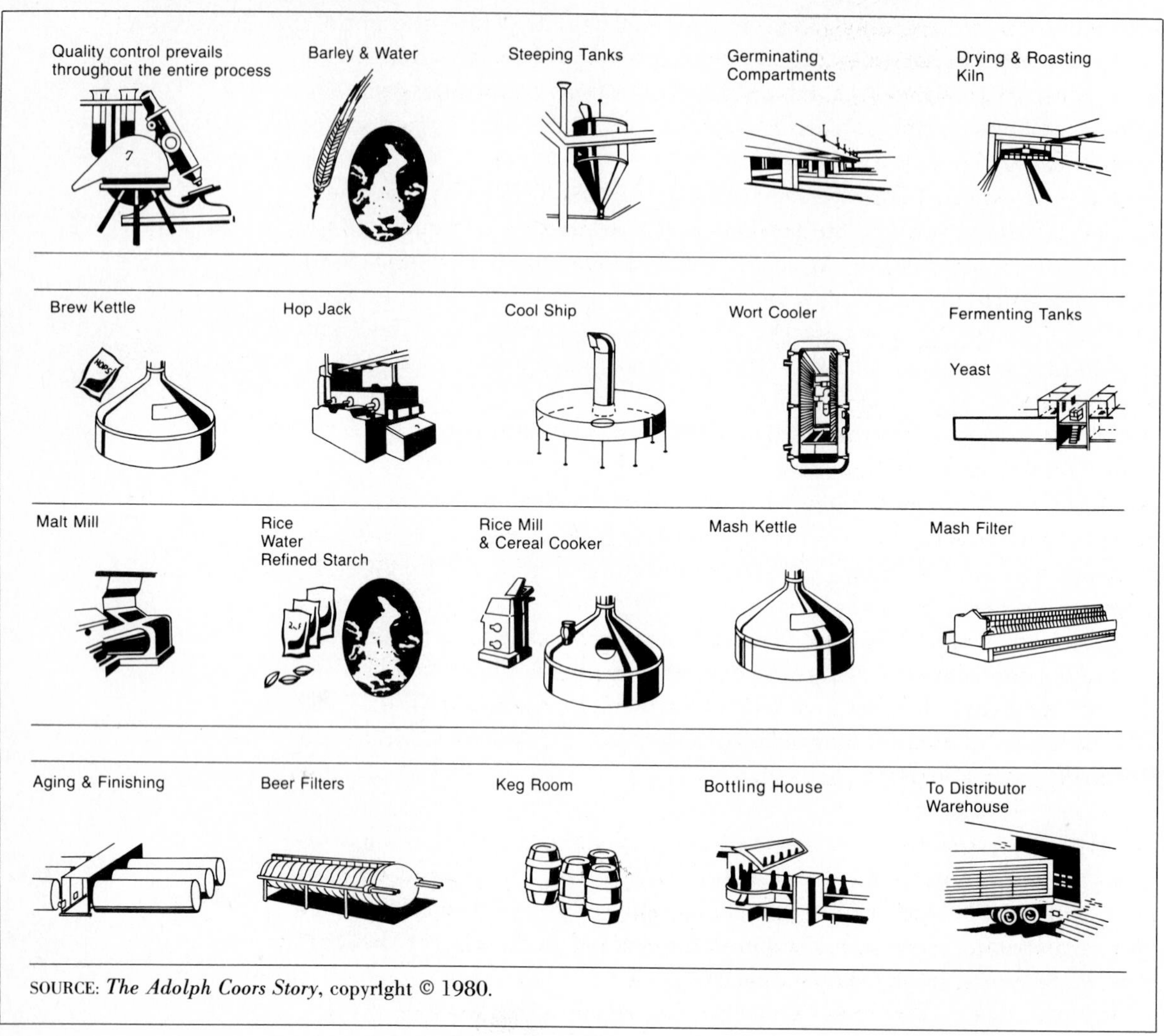

SOURCE: *The Adolph Coors Story*, copyright © 1980.

"Pure Rocky Mountain Spring Water," then allowing it to germinate under carefully controlled conditions, which convert the starch in the barley into a soluble form. The barley is then put into malt kilns, which dry and roast the substance into malt. Coors has continued to attempt to produce better barley strains and has at least one full-time scientist employed at this position.

Coors then grinds the product and mixes it with premium brewers rice, refined starch and spring water in mash kettles. The mash is then converted into fermentable sugars, which are then filtered. Hops are added and the mixture is boiled and purified and then cooled so that the fermenting process can begin after the addition of yeast.

Once complete, the beer is aged for forty-five days under pressure so that it can build up its own natural carbonation. After it is aged, the finishing process is begun by cooling the beer to near freezing where it then achieves the proper alcohol level.

Coors is then packaged into sterile cans and bottles, which are produced by Coors. Flavor tests and other evaluations are made routinely at this stage. Coors became the first brewer to use aluminum cans in 1959, and now besides using its cans for internal use, the company also sells them to other members of the beverage industry.

SUBSIDIARIES

As noted above, Coors produces its own cans, and 90% of its own bottles. This is done through its subsidiary, the Coors Container Company. It expected, in 1979, to sell over a billion cans to outside users in 1979 and 1980. The division currently employs over 2,500 people, and is the world's largest single-site aluminum can manufacturer. It has recently developed a "reverse vending machine" that returns money to people as they insert aluminum cans into it. A division of this subsidiary, the Coors Paper Packaging Division, produces most of the paper products necessary for the brewery.

Another subsidiary, the Coors Energy Company, produces over 90% of Coors's energy needs operating in leaseholds of about 180,000 acres. The firm participated in the drilling of thirty-one wells in 1981, mostly in the Piceance Basin in Colorado. Developed reserves as of 1981 were 29 billion cubic feet of natural gas.

Coors Energy Company also operates the Keenesburg Coal Mine near Denver, which produces coal for the brewery. The mine supplies a majority of the coal needed and it is expected to produce 300,000 tons of coal this year. The mine is expected to meet needs for the next twenty years. Coors expects to continue expansion of its energy company in 1982.

The Coors Food Products Company achieved record sales levels in 1981. This subsidiary operates rice mills in Arkansas and California, with the Arkansas sales increasing 23% over last year.

Research and development efforts have focused on products made from brewery by-products. The firm has developed Brewers Grain 28, a high-protein, high-fiber product with numerous commercial uses. They have also been working on "Coors Cocomost," a cocoa powder replacement made from brewer's yeast. They plan to build a yeast processing plant this year.

Coors's other major subsidiary, the Coors Porcelain Company, which, according to management, helped the firm survive Prohibition, is in a strong position to compete in a worldwide electronic ceramics market. Economic conditions have been weak, but once the economy improves, as Coors's officials hope, the business should boom. The subsidiary is constantly developing new products and improving old ones. For instance, Coors recently developed a new material for dental crowns out of ceramics which is, according to a Harvard scientist who helped develop it, easier to fabricate, less expensive than gold and it does not block x-rays. This is Coors's first venture into the dental field. The estimated market for dental crowns is $850 million per year. (16, 26). The product has not been marketed yet, as it is undergoing voluntary testing by the Food and Drug Administration.

MANAGEMENT

The Adolph Coors Company's leadership is dominated by the Coors family, with the top four positions in the firm held by family members. The office of president is now shared by brothers William K. and Joseph Coors, grandsons of the company's founder and Joseph's sons, Jeffrey and Peter. All four are known by their first names to the Coors employees.

Jeff (age 37) and Peter (age 35) were promoted to the office of President in the May 1982 annual meeting to build "a more cohesive and streamlined management" a spokesman said. The spokesman also stated that "it wasn't the company's intention to 'set up a line of succession' " to the positions held by the elder Coors brothers, Bill (age 65) and Joe (age 64). (17, 23; 1). William Coors said the promotions were "an effort to prepare our company to meet the challenges of the future and assure us the same pattern of success established more than 100 years ago." (4).

However, industry analyst William E. Halliman of Young, Smith and Peacock, Inc., in Phoenix, said that the transition was necessary as the older Coors brothers were nearing retirement age. "Apparently, the Coors company realizes that they've got to have a succession soon" said Halliman. (17, 23; 1).

Coors has no mandatory age for retirement, but once officers reach the age of 65, their contracts are evaluated and renewed on an annual basis by the eight directors, four of whom are family members. Bill is currently serving under a one-year contract. (17, 23).

All of the voting shares are owned by family members and 35% of the 33.8 million publicly held "Class B" non-voting shares is owned by the family. (18, 1558). All of the members of the Board of Directors are officers of the Adolph Coors Company, except R. Derald Whiting, President of the Coors Porcelain Company.

The firm is basically organized into function-related areas (see Exhibit 17.7) and further broken into more specific areas. All of the lower-level officers report to at least one of the four Coors family members who share the office of president.

Exhibit 17.7
ORGANIZATION CHART, ADOLPH COORS COMPANY

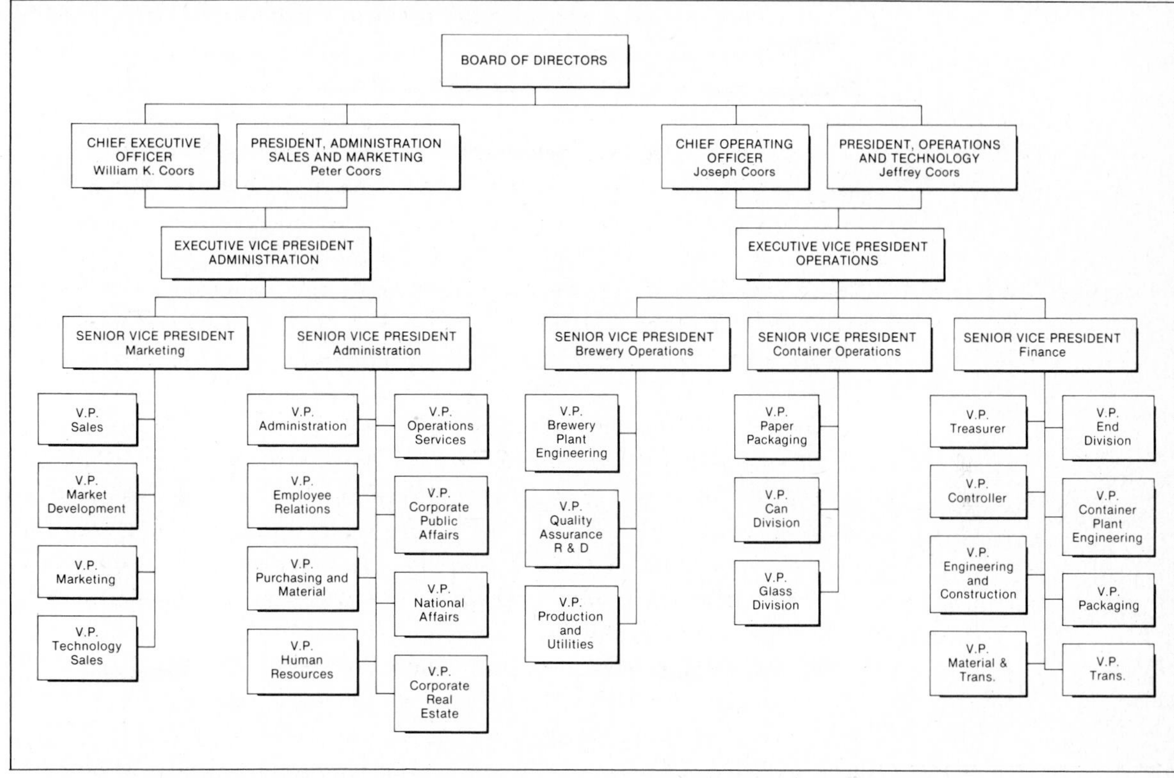

In the past, top management has been slow to react to changes in the market. For example, Coors was reluctant to introduce a beer especially designed to compete with Miller "Lite." Their justification for not doing so was twofold. First, Coors has had a reputation of brewing one product and doing all that they could to make it a high-quality beer. Second, Coors beer was already considered a light beer, being touted as "America's Fine Light Beer."

Joe Coors related this philosophy in 1977 when he noted "Coors beer already has less calories per ounce than regular beer and a few more calories than the light beers. We won't go into production of a special brew which would compete directly with light beers unless it becomes a very significant factor in American public tastes." (3, 92). According to a *Wall Street Journal* article, Bill and Jeff Coors agreed. Jeff said he was "furious" when he found out that company chemists "were secretly experimenting with a light beer after we told them not to." (6, 1; 6).

Peter, however, disagreed. "We had great arguments about whether to try to sell our Banquet beer (regular Coors) as a light beer. A year ago (1978), I was the only one who wanted a light beer. We'd been kicked in the teeth a couple of times, and I was tired of spitting out teeth." (6, 1 and 26).

Coors has, in the past, been reluctant to bring in outside people. Bill Coors once said "We'd rather make our own mistakes." (7, 1; 6).

MANAGEMENT POLICIES

Coors has had its share of problems that are related to its politically conservative posture. Joe Coors, a member of President Reagan's "kitchen cabinet," has been the most active in conservative politics. In 1968, as a Regent of The University of Colorado, he sought to have the ultra-leftwing Students for a Democratic Society removed from the campus, which caused a boycott of Coors beer on the campus. (7, 1; 6). The boycott remained until 1980 when a group of fraternity men pushed a petition to get Coors reinstated. (21, 27; 1).

Coors has had its share of labor troubles, too. In 1959, the brewery workers Union Local Number 366 struck for 118 days, but were unsuccessful in their bid for more pay. (6, 1; 6). However, the most recent and last strike that occurred in 1977 did not involve pay. In fact, even union leaders admitted that they were well paid. "Coors does pay excellent for the area" said Ray Marcouiller, a brewery worker and the Chairman of the Colorado Boycott Committee. (22, 16; 1).

The issues, according to union members, were "human rights." The workers objected to the use of lie detectors for employment screening. The polygraph machines were used to measure responses to questions such as drug use, past felonies, etc. Union workers also disagreed on Coors's requirement that they take an oath which pledged their loyalty to the firm and not to make negative comments about it. The strikers also claimed that Coors was discriminatory in its selection of employees. (22, 16; 1).

These claims first became apparent in 1975 when the Equal Employment Opportunity Commission filed suit against Coors claiming that all females were being used as office workers and employee substitutes and that minorities were placed in unskilled worker programs. (23, 4; 5). However, in 1977, Coors signed an anti-bias pact with the EEOC which promised that no biases will occur, and that caused the suit to be dropped. In the statement, Coors admitted no guilt in past practices. (24, 20; 3).

After the union went on strike, 70% of the workers returned within weeks and the remaining ones were fired. In a letter mailed to the strikers Bill Coors said "This is the toughest decision I have ever made, because it may lead to the loss of your jobs." (24, 18; 2). Coors did, in an effort to smooth the feathers of union workers, pay those strikers who returned to work for the days they were off the job. (24, 36; 4). A month later, the National Labor Relations Board dismissed the union's labor practice suit that had been filed against Coors. (26, 37; 6).

In December 1977, one month later, in a decertification vote, 71% of Coors's workers decided to disband the union. (27, 23; 4). The Coors management had claimed all along that the local union members were pawns of the big labor groups (AFL-CIO) which soon after the strike began, invoked a national boycott of Coors's products which continues today.

The boycott has had some effect upon sales, but the extent on today's sales is not known. In the 1978 annual company meeting, Bill Coors said that the boycott was "having a material effect upon sales." (28, 24; 1). The company has been fighting back, filing lawsuits in Alabama and California. Bill Coors states "This is the kind of war we want to get into, not shy away from." (10, 10).

Allegedly, there were some organized labor groups in California which had been implying that since Coors was not pasteurized, it was not safe to drink and that it causes Legionnaire's Disease. Obviously, such untruths can hurt sales and the Coors family is very bitter about such "lies" as Bill Coors puts it. (29, 20; 3). Such feelings have apparently altered the advertising strategy, with at least Bill Coors wanting to promote the corporate image, righting what he thinks the boycott is, "a bum rap, a smear on the company." (14, 29; 4).

MARKETING

The Adolph Coors Company did not have a Marketing Department until 1975, and then "it was like pulling teeth to get Bill and Joe to do it" according to a former Coors officer. (10, 10). In 1970, an industry analyst stated that the Coors ad agency spends most of "its time looking for streams and waterfalls."

However, through several company reorganizations, Coors now has a Senior Vice-President of Marketing who oversees four other officers. The Executive Vice-President of Administration who oversees the Marketing Division, Robert Recholtz, was formerly head of Marketing for the Joseph Schlitz Brewing Company from February 1980 until November 1981. Recholtz was hired to revitalize the sagging sales and to fight the stiff competition put up by A-B and Miller. (20, 24; 1).

Coors has in the past had conflicts within its Marketing Division. In 1981, Fred Vierra, Vice-President of Sales for two previous years and John Nichols, Vice-President of Marketing, both resigned. Nichols resigned to become a Coors distributor under an agreement he had when he joined the firm, but Vierra resigned because, as Peter Coors put it, "we saw things a bit differently." (14, 29; 4).

Once, Joe Coors, to the horror of marketers and wholesalers, tried to get

Exhibit 17.8

ADVERTISING EXPENSES: ADOLPH COORS COMPANY
(In Thousands of Dollars)

Year	*Amount*
1981	$85,817
1980	66,752
1979	46,400
1978	33,470
1977	15,523

SOURCE: Adolph Coors Company Annual Report.

his wife's friend Zsa Zsa Gabor to promote Coors Light. However, she never did make it to the television screen. (10, 10).

Coors's first advertising campaign was its "Taste the High Country" theme. The theme never was very popular among the Coors people other than the management. Their second theme was aimed at improving the image of the firm, otherwise known as the "We are Coors" campaign. The advertisements featured numerous employees boasting about their company. (See Exhibit 17.8 for a tabulation of Coors advertising expenses.)

Now, Coors has embarked upon a new approach which many hope will help Coors regain market share. The new campaign stresses the high quality of Coors products, by advertising Coors as being made "The way you really want to drink beer." "I used to get madder than a red ant because the brewery wouldn't take our suggestions or allow us to use our imaginations, now

Exhibit 17.9

SELECTED FINANCIAL INFORMATION: BREWING INDUSTRY

Brewer	*Sales (Millions)*	*Operating Margin (%)*	*Net Profit (Millions)*	*Earnings per Share*	*Working Capital (Millions)*	*Long-Term Debt (Millions)*	*Net Worth (Millions)*
Anheuser-Busch	$3,847.2	12.1%	$217.4	$4.79	$45.9	$817.3	$1,208.8
G. Heileman	807.0	11.1%	40.2	3.05	64.1	53.8	158.9
Olympia	337.9	.5%	(1.4)	(.54)	3.8	21.8	72.0
Pabst	691.9	2.7%	(23.5)	(2.88)	13.3	13.3	254.8
Miller	2,236.5	8.1%	N/A	N/A	N/A	N/A	N/A

SOURCE: Value Line Investment Survey.

they finally seem to be listening to us," says James Raymond, a wholesaler from Gearing, Nebraska. (10, 10).

FINANCIAL INFORMATION

Coors has a vast amount of unused resources as it holds no significant long or short-term debt (see Exhibits 17.9 and 17.11). All of its capital structure is composed of stock (and retained earnings).

Coors issued $127 million worth of capital to pay for massive estate taxes

COMPARATIVE INCOME STATEMENTS OF THE ADOLPH COORS COMPANY AND SUBSIDIARIES

Exhibit 17.10

Fiscal Year Ending	**12/27/81**	**12/28/80**	**12/30/79**
Income Statement (*thousands of dollars*)			
Net sales	$ 1,060,345	$ 887,897	$ 740,504
Cost of goods	659,623	629,758	517,748
Gross profit	400,722	258,139	222,756
R & D expenditures	16,848	14,256	11,244
Sell gen & admin exp	311,777	146,293	103,679
Inc bef dep & amort	72,097	97,590	107,833
Non-operating inc	9,137	9,750	8,492
Interest expense	1,601	1,563	1,571
Income before tax	79,633	105,777	114,754
Prov for inc taxes	27,663	40,800	46,305
Net income	51,970	64,977	68,449
Outstanding shares	35,011,624	35,011,624	35,041,624

Segment Data as of December 27, 1981 (*thousands of dollars*)

	Sales	*Operating Income*
Beer business	$787,739	$64,100
Other businesses	142,177	7,997

Five Year Summary

Year	*Sales (thousands of dollars)*	*Net Income (thousands of dollars)*	*EPS*
1981	$929,916	$51,970	1.48
1980	887,897	64,977	1.86
1979	740,504	68,449	1.95
1978	624,804	54,774	1.56
1977	593,120	67,700	1.92

SOURCE: 1981 Annual Report, Adolph Coors Company.

Exhibit 17.11

COMPARATIVE BALANCE SHEETS OF THE ADOLPH COORS COMPANY AND SUBSIDIARIES
(In Thousands of Dollars)

Fiscal Year Ending	**12/27/81**	**12/28/80**
ASSETS		
Cash	$ 11,646	$ 2,629
Mrktable securities	64,968	85,254
Receivables	66,667	57,930
Inventories	115,677	149,504
Raw materials	86,481	115,337
Work in progress	22,383	26,663
Finished goods	6,813	7,504
Other current assets	36,497	34,892
Total current assets	295,455	330,209
Prop, plant & equip	1,023,498	878,052
Accumulated dep	371,408	321,633
Net prop & equip	652,090	556,419
Oth non-cur assets	NA	5,108
Intangibles	2,567	2,649
Deposits & other assets	6,272	NA
Total Assets	956,384	894,385
LIABILITIES		
Notes payable	NA	NA
Accounts payable	40,033	48,923
Cur long term debt	NA	NA
Cur port cap leases	NA	NA
Accrued expenses	67,559	63,744
Income taxes	9,922	3,427
Total current liab	117,514	116,094
Mortgages	NA	NA
Deferred charges/inc	75,968	60,149
Convertible debt	NA	NA
Long term debt	NA	NA
Non-cur cap leases	NA	NA
Other long term liab	9,335	6,042
Total liabilities	202,817	182,285
Common stock net	12,260	12,260
Capital surplus	2,011	2,011
Retained earnings	765,751	724,284
Treasury stock	26,455	26,455
Shareholders' equity	753,567	712,100
Total Liabilities and Net Worth	956,384	894,385

SOURCE: 1981 Annual Report, Adolph Coors Company.

of Adolph Coors, Jr. of over $50 million. (8, 54). Even then, they were very reluctant. The stock that is publicly held (the Coors family owns 35% of it) is non-voting.

In studying the summary of selected financial data (see Exhibits 17.10, 17.11, 17.12, and 17.13), it is apparent that though sales have increased, earnings have fluctuated.

Coors spent $156,157,000 in capital expenditures in 1981, a 41% in-

Exhibit 17.12

SELECTED FINANCIAL DATA OF THE ADOLPH COORS COMPANY AND SUBSIDIARIES

(In Thousands, Except Per-Share Data)	*Fiscal Years Ended in December*				
	1981	**1980**	**1979***	**1978****	**1977**
Barrels Sold	13,261	13,779	12,912	12,566	12,824
SUMMARY OF OPERATIONS					
Net sales	$929,916	$887,897	$740,504	$624,804	$593,120
Cost of goods sold	659,623	629,758	517,748	450,439	413,884
Marketing, general & administrative	181,348	146,293	103,679	79,369	49,842
Research & project development	16,848	14,256	11,244	9,444	13,280
Other expense (income)—net	(7,536)	(8,187)	(6,921)	(7,975)	(3,448)
	850,283	782,120	625,750	531,277	473,558
Income before income taxes	79,633	105,777	114,754	93,527	119,562
Income taxes	27,663	40,800	46,305	38,753	51,862
Net income	$ 51,970	$ 64,977	$ 68,449	$ 54,774	$ 67,700
Per Share of Common Stock:					
Net income	$ 1.48	$ 1.86	$ 1.95	$ 1.56	$ 1.92
Shareholders' equity	$ 21.52	$ 20.34	$ 18.75	$ 17.05	$ 15.73
Dividends	$ 0.30	$ 0.275	$ 0.25	$ 0.25	$ 0.15
Average Number of Outstanding Shares of Common Stock	35,012	35,015	35,042	35,148	35,264
Balance Sheet Summary:					
Working capital	$177,941	$214,115	$201,357	$163,006	$149,177
Properties—net	$652,090	$556,419	$550,196	$475,780	$435,673
Total assets	$956,384	$894,385	$828,945	$751,610	$691,568
Other long-term liabilities	$ 9,335	$ 6,042	$ 5,714	$ 5,237	$ 5,256
Shareholders' equity	$753,567	$712,100	$657,205	$597,516	$554,023

* In 1979, the Company changed to the last-in, first-out method of pricing certain inventories. The effect of this change was to reduce net income by $6,133,000 ($0.18 per share).

** 53 weeks.

Exhibit 17.13

CONSOLIDATED STATEMENTS OF CHANGES IN FINANCIAL POSITION OF THE ADOLPH COORS COMPANY AND SUBSIDIARIES
(In Thousands of Dollars)

	For the years ended		
	December 27, 1981	***December 28, 1980***	***December 30, 1979***
Financial resources were provided by:			
Net income	$ 51,970	$ 64,977	$ 68,449
Add income charges (credits) not affecting working capital:			
Depreciation, depletion & amortization	54,883	49,134	45,261
Increase in accumulated deferred income taxes	15,819	11,083	7,829
Gain on exchange of stock		(431)	
Provision for loss of notes receivable		2,793	
Deferred pension liability	3,122		
Retirements of properties	5,603	5,742	4,948
Working capital provided by operations	131,397	133,298	126,487
Fair market value of investment in common stock exchanged for treasury stock		450	
	131,397	133,748	126,487
Financial resources were used for:			
Additions to properties	156,157	111,099	74,625
Cash dividends	10,503	9,632	8,760
Acquisition of treasury stock		450	
Other—net	911	(191)	4,811
	167,571	120,990	88,196
Increase (decrease) in working capital	$(36,174)	$ 12,758	$ 38,291
Analysis of Changes in Working capital			
Increase (decrease) in current assets:			
Cash and short-term investments	$(11,269)	$(13,330)	$ 12,663
Accounts and notes receivable	8,737	1,453	16,185
Inventories	(33,827)	18,501	15,920
Prepaid expenses and other assets	5,426	5,386	3,923
Accumulated income tax prepayments	(3,821)	(118)	(1,060)
	(34,754)	11,892	47,631
(Increase) decrease in current liabilities:			
Accounts payable	8,890	(14,478)	2,968
Accrued salaries and vacations	(1,811)	(1,806)	(5,635)
Taxes, other than income taxes	1,378	842	(5,458)
Federal and state income taxes	(6,495)	17,326	(3,900)
Accrued expenses and other liabilities	(3,382)	(1,018)	2,685
	(1,420)	866	(9,340)
Increase (decrease) in working capital	$(36,174)	$ 12,758	$ 38,291

crease over the previous year. Most of these were for expansion of brewing facilities and acquiring, exploring and developing natural resource properties. In 1982, the company expects to have $140,000,000 worth of capital expenditures to be financed internally.

Coors attributes the continuously higher sales over the past several years to higher beer prices and an increase in non-beer business sales.

FUTURE OUTLOOK

Peter Coors has determined that the firm faces three separate options for its plans for the future. First, Coors can remain basically a regional brewer and attempt to hold its own against the industry giants, Anheuser-Busch and Miller. Alternatively, the company can slowly phase into the national scene by entering several markets at a time, as it has done in the past, then build the brewery when capacity is reached at the Golden plant. Thirdly, Coors could go national all at once and immediately began construction of the brewery in Virginia.

NOTES

1. *Adolph Coors Company.* Company brochure. Circa 1970.
2. "Adolph Coors Company Sued by U.S. Agency, Bias in Hiring Is Alleged." *The Wall Street Journal,* Eastern ed., September 9, 1975, p. 4.
3. "Adolph Coors Plans to Replace Strikers at Colorado Brewery." *The Wall Street Journal,* Eastern ed., April 11, 1977, p. 18.
4. "Anheuser-Busch Company." *Advertising Age,* September 9, 1982, pp. 32–34.
5. "Anheuser-Busch; The King of Beers Still Rules." *Business Week,* July 12, 1982, pp. 50–54.
6. Boe, Ann, Executive Secretary, Adolph Coors Company. Telephone Interview from Denton, Texas, October 20, 1982.
7. "Brewery That Breaks All the Rules." *Business Week,* August 22, 1970, p. 60.
8. "Brewing Industry." *Value Line Investment Survey,* September 3, 1982, pp. 1555–1563.
9. Bulkeley, William M. "The Brewmasters." *The Wall Street Journal,* Eastern ed., October 26, 1982, p. 1.
10. *Caps Taps 1873–1973,* Company Brochure, Adolph Coors Company, 1973.
11. "Coors Apparently Wins Right to Control Sales." *The Wall Street Journal,* Eastern ed., July 11, 1977, p. 14.
12. "Coors Gets Approval of Pollution Unit." *New York Times,* March 23, 1981, Section IV, p. 4.
13. "Coors Official Says Union Led Boycott Has Hurt Sales." *The Wall Street Journal,* Eastern ed., October 26, 1977, p. 20.

14. "Coors Says NRLB Dismisses Union's Labor Practice Suit." *The Wall Street Journal,* Eastern ed., November 30, 1978, p. 37.
15. "Coors Submits Test Data on Ceramic Dental Crown." *The Wall Street Journal,* Eastern ed., December 12, 1981, p. 26.
16. Garino, David P. "A-B Will Let Bud Light Flow Coast to Coast." *The Wall Street Journal,* Eastern ed., March 1, 1982, p. 16.
17. Getschow, George. "Return of Brew to Student Union Uncaps University of Colorado Anti-Coors Protest." *The Wall Street Journal,* Eastern ed., December 19, 1980, p. 27.
18. Huey, John. "Over a Barrel: Old Men at Coors Beer Find Old Ways Don't Work Anymore." *The Wall Street Journal,* Eastern ed., January 19, 1979, p. 1.
19. Ivens, Molly. "Union's Survival Is at Stake in 14-Month Old Strike at Coors Brewery." *New York Times,* June 16, 1978, p. 16.
20. "Jeffrey, Peter Coors Are Promoted as Part of Firm's Realignment." *The Wall Street Journal,* Eastern ed., May 12, 1982, p. 23.
21. *1981 Annual Report,* The Adolph Coors Company. *1981 Form 10-K,* The Adolph Coors Company.
22. *1982 Second Quarter Report,* The Adolph Coors Company.
23. "Robert Rechholtz Resigns Post at Schlitz to Go to Coors." *The Wall Street Journal,* Eastern ed., November 1, 1981, p. 24.
24. Schlender, Brenton R. "The Beer War; Heady Days Are Over for Coors Wholesalers as Sales Pace Drops." *The Wall Street Journal,* Western ed., October 6, 1982, pp. 1 and 10.
25. Schuster, Linda. "Coors Beer Stumbles in Its Marketing Bid." *The Wall Street Journal,* Eastern ed., July 10, 1981, p. 29.
26. "Stockholder Meeting Briefs; Adolph Coors Company." *The Wall Street Journal,* Eastern ed., May 9, 1978, p. 24.
27. Taylor, Thayer C. "When a Marketer Needs a Plan." *Survey of Buying Power, Sales and Marketing Management Magazine,* July 26, 1982, pp. A-7 to A-35.
28. *The Adolph Coors Story,* The Adolph Coors Company, 1980.
29. "The December Report." *Beer Statistics News.* 8: (March 1982), pp. 1–24.
30. "The Youth Movement in Coors Management." *Business Week,* May, 1982, p. 50.
31. *Value Line Investment Survey,* September 3, 1982, pp. 1555–1563.
32. "Why Coors Finally Had to Take Public Money." *Business Week,* September 22, 1975, p. 54.

Case 18

RICHMOND BRICK COMPANY

Robert N. White

Dick Wood, Director of Industrial Relations, and Sam Verney, Controller, of the Richmond Brick Company, met in the dusty, noisy courtyard encircled by the company's one-story office building, the shipping dock, a warehouse, and the railroad track. It was a hot August morning in 1976. Stopping at the Coke machine, Dick offered Sam a Coke.

"Sam," he said, "I'm getting concerned that our Policy Committee hasn't met for over a month. I've got my job evaluation program and EEOC audit report and some other items that need discussing. And we haven't made progress on our critical issues list."

Sam scuffed some dust over the courtyard bricks and replied throught-fully, "Well, we'll be ready to discuss the preliminary budget numbers with the president in a few days. But budget numbers are one thing—and specific department plans for achieving them are something else. Why can't we get down to cases on our action plans?"

They were joined by Vance McGee, Vice-President for Manufacturing. "Hey, guys," Vance said in his bluff manner, "why don't we just call our own management meeting here and now, and set some corporate objectives? Then I can get some decisions on the new plant project." The three men looked at each other unhappily, finished their Cokes, and moved on to their offices.

BACKGROUND OF THE COMPANY

Richmond Brick Company, founded in 1935 by Simon Todd, began with a small, one-kiln plant in Richmond, Virginia, site of the present executive of-

This case was prepared by Prof. Robert N. White of Babcock Graduate School of Management at Wake Forest University. Reprinted by permission.

fices. The company grew steadily, adding brick plants, expanding facilities, and moving into concrete block as well.

In 1976, Richmond operated six brick plants and four concrete block facilities with a total annual capacity of 305 million bricks and 8.4 million eight-inch concrete block equivalents.

It was the largest brick manufacturer in the Virginia/North Carolina Region. This region produces about 16.2% of all this country's brick. In 1976, Richmond shipped 186 million, or 19% of the regional market.

All of the company's plants were located near major population centers and along interstate highways which go through the middle of the Southeast, the fastest growing area of the United States. Due to freight and transportation costs, plant location is a very important factor to every brick manufacturer. However, since U.S. brick production is concentrated in only a few clay soil regions, there is considerable rail shipment into nonproducing areas.

The regional market accounted for 78% of Richmond's sales; the remaining 22% of sales was distributed throughout the eastern half of the United States. Richmond marketed its brick and block through its own direct sales force of twelve salesmen and three sales managers, who work on commission. In 1976, the average age of the sales force was forty-eight years old.

Five major customers accounted for a total of 9% of sales. No other customer account represented more than 1% of total sales. Home builders and contractors represented 80% of Richmond's sales, while 20% was sold through distributors and dealers. The mix of residential vs. nonresidential sales has been shifting in recent years and was roughly 50–50 in 1976.

The company owned a substantial acreage of clay and shale land in Virginia and North Carolina, sufficient to supply its forecasted needs for a half century in the future. This provided a significant competitive advantage in raw material cost (they have owned the land for many years) and in quality of their clay resources.

The company used natural gas to fire its kilns. While costly, this fuel was still available in early 1976. The company could convert to oil without interrupting production, but fuel costs would rise about 8–10%.

THE INDUSTRY

The brick and concrete block industry was dominated by numerous regional and local companies. In 1976, of an industry total of 8.1 billion bricks produced nationally, 2.1 billion (value, $90 million) were produced in Richmond's regional major market. Because the product is an undifferentiated one, meeting price competition, service, and personal contacts were all important marketing issues. This market had the highest forecast of growth of all regional brick markets.

A perceptible trend was evident in that large companies, both those already in the industry and those from outside, were acquiring regional brick and block companies. General Shale, Justin Industries, and Boren Clay Products Company were examples of acquiring companies which have employed this route to growth.

Richmond's comparative ratios placed it right at the upper range of the better-run companies in the industry.

Starting with the business downturn in 1973, the construction industry in this region suffered through its worst period in many decades. Richmond, like its competitors, laid off workers (but no management people). They cut costs in every conceivable way; price-cutting was used to try to keep the kilns operating.

Exhibit 18.1 provides more detail on the industry and factors significant to its future.

INDUSTRY TRENDS

Exhibit 18.1

EXCERPTS FROM REPORT FROM RICHMOND MARKETING DEPARTMENT

March, 1976

The economic outlook facing the industry was summarized by an industry economist in these terms:

> "The 1976–77 period reflects the most difficult recovery (from 1974–75 recession) that housing has undertaken in the postwar era. The money market squeeze could tighten uncomfortably as the Federal Reserve continues the fight on inflation. Mortgage rates should hover a little below historic heights. New housing will remain disconcertingly expensive. And the consumer will still be trying to get over the worst scare he had since the '30s. The housing industry will have to live with some of these problems for a long time to come. The home building climate has changed, perhaps forever. Two million starts a year may prove the peak, not the norm."

The forecasts indicated that the Southeast would be the most favored section of the country with respect to housing growth. Richmond's brick shipments had traditionally paralleled closely with national private housing starts. A trend toward more emphasis on the industrial and commercial sector of the construction market was identified by industry researchers. Richmond's sales emphasis was still heavily oriented toward residential and the institutional (education, municipal, church) sector.

The economic analysis also pointed out that brick usage over the long term was declining in relation to the trends in housing starts and square footage of walls and floors. It was believed that two factors significant to

(*Continued*)

Exhibit 18.1
(*Continued*)

those trends were periodic brick capacity shortages in times of high demand, and skillful promotion of competing materials.

The industry economists pointed out these favorable indicators:

1. Family incomes are rising faster than construction costs of one-family homes.
2. Brick prices have not increased as much as the price of other building materials.
3. Wage rates for bricklayers are not increasing faster than other building trades.

Richmond's own survey through its sales force reflected the following factors of changes in marketing in its region.

1. More and better media advertising and promotion from competition.
2. Expansion of direct sales forces by competitors.
3. Continued emphasis on new brick colors and new block surface designs.

THE INDUSTRY

Brick and block companies have historically offered products of those materials only. The main efforts at product development were in textures, sizes, and colors of brick, and in surface design of block. Richmond had a fairly wide range of these product offerings. However, some competitors had achieved limited market acceptance with brick and block prefab panels.

Expansion and diversification by industry companies took the form of expanding geographically to compensate for business decline in a regional area, adding ready-mix block operations, centralizing brick and block manufacturing, and combining these with marketing of other "hard materials" (frames, doors, glass, nonwood panels, roofing, etc.). This latter type of diversification had been discussed on several occasions by Phil Todd with his management group; but no study of costs or marketing implications had been made.

Competitive strategies to improve position focused on deviations from price levels, more effective selling and service, limited use of advertising and promotion.

PRESIDENCY OF MR. SIMON TODD

Mr. Simon Todd was a dominant, driving force in the development of the company from a one-kiln plant to leadership in the Virginia/North Carolina brick industry. A tough, abrasive individual, he kept on top of even the smallest details of company operations. Several times a day he would sally forth into the center courtyard to reprimand a worker or collar a passing salesman. He had no truck with new-fangled ideas such as organization charts, salary administration programs, computer controls, and the like. His managers were trained to bring him the problems and implement his decisions—right away. The company grew and prospered under his leadership.

Mr. Todd's son, Phil Todd, started with the company directly out of college. He showed an aptitude for both manufacturing and sales. Under his father's tutelage, Phil learned the business from the ground up. However, he was treated like all the other managers and accorded Mr. Todd the same respect and obedience that was demanded of all company managers.

In 1974, Mr. Todd elevated Phil to President and Chief Executive Officer. He gave Phil his paneled office overlooking the courtyard in which a picture of the stern-faced founder hangs behind the President's chair. Mr. Todd continued as Chairman of the Board.

Profiles of the key management people as of 1976 are shown in Exhibit 18.2. The organization chart is in Exhibit 18.3.

PROFILES OF TOP MANAGEMENT PERSONNEL

Exhibit 18.2

Phil Todd	*President* He is 46 years old with over 24 years of service to the Company. He went to work for the Company after graduating from college, and has worked in every major operation of the Company. Phil Todd is quite active in the industry groups. He is also a director of several companies and a bank.
George Semlow	*Treasurer* He joined the Company as an accountant in 1950 and served as Assistant Secretary, Assistant Treasurer, and Comptroller, prior to becoming Treasurer in 1964. George has a B.S. degree in Accounting from the University of Virginia, and is a Certified Public Accountant. He is also a graduate of the Executive Program at the University of Virginia. He is 58 years old.
Elwood "Teddy" Shanaberger	*Vice-President—Sales* Joined Sampson Brick & Tile Company (Division of Richmond Brick Company) as Sales Manager in 1964. In 1966, he became Regional Sales Manager. He became General Sales Manager in 1969. From 1950 to 1964, Teddy was a District Sales Manager for Merry Brothers Brick & Tile in Georgia. He has an A.B. degree from Clemson University and has done graduate work at Washington and Lee. He is 56 years old with 13 years of service.
Vance McGee	*Vice-President—Manufacturing* He joined the Company in 1961 as an industrial engineer and

(*Continued*)

Exhibit 18.2
(Continued)

	moved up through manufacturing supervision. He was made Vice-President in 1974. He attended South Carolina University and the Executive Program at the University of Virginia. He visited European plants in 1965 and has played an extensive role in bringing automation to the Company.
Richard "Dick" Wood	*Vice-President of Industrial Relations* Dick was employed by Richmond in 1967 as Director of Industrial Relations and was promoted to Vice-President in 1970. For several years he also served as division manager of the Richmond plant. Previously he worked as Director of Industrial Relations for Hanes Hosiery Company. He is a graduate of Hamilton College. He is 50 years old with 7 years of service.
Sam Verney, Jr.	*Controller* Sam joined Richmond Brick Company as Controller in November 1975. Prior to this move, he had held senior accounting positions at Warner & Swazey Company and White Motor Company. He started in public accounting with Arthur Andersen. Sam is 43 years old.
Harry Cannon	*Vice-President—Raleigh Division* Harry has been employed by the Company since 1938. He has worked as a salesman, shipping and payroll clerk, loading foreman, burning superintendent, and plant superintendent before becoming Plant Manager in 1966. He has a degree in business administration from Clemson University. He is 60 years old.

THE OUTSIDE GROUP MOVES IN

Early in 1974, Phil Todd was surprised to receive a phone call from a Harold Ornstein. Mr. Ornstein introduced himself as Vice President of Corporate Development of General Time Corporation, a conglomerate company headquartered in New York City. He explained that his company was interested in investing in Richmond Brick Company.

Phil Todd, who had only nominal stock in his own name, relayed the inquiry to his father and was somewhat taken aback at the extent of the interest shown. Family estate concerns were the motivating factor.

Within two months, the discussions moved into an active stage and in July 1974, a deal was consummated under which General Time took over voting control of Richmond and paid off the Todd family. Exhibit 18.4 details the financing program. This reflects a pattern employed by General Time in previous acquisitions. Phil Todd and six other members of Richmond management were offered (and accepted) the opportunity to buy stock in Richmond.

Exhibit 18.3
ORGANIZATION CHART, JULY 1, 1975

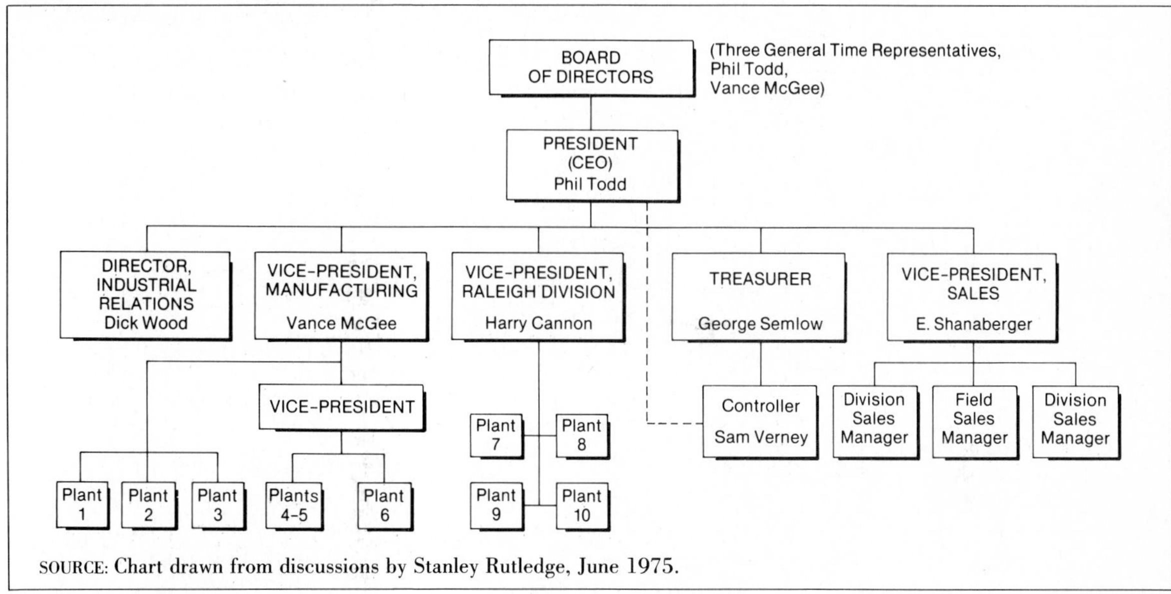

SOURCE: Chart drawn from discussions by Stanley Rutledge, June 1975.

General Time did not seek any changes in Richmond's management and stated they considered their purchase to be an investment. However, they indicated they expected to "actively monitor and participate in the future development of the company." By this they meant receiving informal and formal reports on progress, requiring long- and short-term plans and budgets, and providing financial advice. General Time had stated to Phil Todd that they believed in supporting their acquisitions with capital where the new funds invested could return an ROI higher than the present return on total capital employed in that acquired company, and also that they expected growth in revenue and profit over the long term from all their acquisitions.

DEVELOPMENTS IN MANAGEMENT STARTING IN MID-1975

In May 1975, Dick Wood, Director of Industrial Relations, received his MBA degree from the Graduate School of Management at a nearby university. Dick concluded that the concepts he had been studying could, if properly applied, help Phil Todd and the Richmond Brick Company return to its former prosperous condition and grow over the longer term. He brought Stan Rutledge, his professor in Corporate Planning and Business Policy at the school, and Phil Todd together for discussions. These led to Stan Rutledge becoming a consultant to the company.

FINANCING PROGRAM

Exhibit 18.4

The $26,815,000 required to finance the acquisition to be raised through the issuance of the following securities:

7-Year Senior Bank Notes repayable in equal installments from 1975–1981 @ 1% over prime	$9,000,000
16-Year Senior Notes repayable in equal installments from 1981–1990 @ 10%	9,600,000
16-Year Senior Subordinated Notes repayable in equal installments from 1981–1990 @ 10%	5,500,000
6½% Non-Cumulative Convertible Preferred Stock convertible into 300,000 shares @ $4 per share	1,200,000
Common Equity from the sale of 505,000 shares @ $3 per share	1,515,000
TOTAL RAISED	$26,815,000

Present shareholders to be paid off from corporate cash in amount of approximately $1,700,000.

General Time arranged the following sequence of steps in order to place the debt incurred by the above financing on the books of Richmond Brick Company:

1. General Time established a new subsidiary corporation called RBC Corp., which issued the convertible preferred and common stock (above) and received payment for this stock.
2. RBC Corp. borrowed from financial institutions on the notes (above).
3. RBC Corp. purchased the assets of Richmond Brick Company.
4. RBC Corp. changed its name to Richmond Brick Company, and the old Richmond Brick Company changed its name to Richmond Liquidating Company.
5. Richmond Liquidating Company paid off the stockholders in the old Richmond Brick Company and, a year later, went out of existence.

The consultant's initial step in this arrangement was to conduct a two-day retreat in planning concepts attended by Phil Todd and six of his top men. This session brouught out a number of points:

1. The only formal planning going on was one-year budgeting, initiated the year before.
2. The management group evidenced a strong desire to get on with the job of improving the company, but was not at all sure what should be done first.

3. The management members were hesitant to be critical of company policies and even to take a stand on future directions of the company. Many sidelong glances were cast at Phil Todd during the discussions. He spoke very little.
4. A strong need for a management development program was voiced.
5. There were no organization charts or management job descriptions available.

The group agreed to undertake steps proposed by Stan Rutledge in order to institute a planning system in the company. These were summarized as follows:

1. Develop data on market and competitive trends, advances in processing technology, fuel availability, and other pertinent factors in the external environment.
2. Identify, in specifics, the company's abilities and deficiencies in marketing, production, and other functional areas.
3. Assess internal capabilities in the light of developing external trends to identify strengths and weaknesses; and provide the basis for establishing realistic objectives and strategies for the long term.
4. Develop the annual business plan and conform the budget to the business plan.

Each of these, and their requirements for information development and analysis, were discussed in some depth at the retreat. Phil Todd spoke briefly on the importance of pushing forward with the tasks outlined.

During this same period (mid-1975) Phil Todd was taking other steps to strengthen the management team. First was a series of seminars in management concepts conducted by the university faculty and attended by twenty-six members of Richmond management. The seminars, conducted in late 1975 and early 1976, generated considerable enthusiasm both because of the pertinence of the concepts to Richmond's problems, and because of the evidence they seemed to signify of top management's interests in these concepts.

Phil Todd was advised by the faculty members that his management people would in all likelihood, as a result of the seminars, be putting pressure on him for changes in company policies and operational methods. However, in discussion with Stan Rutledge about this issue, Phil repeated an earlier-voiced concern. "When Simon Todd was running things, none of these fellows had a chance to make their own decisions. Now I'm trying my best to get them to make decisions—and they won't do it. They just wait for me to tell them what to do. I hope they'll start now to do their jobs without asking me. However, I'm not sure they all can change. Mr. Todd left a strong imprint on a couple of them."

Phil also created a Policy Committee of the executives reporting to him, which was to meet monthly. Phil did not put himself on this committee, offering this comment, "I'll come in when they invite me." He also set up a Management Advisory Committee, composed of thirty members of management, to meet monthly. This was conceived of as primarily a sounding board and communications agency.

Late in the fall of 1975 a new member of senior management was added, Sam Verney as Controller. Sam, age forty-four, had had considerable professional experience in other companies, both larger and smaller. His enthusiasm and evident good judgment soon developed respect for his opinions among the management group. Early on, Sam encountered a disturbing situation. He had understood that his boss would be Phil Todd. Upon joining the company, he found that the Treasurer believed that he was Sam's boss. Six months later, this question of who was his boss was still not entirely clear despite two discussions with Phil Todd on the topic.

Sam Verney quickly moved to develop and push through the Policy Committee, a series of accounting policies to replace the outmoded, informal practices that were causing confusion and inefficiency. These moves established some needed groundwork: but Sam had his sights set on a couple of major targets—a modern inventory control program and a computer-based accounting system. Both of these, in his opinion, were badly needed. Sam was an enthusiastic supporter of the long-range planning concept.

During the winter/spring of 1976, business was picking up but not reaching the company's budgeted levels. A salary and wage freeze which Phil Todd imposed in September 1973, was continued into the spring. Top management pressured for increased selling effort. A sales incentive program was developed in the fall and applied in December and January 1975. This program was dropped when two salesmen achieved compensation levels above that of the top marketing executive.

PROGRESS ON LONG-RANGE PLANNING

The long-range planning activity, initiated with enthusiasm at the management retreat, was lagging. Completion of the 1975 budget had tied up the management group generally. Then Stan Rutledge had difficulty mustering staff help to assemble external analysis data on markets, competition, economics, technological developments, etc. This effort was finally launched in late December of 1975, and targets for its completion were moved back several times (see Exhibit 18.5, the planning calendar). It was finished in March 1976.

Since Rutledge had set with Phil Todd a revised target of completing ob-

PLANNING CALENDAR

(Fiscal year September 1–August 31)

Exhibit 18.5

SEPT 1975	OCT	NOV	DEC	JAN 1976	FEB	MAR	APR	MAY	JUNE	JULY	AUG
1	2			3	4	5		6			7

Steps in Planning Process

1. Explain planning to managers.
2. Develop external environment data.
3. Analyze internal capabilities.
4. Assessment.
5. Develop objectives and strategies (long range).
6. Develop action plans (1-year plan).
7. Finalize budget.

SOURCE: Presented at management retreat June 1975 by Stanley Rutledge.

jectives and strategies by mid-April 1976, he launched the internal analysis step while the external analysis effort was still in progress. Members of the management group were asked to submit their views on key issues in the functional areas of the company (manufacturing, sales, personnel, etc.); and on organization and general management. The results of this survey highlighted the major problems of the company. A list of the major problem areas is shown in Exhibit 18.6.

SETTING CORPORATE OBJECTIVES

The stage had been finally been set by May 1976 for establishing corporate objectives. Before meeting with the Policy Committee, Stan Rutledge had several informal discussions with Phil Todd to clarify his views on the future of the company. Phil's concept of the company's future emphasized these issues:

1. Growth in sales volume; but, more important, profitability.
2. Changes in marketing methods to match trends in the construction industry. For example, the full-line building supply houses were gaining position rapidly.
3. Streamlining the organization and freeing him of detail.

COMMITTEE REPORT

Exhibit 18.6

CORPORATE POLICY COMMITTEE REPORT ON MAJOR PROBLEM AREAS DERIVED FROM THE SUMMARY OF STRENGTHS AND WEAKNESSES
(June 8, 1976)

1. Define and communicate structure of the company, as well as responsibilities and corresponding authority.
2. Develop programs in management development, training, and management recruitment to ensure proper utilization of manpower.
3. Define corporate goals and objectives; assign responsibilities for short- and long-range planning to attain these goals.
4. Develop a purchasing policy to achieve maximum savings at the local and corporate level.
5. Establish policy and procedures for production planning, scheduling, and inventory control.
6. Establish an incentive compensation for salaried employees using the Management-by-Objectives concept.
7. Develop policy and procedures for the control and coordination of trucking and transportation.
8. Establish a corporate preventive maintenance program.
9. Develop a quality control policy giving this department new and stronger positions.
10. Establish methods and responsibility for product pricing to achieve maximum profits.
11. Establish better and more effective procedures for communications.

Stan Rutledge felt that these informal discussions had been helpful in getting Phil to voice his opinions on where the company should be heading. But he was concerned that Phil seemed to base his views neither on the external environment data that had been prepared by the Marketing Department, nor on the weakness brought out by the internal analyses. In fact, some of Phil's views seemed to ignore the realities of the problems identified by his own management group in the internal analysis survey.

A meeting with the Policy Committee to define company objectives and strategy was tentatively scheduled by Phil Todd for late June. But further delays developed due to: an EEOC audit; loss of a plant manager; announcement that the company, a major user of fuel, would get no natural gas after September 1976.

PRESENT SITUATION—EARLY AUGUST 1976

Stan Rutledge, the consultant, was puzzled about his progress in introducing planning. It had taken a full year since June 1975 to move through the ground-laying stages of the company's first planning cycle. The management meeting on objectives and strategies was still not firmly scheduled.

The budgeting process, under Sam Verney's direction, was moving steadily forward. September 1 was the target date for finalizing the budget. Shortly thereafter, a meeting was planned with the bankers on the loan repayment schedule. Operations were at 85% of capacity, a level that would normally be producing reasonable profits, but the debt service requirements were draining the cash flow. Exhibits 18.7–18.10 provide the financial data as of this time.

For the second year, the budgets were not being backed up with either marketing or manufacturing plans since action plans were not scheduled for development until after the objectives and strategies had been outlined. Thus attainment of budget targets for revenue and costs were based on commitments by the respective division heads, but not supported by specific plans. The Policy Committee had not met for over a month. Their top priority issue—the need for clarification of organization responsibilities and authorities—was resting with the President. Phil Todd had requested job descriptions from his top people in May; he was to review these, and feed back changes and clarifications to the incumbents. He had not provided this feedback.

In discussing with Stan Rutledge the potential for cost reduction in the company, Sam Verney commented on the performance of a competitor, Virginia Brick Co. "Virginia," Sam said, "just reported year-end figures reflecting a 30% increase in sales and significant improvement in gross margins." Stan responded, "How does that compare with Richmond?" "Well," Sam said, "our sales and gross margins were flat, with a 4% price increase during the year. Virginia had a 8% price increase. They also had a new highly automated brick facility they haven't put on stream yet—and still they increased sales and margins! We seem to be pricing low and falling behind on manufacturing costs. What's even worse, the latest industry figures show our market share has dropped three percentage points in two years—from 22% to 19%. We're still number one in market share by several percentage points but the competition is moving up."

Stan and Phil Todd had confined their discussions primarily to long-range planning steps. On the infrequent occasions when the discussion got into management effectiveness, Phil spoke rather harshly about the ineffectiveness of several of his key people. When Stan asked him what action he planned to take, Phil turned the discussion to other matters.

Phil was meeting every two months with Harry Crowder, the General

Exhibit 18.7
COMPARATIVE BALANCE SHEETS*
(Thousands of Dollars)

	Period Ended									
	7/31 1976	9/30 1975	9/30 1974	7/31 1974	12/31 1973	12/31 1972	12/31 1971	2/28 1971	2/28 1970	2/28 1969
CURRENT ASSETS										
Cash or equivalents[a]	$ 843	$ 919	$ 795	$ 2,786	$ 4,854	$ 6,482	$ 6,021	$ 4,092	$ 3,381	$ 4,220
Receivables—net	3,311	2,471	2,661	3,558	2,355	2,571	2,607	1,931	2,133	2,364
Inventories	3,777	4,334	4,689	3,873	2,645	1,857	2,151	2,835	2,699	1,934
Prepaids & other	102	101	84	81	48	8	29	6	29	39
TOTAL CURRENT ASSETS	8,033	7,821	8,229	10,298	9,902	10,917	10,808	8,864	8,241	8,556
Fixed assets—net	18,833	20,175	21,156	12,830	11,657	8,180	7,899	7,577	7,914	7,838
Other assets	567	615	806	548	767	564	405	332	329	338
TOTAL	$27,432	$28,611	$30,191	$23,675	$22,325	$19,661	$19,112	$16,772	$16,484	$16,731
CURRENT LIABILITIES	$ 4,050	$ 3,855	$ 5,418	$ 3,050	$ 2,237	$ 1,694	$ 2,420	$ 1,472	$ 1,661	$ 2,355
Long-term notes	22,760	24,638	23,303	168	120	321	521	723	819	1,055
Stockholders' equity	623	119	1,470	20,457	19,968	17,646	16,172	14,577	14,004	13,322
TOTAL	$27,432	$28,611	$30,191	$23,675	$22,325	$19,661	$19,112	$16,772	$16,484	$16,731

* See Exhibit 18.10.
[a] Represents cash in checking accounts, savings accounts, certificates of deposit, and marketable securities.

Exhibit 18.8
STATEMENTS OF INCOME*
(Thousands of Dollars)

	Period Ended									
	7/31 1976[a]	9/30 1975	9/30 1974[b]	7/31 1974[c]	12/31 1973	12/31 1972	12/31 1971[a]	2/28 1971	2/28 1970	2/28 1969
Net sales[d]	$19,824	$18,423	$3,395	$13,271	$24,519	$22,277	$17,778	$14,910	$15,114	$14,981
Cost of sales	15,482	13,916	3,129	9,824	15,923	14,643	11,322	10,494	10,359	9,930
Gross profit	4,343	4,508	266	3,447	8,597	7,634	6,456	4,416	4,755	5,051
Selling, general and administrative expenses	2,081	3,339	701	2,135	3,915	3,270	2,639	2,888	2,792	2,529
Operating income (loss)	2,262	1,169	(435)	1,313	4,682	4,364	3,818	1,529	1,964	2,522
Interest expense	1,995	2,592	476	11	29	35	44	57	83	98
Other income (expense)	237	72	(11)	146	441	287	152	227	155	203
Income (loss) before taxes	504	(1,352)	(921)	1,448	5,094	4,616	3,926	1,698	2,036	2,627
Income taxes	—	—	—	597	2,031	2,169	1,805	800	962	1,274
Net income (loss)	$ 504	$ (1,352)	$ (921)	$ 851	$ 3,063	$ 2,447	$ 2,121	$ 899	$ 1,074	$ 1,353

* See Exhibit 18.10.
[a] Ten months.
[b] Two months
[c] Seven months.
[d] Net of discounts, allowances, and delivery costs.

Exhibit 18.9
STATEMENTS OF CHANGES IN FINANCIAL POSITION*
(Thousands of Dollars)

	Period Ended									
	7/31 1976	9/30 1975	9/30 1974	7/31 1974	12/31 1973	12/31 1972	12/31 1971	2/28 1971	2/28 1970	2/28 1969
SOURCE OF FUNDS										
Net income	$ 504	$ —	$ —	$ 851	$3,063	$2,447	$2,121	$ 899	$1,074	$1,353
Initial capitalization	—	—	2,438	—	—	—	—	—	—	—
Depreciation, depletion, and amortization	1,113	1,341	311	717	1,665	1,317	1,022	1,251	1,373	1,424
Deferred taxes & other	311	402	159	219	(6)	66	234	—	24	71
Decrease in working capital	—	—	3,972	417	1,560	—	—	—	—	—
Increase in long-term debt	44	1,395	24,300[a]	171	—	—	—	—	—	—
TOTAL	$1,971	$3,138	$31,179	$2,375	$6,282	$3,830	$3,377	$2,150	$2,471	$2,847
APPLICATION OF FUNDS										
Net loss	$ —	$1,352	$ 921	—	—	—	—	—	—	—
Increase in working capital	1,781	1,155	—	—	—	837	998	809	381	1,203
Capital expenditures	137	473	28,445	1,890	5,172	1,608	1,697	915	990	1,067
Dividends	—	—	—	363	743	572	392	326	392	392
Payment of long-term debt	54	60	1,292	122	201	201	201	95	237	159
Purchase of treasury stock	—	—	—	—	—	398	—	—	—	—
Other	—	99	522	—	167	215	90	6	471	27
TOTAL	$1,971	$3,138	$31,179	$2,375	$6,282	$3,830	$3,377	$2,150	$2,471	$2,847

* See Exhibit 18.10.
[a] Could be included in "Initial Capitalization" of new company.

EXPLANATORY NOTES TO EXHIBITS 18.7, 18.8, 18.9

Exhibit 18.10

FOR VARIOUS PERIODS ENDED AS SHOWN

1. The Company was on a fiscal year ending on February 28. The periods ended February 28, 1969, February 28, 1970, and February 28, 1971 are for full fiscal years (twelve months).
2. A change to a calendar year was made in 1971. The period ended December 31, 1971 is for 10 months. Periods ended December 31, 1972 and December 31, 1973 are for full fiscal years.
3. Sale of the Company was consummated on July 31, 1974; and the transaction represented a sales/purchase of assets. The period ended July 31, 1974 is for seven months.
4. The new company adopted a fiscal year ending September 30; and the period ended September 30, 1974 is for two months. A full fiscal year is represented for the period ended September 30, 1975.
5. The ten months ended July 31, 1976 is the most recent data available for the current fiscal year, which will end September 30, 1976.

Time executive assigned to monitor Richmond. These meetings focused on financial review and outlook, but little advice was offered. So far there was no indication of pressure for changes in Richmond's management approach.

Several members of top management had recently contacted Stan Rutledge, hoping he could help in generating needed decisions on organization and long-term direction of the company. Those who had invested in stock at the time of the takeover were particularly concerned.

A PHONE CALL

On August 22, Phil Todd had a phone call from Harry Crowder's secretary. She said Mr. Crowder wanted an appointment to meet at Phil's office on August 24th. She also passed the message that the subject for discussion was to be "company strategy."

Case 19

XEROX CORPORATION: PROPOSED DIVERSIFICATION

J. David Hunger / Thomas Conquest / William Miller

In the Autumn of 1982, David Kearns was facing some difficult problems as the new Chief Executive Officer of the Xerox Corporation. His company had recently posted a 39% drop in third quarter earnings. This was Xerox's fourth quarterly decline in a row and the picture didn't appear any brighter for the current quarter. Much of the profit decline had been attributed to narrower profit margins brought on by steep price-cutting on many copier models in response to increasing competition, especially from the Japanese. In addition, profits had been reduced by severance costs of trimming its work force; by the strength of the dollar, which eroded dollar values of sales made abroad; and particularly, by the sluggish economy. Xerox had been forced to reduce its work force by 2174 in 1981, down to 120,981 people worldwide. This was the first such reduction in the company's history. Further reductions occurred in 1982 with more predicted for the coming year. Kearns had watched Xerox's share of the plain paper copier market slip from 95% in the early 1970s to about 45% in 1982. In addition, Xerox stock, which had traded for as high as $172 in 1972, was selling for less than $40 in 1982.

Xerox's attempt to lessen its dependence on the competitive copier market by moving into the broader office automation arena had proved less than spectacular. The Office Products Division has had only one profitable quarter in its seven-year history and racked up losses last year totaling approxi-

This case was prepared by Prof. J. David Hunger, Thomas Conquest, and William Miller of the College of Business, Iowa State University, Ames, Iowa as a basis for class discussion rather than to illustrate either effective or ineffective organizational practices. Presented at the Midwest Case Writers Association Workshop, July 1984. This case also appears in C. F. Douds (ed.), *Annual Advances in Business Cases: 1984* (Chicago: Midwest Case Writers Association, 1985), pp. 203–242 and *Journal of Management Case Studies*, Vol. I, No. 1 (Spring 1985), pp. 13–35. Reprinted by permission.

mately $90 million. Kearns recently admitted to analysts that he did not expect the unit to be profitable until 1984.[1] The division had recently been reorganized in an attempt to more effectively deal with some of these problems. Shortly after the reorganization, however, two of the key executives of the Office Products Division resigned to form their own company. Industry reaction to these resignations and Xerox's proposed acquisition of an insurance company has given rise to reports that Xerox may be somewhat less than enthusiastic about the office automation marketplace and its strategies to garner a piece of the market.

Wall Street analysts were puzzled over Xerox's recent offer to acquire Crum & Forster, an insurance holding company, for about $1.65 billion in cash and securities. The proposed acquisition thrusts Xerox, with a mixed record in diversification efforts, into the property-casualty insurance field, where it has no experience. Kearns has defended the proposed acquisition by saying that it could eventually produce a lot of cash, which Xerox needs to support its vigorous research efforts in its core businesses. He maintained that Xerox's entry into the insurance business would not alter its commitment to the office automation market, nor would it sap resources from Xerox's basic businesses.[2] Some analysts felt, however, that the acquisition may have been a defensive move to a rumored offer by GTE in late summer 1982 to acquire Xerox Corporation. The offer had apparently been made on a very quiet, friendly basis. The mere presence of such an offer, nevertheless, might have prompted top management to more seriously consider making itself less attractive to an acquiring firm by diversifying out of the high-tech industry and by taking on more debt.[3]

HISTORY

Xerography, from the Greek words for "dry" and "writing," is basically a process that uses static electricity to make copies instantly on plain paper. Every office worker today takes it for granted, but it took Chester Carlson, a patent attorney and amateur physicist, several years of dabbling in his kitchen to discover the fundamental principles of what he called "electrophotography." By 1927 he had enough of a process to patent it, and he set up a small lab behind a beauty parlor in Astoria, Long Island, to pursue his experiments. His breakthrough came on October 22, 1938, when he duplicated a glass slide on which he had written: "10-22-38 ASTORIA."

Selling his process was more difficult and frustrating than inventing it. During the next six years Carlson was turned down by more than twenty companies, including such notables as IBM, RCA, and General Electric. Finally, in 1944, the Battelle Memorial Institute, a nonprofit research organization in Columbus, Ohio, became interested. It signed a royalty-sharing contract with Carlson and began to develop the process. In 1947 Battelle entered into an agreement with a small photographic paper company in

Rochester, New York, called Haloid, giving the company the right to develop an "electrophotography" machine. Chester Carlson joined Haloid as a consultant.

Haloid's president, Joseph C. Wilson, had grown up with the business. His grandfather had been one of the company's founders in 1906, and his father had worked for the firm from the start. As Haloid and Battelle continued to develop electrophotography, Wilson decided that the process needed a more distinctive name. A Greek scholar from Ohio State University suggested "xeros" (dry) and "graphien" (writing) to form the word "xerography." The machine itself, they decided, would be called Xerox.

Haloid introduced its first copier in 1949, but it was slow and complicated. Haloid found the early models to be better for making lithography masters than for copying documents, but management was sure they were on the right track. In 1958, they changed the name of the company to Haloid Xerox, and in 1959 the firm marketed the first dependable, easy-to-use document copier. The 914 copier, so named because it could copy sheets as large as 9 × 14 inches, was very successful, and within three years the company was ranked among the FORTUNE 500. In 1961, management changed the name of the company to Xerox.

Between 1959, when Xerox introduced the world's first convenient office copier, and 1974, its sales exploded from $33 million a year to $3.6 billion; its profits mushroomed from $2 million to $331 million; and the price of its stock soared from $2 a share to $172. The company had grown by 100 times in fifteen years. In that same short period, photocopying machines dramatically transformed the nature of office work. Xerography made carbon paper and mimeograph machines obsolete and drastically reduced typing time. By year-end 1970, Xerox held a dominant position in the worldwide office plain-paper copier marketplace with more than a 95% share of the market.

This monopolistic market share was seriously eroded in the 1970s due to increased competition from many sources. Xerox had built its business by creating the plain paper copying market and then protecting it with a solid wall of patents, a classic entry barrier to keep out competition. In 1975, however, the company signed a consent decree with the Federal Trade Commission. The decree forced Xerox to license other companies wanting to use its process. The seventeen-year patent protection was also expiring and Xerox's technology could be used increasingly by anyone. Recognizing the mature state of the reprographics industry, Xerox has positioned itself, through both horizontal and vertical integration, to become a major competitor in the *Office of the Future* marketplace. In 1981, Xerox executives stated to stockholders in the company's annual report that the overriding corporate objective over the next decade is to be one of the leading companies in pro-

Exhibit 19.1

XEROX CORPORATION: 1982 TOP MANAGEMENT

Name	*Title*	*Years W/ Xerox*	*Jobs Prior to Xerox*	*Expertise*
D. T. Kearns*	Chief Executive Officer	11	IBM: Vice President of Data Processing	Marketing
W. F. Glavin*	Executive Vice President	12	IBM: Vice President Operations	Operations
W. F. Souders*	Executive Vice President	18		Marketing
J. V. Titsworth*	Executive Vice President	3	Control Data: Executive Vice President, Systems	
M. H. Antonini	Group Vice President	7	Eltra Corp., Group Vice President Kaiser Jeep International, Vice President	Operations
R. D. Firth	Group Vice President	13	IBM: Various Positions	Personnel
M. Howard*	Senior Vice President, Chief Financial Officer	12	Shoe Corp. of America, Vice President	Finance
F. J. Pipp	Group Vice President	11	Ford Motor Co.	Manufacturing
R. M. Pippitt*	Senior Vice President	21		Marketing
R. S. Banks	Vice President & General Counsel	15	E. I. Dupont, Attorney	Legal Affairs
E. K. Damon	Vice President & Secretary	33		Accounting
S. B. Ross	Vice President & Controller	16	Macmillan Publishing Co., C.P.A. Harris, Kerr & Forster, Accountant	Finance
J. S. Crowley*	Executive Vice President	5	McKinsey & Co., Sr. Partner and Director	Administration
J. E. Goldman*	Senior Vice President	14	Ford Motor Co.	Engineering

SOURCE: Xerox Form 10-K Annual Report, 1981.
* Also serve on the Board of Directors.

viding productivity to the office. "In order to accomplish this," asserted top management, "Xerox must maintain and strengthen its position of leadership in reprographics—as we refer to our total copying and duplicating business—*and* emerge from the 1980's as a leading systems company that is a major factor in automating the office."[4]

MANAGEMENT

David T. Kearns, who had served previously as President and Chief Operating Officer of Xerox, succeeded C. Peter McColough as Chief Executive Officer in May 1982. McColough, who had joined Xerox in 1954 and served as chief executive since 1968, continued as Chairman of the Board. Other key executives and related information are shown in Exhibit 19.1. Xerox's top management has generally been promoted from within. Outside help has been recruited when the company has had to deal with significant changes in strategy or the introduction of new products.

There are nineteen directors on the Xerox board, eight of whom are officers of the corporation. The eleven outside directors include a retired executive vice-president of Xerox, two university professors (one from Europe), the chairman of the board of Prudential Insurance, a retired chairman of American Express, the president of the Children's Television Workshop, a managing director of Deutsch Bank AG, the chairman of an investment firm, a president of a university, and two partners in a Washington-based law firm. Together, the corporation's directors and officers own about 1% of the common stock of the firm.

The corporation introduced an executive long-term incentive plan in 1976 under which approximately 5.4 million shares of common stock have been reserved for issue. In December 1981, the board of directors amended the plan to provide for the issuance of incentive stock options as defined in the Economic Recovery Tax Act of 1981. Under the plan, eligible employees may be granted incentive stock rights, incentive stock options, non-qualified stock options, stock appreciation rights, and performance unit rights. Performance rights entitle the employee to receive the value of the performance unit in cash, in shares of common stock, or a combination of the two at the company's discretion. The value of a performance unit is determined by a formula based upon the achievement of specific performance goals. Performance unit rights are payable at the end of a five-year award period.

BUSINESS SEGMENTS

Although Xerox Corporation is organized around a set of groups and divisions, it primarily defines itself in terms of its various businesses. Xerox's principal business segment is reprographics, consisting of the development, manufacture, and marketing of xerographic copiers and duplicators, electronic printing systems, and providing related service. Another significant segment is paper, consisting primarily of the distribution of paper related to reprographic products. The other business segments include electric typewriters, word processors, small computers, facsimile transceivers, toner and other supplies, and publishing education-related materials. Estimated revenues and profits for each product line are shown in Exhibit 19.2.

Reprographics

Xerox manufactures and markets reprographic equipment for lease or purchase. Leasing accounted for over 55% of the company's revenues in 1981. The revenues and profits from this segment depend principally on the number of units of xerographic equipment leased and the usage of these units. In 1981, the Reprographics segment accounted for 72% of revenues.

Exhibit 19.2

XEROX CORPORATION: ESTIMATED REVENUES, OPERATING PROFIT, AND OPERATING MARGINS BY PRODUCT LINE, 1981 (Millions of Dollars)

Product Line	*Revenues*	*Operating Profit*	*Operating Margin*
			%
Copiers			
Rentals	4,805	—	—
Sales	1,135	—	—
Paper & supplies	795	—	—
Total	6,735	1,400	20.8
Office products			
Word processing & small computers	310	(22)	—
Facsimile	95	11	11.6
Total	405	(11)	—
Peripherals			
Printing	125	(15)	—
Xerox computer services	90	10	11.1
Shugart	200	25	12.5
Century data	110	10	9.1
Diablo	130	13	10.0
Versatec	75	7	9.3
Kurzweil	5	0.5	10.0
Total	735	50.5	6.9
Other products			
Publishing	320	805	9.4
WUI	175	26	14.9
Other	310	25	8.1
Total	805	81	10.1
TOTAL	8,680	1,520.5	17.5

SOURCE: *Xerox: A Strategic Analysis* (New York: Northern Business Information, Inc., 1982), p. 6.

Copiers Copying machines have been and still are the largest segment of Xerox's business. However, Xerox has experienced problems in this segment over the past few years. Increased competition from IBM and Kodak in the medium volume market and Japan in the lower volume market has significantly decreased Xerox's market share. Competing now with 40 companies selling at least 240 different models, Xerox's share of the plain paper copier industry in the United States has dropped from 67% to 43% over the past five years. The market, however, has grown in terms of total revenues from $2.8 billion in 1976 to $7.5 billion in 1981. Competitors imported more than a million units into the country in 1981. Analysts expected this number to increase by 50% in 1982.[5] Xerox faces similar competition worldwide. Current estimates of market share data are presented in Exhibit 19.3.

"We really should have been thinking about the market on a much broader basis," says Kearns.[6] Xerox ignored the low-cost coated paper copier that dominated the world copier market before Xerox introduced the first plain paper copier. But the coated paper copiers served a market much larger than anyone knew. Xerox has clearly fought back to regain some of its lost market share. It has cut prices on its lower volume models, concentrating on cutting costs to improve profit margins, and decentralizing the management of the reprographics group to enable more timely and market oriented decision making. Two desk top copiers, the 2350 and 2830, were introduced in 1982 with a selling price of around $3,500 each. A new line of low and medium volume copiers will be introduced in January 1983 labeled the "10" series. These copiers will be imported from Fuji Xerox Co. in Japan. "If you can't beat 'em, join 'em," states Peter McColough.[7] Xerox will also bring in parts and subassemblies from the Japanese affiliate to help lower costs. The new 10 series costs between 40% and 50% less to produce than earlier machines.

Exhibit 19.3

XEROX CORPORATION: ESTIMATED COPIER REVENUES AND MARKET SHARE BY GEOGRAPHIC AREA, 1981

Area	*Market Size*	*Xerox Revenues*	*Xerox Market Share*
U.S.	7,350	$3,160	43%
Europe	4,900	2,200	45%
Japan	1,510	620	41%
Canada	725	410	56%
Other	—	525	—

SOURCE: *Xerox: A Strategic Analysis* (New York: Northern Business Information, Inc., 1982), p. 79.

Another technique used by Xerox to stay competitive is called "competitive benchmarking." This means looking carefully at the lowest priced competing copier, determining exactly how it is being produced for less, and developing a plan to make and sell a competitive product.

In large copiers, Xerox still dominates the industry with a 70% market share. This is due mainly to Xerox's large and experienced sales and service staff. Japanese companies currently lack extensive service support and are not seen to offer Xerox much competition in the higher priced copier market in the near future. Xerox has many models in this market with high output rates and sorting capabilities. Prices range from $25,000 to $125,000.

In a maturing market with high competition, Xerox management realizes that the copier segment will not provide growing profits in the long run the way the company would like. This realization underlies the company's diversification into office automation. Eugene C. Glazer of Dean Witter Reynolds states, "Eventually the company won't make it if they have to depend only on copiers."[8] In the company's annual report, David Kearns notes, "To continue to succeed in the face of strong competition, Xerox must undergo major and lasting change." Robert D. Firth, however, president of the Reprographics group, maintains, "Our copier business is and will remain the main business of Xerox for the projectable future."[9]

Electronic Printing

Listed under Peripherals in Exhibit 19.2, this segment became a dominant product line in 1977 with the introduction of the 9700 electronic printer. Until March 1982, the electronic printing segment reported to U.S. copier operations in Rochester. Now established as the Printing Systems Division, it reports directly to corporate headquarters in Stamford, Connecticut. The traditional computer printout method has been impact printing with ink ribbons and mechanical printing heads on 11 × 17 inch fan-fold computer paper. Although this printing serves many purposes, Xerox management believes that for periodic reports, forms, proposals, or other information stored on electronic computer data files, non-bulky and clear printouts would provide a better alternative. With its electronic printer, Xerox has combined computer technology, lasers, and xerography to design a printer that can print exceptionally clear text on standard 8½ × 11 inch paper. In addition, this printer can print graphics, which cannot be done on most traditional printers, and it has multiple copy and sorting capabilities as well. Xerox management sees electronic printing as playing a large role in the company's future. Customers seem to agree. Jack Jones, Vice-President of the Southern Railway System, states that "the quality of the print is such that everybody is enthusiastic about the smaller page."[10]

In 1980 Xerox developed the 5700 printing system. Priced at $66,000, this unit is designed to be used in an office environment, whereas the 9700 is geared more towards a computer room. The 5700 has the same basic technology as the 9700, but is extremely easy to use with a touch control screen to eliminate operator confusion. It can also be connected to Xerox's Ethernet network system to provide printing from various word processors or computer terminals on the network. A lower priced model has been released on a limited basis with many of the same features as the 9700 and 5700. The 2700, priced at $19,000, is marketed for the small business that can't afford some of the more expensive models.

Xerox has approximately 40% of the global market for electronic printing—slightly behind IBM with Honeywell a distant third in market share. The market in electronic printing may soon be crowded with heavy competition from Japanese companies, such as Canon and Fujitsu. It is also a market where new technology may change things drastically. Ink jet printing and heat transfer processes are already being considered as printing alternatives.

Currently, electronic printing accounts for only 15% of the $8.7 billion computer printing market. Predictions for electronic printing are for a $5.8 billion market by 1986. According to Robert Adams, president of Xerox's Printing Systems Division, "The majority of information generated from host computers and word processors will someday be produced by electronic printers."[11] Although Xerox revenues in 1981 from electronic printing were estimated at $125 million by Northern Business Information, Inc., a New York-based research firm, the newly established Printing Systems Division was hoping for $300 million in revenues in 1982 and $2 billion annually in revenues by 1987.[12]

Office Products

The Office Products Division (responsible for electronic typewriters, word processors, and facsimile telecopiers) and the Office Systems Division manufacture and market information processing equipment for use in the *office of the future.* Although office products accounted for only 10% of the company's revenues in 1981, the commitment was made several years ago to steer Xerox away from a copier-only company to an information company capable of supplying many types of office information and equipment. Current estimates of market share data for both divisions are provided in Exhibit 19.4.

The 860 Information Processing System first marketed in 1979 is a word processing workstation with full text editing capability. It is medium priced and designed for use by professional and clerical personnel. It has limited programming capability. Xerox introduced its 8010 Star Professional workstation in 1981 for a price of $17,000. It is designed for use by managers and professionals to perform word and data processing tasks with a mini-

XEROX CORPORATION: ESTIMATED OFFICE PRODUCTS REVENUES AND MARKET SHARE BY GEOGRAPHIC AREA, 1981 (Millions of Dollars)

Exhibit 19.4

Segment	*Total Xerox Revenues*	*U.S. Xerox Revenues*	*U.S. Market Size*	*U.S. Xerox Share*	*International Xerox Revenues*
Word processing	295	180	1,386	13%	115
Facsimile telecopiers	95	50	165	30%	45
Small business systems	15	10	1,300	1%	5

SOURCE: *Xerox: A Strategic Analysis* (New York: Northern Business Information, Inc., 1982), p. 115.

mum of training. Its ease of use makes it very desirable in preparing presentations and reports.

In 1981, the 820 Information Processor was developed to service a broad range of needs. It can be used as a limited professional workstation for small businesses which cannot afford the Star. It can also be used as a business or personal computer or a word processor. Prices for the microcomputer system start at $3,000 and options for word processing capability bring the price up to $6,500. These prices make the model very competitive with the Apple II or Radio Shack TRS Model III personal computer and also with the IBM Displaywriter and Wang Wangwriter word processors. Xerox also introduced in 1981 a new line of electronic typewriters, called Memorywriters, and an inexpensive (under $1,000) personal computer.

Probably the biggest gamble that Xerox is taking in the office product segment is its *Ethernet* concept. Ethernet is a communication network designed for short physical distances (intra-building) that will connect many pieces of office equipment by coaxial cable together into one information system. This concept allows for several word processors or professional workstations to use common data banks or printing facilities that are in different physical locations within the building. Xerox's marketing strategy is to force its Ethernet network as an industry standard so that all manufacturers of office equipment will be pressured to make their equipment compatible.

Peter McCologh describes the development this way: "We can go into your company and tell you that you don't have to stick with Xerox. You can go to DEC, Intel, or anybody else. The IBM approach says: "We'll put our system in there with IBM equipment, but you won't be able to get much else."[13] This compatibility argument is an extremely effective marketing tool for customers leery of total commitment. The automated office product market is highly competitive and expanding. Major competitors include IBM, Wang, Exxon, Hewlett-Packard, and dozens of smaller companies.

Many problems currently face Xerox's office product divisions. Contributions to profits have been nonexistent for the last several years. Although Xerox has intentionally sacrificed profits to get a jump on competitors, the new products are not selling as management had hoped they would by this time. Of the 300 Ethernet system installations planned for 1981, only 45 were completed. Marketing may be to blame. The company acknowledged the 820 had met with little success in the retail sales environment because many had perceived the machine as an entry into the home computer market, not the office. Software development problems created delays for the full-scale production of the 8010 Star. In addition, the country's prolonged recession has prevented companies from making commitments in office automation.

Disagreements between top management and division management resulted in the resignations of Donald Massaro, president of Xerox Office Systems, and David E. Liddle, Vice-President. The 39-year-old Massaro had founded Shugart Associates, a leading computer memory manufacturer which had been acquired by Xerox in 1977. Liddle, a 10-year Xerox veteran, had worked closely with Massaro to develop the Star and Ethernet. In an interview with *Business Week,* Massaro asserted that he resigned because he wanted complete control of Xerox's office systems effort. He conceded, however, that in a corporation like Xerox where 75% of the revenues and almost all the profits came from copiers and duplicators, "it was frustrating trying to get the attention of top management."[14] Analysts felt that Massaro's resignation was an expected result of the battle between the "old Xerox," epitomized by the conservative East Coast copier group, and the "new Xerox," epitomized by the freewheeling California-type entrepreneurial Massaro. A consultant who had worked extensively with Xerox suggested that a real schism had developed. "The copier people didn't like the idea they were being used as a cash cow and Xerox's office systems people could spend all this money without making any."[15]

In a report from Strategic, Inc., before the Office Products Division was split, the company's president, Michael Killen, boldly predicted, "Xerox will fail because the Office Products Division will fail; and the Office Products Division will fail because Ethernet will fail."[16] Killen's rationale is that Ethernet is built on base band modulation techniques which limit information over the network to interactive data. Broad band modulation techniques, on the other hand, although more complex with which to interface components, allow video and voice communications as well as interactive data.

Ethernet may not become the formal industry standard supported by the Institute of Electrical and Electronics Engineers. Much squabbling is still going on over this issue. Hewlett-Packard, for example, has dropped its support of Ethernet in favor of the slightly different IEEE 802 proposed local-area-networking (LAN) standard. Nevertheless, Xerox management plans to continue working to get Ethernet accepted by the industry as an informal standard even though IBM is said to be working on its own version of Ethernet.

Many people continue to believe that Ethernet is a viable system. John W. King, an industry analyst, says, "Ethernet is alive and well and has excellent prospects through the 1980's." King sees Ethernet and broad band networks working together.[17] Many new electronic components have been developed to simplify connecting equipment to Ethernet. Digital Equipment Corporation (DEC) and Intel agreed to a joint venture with Xerox in May 1980. DEC's role was to provide design expertise in the area of communication transceivers and computer networks. Intel provided expertise in integrated circuits for communications functions. Since Xerox has based all its products in the office segment around Ethernet, its future is of vital strategic importance.

Other Segments

Xerox is one of the largest distributors in the world of standard cut sheet paper used for writing, typing, copying, and other office needs. In addition, it also distributes many types of office chemicals for use with its machines.

Xerox's peripheral subsidiaries are generally composed of acquisitions that helped to vertically integrate the company. Shugart Associates manufactures floppy disk drives, Diablo Systems, Inc. manufactures daisy wheel printers (a substitute technology for IBM's famous typewriter ball), Century Data Systems manufactures rigid disk drives, Versatec manufactures electrostatic printers and plotters, and Kurzweil makes optical scanners. Xerox Computer Services was established in 1970 as an outgrowth of its Scientific Data Systems acquisition and offers timesharing and software packages. Other products and services include published materials, information services, medical systems, and a credit service.

MARKETING

In the past, Xerox has traditionally been a single-product company, selling copiers to large businesses through its own sales and service force. This has changed over the past several years as it has diversified its product lines and redefined its customers. All the company's product lines have been revamped to offer a wide range of products, not only to larger companies, but to smaller businesses as well. With the advent of Ethernet, a systems approach to marketing has become necessary.

To better meet the distribution problems associated with the company's new concepts, Xerox is experimenting with new distribution techniques. Independent distributors and dealers have been contracted to sell products not only to end users, but also to Original Equipment Manufacturers (OEM's) who resell the products as part of a larger system. These distribution channels reduce the company's expenses, thereby increasing profit margins while unburdening the company's own sales force. Xerox also plans to use retail chains as well as its own retail stores to reach small business people. It has already opened approximately thirty retail stores throughout the United States and management has plans to open more nationwide. All outlets are named *The Xerox Store* and are designed to make the small business person comfortable in a store with a familiar name and reputation. In addition to selling Xerox's equipment, these retail outlets also carry brand name equipment of other manufacturers (including competitors) for home and office use. Most of this other equipment complements Xerox's own product line. This supermarket approach includes the selling of Apple Computers, Hewlett-Packard calculators, Matsushita dictating machines, as well as a host of other products.[18]

Xerox is also using new promotions as part of its marketing strategy. Management has cut prices on many products to better compete with Japanese firms for the small business person's dollar. Mail order and telephone campaigns are also being used to reach smaller firms. For the larger customers, Xerox has been offering quantity discounts as an incentive to buy total systems.

According to industry analysts, Xerox has three major marketing strengths. First, its sales and service staff is the largest in the industry. These people have excellent sales skills and are well known in most major companies. Second, the company has large financial resources to fund challenging new product developments. No other company, with the possible exception of IBM, could have tackled the highly complex Star workstation project. Third, the Xerox name is a household word, and gives the business person a feeling of confidence when it comes to getting the product serviced.

If there is any weakness in the company's marketing department, analysts agree it is its lack of expertise in marketing complex office products and systems. There is apparently a world of difference between marketing standalone copying machines and marketing technically more involved information handling and processing systems. In addition, retailing is a new field for Xerox and one in which it has no previous experience. There appears to be some confusion among customers as to the purpose of several particular products. For example, Xerox's efforts to sell the 820 to the retail market through Xerox stores as well as distributors has been costly and somewhat ineffective. Jack Darcy, Senior Vice-President of Kierulff Distributors, an independent distributor who sells equipment from many manufacturers to industrial users, says: "There is such a difference in the mentality to run a successful retail operation and to run a successful industrial business. At Kierulff, we're pointing our effort totally toward the industrial. Xerox, as I understand it, is a consumer product. We're not interested."[19]

FINANCIAL

Consolidated income statements and balance sheets for the 5-year period of 1977–1981 are shown in Exhibits 19.5, 19.6, and 19.7. Although Xerox

Exhibit 19.5

XEROX CORPORATION: CONSOLIDATED INCOME STATEMENTS 1977–1981
(In Millions, Except Per-Share Data)

	1981	1980	1979	1978	1977
Operating revenues					
Rentals and services	$5,279.6	$5,151.6	$4,606.3	$4,130.5	$3,713.8
Sales	3,411.4	3,044.9	2,390.1	1,887.5	1,368.2
Total operating revenues	8,691.0	8.196.5	6,996.4	6,018.0	5,082.0
Costs and expenses					
Cost of rentals & services	2,269.5	2,167.5	1,905.0	1,691.6	1,477.1
Cost of sales	1,570.8	1,435.6	1,075.1	770.6	579.8
Research & development	526.3	435.8	378.1	311.0	269.0
Selling, administrative, & general	3,095.0	2,882.1	2,432.9	2,089.0	1,760.9
Total costs & expenses	7,461.6	6,921.0	5,791.1	4,862.2	4,086.8
Operating income	1,229.4	1,275.5	1,205.3	1,155.8	995.2
Other income less interest expense	(49.5)	3.6	1.7	(64.6)	(82.4)
Income before income taxes	1,179.9	1,279.1	1,207.0	1,091.2	912.8
Income taxes	454.4	611.8	587.2	528.0	440.5
Income before outside shareholders' interests	725.5	667.3	619.8	563.2	472.3
Outside shareholders' interests	127.3	102.4	104.8	86.7	68.3
Net income	$ 598.2	$ 564.9	$ 515.0	$ 476.5	$ 404.0
Average common shares outstanding	84.5	84.4	84.1	84.1	83.9
Net income per common share	$ 7.08	$ 6.69	$ 6.12	$ 5.91	$ 5.15

SOURCE: *Moody's 1982 Industrial Manual,* p. 4672 and 1981 Annual Report, Xerox Corporation, p. 29.

Exhibit 19.6

XEROX CORPORATION: CONSOLIDATED BALANCE SHEETS 1977–1981
(Millions of Dollars)

	1981	1980	1979	1978	1977
ASSETS					
Current assets					
Cash	$ 45.2	$ 86.8	$ 42.2	$ 57.7	$ 73.3
Bank time deposits	234.0	228.8	267.7	412.0	338.4
Marketable securities	148.0	207.3	447.7	269.8	280.3
Trade receivables	1,245.3	1,163.8	1,120.4	927.5	731.0
Receivable from Xerox credit corp.	178.2	196.3	—	—	—
Accrued revenues	403.3	376.8	259.3	211.3	191.6
Inventories	1,131.9	1,090.2	785.8	601.8	525.3
Other current assets	230.2	210.0	180.5	158.7	128.7
Total current assets	3,616.1	3,560.0	3,103.6	2,638.8	2,268.6
Trade receivables due after one year	245.5	199.4	274.2	216.2	104.9
Rental equipment & related inventories	1,905.1	1,966.8	1,736.4	1,501.2	1,397.7
Land, buildings, & equipment	1,438.7	1,410.4	1,222.3	1,111.3	1,029.2
Investments, at equity	319.6	226.6	105.7	67.9	63.2
Other assets	149.4	150.6	111.4	137.7	183.0
Total assets	$7,674.4	$7,513.8	$6,553.6	$5,765.7	$5,046.6
LIABILITIES AND SHAREHOLDERS' EQUITY					
Current liabilities					
Notes payable	$ 224.2	$ 208.4	$ 96.3	$ 64.5	$ 109.6
Current portion of long-term debt	96.3	80.0	40.2	52.4	57.5
Accounts payable	340.2	315.8	325.1	273.2	209.4
Salaries, profit-sharing, other accruals	909.9	907.3	689.5	600.7	475.1
Income taxes	346.5	425.4	426.0	328.8	232.3
Other current liabilities	163.7	147.8	102.2	81.3	61.7
Total current liabilities	2,080.8	2,084.7	1,679.3	1,400.9	1,145.6
Long-term debt	869.5	898.3	913.0	938.3	1,020.0
Other noncurrent liabilities	145.0	133.0	127.9	97.2	46.1
Deferred income taxes	247.0	142.7	110.4	62.7	—
Deferred investment tax credits	108.9	85.6	70.1	63.2	59.6
Outside shareholders' interests in equity of subsidiaries	495.6	539.5	431.5	349.0	315.2

SOURCE: *Moody's 1982 Industrial Manual,* p. 4673 and 1981 Annual Report, Xerox Corporation, pp. 30–31.

Exhibit 19.6 **(*Continued*)**

	1981	1980	1979	1978	1977
LIABILITIES AND SHAREHOLDERS' EQUITY (*Continued*)					
Shareholders' equity					
Common stock, $1 par value authorized 100,000 shares	84.3	84.3	83.9	83.8	80.1
Class B stock, $1 par value authorized 600,000 shares	.2	.2	.2	.3	.3
Additional paid-in capital	306.0	304.9	286.8	286.0	257.3
Retained earnings	3,500.1	3,155.4	2,866.2	2,501.3	2,142.0
Cumulative translation adjustments	(150.1)	98.8	—	—	—
Total	3,740.5	3,643.6	3,237.1	2,871.4	2,479.7
Deduct class B stock receivables	12.9	13.6	15.7	17.0	19.6
Total shareholders' equity	3,727.6	3,630.0	3,221.4	2,854.4	2,460.1
Total Liabilities and Shareholders' Equity	$7,674.4	$7,513.8	$6,553.6	$5,765.7	$5,046.6

management considers the firm to be strong financially, it can be seen that both revenues and profits have been increasing at a decreasing rate. From 1964 to 1974, net income had grown 24% a year on 30% annual revenue gains. From 1975 to 1981, revenues increased 15%, compounded annually, while earnings for the same period increased by slightly over 12% a year. In the first nine months of 1982, Xerox's net income was $370 million, down 24% from the same period the year earlier. Revenues were $6.24 billion, slightly down from $6.28 billion during the same period in 1981.

Data outlining Xerox's common stock performance is given in Exhibit 19.8. The company's stock, which made millionaires of several early investors, has recently traded as low as $27 per share, bringing its P/E ratio to an all-time low. In addition, Xerox stock reacted negatively to the news of the proposed acquisition of Crum & Forster, falling over $3 per share. Investment analysts have recently advised customers to postpone purchases of Xerox stock "until current operations show some sign of life."[20]

Xerox attributes much of the earnings decline to greatly reduced profit margins, as shown in Exhibit 19.9. The company's after-tax profit margin in the third quarter of 1982 was equal to 4.7% of sales, down from 7.9% a year earlier. In the first nine months of 1982, the profit margin was 5.9%, com-

Exhibit 19.7

XEROX CORPORATION: BUSINESS SEGMENT DATA, 1979–1981*
(Millions of Dollars)

	1981	1980	1979
Reprographics			
Rentals and services	$4,974.2	$4,840.9	$4,313.1
Sales	1,419.2	1,224.1	990.6
Total operating revenues	6,393.4	6,065.0	5,303.7
Operating profit	1,355.6	1,326.1	1,243.0
Identifiable assets	5,172.2	5,212.4	4,544.9
Depreciation	717.9	718.6	664.6
Capital expenditures	1,202.3	1,108.0	1,004.0
Paper			
Operating revenues (sales)	554.5	573.6	446.4
Operating profit	34.9	44.2	34.9
Identifiable assets	202.6	220.9	185.5
Depreciation	8.0	8.3	7.7
Capital expenditures	11.0	13.1	11.3
Other Businesses			
Rentals and services	449.3	409.1	357.1
Sales	1,437.7	1,247.2	953.1
Transfers between segments	37.4	34.0	16.6
Total operating revenues	1,924.4	1,690.3	1,326.8
Operating profit	107.8	124.7	106.1
Identifiable assets	1,511.2	1,398.0	1,171.5
Depreciation	96.8	98.3	90.3
Capital expenditures	188.1	192.4	179.7

SOURCE: 1981 Annual Report, Xerox Corporation, p. 36.

* Figures do not sum to data in consolidated income statements because of various adjustments and expenses due to foreign currency gains and losses and general expense items not included in this exhibit.

pared with 7.7% in 1981. Xerox top management attributes the squeeze on profit margins to several factors:

1. Increased competition has forced price reductions on many copier models, especially in the low volume segment where competition has been the fiercest. Reductions of up to 27% have been seen on many models.

Exhibit 19.8

XEROX CORPORATION: STOCK PERFORMANCE, 1973–1982

	1982	1981	1980	1979	1978	1977	1976	1975	1974	1973
High price ($)	41.8	64.0	71.8	69.1	64.0	58.8	68.4	87.6	127.1	170.0
Low price ($)	27.1	37.4	48.6	52.6	40.5	43.1	48.8	46.4	49.0	114.8
Book value ($)	46.45	44.11	42.90	38.29	34.72	30.76	27.30	23.97	22.14	18.89
Earnings per share ($)	—	7.08	7.33	6.69	5.77	5.06	4.51	3.07	4.18	3.80
P/E ratio	—	7.1	8.2	9.0	8.9	9.9	13.2	20.8	22.3	39.0
Dividends per share ($)	3.00	3.00	2.80	2.40	2.00	1.50	1.10	1.00	1.00	.90
Earnings yield (%)	—	14.1	12.2	11.1	11.2	10.1	7.6	4.8	4.5	2.6
Dividend yield (%)	—	5.9	4.7	4.0	3.9	3.0	1.9	1.6	1.1	0.6
Common shares (million)	84.55	84.51	84.48	84.14	80.24	80.37	79.83	79.57	79.24	27.17

SOURCE: *Value Line Investment Survey,* November 12, 1982.

XEROX CORPORATION: AFTER-TAX MARGINS, 1967–1982

Exhibit 19.9

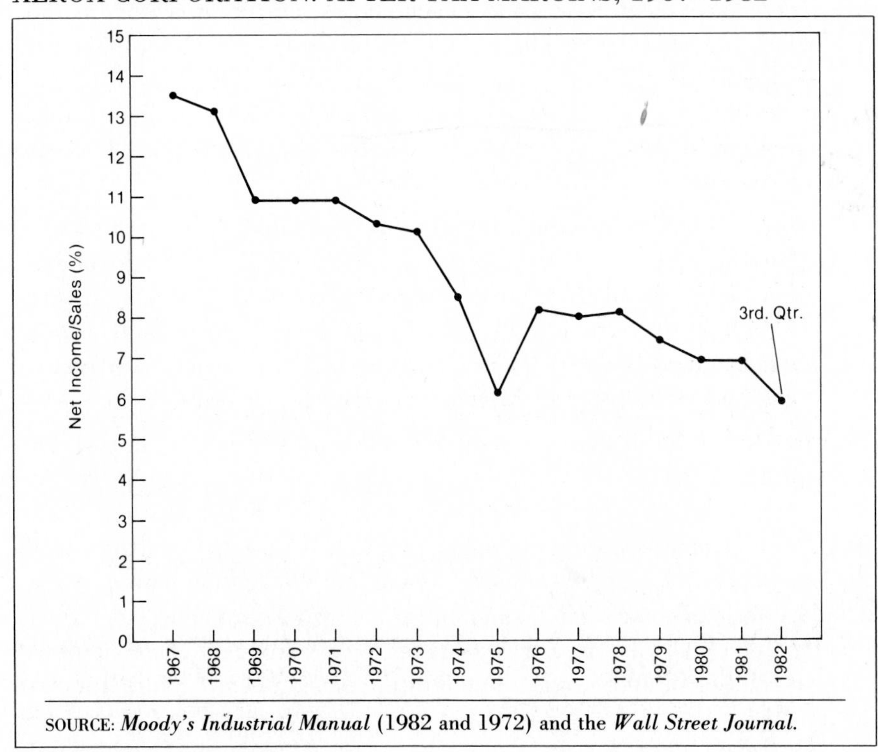

SOURCE: *Moody's Industrial Manual* (1982 and 1972) and the *Wall Street Journal.*

Exhibit 19.10

XEROX CORPORATION: COPIER REVENUES AND OPERATING PROFIT BY MARKET SEGMENT, 1981
(Millions of Dollars)

Segment	*Revenue*	*Operating Profit*	*Operating Margins %*
Low volume	2,020	300	14.9
Medium volume	2,265	700	30.9
High volume	1,835	365	19.9
Paper & supplies	795	70	8.8
TOTAL	6,915	1,435	20.8

SOURCE: *Xerox: A Strategic Analysis* (New York: Northern Business Information, Inc., 1982), p. 80.

2. Increased revenues have occurred in the low-volume copier segment where margins are traditionally lower. (See Exhibit 19.10.)
3. There have been increasing expenditures for research and development, and capital expenditures. In 1981, Xerox spent $526 million and $1.4 billion for these items, respectively. Of the 1981 total for capital expenditures, $1.1 billion was for additions to rental equipment and related inventories, and the balance was for additions to land, buildings, and equipment.
4. Revenues and net income from foreign operations represented 44% and 41%, respectively, of the company's 1981 total. Due to the strong dollar, it is estimated that foreign currency translations created a $64.5 million loss to Xerox in 1981. If unfavorable current impacts were excluded, international revenue growth would have been 13 percent in 1981 over 1980, slightly higher than domestic growth.
5. The reduction of overhead cost the company $63 million in severance costs in 1981.

RESEARCH AND DEVELOPMENT

The Xerox research and development program is directed primarily to the development of new and improved copying and duplicating equipment and supplies, facsimile and digital communications equipment, computer peripheral equipment and services, as well as to the development of new products and capabilities in other areas related to the broad field of information systems.

The company's Palo Alto Research Center (PARC) was established in

Palo Alto, California in 1969 by then-President Peter McColough to provide the technology Xerox needed to become "an architect of information" in the office. Flourishing under a hands-off policy by corporate headquarters, PARC soon developed an excellent reputation within the research community. The Center developed technology in computer-aided design, artificial intelligence, and laser printers. Xerox's ability to design custom chips for use in future copiers comes largely from PARC. Nevertheless, analysts contend that Xerox has been unable to really take advantage of PARC's research on computerized office systems, its original reason for being. Arguing that Xerox's sheer size slows decision making, analysts state that the corporation has trouble translating first-rate research into profitable products. It is simply unable to move quickly into small, fast-changing markets.

Loose management by headquarters also may have encouraged PARC to go into the development of products which were not necessarily in line with the corporation's needs. For example, PARC worked in the mid-1970s to develop the Alto, a computer with some of the attributes of a personal computer, which was supposed to serve as a research prototype. Alto and its software became so popular inside Xerox that some researchers began to develop it as a commercial product. This put PARC into direct conflict with Xerox's product development group which was developing a rival machine called the Star. Since the Star was in line with the company's expressed product strategy of developing complete office systems, the Alto was ignored by top management and emphasis was placed on the Star and the Ethernet concept. The conflict between PARC and Xerox top management has resulted in a number of researchers leaving PARC for firms such as Atari and Apple.

Jack Goldman, Xerox's former research chief, suggests that a big company like Xerox wants every product to be a "home run" in order to justify the costs of marketing and development. Another former employee says that top management "followed the big-bang strategy. They wanted to build absolutely the best office system instead of taking things bit by bit."[21]

In 1981, Xerox incurred $526 million in research and development expenses, approximately 6% of total revenues. Less than $35 million went to PARC. The $526 million represents less than the average percentage of research and development to sales of some of Xerox's major competitors (Hewlett-Packard, 9.7%; Apple Computer, 6.3%; Burroughs, 6.5%; Commodore, 5.9%; Digital Equipment Corp., 9.0%; Honeywell, 7.0%; IBM, 5.5%; Wang, 7.5%; CPT, 5.0%).[22]

OPERATIONS AND INTERNATIONAL

Xerox's principal xerographic facilities are located on a 1047 acre site owned in Webster, New York, a suburb of Rochester. Corporate headquarters were moved to Stamford, Connecticut in 1969 in order that corporate attention would be given not only to xerography, but to xerography overseas, to computers, data processing, education and other extensions of activity generated by acquisitions, mergers, and related research. The Office Products Division, recently reorganized into Office Products and Office Systems, is located in Dallas, Texas. The Office Systems Division, located in Palo Alto, California, is responsible for marketing local network-based office systems to end users. In forming these two divisions, Xerox retained centralized marketing, sales, and manufacturing functions with the Office Products Division in Dallas.

Xerox's largest interests outside the United States are the Rank Xerox Companies—comprising Rank Xerox Limited of London, England, Rank Xerox Holding B.V. of the Netherlands and their respective subsidiaries—and the other subsidiaries jointly owned by Xerox and the Rank Organization. Approximately 51% of the voting power of Rank Xerox Limited and Rank Xerox Holding B.V. is owned directly or indirectly by Xerox and 49% is owned directly or indirectly by the Rank Organization Limited. The earnings of the Rank Xerox Companies are allocated according to an agreement between Xerox and the Rank Organization. For 1981, approximately 66% of the earnings of Rank Xerox was allocated to Xerox. Rank Xerox Limited manufactures and markets most xerographic copier/duplicator products developed by Xerox. Its manufacturing operations are located principally in the United Kingdom.

Fuji Xerox Co., Ltd., of Tokyo, Japan, equally owned by Fuji Photo Film Co., Ltd., of Japan and by Rank Xerox Limited, manufactures in Japan various copiers, duplicators, and supplies which are marketed principally in Japan and in other areas of the Far East. They are also marketed by Xerox in the United States and by Rank Xerox Limited in Europe.

THE PROPOSED CRUM & FORSTER ACQUISITION

In September 1982, Xerox announced an agreement to acquire Crum & Forster, an insurance holding company, for about $1.65 billion in cash and securities. Crum & Forster, the nation's fifteenth largest property-casualty insurer with 1981 premium volume of $1.6 billion, is largely involved in writing insurance for businesses. In 1981, it drew 83% of its premiums from commercial insurance lines. Its biggest line is workers' compensation insurance, which generated 28% of premiums last year. Other lines include commercial casualty, commercial automobile, multiple-peril and fire insurance. In 1981, its operating income was $171 million, up 17% over 1980. Its net income of $176 million increased 24 percent over 1980. (See Exhibits 19.11 and 19.12.) This increase in net income, however, was due almost entirely to an increase in net investment income of $270 million. Pre-tax underwriting losses of over $70 million were somewhat larger than in 1980.

Exhibit 19.11

CRUM AND FORSTER AND SUBSIDIARIES: CONSOLIDATED STATEMENT OF INCOME FOR THE YEARS ENDED DECEMBER 31 (All amounts except per share stated in thousands.)

	1981	1980	1979	1978	1977
INCOME:					
Net premiums written	$1,624,614	$1,660,636	$1,585,022	$1,436,061	$1,283,149
Increase (decrease) in unearned premiums	15,522	(4,473)	50,742	69,891	60,210
Premiums earned	1,609,092	1,665,109	1,534,280	1,366,170	1,222,939
Net investment ncome	270,199	220,957	171,967	132,526	103,400
Commission income	45,203	44,306	38,280	26,564	11,870
Rental income on operating properties	591	627	541	876	566
Total income	1,925,085	1,930,999	1,745,068	1,526,136	1,338,775
EXPENSES:					
Losses	954,844	988,041	881,070	769,907	722,228
Loss expenses	173,907	187,377	183,995	144,423	131,252
Acquisition costs	496,328	507,847	450,936	400,257	339,075
General expenses	65,505	46,315	39,843	26,102	17,509
Dividends to policyholders	62,940	55,371	26,866	24,622	21,895
Total expenses	1,753,524	1,784,951	1,582,710	1,365,311	1,231,959
Operating income before federal and foreign income taxes	171,561	146,048	162,358	160,825	106,816
Provision for (recovery of) federal and foreign income taxes:					
Current	593	3,497	1,032	11,991	1,107
Deferred	(5,185)	(8,911)	13,275	22,912	20,615
Operating income	176,153	151,462	148,051	125,922	85,094
Net realized capital (losses) gains	(160)	(19,790)	(5,968)	(6,627)	4,385
Discontinued operations		9,886	1,265	979	1,135
Net income	$ 175,993	$ 141,558	$ 143,348	$ 120,274	$ 90,614
Earnings per common share					
PRIMARY:					
Operating income	$6.16	$5.39	$5.36	$4.69	$3.23
Net realized capital (losses) gains	(.01)	(.70)	(.22)	(.25)	.17
Discontinued operations		.35	.04	.04	.04
Net income	6.15	5.04	5.18	4.48	3.44
FULLY DILUTED:					
Operating income	6.02	5.26	5.20	4.52	3.11
Net realized capital (losses) gains	(.01)	(.68)	(.21)	(.24)	.16
Discontinued operations		.34	.04	.04	.04
Net income	6.01	4.92	5.03	4.32	3.31
Cash and accrued dividends per share:					
Preferred Series A	2.40	2.40	2.40	2.40	2.40
Common	1.54	1.35	1.15	.905	.80

SOURCE: 1981 Annual Report, Crum and Forster, p. 19.

Exhibit 19.12

CRUM AND FORSTER AND SUBSIDIARIES: CONSOLIDATED BALANCE SHEET AT DECEMBER 31 (All dollar amounts stated in thousands.)

	1981	1980
ASSETS		
Fixed maturities		
Bonds, at amortized cost (market $1,648,849 and $1,575,439, respectively)	$2,376,859	$2,118,257
Preferred stocks, at amortized cost (market $87,705 and $93,895, respectively)	120,344	119,976
Equity securities		
Preferred stocks, at market (cost $28,486 and $36,383, respectively)	21,486	27,746
Common stocks, at market (cost $350,119 and $286,841, respectively)	413,016	455,070
Short-term investments, at cost (market $270,139 and $361,459, respectively)	270,136	361,472
Investment in real estate (net of accumulated depreciation of $13,702)		15,417
Cash	11,689	9,740
Receivables		
Premiums (net of allowance for uncollectible accounts of $6,245 and $6,019, respectively)	439,356	372,904
Other	192,008	99,294
Equity in assets of insurance associations	5,204	8,339
Acquisition costs applicable to unearned premiums	144,939	146,919
Land, buildings, and equipment used in operations (net of accumulated depreciation of $40,832 and $38,492, respectively)	75,591	65,249
Other assets	89,480	60,602
Total assets	4,160,108	3,862,985
LIABILITIES		
Unearned premiums	661,759	646,237
Unpaid losses	1,672,510	1,510,458
Unpaid loss expenses	402,978	300,645
Dividends to policyholders	65,189	54,320
Accounts payable and accrued liabilities	314,981	295,496
Mortgages payable	19,372	12,104
Deferred federal and foreign income taxes		
Unrealized appreciation of equity investments	16,984	46,571
Other	60,945	65,338
Other liabilities	22,000	12,312
Total liabilities	3,236,718	3,003,481
STOCKHOLDERS' EQUITY		
Preferred stock (liquidating value $4,804 and 5,467, respectively)	480	547
Common stock (issued 28,487,085 and 28,071,639 shares, respectively)	17,804	17,545
Additional paid-in capital	39,175	31,858
Retained earnings	827,084	649,911
Net unrealized appreciation of equity investments	38,913	115,021
Less treasury stock at cost (4,000 and 16,000 shares, respectively)	(66)	(378)
Total stockholders' equity	923,390	859,504
Total liabilities and stockholders' equity	$4,160,108	$3,862,985

SOURCE: 1981 Annual Report, Crum and Forster, p. 20.

(See Exhibit 19.13.) In effect, although insurance premiums were insufficient to cover claims and expenses, interest from the investment of these premiums enabled the firm to make a profit. In the first half of 1982, Crum & Forster's operating profit was down 30% to $64.8 million ($2.25 a share) from $92.1 million ($3.24 a share) a year earlier.

Xerox offered $55 for each Crum & Forster share, giving holders the choice of receiving either cash or a combination of Xerox common and a new Xerox preferred stock. At $55 a share, Crum & Forster shareholders will receive about 1.7 times book value, which was $32.33 a share in June, 1982. The Xerox offer is double the pre-offer price and also 40% above the stock's fifteen-year high price.

Xerox plans to finance the cash part of the acquisition, about $800 million, through existing revolving-credit agreements and short term bank loans without touching any cash holdings set aside for its office-products businesses. Xerox claims that the acquisition will be self-funding in that interest costs associated with the takeover will be covered by Crum & Forster's earnings.[23]

Responding to industry puzzlement over Xerox's choice of diversification, Kearns has cited the following reasons for the acquisition:

- Xerox believes the property-casualty insurance lines offer the best growth opportunities in the insurance business. Crum & Forster's lines aren't heavily dominated by a few industries, as in auto coverage.
- Xerox perceives the acquisition as an expansion of Xerox's commercial financial services, pioneered by Xerox Credit Corporation. Formed in 1979, Xerox Credit is expecting to report a profit of about $35 million in 1982, about double 1981's profits.
- The acquisition will provide investment income which Xerox needs to support its vigorous research efforts in copiers, duplicators, electronic typewriters, and other office equipment.
- Xerox foresees a reduction of its tax rate during the down phase of the insurance cycle. Crum & Forster's current underwriting losses, which totaled $110 million before taxes in the first half of 1982, offers potential tax benefits to Xerox. The insurer currently pays relatively little in taxes and says its effective federal income tax rate has ranged from 12% to 14% of operating profit.[24]

Xerox watchers, however, wonder whether the company has lost confidence in its office automation business. Amy Wohl, president of Advanced Office Concepts Corp., responded to the announcement by saying, "This says Xerox doesn't feel its current set of investments gives enough re-

CRUM AND FORSTER AND SUBSIDIARIES:
BUSINESS SEGMENTS
(All dollar amounts stated in thousands.)

Exhibit 19.13

	1981	1980	1979
REVENUES			
Workers' compensation	$ 443,086	$ 431,257	$ 376,349
Casualty	304,454	358,882	357,622
Automobile—commercial	171,586	175,714	161,874
Automobile—personal	167,493	166,699	137,989
Commercial multiple-peril	218,389	217,564	208,049
Fire and allied	133,056	171,154	164,255
Homeowners'	96,246	85,532	77,722
Marine	95,169	79,781	69,743
Fidelity and surety	25,816	23,666	18,957
Investments	277,931	229,383	178,064
Other	591	627	541
Total	1,932,817	1,940,259	1,751,165
OPERATING PROFIT (LOSS)			
Workers' compensation	14,241	2,796	(1,935)
Casualty	9,615	(10,431)	12,386
Automobile—commercial	(17,342)	(12,602)	1,760
Automobile—personal	(20,671)	(15,568)	(11,842)
Commercial multiple-peril	(44,775)	(7,303)	3,141
Fire and allied	(6,912)	(5,952)	6,084
Homeowners'	(8,265)	(9,291)	(3,284)
Marine	(1,324)	(6,978)	(8,781)
Fidelity and surety	2,937	2,919	3,148
Investments	270,199	220,957	171,967
Other	591	627	541
Total	198,294	159,174	173,185
General corporate expenses	(26,733)	(13,126)	(10,827)
Operating income before federal and foreign income taxes	$ 171,561	$ 146,048	$ 162,358

SOURCE: 1981 Annual Report, Crum and Forster, p. 29.

turn."[25] "My hunch," says office automation analyst Patricia Seybold, "is that office products may never be profitable for them. They've lost momentum."[26] Kearns, however, disagrees: "This is a very aggressive strategy to grow this business more rapidly with two market segments very different from each other." As he explains it, Xerox management believes they can maintain their total commitment to office automation and still diversify into a self-funding, high growth area. "We concluded we could leverage the balance sheet at this time to branch out to other areas for a better return to our shareholders."[27]

Xerox, however, has had a mixed record in previous diversification attempts. In 1969, for example, the company purchased Scientific Data Systems (SDS), a manufacturer of mainframe computers, for 10 million shares of Xerox stock worth approximately $908 million. Hoping to compete with IBM, Xerox management hoped that SDS's expertise in computers would be worth giving the SDS stockholders a 73% premium over the stock's market price. Renamed Xerox Data Systems (XDS), the new division's sales fell below $100 million in 1970 and failed to show a profit. By 1972, XDS had lost $100 million before taxes. Losses ranging from $25 to $44 million annually continued until 1975 when the company wrote off the division at an $84 million loss. After six years of effort, XDS still had less than 1% of the mainframe computer market. Analysts reported that Xerox management had been surprised by the lack of R & D capability in Scientific Data Systems.[28]

In 1979, Xerox purchased Western Union International (WUI), an international communications carrier, for $212 million. This represented Xerox's first entry into telecommunications and operating in a regulated environment. Before it purchased WUI, Xerox already had a proposal before the Federal Communications Commission for a domestic data communications network called XTEN. This project was subsequently cancelled because Xerox felt the funds could be better used elsewhere. In December 1981, Xerox announced that it had reached an agreement to sell WUI to MCI Communications Corp. for $185 million, a $27 million loss. Other recent acquisitions, such as Shugart Associates, have been of a smaller nature, less than $50 million, and represent Xerox's attempt to diversify, both horizontally and vertically, in the information processing industry in order to bolster its position in the office automation marketplace.

Just as the current recession has had a negative impact on Xerox's business, the weak economic climate has hurt the insurance industry. Pressures on pricing have cut underwriting profits for property and casualty insurance companies and, with interest rates declining, investment profits may drop. In the last quarter of 1982, the industry looked forward to record underwriting losses offset by also record income from investments. Insurers in recent years have been willing to cut their rates and write policies at a loss in order to generate policyholders' premiums for investment activities. Analysts fear, however, that the industry's underwriting losses may be growing faster than its investment income.[29]

On the other hand, declining interest rates have several positive effects on the insurance business. First, the bonds that comprise the bulk of the companies' portfolios are worth more when rates come down. Second, the insurers' reserves for future claims liabilities are more likely to be adequate when interest rates (and by association, inflation) are lower. Third, lower interest rates raise the prospect of an end to the destructive three-year price war still raging in the industry. Finally, with rates coming down, general economic prospects may brighten enough to increase demand for insurers' services.

Once a turnaround in pricing occurs, industry analysts expect profits to show strong growth over the next three to five years. Between 1975 and 1979, after the last recession, industry profits increased almost eight times. The rebound is not expected to be as strong this time, but considerable growth is predicted. Lower inflation, reduced interest rates, and generally improved economic conditions are predicted to boost the demand for insurance by the mid-1980's.[30]

In reaction to the announcement of the proposed acquisition of Crum & Forster by Xerox, Moody's Investors Service lowered its ratings of several debt issues of Xerox. Moody's said its action "reflects the anticipated additional claim on existing cash flow in support of debt to be issued to acquire Crum & Forster, and the effect of competitive conditions in the company's key markets."[31]

THE OFFICE OF THE FUTURE

The high costs of management, professional, and clerical workers, in combination with continued favorable trends for electronic systems capabilities and costs, establishes Office Automation as a major growth market in the 1980s. The powerful basic reason for automating offices is that white-collar salaries are a huge and intractable cost of doing business. In 1980, 60% of the $1.3 trillion paid out for wages, salaries, and benefits in the United States went to office workers. Meanwhile the prices of electronics have been falling. Computer memory has become cheaper at a compound annual rate of 42% over the last five years, and the price of the logic chips that give computers their intelligence has dropped about 28% a year.

Although in theory office automation makes sense, the market has not developed as quickly as vendors had hoped. According to Wang Laboratories, only 60 or so of the largest industrial corporations have acquired as many as

100 office workstations. A much smaller number have linked them into pervasive networks. Demand has simply developed more slowly than anyone thought it would a few years ago. The current market is so narrow that profits may not appear for years.[32]

Vendors give many reasons for the slow growth of this market. First of all, the recession has cut back capital spending plans of many organizations. Second, the lack of convincing studies on the savings associated with office automation has heightened customers' reluctance to purchase. Third, in developing automation for managers and professionals, there is a problem in specifying exactly what steps or processes these individuals go through in doing their jobs. Fourth, top management does not yet feel comfortable with a computer terminal on their desks. Fifth, the confusion over which networking system will prevail, broad-band or base-band, has made buyers slower to purchase networks. Finally, despite the universal desire of business people to find better ways of doing work, office automation remains poorly understood.[33]

Dataquest, Inc., a California-based market research firm, estimates that U.S. shipments of equipment that can be linked to form electronic offices should grow 34% a year through 1986. Total revenues are predicted to grow between $12 and $15 billion by 1986.[34] Exhibit 19.14 describes the predicted growth in the U.S. market for office automation equipment.

This anticipation of a "booming" market for office automation has brought dozens of companies into the competition. AT&T, IBM, and Xerox have declared the market a key to their futures. In 1981, the top three minicomputer companies—Digital Equipment, Hewlett-Packard, and Data General—launched office automation systems within 30 days of one another. The most successful vendors court the end user and are actually encouraged

Exhibit 19.14

THE U.S. MARKET FOR OFFICE AUTOMATION EQUIPMENT
(Millions of Dollars)

	1981	1986
Word processors	$2,200	$6,000
Electronic typewriters	275	1,200
Professional workstations	5	250
Intelligent copiers	185	900
Digital PBX's	220	4,100

SOURCE: Dataquest, Inc., *Fortune*, May 3, 1982, p. 184.

to do so by most corporate customers. Buyers will designate "preferred" vendors, but leave the final decisions to the line managers and secretaries who have to use the gear. Analysts see IBM, Wang, Digital Equipment, and Xerox as being in the best position to capture large pieces of the growing market. Yet there appear to be enough profitable niches to reward any company that can fill a particular customer need.

Xerox's thrust in office automation has been in directing its equipment to professionals and managers, and in selling complete systems. Its strategy in gaining a share of this market is characterized by the following:

- sacrifice profits for market share until the mid-1980s;
- aim automation at the executive rather than at clerical workers;
- design machines with a multitude of uses;
- provide buyers with the opportunity to use the best available equipment from a range of suppliers;
- be the first to enter new markets;
- make products easy and nonfatiguing to use.

Although it has been the traditionally routine tasks that have been automated so far, manufacturers of this equipment must reach beyond the secretary to managers and professionals for office automation to reach its true potential. These individuals account for 80% of the white-collar salaries. The more complex products, such as professional workstations and intelligent copiers, may not come into their own for some time. Analysts estimate that in 1985 only 6% of managers and professionals are likely to be using sophisticated workstations.[35]

NOTES

1. *Electronic News,* Oct. 4, 1982, p. 22.
2. *Time,* Nov. 1, 1982, p. 67 and *Wall Street Journal,* Sept. 22, 1982, p. 3.
3. *Datamation,* February 1983, pp. 90–98.
4. Annual Report, Xerox Corporation, 1981, p. 3.
5. *Sales and Marketing Management,* Feb. 8, 1982, p. 24.
6. *Forbes,* July 7, 1980, pp. 40–41.
7. *Ibid.*
8. *Sales and Marketing Management,* Feb. 8, 1982, p. 24.
9. *Ibid.*
10. *Infosystems,* January 1981.
11. *Ibid.*
12. *Business Week,* Aug. 23, 1982, p. 80. *Xerox: A Strategic Analysis* by

Northern Business Information, Inc. 66 West Broadway, New York, NY 10007, January, 1982, p. 156.

13. *Forbes,* July 7, 1980, pp. 40–41.
14. *Business Week,* Oct. 18, 1982, p. 134M.
15. *Datamation,* February 1983, p. 92.
16. *Infosystems,* February 1982, p. 26.
17. *Mini-Micro Systems,* February 1982, p. 18.
18. *Business Week,* Apr. 21, 1980, p. 130.
19. *Electronic News,* Dec. 7, 1981, p. 18.
20. *Value Line,* Nov. 12, 1982, p. 1128.
21. *Fortune,* Sept. 5, 1983, pp. 97–102.
22. *Value Line,* Nov. 12, 1982, pp. 1055, 1085, 1087, 1089, 1098, 1102, 1103, 1113, and 1115.
23. *Wall Street Journal,* Sept. 22, 1982, p. 24.
24. *Ibid.*
25. *Business Week,* Oct. 4, 1982, p. 52.
26. *Ibid.*
27. *Ibid.*
28. *Electronics,* Mar. 29, 1981, p. 86.
29. *Wall Street Journal,* Dec. 30, 1982, p. 20.
30. *Value Line,* Oct. 22, 1982, p. 637.
31. *Wall Street Journal,* Oct. 1982.
32. *Fortune,* May 3, 1982, p. 176.
33. *Ibid.*
34. *Ibid.*
35. *Ibid.*

Case 20

APPLE COMPUTERS, INC.

William H. Davidson / Edward E. Colby, Jr.

Chairman Steven Jobs began Apple Computer's annual meeting in January 1983 by introducing President and CEO Mike Markkula, who summarized the past year's financial results. Sales had grown 74% to $583 million, and earnings had risen 55% to $61 million (see Exhibit 20.1). Jobs then returned to introduce two new products. The first, the Apple IIe, was an enhanced version of the highly successful, five-year-old Apple II. Before lifting the cloth that shrouded the much-awaited Lisa personal office system, he said:

> The personal computer was created by a hardware revolution of the 1970s. The next dramatic change will come from a software revolution which Apple is introducing here today.

The two product introductions occurred at a time of rising chaos in the emerging personal computer industry. New competitors appeared weekly; a profusion of software vendors offered an exploding number of software products, and distribution channels were in a state of flux. Apple's position of leadership in the industry was being challenged from a dozen different directions. The IIe and Lisa provided an immediate response to these challenges, but many observers at the annual meeting were secretly concerned about the company's ability to maintain its unprecedented record of success.

Apple management was not resting on its laurels, however. There was a good deal of effort and pressure within the company to improve the company's competitive position. Among the managers present at the annual meeting no one felt that pressure more than Alan Oppenheimer. Alan had left a consumer products marketing position at General Mills to become Apple's director of market research in 1981. He had recently been selected

APPLE COMPUTER COMPANY: FINANCIAL AND OPERATING STATISTICS
(Thousands of Dollars)

Exhibit 20.1

	1978	1979	1980	1981	1982
Sales	$7,883	$47,867	$117,126	$334,783	$583,061
Cost of sales	3,960	27,450	66,490	170,124	288,001
Gross margin	3,923	20,417	50,636	164,659	295,060
Marketing and distribution	1,170	8,802	12,619	55,369	119,945
Research and development	597	3,601	7,282	20,956	37,979
General and administrative	609	2,080	7,150	22,191	34,927
Operating income	1,547	5,933	23,585	66,143	102,209
Interest income	0	0	567	10,400	14,563
Net income	793	3,023	11,698	39,420	61,306
Cash and investments	775	562	2,500	72,834	153,056
Accounts receivable	1,379	5,006	17,400	42,330	71,470
Inventories	1,063	6,348	34,200	103,873	81,229
Net plant and equipment	268	900	4,000	8,453	22,811
Total assets	4,341	17,070	65,400	254,838	357,787
Accounts payable	996	5,411	18,400	26,613	25,125
Notes payable	0	0	0	10,745	4,185
Long-term debt	0	200	700	0	0
Shareholders' equity	1,916	8,155	25,900	177,387	259,402
Apple II unit sales	7,600	35,090	78,100	192,000	350,000
Installed base	8,170	43,260	121,360	313,360	663,360

to head a project to develop Apple's first home computer. Alan's task was to finalize the design for the new home computer and build an organization to manufacture, market and service the product.

Leaving the community college auditorium where Apple held its annual meeting, Alan thought again about the IIe and Lisa systems. Should the home computer be built around Apple II technology and software, or should it incorporate the new Lisa technology? Questions of price and distribution troubled Alan. He also knew that his work in market research was one of the main reasons he had been selected to head this project, yet he was uncertain about the precise segment he should target. If all these issues could be resolved, Alan then had to push the project through the dynamic chaos that characterized organizational life at Apple.

HISTORY OF APPLE COMPUTER, INC.

Nineteen seventy-six was a transition year for Steve Jobs and Steve Wozniak. Both dropped out of college to work in Silicon Valley, Jobs at Atari and Wozniak at Hewlett-Packard. Their spare time was spent in a Los Altos garage experimenting with video games and electronic circuits. Wozniak was particularly intrigued by the potential power of the microprocessor, a programmable computer-on-a-chip invented by Intel in 1971. He began to build a home-made computer system around a microprocessor.

The machine that emerged was crude but effective. Several friends expressed interest in the new computer, and Jobs began to see commercial potential in the product. Jobs' first effort to sell the computer was at the Byte Shop in Palo Alto, the only known store of its time that sold kits for microprocessor-based computers. He showed them Wozniak's machine, which was only a stuffed and wired circuit board. When Jobs asked if they were interested in buying, they replied they would take a hundred, and asked how much they were. Jobs, not quite believing, but without batting an eye, quoted the price of $666.66 each, COD, to be delivered in 30 days. They agreed, and the deal was done.

Jobs rushed back and asked Wozniak what to do next. They had almost no cash, no components, and no one to assemble the boards. Wozniak sold his H-P calculator and Jobs his VW van to raise $1300. Jobs' next step was to call component suppliers to ask for credit on parts purchases. One supplier offered him net 30 terms. Jobs agreed, not knowing what net 30 meant but sensing it gave them some time.

They had their components within a week, and Jobs, Wozniak and Jobs' sister furiously stuffed circuit boards for the next three weeks. They delivered 100 completed boards to the Byte Shop in thirty days, collected and deposited a check for $66,666, and paid their creditors within terms. Jobs and Wozniak were profitable from the time of their first sale.

Jobs sensed the market potential of what he and Wozniak had created. He also acknowledged "we didn't know what the hell we were doing," and sought advice. Wozniak mentioned it to people at Hewlett-Packard, but they turned the design down. Jobs was similarly unsuccessful in interesting Atari in the new product. Jobs then approached Nolan Bushnell, founder of Atari and then a leading Silicon Valley venture capitalist. Bushnell declined any direct involvement, but referred Jobs to a local public relations firm, Regis McKenna, for help. After turning Jobs down twice, the company finally agreed to accept the venture as a client on a pay-later basis.

While doing the rounds of Bay Area venture capitalists, they soon met

A.C. "Mike" Markkula, a successful marketing executive who had recently left Intel. He put up $91,000 of his own funds, helped create a business plan, and secured a line of credit with the Bank of America. In return, Markkula received 20% of the equity in the fledgling company. He later raised $600,000 in venture capital from Venrock Associates and Henry Singleton of Teledyne. Markkula also negotiated terms so that Apple received payment from its dealers in fifteen days, yet paid its suppliers after sixty days.

Jobs, Wozniak and Markkula incorporated their new venture in January of 1977. As the deadline for filing the incorporation papers approached, they still had no name for the company. Finally, Jobs, looking at the apple he was eating, said that if no one could think of anything better, they would call it Apple. No one had a better name and the deadline passed, so Apple Computer, Inc. was born.

Jobs and Markkula used the $600,000 in venture capital equity funds not for product development, but for promotion. Regis McKenna created the colorful Apple logo and the four-color glossy ads that began appearing in magazines. They gave Apple the image of a $100 million company at a time when it had twelve employees. Markkula described this effort as critical because:

> We had to gain recognition in the market fast. We could not start small. We had to dominate the business or go bankrupt trying.

Apple's distribution and promotion policies contributed greatly to its rapid growth. Markkula's marketing plan depended on independent distribution rather than Apple's own salespeople. Apple encouraged electronics retailers to carry its computers by offering high margins, dealer training, cooperative advertising, and point of sale displays. Apple's suggested retail prices incorporated a 45% profit margin for its dealers. The distribution channel, consisting of specialized retail stores, developed simultaneously with Apple. Apple relied on third party wholesalers until 1981, when the company took over its own distribution and service operations.

THE APPLE II

In the meantime, Wozniak continued to improve upon the first computer. Jobs continually pushed him to include additional features. He simplified some of the operating system commands, and incorporated a keyboard and an attachment for a video monitor into his design. They used Markkula's $91,000 for tooling of the high quality, attractive looking outer case Jobs insisted on using. In May of 1977, Apple introduced the Apple II, the first personal computer with a built-in operating system. The operating system manages the computer's internal operations and executes software programs. An Apple II user therefore did not have to program the computer himself. Instead, he could buy software and run programs that had already been written for the Apple.

The early customers for the Apple were hobbyists already familiar with computers and willing to spend money to have their own. What blocked wider sales was the lack of software to run on the Apple. Jobs and Markkula both realized there were lots of hobbyists and enthusiasts, known in the industry as "hackers," who had bought Apples and wanted to write their own programs. Further, they realized that the Apple II would be useful to large numbers of people only if they could choose from a selection of high quality software. Only with this wide selection would a microcomputer become a truly personal computer.

Because they recognized Apple didn't have a monopoly on either smart people or good ideas, they revealed the secrets of the Apple II by publishing its technical specifications. This step was unprecedented in the computer industry. The inner workings of computers had heretofore been cloaked in secrecy; now here was the Apple II for the world to see. A programmer would therefore know exactly how this Apple worked, and he could easily write applications for it.

The results of this action were astounding. New programs and applications for the Apple poured in from every imaginable source. Apple assisted the authors of the more promising software with documentation and publication of their products. Apple's role became one of identifying and communicating these new ideas and uses to potential Apple purchasers.

In 1978 Daniel Bricklin, a Harvard Business School student, and Robert Frankston wrote a program that used a computer to perform lengthy and tedious calculations involved in creating and altering financial spreadsheets. They wrote their program, called Visicalc, for the Apple II. For eleven months, Apple was the only computer that supported Visicalc, and that lead time provided a great competitive advantage over other entrants in the personal computer market. Suddenly, the Apple II offered a broadly based, tangibly valuable application, and sales of Apple and Visicalc soared.

In 1978, Apple became the first personal computer manufacturer to offer a floppy disk drive. This magnetic storage medium was compact, reliable, easy to use, and held the equivalent of thirty-five pages of typed text per disk. An Apple user could simply plug the disk drive into his Apple, and use floppy disks to store his own programs or data, and more significantly, use pre-written programs packaged and sold on floppy disks.

The Apple II was positioned as a personal computer that was easy to use and friendly to the user, whoever the user happened to be. It was small, compact, and neat in appearance. The logo was bright and attractive, and the name connoted a friendly product. Nowhere in the ad copy and promotional material was there the high-technology image and jargon that frightened most people when the word "computer" came to mind.

The written documentation, or instructions and references, that accompanied the Apple II and its software represented a major innovation in the computer industry. The graphics were attractive, the type large and well laid out, the text friendly and humorous, and most importantly, comparatively easy to understand. Heretofore, computer documentation was written in the arcane language of computer professionals—which can be an incomprehensible mystery to the uninitiated. For the first time, a computer manufacturer provided documentation that invited and encouraged the novice.

In January 1983, the Apple II had the largest installed base of any personal computer priced over $1000. Through the end of calendar year 1982 over 650,000 Apple II units had been sold. The Apple II continued its phenomenal sales growth despite obvious shortcomings. The hardware had not been upgraded in six years, while one advance followed another in semiconductor technology. The keyboard was limited to upper case letters, did not contain the full set of characters used in computer programs, and had no up and down arrow key to move the cursor. The Apple II could display only 40 columns on the video monitor, while 80 columns was the standard display. Yet sales continued to rise right up to introduction of the IIe in January of 1983. In fact capacity constraints had limited sales of Apple II systems throughout the company's history.

Apple's manufacturing operations were based in a modern 250,000 square foot plant in Dallas. Operations were oriented towards minimizing cost and maintaining strict quality control. Significant emphasis was also placed on just-in-time inventory management. Since the Dallas plant was primarily an assembly operation, Apple relied heavily on external suppliers. Printed circuit boards were assembled by subcontractors in Singapore. Apple sourced microprocessors from Synertek, other chips from Hitachi, Texas Instrument and Motorola, video monitors from Hitachi, power supplies from Astec in Hong Kong, and printers from Tokyo Electric and Qume. Reliance on outsiders is an Apple trademark. Michael Scott, Chief Financial Officer, stated:

> Fast-growing companies should rely on outside help for the manufacture of nonproprietory components and systems. As long as cost-efficient outside alternatives exist, we won't worry about being innovative in such areas as production procedures. As long as we are protected in terms of quality assurance, there are better things to do with our time here. Our scarcest commodity at Apple isn't cash, it's time.

The Apple II, which retailed for about $2000, contained about $350 in purchased components. Industry observers estimated that the Apple II cost less than $500 to build.

Apple attempted to follow the amazing success of the Apple II with a new personal computer targeted more directly at the business market. This computer was the Apple III, introduced in late 1980. While based on the same relatively slow microprocessor (MOS Technology 6502) as the Apple II, the Apple III featured greater memory and a more sophisticated and simpler operating system. The keyboard offered both upper and lower case type, four directional arrow keys, a separate keypad for entering numerical data, and other improvements over the Apple II.

COMPETITORS

From its beginning in 1977, Apple had very little competition. Not only had Apple invented a new product, it had almost singlehandedly created a new industry. Tandy, which distributed through its vast Radio Shack retail network of over 2000 stores, represented Apple's only rival in its early years. Apple's challenge during that period was to convince people to use personal computers, not to fight the competition for market share.

Stimulating primary demand was the early challenge; in 1983 there was a different threat. More than one hundred manufacturers produced 150 models of personal computers ranging in price from $99 to $37,500. Apple faced the challenge of maintaining leadership in the exploding industry it had helped create.

The players in the personal computer industry in late 1982 comprised a broad representation of businesses from all over the world. Competitors ranged in size from giant computer makers to Silicon Valley start-ups. They included manufacturers of mainframe and minicomputers, such as IBM, DEC, and Data General; semiconductor and electronics firms including Texas Instruments and Hewlett-Packard; Japanese computer and electronic producers such as Sharp, NEC, and Sony; well known office product companies such as Xerox, Wang Laboratories and Olivetti; consumer electronic firms, including Zenith and Atari; and a host of start-ups and young concerns who were strictly in the personal computer business, such as Fortune, Corvus, and Altos Computer (see Exhibits 20.2 and 20.3).

New competitors found it relatively easy to enter the personal computer market (see Exhibit 20.4). The technology was not especially difficult, particularly for anyone who wanted to emulate an existing product. Capital was required to fund product development and marketing activities, but access to capital seemed to be a surmountable problem. Venture capital money was readily available. For example, Fortune Systems was capitalized in 1980 with close to $24 million in venture funds. The largest barrier to entry ap-

APPLE COMPUTER COMPANY: U.S. PERSONAL COMPUTER MARKET SIZE AND SHARES

Exhibit 20.2

	Market Size (billions of dollars)					
	1980	1981	1982	1983(E)	1984(E)	1985(E)
Hardware	1.5	2.9	5.6	8.8	12.8	17.3
Software	0.2	0.5	1.1	2.3	4.3	6.0

Market Share **(1982)**
Price Range

$100–$1,000		Over $1,000	
Commodore	30%	Apple	33%
Atari	24%	Tandy	22%
Texas Instruments	20%	IBM	17%
Tandy	8%	Osborne	9%
Others	18%	Texas Instruments	3%
		Hewlett-Packard	3%
TOTAL Units	2,550,000	Xerox	3%
		Others	10%
		TOTAL	1,150,000

SOURCE: Compiled by the casewriter from a variety of public and private sources.

peared to be access to distribution channels, especially scarce retail shelf space.

Distribution Channels

Distribution channels had evolved together with the personal computer industry. Many retail outlets were owned by independent entrepreneurs, but computer retail chains had expanded rapidly. The largest of these, Computerland, had over 250 outlets in the U.S. Some nationwide department store chains, such as Macy's, opened personal computer centers in many of their outlets. Sears had built 65 free standing Sears Business Centers. Computer manufacturers competed vigorously for shelf space in these stores. A few manufacturers, including IBM, Xerox and DEC, had their own stores, although their personal computers were also sold elsewhere. The IBM product centers sold only IBM products, while the Xerox Stores carried several brands. Most stores carried no more than four or five brands.

Retailers selected the manufacturers they would carry based on several criteria. The profit margin they could earn was an important factor. Retail margins ranged from 25% to over 50%. They relied heavily on the manufac-

Exhibit 20.3

LEADING U.S. COMPANIES' KEY FINANCIAL AND OPERATING RATIOS

	Gross Margin Sales %	*R & D Sales* %	*S,G&A Sales* %	*P,P&E Sales* %	*Debt Equity* %	*Inven-tory Sales* %	*Sales/ Employee* $	*Cash Total Assets* %	*Pre-tax Profit Sales* %	*Profit Total Assets* %	*Divi-dends Profit* %	*AR-AP Sales* %
Apple	50.6	6.5	26.5	5.9	7.8	13.9	171,944	42.8	20.0	32.7	0	7.95
Burroughs	34.8	5.4	25.6	20.0	37.8	13.5	66,053	1.3	1.8	1.8	146.0	14.9
Commodore	47.8	5.8	23.2	16.2	41.8	30.3	121,800	2.9	16.7	21.6	0	9.7
Data General	43.8	10.5	28.3	19.4	32.4	32.6	53,019	24.4	4.5	4.6	0	15.2
DEC	43.6	9.0	19.5	29.5	2.9	29.3	57,836	19.0	17.3	16.7	0	17.2
Hewlett-Packard	52.0	10.0	26.4	27.6	1.7	15.5	62,426	19.7	15.9	19.5	4.4	14.9
IBM	60.2	9.0	27.9	25.5	13.4	10.2	94,201	10.1	23.1	24.4	25.9	12.9
Prime	57.4	8.5	33.2	27.5	7.3	13.2	82,056	7.9	15.0	17.4	0	27.7

APPLE COMPUTER COMPANY: NEW ENTRANTS IN THE PERSONAL COMPUTER INDUSTRY

Exhibit 20.4

	1977	1981
A. Number of Venture Capital Fundings of Firms in Graphics, Computers, and Software	6	99
B. Number of Personal Computer Firms Started	17	62
C. Number of AEA Member Software Firms*	10	140
D. Number of Personal Computer Manufacturers	19	110
E. Number of Personal Computer Models	—	160

SOURCES: A,B,C: Venture, Nov. 1982. D.E.: IDC Report in *Fortune*, Oct. 18, 1982.
NOTE: * AEA is the American Electronics Association.

turer for training materials, point-of-sale displays, brochures, co-op advertising and repair service. Some manufacturers, including Apple, devoted a great deal of time and effort to educating dealers about their products. Both Apple and IBM required prospective dealers to complete product training sessions before they became an authorized dealer. Availability of software and accessories were considered important to dealers, because often a prospective customer would approach a retailer with several applications in mind, and rely on the salesman's recommendation in his purchase decision. If several software packages and hardware accessories were available for a certain computer, the dealer could offer more solutions. Also, margins on software products tended to be higher than for hardware, and dealers would tend to prefer systems with extensive software over a machine with more limited software.

Personal computers were distributed through channels other than computer stores. Some firms used a direct sales force for large volume accounts, while others such as Atari, TI and Commodore sold through mass merchandise outlets. Mail order also accounted for a share of the business. Apple, IBM, and Tandy did not authorize sales of their products through the mail. Apple prohibited the sale of its products by mail in mid-1981. This ban had been generally effective, although several mail order houses were challenging Apple's decision in court. A large amount of software and peripheral equipment was sold through the mail.

Role of Technology

While technical barriers to entry are relatively low, the personal computer business was nonetheless driven by developments in technology. Advances in microelectronics were the primary driving force behind the growth of the industry. Further advances would play a major role in the evolution of personal computers in the next decade. Advances in software also exerted a great influence on the direction of the industry.

Hardware advances were likely to occur in two areas: memory chips and microprocessors. Most microcomputers in 1982 used 16K RAM (Random access memory) chips. However, high quality 64K RAM chips were available at low cost from several American and Japanese suppliers. The Apple II+ required 32 16K RAM chips to achieve 64K of addressable memory, while the IIe used only 8 64K chips to achieve the same capacity.

The pending availability of low-cost 256K RAM chips promised greater capabilities and price-performance for microcomputers. Fewer chips meant lower cost and higher reliability. Greater available memory permitted more sophisticated and powerful software, faster execution time, and higher resolution graphics. For a microcomputer developer, a key challenge was how quickly he could incorporate more memory into his system design.

Advances in technology were not incorporated into personal computers immediately. The lead time from introduction of a new microprocessor until it was designed into a microcomputer was three or more years. For example, the Motorola's 16-bit microprocessor, the MC68000, introduced in 1978 and used in the Lisa, first appeared in personal computers in mid-1982. Most personal computers on the market in 1982 used 8-bit microprocessors. The 8-bits refers to the number of bits, or binary digits, that are processed at one time. The successors to 8-bit systems are based on 16-bit processors, which process 16 bits of data simultaneously. These chips execute instructions faster and can utilize much more memory than 8-bit chips. In 1982, Intel introduced its 32-bit microprocessor with the equivalent computing power of an IBM SYSTEM/370.

Acceptance of the latest technology in the marketplace was constrained by the lead time required to develop software. Machines based on the newest memory or microprocessor technology lacked a broad base of software support. Several years were required to develop peripheral hardware, accessories, and applications software to complement the hardware. The purchase of this equipment and software represented significant investments to their buyers, and therefore made them reluctant to replace that investment quickly. Users purchased systems they felt would be useful for several years. This inertia tended to inhibit quantum leaps in microcomputer applications of the latest electronics technology.

Such constraints on the application of new technology were due largely to one element of software, the operating system. Operating systems, the control programs for the computer, are structured around specific microprocessors, as CP/M was for the Zilog Z80. CP/M (control program for microcomputer) is used in more models of personal computers than any other operating system. Introduced in 1975 by Digital Research, CP/M established an accessible industry standard, and thousands of applications have been written for it. As a result, the Zilog Z80 is the most widely used 8-bit microprocessor. Apple DOS (disk operating system), Tandy's TRS-DOS, and Microsoft's MS-DOS for the IBM PC were other widely used operating systems. Their broad acceptance inhibited development of new operating systems, and encouraged new entrants to build their systems around one of the accepted systems. As of late 1982, software could be written to be used on only one operating system. Translating programs to another operating system was expensive and time-consuming, although developers such as Microsoft were using languages easily transported to many operating systems.

Software strategy was a key issue for all personal computer makers and users. Established companies and users had the large, sunk investment of proven software written around existing operating systems. At the same time more powerful and sophisticated operating systems were being developed. It was conceivable that a new operating system with the ability to run programs of the other systems might emerge. A microcomputer with this capability would contain several microprocessors and could support virtually any application program. All makers and users also had to consider the possibility that a specific operating system would dominate the personal computer market.

The potential for an operating system to gain such broad acceptance depended in part on who owned the rights on it. Apple's DOS was proprietary to Apple, and not available for license. CP/M and MS-DOS were written by software firms who had financial incentives to promote the use of their systems by hardware and software developers.

Technology and Competitive Strategies

Personal computer manufacturers could use several strategies to break into the personal computer market. One was to develop a machine with superior performance, using the latest technology. For example, the Fortune 32:16 used the advanced Motorola MC68000 microprocessor, a highly sophisticated operating system (Bell Labs' UNIX), 1 megabyte of RAM, high resolution graphics, and supported up to nine users. By contrast, the Apple III and IBM PC had slower processing, half the RAM, and lower disk storage. Superior performance could offset a manufacturer's lack of reputation, limited distribution, or small software base.

A company that excelled in hardware engineering, but lacked the resources to distribute its product widely, could sell on an OEM (original equipment manufacturer) basis to systems developers. Convergent Technologies marketed its high-performance workstations this way through Burroughs and Honeywell among others. OEM agreements are not limited to large mainframe makers. Hundreds of small specialized system houses operate on this basis. By integrating and packaging available hardware, systems houses create and install customized turnkey products to user specifications. Sales to such agents, especially in the field of office automation, offered alternative approaches to direct marketing.

Another approach to the market was based on low-price imitation or "knockoff" of a successful computer. Franklin's Ace 100 was a knockoff of Apple II; it looked like the Apple II and was compatible with most Apple II software and hardware accessories. Franklin's ads show a closeup of the Ace 100 keyboard with a shiny red apple perched on top. Its sales grew despite limited distribution and ongoing lawsuits with Apple. Apple had many other imitators. Ads for the Pineapple appeared in the U.S., and Apple has fought the Lemon in Italy, the Orange in Asia and Australia and the Apolo in Hong Kong. A host of knockoffs were offered for the IBM PC as well. This strategy required minimal R&D capabilities and no software development. Success depended on low price, permitted by low engineering costs and an established base of software developed by someone else. Often unable to support a dealer network, knockoffs were commonly distributed through the mail.

For most new entrants, compatibility with a major operating system and software bases was a key element in their strategy. Some firms took this strategy one step further by engineering two microprocessors into the system. These computers were known as dual processor systems. Typically, one of them was the Z80, which ran under CP/M, and therefore guaranteed immediate software availability. However, the Z80 was slower and could address less memory than newer 16-bit processors. The second processor was a faster chip such as Intel's 8086 or Motorola's MC68000. DEC's Rainbow contained the Z80 and the 8088, a scaled-down version of the 8086. IBM's PC has a slot for a second microprocessor of the user's choice. While little software had been developed for these more advanced processors, dual processors allowed the user to upgrade his computing capabilities as new software was published. In the meantime, he could use the full line of software for CP/M. This strategy could become popular, as it hedged against CP/M becoming an industry standard, on the one hand, and against obsolescence of 8-bit systems on the other. The incremental cost of dual processors was relatively small—so it was seen as a powerful means of satisfying both short and longer-term needs.

Market Trends 1983

While the Apple II and III continued to receive excellent response in the market, competition became stiffer by the week. IBM, which introduced its Personal Computer in the summer of 1981, had approached Apple in dollar sales. With its massive financial resources, national sales force, service organization, its brand name and depth of management, IBM was powerful in nearly every aspect of the business. As monthly unit sales passed the 20,000 mark in 1982, IBM was rumored to plan production of one million units in 1983.

Atari, Commodore and Texas Instruments all surpassed Apple in unit sales in 1982. Although the bulk of these sales were in low-priced home computers, each had introduced higher-capacity machines. The Commodore 64, a dual-processor machine priced at $595, ran Apple software and offered greater memory and features than the Apple II. Apple's stock price dropped $2 the day this product was introduced.

Apple's management sensed their customer base was being squeezed from both above and below, in terms of price and technical capability. In addition, the personal computer market had become increasingly segmented. Consumers who once could choose between the Apple II and a few other similar systems could now choose from over 150 models in every range of price and capability. The low-cost home models, led by Atari, offered a cheaper solution for casual users than the Apple II did. Corvus and Altos marketed high-powered 16-bit systems that could out-perform the Apple III in the office. The Grid Compass and Osborne I offered portability, a feature both the Apple II and III lacked. Apple faced the prospect of losing share to more specialized systems employing newer technology that were positioned in more focused ways.

MARKET SEGMENTS

The microcomputer market consisted of five broad segments: the home, education, small business, office and professional categories. The professional market included a range of scientific, engineering and industrial applications. Users in this segment were often very sophisticated in their knowledge of hardware and software and very demanding in terms of processing power, speed and capacity. Such users also often required communications capabilities with other computers, scientific instruments and equipment. Although such users often wrote their own software, several suppliers had recently introduced systems with dedicated software for applications such as computer-aided design, graphics and process control. The professional market was expected to account for about 10% of 1983 microcomputer sales in dollars.

Communications capability was also important in the office market, where electronic mail and data transfer were important functions. Word-processing and electronic filing were also important functions in the office market. The customer base in this segment consisted of medium to large organizations. Given a trend toward the proliferation of computers in many office environments, there was growing concern among many organizations for standardization and central purchasing of microcomputers. The office market was expected to account for 25% of microcomputer dollar sales in 1983.

The small business market consisted of many small business customers. These customers generally had little experience with computers and required assistance in understanding their functions and uses. They had high service and support requirements. Key applications in this market were accounting, spreadsheet analysis, record-keeping billing, and other standard business uses. This segment was expected to represent 25% of the market in 1983.

The education segment ranged from the most simple applications in elementary schools to fairly sophisticated uses in graduate schools. Purchasing often involved bidding procedures in public schools, but high unit volume purchases were common and there was a strong tendency toward standardization in this market, which was expected to account for as much as 10% of 1983 dollar sales.

The home computer market was the least well defined of all the major segments. Many professionals, managers and business people owned or used a computer at home to complement the machine they used at work. These individuals had very different needs than the novice who was interested primarily in games or self-instruction. The home computer market covered a variety of price ranges as well. The bulk of unit sales were in the below $500 range, but home customers accounted for a significant share of sales for more expensive models. While many customers were highly sensitive to price, others demanded ease-of-use, software availability or brand credibility. The home market was expected to account for 33% of 1983 microcomputer sales.

APPLE'S ACTIVITIES IN 1983

Apple's products were used primarily in the business and professional market and to a lesser extent in schools and the home. Although Apple III sales exceeded 50,000 units in 1982, almost all of Apple's sales and profits continued to flow from the Apple II system. The IIe, introduced in early 1983, was the third version of this highly successful product. The IIe offered several advantages over the II+, its predecessor. The IIe offered a base memory capacity of 48k, instead of 32k; it featured upper and lower case letters, cursor keys and other keyboard improvements; it provided an 80-column screen, instead of 40 columns; and it was priced initially at $1595, four hundred dollars below the price of the II+. Sales of the Apple II continued to be broadly based. Thirty percent of unit sales were for the home market. Business, professional and education markets were also important. While the Apple II attracted a wide range of users, it was too expensive for many home computer segments and it could not meet the needs of many professional and office segments. Apple III offered greater power and performance, but it had not met expectations in the office and professional segments. The introduction of Lisa marked a major new initiative in these market segments.

LISA AND MACINTOSH

Apple had two entrants in the office systems market. Lisa, announced at the 1982 annual meeting, was the first entrant. A second project, labeled Macintosh, was headed by Steven Jobs. The Lisa personal office workstation represented a new concept in computers, primarily in the user interface. Lisa incorporated several existing technologies that had never been implemented in the same system. Every element of Lisa's hardware and software design was oriented to facilitating the way a naive user would communicate with the system. The premise behind Lisa's design was to remove the barriers that prevented people from using the computer. Resistance to adoption of computers stemmed from the fact that people were afraid of them; that computers took a long time to learn; that they were difficult to use, and that their software was incompatible. Lisa's features addressed each of these issues. Learning was reduced because Lisa was self-teaching. Each of the six applications programs incorporated in Lisa included an interactive tutorial. Apple claimed the average learning time for one application was close to 20 minutes, as opposed to several hours on other computers.

The screen layout was analogous to a desk top, and the user could arrange it any way he wanted. By using a language called Smalltalk, developed at Xerox Palo Alto Research Center, Lisa enabled the user to create windows to enter or access information from any of the integrated applications programs. Lisa's six integrated applications programs were word-processing (Lisaword), spreadsheet (Lisacalc), list management (Lisalist), business graphics (Lisagraph), free-form graphics (Lisadraw), and critical path and project management (Lisaplan). Parts of one could be included in another. For example, Lisacalc data can be read by Lisagraph to produce a graph, which can be reformatted in Lisadraw, and cut and pasted into a Lisaword document. Additionally, all six programs used the same commands; the user gave instructions to each application in the same way.

Demonstration units of Lisa were being shipped to selected dealers in March, and quantity shipments were expected to begin late in the spring. Lisa was packaged as an entire system, and was priced at $9995. The package included the CPU, one megabyte of RAM, the operating system and six applications software programs, keyboard, mouse, monitor, and 5-megabyte Winchester hard disk storage.

While little was known about Macintosh outside the Mac division, it was said to be based on Lisa technology. Public sources speculated that Macintosh would be a lower priced version of Lisa. The Macintosh project supposedly was scheduled for completion by early 1984. Lisa and Macintosh represented a two-pronged effort to become a significant factor in the office systems market.

THE HOME COMPUTER PROJECT

Apple's thrust in the home market had yet to be defined, but Alan Oppenheimer's project had been formed within the Personal Computer Systems Division (PCSD). Many issues had to be resolved before the home computer thrust could be launched, however. Should the home system be based on Apple II technology, with its huge base of software, or should a Lisa-like product be developed? Should the home system be distributed through Apple's 1400 computer dealers, or should it be carried in chain stores and mass merchandizers? Promotion, pricing, service support, and training policies had to be defined.

With a new product introduction, Apple's management faced the insidious problem of trying to position several new products without cannibalizing others or missing large opportunities. Until 1983, Apple had just two products. Lisa was the third, Macintosh would make four, and the home system, five. The target segments of each overlapped and the problem became more complex as each new system was introduced.

Apple had created a Marketing Council to deal with those and other similar issues. All marketing activities and plans were reviewed by the Council. Alan Oppenheimer commented on the Council and its function:

> We would go to the Marketing Council, which is made up of about ten marketing people, the top marketing person in each division, and get their feedback and recommendations. The Marketing Council exists for interdivisional types of issues, where our division does something that affects others. The Council meets twice a month for about half a day.

Apple's organization and systems were constantly evolving to adapt to the demands of its extraordinary growth. Since its beginning in 1977, Apple had been highly decentralized, reflecting the entrepreneurial nature of its people and industry. As the company grew, it became organized on a product basis. As of January 1, 1983, Apple was organized into five product divisions. Three of the divisions developed and marketed computer systems to end users. The Personal Computer System Division was responsible for the IIe, III and the forthcoming home system; the Personal Office Systems Division developed and marketed Lisa; the Macintosh Division, headed by Steve Jobs, was engaged in developing a low-priced system based on Lisa technology. The two remaining divisions served primarily as suppliers to the systems divisions.

The Peripheral Division designs and manufactures disk drives. The Accessories Division manufactures and sources products such as keyboards, printers, connectors and game controls. In addition to these product divisions, there were separate functional divisions for corporate-wide sales, advertising, system manufacturing, distribution, legal, finance and human resources. There was also a strong functional emphasis within the systems divisions. In the PCSD, for example, managers within each product group were responsible for applications software development, external software vendor relations, hardware engineering, and many other functions. One set of managers performed these functions for the Apple II, and another set of managers handled these responsibilities for the Apple III. In late 1982, the PCSD reorganized formally along functional lines. For example, applications software activities were centralized and personnel from this group worked on programs for both the Apple II and Apple III, and would also work on the home system. One of Alan Oppenheimer's primary efforts involved maintaining a high level of interest and cooperation in the home computer system effort among these functional specialists.

THE MANAGEMENT ENVIRONMENT

Apple's internal management environment had always been distinctive. Suits and ties were never seen inside an Apple facility. A high level of informality was apparent, as well as a high level of energy and activity. There had always been a high level of commitment to the company's "mission" among its employees. Recently, however, several Apple managers have left the company to start ventures of their own, a consequence of the transition from an entrepreneurial organization to a professional orientation. Peter Levy, a young PCSD manager, commented on how the change has been managed:

> I'm impressed with the way it's been handled. There are many people here who are managers, and we're starting to put together a system that lends itself to the process of getting something accomplished; in other words, I don't have to spend my time thinking about *how* to get something done. I have an established system and organization for that. My time is spent thinking what should get done. And for that, I have a manager who listens and provides feedback.

These changes were a response to increasing demands created by Apple's extraordinary growth. As the company grew, management struggled to provide an organizational structure and systems to keep pace. Lines of responsibility were not clear, and communications among divisions were poor. Management spent much of their time figuring out who was supposed to be doing what, instead of putting operating plans together. The reorganization was a major step forward, but information systems lagged behind. Much remained to be done to develop the necessary infrastructure to support Apple's expanding activities in a burgeoning market. As Mike Markkula observed,

> I have a top ten list of priorities for the PCSD, and there are 19 items on it; that should tell you something. That's a real good example of what Apple is.

Case 21

VLSI TECHNOLOGY, INC.

William H. Davidson / Stephen J. Schewe

In February 1983, Alfred J. Stein was reviewing the position of VLSI Technology (VTI) prior to its initial public stock offering. Mr. Stein, who had been President of Arrow Electronics before joining VTI, had just completed his first year as Chairman and CEO of the new company. VTI had been formed in 1979 by Jack Balleto, Dan Floyd and Gunnar Wetlesen, all of whom had left Synertek Corporation after it was acquired by Honeywell.

VTI was formed to design and manufacture custom VLSI chips. VTI also marketed advanced circuit design tools under the name "User-Designed VLSI." These software design tools were intended to shift the function of designing complex integrated circuits from semiconductor makers to original equipment manufacturers themselves. If such a shift occurred, VTI had the potential to grow at a tremendous rate over the next few years. Al Stein's chief concerns were how to encourage the adoption of VTI's services and how to prepare for and manage the company's future growth. His most immediate concern, however, was the stock market's assessment of VTI's prospects.

VTI—THE CONCEPT

Al Stein leaned forward in his chair and spoke softly but intently:

> We have dedicated ourselves uniquely to this business; our whole strategy is based on being a fully integrated "custom" house. We are marketing our design tools and providing training programs to systems companies so they can design their own chips. Other companies in our business want to do custom designs internally. We are of the opposite opinion; we think that industry resources, that is, IC designers, are extremely limited. We want to give the design responsibility to the much larger number of systems engineers. If they design more chips than they have in the past, we hope to reap the benefits by producing those designs in our silicon foundry.

VTI was incorporated on August 1, 1979 in San Jose, California. The founders proposed to greatly reduce lead times for delivery of custom circuits. They planned to slash design time and costs through automation of the design process. VTI's software tools permitted an electrical engineer working at a terminal to design a circuit in graphic form using conventional electrical engineering symbols. The engineer specified the circuit elements and their relationships. The software package then verified the integrity of the circuit design and its efficiency. Once the design was complete, the software package converted the graphic representation into digital code that specified the precise layout of the semiconductor chip.

VTI licensed its design tool software to its customers under agreements which grant the customer a non-transferable, non-exclusive right to use the software for a fixed fee ranging from $58,000 to $160,000. The tools are used on the DEC VAX family of minicomputers or with Apollo Computer workstations (see Exhibit 21.1). A version for IBM mainframe systems was also being developed.

VTI's activities did not end with the completed design. They also planned to provide "quick turnaround" fabrication capability for prototypes and volume production of custom integrated circuits. The digital code generated by the software package would be fed into VTI's wafer fabrication facility to manufacture prototypes and later final products in volume.

Exhibit 21.1

VTI USER-DESIGNED SOFTWARE* AND FUNCTION

Circuit Design Process	*Corresponding Software*
System design	* CELL COMPILERS—Automatic implementation of system building blocks.
Logic design	* VNET—Language to describe logic method. * VSIM—Logic simulator to check function.
Circuit design	* SPICE—Circuit simulator to check performance.
Physical design	* STICKS—Symbolic design for unique cells. * GEOMETRIC EDITOR—Direct creation and modification of layout data base. * PLOT—Graphic output of layout data base.
Verification	* EXTRACT—Circuit extractor to regenerate logic network from implementation. * VSIM—Logic simulator to verify function. * DRC—Design rule check for compatibility with design process.

* Starred software indicates names which have been trademarked by VTI.

ROM OPERATIONS

While anticipating growth in custom chip sales, VTI commenced production of read-only memories (ROMs) in 1982. ROMs were standard products typically manufactured in large volumes. A ROM differed from a RAM, the other primary memory product, in that the data in the ROM was permanently encoded. Data in a RAM is lost when the electric current is turned off. ROMs are typically encoded by the manufacturer. Since ROMs can be uniquely programmed (i.e., can have a unique combination of positive and negative charges within a standard grid), they have some of the characteristics of custom chips. During 1982, the company derived 76% of its revenues from ROM sales to five consumer product manufacturers. Sales to these customers were primarily for use in home video game cartridges. VTI's largest customers were Mattel, Inc. and Coleco Industries, Inc., which accounted for approximately 52% and 17% of revenues, respectively.

VTI contracted with independent companies for most of the fabrication, assembly and test of its read-only memories. These arrangements enabled the development cash flows and important customer relationships before the opening of VTI's wafer fabrication facility in November 1982. Dan Floyd, Vice-President of Programmable Memory Operations (ROMs), planned to continue using subcontractors for his orders, while VTI's fabrication facilities would be used to produce high performance custom circuits designed with the company's software tools.

CUSTOM INTEGRATED CIRCUITS

> I think there are a lot of parallels in this business with the last major electronics revolution, which centered around the microprocessor. A lot of engineers felt the need to learn and use the microprocessor to avoid being pushed aside by younger engineers coming out of college. It's another opportunity/threat.

Wes Patterson, VTI Director of Systems Marketing, was discussing the complicated motivations of potential customers as they decided whether to switch from standard to custom integrated circuits. Although custom circuits had long been available, standard chips accounted for well over 95% of all semiconductor sales.

This usage pattern was due to higher design costs and longer lead times for custom products. Manufacturing realities also limited the development of custom chip usage. The key issues in semiconductor manufacturing had long been the yield of usable chips for a wafer of silicon. Semiconductor manufacturing was a delicate process that required expensive equipment operating at precise tolerances. This process did not reward adjustments of machinery to accommodate production of multiple devices. Fabrication lines usually were set up for large batches of one standard device. Producers invested in research to develop new, more complex devices suitable for wide application, and in plant and equipment designed for long production runs of standard components. These pressures have shaped competitive strategies which emphasize aggressive pricing of standardized components to maximize volume and minimize costs. These industry characteristics had proven extremely attractive to Japanese competitors, who had made major inroads into the U.S. semiconductor market. Japanese suppliers had captured over half of the U.S. market for the latest generation of RAM products (64k units) and were expanding their activities in other high-volume, standardized product segments.

Custom chips began to have an impact in the semiconductor market only in the late 1970s. The custom chip market was stimulated by development of the microprocessor at Intel in 1970. When combined with read-only memory containing a software program, the microprocessor became a device that could be tailored to specific applications. With customized ROM, microprocessors ran products ranging from handheld toys to auto ignition systems and microcomputers. Although flexible, microprocessors themselves were still standard components; they became less effective as higher levels of performance were demanded. Dedicated devices designed for single applications proved to be far more efficient than microprocessors. Although programmable microprocessors have some of the characteristics of custom chips, primary custom products were gate arrays, standard cells, and full custom chips.

Gate arrays are preprocessed layers of silicon containing thousands of logic gates. A gate is an on/off switch in a logic circuit or a bit of information in a memory product. The bottom layers of a gate array are of standard configuration; the top one to three layers are unique for each application. The top layers specify how gates in the other layers will be interconnected to fit a customer's specific requirements. This approach offers superior performance in some applications over microprocessors; gate arrays, however, use silicon space inefficiently. Some of the gates produced in preprocessing will not be wired in the final design. One executive estimated that gate array designs typically waste at least 20% of a chip's gates in this way. Nonetheless, gate arrays have provided fast and flexible system design. IBM gave the technology instant credibility when it used gate arrays in its 4300 series computers in 1978, and more recently in its high-end 308X mainframes. Gate arrays offer quick turnaround time; makers can develop prototypes from customer specifications in twelve weeks. Systems designers in industries with extremely short product lives such as data processing or computer peripherals favor this approach; they can achieve higher density and lower cost than with standard chips. Gate array manufacturers also claim that their technology requires less design time than full custom approaches.

USER ECONOMICS FOR A 2,000 GATE APPLICATION: STANDARD CELLS VS. GATE ARRAYS

Exhibit 21.2

	Gate Array	*Standard Cells*
Tooling costs	$10,000	$40,000
Other development costs	30,000	40,000
Total development costs	$40,000	$80,000
Chip capacity, 4-inch silicon wafer	198 chips	265 to 380 chips
Yield	5%	7–9%
Chip yield	9.9 chips	18.6 to 34.2 chips
Cost of wafer fabrication	$100	$100
Cost per chip processed	$10.10/chip	$2.92 to $5.38/chip
Breakeven requirements	5,571 to 8,475 units	

SOURCE: *Electronics,* February 10, 1983.

Standard cells can provide a more economical solution than gate arrays for users less constrained by product design deadlines. These cells are complete functional blocks drawn from a computerized "library"; they include logic functions, memories, processors and peripheral components. These cells are put into position and connected on a silicon chip in a process similar to putting standard components onto a printed circuit board. Standard cells are more efficient than gate arrays because only necessary functions are included in the design. If standard cells and gate arrays are the same size, the greater density of standard cells will allow for higher operating speed. Furthermore, because of smaller size, standard cells will realize higher yields and lower unit fabrication costs. These benefits must be weighed against the lower development costs for gate arrays; for a typical application, standard cells become more attractive at higher production volumes. (See Exhibit 21.2.)

The Structured Design Approach for Full Custom Chips

Developments in circuit design methodology in the late 1970s reduced the time and cost needed to design a custom VLSI circuit. A design methodology known as "Hierarchical VLSI" was developed by Professor Carver Mead of Cal Tech and Lynn Conway of the Xerox Research Center in Palo Alto. Their approach applied systems concepts to circuit design. It could be used by application engineers to lay out a simplified "floor plan" of a circuit and then to lay out individual cells in detail using design tools. Using these tools, a systems engineer could improve circuit density, put more functions on a

Exhibit 21.3

USER ECONOMICS FOR A 20,000 GATE APPLICATION: STANDARD, SEMI-CUSTOM, AND CUSTOM

	Standard Parts	*Semi-Custom (Gate Array)*	*User-Designed*
Number of chips	1,667	27	13
Number of circuit boards	33	2	1
Development cost	$165,000	$550,000	$395,000
Total Cost for 10,000 units	$56 million	$15.2 million	$8.7 million

SOURCE: *Dataquest,* December 1982.

chip, and reduce the number of components needed in a system. For example, the Apple II+ had 110 components on its printed circuit board; the next generation Apple IIE was redesigned with VLSI technology to use only thirty-one components. Custom chips become more attractive with larger unit requirements. Exhibit 21.3 shows an estimate of user economics for a state-of-the-art 20,000 logic gate system.

The user-designed chip had lower development costs because of the new availability of computer-aided design (CAD) tools and made more efficient use of silicon, which cut material and overhead costs.

Past Objections to Custom Circuits

Although the economics appeared attractive, certain risks attended the potential user of custom chips. The design process in the past had been subject to frequent errors and many manual procedures, such as verifying circuit design or the debugging of prototypes. Intricate devices such as VLSI logic circuits ran the risk of eating up man-years of design resources using traditional methods. Skilled IC design engineers available to complete these designs were scarce; there were only about 2,000 IC engineers in the United States, compared to 200,000 or more systems-level engineers. The supply situation promised to become worse in the future; the American Electronics Association projected demand for 51,300 electrical engineers in 1985. At the same time, product lives have shortened as OEMs push to use the latest chips in their systems, increasing demand.

In the past, potential users of custom chips have had three alternatives to solve these problems. To obtain chips, they could develop an internal or "captive" production capability, acquire a minority interest or complete ownership of an existing IC manufacturer, or request custom service from one of the large semiconductor manufacturers. The first option had been widely pursued; the industry had witnessed a dramatic surge of new entrants in the past twenty-five years. While some were ventures formed to exploit new technology, others were large users of chips who formed their own in-house or "captive" suppliers of semiconductors. Captive production of integrated circuits was estimated to have accounted for one third of total U.S. production in 1980 and 90% of all custom chip production. (See Exhibit 21.4.)

The relative advantages of vertical integration were being debated hotly in the industry. Recently, Hewlett-Packard used its captive operations to develop a 32-bit microprocessor for use in its 9000 series of minicomputers. Development took $100 million and five years; the device will be used only in HP products. In an interview with Electronic News, George Bodway, the general manager of HP's Computer Integrated Circuits Division, explained

Exhibit 21.4

NUMBER OF INTEGRATED CIRCUIT MANUFACTURERS, U.S. MARKET

Years	*Merchant Manufacturers*	*Captive Manufacturers*
1960	27	6
1965	44	11
1970	92	18
1975	108	31
1980	95	60
1983	107	65

TOP 10 U.S.-BASED CAPTIVE SUPPLIERS OF INTEGRATED CIRCUITS

Company	*Estimated 1982 Production (millions of dollars)*
IBM	2100
Western Electric	385
Delco (General Motors)	185
Hewlett-Packard	160
NCR	70
Honeywell	70
DEC	60
Burroughs	40
Data General	30
Tektronix	25

SOURCE: *Integrated Circuit Engineering.*

that HP's device would provide a substantial lead over competitors, since no equivalent product was available from merchant vendors.

Many companies have acquired semiconductor makers; major recent purchasers of chip manufacturers included GE (Intersil), Honeywell (Synertek), and IBM (30% investment in Intel). For others, the choice was to request service from the semiconductor houses like Motorola, TI, and Intel. Douglas Fairbairn, VTI Director of User-Designed VLSI software, explained that large amounts of demand were not being satisfied by such manufacturers because of economic pressures:

> In the past, only customers who needed a very high volume of product could get someone to design a chip for them—say, 10,000 units and up. Below 10,000 it was not cost effective to use scarce engineering talent.

In contrast, qualified design houses were difficult to find and low volume production facilities were scarce. Moreover, timetables and performance levels for custom chips were viewed with uncertainty by most users. An effort at ITT to develop a custom chip for use in portable telecommunications gear in 1975–1976 was abandoned after two years of effort. The ITT users contracted the design process to a specialty custom producer, which was unable to design a chip that worked in the overall system. Although the custom chip prototypes were half the size of the chosen approach, the design process burned up almost two years before ITT cancelled the custom project; they were unwilling to delay the product's market entry to obtain a more efficient chip. Such "horror stories" had been a major barrier to user acceptance of custom. In addition, custom chips were by their nature difficult or impossible to second-source (i.e., to develop alternative supplier relationships), so that dependence on suppliers was a problem.

Potential Advantages of Full Custom

Full custom circuits were extremely efficient in their use of silicon space, yielding higher density and fewer components per application. On a system-wide basis, this advantage created an opportunity to design products with less circuit board space, fewer unique components, lower power requirements, and a smaller cooling system. In addition, fewer components meant overhead savings in packaging, testing, inventory, and documentation costs. For customers who required enough units to cover design and development costs, these advantages could provide a competitive edge over rivals using alternative technologies.

One example of full-custom's advantage in this area was the experience of Network Systems, a manufacturer of high-speed data communications equipment. The company originally approached VTI for a custom solution to cut the size of its communication hook-up for terminals, which required two printed circuit boards of 8.5 × 11 inches. These boards, which utilized a variety of standard components, cost about $250 each. A gate array manufacturer developed a solution using three large gate array circuits for a total cost of $300. VTI's approach called for one chip priced at $100. The cost of materials in the VTI chip was $25 compared to $150 for the standard component solution. Interviewed for an article on future computer technology, James Thornton, founder of Network Systems, firmly supported the trend to application-specific ICs:

> I believe the advances in semiconductors and gate densities are driving the push toward new equipment. We can now exploit the idea of really specializing . . . Chip design is undergoing standardization in that certain cell designs are being put in a library and can be called up for use in various designs. Basically, you won't have to know how to design the circuit, only how to use the circuit or the software that is embedded in it. There will be a shift from the classic semiconductor supplier to a new silicon foundry. The ideal way is to put the design tube (CRT) in the hands of the user and let the user design the custom chip.

Decisions by users on whether to use custom chips and which type to employ would be decided by the requirements of each application. Customers in the video games market might choose ROMs with microprocessors because they were cheap, rapidly available in high volume, and the customized ROM provided some commercial security. Data processing equipment makers might choose gate arrays because of the quick turnaround time, and the higher density and lower costs relative to standard components. Military or telecommunications applications might have power and space constraints or demand unusually high performance, with a full custom chip being the appropriate technology. Users whose products had short product life cycles might require a chip with a shorter development cycle. Users desiring design security would prefer custom approaches.

Market Projections—Custom Chips

Exhibit 21.5 shows custom and semi-custom chips as a percent of total integrated circuit consumption. Improvements in design techniques, computer-aided engineering, support, and silicon foundry availability are expected to increase custom and semi-custom chips to 18.5% of total IC sales in 1986.

VTI—MARKETING

VTI's primary marketing effort was its six week design course. To acquaint potential customers with the design system, VTI conducted six week courses in VLSI circuit design in which students designed an actual circuit using VTI's design methodology and tools. The course fee of $6,000 included the fabrication and packaging of student prototype circuits. Companies found that tuition was often recouped by this "class project." Through the end of 1982, approximately 80 students from 35 companies had taken the course. VTI had also entered into three joint design projects where company and

Exhibit 21.5

CUSTOM IC CONSUMPTION AS A % OF TOTAL IC CONSUMPTION
(U.S. Merchant Sales Only, Millions of Dollars)

	1981	1982	1983E	1986E
Full-custom	15.7	25.9	49.6	790.0
Gate arrays	36.1	45.8	59.9	530.0
Standard cells	9.5	19.0	38.8	1215.0
Total custom	61.3	90.7	148.3	2535.4
Total ICs	5140.7	5942.2	7487.2	13705.3
Custom as a % of ICs	1.2%	1.5%	2.0	18.5

SOURCE: *Electronics*, January 13, 1983.

customer engineers worked together to meet tight design schedules. VTI planned to expand its training capacity by opening Technology Centers in Boston, Dallas, Chicago, and one European city in 1983.

According to Wes Patterson, VTI's major marketing goal for 1983 was to gain new bookings and accounts and to broaden its customer base:

> As we try to diversify our customer base and to introduce our design tools, we're in a tough spot. We can't bring on a direct sales force fast enough, and the salesmen typically aren't technical enough. We're having to create our own market through the design course. Nearly every tool sale we've made to date is directly traceable to an engineer who has been through the course. With a little pre-screening, we think we can expect 15% or more of the companies who send employees to the course to buy the tools.

Major motivations for VTI customers included security, special design requirements, and the growing need of systems designers to become intimately involved in the design process. As Patterson explained:

> A lot of our customers need proprietary protection for design ideas from imitators. The standard products look more and more the same; for example, there must be 20 producers of UNIX-driven 16-bit minicomputers; there's no product protection except for the software.

These pressures were nowhere more evident than in the viciously competitive video games market. The industry leader, Atari, had just completed layoffs of 1,700 workers and had moved assembly operations overseas in an effort to cut costs.

VTI—DESIGN OPERATIONS

The nature of the custom chip design process required a close working partnership between systems designers and their design and fabrication resources. Such a relationship could not always be provided by one of the standard components manufacturers or by vendors of semicustom approaches like gate arrays or standard cells. As Patterson explained:

> In each of these cases, he (the designer) carries his design up to a certain point, then throws it over the transom to these other companies. He doesn't know or understand them, yet he's dependent on their guarantees for delivery on time and a prototype that works.

VTI's service orientation included a willingness to produce small volume runs (e.g., 5,000 to 10,000 chips per year) unwanted by large standard components producers, and to cheaply and quickly produce prototypes. Al Stein commented:

> If you design a chip, you want to know whether the damn thing works and you want to know in a hurry. We offer a multi-product wafer capability which consolidates a whole host of designs on one wafer for one process run. The costs of tooling for masks are $15,000 to $20,000 per mask.* By sharing the costs of that run, your costs are dramatically lowered. That service is run once a month and is an integral part of being a full-service custom house.

VTI has been able to go from masks to prototypes in as little as two weeks, compared to fourteen weeks for large semiconductor manufacturers.

Under some customer contacts, VTI performed the entire design function. Completed design projects included a custom logic circuit for a coin operated video game, a shift register for a telecommunications application, and a RAM circuit for video arcade games. At the end of 1982, VTI was working on design contracts for six customers relating to a total of fifteen circuits. During 1982, VTI completed five custom design circuits, of which two were in production at year end. Most design contracts took sixteen to twenty-two weeks to complete.

VTI—FOUNDRY OPERATIONS

The trend to custom chips had been assisted by the evolution of the silicon foundry, a wafer processing facility emphasizing quick turnaround time (QTAT) and standardized design-manufacturing data interchange rules. VTI's fabrication facility, or "silicon foundry," was designed for quick turnaround manufacturing. For prototype and small volume runs, VTI's use of multi-project wafers (MPWs) allowed wafer fabrication costs to be shared among several designs. Compared to conventional fabrication techniques, this approach reduced mask tooling costs substantially for small production lots.

* Masks are transparent glass units that contain circuitry patterns to be etched into silicon. The mask is transparent except for the circuit patterns drawn on its surface. The mask is placed over silicon coated with photo-sensitive material. When exposed to light, the silicon is "exposed," except in areas where the mask is not transparent (the circuit patterns). The resulting patterns form the basis for all silicon circuitry.

VTI also established an electronic network known as "VTINet." VTINet allowed customers to submit chip design codes from their remote locations. When fully operational, this system would permit customers to submit circuit layouts of custom chips and to use a computer terminal to determine the status of their orders in the production cycle.

VTI's fabrication facility was still under construction in early 1983, although several processing lines were in operation. Output at full capacity would be 1,000 wafers per day. Current output during the startup phase in January 1983 was 100 wafers per week. Gunnar Wetlesen, director of foundry operations, estimated that an additional investment of $22 million would be required to bring the facility to full capacity.

VTI's managers believed that their long-term profitability depended on convincing users to give VTI high-volume fabrication contracts for custom chips. Wes Patterson said:

> We believe we can get the silicon business, which is the nice difference between our strategy and just being a tools company. When the guy designs a circuit that hits his own market niche and sells by the hundreds of thousands, we get to participate in that success.

To aid in securing fabrication runs, the company planned to provide a steady stream of enhancements to its proprietary design tools. As Wes explained:

> We plant a hook in these tools that brings the guy back to our foundry in the form of what we call a cell compiler library. The library contains a set of specific circuit functions. It uses parameters to provide an exact fit for the guy's requirements; nobody else can do that. The cell compiler and other enhancements can further cut design time by a factor of 3 or 4 times. To obtain a license for the enhancements, we ask for a commitment of the production from designs done with these tools, typically 80% in the first year and decreasing after that.

In 1982, ROM sales provided 76% of VTI revenues, with design tools and foundry operations making up the balance. By 1985, VTI's management hoped to reverse that ratio, so that design tools and custom foundry runs would generate 60 to 80% of sales. ROM sales were expected to continue expanding at 15% per year.

PROGRAMMABLE MEMORY OPERATIONS

"We see ROMs as our lead horse and our cash cow," commented Dan Floyd, Vice President, Programmable Memory Operations. VTI's ROM business addressed a broad segment of the market and emphasized high performance and density. The company offered five types of ROMs: standard 32K and 64K, "fast" 64K and 128K, and a 256K device. The majority of sales came from the standard 32K and 64K products. In addition, VTI designed "custom" ROMs, which incorporated random access memory and logic onto the same chip with the ROM circuitry.

The logistics of selling ROMs were relatively easy, since there were a small number of significant potential customers. According to Wes Patterson, the business was based on close relationships and assurance of delivery.

> The customers knew they had our attention and that we'd jump through hoops for them. The big companies can't turn on a dime and deliver product (ROMs) inside four weeks.

VTI expanded these relationships through joint design projects for custom logic chips. The ROM strategy also meshed nicely with the tiny sales force of seven, which could cover the major customers without difficulty.

Besides generating revenues, the ROM business provided pressure to improve technological processes and reduce costs. Gunnar Wetlesen, Vice-President of Wafer Fabrication, said:

> No company has been able to develop state of the art processes for building logic unless they are also in the memory business. They need the volumes and densities to keep the technologies current. The learning curve is nothing more than continuous experimentation on a fixed data base of production runs; the more runs you have, the more opportunities to reduce costs.

VTI's manufacturing policy to date had been to subcontract ROM production in a complicated international network. After chips were designed internally, masks for the photolithography process were produced under subcontract by U.S. specialty houses. Completed masks were then flown to Japan for wafer fabrication by Ricoh and to Korea for assembly and test. At the end of the processing, completed chips were drop-shipped to customers. This strategy allowed VTI to accept ROM contracts before completing its own processing facilities and helped to fund custom chip research and development.

Now that VTI's own wafer processing facility had begun operations, Floyd expected to move the most sophisticated segment of the ROM business to it. The 128K and 256K chips would be used to drive the process technology; shared benefits would accrue in the costs, quality and capacity of custom production. A separate line within the "clean room" where the chips were fabricated would be maintained for quick turnaround of custom prototypes; this line would have only four common operations with the rest of the facility. Floyd hoped to add a packaging operation next to the wafer processing facility in 1983. The standard "jelly bean" ROMs like the 32K and the 64K would continue to be subcontracted.

COMPETITION—ROMs

Competition in the ROM market was intense because of a large number of established competitors and readily available substitutes. VTI competed with over thirty ROM suppliers, including: Synertek, a division of Honeywell

Exhibit 21.6

PRICE FORECAST FOR ROMs

Product	1982	1983E	1984E	1985E
32K	$2.21	$1.53	$1.07	$0.82
64K	4.42	3.06	2.14	1.64
128K	8.86	6.12	4.28	3.28
256K	NA	12.24	8.56	6.56

founded by current members of VTI management; National Semiconductor; NEC; American Microsystems (a division of Gould); and General Instrument. Competition was based on price. Many competitors had shared costs with other product lines; entry decisions could be made on an incremental basis. Exhibit 21.6 shows projected prices for ROMs for the next three years.

In many low-volume applications, and in products where software revisions were required, erasable programmable memories (EPROMs) had replaced ROMs. EPROMs can be reprogrammed in the field using ultraviolet light to erase previous instructions. These circuits are generally more expensive than ROMs, however, and ROMs are thus more likely to be used in consumer products where the circuit features are not alterable by the user. Although price is an important competitive factor in this market, service and delivery are also important because ROMs cannot be sold from inventory; they must be manufactured to meet the customer's pattern or program.

Mask ROMs, supported by the toy and game markets, were expected to grow from $414.7 million in 1982 to 492.9 million in 1983, an increase of 19%. Sales had increased 22.6% in 1982. It was estimated that five producers (TI, Motorola, Intel, National, and Advanced Micro Devices) held 53% of the $869 million ROM and EPROM market.

COMPETITION—SEMICUSTOM

Nearly 100 companies were currently competing in the semicustom IC market. Gate array and standard cell design approaches continued to battle for market acceptance as the industry standard; as explained above, each had specific strengths and shortcomings. Six firms currently were offering cell-library design, including American Microsystems, startups International Microelectronic Products and Zymos, Synertek, NCR's Microelectronics Division, and Harris Corporation's Semiconductor Division. No Japanese suppliers had yet announced standard cell libraries in the United States. Fifty to sixty companies compete in the gate arrays market, including industry giants such as Motorola, Texas Instruments, Toshiba, and Fujitsu.

Gould's American Microsystems was the largest company devoted exclusively to custom semiconductor devices and was a major participant in gate arrays.

COMPETITION—CUSTOM DESIGN TOOLS

Competition among manufacturers of integrated circuit design tools was intense. The market consisted of several large manufacturers of CAD workstations (IBM, Calma/GE, Applicon/Schlumberger, Computervision) and dozens of software suppliers who offered packages to run on these machines. Most of these companies were small startup ventures concentrating on the simulation and verification aspects of chip design. These companies included Avera, CADTEC, CAE Systems, Daisy Systems, Mentor Graphics, Metheus, and Valid Logic Systems.

The natural progression of the industry was toward further integration of the design process within one system. Although VTI's system of design tools had not yet gained significant commercial acceptance, its approach was unique in that it integrated most stages of the design process. The user could construct an electrical engineering diagram with the aid of a sophisticated graphics package and cell library. VTI's system automatically tested, optimized, and converted the electrical engineering diagram to a semiconductor circuit design. The user could then transmit the resulting data via VTINet to the fabrication facility. Although VTI's system was unique, management believed they had only a nine-month lead on the competition. New packages were being offered weekly.

In its custom design business, the company competed with many large custom circuit manufacturers, as well as the internal design centers of several original equipment manufacturers. In addition, the custom design process competed with the gate array, standard cell, and field-programmable devices (microprocessors with ROMs) mentioned above.

COMPETITION—SILICON FOUNDRIES

In the latest survey published in VLSI Design, a trade journal for the industry, thirty-eight companies reported that they were offering silicon foundry service, up from twenty-six the year before. Competitors included small startups like VTI, successful semicustom chip makers like American Microsystems which specialized in gate arrays and established standard components manufacturers. The commitment of these firms to the concept of the silicon foundry was unclear in January 1983. The larger houses seemed to be searching for ways to fill capacity idled by the recession, while many of the smaller firms did not yet have a complete processing facility.

> The competitor that scares me to death is Intel, exclaimed Wes Patterson. They've got the foundry, the technology and the sales force, and they still have enough entrepreneurial spirit to go after this market. Motorola and TI don't.

Intel had recently concluded an agreement with Zymos to buy a cell library for its newest high performance fabrication process. According to press reports, they hoped that the agreement would generate new business from small volume users for its silicon foundry while avoiding a company investment in design support operations.

Al Stein believed that his company's emphasis on quick turnaround time, its advanced software and design capability, and its fully integrated service-oriented approach provided it a distinct market advantage.

> There are CAD companies that sell the design tools, and companies that just do wafer processing. We're a one-stop shop.

RESEARCH AND DEVELOPMENT

VTI spent $4.2 million on research and development since its founding, including $3.3 million in 1982. Major areas of emphasis include:

- Advanced software design tools for integrated circuits.
- Advanced networking and communications to provide an interface between customers and the VTI silicon foundry.
- Read-only memory circuits.
- Semiconductor manufacturing processes.

The company's research expenditures were focused on increasing circuit density and quick turnaround time. During 1983, VTI planned to expand its VTINet capabilities to include transmission and processing of custom circuit data bases, and remote inquiry systems to allow customers to track jobs in progress.

HUMAN RESOURCES

At the end of 1982, VTI employed 193 people: 62 in research and development; 20 in manufacturing engineering; 76 in manufacturing; 18 in marketing; and 17 in general management and administration. Al Stein saw his major task as managing this group of highly talented and diverse people:

> The success of any organization, whether it's a high technology company or a football team, is dependent on the people you have in your company. My major efforts are directed at putting together a highly talented group of people who work together well and get the job done.

In turn, Al Stein's move to VTI as Chairman and Chief Executive Officer in February 1982 brought an important level of business and financial credibility to the company. VTI was founded by Jack Balletto, Gunnar Wetlesen, and Dan Floyd. The positions and backgrounds of company officers are shown in Exhibit 21.7. According to Doug Fairbairn, Vice-President of User Designed VLSI and a co-founder, Stein's strengths were his business skills and his track record:

> He's doing here the same things that made him successful at TI and Motorola. He's concentrating on getting product out. He's burdening the

VLSI TECHNOLOGY INC.: LIST OF OFFICERS AND DIRECTORS

Exhibit 21.7

Name	*Age*	*Position and Background*
Alfred J. Stein	50	Chief Executive Officer, President, and Chairman of the Board. With VTI since March 1982. Previously CEO Arrow Electronics, 1981–1982; Corporate VP of Motorola, Assistant Gen. Mgr., Semiconductor Group, Gen. Mgr., Integrated Circuits Division, 1977–1981; various positions with Texas Instruments, most recently Corporate VP, 1958–1976. Also Director of: Tandy Corporation, Applied Materials, Inc.
John G. Balletto	42	Senior Vice President and Director. President and CFO, VTI, 1979–1983; Director of Marketing, Synertek, 1973–1979; Assistant to President, Ricoh Electronics, various positions at Fairchild Camera and Instrument, 1962–1973.
Daniel W. Floyd	42	Vice President, Programmable Memory Operations and Director. With VTI since 1979. Previously Vice President of Manufacturing, Synertek, 1973–1979; Director of Wafer Fabrication, American Microsystems, and Director of Standard Products, Harris Semiconductor, 1963–1973.
Gunnar A. Wetlesen	35	Vice President, Wafer Fabrication, Technology, and Foundry Activities and Director. With VTI since 1979. Previously Director of Technology Development, 1974–1979, and Director of Memory Products, 1976–1979, Synertek; Manager of Process Technology, American Microsystems, 1968–1974.
Douglas G. Fairbairn	34	Vice President—User-Designed Technology. With VTI since December 1980. Research Staff, Xerox Corporation's Palo Alto Research Center, 1972–1980.
Kenneth A. Goldman	33	Vice President—Finance, CFO and Secretary. With VTI since 1981. Previously Group Controller, Consumer Products Group, 1979–1981, Manager of Budgeting and International Planning, 1977–1979, Memorex Corporation; Controller of MOS Division, Fairchild Camera and Instrument and other positions, 1974–1977.
Ronald C. Kasper	40	Vice-President, Sales. With VTI since 1981. Previously Managing Director, European Sales, 1978–1981, and Western Area Sales Manager, 1976–1978, Synertek; various sales positions, Electronic Memories and Magnetics, 1967–1976.

(Continued)

Exhibit 21.7
(Continued)

Name	*Age*	*Position and Background*
David C. Evans	58	Director. President, CEO, and Chairman of the Board, Evans and Sutherland Computer Corporation, 1968-present. Previously Director of Engineering, Research and Development, Bendix Corporation.
William R. Hambrecht	47	Director. President, CEO, and Director of Hambrecht and Quist, 1968-present. Also Director of: ADAC Laboratories, Auto-trol Technology, Computer and Communications Technology, Evans & Sutherland, Granger Associates, Magnuson Computer Systems, NBI, People Express Airlines, Silicon General, and Xidex Corporation.
James J. Kim	47	Director. Chairman of AMKOR Electronics, Inc., and President of The Electronics Boutique, 1978-present.
William J. Perry	55	Director. Senior Vice President of Hambrecht & Quest, 1981-present. Undersecretary of Defense for Research and Engineering, 1977–1981; President and Chief Executive Officer, ESL, Incorporated (now a division of TRW), 1964–1977. Also director of: ARGO Systems, Avantek, and Technology for Communications International.

company with a minimum amount of overhead for things like administration, and he's demanding absolute perfection, or as close to it as he can, from everybody in the company. Al is well-respected by the financial community and his presence has focused a lot of attention on us. There's a perceived quality of assumed success rather than assumed failure.

FINANCES

VTI had grown at a rapid pace; revenues were $82,404 in 1980, $552,553 in 1981, and $21,229,251 in 1982. Net revenues in 1981 resulted primarily from course fees and rentals from the related video tape lecture series. The sharp increase in revenues realized in 1982 resulted from initial sales of ROM circuits, which accounted for 76% of revenues. VTI's management expected another sizeable increase in sales in 1983. The company's design tools were first offered to customers in 1982, and the first production runs from custom chips designed with the VTI design methods were expected at the end of 1983. These revenue gains were accompanied by heavy expenses resulting from the staffing of engineering teams, product development and marketing activities during 1981, and large capital expenditures

VLSI TECHNOLOGY, INC.: STATEMENT OF OPERATIONS

Exhibit 21.8

	Years Ended		
	December 31, 1980	***December 31, 1981***	***December 26, 1982***
Net revenues	$ 82,404	$ 552,553	$21,229,251
Cost and expenses:			
Cost of sales	73,811	139,942	14,238,656
Wafer processing start-up	—	—	2,761,547
Research and development	—	809,257	3,319,959
Marketing, general and administrative	32,453	1,229,198	3,299,819
Operating costs and expenses	106,264	2,178,397	23,619,981
Operating income (loss)	(23,860)	(1,625,844)	(2,390,730)
Interest income	2,010	151,666	831,057
Interest expense	—	(3,456)	(530,302)
Net income (loss)	$ (21,850)	$(1,477,634)	$(2,089,975)
Income (loss) per common share	$(.01)	$(.72)	$(.53)
Weighted average common shares outstanding	1,563,000	2,054,600	3,967,507

and startup costs for the wafer processing facilities in 1982. As a result of these expenses, VTI had lost a total of $3.6 million during its first three years of operations. Exhibits 21.8, 21.9, and 21.10 show the income statements, balance sheets, and statement of sources and uses of VTI for the years 1980–1982.

Funds needs were expected to remain high in the foreseeable future. VTI's business strategy required a large up-front investment in equipment for the silicon foundry and in development outlays for the design tools. The company's operating plan estimated that $20 million would be required in plant and equipment investment over the next eighteen months. Rapid technological change in chip fabrication and circuit design software indicated the need for sustained development expenditures and equipment investments of this magnitude. Dataquest estimated that the industry was becoming more capital intensive each year and projected an increase in net plant over sales to 70% by 1985.

Exhibit 21.9

VLSI TECHNOLOGY, INC.: BALANCE SHEET

	December 31, 1981	*December 26, 1982*
ASSETS		
Current assets		
Cash and cash equivalents	$ 757,928	$10,552,577
Accounts receivable, net of allowance for doubtful accounts, and customer returns of $338,000 in 1982	99,212	4,246,640
Inventories	—	1,093,304
Prepaid expenses and other current assets	49,220	58,375
Preferred stock subscriptions receivable due within 1 year	8,016,000	—
Total current assets	8,922,360	15,950,896
Plant and equipment		
Machine equipment	17,287	874,788
Leasehold improvements and equipment leased under capital leases	577,676	12,424,381
	594,963	13,299,169
Accumulated depreciation and amortization	(26,801)	(993,666)
Net plant and equipment	568,162	12,305,503
Deposits and other assets	119,220	49,286
	$9,609,742	$28,305,685
LIABILITIES AND SHAREHOLDERS' EQUITY		
Current liabilities		
Accounts payable	$ 390,925	$ 5,914,776
Accrued liabilities	197,977	1,377,640
Deferred income	147,628	761,845
Current portion of capital lease obligations	31,144	1,009,866
Total current liabilities	767,674	9,064,127
Noncurrent obligations under capital leases	318,135	10,783,129
Shareholders' equity		
Series A Preferred Stock, no par value; 6,000,000 shares authorized;		
Issued: 6,000,000 in 1982, 1,200,000 in 1981	1,973,750	9,989,750
Subscribed: 4,800,000 in 1981	8,016,000	—
Series B Preferred Stock, no par value; 2,600,000 shares authorized;		
Issued: 598,803 in 1982	1,000	1,976,102
Common Stock, no par value, 30,000,000 shares authorized;		
Issued: 4,874,464 in 1982, 2,504,000 in 1981	50,080	99,449
Retained earnings (deficit)	(1,516,897)	(3,606,872)
Total shareholders' equity	8,523,933	8,458,429
	$9,609,742	$28,305,685

Exhibit 21.10

VLSI TECHNOLOGY, INC.: STATEMENT OF CHANGES IN FINANCIAL POSITION

	Years Ended		
	December 31, 1980	***December 31, 1981***	***December 26, 1982***
Working capital was applied to:			
Net loss from operations	$ 21,850	$1,477,634	$ 2,089,975
Less charges to operations not involving the current use of working capital—depreciation and amortization	—	(26,801)	(966,865)
Total working capital applied to operations	21,850	1,450,833	1,123,110
Additions to plant and equipment	—	594,963	12,704,206
Increase in deposits and other assets	—	119,220	(69,934)
Total working capital applied	21,850	2,165,016	13,757,382
Working capital was provided by:			
Issuance of common stock	2,500	17,580	49,369
Issuance of preferred stock	971,750	1,002,000	9,991,002
Preferred stock subscribed	9,018,000	(1,002,000)	(8,016,000)
(Increase) decrease in preferred stock subscriptions receivable due after one year	(8,016,000)	8,016,000	—
Issuance of warrant	—	1,000	100
Increases in noncurrent obligations under capital leases	—	318,135	10,464,994
Total working capital provided	1,976,250	8,352,715	12,489,465
Increase (decrease) in working capital	$1,954,400	$6,187,699	$(1,267,917)
Increase (decrease) in working capital by component:			
Cash and cash equivalents	$ 984,025	$ (238,684)	$ 9,794,649
Accounts receivable	13,203	86,009	4,147,428
Inventories	—	—	1,093,304
Prepaid expenses and other current assets	—	49,220	9,155
Preferred stock subscriptions receivable due within one year	1,002,000	7,014,000	(8,016,000)
Accounts payable	(26,328)	(364,597)	(5,523,851)
Accrued liabilities	(18,500)	(179,477)	(1,179,663)
Deferred income	—	(147,628)	(614,217)
Current portion of capital lease obligations	—	(31,144)	(978,722)
Increase (decrease) in working capital	$1,954,400	$6,187,699	$(1,267,917)

Cash flows from custom chip fabrication would increase slowly because of the long development cycle typical of VTI's OEM customers. Industry observers compared the development cycle to a "two-year wheat crop": the OEMs needed additional time for the design and development of new systems after receiving working prototypes of the custom chips; volume production runs that generated large demand for foundry services would only occur at "harvest," once the product was in the market. When volume orders for foundry business came in, VTI would have a comfortable margin; variable costs were estimated at only 20 to 30% of total costs.

For a startup venture, VTI had experienced unusual success in obtaining funds during its early years. Originally, funding was provided in December 1980 by sales of preferred stock to five venture capital firms and Evans and Sutherland Computer Corporation. The venture capitalists were among the most successful firms in the business, including Hambrecht and Quist, Rothschild, Advanced Technology Ventures and Kleiner, Perkins, Caufield & Byers. A list of major shareholders is given in Exhibit 21.11. William Hambrecht and William Perry of Hambrecht and Quist were directors of the company. Further funding was provided by capitalized leases and favorable terms by customers and suppliers. With the assistance of Bendix Corporation, VTI leased the first $13.6 million of equipment and leasehold improve-

VLSI TECHNOLOGY, INC.:
Major Shareholdings

Exhibit 21.11

	Number[1]	*Percent*
Evans & Sutherland Computer Corporation	1,800,000	15.7%
Advanced Technology Ventures	1,154,791	10.1
Accounts advised by Rothschild	1,154,791	10.1
The Bendix Corporation	908,267	7.9
Olivetti Realty	598,803	5.2
Kleiner, Perkins, Caufield & Byers II	577,545	5.0
Officers and directors (11 total)[2]	3,125,869	27.2
Other shares[3]	2,153,201	18.8
Total shares outstanding	11,473,267	100.0

NOTES: 1. Includes all common stock and all preferred shares; preferred is convertible into common; the preferred is convertible into common at a price of $1.67 per share. Cost basis for the common is $0.025 per share. 2. Major individual shareholders include: Alfred J. Stein, 936,889 shares; John G. Balletto, 500,000 shares; Daniel W. Floyd, 500,000 shares; and Gunnar Wetlesen, 485,000 shares. 3. Includes shares beneficially owned and held in trust.

ments associated with its facilities. Bendix also purchased Series B preferred stock from VTI. At the end of 1982, VTI's unused sources of funds consisted of $10.553 million in cash and equivalents, $3.5 million in net available capital lease financing, and $500,000 in research and development funds available from Bendix. In addition, the company possessed $2.7 million in tax carryforwards, including net operating losses, investment tax credits, and research and development credits.

PUBLIC OFFERING

VTI filed for a public offering of common stock on January 25, 1983. The preliminary prospectus estimated that three million shares would be sold at a price between $10 and $12 per share. VTI said the proceeds would be used for capital expenditures and working capital. Currently, 11.5 million shares were outstanding.

Al Stein recognized that VTI's growth potential depended on his company's access to the capital markets:

> We need to raise a good amount of additional capital if we're going to grow at this rate. We think a public offering is the way to go because Wall Street is enthusiastic and our financial performance to date has been better than expected.

New registrations for initial public offerings had surged to a 1982 peak of 31 in the month of December; in the first 11 months of 1982, 186 companies had gone public, raising more than $1.1 billion. Industry participants believed that the market would continue to strengthen; for example, Morgan Stanley announced plans to manage the initial public offering for Apollo Computer in early 1983. Other new issues rumored to be imminent included offerings for: the robotics manufacturer, Automatix; Diasonics, Inc., a supplier of ultrasound imaging systems to radiologists and cardiologists; and desktop computer maker Fortune Systems. Exhibit 21.12 lists selected statistics on recent public offerings.

THE FUTURE

1983 would be an important year for VTI. Stein still saw the company in its startup phase; the wafer processing facility would require several quarters to reach efficient operation and would cause continued losses. The company also needed to build acceptance for its design tools and lessen its dependence on the ROM business by adding customers for custom chips. "The thing that's holding us back is a few solid references," said Wes Patterson. "That cycle takes a couple of years. We won't have testimonials from our earliest customers until the end of 1983."

VTI needed to firmly publicize its claimed advantages in cost and performance to reach its goal of 1000 customers by 1986. As Gunnar Wetlesen explained:

Exhibit 21.12
STATISTICS ON SELECTED INITIAL PUBLIC OFFERINGS

Company	Galileo Electro-Optics	Quantum Corp	ARGO Systems, Inc.	IMAGIC	Altos Computer Systems	Systems & Computer Technology Corp.	Convergent Technologies Inc.	VTI, Inc.
Date Offer Filed	12/28/82	11/9/82	10/27/82	11/3/82	10/14/82	10/5/82	4/14/82	
Line of Business	Manufacturer of electro-optic components	Designs and mfg. rigid disk drives	Designs and mfg. elec. reconnaisance systems	Designs and mfg. home entertainment systems	Designs and mfg. microcomputer systems	Provides application software products and services	Manufactures computer systems	Custom i/c vendor
FINANCIAL INFORMATION (IN THOUSANDS OF DOLLARS EXCEPT PER-SHARE DATA)								
Revenues	14,268	29,968	32,187	35,044	57,443	26,792	19,692	21,229
Net Income	774	4,928	2,462	6,108	6,359	3,225	1,881	−2,090
Earnings Per Share	.57	1.13	1.08	.43	.55	.29	.15	−.53
Total Assets	8,187	18,448	28,014	29,352	27,033	12,166	20,247	9,610
Shareholders' Equity	1,060	13,981	9,442	8,597	14,553	8,337	13,165	−3,607
Offering Data								
Underwriter	L.F. Rothschild	Morgan Stanley	Hambrecht & Quist	Merrill Lynch	L.F. Rothschild	L.F. Rothschild	L.F. Rothschild	L.F. Rothschild
Securities Offered	700,000 com.	2.5 million com.	606,390 com.	2.7 million com.	3.3 million com.	2.58 million com.	4 million com.	3 million com.
Price Range	\$8.00–\$10.00	\$20.50	\$16.00–\$18.00	\$15.00–\$17.00	\$21.00	\$16.50	\$12.00–\$15.00	\$10.00–\$12.00
Value of Offering	\$7 million	\$51.25 million	\$10.915 million	\$45.9 million	\$69.3 million	\$42.57 million	\$60 million	\$36 million
P/E Ratio	17.5x	18.1x	16.7x	39.5x	38.2x	56.9x	100.0x	negative
Offerings as a % of Pro Forma Shares Outstanding	38.4%	28.1%	22.2%	16.9%	23.3%	20.2%	20.8%	20.7%
Mkt. Value at Initial Price	\$18.22 million	\$182.34 million	\$49.272 milion	\$272.3 million	\$297.0 million	\$210.8 million	\$288.7 million	\$173.7 million
AFTERMARKET								
Bid on 1/21/83 (Day before VTI filed offering)	NA	24.75	34.75	NA	26	NA	NA	
% Change From Initial Price		18.3	104.4		23.8			

The design cost, production cost, and performance are all dynamic and must achieve a new equilibrium now that CAD techniques are on the scene. It takes time to realize what's happening and switch over.

Stein was confident that VTI was in the right place at the right time:

A little semiconductor company has to find a strategy and a market niche so that it's not competing with the Motorolas, TIs and Fairchilds. There's no way from a financial or people-resources point of view that it can compete successfully with such companies. You have to have something unique. I think we do indeed have something that is different and that will, over time, change the whole semiconductor industry.

Case 22

HEWLETT-PACKARD, 1978–1981: THE EVOLUTION OF LEADERSHIP

Roger M. Atherton

In May 1978, one day before his sixty-fifth birthday, Bill Hewlett resigned from his position as Chief Executive Officer of Hewlett-Packard, the company he had helped found in 1939. He was appointed Chairman of the Executive Committee and joined David Packard, Chairman of the Board of Directors, in semi-retirement. John Young, who had succeeded Bill Hewlett as President and Chief Operating Officer in November 1977, was promoted to the vacated C.E.O. position. For the first time in its 39-year history, H-P was to be directed by an executive who had been developed from within the organization rather than being led by its original, almost legendary founders.* It had become John Young's responsibility to manage the rapidly growing company as it headed deeper and deeper into the unfriendly territory of computational technology, where the competition was both bigger and tougher than in H-P's traditional businesses—electronic test and measurement, medical electronic equipment, and analytical instrumentation. The question raised by the trade press, Wall Street analysts, and some employees was whether John Young could provide the needed strategies and leadership in this more hostile environment for continued successful growth.

* See earlier cases on Hewlett-Packard in Thomas L. Wheelen and J. David Hunger, *Strategic Management and Business Policy* (Reading, Mass.: Addison-Wesley Publishing Company, 1983). "Hewlett-Packard Company (A): Problems of Rapid Growth" describes the company from 1972 to 1975; "Hewlett-Packard Company (B): A 1975–1978 Review" describes the company from 1975 to 1978.

This case was prepared by Prof. Roger M. Atherton of Northeastern University. Reprinted by permission.

STRATEGIC CHANGES

Electronic Office Systems

By 1981 H-P had become the world's third largest minicomputer manufacturer, exceeded only by IBM and Digital Equipment Corporation. In October 1981, the *Wall Street Journal*[1] reported that H-P had decided to expand from its traditional base of data-processing equipment for business, factory, and scientific purposes into the word-processing and office terminal field dominated by IBM and Wang Laboratories. John Young indicated that H-P's strategy would be to place computer power in the form of interactive, information-processing networks directly into the hands of all office professionals, specialists, and managers, as well as secretaries and the data-processing staff. To implement this strategy, H-P introduced twenty-seven new office products, including two new minicomputers, new word-processing terminals, improved computer terminals for creating graphic representations of numbers, new low-cost disc memories, and four new data communications products to tie all these elements together. Electronic mail and electronic filing packages were due to be introduced within a year. Combined with its previously announced products such as laser printers and a low-cost personal computer, these new products gave H-P a fully integrated office system. For the first time, H-P had the potential to penetrate the full spectrum of business computer uses.

Although in 1979 and 1980 Hewlett-Packard had enjoyed an average annual growth rate of 45% in electronic data products revenues, that growth rate dropped in 1981 to 17%. According to *Business Week*,[2] a growing number of their data processing customers had begun to purchase equipment from such companies as Wang Laboratories, Datapoint, and Lanier Business Products, which offered systems aimed directly at the automated office. Growth in the market for conventional minicomputers had slowed to 25%, so that H-P needed to tap into the market for the larger so-called super-minis and the market for office systems, since both were expanding at about 40% a year, if it wanted to continue its healthy growth rate.

A major target for H-P's thrust into office systems would be manufacturing companies. H-P had focused its efforts in minicomputers on this market segment, which accounted for 40% of the company's business computer sales. H-P wanted to offer these same customers systems that integrated everything from measurement instruments and data collection terminals on the factory floor to word processors in the front office in a single data processing network.

The office market presented H-P with new marketing challenges. Minicomputer makers traditionally sold to data processing departments, but to sell office equipment they would have to identify a whole new set of buyers among their large corporate customers. H-P had developed plans to expand its business computer marketing force by 25% and service force by one third. It also intended to go after new customers in financial services, retailing, and other non-manufacturing sectors. John Young has indicated that H-P would not aggressively go after new customers in these other areas except as there were spare resources to do so. These markets were seen as highly opportunistic sectors of the market, where perhaps some additional business could be picked up, but they were not seen as part of the basic strategic program.

Whether H-P could win sales outside its own manufacturing customer base remained to be seen. But few industry watchers doubted the company's new products would appeal to a large proportion of their regular customers. One competitor believed that if they could execute their strategies and followed them up with service and support, there was no question that H-P would gain market share at the expense of word processor vendors with narrower offerings. Conversely, a Wang Laboratories vice-president indicated that H-P didn't concern them that much because H-P's strength was selling to data processing managers. Wang and IBM had much more experience selling directly into the office.

The office automation market was expected to triple to $36 billion by 1990, according to a market research report released in October, 1981 by International Resource Development, Inc. No doubt the major contenders would compete fiercely to dominate the market while the multitude of small firms, which had just entered the new market, would have to scramble to survive. But in 1981, no single company had managed to secure for itself a corner on the market. *Electronics,*[3] a major trade journal, predicted that the main contenders would be IBM, AT&T, Xerox, and very possibly Wang and Datapoint. It also indicated that DEC and H-P had the background for especially good chances of success. The unanswered question was whether Hewlett-Packard could manage this new growth and whether the company could manage to remain technologically competitive in this new business and its traditional businesses at the same time.

ELECTRONIC CALCULATORS

In sharp contrast to the rapid-growth market in electronic office equipment, the market for electronic hand-held calculators was largely saturated. Texas Instruments had been the pioneer in inexpensive hand-held calculators and dominated the market for years, until low-priced Japanese models had taken over the lower end of the market. In 1981–1982 the different calculator makers were attempting to develop specific market niches that they believed would provide opportunities for further growth. The big Japanese producers had added gimmicks like solar calculators and games such as boxing matches and electronic cube puzzles. Casio was trying to get more business by driving prices still lower. It was also offering low-cost printer calculators that could fit in a shirt pocket. At the high-priced end of the market, companies were developing—or were already producing—products that could compete in the newly formed hand-held computer market. This market had only developed recently when Tandy (Radio Shack), Casio, and others introduced their pocket computers. In fact, *Business Week*[4] even questioned whether there was still a market for calculators with $300 price tags since the Japanese and Radio Shack had begun to sell hand-held computers that cost less. One consultant asserted that hand-held computers would replace programmable calculators in the following three to five years. Other experts felt that the market might flatten out, but that the market for programmable calculators would die slowly and hard.

The essential difference between hand-held calculators and computers is the way the units are programmed. On advanced calculators, programs are written by pressing a series of fixed-function keys in the order needed to step through calculations. Hand-held computers, however, use a conventional programming language which consists of short statements that tell the machine what to do. Both TI and H-P were working to reposition their products in this developing market segment.

Hewlett-Packard had dominated the top end of the market from the beginning with its highly successful scientific calculator, the HP-35, introduced in 1972. With its late 1981 introduction of several new products, H-P put its calculator somewhere in the increasingly gray border between programmable calculators and hand-held computers. For example, the Hewlett-Packard Interface Loop (HP-IL) provided a link that let the HP-41 calculator control and communicate with other machines and computers, including the company's HP-80 personal computer. Complementary products included a battery-operated printer, a digital cassette drive, cassettes that significantly expanded the calculator's memory, and a device that other companies could build into their computers to make them compatible with the system. The company aimed the new system at its favorite customers: engineers and scientists. The products would allow H-P to sell accessory products to people who already owned the popular HP-41 series calculators, and to attract new customers who would prefer to pay $325 and add components later, instead of paying $2000 or more for a personal computer.

Analysts expected both Texas Instruments and Tandy Corporation (Radio Shack) would be strong competitors, especially at the high-priced end of the market. However, as *Business Week*[5] and the *Wall Street Journal*[6] were quick to point out, the Japanese producers were not limiting their horizons to the high end of the calculator market. They were clearly working on strategies and products that would expand pocket computers to the mass market. One of Casio's vice-presidents eventually expected to have a pocket computer low enough in price to do away with all the scientific calculators in the market. It seemed clear that H-P would have to be both technologically innovative and cost-effective if it intended to be competitive in this market.

Business Segment Performance (1978–1981)

Hewlett-Packard reported data by business segment, with both electronic office systems and hand-held calculators and computers included in electronic data products. The other business segments were electronic test and measurement, medical electronic equipment, and analytical instrumentation. Exhibit 22.1 provides data on net sales, earnings before taxes, identifiable

Exhibit 22.1
SELECTED DATA ON BUSINESS SEGMENTS
(Millions of Dollars)

	1978	1979	1980	1981	*Percent Average Annual Growth* 1978–1981
Net Sales					
Electronic data products	$715	$1,060	$1,510	$1,771	36
Electronic test and measurement	731	986	1,200	1,349	23
Medical electronic equipment	163	193	230	273	19
Analytical instrumentation	98	122	159	185	24
Earnings Before Taxes					
Electronic data products	$124	$ 183	$ 285	$ 319	38
Electronic test and measurement	180	242	271	284	17
Medical electronic equipment	26	27	37	50	25
Analytical instrumentation	16	16	24	32	28
Identifiable Assets					
Electronic data products	$587	$ 767	$1,000	$1,169	26
Electronic test and measurement	452	594	709	817	22
Medical electronic equipment	120	131	146	175	14
Analytical instrumentation	71	83	94	99	16
Capital Expenditures					
Electronic data products	$ 90	$ 115	$ 148	$ 174	25
Electronic test and measurement	49	46	85	89	28
Medical electronic equipment	7	5	11	18	52
Analytical instrumentation	7	6	11	9	17

SOURCE: Hewlett-Packard *Annual Reports.*

assets, and capital expenditures for these four business segments. Exhibit 22.2 compares electronic data products with the other business segments combined together to provide a summary comparison of their comparatively newer, more competitive, and higher risk line of business with their basic and more traditional business activities. The electronic data products appeared to have provided greater growth in profit margins (ebt/sales), asset

Exhibit 22.2

COMPARISON OF ELECTRONIC DATA PRODUCTS AND OTHER BUSINESS SEGMENTS COMBINED[1]

Summary Data	**1978**	**1979**	**1980**	**1981**	***Percent Average Annual Growth* 1978–1981**
Net Sales (millions)					
Electronic data products	$ 715	$1,060	$1,510	$1,771	36
Other segments combined	992	1,301	1,589	1,807	22
Earnings Before Taxes (millions)					
Electronic data products	$ 124	$ 183	$ 285	$ 319	38
Other segments combined	222	285	332	366	18
Identifiable Assets (millions)					
Electronic data products	$ 587	$ 767	$1,000	$1,169	26
Other segments combined	643	808	949	1,091	19
Capital Expenditures (millions)					
Electronic data products	$ 90	$ 115	$ 148	$ 174	25
Other segments combined	63	57	107	106	26
Strategic Ratio Analysis					
EBT/Sales (percent)					
Electronic data products	17.3	17.3	18.9	18.0	2
Other segments combined	22.4	21.9	20.9	20.3	−3
Sales/Identifiable Assets (times)					
Electronic data products	1.22	1.38	1.51	1.51	8
Other segments combined	1.54	1.61	1.67	1.66	3
EBT/Identifiable Assets (percent)					
Electronic data products	21.1	23.9	28.5	27.3	9
Other segments combined	34.5	35.3	35.0	33.5	−1

[1] Electronic Test and Measurement, Medical Electronic Equipment, and Analytical Instrumentation.

turnover (sales/assets), and return on assets (ebt/assets), although the level of returns was higher in the more traditional businesses.

STRATEGIC IMPLEMENTATION

Structural Changes

The January 1982 Hewlett-Packard Corporate Organization Chart (Exhibits 22.3 and 22.4) shows that a number of changes have been made since Mr. Young became Chief Executive Officer. Ralph Lee, Executive Vice-President-Operations, retired in 1980 after thirty-five years with H-P. Paul Ely, Vice-President and General Manager-Computer Systems, and Bill Terry, Vice-President and General Manager-Instruments, were subsequently made Executive Vice-Presidents-Operations.

Bill Doolittle had been promoted from Vice-President-International to

HEWLETT-PACKARD CORPORATE ORGANIZATION
JANUARY, 1982

Exhibit 22.3

Viewed broadly, Hewlett-Packard Company is a rather complex organization made up of many business units that offer a wide range of advanced electronic products to a variety of markets around the world. Giving it common direction and cohesion are shared philosophies, practices and goals as well as technologies.

Within this broad context, the individual business units—called product divisions—are relatively small and self-sufficient so that decisions can be made at the level of the organization most responsible for putting them into action. Consistent with this approach, it has always been a practice at Hewlett-Packard to give each individual employee considerable freedom to implement methods and ideas that meet specific local organizational goals and broad corporate objectives.

Since its start in 1939, the HP organization has grown to more than 40 product divisions. To provide for effective overall management and coordination, the company has aligned these divisions into product groups characterized by product and/or market focus. Today there are ten such groups or segments. Six sales-and-service forces, organized around broad product categories, represent the product groups in the field.

HP's corporate structure is designed to foster a small-business flexibility within its many individual operating units while supporting them with the strengths of a larger organization. The accompanying chart provides a graphic view of the relationship of the various groups and other organizational elements. The organization has been structured to allow the groups and their divisions to concentrate on their product-development, manufacturing and marketing activities without having to perform all the administrative tasks required of a company doing business worldwide. Normal and functional lines of responsibility and communication are indicated on the

SOURCE: Hewlett-Packard 1981.

Exhibit 22.3
(Continued)

chart; however, direct and informal communication across lines and between levels is encouraged.

Here is a closer look at the company's basic organizational units.

PRODUCT DIVISIONS

An HP product division is a vertically integrated organization that conducts itself very much like an independent business. Its fundamental responsibilities are to develop, manufacture and market products that are profitable and which make contributions in the marketplace by virtue of technological or economic advantage.

Each division has its own distinct family of products, for which it has worldwide marketing responsibility. A division also is responsible for its own accounting, personnel activities, quality assurance, and support of its products in the field. In addition, it has important social and economic responsibilities in its local community.

PRODUCT GROUPS

Product groups, which are composed of divisions having closely related product lines, are responsible for coordinating the activities of their respective divisions. The management of each group has overall responsibility for the operations and financial performance of its members. Further, each group has worldwide responsibility for its manufacturing operations and sales/service forces. Management staffs of the four U.S. sales regions and two international headquarters (European and Intercontinental Operations) assist the groups in coordinating the sales/service functions.

The group management structure provides a primary channel of communication between the divisions and corporate departments.

CORPORATE OPERATIONS

Corporate Operations management has responsibility for the day-to-day operation of the company. The executive vice presidents in charge of Corporate Operations are directly responsible to HP's president for the performance of their assigned product groups; they also provide a primary channel of communication between the groups and the president.

CORPORATE ADMINISTRATION

The principal responsibility of Corporate Administration is to ensure that the corporate staff offices provide the specialized policies, expertise and resources to adequately support the divisions and groups on a worldwide basis. The executive vice president in charge of Corporate Administration also reports to the president, providing an important upward channel of communication for the corporate staff activities.

The Marketing and International offices, through the U.S. sales regions and two international headquarters, ensure that—on a worldwide basis—all corporate policies and practices are followed and that local legal and fiscal requirements are met.

(*Continued*)

Exhibit 22.3
(*Continued*)

CORPORATE RESEARCH AND DEVELOPMENT

HP Laboratories is the corporate research and development organization that provides a central source of technical support for the product-development efforts of HP product divisions. In these efforts, the divisions make important use of the advanced technologies, materials, components, and theoretical analyses researched or developed by HP Labs. Through their endeavors in areas of science and technology, the corporate laboratories also help the company evaluate promising new areas of business.

BOARD OF DIRECTORS

The Board of Directors and its chairman have ultimate responsibility for the legal and ethical conduct of the company and its officers. It is the board's duty to protect and advance the interests of the stockholders, to foster a continuing concern for fairness in the company's relations with employees, and to fulfill all requirements of the law with regard to the board's stewardship. The board counsels management on general business matters and also reviews and evaluates the performance of management. To assist in discharging these responsibilities, the board has formed various committees to oversee the company's activities and programs in such areas as employee benefits, compensation, financial auditing, and investment.

PRESIDENT

The president has operating responsibility for the overall performance and direction of the company, subject to the authority of the Board of Directors. Also, the president is directly responsible for corporate development and planning functions, and for HP Labs.

EXECUTIVE COMMITTEE

This committee meets weekly for the purpose of setting and reviewing corporate policies, and making coordinated decisions on a wide range of current operations and activities. Members include the Executive Committee chairman, the chairman of the Board, the president and the executive vice presidents for Operations and Administration. All are members of the Board of Directors.

OPERATIONS COUNCIL

Primary responsibilities of this body are to review operating policies on a broad basis and to turn policy decisions into corporate action. Members include the executive vice presidents, product group general managers, the senior vice presidents of Marketing and International, the vice president—Europe, and the managing director of Intercontinental.

Exhibit 22.4
HEWLETT-PACKARD CORPORATE ORGANIZATION, JANUARY 1982

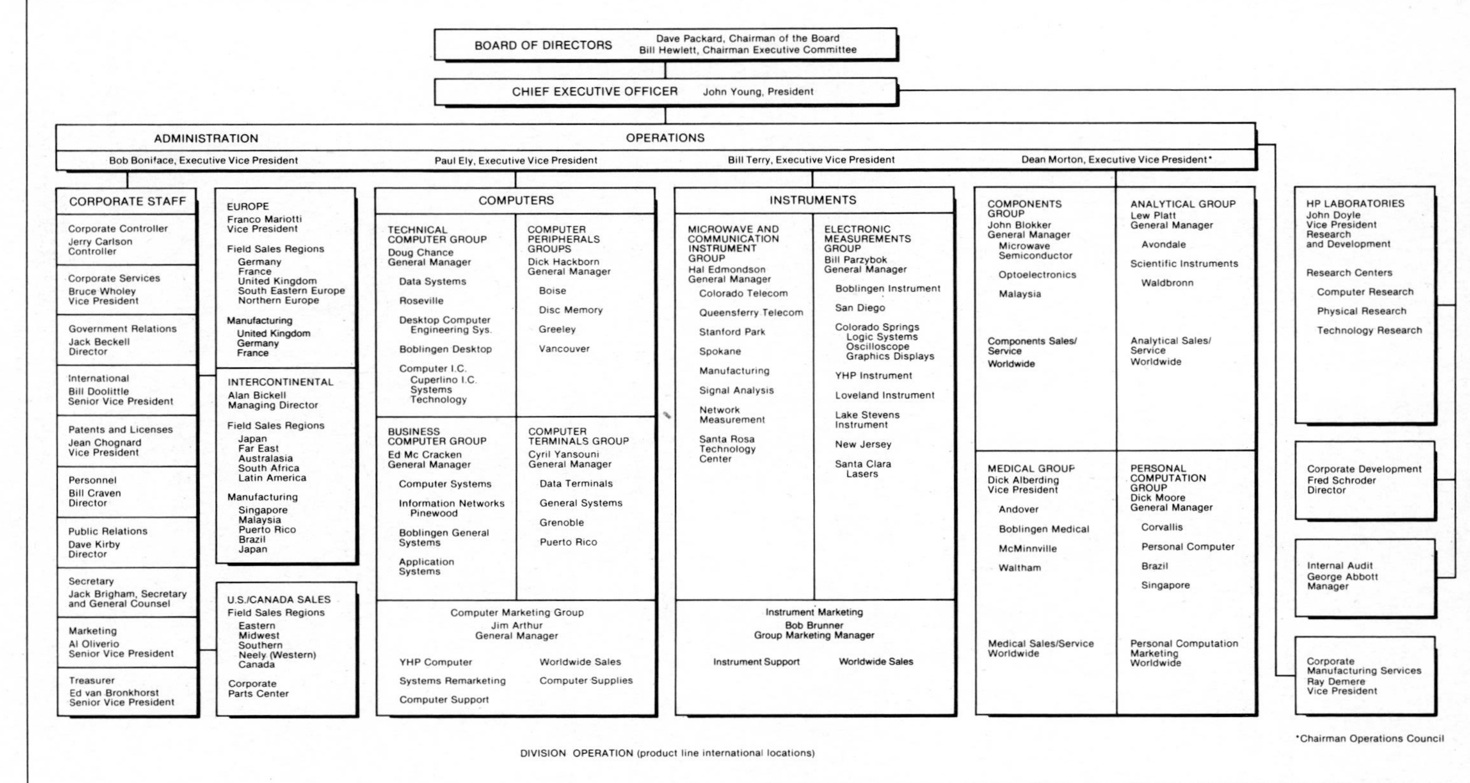

Senior Vice-President-International. Al Oliverio had been promoted from Vice-President-Marketing to Senior Vice-President-Marketing. Ed van Bronkhorst had been promoted from Vice-President to Senior Vice-President, Corporate Treasurer, and Chief Financial Officer. Franco Mariotti had been promoted from Managing Director-Europe to Vice-President-Europe. Dick Alberding had been promoted from General Manager-Medical Group to Vice-President-Medical Group. Dr. Bernard Oliver retired as an officer and director of the company in May 1981. He had been with H-P for twenty-nine years as head of corporate research and development activities. John Doyle, Vice-President of Personnel, replaced Oliver as Vice-President, Research and Development. Appointed Director of Personnel, succeeding Doyle, was Bill Craven, General Manager of the McMinnville Division (Medical Group) since 1976. Exhibit 22.5 provides background information on these executive officers.

Corporate Manufacturing Services had been shifted from being part of corporate staff reporting to administration to having a direct reporting relationship to operations. An Internal Audit department had been set up and reported directly to John Young. The Computer Systems Group had been split into four separate entities: the Technical Computer Group, the Business Computer Group, the Computer Peripherals Group, and the Computer Terminals Group. The products of these four groups continued to be marketed through one organization, the Computer Marketing Group. The Instruments Group had been divided into the Microwave and Communication Instrument Group and the Electronic Measurements Group. The products of these two groups continued to be marketed through one organization, Instrument Marketing. The hand-held calculator and personal computer activities had been elevated to product group status, the Personal Computation Group. As a result, there were ten product groups instead of the six in 1978. There remained however, the same six marketing organizations.

Exhibit 22.5

EXECUTIVE OFFICERS OF HEWLETT-PACKARD

David Packard; age 69; Chairman, HP. Mr. Packard is a co-founder of the Company and has been a director since 1947.[1] He has served as Chairman of the Board of Directors since 1972 and was the Company's President from 1947 to 1964. Mr. Packard also served as Chairman of the Board and Chief Executive Officer from 1964 to 1968 when he was ap-

SOURCE: Hewlett-Packard 1981 Form 10-K.

[1] Mr. Packard did not serve as a Director during his service as United States Deputy Secretary of Defense from January 1969 to December 1971.

Exhibit 22.5
(*Continued*)

pointed U.S. Deputy Secretary of Defense. Mr. Packard is a Director of Caterpillar Tractor Company; Standard Oil Company of California; The Boeing Company; and Genentech, Inc.

William R. Hewlett; age 68; Chairman of the Executive Committee, HP. Mr. Hewlett is a co-founder of the Company and has served on its Board of Directors since 1947. Mr. Hewlett served as Executive Vice President of the Company from 1947 to 1964 when he was appointed President. He served as President and Chief Executive Officer from 1969 to 1977 and was Chief Executive Officer and Chairman of the Executive Committee from November, 1977 to May, 1978 when he retired as Chief Executive Officer. Mr. Hewlett remains the Chairman of the Company's Executive Committee. He also is a Director of Chrysler Corporation and Utah International, Inc., a mining company.

John A. Young; age 49; President and Chief Executive Officer, HP. Mr. Young has served as President and Chief Executive Officer of the Company since May 1978. He was appointed President and Chief Operating Officer of the Company as of November 1, 1977 and has been a member of the Company's Board of Directors since 1974. Prior to his appointment as President and Chief Operating Officer, Mr. Young served as Executive Vice President from 1974. Mr. Young is a Director of Wells Fargo & Company; Wells Fargo Bank, N.A.; Dillingham Corporation; and SRI International. He also serves on the Board of Trustees of Stanford University.

Robert T. Boniface; age 57; Executive Vice President, HP. Mr. Boniface has been a Director of the Company since 1974. He has served as an Executive Vice President of the Company since 1975 and was Vice President, Administration from 1974 to 1975. Mr. Boniface served as Vice President, Marketing from 1970 to 1974.

Paul C. Ely, Jr.; age 49; Executive Vice President, HP. Mr. Ely was named an Executive Vice President of the Company in July 1980 and was elected to the Board of Directors effective Ssptember 1980. Mr. Ely is responsible for the Company's Computer Groups. Prior to his appointment as Executive Vice President, Mr. Ely served as Computer Group General Manager from 1974 and as Vice President from 1976.

Dean O. Morton; age 49; Executive Vice President, HP. Mr. Morton was elected a Director of the Company in September 1977. He was appointed a Vice President of the Company in 1973 and was also appointed General Manager of the Company's Medical Products Group in 1974. Mr. Morton served in those dual capacities until he assumed his present position in November 1977. Mr. Morton is also a Director of State Street Investment Corporation and Cobe Laboratories, Inc.

William E. Terry; age 48; Executive Vice President, HP. Mr. Terry was named an Executive Vice President of the Company in July 1980 and

(*Continued*)

Exhibit 22.5
(*Continued*)

was elected to the Board of Directors effective September 1980. Mr. Terry is responsible for the Company's Instrument Groups. Prior to his appointment as Executive Vice President, Mr. Terry served as Vice President and General Manager of the Company's Instrument Group from 1974. Mr. Terry served as General Manager of the Company's Data Products Group from 1971 to 1974. Mr. Terry is a Director of Applied Magnetics Corporation; Altus Corporation, a manufacturer of lithium batteries; and Kevex Corporation, a manufacturer of x-ray spectrometers.

William P. Doolittle; age 63; Senior Vice President, International, HP. Mr. Doolittle has been a Director of the Company since 1971 and served as Vice President, International from 1963 until he assumed his present position in July 1981. Mr. Doolittle is also a director of Machine Intelligence Corp. and Creative Strategies International.

Alfred P. Oliverio; age 54; Senior Vice President, Marketing, HP. Mr. Oliverio served as Vice President, Marketing from 1974 until he assumed his present position in July 1981.

Edwin E. van Bronkhorst; age 57; Senior Vice President, Treasurer, HP. Mr. van Bronkhorst served as Vice President and Treasurer of the Company from 1963 until his appointment as Senior Vice President and Treasurer in July 1981. He also serves as the Company's Chief Financial Officer. He was named a Director of the Company in 1962 and currently serves as a Director of ROLM Corporation, a manufacturer of computerized communication systems; Northern California Savings and Loan Association; and TRIAD Systems Corporation, a manufacturer of microcomputer-based data processing systems primarily for the auto parts distribution industry.

Richard C. Alberding; age 50; Vice President, Medical Products Group, HP. Mr. Alberding was appointed to his present position in July 1981, and has served as general manager of the Company's Medical Products Group since 1977. Mr. Alberding was director of the Company's European operations from 1970 until 1977.

Jean C. Chognard; age 57; Vice President, Patents and Licenses, HP. Mr. Chognard has been Patent Counsel for the Company since 1958 and has been a Vice President of the Company since May 1976.

Raymond M. Demere, Jr.; age 60; Vice President, Manufacturing Services, HP. Mr. Demere has been a Vice President of the Company since 1971 and served as operations manager of the Instrument Group of the Company from 1974 until September 1977 when he was appointed Vice President, Manufacturing Services.

John L. Doyle; age 48; Vice President, Research and Development, HP. Mr. Doyle was appointed Corporate Director of Personnel in June 1976

Exhibit 22.5 (Continued)

and thereafter elected Vice President, Personnel in July 1976. In June 1981 Mr. Doyle assumed his present position as Vice President, Research and Development.

Franco Mariotti; age 46; Vice President, Europe, HP. Mr. Mariotti was appointed to his present position in July 1981 and has served as managing director of the Company's European operations since 1977. From 1976 to 1977 Mr. Mariotti served as marketing manager for Europe.

W. Bruce Wholey; age 60; Vice President, Corporate Services, HP. Mr. Wholey has been Vice President, Corporate Services since January 1973.

S.T. Jack Brigham III; age 42; Secretary and General Counsel, HP. Mr. Brigham was elected Assistant Secretary of the Company in May 1974. He served in that capacity as well as General Attorney of the Company until May 1976 when he was elected Secretary and General Counsel of the Company.

Leadership

According to the *San Jose Mercury*[7] John Young's team of employees was learning to play the electronics game by Young's rules, which demanded diligent planning, close attention to cost-effectiveness, and no last-minute surprises. Although many had originally doubted that he could fill the shoes of the two founders, these critics have since admitted they like the way Young has changed and redirected the firm. He has placed added emphasis on manufacturing and marketing, dropped technological programs when they weren't cost-effective, and monitored day-to-day details to correct problems before they have snowballed. At the same time he has balanced his approach by stimulating efforts on new products and technologies, such as electronic office systems and hand-held computers with the associated H-P integrated loop. Young has not emphasized formal planning done by corporate planners. Instead, he has pushed a pragmatic system with the operating people doing the planning. Young believed his contribution was having put emphasis on having a lot more time spent in thoughtful consideration of what the company was doing, but not in a formal planning regime.

John Young was reported to be a serious chief executive with a dry sense of humor, a logical thinker who often asked leading questions to get his managers to come around to his way of thinking, and an efficient worker who did not tolerate incompetence. Associates saw him as a "numbers man" with a top priority of profits. Despite his devotion to numbers and planning, Young also followed two basic and more subtle tenets of the H-P way of life: managing by wandering around and showing respect and empathy for employees. Exhibit 22.6 provides a brief outline of "The HP Way." For all his formal position power, Young has relied heavily on consensus-style management. He has met often with his executive committee, and few major decisions have been made without the agreement of everyone around the table. Members of the committee were expected to be independent thinkers, but Young has used a subtle approach based on logic to bring people around to his point of view. When Young has not agreed with a colleague's opinion, he has asked questions. These were not confrontational kinds of questions, but they were penetrating. Young would then go along with whatever course the executive eventually recommended. Young saw himself as being good at the non-directive approach and worked hard at being a good coach.

THE HP WAY

Exhibit 22.6

BUSINESS PRACTICES

Pay as We Go—No Long-Term Borrowing

- Helps to maintain a stable financial environment during depressed business times.
- Serves as an excellent self-regulating mechanism for HP managers.

Market Expansion and Leadership Based on New Product Contributions

- Engineering excellence determines market recognition of new HP products.
- Novel new-product ideas and implementations serve as the basis for expansion of existing markets or diversification into new markets.

Customer Satisfaction Second to None

- Sell only what has been thoroughly designed, tested, and specified.
- Products must have lasting value, having high reliability (quality) and customers discover additional benefits while using them.
- Offer best after-sales service and support in the industry.

Honesty and Integrity in All Matters

- Dishonest dealings with vendors or customers (such as bribes and kickbacks) not tolerated.
- Open and honest communication with employees and stockholders alike. Conservative financial reporting.

PEOPLE PRACTICES

Belief in Our People

- Confidence in, and respect for, HP people as opposed to dependence on extensive rules, procedures, etc.

SOURCE: *Measure*, September-October, 1981, p. 14.

Exhibit 22.6
(Continued)

not set-up for low-cost producers

- Trust people to do their job right (individual freedom) without constant directives.
- Opportunity for meaningful participation (job dignity).
- Emphasis on working together and sharing rewards (teamwork and partnership).
- Share responsibilities; help each other; learn from each other; provide chance to make mistakes.
- Recognition based on contribution to results—sense of achievement and self-esteem.
- Profit sharing; stock purchase plan; retirement program, etc., aimed at employees and company sharing in each other's success.
- Company financial management emphasis on protecting employees' job security.

A Superior Working Environment

- Informality—open, honest communications; no artificial distinctions between employees (first-name basis); management by wandering around; and open-door communication policy.
- Develop and promote from within—lifetime training, education, career counseling to give employees maximum opportunities to grow and develop with the company.
- Decentralization—emphasis on keeping work groups as small as possible for maximum employee identification with our businesses and customers.
- Management-By-Objectives (MBO)—provides a sound basis for measuring performance of employees as well as managers; is objective, not political.

MANAGEMENT STYLE

Management By Wandering Around

- To have a well-managed operation, managers and supervisors must be aware of what happens in their areas—at several levels above and below their immediate level.
- Since people are our most important resource, managers have direct responsibility for employee training, performance and general well being. To do this, managers must move around to find out how people feel about their jobs—what they think will make their work more productive and meaningful.

Open Door Policy

- Managers and supervisors are expected to foster a work environment in which employees feel free and comfortable to seek individual counsel or express general concerns.

(Continued)

Exhibit 22.6
(*Continued*)

- Therefore, if employees feel such steps are necessary, they have the right to discuss their concerns with higher-level managers. Any effort through intimidation or other means to prevent an employee from going "up the line" is absolutely contrary to company policy—and will be dealt with accordingly.
- Also, use of the Open Door policy must not in any way influence evaluations of employees or produce any other adverse consequences.
- Employees also have responsibilities—particularly in keeping their discussions with upper-level managers to the point and focused on concerns of significance.

High on Young's list of priorities for the 1980s was for H-P to become a low-cost manufacturer. Young admitted this had not been one of H-P's strengths. His concern for cost-effectiveness was almost legendary. When he initially assumed the presidency, he put a lot of effort into convincing his management team that the company could do a better job of managing assets, particularly inventory and accounts receivable. One of the first things he axed was research for research's sake. Yet about 70% of total company product orders in 1981 resulted from products developed after 1977. Under Young, technology has received more of a profit-and-loss kind of consideration and evaluation. In 1981, research and development was increased to 9.7% of sales, an increase of 1.1% over the previous year. Further, John Young has restructured H-P Laboratories entirely. He has also created over the last three years a computer and semiconductor research facility staffed with 100 professionals. He thought this would become one of the top such facilities in the United States.

In September 1979, an attitude survey was taken in which 7,966 employees were asked to evaluate more than 100 topics at H-P, including pay, benefits, supervision, management, job satisfaction, and many other items. Exhibit 22.7 provides results on major items and a comparison to national norms. With a 67% favorable response, employees rated H-P management well above the national norm of 46%. The rating covered such questions as the fairness of management decisions and the concern of managers for the well-being of the people they managed. As reported in the March-April issue of *Measure*[8] (HP's magazine), four of the top twenty-two issues generated by the survey analysis showed concern about top management and the application of management philosophy. The quality of some managers was questioned; management-by-objectives and management-by-wandering-around were criticized for not being used widely enough; and the use of the Open Door Policy was sometimes frustrated by a feeling of threat of retribution.

H-P ATTITUDE SURVEY

Exhibit 22.7

	Percent Favorable Responses	
	HP Employees	*National Sample*[1]
Work organization	70	65
Work efficiency	67	63
Management	67	46
Job training and information	61	56
Work associates	81	78
Supervision	70	61
Overall communications	58	41
Performance and advancement	75	58
Pay	52	39
Benefits	70	53
Job satisfaction	76	66
Organizational identification	84	59
Organization change	28	25
Working conditions	59	44
Job stability	56	60
Policies and practices	81	69
Reactions to the survey	77	55

SOURCE: *Measure,* "Open Line," March-April 1981, p. 12b.
[1] 200 top U.S. companies.

The fundamental responses to these concerns were seen by top management as chiefly matters of local responsibility and action, although corporate support in the form of training, communication, and management evaluation was believed to be important. The startup of more than 300 quality teams at many locations was believed to improve both productivity and the practice of MBO. The Open Door Policy as well as MBWA were topics of messages by Young in various issues of *Measure.* Both of these policies were seen by John Young as important to the creation of a feeling of openness and providing information opportunities for everyone to hear and be heard. He believed the desired result was to achieve mutual trust and respect for both the people and the process involved. He has tried to make it clear both in his communications and his actions that the H-P manager has no greater responsibility.

Performance (1978–1981)

Since 1978, when John Young became CEO, Hewlett-Packard has grown rapidly. The annual growth rate of net sales has averaged 27.4% and that of net earnings has averaged 26.9%. The growth rates for 1980–1981, how-

Exhibit 22.8

FOUR-YEAR CONSOLIDATED SUMMARY*
FOR THE YEARS ENDED OCTOBER 31
(Millions of Dollars Except for Employee and Per-Share Amounts)

	1978	1979	1980	1981
Net sales	$1,737	$2,361	$3,099	$3,578
Costs and expenses				
Cost of goods sold	808	1,106	1,475	1,703
Research and development	154	204	272	347
Marketing	264	362	459	526
Administration and general	215	291	370	422
	1,441	1,963	2,576	2,998
Earnings before taxes	296	398	523	580
Provision for taxes	143	195	254	268
Net earnings	$ 153	$ 203	$ 269	$ 312
Per share:*				
Net earnings	$ 1.32	$ 1.72	$ 2.23	$ 2.55
Cash dividends	$ .12	$ .17	$ .20	$ .22
At year-end:				
Total assets	$1,462	$1,900	$2,337	$2,758
Long-term debt	$ 10	$ 15	$ 29	$ 26
Common shares outstanding*	116	118	120	123
Thousands of employees	42	52	57	64

SOURCE: Hewlett-Packard *Annual Reports.*
* Reflects the 2-for-1 stock splits in 1979 and 1981.

Exhibit 22.9
SELECTED FINANCIAL INFORMATION

	Percent Increase from Prior Year				*Percent of Net Sales*			
	1978	1979	1980	1981	1978	1979	1980	1981
Net sales	27.0	35.9	31.3	15.5	100.0	100.0	100.0	100.0
Cost of goods sold	29.3	36.9	33.4	15.5	45.7	46.8	47.6	47.6
Research and development	23.2	32.5	33.3	27.6	8.9	8.6	8.8	9.7
Marketing	26.9	37.1	26.8	14.6	15.2	15.3	14.8	14.7
Administrative and general	18.8	35.3	27.1	14.1	12.4	12.3	11.9	11.8
Earnings before taxes	29.3	34.5	31.4	10.9	17.0	16.9	16.9	16.2
Provision for taxes	32.4	36.4	30.3	5.5	8.2	8.3	8.2	7.5
Net earnings	26.4	32.7	32.5	16.0	8.8	8.6	8.7	8.7

CONSOLIDATED BALANCE SHEET
(In Millions of Dollars, for Fiscal Years Ending October 31)

Exhibit 22.10

	1978	1979	1980	1981
CURRENT ASSETS				
Cash and temporary cash investments	$ 189	$ 248	$ 247	$ 290
Accounts and notes receivable	371	491	622	682
Inventories:				
Finished goods	99	120	148	186
Purchased parts and fabricated assemblies	257	358	397	456
Other current assets	36	52	77	91
Total current assets	952	1,269	1,491	1,705
Property, plant, and equipment:				
Land	44	53	69	78
Buildings and leasehold improvements	405	491	645	789
Machinery and equipment	272	348	447	581
	721	892	1,161	1,448
Accumulated depreciation	245	301	372	469
	476	591	789	979
Other assets	34	40	57	74
	$1,462	$1,900	$2,337	$2,758
CURRENT LIABILITIES				
Notes payable and commercial paper	$ 85	$ 147	$ 143	$ 144
Accounts payable	71	109	104	143
Employee compensation, benefits, and accruals	171	237	297	308
Accrued taxes on income	88	106	147	109
Total current liabilities	415	599	691	704
Long-term debt	10	15	29	26
Deferred taxes on earnings	35	51	70	108
SHAREHOLDERS' EQUITY				
Common stock	29	59	60	123
Capital in excess of par	247	267	333	358
Retained earnings	727	909	1,154	1,439
Total shareholders' equity	1,002	1,235	1,547	1,920
	$1,462	$1,900	$2,337	$2,758

SOURCE: Hewlett-Packard *Annual Reports.*

CONSOLIDATED STATEMENT OF CHANGES IN FINANCIAL POSITION
(In Millions of Dollars, for Fiscal Years Ending October 31)

Exhibit 22.11

	1978	1979	1980	1981
Funds provided:				
Net earnings	$153	$203	$269	$312
Items not affecting funds:				
Depreciation and amortization	56	72	93	120
Other, net	11	27	27	53
Total from operations	220	302	389	485
Proceeds from sale of stock	29	37	50	67
Increase in accounts payable and accrued liabilities	59	104	55	50
Total funds provided	308	443	494	602
Funds used:				
Investment in property, plant, and equipment	159	191	297	318
Increase in accounts and notes receivable	99	120	131	60
Increase in inventories	77	122	67	97
Increase in other current assets	8	16	25	14
Decrease (increase) in accrued taxes	(26)	(18)	(41)	38
Dividends to shareholders	14	20	24	27
Other, net	(1)	(5)	(12)	6
Total funds used	330	446	491	560
Increase (decrease) in cash and temporary cash investment, net of notes payable, and commercial paper	$ (22)	$ (3)	$ 3	$ 42
Net cash at beginning of year	126	104	101	104
Net cash at end of year	$104	$101	$104	$146

SOURCE: Hewlett-Packard *Annual Reports.*

ever, were substantially lower than previous years, 15.5% and 16.0% respectively. The 1981 *Annual Report*[9] indicated that the major cause of the reduced growth was the adverse economic conditions in the United States and abroad. Net sales were somewhat below projections, and incoming orders were considerably lower than expectations. These shortfalls, coupled with a high level of committed expenses for new product development and product introductions, put heavy pressure on operating profit. Two changes were made in 1981 that somewhat modified earnings. The first was a $14 million reduction in accrued pension expense for the year, which increased net earnings by $7 million. This change resulted from a scheduled five-year review of the initial funding assumptions used for the U.S. Supplemental Pension Plan begun in 1976. The second was an $8 million reduction in income taxes, resulting from the Economic Recovery Tax Act of 1981. Without these two adjustments, the company's net earnings would have been $297 million, up only 10.4% from 1980. Exhibit 22.8 provides a four-year consolidated summary of various measures of performance. Exhibit 22.9 provides an analysis of operating results. Exhibit 22.10 is a consolidated balance sheet. Exhibit 22.11 is a consolidated statement of changes in financial position, showing how funds were provided and how they were used. Exhibit 22.12 provides a strategic ratio analysis of H-P's performance during this period. Exhibit 22.13 includes information on sales, profits, and research and development expenses for selected companies and industries.

A TIME FOR EVALUATION

John Young had just reviewed the changes made in strategy and strategic implementation while he had served as chief executive officer. He wondered whether the strategic changes made had been the right ones and whether any additional changes might be needed. He believed the performance of the

Exhibit 22.12

STRATEGIC RATIO ANALYSIS

Fiscal Year	***Profit Margin*** *Earnings per Sales (Percent)*	***Asset Turnover*** *Sales per Assets (Times)*	***Return on Assets*** *Earnings per Assets (Percent)*	***Financial Leverage*** *Assets per Net Worth (Times)*	***Return on Net Worth*** *Earnings per Net Worth (Percent)*
1978	8.81	1.19	10.5	1.46	15.3
1979	8.60	1.24	10.7	1.54	16.4
1980	8.68	1.33	11.5	1.51	17.4
1981	8.72	1.30	11.3	1.44	16.3

Exhibit 22.13

SALES, PROFITS, AND R&D DATA ON SELECTED COMPANIES AND INDUSTRIES

	Sales		Profits		R & D Expense			
	1981 millions of dollars	Percent annual change (1977–1981)	1981 millions of dollars	Percent annual change (1977–1981)	1981 millions of dollars	Percent of Sales	Percent of Profit	Dollars per Employee
Selected Companies								
AT&T	58,214	12.2	6,888	10.6	507.2	0.9	7.4	594
Datapoint	396	40.1	49	53.8	34.7	8.8	71.2	5,091
Digital Equipment	3,198	31.1	343	33.2	251.2	7.9	73.2	3,987
Hewlett-Packard	3,578	28.4	312	27.9	347.0	9.7	111.2	5,422
Lanier Business Products	303	35.9	26	39.4	4.7	1.5	18.4	1,163
IBM	29,070	12.3	3,308	5.4	1,612.0	5.5	48.7	4,542
Texas Instruments	4,206	21.0	109	2.7	219.4	5.2	202.2	2,621
Wang Laboratories	856	60.2	78	73.3	66.9	7.8	85.7	4,240
Xerox	8,691	14.3	598	8.4	526.3	6.1	88.0	4,350
Industry Composites								
Instruments	14,106	18.6	740	17.4	647.5	4.6	87.5	2,571
Information processing								
Computers	60,057	15.5	5,311	9.4	3,845.5	6.4	72.4	4,231
Office equipment	14,716	17.9	771	13.2	729.2	5.0	94.6	3,324
Peripherals & services	5,800	29.3	365	35.7	344.1	5.9	94.2	3,284

SOURCE: *Business Week*, "R & D Scoreboard," July 5, 1982, pp. 54–72.

various business segments might offer a valuable point of departure for his analysis. He also felt that this seemed like an appropriate time to review the changes made in organization structure, his management and leadership of the company, and the organization's overall corporate performance during these recent years of growth and strategic change. He believed that enough time had passed that a reasonably objective assessment could be made as to whether he had provided the necessary strategies and leadership to the Hewlett-Packard Company during this difficult transition period.

NOTES

1. *Wall Street Journal,* "Digital Equipment and Hewlett-Packard Enter Electronic Office Systems Market," October 30, 1981, p. 48.
2. *Business Week,* "Two Giants Bid for Office Sales," November 9, 1981, pp. 86–96.
3. *Electronics,* "H-P: A Drive into Office Automation," November 3, 1981, pp. 106–110.
4. *Business Week,* "When Calculator Is a Dirty Word," June 14, 1982, p. 62.
5. Op. cit.
6. *Wall Street Journal,* "Calculator Makers Add Features and Cut Prices To Find a Niche in a Crowded Market," December 21, 1981, p. 23.
7. *San Jose Mercury,* "H-P—Now It's the House That Young Built," August 24, 1981, pp. 1D and 7D.
8. *Measure,* "Open-Line," March–April, 1981, pp. 12 a–h.
9. *Hewlett-Packard Company,* "1981 Annual Report," pp. 2–4.

Case 23

TANDY, INC.

Sexton Adams/Adelaide Griffin

The Tandy Corporation, which controls the largest number of retail electronics outlets in the world, and produces over $2.4 billion in sales was, as of 1984, "the world's leading distributor of electronic technology to the individual."[1] The span of products sold through the Tandy system is almost overwhelming, ranging from sophisticated computer and telecommunicative systems at one extreme to diodes and transistors at the other. The incredible size Tandy has achieved becomes that much more amazing when one considers its humble beginnings only a short time ago.

As with any organization that has experienced extraordinary early growth, the environmental forces facing the firm and the resulting choices made in response to those forces, require constant review, and Tandy is no exception. Tandy presently faces many challenges in many new markets. How these challenges are dealt with will determine whether Tandy can maintain its past growth rate and remain a "star" or simply become another company "has been."

HISTORY

Since 1960 the Radio Shack chain had grown from a small, money-losing, Boston-based company to an electronics powerhouse whose after-tax income rivals those of the country's largest retailers. The man who oversaw much of that transformation was Charles Tandy, a Harvard Business School drop-out who converted common sense, salesmanship, and employee motivation into a spectacular business success.

Tandy had practice at turning local operations into national ones. During the 1950s he had turned his family's small leathercraft business, Tandycrafts, Inc., into a national chain. He then sold Tandycrafts to a leather and

This case was prepared by Paul Trobaugh, Greg Dufour, Michelle Little, Alex Blair, Sally Dehaney, and Alan Moore under the supervision of Prof. Sexton Adams, North Texas State University and Prof. Adelaide Griffin, Texas Woman's University. Reprinted by permission.

sportswear company, but shortly afterwards reacquired it, along with the leather and sportswear firm, in a proxy fight.

In 1960, Tandy bought an option of 51% of Radio Shack stock. He paid $5,000 cash and took out a $300,000 loan for the option, which allowed him to purchase the stock at book value. Book value, as the auditors later determined, was a negative $1.5 million. The loan was later converted to stock, and Charles Tandy was left with control of Radio Shack on a personal investment of only $5,000.

Some would say that the purchase of a losing proposition at any price is not a bargain. There was little doubt that Radio Shack was a losing proposition. In addition to its huge debts, the chain had posted a $4.0 million loss the year before Tandy took control. Tandy, however, felt that the firm, which at the time was selling electronic equipment to ham operators and other electronics buffs, would compliment his recent acquisition of the Electronic Crafts Company of Fort Worth. In addition, Tandy was attracted by the chain's $9.0 million annual sales and by the high quality of its personnel, a characteristic that he considered essential for growth in the electronics area.

Charles Tandy set out to prove his doubters wrong "with a vengeance." The first order of business was to reduce the ailing firm's accounts receivable balance. Radio Shack had a policy of selling on a no-money down, two-years-to-pay basis which had resulted in a large number of bad debts. Tandy quickly eliminated this problem by hiring a legal team to "go after Radio Shack's dead beats."

Also of concern to Tandy was the excessive number of products offered and high inventory levels. Tandy reduced inventory and whittled the product lines down from over 25,000 to just 2,500 using aggressive direct mail advertising campaigns and sidewalk sales. Products that had a low turnover were cut, as well as those that generated anything less than a 50% gross profit margin. Radio Shack was eventually left with a relatively small group of diverse, but highly profitable products.

Tandy also decided to eliminate brand name items, realizing that larger profits could be made by marketing private-label merchandise. He was particularly successful in negotiations with Japanese manufacturers, who at that time were actively seeking an opening into U.S. markets.

Tandy felt that the company's overhead costs should be spread out over as many stores as possible. That belief led to the rapid expansion of Radio Shack's retail outlets. In less than ten years, the company was opening new stores at the rate of one a day. By 1969, the firm was ready to begin producing its own goods, and the first of twenty-six manufacturing plants was built.

But the development of Radio Shack was not Tandy's only concern during the sixties. The company acquired, developed, and eventually spun off Color Tile, Inc., and Stafford Lowden, Inc., a printing firm. Tandycrafts and Tandy Brands were also spun off. The Radio Shack division, however, remained, and became one of the world's leading distributors of technology to the individual consumer.

The firm was more than ready for the CB radio boom of the mid-1970s. "As consumers stampeded to get the chance to say 'breaker one nine,' Tandy saw its net income rise from $26.8 million in 1975 to $69 million in 1977, a 157% increase."[2] But CB's proved to be a passing fad and "Tandy had to scramble in 1977 to switch from its heavy commitment to CB manufacturing."[3]

In 1977 the firm began developing its first home computer. Tandy was among the first companies to enter that market, and the move was to provide much of the firm's growth in the early part of the eighties.

MANAGEMENT

Tandy had an extremely young management team who relied, for the most part, on Charles Tandy's tried and true management techniques. In 1983 the average age of the company's vice-presidents was forty-eight, and more than two-thirds had spent fifteen years or more with Tandy.

Charles Tandy

Charles Tandy had been described as the "founder, architect, and driving force behind the corporation that bears his name."[4] Tandy was still a strong influence at Tandy more than five years after his death. According to one source, "even today, Radio Shack executives characterize their performance by saying, 'Charles Tandy would have been proud of what we've done.' "[5]

Tandy's rise to the top closely paralleled that of his company. "He had no hobbies, no children," said one Tandy executive, "He ate, drank and slept business, from dawn until as late as anyone was willing to talk about his business with him." Executives described him as "larger than life . . . throwing off boundless energy, laughing into his ever-busy phone, while waving a 30-cent cigar with his free hand . . ."[6]

Tandy, in his own unique style "set the rules and pattern successors have carried on since he died . . ." Among his favorite Tandyisms were: "You can't sell from an empty wagon" (a conviction that led the firm to stock high levels of inventory in its retail outlets); "Who wants dividends when they can have capital gains?" (thus the firm never paid dividends, using all earnings for growth); and "If you want to catch a mouse, you have to make a noise like a cheese" (the philosophy that justified an exceptionally large advertising budget). He also emphasized gross profit: "Tandy never entered a market or sold a product without a 50% gross margin."[7]

Vertical integration was another important part of Tandy's management philosophy. Everything from production to distribution to retailing to advertising was kept in-house whenever possible. By 1982, one observer was moved to remark, "No retailer—not even Sears—has that kind of vertical integration."[8]

Charles Tandy's real genius was in motivation. Store managers were offered large bonuses and profit sharing plans based on their store's performance. Former chairman Phil North recounted, "Charles would call the employees into a room when it was time to hand out the bonus checks. He wouldn't let them out until they bought Tandy stock."[9] He was so successful at convincing employees to invest in the company that today nearly 25% of Tandy's stock is estimated to be owned by employees.

Charles Tandy's fatal heart attack could hardly be said to mark the end of an era at the Tandy Corporation. "I miss him," says one executive, "but the company won't, because he taught enough people to do it right."[10] Another observer agrees, "Tandy's personal influence on the development of the corporation cannot be understated. He developed a top management team that understood and appreciated his business philosophy."[11]

Journalist Harold Seneker described Tandy's death: "Charles D. Tandy, 60, lay down for a nap one Saturday afternoon in November and never got up. He couldn't have timed his passing much better if he had planned it." The firm's directors and top officers were in Fort Worth for a stockholders' meeting, and by the time the stockmarket opened on Monday they had decided on their course of action—business as usual—and on Charles Tandy's successor, Phil North.[12]

Phil North

Phil North was named president and chairman of Tandy when his long-time friend and business associate, Charles Tandy, passed away. As a young man, North had been a reporter on his family's newspaper, the *Fort Worth Star Telegram.* During World War II, he served as General Douglas MacArthur's personal press secretary. In 1964, Tandy convinced him to invest $100,000 in his firm, and in 1966, North became a member of Tandy's board of directors.

North was less than delighted by the prospect of taking control of the firm. "I'd rather be perfecting my duplicate bridge or seeing friends around the world," he said. He agreed to accept the position only "to provide a smooth transition of management for an interim period," saying that it was "one of the last things I can do for Charles, and by God, I'm going to do it."[13]

North, who described himself as "the company philosopher," was described by others as "Charles Tandy's alter ego." He was determined to carry on the Tandy philosophy, saying, "we will achieve the goals Charles set."[14]

As soon as practical North relinquished the presidency to John Roach, and in 1982 Roach also took over as chairman of the board. Phil North returned to his position as a director, and presumably, to his bridge.

John Roach

John Roach, Chairman and CEO, took charge of Tandy Corp. at the age of forty-three. Roach was born and raised in Texas, as were the majority of Tandy's executives, and had received his MBA from Fort Worth's Texas Christian University. Roach came to Tandy in 1967 as a data processing specialist and embarked on what was to become his pet project, the development of a home computer. Ten years later, after rapidly rising within the firm, his project was complete. One day in early 1977 Charles Tandy came down to his office to see it and was hooked. The computer was a resounding success and Roach's future with the company assured.

In spite of his youth, Roach was awarded the 1982 Chief Executive of the Year Award by Financial World. Roach's management philosophy smacks of Tandy's: "We are continuing to build Tandy's business on the strong fundamentals that have yielded extraordinary operating results for a retailer in one of the most competitive segments of the retail industry. Our basic philosophies of private label merchandising, strong promotion . . . convenient locations, vertical integration and the institutionalization of individual entrepreneurship truly make Tandy and Radio Shack unique."[15]

The Executive Vice-Presidents

Roach's two primary executives in the Radio Shack division are Bernard Appel, Executive Vice-President for Marketing, and Robert Keto, Executive Vice-President for Operations (see Exhibit 23.1). Appel, who had been with Tandy for twenty-four years, was also strongly committed to the Tandy philosophy. As Appel puts it, "Charles Tandy was a genius."[16] Appel's approach, like Tandy's, was that "our own product line, sold through our own distribution system via our own marketing plan . . . will enable us to remain the Number One retailer of electronics to the world."[17] Robert Keto added, "Providing our customers with products they want at a convenient location and then giving them the after-the-sale service they have come to expect, is why Radio Shack continues to be the leader in consumer electronics." Keto was forty-two years old in 1983 and had been with Radio Shack for nineteen years.[18]

MARKETING

The Tandy marketing effort was a reflection of the size and diversity of the company as a whole. The marketing effort cannot be discussed in terms of stores alone, because to do so would drastically oversimplify the nature of the organization. As a result this section is subdivided into two sections: internal and external. Each of these is in turn further subdivided into stores and products. In this way, the major internal operations and external forces affecting those operations are singled out for more thorough analysis.

Exhibit 23.1
TANDY CORPORATION ORGANIZATION CHART

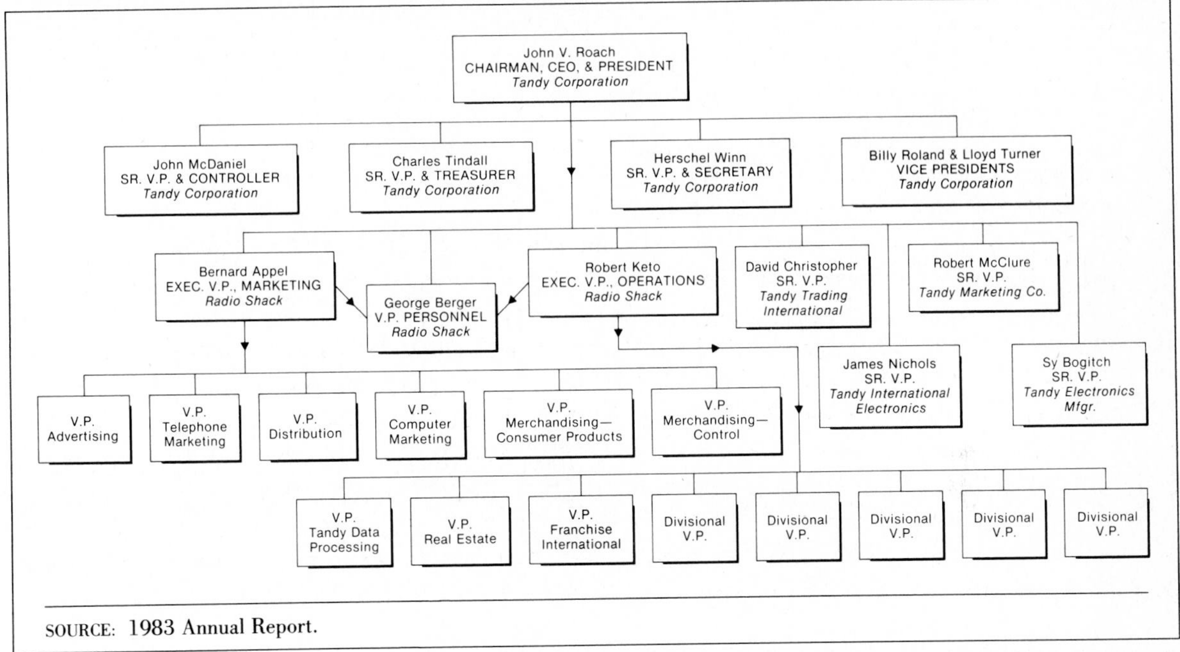

SOURCE: 1983 Annual Report.

Internal

Store Operations

John Roach described the Tandy Store concept better than anyone else when he said, "Tandy is a distribution system for the products of technology. Sometimes we are innovators, sometimes not, but we do have the capability to move a lot of products."[19] As of 1983 the Tandy distribution system was comprised of more than 6,400 individual stores.

Out of these 6,400 stores approximately 4,300 are corporate owned and managed, while some 2,000 are privately franchised. In fiscal 1983 Tandy opened the 500th full-service computer center worldwide. More than 400 of these are in the United States. In addition to the stand-alone Computer Centers, more than 775 Radio Shack stores have Computer departments. Six hundred of these are in the United States. Through expansion of both stand-alone Computer Centers and computer departments within Radio Shack stores, Tandy anticipated having more than 1,400 computer centers and computer departments by the end of 1984. For many retail organizations, this number of stores would be considered unmanageable. However, Tandy had always considered a large number of stores crucial to their strategy of insuring distribution.

Although generally lost in the intense interest in computers, Tandy has always been primarily a full line electronics retailer. As Exhibit 23.2 illustrates, the lines that Tandy stores have carried ranged from computers to

Exhibit 23.2
WORLDWIDE WAREHOUSE SHIPMENTS (UNAUDITED)

	Year Ended June 30				
Class of Products	**1983**	**1982**	**1981**	**1980**	**1979**
Radios, phonographs, and televisions	8.6%	9.4%	11.6%	12.1%	13.3%
Citizens band radios, walkie-talkies, scanners, and public address systems	4.9	6.0	6.8	9.3	13.2
Audio equipment, tape recorders, and related accessories	18.2	21.5	25.4	29.5	33.8
Electronic parts, batteries, test equipment, and related items	13.2	13.9	14.5	15.8	16.4
Toys, antennas, security devices, timers, and calculators	12.5	12.0	14.1	12.6	10.3
Telephones and intercoms	8.0	6.5	5.8	5.6	3.5
Microcomputers, software, and peripheral equipment	34.6	30.7	21.8	15.1	9.5
	100.0%	100.0%	100.0%	100.0%	100.0%

SOURCE: 1983 Annual Report.

diodes and almost everything in between. Again, reviewing Exhibit 23.2, significant trends appear in this data. The first, and most notable, was that computers and computer related sales were steadily becoming a much larger and more substantial part of the business. Along with this, areas of historical strength (such as stereos and CB's) had become much less significant. Second, telephone and telephone related sales, while not substantial, had been growing very rapidly.

As a result of these trends, Tandy aggressively pursued both the computer and the telecommunications business. Exhibit 23.3 provides a breakdown of computer related sales by product group. Although telecommunications was still in its infancy, Tandy pursued the same formula for these lines of business as with computer systems. That formula consisted of providing full line "Tandy" computer or telephone centers in large metropolitan areas (thereby disassociating these products from the Radio Shack name) and using add-on departments in those areas too small to support free standing specialty stores. The free standing store was typically about 3,000 square feet and incorporated a sales area, training room, repair service, storage space, and offices. A typical staffing arrangement includes a store manager, one manager trainee, three full time sales representatives, a full time instructor, and a repair service technician.

The altering of traditional merchandise lines was tied directly to changes taking place in Tandy's customer base. In the past, Tandy was essentially a

COMPUTER-RELATED SALES BY PRODUCT GROUP

Exhibit 23.3

	Year Ended June 30		
(*Unaudited*)	**1983**	**1982**	**1981**
Model I/III/4	28.1%	27.2%	30.5%
Model II/12/16	21.4	25.7	25.3
Color computers	9.8	7.2	3.3
Portable/pocket computers	3.1	2.5	2.7
Printers	16.5	16.7	17.5
Software	9.2	8.5	7.5
Other	11.9	12.2	13.2
	100.0%	100.0%	100.0%

SOURCE: 1983 Annual Report.

consumer electronics "hobby shop," which catered to electronics hobby buffs. This group represented a substantial customer base. The Tandy of 1984, however, was moving toward the commercial consumer of computer and telecommunications products. This resulted in the customer base being segmented into two broad classes: consumer and commercial.

Tandy experienced problems with this shift in customer groups stemming from its carefully developed image as an electronics hobby shop. Commercial customers tended to view Radio Shack equipment as more appropriate to the home than the office. For this reason new computer and telecommunications products were marketed under the brand name of Tandy rather than Radio Shack. In addition, free standing computer and telephone stores carried the name "Tandy" versus Radio Shack.

One of Tandy's great strengths had been their ability to hold customers through heavy, targeted advertising. At the core of the advertising program was the direct mail catalog. Each month Radio Shack sent a 24 page pamphlet (32 page in November and 48 page in December) to more than 25 million previous customers. The mailing list used for these mailings had been assembled over many years at checkout centers in Radio Shack stores all over the United States. The objective of the catalogs was that the "Complex nature of the electronic equipment and gadgetry sold through the Radio Shack stores is distilled and presented in an easy-to-understand form."[20] This philosophy was apparent in the manner that computers were marketed through the catalog. The catalogs stressed a computer for every walk of life, for every use, whether it be a computer for the home or business. This was done in a style that stressed plain English and deemphasized technical descriptions. The catalogs also served to standardize (or police) pricing in all stores (franchised or company owned), and promote Radio Shack's nationwide distribution and service network.

Although catalogs were the primary advertising vehicle, they were still only a part of the program. Catalogs were closely linked to free standing inserts and ROP (Run-of-the-paper) newspaper advertising. Free standing inserts consisted of eight- and twelve-page inserts circulated at least fifteen times a year. Magazines played an increasing role in advertising to more specialized markets, such as computer and telecommunications users. Television was considered the least important medium, and was used primarily for status or "class" exposure.

An in-house agency named Radio Shack National Avertising Agency was responsible for all advertising programs. This agency, which employed 145 people and took up one floor of the corporate headquarters, was given the company's total advertising budget of over $160 million. Notes Bernard Appel, Executive Vice-President of Marketing, "Keeping the agency inside allows us to have tighter control and ultimately better input over our advertising. It would also be much more costly to go outside."[21] Although the agency was in-house, its relationship to the company was similar to that of an outside agency, with the client being Radio Shack. All of the advertising for a product was the responsibility of the buyer. The buyer acted as the client and the agency had to obtain his approval.

The total cost of advertising was $199.1 million in 1983, a 23% increase from the expenditure of $160.9 million in 1982. For the first time since 1979 the percentage increase in advertising expense was greater than the sales increase. Even so the advertising expense as a percent of sales had been declining since 1979. This percentage was 9.4%, 9.0%, 8.1%, 7.9%, and 8.0% in 1979, 1980, 1981, 1982, and 1983, respectively.

The merchandising of the Radio Shack stores was guided primarily by information gathered at the store level. One type of information previously noted was the customer names that supported the mailing list. An even more critical type of information was that gathered through the Radio Shack operating system (SOS). Through this system, each retail store was able to transmit daily sales, financial data, payroll, inventory, and merchandise orders. This system has served to provide up to date merchandising data, streamline stores and central office accounting and warehouse operations. Through a joint venture with Citibank Tandy began offering a national credit card good for purchases of more than $225.00 at all Radio Shack stores nationwide. This provided a source of information on large credit purchasers that Tandy had not had access to in the past.

Tandy put this information to good use judging by the financial status of its stores. Year-to-year sales gains of 22%, 20%, 22%, 14%, and 15% were

Exhibit 23.4

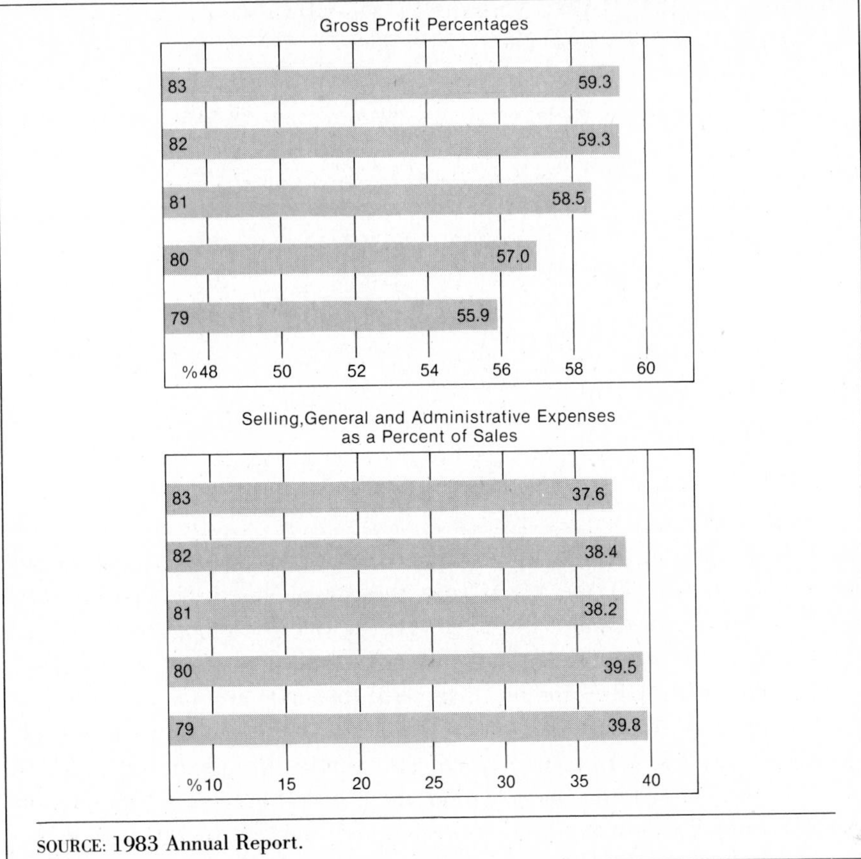

SOURCE: 1983 Annual Report.

recorded in 1983, 1982, 1981, 1980, and 1979. This sales growth came through the expansion of the store system, increases in sales of old stores, new product categories and international operations. As can be seen from Exhibit 23.4, none of these gains were at the expense of gross profit or general overhead expenses.

Gross profit as a percent of sales remained steady for fiscal 1983 and 1982 after four years of increases. Factors that favorably influenced the gross profit were the continuing increases in the volume of self manufactured products and the increase in manufacturing profits. The factors that limited gross margins were adverse conditions in international operations caused by the strong dollar and foreign market restrictions.

Through a continuous improvement in financial position, Tandy had become a retail powerhouse rivaling the traditional giants of the industry.

As can be seen from Exhibit 23.5, Tandy's return on equity was still one of the highest of the nation's retail giants.

Exhibit 23.5

FINANCIAL INFORMATION FOR RETAIL CHAINS

	Twelve Months Ending	*Total Sales (millions)*	*Retail Income (millions)*	*Return on Equity*
K Mart	10/28/81	$15,759	$232	9.9%
JC Penney	1/31/82	11,860	156	12.9
Sears, Roebuck	12/31/81	27,357	285*	6.6
Tandy	12/31/81	1,886	200	40.8
Toys R Us	11/01/81	687	36	19.4
Wal Mart	1/31/82	2,445	83	27.9

SOURCE: *Forbes*, March 1982.

* After capital gains and before unassigned corporate costs of $108 million.

Products The primary strategy Tandy had pursued was to develop the largest retail distribution system in the electronics industry. The distribution system Tandy developed became enormous, presenting both opportunities and problems. One way that Tandy had chosen to capitalize on these opportunities and cope with these problems had been through self-manufacturing.

Tandy produced some products within all of the product categories sold in the Radio Shack stores. The percentage manufactured in-house varied by product line, the largest concentration being in the area of computers and related peripheral devices. One area of rapidly increasing production was that of telephone and telecommunications equipment. This was particularly true of those product areas that combined the features of computer and telephone equipment. In addition to production in-house, a large number of products were manufactured under contract in production facilities not owned by Tandy. These products carried private labels, such as Realistic.

Tandy saw many opportunities in self-production. The first was the positive effect manufacturing in-house had on gross profit. As can be seen from Exhibit 23.4 gross margins had been increasing in direct relation to the percentage of private label merchandise sold through the Radio Shack stores. The percentage of private label merchandise was limited, however. Since the early eighties, Tandy had been mainly building computer manufacturing capacity and President John Roach estimated that because of this Tandy might get up to 65% self production, but no further.[22] Margins were assisted through both the ability to control vendor profit, and the ability to develop products designed to fit the unique needs of the Radio Shack stores. One of the major advantages of in-house production was the result of one of the problems arising out of maintaining a large distribution system. The sheer size of the Tandy system made it difficult to find suitable suppliers. Manufacturing in-house reduced Tandy's dependence on outside suppliers. Other advantages were obvious. Tandy had the ability to keep in close contact with technological developments. Tandy had continuous merchandising input to guide and quickly implement product development. In summary, Tandy had reduced their overall dependence on outside suppliers and increased control over the products sold in Radio Shack stores.

Tandy also experienced a number of disadvantages with this system. One of the more substantial was the problem of attempting to play the dual roles of both the manufacturer and retailer. As Equil Juliussen, computer marketing analyst, states, "If you have your manufacturing hat on, you want as many outlets as possible; but if you have your retail hat on, you may not, since you could be taking sales from our own stores."[23] This had never been a problem until Tandy became heavily committed to computers. Computer sales had become such a substantial portion of the business in terms of retail and manufacturing sales that neither one could be thought of as subservient to the other.

Tandy, in late 1983, realizing that more outlets were needed in order to maintain market share in computers, began for the first time using independent distributors. Sixty distributors were signed up, who would sell to over 2,000 retail outlets. Although the move had been promoted as "experimental," Tandy management had clearly become aware that they would have to expand distribution if they were to maintain their position in the computer market. Tandy was being slowly forced into a position of having to set priorities. "The company could be forced to choose which role is more important if its competitors pushed strategies of heavily discounting their computers to win customers, and aggressively pursuing the highly profitable software and peripheral markets."[24]

Radio Shack's computer and electronic equipment prices had been traditionally thought of as being low, when compared to competitors' products. Radio Shack's low pricing strategy was developed in 1977 when the TRS-80 was first brought into the market. The primary reason Tandy chose a low pricing strategy was that in order to sell through their Radio Shack stores, the computer price had to be in line with other consumer electronic products. It was in Radio Shack's strategy to keep the TRS-80 at a reasonable level ($599.95) so that more of their current customers could afford to buy one.

Since that time, however, competition in the home and personal computer market had become intense. This had served to place extreme pressure on gross margins which had placed Tandy in a serious dilemma. Tandy's strategy had always been to drop lines that did not produce at least a 50% gross margin. Tandy was now far too dependent upon computer systems to simply drop them. This problem was not acute when Tandy never had to compete head to head with the products in non-Radio Shack stores. However, with wider distribution, Tandy no longer had this luxury. This problem was further aggravated by the fact that costs have not come down as fast as prices, and that Tandy had a high manufacturing cost. As one article on the subject points out, "It seems no accident that the home computer company with the highest prices in the U.S.—Tandy—also performs most of its assemblies in the U.S."[25] This situation had the effect of forcing price discounting on the independent retailers that were now carrying Tandy computers. This had been unheard of in the past and had the effect of putting more price pressures on Tandy products in Radio Shack stores.

The name "Radio Shack" corresponded with a hobby shop image in the minds of many consumers. This was a desirable image for most of the product areas that Tandy serves. However, computer systems was not one of those areas. To many computer buyers, Tandy maintained the image of a peddler of cheap electronics goods. The TRS-80 model 16 was developed primarily to counteract this image. The unit, which initially cost $4,999, was aimed at the sophisticated user, such as large corporations. In further moves to change their image, Tandy was replacing Radio Shack with the Tandy name on all computer products, and full service computer stores. Probably more important was the manner in which Tandy modeled themselves after IBM stressing support and systems, as selling points. This had been an area of needed improvement which had become especially apparent to independent retailers who had complained of weak and indecisive support from Tandy.

External

Stores

Tandy, as discussed earlier, marketed a wide range of electronics products. These products essentially fell into four general areas; consumer electronics (radios, stereos, etc.), electronic components (diodes, transistors, etc.), computer related (computers and peripheral devices), and telephone related (telephones and related peripheral devices). The first two of these product areas were entered when they were considered high growth markets. As these markets began to mature and stagnate, efforts were made to replace them with products aimed at new growth markets. It was at this time that Tandy entered the computer market. When that growth in the computer markets began to slow and competition became more intense Tandy began to invest in the development of telephone and telecommunications equipment. This was the pattern that led to the market structure facing Tandy, in addition to providing a basis on which to understand its retail competition.

Tandy's original product line was that of electronic components aimed at the home electronics buff. These components were carried in all Radio Shack stores except those that were full line computer or telephone stores. Competitors in this area were generally in the form of small independent retailers or small regional chains.

The next market was that for consumer electronics. This category covered a wide range of products from expensive component stereos to walkie-talkies. These products were carried in all stores except those devoted exclusively to computers or telephone systems. Tandy's primary competition in this market could generally be considered the large mass merchandising chains such as Sears, Penney, and Target on the one hand and the large stereo/electronics specialty chains such as Pacific Stereo, on the other.

The next market, and the one that was responsible for the strongest recent growth and largest percentage of total sales, was that for computers and related equipment. Tandy faced strong competition in three areas: mass merchandisers, computer specialty stores, and manufacturers who sold directly.

It was estimated that in 1983 there were approximately 20,000 mass merchandisers selling lower priced home computers (less than $1,000). As a result, margins on these units had been squeezed to the point where most computer specialty stores were being forced out of this market into professional business systems.

The strongest competition for Tandy came from computer specialty stores. In 1982 there were an estimated 1,800 computer dealers in the United States who controlled over 50% of the micro-computer market. This number was expected to grow to over 6,500 stores in 1988 and control 35% of the products in the personal computer market alone. As the number of stores grew their markup was also changing, as can be seen in Exhibit 23.6. Independent retailers were gradually losing ground as chains began to dominate the market. The largest of the competing chains was Computer Land which had over 500 franchised stores, followed by Sears with over 100 stores, and IBM with over 60 stores and Computer Craft with over 30.

This trend toward chains was being motivated by shifts in market structure. Smaller stores were having a difficult time competing with the same recognition, buying power, capital formation abilities, and advertising of the larger chains. In addition, there was a shift toward standardization and a deemphasis on technology in favor of marketing, value-added services, and price cutting. This translated into retail chains that operated on minimum margins, maintained outside sales personnel, and high levels of service.

One chronic problem of many chains and independent wholesalers alike was lack of adequate cash flow. High ticket merchandise coupled with a high

Exhibit 23.6

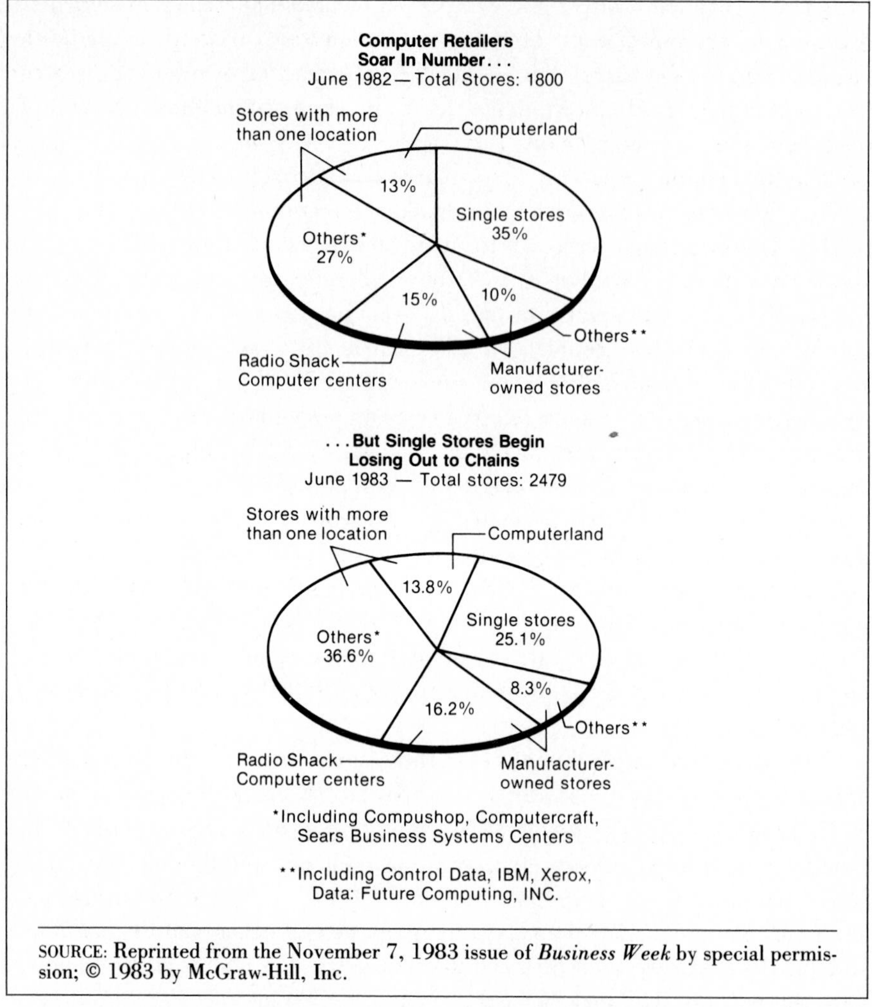

SOURCE: Reprinted from the November 7, 1983 issue of *Business Week* by special permission; © 1983 by McGraw-Hill, Inc.

growth market had created severe cash flow problems for many dealers. Tandy had not had any serious difficulties with this problem.

Tandy was meeting the competition from other computer retail organizations in several ways. Tandy's primary strategy was to blanket the nation with a large number of stores in order to guarantee stable national distribution. As of 1983 Tandy had 412 free standing computer centers, and 632 Radio Shack stores containing computer departments, in addition to plans to add 100 centers and 50 combined stores by the end of the year. In order to further enhance distribution, Tandy had signed up at least 60 distributors to market its computers to independent retailers. Aware of the need to sell to corporate customers directly, Tandy had begun the formation of a direct field sales force. This sales force had embarked upon a campaign of seminars and direct mail advertising to data processing managers in order to acquaint professional users with the capabilities of Tandy equipment. Lastly, Tandy was beginning to provide comprehensive service in terms of repair and training throughout the entire Tandy store system.

The last market, and the one that Tandy looked to for further growth, was that for telephones and related equipment. Tandy was, at this time, considered the largest independent retailer of telephones in the United States. Telephones were marketed through all Tandy stores except computer centers. In 1984, Tandy opened a group of experimental telephone centers designed to carry nothing but telephone equipment. The telephone centers were designed to fulfill a similar role to that of the stand-alone computer centers in that they carried lines appropriate to the small business user such as business phones and key systems.

Tandy's interest in telephones was based on two factors. The first was that the telephone market was projected to reach over $5 billion annually by the latter part of the decade. The second was that developing technology was giving the telephone substantial new capabilities that would include integration with such devices as personal computers and home electronics. Lastly, telephones and related products were the fastest growing segment of Tandy's business.

Tandy was not alone in its interest in this market. AT&T already had over 461 phone centers and had announced plans to open more in major Sears mall locations. GTE was also a major retailer through freestanding phone centers as were most other national mass merchandisers.

Products

The consumer electronics industry, of which Tandy was a part, represented an estimated $20 billion dollars in 1983. Tandy's sales, while dominated by the computer, had shown comfortable growth in nearly all "traditional" product areas. As a result, only two areas will be reviewed in depth: computers and telecommunications: Computers, because of the fact that they dominate sales and had become substantially more competitive; telecommunications, because this market represented future growth.

Computer Systems The conditions facing Tandy in the computer markets were the result of the two markets Tandy was in: home, and small business and personal computers.

The vast majority of people for whom a computer is a necessity already owned a computer. As a result, the order of the day was to create a mass market for home computers.

Atari's Senior Vice-President of marketing, Ted Vass, put the situation clearly when he said, "The people who pioneered this field were technology-orientéd. But now the essence of the business is consumer marketing."[26] The drive toward mass merchandising accurately described the nature of the home computer market in 1984.

The most significant factor that faced both the home and small business computer market was intense competition. The inner workings of most small computers were the same with key ingredients provided by the same handful of suppliers. Much of the software was also the same. Although manufacturers had tried to distinguish themselves by providing innovative features, these were rapidly copied by competitors. The result was that no computer really had a substantial technological advantage. As a result, the real differences were found in price, service, compatibility, distribution networks, and image.

"Clearly, the industry had grown out of its initial, entrepreneurial stage and is reaching for maturity," said David Lawrence, an analyst with Montgomery Securities in San Francisco.[27] With the change from an entrepreneurial to a mature market, the critical factors for success also changed. To succeed, personal computer makers would need to monitor these critical areas:

1. *Low cost production:* As personal computer hardware became increasingly standardized, the ability to provide the most value for the dollar greatly influences sales.
2. *Distribution:* Only those makers that could keep their products in the customer's line of sight would survive.
3. *Software:* Computer sales would suffer unless a wide choice of software packages was offered to increase the number of applications.[28]

In summary, the market became saturated with undifferentiated manufacturers, crowded distribution channels and heavy price discounting. As a result even though worldwide sales were expected to grow from $6.1 billion in 1982 to $21 billion in 1986 there was little doubt that a shakeout would gradually occur over the next three to five years. By 1986, it has been predicted there could be only one dozen microcomputer vendors left.

Exhibit 23.7 provides an overview of the general position Tandy held as compared to the competition.

Tandy's strengths were guaranteed distribution, financial muscle, and service through Radio Shack stores. However, as Cleve G. Smith, an analyst for the Yankee Group, says, "Tandy's advantage in distribution has disappeared," and further stated that "the company will slip to fourth this year

Exhibit 23.7
COMPETITION IN PERSONAL COMPUTERS

	Current Strengths							
Companies	*Applications Software*	*Brand Image*	*Depth of Management*	*Financial Muscle*	*Low-cost Production*	*National Sales Force*	*Retail Distribution*	*Service and Support*
Apple Computer	*	*					*	
Atari (Warner)	*	*		*			*	
Commodore International					*		*	
Digital Equipment			*	*	*	*		*
Fortune Systems	*							
International Business Machines	*	*	*	*	*	*	*	*
Japan Inc.			*	*	*			
Radio Shack (Tandy)	*	*		*			*	*
Texas Instruments			*	*	*		*	*

SOURCE: Reprinted from the November 22, 1982 issue of *Business Week* by special permission; © 1982 by McGraw-Hill, Inc.

NOTE: *Business Week* interviewed more than forty leading hardware, software, and peripheral equipment makers; industry consultants; and analysts to come up with a list of expected survivors and their current strengths.

(1982) in home computer sales."[29] Tandy also had a notable weakness in that it lacked a national outside sales force and that it had relied entirely on in-house programmers for software development. Moving to correct these deficiencies, Tandy began to staff full line computer centers with field sales personnel, in addition to allowing software companies to sell products under the Tandy name. Finally, Tandy had begun to respond to price pressures by reducing prices on many items, particularly those that are more price-sensitive such as low priced home computers.

Tandy's largest competitor was without a doubt IBM. In fact, it could be said that IBM had virtually defined the competition. As can be seen from Exhibit 23.7, they had no obvious weaknesses. IBM was known for their aggressive marketing, superb sales force, financial power, and an impeccable brand image. They had combined all of these abilities to create one of the most incredible marketing success stories of this century, the introduction of the IBM-PC. As Exhibit 23.8 illustrates, the growth of the PC had been nothing less than phenomenal.

Following the introduction of the PC, IBM had introduced the PC Jr. With both of these IBM had followed a strategy of aggressive distribution and pricing, designed to make them the dominant producer in these markets. Declares David G. Jackson, president of Altos Computer Systems, "IBM is moving faster than anything I've ever seen. It is being absolutely predatory."[30]

New sales did not necessarily represent the whole picture as Exhibit 23.9 demonstrates. IBM, while certainly a powerful new force, was far behind in terms of units in place.

Exhibit 23.8

WHICH COMPANIES ARE TAKING THE BIGGEST BYTE OF THE PIE?

Personal Computer Market Shares

	1980	1981	1982	1983
Apple	29.3%	41.8%	28.5%	22.0%
IBM	0%	5.0%	22.2%	28.0%
Tandy	37.6%	22.5%	10.1%	7.0%
Hewlett-Packard	5.3%	6.1%	4.7%	3.5%
Commodore	15.9%	10.6%	3.6%	3.5%
Franklin	0%	0%	2.5%	3.5%
Others	11.9%	12.6%	20.2%	29.0%

 Source: *Dataquest*.

Exhibit 23.9

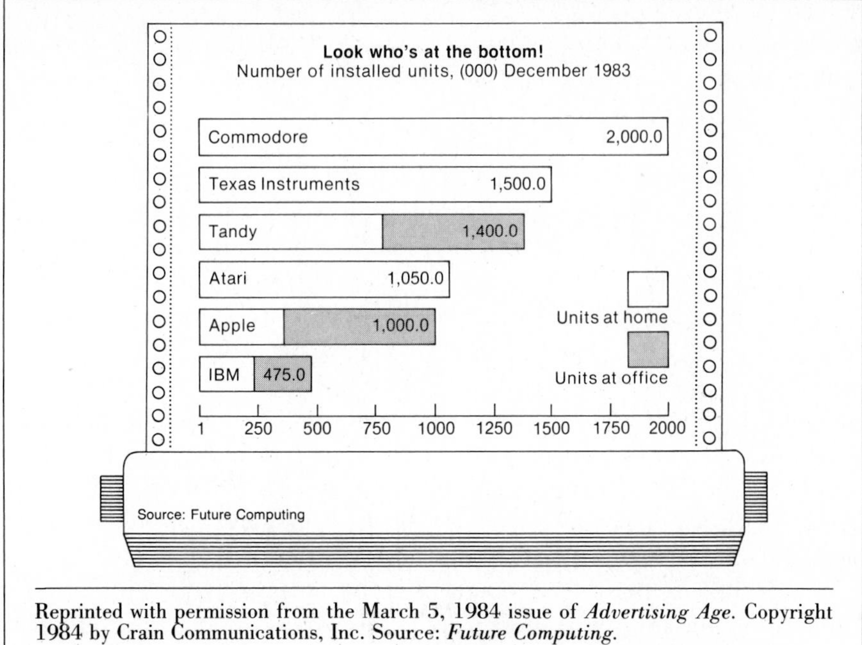

Reprinted with permission from the March 5, 1984 issue of *Advertising Age*. Copyright 1984 by Crain Communications, Inc. Source: *Future Computing*.

As a result of the IBM PC, Apple Computer was being unseated from the number one spot in personal computers. Apple (referring again to Exhibit 23.7) had many areas of weaknesses, the primary one being their inability to come up with a cohesive product and marketing strategy. However, under the direction of their new president John Sculley, who resigned as president of Pepsi-Cola to join Apple, these flaws were being rapidly corrected. Apple brought out a whole new series of products aimed directly at IBM, in addition to cutting prices and redirecting marketing efforts on their current lines.

Of the remaining competition, the most significant fell into the area of inexpensive home computers. These makers included Commodore, Atari, and Texas Instruments. Of this group, Commodore was probably the most significant to Tandy. Of the larger computer manufacturers, Commodore alone had yet to be scathed in the home computer price wars. This had largely been a result of the low cost production Commodore enjoyed in the Far East. Atari, following suit, had completely eliminated assembly operations in the United States, hoping to achieve cost parity through foreign assembly operations.

These computer manufacturers had been at the forefront of the effort to mass merchandise home computers. They had pursued this effort through extensive distribution, low service, and heavy price discounting. It was because of these companies that Tandy decided to begin using independent distributors, and a more flexible pricing policy.

Telecommunications Arthur D. Andersen expected the world telecommunications market to grow from $40 billion in 1980 to about $87.5 billion by the end of the decade.[31] The telephone market alone in 1982 was growing at a rate of 40% a year.

Quite understandably, U.S. manufacturers and those abroad were rapidly moving into what was shaping up to be a very lucrative market.

At the heart of this growth were three factors; the break up of AT&T; demand for new service; and new technology. The breakup of AT&T provided an opening for new competitors in what was once a monopolistic market. Second, much of the future demand would be for services aimed at moving computer data. Lastly, new technology was providing systems for applications never before possible.

Tandy focused on two markets in this industry: the basic telephone and data systems. Tandy pursued the first market area through products such as telephones, pagers, answering machines, and the like. More focus, however, was being placed on combining computer and communications technologies into a "symbiotic connection."

Tandy already faced competition from an array of large corporations. The most significant of these was AT&T. Already AT&T had distribution of its products through 4,500 retail stores and at least half of their sales through another group of mail order houses, and catalog companies.

In addition, AT&T was developing an entirely new line of small office, data, and computer systems, all of which integrated telecommunications and data processing functions.

The potential of this market had not been lost on IBM, which had bought a 15% interest in Rolm Corp., a maker of telecommunications equipment. Thanks to the IBM connection Rolm was the safe choice of buyers of telecommunications equipment, the way the phone company used to be. This development, of course, placed Tandy in direct competition with IBM in the telecommunications market as well as the computer market.

The International Telephone & Telegraph Corporation (ITT) was the second largest telephone company in the world; in 1982 it had a net income of $702.8 million and a 21% market share in the total electronics industry. ITT was aggressively pursuing the market because of the void created by the deregulation of AT&T. Unlike Tandy, ITT was known for its aggressive pricing policies, and in addition, spent over $750 million in telecommunications research in 1982.

PRODUCTION

Tandy operated twenty-nine wholly owned factories in the United States, Asia, and Canada, that produced products for Radio Shack stores. This was in addition to the products manufactured under contract by independent producers and sold under private labels through Radio Shack stores.

The company had been consistently increasing the percentage of products made internally over the years. However, John Roach, the president and CEO, forecasted Tandy might get up to 65% self-production, but no further. This was due to the fact that most self-production was dedicated to computer related products, and there was a limit to the total percentage of these that could be economically produced in-house. Another reason was the criteria applied to an in-house production decision. If Tandy could not offer the best possible product at competitive prices and make an adequate profit, merchandising would be from the outside sources. If the decision was made to produce in-house the sampling and quality control procedures were the same that outside vendors were required to follow.

Percentage Private Label Merchandise to Total Sales

1981	1982	1983
<50%	54%	57%

One of the major problems with this arrangement had been the conflict between the needs of the retail and the manufacturing operations. This was particularly true since Tandy had begun selling to independent distributors. In response to this problem Tandy split the top management of its International Manufacturing Operations into Tandy Division. The latter was eventually split giving one-half responsibility for manufacturing of all products sold through the Radio Shack store chain, and the other half responsibility for products sold to the general retail market. These divisions were called Tandy Electronics Manufacturing and Tandy Marketing Co., respectively.

Although Tandy's greatest strength was its distribution system, manufacturing operations were taking on much greater importance. Because of this, Tandy was constantly on the lookout for possible acquisitions of manufacturing plants, in order to improve its already high degree of vertical integration and ability to capture additional manufacturing margins. For example, on September 27, 1983, Tandy announced its intentions of acquiring Datapoint's half of a joint disk manufacturing venture. In fiscal 1982, video tape manufacturing capabilities were added through the purchase of the domestic portion of the Consumer Products Division of Memorex. The international operations of this division were being acquired on a country by country basis. Also, Tandy has agreed to a joint manufacturing venture with Matra S.A. of France in order to produce microcomputers. On August 18, 1983, Tandy made public its plans to acquire O'Sullivan Industries, Inc., a subsidiary of Conroy Inc. O'Sullivan was a manufacturer of consumer electronic stands, racks, desks, and accessories.

These production facilities were supported by efforts of two major design centers: one in Fort Worth and one in Tokyo. These design centers, along with those attached to specialized production facilities, were responsible for all product design from car radios to computers. These groups included not only hardware designers but also a 180-person team engaged in software development for the Tandy computer line.

Even with this R&D capability Tandy did not strive to be an innovator, which was revealed by the fact that R&D costs were considered financially "immaterial." The Tandy product design effort was set up to create applications not technologies.

One of the major tasks of these groups was to reduce production costs. This had become a substantial problem in recent years because of the strong dollar and high domestic production costs. Most of Tandy's computer products came from domestic plants which were considered to be high cost production facilities. At the same time these products were competing against imports (Commodore) which had a price advantage because of the strong dollar.

WORKING CAPITAL

In 1983 operations generated $321 million in working capital, an increase of over 23% as compared to 1982 (see Exhibit 23.10). The 1983 working capital amount was approximately twelve times the amount generated in 1974.

Tandy utilized its working capital for capital expansion as Tandy did not issue any long-term debt in 1983. The total capital expansion budget for

Exhibit 23.10

WORKING CAPITAL PROVIDED BY OPERATIONS
(In Millions of Dollars)

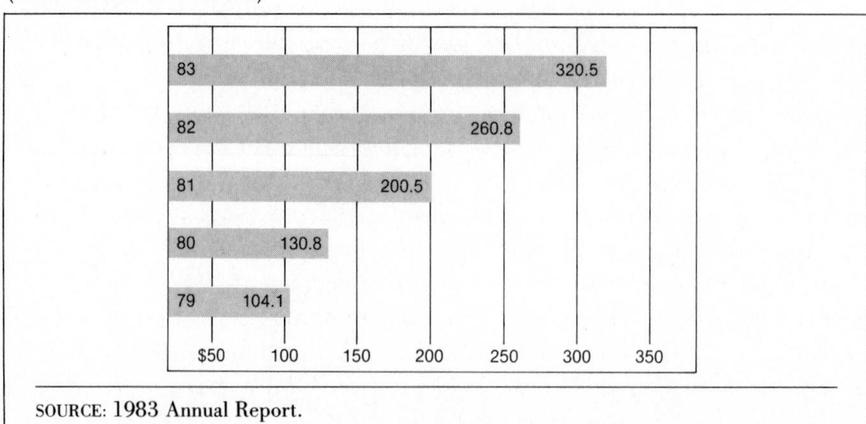

SOURCE: 1983 Annual Report.

1983 was $75 million. This included the expansion of manufacturing facilities, the opening of 350 new retail stores and the remodeling of 600 existing retail stores.

Cash Flow

In 1983 Tandy's net income increased by 24.3% on a sales increase of 21.8%. Tandy had recorded similar gains such as the one in 1976 when sales increased 40% because of the CB radio craze. The lowest sales increase Tandy ever experienced since 1973 was in 1978 when sales only grew 12% after the CB radio craze ended (see Exhibits 23.11 and 23.12).

The effect of the CB radio craze is shown through an Operational Cash Flow analysis that was performed by Paul Pappadio, a professional analyst. Pappadio defined operational cash flow (OCF) as net income, plus depreciation, plus changes in working capital, less investments in property, plant and equipment, and debt. OCF can be thought of as the uncommitted cash Tandy has on hand at the end of the year.[32]

Through his analysis, Pappadio found that in 1977, when the CB radio craze ended, Tandy's OCF fell to negative $30 million. In the years following, due to Tandy's rebound brought about by entering the microcomputer market, OCF rose to a high of $70 million. Pappadio also found that in 1982 Tandy's OCF fell again to negative $78.5 million. Pappadio credits this drop to the accumulation of huge inventories.

In response to this OCF analysis, Garland Asher, a Tandy financial officer, stated that by putting cash into inventory, rather than simply holding it, it earns a better return, making it the better strategy. Substantiating this, Asher stated that in 1982 Tandy's after tax return on non-cash assets was 25.5%. Further, Asher concluded that the success of the company lay largely in the fact that its customers were never faced with empty shelves.[33]

International Financial Markets

The strength of the U.S. dollar in the 1981–1983 period affected Tandy in three major ways. First, foreign-produced products imported into the United States carried a favorable price advantage. In fact, Robert Miller, Vice-President of Merchandising, Consumer Products, said, "The strong U.S. dollar improved technology and manufacturing efficiencies continue to bring our customers more advanced products at lower retail prices."[34]

Second, the strong dollar raised the costs of Tandy's exported products in the international markets. This means that exported American-made products carried a price disadvantage abroad.

Finally, the profits the international division generated were greatly reduced due to currency translation charges. These charges reflect the costs of translating foreign currency denominated profits into U.S. dollars. In 1983, the international division yielded $527 million of profits but lost over $590 million in foreign currency translation.

Exhibit 23.11
TEN-YEAR CONSOLIDATED STATEMENTS OF INCOME
TANDY CORPORATION AND SUBSIDIARIES
(In Thousands of Dollars Except Per-Share Amounts)

	Year Ended June 30									
	1983	1982	1981	1980	1979	1978	1977	1976	1975	1974
NET SALES (see Notes 1 and 2)	$2,475,188	$2,032,555	$1,691,373	$1,384,637	$1,215,483	$1,059,324	$949,267	$741,722	$528,286	$411,241
Other income	38,109	28,657	15,697	11,360	11,403	5,629	3,763	2,649	3,963	2,153
	2,513,297	2,061,212	1,707,070	1,395,997	1,226,886	1,064,953	953,030	744,371	532,249	413,394
Costs and expenses:										
Cost of products sold	1,008,187	826,842	701,777	594,841	535,549	491,509	434,031	331,400	249,006	198,067
Selling, general and administrative, net of amounts allocated to spun-off operations in fiscal 1976 and prior	930,244	780,378	645,934	546,325	484,249	403,173	350,878	270,308	204,107	158,792
Depreciation and amortization	38,679	29,437	23,288	19,110	17,121	13,879	11,140	8,034	7,392	5,461
Interest expense, net of interest income and interest allocated to spun-off operations in fiscal 1976 and prior	8,905	1,168	15,454	25,063	28,466	30,260	15,192	7,282	14,044	8,544
	1,986,015	1,637,825	1,386,453	1,185,339	1,065,385	938,821	811,241	617,024	474,549	370,864
Income from continuing operations before income taxes	527,282	423,387	320,617	210,658	161,501	126,132	141,789	127,347	57,700	42,530
Provision for income taxes	248,761	199,302	151,015	98,423	78,272	59,986	69,970	63,066	29,078	20,669
Income from continuing operations	278,521	224,085	169,602	112,235	83,229	66,146	71,819	64,281	28,622	21,861

Loss from discontinued operations, net of income taxes	—	—	—	—	—	—	(2,777)	—	(1,820)	(7,072)
Net income before income from operations spun off	278,521	224,085	169,602	112,235	83,229	66,146	69,042	64,281	26,802	14,789
Income from operations spun off, net of income taxes	—	—	—	—	—	—	—	3,243	7,794	5,657
NET INCOME	$ 278,521	$ 224,085	$ 169,602	$ 112,235	$ 83,229	$ 66,146	$ 69,042	$ 67,524	$ 34,596	$ 20,446
Income (loss) per average common share and common share equivalent:										
Continuing operations	$2.67	$2.17	$1.65	$1.12	$ .81	$ .69	$ .54	$ .44	$ .20	$ .13
Discontinued operations	—	—	—	—	—	—	(.02)	—	(.01)	(.04)
Spun-off operations	—	—	—	—	—	—	—	.02	.05	.03
NET INCOME	$2.67	$2.17	$1.65	$1.12	$ .81	$ .69	$ .52	$ .46	$ .24	$ .12
Average common shares and common share equivalents outstanding	104,335	103,395	102,578	103,644	106,004	96,136	132,336	144,824	145,408	169,992

SOURCE: 1983 Annual Report.

NOTES: 1. Per share amounts restated for two-for-one stock splits in May 1981, December 1980, June 1978, and December 1975. 2. Fiscal 1983 and 1982 amounts reflected the adoption of FAS No. 52, Foreign Currency Translation.

CONSOLIDATED BALANCE SHEETS, TANDY CORPORATION AND SUBSIDIARIES
(In Thousands of Dollars)

Exhibit 23.12

	June 30 1983	June 30 1982
ASSETS		
Current assets:		
Cash and short-term investments	$ 279,743	$ 167,547
Accounts and notes receivable, less allowance for doubtful accounts	107,530	83,616
Inventories	844,097	670,568
Other current assets	31,928	27,000
Total current assets	1,263,298	948,731
Property and equipment, at cost:		
Consumer electronics operations, net of accumulated depreciation	194,004	158,678
Tandy Center, net of accumulated depreciation	63,616	66,317
	257,620	224,995
Other assets	60,990	53,918
Total	$1,581,908	$1,227,644
LIABILITIES AND STOCKHOLDERS' EQUITY		
Current liabilities:		
Notes payable	$ 55,737	$ 24,942
Accounts payable	64,640	63,641
Accrued expenses	115,054	92,125
Income taxes payable	50,668	52,160
Total current liabilities	286,099	232,868
Notes payable, due after one year	15,482	20,642
Subordinated debentures, net of unamortized bond discount	122,938	122,666
Store managers' deposits	8,490	9,306
Deferred income taxes	17,682	18,886
Other non-current liabilities	10,345	10,599
Total other liabilities	174,937	182,099

Exhibit 23.12
(Continued)

	June 30	
	1983	**1982**
Stockholders' equity:		
Preferred stock, no par value, 1,000,000 shares authorized, none issued or outstanding	—	—
Common stock, $1 par value, 250,000,000 shares authorized with 105,645,000 shares issued	105,645	105,645
Additional paid-in capital	68,111	39,627
Retained earnings	969,626	691,105
Foreign currency translation effects	(16,297)	(12,317)
Common stock in treasury, at cost, 976,000 and 1,789,000 shares, respectively	(6,213)	(11,383)
Total stockholders' equity	1,120,872	812,677
Commitments and contingent liabilities	—	—
Total	$1,581,908	$1,227,644

NOTES

1. 1983 10-K Tandy Corp., p. 2.
2. Borenstein, Paul, "Can Tandy Stay on Top?" *Forbes,* April 11, 1983, p. 43.
3. *Ibid.*
4. *Business Week,* "A Computer That Builds Radio Shack Image," February 1, 1982, p. 23.
5. Appel, Bernard, *Marketing and Media Decisions,* "Advantages of Being Self Contained," Spring 1982, special, p. 71.
6. Seneker, Harold, "What Do You Do after You Bury the Boss?" *Forbes,* March 3, 1979, p. 7.
7. Rudnitsky, Harold, and Mach, Toni, "Sometimes We Are Innovators, Sometimes Not," *Forbes,* March 29, 1982, p. 66.
8. *Ibid.,* p. 68.
9. Seneker, p. 7.
10. Rudnitsky and Mach, p. 66.
11. Appel, p. 71.
12. Seneker, p. 118.
13. *Forbes,* "Tandy Man," December 11, 1978, p. 118.
14. *Ibid.*
15. 1983 Annual Report, p. 3.
16. Appel, p. 71.

17. 1983 Annual Report, p. 5.
18. *Ibid,* p. 15.
19. Rudnitsky and Mach, p. 66.
20. Annual Report 1983, p. 14.
21. Madeleine and Dreyfack, "Do It Yourself," *Marketing and Media Decisions,* May 1983, p. 60.
22. Rudnitsky and Mach, p. 68.
23. *Business Week,* August 30, 1983, p. 30.
24. *Business Week,* "Rivals Crowd Tandy's Computer Niches," August 30, 1982, p. 30.
25. Halper, Mark, "Losses Mount in Home Computers as Suppliers Assess 2nd. Half," *Electronic News,* p. 60.
26. "Computer Marketing: No Longer Fun and Games," *Advertising Age,* March 5, 1984, M-1.
27. "Painful Adolescence: A Hot Market Meets a Shake-Out," *Electronic Business,* December 1983, p. 30.
28. *Business Week,* "The Coming Shakeout in Personal Computers," November 22, 1982, p. 74.
29. *Business Week,* "Rivals Crowd Tandy's Computer Niches," August 30, 1982, p. 28.
30. *Business Week,* "Personal Computers and the Winner is IBM," October 3, 1983, p. 78.
31. "World Telecommunication: Study II 1980–1990," A. D. Little, Inc., Cambridge, MA.
32. "Tandy to Acquire Datapoints Half of Disk Venture," *Electronic News,* September 27, 1983, p. 16.
33. *Ibid.*
34. *Ibid.*

Case 24

COMSHARE, INC. (A): STRATEGIC ACTIONS IN THE COMPUTER SERVICES INDUSTRY

Donald W. Scotton/Allan D. Waren

Bernard C. Reimann

Comshare, Inc. was a computer service firm that began operations in 1966. It was a "high tech" company offering timesharing services to industry, government, and other non-profit organizations. These services included network access to computers owned and operated by Comshare. Users were able to communicate with the Comshare computers, located at Ann Arbor, Michigan, via sophisticated communication networks of telephone lines. The system was designed to provide very rapid, apparently instantaneous, response to most simple requests. It appeared to the user that he had access to his own computer. All of the usual data processing and accounting functions could be performed on data stored at the computer center. Users could access their data from any of their plant locations for use in dealing with organizational problems.

During the period from 1966 until 1982, many advances occurred in the use of timesharing and in the services offered by Comshare. These included the addition of sophisticated data bases, better methods for retrieving information, and the development of modeling methods for solving business and financial problems. Comshare was a leader in the industry in developing con-

Prepared by Profs. Donald W. Scotton, Allan D. Waren, and Bernard C. Reimann of Cleveland State University. This case was presented at the Case Research Association Meeting, 1984. Distributed by the Case Research Association. This case also appeared in the *Case Research Journal, 1985,* pp. 175–195.

cepts and products to make possible this advanced technology for problem solving.

The latest, and most significant of these developments, was System W, an advanced Decision Support System (DSS) software product, which Comshare introduced late in 1982. This software made it possible for executives to enter or retrieve data from either mainframe or personal computers, build models to simulate their businesses, make forecasts, do statistical analyses, test assumptions or alternative "scenarios," and even display their results in customized reports or graphs. While a substantial number of competitive products existed, Comshare executives considered System W to be a technological breakthrough in that it greatly facilitated modeling in multiple dimensions. Most of the competitive products were either limited to two-dimensional "spreadsheets," or required extremely complex programming to achieve multidimensional modeling and analysis.

Comshare had recently signed a marketing arrangement with IBM concerning System W. IBM was interested in making highly sophisticated software available to its customers to complement its offerings of mainframe and personal computers. The arrangement included the agreement for IBM salespeople to recommend that users and prospects interested in DSS software consider System W. When feasible and desirable, IBM representatives could make joint sales calls with Comshare salespeople.

Shortly after this arrangement was made, Comshare executives were reflecting upon this action and its implications. Richard L. Crandall, President of Comshare, indicated:

> We will utilize our complete organization to make this arrangement successful; and we will modify and adapt System W to the changing needs of users. We are no longer only a computer based timesharing corporation. An important part of our future lies in the development of Decision Support Systems that permit business executives to make better decisions through the interactive use of mainframe and personal computers.

THE INDUSTRY

Product Evolution

Initially computers were developed primarily for scientific computing. Their ability to store and manipulate any information was recognized and led to more and more business-oriented applications. Information could be stored, processed, and returned to users in manageable and meaningful reports and graphs. The rapid acceptance of computers led to the development of improved computers and ancillary equipment, such as terminals for entering data and calling it out, printers and plotters to provide "hard copy" output, and supporting networks and hardware to transmit and receive information. A vital complement to the hardware configuration was the appropriate software (program) to tell computers how to process the information.

An early trend toward specialization in the computing industry occurred in the mid-1960s, at which time it was recognized that not every firm or branch operation needed its own large mainframe computer. Rather, access through a communications network to a remote computer could meet user needs more economically, with little or no capital investment. Specialists developed the timesharing concept whereby many different firms, as well as the many branches of each firm, could share a common computer in such a fashion that it appeared to each individual user that he had sole access to the machine. Initial reception of this approach was best among the scientific and engineering community, and these groups were initially seen as the natural market for timesharing.

Concurrent with this phase was the development of communication networks that utilized telephone lines and supporting hardware to transmit and receive data.

By the late 1960s, it was recognized that it was the business needs of private firms, nonprofit groups, and government that comprised the most significant market for computer services. There was a growing requirement for better ways to record, store, retrieve, and manipulate information about organization functions such as accounting, finance, production, personnel, marketing, and research. Therein lay the challenge for developers of software packages: To provide the means to perform these functions with the aid of computers. Software specialist firms emerged to supplement the efforts of the large hardware developers such as IBM and Digital Equipment Corporation.

Since hardware manufacturers tended to focus their efforts on systems software, a profitable and growing niche became available in the area of applications software. As a result, a variety of "software houses" emerged to provide high quality applications software with an emphasis on "user friendliness," or ease of use, as well as on efficiency. Typical applications included material requirements planning, accounting and financial reporting, and data base management.

Another important factor contributed to the accelerating growth of this specialized software market in the 1970s. This was the inability of the data processing function, in most firms, to keep up with the burgeoning demand for its services. The resulting backlog of data processing projects led to an urgent need for highly sophisticated software which would be so easy to use that non-programmers, such as financial or marketing executives and their staffs, could develop their own, custom-made applications.

At the same time, the increasing competitiveness and uncertainty of the business environment were creating a growing interest in strategic planning. This in turn led to a strong need for information systems to help top executives and strategic planners make decisions. One answer to this need was DSS (Decision Support System) applications software. This highly sophisticated software made possible the bringing together of relevant information from both internal and external data bases, and the use of complex models to simulate and analyze strategic alternatives before they were implemented.

The Market

There were fewer than 2,000 international computer software and service firms as reported in the 1982 Comshare Annual Report. Comshare, Inc. was one of the largest of these firms involved in the marketing of DSS software, which included data management, financial modeling, forecasting, analysis, reporting, and graphics. These DSS products were used by timesharing customers via a worldwide computer network, as well as by customers who licensed the products for use on their mainframe computers and/or microcomputers.

The market for corporate and financial planning DSS software and processing services was reported as follows in the 1983 Comshare Annual Report:

1981 Sales	$549 million
1982 Sales	729 million
1987 Forecast	3.1 billion

The report also indicated that 1981 industry sales of all types of software totalled $4.2 billion. Richard L. Crandall, President of Comshare, reported in an interview that 17%, or $714 million, came from data management and financial software sales, the two main predecessors of DSS. He indicated also that "in 1975 barely one-half billion dollars of industry sales were in software." *Business Week,* in its February 27, 1984 issue, published a special report on "Software: the New Driving Force." In it, they forecast that software sales in the U.S. would "keep on growing by a dizzying 32% a year, topping $30 billion in 1988."

Competition

Kevin O. N. Kalkhoven, Group Vice-President, estimated that the 1983 DSS industry leaders, their products, and sales were as follows:

Execucom	IFPS	$20 million
Management Decision Systems	Express	7–8 million
Comshare	System W	7–8 million
EPS, Inc.	FCS/EPS	6–7 million

It should be noted that, prior to the introduction of System W, Comshare had been a vendor of FCS/EPS on its timesharing service. It still supported those timesharing customers who were not willing to switch to System W.

There were more than sixty other competitors, at least twenty of whom had entered the business in the last two or three years. Two software products were identified as being particularly significant to Comshare. These were IFPS, a product originally developed for financial risk analysis, and Express, which was developed originally for marketing research functions. Both products had subsequently been enhanced and were being marketed as full function DSS systems. Comshare viewed IFPS as being particularly easy to use but lacking integrated functionality in areas such as data management, whereas Express was seen as a very hard to use product which was functionally well integrated and quite powerful.

In order to compete effectively in this market, Comshare felt it was essential to develop a product which was easier to use than Express and had more capabilities and was better integrated than IFPS. Thus System W was designed to take advantage of this opportunity for product positioning relative to the industry leaders.

Another potential threat that Comshare management had noticed was that a number of other firms were waking up to the huge potential of the market. These firms were redoubling their efforts both in improving their products and in marketing them. Several firms had decided to "unbundle" their prices for total systems in order to be more competitive. Thus a customer interested only in modeling, for example, could buy a "starter" system for as little as $10,000. If other capabilities, such as forecasting or graphics were desired, each of these additional modules could be purchased separately for $5,000–15,000 each. Another aspect of product pricing was the increasing willingness of some vendors to discount the prices of their software, especially for multiple purchases.

Life Cycle

Timesharing sales were of continuing importance to Comshare. A recent issue of *Data Communications* revealed that timesharing expenditures in the United States were $3.1 billion in 1982 and $3.8 billion in 1983. Projected expenditures in 1984 were $4.2 billion. The bulk of Comshare's revenue continued to be realized from timesharing services.

Mr. Kalkhoven made the following comments about the timesharing portion of the industry:

> In the mid and late 1960's there were 800 timesharing companies and now there are less than 100. There are 600 microcomputer manufacturers today and they will follow the same pattern as timesharing. There will be very few in the future. I have been involved in this industry (high computer technology) since 1970. It has undergone an interesting life cycle pattern.

He proceeded to draw the following diagram on a blackboard:

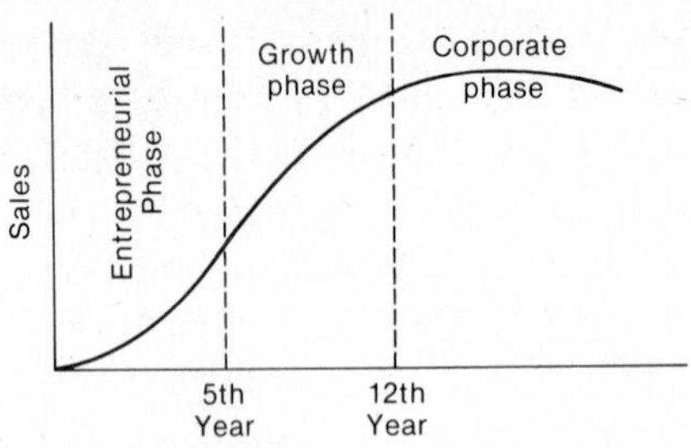

He described the three phases in the life cycle of a high technology computer oriented firm as follows:

1. *Entrepreneurial Phase.* Normally the computer high tech firm remains in this phase for about five years. It takes from three to five years to realize a profit. There is a fast change in products; and a heavy capital investment is required. Management is largely drawn from technological people who are involved in the innovation of the products and concepts, for example from engineering. A large number of firms fail and drop out because they run out of capital and cannot meet the rapidly changing technology.
2. *Growth Phase.* This period extends from about year six through twelve. Market leaders evolve. The number of competitors is reduced dramatically. For example, in the timesharing portion of the computer field, the number of firms was reduced from approximately 800 to 100. During this period, technical and management stabilities emerge. The firms begin to develop corporate missions and policies; they establish planning and marketing management approaches to guide their destinies.

   However, signs of what will happen later also emerge. These include a technological slow down where profit is realized on existing technology rather than on new product developments. As an example, Comshare enjoyed profits and the fruits of a number of innovations associated with timesharing networks. The need for significant capital becomes urgent in this phase. Furthermore, the economic climate is likely to suffer a recession at some point over this period of years. By the latter 1970's timesharing technology had passed its period of rapid development, and the onset of a recession confronted young management with new and unanticipated conditions.
3. *Corporate Phase.* During the Corporate Phase the strategic management and marketing process, initiated in the Growth Phase, is implemented fully. Marketing opportunities are identified more specifically. Strategic and tactical planning reach maturity. Operational programs

> and controls are developed as the bases for achieving objectives. At this stage the firm must pick a product and go . . . you must pay for its development and introduction with the cash cows. The initial mission, technology, and products may change. For many members of the industry the Corporate Phase is just emerging. They must decide whether they will be hardware manufacturers, specialists in mainframes and/or microcomputers, timesharing providers, systems consultants, limited software developers and purveyors, or decision support systems businesses.

COMSHARE BACKGROUND

Antecedents

The firm was founded in 1966 at Ann Arbor, Michigan. The founding president was Robert F. Guise, an independent consultant. He was joined in this venture by Richard L. Crandall, at that time a graduate student at the University of Michigan, and by four other persons.

Mr. Crandall studied computer applications under Professor Westervelt and taught computer courses at the university. In 1965, he learned about some exciting developments at Berkeley involving the design of a timesharing operating system. He joined a group with members from Tymshare and from the University of California at Berkeley to work on this project. Crandall said:

> This was a stimulating group with which to work. We completed the operating system development and then I returned to Ann Arbor in 1966 to rejoin Comshare. (He returned as Research Director.)

Timesharing was the first service to follow Comshare's consulting activities. Their first network consisted of direct dial access from customers to the Comshare computer. Mr. Crandall was involved in the technical aspects of developing timesharing and the facilitating network hardware. In 1967 he became Vice-President of Research and Development and also assumed operating responsibilities, including marketing. Mr. Crandall continued his remarks:

> We went public in 1968 and took in over $5 million. It was used within one year to open offices around the country. By January 1970 we had $3–4 million sales volume but were losing so much money that there was concern about the employees and the future of the firm. At the time of our March 1970 board meeting, I was chief operating officer and serious discussions took place as to the survival of the company. In August 1970 I was given the Presidency. We were $6 million in debt and losing $3 million a year.

Acquisitions and Divestitures

Comshare reacted to its changing environment through a variety of strategies. First there was a series of acquisitions and divestitures as indicated in Exhibit 24.1. These were carried out in the desire to gain new, related prod-

Exhibit 24.1

CHRONOLOGICAL ACTIVITIES: COMSHARE, INC.

1965	Start-up and time sharing operating system development
1966	Incorporation as a Michigan company
1968	Public offering of stock (traded over the counter)
	Start up of Canadian affiliate (Comshare, Ltd.)
1970	Start up of European operations as Canadian subsidiary (Comshare International, BV)
1974	Purchase of 30% interest in Comshare International, BV
	License agreement to provide services in Japan (Japan Information Service, Ltd.)
1977	Acquisition of Systematic Computer Systems Inc. (individual income tax processing services)
1978	Acquisition of Valuation Systems Corporation (consultants in current measurement systems)
	Acquisition of Trust Management Systems Inc. (Bank Trust Department services)
	Acquisition of 100% Comshare International BV
1979	Acquisition of Digitax, Inc. (individual and fiduciary tax return processing services)
	Stock split (three for two)
1980	Acquisition of Computer Research Company (supplier of large-scale IBM computer processing services)
	Expansion into France with a wholly owned subsidiary (after receiving French government permission)
	Start up of Hardware Systems Division (to provide services to users of large-scale Xerox computer systems)
	Secondary public offering of shares (net $10.1 million)
1981	Sale of individual income tax processing services (including those of Systematic Computer Systems and Digitax)
	Acquisition of Advance Management Strategies Inc. (microcomputer software now sold as COMSHARE Target Software)
	Increase in ownership of Comshare Ltd. (now owns 37.3% of Canadian affiliate)
1982	New product release: Planner Calc and Target Financial Modeling (microcomputer based DSS products)
	Sale of the fiduciary income tax processing services
1983	New flagship product release: System W (DSS system for large-scale IBM computers)
	Sale of Trust Management Systems (accounting software for bank trust departments)
	Sale of Trilog Associates (balance of bank trust department services)
1984	Consummation of marketing agreement with IBM

SOURCE: Comshare, Inc., *Annual Reports.*

ucts, market entry, and knowledge about technical products and their adaptation to the markets.

Opportunities and complexities occurred with some acquisitions. Mr. Crandall commented:

> Computer Research Company was acquired in 1980 to learn about their use of IBM equipment and software. They were essentially a vendor of raw computer time and we did not understand the myriad of implications and options, including such items as pricing and IBM operating systems. Initially there was a culture shock between the two firms. Integration was difficult and eventually was achieved by absorbing the entire operation into the main business of the parent, Comshare. We finally learned the IBM environment, from the executive office through to the salesmen. In the meantime, Computer Research Company has been completely integrated.

T. Wallace Wrathall, Group Vice-President, Finance and Administration discussed some of the acquisitions and divestitures as follows:

> The 1978 acquisition of Valuation Systems Corporation gave us their software for computing the current values of assets based on replacement costs. These financial systems products fit into the Comshare family of products and thus made the merger attractive. The corporation was eventually merged into Comshare. Currently these specific financial reports are no longer required by the Securities and Exchange Commission. However, the merger was successful.
>
> Trust Management Systems, Inc. was bought to tie into our human resources (personnel) product lines. Later it was evaluated as belonging to the bank market rather than in the domain of human resources, and it was sold.
>
> We were in the tax processing business and had purchased Systematic Computer Services to add to our line of services for CPA firms and their needs. To provide national coverage for our income tax processing services we then acquired Digitax in 1979. These firms were then sold in 1981. They were not profitable and, to offset this trend, more product development effort would have been required.

Mr. Crandall commented that the acquisitions of the Canadian, British, and European affiliates had been highly beneficial in extending markets, integrating operations, and furthering innovation and product development. As shown in Exhibit 24.1 this effort has extended from 1968 forward.

STRATEGY LEADING TO SYSTEM W

Introduction

Comshare had been a planning oriented company since the early seventies. In 1972 they first formulated a long-range strategic plan. This plan enumerated corporate goals in broad terms and specified detailed objectives that were as quantified as possible. Strategies were developed to meet these objectives and thus the corporate goals. In general terms, these goals were: (1)

to be a profitable growth company, and (2) to be the best firm in their market segment.

As a direct result of this planning process, Comshare changed its emphasis from general purpose timesharing sales to providing more specialized, business problem solving assistance. This was achieved by: (1) making appropriate software tools available on their timesharing network and (2) utilizing their customer support representatives to help customers solve business problems using these software tools. As Kevin Kalkhoven stated, "It was no longer appropriate to be everything to everyone."

In 1979 Comshare undertook a major review of their current plans and strategies. Mr. Kalkhoven further commented:

> We saw three important things in 1979: (1) we had not changed—we were still primarily a timesharing company, (2) we had not anticipated the rapid changes in hardware costs and performance and (3) we had not anticipated the market place being dominated by the demand for microcomputers and software. Moreover, Comshare was experiencing the effects of the recession and the accompanying reduced revenues. Although we were one of the market leaders, we were in a period of technological stagnation.

Richard L. Crandall, reflecting on the results of this review, said, "We were satisfied that the corporate goals spelled out in 1972 were still valid; however, the environment had changed and we needed to reassess it and its impact on our strategies.

Environmental Review

The environment and company position was reviewed in terms of strengths, weaknesses, opportunities, and threats, and the following were found:

A. *Strengths*
   1. The firm was well developed and represented on the international market. Its international sales force provided a strong competitive advantage.
   2. The talent existed to solve business problems. Experienced people had worked on these problems in the sale of timesharing services.
   3. Market position was established in timesharing.
   4. A product gap in inquiry and analysis software had been identified, and Comshare had the research and development capability to resolve it.
   5. The firm had a good cash flow and cash position. It could operate at a breakeven position for several years.

B. *Weaknesses*
   1. Comshare had no identifiable image in software.

2. The marketing organization did not have selling skills in software.
3. The business recession and lack of a software product prevented Comshare from taking immediate market action.

C. *Threats*

1. As software firms and products became more prevalent for in-house computer use, the demand for timesharing services diminished.
2. Service firms reduced prices to compete for market share.
3. The advent of personal computers caused both computers and software to become available to users at lower costs.

C. *Opportunities*

1. There was an increased demand for productivity software. Certain packages were available for data management applications. Also there were "first round" relatively unsophisticated financial modeling packages. There was a need for a more functional product to solve a variety of problems for a broader group of users.
2. Existing software was relatively difficult to use and not as integrated and functional as it could be. Thus, Comshare had a market opportunity for a more functional and easier to operate DSS.

New Strategies

The environmental review led to a number of conclusions that were significant for the development of new strategies to achieve corporate goals. Comshare realized that:

1. Its value and importance to the customer was based on the skills of the Comshare employees and on the capabilities of the software it provided.
2. Timesharing was only a delivery mechanism for providing access to software, which was used to solve business problems.
3. Software could also be delivered to the customer by selling mainframe software for use on customers' computers.
4. Personal computers were potentially important software delivery vehicles.

As a result of further analysis, Comshare decided that Decision Support Software was its primary product and should be delivered to customers in as many ways as possible. Timesharing, as a delivery mechanism, remained an important aspect of the business; however, future development emphasis would be on DSS software.

To provide a finer focus for these efforts, Comshare determined that its best approach lay in the development and marketing of DSS software specifically designed for IBM computers. Thus the decision was made to develop a comprehensive, easy-to-use decision support system optimized to run on IBM systems.

The developmental work was carried out in the European Headquarters in London and resulted in a software product named Wizard. Presently this DSS is marketed in Europe under the name of Wizard and in the United States as System W. Comshare had planned to use the name Wizard in the U.S. However, they discovered that a small software vendor had obtained an earlier trade mark of Wizard for his product. To avoid infringement, Comshare was forced to change the name, at considerable expense, because sales brochures and other documentation had been printed bearing the designation Wizard.

Complementary Marketing Arrangement with IBM

A letter was received from IBM in September 1982 in which an invitation was extended to approximately 100 computer firms to attend an IBM-hosted conference. The purpose of the conference was to consider strategy for dealing with end users of computers and related services. The emphasis was on application software rather than data management and operating system software. Mr. Crandall attended the conference and noted that most representatives of attending firms did not seem to take the new IBM direction seriously.

However, he felt that IBM was very serious in its desire to have outsiders provide application software, while IBM concentrated on further developing its hardware—both mainframe and personal computers. This was a central part of IBM's new "Information Center" strategy, conceived to meet the pent-up demand among executives to use computers to satisfy their needs for relevant information. This concept required the development of "user friendly" software which would allow nonprogrammer executive users to develop their own decision support systems. Since IBM did not itself have any strong offerings in this type of DSS software, Mr. Crandall envisioned a desire on the part of IBM to work closely with a firm capable of developing and marketing superior DSS software.

Discussion continued between IBM and Comshare, and in early January 1984 a two-year complementary marketing arrangement was reached. As indicated in the January 9, 1984, issue of *Computerworld,* IBM would recommend System W for use in Information Centers using IBM 4300 computers. IBM and Comshare sales representatives would refer prospects to each other. In addition, provision was made for joint sales calls of IBM and Comshare personnel to prospective users of DSS. The potential advantage to IBM was the prospect of increased hardware sales resulting from the availability of Comshare's DSS software. Finally, Comshare would continue its responsibility to users to install System W and conduct training programs.

FINANCIAL CONSIDERATIONS

Comshare was founded much as other entrepreneurial firms. Capital contributions by the six founders and the Weyerhauser family provided the im-

Exhibit 24.2

COMSHARE'S SIX-YEAR TREND: SELECTED FINANCIAL INFORMATION
(In Thousands of Dollars Except Per-Share Data)

Year Ended June 30	1983	1982	1981	1980	1979	1978
Revenue	$76,337	$78,453	$79,837	$68,579	$46,049	$23,404
Income from operations	2,453	1,406	8,163	10,672	8,292	3,791
Interest expense	1,039	1,240	1,291	1,486	752	450
Interest income	1,052	1,278	370	156	116	70
Income before taxes	2,458	1,591	7,535	9,146	7,711	3,943
Income from continuing operations	1,331	829	4,374	5,346	4,383	2,682
Per share	.31	.18	1.03	1.41	1.31	1.00
Average number of shares outstanding (thousands)	4,340	4,542	4,251	3,791	3,334	2,675
Research and development	6,135	6,109	5,916	4,539	3,289	1,857
As a % of revenue	8.0%	7.8%	7.4%	6.6%	7.1%	7.9%
Working capital	9,378	12,350	12,224	5,584	3,208	1,107
Capital expenditures	6,377	8,684	10,516	13,685	11,277	3,081
Total assets	59,381	66,842	70,919	62,581	47,275	21,663
Long-term debt	2,067	9,960	8,485	14,415	9,553	3,825
Shareholders' equity	38,192	37,745	40,735	27,736	22,086	12,537
Number of employees at year-end	1,084	1,164	1,215	1,282	1,100	538

SOURCE: Comshare 1983 Annual Reports.

NOTES: In fiscal 1982, the Company, in compliance with Statement No. 52 of the Financial Accounting Standards Board, changed its method of accounting for foreign currency translation adjustments. Financial data for periods prior to fiscal 1982 have not been restated for this change in accounting principle. Information regarding Results of Operations excludes discontinued operations. The average number of shares outstanding and income per share data have been adjusted to reflect a three-for-two stock split in July 1979.

petus for the firm's start. There was a public offering of the firm's stock in 1968 and it was followed by a secondary offering in 1980 which netted $10 million. Exhibits 24.2 and 24.3 contain income and balance sheet data from 1978 through fiscal year 1983. These data reveal revenue increases until 1981, at which time recessionary influences were evident.

T. Wallace Wrathall, Group Vice-President, Finance and Administration, commented:

> There are notable differences in the financial management of Comshare versus industry at large. Some of these include:

Exhibit 24.3

COMSHARE, INCORPORATED: CONSOLIDATED BALANCE SHEET

As of June 30	1983	1982
ASSETS		
Current assets		
Cash	$ 3,407,500	$ 3,059,300
Temporary investments, at cost	4,413,800	7,507,000
Accounts receivable, less allowance for doubtful accounts of $570,700 in 1983 and $550,400 in 1982	13,221,900	13,301,000
Prepaid expenses	2,154,200	2,512,900
Total current assets	23,197,400	26,380,200
Property and equipment at cost		
Land	964,400	999,200
Computers and other equipment	42,983,700	42,408,200
Building and leasehold improvements	6,221,800	6,152,000
Property and equipment under construction	2,518,800	3,530,700
	52,688,700	53,090,100
Less accumulated depreciation	26,605,200	23,694,200
Property and equipment, net	26,083,500	29,395,900
Other assets		
Investment in affiliate	1,905,700	2,020,500
Goodwill, net of accumulated amortization of $766,200 in 1983 and $567,300 in 1982	6,242,800	6,486,300
Purchased software, net of accumulated amortization of $1,101,600 in 1983 and $496,000 in 1982	1,521,100	1,948,600
Deposits and other	430,600	610,700
Total other assets	10,100,200	11,066,100
	$59,381,100	$66,842,200

SOURCE: Comshare 1983 Annual Report.

1. We have no inventory—only software tapes with low unit production cost. (This does not include the cost of research and development.)
2. There is a short life cycle of plant and products because of the rapidly changing technology.
3. Investment decisions have a short life cycle. So we need a high rate of return.
4. Research and development expenditures are high compared to other industries.

Exhibit 24.3
(Continued)

As of June 30	1983	1982
LIABILITIES AND SHAREHOLDERS' EQUITY		
Current liabilities		
Current portion of long-term debt	$ 345,200	$ 1,039,000
Notes payable	1,857,700	1,151,700
Accounts payable	3,709,600	3,437,200
Accrued liabilities		
Payroll	2,722,600	2,391,600
Taxes, other than income taxes	992,400	1,162,400
Discontinued operations	98,500	1,720,500
Other	3,186,100	2,601,300
Total accrued liabilities	6,999,600	7,875,800
Accrued income taxes	907,500	526,300
Total current liabilities	13,819,600	14,030,000
Long-term debt	2,067,300	9,959,900
Deferred income taxes	5,302,500	5,086,900
Deferred credits	—	20,900
Shareholders' equity		
Common stock, $1.00 par value; authorized 10,000,000 shares; outstanding 4,281,414 shares in 1983 and 4,599,604 shares in 1982	4,281,400	4,599,600
Capital contributed in excess of par	24,368,400	25,871,200
Retained earnings	12,624,200	10,415,200
Currency translation adjustments	(3,082,300)	(2,377,200)
	38,191,700	38,508,800
Less treasury stock, at cost (119,000 shares in 1982)	—	764,300
Total shareholders' equity	38,191,700	37,744,500
	$59,381,100	$66,842,200

5. Capital requirements are declining and are relatively low compared to the remainder of industry.
6. Operating, selling, and development costs are largely people costs and will go up more rapidly than industry averages.

Mr. Wrathall reflected on other aspects that affect the firm:

1. Accounting rules can cause us to buy rather than make . . . the manner in which we are required to report research and development costs is all-important.
2. One-third of our sales are in markets outside of the United States. Be-

cause of the declining value of the British pound sterling, transferred earning and investments are reduced. Continued decline in the value of the pound could result in a real loss.

3. System W was developed in the United Kingdom (under the name of Wizard) and sold to Comshare in the U.S. This developmental policy can result in the parent firm paying less for R and D because of favorable exchange rates and possibly more favorable tax rates.

Mr. Kalkhoven spoke on the necessity for a combination of product and financial policy to finance the marketing of System W and other new products. He alluded to the Boston Consulting Group's explanation of classifying products according to their growth and market share rates. Those products that no longer have a high growth rate but have retained a favorable market share can be marketed successfully for revenues to support the introduction and market development of new products under the so-called cash cow strategy. The executives of Comshare had its timesharing product line as a cash cow that would be useful in supporting the introduction of System W, its development, and the development of other DSS products as well. Moreover, Comshare's substantial timesharing customer base gave it an easily accessible and somewhat captive market for System W and related products.

MANAGEMENT CONSIDERATIONS

Early in 1984, the top management group consisted of the following relatively young, but highly qualified executives:

Richard L. Crandall, 41, became president and Chief Executive Officer in 1970. He was one of the original six founders of the firm in 1966. In 1978 he had served as president of the Association of the Data Processing Service Organizations. He was also a frequent speaker and author of numerous articles related to issues pertinent to the computer industry.

Kevin O. N. Kalkhoven, 39, was Group Vice-President in charge of marketing product development and sales. He had been with the company since 1971. Prior to that he worked for IBM as an analytical services manager, and in sales management for SIA, Ltd. in the U.K. He lectured frequently on the subject of decision support systems to such groups as the American Marketing Association and the Planning Executives Institute.

T. Wallace Wrathall, 47, Group Vice-President of Finance and Administration had joined Comshare in 1975. Prior to that he had seventeen years of broad experience in finance and accounting. His previous employer, Varian Associates, was also in the computer high technology business and also had extensive foreign operations. Other employers included Del Monte Corporation, Optical Coating Laboratory, and Eldorado Electrodata.

Ian G. McNaught-Davis, 54, became Group Vice-President in 1978 and managed the European Operations. He was also a director of Comshare Limited. Mr. Davis was the founding chief executive of Comshare Limited (U.K.) in 1970. He was employed earlier for nine years with General Electric Information Systems. His last position with G.E. was Director of Marketing. He has been the moderator of approximately twenty one-hour television programs for the British Broadcasting Corporation concerning computers and their uses. Also, he lectured throughout the United Kingdom and Europe at universities and professional conferences.

These men exercised management and intellectual leadership throughout the organization. They were innovative in the development of solutions to everyday business problems and issues. During the early years the overriding concern was bringing together people who were innovative, self-reliant, and results-oriented. In this way computer services and software could be developed by a group of imaginative and dedicated people.

Richard Crandall was a leader and model for personnel involved in this activity. He became involved at the age of 18. He was president at the age of 26. This was a young man's sphere of activity populated by those who shared common levels of intelligence, curiosity, innovativeness, and the pleasure of working diligently to achieve results to be enjoyed psychologically and materially. In 1983 the average ages of Comshare employees were:

Non-managers	26 years
Managers	32 years
Executives	38 years

It was found that successful persons were socially adept, got on well with others, and had excellent senses of humor. They had a natural curiosity about management practices. This led them to study and adapt business management approaches to planning, programming, operating, and controlling the firm's activities.

Mr. Crandall summarized the management philosophy and direction of Comshare as follows:

> The future of our business is in knowledge based software, and we must organize and operate properly to maintain success. We are a marketing oriented company. Our Research and Development effort is directed to meeting market needs in creative ways. New technology can spur innovation and creativity. We must attract talented people to Comshare who can work successfully in our environment. Top management is the key to innovation and the strategic management and marketing process. The approach and philosophy must permeate from the top of the organization.

Case 25

SOUTHEASTERN VIDEO SERVICES, INC.

Jo Ann C. Carland/James W. Carland

> Ours is a young industry and for those few firms, like ourselves, who are successfully and profitably operating cable commercial insertion systems, the immediate potential is tremendous. As the value and impact of this rapidly growing industry continues to increase nationwide, so will the success and profits of SVS in the systems we operate!

Thomas J. Robson stretched and leaned back in his chair. He was pleased with himself, but not altogether carefree about the future. Southeastern Video Services, Inc. (SVS) is the latest in a long series of business ventures for the forty-six-year-old Robson. Real-estate, building, and land development occupied his time for twenty years. This latest venture is in the wake of a series of business setbacks which ruined all but a few of Robson's other investments. This business must succeed, or Robson will have nowhere to turn. Despite his outward confidence, Robson knows that his latest equipment lease request has been declined. Finding another lender has proved harder than expected.

THE BUSINESS OF CABLE ADVERTISING

Cable television systems have long had available insertion spots for local commercials on the major satellite networks. Most cable systems concentrate on selling more subscribers so that they more or less ignore sales of local commercials. This results in considerable loss of advertising revenues. Exhibit 25.1 displays a typical advertising profile for a locally owned and

This case was prepared by Prof. Jo Ann C. Carland and Prof. James W. Carland of Western Carolina University. Presented at the Case Research Association Meeting, 1984. Distributed by the Case Research Association.

SAMPLE ADVERTISING PROFILE

Exhibit 25.1

Company Name: Home View Systems
Owner(s): Roger G. McMahan
Market: Central James County, Georgia
Homes Passed: 9,000
Basic Subs: 3,600
Pay Units: 4,680 (130%)
Channel Capacity: 52, 31 in use
Basic Channels/Pay Channels: 28/3 HBO, Showtime, Prism
Ad Rep: None
Media Competition: Radio: 1 local AM, 7 regional AM, 9 regional FM
Newspapers: 1 daily, 1 weekly
System Began: June 1979
Ad Sales Began: October 1981
Sales Personnel: 1 sales coordinator, 2 part-time salespersons
Source of Avails: CNN, ESPN, MTV, Cable Health Network
Rate Cards: Grid cards used. Rates range from $5 to $20 per 30 sec spot. All spots are run of station. Minimum purchase is $500. Frequency discount applies, unsolds avails used for existing clients.
Ad Revenues: $65,000 in 1982 (20% of Avails)
Ad Sales Projections: $175,000 for 1983

operated cable TV system. Such profiles are prepared by advertising bureaus and can be purchased for most of the cable systems in the country.

As the exhibit shows, there are considerable revenue opportunities in the more effective exploitation of the available commercial insertion spots. This lack of pursuit of advertising is especially commonplace among smaller cable systems.

THE DEVELOPMENT OF SOUTHEASTERN VIDEO SERVICES

SVS, like a small number of other firms in early 1982, recognized the potential for a commercial facilitator. Robson and his partner Jack Higgins observed that local cable systems had neither the staff nor the resources to market effectively cable TV advertising. Such commercials require production facilities, which are expensive and require highly skilled personnel for operation. In addition to the problems associated with production of commercials, SVS had to train an active sales force for marketing the commercial slots. SVS was intended to sell, produce, and schedule commercial insertions for cable systems throughout the southeastern United States.

Robson owns 51% of SVS, and Higgins owns 30%. The remaining stock is owned by the other officers of the corporation. Exhibit 25.2 contains a list of management personnel and synopses of their backgrounds. The corporation began business early in 1983. Robson and Higgins took no salaries in

MANAGEMENT PERSONNEL

Exhibit 25.2

Thomas J. Robson, 46, President. Has been an independent business owner in the Hickory area for the last 20 years. Past President of the Board of Realtors, Past President of the Western North Carolina Home Builders Association, past member of the board of the National Home Builders Association.

Jack W. Higgins, 38, Vice President. Former partner in a sound recording studio in Atlanta, Ga. Former manager of performing artists and groups. Promoter of concert tours. Producer of radio and TV commercials. Newspaper and radio advertising sales.

William K. Johnathon, 27, Production Manager. BA, Broadcasting, University of Florida. Former instructor of video production at Norfolk Technical Institute. Experienced in all phases of video production, writing, directing, and producing.

Douglas A. Rowell, 32, Director of Marketing—N.C. Former general manager of weekly newspapers in the South, North and Southeast. Former general manager of a small town daily newspaper.

Roscoe J. Coggins, 41, Director of Marketing—S.C. Production manager for Metal Products Company. Vice President of Marketing for the largest Valvoline distributor in the Southeast.

1983 while they attempted to build up the business. The first contract with a cable system was closed in August 1983 and commercial insertions began. The remaining management staff came aboard in late 1983 and early 1984 as the company's sales volume picked up. The second cable system was brought on line in December 1984. Both of these systems operate in North Carolina. The company now employs sixteen people and plans to add six more to support the South Carolina systems which have recently been contracted.

SVS operations are conducted from Hickory, N.C., in a building rented from Robson. The facilities include broadcast-quality production studios employing the latest technology in three-quarter inch professional video production equipment. All of the equipment is leased. A second office is located in Greenville, S.C., but is not yet fully equipped with production equipment. SVS is currently attempting to find a lessor willing to handle this equipment need and is seeking working capital to fund the penetration into new markets. The authors were called in as consultants to assist in preparing a financial package.

The company's financial statements for 1983, its first year of operations, and for the first four months of 1984, are included in Exhibit 25.3. The financial statements were compiled by the firm's CPA and accordingly include no expression of opinion or any other form of assurance by the CPA. The books were closed on April 25 because there were no remaining billings and because the management of the firm desired financial reports as recent as possible. The Stockholders' Equity section of the balance sheet shows a large retained deficit dating from years before 1983. This condition exists because Robson used an existing corporation as the vehicle for this venture changing its name to SVS. The old company had been inactive during 1983 but still possessed substantial loss carryforwards for tax purposes which Robson did not want to lose.

SVS now has contracts with five cable TV systems, having sold contracts to three South Carolina firms in 1984. Commercial insertions began for the three new systems in April. Its contract provides SVS with exclusive access to the commercial insertion slots and guarantees the cable system a flat fee based on the number of subscribers and a commission on the actual advertising revenues generated by SVS in that cable system. A sample of the contract appears in Exhibit 25.4. SVS provides all equipment and handles all production and marketing of commercials. SVS is currently negotiating with two additional cable systems. Those contracts, if closed, will require additional financial support for implementation.

Advertising rates are largely a function of the number of subscribers in a cable system. A rate card is displayed in Exhibit 25.5 portraying the weekly rates for various combinations of advertising slots and periods. In addition to the advertising rate, a commercial that SVS produces will incur production costs. Advertisers are free to provide or produce their own commercials if they prefer. The production rates of SVS are competitive. SVS attempts to maximize its advertising revenues by insuring that production fees are not an obstacle to a sale. Consequently, production revenue is minor.

Two of the five cable systems currently under contract have large numbers of subscribers. The Hickory and Asheville systems in North Carolina reach a total of 25,000 homes. Two of the three systems in South Carolina are in small towns, Laurens and Camden. The third system is currently small but has excellent growth potential since it is a suburb of Greenville. April 1984 advertising revenues for each of the five systems is shown in Exhibit 25.6. Note that the South Carolina systems were in operation only one to two weeks in April 1984.

Exhibit 25.6 also displays the seasonality of the business. There is a decline in sales for May and June. This loss of revenue is normal because summer is the off-season for television advertising.

THE SITUATION

The hour was late and the atmosphere tense. The evening began with a sense of excitement and anticipation. The five officers involved in the new and interesting enterprise were meeting to discuss their plans and needs with a consultant. They hoped to convince their new consultant that the venture

Exhibit 25.3

	December 31, 1983	April 25, 1984
ASSETS		
Current assets		
Cash in banks	$ 432	$ 3,194
Accounts receivable	49,930	46,735
Loans receivable from employees	14,277	20,276
Other receivables	—	4,000
Advances to salespersons	4,312	15,824
Prepaid expenses	—	7,250
Total Current Assets	68,951	97,279
Property and equipment		
Vehicles	—	16,095
Furniture and fixtures	3,530	11,874
Video equipment	36,086	59,046
Leasehold improvements	—	1,392
Land	—	27,500
	39,616	115,907
Accumulated depreciation	5,931	12,273
Net Property & equip	33,685	103,634
Other assets		
Deposit on equipment	—	12,093
Lease deposits	818	5,069
Total Assets	$103,454	$218,075
LIABILITIES AND STOCKHOLDERS' EQUITY		
Current liabilities		
Accounts payable	$ 3,300	$ 27,125
Notes payable (see note 1)	37,352	18,403
Income tax payable	673	1,107
Other taxes payable	461	2,931
Total liabilities	41,786	49,566
Stockholders' equity		
Common stock subscribed	—	20,000
Common stock: $1,000 par; 100 shares authorized	52,000	60,000
Paid in capital	—	72,000
Retained deficit from prior years	(31,537)	—
Retained earnings	41,205	16,509
Total Equity	61,668	168,509
Total Liabilities and Equity	$103,454	$218,075

NOTES: 1. All notes payable at December 31, 1983 and April 25, 1984 are due to stockholders and are unsecured and due on demand.

2. The company is obligated for payments under non-cancellable lease agreements as follows:

April 26, 1984 through December 31, 1984	$ 35,528
January 1, 1985 through December 31, 1985	44,978
January 1, 1986 through December 31, 1986	44,978
January 1, 1987 through December 31, 1987	38,978
January 1, 1988 through December 31, 1988	22,005
January 1, 1989 through December 31, 1993	41,250
Total Future Minimum Payments	$227,717

Exhibit 25.3
(Continued)

	Income Statement	
	January 1, 1983 to December 31, 1983	*January 1, 1984 to April 25, 1984*
Income		
Advertising income	$128,447	$92,844
Production income	2,636	1,735
Total Income	131,083	94,579
Cost of revenue		
Cablevision system fees	17,153	23,272
Equipment lease expense	3,267	6,345
Sales commissions	8,563	11,503
Depreciation on video equipment	5,931	3,864
Total Cost of Revenue	34,914	44,984
Gross profit	96,169	49,595
General and administrative expenses		
Salaries	1,800	11,010
Payroll taxes	4	844
Rent expense	14,082	4,824
Telephone	6,501	2,440
Utilities	23	337
Office supplies	1,438	1,641
Bank charges	156	291
Interest expense	498	325
Automobile expense	4,281	1,961
Lease expense—Van	3,003	501
Travel and entertainment	8,691	9,985
Postage and freight	741	357
Dues and subscriptions	288	565
Insurance	1,415	2,941
Advertising	5,383	270
Equipment repair	648	433
Talent and dubbing fees	712	232
Accounting and legal	963	500
Employee relations	413	721
Training	143	125
Depreciation	3,108	2,017
Total Expenses	54,291	42,320
Operating profit	41,878	7,275
Income taxes	673	434
Net income	41,205	6,841

3. The financial statements are based on operations from January 1, 1983 to December 31, 1983 and January 1, 1984 through April 25, 1984, respectively. Three new cable system divisions were added in 1984. The Camden, S.C. division is not yet operational. Operations of the remaining systems were included for the following dates:

Hickory & Asheville, N.C.	January 1, 1984–April 25, 1984
Greenville, S.C.	March 19, 1984–April 25, 1984
Laurens, S.C.	March 26, 1984–April 25, 1984

SAMPLE CABLE SYSTEM CONTRACT

Exhibit 25.4

This agreement, made and entered into this ______ day of ______, 1984, by and between SOUTHEASTERN VIDEO SERVICES, INC., hereinafter called SVS, and ______, hereinafter called SYSTEM;

WHEREAS, SYSTEM operates in and around the ______ county area a cable television system which includes the satellite networks known as ESPN, CNN, ______, and others making local commercial time available; and

WHEREAS, said satellite networks provide opportunities for the sale of local advertising spots, hereinafter called insertions; and

WHEREAS, SVS is in the business of marketing, and production of videotaped commercials and other services related thereto; and

WHEREAS, the parties desire to enter into an agreement providing for the use of the insertions by SVS and payment by SVS to SYSTEM.

NOW, THEREFORE, in consideration of the promises, obligations, and covenants contained herein, the undersigned parties do hereby contract and agree as follows:

1. SYSTEM hereby grants to SVS the exclusive right to use the advertising insertion times provided by ESPN, CNN, ______, and other satellite television networks making local commercial time available to SYSTEM during the term of this contract. These rights include the right to sell, produce, and control the local commercial time pursuant to the terms and conditions of this contract.
2. SYSTEM will provide access to SVS during normal business hours for the installation, operation, and maintenance of advertising insertion equipment, and such other equipment which may be required to provide the services described herein.
3. SVS will provide all equipment necessary for advertising insertions and will maintain, service, and insure all such equipment.
4. SVS shall pay to SYSTEM:
   A. A sum equal to the total number of subscribers connected to each network offered by SYSTEM multiplied by $.05 per month, per network used. Such amounts will be payable on the 20th day of each month based on the enrollment on the 1st day of the month. SYSTEM shall advise SVS of the number of enrollees.
   B. A sum equal to 10% of all advertising revenues received by SVS for the sale of insertions. Such amounts will be payable on the 5th day of each month based on the revenue actually received by SVS during the preceding month.
5. SYSTEM reserves the right to change or delete commercial material when, in its sole opinion, such material would be objectionable to its subscribers, or violate community standards.
6. SVS will provide to SYSTEM a monthly report of gross advertising sales and receipts, and an annual report of the same audited by an independent CPA.
7. Either party may terminate this agreement with 30 days' written notice to the other party.
8. The term of this agreement shall be from the date hereof until ______.

SVS RATE CARD

Exhibit 25.5

Hickory		Ashville		Combined	
ESPN 20 commercials		ESPN 20 commercials		ESPN 20 commercials	
20 commercials/wk		20 commercials/wk		40 commercials/wk	
6 wk schedule	$209	6 wk schedule	$109	6 wk schedule	$289
13 wk schedule	159	13 wk schedule	84	13 wk schedule	219
26 wk schedule	149	26 wk schedule	79	26 wk schedule	199
ESPN 20 commercials		ESPN 20 commercials		ESPN 20 commercials	
CNN 20 commercials		CNN 20 commercials		CNN 20 commercials	
40 commercials/wk		40 commercials/wk		80 commercials/wk	
6 wk schedule	$359	6 wk schedule	$189	6 wk schedule	$499
13 wk schedule	279	13 wk schedule	149	13 wk schedule	369
26 wk schedule	259	26 wk schedule	139	26 wk schedule	339

Greenville		Laurens or Camden		Combined	
ESPN 21 commercials		ESPN 21 commercials		ESPN 21 commercials	
USA 14 commercials		USA 14 commercials		USA 14 commercials	
or		*or*		*or*	
CNN 25 commercials		CNN 25 commercials		CNN 25 commercials	
CBN 10 commercials		CBN 10 commercials		CBN 10 commercials	
35 commercials/wk		35 commercials/wk		105 commercials/wk	
6 wk schedule	$129	6 wk schedule	$125	6 wk schedule	$340
13 wk schedule	109	13 wk schedule	105	13 wk schedule	289
26 wk schedule	99	26 wk schedule	95	26 wk schedule	260

Greenville		Laurens or Camden		Combined	
ESPN 21 commercials		ESPN 21 commercials		ESPN 21 commercials	
USA 14 commercials		USA 14 commercials		USA 14 commercials	
CNN 25 commercials		CNN 25 commercials		CNN 25 commercials	
CBN 10 commercials		CBN 10 commercials		CBN 10 commercials	
70 commercials/wk		70 commercials/wk		210 commercials/wk	
6 wk schedule	$224	6 wk schedule	$217	6 wk schedule	$592
13 wk schedule	189	13 wk schedule	182	13 wk schedule	521
26 wk schedule	172	26 wk schedule	165	26 wk schedule	468

was verging on success and to get some much-needed advice about finances. But no one wanted to hear any negative comments.

The meeting began with an excellent meal and much flattery for all participants. The five officers continued to encourage and compliment each other on jobs well done. Then with dessert came the business discussion. The consensus was rapidly reached: What was needed was a source of venture capital. Names of venture capitalists known by the participants were bandied about and omens of successful agreements were prophesied. It was obvious

Exhibit 25.6

REVENUES BY SYSTEM

	Advertising Revenues			
System	*April*	*May*	*June*	*Total*
Hickory, N.C.	$23,432	$14,189	$ 6,549	$44,170
Asheville, N.C.	10,655	7,171	3,089	20,915
Greenville, S.C.	8,016	4,320	NA	12,336
Laurens, S.C.	5,694	3,341	2,154	11,189
Camden, S.C.	953	1,906	1,031	3,890
Totals	$48,750	$30,927	$12,823	$92,500

that anyone understanding this business could not avoid being moved by its promise of largess. Each member had visions of success in his own way.

The primary concern was for sufficient capital to buy or lease equipment necessary for the actual functioning of the enterprise. The opening of the South Carolina operation created an immediate need for more equipment and for working capital to support the sales effort in the new territories. Second, the company sought capital to support expansion while the field was ripe. The consultant pointed out that the cable TV industry, while presently thriving, might reach its zenith soon. Pressure on cable operators from the rapidly growing home-satellite-receiving stations might cause them to turn to control of their own insertion spots to alleviate profit squeezes. While the SVS group verbally acquiesced to this idea, it was evident that they felt riches would be theirs long before such events occurred. Their real problem was to jump now before other firms of similar nature could begin to compete. The southeastern United States was ripe. A major portion of the cable systems in the region could be closed within two years if only sufficient capital existed! Already negotiations with two more systems were underway with excellent prospects for closure. The consultant's role was clear: Look at the statements and the pro formas and structure a package to obtain the immediate equipment financing. Following that, the consultant should concentrate on working capital and growth capital sources.

The business was fascinating and the venture sounded potentially successful. The company was already existent and profitable. The principal owner, Thomas Robson, had been successful in the past and had recruited knowledgeable people to do the work: a technician who appears well-qualified and provides a thorough explanation of his function, and a marketer who seems proficient although a bit abrasive. Robson, who is suave and intelligent, also has controlling interest and is therefore able to make decisions for the group without question. The management team appears well-qualified and has had successful business experience in the past. But there are problems!

The company needs an immediate $80,000 to pay for equipment, which has already been ordered and delivered. The company had been counting on a lease for this equipment from a local bank which had provided leases for the previous equipment. The lease request had been declined. The company followed that failure with a loan request from another local bank. That request was also declined. These failures were disconcerting. Most bankers should be willing to extend loans when they are so fully collateralized. The equipment will have to be returned within a few days if payment is not forthcoming. An additional $20,000 is needed to provide working capital for the exploitation of the new markets. The reason for calling in a consultant is now clear.

Because of a recent real-estate recession, the principal owner had lost considerable business and personal funds. Robson was no longer considered the strong credit risk he once was by the local banks. The remaining owners did not have sufficient personal worth to stand for so large a loan. The initial lease had been approved principally on Robson's remaining worth. He was required to guarantee the transaction personally. Robson's worth was insufficient to support additional extensions.

The need for expansion was immediate. While rapid expansion may frequently be considered a negative attribute to a new venture, the nature of this particular industry was such that if expansion is not rapid, competitors will flood the field. SVS has been fortunate in being there first. To maintain their momentum, they must continue to penetrate the market. If the momentum is lost, competition will effectively constrain the company to a local enterprise and destroy the owners' dreams of growth. Present plans call for solicitation of the cable systems surrounding existing service areas in an ever-widening circle. SVS would like to bring a new cable system on line each month from August 1984 through the end of 1985.

However, rapid expansion—even when desired—brings with it problems. SVS was concerned about its reputation in its outlying market areas because of a problem with a recently hired salesperson. The person was promising the moon and delivering air. After learning of the salesman's techniques, the company immediately terminated him. SVS did attempt to deliver on the salesman's promises at some financial loss. Increasing numbers of competent supervisors will be required as well as capable technical and sales people if growth is to be beneficial. In addition, if growth is to be funded by debt, then new markets must be able to service that debt.

Exhibit 25.7 contains pro forma income statements for the remainder of

PRO FORMA INCOME STATEMENT

Exhibit 25.7

	May 1, 1984 to December 31, 1984	*January 1, 1985 to April 25, 1985*
Income		
Advertising income, N.C.	$316,000	$ 661,000
Production income, N.C.	6,320	13,220
Advertising income, S.C.	327,000	763,000
Production income, S.C.	7,875	21,000
Total income	657,195	1,458,220
Cost of revenue		
N.C. cablevision system fees	53,700	134,800
N.C. equipment lease expense	14,760	22,140
N.C. sales commissions	41,960	115,920
S.C. cablevision system fees	49,968	40,052
S.C. equipment lease expense	17,280	28,800
S.C. sales commissions	93,290	225,085
Total Cost of Revenue	270,958	566,797
Gross profit	386,237	891,423
General and administrative expenses		
N.C. salaries, payroll tax and fringes	75,667	131,562
S.C. salaries, payroll tax and fringes	49,800	89,729
Travel and entertainment, N.C.	19,600	30,000
Travel and entertainment, S.C.	3,300	6,600
Rent, N.C.	11,000	16,500
Rent, S.C.	4,900	7,200
N.C. automobile expense	4,808	7,812
S.C. automobile expense	5,250	10,200
Other expense, N.C.	23,509	37,980
Other expense, S.C.	20,312	38,304
Total Expenses	218,146	375,887
Operating profit	168,091	515,536

NOTES: 1. Depreciation expenses have been omitted from the pro forma statements. 2. Income taxes have been omitted from the pro forma statements. Sufficient loss carry-forwards and investment tax credits exist to effectively eliminate income tax liability for the year 1984. Tax liability will exist for 1985 if the forecast for 1984 is accurate.

1984 and for all of 1985. These statements were prepared by the management of the firm and were presented to the consultant for evaluation. The statements were prepared assuming no new cable systems. The forecasts reflect a utilization factor in the South Carolina systems of 20% in the early months of 1984, growing to 50% by the end of the year. The North Carolina systems are presently at a utilization level of 50%, and predictions for the rest of 1984 involve selling up to a maximum of 80% of the potential commercial insertion spots available. The 1985 forecasts for North Carolina reflect the 80% utilization maximum, with the South Carolina systems expected to grow to the 80% level by the end of 1985. Expenses are based on budget preparations by the management. The statements assume that the new equipment has been obtained by lease.

The consultant is expected to study the financial statements and pro formas and to draw conclusions about Southeastern Video Services, Inc., the validity of its forecasts, and its prospects for success.

Case 26

SOUTHERN CABINET COMPANY

Timothy M. Singleton/Robert McGlashan/Mike Harris

Mike Norris leaned back in his chair and stared alternately between the computer screen spreadsheet and the view through the front window of his suburban home. The view out the window was only a blur, however, as Mike's attention and energy were focused on the information in front of him on the screen. The numbers represented a profit-cost-volume analysis of Southern Cabinet Company (SCC), a manufacturer of kitchen and bathroom cabinets located in a large metropolitan area in the Sunbelt. The President and Chairman of the Board of the small firm was Mike's father-in-law, Bill Martin. Mike and Bill had often discussed the business over the years when convenience and time permitted. Mike's interest was now more serious, however, as he was considering an offer by Bill to go to work in the business. Mike was a recent MBA graduate while Bill's formal education did not extend beyond high school. But they were both impressed that they often came to the same conclusions regarding various aspects of the business despite different analytical approaches and perspectives.

Southern Cabinet Company was founded in 1956 by Bill Martin, the current President and Chairman of the Board. In the early days, there were times when Bill was literally the only employee of the company. By 1984 there were 32 people in the shop and six full-time office personnel, including Bill's wife Laura. SCC builds kitchen and bathroom cabinets for new residential construction only, including townhouses and condominiums. Several characteristics of SCC are believed to make it unique with respect to the competition:

This case was prepared by Prof. Timothy M. Singleton, Prof. Robert McGlashan, and Mike Harris of the University of Houston-Clear Lake as a basis for class discussion. This case was presented at the Case Research Association Meeting, 1984. Distributed by the Case Research Association.

1. The product, although not strictly a custom cabinet, is of better quality than that built by its major competitors.
2. The price of SCC's products is slightly higher than the competition.
3. SCC is smaller (sales volume) than its competitors.
4. SCC builds a wider variety of cabinet sizes and types than its competitors, with over 800 unique pieces.
5. SCC does not carry a finished goods inventory, that is, cabinets are manufactured after they are ordered by the customer.

RECENT BUSINESS HISTORY

The nature of SCC's operations in the past four years changed rather dramatically. (See Exhibits 26.1 and 26.2.) Even with relatively good economic fortune in many areas of the Sunbelt, many builders and SCC's competitors were hurt badly due to a combination of high interest rates and heavy debt. In contrast, SCC had its best years ever during the early 1980s recession. Operations provided the cash flow to support an increase in sales, and the computer acquired in 1980 made it possible to handle the additional administrative and management burden necessary to support increased volume.

PLANT OPERATIONS

SCC manufactures cabinets with three different wood finishes, although all contain certain common wood products for the shelves and back. The manufacturing process begins after an order has been received, the dimensions of the kitchen at the construction site have been carefully measured, and the order placed on a schedule. A list of individual pieces (cabinets) which make up an order is produced by the sales department using a detailed hand drawing of the installation site. This list is entered into a computer program, and "cutting lists" are output from the computer and given to various departments in the plant. These lists describe the parts that must be cut to satisfy a particular job order which may contain several work orders. For example, a job may entail building cabinets for several kitchens.

Although there are many steps in the assembly-line-like manufacturing procedure, there are a few key steps which give one a feel for the process. There are six major departments. One cuts the parts for the face frame, the frame that fits to the front of the body of the cabinet. A second department, the Cutting Department, cuts parts for the body of the cabinet. Some of the cut parts require more finishing in the Sanding Department before they are gathered in one location so that an audit can be made to verify that all the parts necessary for completion of the work order have been produced. The collection of parts is then moved to the Assembly Department. The cabinets are assembled with staple guns and glue, and the Hardware Department installs the drawer guides and doors. The assembled cabinets are then placed on a dolly and moved to the Paint Department. After staining and finishing, cabinets are stacked until the customer can take delivery.

Exhibit 26.1
BALANCE SHEET
(Fiscal Year Begins October 1)

(In dollars)	1979	1980	1981	1982	1983	1984 Year to Date April 30
ASSETS						
Current assets						
Cash	53,314	152,524	236,391	277,507	264,094	308,489
Accounts receivable	221,582	160,568	213,671	175,917	248,592	238,887
Merchandise inventory (doors and hardware)	121,419	116,902	180,070	180,886	195,020	214,635
Prepaid expenses	12,789	22,341	20,040	19,044	22,333	23,440
Total	409,104	452,335	650,172	653,354	730,039	785,451
Fixed assets (net)						
Land & building	—	—	—	—	90,941	153,508
Office furniture	3,359	16,915	13,126	25,088	32,695	28,646
Plant equipment	18,662	17,360	22,386	22,490	16,926	15,528
Auto equipment	7,406	47,709	39,215	32,063	21,477	14,766
Other	467	1,582	500	5,000	—	—
Total	29,894	83,566	75,227	84,641	162,039	212,448
Other assets (Including prepaid tax)	1,710	54,027	10,321	24,331	563	45,055
TOTAL ASSETS	440,708	589,928	735,720	762,326	892,641	1,042,954
LIABILITIES						
Current liabilities						
Accounts payable	76,718	34,282	36,993	30,759	31,824	34,898
Notes payable	35,164	15,281	13,677	13,229	6,745	6,196
Accrued wages, sales commissions, and salary bonuses	46,879	77,995	113,800	74,720	92,935	9,705
Other	6,859	57,523	29,472	12,859	18,768	11,182
Total current liabilities	165,620	185,081	193,942	131,567	150,272	61,981
Long-term liabilities	594	28,518	15,235	2,804	—	—
NET WORTH						
Capital stock	14,590	14,590	14,590	15,000	15,000	15,000
Treasury stock	—	—	—	410	410	410
Capital surplus	28	28	28	28	28	28
Retained earnings	162,448	256,183	358,096	460,449	548,926	724,404
Net profit, year to date	97,428	105,528	153,829	152,068	178,005	241,131
Total	274,494	376,329	526,543	627,955	742,369	980,973
TOTAL LIABILITIES AND NET WORTH	440,708	589,928	735,720	762,326	892,641	1,042,954

Exhibit 26.2
INCOME STATEMENTS

(In Dollars)	1979	1980	1981	1982	1983	1984 *Year to date* *April* 30, 1984
Sales	1,541,133	1,414,931	1,913,990	1,914,553	1,967,429	1,514,975
Cost of sales	1,195,531	998,568	1,304,707	1,414,781	1,393,861	1,059,338
Gross profit	345,602	416,363	609,283	499,772	573,568	455,637
Operating expenses						
Office and administration	143,262	116,075	138,489	181,542	208,178	134,016
Selling and advertising	48,551	48,092	60,935	62,306	76,023	59,214
Delivery expense	55,585	42,907	63,082	60,101	47,651	36,321
Total operating expense	247,398	207,074	262,506	303,949	331,852	229,551
Net profit from operations	98,204	209,289	346,777	195,823	241,716	226,086
Installation Income (Exp)	(776)	415	2,344	1,455	1,371	3,669
Other Administrative Income	8,341	7,017	8,819	24,153	19,128	11,377
Net operating profit	105,769	216,721	357,940	221,431	262,215	241,132
Incentive bonuses*	16,694	68,090	112,111	69,362	84,210	—
Net profit for federal taxes	89,075	148,631	245,829	152,069	178,005	241,132
Provision for federal taxes	15,911	43,101	91,998	47,871	59,986	—
Net profit after taxes	73,164	105,530	153,831	104,198	118,019	241,132

* Office personnel bonuses based on net operating profit.

All the manufacturing processes are relatively simple tasks, and with the exception of painting, require no special skills. Most of the labor is unskilled, and from time to time workers are able to be shifted from one job to another if a worker quits or is ill. Many of the workers in the plant have been with the company over ten years, and a few for over twenty years. Though the average pay is about $6.50 an hour, all workers in the plant participate in a piece count bonus program on a weekly basis. Starting at 500 pieces, the entire crew receives extra pay for each piece produced. The incremental pay for each piece increases gradually for each 100 pieces up to 1,000. For 1,000 pieces and up, the incremental pay per piece is constant. Mike has noted in looking over the past few months production and pay statistics that the unit labor cost decreases despite the bonus pay until production reaches around 800 to 900 pieces per week. At that point, overtime pay expense begins to be incurred which offsets the benefits of increased volume, and unit labor costs begin to increase. The increase in pay at 1,000 pieces, not counting overtime, is $100 per week per employee if the employee has perfect attendance for the week.

CAN'T LIVE WITH 'EM, BUT CAN'T LIVE WITHOUT 'EM

Like most small companies that have been initiated to the uses of microcomputers and minicomputers, SCC has had its share of problems. Overall, however, SCC has benefited significantly from the use of first a microcomputer and now its Texas Instruments minicomputer. The primary use continues to be the creation of "cutting lists" for use in the plant as mentioned previously. The accounting system has gradually been placed on the computer over the past year with limited success. The accounting package was built from scratch by Linda Sharp's assistant, Bud Melman, who happens to have extensive programming experience but little actual accounting experience. In fact, Bud took a course in accounting to facilitate the program development. Most of the "bugs" seem to be out of the system at this point, though occasional problems still occur which lead Laura to have little confidence in the system. A further potential problem with the software is that it is written in a language called TPL which is unique to Texas Instruments systems, and consequently the average programmer who has developed business software has never heard of TPL. This makes it much more difficult to modify the software when necessary than if it were written in a more common language. In addition, TPL is not an easy language to use in "database" development, a feature that usually makes business software development much easier. Mike has also noticed that the current software is not documented. There is no explanation within the code the programmer had developed to facilitate a subsequent programmer's attempts to modify the current software. SCC's latest system, however, does have a new operating system with the ability to run COBOL, a common computer language used in business. SCC has currently invested about $50,000 in computer hardware and software in the past four years. The question now is what to do about the current software, particularly the accounting software.

KEY PEOPLE AT SCC

If entrepreneurs tend to "march to their own drummer," Bill Martin is no exception. He was born in a small Southern town in 1920. Despite being brought up in what some call a "Bible Belt" region, Bill did not care much for the local religion. He developed an interest in other religious philosophies through the years, as well as an interest in movies and film making. Bill still has color film of Hawaii that he took during the Second World War when he was stationed at Hickam Field. He was learning to fly B-17s when the Japanese attacked in 1941, and later piloted a B-17 with the 8th Air Force over Germany. In the past ten years, he has produced two full-length films of the homemade variety, and if not for the demands of the business, which he also continues to enjoy, Bill would gladly spend more time with the movie equipment and other hobbies.

Bill had acquired experience in the construction industry while he was growing up and decided to start his own business, motivated primarily by a desire to be his own boss rather than to make a lot of money. Bill runs the company in what most would consider a very relaxed manner, and with an "open door" policy. If he ever gets very excited about anything, he disguises it well. Most people would probably describe him as patient and deliberate. Bill is not at all impulsive, and likes to mull things over carefully before making decisions—a habit that for the most part seems to have served him well.

Laura Martin, Bill's wife of forty-three years, handles the accounting and office administration. Laura seems to enjoy the work as much as Bill and often serves as a sounding board for office and plant employees who discuss business as well as personal matters. Laura is from Bill's home town, and left home after high school to marry Bill in Hawaii in 1941.

Harry Wood, 42, holds the title of VP of Sales, and has been with the company for over ten years. He has an assistant, but Harry does all the direct selling to the customer. Harry has a knack for satisfying the customer before and after the sale, and an excellent ability to qualify potential customers. Bad debts were less than one-half of 1% of sales in 1983.

Linda Sharp, 32, serves as an administrative assistant to Bill and Laura. Linda does a little of everything, and through the years has gradually assumed more and more administrative responsibility around the office. She has consistently done a good job and demonstrated talent in many areas, including public relations. Harry has even mentioned that he would like to have her in sales. Linda now has an assistant, but she still often handles the front desk and other general office duties such as answering the phone. Linda has been with the company for eight years, and she and Harry are considered to be loyal and invaluable employees.

The key people in the plant have been with the company over twenty-five years. Jim Mayo, 70, manages the materials flow and performs maintenance on most of the plant equipment. Despite his age, Jim seems to have more energy than almost anyone in the plant. Oscar Wyatt, 58, is general shop foreman and supervises the lead people in the plant who oversee the six departments.

Mike Norris, 34, has worked for six years as a senior systems engineer for an aircraft simulator manufacturer and has a Masters degree in Mathematics as well as the MBA. Mike's previous experience around construction has been limited to part time work for a painting contractor during summers when he was an undergraduate student. His recent experience is primarily in software design of various aircraft systems, and he has approximately three years' experience as a department supervisor with fifteen people. In this capacity, his duties included customer contact, report generation, planning, hiring new employees, and employee evaluation. He began the MBA program at a local university primarily as a diversion from the normal day to day activities and because he felt it was a good use of his extra time. As he began to accumulate hours in the business program, he began to think more seriously about changing careers and going to work for Southern Cabinets.

RECENT DEVELOPMENTS

Sales have been growing steadily over the years, with the last five years sales history shown in the operating statements in Exhibit 26.2. Though sales leveled off in 1983, projected sales for the current fiscal year are around $2.5 million. The average price per piece in 1983 was around $63, with a volume of 31,000 pieces. With a lack of space to store the finished product a recurring problem, Bill sees this as a hindrance to increasing sales much beyond current levels. Though the customer takes delivery fairly soon after the order is completed, more sales mean more product to store at one time, and this can be particularly troublesome during winter if the weather is bad and the customer cannot take delivery readily. Bill leases space on a monthly basis to help alleviate this problem. This leads to increases in fixed as well as variable costs that need to be carefully analyzed. Recent cost of the leased storage space was $1,000 per month. This high level of business is a new experience for SCC, and it has not been necessary until recently to give these problems close attention.

The lease on the current building has increased dramatically over the past two years from $3,500 to $5,600 per month, and the current lease runs out within six months. Seeing these problems coming on, Bill bought three acres of land near the present building a little over a year ago for $90,000 with the intention of eventually building his own facility. Architectural and engineering plans have been completed, bringing the total current investment to $150,000. The cost of the new building is estimated at around $800,000, down from about $1 million in the original estimate. In addition to solving the problems with space (the new building plans show an increase of 40% in floor space) Bill has plans for a conveyor in the new building that will more efficiently transfer the assembled products to the paint department, and greatly simplify the paint department operations. Materials handling and storage, scheduling, and a myriad of other problems would also be alleviated with the extra space in the shop. A 40% increase in floor space will also satisfy a need for increased office space. The computer, which is housed in a 6 foot tall cabinet, and a printer currently occupy a space of less than 75 square feet that also serves as a coffee room and lunch time gathering place for plant employees who use a microwave oven in the same room. In addition, all employees also share two restrooms that are located in the office portion of the building. Bill will have to borrow heavily to finance the new building and feels he ought to hold on to as much cash as possible to provide a safe level of working capital necessary to support current or increased sales levels. The monthly payment on the new building with a thirty-year loan is expected to be around $10,000. Bill has not borrowed any money for about three years and has not aggressively sought a loan, but he foresees no serious problem in getting the money. His major concern is whether to actually go ahead with the building at the present time. Business for the current year could produce an increase in profit from operations of around 100% with an increase in sales volume of 25%. Prospects for the next fiscal year are considerably more uncertain, with many economists predicting a downturn in housing starts. Complicating the decision are strong indications that the land Bill purchased for the building may have tripled in value due to rapid development of surrounding property. The land may be worth more in the long run without a building on the property.

In past years, Bill has often wished the company had the financial and physical capacity to carry some finished inventory. He has always considered this a very risky business, however, due to the fact that it would require more debt than he wanted or could carry, or because of the space limitations mentioned previously. The average material cost in a piece in 1983 was about $24 out of a total variable cost per piece of around $32. The $32 includes variable selling and administrative costs as well as manufacturing costs. Bill's work force is rather stable throughout the year despite rather wide fluctuations in production, and Mike compiled these cost figures assuming direct labor as a fixed cost. Clearly, it would not be possible to carry inventory on every cabinet. A decision would have to be made about which cabinets to build for the finished goods inventory. Complicating this decision is the fact that SCC uses several types of paint finishes on the cabinets, which would seem to make it impractical to actually store the cabinets in a completely finished condition. A considerable portion of the assembled cabinets, however, are shipped without paint finishing.

Several factors intrigued Mike about leasing extra space as a temporary measure rather than building a new facility, as well as possibly carrying some finished goods inventory:

1. Harry Wood has indicated that if the price of the product was a little more in line with the competition, sales could increase significantly.
2. The current work force, which in 1984 has shown the capacity to produce 60% over the average 1983 monthly production, might be more efficiently utilized by spreading the work more evenly over the year, decreasing the level at peak activity with the potential of increasing overall production.
3. It appears that profit from operations could increase substantially with only a moderate increase in sales volume from current levels.
4. Customer uncertainty concerning SCC's ability to provide the product quickly and reliably would be reduced.

Mike is uncertain about the desirability of financing extra inventory for other reasons:

1. A more sophisticated inventory control system would have to be implemented, possibly affecting current computer software needs.
2. Sales volume across the industry is highly dependent on swings in the economy, and it might be difficult to avoid getting stuck with unwanted inventory.
3. The sudden growth in the level of operations is beginning to strain the administrative capacity of management.

The current successful profit picture may indicate SCC should only seek to maintain current sales level while the entire organization adjusts to the growth in the level of operations—adopt a temporary philosophy of "if it ain't broke, don't fix it." If operations continue to produce similar results over the next year or two, the financial flexibility of the company will be greatly enhanced.

TO SELL OR NOT TO SELL

On a recent trip to the plant, Mike was asked by Bill to sit in on a meeting between Bill and Charlie White, a local business broker. Charlie had in the past discussed with Bill the possibility of selling the business. Though Bill was not considering the idea seriously, he liked Charlie, and was interested in what he had to say about the value of the business. In particular, on this day, Charlie was bringing some figures that he had analyzed with the help of a "young man" with a degree in finance. Mike had done his own analysis, and was interested that Charlie had valued the business from the point of view of projected cash flow as well as current asset value. Mike's figures closely matched Charlie's in measuring the estimated present value of cash flow. There was apparently an interested buyer who had seen the last five years operating statements and had ideas about continuing the cabinet operation as well as using the equipment for other purposes. Though the tax consequences for Bill of a sale had not been analyzed, the amount mentioned was sufficient enough to provide Bill and Laura with a comfortable retirement. The figure mentioned did not include the current cash in the business, which Bill would keep, nor did it allow for the appreciation of the land Bill had purchased the year before. Bill and Laura, however, feel they would have a hard time being comfortable with the retired life. Laura has often said the business "keeps us young." Furthermore, they are naturally concerned about the fate of some of the people in the plant who have been loyal to them for almost three decades.

WHAT'S NEXT?

Bill Martin wants to continue operating SCC for several years. He currently sees SCC as being on the threshold of becoming a much larger company if some of the opportunities and obstacles described above are handled skillfully. Though there seem to be strong indications that SCC may have found a niche in the market with builders who seek to put extra quality in their homes, the size and stability of this market are uncertain. Meanwhile, Bill and Laura have the feeling that a company must change and grow to remain viable.

Case 27

THE CRAFT COTTAGE

Wayne H. Decker/Thomas R. Miller

In late 1979 Fred Randall[1] was puzzled about what he should do. He had been considering the possibility of expanding his arts, crafts, prints, and picture framing business through purchase of the Frame Shoppe and/or Jefferson City Art and Frame, two local firms in the business district of the city. If he acquired either of these firms, he knew he would need to secure management personnel to operate the new units for him. He anticipated continuing to manage his present store, the Craft Cottage, regardless of the decision to acquire the other firms. As he reflected, he thought the prospect of financing the acquisitions really bothered him less than the thought of managing these units. After all, he realized he had some problems to solve in just operating the Craft Cottage, as small as it was. The business had not generated a profit in its first four years and probably would not this year. And wouldn't the expansion of his business result in more headaches? But, on the other hand, maybe this was a unique opportunity that he should not forego. He wondered . . .

BACKGROUND

The Craft Cottage is a small store in Jefferson City, a small southeastern city located about 35 miles from a major metropolitan center. Jefferson City has about 30,000 residents and is the county seat of Jefferson County, which has a population of nearly 80,000. Jefferson County is one of the fastest growing counties in the state, having increased an estimated 30% in population from 1970 to 1979. The major types of industries in the area are manufacturing, retailing, and agriculture. Manufacturing employs more workers than any other type of industry, providing about one-third of the employment in the

This case was prepared by Prof. Wayne H. Decker and Prof. Thomas R. Miller of Memphis State University as a basis for class discussion. This case was presented at the Case Research Association Meeting, 1982. Distributed by the Case Research Association.

county. The average income for the county exceeds the statewide average.

Educational and cultural activities are quite prevalent in the Jefferson City area. The city is the home of Chancellor State University, which has over 10,000 students and over 400 faculty members. The presence of Chancellor State contributes to the educational level of the area population, which is substantially higher than the statewide average. The county and city feature several historical sites which are not only tourist attractions but also sources of civic pride. Also located in the community are many antique shops, a community theater, and an outdoor amphitheater.

Mr. and Mrs. Fred Randall established the Craft Cottage by converting their garage into a store and adding a woodworking shop to the back of their home. Their home is located on a corner lot about one mile from Chancellor State and one block from a four-lane state highway, which links the Chancellor State area with several shopping and industrial areas. The Randalls' neighbors are primarily educators and other professionals whose homes are well-kept, modern houses built among mature trees.

The Craft Cottage opened in October 1975, although inventory accumulation began during the preceding summer. Mr. Randall stated that he had started the business more for enjoyment than for money. Products initially offered were hand-made crafts, tole-painting[2] supplies, and tole-painting lessons. In fact, the business originally centered around his wife's skills in teaching tole painting. However, Mr. Randall has stated that he "did not want to have all his eggs in one basket." He felt he needed to diversify in case his wife's health were to prevent her from continuing in an active role in the business. Recently an increased emphasis has been placed on the sale of original prints[3] and picture framing. While the store has prints that are quite inexpensive, most of the prints stocked are in the $150 range. Tole painting is still a major part of the business, but hand-made crafts are being deemphasized.

OPERATIONS

Craft Cottage has six employees: Mr. and Mrs. Randall and four part-time workers. Mr. Randall, a retired military officer, also teaches half time in the Industrial Studies Department of Chancellor State University and has turned down an offer of full-time employment at the university. He also has completed all work except the dissertation toward a doctoral degree in health, physical education, and recreation. Mrs. Randall had earlier received her doctorate in the teaching of English from the university.

In discussing his employee situation, Mr. Randall has expressed the view that "it is difficult to get good help." His part-time employees engage in various activities, including bookkeeping, woodworking, matting and framing, cleaning, and yard work. The bookkeeper is a doctoral candidate in history who has had no formal training in bookkeeping. She works no regular hours but works at her convenience. Two of the other employees are also university students.

From his observations of customers, Mr. Randall has identified his primary market as educators' families and families of other professionals, in particular, middle-class women in the 25–35 age range. Mr. Randall believes women who buy prints do so more for the appearance of the print than for its investment value. While not located in a business district, the Craft Cottage is close to many of its customers' residences or routes that they travel for other reasons. The store has an appeal to customers because of its informal "non-commercial" atmosphere and environment. Mr. Randall views word-of-mouth and direct mail as his most effective forms of advertising. The latter consists of a full-color newsletter published by a print distributor, which carries the name of the Craft Cottage on each issue. It is distributed about every two months chiefly to people who have previously been in the shop. In addition to the daily newspapers and local radio, advertising has included high school and campus papers and the Yellow Pages telephone directory. In the Yellow Pages, the Craft Cottage is listed under "Picture Frames—Dealers," "Art Galleries and Dealers" and "Art Goods." Although several of its competitors use display ads, the Craft Cottage is listed in the smallest type. However, Mr. Randall plans to drop his listings next year, since he believes they are not effective and that people call and ask for "stupid things."

Those products not made in the shop at the Craft Cottage are generally purchased from distributors. However, Mr. Randall has also obtained some goods from vendors on a consignment basis. Prices at the Craft Cottage tend to be lower than those of the larger shops located in the Jefferson City business district. Mr. Randall sets his prices according to his costs for an item and attributes his lower prices to lower overhead.

Mr. Randall stated that upon starting the business his goals were to generate sales of $1,000 per month within three years and to break even within five years. His current goal is to increase annual gross sales to $20,000 by the seventh year of operation. A balance sheet for all years of operations is presented in Exhibit 27.1 and an income statement appears in Exhibit 27.2. The figures for the first nine months of 1979 are not exact because depreciation has not been taken off, nor has the amount of inventory sold been deducted.

The bookkeeper does not have access to the file system, nor does she send out statements. She pays bills as they are given to her by Mr. Randall. Frequently, purchase discounts are missed because invoices are misplaced. Another aspect of the bookkeeper's job is to match sales tickets with the appropriate listings in the inventory book. Since the items in inventory are not

Exhibit 27.1
BALANCE SHEET FOR YEARS 1975–1979
(Year ends December 31; 1979 data as of September 30)

	1979	1978	1977	1976	1975
ASSETS					
Current assets					
Cash	98.10	572.39	221.49	89.62	484.26
Accounts receivable	85.09	569.31	708.32	—	59.36
Supplies, selling	906.83	382.97	323.37	279.04	309.65
Supplies, manufacturing	8,949.60	4,812.96	4,276.69	3,330.96	1,983.72
Merchandise	41,406.00	16,351.98	8,111.43	4,083.12	2,759.85
Total Current Assets	51,445.62	22,689.61	13,641.30	7,782.74	5,596.84
Fixed assets					
Delivery equipment	400.00	400.00	163.00	245.00	367.00
Store equipment	1,803.22	1,487.81	977.64	802.73	795.04
Office equipment	1,181.31	784.92	357.60	347.97	266.85
Manufacturing equipment	9,053.70	7,595.40	5,591.33	2,999.74	2,334.44
Building	7,969.05	7,016.98	5,566.27	5,575.42	4,502.70
Total Fixed Assets	20,407.28	17,285.11	12,655.84	9,970.86	8,266.03
TOTAL ASSETS	71,852.90	39,974.72	26,297.14	17,753.60	13,862.87
LIABILITIES AND CAPITAL					
Current liabilities					
Accounts payable	93.55	399.85	1,048.61	757.51	680.11
Sales tax payable	60.24	137.94	79.68	46.04	35.81
Total Current Liabilities	153.79	537.79	1,128.29	803.55	715.92
Capital	71,699.11	39,436.93	25,168.85	16,948.05	13,146.95
TOTAL LIABILITIES AND CAPITAL	71,852.90	39,974.72	26,297.14	17,751.60	13,862.87

numbered, it may take the bookkeeper fifteen to twenty minutes to find a 50-cent item in the book. Descriptions and prices on sales tickets often do not match those in the inventory book and many items get into inventory without being listed in the book. The bookkeeper sees no record of items that are on consignment.

No sales-by-product or sales-by-month breakdowns are available. Although he has not done any monthly analysis, Mr. Randall is relatively certain that July and August are his slowest months. Sales on credit are given on

Exhibit 27.2

INCOME STATEMENT FOR YEARS 1975–1978

	1978	1977	1976	1975
Revenues				
Sales	11,227.82	10,583.95	3,200.33	1,162.44
Miscellaneous revenues	11.73	10.22	3.09	.37
Total	11,239.55	10,594.17	3,203.42	1,162.81
Cost of goods sold	7,622.93	5,937.69	1,488.58	461.36
Gross profit	3,616.62	4,656.48	1,714.84	701.45
Operating expenses				
Salaries	625.25	267.75	214.50	18.00
Supplies	2,029.68	1,110.27	1,048.92	331.71
Rent	628.14	628.08	628.08	336.38
Depreciation	1,909.48	1,274.57	930.79	797.34
Trips	854.66	424.67	1,085.98	699.65
Utilities/taxes	594.36	541.05	402.34	200.98
Miscellaneous expenses	3,706.97	3,189.29	2,603.13	1,663.44
Total	10,348.54	7,435.68	6,913.74	4,077.50
Net income (loss)	(6,731.92)	(2,779.20)	(5,198.90)	(3,376.05)

a relatively informal basis and only to persons known well by the Randalls. There are no set policies on the amounts of down payments for monthly installments. However, a 1% per month finance charge is applied after three or four months.

Most of the recent inventory growth consists of acquisitions of prints. Almost every room in the house contains stacks of prints. In fact, Mrs. Randall has expressed concern over the amount of money now invested in prints. According to Mr. Randall, there have been "no conscious decisions" guiding inventory levels. Purchasing has been determined mainly by his feelings that there are shortages of particular kinds of prints (e.g., subjects or artists).

COMPETITION

Mr. Randall views his major competition to be the Frame Shoppe, the apparent leader in sales of prints in Jefferson City. The other major picture frame business in town is Jefferson City Art and Frame. Mr. Randall has stated that both of the above businesses would like for him to buy them out. He believes that these establishments would be more suitable outlets for print sales than the Craft Cottage.

The Frame Shoppe owner wants about $125,000 for his business, $35,000–$40,000 of which Mr. Randall estimates to be for goodwill. The owner of the Frame Shoppe estimated his annual gross sales as over $100,000 and his inventory turnover to be 2.0 times. The business is located in a leased building in downtown Jefferson City. Mr. Randall would be willing to lease the building for a year, but then he would want to buy another. He believes a proprietor should generally own his building unless located in a shopping center.

Mr. Randall estimates that Jefferson City Art and Frame could be purchased for $35,000–$40,000. In addition the owners are asking $300,000 for their building, which is located at the edge of the city on a heavily traveled and commercialized state highway and adjacent to a proposed loop around the city. Jefferson City Art and Frame's annual sales are reported to be about $80,000 with an inventory turnover of 2.5 to 3.0 times.

NOTES

1. Names of persons and places are disguised.
2. Decorative painting or lacquering of metalware popular in the eighteenth century and reproduced today for trays, lamps, etc.
3. The Print Council of America considers a print original when the "artist alone" has created the image on the copper plate, stone, wood block, or other medium from which the print is produced and the finished product is approved by the artist. However, many dealers and curators do not feel the artist has to do the above entirely alone for the print to be considered original.

Case 28

THE THERMOMETER CORPORATION OF AMERICA: DIVISION OF FIGGIE INTERNATIONAL, INC.

Ken Burger/Per Jenster/Henry Odell

INTRODUCTION

It is late November 1982, and Harry Figgie, Jr., Chairman of Figgie International, and Joe Skadra, Group Vice President and Treasurer, are meeting in the company's new headquarters complex in Richmond, Virginia. Figgie International (FI) is a diversified company which has forty different businesses ranging from fire engines to clothing. Included in these businesses is the manufacture of thermometers, which is conducted under the name of Thermometer Corporation of America (TCA). The TCA plant is located in Springfield, Ohio, a city of 86,000 in the middle western part of the state.

FI recently received a proposal from Ohio Thermometer Co. (OTC) dated November 17, 1982 and entitled "An Analysis of a Merger and Future Between TCA and OTC" (Exhibit 28.1). The proposal was presented by Charles L. Wappner and Jerome P. Bennett, President and Vice President, respectively (and co-owners), of OTC. OTC is a competitor in the thermometer business and is also located in Springfield, Ohio. The meeting between

This case was prepared by Profs. Ken Burger, Per Jenster, and Henry Odell of the McIntire School of Commerce, University of Virginia. This case was used in the fourth McIntire Case Competition (MCI IV) held at the University of Virginia on February 9–11, 1985. We gratefully acknowledge the General Electric Foundation for support of the MCI and the writing of this case. This case also appeared in the *Case Research Journal, 1985,* pp. 123–155.

AN ANALYSIS OF A MERGER AND FUTURE
BETWEEN TCA AND OTC
(Presented to Harry E. Figgie, Jr.
By Jerome P. Bennett and Charles L. Wappner
November 17, 1982)

Exhibit 28.1

We at Ohio Thermometer are of the opinion that our company's growth is tied to the economy. When times are good, sales are good and when times are bad, sales drop. The reason is our product base. Ohio Thermometer is very weak in the inexpensive category, kitchen or cooking category and almost nonexistent in the gift and decorator field. Without these three areas it is impossible for us to replace another thermometer company. We don't have the necessary capital to tool for all of these areas, hence our need for TCA's products. We feel, as competitors to TCA, that they have the same problems in the housewares field, only more severe. They have been unable to come up with a dial that is competitive with Ohio's; consequently they have no ammunition to replace any other company. Companies such as TCA are being replaced by Springfield or Taylor. Ohio Thermometer is, however, not being replaced mainly because everybody has to have our dials. We can't see TCA making much movement in the housewares industry because of the above problems. We feel TCA is also tied to the economy in this particular area.

In other areas of thermometry Ohio Thermometer has the advertising thermometer business locked up. This is an area that's up and expanding and profitable. TCA is in the auto field and scientific area, which are areas that we don't get into, so we really don't know how they are doing in those areas. They also have a gourmet thermometer line that we feel has tremendous potential, but they lack the customer base that we have. If they had our customer base, those items could perform miracles. In addition to the mentioned areas, Ohio has the Detroit automobile business under control, in our pocket, and we are the dominant people in the poultry industry.

Put the two companies together and you wind up with the most balanced thermometer company in the country. Together the companies would be the answer to many of our customers' problems. Most purchasing agents at this time want to cut down the list of vendors. In the thermometer field, if you talk to them, they say they must carry Taylor because of their name, and they must have Ohio because of their dials. Most have Springfield and they usually have a fourth vendor, which is either Chaney, Cooper or TCA, but very, very seldom do they ever have a fifth vendor, so they take their pick between one of the three, either Chaney, Cooper or TCA. With a combined company, TCA and Ohio, we certainly would be in a position to eliminate the fourth vendor and very possibly eliminate the third vendor. I am not too sure that, at certain areas, you couldn't really take a good shot at Taylor. We know Chaney's and Cooper's customers and we know their weaknesses and we know their strengths. I think a com-

(*Continued*)

Exhibit 28.1
(*Continued*)

bined company would have a field day or a Marianna's turkey shoot in the foreseeable future.

Looking at both sides, if Ohio could buy TCA, and I might add we have tried to do this in 1973, at this point it would probably stretch our finances. We feel that our borrowing would be somewhere close to $1,000,-000. This would cover our current borrowing, allow $500,000 to be paid to Figgie International, with the rest going toward working capital. We would have to have some other type of financing for the remainder of the purchase price of TCA, and pay these off over a number of years. Could we get this financing? Questionable.

If Figgie International takes over Ohio these problems are eliminated and with Kiefer running a lean operation, we see immediate profits and probably large profits.

I, personally, feel that by taking the best sales reps from Ohio and the best sales reps from TCA and combining them—figures don't lie—we would have one of the strongest sales operations in the thermometer field. I feel that because of our contacts and our personal relationships with all of our customers, we would keep all of them and be able to expand the entire base thermometer business. In addition, we sell to almost all of TCA's housewares accounts, so I can't see where we would lose any of that business. Quite frankly, with the two companies, the housewares end of the business would be a bonanza to the customers, at the same time solving their problems of too many vendors.

Our four or five year sales forecast would be in the $10 million plus range. Even if the economy didn't bounce back, we could still project many inroads in the thermometer business, and even if the economy stays as it is today, we would project a 10% to 15% to 20% sales increase per year. Again, with these sales and with the idea of running a lean company, there would be enough profit to go into the thermometer business with new items in depth. We look at weather stations that Taylor sells in the $300 to $400 range and it makes our mouths water. We sell to the same accounts that they sell to, only we can't compete with them, as we don't have the product.

Lastly, whether together or separately, both TCA and Ohio are going to have to get into the electronics area. Obviously TCA would have the jump on us, because they could use other Figgie operations. However, individually, we doubt that they would have the necessary profits to make the expenditures to do this.

A HAPPY MARRIAGE!

INTANGIBLES THAT OHIO HAS TO SELL:

1. *DIAL THERMOMETER BUSINESS*
   Making TCA the major factor in the dial thermometer business with $2,750,000 in existing business, this is the heart of the thermometer business today.

Exhibit 28.1
(Continued)

2. *ADVERTISING THERMOMETER BUSINESS*
   This would make TCA the major and dominant supplier in the advertising and point of sale thermometer business with $550,000 of existing business. Ohio now supplies almost all of the major corporations with their advertising thermometer needs, controlling an estimated 95% of this business.
3. *INDUSTRIAL AND SPECIAL PRODUCTS*
   This would make TCA the dominant company in the automobile thermometer business and the major supplier of thermometers and instruments to the poultry industry, both in the United States and Canada.
4. *CUSTOMER BASE*
   Ohio now has a very broad base of customers because all major accounts carry Ohio dials. The list of Ohio's customers is attached. This would automatically expose all TCA products to the major discounters, distributors, department and variety stores, hardware chains, drug chains, food chains, and catalog and catalog showrooms.
5. *OHIO EXPERTISE IN THERMOMETER BUSINESS*
   Ohio Thermometer is about to start its fiftieth year in the thermometer business. Over the years we have consistently ranked number one or two with Taylor Instrument in accuracy and quality, according to past published consumer reports.
6. *SALES OPERATION*
   In looking over our customer base, it should be obvious that Ohio has the dominant sales rep organization between the two companies. In addition, Bennett and Reeder know the buyers on a first name basis at the major accounts such as K-Mart, Sears, Penney's, etc. We feel this will automatically prevent the loss of customers and would actually increase the thermometer base. Almost all accounts that Ohio now sells are TCA's accounts, which would add to protecting our business.

Figgie and Skadra was arranged to discuss the November 17 proposal. The conversation begins as follows:

FIGGIE: As you know, I met with Charlie [Wappner] and Jerry [Bennett] on November 17th at their request. At this meeting they presented their proposal, which calls for Figgie [International] to purchase OTC.

SKADRA: As I recall, they [OTC] had tried to acquire TCA from us back in 1978.

FIGGIE: Yes, at that time we felt that the growth potential for TCA was too good to consider divesting. I have kept in touch with Charlie and Jerry since then, so their proposal was not a complete surprise.

SKADRA: How did the meeting go?

FIGGIE: The atmosphere was very friendly. I pointed out as best I could that, while we regard ourselves as a good parent company to work with, a number of changes would have to be made if we assimilated OTC. I am sure from the comments they made that they understand this and would be willing to work with us.

SKADRA: Living and working in the same community, they must know Bill Kiefer [TCA President].

FIGGIE: They know him and apparently have considerable respect for him and for his abilities as a manager, as do we. In the proposal they specifically refer to his [Kiefer's] "running a lean operation." This tells me that if a merger of TCA and OTC were to take place, they would be willing to accept Kiefer as their leader.

SKADRA: In terms of return on investment TCA has been one of our top businesses (until recently).

FIGGIE: True enough, but we have not been able to get the sales growth we had hoped for. Bill [Kiefer] has on several occasions asked me for help in acquiring businesses that would help us expand the thermometer business and help him in getting that growth.

SKADRA: I remember looking at a couple that just couldn't be justified.

FIGGIE: Despite the recent decline in sales at TCA I still think it has potential, and I don't want to consider selling it. We have a proven manager in Bill and a good operation. We are not fully utilizing the managerial capabilities of Bill and his team.

SKADRA: The proposal indicates a number of possible synergies that might be realized by combining the two operations.

FIGGIE: Yes, and I also keep thinking about that idle manufacturing plant we have in Springfield which is now being used for storage.

SKADRA: As I recall that plant has 65,000 square feet on the floor.

FIGGIE: Charlie said that their present plant has 100,000 square feet on one floor. Apparently it is not being fully used now. Charlie and Jerry own it personally.

SKADRA: From a quick look at the figures, their asking price of $1,500,000 (Exhibit 28.2) seems very high. I would like to take a closer look at the whole situation, especially the financial aspect.

FIGGIE: I agree. Let's analyze the offer from a strategic and financial standpoint, looking at all the angles.

SKADRA: Since both TCA and OTC have had declining sales and profits in the last couple of years, I think we should pay special attention to costs.

Background

In late 1963, Harry E. Figgie, Jr., acquired the controlling interest in "Automatic" Sprinkler Corporation of America, a family-owned firm with sales of $22 million. Harry Figgie recalls:

On January 2, 1964, I drove 90 miles to Youngstown, Ohio, to take over a company I'd never seen. Their top officer said to me, "You've got to be the dumbest man alive." I said, "I'm the second dumbest. You sold it!"

Since then, H. H. Figgie, Jr. and his executive team have expanded the corporation to a multidivisional firm with sales of $770 million in 1981. This growth came through an aggressive acquisition phase to obtain what Mr. Figgie saw as a "critical mass" of $300 million in annual sales. To do this, he applied a management concept of a lean organization with a small, highly mobile corporate staff. According to Harry Figgie:

In those days, it was not uncommon for the team to look over as many as fifty companies a month. In one rush of buying (in 1967), they closed five deals in just twenty-five days.

PROPOSED TERMS OF SALE OF ASSETS OF OHIO THERMOMETER TO FIGGIE INTERNATIONAL

Exhibit 28.2

	Net Sound Value
Lloyd-Thomas Appraised Values May 31, 1982	
Machinery	$ 555,985
Furniture and fixtures	135,361
Office furniture and fixtures	39,921
Office machines	19,808
Industrial power trucks	10,758
Dies*	213,473
Tools and trucks*	4,000
	979,306
Inventories—complete—at cost—September 30, 1982 values	513,740
Total value	$1,493,046

Acceptable terms:

1. $1,493,000 cash at closing or at your option: $500,000 cash at closing and balance in acceptable securities or notes.
2. Jerry Bennett and Charles Wappner would agree to stay for at least two years.
3. We would agree to lease our 100,000 sq. ft. factory and office building to Figgie International for two years at $5,000 per month on a net net basis.
4. Our NCR 8271 computer system is leased from U.S. Leasing. There are thirty months remaining at a rental of $1,672 per month. We would agree to transfer this lease to Figgie International if desired.

* Owners' valuation.

This strategic phase ended in 1970, after Figgie had acquired more than fifty new divisions. Among these acquisitions was Mid-Con, Inc., a minor conglomerate which consisted of a number of smaller companies in the Ohio Valley, one of which was the Thermometer Corporation of America. Most of the other small firms obtained in this particular acquisition have been divested since then.

During the next ten years the company grew from $356 million in sales to $770 million with 99% internal growth. Harry Figgie recalls:

> Such growth was not without problems as we chewed up working capital and sent our debt-to-equity ratio up to 1.36 to 1 [1979].

In 1981, the company changed its name to Figgie International, Inc. and prepared itself for a new period of aggressive growth. As the recession hit the company in 1982 and overall sales dropped 8% (est.), cost reduction (Harry Figgie's forte) became the number-one priority in 1982 (Balance Sheet and Income Statement Data, Exhibit 28.3).

Organization

Figgie International is organizationally divided into five groups: Consumer, Fire Protection/Safety, Machinery, Technical, and Service. The contribution by group is as follows:

***Business Group* (1982)**	***Sales***	***Profits***
Consumer	18%	8%
Fire protection/safety	43%	41%
Machinery and products	19%	−6%
Technical	19%	21%
Services	1%	36%

NOTE: Sales to the U.S. Government accounted for an estimated 21% of the total in 1982.

- The Consumer Group includes Rawlings sporting goods (baseballs, baseball gloves, basketballs, footballs, golf clubs, and related equipment), Adirondack baseball bats, Fred Perry sportswear (tennis clothing and other sportswear), home fire alarms, vacuum cleaners, and thermometers (TCA).
- The Fire Protection/Safety Group consists of custom-made fire engines, sprinkler systems, chemical fire extinguishers, aerial-type water delivery systems for fire-fighting apparatus, protective breathing equipment, and security systems and equipment.
- The Machinery and Products Group encompasses capping, sorting and sealing machinery, high-speed automatic bottling equipment, road-building and maintenance equipment, hydraulic pumps, vibrating road rollers, material-handling systems, battery-powered vehicles, and mortar and concrete mixers.

Exhibit 28.3

FIGGIE INTERNATIONAL, INC.: BALANCE SHEET AND INCOME STATEMENT DATA

Income Data (Millions of Dollars)

Year Ended Dec. 31	Revs.	Oper. Inc.	% Oper. Inc. of Revs	Cap. Exp.	Depr.	Int. Exp.	Net Bef. Taxes	Eff. Tax Rate	Net Inc.	% Net Inc. of Revs.
1982[1]	708	51.0	7.2%	31.9	14.9	21.4	38.6	32.4%	26.1	3.7%
1981[2,3]	770	72.3	9.4%	28.1	14.5	22.2	48.1	46.6%	25.7	3.3%
1980[2]	760	65.2	8.6%	22.4	13.8	23.6	40.3	48.8%	20.6	2.7%
1979	691	62.0	9.0%	24.0	16.1	21.3	33.8	48.0%	17.6	2.5%
1978	628	52.4	8.3%	29.1	12.9	16.8	30.4	49.0%	15.5	2.5%
1977	568	40.5	7.1%	34.4	9.7	12.5	21.8	47.1%	11.5	2.0%
1976	518	41.4	8.0%	12.7	8.1	9.5	25.7	48.7%	13.1	2.5%
1975	480	40.2	8.4%	13.5	7.7	9.9	23.7	48.2%	12.2	2.5%
1974	476	41.1	8.6%	14.8	6.6	13.3	22.9	48.6%	11.2	2.4%

Balance Sheet Data (Millions of Dollars)

Dec. 31	Cash	Current Assets	Current Liab.	Current Ratio	Total Assets	Ret. on Assets	Long-Term Debt	Common Equity	Total Cap.	% LT Debt of Cap.	Ret. on Equity
1982[1]	15.6	268	111	2.4	465	5.5%	122	164	343	35.7%	15.9%
1981	6.8	298	131	2.3	475	5.4%	127	146	335	37.8%	17.6%
1980	10.6	318	141	2.3	485	4.3%	140	128	335	41.7%	15.7%
1979	7.0	316	143	2.2	478	3.8%	145	111	326	44.5%	15.2%
1978	9.8	285	111	2.6	436	3.8%	154	98	315	48.7%	14.7%
1977	9.2	256	108	2.4	376	3.5%	117	90	260	45.0%	11.5%
1976	8.8	217	63	3.4	312	4.3%	110	88	244	45.0%	13.8%
1975	15.2	213	63	3.4	300	4.0%	112	79	232	48.2%	13.9%
1974	14.8	228	80	2.9	309	3.8%	113	72	224	50.6%	14.1%

NOTES: 1. Estimated. 2. Reflects acquisitions. 3. Reflects accounting change.

- The Technical Products Group consists primarily of aircraft and missile components, aircraft display instruments and armament control systems, telemetry and electronic instrumentation systems, and electronic access control and monitoring systems.
- The Service Group includes sales financing, computer software, real estate, and natural resources investments.

Future Plans

In a recent interview in *The Craftsman,* an internal publication of FI, Harry Figgie discussed his ambitious plan of growth for the future. The plan entails a new phase of acquisitions that will build on the company's present nucleus groups. The goals for the future include:

- Further reduce the company's debt-to-equity ratio.
- Top $1 billion in sales and start building toward $2 billion through an aggressive acquisition program.
- Continue to emphasize internal consolidation, bringing the minimum divisional size up to $25 million in sales.
- Pursue high technology and bring robotics and CAE/CAD/CAM into the workplace by adapting new techniques and strategies.
- Remain faithful to the company's commitment of producing quality products at competitive prices.

Harry E. Figgie, Jr. and His Management Philosophy

Most people would probably say that Harry Figgie was well prepared when he took over the small, troubled Automatic Sprinkler Corp. in 1964. After earning his BS in metallurgical engineering at Case Institute of Technology, Harry Figgie earned an MBA at Harvard Business School, a JD at Cleveland Marshall Law School, and a MS in industrial engineering at Case. Later, as a partner with Booz, Allen & Hamilton, a management consulting firm, Harry Figgie was exposed to a wide range of business situations in smaller and medium-size firms. The experience he gained in management consulting as well as in his capacity as chairman and chief operating officer of Figgie International has made him known as one of the foremost cost-reduction authorities in the world. In his book, *The Cost Reduction and Profit Improvement Handbook,* he stresses the importance of a lean organization:

> The first point to remember about the concept of cost reduction is that it can be used interchangeably with the term "profit improvement." If profit improvement is the glass of water half full, then cost reduction is the glass half empty [p. 1] . . . As will be demonstrated, a 10% reduction in costs can increase profits by 25% to 50%, or more if the savings can be preserved . . . [p. 3].

Harry Figgie's management concept also places responsibility for profit-making decisions at the basic profit center level, that is, the division president. Accordingly, each president has "entrepreneurial" control of his division's profit and growth performance. He reports to a group vice-president, who in turn, reports directly to Figgie. One subdivision president comments:

> I have full responsibility for my division, but will receive help from corporate headquarters if I ask. And you'd better ask before the trouble arrives; they [corporate headquarters] don't like surprises. . . . Figgie International is our banker and advisor.

Management Systems

Cash is managed centrally at Figgie International, and divisions submit all receivable collections to headquarters. Conversely, cash for payables is sent to divisions upon request. Corporate capital and headquarters expenses are paid for in two ways: "payment for debt services" (assets less certain liabilities at cost of capital rate [Beta = 1.10]), and "incremental costs of working capital" which are charged at slightly over prime for changes in working capital calculated on a monthly basis.

The capital budgeting procedure runs parallel to the allocation of working capital. Here, a division manager can make discretionary decisions up to $1,000, and a group vice-president up to $5,000. All other capital investments must be encompassed in the budget or submitted for Harry Figgie's approval.

Planning is also an integral part of the management process. In line with the management philosophy of keeping things simple, divisional presidents present with their group officer the annual business plan between October 1 and November 30 to Harry Figgie and the corporate staff. The plan includes a detailed budget for the coming year and a summary for the following four years. As one corporate officer noted: "Three things can happen to a plan at the annual meeting, and two are not good." Operational performance (actual) and a rolling five-month forecast are reported by divisions on a monthly basis.

The reward system is a central part of the management system at Figgie International and is highly integrated with the planning and budgeting process. It is particularly worth mentioning that the division presidents receive bonuses based on their achievement of pretax return on sales (50%) and pretax return on assets (50%).

OPERATIONS OF TCA AND OTC

Operations of TCA

The operations of TCA are in a 35,000 square foot, two-story plant in the southern part of the city of Springfield. The office consists of 2,500 square feet on the second floor. A wide variety of thermometer products is manufactured, including scientific houseware products. The main manufacturing processes are as follows:

1. The blowing of glass tubes to modify them by adding bulbs, joining tubes of different diameters, etc. Standard lathes have been customized so that the glass tubes can be heated and rotated as the blowing takes place.
2. Etching of glass tubes is needed to provide the degree markings for the scientific and other special use thermometers. The tubes are coated with wax and a special machine forms slits through which acid can reach the glass surface.
3. Calibration of the thermometer requires the right combination of tube bore and bulb size, amount of liquid enclosed (mercury or alcohol-based), and degree marking (etched on the glass or printed on an enclosure in the tube or on a mounting). The operators work with controlled temperature baths and make the adjustments.

Since the operations do not lend themselves to automation, the machines require full-time operators to load each piece and perform the operation. Considerable manual skills are required, especially in the glass-blowing. Most operations with the glass require it to be in a heated semimolten state so that the machines usually have heating attachments, some of which have been designed by TCA.

Many of the machines are "dedicated," that is, they are set up for a particular operation and are not changed. As a result these machines remain idle for much of the time; they are typically older machines but are deemed to be as effective as newer models. The plant is operating at 40% of capacity. About 50% of the total cost of sales is raw materials and purchased parts.

There are thirty-one hourly paid employees in the plant, most of whom are women. They belong to the United Auto Workers union. The average hourly wage rate is $4.39 plus $1.48 in fringe benefits. There has been one brief strike in recent years. The relationship between management and workers seems good; many of the employees have been with TCA for many years, and turnover is low.

Salaried workers are shown in the organization chart (Exhibit 28.4). A manual accounting system is used, which Mr. Kiefer considers adequate for generating needed information for his operating purposes and for the required reports to FI headquarters. He indicated that he would want to study the situation very carefully and find just the right hardware before shifting to computerization.

Financial information is shown in Exhibits 28.5, 28.6, 28.7, and 28.8.

Operations of OTC

OTC is located in a one-story, 100,000-square-foot building in Springfield. The plant is about 5 miles from the TCA plant. The current operation

THERMOMETER CORPORATION OF AMERICA
ORGANIZATION CHART, NOVEMBER 1982

Exhibit 28.4

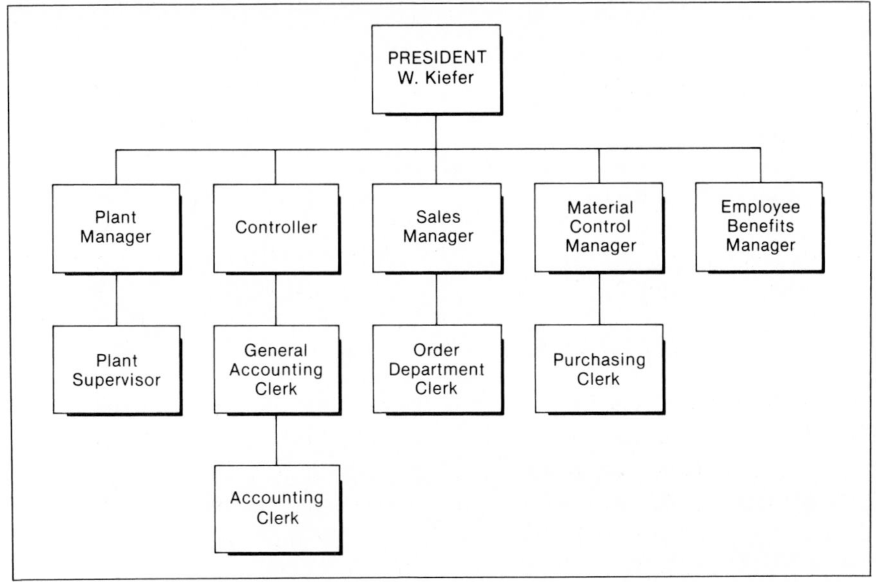

(equipment and storage) uses 60% of the floor space. The primary product is dial thermometers of 12″ and 18″ diameters. The primary parts are the coated steel dial face (which is printed with the thermometer readings and other desired backgrounds), the aluminum outer band, brass bushings and shaft, temperature indicator, clear acrylic plastic dial cover (lens), and the bimetallic coil (which moves the indicator as the temperature varies). OTC uses more durable materials than competitors. The total material purchases including raw materials and purchased parts, such as coils and indicators, are about 50% of total cost of sales.

The plant operations are divided into three areas. One area contains the punch presses which cut out the dial faces and the outer bands from sheet metal. A second area holds the printing line with various printing presses and a drying oven connected by a circular conveyor belt. The third area is where the assembly takes place. The punch presses are the only metalworking equipment used and are standard models.

There are 70 hourly paid shop employees who belong to the International Association of Machinists union. The average wage rate is $4.92 per hour. Fringe benefits are $1.60 per hour. The work in the plant is not highly skilled. As shown in Exhibit 28.9 the plant has five supervisors.

OTC has an art department which generates a wide variety of advertising

Exhibit 28.5

THERMOMETER CORPORATION OF AMERICA: COMPARATIVE BALANCE SHEETS AT DECEMBER 31, 1981, 1980, AND 1979

	1981	1980	1979
ASSETS			
Current assets			
Cash	$ (27,000)	$ —	$ —
Accounts receivable (net)	162,000	211,000	193,000
Inventory	869,000	642,000	638,000
Prepaid expenses	6,000	2,000	1,000
Total current assets	$1,010,000	$ 855,000	$ 832,000
Property and equipment			
Land	9,000	9,000	9,000
Machinery and equipment	1,192,000	1,176,000	1,164,000
Total	$1,201,000	$1,185,000	$1,173,000
Less: Accumulated depreciation	1,088,000	1,072,000	1,046,000
Total property and equipment	$ 113,000	$ 113,000	$ 127,000
Other assets			
Patents	36,000	42,000	47,000
Other assets	1,000	1,000	1,000
Total other assets	$ 37,000	$ 43,000	$ 48,000
Total assets	$1,160,000	$1,011,000	$1,007,000
LIABILITIES & STOCKHOLDERS' EQUITY			
Current liabilities			
Accounts payable	$ 100,000	78,000	23,000
Unpaid withheld taxes	33,000	30,000	25,000
Accrued expenses	225,000	186,000	165,000
Total current liabilities	$ 358,000	294,000	213,000
Long-term debt	—	—	—
Total liabilities	$ 358,000	294,000	213,000
Stockholders' equity			
Original investment	151,000	151,000	151,000
Retained earnings	1,121,000	1,015,000	93,000
Intra-company current	(470,000)	(449,000)	550,000
Total stockholders' equity	$ 802,000	$ 717,000	$ 794,000
Total liabilities and stockholders' equity	$1,160,000	$1,011,000	$1,007,000

THERMOMETER CORPORATION OF AMERICA: COMPARATIVE INCOME STATEMENTS FOR THE YEARS ENDED DECEMBER 31, 1981, 1980, AND 1979

Exhibit 28.6

	1981	1980	1979
Net sales	$1,677,000	$1,730,000	$1,762,000
Cost of sales	1,096,000	1,193,000	1,220,000
Gross profit	581,000	537,000	542,000
Operating expenses			
Selling	134,000	123,000	124,000
Administrative	172,000	153,000	160,000
Debt service	72,000	80,000	78,000
Other	7,000	(3,000)	8,000
Total operating expenses	385,000	353,000	370,000
Income (loss) from operations	196,000	184,000	172,000
Provision for income taxes	90,000	85,000	79,000
Net income (loss)	$ 160,000	$ 99,000	$ 93,000

for printing on the dial face. The equipment provides photographic and silk screening capabilities.

Exhibit 28.9 shows twenty-three salaried employees, including the three officers, Charlie Wappner (President), Jerry Bennett (Vice-President, Sales), and V. Bennett (Secretary). V. Bennett is Wappner's sister and Bennett's wife and fills the position of secretary on a part-time basis at a salary of $3,000 annually. Aside from these corporate officers the average annual salaries are as follows:

Managers and engineers	$25,000
Supervisors, technicians, and artists	$18,000
Clerks, computer operators, and secretaries	$14,000

Fringe benefits are about 35% of salaries.

The NCR 8271 computer (leased) is used for accounting, inventory, and production control. It has far larger capabilities than are needed for the operation.

Financial information is shown in Exhibits 28.10, 28.11, 28.12, and 28.13. Sales and profits since the fiscal year end on June 30 (1982) are off about 10% from the prior year's pace.

Exhibit 28.7

THERMOMETER CORPORATION OF AMERICA: SCHEDULE OF COST OF GOODS SOLD FOR THE YEAR ENDED DECEMBER 31, 1981

	1981
Materials	$ 467,992
Direct labor	211,066
Manufacturing expenses	
Indirect labor	$ 60,497
Supervision	59,760
Vacation and holiday	39,996
Payroll taxes	42,439
Industrial welfare	550
Employees' insurance	43,534
Supplies	32,110
Maintenance and repairs	10,269
Truck	5,896
Freight	41,816
Utilities	49,161
Depreciation	12,352
Insurance	39,450
Taxes	—
Scrap	17,584
Travel	221
Rentals	17,018
Miscellaneous	—
	$ 472,653
Burden (absorbed)	(363,601)
Burden from inventory	307,593
Total cost of goods manufactured	$ 416,645
Decrease in finished goods inventory	—
Cost of goods sold	$1,095,703

THERMOMETER CORPORATION OF AMERICA: SCHEDULE OF SELLING AND ADMINISTRATIVE EXPENSES FOR THE YEAR ENDED DECEMBER 31, 1981

Exhibit 28.8

	1981
Selling expenses	
Salaries	$ 9,586
Commissions	61,295
Travel	715
Advertising	31,172
Samples	2,917
Telephone	4,037
Show expense	20,460
Payroll taxes	899
Depreciation	2,439
Supplies	131
Miscellaneous	—
	$133,651
Administrative expenses	
Salaries	$110,443
Payroll taxes	9,301
Pension	11,000
Travel	4,278
Office supplies	3,892
Telephone	2,422
Legal and professional	2,800
Depreciation	1,595
Dues and subscriptions	3,572
Insurance	1,274
Bank charges	4,106
Contributions	914
Data processing	4,238
Rent—autos	3,643
Amortization patents	5,700
Bad debt expense	3,000
Miscellaneous	386
	$172,554

Exhibit 28.9
OHIO THERMOMETER ORGANIZATION CHART, NOVEMBER 1982

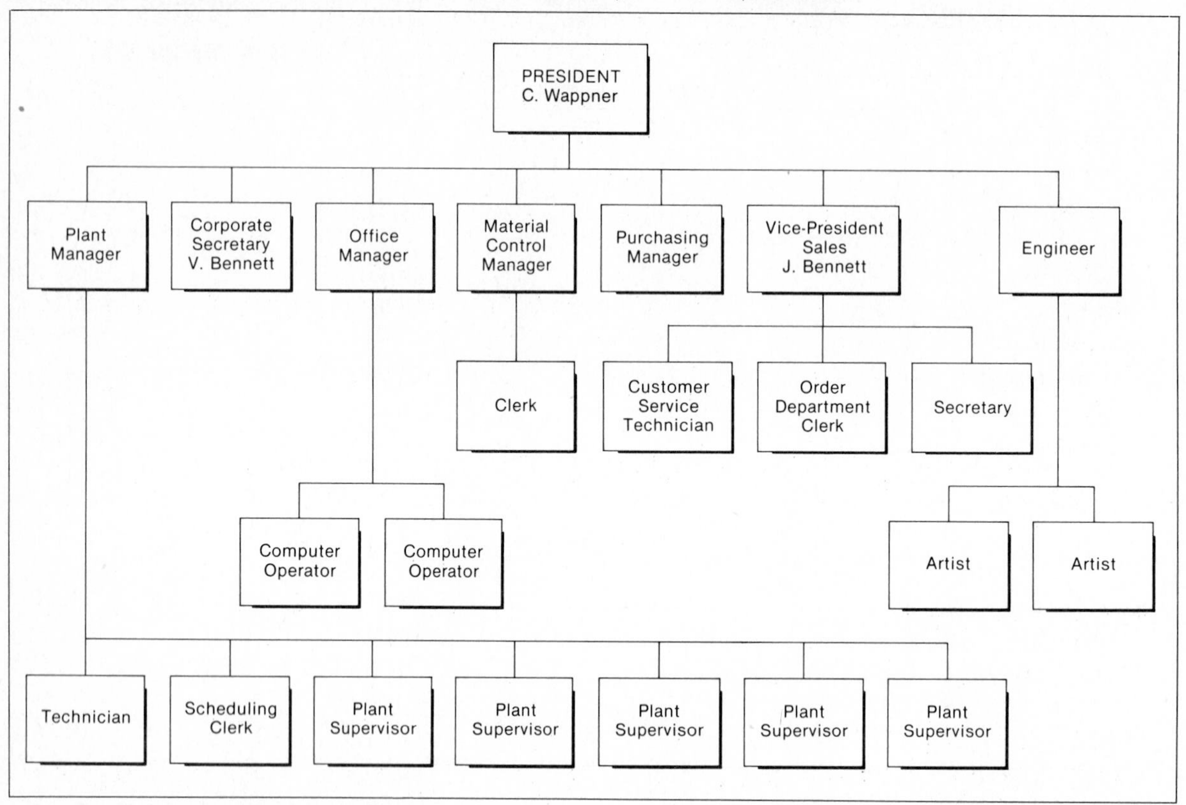

THE THERMOMETER INDUSTRY

Market Structure

In the early 1980s, the thermometer industry was composed of two major segments: the consumer market and the industrial market. While TCA maintained an interest in both, OTC was focused predominantly in the consumer segment, especially the weather components of that market which comprised over 80% of their total thermometer sales.

Marketing information for the industrial sector is generally not available on a per company basis or by type of thermometer instrument. This situation is due to the fact that the production of thermometers in most companies is but a small part of a huge product line of all types of recorders, gauges and instruments. Therefore, it is virtually impossible to isolate meaningful information on the industrial market.

Therefore, the majority of information will focus on the competitive activities within the consumer market. The product lines in this market include weather, houseware/decorator, cooking, and a miscellaneous line which includes medical, automobile, and other small uses of thermometers. The total

Exhibit 28.10

THE OHIO THERMOMETER COMPANY: COMPARATIVE BALANCE SHEETS AT JUNE 30, 1982, 1981, 1980, 1979, AND 1978

	1982	1981	1980	1979	1978
Current assets					
Cash	$ 7,939	$ 4,934	$ 4,330	$ —	$ —
Federal income tax refundable	—	55,216	90,546	—	—
Accounts receivable (net)	247,087	282,055	339,342	559,238	481,374
Inventory	626,796	708,409	853,579	903,762	795,181
Prepaid expenses	24,513	20,808	19,737	45,392	23,552
Total current assets	$ 906,305	$1,071,422	$1,307,534	$1,508,392	$1,300,607
Property and equipment					
Land	51,851	51,851	51,851	51,851	51,851
Building	308,418	308,418	308,418	308,418	308,418
Machinery and equipment	380,362	356,235	353,300	320,180	281,792
Trucks	9,518	9,518	9,518	9,518	9,518
Furniture	97,717	87,570	86,480	85,320	83,790
Total	$ 847,866	$ 813,592	$ 809,567	$ 775,287	$ 735,369
Less: Accumulated depreciation	691,896	663,478	635,337	610,816	577,634
Total property and equipment	$ 155,970	$ 150,114	$ 174,230	$ 164,471	$ 157,735
Other assets					
Cash value life insurance	21,860	21,679	109,958	135,833	135,833
Advances to employees	1,544	12,912	10,635	—	—
Deposits on leased equipment	1,202	2,220	2,220	5,256	5,410
Total other assets	$ 24,606	$ 36,811	$ 122,813	$ 141,089	$ 141,243
Total assets	$1,086,881	$1,258,347	$1,604,577	$1,814,452	$1,599,585
Current liabilities					
Notes payable	$ 300,000	$ 175,000	$ 185,000	$ 175,000	$ 85,000
Current maturities on L-T debt	9,993	10,290	8,728	5,753	5,255
Accounts payable	418,671	519,981	418,566	506,937	450,094
Accrued expenses	73,390	67,136	83,414	106,679	132,510
Total current liabilities	$ 902,054	$ 772,407	$ 698,708	$ 794,369	$ 672,859
Long-term debt	20,473	53,374	159,173	187,464	196,197
Total liabilities	$ 822,527	$ 825,781	$ 854,881	$ 981,833	$ 869,056
Stockholders' equity					
Common stock	250,000	250,000	250,000	250,000	250,000
Retained earnings	111,634	279,844	596,976	679,899	577,809
Less: Treasury stock	97,280	97,280	97,280	97,280	97,280
Total stockholders' equity	$ 264,354	$ 432,466	$ 749,696	$ 832,619	$ 730,529
Total liabilities and stockholders' equity	$1,086,881	$1,258,347	$1,604,577	$1,814,452	$1,599,585

Exhibit 28.11

THE OHIO THERMOMETER COMPANY: COMPARATIVE INCOME STATEMENTS FOR THE YEARS ENDED JUNE 30, 1982, 1981, 1980, 1979, AND 1978

	1982	1981	1980	1979	1978
Net sales	$3,654,311	$3,649,931	$4,286,345	$4,735,234	$4,367,128
Cost of sales	2,788,718	2,882,232	3,337,012	3,538,663	3,248,270
Gross profit	865,593	767,699	949,333	1,196,571	1,118,858
Operating expenses					
Selling	513,136	593,627	654,647	615,489	525,870
Administrative	441,451	472,730	435,530	422,065	334,121
Interest	63,317	56,546	40,668	30,706	18,461
Bad debts	15,206	15,241	—	—	—
Other	—	—	(4,976)	(4,474)	41,950
Total operating expenses	1,033,110	1,138,144	1,125,869	1,063,786	920,402
Income (loss) from operations	(167,517)	(370,445)	(176,536)	132,785	198,456
Provision for income taxes	—	—	—	30,000	78,000
Tax benefit of net oper. loss carry-backs	—	54,010	70,546	—	—
Net income (loss) before special items	(167,517)	(316,435)	(105,990)	102,785	120,456
Insurance proceeds on deceased officer	—	—	23,762	—	—
Net income (loss)	$ (167,517)	$ (316,435)	$ (82,228)	$ 102,785	$ 120,456

market for thermometers (consumer and industrial) was estimated at $100 million in 1982. This total market is expected to expand between 10% and 20% annually. This estimate does not distinguish between consumer and industrial markets.

Market Conditions

The sale of consumer thermometer lines generally fluctuates with the economy (see Exhibit 28.14). A number of items within the decorator line, for example, are positioned as gift ideas, and sales correspond to the general consumer buying mood, especially during holidays.

Products within all categories range from low-price, mainly discount items to high-quality, high-price specialty items. Most of the seven major competitors within the consumer market have at least one strong product which acts as the anchor for the rest of their lines.

Distribution of consumer thermometer products is generally accom-

THE OHIO THERMOMETER COMPANY: SCHEDULES OF COST OF GOODS SOLD FOR THE YEARS ENDED JUNE 30, 1982, AND 1981

Exhibit 28.12

	1982	1981
Materials	$1,423,055	$1,462,728
Direct labor	$ 513,231	$ 555,098
Manufacturing expenses		
Indirect labor	$ 63,303	$ 59,041
Production office	3,157	4,034
Engineers	41,780	41,984
Supervision	120,874	112,258
Vacation and holiday	88,482	91,659
Retirement	29,372	33,198
Payroll taxes	81,298	87,391
Industrial welfare	210	2,527
Employees' insurance	109,956	94,604
Supplies	104,784	106,549
Maintenance and repairs	66,883	69,858
Truck	2,645	2,780
Freight	16,465	17,090
Utilities	58,373	50,676
Depreciation—building	9,850	9,850
Depreciation—other	14,918	11,312
Insurance	5,125	7,234
Taxes	5,616	5,788
Dues and subscriptions	420	1,148
Travel	222	267
Rent	490	442
Miscellaneous	2,236	2,187
	$ 826,459	$ 811,877
Total cost of goods manufactured	$2,762,745	$2,829,703
Decrease in finished goods inventory	25,973	52,529
Cost of goods sold	$2,788,718	$2,882,232

Exhibit 28.13

THE OHIO THERMOMETER COMPANY: SCHEDULES OF SELLING AND ADMINISTRATIVE EXPENSES FOR THE YEARS ENDED JUNE 30, 1982, AND 1981

	1982	1981
Selling expenses		
Salaries	$135,936	$157,883
Commissions	159,211	202,616
Travel	18,088	23,873
Advertising	20,662	15,219
Prospect	10	32
Samples	3,657	6,392
Freight	167,595	179,743
Telephone	5,818	4,780
Dues and subscriptions	2,159	3,089
	$513,136	$593,627
Administrative expenses		
Executive salaries	$ 99,611	$ 88,299
Office salaries	124,401	126,898
Payroll taxes	36,584	24,862
Executive pension	28,293	60,638
Director fees	3,300	2,400
Travel	9,139	4,625
Postage	5,872	6,132
Office supplies	30,610	50,332
Telephone	8,109	7,194
Legal and professional	19,077	19,133
Depreciation	3,649	6,980
Dues and subscriptions	2,056	2,354
Insurance	17,007	14,468
Life insurance on officers	10,398	8,564
Contributions	3,520	753
Taxes	15,458	21,961
Rent—computer	20,064	20,064
Rent—autos	4,303	7,073
	$441,451	$472,730

Exhibit 28.14
ECONOMIC INDICES

Title	*Unit of Measure*	*Fourth Quarter 1982*	*October 1982*	*Est. of November 1982*	*Est. of December 1982*	*Average* 1980	*Average* 1981	*Average* 1982 (*Est.*)
Twelve leading indicators	1967=100	131.4	130.6	130.8	132.8	131.2	133.3	128.4
Four coincident indicators	do.	128.3	128.5	128.3	128.2	140.3	141.3	132.2
Six lagging indicators	do.	165.1	168.4	165.0	161.9	176.8	187.7	177.4
Total unemployed	Thousands	11,839	11,576	11,906	12,036	7,448	8,080	10,678
Unemployment rate, total	Percent	10.7	10.5	10.7	10.8	7.1	7.9	9.7
New private housing units started, total	A.r., thous.	1,253	1,126	1,404	1,229	1,292	1,087	1,061
Change in business inventories, 1972 dollars	do.	(17.7)				(2.9)	8.2	(8.5)
Change in money supply	Percent	1.29	1.72	1.41	0.74	0.52	0.52	0.69
Federal funds rate	Percent	9.29	9.71	9.20	8.95	13.36	16.38	12.26
Treasury bill rate	do.	7.93	7.75	8.04	8.01	11.61	14.08	10.72
Bank notes on short-term business loans	do.	11.26				15.17	19.56	14.69
Average prime rage charged by banks	do.	11.96	12.52	11.85	11.50	15.27	18.87	14.86
Consumer prices (CPI), all items	1967=100	293.4	294.1	293.6	292.4	246.8	272.4	289.1
Producer price index (PPI), all commodities	do.	300.3	299.9	300.4	300.6	268.8	293.4	299.3

Title	*Unit of Measure*	*Average* 1979	*Average* 1980	*Average* 1981	(*Est.*) 1982	*First Quarter* 1982	*Second Quarter* 1982	*Third Quarter* 1982	*Fourth Quarter* 1982 (*Est.*)
GNP in 1972 dollars	A.r., thous.	1,483.0	1,474.0	1,502.6	1,475.5	1,470.7	1,478.4	1,481.1	1,471.7
GNP in current dollars	do.	2,413.0	2,633.1	2,937.7	3,057.5	2,995.5	3,045.2	3,088.2	3,101.3
Personal saving rate	Percent	5.2	5.8	6.4	6.5	6.6	6.7	6.9	5.8

plished through retailers of all types, including department/variety, hardware, discount, drug, grocery, and showroom and catalog stores. An example of retail outlets by type that commonly carry thermometer products is shown at Exhibit 28.15. Because of shelf space limitations and high costs of dealing with multiple vendors, most retail outlets prefer to do business with vendors who represent manufacturers that produce a wide variety of thermometers. Historically, most retailers limit the number to three or, at most, four separate vendors. Most would welcome the opportunity to reduce that number if a manufacturer could expand to include thermometers from more of the standard lines.

Competitive Situation

The largest share of the thermometer market is held by *Taylor* (30%). Not only does this company have a balanced array of products which spans all of the consumer lines; it is also strongly positioned in the industrial market. Its industrial line includes all types of sensing, recording, and control devices.

Taylor has used its expertise in the industrial sector to develop specialized, high-quality products which compete at the high end of the consumer market. Decorator units include "top-of-the-line" thermometers and hydrometers as well as recording devices for amateur meteorologists. Taylor has positioned most of its products as specialty items or heterogenous shopping good items.

Springfield holds the second largest share of the market (15%). This company concentrates on the price-sensitive consumer. It emphasizes high-volume, limited product lines, low raw material costs, and large production runs to hold down production costs. Springfield has strong positions in the weather, cooking, and decorator components of the consumer market.

Airguide has a narrow product line (6% market share). Its initial entry into the consumer market was through its compass line. Since then, the company has diversified into consumer weather thermometers. Airguide actively pursues international markets and currently imports many of its products.

Cooper maintains fourth position in the consumer market (5%). This company has products in the weather segment; however, its main strength is its line of bimetal cooking thermometers. Patents on manufacturing processes provide a competitive edge in terms of best quality combined with the lowest production costs in the industry for these types of thermometers.

OTC occupies fifth position by virtue of its strength in round dial thermometers (3.5%). Springfield has captured the low end of this segment; however, OTC produces higher quality products and has an established reputation as the most reliable name in this segment of the market. In addition, OTC has captured the market dealing in promotional and scenic display thermometers (12″ and 18″ round dial types). Its Achilles heel is the lack of

Exhibit 28.15

EXAMPLES OF RETAIL OUTLETS BY TYPE

Discounters	*Department & Variety*	*Foods*	*Distributors*
K-Mart	Sears	Certified	Dutch Peddler
Woolworth	Montgomery Ward	Kroger's	Washington
Target	Penney's	T.G. & Y.	Peyton's
G. C. Murphy	Alden's	Lucky (Ch.)	Mid States
Shopko	Hammacher-Schlemmer	Von's	Invento—H & S
Fedco	Hoffritz	Publix	Benny's
Wilson's	Mercantile	Safeway	Manor Sales
Frank's Nursery	Allied	National Tea	Edwin Jay
Hill's	Ben Franklin	Gemco	Comer-Hanby
Western Auto	Neiman-Marcus	Albertson's	Superior Merchandise
Rink's		Western Grocers	Ely
Meijer-Thrifty Acres		National Grocers	Ideal School Supply
		Lucky (L.A.)	Orchard Supply
		Super Valu	Mid States Distributing
		Spartan's	
Hardware	***Drug Stores***	***Advertising and Premium***	
American	Walgreen	General Motors	Jack Daniels
Ace	Super X	Ford	Standard Oil
Cotter-True Value	Skaggs	Coca-Cola	Firestone
Geo. Worthington—Sentry	Eckerds	Pepsi	Calverts
HWI	Rexall	Seagram's	Dupont
S & T	Cunningham	National Distributors	Cargill
Bostwick-Braun-Pro	Skillern	Seven Up	Goodrich
Clark-Siviter	Osco	Dr. Pepper	RCA
S. B. Hubbard	Fays	E. H. Lilley	Fram
Stratton-Baldwin	K & B	Monroe	Homelite
Woodward-Wight	Affiliated	R. C. Cola	Chrysler
Farwell, Ozmun, Kirk	Long's	Coors	Briggs & Stratton
Our Own Hardware	Zahn	Anderson Anco	Bolens
Coast to Coast	Kerr	Bendix	Stihl
United	McKesson	Plough	
Central	Thrifty		
	Payless		
	Catalog & Show Rooms		
E. F. Macdonald	Southern States	Gander Mountain	Bolinds
Top Value	Edmund Scientific	Sportsman's Guide	Harriet Carter
Premium Corporation	Edward Don	Gokey's	Miles Kimball
L. L. Bean	Joan Cook	Johnny Appleseed	Eastern Mountain Sports
Century	Taylor Gifts	Brookstone	Orvis Stitchery

Exhibit 28.16

RELATIVE MARKET POSITION AND BREADTH OF PRODUCT LINES

		Segments of Consumer Sector			
Company	*% of Total Thermometer Market*	*Weather*	*Houseware & Decorator*	*Cooking*	*Misc.*
Taylor	30.0	Y	Y	Y	Y
Springfield	15.0	Y	Y	Y	N
Airguide	6.0	Y	N	N	Y
Cooper	5.0	Y	Y	Y	N
OTC	3.5	Y	N	Y	Y
TCA	1.5	Y	Y	Y	Y
Chaney	1.0	Y	N	Y	N

competitive products across all parts of the consumer market. Over 80% of OTC's total thermometer sales are concentrated in their dial thermometers. They do manufacture thermometers for miscellaneous uses such as automobiles, but these areas are considered to be rather limited in terms of growth potential. OTC has, however, compensated for its lack of a wide product selection by developing one of the best vendor representative groups in the consumer thermometer industry. This network of vendor representatives provides excellent breadth and depth of reach into all retail markets.

TCA struggles in sixth place in the total consumer market (1.5%). Most of its revenues (80%) originate from weather and cooking thermometers. In addition, TCA maintains a small presence in the industrial market (15% of revenues) as well as the housewares and miscellaneous markets.

Although TCA has managed to maintain product lines which cross all consumer markets, it has failed to dominate in any of these markets. Consequently, it is experiencing low market share across the board and has no flagship product that can ultimately provide a dominant level of consumer awareness and interest in its products. TCA also appears to have somewhat weak representation in the marketplace due to its inability to develop a strong, comprehensive vendor network.

Chaney is seventh among the top competitors and is really focused in only two areas (1%). Its major strength is based on strong candy and meat thermometer products. The company does offer weather instruments but none of its weather products are well known.

Exhibit 28.16 summarizes the relative positions of each of the seven top competitors in the consumer market and indicates which segments are served by their products.

EXAMPLES OF PRODUCTS INCLUDED IN EACH OF THE PRODUCT LINES

Exhibit 28.17

Weather
- 12″ and 18″ dials—plain and decorated
- Window units
- Remote reading units
- Wall weather units
- Patio units

Houseware—decorator
- Gift lines
- Clock component
- Oven-refrigerator units

Cooking
- Meat units
- Candy units
- Thermo spoon/fork units
- Cheese/yogurt units

Miscellaneous
- Mercury units
- Car units
- Dairy and poultry units
- Laboratory/hobby units

In addition, Exhibit 28.17 provides a summary of various types of thermometers within each of the four product lines.

Distribution Channels

Most of the companies have comparable channel configurations. For example, all of the seven competing manufacturers use vendor systems in which manufacturers' reps contact all types of retail outlets.

Taylor, Springfield, and OTC have the strongest network of reps. Since most retail outlets prefer to do business with only those reps that carry broad, well-established product lines, it is difficult for the other companies to break into the retail marketplace. Thus, TCA uses a combination of manufacturers' reps and its own sales reps to maintain a stronger presence in the marketplace. Normally their sales force reps concentrate on key accounts (based on geographical location and size).

CONCLUDING DIALOGUE

The conversation between Figgie and Skadra continues:

FIGGIE: Jerry Bennett told me that he thought the addition of TCA products for his present OTC manufacturers' reps would immediately increase the rate of sales by $500,000 annually. He also thinks that within five years the combined companies would have a sales potential of $10,000,000.

SKADRA: Very optimistic! He sounds like a salesman.

FIGGIE: I had a chance later to talk with Bill Kiefer. He has concerns about working with the OTC plant personnel. He thinks they are used to doing things in their own way and may be difficult to change. And he thinks that their processes can be made more efficient.

SKADRA: Do you think we can assimilate Charlie and Jerry into TCA without losing their interest and effort?

FIGGIE: We'll have to do some thinking about that.

SKADRA: By agreeing to cut their salaries by a combined total of $72,000 per year and by agreeing to work for two years they are demonstrating support for the continuing operation.

FIGGIE: Charlie and Jerry have apparently taken title to the building in their own names and would like to rent the building to us as part of a merger.

SKADRA: With FI's vacant plant we may have an alternative to renting from them.

FIGGIE: Springfield is a small town and we have little chance of leasing the vacant plant. How much do you estimate we would have to spend for improvements to make the plant usable for manufacturing?

SKADRA: About $100,000.

FIGGIE: The possible loss carry forward does not justify assuming the risk of potential liabilities that would accompany the purchase of the stock of OTC Corporation.

There are a number of factors to consider here, Joe. Will you and your staff take a good look at the November 17th offer and prepare a complete counter proposal with supporting justification. Also I would like to have a strategy for conducting the negotiations.

Case 29

MUSE AIR CORPORATION

Robert McGlashan/Timothy M. Singleton

En route to the Love Field airport in Dallas in one of the company's planes, Michael Muse had many things on his mind. He deeply wanted his company, Muse Air Corporation, to be profitable. There was more at stake here than money; it was a matter of pride. "How could anyone have the misfortune to start an airline just a few weeks before the air traffic controllers' strike?" Michael asked his father, Lamar Muse, who was in the next seat. "It's just not possible to control everything at all times. You just have to make the best of things," Lamar responded. "Well it's time we took control again," Michael said firmly. "Let's map out our revised strategy for expansion." Lamar knew that he was going to have to review the major factors facing Muse Air to resolve things in Michael's mind.

THE AIRLINE INDUSTRY

Regulation

The major issues facing the airline industry today (April 1984) stem from its continuing struggle to adjust to the changing environment created by the Airline Deregulation Act of 1978. Under deregulation, the control of the Federal Aviation Administration (FAA) and the Civil Aeronautics Board (CAB) over airlines was drastically reduced. As controls over routes and fares were lifted, the industry faced rapidly changing market conditions in which competition increased significantly. The immediate result for the major established airlines was a dramatic drop in corporate earnings as new low-priced entrants forced price wars. The industry continues to be plagued by financial losses and excess passenger capacity. From 36 certified carriers

This case was prepared by Profs. Robert McGlashan and Timothy M. Singleton of the University of Houston—Clear Lake as a basis for class discussion. Research was prepared by Sheryl Dawson, Frederick Mullin, David Olson, and Margaret Parish, MBA students at the University of Houston—Clear Lake. This case was presented at the Case Research Association Meeting, 1984. Distributed by the Case Research Association.

prior to deregulation, the industry has mushroomed to about 125 airlines today. But the rate of failure has increased also as 28 carriers have gone out of business since 1978.

The primary long-term result of deregulation and increased competition is a stronger and more efficient industry. Overall inflation-adjusted ticket prices, because of discount fares, are now 10–20% lower than in 1974. Departures at major hub cities in 1983 were up 15.7%, and at medium hubs were up 22.5% from 1978. The number of interstate carriers has risen from thirty-six to ninety-eight with big airlines now controlling 79% of the market, versus 91% before deregulation. Although since 1978, the major carriers have reduced their work forces by 24,000 employees, nearly that many jobs have been created by the smaller airlines.

The FAA continues to exercise regulatory authority over airlines in regard to ground facilities, communication, training of pilots and other personnel, and aircraft safety. Airlines must obtain an operating certificate, subject to compliance with all regulations in these areas. Environmental regulation is also imposed to control noise and engine emissions. Local pressure groups may exert influence on airports to limit flights over certain areas in order to control noise pollution. One special regulation imposed by the International Air Transportation Competition Act of 1979 is the limitation on flights out of Love Field in Dallas. Destinations from Love Field may include locations only in the four states neighboring Texas: Arkansas, Oklahoma, New Mexico, and Louisiana.

When the CAB is dissolved on January 1, 1985, the regulatory authority over mergers and interlocking relationships will be transferred to the Justice Department, under which the FAA operates. For other businesses, this regulatory authority is the jurisdiction of the Federal Trade Commission. Other responsibilities which the CAB handles, such as selection of carriers for international route operations, have been reassigned to the Department of Transportation. Since both of these departments are in the Executive Branch, there is congressional debate as to whether sufficient control over the airline industry can be retained without the CAB or another congressional agency. Re-regulation considerations will continue to surface as the CAB deadline approaches.[1]

Air Traffic Control

Airlines are still dealing with the effects of the August 2, 1981, union strike of the Professional Air Traffic Controllers Organization (PATCO). The air controller's job is to keep airplanes moving at a safe distance from one another as they are passed along from one tower to another. As planes taxi, take off, fly and land, they stay in touch with the pilots by radio and follow their progress on radar screens. These screens display each plane's location, altitude, speed and any problems, such as two planes moving too close together. The screens are all computer-generated.

When 12,000 of the 17,000 controllers walked out at the start of the strike, the traffic control system was thrown into confusion. Under FAA emergency controls, which reduced flight frequencies, nearly 75% of the 22,000 daily flights were kept flying. All the major airlines experienced a decrease in revenues and available slots, both airport and en route, which reduced flexibility in route structuring despite deregulation. Once the initial pandemonium over the strike abated, the airlines began to tailor their operations to meet the new environment. Steps taken included grounding of the least fuel-efficient planes, concentration on the more important routes, reduction in the work force and restrictions placed on discount fares. A drop in revenue of 12% was reported by TWA and 15% by United Airlines. These figures were typical for the airline industry.

Only since October 30, 1983, has the FAA eliminated most slot restrictions, enabling airlines to determine destinations without having to negotiate and trade for landing slots. Because of continued air traffic control problems in Chicago, Los Angeles, New York and Denver airports, restrictions have not as yet been lifted in these high-density cities. The post-strike rules are slated to expire April 1, 1984, in Denver, but will remain in effect in Los Angeles until after the Olympics. Expiration of the rules in New York and Chicago has been delayed until January 1985, however, based on the FAA's assessment of air control's inability to handle unrestricted air traffic at these airports. The temporary preferential route system requires that aircraft fly specific mandatory routes to circumvent congested airspace, but the routes are often considerably longer in distance than airlines would normally fly. Costing time and fuel, these restrictions have affected airlines' cost reduction efforts, especially for the majors who serve longer hauls. It is expected that the FAA finally will eliminate the preferential route system early in 1984.[2] The future of air traffic control is enhanced by the long awaited decision to modernize the system. The FAA has embarked on a ten-year, $10 billion effort to upgrade air traffic control in order to cope with the projected 26.5% growth in aviation by the year 2000.

Cooperative Routing

The flexibility in routing brought about by deregulation has given rise to the hub and spoke system with its central exchange point. This system enables airlines to carry passengers to their final destinations without having to share revenues, as is necessary in interlining agreements. This prederegulation system of interlining is beginning to fall apart as the majors reevaluate their benefit. Under multi-lateral, open-ended agreements which have created an integrated national air transportation system, the major airlines provide passengers with interchangeable ticketing and baggage service to final destination. United, American, and Delta are now advising interlining partners that their agreements will be on a bilateral basis with periodic review. The change is contemplated by the majors because of Continental Airlines' action in seeking protection under bankruptcy regulations in 1983. Because Continental did not cease operations completely and resumed service within two days, the bankruptcy court judge ruled that Continental's partners should continue to honor the interline agreement and yet would not be able to collect money owed for services prior to the bankruptcy. At issue, too, is the industry's default protection plan which protects ticket-holders in the event of airline bankruptcy. The end to either system would place new competitive pressures on financially weak airlines.[3]

A new form of cooperative routing has developed in which airlines agree bilaterally to link their route systems in an effort to strengthen their individual hub and spoke networks. Muse Air has such an arrangement with Air Cal. Cooperative routing could be achieved by other means such as arrangements similar to franchise service exchange agreements or outright acquisition of commuter carriers by larger airlines.

Economy

The airline industry is highly affected by the business cycle. The current upturn in the economy has brought increases in revenue passenger miles to help reduce the pressures of overcapacity which plagued the industry throughout the recession of 1981 and 1982. As disposable income grows and air travel increases during the favorable economy, airlines will experience increasing revenues. The temptation in an upturn is to be less vigilant regarding rising costs. Whether these increased revenues translate into increased profits or not depends on the ability of airlines to keep costs down.

In fact, cost control is the primary key to profitability in the airline industry. With labor cost representing 37% of the total expenses of the established major and national carriers, in contrast to the new entrants' 18%, there is a significant disequilibrium in the industry that market forces will inevitably eliminate. Entering into this equation is the labor relations dilemma facing the industry. Recognizing that a favorable employee attitude is essential to high-quality service, how airlines achieve labor cost control directly impacts effectiveness as well as efficiency. Two advantages that new entrants have in labor productivity are: (1) established airline employees and their unions have little understanding or sympathy for the effects of deregulation and (2) employees of new airlines have no allegiance to the preregulation structure and possess the enthusiasm of sharing in a new enterprise. There have been several approaches to labor cost control including employee ownership programs, establishment of new subsidiary carriers, revocation of labor contracts through declaration of bankruptcy, and a two-tiered wage system for old and new employees.

The second major cost factor is fuel availability. The sporadic shortages, political instability in oil-producing countries, and decontrol of oil prices are uncontrollable external conditions that directly impact profitability of airlines. When fuel costs rose dramatically in 1979–1980, competitive pressures prevented airlines from passing on those increases to passengers. Although fuel costs have declined for the past three years, they still represent 25% of total airline costs. Fuel-efficient aircraft have become an important consideration as a result of high fuel costs.

Beyond operating expenses, the major cost of airlines is the aircraft itself. The high cost of new aircraft has made their acquisition economically prohibitive in spite of their greater fuel efficiency. At current fuel costs, the savings is not sufficient to cover the cost of buying expensive new aircraft. One of the reasons for the high price of aircraft is the fact that manufacturers produce aircraft on an individual job-order basis rather than by mass-production. This nonstandardized production not only increases the original cost but reduces the residual value of aircraft.

Additionally, the fragmentation of the market has reduced opportunities to use larger aircraft. The per seat cost savings on a 150 vs. 100 seat aircraft, for instance, can only be realized if the extra capacity is utilized. This is difficult to achieve in a competitive market already facing overcapacity. Once again, the impact of deregulation seems to be responsible for setting a new trend. In an effort to reduce capacity, airlines are seeking smaller aircraft. The transition to the downsized transport will be costly to airlines and place new competitive pressures on aircraft manufacturers who have suffered decreased sales for five years. As airlines return to profitability, fleet acquisition will be a priority in order to gain competitive position.[4]

Reservation Systems

The distribution of airline ticketing is dominated by travel agents utilizing computerized reservation systems. In fact, 65% of airline reservations are handled by travel agents. Airlines subscribe to one of the majors' computerized systems of which American's Saber is dominant in Texas markets. There are two advantages to the owners or host carriers of the reservation systems. One is a computer bias in which the host is given priority listing among available flights with more information listed than for other airlines. This tends to encourage the choice of the host by travel agents in reserving flights, resulting in increased market share for the host. Secondly, it is commonplace for travel agents to book (or plate) tickets to the servicing carrier, which is the computer host. Since there is a four- to ten-week ticket settlement period, in effect this gives the host utilization of the amounts "plated away" from airline subscribers who are denied cash settlement for that period. It is estimated that the float created by this plating process amounts to $3 billion and costs the airlines financing that float $360 million a year in new interest expense. The Justice Department has asked CAB to adopt rules to reduce competitive abuses of the computerized systems.[5]

With agent commissions representing 6.7% of total airline operating expenses, the CAB's plan to abolish travel agent exclusivity at the end of 1984 will increase competitive initiatives in retail marketing. By breaking up the travel agent monopoly, new innovations in the distribution of airline ticketing are possible. For instance, direct reservations by individuals through cable television may be implemented, discount houses for airline ticket sales could develop, and business travel departments may gain access to direct reservation systems. New economies may also be realized if the practice of "plating away" from airlines, which attempt to reduce travel agent commissions, is eliminated.[6]

COMPANY HISTORY

The Beginning

Muse Air Corporation was organized in early 1980 by two ex-Southwest Airlines employees, Lamar and Michael Muse. The airline was organized to provide high-frequency, single class, low-cost air transportation for the general public. It was one of the many new regional airlines entering the market after deregulation of the airline industry.

Lamar Muse, one of Southwest Airline's founders and former chief executive officers, left Southwest Airlines after a bitter policy dispute in 1978. His two year no-competition agreement with Southwest ran out in October 1980, when he joined his son, Michael, to operate Muse Air. Michael was a former chief financial officer for Southwest Airlines.

Muse Air began service on July 15, 1981, with two DC-9 Super 80s flying between Dallas and Houston. The plans were to compete directly with Southwest on their most lucrative route. Muse had an aggressive expansion program laid out for the next several years, planning to become a major airline as quickly as possible. Fate had no intention of allowing Muse's plans to run smoothly.

Air Traffic Controllers' Strike

On August 2, 1981, just eighteen days after Muse began service, PATCO went out on a nationwide strike, causing the FAA to place restrictions on landing slots.

With the delivery of two McDonnell Douglas DC-9 Super 80s, Muse Air planned to expand its routes to include Midland-Odessa and Tulsa by May 1982. Even though the FAA planned to increase the air traffic system's capacity to 90% of normal (before strike) by September 1982, no changes or increases in landing slots were authorized for Dallas or Houston. This was at a time when airline officials were expressing strong dissatisfaction with the FAA's continued use of emergency powers to allocate the additional capacity, instead of switching to normal administrative procedures. Many airlines felt the allocation of additional slots and routes was not being handled fairly.

Planned expansion by Muse into these two new markets in May 1982 and two additional markets in July 1982 was being delayed because of Federal Aviation Administration restrictions on operating slots at Love Field in Dallas and Hobby Airport in Houston. Muse Air had applied for permission to provide Houston-Dallas-Tulsa with seven daily round trips and six daily round trips from Dallas to Midland-Odessa. Refer to Exhibit 29.1.

The FAA approved Muse Air for operation of one evening offpeak round trip to Tulsa and denied all other requested slots. The FAA also denied a request for thirteen flights daily between Love Field and Austin and fourteen flights between Love Field and San Antonio. Muse Air officials argued that the slot restrictions were contrary to the meaning of the deregulation act,

MUSE AIR CORPORATION: AIRCRAFT DELIVERY SCHEDULE

Exhibit 29.1

	Aircraft			
Delivery Date	***Type***	***Quantity***	***Seating***	***Cities Served***
July 1981	DC9-80 (Super 80)	2	155	Dallas, Houston
May 1982	DC9-80	2	155	Midland, Odessa, Tulsa
Oct. 1982	DC9-80	2	155	Los Angeles
Aug. 1983	DC9-51 (Super 50)	1	130	Lubbock*
Nov. 1983	DC9-51	2	130	Austin
Feb. 1984	DC9-51	1	130	Ontario, CA, New Orleans
Projected Delivery Date				***New Cities***
Apr. 1984	DC9-51	1	130	Little Rock** Las Vegas
Mar. 1985	DC9-51	2	130	San Antonio Chicago
Mar. 1986	DC9-51	2	130	Atlanta Florida

SOURCE: 1983 Muse Air Annual Report and Muse Air News Release.

* Service discontinued in February 1984.

** Service start-up cancelled February 1984.

tending to favor established carriers over new entrants. Obtaining the slots was vital for Muse Air, not only to prevent grounding of the two DC-9s that were being received, but to boost the load factors systemwide as the result of traffic the new cities would give to its present operation.

The Collapse of Braniff

In May 1982, Braniff Airlines ceased operations and filed for bankruptcy-court protection under Chapter 11 of the Federal Bankruptcy Code. Braniff needed protection from creditors' lawsuits as it tried to work out a plan to repay all debts. This opened up many slots for other airlines to pick up and expand service. Muse Air was one of the first to present its request to the FAA for some of the Braniff slots.

Of all the new slots received by Muse Air, they were able to finally begin service to Midland-Odessa and Tulsa in late May 1982. Attention was then turned toward the next planned expansion, that of Austin and San Antonio. Muse Air felt they still had enough Dallas slots to accomplish this expansion on schedule.

The FAA gave Muse Air seven en-route slots and eight airport slots at Dallas on a temporary basis. These slots were former Braniff slots which the FAA later rescinded away and allocated to other airlines by lottery. This left Muse in a position of negotiating for needed slots at Dallas in exchange for slots it did not want, such as at New York LaGuardia. So, again in August 1982, Muse Air was in a position of having to ground newly acquired aircraft for lack of available slots.

The West Coast

On October 1, 1982, as a way to keep from grounding aircraft, Muse Air began service to Los Angeles, California. This was a complete shift in original expansion plans. While the continuing restrictions on landing rights imposed by the FAA forestalled planned expansion to Austin and San Antonio, the new service to California achieved a breakeven level of operations by December 1982.

During the first part of 1983, Muse Air worked very hard at strengthening existing routes and increasing market share. For the first eight months of 1983, passenger traffic, as measured by revenue passenger miles, was up 195%. The fact that gains in traffic outpaced any increase in capacity was due to growing passenger load factors, the percentage of seats filled. Growing identity with the traveling public, as much as anything else, was a major reason for these gains. This was accomplished by increasing the number of flights serving a particular market (the Dallas-Houston route was increased to seventeen round trip flights daily), and attracting a larger portion of the business community as passengers, since these are the people who travel most frequently.

Continuing Expansion

In late 1983, Muse Air began the expansion again, with service to Lubbock in August and Austin in November 1983. A major factor that made this possible was the elimination of most FAA slot restrictions on October 30, 1983. Muse's new $3 million dollar terminal at Hobby airport was completed in November 1983, thus adding another large upgrade to the system.

Muse Air continued with expansion in early 1984, with the opening of the New Orleans market in February. The Madri Gras festival in the Spring and the World's Fair opening in the Summer meant increased traffic to the New Orleans area. Muse Air fully expected to take advantage of this increased traffic flow and become very quickly established in the area.

Service was also begun to Ontario International in California in February, 1984, and a selective joint marketing agreement was signed with Air Cal. Through these two "gateway" locations, Muse Air passengers can quickly connect to eight of Air Cal's markets. In essence, this agreement represents a doubling of marketing destinations available to Muse Air customers. All the conveniences of expanded service to eight new West Coast markets were achieved without the costly capital outlays required for opening individual, on-site operations.

In late February 1984, Muse Air discontinued service to Lubbock as it had proven to be unprofitable for the company. Plans for new service to Little Rock, Arkansas were abandoned the following month. Southwest Airlines moved into Little Rock first and saturated the market with flights.

In response to this, Muse Air opened up non-stop service between Dallas and New Orleans, began service to Las Vegas from Houston in April of 1984 and began special discount fares and Olympic tour packages. At this time, all eleven of their planes were being fully utilized and earning a profit for Muse.

COMPANY MANAGEMENT

Management Organization

The organization of Muse Air's top management is a straightforward top-down style (see Exhibit 29.2). Lamar Muse is Chairman of the Board and Michael is President and Chief Executive Officer. There are nine vice-presidents who report to Michael Muse, covering all the major areas of company operation. These people are:

Vice President-Flight Operations
Mr. Ferguson served as a senior captain for Texas International Airlines and is now responsible for all operations and pilots.

Vice President-Maintenance & Engineering
Mr. Minter worked previously for Braniff in their maintenance department and as Staff Vice-President.

Vice President-Purchasing & Stores
Mr. Lane came from Southwest Airlines as Director of Purchasing.

Exhibit 29.2

MUSE AIR CORPORATION: CORPORATE ORGANIZATION CHART

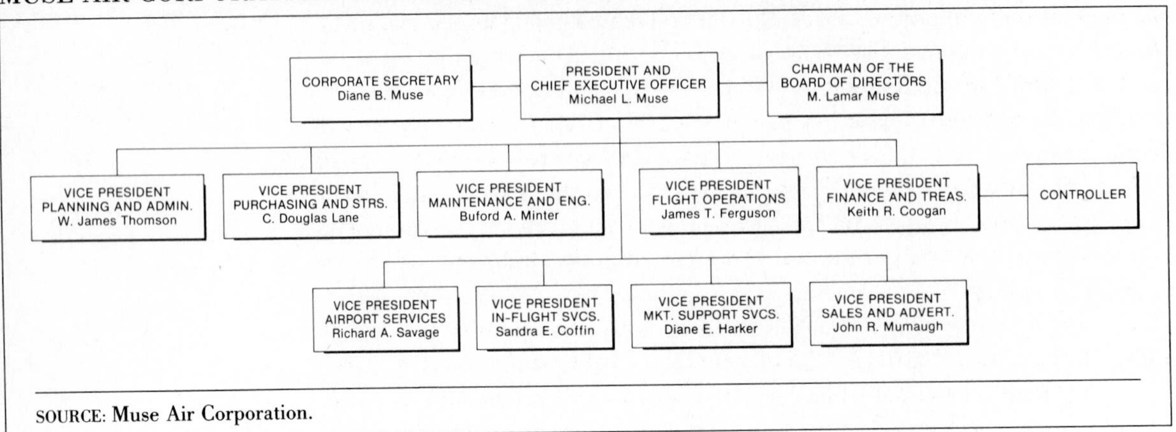

SOURCE: Muse Air Corporation.

Vice President-Planning & Budgeting

Mr. Thomson is another former Southwest Airlines employee. He was Director of Treasury Operation.

Vice President-Finance & Treasurer

Mr. Coogan, a former Audit Manager for Price Waterhouse, has been with Muse Air two years.

Vice President-Airport Services

Mr. Savage has worked for Texas International, Air Couriers International and TWA, managing airports and airport facilities.

Vice President-Sales & Service

Ms. Harker was a manager of Marketing and Financial support for American Airlines previously.

Vice President–In-Flight Services

Ms. Coffin has worked as a flight attendant and as Director of Training and Support for Eastern Airlines.

Vice President-Sales Advertising

Mr. Mumaugh worked for United Airlines previously in sales, marketing, in-flight operations and customer service.

The Muse Air management team contains a great amount of experience and expertise concerning the airline industry from a wide variety of sources and companies.

Employee Benefits Muse Air has no pension plan for their employees but does have a profit sharing plan. When operating profits exceed a set amount for a quarter, 20% of these excess profits are distributed to the employees as cash. This is only for employees who have been with the company for a set period of time.

Muse Air will also adopt a stock purchase plan for their employees and highly encourage participation in the program. With the employees having a portion of ownership in the company, they will be more inclined to keep productivity up and costs down.

At present, there is a stock option plan for employees as far down in the company as mid-management. The employee's position with the company determines how many shares he or she may purchase and at what price. An employee must have one year of service with Muse Air to participate and can only purchase one-third of the option shares within a given year. The employee has five years to purchase all the stock available to him or her under the option agreement.

A nonmonetary benefit of Muse Air is the rotation of employees within different ground operation positions. This allows the employees to become well-cross-trained in various jobs while keeping their interest rate at a high level. Cross-training helps keep productivity up while keeping costs down for Muse Air since they do not have to keep excess people on the payroll.

AIRCRAFT AND FACILITIES

Muse Air uses the McDonnell Douglas DC-9, Super 80 and DC-9, Super 50 aircraft. These planes both use the cost-efficient two-engine design and require only two pilots, instead of three, as needed by other aircraft. All planes are set up for single class service with a distinguished, club-style atmosphere. The exterior is white with the Muse Air signature in blue on the side of the plane.

The corporate signature of Muse Air as analyzed by Ray Walker, handwriting expert, announces strength and character. The backstroke on the letter "M" shows an awareness of the past, complemented by a powerful forward sweep that indicates confidence in the future. The "A" is an indication of pride. The dot over the "I" is close to the stem, showing an appropriate caution with emphasis on the safety and well-being of others.

Muse Air has implemented a cost efficient work force. Employees are non-union, which helps keep wage levels moderate. Also, employees are cross-utilized between various jobs, eliminating the work restriction rules that plague many major carriers and raise their effective labor costs. Finally, because Muse Air is such a young company, there are no long-time employees, meaning lower overall wage levels.

Within the air terminals, Muse Air uses cash register type ticketing and standardized check-in and baggage handling procedures. Operating costs are substantially reduced and passenger arrival-departure time kept to a minimum.

Keeping the comfort and convenience of passengers in mind, all flights are non-smoking. The DC-9 Super 80 carries 155 passengers while the

Super 50 carries 130. This, plus the 3-2 style of seating that has been installed, means more room and comfort for the passengers. The DC-9 gives the passenger a very quiet and smooth ride.

COMPETITION

General

The airline industry is divided into three segments: the major airlines; the national airlines; and the regionals, such as Muse Air. The market share of the majors has been declining since deregulation. At the same time, market share for the regionals has been increasing, picking up what the majors have lost. The load factors of the major airlines have stabilized over the past few years, neither growing nor decreasing. Muse Air's competition consists of three types. The first is Southwest Airlines, with whom Muse Air initiated head-on competition. Second are the regionals that have come into existence following deregulation. Last are the majors who are reestablishing on a much smaller scale, including Braniff and Continental Airlines.

Southwest Airlines

Southwest Airlines provides a single class, high-frequency air service to cities in Texas and surrounding states. The company concentrates on short-haul markets and stresses high level of aircraft utilization and employee productivity. The principal hubs of Southwest's systems are Dallas' Love Field and Houston's Hobby Airport, with a new hub established in Phoenix. These airports are located substantially closer to downtown business centers than the major airports.

Southwest is considered one of the best run airlines in the country. Revenues and revenue passenger miles rose all during 1983. The airline has a load factor around 62%, well above its breakeven point. Southwest will be expanding into the longer haul routes with the delivery of new Boeing 737-300 aircraft in 1984. With a young and efficient fleet, the company is well positioned to benefit from any improvement in the domestic economic activity.

Regional Airlines

People Express began operating in April 1981, and intends to triple its size by mid-1985 through the purchase of several Boeing 727s. It also began offering transatlantic service during the summer of 1983, with a leased 747-200. People Express services seventeen cities domestically, mostly in the Northeast. It flies from its base at Newark, New Jersey, as far as Houston's Hobby. It was one of the few airlines to report a profit in 1982.

New York Air initiated service in late 1980 in the New York, Boston, Washington, D.C. corridor, competing directly with Eastern's shuttle service. Since then it has added cities in the Southeast. The airline experienced an increase of profitability in 1983. New York Air pioneered the concept of business class service at coach class rates. Passengers have been lured with such items as two-by-two seating, more leg room, bagels and the *New York Times.*

In February 1984, Air Atlanta began service between Atlanta, Memphis and New York. The airline is using fewer seats, bigger chairs, more legroom, shorter ticket lines and waiting areas with telephones and refreshments to lure full fare business passengers. Air Atlanta plans to specialize totally for this market. The planes and waiting areas have been completely redesigned for the business passenger to move on and off the plane quickly. Air Atlanta intends to cater to business passengers.

St. Louis-based Air One began operations in April 1983, with flights to Dallas, Kansas City, Washington, D.C. and Newark, N.J. Air One is another airline that caters to the business traveler, offering first class service at coach class prices. In February 1984, Air One began service between St. Louis and Houston's Hobby, the first of twenty-two cities it eventually plans to include in its route system. Air One currently has seven Boeing 727s and will add five more in late 1984.

Rebirths

Like the "Phoenix" that rose from the ashes, Braniff Airlines began flying again on March 1, 1984. It plans to operate a premium-service, low cost airline, aimed strictly at the business travel market. From its Dallas hub, Braniff will serve seventeen cities, including Houston, Austin, Los Angeles, New Orleans, San Antonio, and Tulsa. Braniff is flying from Dallas–Forth Worth Regional Airport and Houston's Intercontinental. Estimates are that it will take several years for the airline to regain the market share it lost in the Houston market.

Braniff restructured itself with the financial backing of the Hyatt Corporation. It has reduced salaries, employees and operating costs to the bare minimum. Even at these low levels, Braniff needs a 47% load factor to break even. The first stock offering by Braniff indicated moderate public confidence in the reborn airline.

Continental Airlines filed to reorganize under Chapter 11 of the Federal Bankruptcy Code during the third quarter of 1983. In February 1984, the airline reappeared with bare bones pay scales, unrestricted low air fares, and employees with a stake in the airline's profitability. Like many of the new airlines, Continental is aiming for the single class business market with competitive fares and many special services.

MARKETING STRATEGY

Muse Air endeavors to provide the highest quality air line service to its target market, primarily businessmen and women. The marketing strategy is based on service, price, name recognition, and expansion of routes.

Service Quality service on Muse Air includes many features: a quiet, comfortable ride on a Super 80 or Super 50 aircraft, with comfortable, large, leather seats in a clean, smoke-free environment; dependable service with convenient close-in airport locations and convenient departure times; the convenience of reserved seating to prevent the crush to board; the best service provided by motivated employees; easy booking for travel agents through American Airlines' computerized SABRE system.

Price The air transportation market is growing, as the economy improves. Muse Air must gain its share of this market growth. To accomplish this goal, it uses competitive prices to attract customers. In March 1983, Muse Air offered the "lowest" discounted fare to Los Angeles of $88.

Off-peak pricing is used to attract more customers and keep more planes flying at higher occupancy. Muse Air primarily utilizes a two-tier fare structure: business class providing low cost, first class air transportation during prime time; and leisure class providing an economically competitive alternative to various forms of ground transportation.

Muse Air has always had to meet or beat the low fares of their major competitor, Southwest Airlines. The recent revival of Continental and Braniff Airlines in March 1984 increased competition on most of the Muse Air routes. This competitive environment may spark another round of price slashing. Braniff has already announced reduced economy fares during March 1984.

The reborn Continental Airlines precipitated fare discounting as a means to fill seats and gain the customers it lost after filing to reorganize under Chapter 11. Additionally, Delta Air Lines, Pan Am, American, Eastern and TWA have joined in with their own discounting in order to remain competitive. Of these majors, Delta began service on March 1, 1984, from Houston's Hobby Airport to seven cities including Dallas–Ft. Worth, the major market for Muse Air.

Because of deregulation and the Chapter 11 alternative, the airline industry is becoming more efficient. Everyone is trying to keep costs low, so their rates can be competitive. It is with Southwest that Muse Air must be competitive in order to gain the needed traffic. Muse Air has a lower average cost than Southwest (5.2 cents a seat mile against Southwest's 6 cents and the industry average of nearly 11 cents). Since overhead is almost identical, Muse Air must differentiate itself from Southwest in order to "break the Southwest habit" to which the frequent flier has become accustomed.

Name Recognition Lamar Muse feels that name recognition is critical to success. Therefore, Muse Air devotes a lot of effort to promote a premium product with a reserved and sophisticated image.

PROPOSED EXPANSION OF MUSE AIR ROUTES
(Effective April 29, 1984)

Exhibit 29.3

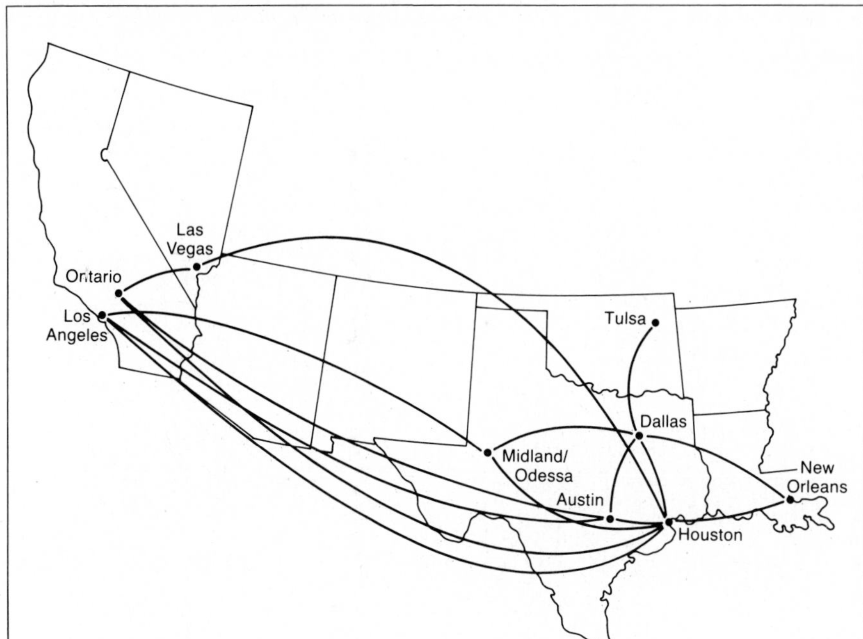

SOURCE: Muse Air Corporation.

To enhance the club car image, they provide many in-service extras, including drinks on afternoon flights and a complimentary copy of the *Wall Street Journal.*

To encourage repeat customers, Muse Air has developed several packages and clubs that provide benefits for frequent flyers. For example, the Muse Air Club is for travel coordinators, secretaries, and people in business and government who are responsible for travel arrangements. Club members can earn free trips, participate in monthly drawings for special prizes, receive the Muse Air magazine, and invitations to special receptions.

Muse Air continues to spend heavily for advertising. In 1982, expenditures were over $6 million, or 16% of all operating expenses, for marketing. The initial ad campaign, "Big Daddy Is Back," emphasized their leader, Lamar Muse, and his experience in the airline industry. The next campaign was testimonials from customers.

The latest advertising effort on radio and television is intended to reach a wider group of potential passengers by using people of various ages and occupations. The campaign also attempts to entice the customer with a mystical, indescribable, beautiful experience. The themes are "You just gotta fly

Exhibit 29.4

MUSE AIR STRATEGIC ROUTE PLAN, 1980

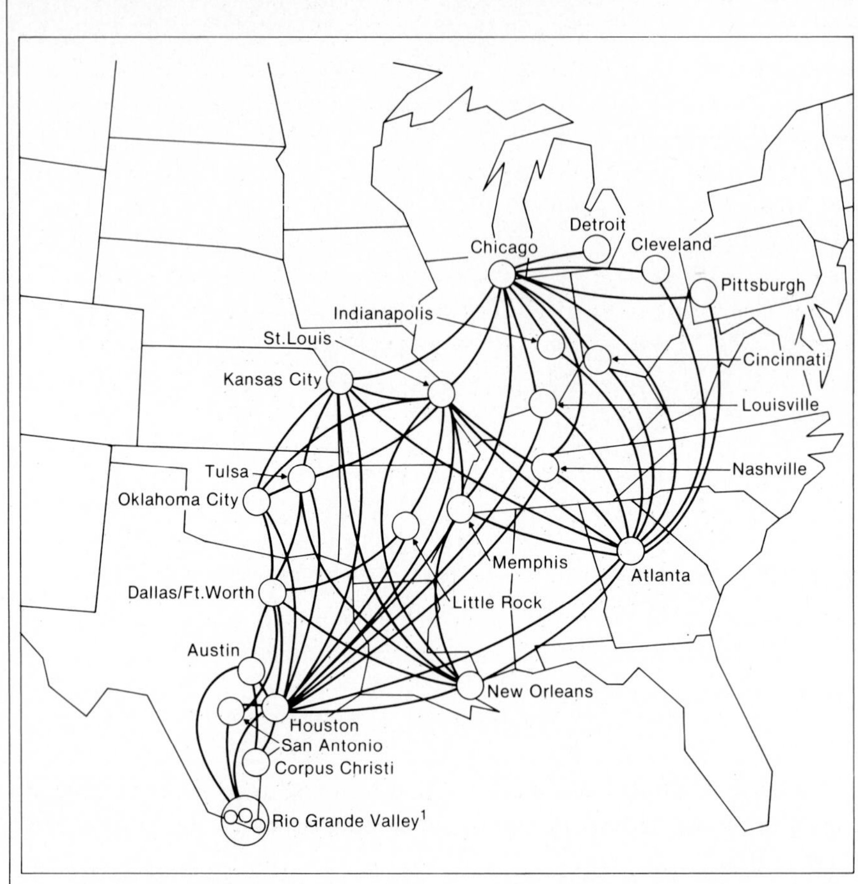

[1] Includes airports at Brownsville, Harlingen and McAllen, Texas.

Note: Long-range plan of Muse Air is to expand its initial Dallas-Houston service to cover a total of 24 markets from hubs at Houston, Chicago and Atlanta, matching Southwest Airlines' fares in its markets and undercutting any other competition.

SOURCE: Reprinted from *Aviation Week and Space Technology*, August 17, 1981. Used by permission.

it," and "See how beautiful Muse Air can be." Initial response to this campaign has been very positive.

Route Expansion The fourth component of the Muse Air marketing strategy is expansion of routes. Muse Air began service in July 1981 between Dallas (Love Field) and Houston (Hobby Airport). As of February 1984, Muse Air flies seventeen round trips daily on the Dallas-Houston route, which is its most popular.

From 1982, Muse Air has expanded service to Midland-Odessa, Texas; Tulsa, Oklahoma; Los Angeles, California; Lubbock, Texas; Austin, Texas; Ontario, California; and New Orleans, Louisiana. As of April 29, 1984, Muse Air will be offering service to Las Vegas. See Exhibit 29.3 on page 867 for a map of the expanded service area. Plans for future expansion include San Antonio, St. Louis, Chicago, New York, Atlanta, and Florida.

Originally, Muse Air expansion plans were to fly to the South and Midwest. Exhibit 29.4 is a map of the initial strategic plan of Muse Air as formulated in 1980. There are indications that the westward air travel market is served to over capacity. Muse may try to return to these original plans to increase profitability. Houston will become the center of operations.

At the end of February 1984, Muse Air had to cancel plans for beginning service to Little Rock, Arkansas. Muse's service to Little Rock had been announced in January and was to begin April 19, 1984. After the announce-

Exhibit 29.5
MUSE AIR AND AIRCAL ROUTES
(Effective March 1, 1984)

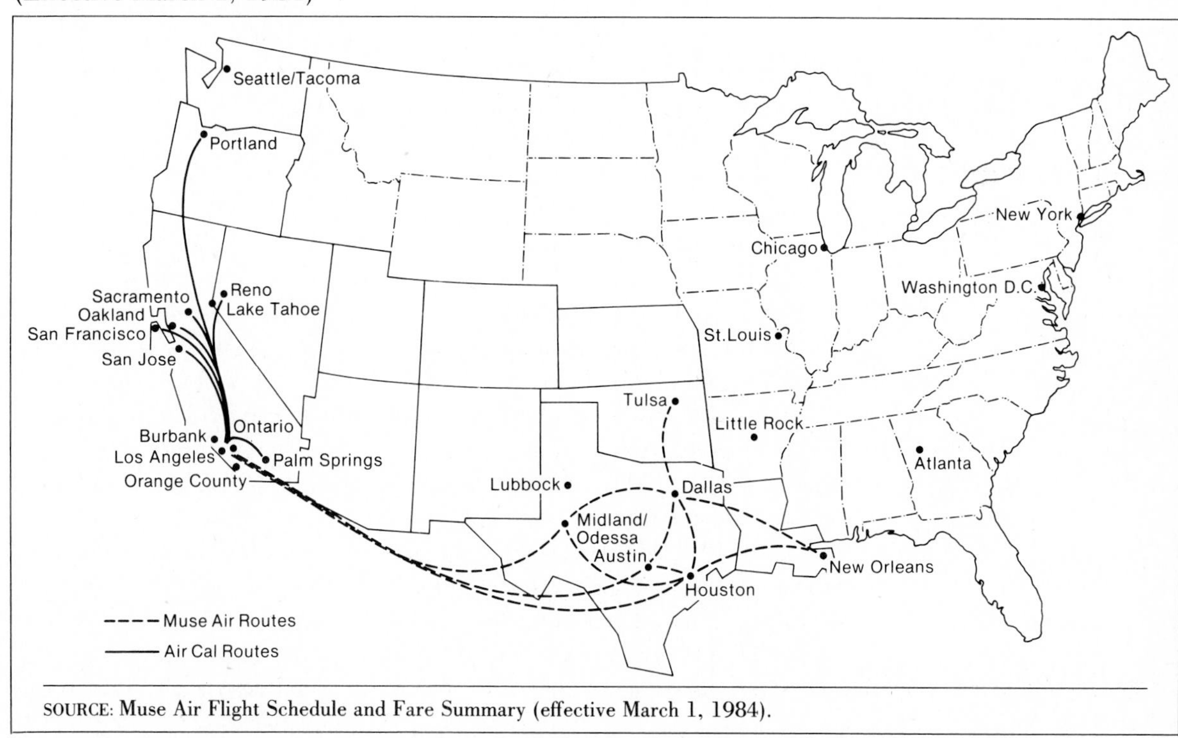

SOURCE: Muse Air Flight Schedule and Fare Summary (effective March 1, 1984).

ment, Southwest Airlines flooded the Little Rock market with new flights forcing Muse Air out before service began.

Muse Air will face other competitors as it tries to expand. Delta has already started service to Atlanta from Houston's Hobby Airport, the same route proposed by Muse for service in March 1986.

Not only is Muse Air being crowded out of expansion routes but existing routes as well. After several months of service, Muse Air discontinued flights to Lubbock, Texas. Delta, American, and Southwest Airlines all service Lubbock. This is the first route that Muse Air has ever had to discontinue.

Besides planned route expansion, an innovative joint marketing program with Air Cal should help Muse Air grow beyond its strictly regional status. The Muse Air/AirCal joint marketing agreement began February 5, 1984. Muse Air passengers can connect quickly to eight of AirCal's markets including San Francisco, Sacramento, San Jose, Palm Springs, and Oakland, California; Seattle, Washington; Portland, Oregon; and Reno, Nevada. See Exhibit 29.5 for a map of AirCal routes.

This selective joint marketing agreement represents a doubling of market destinations available to Muse Air customers virtually overnight. All the conveniences of expanded service to eight new West Coast markets were achieved without the costly capital outlays required for opening individual airline on-site operations. According to John Mumaugh, Vice-President, Sales and Advertising, this joint marketing program illustrates clearly how deregulation has freed carriers to pursue creative marketing techniques in a cost-effective manner to ultimately benefit the traveling public.[7]

FINANCES

Equity

The company was initially capitalized in February 1980 through the issuance of 31,250 shares of common stock to Michael L. Muse for $25,000 in cash. In October 1980, the company issued and sold an aggregate of 318,750 shares of common stock to five members of the Muse family and Cole, Brumley & Eichner, Inc. for cash payment of $.80 per share. In October 1980, the company also issued and sold to five members of the Muse family an aggregate of $190,000 principal amount of its 12% convertible subordinated debentures at the face amount. In February 1981, 237,500 shares of common stock were issued to the five members of the Muse family upon conversion of the debentures. On March 20, 1981, the company's stock was split five-for-four.

On April 30, 1981, the company made a public offering of 2,200,000 shares of common stock with warrants to purchase 1,100,000 shares of common stock priced at $17.50 per unit (one share of common stock and one-half warrant). The proceeds of this offering were used as a deposit and fee relating to the future acquisition of four new DC-9 Super 80 aircraft, the

MUSE AIR CORPORATION: BALANCE SHEET

(For Year Ending December 31)

Exhibit 29.6

	1983	1982
ASSETS		
Current assets		
Cash and temporary investments of $16,931,000 in 1983 and $7,250,000 in 1982	$ 18,404,116	$ 7,488,653
Accounts receivable	6,600,356	3,068,720
Inventories of parts and supplies	513,582	412,833
Prepaid expenses	1,001,455	555,246
Total current assets	26,519,509	11,525,452
Property and equipment at cost		
Flight equipment—aircraft	130,187,529	109,700,751
Aircraft purchase deposits	8,672,808	
Leasehold improvements	3,454,387	1,026,286
Other flight and ground equipment	14,100,401	9,325,544
	156,415,125	120,052,581
Less: Accumulated depreciation and amortization	(10,593,431)	(3,255,798)
	145,821,694	116,796,783
Other assets, net	445,502	2,470,381
	$172,786,705	$130,792,616
LIABILITIES AND STOCKHOLDERS' EQUITY		
Current liabilities		
Accounts payable	$ 4,352,121	$ 1,081,662
Unearned transportation revenues	1,637,359	681,535
Accrued liabilities	6,957,066	3,389,432
Current maturities of long-term debt	9,615,541	2,460,000
Total current liabilities	22,562,087	7,612,629
Long-term debt less current maturities	83,594,659	76,440,000
Deferred federal income taxes	263,501	715,740
Other long-term liabilities		1,013,790
Total liabilities	106,420,247	85,782,159
Stockholders' equity		
Common stock, $1.00 par value; 20,000,000 shares authorized; issued and outstanding 4,636,750 shares in 1983 and 3,100,000 shares, $.10 par value, in 1982	4,635,750	310,000
Additional paid-in capital	56,183,993	37,196,245
Retained earnings	5,545,715	7,504,212
Total stockholders' equity	66,366,458	45,010,547
Commitments and contingencies	$172,786,705	$130,792,616

SOURCE: Muse Air Corporation 1983 Annual Report.

Exhibit 29.7

MUSE AIR CORPORATION: STATEMENT OF OPERATIONS

(For Year Ending December 31)

	1983	1982	1981
Operating revenues			
Passenger	$68,976,808	$32,211,861	$ 6,217,593
Other	3,951,150	844,063	78,268
Total operating revenues	72,927,958	33,055,924	6,295,861
Operating expenses:			
Fuel and oil	20,940,064	12,182,590	3,201,335
Flight operations	8,360,307	6,130,036	2,871,844
Marketing	13,292,021	6,112,769	2,251,081
Maintenance	3,827,987	2,211,586	941,113
In-flight service	4,479,305	2,001,974	545,566
Terminal operations	5,109,215	2,889,318	832,069
Insurance and taxes	2,819,025	1,572,725	277,684
General and administrative	2,136,772	1,578,310	714,538
Depreciation and amortization	7,347,628	3,114,827	197,620
Total operating expenses	68,312,324	37,794,135	11,832,850
Operating income (loss)	4,615,634	(4,738,211)	(5,536,989)
Non-operating income (expense)			
Interest income	1,647,481	897,928	1,569,469
Interest expense (less interest capitalized at $797,967 in 1983 and $1,353,943 in 1982)	(8,556,268)	(4,309,216)	
Other income	499,985	21,835,019	
Other expense	(617,568)	(1,502,186)	
Net non-operating income (expense)	(7,026,370)	16,921,545	1,569,469
Income (loss) before provision for federal income taxes and extraordinary item	(2,410,736)	12,183,334	(3,967,520)
Federal income tax provision (benefit)	(452,239)	2,540,800	
Income (loss) before extraordinary item	(1,958,497)	9,642,534	(3,967,520)
Extraordinary item—utilization of net operating loss carry-forwards		1,825,060	
Net income (loss)	$ (1,958,497)	$11,467,594	$ (3,967,520)
Income (loss) per common share			
Income (loss) before extraordinary item	$(.49)	$3.25	$(1.86)
Extraordinary item		.62	
Net income (loss)	$(.49)	$3.87	$(1.86)
Weighted average shares outstanding	4,030,113	2,963,151	2,136,781

SOURCE: Muse Air Corporation 1983 Annual Report.

prepayment of a one-year lease on the two Super 80 aircraft that were in operation, the acquisition of aircraft spare parts and engines, the purchase of ground equipment and leasehold improvements, and the unrestricted addition to working capital. The stock was traded in the over-the-counter market under the symbol "MUSE." The warrants provide for the purchase of common stock at $16.00 per share and expire on April 30, 1986, or as early as January 1, 1984, if certain conditions are satisfied and the company chooses to accelerate the expiration date. No warrants have been exercised to date.

On May 24, 1983, the company made another public offering of 1,540,000 shares of common stock at $16.25. The net proceeds of this offering were used to prepay a secured bank note due in July, 1984, and to increase the equity base and working capital position of the company to support future expansion. The common stock commenced trading on the American Stock Exchange under the symbol "MAC" on April 18, 1983 at which time it ceased trading in the over-the-counter market.

With this last equity offering, no further financing is expected in 1984. A cash flow of $12.5 million in 1983 and $25 million in 1984 should pose few difficulties requiring further equity. In addition, the company will likely force

MUSE AIR CORPORATION: SUMMARY OF BOOK VALUE/TRADING PRICE PER SHARE

Exhibit 29.8

		Book Value Per Share	*Trading Price per Share*	
Year	*Quarter*	*Price*	*High*	*Low*
1980	4th	$ .81	—	—
1981	1st	—	—	—
	2nd	12.19	15	11½
	3rd	11.26	15¼	7¼
	4th	10.83	12⅝	7⅜
1982	1st	10.35	8⅞	5½
	2nd	9.81	7⅜	3½
	3rd	11.05	9	4⅜
	4th	14.52	13⅝	6⅝
1983	1st	14.09	15	10⅜
	2nd	13.64	19⅜	14¼
	3rd	14.27	17¾	13½
	4th	14.31	16¾	14

SOURCE: 1981, 1982, 1983 Muse Air Corporation Annual Report.

MUSE AIR CORPORATION: STATEMENT OF OPERATIONS
(In Thousands of Dollars Except Per-Share Amounts)

Exhibit 29.9

	1984E	1983	1982	1981
Revenue	$135,000	$72,928	$33,056	$ 6,296
Operating expenses	110,000	68,312	37,794	11,833
Operating income	25,000	4,616	(4,748)	(5,537)
Non-operating income	(16,000)	(7,026)	16,922	1,569
Earnings before taxes	9,000	(2,410)	12,184	(3,968)
Taxes	2,000	(452)	2,541	—
Earnings before extraordinary items	7,000	(1,958)	9,643	(3,968)
Extraordinary items	—	—	1,825	—
Net income	$ 7,000	$ (1,958)	$11,468	$ (2,941)
Primary shares	4,640	4,030	2,963	2,131
Earnings per Share				
Earnings before taxes	$ 1.95	$ (0.49)	$ 4.11	$ (1.86)
Earnings before extraordinary items	—	—	$ 3.25	—
Net income	$ 1.50	$ (0.49)	$ 3.87	$ (1.86)

SOURCE: 1983 Muse Air Annual Report and Analyst Estimates.

the conversion of the 1.1 million warrants at $16 per share if the common stock trades at or above $24 per share for 30 consecutive trading days. Market capitalization on December 31, 1983, stood at 4,030,113 common shares. The company's balance sheet and statement of operations are included as Exhibits 29.6 and 29.7, respectively.

In 1982, Muse sold tax benefits of depreciation and investment tax credits on four of its DC-9 Super 80 aircraft producing net proceeds to the company of approximately $21.6 million. This item was treated as "other" income and accounted for the net earnings of $3.87 per share during fiscal 1982. Without these tax related benefits, the company would have reported a 1982 full-year net loss of $3.17 per share.

Capital Stock Valuation

Because of the various crisis situations Muse has encountered, the stock's price has fluctuated widely from a high of 19⅜ to a low of 3½ during its short life (see Exhibit 29.8). While the stock price has changed with the outlook for the company's future, the book value has steadily increased. Currently, the stock is selling at a 25% discount from book value and about seven times estimated 1984 earnings. As a comparison, Southwest Airlines sells at three times book value and 20 times earnings; Midway and People Express sell at comparable or higher multiples. Also, the earnings leverage is considerable because passenger traffic should increase more rapidly than growth in capacity and net loss carryforwards. Additionally, investment tax credits will be available to offset future income tax.

Based on estimates, Muse Air has the potential to earn $1.50 per share in fiscal year 1984 (see Exhibit 29.9). If these earnings estimates prove correct and are based on a valuation of twelve times earnings, a value for Muse common of $18 per share is possible. The potential for substantial price appreciation is within reason. Since warrants move, percentage wise, to a greater extent than does the common, the excellent leverage provided by this vehicle would reward investors even more handsomely.

Muse Air reported its first operating profit of $780,000, or $.17 per share, in the third quarter of 1983. In the 1983 fourth quarter, the company again reported an operating profit of $202,000 or $.04 per share. Both quarters of operating profits helped reduce the 1983 operating net loss to $1,959,000 or $.49 per share. Mr. Michael L. Muse stated that the positive results of the third and fourth quarter ". . . provided Muse Air a solid launching pad for what should prove to be a very successful 1984."[8]

Aircraft Acquisition

The company began service on July 15, 1981, with two Super 80 aircraft leased from McDonnell Douglas Corporation (MDC). The first equity offering in April 1981 provided the funds for the lease of these two aircraft as well as the purchase of four new aircraft. In August 1982, the company repaid the subordinated debt of $4.1 million to MDC from proceeds received from the sale of tax benefits on one of these aircraft.

The company purchased two additional Super 80 aircraft in September 1982, and one in November 1982, with $42 million provided from bank financing and with approximately $14 million of the proceeds from the sale of tax benefits associated with these aircraft. In December 1982, the company leased a sixth Super 80 aircraft under a long-term operating lease agreement from the McDonnell Douglas Finance Corporation (MDFC). As of this date, Muse Air owns five of its Super 80 aircraft and holds a long-term lease for the sixth. Exhibit 29.1 shows the aircraft delivery schedule.

In August 1983, Muse Air negotiated the purchase of ten used McDonnell Douglas DC-9-51 aircraft, five of those from SwissAir and the other five from Austrian Air. The total cost of this acquisition is approximately $100 million. The first two aircraft were delivered in October 1983, the third in February 1984. Two more are to be placed in service during late April or early May 1984. Three additional aircraft are to be delivered in the first quarter of 1985 and the final two in the first quarter of 1986. Muse Air intends to use the smaller aircraft on its shorter hauls with less passenger demand while using the Super 80s on longer and more heavily traveled flights. Approximately $11 million from the second equity offering was used as a deposit on the aircraft with the balance to be financed with bank debt of $65 million as the planes are delivered through 1986.

THE PREDICAMENT

Lamar and Michael Muse were weary from reviewing all of the relevant information pertaining to their situation. The airline industry is going through a time of change. What is the best strategy for Muse Air Corporation to pursue in this rapidly changing environment? Is the time right to expand? Should expansion be regional or national? These were all important questions that Michael Muse felt required definite answers.

NOTES

1. Joan M. Feldman. "Deregulation Loose Ends Spark Debate about Regulation after 1984." *Air Transport World* 20 (May 1983): p. 23.
2. "FAA Nears Ruling on Preferential Routes." *Aviation Week & Space Technology* 119 (April 18, 1983) p. 34.
3. "Airline Cooperation Starts to Break Apart." *Business Week,* November 29, 1983, p. 45.
4. James Ott. "Airlines Gear for New Challenges." *Aviation Week & Space Technology* 118 (November 14, 1983): p. 48.
5. Michael Cieply. "Hardball." *Forbes* 132 (February 28, 1983): p. 33.
6. James Ott. "House Questions Agent Decision." *Aviation Week & Space Technology* 118 (May 30, 1983): p. 57–58.
7. John Mumaugh. "Executive Corner," *Muse Air Monthly,* October 1983, p. 7.
8. "Muse Air Reports Substantial Fourth Quarter Operating Profit; Finishes 1983 with Back-to-Back Quarterly Net Profits as Well," *News Release Muse Air,* January 1984.

Case 30

THE STANDARD OIL COMPANY OF OHIO: GROWING PAINS IN THE EIGHTIES

J. David Hunger

BACKGROUND

Standard Oil of Ohio was officially established as an independent firm in 1911 when the United States Supreme Court ordered the giant Standard Oil of New Jersey to divest itself of holdings in thirty-three other companies. The largest, Standard of New Jersey, became the successful Exxon Corporation. Standard Oil of Ohio, in contrast, was established as a one-state marketer with obsolete and inadequate refining capacity. The company owned no crude oil and no pipelines. Its assets were only $6.6 million, consisting of Rockefeller's original Cleveland refinery, some storage tanks, and wagons. Reduced to the status of buying and selling other companies' oil, Sohio concentrated on marketing gasoline to the developing automobile market. Its red, white, and blue signs shone from attractive service stations located on the most desirable intersections throughout Ohio. Sohio's marketing expertise made the firm a very strong competitor within the state. In the past few years, for example, Texaco, Exxon, and Atlantic Richfield pulled their stations completely out of Ohio. Nevertheless, until 1970, Standard Oil of Ohio, or Sohio, as it refers to itself, was a very minor player in the global petroleum industry.

This case was prepared by Prof. J. David Hunger with the assistance of Koh Tong Boon, Jeff Dingeman, Brad Niland, and Greg Seiler of the College of Business, Iowa State University. This case also appeared in the *Journal of Management Case Studies* (Vol. I, no. 4, 1985).

In 1970, Sohio traded 53% of its equity to British Petroleum Company in exchange for a major share of the 1.5 million barrel-a-day Prudhoe Bay oilfield. In return, the British company (32% of which is owned by the British government) obtained three seats on Sohio's fifteen-person board of directors, a voice in Sohio's capital spending plans, a healthy annual infusion of cash in the form of dividends from Sohio, and an experienced U.S. marketer for its Alaskan oil.

The huge cost of environmental battles and technical mistakes increased the price of the Prudhoe Bay oil pipeline from $900 million to $9.3 billion, thus forcing Sohio to borrow approximately $4.6 billion to pay its share of construction costs. Nevertheless, world oil prices began to soar with the 1973 OPEC oil embargo. The bold gamble paid off when the oil started flowing from Alaska. Sohio suddenly found itself in 1978 among the major oil companies, ranking ninth in total assets. Prudhoe Bay, however, accounted for 80% of its assets and contributed more than 85% of its profits.

Realizing that the flow of oil coming from Prudhoe Bay will likely begin declining in the late 1980s, Alton W. Whitehouse, chairman and chief executive officer of Standard Oil of Ohio, addressed himself in the 1978 annual report to the problem of spending anticipated profits of more than $1 billion per year.

> . . . Sohio is developing plans to reinvest much of the cash generated by the Alaskan investment in energy-related programs and projects. These include increasing production, improving the profitability of our refining and marketing operations, and investing in further chemical expansion.
>
> However, Sohio intends to develop contingency plans to pursue alternate strategies that include diversification, if the economic or political environment becomes unduly hostile.
>
> Our plans also provide for retiring debt and improving our financial position in order to give us flexibility to invest in energy or other businesses in a changing business environment. We also plan to increase dividends to shareholders periodically, in keeping with our stated long-range objective of increasing our payout ratio.

POST-PRUDHOE BAY DEVELOPMENTS

In keeping with its stated strategy of expanding oil and gas exploration and investing in other forms of energy, Sohio spent money on a number of unprofitable ventures as well as on some that may be profitable in the long run. Exploration was expanded into the lower forty-eight states. "We want to avoid having too many eggs in the Alaska basket," explained Richard A. Bray, President of Sohio Petroleum Company—Sohio's exploration and production unit.[1] As of the beginning of 1983, Sohio was dependent on Alaskan reserves for 97% of its production. Spending billions of dollars for exploration rights, the company acquired an interest in eighty-seven lease tracts in the Gulf of Mexico resulting in five commercial discoveries by end-1983. Two more discoveries were made in 1984. A spokesman for the company said Sohio isn't yet sure that the two recent Gulf of Mexico discoveries contain enough oil to make commercial production feasible.[2] In 1979, Sohio merged with Webb Resources, Inc. and Newco Exploration Company of Denver to gain access to the Rocky Mountain Overthrust region in Colorado. It also bought leases in the gas-rich Anadarko Basin in Oklahoma. From 1977 when Sohio spent only $20 million on exploration to 1982 when its exploration/production budget was $1.96 billion, Sohio has become a very active seeker of new oil resources. In December 1983, the corporation entered an exploratory agreement with Weyerhaeuser Company giving Sohio the exclusive right to lease up to 592,000 acres in the southwestern Arkansas portion of the Ouachita Overthrust.

A partnership with Energy Conversion Devices (ECD) in 1981 gave Sohio an interest in solar energy. Working with ECD and the Japanese company Sharp, the firm is involved in the development of a new solar energy device. Other promising projects with big earnings potential are its work in specialized ceramics and sulfur-reducing coal boilers. Its Chase Brass and Copper Company subsidiary has a new continuous-production process for narrow copper and brass strips used in household wiring and auto parts. The company plans a series of mills using the process, from which it expects excellent earnings growth.[3]

Disappointing Kennecott Acquisition

By far, however, the company's two largest investments have been unsuccessful. In 1981, Sohio purchased the nation's largest copper producer, Kennecott Corporation, for $1.77 billion. In the three years since the acquisition, Kennecott has lost $354 million. Analysts believe that the losses were primarily a result of poor worldwide economic conditions resulting in a large drop in the price of copper. Fighting to stem the losses, Sohio's top management decided in 1983 to close Kennecott's abrasive operations. These operations had been a part of Carborundum, a firm purchased earlier by Kennecott, and were responsible for a 1982 operating loss before income taxes of $27 million on sales of $242 million. In 1984, Kennecott cut operations by two-thirds at its Utah Copper Division following an announcement by Kennecott's president, G. Frank Joklik, of a first quarter loss of $45 million and an expected second quarter loss of $20 million. The fundamental problem is oversupply, said Mr. Joklik, aggravated by overproduction by foreign producers. Zaire's Gecamines copper mine, for example, was still able to earn a 25% profit margin in 1984 even with low world prices.[4]

By keeping output high, Third World competitors have kept prices around 60 cents per pound versus the 82 cents per pound average cost of

U.S. production. As a result, the twelve major U.S. copper producers are now operating at 60% of capacity and employ only 25,000 workers. In September, the Reagan Administration turned down a recommendation by the International Trade Commission to grant the copper industry protection by limiting or taxing foreign copper entering the country.[5] The steel industry, in contrast, which employs 240,000 unionized steelworkers, did receive some administration support for voluntary quotas.

Costly Mukluk Exploration

During the period 1978 to 1984, Sohio continued to look for more oil in Alaska. Realizing that it needed a big oil strike to replace the $6 billion in annual revenues from Prudhoe, Sohio invested heavily in a prospect called *Mukluk* in the Beaufort Sea. After an estimated cost of $1.7 billion for leases and drilling 14 miles off Alaska's north coast, the exploratory well was found on December 3, 1983 to contain water, not oil. Even though this was the most expensive "dry well" in history, Sohio's top management continued to push for continued exploration both in Alaska and in the lower forty-eight. "Because we want to replace Prudhoe, we need to do some elephant-hunting," said Mr. Bray. "But because most times you don't bag one, you also need to go after rabbits, squirrels, anything that's out there."[6]

THE OIL INDUSTRY

In 1984, one decade after the Arab oil embargo, the worldwide oil industry was suffering from depressed world energy demand and abundant crude oil supplies. Since 1982, members of the Organization of Petroleum Exporting Countries (OPEC) have been reducing per barrel prices to sell their petroleum. United States oil demand of 15.2 million barrels per day in 1983 was 20% below the 1978 level.[7] This caused a substantial underutilization of the industry's refining, distribution, and retailing capacities, which had been built on the assumption that consumption would rise. Exploration and drilling companies, such as Blocker Energy Corporation and MGF Oil, lost millions of dollars in 1982 when prices suddenly fell.

With revenues tumbling nearly $20 billion during 1982 and 1983, Exxon Corporation reacted by closing nine refineries, reducing tanker capacity by 25%, selling or closing more than 10,000 service stations, and laying off more than 24,000 employees. A dozen of the industry's biggest employers followed Exxon's example by cutting their workforces by about 14% compared to 1981. Layoffs were especially heavy in the refining and marketing operations.[8] In commenting on the collapse of prices in 1982, T. Boone Pickens, Jr., chairman of Mesa Petroleum said, "I've never seen a collapse as dramatic as this has been. It's an unbelievable situation."[9]

Depressed Prices

During 1983, oil prices continued to be low. A survey of the leading 400 publicly traded U.S. oil and gas firms found that the largest corporations tended to be profitable while the smaller ones were not. Of the top 100 firms (ranked by assets), only 5 lost money during 1983. In contrast, 71 of the bottom 100 lost money during the same year.[10] (Refer to Exhibit 30.1 for summary statistics on the top twenty U.S. oil and gas firms at year-end 1983.)

Strong economic recoveries in the United States and Japan led a worldwide increase in oil consumption during the first half of 1984 of around 3% over the same period in 1983. Unfortunately, global production of oil increased 7% during the same time frame. Prices for spot market oil, which trades without long-term binding contracts, hit a seventeen-month low in July 1984.[11] Although the large, integrated oil firms tended to improve their profits over the first half of 1983 due to a series of economy measures taken in 1982 and 1983, smaller independents still faced crippling cash flow problems and difficulties in raising outside funds. For example, Crystal Oil announced in September 1984 that due to the "economic uncertainties in the energy business," it was laying off 18% of its workforce and reducing its drilling rigs on contract from ten to twelve down to one or two.[12] Apex Oil, owner of Clark Oil, one of the Midwest's largest gasoline chains, was being forced to curtail refining activities, lay off workers, and close retail gasoline outlets. Apex had difficulty meeting Clark's current debt of more than $600 million.[13]

Problems with Diversification

A number of the major integrated oil companies have found the industry-wide problems to be aggravated by their experiences in diversifying outside the energy-related field. Standard Oil of Ohio's poor experience with its Kennecott acquisition was paralleled by Mobil's problems with its cash-hungry Montgomery Ward subsidiary, Ashland Oil's unsuccessful move into insurance, and Exxon's string of bad investments. In particular, Exxon's purchase of Reliance Electric in 1979 for $1.2 billion was recently selected by *Fortune* as one of the decade's seven worst mergers.[14] The list of oil firms diversifying out of oil during the 1970s had become quite a long one by 1980. Not all of these, however, could be called unsuccessful.

Threat of Takeovers

Adding to the pressures facing the major oil firms in 1983 and 1984 was the increasing threat of a takeover. The acquisitions of Cities Service by Occidental Petroleum, Getty Oil by Texaco, Superior Oil by Mobil, and Gulf by Standard Oil of California (Chevron) shook the industry. Other companies rumored to be potential takeover or proxy fight candidates during 1984 were Phillips Petroleum, Sun, Occidental Petroleum, Pennzoil, and Louisiana Land and Exploration. Forces leading to the intense merger activity included undervalued stock prices, high cash positions, and declining U.S. oil deposits. With growth in world demand for refined oil products projected at

Exhibit 30.1

SITUATION OF TOP TWENTY U.S. OIL AND GAS FIRMS AT YEAR-END 1983

The Top 20 in Total Assets and in Total Revenue

Rank	*Company name*	*Total assets* ($000)	*Rank*	*Company name*	*Total revenue* ($000)
1	Exxon Corp	62,962,990	1	Exxon Corp	94,733,971
2	Mobil Corp	35,072,000	2	Mobil Corp	58,998,000
3	Texaco Inc	27,199,000	3	Texaco Inc	41,147,000
4	Standard Oil Co (Indiana)	25,805,000	4	Standard Oil Co (Indiana)	29,494,000
5	Chevron Corp	24,010,000	5	Chevron Corp	29,182,000
6	Atlantic Richfield Co	23,282,307	6	Gulf Corp	28,887,000
7	Shell Oil Co	22,169,000	7	Atlantic Richfield Co	26,279,250
8	Gulf Corp	20,964,000	8	Conoco Inc	23,775,000
9	Tenneco Inc	17,994,000	9	Shell Oil Co	19,883,000
10	Standard Oil Co (Ohio)	16,362,000	10	Occidental Petroleum Corp	19,115,667
11	Phillips Petroleum Co	13,094,000	11	Sun Co	15,523,000
12	Sun Co	12,466,000	12	Phillips Petroleum Co	15,411,000
13	Occidental Petroleum Corp	11,775,351	13	Tenneco Inc	14,449,000
14	Conoco Inc	11,565,000	14	Standard Oil Co (Ohio)	12,215,000
15	Getty Oil Co	10,385,050	15	Getty Oil Co	12,017,028
16	Marathon Oil Co	9,332,000	16	Unocal Corp	10,690,500
17	Unocal Corp	9,228,000	17	Marathon Oil Corp	9,262,000
18	Amerada Hess Corp	6,217,098	18	Amerada Hess Corp	8,442,076
19	Diamond Shamrock Corp	6,024,441	19	Ashland Oil Inc	8,258,809
20	Houston Industries Inc	5,678,076	20	Coastal Corp	5,963,074

The Top 20 in Net Income and in Stockholders' Equity

Rank	*Company name*	*Net income* ($000)	*Rank*	*Company name*	*Stockholders' equity* ($000)
1	Exxon Corp	4,977,957	1	Exxon Corp	29,443,095
2	Standard Oil Co (Indiana)	1,868,000	2	Texaco Inc	14,726,000
3	Shell Oil Co	1,633,000	3	Chevron Corp	14,106,000
4	Chevron Corp	1,590,000	4	Mobil Corp	13,952,000
5	Atlantic Richfield Co	1,547,875	5	Standard Oil Co (Indiana)	12,440,000
6	Standard Oil Co (Ohio)	1,512,000	6	Conoco Inc	11,472,000
7	Mobil Corp	1,503,000	7	Shell Oil Co	11,359,000
8	Texaco Inc	1,233,000	8	Atlantic Richfield Co	10,888,138

9	Gulf Corp	978,000	9	Gulf Corp	10,128,000
10	Phillips Petroleum Co	721,000	10	Standard Oil Co (Ohio)	8,094,000
11	Tenneco Inc	716,000	11	Tenneco Inc	7,004,000
12	Unocal Corp	625,900	12	Phillips Petroleum Co	6,149,000
13	Conoco Inc	621,000	13	Getty Oil Co	5,402,707
14	Occidental Petroleum Corp	566,699	14	Sun Co	5,236,000
15	Marathon Oil Co	522,000	15	Unocal Corp	5,180,100
16	Getty Oil Co	494,314	16	Occidental Petroleum Corp	4,642,051
17	Sun Co	453,000	17	Diamond Shamrock Corp	2,743,327
18	Union Texas Petroleum	413,000	18	Amerada Hess Corp	2,525,663
19	Texas Oil & Gas Corp	295,703	19	Superior Oil Co	2,467,790
20	Superior Oil Co	241,755	20	Houston Industries Inc.	2,070,470

The Top 20 in U.S. and World Liquid Reserves

Rank	*Company name*	*U.S. liquid reserves* (000 *bbl*)	*Rank*	*Company name*	*World liquid reserves* (000 *bbl*)
1	Standard Oil Co (Ohio)	2,818,400	1	Exxon Corp	6,478,000
2	Exxon Corp	2,782,000	2	Standard Oil Co (Ohio)	2,818,400
3	Atlantic Richfield Co	2,573,000	3	Atlantic Richfield Co	2,783,000
4	Shell Oil Co	2,166,000	4	Standard Oil Co (Indiana)	2,632,000
5	Standard Oil Co (Indiana)	1,706,000	5	Shell Oil Co	2,237,000
6	Getty Oil Co	1,189,000	6	Mobil Corp	2,148,000
7	Chevron Corp	1,182,000	7	Gulf Corp	2,046,000
8	Texaco Inc	967,000	8	Getty Oil Co	1,881,000
9	Mobil Corp	855,000	9	Texaco Inc	1,840,000
10	Gulf Corp	791,000	10	Chevron Corp	1,643,000
11	Unocal Corp	662,000	11	Conoco Inc	1,539,000
12	Sun Co	655,000	12	Marathon Oil Co	1,096,086
13	Marathon Oil Co	574,336	13	Phillips Petroleum Co	1,048,000
14	Phillips Petroleum Co	553,000	14	Occidental Petroleum Corp	920,000
15	Conoco Inc	366,000	15	Unocal Corp	856,000
16	Tenneco Inc	254,000	16	Sun Co	780,000
17	Occidental Petroleum Corp	242,000	17	Amerada Hess Corp	740,000
18	Amerada Hess Corp	237,000	18	Tenneco Inc	380,000
19	Superior Oil Co	180,034	19	Superior Oil Co	314,305
20	Champlin Petroleum Co	154,100	20	Texas Eastern Corp	168,292

(*Continued*)

Exhibit 30.1 *(Continued)*

The Top 20 in U.S. and World Liquid Production

Rank	*Company name*	*U.S. liquids production* (000 *bbl*)	*Rank*	*Company name*	*World liquids production* (000 *bbl*)
1	Exxon Corp	285,000	1	Exxon Corp	557,000
2	Atlantic Richfield Co	238,000	2	Standard Oil Co (Indiana)	288,000
3	Standard Oil Co (Ohio)	223,800	3	Atlantic Richfield Co	253,000
4	Shell Oil Co	191,000	4	Texaco Inc	232,000
5	Standard Oil Co (Indiana)	149,000	5	Standard Oil Co (Ohio)	223,800
6	Texaco Inc	124,000	6	Shell Oil Co	197,000
7	Chevron Corp	116,000	7	Gulf Corp	196,000
8	Getty Oil Co	104,000	8	Mobil Corp	191,000
9	Mobil Corp	102,000	9	Chevron Corp	174,000
10	Gulf Corp	100,000	10	Getty Oil Corp	149,000
11	Sun Co	74,000	11	Conoco Inc	143,810
12	Unocal Corp	64,000	12	Occidental Petroleum Corp	121,000
13	Marathon Oil Co	57,410	13	Phillips Petroleum Co	106,000
14	Phillips Petroleum Co	57,000	14	Unocal Corp	92,000
15	Conoco Inc	42,340	15	Marathon Oil Co	85,709
16	Tenneco Inc	33,000	16	Sun Co	85,000
17	Occidental Petroleum Corp	31,000	17	Amerada Hess Corp	56,000
18	Amerada Hess Corp	27,000	18	Tenneco Inc	47,000
19	Champlin Petroleum Co	22,198	19	Union Texas Petroleum	31,598
20	Superior Oil Co	19,557	20	Superior Oil Co	28,693

The Top 20 in U.S. and World Gas Reserves

Rank	*Company name*	*U.S. gas reserves* (*MMcf*)	*Rank*	*Company name*	*World gas reserves* (*MMcf*)
1	Exxon Corp	17,433,000	1	Exxon Corp	29,279,000
2	Atlantic Richfield Co	14,065,000	2	Mobil Corp	18,327,000
3	Standard Oil Co (Indiana)	9,391,000	3	Standard Oil Co (Indiana)	15,190,000
4	Shell Oil Co	7,434,000	4	Atlantic Richfield Co	14,741,000
5	Mobil Corp	6,275,000	5	Texaco Inc	8,528,000
6	Standard Oil Co (Ohio)	6,246,500	6	Shell Oil Co	7,688,000
7	Texaco Inc	5,481,000	7	Phillips Petroleum Co	6,859,000
8	Unocal Corp	5,049,000	8	Chevron Corp	6,658,000
9	Chevron Corp	4,877,000	9	Unocal Corp	6,365,000

10	Gulf Corp	3,772,000	10	Standard Oil Co (Ohio)	6,246,500
11	Phillips Petroleum Co	3,548,000	11	Gulf Corp	5,659,000
12	Tenneco Inc	3,402,000	12	Superior Oil Co	4,250,000
13	Sun Co	2,931,000	13	Sun Co	3,410,000
14	Burlington Northern Oil & Gas Div	2,554,000	14	Tenneco Inc	3,408,000
15	Occidental Petroleum Corp	2,436,000	15	Marathon Oil Co	3,315,701
16	Getty Oil Co	2,203,000	16	Conoco Inc	3,028,000
17	Conoco Inc	2,198,000	17	Getty Oil Co	2,820,000
18	Superior Oil Co	1,929,000	18	Burlington Northern Oil & Gas Div	2,554,000
19	Champlin Petroleum Co	1,807,900	19	Occidental Petroleum Corp	2,534,000
20	Marathon Oil Co	1,765,366	20	Amerada Hess Corp	1,998,000

The Top 20 in U.S. and World Gas Production

Rank	*Company name*	*U.S. gas production (MMcf)*	*Rank*	*Company name*	*World gas production (MMcf)*
1	Exxon Corp	946,000	1	Exxon Corp	1,516,000
2	Texaco Inc	674,000	2	Standard Oil Co (Indiana)	945,000
3	Standard Oil Co (Indiana)	637,000	3	Mobil Corp	860,000
4	Shell Oil Co	539,000	4	Texaco Inc	776,000
5	Atlantic Richfield Co	481,000	5	Shell Oil Co	543,000
6	Gulf Corp	466,000	6	Gulf Corp	534,000
7	Mobil Corp	448,000	7	Atlantic Richfield Co	526,000
8	Chevron Corp	422,000	8	Chevron Corp	496,000
9	Tenneco Inc	360,000	9	Phillips Petroleum Co	468,000
10	Unocal Corp	301,000	10	Unocal Corp	361,000
11	Phillips Petroleum Co	289,000	11	Tenneco Inc	360,000
12	Sun Co	271,000	12	Sun Co	302,000
13	Getty Oil Co	267,000	13	Superior Oil Co	300,000
14	Occidental Petroleum Corp	237,000	14	Getty Oil Co	276,000
15	Superior Oil Co	235,000	15	Conoco Inc	274,480
16	Conoco Inc	213,160	16	Occidental Petroleum Corp	262,000
17	Texas Oil & Gas Corp	149,507	17	Marathon Oil Co	196,575
18	Marathon Oil Co	129,515	18	Amerada Hess Corp	178,000
19	Pennzoil Co	120,000	19	Texas Oil Gas Corp	149,507
20	Consolidated Natural Gas Co	101,000	20	Pennzoil Co	132,000

(Continued)

Exhibit 30.1 (*Continued*)

The Top 20 in Spending and in Net U.S. Wells Drilled					
Rank	*Company name*	*Capital & exploratory spending ($000)*	*Rank*	*Company name*	*U.S. net wells drilled*
1	Exxon Corp	9,000,000	1	Exxon Corp	1,035.0
2	Standard Oil Co (Indiana)	4,091,000	2	Standard Oil Co (Indiana)	840.0
3	Texaco Inc	3,833,000	3	Sun Co	794.0
4	Mobil Corp	3,771,000	4	Gulf Corp	737.0
5	Atlantic Richfield Co	3,355,384	5	Texas Oil & Gas Corp	704.8
6	Chevron Corp	3,067,000	6	Getty Oil Co	597.6
7	Shell Oil Co	2,850,000	7	Shell Oil Co	595.0
8	Gulf Corp	2,770,000	8	Texaco Inc	555.0
9	Standard Oil Co (Ohio)	2,298,000	9	Atlantic Richfield Co	480.0
10	Unocal Corp	1,751,000	10	Mobil Corp	437.0
11	Conoco Inc	1,744,700	11	Chevron Corp	428.0
12	Tenneco Inc	1,609,000	12	Conoco Inc	343.0
13	Sun Co	1,294,000	13	Quaker State Oil Refining Corp	333.9
14	Getty Oil Co	1,223,319	14	Marathon Oil Co	268.0
15	Phillips Petroleum Co	1,141,000	15	Unocal Corp	259.0
16	Superior Oil Co	1,016,855	16	Phillips Petroleum Co	254.0
17	Marathon Oil Co	969,000	17	Consolidated Natural Gas Co	249.3
18	Occidental Petroleum Corp	951,019	18	Occidental Petroleum Corp	199.0
19	Amerada Hess Corp	726,365	19	Champlin Petroleum Co	190.0
20	Texas Oil & Gas Corp	662,332	20	Houston Natural Gas Corp	187.0

SOURCE: "The OGT 400," *Oil and Gas Journal*, September 10, 1984, pp. 103–110. Reprinted by permission.

a rate of only 1 to 2% annually for the next several years, stocks of the big oil firms were trading at substantial discounts to the value of the wealth they had amassed to date.[15] The generation of huge cash flows coming from the production and sales of oil and gas reserves was generally far larger than could be prudently spent on new drilling prospects. After noting the bad experiences of Mobil, Sohio, Ashland Oil, and Exxon, among others, in investing outside of the energy industry, and considering the depressed nature of coal and nuclear energy, almost all of the large firms had been raising their dividends.

U.S. crude oil reserves have dropped every year since 1971. In 1983, the twenty largest U.S. oil companies found only 60% as much domestic petroleum as they produced. Exploration expenditures, however, rose from $5.4 billion in 1973 to $30.7 billion in 1981 with the average number of exploratory wells more than doubling. When the average finding costs of over $15 per barrel for the major firms were discounted to present value, they were only marginally profitable at a March 1984 world price of $29 per barrel.[16] It therefore made sense for oil firms to supplement their exploration activities by buying other companies' reserves. Noting that the industry was not heavily concentrated by Federal Trade Commission and Justice Department standards, the U.S. Congress in March 1984 rejected a proposed eleven-month moratorium on further oil industry mergers. A green light was thus given to further merger activity for the foreseeable future.

Recent Actions

Companies like Exxon, Standard Oil of Indiana, and Standard Oil of Ohio were actively buying back their own stock in 1984. Such a move served several functions. Assets were acquired with excess cash at low risk without a takeover premium. By reducing stock outstanding, earnings per share was increased. The company's stock price was also supported.

Most large oil companies in 1984 appeared to be seriously considering cutting back the activities or even selling their nonrelated acquisitions. Ashland, for example, announced in September 1984 its proposed sale of Integon Corporation, its insurance holding company, and a number of units of the U.S. Filter Corporation it had acquired in 1981. "This is really a return on Ashland's part to businesses that we historically have operated and are skilled in," said John R. Hall, chairman and chief executive officer of Ashland Oil. "We felt that we were trying to do too many different things."[17] Ironically, Ashland sold most of its oil reserves in the 1970s and used the proceeds for its ill-fated diversification.

Additional Concerns

Even with various belt-tightening and refocusing efforts, oil companies will continue to face some difficult times. John Neerhout, Jr., President of Bechtel Petroleum, Inc., concluded in late 1984, "We've just weathered one of the toughest storms in our history. There won't be another boom like the one during 1979–81."[18] In addition to the knowledge that oil and gas are nonrenewable resources which may become impractical to recover in sixty more years, are several short-term challenges. One is likely long-term glut of world refining capacity aggravated by a continuing push by oil producing nations such as Saudi Arabia and Indonesia to develop their own "downstream" facilities.

Another concern is the recent requirement by the U.S. Environmental Protection Agency that the lead content of leaded gasoline be reduced from its present 1.1 gram per gallon to 0.1 gram per gallon by January 1, 1986. Although most refiners seem to agree with ARCO's announced statement accepting the agency's view that lead in gasoline must be reduced as soon as possible because of public health considerations, they are very concerned with the lack of time and the likely cost of refinery conversions. Dallas consulting engineers Turner, Mason, and Associates predict that the proposed phasedown would cost refiners $995 million a year in operating costs.[19] Given the precarious financial position of many independent refiners, such a requirement might force them to cease operations. Severe gasoline shortages could result in 1986 until the industry is able to adjust.

SOHIO'S OPERATIONS

Taking over from Charles Spahr in 1978 as chief executive officer, Alton W. Whitehouse, Jr. has worked hard to transform Sohio from a small regional marketer/refiner into a major integrated oil company. Coming to the company in 1968 as the firm's first chief legal counsel, Mr. Whitehouse represented Sohio in the negotiations with British Petroleum. He subsequently became Sohio's president in 1970 and its vice-chairman in 1977. Admitting his lack of technical knowledge of the oil industry, Mr. Whitehouse divided the company into five business groups and delegated most operating responsibility to the unit heads. He emphasized exploration activities (an area of traditional weakness at Sohio), the hiring and promoting of experienced managers and professionals, and increased research and development. From a staff of 60 exploration engineers and staff in 1977, the number had increased to nearly 1,000 by the end of 1983. At Sohio's annual top management conference in February 1984, 38 of the 80 executives present had joined the company since 1980, according to Glenn Brown, senior vice president for technology and planning.[20] (For further information on Sohio's board of directors, key officers, and operating executives, refer to Exhibit 30.2.) Research and development expenditures were increased from $15.1 million in 1978 to $54 million in 1981 and $109 million in 1983. A $35 million program completed in 1983 doubled the Cleveland laboratory space.

A second "major technology campus" is to be located in Dallas, Texas to focus on exploration and production research and development.

Standard Oil of Ohio is presently organized into five business units: *Exploration and Production* (Sohio Petroleum Company), *Petroleum Trading, Transportation, Refining and Marketing* (Sohio Oil Company), *Chemicals and Industrial Products* (SCIPCO), *Metals Mining* (Kennecott Corporation), and *Coal* (Old Ben Coal Company). In 1983, petroleum comprised 78.2% of sales and operating revenue (80.3% in 1982); coal 3.0% (2.6% in 1982); metals mining 6.0% (4.4% in 1982); chemicals 4.7% (4.1% in 1982); and industrial products 8.1% (8.6% in 1982).[21]

Exploration and Production

At year-end 1983, Sohio's proved reserves (total developed and undeveloped liquids) totaled 2.8 billion barrels of crude oil, condensate, and natural gas liquids plus 6.2 trillion cubic feet of natural gas. These are the largest domestic and second largest total liquids reserve held by a U.S. oil company. Weak prices have thus far ruled out building the costly pipelines needed to bring the natural gas to market. Sohio's largest oil producing area, Prudhoe Bay, produced 589,200 barrels per day in 1983 compared to 673,200 barrels per day in 1982. This decrease was due to an agreement reached with Sohio's Prudhoe partners (Atlantic Richfield and Exxon) to make a final adjustment concerning ownership of the field. Under the agreement, Sohio's participating interest in the oil reservoir declined from 53.0 to 50.4%, resulting in a maximum allowable production of 661,700 barrels per day. In order to adjust for production in previous years, Sohio agreed to reduce its allowable production by 76,000 net barrels a day for a two-year period ending September 3, 1984. A total of 224 million barrels of crude oil and natural gas liquids were produced in 1983. Of these, approximately 96% were produced by Sohio in the Prudhoe Bay area.

The Kuparuk field, 40 miles west of Prudhoe Bay, averaged 109,200 gross barrels per day during its second year of operation. With its 9.6% interest in the field, Sohio's net production was 5,600 barrels per day. This amount should increase over the next few years as the field moves to full production in 1987.

Sohio has five producing wells in the Rocky Mountains plus others in Nebraska, Oklahoma, Texas, and Arkansas. Although these wells do not produce a great deal of oil, they are very stable and easily accessible. The company's first platform began production in the Gulf of Mexico in 1984. Four more are planned by 1987.

As a result of its aggressive search for promising oil leases, Sohio had about five million undeveloped acres by the end of 1983. Exploratory drilling expenditures totaled $132 million in 1983 and are expected to more

Exhibit 30.2

BOARD OF DIRECTORS AND TOP MANAGEMENT, STANDARD OIL OF OHIO

BOARD OF DIRECTORS

E. E. Bailey
Dean, Graduate School of Industrial Administration
Carnegie-Mellon University

T. D. Barrow
Vice Chairman

R. Bexon[3]
Deputy Chairman
The British Petroleum Company p.l.c.
(an International Oil Company)

G. R. Brown
Senior Vice-President
Technology and Planning

D. W. Buchanan, Jr.[2, 4]
Retired President
Old Ben Oil Company

[1] Member of Executive Committee
[2] Member of Audit Committee
[3] Member of Compensation Committee
[4] Member of Pension Committee

W. J. DeLancey[1, 3]
Retired Chairman of the Board and Chief Executive Officer
Republic Steel Corporation
(Steel Manufacturer)

J. J. Hangen[2, 4]
Chairman of the Board and Chief Executive Officer
Appleton Papers Inc.
(Paper Manufacturer)

R. B. Horton
Managing Director
The British Petroleum Company p.l.c.
(an International Oil Company)

C. F. Knight[2]
Chairman of the Board and Chief Executive Officer
Emerson Electric Co.
(Electrical and Electronic Products and Systems Manufacturer)

W. A. L. Manson[4]
President
BP North America, Inc.
(Subsidiary of the British Petroleum Company p.l.c., an International Oil Company)

R. C. McPherson[1, 3]
Corporate Director

J. R. Miller
President and Chief Operating Officer

F. E. Mosier
Senior Vice President—
Petroleum Trading, Transportation, Refining, and Marketing

W. P. Rogers[3]
Senior Partner
Law Firm of Rogers & Wells

A. W. Whitehouse[1]
Chairman of the Board and Chief Executive Officer

OFFICERS

A. W. Whitehouse*[1, 2, 3]
Chairman of the Board and Chief Executive Officer

T. D. Barrow*[1, 2, 3]
Vice Chairman

J. R. Miller*[1, 2, 3]
President and Chief Operating Officer

R. A. Bray[3]
Senior Vice President—
Exploration and Production

G. R. Brown[1, 3]
Senior Vice President—
Technology and Planning

A. H. Ford[1, 3]
Senior Vice President—
Finance and Control

G. F. Joklik[3]
Senior Vice President—
Metals Mining

C. H. King[2, 3]
Senior Vice President—
Administration

W. P. Madar[3]
Senior Vice President—
Chemicals and Industrial Products

F. E. Mosier[3]
Senior Vice President—
Petroleum Trading, Transportation, Refining, and Marketing

D. J. Atton
Vice President—
Corporate Planning

R. M. Donaldson
Vice President—Government and Public Affairs

G. J. Dunn[3]
Vice President and General Counsel

D. C. Haley
Vice President—Control

R. A. Meierhenry
Vice President—Finance and Treasurer

E. H. Nielsen
Vice President—Human Resources

V. J. Carbone
Controller

W. P. Ginn
Corporate Secretary

SOURCE: *1983 Annual Report,* Standard Oil Company (Ohio), pp. 62–63.
* Member of Office of the Chairman
[1] Member of Strategy Review Committee
[2] Member of Human Resources Committee
[3] Member of Operations Committee

Exhibit 30.2 ***(Continued)***

KEY OPERATING EXECUTIVES

Exploration and Production

R. A. Bray
Sohio Petroleum Company President

J. J. Hohler
Exploration

D. D. Lybarger
Production

R. A. Flohr
Western Region

R. D. Wilson
Central and Southern Region

G. N. Nelson
Alaska

H. D. Yorston
Construction

Petroleum Trading, Transportation, Refining, and Marketing

F. E. Mosier
Sohio Oil Company President

J. G. McDonald
Petroleum Products and Refining

R. A. McGimpsey
Crude Trading and Transportation

H. D. Hanna
Retail Marketing

D. R. Brinkley
Transportation

J. D. Campbell, Jr.
Wholesale Marketing and Distribution

J. L. Locker
Refining

Chemicals and Industrial Products

W. P. Mader, Jr.
Sohio Chemicals and Industrial Products Company President

E. J. Finn
Sohio Chemicals and Industrial Products Company Executive Vice President

W. W. Colville
Processed Minerals Sector

J. E. Goodell
Process Systems and Equipment Sector

L. F. Kahl
Engineered Materials Sector and Carborundum Company

R. R. Mesel
Chase Brass and Copper Company

L. A. Pagliaro
Sohio Chemical Company

C. J. Barton
Dorr-Oliver Incorporated

B. J. Grierson
QIT-Fer et Titane Inc.

W. A. Himmler
The Pfaudler Co.

J. E. Jackson
Pangborn

Metals Mining

G. F. Joklik
Kennecott President

R. C. Cereghini
Control, Planning and Administration

J. R. Cool
Human Resources, Government and Public Affairs

T. S. Murphree
Kennecott Sales

J. B. Winter
Operations

Coal

G. Blackmore
Old Ben Coal Company President

M. M. O'Brien
Operations

T. G. Norris
Business Development

H. E. Sergent
Marketing

H. M. Sartin
Administration

than double by 1985.[22] (For additional statistics on exploration and production, see Exhibit 30.3.)

Petroleum Trading, Transportation, Refining and Marketing

Sohio owns 2,500 miles of crude oil and product pipelines and has varying interests in 8,500 more miles of pipelines. In addition to its interest in the Trans-Alaska Pipeline System (TAPS), Sohio has formed a partnership with two other companies to transport expected increased oil production from the Kuparuk field to TAPS. Its share of the pipeline cost is estimated at approximately $15 million. The pipeline is to be completed late 1984.

Sohio currently owns three refineries with a total rated capacity of 456,000 barrels of crude oil per day. These refineries are located in Marcus

Exhibit 30.3

EXPLORATION AND PRODUCTION FIGURES FOR 1982 AND 1983, STANDARD OIL OF OHIO

	1983	1982
Liquid reserves—year-end (million net barrels)		
Alaska	2,772.8	2,807.1
Lower 48 states	45.6	48.5
	2,818.4	2,855.6
Natural gas reserves—year-end (billion net cubic feet)		
Alaska	6,002.0	6,125.2
Lower 48 states	244.5	265.8
	6,246.5	6,391.0
U.S. drilling (net wells)		
Exploratory		
Productive	3.2	4.4
Dry	17.6	11.2
Development		
Productive	69.3	96.4
Dry	5.6	3.4
U.S. undeveloped acreage (net acres)		
Alaska	263,950	248,688
Lower 48 States	4,870,179	4,655,543
Net production crude oil and liquids (barrels per day)		
Alaska	594,800	676,700
Lower 48 states	17,200	18,200
	612,000	694,900
Natural gas sales (million cubic feet per day)		
Alaska	14.9	14.3
Lower 48 states	80.7	76.4
	95.6	90.7
Average crude oil wellhead prices per barrel		
Alaska	$18.26	$20.61
Lower 48 States	29.06	31.86
Average natural gas prices per thousand cubic feet	$2.61	$2.38

SOURCE: *1983 Annual Report,* The Standard Oil Company (Ohio), p. 7.

Hook, Pennsylvania; Lima, Ohio; and Toledo, Ohio. These plants were operated at 86% of total distillation capacity in 1983 compared to an industry average of around 78%.[23]

Sohio's marketing consists mostly of retail outlets selling petroleum products in Ohio and parts of the East Coast and Midwest under the Sohio, BP, and Boron names. Facing continued forecasts of decreasing gasoline demand while station expenses continue to rise, the company is responding by increasing the number of self-service stations. These self-service outlets accounted for 72% of Sohio's retail gasoline sales in 1983. Adding to its present total of seventeen truck stops, the company is acquiring Truckstops of America, a subsidiary of Ryder Systems. This will bring the total number of Sohio truck stops to forty.

Chemicals and Industrial Products

Sohio Chemicals and Industrial Products Company (SCIPCO) was formed in 1982 by joining Sohio's chemical business with the manufacturing and mineral processing businesses acquired as part of Kennecott in 1981. With combined 1983 sales of $1.5 billion, SCIPCO's businesses had an operating loss of $150 million including a one-time abrasives pretax writeoff of $137 million. In 1982 SCIPCO had an operating loss of $20 million on sales of $1.7 billion. Many units have been consolidated and reorganized to make SCIPCO smaller and more efficient. Manufacturing operations, for example, were reduced from ninety-two locations in 1982 to sixty-four in 1983.

At this point, SCIPCO is considered "a sleeper," says Glenn Brown, Sohio's senior vice-president for technology and planning. Many of its high potential products, such as high-performance ceramics, photovoltaics (for solar energy conversion to electricity), and Chase Brass' narrow brass strip, are still under development. Investment in R&D for SCIPCO increased 18% in 1983 with a further increase in 1984.

Metals Mining

Kennecott, the nation's largest copper producer, has three open-pit mining and processing operations, with total capacity to produce about 440,000 tons of refined copper annually. In addition to copper, Kennecott produces by-product metals including gold, silver, lead, and molybdenum. Sohio expects an increasing demand for copper in the future because of copper's outstanding qualities as an electrical conductor and because of the recent improvement in the economy. The modernization of facilities plus a cost reduction program resulted in 1983 in an increase in copper production of 11% and a reduction of Kennecott's operating losses by 50%. During 1983, Kennecott acquired three "promising" gold projects in western Nevada, central Brazil, and New Guinea. The company also owns a 49% interest in a Mexican mining company which found a new silver vein in its Bolanos mines in Mexico. Nevertheless, Kennecott faces another year of losses in 1984 as world copper prices continued to fall through July.

Coal

The Old Ben Coal Company produces bituminous coal obtained from surface and underground mines. Most of the coal is mined in Illinois and Indiana with the rest in West Virginia's eastern panhandle. Operating improvements in 1983 reduced costs and resulted in higher operating income in spite of depressed industry conditions. Old Ben reported operating income of $21 million in 1983 compared to a loss of $1 million in 1982. The company was able to be more efficient by operating some mines at or near capacity while letting some others lie idle.

Old Ben's proved and probable coal reserves total 1.7 billion saleable tons. Its principal customers are electric utilities. These utilities, which burn approximately 83% of the coal consumed in the United States, bought 5.5% less coal from 1981 through 1983 from all sources. As more utilities convert to coal from petroleum and natural gas, coal consumption should increase unless increasing concerns with acid rain curtail its use.

Sohio's top management is very optimistic about the long-term prospect for coal. They believe that long-term demand will soon grow faster than real gross national product. Old Ben is located well geographically, has excellent transportation alternatives, and a diverse reserve base (coal reserves located throughout Appalachia and the Midwest of various grades).

COMMUNITY RELATIONS

Sohio's Alaskan venture and the resultant rapid growth made the corporation a target of protests in its hometown. At a time when gasoline lines and steep prices were aggravating motorists, and unemployment was growing in northeastern Ohio, Sohio was earning millions of dollars from its Prudhoe Bay oil. In 1982, the company abruptly halted its annual meeting of shareholders after the first five minutes because of protestors. During that same year, demonstrators asking Sohio for a billion-dollar contribution to a fund to pay energy bills for the poor staged a weekend protest at the Chagrin Valley Hunt Club, a social club attended by Cleveland executives, including Alton Whitehouse. Shouting, "We want Whitehouse," the demonstrators surged across the club's lawns and were given heavy coverage by a local Cleveland television station.

In a recent interview, Mr. Whitehouse commented that the company has learned a lot since then. "The industry was perceived as being very arrogant, and that may have been true at one time, but I don't think it's true anymore." Sohio's problem, he says, is that "success in a depressed part of the country can create some negative reactions which I think are understandable."[24] Ms. Geraldine Brooks, a *Wall Street Journal* reporter, comments that the company is no longer an activist target, partly because its recent failures have been more conspicuous than its successes.

Sohio is presently erecting a new corporate headquarters building on Public Square in downtown Cleveland. Referring to its new forty-five story office building as a "symbol of downtown renaissance and Sohio's commitment to its hometown," management sees the new building as part of the revitalization of Cleveland's decaying downtown area. Sitting on the eastern edge of Public Square across from the fifty-two-story Terminal Tower, the "Sohio Building" will include an atrium housing shops, restaurants, and a skylit public garden. Scheduled for completion in 1985, the building has already been cited as the reason Cleveland's Downtown Business Council named Sohio in 1984 the recipient of its sixth annual Downtown Recognition Award for physical development.

FINANCIAL

Financial data for Sohio covering the past five years is presented in Exhibits 30.4 through 30.8. During 1984, Sohio offered to pay $47.50 a share for

Exhibit 30.4

SELECTED FINANCIAL DATA, STANDARD OIL OF OHIO

(Millions of Dollars)

	1983	1982	1981	1980	1979
Sales and operating revenue	$12,067	$13,529	$14,140	$11,367	$8,241
Income before interest and income taxes	2,909	3,697	4,068	3,868	2,434
Net income	1,512	1,879	1,947	1,811	1,186
Per share of common stock					
Net income	6.14	7.63	7.92	7.37	4.91
Cash dividends	2.60	2.55	2.25	1.40	.61
Cash provided from operations	2,946	3.091	1,930	3,886	2,463
Capital expenditures	2,298	2,708	4,501	1,007	602
Total assets	16,362	16,016	15,743	12,080	9,209
Long-term debt and capital lease obligations	3,843	4,185	3,878	3,529	3,822
Debt to borrowed and invested capital*	30%	34%	37%	42%	51%

SOURCE: *1983 Annual Report,* The Standard Oil Company (Ohio), p. 39.

* Debt includes long-term debt (excluding borrowings under reverse repurchase agreements, if any), capitalized lease obligations, and current maturities of long-term obligations. "Borrowed and invested capital" includes debt, deferred income taxes, and shareholders' equity.

STATEMENT OF INCOME, STANDARD OIL OF OHIO
(Millions of Dollars—Year Ended December 31)

Exhibit 30.5

	1983	1982	1981
Revenues			
Sales and operating revenue (including excise taxes)	$12,067	$13,529	$14,140
Interest income	148	313	527
	12,215	13,842	14,667
Costs and expenses			
Costs of products sold and operating expenses	5,342	5,810	5,601
Windfall profit tax	169	620	1,438
Other taxes, excluding income taxes	1,343	1,432	1,406
Depreciation, depletion, and amortization	767	727	625
Oil and gas exploration expenses, including amortization of unproved properties	834	486	368
Selling, general, and administrative expenses	703	757	634
Interest expense	402	613	573
	9,560	10,445	10,645
Income before income taxes	2,655	3,397	4,022
Income taxes	1,143	1,518	2,075
Net income	$ 1,512	$ 1,879	$ 1,947

SOURCE: *1983 Annual Report,* The Standard Oil Company (Ohio), p. 40.

eleven million of its shares of common stock. By August 20, approximately 22.9 million (20 percent of the company's 116 million publicly traded shares—not counting British Petroleum's share equivalents) were tendered. Top management announced that it would buy 48% of the tendered shares on a pro rata basis, paying a total of $525.5 million. On August 17, the stock was selling for $45.25 a share. Management further commented that it intends to buy its common stock from time to time as market conditions warrant. A company spokesperson said that the company was not surprised by the large number of shares tendered. "We just don't have as many long-term loyal investors as we used to."[25]

RECENT DEVELOPMENT

On September 27, Chevron Corporation (Standard Oil of California) announced that it had accepted Sohio's bid to purchase Gulf's service stations in the Southeast plus Gulf's 200,000 barrel-a-day refinery in Louisiana. The sale includes all of Gulf's wholesale and retail petroleum businesses in Kentucky, Tennessee, Alabama, Mississippi, Georgia, Florida, South Carolina, and North Carolina. Sohio outbid an international field of competitors including Mobil Corp. and Kuwait Petroleum Corp. The contract calls for Sohio to pay $340 million for the marketing businesses and the refinery plus another $350 million for about 10 million barrels of petroleum inventories. The funding for the acquisition is to come from "a combination of internally generated funds and short-term borrowings," stated a spokesperson for Sohio. The spokesperson also remarked that the addition of the Louisiana refinery will allow the company to refine more of its crude oil instead of having to sell it.[26] The sale of these units is one of the steps being taken by Chevron to complete its acquisition of Gulf Oil, the largest takeover in corporate history.

LOOKING TO THE FUTURE

Now producing at the maximum rate permitted by the state of Alaska—1.5 million gross barrels of oil a day—the Prudhoe field is expected by Sohio's top management to begin its natural production decline in 1987. It may decline to approximately 750,000 barrels a day by 1992. As of the fourth quarter of 1984, Sohio's share of production is 661,700 barrels a day. With various planned oil recovery techniques, such as the injection of enriched gas into the oil reservoir, Sohio hopes that it may be able to maintain its 600,000 barrel-a-day production until the end of the century.

In a letter to the stockholders dated February 24, 1984, Mr. Whitehouse stated that 70% of the capital expenditures planned for 1984 will be energy related. Of this spending, 94% will be for oil and gas activities. "This action reaffirms our intention to remain primarily a domestic energy company with emphasis on oil and gas."[27] James Hohler, Executive Vice-President for exploration, contends, however, that Sohio should do more hunting abroad because of the decreasing chance of another big strike in the United States. His superior, Richard Bray, is skeptical of this idea and is wary of exploring for oil in Central America, Antarctica, or other foreign lands because of the political hazards. Top management's main exploration concerns therefore lie in the Gulf of Mexico and in the Beaufort Sea, Prudhoe Bay, and Bering Sea areas of the Arctic. Bray comments that Sohio is "constantly crunching the numbers" on possible acquisitions, but prefers to find the oil rather than to buy it. "Exploration, if you do it right, isn't all that exorbitant," he adds.[28]

At its forthcoming meeting on September 27, 1984, Sohio's board of directors will consider the funding of expenditures estimated at around $900 million by one analyst to bring the Endicott oil field in Alaska into production. Located northeast of Prudhoe Bay, Endicott has about 350 million recoverable barrels of oil—approximately one-tenth the size of Prudhoe. Sohio, owning a 57% interest, would be operator of the field. Standard Oil of Indiana, Exxon, Atlantic Richfield, and Union Oil each hold a 10% stake with an Alaskan native group holding the remainder. An oil analyst commented that Endicott could produce oil at a rate of 100,000 barrels a day over five years and that it could be operating by 1988.

The board will also be asked at its September meeting to approve funding

BALANCE SHEET, STANDARD OIL OF OHIO
(Millions of Dollars—Year Ended December 31)

Exhibit 30.6

	1983	1982
ASSETS		
Current assets		
Cash and short-term investments	$ 91	$ 163
Accounts receivable, less allowance	1,169	684
Inventories	1,154	1,439
Prepaid expenses and deferred charges	72	144
	2,486	2,430
Other assets		
Investments	781	1,436
Long-term receivables	407	380
Prepaid expenses and deferred charges	131	102
	1,319	1,918
Property, plant and equipment		
Petroleum		
Exploration and production	11,742	10,127
Refining and marketing	1,292	1,238
Coal	1,158	1,137
Metals mining	1,967	1,824
Chemicals	596	511
Industrial products	424	465
Corporate and other	294	223
	17,473	15,525
Less accumulated depreciation, depletion, and amortization	4,916	3,857
	12,557	11,668
	$16,362	$16,016

Exhibit 30.6
(Continued)

	1983	1982
LIABILITIES AND SHAREHOLDERS' EQUITY		
Current liabilities		
Notes payable	$ 25	$ 236
Accounts payable	1,418	1,217
Accrued income and other taxes	296	623
Accrued interest	120	124
Other accrued expenses	522	480
Current maturities of long-term obligations	128	297
	2,509	2,977
Long-term obligations		
Long-term debt	3,474	3,805
Capital lease obligations	369	380
Other	701	665
	4,544	4,850
Deferred income taxes	1,215	968
Shareholders' equity		
Capital Stock		
Common—$1.25 stated value, 300 million shares authorized, shares issued: 1983—121,796,171; 1982—121,421,389	152	152
Special—stated value, 1,000 shares authorized and issued	25	25
	177	177
Additional paid-in capital	789	787
Retained earnings	7,128	6,257
	8,094	7,221
	$16,362	$16,016

SOURCE: *1983 Annual Report,* The Standard Oil Company (Ohio), pp. 42–43.

for two other Alaska projects. One is to inject enriched gas into Prudhoe wells to increase the recovery of oil by about 149 million barrels. The other project is to develop the Lisburne oil pool underneath the northeastern part of the Prudhoe field.[29]

In an interview with the *Wall Street Journal,* Sohio's top management emphasized its primary concern with exploring for new petroleum resources in Alaska. In response to a question asking if the costly Mukluk project has caused him to lose his nerve, Mr. Whitehouse responded: "If those guys come in with another (enticing prospect like Mukluk) tomorrow, I'll have my neck right back out there."[30]

Exhibit 30.7
BUSINESS SEGMENT DATA, STANDARD OIL OF OHIO (Millions of Dollars)

Business Segment Information	1983	1982	1981	1980	1979
Sales and operating revenue					
Petroleum	$ 9,438	$10,875	$11,953	$10,593	$7,582
Coal	361	346	293	274	231
Metals mining	727	596	539	—	—
Chemicals	566	554	491	486	409
Industrial products	982	1,166	833	—	—
Corporate and other	(7)	(8)	31	14	19
	$12,067	$13,529	$14,140	$11,367	$8,241
Income before interest and income taxes					
Petroleum					
Exploration and production	$ 2,848	$ 3,647	$ 3,900	$ 3,605	$2,239
Refining and marketing	453	390	266	259	191
	3,301	4,037	4,166	3,864	2,430
Coal	21	(1)	(8)	9	4
Metals mining	(91)	(187)	(99)	—	—
Chemicals	(3)	(22)	44	64	37
Industrial products	(147)	2	51	—	—
Corporate and other	(172)	(132)	(86)	(69)	(37)
	$ 2,909	$ 3,697	$ 4,068	$ 3,868	$2,434
Assets					
Petroleum					
Exploration and production	$ 8,536	$ 8,023	$ 7,034	$ 6,159	$6,016
Refining and marketing	1,492	994	1,512	1,500	1,454
	10,028	9,017	8,546	7,659	7,470
Coal	1,103	1,113	932	269	241
Metals mining	2,375	2,450	1,946	—	—
Chemicals	642	534	525	378	216
Industrial products	1,033	1,233	1,179	—	—
Corporate and other	1,181	1,669	2,615	3,774	1,282
	$16,362	$16,016	$15,743	$12,080	$9,209
Capital expenditures					
Petroleum					
Exploration and production	$ 1,795	$ 1,996	$ 1,447	$ 761	$ 500
Refining and marketing	84	102	113	48	40
	1,879	2,098	1,560	809	540
Coal	23	168	666	42	22
Metals mining	156	202	1,668	—	—
Chemicals	87	87	138	110	33
Industrial products	70	71	440	—	—
Corporate and other	83	82	29	46	7
	$ 2,298	$ 2,708	$ 4,501	$ 1,007	$ 602

SOURCE: *1983 Annual Report,* The Standard Oil Company (Ohio), p. 60.

Exhibit 30.8
OPERATING AND OTHER STATISTICS, STANDARD OIL OF OHIO
(Millions of Dollars)

	1983	1982	1981	1980	1979
Petroleum					
Crude oil and natural gas liquids produced (net)—barrels per day					
Alaska	594,800	676,642	698,150	696,377	590,793
Lower 48 states	17,202	18,227	19,141	19,407	20,183
Foreign	—	—	—	—	—
	612,002	694,869	717,291	715,784	610,976
Natural gas sold (net)—thousands of cubic feet per day	95,604	90,678	83,965	79,832	80,563
Refinery runs—barrels per day	393,700	360,100	362,012	400,900	428,552
Refinery capacity (year-end)—barrels per calendar year	456,000	456,000	452,000	452,000	452,000
Refined petroleum products sold—barrels per day					
Gasoline	267,267	243,641	246,117	260,531	269,988
Distillates	90,731	91,248	95,530	98,093	96,823
Residuals	29,269	22,130	21,815	39,282	53,073
Other	17,410	13,922	14,968	16,604	10,232
	404,677	370,941	378,430	414,510	430,116
Marketing retail outlets*	2,100	2,200	2,300	2,300	2,600
Minerals					
Coal sold—thousands of tons	10,661	10,861	9,546	11,082	10,084
Produced copper sold—thousands of tons	316	268	216	—	—
Operating results					
Sales and operating revenue (millions)	$ 12,067	$ 13,529	$ 14,140	$ 11,367	$ 8,241
Net income (millions)	$ 1,512	$ 1,879	$ 1,947	$ 1,811	$ 1,186
Rate of return on borrowed and invested capital	13.4%	17.9%	22.0%	24.3%	19.8%
Ratio of earnings to fixed charges	5.7	5.3	7.2	10.3	5.1
Per share of common stock					
Net income	$ 6.14	$ 7.63	$ 7.92	$ 7.37	$ 4.91
Dividends paid	$ 2.60	$ 2.55	$ 2.25	$ 1.40	$ .61
Market price, high-low	$ 59–35	$ 42–26	$ 73–36	$ 92–40	$ 47–20

SOURCE: *1983 Annual Report,* The Standard Oil Company (Ohio), p. 61.
* Excludes outlets supplied by jobbers, automobile dealers, marine dealers, etc.

(Continued)

Exhibit 30.8 **(*Continued*)**

	1983	1982	1981	1980	1979
Other data					
Average number of shares outstanding (millions)	246	246	246	246	241
Shareholders of record of common stock	62,797	63,339	58,918	51,162	45,679
Employees at year-end	43,984	49,837	56,672	22,938	22,103
Wages, salaries, and employee benefits (millions)	$ 1,510	$ 1,612	$ 1,268	$ 629	$ 541
Research and development expense (millions)	$ 109	$ 71	$ 54	$ 25	$ 18
Maintenance and repairs (millions)	$ 486	$ 583	$ 490	$ 259	$ 218
Exploration expenses (millions)	$ 834	$ 486	$ 368	$ 176	$ 35

NOTES

1. "Sohio Barrels into the Lower 48," *Business Week,* December 13, 1982, p. 56.
2. 1983 Annual Report, p. 9 and "Sohio Discovers Oil at 2 Test Drill Wells in the Gulf of Mexico," *Wall Street Journal,"* September 9, 1984, p. 10.
3. G. Brooks, "After Mukluk Fiasco, Sohio Strives to Find, or Perhaps to Buy, Oil," *Wall Street Journal,* April 19, 1984, p. 22.
4. A. Sullivan, "Sohio Unit to Cut Copper Division by Two-Thirds," *Wall Street Journal,* June 18, 1984, p. 2.
   S. Mufson, "Sagging Copper Prices Are Tarnishing Economies of 2 Big African Producers," *Wall Street Journal,* October 16, 1984, p. 32.
5. "No Pretty Penny for Copper," *Time,* September 17, 1984, p. 70.
6. G. Brooks, p. 22.
7. J. H. Lichtblau, "There's No Need to Crimp Oil Mergers," *Business Week,* April 16, 1984, p. 21.
8. R. B. Schmitt, "Major Oil Firms Are Slashing Jobs as Takeovers Rise, Demand Sags—Most Cuts Borne by Managers," *Wall Street Journal,* April 19, 1984, p. 29.
9. "Coming Up with Dry Holes," *Time,* April 18, 1983, p. 70.
10. "Big Firms Do Well; Most Small Ones Don't," *Oil and Gas Journal,* September 10, 1984, p. 103.
11. "World Oil Output Rose 7% in 1984 First Half, Industry Estimates," *Wall Street Journal,* August 15, 1984, p. 43.
12. "Crystal Oil Lays Off 18% of Its Work Force," *Wall Street Journal,* September 19, 1984, p. 6.

13. J. Curley, "Apex Is Hurt by Problems in Oil Industry," *Wall Street Journal,* September 20, 1984, p. 31.
14. *Fortune,* April 30, 1984.
15. "Ratings and Reports," *Value Line Investment Survey,* Vol. XXXIX, No. 42, July 13, 1984, p. 402.
16. "Why Gulf Lost the Fight for Life," *Business Week,* March 19, 1984, p. 77.
17. R. E. Winter, "Ashland Sets $270 Million Charge, Cites Plan to Sell Units; Fiscal 1984 Loss Seen," *Wall Street Journal,* September 21, 1984, p. 5.
18. "Neerhout: Industry Shifting Emphasis to Upstream Action," *Oil and Gas Journal,* September 17, 1984, p. 160.
19. P. Crow, "Shortages Seen if EPA Enacts Rapid Gasoline Lead Level Cuts," *Oil and Gas Journal,* September 10, 1984, pp. 73–74.
20. G. Brooks, p. 1.
21. *Standard Corporation Descriptions,* Standard and Poor's Corporation, Publishers, Vol. 45, No. 11, June, 1984.
22. 1983 Annual Report, Standard Oil of Ohio, pp. 8 and 9.
23. 1983 Annual Report, p. 18.
24. G. Brooks, p. 22.
25. "Sohio to Buy Back 48% of Shares Tendered for $522.5 Million," *Wall Street Journal,* August 20, 1984, p. 10.
26. M. Chase, "Chevron Agrees to Sell to Sohio Some Gulf Units," *Wall Street Journal,* September 28, 1984, p. 2.
27. 1983 Annual Report, Standard Oil of Ohio, p. 4.
28. G. Brooks, p. 22.
29. "Sohio Board to Vote on Outlays to Start Endicott Production," *Wall Street Journal,* September 14, 1984, p. 7.
30. G. Brooks, p. 22.

SECTION D

MULTINATIONAL

Case 31

THE EUROPEAN ECONOMIC COMMUNITY

H. Landis Gabel/Anthony E. Hall

The European Economic Community was founded in 1957 with the signing of the Treaty of Rome (see Exhibit 31.1). The original signatories of the treaty were France, Germany, Italy, Belgium, Holland, and Luxembourg. The hope of the founders was expressed in Article 2 of the Treaty which read:

> The Community shall have as its task, by establishing a common market and progressively approximating the economic policies of Member States, to promote throughout the Community a harmonious development of economic activities, a continuous and balanced expansion, an increase in stability, an accelerated raising of the standard of living and closer relations between the States belonging to it.

But by 1983, there was virtually universal abandonment of any such hope. Indeed, some observers were questioning whether the EEC would survive another year. National self-interest had, since the various crises of the 1970s, become a progressively greater impediment to Community-wide cooperation, agricultural programs had grown to consume 80% of the EEC budget, and Britain refused to agree to the 1984 budget without a major restructuring of the Community's finances. The state of the automobile industry exemplified many of the EEC's problems.

This case was written by Associate Professor H. Landis Gabel and Research Associate Anthony E. Hall, INSEAD. Revised January 1985. This case also appeared in the *Journal of Management Case Studies,* Vol. 1, No. 3, Fall 1985, pp. 191–195.

Exhibit 31.1

TREATY OF ROME
Article 3

For the purposes set out in Article 2, the activities of the Community shall include, as provided in this Treaty and in accordance with the timetable set out therein

(a) the elimination, as between member states, of customs duties and of quantitative restrictions on the import and export of goods, and of all other measures having equivalent effect
(b) the establishment of a common customs tariff and of a common commercial policy towards third countries
(c) the abolition, as between member states, of obstacles to freedom of movement for persons, services, capital
(d) the adoption of a common policy in the sphere of agriculture
(e) the adoption of a common policy in the sphere of transport
(f) the institution of a system ensuring that competition in the common market is not distorted
(g) the application of procedures by which the economic policies of member states can be coordinated and disequilibria in their balances of payments remedied
(h) the approximation of the laws of member states to the extent required for the proper functioning of the common market
(i) the creation of a European social fund in order to improve employment opportunities for workers and to contribute to the raising of their standard of living
(j) the establishment of a European investment bank to facilitate the economic expansion of the Community by opening up fresh resources

SOURCE: Treaties Establishing the European Communities, 1978.

EUROPEAN INDUSTRIAL POLICY

The European Economic community was governed by the Treaty of Rome, and the European Commission was the official custodian of the articles of the Treaty. The work of the Commission was divided into nineteen directorates which were allocated to fourteen Commissioners who came from the ten member states. (Denmark, Eire, and the United Kingdom joined in 1973, and Greece was admitted to membership after its return to democracy in 1979.)

European industrial policy was the responsibility of the Industry Directorate of the EEC Commission. The head of the Directorate—known as DG III—was Viscount Etienne Davignon, who was also a Vice-President of the Commission. Davignon, a Belgian national, was widely regarded as the most able politician in Brussels and would be a contender for the presidency of the Commission when Gaston Thorn left that office in 1984.

Since the late 1970s, DG III had been moving toward a sectoral approach, as one major industrial sector after another experienced crises brought on, at least in part, by the worldwide recession. Steel, shipbuilding, and textiles were prominent cases of structural adjustment programs. In essence, these programs were attempts to sustain price levels while excess capacity was eliminated by multinationally negotiated agreements.

Japanese imports were a frequent target of EEC sectoral industrial policy, and by 1983, Viscount Davignon had led three major deputations to Japan. The result was that slightly less than 40% of all Japanese imports into the EEC were subject to some form of restriction (often a "voluntary" one). Product categories with import restrictions included automobiles and vans, motorcycles, forklift trucks, color televisions and picture tubes, machine tools, hi-fi equipment, quartz watches, and video tape recorders.

THE EUROPEAN AUTOMOBILE INDUSTRY AND THE STATE

There are major state-owned producers in each of the EEC's major markets: British Leyland in the UK, Renault in France, Alfa-Romeo in Italy (through the holding company of IRI), and Volkswagen in West Germany (40% of which was owned by the federal government and the Lander of Saxony). This has given EEC member-state governments a special interest in their own national producer that goes beyond each government's concern for the contribution that any company's automobile production could make to its domestic economy.

Each country has looked to the automobile industry for regional job creation. Chrysler (later to become Talbot) was persuaded to invest in a plant at Linwood, Scotland; both Peugeot and Renault had been encouraged to invest in new component plants in Alsace and Lorraine; an Alfa-Sud plant was built in depressed Southern Italy; and even the German government offered attractive incentives to locate in high-priority areas such as West Berlin. These national efforts to attract automobile investments as part of regional development schemes led to intense competition between countries for producers' investments. Since 1971, the EEC Commission has tried, with limited success, to coordinate the incentives that member countries have offered and in particular to limit competitive bidding for industry. Looking back at some of the controversial cases of heavy government investment subsidies, the picture is not one of success. Chrysler's Linwood plant closed in 1982, the De Lorean plant in Northern Ireland was closed with the company's bankruptcy, Ford's Halewood facility continues to experience productivity problems, and GM has significantly reduced the output from its UK operations.

Many industry observers believe there is an inherent conflict between an employment objective and an objective of establishing a successful plant. Efficient new plants are very capital intensive with CAD/CAM and robotic techniques used widely. Already enormous progress with these techniques had been made in Europe. For instance, Ford had installed 450 robots in Europe by 1982, and Fiat had made huge strides in automating production lines with consequent gains in productivity and quality.

EEC COMPETITION POLICY AND THE AUTOMOBILE INDUSTRY

One of the most basic principles of the EEC was that goods and resources should move freely within the Common Market. The Directorate of Competition—DG IV—was responsible for ensuring that anti-competitive business conduct did not block such free movement. In October 1983, the Directorate issued two draft proposals intended to ensure first that any type of car available in one country would be made available in all, and second that price differences across member countries would not exceed 12%, net of taxes.

Prior to these draft proposals, automobile manufacturers could establish exclusive distribution agreements with selected dealers in national markets. From 1967 to 1983, exclusive distribution and exclusive purchasing agreements qualified to block exemption from prosecution under the EEC antitrust laws. The exclusivity of the agreements gave manufacturers the power to maintain price differences between different countries by withholding cars from anyone trying commercial arbitrage. But DG IV's new proposals included provision for "parallel imports" from nonauthorized dealers if pretax price differences exceeded 12% for more than six months.

The reaction of European producers and dealers was immediate and hostile. Both the CCMC and the CLCA (The Committee of Common Market Automobile Constructors and the Liaison Committee for the Motor Industry in the EEC) filed objections to the proposals. Mr. Victor Dial, Marketing Director of Peugeot S.A., said at a Data Resources International conference in November 1983 that the proposals jeopardised the whole distribution system and that if they were carried out they would cause poor levels of servicing and safety.

Regarding the issue of model availability, in 1983 Ford was ordered under Article 85(1) of the Treaty of Rome (an antitrust article) to supply 4,800 right-hand-drive cars to the Common Market; Ford had stopped supplying right-hand-drive cars to Germany in 1981. At that time there was a 30% price difference between the German and UK markets prompting significant private purchase of right-hand-drive Fords in Germany for export to the United Kingdom. Ford claimed that the cut-off was done to protect its UK dealers.

Another significant barrier to international trade in automobiles within the EEC was the difference in technical standards from country to country. Although the EEC had been working on technical standardization (homologation), by 1982 it had only achieved it in tires, windshields, and safetybelts.

EEC INDUSTRIAL POLICY TOWARD THE AUTOMOBILE INDUSTRY

In 1983, the state of the European automobile industry could be described as in crisis. Umberto Agnelli, President of Fiat, made a widely reported prophecy in the late 1970s that by 1985 there would only be five major manufacturers in Europe. (He presumably included Fiat.) The shake-out was still to come. Some industry experts thought that there were as many as 2 million units of excess capacity in Europe. A price war was underway and only Ford of Europe and Mercedes made significant profits in 1982.

Yet huge sums were required to finance the development of the industry in the 1980s. Data Resources International estimated the requirement to be $80 billion. Ed Blanch, Chairman of Ford of Europe, said in the *Financial Times* in October 1983, "If the profit is not there, the industry will not be able to support its long term investment program. Then the problem will become a jobs problem."

The threat was not only to the EEC manufacturers (who employed about 2 million, compared to 2.2 million in the United States and 250,000 in Japan). Component suppliers such as Robert Bosch (West Germany), Lucas (UK) and Ferodo (France) had also suffered with the downturn in the industry.

In January 1981, the European Parliament passed a resolution criticizing the American producers and Japanese importers in Europe and urging action from the Commission. In June 1981, the Commission presented a report to the Council of Ministers which attempted to analyze the industry, especially in the context of its global competition. The report called for an evolutionary change in the structure of the industry controlled by a dialogue with the world's other two major producing nations. In its tone, the report was more supportive of the British approach of collaborative agreements with Japanese producers than it was supportive of protectionism and isolation. Many observers felt the report lacked specific proposals, however.

One problem that the report did foresee was the entry of Spain and Portugal into the Community. Negotiations were underway by 1983 and were proceeding slowly. The two countries hoped to be full members by 1987. Both countries had significant car assembly operations. Seat was Spain's nationalized producer and was linked to Fiat. Ford and GM had major plants in Spain building small cars. The Ford plant was built in 1976 and GM's in 1982. Spain has relaxed its local content rules to attract these investments, but the plants were still subject to export performance requirements. Portugal, a member of EFTA, had penal tax rates on imported cars allowed as a transitional concession to protect its industrial base. Thus, most manufacturers had assembly plants in Portugal building cars for the local market. Renault, however, had a plant building Renault 5s for export.

THE EEC'S POLICY DISCRETION

The EEC wanted to present a unified trade policy to the outside world rather than to confront it with a set of disparate national policies. But despite the fact that under the Treaty of Rome all member states had surrendered their sovereignty over trade matters to the EEC, there was in fact little that the EEC could do to impose its objective on uncooperative member states.

In the case of Italy, the 2,200 unit annual Japanese import limit was a bilateral treaty signed in 1956 by both countries before the Treaty of Rome and the General Agreement on Tariffs and Trade (GATT) were established. Thus the EEC had no jurisdiction in Italy, and the Italian government showed no willingness to abolish the treaty. In the other countries, the Japanese car import limits were either agreements between national vehicle manufacturers' associations and the Japanese Association of Motor Assemblers (JAMA) or negotiated voluntary agreements between countries' governments.

Were the EEC to unify these disparate quantitative restrictions, it would need the unanimous agreement of all member countries. And then any single EEC trade position would have to be agreed to voluntarily by Japan to avoid a clear violation of the GATT. Yet unanimity within Europe seemed an unlikely prospect in the light of conflicting national objectives. The Germans generally preferred relatively open markets, the British wanted to export cars of questionable origin to the Continent, and the French and Italians wanted tight controls.

While all these problems loomed ahead of the EEC, a new problem just surfaced. The German government announced that it would introduce U.S.-style antipollution measures for all cars sold in the German market. This involved the use of lead-free gasoline and catalytic converters. It said that it was taking the action because of increasing atmospheric pollution and acid rainfall which threatened the German forests. The Germans took unilateral action because agreement could not be reached in Brussels for a common policy. However, the French and Italian producers announced that they would not comply with the regulations.

Case 32

UNITED KINGDOM: INDUSTRIAL POLICY TOWARDS THE AUTOMOBILE INDUSTRY

H. Landis Gabel/Anthony E. Hall

INTRODUCTION

In many ways, the decline of the United Kingdom (UK) automobile industry since 1945 mirrors the decline of the global strength of the UK's manufacturing base and overall economic performance. This decline has occurred despite (or because of) a wide variety of policies which directly or indirectly affected the fortunes of the automobile sector.

The UK automobile industry emerged from World War II with a high degree of modern plant and equipment. With the end of rationing of essential raw materials in the early 1950s, the industry rapidly became the world's leading car exporter and its second largest producer (after the U.S.). In 1953 the UK exported nearly 400,000 units, and exports peaked at 617,000 units in 1963. Domestic automobile registrations reached 300,000 in 1953, then 500,000 in 1955, and topped 1,000,000 in 1963. Import penetration was low. Even by the early 1970s, imports had not exceeded about 10% of the UK market.

After 1964, domestic demand stagnated as the country suffered the consequences of a series of balance of payments crises. Then in 1971, the Conservative government of Edward Heath introduced a number of policies (e.g., the easing of hire-purchase conditions and the reduction of indirect taxes on automobiles) which led to a boom in automobile sales. Domestic producers were unfortunately unable to satisfy this demand, and in 1973 imports jumped to 31% of the market.

By the end of the 1970s, the import penetration rate approached 65% of the UK market, principally as a consequence of two factors. One was a series of problems at British Leyland and Chrysler UK about which more will be said below. The other was Ford's and General Motors' gradual rationalization of automobile assembly on the Continent.

THE STRUCTURE OF THE UK AUTOMOBILE INDUSTRY

There were dramatic changes in the structure of the UK automobile industry from 1950 to 1980. In 1952, Morris and Austin combined to fight the growing influence of Ford. This established the "Big Five" producers—BMC, Ford, Rootes, Vauxhall (owned by GM since 1925), and Standard-Triumph.

Again, to counter the growth of Ford in the UK, Leyland (a relatively small specialist truck producer) bought Standard-Triumph in 1957. With the sponsorship of the Industrial Reorganization Commission (IRC), Leyland acquired BMC in 1968 to become British Leyland which was nationalized in 1975. Finally, Chrysler acquired 30% of Rootes in 1964, control of the company in 1967, then sold it and all other European operations to Peugeot-Citroen in 1978.

In the decade of the 1970s, Ford steadily increased its share of UK production from 27% to 37%. By this measure it was second to British Leyland, which held a stable 45–50% share throughout the decade. But by importing cars from Belgium, Spain, and Germany, Ford attained the leading sales share (rising to 30% by the end of the 1970s). British Leyland was second in sales share (which fell through the decade to 18%). Chrysler (Rootes) and Vauxhall both had shares of production below 10%, and had habitually lost money.

GM's fortunes improved in the 1980s with its Vauxhall "Cavalier" (especially popular in the important fleet market), the "Corsa" (produced in Spain), and its Opel imports. These cars, coupled with acceptance problems that troubled the "wedge" shape of the Ford "Sierra," boosted GM's share of UK sales to 14% in 1982.

TOOLS OF POLICY

Import tariffs were a key factor in the post-war development of the European automobile industry. In the UK in the 1950s, the level for finished cars was 33.3%. This contrasted with a level in France at the same time of almost 70% and in Germany of only 13%. After the establishment of the EEC and the GATT, tariffs fell quite rapidly, and for the UK reached 18% by 1970.

Japan was the first country to completely eliminate tariffs on imports (in 1978), and all tariffs on trade within the EEC were due to be eliminated by January 1984.

The UK had three main forms of taxation on cars. Prior to 1973 a purchase tax was levied on the wholesale price. This was replaced by a value-added tax in 1973 (as an entry requirement of joining the EEC). It was supplemented by a special car tax on the wholesale price, designed partly to keep the tax burden on cars at its original level and thus prevent stimulating demand. There was also a tax on fuel and a road tax levied at a fixed rate on each vehicle.

Major factors affecting car sales in the UK included the terms and conditions of hire-purchase agreements. Government policy traditionally set the minimum down payment percentage and the maximum repayment period, but this was abolished in 1971. After this policy change, there was a major shift of auto sales from the household market to the corporate market. A company car became an accepted part of an employee's remuneration. The percentage of car sales made to companies rose to 67% by 1978.

Demand management policies employed by the government repeatedly disrupted the automobile industry in the UK in the 1960s and 1970s. Between 1960 and 1975 the tax rates on cars changed twenty-five times resulting in abrupt and substantial swings in consumer demand.

Plant location strategy was also heavily influenced by the government. The traditional center for car production was the Midlands of England around Birmingham, although Ford and GM had established plants near London (Ford at Dagenham, 20 miles east of London, and GM at Luton, 30 miles north of London). In the early 1950s, the government started to try to disperse the industry. Mersyside, Liverpool and Scotland were favored locations. Policy was enacted by means of Industrial Relocation Certificates. In essence, permission to relocate was refused unless a company chose a location favored by the government. Additional incentives offered after 1965 were investment grants and tax incentives for investments in the underdeveloped regions of the North and West. These could be supplemented by discretionary grants. For example, Ford received direct aid totalling £180 million to locate the "Erika" ("Escort") engine facility at Bridgend in South Wales, and the Welsh Development Authority provided all of the infrastructure, roads, and rail links, free of cost. (The UK had to bid against Berlin for the facility.) The ill-fated DeLorean plant in West Belfast, Northern Ireland, is another example. £52 million was granted out of a total investment of £65 million to produce an aluminum-bodied sports car for the American market. The company collapsed in 1982 in scandal and publicity. These incentives were directly comparable to those offered by the West German government to locate industry in Berlin, by the Italians in Southern Italy, and by the French in Alsace and Lorraine.

Two final areas of public policy that had significant impacts on the automobile industry were incomes policies and industrial relations policies. Until the Thatcher government in 1979, various pay policies had been in force for most of the time since 1961 when the Chancellor of the Exchequer mapped out pay norms for the public sector. Wage freezes and percentage limits on wage increases became a feature of government policy under both Labor and Conservative administrations. These were coupled with two attempts to curb trade union power. The first came under the Tories in 1971 with their Industrial Relations Act, and the second under Labor in 1978 with "In Place of Strife." Both resulted in widespread disruption, especially in the automobile industry.

Margaret Thatcher swept away nearly all specific policy tools for controlling the automobile industry after her election in 1979. The National Enterprise Board was abolished, as were wage and price controls. Taxes were abandoned as a device to manage automobile demand. The Tories also reduced the scale of regional grants and incentives and narrowed their geographic scope.

CHRYSLER UK Three times in the 1960s and 1970s, Labour administrations faced policy crises over the Rootes operations. In 1963, Rootes launched a new car model called the Hillman "Imp" to counter the very successful BMC "Mini." Although Rootes had long been located in Coventry in the Midlands, the government's redevelopment policy forced it to locate its new "Imp" plant at Linwood, near Glasgow, Scotland. The project was a failure and by 1966 Rootes was in deep financial trouble. Chrysler was then undertaking a massive global expansion program to try belatedly to match the international operations of its U.S. rivals. The Labour administration initially rejected a Chrysler takeover of Rootes, but after BMC and Leyland refused to help, the government agreed to Chrysler expanding its 30% minority stake in the company to 85% in 1964. The government, through the IRC, bought 15% of the shares. Chrysler agreed to preserve the Rootes operations and to expand employment, especially at Linwood.

Late in 1975 (only six months after the nationalization of British Leyland) Chrysler UK appealed to the UK government for financial assistance. Before the Department of Industry could reply, John Riccardo, Chairman of Chrysler U.S., demanded and got an appointment with the Prime Minister, Harold Wilson. Riccardo offered three alternatives: (1) liquidation of the UK operation in three months; (2) donation of Chrysler UK to the government; or (3) donation of 80% to the government, with Chrysler U.S. keeping a minority stake. After frantic negotiations, the government agreed to bail out Chrysler. This was against the advice of the Industry Minister, Eric Varley, and a Central Policy Review Staff report urging further nationalization of the industry. £162.5 million was loaned to Chrysler UK in return for a Chrysler U.S. investment of £64 million and a declaration of intent to introduce new models and to integrate the UK operation with its European operations in Spain and France.

In 1978, Chrysler went back to the Labour government and announced its intention to sell its entire European and UK operation to Peugeot-Citroen. Despite union opposition, the cabinet under James Callaghan agreed to the sale in September 1978, after Peugeot made similar undertakings as Chrysler U.S. to the government. However, after the election of the Conservative Administration in 1979, Peugeot closed the Talbot Linwood operation in Scotland and concentrated assembly at Ryton, near Coventry.

BRITISH LEYLAND

The problems that confronted British Leyland (BL) in the 1970s arose from its inability to rationalize the proliferation of models and assembly plants it inherited from its various mergers since the 1950s. By 1974 it was clear that BL was bankrupt.

In December 1974, the Labour government's Industry Minister, Tony Benn, declared that because of "the company's position in the economy as a leading exporter and its importance to employment directly and indirectly," the government would assist BL.

A formal investigation of BL's problems culminated in the Ryder Report, which blamed BL's difficulties on inappropriate organization, low investment, excessive dividends, incompetent management, and poor productivity from outdated plants. The report recommended an immediate investment of £265 million to buy out the equity, and then subsequent investments of £1.4 billion over eight years to be paid on a tranche system subject to satisfactory performance. The National Enterprise Board (a government holding authority set up in 1974) was to supervise BL.

By 1977, it was clear that British Leyland was still in trouble. Little progress had been made with new model introductions, losses approached £500 million each year, and public confidence was at an all-time low following repeated disputes and strikes at the company. A new head of the National Enterprise Board, Leslie Murphy, was appointed to replace Ryder, and he quickly appointed Michael Edwardes as BL Chairman. Edwardes insisted on a free hand, and he got it.

Edwardes' plan was a radical departure from Ryder's. Within a month most of the previous senior management had left the company. The plan called for 12,500 redundancies, decentralization of decision making, and an end to the tranche system of funding. £450 million was immediately injected as further equity capital. After almost five years of tough—almost confrontational—management, Edwardes succeeded in reducing the number of assembly plants from nine to two, in launching the successful "Metro" and "Maestro," and in establishing strong links with Honda. BL began making the Triumph "Acclaim" (Honda "Ballade") under license and was jointly developing a new executive-class car with Honda for production in Japan, the U.S. and the UK. The company will return to profitability (albeit insignificant) in 1983.

JAPANESE PENETRATION OF THE UK MARKET

Import penetration stayed at very low levels in the UK until 1971. The sudden upsurge in demand that year surprised the domestic suppliers and was satisfied by imports. Nissan, in particular, launched a major marketing effort at this time, and both the Japanese and Continental European suppliers succeeded in acquiring discontented BL and Chrysler dealers.

The leaders of BL, Chrysler, and the trade unions repeatedly called for controls on imports in the 1973–1975 period. Although most of the import pressure originated from the Continent, it was unrealistic to hope to control those imports since the UK had just joined the EEC in 1973. Rather, an attack on imports had to be an attack on the Japanese.

During a House of Commons inquiry into the automobile industry in 1975, Sir Peter Carey, the head of the Department of Industry, described the Japanese competition as "not unfair." He attributed the problems of the UK industry to underinvestment and too many strikes. However, he recognised an imbalance in trade and asked for Japanese "self-restraint."

The Japanese accepted the suggestion, and JAMA (Japanese Association of Motor Assemblers) agreed to limit 1976 sales to 1975 levels. The Japanese had been shocked in Australia in 1975 when unheeded Australian government calls for restraint resulted in a unilaterally imposed quota on Japanese imports. This rapidly led to direct investments by Nissan and Toyota in Australia.

The self-restraint that the Japanese practiced was unsatisfactory to the British because the Japanese share of the UK market continued to rise. Part of the increase was due to two new Japanese entrants to the UK market (Subaru and Suzuki) but part resulted from continued domestic UK production problems. The British Ambassador to Japan argued with MITI (Ministry of International Trade and Industry) that further "forms of words" would be "unsatisfactory" and that it was time for "effective restraint." MITI undertook to establish administrative controls for the UK market, "recognising the special circumstances of British industry." Japan was thus effectively limited to 11% of the UK market—its approximate market share at the time.

Nissan then announced its intention to build an automobile assembly plant in the UK in 1981. The project was still under consideration in 1983, and negotiations were underway with the Department of Industry over financing arrangements and the level of the local content. Nissan had problems with its own union in Japan which was opposed to any further overseas investment. Concern was also expressed by the French and Italian governments to "backdoor" Japanese imports. The objections of both governments to BL's Triumph "Acclaim" were only mollified by high-level UK diplomatic representations in both Paris and Rome.

THE POLITICAL APPRAISAL

In UK political circles there were two competing views of the prospective Nissan plant. The British government was obviously very keen to see the Nissan plant built in the UK. The government was developing a strategy of supporting British Leyland in its new slimmer form while at the same time hoping that Nissan would show how (and that) a state-of-the-art facility could be run in Britain. The government's hope (and its economic ideology) was that vigorous competition would revitalize not only the assembly industry but the component supply industries as well where there were severe problems of excess capacity.

The opposition believed that in the long run neither BL nor Ford, with their older plants and traditional union agreements and work practices, would be able to compete with a new Japanese greenfield operation. Were Nissan to go ahead with the investment, the two models it would be most likely to make would compete directly with BL's forthcoming LM 10 range and Ford's "Escorts" and "Cortinas." Although the new plant might employ 4,000–5,000 workers, a Ford-produced scenario suggested that under some admittedly pessimistic assumptions there could be a net loss of 50,000 jobs in the industry.

The health of the component industry was also worrisome to critics of Nissan's investment. Mr. Jeffrey Wilkinson, Chairman of the Independent Original Equipment Manufacturers' section of the Society of Motor Manufacturers and Traders, claimed that unless Nissan produced cars with 80% European content (at ex-works value) the component producers would face a net job loss. Going farther than that, there was a widely held theory that the next target of "Japan Inc." was the worldwide automobile component industry. The issue of required local content was clearly central to all this.

There was some speculation in the UK press that Nissan and the government would strike a deal whereby Nissan would substantially reduce its auto exports to the UK (running at about 100,000 units yearly) in return for lower local content requirements. This plan would mean slower buildup of Nissan's British plant (which would please those on Nissan's board who were cautious about rapid expansion at a time of stagnant world demand). Of course, to the UK component industry, such a deal would be seen as a sellout of their interests.

In late 1983 it was not at all clear whether the government's strategy would work. Nissan had still not announced the go-ahead of a UK plant. British Leyland had stopped its cash hemorrhage but was hardly a success yet. It had less than 20% of its domestic market and had made little headway on the Continent. Ford and GM continued to move assembly from the UK to the Continent while expanding their UK market shares by exporting the assembled cars back to Britain. Meanwhile, in 1983 a fierce price-cutting war had broken out in the market as companies fought for market share. BL's viability was still threatened.

Case 33

FORD OF EUROPE AND LOCAL CONTENT REGULATIONS

H. Landis Gabel/Anthony E. Hall

In mid-1983, the Management Committee of Ford of Europe (the company's senior decision-making committee) was once again examining the trends, opportunities, and threats offered by the European market (see Exhibits 33.1, 33.2, and 33.3). The principal threat perceived by management was the growing Japanese presence in Europe. Japanese manufacturers had increased their car sales in Western Europe from 750,000 units in 1979 to almost one million in 1983 and were beginning to establish a manufacturing foothold in Europe. Nissan, for example, was just beginning to produce automobiles in Italy, it would soon increase its production of vehicles for Europe from a Spanish plant, and, most worrisome, the company was expected to announce imminently a decision to proceed with a previously shelved plan to construct a new and very large assembly plant in the United Kingdom (UK). Although Ford competed very successfully against the other European producers—and for the first time had captured the number one European market share position in the second quarter of 1983—Japanese producers' plants in Europe would constitute a new and severe challenge. What especially worried Ford was the possibility that Nissan's new UK plant would import major automobile components into Europe from Japan, as-

This case study was developed after discussions with certain Ford personnel but does not necessarily reflect the actual scope or manner of deliberations undertaken by Ford management or the conclusions of Ford management. The case study was not formulated by Ford and is solely the responsibility of INSEAD. This case was written by Associate Professor H. Landis Gabel and Research Associate Anthony E. Hall, INSEAD. Also appearing in the *Journal of Management Case Studies*, Vol. 1, No. 1, pp. 38–59.

semble them into finished vehicles, and then claim that the vehicles were European in origin and thus not subject to any existing European–Japanese trade agreements or understandings.

This worry had led Ford executives back in 1981 to consider seriously local content regulations as a way of reducing this risk and helping to stem the growth of the Japanese producers' share of the European market. Local content regulations, most commonly employed by developing countries against multinational firms based in developed countries, define the percentage of a product that must be produced in a specified geographical region as a precondition of sale in that region.

Although local content regulations had been discussed occasionally in the Management Committee for the past two years with no conclusions reached, pressure was building to push the discussion through to a definitive policy stance. If the Committee were to decide to favor local content regulations, it

Exhibit 33.1

CONSOLIDATED BALANCE SHEET

December 31, 1982 and 1981 (In Millions of Dollars)
Ford Motor Company and Consolidated Subsidiaries

	1982	1981
ASSETS		
Current assets		
Cash and cash items	$ 943.7	$ 1,176.5
Marketable securities (including $500 million of commercial paper of Ford Motor Credit Company in 1981), at cost and accrued interest (approximates market)	611.7	923.5
Receivables	2,376.5	2,595.8
Inventories	4,123.3	4,642.9
Other current assets	743.7	838.2
Total current assets	8,798.9	10,176.9
Equities in net assets of unconsolidated subsidiaries and affiliates	2,413.4	2,348.2
Property		
Land, plant, and equipment, at cost	17,014.9	16,395.7
Less accumulated depreciation	9,546.9	8,959.4
Net land, plant and equipment	7,468.0	7,436.3
Unamortized special tools	2,668.3	2,410.1
Net property	10,136.3	9,846.4
Other assets	613.1	649.9
Total Assets	$21,961.7	$23,021.4

Exhibit 33.1
(Continued)

	1982	1981
LIABILITIES AND STOCKHOLDERS' EQUITY		
Current liabilities		
Accounts payable		
Trade	$ 3,117.5	$ 2,800.2
Other	1,002.1	1,089.8
Total accounts payable	4,119.6	3,890.0
Income taxes	383.0	208.9
Short-term debt	1,949.1	2,049.0
Long-term debt payable within one year	315.9	128.7
Accrued liabilities	3,656.4	3,663.7
Total current liabilities	10,424.0	9,940.3
Long-term debt	2,353.3	2,709.7
Other liabilities	1,922.7	1,856.2
Deferred income taxes	1,054.1	1,004.8
Minority interests in net assets of consolidated subsidiaries	130.1	148.2
Guarantees and commitments	—	—
Stockholders' Equity		
Capital Stock, par value $2.00 a share		
Common Stock, shares issued: 1982—108,870,062; 1981—107,859,065	217.8	215.7
Class B Stock, shares issued: 1982—11,717,738; 1981—12,717,003	23.4	25.5
Capital in excess of par value of stock	522.4	526.1
Foreign-currency translation adjustments	(623.2)	—
Earnings retained for use in the business	5,937.1	6,594.9
Total stockholders' equity	6,077.5	7,362.2
Total Liabilities and Stockholders' Equity	$21,961.7	$23,021.4

would then have to decide on strategy and tactics. Regulations could take various forms, some of which might be more advantageous to Ford than others. And, of course, Ford would have to decide how to represent its position to the governmental bodies which would have to introduce, monitor, and enforce the regulations.

FORD OF EUROPE

Ford's European headquarters are based at Warley near Brentwood in Southeast England. The sixth floor of its 2,500-person office building houses Ford of Europe's executive suites, where trade policy is a frequent—and

Exhibit 33.2

TEN-YEAR FINANCIAL SUMMARY

(In Millions of Dollars)

Ford Motor Company and Consolidated Subsidiaries (Worldwide)

Summary of Operations	1982[1]	1981	1980	1979	1978	1977	1976[2]	1975	1974	1973
Sales	$37,067.2	38,247.1	37,085.5	43,513.7	42,784.1	37,841.5	28,839.6	24,009.1	23,620.6	23,015.1
Total Costs	37,550.8	39,502.9	39,363.8	42,596.7	40,425.6	35,095.9	27,252.7	23,572.7	23,015.4	21,446.1
Operating income (loss)	(483.6)	(1,255.8)	(2,278.3)	917.0	2,358.5	2,745.6	1,586.9	436.4	605.2	1,569.0
Interest income	562.7	624.6	543.1	693.0	456.0	299.1	232.6	155.8	171.4	189.9
Interest expense	745.5	674.7	432.5	246.8	194.8	192.7	216.6	301.0	281.5	174.7
Equity in net income of unconsolidated subsidiaries and affiliates	258.5	167.8	187.0	146.2	159.0	150.0	136.3	107.0	58.5	48.5
Income (loss) before income taxes	(407.9)	(1,138.1)	(1,980.7)	1,509.4	2,778.7	3,002.0	1,739.2	398.2	553.6	1,632.7
Provision (credit) for income taxes	256.6[3]	(68.3)[3]	(435.4)[3]	330.1	1,175.0	1,325.6	730.6	151.9	201.5	702.1
Minority interests	(6.7)	(9.7)	(2.0)	10.0	14.8	3.6	25.5	18.8	25.0	24.1
Income (loss) before cumulative effect of an accounting change	(657.8)	(1,060.1)	(1,543.3)	1,169.3	1,588.9	1,672.8	983.1	227.5	327.1▲	906.5▲
Cumulative effect of an accounting change[4]	—	—	—	—	—	—	—	95.2	—	—
Net income (loss)	(657.8)	(1,060.1)	(1,543.3)	1,169.3	1,588.9	1,672.8	983.1	322.7	327.1	906.5
Cash dividends	—	144.4	312.7	467.6	416.6	359.3	263.4	242.6	298.1	317.1
Retained income (loss)	$ (657.8)	(1,204.5)	(1,856.0)	701.7	1,172.3	1,313.5	719.7	80.1	29.0	589.4
Income before minority interests as percentage of sales	*	*	*	2.7%	3.7%	4.4%	3.5%	1.4%	1.5%	4.0%
Stockholders' equity at year-end	$ 6,077.5	7,362.2	8,567.5	10,420.7	9,686.3	8,456.9	7,107.0	6,376.5	6,267.5	6,405.1
Assets at year-end	$21,961.7	23,021.4	24,347.6	23,524.6	22,101.4	19,241.3	15,768.1	14,020.2	14,173.6	12,954.0
Long-term debt at year-end	$ 2,353.3	2,709.7	2,058.8	1,274.6	1,144.5	1,359.7	1,411.4	1,533.9	1,476.7	977.0
Average number of shares of capital stock outstanding (in millions)	120.4	120.3	120.3	119.9	119.0	118.1	117.6	116.6	116.8	124.1

(Continued)

A share (in dollars)										
Income (loss) before cumulative effect of an accounting change	$ (5.46)	(8.81)	(12.83)	9.75	13.35	14.16	8.36	1.95	2.80▲	7.31▲
Cumulative effect of an accounting change[4]	—	—	—	—	—	—	—	0.82	—	—
Net income (loss)[5]	$ (5.46)	(8.81)	(12.83)	9.75	13.35	14.16	8.36	2.77	2.80	7.31
Net income assuming full dilution	—	—	—	$9.15	12.42	13.08	7.74	2.65	2.69▲	6.86▲
Cash dividends	—	$ 1.20	2.60	3.90	3.50	3.04	2.24	2.08	2.56	2.56
Stockholders' equity at year-end	$ 50.40	61.06	71.05	86.46	80.77	71.15	60.14	54.09	53.58	51.66
Common Stock price range (NYSE)	$ 41½	26	35¾	45⅜	51⅞	49¼	49½	36¼	43½	65⅞
	$ 16¾	15¾	18⅛	29⅜	39	41⅜	34⅞	25⅞	23	30⅞
▲ *Pro forma* amounts assuming the investment tax credits accrued after 1970 flowed through to income in the year the assets were placed in service:										
Net income (in millions)	—	—	—	—	—	—	—	—	$363.9	938.9
Net income a share	—	—	—	—	—	—	—	—	$ 3.12	7.57
Assuming full dilution	—	—	—	—	—	—	—	—	$ 2.98	7.10
Facility and Tooling Data										
Capital expenditures for expansion, modernization, and replacement of facilities (excluding special tools)	$ 1,605.8	1,257.4	1,583.8	2,152.3	1,571.5	1,089.6	551.0	614.2	832.5	891.7
Depreciation	$ 1,200.8	1,168.7	1,057.2	895.9	735.5	628.7	589.7	583.8	530.8	485.1
Expenditures for special tools	$ 1,361.6	970.0	1,184.7	1,288.0	970.2	672.7	503.7	342.2	618.7	594.3
Amortization of special tools	$ 955.6	1,010.7	912.1	708.5	578.2	487.7	431.0	435.3	392.7	463.1
Employee Data—Worldwide										
Payroll	$ 8,863.0	9,380.1	9,519.0	10,169.1	9,774.9	8,338.3	6,639.2	5,629.2	5,892.6	5,769.2
Total labor costs	$11,756.7	12,238.3	12,417.3	13,227.2	12,494.0	10,839.2	8,653.3	7,165.7	7,317.3	7,108.2

(*Continued*)

Exhibit 33.2 *(Continued)*

Summary of Operations	1982[1]	1981	1980	1979	1978	1977	1976[2]	1975	1974	1973
Average number of employees	379,229	404,788	426,735	494,579	506,531	479,292	443,917[6]	416,120	464,731	474,318
Employee Data—U.S. Operations										
Payroll	$ 5,352.7	5,507.5	5,248.5	6,262.6	6,581.2	5,653.4	4,380.4	3,560.5	3,981.9	4,027.0
Average hourly labor costs per hour worked[7] (in dollars)										
Earnings	$ 13.57	12.75	11.45	10.35	9.73	8.93	8.03	7.10	6.61	6.12
Benefits	9.80	8.93	8.54	5.59	4.36	3.91	3.98	3.86	2.88	2.31
Total	$ 23.37	21.68	19.99	15.94	14.09	12.84	12.01	10.96	9.49	8.43
Average number of employees	155,901	170,806	179,917	239,475	256,614	239,303	219,698[6]	203,691	235,256	249,513

SOURCE: Ford of Europe.

Share data have been adjusted to reflect the five-for-four stock split that became effective May 24, 1977.
* 1982, 1981 and 1980 results were a loss.
[1] See Note 1 of Notes to Financial Statements.
[2] Change to LIFO reduced net income by $81 million.
[3] See Note 5 of Notes to Financial Statements.
[4] Cumulative effect of change (as of January 1, 1975) to flow-through method of accounting for investment tax credit.
[5] See Note 7 of Notes to Financial Statements.
[6] Excludes effect of UAW strike.
[7] Excludes data for subsidiary companies.

often emotional—topic of conversation. The Ford Motor Company had a long tradition of favoring unrestricted international trade. Henry Ford declared in 1928 that, "I don't believe in anything else than free trade all 'round." Indeed, he exported the sixth car he made (to Canada). But the international trade environment of the 1920s was not that of the 1970s and 1980s, and although Henry Ford II was a strong free-trader like his grandfather, Ford U.S. had altered its official policy position in 1980 away from free trade toward fair trade with an element of protectionism. The management of Ford of Europe could follow this lead by lobbying for local content regulations, but they did not feel obliged to do so. They were sufficiently independent of their American parent that the decision was theirs to make.

Ford of Europe was a product of the Ford Motor Company's traditional internationalism. It was created in 1967 when the managing director of Ford of Germany, John Andrews, convinced Henry Ford II of the need to coordinate the design, development, production and marketing operations of the Ford European national operating companies within the framework of the European Economic Community (EEC).

Ford now has twenty-five manufacturing sites in six European countries, and it is the most geographically integrated car producer in Europe (see Exhibit 33.4). In the last five years the company spent more than $5 billion on automation and common design of its European cars, with the objective of making at least half the parts used in its European line interchangeable (see Exhibit 33.5). Ford's European integration and focus and its image as a national producer in each national market is an important advantage with growing nationalistic car buying. The company proudly claims that 95% of the content of its European cars is European in origin.

Ford in Europe had sales of $9.9 billion in 1981 and would have ranked thirty-fourth on the *Fortune* 500 listing. From 1980 through 1982—one of the worst periods for the auto industry since the 1950s—Ford of Europe earned $1 billion in profit. (See Exhibits 33.6 and 33.7 for production information on world automobile manufacturers.)

THE GROWING JAPANESE PRESENCE IN EUROPE

Ford of Europe had identified Japanese automotive products as the principal threat in the 1980s. To respond to that threat, Ford's European companies launched a major education and development program in the late 1970s called "After Japan." The program had started with trips by management to Japan to tour Japanese automobile assembly plants. By 1983, "After Japan" was well established with emphasis on robotics, quality circles, "just in time" inventory controls, and other work practices imported from Japan. Already, over 700 robots were at work in Ford's European plants with 1,500 planned by 1986.

Exhibit 33.3

TEN-YEAR SUMMARY OF VEHICLE FACTORY SALES

Ford Motor Company and Consolidated Subsidiaries (Worldwide)

	1982	1981	1980	1979	1978	1977	1976	1975	1974	1973
U.S. and Canadian Cars and Trucks*										
Cars										
United States	1,270,519	1,385,174	1,397,431	2,044,461	2,632,190	2,625,485	2,197,039	1,867,713	2,336,415	2,685,423
Canada	118,721	148,515	162,576	236,437	248,285	247,427	210,049	225,293	258,980	231,598
Total cars	1,389,240	1,533,689	1,560,007	2,280,898	2,880,475	2,872,912	2,407,088	2,093,006	2,595,395	2,917,021
Trucks*										
United States	803,484	716,648	753,195	1,183,016	1,458,132	1,345,282	1,017,736	809,360	991,447	1,086,281
Canada	70,120	104,136	109,006	160,160	153,955	149,756	131,186	131,104	143,079	98,326
Total trucks	873,604	820,784	862,201	1,343,176	1,612,087	1,495,038	1,148,922	940,464	1,134,526	1,184,607
Total cars and trucks	2,262,844	2,354,473	2,422,208	3,624,074	4,492,562	4,367,950	3,556,010	3,033,470	3,729,921	4,101,628
Cars and Trucks Outside the United States and Canada*										
Germany	797,850	737,383	657,258	880,325	847,529	891,390	815,279	636,799	496,780	728,514
Britain	423,073	418,629	468,472	555,496	433,191	563,384	515,368	468,255	559,534	615,276
Spain	229,839	254,006	266,522	252,917	247,408	212,855	16,448	—	—	—
Brazil	145,110	125,346	165,703	169,631	158,935	129,466	169,707	172,235	177,698	144,739
Australia	141,990	127,181	93,490	115,148	107,389	112,376	108,549	124,600	131,393	130,881
Mexico	90,478	107,312	84,668	74,703	68,009	49,216	45,498	55,909	54,649	44,242
South Africa	59,171	66,962	52,671	40,447	46,201	34,156	33,638	36,878	40,155	35,473
Argentina	52,764	78,671	106,463	89,669	52,702	52,466	35,318	39,793	53,810	61,373
Other countries	51,790	43,225	10,995	7,894	8,139	9,042	8,629	9,833	14,993	8,902
Total outside United States and Canada	1,992,065	1,958,715	1,906,242	2,186,230	1,969,503	2,054,351	1,748,434	1,544,302	1,529,012	1,769,400
Total worldwide—cars and trucks	4,254,909	4,313,188	4,328,450	5,810,304	6,462,065	6,422,301	5,304,444	4,577,772	5,258,933	5,871,028
Tractors*										
United States	24,258	31,517	35,286	51,361	35,789	39,650	34,643	38,342	41,090	40,223
Overseas	48,905	57,757	62,415	82,267	59,448	90,880	83,177	73,981	68,202	61,624
Total worldwide—tractors	73,163	89,274	97,701	133,628	95,237	130,530	117,820	112,323	109,292	101,847
Total worldwide factory sales	4,328,072	4,402,462	4,426,151	5,943,932	6,557,302	6,552,831	5,422,264	4,690,095	5,368,225	5,972,875

(*Continued*)

Ford Shares of Major Car and Truck Markets

	Cars				Trucks			
	1982		1981		1982		1981	
	Industry Unit Sales	*Ford Market Share*	*Industry Unit Sales*	*Ford Market Share*	*Industry Unit Sales*	*Ford Market Share*	*Industry Unit Sales*	*Ford Market Share*
United States	7,955,970	16.9%	8,514,956	16.6%	2,584,989	30.6%	2,281,879	31.4%
Canada	713,005	15.8	903,536	15.2	205,409	26.7	287,290	30.2
Germany	2,091,297	11.3	2,264,634	11.8	187,789	8.1	214,261	7.7
United Kingdom	1,552,926	30.5	1,484,250	30.9	229,346	36.6	213,832	30.5
Other European markets†	6,171,231	8.2	5,913,692	7.8	874,626	6.1	842,626	7.0
Brazil	556,596	17.6	448,256	19.2	134,621	23.2	132,677	17.9
Mexico	288,253	12.9	342,724	15.9	181,948	27.7	230,939	25.6
Argentina	114,455	33.9	172,640	31.8	29,484	54.1	56,965	46.4
Other Latin American markets†	288,423	15.9	439,635	11.1	171,138	17.5	249,266	13.8
Australia	454,250	26.0	453,806	23.0	162,104	13.0	152,476	13.1
South Africa	283,427	14.5	301,528	16.7	142,696	10.3	152,013	10.7
All Other Markets†	4,673,287	2.0	4,630,160	1.8	3,288,457	1.0	3,437,096	0.8
Worldwide Total†	25,143,120	12.5%	25,869,817	12.4%	8,192,607	14.6%	8,251,320	14.0%

SOURCE: Ford of Europe.

* Factory sales are by source of manufacture, except that Canadian exports to the United States are included as U.S. vehicle sales and U.S. exports to Canada are included as Canadian vehicle sales. Prior year data have been restated for reclassification of Club Wagons from cars to trucks.

** Includes units manufactured by other companies and sold by Ford.

† 1982 data estimated.

Exhibit 33.4

FORD IN EUROPE

1 **BELFAST** (N Ireland) plant produces carburetors and distributors for European Ford petrol engines.

2 **CORK** (Ireland) assembles Sierras.

3 **HALEWOOD** (England) assembles Escorts and produces trim and body-panels, transmissions, transaxles, engine gears and suspension components.

4 **TREFOREST** (South Wales) makes sparking plug insulators.

5 **SWANSEA** (South Wales) produces rear axles for Sierra, Capri, and Transit, As well as Cargo Truck rear axle gear set, and gearboxes, plus car and truck brake parts.

6 **BRIDGEND** (South Wales) builds the CVH engine for the Escort.

7 **LANGLEY** (England) assembles Cargo and A Series trucks, and R Series bus chassis; also produces cabs, axle, and suspension parts for trucks.

8 **LEAMINGTON** (England) produces components for all Ford Petrol engines in its foundry and also makes brake parts and transmission cases and truck hubs and drums. Has also a machine shop one mile from the foundry for machining operations.

9 **DAVENTRY** (England) main supply point for Ford and Motorcraft parts in Britain. Holds 85,000 product lines.

10 **SOUTHAMPTON** (England) builds the Transit van and bus range and produces Cargo cab panels, and light truck cabs.

11 **DAGENHAM** (England) assembles Fiestas and Sierras, can build up to 600,000 engines a year and its seven plants include a metal stamping and body plant, foundry, and forge.

12 **ENFIELD** (England) makes instrument clusters, windscreen wiper motors, fuel pumps, and sparking plugs for all Ford vehicles.

13 **WOOLWICH** (England) makes engine and transmission parts.

14 **BASILDON** (England) has two plants, a tractor plant and a radiator plant.

15 **OSLO** (Norway) National sales company office and parts distribution centre.

16 **STOCKHOLM** (Sweden) National sales company office and parts distribution centre.

17 **HELSINKI** (Finland) National sales company office and parts distribution centre.

18 **COPENHAGEN** (Denmark) National sales company office and parts distribution centre.

19 **AMSTERDAM** (Holland) National sales company office and parts distribution centre.

20 **ANTWERP** (Belgium) assembles tractors and has a parts distribution centre.

21 **LOMMEL** (Belgium) proving ground with a variety of test circuits.

22. **BRUSSELS** (Belgium) Ford Marketing Institute and Government Affairs offices.

23. **WUELFRATH** (Germany) makes transmission, steering, and suspension components.

24. **COLOGNE** (Germany) builds Granada, Capri and Fiesta, makes trim, engines, forging, and die castings for transaxle, transmission, and clutch cases and incorporates Merkenich Research and Engineering Centre.

25 **GENK** (Belgium) manufactures Sierras and Transits.

26 **DUEREN** (Germany) makes rear axles and hubs.

27 **CHARLEVILLE** (France) builds 4WD shovel-loaders.

28 **PARIS** (France) National sales company office and parts distribution centre.

29 **SAARLOUIS** (Germany) builds Escorts and produces trim and body panels for cars and trucks.

30 **ZURICH** (Switzerland) National sales company offices.

31 **BORDEAUX** (France) two plants building C3 automatic transmissions and transaxles for Fiesta and Escorts.

32 **MADRID** (Spain) National sales company office.

33 **LISBON** (Portugal) assembles Transit van and Cargo truck.

34 **VALENCIA** (Spain) final assembly of Fiesta and Escort, produces Fiesta and Escort engines.

35 **VIENNA** (Austria) Office building.

36 **SALZBURG** (Austria) National sales company office and vehicle preparation centre.

37 **ROME** (Italy) National sales company office and parts distribution centre.

38 **BERLIN** &(Germany) New plastics plant.

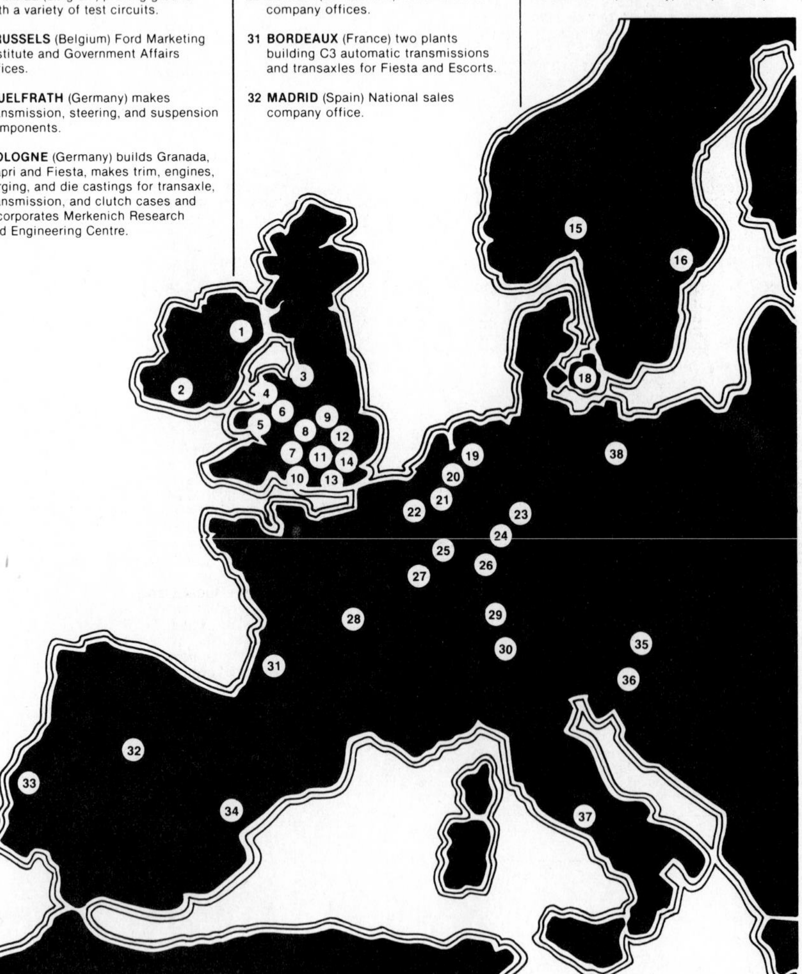

SOURCE: Ford of Europe.

Exhibit 33.5

AUTOMOBILE COMPONENT BREAKDOWN

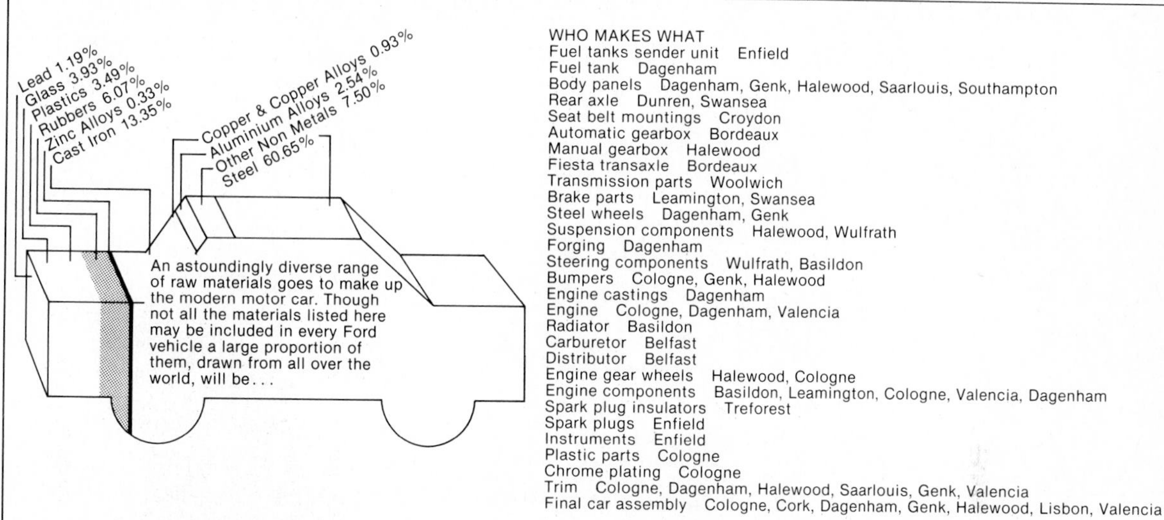

WHO MAKES WHAT

Fuel tanks sender unit	Enfield
Fuel tank	Dagenham
Body panels	Dagenham, Genk, Halewood, Saarlouis, Southampton
Rear axle	Dunren, Swansea
Seat belt mountings	Croydon
Automatic gearbox	Bordeaux
Manual gearbox	Halewood
Fiesta transaxle	Bordeaux
Transmission parts	Woolwich
Brake parts	Leamington, Swansea
Steel wheels	Dagenham, Genk
Suspension components	Halewood, Wulfrath
Forging	Dagenham
Steering components	Wulfrath, Basildon
Bumpers	Cologne, Genk, Halewood
Engine castings	Dagenham
Engine	Cologne, Dagenham, Valencia
Radiator	Basildon
Carburetor	Belfast
Distributor	Belfast
Engine gear wheels	Halewood, Cologne
Engine components	Basildon, Leamington, Cologne, Valencia, Dagenham
Spark plug insulators	Treforest
Spark plugs	Enfield
Instruments	Enfield
Plastic parts	Cologne
Chrome plating	Cologne
Trim	Cologne, Dagenham, Halewood, Saarlouis, Genk, Valencia
Final car assembly	Cologne, Cork, Dagenham, Genk, Halewood, Lisbon, Valencia

Material	Uses
Aluminium	Engine parts, transmission parts, spark plugs, casting, trim mouldings
Asbestos	Brake linings, gaskets, sound deadeners
Barite	Fillers for paints, rubber, plastics
Bauxite	Ore for metal aluminium
Beeswax	Wire insulation, adhesives
Bismuth	Hardens lead, tin, steel
Borax	For smelting and special steels
Cadmium	Alloy to harden copper, electropainting, paints
Carbon	Rubber making, paints, electrodes, graphite seals, electrical brushes
Cattle	Glue, glycerines, hides, hair for air cleaners
Chemicals	Nylon, synthetic rubber, plastics
Chromite	Ore produces chromium used for plating, alloys
Clay	Rubber filler, modelling
Coal	Iron and steel making, nylon, solvents, tars, fuel
Cobalt	Steelmaking
Coconut Oil	Paints, lacquers
Columbium	Stainless steel
Copper	Electrical system, radiator, plated parts, alloys
Cork	Gaskets, insulation
Cotton	Wadding, padding, felt tyres, insulation, thread
Diamonds	Cutting, grinding, drilling metals
Flaxseed	Linseed oil for paint, sand binder in foundry
Fluorspar	Flux in iron and steelmaking
Glass	Windscreen, windows, headlights and spun insulation
Hides	Upholstery
Iron Ore	Steel, castings for engine and chassis parts
Jute	Fabric, floor coverings
Lead	Batteries, petrol, solder, plating
Lime	Flux in steelmaking, lubricant in wire making
Magnesite	Mineral ore of magnesium
Magnesium	Light alloys for engine parts
Manganese	Steelmaking
Mercury	Mirrors, amalgams with other metals, switches
Mica	Electrical insulators
Mohair	Upholstery, carpets
Molybdenum	Steel alloys, fine wire, grease, paint
Nickel	Alloyed with steel, copper, other metals, plating
Paint	Body and interior finish
Paper	Insulation, gaskets, soundproofing, filters
Petroleum	Petrol, oil, lubricants, synthetics, solvents
Plastics	Body and engine parts, trim, upholstery
Platinum	Alloy for special wire, electric contact points, transistors
Rubber	May be natural or synthetic. Tires, weatherproofing, vibration damping, belts, insulation, hoses, wipers
Silver	Electrical system, plating, brazing
Sisal	Padding
Soya Beans	Used in paints and solvents, and for hardening steel
Steel	Frame body, wheels, engine parts, gears, springs, hardware
Sugar Cane	Alcohol, cellulose for safety glass, solvent in varnishes
Sulphur	Vulcanising rubber, lubricant, additives, steel
Textiles	Upholstery, lining, tires
Tin	Plating, alloys, solder
Tungsten	Special steel, lamp filaments
Turpentine	Paints
Vanadium	Special steel
Wheat Straw	Strawboards, panels
Wood	Cellulose for safety glass, packing cases, paper, fibre board, truck body parts, veneer trim
Wool	Upholstery, carpeting, felt
Zinc	Batteries, alloy for die-cast parts, plating
Zirconium	Alloy in steel and copper making, aluminium castings

SOURCE: Ford of Europe.

AUTOMOBILE PRODUCTION BY PRODUCER 1975, 1980, 1982
(In Thousands of Units)

Exhibit 33.6

Producer	1975	1980	1982
1. General Motors (USA)	4,649	4,753	4,069
2. Toyota (Japan)	2,336	3,293	3,144
3. Gr. Nissan (Nissan-Fuji)	2,280	3,117	2,958
4. Volkswagen-Audi	1,940	2,529	2,108
5. Renault-RVI (F)	1,427	2,132	1,965
6. Ford Motor (USA)	2,500	1,888	1,817
7. Peugeot-Talbot-Citroën (F)	659	1,408	1,574
8. Ford Europe	1,099	1,395	1,450
9. Fiat-Autobianchi-Lancia-OM	1,231	1,554	1,170
10. Toyo-Kogyo (Mazda)	642	1,121	1,110
11. Honda	413	956	1,020
12. Mitsubishi	520	1,104	969
13. Chrysler Co. (USA-Canada)	1,508	882	967
14. Opel (General Motors)	675	833	961
15. Lada (FIAT-USSR)	690	825	800
16. Daimler-Benz	556	717	700
17. Suzuki	184	468	603
18. General Motors (Canada)	598	763	560
Talbot (F, GB, E)	719	642	—
19. British Leyland	738	525	494
20. Isuzu	244	472	404
21. BMW	221	341	378
22. Ford Canada	481	434	374
23. Volvo (Sweden-Netherlands)	331	285	335
24. Seat (Fiat)	332	297	246
25. Polski Fiat	135	330	240
26. Moskvitch	300	230	205
27. American Motors	463	252	194
28. Alfa Romeo	191	221	189
29. Vauxhall	190	151	164
30. Saporoskje (USSR)	130	150	150

SOURCE: *L'Argus de l'Automobile.*

Exhibit 33.7

AUTOMOBILE INDUSTRY IN LEADING COUNTRIES
(Data in Thousands of Units)

	1973	1980	1982*
Worldwide production	29,793	29,244	27,197
Fed. Rep. of Ger.			
New car registrations	2,031	2,426	2,156
Imports	763	1,013	824
Exports	2,173	1,873	2,194
to Europe	1,150	1,381	1,785
to US	786	335	257
Production	3,650	3,521	3,761
France			
New car registrations	1,746	1,873	2,056
Imports	461	675	972
Exports	1,446	1,530	1,464
to Europe	1,222	1,203	1,095
Production	2,867	2,939	2,777
Great Britain			
New car registrations	1,664	1,516	1,557
Imports	505	863	934
Exports	599	359	313
to Europe	296	143	140
Production	1,747	959	888
Italy			
New car registrations	1,449	1,530	1,900
Imports	419	908	868
Exports	656	511	437
to Europe	505	385	383
Production	1,823	1,445	1,297
Spain			
Exports	158	492	495
Production	706	1,029	928
USSR			
Production	917	1,327	1,307
Japan**			
New car registrations	2,919	2,854	3,038
Imports	37	46	35
Exports	1,451	3,947	3,770
to Europe	357	1,003	896
to US	601	1,887	1,741
Production	4,471	7,038	6,882
US			
New car registrations	11,351	8,761	7,754
Imports	2,437	3,248	3,091
Exports***	579	560	353
to Europe	15	24	6
Production	9,667	6,376	5,073

SOURCE: Daimler-Benz.

* Figures are partly estimated.
**From 1978 on, actual figures excluding major components.
***Including exports to Canada.

Ford's top management believed, however, that it would still take at least five to ten years for their European plants to establish the cost and productivity levels necessary to match the landed price of Japanese imports. The Japanese cost advantage has been estimated to be about $1,500 ex-works per automobile.

A series of bilateral trade agreements between individual European countries and Japan currently capped Japanese automobile imports into Europe. A reciprocal trade treaty between Italy and Japan (ironically initiated by the Japanese in the 1950s) restricted exports to each other's market to 2,200 units annually. Japan's shares of the French and UK markets were informally limited to 3% and 11%, respectively. The French quota was imposed by President Valéry Giscard d'Estaing in 1976 after an abrupt increase in Japan's share of the French market. The UK quota was negotiated with the Japanese Ministry of International Trade and Industry (MITI) in 1978 after a previous, less formal agreement on export restraint failed. The Benelux countries and West Germany were technically open to the Japanese after the lapse of a 1981 informal one-year agreement in those countries establishing a maximum share of 10% of each market for the Japanese. Although there was no evidence that the Japanese were moving quickly to exploit this opening into Europe, Ford executives feared that the whole structure of trade understandings could be very fragile.

Ford also perceived an import threat from the emerging automobile industries of Eastern Europe. Many of the countries of Eastern Europe had established their industries with the help of Western European producers (e.g., Fiat in Russia and Poland, and Renault in Romania). The cars now produced in Eastern Europe were of outdated design, however, and with rapidly growing domestic demand, Eastern European countries were not expected to be a challenge in Western European markets on a scale close to that of the Japanese.

It was not only by exporting vehicles that the Japanese were making their presence felt in Europe, threatening European producers, and prompting European government concern. In 1981, British Leyland launched its Triumph "Acclaim." The "Acclaim" was a Honda "Ballade" assembled under licence from Honda. Mechanical components were imported from Japan, and a royalty was paid to Honda on each car. The "Acclaim" was introduced to plug a gap in British Leyland's model range and it precipitated a considerable outcry by some European governments. For example, although British Leyland argued that 70% of the car was British in origin, the Italian government refused to allow the first consignment of "Acclaims" to enter their country from Britain in 1982. The Italians classified the car as Japanese and thus subject to the strict quota agreement between Italy and Japan. British Leyland successfully mobilized support from the UK government and the

EEC, and the Italians eventually backed down. Nonetheless, the nature of the future battle was becoming clear.

In August 1983, the French government announced that starting in 1984 the "Acclaim" would be subject to the French "voluntary" agreement with Japan. Or rather 40% of it would be. That was the percentage that the French government deemed to be of Japanese origin. Again the threat to the "Acclaim" was withdrawn after a visit to Paris by the UK Trade Minister, Mr. Cecil Parkinson, in August 1983.

The UK also experienced a similar situation on the import side. In 1983 a Mitsubishi automobile named the "Lonsdale" was imported for the first time into the UK from Australia, where it was assembled from Japanese components. Strong industry concern was again expressed about hidden loopholes in the network of orderly marketing agreements, but no action was taken.

Japanese components were also beginning to appear on the European market in the 1980s in what had been until then strictly European automobiles. In Milan, Innocenti replaced the old British Leyland mini engine in its small car with a Japanese Daihatsu engine. And in 1981 General Motors started to purchase gearboxes from Japan for its "Cavalier" (UK) and "Rekord" (Germany) models. GM was thought by many industry observers to be pursuing a policy of increasing the percentage of Japanese components in its European and U.S. models.

In addition to their direct exports of vehicles, and their indirect exports through cooperative agreements with some European producers, the Japanese were beginning to explore direct foreign investment in Europe. Nissan (Datsun) had for some time been actively looking at sites for overseas automobile assembly plants. In 1981, Nissan commissioned the consulting firm of McKinsey and Co. to undertake a feasibility study for the location of an assembly plant in the United Kingdom. It was to produce up to 200,000 units annually by 1986, rising possibly to 500,000 by 1990. Employment on a greenfield site was to be 4,000–5,000, rising to perhaps 12,000 workers. The scheme would be eligible for government grants of £50–£100 million.

Included in the negotiations between Nissan and the UK government was a discussion of the degree of voluntary local content. It was widely rumored at the time that Nissan was prepared to accept an EEC content level of 60% by value from the outset, rising to 80% later. The UK Department of Industry was rumored to want these percentages to apply to the ex-works price, after classifying Nissan's profit after tax on the operation as an import. British Leyland and Ford lobbied hard for an immediate 80% local content. Further uncertainty revolved around the impact of the new plant on the understanding between the UK Society of Motor Manufacturers and Traders and the Japanese Association of Motor Assemblers which restrained the Japanese share of the UK market to 11%. The project had been shelved temporarily in 1982 due to uncertainty about future car sales, possible hostility from European governments (notably Italy and France), and fears of poor labor relations. It now threatened to come off the shelf.

Although the UK project was at least temporarily stalled, the first cars had just begun to roll off the line from a factory in Southern Italy that Nissan built jointly with Alfa Romeo. This plant was a 50/50 joint venture in which Alfa Romeo mechanical components were installed in a Nissan "Cherry" body coming from Japan. Alfa Romeo ran the assembly operation. Half of the finished vehicles went to Alfa Romeo and half to Nissan. The production rate planned was 60,000 units annually. The Italian government was said to be satisfied that no more than 20% of the value of the cars was being imported into Italy.

Finally, Nissan was sending four-wheel drive vehicles into the EEC from a Spanish plant in which it held a two-thirds share. In 1980 Nissan bought 36% of Motor Iberica and later increased that share to 66%. Next year, panel vans would follow.

THE U.S. SITUATION

Much of what might be envisioned in Europe's future was already taking place in the United States. Japanese imports had been taking a progressively larger and larger share of the market until a voluntary limit of 1.68 million vehicles was negotiated between Washington and Tokyo in 1981. That agreement was due to expire in March 1984, and there was widespread speculation that the Japanese wanted at least a substantially higher ceiling in the future. In the meantime, Ford's share of the U.S. market had dropped alarmingly from 26% in 1976 to 16% in 1982. Analysts blamed much of this on a 1975 decision by Henry Ford II to postpone a major U.S.-based small car program. (A U.S.-based "Fiesta" had been planned.) Ford reengineered and restyled their existing "Pinto" line instead and relied on that for the small car market.

Regardless of the question of fault, Ford's deteriorating position in the late 1970s led the company in 1980 to reverse its historic free trade policy, arguing for what was called "fair trade" instead. "Fair trade" was defined by its proponents as trade between countries with similar social and industrial infrastructures and similar national trade policies (e.g., similar wage rates, indirect tax burdens and export incentives).

In November 1980, Ford and the United Auto Workers Union lost a petition they had filed in June with the U.S. International Trade Commission seeking protection from imports. The International Trade Commission is an advisory commission with the role of determining whether a given industry was substantially injured by foreign imports, and if so, making recommendations to the President. Traditionally, the Commission has been viewed as a valuable ally of beleaguered U.S. industries in the Executive branch of the government. Thus, its decision in this case was a surprise to everyone. A three-to-two majority of the commissioners ruled that imports were not the major cause of the industry's problems. The causes, according to the majority, were the recession and Detroit's own mistakes.

Ford had requested in its statement to the International Trade Commission that imports from Japan be limited to 1.7 million cars—the 1976 import level. Ford's setback by the Commission was short-lived, however. In April 1981, President Reagan announced the voluntary export restraint agreement with MITI. Automobile imports would not exceed 1.68 million units for the next three years.

In spite of the voluntary export restraint, Ford continued lobbying for legislative relief from the pressure of Japanese imports. Ford favored a policy which combined a continuing cap on Japanese imports, a better yen/dollar exchange rate, and tax incentives. The United Auto Workers Union, fearful of the threat to American jobs, was lobbying hard for domestic content legislation.

In February 1983, a bill was introduced in Congress entitled "Fair Practices in Automotive Products Act" (see Exhibit 33.8). If passed, the bill

SELECTED TESTIMONY ON "FAIR PRACTICES AND PROCEDURES IN AUTOMOTIVE PRODUCTS ACT OF 1983"

Exhibit 33.8

Over one million jobs have been lost in the auto industry and its supplier industries since 1978. In many parts of our country, this has contributed to unemployment unheard of since the Great Depression.

Quite simply, this bill requires that the more cars a company wants to sell in our country, the more they would be required to build here. If a company takes advantage of the biggest automobile market in the world, it ought to make some effort to put some of its manufacturing in that market—the economic times demand it, and so does the American worker.

These are tough times—and much of the industrial base of our country has eroded. Without reviving this base, our national security is jeopardized and economic recovery will be stifled. We must act now, before our jobs and industrial base are permanently lost.

Congressman Richard Ottinger (D–N.Y.)
(sponsor of the Bill)

It is our belief that this legislation will (1) have a negative effect on U.S. employment, (2) impose substantial costs on consumers, (3) violate our international agreements, (4) invite retaliation by our trading partners against United States exports, (5) undermine the competitiveness of the domestic auto manufacturers, and (6) discourage foreign investment in the United States.

(Continued)

Exhibit 33.8
(*Continued*)

When the Congressional Budget Office reviewed this legislation last September, it determined that, by 1990, this legislation would create 38,000 auto jobs but 104,000 jobs would be lost in the U.S. export sector. This would mean a net loss in American jobs of 66,000.

The direct effect of H.R. 1234 would be to increase substantially the automobile prices paid by American consumers by reducing both the number of automobile imports and the competitive pressures that they exert on domestic manufacturers.

A 1980 Commission staff analysis—commenting on a proposal to reduce foreign car imports from 2.4 million to 1.7 million units per year—estimated that prices of small cars would increase by between $527 and $838 per unit, and increase total consumer expenditures on the purchase of automobiles by $1.9 to $3.6 billion per year.

Statements by opposing Congressmen

(The Bill) would severely damage America's trading position, flout our international obligations under the General Agreement on Tariffs and Trade (GATT), subject us to challenge under bilateral Treaties of Friendship, Commerce and Navigation with many of our trading partners, and be of great cost to the American consumer and to the nation.

Secretary of State George Schultz

In addition to competitive pressures on price, foreign competition has also provided important incentives for U.S. manufacturers to engage in research efforts and to invest in new technologies. American car makers have been moving rapidly toward smaller "world cars" that are very similar to those produced abroad, and United States companies are already importing engines, transmissions, and other components. Confronted with the enormous cost of downsizing American cars and the lower production costs of many foreign companies, United States auto makers are reportedly planning even greater reliance on foreign sources for major components. The enactment of legislation requiring vehicles sold in the United States to be 90 percent "American-made" by 1987 would disrupt established supply lines and aggravate the demands upon scarce domestic capital resources now faced by the United States automobile industry and the economy as a whole. The resulting supply effects would increase car prices, leading to reduced sales and employment in the auto industry.

United States Federal Trade Commission

The difficulties of our industry ultimately will not be resolved in legislative halls, but rather in the marketplace where success is earned by offering superior products at competitive prices. Rather than seek shelter from competition—even temporarily—in laws and regulations, U.S. automakers must continue their efforts to meet and exceed foreign competition.

General Motors Corporation

would impose a graduated minimum domestic content percentage for automobile importers which depended on the total volume of the importer's sales. The percentages ranged from zero for foreign producers with U.S. sales of less than 100,000 units per year to an upper limit of 90% for those with annual sales of more than 500,000 units.

The conflicting positions on trade policy of GM on one hand and Ford, Chrysler, and AMC on the other were brought into the open by the proposed bill. GM lobbied against the bill, arguing that any moves toward protectionism could cause a cascade of restrictive measures that would threaten global traders such as itself. Said Thomas R. Atkinson, GM's Director of International Economic Policy:

> Local content and other performance regulations decrease our flexibility as a corporation, and force us to do things we otherwise might not be doing. We wish these laws had never been invented, and would not like to see them increased or created in countries where they don't exist now.[1]

General Motors' position was particularly suspect in the eyes of the other major U.S. manufacturers given the 1982 announcement by GM and Toyota of a cooperative plan to produce 450,000 small cars annually by 1985 from a mothballed GM plant in Freemont, California. GM and Toyota would have equal shares in the venture, and half of the output would be sold under the Toyota name, half under the GM name (to replace GM's "Chevette"). Ford and other U.S. manufacturers were strongly opposed to the deal, fearing that it was a precedent that could end up threatening the native U.S. industry. The implications of a joint venture by the world's first and third largest automobile manufacturers were plain to see by all their competitors.

Of course, there were other risks involved in the proposed U.S. domestic content law that went beyond those cited by GM. The more restrictive the import regulations in the United States, for example, the greater the pressure on Europe from Japanese exports diverted away from U.S. shores. And some analysts within Ford felt that the bill would stimulate Japanese direct investment in the United States, perhaps constituting a greater threat to the U.S. manufacturers than some limited degree of imports. On this point the interest of the U.S. labor unions and manufacturers could conflict. Finally, there was the general realisation that the government could exact a "price" in return for protectionist favors granted the industry.

The bill was currently being debated in Congress where it was felt to have a reasonable chance of passage. Whether it would pass the Senate and survive a threatened presidential veto would likely depend on Japanese export pressure. A Data Resources International analyst argued that the passage of the bill would be a real possibility if the Japanese were to take much more than their current 20% of the U.S. market.

LOCAL CONTENT REGULATIONS

Local content regulations have long been a device used by developing countries to force multinational companies to increase the rate at which they transfer technology and employment to their local operations. With respect to automobiles, these regulations typically require that a certain percentage of a vehicle's content be produced in the country of sale. This percentage may be defined by value or by weight. Weight is generally thought to be a stricter criterion since it is not susceptible to manipulation by transfer pricing. Yet it can lead to only low-technology, high-weight items being produced locally (e.g., steel castings and chassis components).

Although simple in concept, local content regulations can often be quite complicated in practice. The treatment of overhead and profit is often a problem (see Exhibit 33.9). Some countries apply the regulations on the basis of fleet averaging, others to specific models. Mexico, where at least 50% of the value of all cars sold must be produced locally, strengthened its regulations by also requiring that the value of all component imports must be matched by component exports for each assembler. This led to a flurry of investments by Chrysler and Ford in engine facilities in Mexico.

Until recently, Spain had a 95% domestic content rule. All component

Exhibit 33.9

ANALYSIS OF AUTOMOBILE CONSTRUCTION COST

		Percentage of Ex-Works Price
Freight		2
Administration, selling cost, warranty, and profit		7
Production and assembly overheads		22
Variable manufacturing costs		69
Engine	10.4	
Gearbox	4.8	
Axles	6.9	
Other mechanical parts	8.3	
Body stamping	5.5	
Body assembly	6.9	
Accessories and seating	7.6	
Final assembly and painting	18.6	
Total	69.0	100%

SOURCES: Yves Doz, "Internationalization of Manufacturing in the Automobile Industry," unpublished paper, and Ford of Europe estimates.

NOTES: 1. The labor content of variable manufacturing costs accounts for 14% of the total ex-works price. 2. For a typical medium-size saloon at a production level of 200,000 annually. 3. Final Retail Price is usually 22% higher than the ex-works price.

imports were assessed a 30% customs duty, and 50% of all local manufacturing operations had to be Spanish-owned. All this was changed in the 1975 negotiations between the Spanish government and Ford over Ford's "Bobcat" (or "Fiesta") project in Valencia. Contemplating the attractive prospect of a plant producing 225,000 cars annually, the Spanish government settled for 100% Ford ownership, 75% Spanish content, and 5% import duty on component parts. Concessions on import duty were also granted for machine tools and equipment unavailable in Spain. But two-thirds of automobile production had to be exported from Spain, and Ford's sales in Spain could not exceed 10% of the previous year's total Spanish market size. General Motors arranged a similar deal for a plant in Zaragoza, Spain, producing 280,000 small "S-cars" ("Corsas") annually. Spanish accession to the EEC would phase out much of its protective legislation.

Local content regulations did not exist in any EEC or European Free Trade Association (EFTA) country except Portugal and Eire. (The European Community's trade regime did have a scheme for defining local assembly with the EFTA countries for the purpose of trade classification—60% of value added had to be locally produced.) Nevertheless, there was a variety of statutory powers in the EEC and the General Agreement on Tariffs and Trade (GATT) which could protect specific industries. For example, Regulation No. 926 of the EEC allowed for the protection of specific industries and could be triggered by the Commission of the EEC after advice from the Council of Ministers.

At the GATT level, any member country could ask for temporary protection from imports from another member (under Articles 19–23) if those imports severely endangered national industry (see Exhibits 33.10 and 33.11). These "escape clause" articles were difficult for EEC countries to use, however, since each country delegated responsibility for all trade negotiations to the EEC Commission in Brussels. Thus, the European automobile industry would have to coordinate campaigns in a number of EEC member countries before it could approach the EEC Commission. Even then, there was no guarantee that the Commission would agree to take a case to the GATT. Not surprisingly, existing import restrictions were essentially bilateral diplomatic agreements—varying widely from country to country—rather than statutory enactments.

FORD'S DELIBERATIONS

At least on the surface, informal local content regulations in Europe looked very attractive to Ford's executives. The Japanese threat was surely very real. Production levels in Europe in 1980 were about the same as they had been in 1970, and in the last decade, while European exports to non-European markets fell 42%, Japanese worldwide exports rose 426% (see Exhibits 33.12 and 33.13). Ford's market analysts forecast slow growth for the

Exhibit 33.10

EEC MARKET SHARE ANALYSIS: 1973/1980/1982

(Percent of Total Registrations)

Make	*Germany*	*Belgium*	*Denmark*	*France*	*United Kingdom*	*Italy*	*Holland*	*Total*[6]
Fiat[1]	7.2/3.6/4.3	9.1/5.4/5.7	7.1/8.7/4.9	4.8/3.7/4.9	3.0/3.3/3.0	64.6/49.4/51.7	8.8/4.1/5.5	16.9/12.2/14.9
Ford[2]	12.8/10.4/11.3	14.7/8.5/8.6	11.7/10.6/16.1	4.6/3.7/6.5	24.2/30.7/30.1	3.6/4.8/5.6	9.3/9.1/10.4	11.5/11.4/12.1
GM[3]	21.6/16.9/18.2	13.4/10.2/10.3	12.8/11.6/14.3	2.5/1.8/2.5	9.8/8.8/12.0	3.3/3.5/3.7	13.0/15.3/16.1	10.4/9.1/9.5
Renault	7.1/4.7/3.9	9.7/8.9/9.4	5.3/1.9/1.0	28.9/40.5/39.1	3.6/5.8/4.1	3.3/10.5/11.1	7.5/8.7/8.0	10.6/14.3/14.4
Peugeot[4]	6.7/4.7/4.0	24.3/15.2/13.8	11.6/8.6/7.4	51.8/36.4/30.2	12.4/5.1/4.4	10.2/11.0/8.5	27.8/12.9/11.8	20.6/14.1/12.2
Volkswagen[5]	24.9/21.7/23.5	10.3/8.9/10.4	19.1/5.1/5.3	2.4/4.0/4.9	4.1/3.4/4.5	3.8/4.4/5.3	8.4/7.5/8.2	9.9/9.6/10.0
Nissan	−/2.1/2.0	−/3.8/3.7	−/5.0/5.2	−/0.9/0.9	−/6.1/5.9	−/.03/.01	−/5.3/4.6	−/2.5/2.2
Honda	−/1.8/1.5	−/4.4/3.3	−/2.4/0.9	−/0.4/0.4	−/1.5/1.1	−/.03/.01	−/5.5/3.5	−/1.4/1.0
Mazda	−/1.9/1.9	−/3.2/3.6	−/8.9/9.4	−/0.7/0.7	−/1.0/1.0	−/.02/.01	−/3.9/3.7	−/1.4/1.3
Mitsubishi (Colt)	−/1.7/1.9	−/3.5/3.4	−/3.4/1.2	−/0.2/0.2	−/0.7/0.6	−/.02/.02	−/4.8/3.5	−/1.1/0.9
Toyota	−/2.4/1.9	−/9.1/6.1	−/8.2/7.1	−/0.7/0.7	−/2.3/1.8	−/.02/.03	−/6.0/4.4	−/2.1/1.5
For 1973—all Japanese vehicles	0.8	13.4	7.1	0.6	4.6	0.1	10.1	2.5

SOURCE: L'Argus.

NOTES:

[1] Fiat includes Lancia and Autobianchi.
[2] Ford includes all sourced vehicles, e.g., Spain and Belgium.
[3] GM includes both Vauxhall and Opel.
[4] Peugeot includes for 1973 Chrysler and Citroen, bought in 1979 and 1974, respectively.
[5] Includes Audi.
[6] Eire and Luxembourg are ignored (about 100,000 units).

Exhibit 33.11
EUROPEAN MOTOR INDUSTRY: NET PROFITS
(In £m, Unless Otherwise Stated)

Make	1977	1978	1979	1980	1981	1982
Peugeot	226	526	1,800	–150	–184	–336
Renault	31**	19**	133**	140	–55	–112
Ford UK	116	144	347	204	165	192
Ford Werke	143	143	124	11	32	76
Ford Europe*	1,045	1,271	1,219	323	289	451
Vauxhall	–2	–2	–31	–183	–57	–29
Opel	84	128	65	–97	–130	22
GM Europe*	277	376	338	–359	–427	6
BL	–52	–28	–145	–536	–497	–293
VAG	103	149	172	76	20	–11
Daimler Benz	145	154	164	261	181	217
BMW	31	39	45	28	32	47
MAN	—	17	18	13	12	7
Alfa-Romeo	–98	–77	–52	–28	–51	–29
Fiat	41	46	22	26	39	58
Seat	n/a	n/a	n/a	–106.6	–104.7	–122.6
Motor Iberica	5.8	6.6	4.2	–2.3	–13.4	–17.2
Volvo	25	36	46	4	45	45
Saab	23	23	26	36	39	43

SOURCES: Company accounts and University of East Anglia, finance and accountancy department. Krish Bhaskar.

NOTES:
*US$m.
**Unconsolidated.
n/a = not available.

European market in the future, indicating that higher Japanese sales in Europe would come directly from those of the established European producers. The existing structure of voluntary agreements to limit Japanese imports into individual European countries was fragile. Although "voluntary" was clearly a euphemism, any cracks in the agreements could quickly lead to more Japanese imports before new and possibly more lenient agreements were negotiated. West Germany and Belgium were thought to be the weak spots.

If a European local content rule were to be established on the basis of local sales (i.e., if a specified percentage of each manufacturer's European

Exhibit 33.12

SHARE OF JAPANESE EXPORTS IN REGISTRATIONS BY IMPORTING COUNTRY IN EUROPE

Country	1966	1970	1975	1979	1981
Belgium	0.3	4.9	16.5	18.0	28%
France	0	0.2	1.6	2.2	2%
Germany	0	0.1	1.7	5.6	10%
Italy	0	0	0.1	0.1	—
Netherlands	0.6	3.2	15.5	19.5	26%
UK	0.1	0.4	9.0	10.8	10%
Denmark	0.5	3.4	14.7	18.1	28%
Ireland	0	0	8.9	25.2	30%
Austria	0	0.9	5.4	12.4	23%
Switzerland	0.1	5.6	8.4	16.0	26%
Portugal	0	10.7	11.8	7.8	11%
Finland	14.4	18.3	20.8	23.9	26%
Norway	1.9	11.4	28.4	24.2	36%
Sweden	0.2	0.7	6.5	10.0	14%

SOURCE: G. Sinclair, *The World Car.*

sales had to be produced in Europe), then the existing system of individual national voluntary trade agreements would become redundant. Alternatively, if a local content rule were to be applied to local production (i.e., if a specified percentage of the content of each manufacturer's cars assembled in Europe had to be sourced in Europe), then some controls on automobile imports would still be needed. A local content rule of this type would prevent the Japanese from circumventing the intent of import controls by importing the bulk of their components from Japan while establishing only token assembly operations in Europe.

Yet there were many potential negative consequences for European producers if local content regulations spread across Europe. It was not obvious that European producers should object to Japanese imports, even at a substantially higher level than at present, if the alternative was to be new Japanese greenfield plants in Europe. Even if they complied scrupulously with local content rules, these new plants, employing the most advanced production technology and work methods, could be tough competitors, unshackled from any form of constraint. At the very least, they would add production capacity to a market already suffering from 20% excess capacity. A price war was certainly not impossible to imagine. And Ford, among others, was wor-

RESTRICTIONS ON JAPANESE CAR SALES IN DEVELOPED COUNTRIES, 1981/1982

Exhibit 33.13

United Kingdom	10–11% market share ceiling, dating from 1975 package to nationalize BL
Federal Republic of Germany	Growth limit of 10% pa on 1980 sales (252,000 units)
Netherlands	No increase on 1980 level
Luxembourg	No increase on 1980 level
Italy	Quota of 2,200 units
France	3% market share ceiling
Belgium	Reduction of 7% on 1980 sales
EEC as a whole	Common External Tariff is 10.9%.
Canada	Shipments of "around 174,000" units as against 158,000 in 1980
Australia	All imports restricted to 20% of market. Tariff of 57%. Local content must be 85% to count as home-produced.
USA	Shipments of 1.68 mn for 1981 (Japanese fiscal year). Subsequent shipment limits to be calculated taking account of US market conditons. Tariff is 2.9%.
Denmark Greece Ireland	No restrictions
Japan	No quotas or tariffs on assembled cars, but internal taxes, depending on engine size. Distribution and administrative checking systems alleged to operate as non-tariff barriers.

SOURCE: G. Sinclair, *The World Car.*

NOTE: The Benelux and Canadian restrictions are supposed to last only for 1981. The others appear to be more permanent.

ried about the impact that these plants could have on fleet sales, particularly in the high-margin UK market, if nationalistic customers began to think of Nissan, for example, as a "national" producer.

Another problem was that local content rules could limit Ford's own manufacturing flexibility. The key new concept in the automobile industry in the 1970s was that of a "world car." A world car is assembled in local markets (tailored to local consumers' tastes) from a common set of components. Each component is produced in very high volume at one site, where it can be done cheapest, and then shipped around the world to the scattered assembly plants. Local content rules and world cars were seemingly incompatible.

Ford's "Erika" project (the 1981 "Escort") was the first of the world cars. In actual practice, the world car concept was of questionable success. The "Escort" that was marketed in the United States differed so much in style and design from its European sibling that there was little parts commonality, and transportation costs ate away at the efficiency gains from large scale production of the parts that were common. The result was that although there was some international trade in components within Ford, most movement of parts was either within Europe or within the United States.

General Motors had similar problems with their "J-car" (the Vauxhall "Cavalier" in the UK and Opel "Rekord" in West Germany) and "X-car" (the Vauxhall "Royale" in the UK and Opel "Senator" in Germany). GM seemed to have been more successful than Ford, however, in standardising components, and whereas Ford had primarily maintained an approach of European sourcing for European markets, GM had already moved to exploit its global reach.

To make matters even more complex, Ford had a 25% share in Toyo Kogyo (Mazda) and thus an option of working with Mazda to import inexpensive Japanese vehicles (see Exhibits 33.14 and 33.15). Indeed, a Mazda pickup truck was sold in the United States and Greece as a Ford truck, and the very successful Ford "Laser" in the Far East was a version of the Mazda 626 made in Japan. (In July 1983, Ford was threatening such a policy to counteract the proposed GM-Toyota production plant in California.)

TECHNICAL ASPECTS OF LOCAL CONTENT REGULATIONS

If the management of Ford of Europe were to support local content regulations, they felt they would have to answer four technical questions.

1. How should "local" be defined geographically?
2. How was local content to be measured?
3. To what should local content regulations be applied—individual cars, models, or a producer's entire fleet?
4. What should the minimum percentage of local content be?

The company had already done some thinking about each question.

Of all the producers, Ford was the most geographically integrated in Europe. It would therefore be important to encompass most or all of Europe in the term "local." A definition restricted to the EEC would exclude Ford's big Valencia plant in Spain and a 200,000 unit per year plant contemplated for Portugal. These plants represented critical low cost sources for small cars for the other European markets. (Both Spain and Portugal had applied for admission to the EEC, however.) Ford regarded a nation–state definition as impractical and intolerable.

The question of how to define local content was a very difficult one to answer. One proposal was to define content by weight. This had the advantage

Exhibit 33.14
RELATIONSHIPS BETWEEN AUTOMAKERS IN JAPAN, UNITED STATES, AND EUROPE, 1982

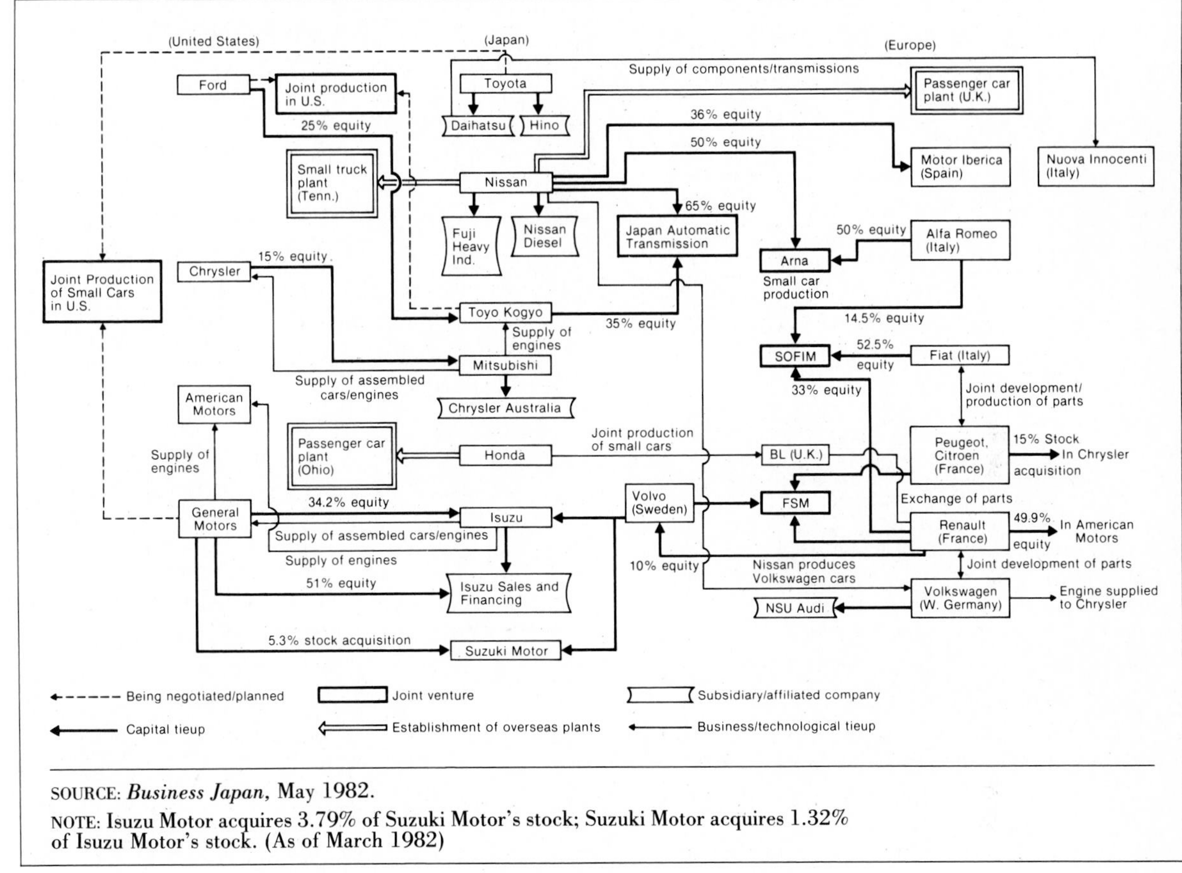

SOURCE: *Business Japan*, May 1982.

NOTE: Isuzu Motor acquires 3.79% of Suzuki Motor's stock; Suzuki Motor acquires 1.32% of Isuzu Motor's stock. (As of March 1982)

of being difficult to manipulate by transfer pricing, but it might allow the importation of high value, high technology components that were light in weight.

The other common definition of local content was by value. Essentially, the percentage of local content was established by subtracting the value of the imported components as declared on customs documentation from: (a) the distributor's price or (b) the ex-works price or (c) the ex-works price minus the labor and overhead content of the car. Then the local content residue was divided by the corresponding denominator.

Clearly the percentage of the imported components gets larger from (a) to (c) as the value of the domestic content gets smaller. Ford had not decided

Exhibit 33.15

FOREIGN SOURCING—RECENTLY ANNOUNCED COMMITMENTS BY U.S. AUTOMOBILE MANUFACTURERS TO PURCHASE FOREIGN-MADE COMPONENTS FOR USE IN DOMESTIC VEHICLES PRODUCTION

Automobile Manufacturer	*Description of Component*	*Intended Use*	*Manufacturing Source*	*Approximate Number of Components*	*Period*
GM	2·8 lit V-6	Cars	GM Mexico	<400,000/year	1982–
	2·0 lit L-4 with transmission	Mini trucks	Isuzu (Japan)	100,000/year	1981–
	1·8 lit diesel L-4	Chevette	Isuzu (Japan)	small numbers	1982–
	1·8 lit L-4	J-car	GM Brazil	250,000/year	1979–
	THM 180 automatic transmission	Chevette	GM Strasbourg (France)	−250,000/year	1979–
Ford	2·2 lit L-4	Cars	Ford Mexico	<400,000/year	1983–
	Diesel L-4	Cars	Toyo Kogyo	150,000/year	1983–
	2·0 lit L-4	Mini trucks	Toyo Kogyo	<100,000/year	1982–
	2·3 lit L-4	Cars	Ford Brazil	−50,000/year	1979–
	Diesel 6 cyl.	Cars	BMW/Steyr	100,000/year	1983–
	Turbo-diesel/ 4 cyl.	Cars	BMW/Steyr	—	1985–
	Manual trans-axles	Front disc cars	Toyo Kogyo	100,000/year	1980–
	Aluminum cylinder heads	1·6 lit L-4	Europe, Mexico	—	1980–
	Electronic engine control devices	Cars	Toshiba	100,000+/year	1978–
	Ball joints	Cars	Musashi Seimibu	1,000,000/year	1980–84

Chrysler	L-6 and V-8 engines	Cars	Chrysler Mexico	<100,000/year	early 1970
	2·2 lit L-4	K-body	Chrysler Mexico	<270,000/year	1981
	2·6 lit L-4	K-body	Mitsubishi	1 million	1981–85
	1·7 lit L-4	L-body (Omni)	Volkswagen	1–2 million	1978–82
	1·6 lit L-4	L-body	Talbot (Peugeot)	400,000 total	1982–84
	2·0 lit Diesel	K-body	Peugeot	100,000/year	1982–
	V-6				
	1·4 lit L-4	A-body (Omni replacement)	Mitsubishi	300,000/year	1984–
	Aluminum cylinder heads	2·2 lit L-4	Fiat		
AMC	Car components and power train	AMC-Renault	Renault in France and Mexico	300,000/year	1982–
VW of America	Radiators, stampings	Rabbit	VW Mexico	250,000/year	1979–
	L-4 diesel and gas	Cars	VW Mexico	300,000+/year	1982–

SOURCE: Bulletin of the European Communities, *The European Automobile Industry: Commission Statement.*

its position with regard to this issue, except that it did not want specific components identified for mandatory local production. It was also possible to devise other hybrid methods of valuing local content, but they were generally not under discussion.

Regarding the question of to what should the local content rules be applied, Ford favored applying them to the average of a producer's entire line of cars, rather than to each individual car or model. The former would jeopardise Ford's current importation from South Africa of small quantities of their P100 pickup truck (based on the "Cortina").

There was also a related question of whether automobile production or regional sales should form the basis of measurement. Ford preferred that a specified percentage of a producer's European sales be made in Europe, since such a rule was insurance against circumvention of the current import quotas. A production-based local content rule would only prevent circumvention of the intent of import quotas by token local final assembly.

Finally there was the question of what the appropriate percentage should be. Figures currently under discussion ranged from 60% to 80%, although the percentage clearly depended on the format of the specific proposals. Of particular significance in terms of these percentages was the fact that a 60% rule might allow importation of engines and major parts of the drive train which would all be excluded by an 80% rule. Also, it might be very difficult for the Japanese to start up a new plant with an immediate 80% local content (even if that percentage were to be achieved with more time). Startup at 60% would be substantially easier.

THE POLITICAL OPTIONS

Should Ford decide to support local content regulations and then find answers to the technical questions, it would still have to determine the best way to carry its case to the appropriate government body. And here again, the way was not clear.

Ford definitely did not want to act on its own. It would be much better to act in concert with the other European producers. (Despite the all-American image of the founder and his name, Ford of Europe unquestionably considered itself "European.") Not only was this desirable on general principles, but for one quite specific reason Ford preferred not to lobby the EEC directly. It had recently fought and was currently fighting other battles with the European Commission. In 1982, the Commission had issued an interim order to Ford under Article 85 of the Treaty of Rome (an antitrust statute) requiring the company to offer right-hand-drive cars to the West German market. The background to this directive was that most European automobile producers charged significantly higher prices in the United Kingdom than on the continent. To prevent customers from ordering right-hand-drive cars in Germany and importing them to the UK, Ford had refused to make the models available on the continent. This provoked a consumer response to which the EEC Commission had responded.

In June of 1983 the Commission issued a draft regulation applicable to the distribution systems of all motor manufacturers operating in Europe. The regulation aimed at harmonizing vehicle availability and prices across Europe. Any model of vehicle sold in any EEC member state would have to be made available in all other member states. And if price differences exceeded 12% (net of taxes) between any EEC markets, new importers (not authorized by the manufacturer) could enter the market. Ford, along with all other European motor manufacturers, was opposing this proposal vigorously.

Although Ford preferred to have a common industry position to press on the governmental authorities, there was little likelihood of unanimity among the European producers even on the most basic question of whether local content rules were desirable. General Motors was an almost certain opponent to local content rules despite the fact that it too might welcome relief from Japanese competition. Fiat, Renault, and British Leyland, on the other hand, might be strong allies who could perhaps rally the support of their respective governments. They appeared to have much to gain from local content rules since they had most of their operations in Europe and they purchased most of their components locally.

There were a number of sourcing arrangements, however, which could undermine the support of some of these firms. Japanese cars assembled in Australia were entering the UK with a certificate of origin from Australia. British Leyland's "Acclaim" was of questionable origin. Fiat was bringing in "Pandas" from Brazil, and VW "Beetles" came into Europe from Mexico. Renault had extensive operations in the United States which could alter the company's outlook. And on July 27, 1983, *The Wall Street Journal* reported that Fiat was being indicted by the Italian authorities for selling cars made in Spain and Brazil under the guise of Italian manufacture. Fiat denied the charge.

Ford executives believed, nonetheless, that with the exception of GM, Ford was likely to find general support within the industry. In fact, in a 1981 draft paper, the CLCA (Committee de Liaison des Constructeurs Associations, basically a political liaison committee of the national automotive trade associations of France, the United Kingdom, Germany, Belgium, Holland, and Italy) stated that:

> The establishment of Japanese motor vehicle manufacturing plants should be subject to the following durable conditions:

a) the CIF value of the components not originating from the EEC should not exceed 20% of the price ex-works of the vehicle.
b) the manufacturing and assembly of mechanical components (engines, gearboxes and drive train) should be performed within the EEC.

THE EUROPEAN COMMISSION

Ford executives believed that the European Commission was prepared to take some action on the automobile imports issue. In January 1983 the Commission had held discussions with the Japanese in Tokyo and had obtained a non-binding commitment to moderate vehicle exports to the EEC. The Commission was currently monitoring the agreement. Beyond this it was unclear what action the European Commission was considering. In principle, the EEC should be expected to favor relatively free trade between its member countries and the rest of the world. The history of international trade since World War II—a history in which the EEC featured prominently—was one of declining tariffs (from an average of 20% on manufactured goods in the 1950s to 8% in the mid-1970s), dramatically growing trade volumes, and greater interdependence of national economies. Two other principles dear to the EEC were that all member countries maintain a *common* trade policy vis-à-vis non-EEC countries, and that there be no barriers to trade between member countries. Clearly, the existing set of non-uniform bilateral trade agreements with the Japanese offended these principles.

Although the principles underlying the EEC were relatively unambiguous, the EEC often resorted to protective policies, and it was not immune to pressures to maintain jobs in the automotive sector. But granted this observation, it was still not evident just how job preservation might best be achieved. Formal local content rules would be inconsistent with EEC law and would violate the GATT. Thus any local content measures would have to be informal, such as those which currently existed between the Japanese and the British. Would the EEC prefer to see a uniform (albeit informal) external quota and internal production-based local content rule? Or would it rather see a uniform internal sales-based content rule and no quota? Would its preference in either case be less restrictive than the status quo, shaky though it might be? And was it realistic to expect that an informal negotiating process could create a common position among the different EEC member states? A weak, contentious, and non-uniform set of local content rules established and enforced by each EEC member country could be the worst of all the imaginable alternatives.

The Japanese, of course, would have some influence on EEC thinking on this matter. Any EEC action would probably come in the context of trade negotations—not simply unilaterally-imposed trade sanctions. And what position might the Japanese take? It is conceivable that they might agree to some reasonable export restraints into the EEC in return for open markets within the EEC. That would give them access to the two big markets from which they were currently virtually excluded—France and Italy. But would those two countries agree? Each would face greater Japanese competition in its home market but less in its export markets in other EEC countries.

The executives on the Management Committee considered their alternatives. If they were to have any role in determining the public policies that would undoubtedly have a significant impact on their company, they would have to act quickly.

NOTE

1. *New York Herald Tribune*, June 27, 1983.

Case 34

COTTON BELT EXPORTERS

Paul N. Keaton/Patricia A. Watson-Kuentz

While John Welch was growing up in Texas, he was an excellent student. His parents and teachers thought of him as "college capable"; in fact, he never seriously considered any option other than college. He chose to major in marketing because one of his goals was, in his own words, "not to get stuck in Civil Service like my dad did. Private industry is the place for me where I have more of an opportunity to be promoted on my own merits and not necessarily on seniority." John entered college and, as usual, did well scholastically.

As college graduation neared, John began to interview with a number of companies. The college placement counselor advised John to make a list of aspects that he would find desirable or undesirable in a job. One of the items on his list was that the company and its product or goal had to be socially justifiable. This item had come to mind because many of his classmates were going to work for oil companies. John believed that in spite of the oil companies' slightly higher pay scale, he would not want to work for a company that made its money selling a non-renewable resource.

Another of the items on his list was that he wanted to travel in his job. His family had traveled in the United States on vacations when he was a child and he had been to Mexico and Canada, but he wanted to see something of other parts of the world. Although John did not care to live in another country, he did think that a job which took him periodically to other countries for short trips would be desirable.

One day during the spring semester of his senior year, John talked with

This case was prepared by Prof. Paul N. Keaton of the University of Wisconsin-La Crosse and Ms. Patricia A. Watson-Kuentz. Presented at Midwest Case Writers Association Workshop, 1982. Reprinted by permission.

one of his marketing professors, Dr. Mayfield, about his career goals, and Dr. Mayfield suggested that perhaps John should look into the exporting business. Dr. Mayfield said he had a friend in Memphis who was a vice-president in a cotton exporting firm, Cotton Belt Exporting. Things fell into place and John received and accepted an offer of a job in the firm.

For the first couple of years, John's responsibilities included traveling throughout the Southern United States and California buying cotton from farmers and gins, but the company promised that once he had proven himself in a couple of positions he would be promoted into a position where he would be dealing directly with people in foreign countries. After about six years and two positions with the firm, he was promoted to Manager of Export Sales to Japan.

It took John some time to become accustomed to dealing with Japanese businesspeople, but in doing so he became fascinated by the differences in customs. He learned to understand that just because a Mr. Tanaka said "yes" while John was talking to him, he did not mean that he agreed to what was being said—instead, he meant merely that he understood what was being said. Each trip to Japan was a learning experience.

John also became acquainted with the mechanics of selling cotton to Japan. He learned that disagreements between cotton sellers in the United States and cotton buyers in Japan were arbitrated to a large degree by two associations, one in the United States (the American Cotton Shipping Association) and one in Japan (the Cotton Trade Association). The two associations agreed on many rules for trade but when their rules conflicted, the cotton contracts themselves specified which rules would apply.

On one trip to Japan, John heard rumors from importers that the Cotton Trade Association was contemplating some rule changes in the near future that could affect his company's ability to trade with Japan. He paid a visit to the Association but his usual contact was on vacation in Hawaii, so he had to see another gentleman, Mr. Kodama. Mr. Kodama said that he knew little about the pending changes but he intimated that, although he was a busy man, for a small fee he could probably find out "many" details. John left the office promising to get back to Mr. Kodama.

John considered his options. He decided that although he had never approved of paying to obtain such information, the urgency of the situation and the probable need for immediate action dictated that he should make the payment. The next day he returned to Mr. Kodama's office with an envelope containing 22,170 yen (equivalent to about $100 U.S.) which was, from his experience, the going rate for such payments.

Mr. Kodama told John that a middle-level government official, Mr. Nakamura, was pressuring the cotton importing people to diversify their source of cotton in order to reduce Japan's dependency on any one country. The Association reacted by considering rule changes that would encourage importers to buy from sources other than their largest ones. Since the United States was the largest supplier of cotton to Japan, this action was certain to reduce the total amount of cotton it could sell to Japan.

John checked with his company, and his boss approved John's suggestion that he do some lobbying while he was in Japan. After obtaining the appropriate introductions John arranged to have lunch with Mr. Nakamura. At the restaurant, John explained his company's situation, giving Mr. Nakamura facts about the promise of larger crops in the United States, reduced prices because of technological advances in production, improved strains of cotton, and so on. After much discussion, Mr. Nakamura indicated that, having given some thought to the specifics of the problem, he believed he might be able to see John's side of the argument.

Later in the conversation, Mr. Nakamura began to discuss the increasing cost of living, especially since his son had been admitted to Harvard. He wondered if John's company might see fit to give the boy some type of scholarship: According to the Harvard catalog, his son would need about $20,000 per year to attend school. Mr. Nakamura subtly (but unmistakably) intimated that financial aid to his son might help him see the cotton situation more clearly.

John found himself in a dilemma. He had rationalized the payments for information, but somehow this situation seemed different.

Case 35

UNION CARBIDE OF INDIA, LTD.: THE BHOPAL TRAGEDY

Arthur Sharplin

December 2, 1984 began as a typical day in the central Indian city of Bhopal. Shoppers moved about the bustling, open-air market; here and there a customer haggled with a merchant. Beasts of burden, donkeys and oxen, pulled carts or carried ungainly bundles through the partly paved streets. Children played in the dirt. In the shadow of a Union Carbide pesticide plant, tens of thousands of India's poorest citizens milled about the shanty town they called home. Further away, wealthy Indians lived in opulence rivalling that of the first-class districts of London or Paris. Inside the plant, several hundred Indian workers and managers went about their duties, maintaining and operating the systems which produced the mildly toxic pesticide, Sevin. Most of the plant was shut down for maintenance and it was operating at far below capacity.

At about 11 o'clock that evening, one of the operators noticed that the pressure in a methyl isocyanate (MIC) storage tank read 10 pounds per square inch—four times normal. The operator was not concerned, thinking that the tank may have been pressurized with nitrogen by the previous shift. Around midnight several of the workers noticed that their eyes had begun to water and sting, a signal experience had taught them indicated an MIC leak. The leak, a small but continuous drip, was soon spotted. The operators were still not alarmed because minor leaks at the plant were quite common. It was time for tea and the crew retired to the company canteen, resolving to correct the problem afterward.

This case was prepared by Prof. Arthur Sharplin of Northeast Louisiana University. Reprinted by permission. This case also appeared in the *Case Research Journal, 1985,* pp. 229–248.

By the time the workers returned it was too late. The MIC tank pressure gauge was pegged. The leak had grown much larger and the entire area of the MIC tanks was enveloped in the choking fumes. The workers tried spraying water on the leak to break down the MIC. They sounded the alarm siren and summoned the fire brigade. As the futility of their efforts became apparent, most of the workers panicked and ran upwind—some scaling the chain-link and barbed-wire fence in their frantic race for survival.

By 1 o'clock, only a supervisor remained in the area. He stayed upwind, donning his oxygen breathing apparatus every few minutes to check the various gauges and sensors. By that time the pressure in the MIC tank had forced open a relief valve and the untreated MIC vapor could be seen escaping from an atmospheric vent line 120 feet in the air.

The cloud of deadly white gas was carried by a southeasterly wind toward the Jai Prakash Nagar shanties, where some of India's poorest citizens lived. Because MIC is much heavier than air, it drifted downward. As the gaseous tentacles reached into the huts there was panic and confusion. Many of the weak and elderly died where they lay. Many who made it into the streets were blinded. "It was like breathing fire," one survivor said. As word of the gas leak spread, many of Bhopal's affluent were able to flee in their cars. But the poor were left behind. When the gas reached the railroad station, word was sent out along the tracks and the incoming trains diverted, cutting off another means of escape.

Of Bhopal's total population of 1,000,000, an estimated 500,000 fled that night, most on foot. The surrounding towns were simply unprepared to accept the gasping and dying mass of people. Thousands waited outside hospitals for medical care. There was no certainty about how to treat the gas victims and general purpose medical supplies were in hopelessly short supply. Inside the hospitals and out, screams filled the air. Food supplies were inadequate and people were afraid to drink the water, not knowing if it was contaminated.

During the second day, relief measures were better organized. Several hundred doctors and nurses from nearby hospitals were summoned to help medical personnel in Bhopal. Disposing of the dead was a major problem. Mass cremation was necessary. Islamic victims, whose faith allows burial rather than cremation, were piled several deep in hurriedly dug graves. Bloated carcasses of cattle and dogs littered the city. There was fear of a cholera epidemic. Bhopal's mayor said, "I can say that I have seen chemical warfare. Everything's so quiet. Goats, cats, whole families—father, mother, children—all lying silent and still. And every structure totally intact. I hope never again to see it."

By the third day, the city had begun to move toward stability, if not normalcy. The Union Carbide plant had been closed and locked. A decision was made to consume the 30 tons of MIC that remained by using it to make pesticide. Most of the 2,000 dead bodies had been disposed of, however inappropriately. The more than 100,000 injured were being treated as rapidly as the limited medical facilities would allow, although many simply sat in silence, blinded and maimed by an enemy they had never known well enough to fear. For them, doctors predicted an increased risk of sterility, kidney and liver infections, tuberculosis, and brain damage. The potential for birth defects and other long-term effects was not yet known.

COMPANY BACKGROUND

Union Carbide's predecessor, the Ever-Ready Company, Ltd. (of Great Britain), began manufacturing flashlight batteries in Calcutta in 1926. The division was incorporated as the Ever-Ready Company (India), Ltd. in 1934 and became a subsidiary of Union Carbide Corporation of New York. The name of the Indian company was changed to National Carbide Company (India), Ltd. in 1949 and to Union Carbide (India), Ltd. (UCIL) in 1959. The 1926 capacity of 40 million dry cell batteries per year was expanded to 767 million by the 1960s. In 1959, a factory was set up in India to manufacture the flashlights themselves.

By the 1980s, UCIL was involved in five product areas: batteries, carbon and metals, plastics, marine products, and agricultural chemicals. Exhibit 35.1 provides production statistics for UCIL products. The company eventually operated fourteen plants at eight locations, including the headquarters operation in Calcutta. Union Carbide's petrochemical complex, established in Bombay in 1966, was India's first.

UCIL began its marine products operation with two shrimping ships in 1971. The business is completely export oriented and now employs fifteen deep-sea trawlers with processing facilities off the east and west coasts of India. The trawlers now harvest deep sea lobsters in addition to shrimp.

In 1979, UCIL initiated a letter of intent to manufacture dry cell batteries in Nepal. Construction of an Rs. (rupees) 18 million plant was begun in 1982.

UCIL's assets grew from Rs. 558 million in 1974 to Rs. 1,234 million in 1983 (the conversion rate stayed near 9 rupees to the dollar during this period, moving to about 13 as the dollar strengthened worldwide during 1984 and 1985). The *Economic Times* of India ranks UCIL number twenty-first in terms of sales among Indian companies. Union Carbide Corporation (USA) owns 50.9% of UCIL's stock and Indian citizens and companies own the remainder. When Indira Gandhi was voted out of office in 1977, the Janata (Peoples') Party obtained passage of a law requiring majority Indian ownership of multinational subsidiaries in the country. As a result, IBM, Coca-

Exhibit 35.1
PRODUCTION STATISTICS

Class of Goods	**1982** *Capacity*	*Production Levels* **1977**	**1978**	**1979**	**1980**	**1981**	**1982**
Batteries (millions of pieces)	767	363.3	430.3	460.3	458.8	411.3	512.2
Flashlight cases (millions of pieces)	7.5	5.0	5.7	6.4	6.9	7.4	6.7
Arc carbons (millions of pieces)	9.0	6.3	6.1	6.2	6.7	7.0	7.0
Industrial carbon electrodes and shapes (millions of pieces)	2.5	0.5	0.2	0.5	0.3	0.5	0.5
Photo-engravers' plates/strips for printing (tonnes*)	1,200	476.0	506.0	469.0	399.0	431.0	478.0
Stellite castings, head facings, and tube rods (tonnes)	150	13.7	18.2	15.8	14.5	16.4	12.7
Electrolytic manganese dioxide (tonnes)	4,500	650	2,700	2,605	2,803	3,000	3,085
Chemicals (tonnes)	13,600	11,783	8,069	8,511	7,550	6,865	6,331
Polyethylene (tonnes)	20,000	15,337	12,059	16,324	19,198	19,928	17,290
MIC based pesticides (tonnes)	5,000	321	367	1,496	1,542	2,704	2,308
Marine products (tonnes)	5,500	607	731	648	601	642	649

SOURCE: The Stock Exchange Foundation, Bombay, India, *The Stock Exchange Official Directory*, Vol. XVII/29, July 18, 1983.

* 1 tonne = 2240 lbs.

Cola, and several other international companies pulled out of India. UCIL received a special exemption from this law. Since 1967 the chairman of the board of UCIL has been an Indian and foreign membership on the eleven-member board of directors has been limited to four. One expert on Indian industry affairs said, "Though the foreigners on the board are down to four from six in previous years, they continue to hold sway over the affairs of the company."

The agricultural products division of UCIL was started in 1966 with only an office in Bombay. Agreement was reached with the Indian government in 1969 to set up a pesticide plant at Bhopal. Land was rented to UCIL for about $40 per acre per year. The initial investment was small, only $1 million, and the process was simple. Concentrated Sevin powder was imported from the United States, diluted with non-toxic powder, packaged, and sold. Under the technology transfer provisions of its agreement with the Indian government, Union Carbide Corporation (USA) was obligated to share its more advanced technologies with UCIL. Eventually the investment at Bhopal grew to exceed $25 million and the constituents of Sevin were made there. Another Union Carbide insecticide, called Temik, was made in small quantities at Bhopal.

OPERATIONS AT BHOPAL

On the surface, the UCIL insecticide factory is a typical process plant. A wide diversity of storage tanks, hoppers, and reactors are connected by pipes. There are many pumps and valves and a number of tall vent lines and ducts. Ponds and pits are used for waste treatment. And several railway spur lines run through the plant. Exhibit 35.2 is a diagram of the factory.

Sevin is made through a controlled chemical reaction involving alpha-naphthol and MIC. Alpha-naphthol is a brownish granular material and MIC is a highly reactive liquid which boils and becomes a gas at usual daytime temperatures. When plans were first made to begin production of alpha-naphthol at Bhopal in 1971, a pilot plant was set up to manufacture the product. Because the pilot plant was successful, a full-size alpha-naphthol plant (in fact, the world's largest) was constructed and placed in operation in

Exhibit 35.2

UNION CARBIDE (INDIA), LTD.: PESTICIDE PLANT AT BHOPAL

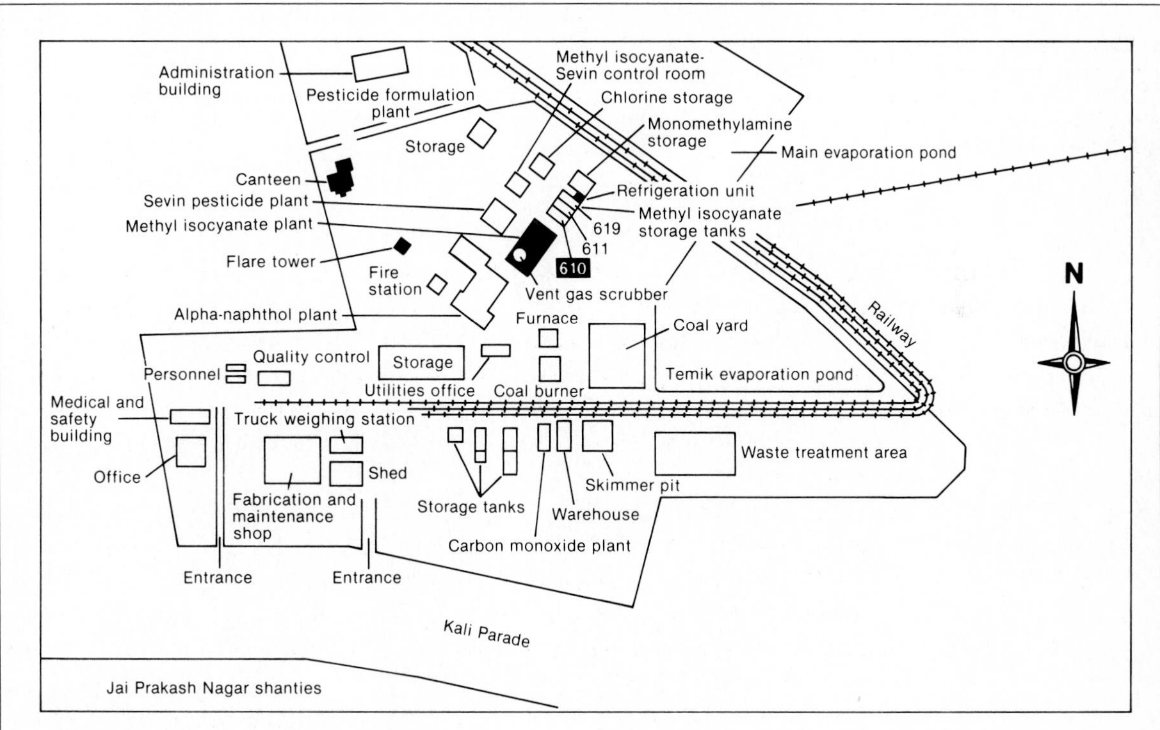

NOTES: MIC Tank 610 is tank that leaked.
Major discharge occurred above vent gas scrubber 120 feet high.
Wind was variable, three to seven miles per hour in a southeasterly direction when leak occurred.

1977. Mr. V.P. Gokhale, managing director of UCIL, called the alpha-naphthol plant a "very large mistake." But he said the company was forced to build it to keep its operating license from the Indian government.

In the meantime, work had begun on the ill-fated MIC plant. But even before the MIC plant was completed in 1979, problems began to crop up with the alpha-naphthol plant, resulting in a shutdown for modifications in 1978. In February 1980, the MIC plant was placed into service. The alpha-naphthol plant continued in various stages of shutdown and partial operation through 1984. The Bhopal factory was designed to produce 5,000 tons per year of Sevin but never operated near capacity.

FINANCE Exhibits 35.3, 35.4, 35.5, and 35.6 provide financial facts and figures for UCIL. As mentioned earlier, Union Carbide Corporation (USA) holds 50.9% of UCIL's common shares. The remainder are publicly traded on the Bombay stock exchange. Most of these shares are held by about 24,000 individuals. However, a number of institutional investors, such as life insurance companies and pension funds, hold substantial blocks. The Indian govern-

Exhibit 35.3
SUMMARY OF INCOME STATEMENTS
(In Thousands of Rupees Except Per Share Data)

	1982	1981	1980	1979	1978
Net sales	2,075,282	1,854,214	1,615,926	1,449,664	1,111,244
Cost of goods sold	1,720,303	1,518,538	1,307,042	1,190,242	926,958
Operating expenses	136,834	115,550	103,318	83,501	54,592
Profit from operations	218,145	220,126	205,566	175,921	129,694
Other income	27,426	26,955	23,528	13,685	10,187
Profit from operations plus other income	245,571	247,081	229,094	189,606	139,881
Interest expense	57,082	30,950	31,468	19,871	15,131
Depreciation expense	41,614	40,913	36,524	32,016	33,340
Earnings before taxes	146,875	175,218	161,102	137,719	91,410
Provisions for taxes	50,200	80,300	80,000	73,000	41,000
Net earnings	96,675	94,918	81,102	64,719	50,410
Earnings per share	2.95	2.91	2.49	2.98	2.32
Earnings as % of price	11.73	10.96	10.20	11.46	8.97
Cash dividends per share	1.50	1.50	1.40	1.60	1.60

NOTE: Average conversion rate for 1978–82, \$1 = RS. 9.00; for 1985, \$1 = Rs. 13.00.

Exhibit 35.4
SUMMARY OF BALANCE SHEETS
December 25, Respective Years (In Thousands of Rupees)

	1982	1981	1980	1979	1978
ASSETS					
Current assets					
Cash	52,285	52,173	56,589	53,026	94,482
Receivables	375,672	244,158	169,015	121,718	78,974
Inventories	327,317	368,606	311,612	292,935	231,945
Other current assets	6,088	9,230	9,277	11,237	12,738
Total curret assets	761,362	674,167	546,493	478,916	418,139
Net fixed assets	449,546	393,516	405,890	401,422	389,252
Miscellaneous assets	21	21	57	57	57
Intangible assets	3,000	3,000	3,000	3,000	3,000
TOTAL ASSETS	1,213,929	1,070,704	955,440	883,395	810,448
LIABILITIES & OWNERS' EQUITY					
Current liabilities					
Accounts payable & accruals	530,641	390,990	341,956	320,942	312,116
Provision for taxes	57,739	63,266	60,216	49,000	38,799
Total current debt	588,380	454,256	402,172	369,942	350,915
Long-term liabilities					
Debentures	29,340	54,823	31,315	20,300	—
Long-term loans	20,836	34,049	40,420	46,306	33,440
Total long-term debt	50,176	88,872	71,735	66,606	33,440
Stockholders' equity					
Common stock	325,830	325,830	325,830	217,220	217,220
Retained earnings & surplus	249,543	201,746	155,703	229,627	208,873
Total owners' equity	575,373	527,576	481,533	446,847	426,093
TOTAL LIABILITIES & OWNERS' EQUITY	1,213,929	1,070,704	955,440	883,395	810,448

ment does not directly own any UCIL stock, although the Life Insurance Corporation of India, the country's largest insuror and owner of many UCIL shares, is an arm of the Indian Government. During the months before the Bhopal disaster UCIL's common shares hovered around Rs. 30, but dropped to a low of Rs. 15.8 on December 11, recovering only slightly in succeeding weeks.

Exhibit 35.5
SUMMARY OF COMMON STOCK ISSUES

	Paid-Up Common Stock			
Year	*# of Shares*	*Paid Up per Share Rs.*	*Total Amount Rs.*	*Remarks*
1959–1960	2,800,000	10	28,000,000	800,000 right shares issued premium Rs. 2.50 per share proportion 2:5.
1964	3,640,000	10	36,400,000	840,000 right shares issued at a premium of Rs. 4 per share in the proportion 3:10.
1965	4,095,000	10	40,950,000	455,000 bonus shares issued in the proportion 1:8.
1968	8,190,000	10	81,900,000	2,047,500 right shares issued at par in proportion 1:2. 2,047,500 bonus shares issued in proportion 1:2.
1970	12,285,000	10	122,850,000	4,095,000 bonus shares issued in the proportion 1:2.
1974	18,427,500	10	184,275,000	6,142,500 bonus shares issued in the proportion 1:2.
1978	21,722,000	10	217,220,000	3,294,500 shares issued at a premium of Rs. 6 per share to resident Indian shareholders, the company's employees, and financial institutions.
1980	32,583,000	10	325,830,000	10,861,000 bonus shares issued in proportion 1:2.

In 1975, the United States Export-Import bank, in cooperation with First National Citibank of New York, agreed to grant loans of $2.5 million to buy equipment for the MIC project. Also, the Industrial Credit and Investment Corporation of India (ICICI) authorized a Rs. 21.5 million loan, part of which was drawn in 1980. Finally, long-term loans were provided by at least seven Indian insurance companies. Some of these loans were guaranteed by the State Bank of India.

Profits of several million dollars from the Bhopal facility were predicted for 1984. Several factors kept these expectations from being realized. First, an economic recession made farmers more cost conscious and caused them to search for less expensive alternatives to Sevin. Second, a large number of small-scale producers were able to undersell the company because they were exempt from excise and sales taxes. Seventeen of these firms bought MIC from UCIL and used it to make products virtually identical to Sevin and Temik. Finally, a new generation of low-cost pesticides was becoming available. With sales collapsing, the Bhopal plant became a money loser in 1981.

FINANCIAL CHARTS

Exhibit 35.6

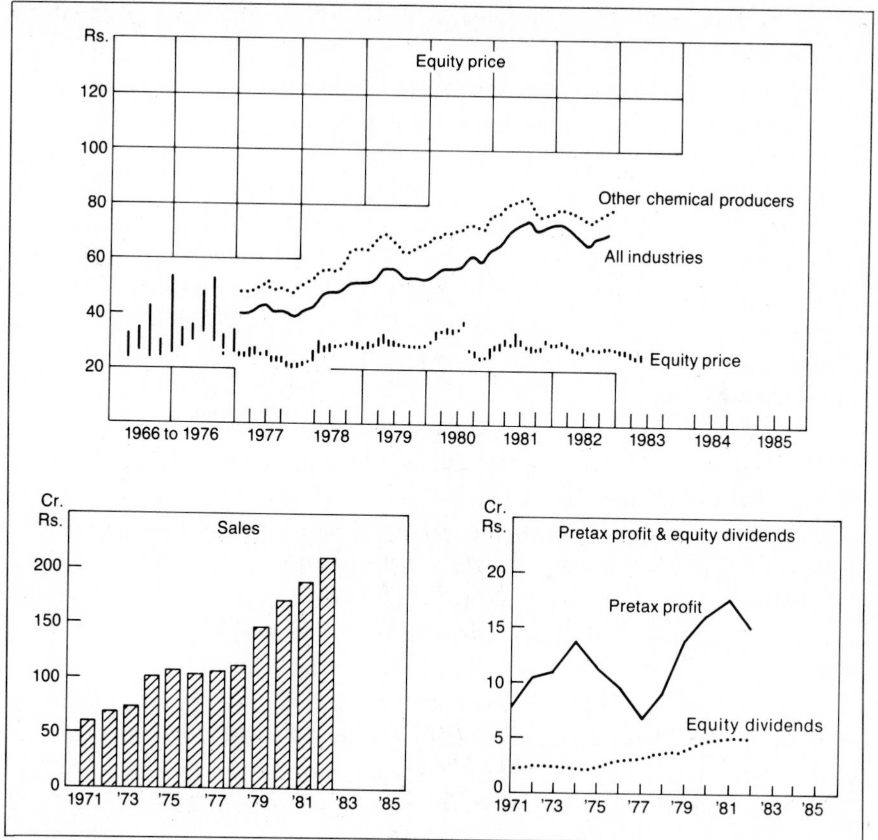

The prediction for 1984 was for a loss of $4 million based on 1,000 tons of output, one-fifth of capacity.

To forestall what may have seemed inevitable economic failure, extensive cost-cutting efforts were carried out. The staff at the MIC plant was cut from twelve operators on a shift to six. The maintenance team was reduced in size. In a number of instances, faulty safety devices remained unrepaired for weeks. Because a refrigeration unit, designed to keep the methyl isocyanate cool, continued to malfunction, it was shut down. Though instrumentation technology advanced at Union Carbide's other pesticide plants, the innovations were only partly adopted at Bhopal.

PERSONNEL

Until 1982, a cadre of American managers and technicians worked at the Bhopal plant. The Americans were licensed by the Indian government only for fixed periods. While in India they were expected to train Indian replacements. From 1982 onward, no American worked at Bhopal. While major decisions, such as approval of the annual budget, were cleared with Union Carbide, USA, day-to-day details such as staffing and maintenance were left to the Indian officials.

In general, the engineers at the Bhopal plant were among India's elite. Most new engineers were recruited from the prestigious Indian Institutes of Technology and paid wages comparable with the best offered in Indian industry. Successful applicants for engineering jobs with UCIL were provided two years of training before being certified for unsupervised duty.

Until the late seventies, only first-class science graduates or persons with a diploma in engineering were employed as operators at Bhopal. New hires were given six months of theoretical instruction followed by on-the-job training. As cost-cutting efforts proceeded in the eighties, standards were lowered significantly. Some operators with only a high school diploma were employed and training was much less rigorous than before. In addition, the number of operators on a shift was reduced by about half and many supervisory positions were eliminated.

The Indian managers developed strong ties with the local political establishment. A former police chief became the plant's security contractor and a local political party boss got the job as company lawyer. *Newsweek* reports that a luxurious guest house was maintained and lavish parties thrown there for local dignitaries.

In general, wages at the Bhopal plant were well above those available in domestic firms. A janitor, for example, earned Rs. 1,000 per month compared to less than Rs. 500 elsewhere. Still, as prospects continued downward after 1981, a number of senior managers and the best among the plant's junior executives began to abandon ship. The total work force at the plant dropped from a high of about 1,500 to 950. This reduction was accomplished through attrition, with those having the best job prospects tending to leave first.

MARKETING

The population of India is over 700 million persons, while its land area is about one-third that of the United States. Three-fourths of India's people depend on agriculture for a livelihood. Fewer than one-third are literate. Modern communications and transportation facilities connect the major cities but the hundreds of villages are largely untouched by twentieth century technology. English tends to be at least a second language for most Indian professionals but not for ordinary Indians. There are sixteen official languages in the country. The most common official language, and the one supported by the Indian central government, is Hindi, which is dominant in five of India's twenty-two states. The working classes speak hundreds of dialects, often unintelligible to citizens just miles away.

India's farmers offer at best a challenging target market. They generally eke out a living from small tracts of land. Most have little more than subsistence incomes and are reluctant to invest what they have in such modern innovations as pesticides. They are generally ignorant of the right methods of application and, given their linguistic diversity and technological isolation, are quite hard to educate. UCIL has used billboards and wall posters as well as newspaper and radio advertising.

Radio is the most widely used advertising medium in India. The state-owned radio system includes broadcasts in local languages. Companies can buy advertising time on the stations but it is costly to produce commercials in so many dialects. Much of the state-sponsored programming, especially in rural areas, is devoted to promoting agriculture and instructing farmers about new techniques. Often the narrators mention products such as Sevin and Temik by name.

Movies provide another popular promotional tool. Most small towns have one or more cinema houses and rural people often travel to town to watch the shows. Advertisements appear before and after main features and are usually produced in regional languages (not in local dialects).

Until recently, television was available only in the cities. During 1984, a government program spread TV relay stations at the rate of more than one each day, with the result that 80% of the population was within the range of a television transmitter by the end of the year. Still, few rural citizens have access to television receivers.

Pesticides sales are highly dependent on agricultural activity from year to year. In years of drought, like 1980 and 1982, UCIL's pesticide sales have suffered severe setbacks. In 1981, abundant rains help spur pesticide sales.

India has a very extensive network of railways. The total track mileage in India is second only to the USSR. The road and highway system crisscrosses the areas in between railway lines. The railway system is especially significant to UCIL's pesticide operation because Bhopal lies near the junction of the main east–west and north–south tracks in India. Exhibit 35.7 is a map of India. Bhopal is also just south of the vast Indo-Gangetic plain, the richest farming area in India. Much of UCIL's pesticide is marketed through government agricultural retailing offices which sell seed, fertilizers, and pesticides. An Indian familiar with the agricultural economy remarked, "Overall, physical distribution of pesticides is not too monumental a task. Getting farmers to use them and teaching them how are the real problems."

PROSPECTS FOR THE FUTURE

Following the disaster, the government of India cancelled the license issued to the Bhopal plant, clearing the way for the plant's dismantlement. The likelihood that this would happen provoked a Bhopal political leader to remark, "We've lost 2,000 lives, now must we lost 2,000 jobs?"

Manslaughter and other charges have been filed against UCIL execu-

Exhibit 35.7

MAP OF INDIA

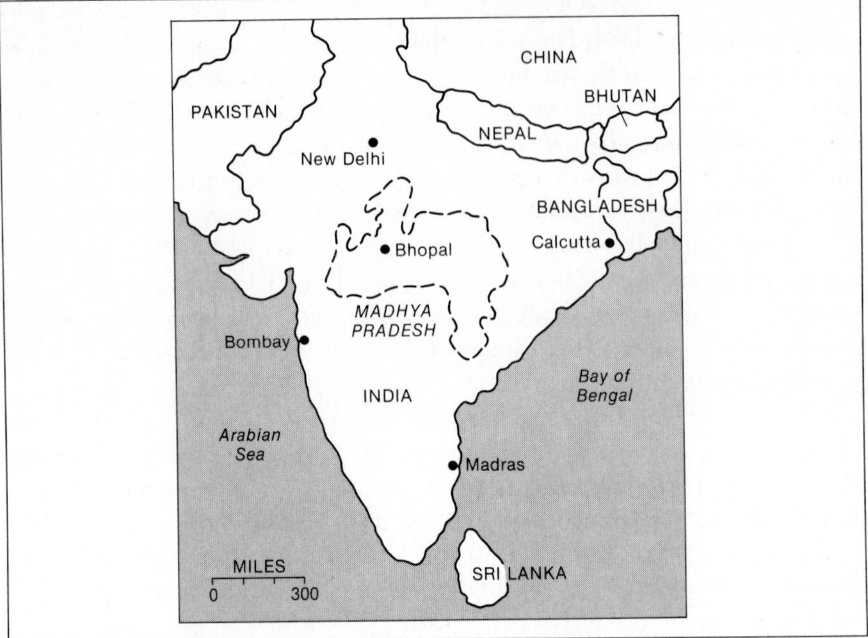

tives. Union Carbide, USA, Chairman Warren Anderson, was briefly detained by Indian officials. Still, the companies continue to enjoy good relations with the Indian government. Many leading citizens and institutions have a financial interest in UCIL. And, except for the Bhopal incident, Union Carbide has an excellent safety record in India.

Warren Anderson has said, "The name of the game is not to nail me to the wall but to provide for the victims of the disaster." Union Carbide, USA, has begun construction of a hospital to provide treatment to the Bhopal victims. The company has also contributed at least $2 million to a victims' relief fund. Finally, plans have been made for a new plant at Bhopal, one which does not use poisonous inputs and which will provide employment to the workers displaced by the destruction of the Sevin plant.

Union Carbide, USA, faces lawsuits in amounts far exceeding the company's net worth. A dozen or more U.S. attorneys signed up thousands of Bhopal victims and relatives of victims and filed suits in the United States purporting to represent them. The Attorney General of India was authorized to sue Union Carbide in a U.S. court. He stated that compensation had to be in accordance with U.S. standards. A Minneapolis law firm which specializes in product liability cases was retained to represent India. Union Carbide publicly opposed trying the lawsuits in U.S. courts. The company clearly would benefit from Indian trials, where punitive damages are almost never allowed and wrongful death judgments often amount to only a few thousand rupees.

By March 1985, the streets of Bhopal were bustling again. There were cars, cattle, and crowds of people. But everywhere there were reminders of the disaster. Many wore dark glasses and covered their faces with shrouds to protect their injured eyes from the sunlight or to keep others from seeing their blindness. At the city's main police station, women and children continued to seek help. Vegetables shriveled by the poison gas were putting forth green shoots here and there. Occasionally, someone still fell sick from eating fish contaminated by MIC.

In the modernistic masonry-and-glass headquarters in Danbury, Connecticut, Union Carbide officials looked out on the beautiful countryside and wondered how best to manage the company's public affairs and how to grapple with the needs in India. Half a world away, in geographical as well as philosophical distance, the poor of Jai Prakash Nagar, now poorer than ever, peered out from their shanties on dusty streets and pondered quite different questions: From where will tomorrow's food come? How long will the pain inside and the dimming of vision last? And, just as importantly, what source of wealth will replace the pesticide plant? And how long will it be before its effects are felt?

BIBLIOGRAPHY

"Bhopal." *Chemical and Engineering News,* February 11, 1985, pp. 3, 14–65.

"The Bhopal Disaster" (and other related articles). *The New York Times,* January 28, 30, 31, February 3, 1985.

"Carbide's Anderson Explains Post-Bhopal Strategy." *Chemical and Engineering News,* January 21, 1985, pp. 9–15.

"City of Death" (and other related articles). *India Today,* December 31, 1984, pp. 4–25.

"Gassed." *The Week,* December 16, 1984, pp. 15–27.

"India's Night of Death" (and other related articles). *Time,* December 17, 1984, pp. 22–31.

"It Was Like Breathing Fire . . ." *Newsweek,* December 17, 1984, pp. 26–32.

The Stock Exchange Foundation, Bombay, India. *The Stock Exchange Official Directory* Vol. XVII/29, July 18, 1983.

"Union Carbide Fights for Its Life." *Business Week,* December 24, 1984, pp. 52–57.

"Whose Life Is It Anyway?" (and other related articles). *The Illustrated Weekly of India,* December 30, 1984, pp. 6–17.

A number of articles from *The New York Times, Wall Street Journal, India Abroad,* and the Indian newspapers *The Indian Express, The Financial Express, The Times of India, The Economic Times,* and *The Hindustan Times.*

SECTION E

NOT FOR PROFIT

Case 36

THE CLASSIC CAR CLUB OF AMERICA

Matthew C. Sonfield

THE "COLLECTOR CAR" HOBBY

The "collector car" hobby in the United States is a broad and wide-reaching activity involving a large number of Americans. Basically, a "collector car" is any automobile owned for purposes other than normal transportation. The most widely read collector car magazine, *Hemmings Motor News,* had a circulation of over 210,000 in March 1984, and its circulation had been steadily growing for many years. Thus, a figure of 250,000–300,000 would probably be a conservative estimate of the number of Americans engaged in this hobby.

"Collector car" is a loose term, ranging from turn-of-the-century "horseless carriages" to currently built but limited-production cars, such as Italian super-sports cars and American convertibles. Naturally, owners of collector cars enjoy the company of other persons with similar interests, and thus a wide variety of car clubs exist to suit almost any particular segment of this vast hobby. The largest of these clubs, the Antique Automobile Club of America, caters to owners of virtually all cars 25 years old or older, and in 1984 was close to achieving a membership level of 50,000.

HISTORY AND BACKGROUND

The Classic Car Club of America, Inc. (CCCA) was formed in 1952 by a small group of enthusiasts interested in the luxury cars of the late 1920s and 1930s. A listing of certain high-priced, high-quality, and limited production cars were designated as "Classic Cars," and the period of 1925–1942 was chosen as the limits of the "Classic Era." It was felt that cars built prior to 1925 had not yet reached technical maturity, and that after World War II

This case was prepared by Prof. Matthew C. Sonfield of Hofstra University. Reprinted by permission.

the quality of most so-called luxury cars had succumbed to the economic pressures of mass-production.

Over the years, the list of CCCA-recognized Classics was modified and expanded, and the time period was extended to 1948 to include certain pre-WWII models that continued in production for a few years after the war. While all cars included on the list were of considerably higher price and quality than the mass-production cars of this era, there was also a wide variance in original price and quality of these recognized Classics. For example, in 1930 a new Ford Model A (not a Classic) cost about $450. Two of the many CCCA-recognized Classics of that year are the Auburn Eight, priced as low as $1195, and the Duesenberg Model J, which sold in the $12,000–$14,000 range. The Auburn, although a car of middle price and quality, is considered a Classic because its styling was exceptional at the time; while the Duesenberg was the highest priced and most exotic American car of the era, carrying custom-built bodies and bought by an exclusive clientele of movie stars, playboys, and other super-rich personalities. Most Classics fell somewhere between these two extremes, with original prices in the $2,000–$5,000 range. Exhibit 36.1 lists those cars recognized as Classics by the CCCA in 1984.

CCCA ACTIVITIES AND ORGANIZATION

When the CCCA's fiscal year ended on October 31, 1983, the club had 4,560 members as indicated below:

Active (regular membership—1983 dues $25/yr)	3796
Associate (for spouses, no publications—$3/yr)	578
Life (one-time charge of $350, after 10 years)	142
Life Associate (spouse of Life—$35)	37
Honorary (famous car designers, etc)	7
	4,560

CCCA members receive a variety of benefits from their membership. A high-quality magazine, *The Classic Car,* is published four times a year. It features full-color photos of Classics on the front and back covers, and forty-eight pages of articles and black-and-white photos of Classics and CCCA activities within. A CCCA *Bulletin* is also published eight times per year, and contains club and hobby news, technical columns, and members' and commercial ads for Classic Cars, parts, and related items. A further publication is the club's *Handbook and Directory,* which is published annually. It contains the CCCA by-laws, judging rules, and so on, as well as a listing of current members and the Classic Cars they own.

The CCCA also sponsors three national events each year. The Annual Meeting in January includes business meetings and a car judging meet, and

Exhibit 36.1

CCCA RECOGNIZED CLASSIC CARS

A.C.
Adler*
Alfa Romeo
Alvis*
Amilcar*
Armstrong-Siddeley*
Aston Martin*
Austro-Daimler
Auburn*
Ballot*
Bentley
Benz*
Blackhawk
B.M.W.*
Brewster*
Brough Superior*
Bucciali
Bugatti
Buick 90
Cadillac*
Chrysler*
Cord
Cunningham
Dagmar*
Daimler*
Darracq*
Delage*
Delahaye*
Delaunay Belleville*
Doble
Dorris
Duesenberg
du Pont
Excelsior*
Farman*
Fiat*
Franklin*
Frazer-Nash*
Graham-Paige*
Hispano-Suiza
Horch
Hotchkiss*
Hudson*
Humber*
Invicta
Isotta-Fraschini
Itala
Jaguar*
Jensen*
Jordan*
Julian*
Kissell*
Lagonda*
Lancaster*
Lancia*
La Salle*
Lincoln*
Lincoln Continental
Locomobile*
Marmon*
Maserati*
Maybach
McFarlan
Mercedes
Mercedes-Benz*
Mercer
M.G.*
Minerva*
Moon*
Nash*
Packard*
Peerless*
Peugeot*
Pierce-Arrow
Railton*
Raymond Mays*
Renault*
Reo*
Revere
Riley*
Roamer*
Rohr
Rolls-Royce
Ruxton
Squire
S.S. Jaguar
Stearns-Knight
Stevens-Duryea
Steyr*
Studebaker*
Stutz
Sunbeam*
Talbot*
Talbot-Lago
Tatra*
Triumph*
Vauxhall*
Voisin
Wills Ste Claire*
Willys-Knight

* Indicates that only certain models of this make are considered Classic and/or post-WW II models require individual approval from the club for Classic status.

is held in a different location in the United States each year. In July a series of "Grand Classic" judging meets are held simultaneously in a number of locations around the country. In 1983, 365 Classics were judged or exhibited at six different Grand Classics from coast to coast. At CCCA judging meets, cars are rated by a point system which takes into account the authenticity of restoration and the general condition of the car, both cosmetically and mechanically.

Each summer the club sponsors one or more "Classic CARavans" in various parts of the U.S.A. and Canada. The CARavan is a tour in which more than 100 Classics join together in a week-long planned itinerary.

The CCCA also has technical advisors available to assist members and makes available for sale to members certain club-related products, such as hats and ties with a Classic Car design.

The club is managed by a fifteen-person Board of Directors, with President, Vice-Presidents, Treasurer, Secretary, and so on. All are club member volunteers (from all over the U.S.A.) who have shown a willingness and ability to help run the CCCA and have been elected by the total membership to three-year terms of office. They are not reimbursed for their expenses, which include attending monthly board meetings, most of which are held at headquarters offices which are rented in Madison, New Jersey. The only paid employees of the club are a part-time secretary and the publications editor. An organization chart of the CCCA is shown in Exhibit 36.2.

In addition to belonging to the National CCCA, the majority of members also pay dues and belong to a local CCCA Region. In 1984 there were twenty-four regions throughout the U.S.A. (See Exhibit 36.3.) Each region sponsors a variety of local activities for members and their Classics and also

Exhibit 36.2

CLASSIC CAR CLUB OF AMERICA—ORGANIZATION CHART

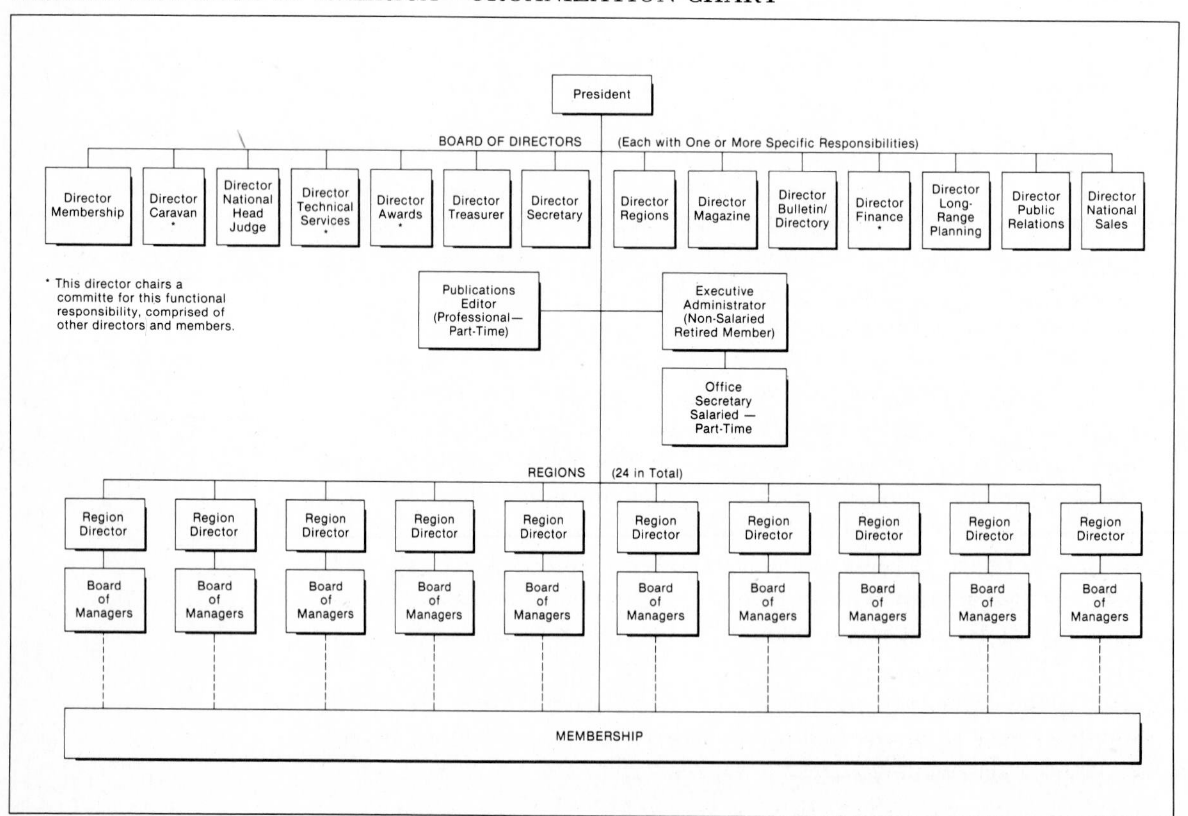

Exhibit 36.3
MAP SHOWING BOUNDARIES OF REGIONS OF CLASSIC CAR CLUB OF AMERICA

publishes its own magazine or newsletter. Many of the regions also derive revenues from the sale of Classic Car replacement parts or service items, which are offered to all members of the national club.

CURRENT PROBLEMS THAT FACE CCCA

While the officers and directors of the CCCA believe the club to be strong, both financially and in its value to its members, a variety of concerns about the future exist. As indicated in the financial statements provided in Exhibit 36.4, the CCCA experienced a small negative cash flow for the 1983 fiscal year.

Of primary concern is the effect of inflation upon the club's ability to maintain its current level of service and benefits to the membership. In particular, the cost of publications and headquarters office administration and rent have risen considerably in recent years. The board of directors has responded by both watching costs carefully and raising dues several times, but it recognizes that certain cost increases are unavoidable and that raising dues too high will result in a loss of members.

One way to overcome this problem is to increase the number of members

Exhibit 36.4
CCCA FINANCIAL STATETMENTS

	FY 1983	*FY* 1982	*FY* 1981
Receipts			
Active dues (dues received for current fiscal year)	$ 47,950	$ 43,900	$ 41,199
Prepaid active dues (received for next fiscal year)	54,975	47,370	33,440
Associate dues ($3.00/yr '83, '82, '81)	972	978	801
Prepaid associate dues (for next fiscal year)	1,227	762	648
Life membership ('83: $350; '82 & '81: $250)	7,310	5,375	6,775
Publications (back issue, individual copy sales)	3,429	3,472	4,202
Bulletin advertising	3,663	3,396	1,459
Magazine advertising	3,567	1,658	2,752
Awards (payments from members for judging meets and meetings)	5,240	5,091	5,230
CARavan (current years)	5,300	5,646	5,900
CARavan (prepaid for next fiscal year)	6,360	1,500	1,550
National sales items (badges, jewelry, clothing)	5,235	4,045	609
Interest earned	10,416	8,750	9,957
Regional insurance (reimbursements from regions)	1,100	1,550	1,300
Misc. & foreign exchange	887	2,330	322
Total receipts	$157,631	$135,823	$116,144
Disbursements			
Bulletin	$ 18,961	$ 17,036	$ 13,739
Magazine	52,123	42,099	33,756
Directory	16,181	9,277	9,237
Awards (judging, meetings, trophies, etc.)	8,888	9,648	10,025
General administration	8,786	7,573	10,843
Office (salaries, rent, utilities, etc.)	28,573	21,824	16,934
CARavan	5,069	5,564	4,252
National sales items	1,710	4,123	126
Membership (recruitment)	5,670	3,401	1,619
Regional insurance	1,600	1,177	1,279
Regional relations	454	462	431
Computer services	3,678	3,611	8,011
Misc. & foreign exchange	2,562	1,972	1,142
Total disbursements	$159,255	$127,767	$111,394
Surplus	$(−1,624)	$ +8,056	$ +4,750
Assets			
Bank Balance	$ 5,356	$ 1,891	$ 5,485
Investments (at cost; notes, C.D.'s. money market funds)	96,566	88,997	85,236
(Includes life membership funds)	(37,245)	(29,800)	(24,255)
Liabilities			
None			

Notes to Financial Statements:

[1] Cash basis reporting.
[2] Security transactions not included.
[3] Other assets not included (furniture, fixtures, sales items, trophies, deposits, etc.).

and thus create greater revenues for the club. The directors know that many Classic owners do not belong to the CCCA. While CCCA members owned about 6,500–7,000 Classics in 1983, no one really knows how many Classics and owners are not in the club. Club efforts in recent years to increase membership have been targeted at these Classic-owning non-CCCA members. Letters have been sent to past members who failed to renew their CCCA membership (about 5%–10% each year), region officers have contacted local non-CCCA members known to own Classics, and a few articles about CCCA activities as well as paid CCCA membership advertisements have been placed in old car hobby magazines.

Furthermore, while some CCCA members do not own Classics, most do, for much of the pleasure of belonging to the club derives from participating in the various activities with a Classic Car. Thus, while Classic enthusiasts who do not own a Classic might also be an appropriate target for CCCA new membership efforts, the primary focus has been on persons currently owning a Classic.

Yet, unless the listing of unrecognized Classics is expanded, the number of Classics in existence is fixed, and with it, by and large, is the number of Classic owners. There are varying opinions within the CCCA with regard to expanding the current listing of Classics. While there is some debate over adding further makes and models within the current 1925–1948 year limits, the main controversy concerns whether or not to add cars built after 1948.

The minority of members who favor this post-1948 expansion make several arguments. They say that some high quality cars were built after 1948 and these should also be considered "Classic." Furthermore, they argue that the club is currently not attracting young members (only 20% of CCCA members are under forty-five), and this is because younger people are less able to afford the cost of a Classic and are unable to "identify" with a 1925–1948 car as they can with a car of the 1950s or 1960s. While prices of Classics vary greatly, depending upon the make of car, its condition, and type of body, all prices rose significantly in the 1970s. Also it is true that many current CCCA members own Classics because of nostalgia for the cars of their youth.

On the other hand, most members of the board of directors, along with a clear majority of the membership, argue against expansion of the list of Classics past 1948. The primary argument is that a Classic Car is more than just a high-quality luxury car. Rather, it is the product of a "Classic Era," when the truly wealthy lived a separate life-style from the rest of the population, and when an elite group of automakers and custom body craftsmen were willing and able to produce cars to meet this upper-class life-style. By the end of World War II, it is argued, social upheavals ended this life-style, and economic pressures closed down the custom body builders and most of the independent luxury car makers, with the remaining luxury cars generally becoming simply bigger, heavier, and better-appointed versions of other cars made by multi-line manufacturers.

Furthermore, it is argued, while a few truly special car models were made after 1948, the quantities produced were small, and the addition of these cars to the list would bring in few new members to the CCCA.

Beyond the board's concerns about the future financial strength of the club, there is a concern about the use of members' Classics and the nature of CCCA activities. As previously mentioned, the value of Classics has risen significantly over the years. In 1952 when the club was founded, most people viewed Classics as simply "old cars," and they could generally be bought for a few hundred to a few thousand dollars. Today, Classics are viewed as a major investment item, with professional dealers and auctions a significant factor in the marketplace. While some less exotic and unrestored Classic models can be found for under $10,000, most sell for $10,000–$75,000, and the most desirable Classics (convertible models with custom bodies, 12 and 16 cylinder engines, etc.) can sell for $100,000 and more. Furthermore, judging meets have become very serious events, with high scores adding significantly to a Classic's sales value. Thus, many top-scoring Classics are now hardly driven at all and are trailered to and from judging meets. While most Classic owners still enjoy driving their cars, the emphasis in the club is definitely moving from the driving to the judging, and this upsets many CCCA members.

Still another concern of some members involves possible future gasoline shortages in the United States. If such a shortage arose, how would the public view Classic Cars and the old-car hobby in general? Would the ownership and driving of cars for non-transportation purposes be considered unpatriotic or anti-social?

MEMBERSHIP SURVEY

In response to these various concerns, the CCCA board established a Long Range Planning Committee to study issues about the future of the club, and to make recommendations to the board. In late 1983 a membership questionnaire was developed and sent to all members along with their 1984 membership renewal material. The response rate was excllent—about 75% of the club's members returned a completed questionnaire with their 1984 dues. Exhibit 36.5 presents this questionnaire and a tabulation of quantifiable responses.

It is more difficult to summarize the responses to the open-ended questions. While no one sentiment represented a majority or even a large minority of the membership, some themes were frequently repeated:

Exhibit 36.5

CLASSIC CAR CLUB OF AMERICA

MEMBERSHIP QUESTIONNAIRE

Please help your National Board of Directors guide the CCCA in the path that you desire by completing this questionnaire and returning it with your membership renewal.

1. I have been a member of the CCCA
   ☐ less than 2 years 11% ☐ 2 - 5 years 20% ☐ 5 - 10 years 18% ☐ more than 10 years 51%
2. I live in the ______________ region (or state if there is no region)
3. My age is ☐ under 25 1% ☐ 25 - 34 3% ☐ 35 - 44 17% ☐ 45 - 54 30% ☐ 55 - 64 28% ☐ 65 and over 22%
4. I am a member of a CCCA Region ☐ yes 69% ☐ no 31%
   If not, why not? ______________
5. I have attended
   64% ☐ One or more Grand Classics
   19% ☐ One or more National CCCA CARavans
   24% ☐ One or more Annual Meetings
   52% ☐ One or more Regional Events
6. I belong to ______(how many) other car clubs.

0	1	2	3	4	5	6	7	8	9	10 & +
9%	19%	23%	17%	12%	7%	5%	2%	2%	1%	3%

   I am more active in some of these clubs than I am in the CCCA. ☐ yes 44% ☐ no 56%
   If "yes," why? ______________
7. Compared to other car clubs, the CCCA is
   ☐ the best 31% ☐ better than most 47% ☐ average 21% ☐ poor 1%
8. Compared to other car clubs, the value I receive for my CCCA dues is
   ☐ the best 27% ☐ better than most 40% ☐ average 31% ☐ poor 3%
9. Overall, I rate *"THE CLASSIC CAR"* magazine ☐ excellent 74% ☐ good 24% ☐ fair 1% ☐ poor 0%
10. Overall, I rate the *"CCCA BULLETIN"* ☐ excellent 35% ☐ good 51% ☐ fair 13% ☐ poor 1%
11. In *"THE CLASSIC CAR"*, the types of articles I enjoy most are:
    Rate each: 3 = enjoy a great amount 2 = enjoy a fair amount 1 = enjoy a little 0 = do not enjoy

Rating	Article type	Rating	Article type
2.3	Grand Classic articles	2.4	Articles on classic car designers
1.5	Annual Meeting articles	2.7	Car photos from the Classic Era
2.1	CARavan articles	2.3	Reprints from classic era publications
2.7	Stories and photos of members' cars	1.5	Book reviews
2.8	Historic articles on classic cars or coachbuilders	1.6	Articles on regional events
2.4	Technical articles	1.3	Articles on non-CCCA car events
2.5	Restoration articles	1.7	Classic car humor
2.4	Articles on car collections or car museums	1.8	Letters to the editor
____	Other: ______________		

12. I would prefer
    28% ☐ to continue to have the *HANDBOOK-DIRECTORY* published every year
    72% ☐ to have it published every other year if a significant savings to the club would result
13. Currently the club's By-Laws require that 7 candidates run each year for election to 5 open National Board positions. While this gives the membership a choice in their voting, it also means that the two least-known candidates generally lose and will not seek election to the Board again.
    I think it is important to continue the system of 7 candidates for 5 positions. ☐ yes 64% ☐ no 36%

(Please continue on other side)

***Exhibit 36.5** (Continued)*

14. With regard to the CCCA's listing of recognized Classic Cars,
69% ☐ I basically think the current listing is good
28% ☐ I think the listing should be expanded
3% ☐ I think the listing should be reduced
Comments:____________________

15. With regard to the CCCA 100-point judging system,
86% ☐ I basically think the current system is good
14% ☐ I think the system could be improved
If so, how? ____________________

16. Overall, I would rate the Grand Classics as
☐ excellent 50% ☐ good 30% ☐ fair 2% ☐ poor 1% ☐ don't know 17%

17. Overall, I would rate the Annual Meetings as
☐ excellent 15% ☐ good 22% ☐ fair 5% ☐ poor 0% ☐ don't know 59%

18. Overall, I would rate the CARavans as
☐ excellent 28% ☐ good 16% ☐ fair 2% ☐ poor 0% ☐ don't know 54%

19. I think the CCCA should have additional National Judging Meets. ☐ yes 23% ☐ no 77%
If "yes," what type? ____________________

20. I think the CCCA could be improved by:
____

Other comments: ____________________

Thank you for your assistance.

- A concern about trailered cars and professionally restored cars competing with other Classics in judging.
- Too much emphasis in the CCCA on judging, and not enough emphasis on driving. A focus on cosmetics rather than mechanics.
- To attract younger members, the club must expand the listing of Classics beyond 1948.
- "The _______ (which I happen to own) should be recognized as a Classic. It is as fine a car as the _______, which is recognized by the CCCA as a Classic."
- The CCCA should not dilute the meaning of "Classic." Hold fast to the 1925–1948 limits.

FUTURE DIRECTION OF CCCA

In 1984 the CCCA Board of Directors was studying these issues. The board members knew that they could not ignore the problem of rising costs, and that the response must be beyond raising dues. While the survey clarified some of the opinions of the membership, the board did not view this survey as a ballot, with the board obligated to follow the majority preference in every question area.

As they met for their monthly Board of Directors meeting, the fifteen officers and directors of the CCCA asked themselves the following questions:

1. How do we deal with rising costs to the club?
2. What should be our policy with regard to future dues increases?
3. Should we consider the reduction of CCCA services to our membership in the future?
4. Is expansion of the listing of recognized Classic Cars desirable?
5. What are the alternative ways to increase membership in the club?
6. How can younger people be attracted to the CCCA?
7. Are there other sources of revenue for the club?
8. Were important questions not included in the 1983 membership survey that should be included in a future survey?
9. Are there other long-range issues or concerns that the club has not yet addressed?

Case 37

CERVANTES EQUESTRIAN CENTER

Melvin J. Stanford

> Have you ever wondered how we landed on the whopper of a name, CERVANTES EQUESTRIAN CENTER, RIDING FOR THE HANDICAPPED?? Well . . . Mr. Cervantes was the author of the book "Don Quixote" from whence the song the "Impossible Dream" came. We felt it appropriate to name our program of riding therapy for the handicapped after the man who inspired us to "dream impossible dreams," and "to reach unreachable stars." Romantic? Idealistic?? You Bet!!! But CERVANTES was an impossible dream—and the idea that Ronnie or Jennifer, two of our cerebral palsy students, could ever leave their wheelchairs and ride horses was for them, an impossible dream—and yet it is happening!!
>
> So we will continue to dream impossible dreams and reach for unreachable stars. You can be sure that we will continue to inspire our students to dream their impossible dreams and to reach out after their unreachable stars. We're betting—and working—and praying—that they will make it.

This is how Linda Smith described the selection of the name "Cervantes" in a newsletter to her students, volunteer staff members, and friends. Linda founded the Cervantes Equestrian Center in the summer of 1979 for the purpose of teaching both handicapped and normal children to ride horses.

Linda Smith grew up in Rockford, Illinois. At an early age she learned to ride horses and began to participate in horse shows, where she later won a number of awards with her horses. She majored in physical education in college and became a certified instructor (one of only twelve people so certified by NARHA) for teaching horseback riding to the handicapped. After graduation from college, she worked on an assembly line in a manufacturing plant in the Rockford area in order to save some money for her riding school.

This case was prepared by Dean Melvin J. Stanford, Mankato State University. Reprinted by permission.

Linda became a member of the North American Riding for the Handicapped Association. NARHA was a non-profit, tax-exempt organization which had been organized in 1969. The stated aims of NARHA were:

- to establish standards and techniques for teaching riding to the handicapped.
- to advise and certify existing programs that wish to be members.
- to approve training programs and provide certification of instructors who plan to teach the handicapped.
- to maintain contact with members of the medical profession in order to insure the safety and well-being of handicapped riders and to gain approval and recognition of riding as a valuable therapeutic activity.
- to make periodic inspection of those centers in operation and to visit affiliated programs regularly.
- to provide experienced consultants for lectures and discussions.
- to promote responsible research, and to make the resulting data generally available.

Normal children as well as handicapped were accepted as students by Cervantes because Linda believed that both groups of children could learn from each other. Moreover, the lessons for the normal children helped bring in enough revenue to get Cervantes started without relying solely on a clientele of handicapped students. There were three other riding schools in the county in which Linda lived. Two of them gave riding lessons, but neither of them had any handicapped students. There were several riding stables and riding schools in a more populous adjoining county. Some of them gave lessons, but so far as Linda knew, none of them was certified to teach handicapped students.

Volunteers consisting of students from a nearby university and neighbors in Linda's community helped her get Cervantes started. She received a very positive response to requests for donated help because of the nature of what was being done for handicapped children. The progress that those children made was rather dramatic in some cases. Linda described her experience with a student, Peter, as follows:

> I remember well the first time I worked with Peter. I heard Peter before I saw him. He came into the arena screaming and crying because he was afraid.
>
> Peter is autistic. He lived isolated in his own little world devoid of emotion, happiness, and human contact. He was afraid of everything and would not speak or communicate in any way with other people except to push them away or to cry.
>
> It took one man and three women to put ten-year old Peter, kicking, screaming and pushing us away, up on the back of patient "Little Mike." Little Mike never even batted an ear while all of this was happening. An

interesting thing occurred as Peter was walked around on Little Mike's back. Peter realized his world was changed. He was up on the back of some warm and fuzzy creature who was moving. This change and movement caused Peter to focus his mind, to concentrate, and to get in touch with what was happening in the world around him. He stopped crying. He was unable to participate that first evening as member of a team in the relay race, so we had him go solo. Encouraged by the clapping and cheering of his teammates and volunteers, Peter was led to the end of the arena where he was given a piece of red paper and led back down the home stretch of the race, amid clapping and cheers of "come on Peter!" A faint smile flickered across his face.

I was talking to my volunteers just before Peter's second lesson, telling them not to be upset if Peter struggled as we put him on the pony. Just then the bus pulled up with the students. Peter was the first one off the bus. He came galloping into the arena, grabbed my hand, and pulled me over where Little Mike, his pony, was tied. I was shocked! My mouth hung open and tears filled my eyes as I helped Peter pet Little Mike. Peter wanted to get on. He would start to climb on and then lose his courage. The little boy, who last week had required four people to put him up on the pony's back, this week only required mild encouragement and the helping hand of one person.

National studies have shown that the use of animals can be effective in bringing patients out emotionally so they think better of themselves and interact more effectively with others. The use of horses can also bring students out physically because they want to ride, lead, brush, pet, feed, and play with their horses and ponies. This has certainly been the case with Peter. Peter has made steady improvement from the first day on. He has formed a strong friendship and trust in his pony and his volunteers. He now participates in the games and gets on and off and controls his pony by himself. He loves to feed Little Mike carrots and pet him.

Probably the most exciting event so far occurred about a month ago. We were playing a game of tag on horseback. This exciting game is a favorite of the children and they giggle all the way around the arena. Peter was tagged "it." He laughed and yelled, "attack!" His volunteer was so shocked at Peter speaking that she stopped the pony and in amazement said, "Peter, what did you say?" Peter was excited to chase his classmates. He kicked Little Mike and yelled again, "ATTACK!!" Peter spoke several words that day, among them were: whoa, carrots, go, thank-you, and good-bye.

It fills the hearts of all of us with joy as Peter laughs and interrelates with his volunteers, his pony, and his classmates. He is experiencing happiness and joy—a strong contrast to the lonely, self-isolated Peter of a few months ago.

We at CERVANTES feel each student is important. There is great joy as we see each student progressing and reaching goals that will help them enjoy life more. We feel confident that Peter will continue to progress, and we are grateful that for one hour on Saturday we can be part of his life.

Favorable publicity soon began to result from the work done at Cervantes. Several feature articles with photographs were run in some of the larger newspapers in the area. By early summer of 1980, enrollment had built up to nearly fifty students, each taking one riding lesson per week. Linda had a roster of eighty volunteer workers, about thirty of whom were spending four to five hours per week with Cervantes. Linda also had eleven horses, four of which had been donated to Cervantes. Four of her horses were bearing foal. Cervantes operated in a donated facility that included a stable, outdoor arena, and pasture. During the winter, an indoor arena was used at a cost of $1 per student per hour. The first facility used by Cervantes was also donated rent-free; however, after Linda and her volunteers had cleaned and fixed it up and used it only for a short period of time, the owner said he wanted to do something else with it. Linda was thus obliged to find another facility and repeat the cleanup and repair process. Then in late July of 1980, she was told that her present facility was needed by the owner and that Cervantes would need to vacate it by August 18.

Parents of some of her students offered pasture for Cervantes' horses and for riding lessons if needed temporarily. However, Linda wanted to find a new facility she could stay in. She thought of buying a stable or buying some land and building a stable. With this in mind, she reviewed her financial situation.

When Cervantes was started in August 1979, Linda had $1,500 cash she had saved. She also had five horses and some equipment. In September, Linda applied for a loan from a local bank. She prepared for the banker a list of her assets offered as collateral and a list of what the loan would be used for (see Exhibit 37.1). She also made a list of projected expenses and income for each month for twelve months (see Exhibit 37.2). The bank then loaned

CERVANTES EQUESTRIAN CENTER

Exhibit 37.1

List of collateral for bank loan	
1977 AMC Pacer	$ 3,800
1974 Chevrolet ¾-ton pick-up	2,500
1971 Champion 6-horse trailer	2,800
5 horses	17,850
5 saddles	500
Miscellaneous equipment	250
Use of loan	
Insurance	$2,000
6 saddles at $200 each	1,200
3 horses at $500 each	1,500
Working capital	2,000
	$6,700

Exhibit 37.2

CERVANTES EQUESTRIAN CENTER: PROJECTED EXPENSES AND INCOME

September 1979 to August 1980

Projected Expenses	**1979** *September*	*October*	*November*	*December*	**1980** *January*	*February*	*March*	*April*	*May*	*June*	*July*	*August*
Taxes	$ 0	$ 0	$ 0	$ 0	$ 0	$ 0	$ 0	$ 0	$ 0	$ 0	$ 0	$ 0
Rent	0	0	0	100	100	100	100	0	0	0	0	0
Repairs	120	5	5	0	5	5	5	5	5	5	5	5
Payroll	100	200	200	200	200	200	250	300	300	400	400	400
Insurance	0	85	85	85	85	85	85	85	85	85	85	85
Legal fees	0	0	0	0	0	0	0	0	0	0	0	0
Bank payment —truck loan	78	78	78	78	78	78	78	78	78	78	78	78
Veterinarian and worming	10	40	10	40	10	40	10	40	10	40	10	40
Blacksmith	36	0	36	0	36	0	36	0	36	0	36	0
Feed	112	137	137	152	162	162	162	162	162	137	137	137
Tack	400	200	200	200	200	0	0	10	10	0	0	10
Advertising	70	70	0	0	70	50	50	50	0	0	0	0
Telephone	6	15	15	15	15	15	15	15	15	15	15	15
Gas	50	50	50	50	50	50	50	50	50	50	50	50
Misc.	25	25	25	25	25	25	25	25	25	25	25	25
Totals	$1007	$905	$841	$945	$1006	$ 810	$ 866	$ 820	$ 776	$ 835	$ 841	$ 845
Projected Income												
Lessons	$ 120	$600	$900	$720	$1200	$1080	$1320	$2250	$1800	$1920	$2700	$2160
Stud service						600	600	600	600	0	0	0
Boarding						150	150	150	150	150	150	150
Training						250	250	250	250	250	250	250
Totals	$ 120	$600	$900	$720	$1200	$2080	$2320	$3250	$2800	$2320	$3100	$2610

her $6,700 at 16% interest, with monthly payments of $184.49 for five years.

All income was deposited in the bank, and all expenses were paid by check. For several months, Linda summarized her income and expenses. Actual income was $91 in September 1979; $104 in October; and $229 in November. Actual expenses were $607 in September; $1,617 in October; $1,662 in November; and $499 in December. Thereafter, she didn't summarize her income and expenses, but she tried to be very careful with her money. Typically, Linda withdrew only $50 to $100 per week for living expenses. By July 1980, she still had $3,000 of the original bank loan on hand, which she kept in an interest-bearing saving account, making withdrawals only when needed. Linda had estimated that if she took in $360 per week and drew $100 for herself, Cervantes would break even financially. Earlier in the summer of 1980, she had been grossing $1,200 per month, with expenses (other than her draw) running about $600 per month. In July, however, she raised the price of a one-hour lesson for a handicapped student from $5 to $6. As a result, a local handicapped school discontinued sixteen of its eighteen students that had been coming for a weekly riding lesson. It appeared that this change would reduce Cervantes' gross to $800 for July.

The reason the school gave for discontinuing that many students was that they had to pay for the riding lessons out of a personal money allowance of $25 per month. She wondered how she might get institutions or schools to budget for riding lessons as therapy or recreation. Cervantes' price for a one-hour lesson for a normal child was $7.50. Linda believed that price to be comparable for other stables in the area.

In addition to the eleven horses, valued at $30,000 to $40,000 (depending on the value of the foals, when born), Cervantes had its original equipment, plus three more saddles. Payments on both loans were current, with a principal balance due of $4,356 on the bank loan and $783 on the truck loan.

The local Junior Chamber of Commerce had helped Cervantes with volunteer cleanup projects. Linda wondered whether they could help her find a new facility. Could she make Cervantes profitable as a business without volunteers or donated facilities? If so, were there other locations in the country where a Cervantes Equestrian Center could serve both handicapped and normal children and make enough profit to justify the investment? There were about 100 riding centers for the handicapped in the United States. All of them were non-profit, and none of them had non-handicapped students. Linda Smith wanted to control her own operation, and she wondered how she could best develop Cervantes toward success and stability.

Case 38

CASCADIA COLLEGE: IMPLEMENTING A STUDENT RETENTION PROGRAM

Larry D. Alexander

Cascadia College is a medium to small-sized college of 6,407 students located in the beautiful Pacific Northwest region. It is located in Greensville which is a "college town" of about 25,000 population. Greensville is 20 miles from the nearest similar-sized city and over 100 miles from the major metropolitan area in the state. The college is a land grant public institution that was founded in 1912. About 90% of the students are working toward various bachelor's degrees. The remaining 10% of the students are all working on master's degrees since the college does not offer any doctorate degrees.

The various academic programs and student majors are grouped under five basic schools. These schools, along with their current student enrollment figures, are as follows: School of Liberal Arts (1,476 students), School of Business (1,807 students), School of Engineering (1,209 students), School of Science (1,357 students), and School of Education (558 students). Each school, in turn, is subdivided into a number of distinct departments. For example, the School of Science is broken down into the biology, chemistry, physics, geology, zoology, and mathematics departments. Similarly, the School of Business is divided into the marketing, finance, production, accounting, and management departments.

The academic portion of the college has fairly clear lines of reporting re-

This case was preprared by Prof. Larry D. Alexander of Virginia Polytechnic Institute and State University. Reprinted by permission. This case was prepared from generalized experience; thus the college name in this case does not exist in real life.

lationships to superiors. The faculty of 288 full-time professors and 57 part-time instructors report directly to their respective department chairmen. Department chairmen, or chairwomen in some instances, report directly to the dean that heads their school. The five deans of these major schools all report to the Vice-President for Academic Affairs, Dr. Hal Wood. Finally, Vice-President Wood reports directly to the President, Dr. John Turner. Exhibit 38.1 shows these and other reporting relationships in a simplified organizational chart of Cascadia College.

CASCADIA COLLEGE ORGANIZATION CHART

Exhibit 38.1

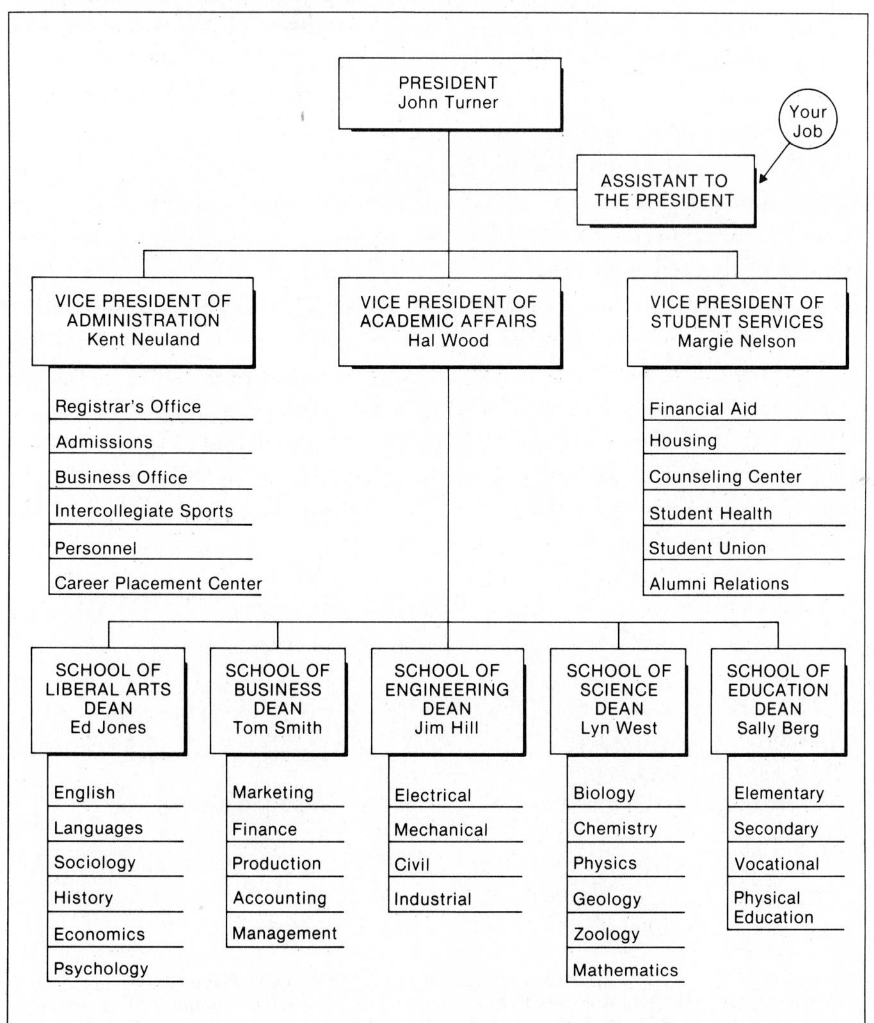

YOUR NEXT ASSIGNMENT

Your position at Cascadia has been as an Assistant to the President, Dr. Turner, for some fifteen months. Before that time, you had been working at Reed College in Portland, Oregon on some new program developments for several of their degree offerings. Here at Cascadia, Dr. Turner has had you working on a wide variety of administrative assignments and special projects. Your job has brought you into contact with the three vice-presidents, all of the deans, and some of the many department chairmen. Thus far, you have developed fairly good working relationships with most of these people, except Kent Neuland, the Vice-President of Administration.

Yesterday afternoon, you met with your boss for several hours about a major program he wants you to help set up and implement. President Turner has made the decision that Cascadia College will quickly start up a formal student retention program. He hopes that such a program will increase the likelihood that incoming students will remain at Cascadia until they graduate. He further believes that a successful program will help stabilize student enrollment figures which have been declining for some time. Since the college reached its all time high of 8,100 students, some eight years ago, the student population has steadily declined to its present figure of 6,407 students as of this fall semester.

Dr. Turner is convinced that retaining present and future students is the best strategy to help resolve the problem of declining student enrollments. As John put it, "Every student that stays at Cascadia for four years helps stabilize and even increase our enrollment figures." Dr. Turner's interest in student retention was rekindled when he recently came across a reprint of an article on the subject. That article explained what several colleges have done to successfully implement their student retention programs. A copy of the article that the president forwarded on to you appears in Exhibit 38.2.

WITH FRESHMEN SCARCER, EMPHASIS SHIFTS TO KEEPING PRESENT STUDENTS

Exhibit 38.2

At least 40 per cent of every new class entering North Carolina State University over the past quarter of a century failed to stay around long enough to receive a degree.

That figure, which comes from a recently completed historical study of graduation patterns at North Carolina State, used to raise few eyebrows. Compared to attrition rates at other four year public universities around the country, it is not excessively high. And there have always been new freshmen to replace the dropouts.

SOURCE: Lorenzo Middleton, "With Freshmen Scarcer, Emphasis Shifts to Keeping Present Students," *The Chronicle of Higher Education*, October 30, 1978, pages 1, 6.

Exhibit 38.2
(*Continued*)

This year, however, in light of predictions that there will be a nationwide shortage of college freshmen over the next decade, officials at North Carolina State are trying to find a way to hold on to more students.

"Like everybody else," says Ronald C. Butler, associate dean for student affairs, "we began to look down the road toward enrollments in the future, and we were suddenly jolted into saying, Hey! Are we doing everything we could be doing in terms of retention?"

Mr. Butler and other members of the student affairs office began working on a plan to increase student retention this fall, after realizing, Mr. Butler says, that "retention is sort of like recruitment in reverse. Why spend all your time and money going out and recruiting additional students and not doing anything to keep the ones that you have?"

Retention is becoming an increasingly popular subject of discussion on campuses around the country, reflecting a changing attitude among college administrators and faculty members, who are just beginning to see financial benefits in keeping students from dropping out of their institutions.

It used to be that most colleges, like North Carolina State, accepted their student attrition figures and planned accordingly. Residence halls were deliberately overbooked during the enrollment boom of recent years, with college housing officials cramming students into overcrowded, makeshift quarters for the first few weeks of the fall term while waiting for the predicted number of early dropouts to depart.

But now many colleges are beginning to change their strategies.

Orientation programs are being overhauled to make new students more comfortable. Faculty members are being asked to be more sensitive to potential dropouts from their classes. Counseling and advising programs are getting more support. And in some cases entire university staffs, from provosts to campus policemen, are being told to think of students as customers—persons who should be encouraged not to take their business elsewhere.

PUSH TO KEEP CLASSROOMS FULL

Much of the concern stems from demographers' predictions of a 19 per cent decline in the number of high-school graduates over the next decade. Experts are divided over whether the declining number of 18 year olds will lead to a significant slump in college enrollments, but people whose jobs depend on maintaining the population of "full-time-equivalents" are worried.

Crash programs to increase retention are part of a major push at many universities to keep classrooms full. Other efforts include the addition of attractive courses and extra hours in an attempt to reach the growing pool of older students.

But, argue many college administrators who are devoting more and

(*Continued*)

Exhibit 38.2
(*Continued*)

more time and money to retention, evening and part-time students will not fill the holes caused by the shortage of full-time freshmen during the 1980's.

"There is no question that the emphasis has switched to retention," says Lee Noel, a vice-president of the American College Testing Program, who was a pioneer in his field when he began to conduct national seminars on student retention in 1974.

Few colleges, Mr. Noel says, took their retention problems seriously when he began talking about the need for improving student services four years ago.

But now, he says, "institutions are looking at retention as a base for keeping up their F.T.E.'s. They're looking at it with dollar signs in their eyes."

"The concept of increasing service to students didn't take, but the idea of increasing enrollment did take. We really did not get sensitive to the needs of students until we felt it in the budget!"

At Drake University, Everett E. Hadley, director of admissions and retention programs, has encouraged university employees to join the retention bandwagon with the slogan, "The job you save may be your own."

Students may be prompted to drop out by unthinking members of the staff at any level. Mr. Hadley says, "It may be a snappy cashier, or it may be the witch in the registrar's office."

The campus-wide effort at Drake, which has included training sessions to help faculty members become more effective advisers, has helped reduce its dropout rate from 31 per cent to 24 per cent over the past five years, Mr. Hadley says, and has saved the university about $250,000 a term.

Other successful retention programs have been launched at:

- Reed College, in Portland, Ore., where improved freshman orientation programs have helped the retention rate climb from 72 per cent in 1973 to 82 per cent in 1977.

  The college tries to improve its orientation program every year, a spokesman says. This year, for example, the orientation office has been redecorated with throw rugs and overstuffed furniture to make new students feel more at home, and the college is picking up the tabs for faculty members who invite freshmen to dinner.

- Central Washington University, where faculty members have been encouraged to carry students' luggage and serve them meals in the cafeteria as part of a freshman "preview week."

  "The idea is to encourage more positive faculty-student interaction outside the classroom," says Gregory Trujillo, assistant dean of students. He says 66 per cent of the students who attended the orientation

Exhibit 38.2
(*Continued*)

session last year returned this year, compared to a usual loss of about 50 per cent of the freshman class in the first year.

- The University of Maryland, which has concentrated on reaching students who might drop out for academic reasons with a system called the "data-drive retention model for faculty/administrators serving minority and nontraditional students in predominantly white universities." Under this system, developed by Andrew Goodrich, formerly the director of the office of minority student affairs, a computer identifies students who fall below certain grade levels and sends them invitations to counseling sessions with faculty members. Chancellor Robert L. Gluckstern says the program has helped increase the retention rate among minority groups at College Park from 52 per cent in 1974 to 61 per cent in 1977, and has begun to expand it in an attempt to reduce attrition among white students.

Much of the emphasis on reducing attrition rates is coming from admissions officers, says Stephen L. Yale, president of Enrollment Analysis, a consulting firm, which is currently conducting a series of student-retention seminars around the country.

"The poor admissions officer is increasingly being put in the role of seducer, making promises to prospective students that can't be kept once they get on the campus," Mr. Yale says. And often, the admissions officer is blamed when significant numbers of disappointed students decide to leave.

"A REAL SORE SPOT" AT LINDENWOOD

Amy Basore, director of admissions at the Lindenwood Colleges in St. Charles, Mo., says the loss of half of the college's resident students last year has become "a real sore spot" on her campus.

"The deans think it's an admissions problem," she says. "The administration is blaming the faculty. No one wants to say, it's my fault."

However, Alexander W. Astin, a professor of education at U.C.L.A. says: "The biggest factor in student attrition is the kind of students coming into the institution, not anything the institution does."

In 1975, Mr. Astin wrote what some refer to as the bible of student retention, *Preventing Students from Dropping Out,* in which he identified potential dropouts as students who (among many other factors): have poor high-school records, low grades and bad study habits; were raised by low-income and poorly educated, Protestant parents; are married females; are habitual smokers.

Mr. Noel believes, nonetheless, that most colleges can reduce student attrition by 6 to 8 per cent. Many students will drop out no matter what the institution does, he says, "because they selected the college for the wrong reasons."

Exhibit 38.3

STUDENT TURNOVER RATES BY YEAR IN COLLEGE*

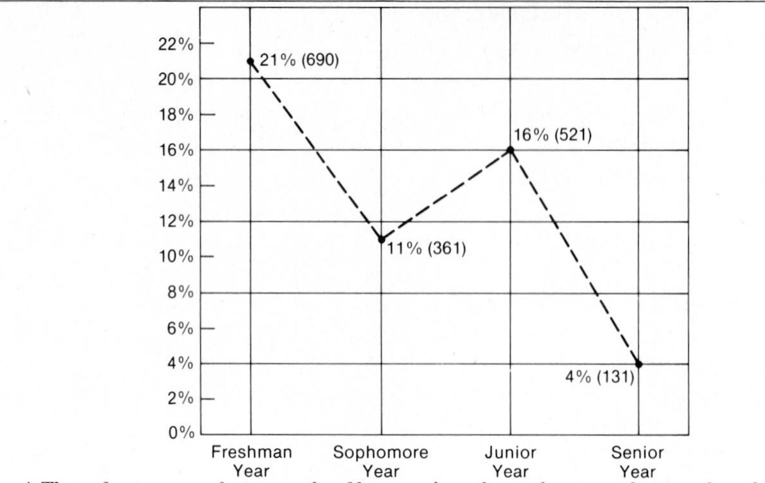

* These figures come from a study of last year's undergraduate, graduating class throughout their four years at Cascadia. It shows, for example, that during their freshman year, four years ago, 21% (690) of the 3,287 entering freshmen dropped out of Cascadia College. Students who transferred to Cascadia from other two- and four-year colleges are excluded from this study to keep the study simple and free from complicating factors. The low dropout rate during last year, this class's expected senior year, is somewhat understated. Perhaps some students who are taking more than four years to graduate (estimated at about 20%) will drop out during this year, their fifth year in college.

STUDENT TURNOVER AT CASCADIA

This morning you arrived at your office at 6:45 A.M. to get caught up on some pressing paperwork and back reading. It is now 11:00 A.M. and you have just finished reading the results of a recent study of student turnover at Cascadia. You are shocked at its findings. About 52% of the particular freshman class studied left Cascadia before four years of college were up. Exhibit 38.3 breaks this alarming figure down by the year in school. Thus, 21% of the students left during their freshman year, 11% left as sophomores, 16% as juniors, and a low 4% as seniors. The results of this informative, but somewhat crude, study were completed last week by Dr. Margie Nelson, the fairly new Vice-President of Student Services.

Another study done by Dr. Nelson sought to determine why students left Cascadia College last year. A total of 113 students who left Cascadia (before graduation) during the past academic year were interviewed before they left by the Counseling Center. The seven main reasons that students gave for leaving the college are shown in Exhibit 38.4. These key reasons are as follows: (1) poor grades and lack of progress toward a degree, (2) impersonal atmosphere in the dorms, classes, and on campus in general, (3) inadequate advising of students about courses, majors, and career opportunities, (4) dis-

REASONS STUDENTS GAVE FOR LEAVING CASCADIA COLLEGE LAST YEAR*

Exhibit 38.4

Reasons	*Number of Students*	*Percent of 113 Students Leaving*
Poor grades and lack of progress toward a degree	43	35.5
Impersonal atmosphere in the dorms, classes, and on campus in general	28	23.1
Inadequate advising of students about courses, majors, and career opportunities	19	15.7
Dissatisfaction with the teaching ability of some professors	42	34.7
Financial difficulties and the increasing cost of college	15	12.4
Personal problems (emotional, family, roommates, boyfriends or girlfriends, etc.)	38	31.4
Miscellaneous	12	9.9

* These reasons came from interviews with freshman, sophomore, junior, and senior students who left Cascadia during the last academic year. A total of 113 students were interviewed in the Counseling Center to try to determine why they were leaving the college. The "number of students" column adds up to more than 113 because many students gave more than one reason for leaving. In fact, 42 students gave one reason, 58 gave two reasons, and 13 gave three reasons. The "percent of 113 students leaving" column adds up to more than 100% for the same reasons.

satisfaction with the teaching ability of some professors, (5) financial difficulties and the increasing cost of college, (6) personal problems (emotional, family, roommates, boyfriends or girlfriends, etc.), and (7) miscellaneous.

Many former students indicated that they had left Cascadia for a combination of the above reasons. In fact, 63% of the 113 students interviewed mentioned two or more reasons. Several other reasons were mentioned by some students but they varied quite a bit. Surprisingly, a few students even indicated that they were going to attend another college in the region that had a much stronger football team. Apparently, these football fans had become depressed each fall sitting in the rain at Alumni Stadium witnessing the "fighting Bulldogs" getting beaten week after week.

CASCADIA'S THREE KEY FUNCTIONAL AREAS

Before deciding on what your student retention program will be, it might be helpful to review the three major functional areas of the college's organizational structure. These three "arms of the college" are Academic Affairs, Student Services, and Administration.

Academic Affairs Academic Affairs, which was discussed earlier, is headed by Hal Wood, a powerful Vice-President. His five key subordinate managers are the deans of the Schools of Liberal Arts, Business, Engineering, Science, and Education. Although not shown on Exhibit 38.1, several other key people also report to Hal Wood. They are the Dean of Undergraduate Programs and the Dean of the Graduate Division. These two people are responsible for insuring quality control standards for the various degree programs offered throughout the five schools. In addition, a Dean of Research reports directly to Wood. She is responsible for administering all research funding that the faculty have been able to bring in from external sources. The Dean of Research also allocates a limited budget for faculty research that comes from Cascadia's operating budget. Finally, the head of Baker Library reports directly to the Academic Affairs Vice-President. Thus, nine people report directly to this powerful position in Cascadia's organizational structure.

Dr. Wood is an experienced administrator who has come up through the ranks of the faculty at Cascadia College. Early in his career at Cascadia, he taught in the biology department. He became known in that field for his successful textbook, *An Introduction to Biology,* which has been used by a number of different colleges in the United States and some foreign countries. He was Department Chairman of the Biology Department for seven years and then promoted to the Dean of the School of Science. He is 57 years old and has been in his present position as Vice-President for Academic Affairs for approximately eight years now.

He is considered to be a powerful administrator for a number of reasons. First of all, he heads up the academic arm of the college; thus, all of the faculty indirectly report to him through intermediate levels in the hierarchy. Second, he is very respected by the faculty for still remaining active in research and writing, even though his job as Vice-President makes tremendous demands on his time. As a side note, he is now working on revisions to the upcoming fifth edition of his bestselling textbook. Third, he is the head of the academic committee that basically decides which faculty members get promoted to tenured status positions. Fourth, his effective matter of fact administrative style, backed up by personal competence, has helped to reinforce his ability to get things done.

Since assuming his office, Wood has continued to stress the importance of faculty members doing course related research. Although he is not anti-teaching, he clearly has expressed his doubts about the validity of judging a professor's worth by what an 18-year-old student has to say in instructor evaluations. It should be pointed out, however, that all classes are asked to complete computer scored forms on the professors' teaching ability, but Dr. Wood has made little use of them to date. Thus, research publications have been given top priority over teaching ratings in deciding who gets tenure.

Student Services

Dr. Margie Nelson is the Vice-President of Student Services at Cascadia. Although she is only 37 years old, Margie already has an impressive background. Educationally, she has both a B.S. in business administration, with a marketing concentration, and a Ph.D. in College Student Services Administration from Oregon State University. After receiving her Bachelor of Science degree, she worked in marketing research for a Fortune 500 firm for two years. She then enrolled in an M.S. program in psychological counseling at Washington State University. When she graduated, Margie worked as a full-time counselor at Washington State in their Psychological Counseling Center for four years. The last two years, she was the head of that center.

Vice-President Nelson came here two years ago right after completing her Ph.D. in College Student Services Administration with honors. It has taken her two years to really get her job under control because of limited staff in her various support departments. For example, she also acted as the interim head of the counseling center for the last year in addition to her main position as a Vice-President. The other departments, fortunately, all have separate supervisors with the exception of Alumni Relations, which is just getting organized.

Margie got concerned about student turnover at Cascadia College even before she started working here. During her interview for her job, she was shocked to learn from Dr. Turner about the high student turnover rate and declining student enrollment trend. While she filled in as interim head of counseling last year, she had an opportunity to examine student turnover more directly. She set up formal exit interviews with students about to leave Cascadia while working at the counseling center. Out of the 113 interviews that she and other counselors conducted emerged the various reasons why students leave Cascadia shown in Exhibit 38.4.

Dr. Nelson is a warm, personable individual who seems to be ideally suited for her role as head of Student Services. She has been openly critical of the other two vice-presidents at Cascadia. Margie takes exception with Wood's overemphasis on research as the number one criteria for granting of tenure to the junior faculty. However, she does get along with him despite their agreement to disagree on the proper priority that teaching and research have for the faculty. She considers Vice-President Neuland to have already retired on the job and tries to avoid interaction with him as much as possible.

Departments

The six departments under Nelson are Financial Aid, Housing, the Counseling Center, Student Health, the Student Union, and Alumni Relations. The primary responsibilities of each of these important student services are summarized below.

The *Financial Aid Department* attempts to provide assistance to students whose families cannot afford the increasing cost of a college education. Some of the programs it administers are scholarships, student loans, grants-in-aid, work-study programs, and some outside part-time jobs in the community. A prime responsibility of employees working in this department is to make students aware of all the various sources of financial assistance. In addition, they provide technical assistance in the completion and timely submission of the various forms and financial statements needed to apply for financial aid.

The *Housing Department* primarily oversees the staffing and operating of the various dorms on campus. Because student enrollments have been declining in recent years at Cascadia, a policy was established two years ago requiring all freshman students to live in the dorms. This decision has helped to keep down dorm price increases somewhat by spreading overhead costs over a "full house" of students. All sophomores must also live in the dorm unless they are (1) over the age of 21, or (2) have written proof they have been accepted to live in a recognized fraternity or sorority house. Housing also maintains a list of various apartments and rental houses in the community. These living accommodations are open to all juniors, seniors, graduate students, married students, or students at least 21 years old.

The *Psychological Counseling Center* provides free professional and paraprofessional counseling to all students. Counselors try to work with students and their specific problems, no matter what they may be. They may concern personal problems, career or life goals, family pressures, interpersonal relations with other students, and so on. Margie Nelson, acting as interim head, has recently implemented a policy that all of the center's records on students are strictly confidential; therefore, they are off limits to any faculty member or administrator who might want to completely understand a particular student's problem.

Student Health Services is available for students who have physical, rather than psychological problems. The staff doctors and nurses try to tactfully refer students to the counseling center when they suspect that emotional problems are the cause of psychosomatic symptoms. Office visits at student health are free, prescription drugs cost the student only 20% of their retail price, and hospital stays are covered in full for those students who purchase a reasonably priced extended benefits medical plan. Referrals are made to Greensville Memorial Hospital for many illnesses requiring a specialist's opinion since the staff physicians at Cascadia are all general practitioners.

The *Student Union* serves as the informal congregating point for many students and faculty members at Cascadia. This department manages the bookstore, cafeteria, snack bar, lounges, recreational rooms, and so on that are located in the Student Union building. Almost all of the various school clubs and formal activities have limited office space located in the Union's basement. The main cafeteria serves as a gathering place for many administrators, faculty members, and students at lunch time. A separate, larger dining room in the Union provides breakfast, lunch, and dinner for all students living in the dorms.

The final department under student services is strangely *Alumni Relations.* Typically this department is organized structurally under the Vice-President of Administration at most colleges. Dr. Nelson has been working to strengthen this area, which only existed as a token effort before her arrival. From a pragmatic viewpoint, an effective alumni relations program has the potential for raising additional external money from annual dues of members in alumni clubs. Occasionally, it is possible to receive a major donation from a former student who has become successful or some wealthy individual in the state.

Administration

Kent Neuland, the Vice-President of Administration, has held this position for well over twenty years. Dr. Neuland is 63 years old, a little hard of hearing, and speaks with a thick European accent. He received a Ph.D. in Public Administration from the University of Heidelberg, in Germany, many years ago. He immigrated to the United States after World II, and has lived in the scenic Pacific Northwest for the last twenty-eight years.

Since Dr. Neuland will be retiring in two years, President Turner has decided not to try to change Kent's approach to administration. As it stands, many of the other administrators and faculty members feel that he is thoroughly entrenched in his thinking and unwilling to change with the times. One structural change President Turner has vowed to make, once Neuland does retire, is to shift the Career Placement Center to student services where it rightfully belongs. Almost every other college has it located there because it is clearly a student service. Unfortunately, Kent got an employment office started quite some time ago and it has been next to impossible to get him to let go of it since Turner assumed the Presidency three years ago.

The six departments under Neuland are the Registrar's Office, Admissions, the Business Office, Intercollegiate Sports, Personnel, and the Career Placement Center. Again, let's briefly summarize the primary responsibilities of these departments.

Departments

The *Registrar's Office* performs a variety of administrative support activities. It maintains student academic records, issues grade reports each semester, prepares the college catalog, issues the schedule of classes for each semester, and mails out a number of other official documents and publications. This office also functions as a central information point for students and faculty who may not know where to go to get an answer to an academic question. A number of students, however, feel that the clerks working in this office treat them like children. Frequently, they are sent off on a wild goose chase that leads nowhere.

Admissions, as the name implies, processes and evaluates all applicants seeking entrance to Cascadia College. It insures that all incoming freshmen or transfer students satisfy the entrance requirements. For incoming freshmen, these standards are a 2.25 grade point (a little above a C average) from any recognized high school in the state. Only a 2.00 grade point average, in all college courses, is required for students transferring from another college. Only an average score on the S.A.T. (Scholastic Aptitude Test) is needed. As a side note, because of significantly higher out-of-state tuition, Cascadia does not attract many students from nearby states. Admissions is also responsible for doing the tedious task of evaluating each incoming student's record to determine advanced standing, approved credits, and so on.

The *Business Office* groups together a number of different administrative activities. Some of these activities include processing the payroll for faculty and staff, preparing various accounting reports, coordinating the budgets in all academic departments, collecting all student fees at the cashier's window, and overseeing building maintenance. For some reason, Neuland spends much of his time doing this portion of his job.

Intercollegiate Sports, headed by the Athletic Director, also reports to the Vice-President of Administration. This arrangement is best described as unique when compared to other colleges and universities. Cascadia participates in Division II of the N.C.A.A. (National Collegiate Athletic Association) for men and a similar group for the women's sports program. The college made a conscious decision a number of years ago to get out of Division I, which is described as the "major league of collegiate sports." This was done to avoid embarrassing losses to such strong schools in the western states as the University of Washington, the University of Oregon, and the University of California at Berkeley. It was also done to avoid the tremendous financial cost of supporting teams capable of winning at that level of competition. Nevertheless, Cascadia College does participate in football, basketball, track, tennis, baseball, gymnastics, swimming, and golf for both men and women.

The *Personnel Department* is responsible for the recruitment and filling of all nonteaching job openings on campus. For the teaching positions, each academic department hires who they want as long as they satisfy affirmative action requirements that they made an effort to locate women and racial minority candidates. Personnel also administers the various employee benefit programs, handles affirmative action matters, and conducts wage and salary surveys of comparable colleges for all positions. Most academic and staff employees find the people working in this department to be friendly and helpful. Many employees, however, do complain about the poor coverage provided by the major medical insurance plan.

Cascadia's *Career Placement Center* is the last major department reporting to Vice-President Neuland. This is under administration, rather than student services, because Margie Nelson's predecessors never got one started. Finally, in desperation, Dr. Neuland set one up under administration some years ago. Most students find the career planning sessions, resume-writing lectures, and videotaped practice interviews to be very helpful. Likewise, for a college of Cascadia's size, the high number of organizations that regularly interview on campus to fill entry-level jobs is particularly pleasing to almost everyone at Cascadia. Still, it does seem rather strange for a Career Placement Center to be organized under administration.

HOW PROFESSORS EARN TENURE

It might also be helpful to understand what tenure is and how faculty members get it. An appreciation of this almost sacred idea that almost all colleges follow may or may not affect the design of your student retention program.

Tenure amounts to the granting of a permanent job for life to a faculty member. As a result, when a faculty member receives tenure, it means that he or she has earned a secure job with that specific college. It is believed that tenure promotes a secure situation for faculty members to practice academic freedom by expressing their own opinion on any subject without fear of reprisals. About the only grounds for dismissing a tenured faculty member are (1) extremely inappropriate personal conduct, and (2) adverse economic conditions requiring faculty members to be laid off. In the latter situation, all untenured faculty in the same department would first have to be terminated before any tenured ones could be laid off. Obviously, such job security as tenure is something that almost all faculty members want to achieve.

The official title that a faculty member has generally indicates his tenure status. Faculty members with the title of Lecturer or Assistant Professor are untenured faculty. Thus, they can be more readily let go after limited notice if their performance is not satisfactory. Typically, these junior faculty members have to work hard for five to six years before they are reviewed for tenure at Cascadia. If a faculty member is granted tenure at that time, he would be promoted to Associate Professor with a salary increase as well. If the tenure review showed that the faculty member had not done enough research or a poor job of teaching, then he would be denied tenure. He would be forced to leave Cascadia College and look for a teaching position elsewhere. Associate Professors that continue to do a good job in research are promoted to a higher paying status called "Full" Professor after another five or six years.

As briefly mentioned earlier, research is clearly given the highest importance for the granting of tenure at Cascadia. This emphasis on writing has been given added importance ever since Hal Wood became the Vice-President of Academic Affairs. The college does expect its faculty members to be good classroom teachers; however, good teaching by itself will not earn tenure. For example, a faculty member that is rated excellent in the classroom, based on student evaluations, won't earn tenure without doing some research. On the other hand, another Assistant Professor who is very active in publishing articles in peer-refereed journals will get promoted quickly, even if students rate him only adequate as a teacher. Thus, while Cascadia College may not be a "publish or perish" institution, research is given more importance in faculty promotion decisions than teaching ability.

THE FACULTY: OVERWORKED AND UNDERPAID

The typical faculty member at Cascadia works in excess of 50 hours per week. The breakdown of how the average Assistant Professor spends his or her time is as follows:

9 hours—teaching in the classroom (three classes per semester)

3 hours—formal posted office hours

6 hours—preparation for classes

10 hours—preparing exams, grading, etc.

8 hours—department and school meetings and assignments

16 hours—research, writing, and reading in one's field

52 total hours per week

These estimates come from forms required of faculty members stating how they spend their time; these forms are turned in each semester. The distribution of hours for tenured faculty (Associate and Full Professors) may differ by category, but the total hours are about the same. For example, some tenured faculty members choose to no longer do research but most are more involved with time consuming campus-wide committees and administrative matters.

In addition to working long hours, the faculty as a whole is becoming increasingly dissatisfied with their salary for a number of reasons. First, their average annual salary ranks next to the bottom among the seventeen comparable colleges reviewed each year by the personnel department's wage and salary survey. Second, the administration seems to reinforce low pay with an attitude that a "faculty member should be willing to take a four or five thousand dollar cut in pay for the privilege of living in the great Pacific Northwest." Third, yearly pay increases have lagged considerably behind the U.S. inflation rate resulting in an actual loss in real wages. Fourth, pay increases have been awarded pretty much across the board with little difference based on actual faculty performance. Finally, because of budget constraints, new faculty members one year are often brought in at higher salaries than those hired the year before. This practice is done to stay competitive with other colleges offering more money in order to attract the best possible faculty.

In addition to teaching and research, many faculty members also get involved in the time consuming process of advising students. Some academic departments use a decentralized advising system which assigns all incoming students to a faculty member. In these departments, students are supposed to go to their advisors whenever they have academic problems, although many students never do. Other departments use a centralized advising system. In this system, all students see professional advisors, rather than any faculty members, for all advising matters. Finally, a few departments utilize a mix of centralized and decentralized advising. For example, all departments in the large School of Business use this system. Each year, some of the business faculty members are "drafted" to do advising for a couple of days at the start of each semester. However, a small centralized advising office processes all of the detailed paperwork. This office also answers questions that students have about degree requirements and that faculty advisors pose to handle specific situations.

WHAT SHOULD YOUR IMPLEMENTATION PLAN CONSIST OF?

As another light rain begins to fall, you sit in your office examining the statistics for student turnover according to Cascadia's schools as shown in Exhibit 38.5. You finally put that paper down and wonder what to do next. The president has made this decision to set up a program to retain students once they do start attending Cascadia. The idea sounds great but how do you begin to implement it? What actions will be needed by the faculty members who have daily contact with the students? How will the department chairmen and deans help administer such a program? What exactly will the program consist of? How can the various departments within Student Services be of help? How can the Administration departments help solve this student turnover problem? What actions will you recommend that President Turner take himself? How can you as a staff assistant, rather than a line administrator, help coordinate such a program? Will it be possible to retain students without lowering academic standards, which the president insists must be maintained? These and other questions are still coming into your mind as you begin to prepare a plan to implement a student retention program at Cascadia College.

Exhibit 38.5

STUDENT TURNOVER BREAKDOWN BY CASCADIA'S SCHOOLS*

	Number of Freshman Students by School	*Number Who Left Cascadia before Graduation*	*Student Turnover Rate by School*
School of Liberal Arts	767	435	56.7%
School of Business	982	601	61.2%
School of Engineering	603	289	47.9%
School of Science	675	294	43.6%
School of Education	260	84	32.3%
Totals	3,287	1,703	51.8%

* The "number of freshman students by school" column shows the initial majors of last year's graduating class some four years earlier. The "number that left Cascadia before graduation" column, however, shows how many students left our college that originally majored in each of the five schools. For example, 435 students left Cascadia before graduation who originally started in the School of Liberal Arts. It must be pointed out that some students who subsequently left Cascadia had changed majors before they dropped out of our college. The "student turnover rate by school" column is determined by dividing the middle column figure by the corresponding left hand column figure. Thus, the 56.7% student turnover rate for the School of Liberal Arts is calculated by dividing 435 by 767.

As a final note, it must be pointed out that the college is facing a financial problem. The state legislature has granted very limited increases to Cascadia's annual budget during the past three years. In fact, these limited increases have not quite kept up with the yearly inflation rate. This situation helps to put in perspective a comment that President Turner made to you yesterday. As Dr. Turner put it, "I want an effective, but realistic, student retention program put into effect at once." He added, "I can't give you a blank check to do a lot of fancy, high-priced things. But I think I could come up with $80,000, maybe even $100,000, if I transferred some discretionary funds around in our current year's budget. But you would have to clearly convince me that this investment would actually bring about a reduction in student turnover."

CASE INDEX

NAME INDEX*

* For people and companies mentioned or noted in Chapters 1–11 only. Case contributors are listed on pages xxiii–xxvii.

SUBJECT INDEX*

* For Chapters 1–11 only.